PE⊕PLE
in Time and Place

PROFESSIONAL GUIDE

WEDNESDAY

THURSDAY

FRIDAY

What's Happening in Social Studies...

History: *Exciting new ways to let* <u>*ALL*</u> *students see themselves as makers of history*

Geography: *Effective new ways to help* <u>*ALL*</u> *students grow up to be geographically literate in a chan...*

Citizen...
ways to ... actively in citizens... starting ***now***

And more ...

SILVER BURDETT & GINN

We Bring It All Together

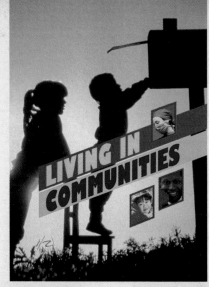

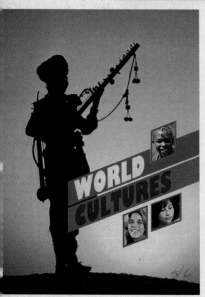

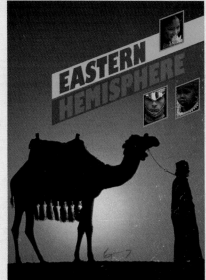

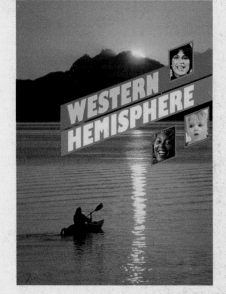

PE●PLE
in Time and Place

Silver Burdett Ginn

Our Bill of Beliefs

1. **We believe that every moment spent on social studies education is precious time well spent, for it is primarily through social studies that students learn the knowledge, skills, and values they need for a lifetime of full and productive citizenship.**

   …That is why we provide a social studies program that reaches **ALL** students.

2. **We believe that the twin cornerstones of social studies are history and geography.**

   …That is why our authors are talented historians and geographers, capable of presenting solid content as an engaging story of people in time and place.

3. **We believe that citizenship education must emphasize active participation in school and community.**

   …That is why we provide ample opportunities for students to put into practice the knowledge, skills, and values they are learning.

4. **We believe that social studies reaches ALL students through a multicultural perspective.**

   …That is why we have structured the program so that every child feels dignified as an active participant in the ongoing story of people in time and place.

5. **We believe that the story of people in time and place is enriched by the social sciences, fine arts, and humanities.**

   …That is why we have integrated appropriate literature passages, fine arts reproductions, and other primary and secondary materials.

6. **We believe that social studies must provide each child with the opportunity to grow in self-awareness and self-confidence.**

...That is why we have built in opportunities for learning, practicing, and applying thinking and other skills, including skills for effective interpersonal relationships.

7. **We believe that the story of people in time and place becomes more memorable and exciting when students are actively involved.**

...That is why we have included a variety of "hands-on/minds-on" activities, cooperative learning, and ways to make thinking more visual.

8. **We believe that social studies takes on added meaning, maximizing time spent on social studies, when students make connections between social studies and other subjects.**

...That is why we have incorporated content-area reading strategies, writing across the curriculum, and multidisciplinary activities.

9. **We believe that the textbook program comes to life through the classroom teacher.**

...That is why we have involved classroom teachers in every step of the development of this program and in the writing of the Teacher-to-Teacher Edition.

10. **We believe that classroom teachers have the right to expect the very best support when they teach social studies.**

...That is why we have brought together in one program everything teachers need to make social studies a successful experience for ALL students: textbook, ancillary materials, and personnel committed to providing top-quality in-service.

PE●PLE
in Time and Place

Silver Burdett Ginn

HISTORY
as a Well-Told Story

How good writing draws students into the study of history

Dr. Herbert J. Bass

All teachers know that getting students involved is a key to learning. Well-written history helps teachers do just that. Writing that is clear and direct, that employs eye-catching detail to flesh out characters and relate events, that helps young readers create mental images of the past — that kind of writing brings history to life for students.

History brims with suspense and drama

Someone once described history as a "cracking good story." That's the way it should be written. Certainly history

doesn't lack for rich story materials. Who could imagine a more wildly improbable tale than that of Pizarro and his band of 168 men conquering the huge empire of the Incas? Is there a more inspiring story than that of the American colonists' struggle for independence against the greatest military power of the age? Or a more suspenseful one than Harriet Tubman's risking her life to guide slaves to freedom? Surely the true stories of the explorers and the pioneers rival the best adventure novels. Such stories have a vast potential for involving the young reader.

Well-written history encourages acts of imagination

To understand history, students have to put themselves into a time very different from their own. That's not easy to do. There is no time machine to carry young readers back to the first Thanksgiving, the American Revolution, or life in the early days of their communities. No time machine, that is, except the one that is within ALL students — imagination.

We encourage acts of imagination when we present history not as a collection of dry, isolated facts but as a story filled with vivid descriptions of what the eye would have seen and the ear would have heard. For example, we could simply state, *City streets in America in 1850 were crowded.* Or we might write this instead:

> *If you visited an American city in the year 1850, you would quickly notice how crowded the streets were. Soon after the sun rose, wagons, carriages, horses, and mules jammed the streets. Few cities had sidewalks, so people walked in the street or along the side of it with the rest of the traffic. There were no laws about which side of the street to ride on, so people traveled on both sides of the street in both directions!*

Each version conveys the facts about crowded city streets, but the second one can also get students' time machines "up and running."

Visuals support the well-told story

Today's "visual generation" is used to getting information from TV and other visual images. Making use of well-chosen visuals such as photographs and paintings, along with plenty of maps and well-constructed time lines, can capitalize on that fact. Teachers will often use films, slides, and videos to stimulate thinking and discussion. That is all to the good.

But in the end, it is the written word that matters most in learning history. And since that is so, it is the well-told story that offers us the greatest opportunity to turn students into interested, active learners.

Dr. Herbert J. Bass, Professor of History, Temple University, Philadelphia, Pennsylvania, has written or edited a half dozen books on American history, several of them for use by elementary students. A recipient of an award for outstanding teaching, Dr. Bass is one of the professional historian-authors of **PEOPLE IN TIME AND PLACE.**

PEOPLE IN TIME AND PLACE
helps to draw students into the study of history.

- **An engaging writing style** presents history as the story of people in time and place

- **Understanding Source Material** engages students in learning about the past and present through interesting print and nonprint sources of information

- **Literature excerpts and selections** *about* historical periods and *of* historical periods give students an illuminated view of the people, places, and events they are learning about

- **Quotations** from people who lived in a particular time and place, as well as quotes about those people, when woven into the text, provide students with a sense of historical perspective

- **Historical maps, time lines, graphs, diagrams, tables, and other graphics** provide integrated visual support for the text, as well as another mode of presentation for historical information

- **Citizenship and American Values** features enable students to understand the history of democracy

- **Five Themes of Geography questions** in the teacher edition help students connect history and geography, time and place

- **Comprehensive vocabulary treatment** provides students with a knowledge of the key terms that bring more understanding to their reading about history

- **Skillbuilders** provide opportunities for students to learn skills that help them unlock the story of people in time and place

- **Current Events** activities in the teacher edition increase student interest in history-in-the-making

- **Multidisciplinary Activity** features help students connect history with the social sciences and other subject areas

History

as a well-told story of people in time and place inspires ALL students to see themselves as makers of history.

From *Our Country*, p. 289

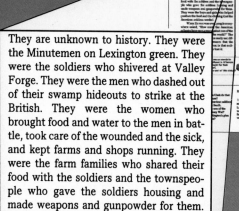

They are unknown to history. They were the Minutemen on Lexington green. They were the soldiers who shivered at Valley Forge. They were the men who dashed out of their swamp hideouts to strike at the British. They were the women who brought food and water to the men in battle, took care of the wounded and the sick, and kept farms and shops running. They were the farm families who shared their food with the soldiers and the townspeople who gave the soldiers housing and made weapons and gunpowder for them. They were the boys and girls who helped produce the food and the clothing that the American soldiers needed.

When the war was over, people everywhere asked, "How could the American colonies have won a war against one of the great military powers in the world?" The answer to this question was really not difficult to find. The main reason that the Revolutionary War was won is that ordinary Americans refused to lose it.

for more HISTORY look for
- **Visuals with captions**
- **Using Source Material**
- **Literature excerpts and selections**
  and in the Teacher-to-Teacher Edition
- **Current Events**

PE PLE
in Time and Place

We bring it all together

Promoting Geography Literacy

The five themes of geography help all students make more sense out of their world

Dr. Gail S. Ludwig

Geographers, teachers, and parents share a common goal: to make students more geographically literate. To help make this happen, professional geographers have shared with classroom teachers a conceptual framework to use in discussing geography. That framework is called the five themes of geography.

The following description of the five themes includes sample discussion questions based on Timbuktu, an African city that I enjoy using to illustrate the five themes of geography in presentations to teachers and students.

The Five Themes of Geography

Theme 1. Location

Location consists of **absolute location** and **relative location.** Every place has an absolute location that can be pinpointed on a map, using latitude and longitude. Every place also has relative location in relation to its surroundings.

To help students think in terms of absolute location, discuss in reference to latitude and longitude on a map or in a gazetteer: *What is the latitude and longitude of Timbuktu?* To help students understand relative location, discuss in reference to a map or globe: *Where is Timbuktu in relation to the Sahara Desert?*

Theme 2. Place

The sense of place includes the combination of physical and human characteristics that makes one location unique from all others. Physical characteristics include climate, soil, and vegetation; human characteristics include values, ideas, and architecture.

To help students think in terms of place, discuss with them in relation to maps, text, and visuals: *There is only one Timbuktu. What are some physical and human characteristics that make Timbuktu different from every other place?*

Theme 3. Human – Environment Interactions (Relationships Within Places)

Relationships within places include the ways humans have been affected by their physical environment. It also includes the ways humans have affected their physical environment.

To help students think in terms of relationships within places, both past and present, discuss in reference to maps, text, and visuals: *Why did Timbuktu grow and develop where it did? In the past, how have the people of Timbuktu changed their environment? What environmental problems do the people of Timbuktu face today? What solutions are they trying?*

Theme 4. Movement

Movement relates to the flow of people, goods, and ideas. The most obvious signs of movement are transportation systems — rivers, railroads and roads — and communication systems — word of mouth, television, newspapers, and so on.

To help students think in terms of movement, discuss in relation to maps, text, and visuals: *How do goods, people, and ideas travel within and in and out of Timbuktu?*

Theme 5. Regions

As a basic unit of study, regions are areas that can be defined on the basis of unifying characteristics, either physical or human (cultural, economic, social, and/or political).

Help students think in terms of regions by discussing: *To which region — or regions — does Timbuktu belong? How is this region different from the region where you live?*

Teaching with the Five Themes of Geography

Strategies For many years, classroom teachers have been using the five themes intuitively as a questioning strategy. Today, classroom teachers are using them more consciously in connection with a strong map and globe skills program. Because they overlap, the five themes do not have to be used in strict order, although the location theme logically is a good starting point. You may adapt the five themes to fit your teaching style and the needs of all your students.

Benefits The five themes can help ALL students, especially students at risk of failing, make more sense out of the world around them. Thinking like geographers, students can use the five themes to see connections among history, geography, the social sciences, the arts, and the humanities. These connections help students remember information, observe, analyze, speculate, and do other kinds of critical thinking that enhances geography literacy.

Dr. Gail S. Ludwig currently serves as the Geographer-in-Residence for the National Geographic Society's Geography Education Program. An experienced social studies classroom teacher, Dr. Ludwig coordinated the first state-level National Geography Bee and has served as president of the National Council for Geographic Education. Dr. Ludwig is one of the professional geographer-authors of PEOPLE IN TIME AND PLACE.

PEOPLE IN TIME AND PLACE builds geography literacy.

- **Consistent map and globe skills program** is integrated throughout the text:
  - Maps have a caption question in the student text and a five-themes discussion question in the teacher edition, provoking geographic thinking
  - End-of-lesson map skills checks provide constant reinforcement

- **Built-in reference tools** support geographic exploration:
  - Map Skills Handbook, strategically positioned at the start of the text, reviews and previews important map skills and provides reference throughout the course of study
  - Atlas, Gazetteer, and Dictionary of Places in the Resource Section in the back of the student texts provide ready access to geographic information

- **Extensive variety of clearly detailed special-purpose maps, including** relief, physical, political, product, population, historical, and transportation maps, provide a rich basis for five-themes discussions

- **Wealth of other graphic resources** — charts, tables, photographs, and drawings — support five-themes discussions

- **Content-rich geography, integrated with history and the other social sciences, the arts, and the humanities,** provides the solid information and cultural literacy background that students need to discuss the five themes

Geography

literacy is built when maps, content, and skills come together through reading, thinking, and discussing.

From World Cultures, p. 286

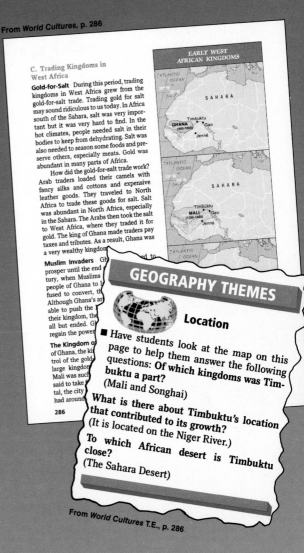

From World Cultures T.E., p. 286

for GEOGRAPHY tools look for
- Gazetteer
- Map Skills Handbook
- Atlas
- Dictionary of Places

PE**O**PLE
in Time and Place

We bring it all together

What's New in Citizenship Education?

Seven Strands Support Real-life Citizenship Participation

Dr. Theodore Kaltsounis

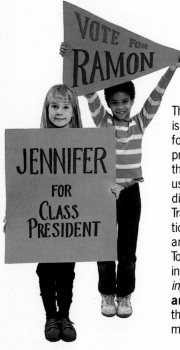

The goal of citizenship education is clear: to prepare all youngsters for their future roles as full and productive citizens, committed to the American values that protect us as a nation rich in individual differences and ethnic diversity. Traditionally, citizenship education has focused on teaching *for* and *about* adult citizenship. Today, the emphasis is on actively involving youngsters in *participating* in citizenship, **both in school and in their communities.** In this way, citizenship education is more than a dress rehearsal!

Seven Strands of Citizenship

The following seven basic strands of citizenship provide a framework for structuring activities that enable students to participate in real-life citizenship while learning the traditional information, skills, and values that provide the foundation for citizenship education.

1. **Participate in the democratic process**

2. **Develop patriotism and American values**

3. **Develop an awareness of and skills in interdependence**

4. **Develop an awareness of and skills in resolving social issues**

5. **Develop an awareness of and skills in relating to public officials**

6. **Learn how to use resources wisely**

7. **Develop strong personal integrity and positive self-image**

Real-life Citizenship Activities

Here are some examples of easily manageable real-life activities that illustrate seven basic strands of citizenship. Through these and similar activities, teachers play a vital role in preparing students for full adult citizenship by providing them with the opportunity, guidance, and encouragement they need to be active citizens **today.** Students don't just read about citizenship, they participate in it in ways that are commensurate with their ages, abilities, and interests.

1. Participate in the democratic process by	• Holding class elections • Writing classroom rules • Conducting mock trials
2. Develop patriotism and American values by	• Celebrating patriotic holidays • Pledging allegiance
3. Develop an awareness of and skills in interdependence by	• Engaging in cooperative learning • Making a farm-to-table foods flowchart
4. Develop an awareness of and skills in resolving social issues by	• Discussing current events • Conducting debates • Writing letters to the editor
5. Develop an awareness of and skills in relating to public officials by	• Writing to public officials • Interviewing public officials • Visiting town hall

8

6. Learn how to use resources wisely by
- Participating in recycling
- Holding a conservation-theme social studies fair

7. Develop strong personal integrity and positive self-image by
- Serving as a safety patrol
- Volunteering as a peer tutor
- Participating in scouting, 4-H

Dr. Theodore Kaltsounis, Professor of Social Studies, College of Education, University of Washington, Seattle, Washington, is an experienced elementary teacher and author of a methods book on citizenship education. A former president of the National Council for the Social Studies, Dr. Kaltsounis is the social studies series consultant for PEOPLE IN TIME AND PLACE.

PEOPLE IN TIME AND PLACE provides built-in ways to activate citizenship participation.

- **Citizenship and American Values** models for students seven citizenship strands including developing patriotism and American values and developing strong personal integrity

- **Citizenship and American Values: You Decide** enables students to evaluate alternatives, weigh evidence, and make decisions — skills that are needed for resolving social issues

- **Cooperative Learning** activities help students develop skills in interdependence, while also developing positive self-image

- **Skillbuilder** lessons enable students to practice a variety of thinking, social studies, and communication skills needed for citizenship, including skills for interdependence, resolving social issues, and relating to public officials

- **Current Events** activities in the teacher edition provide opportunities for students to develop an awareness of interdependence, resolving social issues, and relating to public officials

- **Five-themes-of-geography discussion questions** in the teacher edition encourage students to use resources more wisely

- **How To** features in the teacher edition provide guidelines for conducting activities that help students learn to participate in the democratic process

Citizenship

education puts the accent on active involvement by ALL students.

From *Living in Communities,* p. 184

CITIZENSHIP AND AMERICAN VALUES

Conserving Natural Resources

Adam wanted a drink of water. He turned on the faucet. He let the water run and run. Adam's mother heard the water running.

"Why is the water running for so long?" asked his mother.

"I want it to get cold before I drink it," replied Adam.

His mother said, "Water is an important resource. We must use only what we need. This way we can conserve it."

"What does conserve mean?" asked Adam.

"Conserve means we must not spoil or waste, but use wisely," said his mother.

Then Adam's mother gave him water from the refrigerator. She told Adam how it is important to conserve all of our resources.

Water is one of our most important natural resources. Air, land, and forests are also very important. We use many natural resources every

Current Events Activity

Ask students to bring in newspaper or magazine articles about organizations or individuals trying to conserve natural resources. Make a bulletin board and classify articles by the natural resources in question. Discuss ways students in the class can help specifically to preserve each of the resources mentioned.

From *Living in Communities* T.E., p. 184

for more CITIZENSHIP look for
- ## Skillbuilder
- ## Using Source Material

and in the Teacher-to-Teacher Edition
- ## How To
- ## Cooperative Learning

PE PLE
in Time and Place

We bring it all together

MULTICULTURAL PERSPECTIVES
in
Social Studies

Addressing content issues, process issues, and equity issues helps make ALL students winners

Dr. James A. Banks

A respected authority on multicultural education, Dr. James A. Banks served as chairperson and senior author on the National Council for the Social Studies Task Force that issued "Curriculum Guidelines for Multi-ethnic Education." A former elementary teacher, Dr. Banks has authored numerous books and articles on strategies for teaching multicultural education in the social studies. Dr. Banks is Professor of Education, University of Washington, Seattle, Washington.

Nowhere else are more of the world's culturally diverse people housed under one roof, so to speak, than in our own country. More than any other society, Americans have the opportunity to enjoy the full richness of cultural diversity — customs, traditions, values, and literature. Multicultural education brings that richness into the classroom, creating equal educational opportunities for students from different racial, ethnic, cultural and gender groups. The social studies classroom — where the story of people in time and place is told — provides the ideal setting to engage students in the practice of multicultural education in terms of (1) content issues; (2) process issues; (3) equity issues.

Content Issues

Content issues deal with the extent to which examples from a variety of cultures and groups are used to illustrate key concepts that are part of the social studies curriculum, such as culture, family, community, and nation. When families are studied, the examples in the textbook and other student materials can be extended by asking the students to prepare reports on the histories and cultures of their families. When preparing their reports, the students can interview their parents and other relatives. By asking the students to share the stories of their families, the teacher can highlight, dignify, and celebrate the diverse cultures and family experiences represented in the classroom, the school, or the community.

Process Issues

Process issues relate to the extent to which a multicultural approach is used — that is the extent to which students are helped to view concepts, issues, problems, and events from the points of view of ALL the groups involved: racial, ethnic, and gender. For example, in the study of United States history, students can be helped to view the westward movement from the point of view of the American Indian groups that were already living in the West as well as from the perspective of the European American settlers. By helping the students to view the westward movement from the perspectives of both groups, the teacher can help the students to develop a more accurate and compassionate understanding of the development of our nation.

Equity Issues

Equity issues relate to teaching and instructional strategies that facilitate the academic achievement of students

from diverse racial, ethnic, and cultural groups. While some researchers suggest that certain groups of students respond more positively when instruction is personalized, cooperative, and actively engaging, the reality is that the same strategies can help **ALL** students to increase their academic achievement and develop more interest in the social studies. Thus, implementing content issues, process issues, and equity issues in multicultural education is an effective strategy for making **ALL** students winners.

PEOPLE IN TIME AND PLACE
addresses content, process, and equity issues to provide a multicultural perspective.

- **Content rich in the story of ALL people in time and place** — their history, geography, social institutions, customs, religion, music, art, literature, government and so forth — enable students to appreciate cultural diversity among the earth's peoples

- **Visuals** such as fine arts reproductions, pictures of artifacts, and photographs of ethnic celebrations that integrate with the text help students recognize and appreciate the contributions of culturally diverse peoples

- **Pen Pals** provide an opportunity for students to learn about the lifestyles of children in other countries

- **Using Source Material** questions engage students in looking at the experiences of people in time and place from the viewpoints of those who actually had the experiences

- **Thinking About Literature** questions stimulate students to reflect on the experiences of men, women, and children of different racial, religious, and ethnic groups

- **Citizenship and American Values** features help students appreciate the cultural diversity of our nation's people by presenting American democracy in terms of its history, its procedures, and its ideals

- **Citizenship and American Values: You Decide** features provide students with an opportunity to examine both sides of an issue

- **Meeting Individual Needs** activities ensure that **ALL** students have an opportunity to learn difficult concepts

- **Cooperative Learning** activities in the student text and teacher edition provide opportunities for **ALL** students to experience increased self-esteem and growth in positive interdependence

- **Writing skills check** questions in the student text and **Writing to Learn** activities in the teacher edition provide opportunities that enable students to personalize social studies

- **Multidisciplinary Activity** features, **How To** projects and activities, and a wide variety of **Optional Activities** in the teacher edition actively engage **ALL** students in learning social studies

Multicultural
perspectives enable ALL students to identify with the story of people in time and place.

From *Living in Families*, pp. 18/19

for more MULTICULTURAL perspectives look for

- **Visuals with captions**
- **Literature excerpts and selections**

  and in the Teacher-to-Teacher Edition

- **Meeting Individual Needs**
- **Current Events**

PE●PLE
in Time and Place

We bring it all together

READING IN THE CONTENT AREAS

Key Before-Reading Strategies That Prepare Your Students for Success in Social Studies

Dr. James F. Baumann

"I think social studies is boring," says Miguel.
"And I never do well on the tests," admits Susie.

Chances are these students are struggling content-area readers — perhaps because they haven't recalled what they already know, don't see the point of what they're reading, or haven't gotten a handle on critical vocabulary. We can help turn things around for them; we can set the stage for reading success in social studies. How? By helping students learn some key before-reading strategies that will provide a rich backdrop against which the content information will make a lot more sense — and be much more enjoyable!

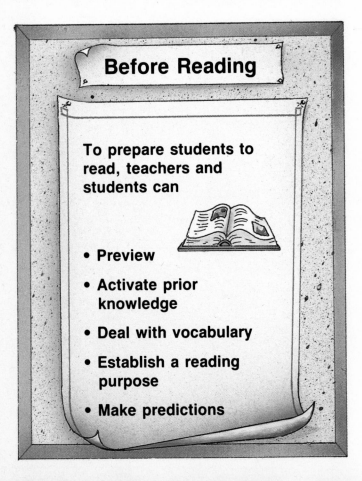

Before Reading

To prepare students to read, teachers and students can

- **Preview**
- **Activate prior knowledge**
- **Deal with vocabulary**
- **Establish a reading purpose**
- **Make predictions**

Five Before-Reading Strategies

Preview the Lesson

One nonthreatening before-reading strategy is previewing. You may help students preview by directing their attention to the lesson title and the boldfaced headings and subheadings. Then have students look at the graphic materials — the photographs, maps, charts, illustrations, and so forth — and have them read the accompanying caption questions. Previewing gives students an overall sense of what the lesson is about and provides a general context for the information they will be reading.

Activate Prior Knowledge

Another strategy for preparing students for reading is to help them activate their prior knowledge. One way to accomplish this is to ask questions that help students think about what they already know about the lesson topic. Activating prior knowledge enables students to link existing knowledge to new information. Having such a link provides students with a reference point for assimilating new material, thus adding greater meaning to the new content.

Deal with Vocabulary

Unlocking the meaning of unfamiliar specialized vocabulary terms is critical in preparing students to comprehend what they will be reading. Definitional, contextual, and associational activities provide sound ways to familiarize students with key new vocabulary terms. Helping students deal with key vocabulary terms prior to reading increases comprehension and motivation and decreases frustration and confusion.

Establish a Reading Purpose

Reading makes more sense when students know why they are reading — when their reading has purpose. You can involve students in setting the purpose for their reading or you can provide the reason for reading by providing a question for them to keep in mind.

Make Predictions

Having a stake in the reading increases student interest and motivation. Encouraging students to make predictions about the lesson content is one way to provide such a stake. You can help students make predictions by having them use section headings and visuals.

Is it necessary to use all the before-reading strategies every time my students read in the content areas?

Absolutely not! Based on the type of information being presented in a particular lesson, the overall purpose for reading the lesson, and the students' unique reading abilities and needs, you should select only the most appropriate before-reading strategies that will help your students become better content-area readers.

Dr. James F. Baumann, Professor and Head of the Department of Reading Education, College of Education, The University of Georgia, Athens, Georgia, is a former elementary teacher whose research on strategies that improve reading comprehension have helped classroom teachers teach reading in the content areas. Currently serving as editor of The Reading Teacher, *Dr. Baumann is the reading-language arts series consultant for* PEOPLE IN TIME AND PLACE.

PEOPLE IN TIME AND PLACE makes it easy to use before-reading strategies.

- **Carefully worded titles and headings** provide a sense of the lesson content, prompting students to preview and make predictions.

- **A variety of highly appealing visuals and caption questions,** and **Visual Thinking skill** questions provide a highly motivating way to get all students, particularly reluctant readers, to preview and make predictions.

- **Think About What You Know** questions and **Motivation** activities help students activate prior knowledge

- **Key new vocabulary words are thoroughly developed:** identified before each lesson, highlighted and defined in context the first time they appear in the lesson, defined in the **Glossary** and the **Picture Glossary,** extended through activities in the teacher edition, practiced on worksheets, and assessed in tests

- **Focus Your Reading** questions help students establish a reading purpose

Reading Strategies

build success in social studies for ALL students — right from the start of the lesson.

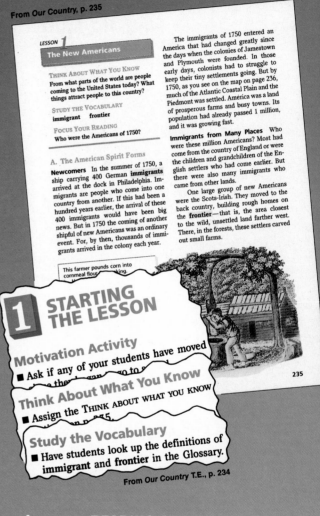

From Our Country, p. 235

From Our Country T.E., p. 234

for more READING STRATEGIES look for
- **Visuals with caption questions**
- **Skillbuilder**

  and in the Teacher-to-Teacher Edition
- **Thinking Critically**
- **Read and Think**

PE PLE
in Time and Place

We bring it all together

Sharpen Thinking Skills —

with

Graphic Organizers

Help ALL students visualize their thinking

Dr. James F. Baumann

Date: Election Day, 2020
Setting: Voting booths across America

The children currently sitting in your class are casting their votes, making decisions that will to a large extent shape American life in the upcoming years. Are they ready? Can they analyze the issues? Can they make accurate observations about the candidates, and summarize the stance of each? Do they know how to compare the platforms? Can they infer the probable effects of each plank?

As teachers of social studies, we can do a great deal to increase the likelihood that the answer to each of these questions is a resounding Yes, for social studies is the ideal arena for building the thinking skills that effective citizens need.

Getting the Big Picture

How do we teach youngsters to think clearly? A crucial step is to show them how to organize information, a prerequisite to making considered decisions. An easy way for children to get the hang of organizing ideas is to teach them to use graphic organizers. Graphic whats? Relax — they're really old friends: time lines, tables, and flowcharts are a few. *Graphic organizers* are simply visual displays that show relationships among ideas, conveying "the big picture." In addition, they allow users to see their thoughts unfolding in patterns as they construct them. Youngsters who learn to use graphic organizers become more aware of their own thinking processes, more metacognitive.

A Variety of Visuals

Specific types of graphic organizers facilitate particular kinds of thinking. For instance, wheels with spokes, as shown in the diagram that follows, help children make observations about things. In this case, on the spokes of each wheel students add observations about the colony indicated in the middle of the wheel.

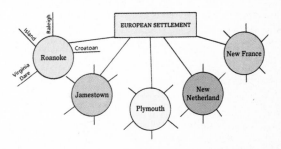

Branch diagrams assist children in selecting important ideas and analyzing the relationships among them. The graphic organizer shown below, for example, helps students process information about colonial life in the South.

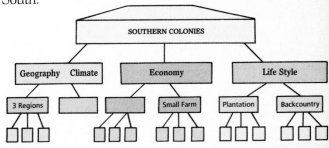

Geometric shapes connected with arrows work well for summarizing cause-and-effect relationships, while numbered boxes help youngsters sequence events. The diagram below combines both of these devices. An alternative graphic organizer for placing events in sequential order is the time line.

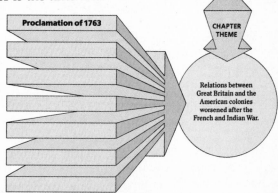

Active Learning, Enjoyable Teaching

As you can see, graphic organizers actively engage learners; children have to process information to complete

14

them. Most youngsters enjoy fitting ideas into "pictures." Further, the use of graphic devices is a real plus for youngsters with language difficulties because they call into play nonverbal, visual faculties.

Graphic organizers offer you plusses, too. As you circulate among children working with them, you can acquire insight about each child's thinking process and offer assistance as needed. What's more, these learning devices can stimulate discussion, enhance motivation, and increase interest in social studies, making the subject even more fun to teach.

Dr. James F. Baumann is an authority on instructional design options, including teaching techniques that use graphic organizers to help students assume greater responsibility for their learning. Professor and Head of the Department of Reading Education, College of Education, The University of Georgia, Athens, Georgia, Dr. Baumann is the reading-language arts series consultant for PEOPLE IN TIME AND PLACE.

PEOPLE IN TIME AND PLACE
helps to sharpen thinking skills.

- **Graphic organizers** in the chapter review section of the student text, on review masters, and in the optional activities section of the teacher edition help students visualize their thinking

- **Lesson review questions** engage students in recalling, analyzing, inferring, synthesizing, evaluating, and hypothesizing

- **Thinking skills check** questions at the end of the lesson provide opportunities for practicing thinking skills

- **Thinking Critically** questions at the end of the chapter activate higher-level thinking

- **Understanding Source Material** questions engage students in thinking critically about print and nonprint sources of information

- **Skillbuilders** motivate students to learn, practice, and apply thinking skills

- **Thinking About Literature** questions in the teacher edition help students articulate the social studies-literature connection by having students relate literary excerpts to social studies content

- **Citizenship and American Values: You Decide** features enables students to evaluate alternatives, weigh evidence, and make decisions

- **Five Themes of Geography** questions in the teacher edition help students draw conclusions about the world around them

- **Highly appealing graphics with caption questions** in the student text and **Visual Thinking Skills** questions in the teacher edition get students to analyze visuals

Thinking Skills

are sharpened when students use graphic organizers to help visualize their thinking.

From *Our Country*, p. 269

SUMMARIZING THE CHAPTER

On a separate sheet of paper, draw the graphic organizer shown here. Copy the information from this graphic organizer to the one you have drawn. Fill in the blank boxes with important events from the chapter that support the chapter theme. Put the events in the correct sequence. The first box has been filled in for you. Be prepared to explain why you chose the events you did.

Proclamation of 1763

CHAPTER THEME

Relations between Great Britain and the American colonies worsened after the French and Indian War.

Graphic Organizer

To help the students recognize the different community workers whose help they depend on every day, draw the graphic organizer on the chalkboard. Have the students name as many community workers as they can. Add their responses to the board.

From *Living in Communities* T.E., p. 105

for more THINKING SKILLS look for
- Thinking skills checks
- Citizenship and American Values: You Decide

and in the Teacher-to-Teacher Edition
- Thinking Critically
- Visual Thinking Skill

PE●PLE
in Time and Place

We bring it all together

Writing to Learn
Social Studies

A conversation with **Dr. Marian Davies Toth,** whose research on Writing to Learn and tireless efforts to bring improved writing instruction across the curriculum to **ALL** students have earned her national recognition as an educational leader and writing consultant.

❝Writing is a powerful tool for learning. . . . The social studies classroom provides a perfect time and place for exploring our world through an abundance of writing opportunities.❞
— Marian Davies Toth

Q: Traditionally we think of writing instruction as an English teacher's responsibility. What is the connection between writing and social studies?

A: Rather than teach writing, I suggest that social studies teachers **use** writing. Writing is a powerful tool for learning. It motivates thinking. The social studies classroom provides a perfect time and place for exploring our world through an abundance of writing opportunities. If writing is used in a nonthreatening way, the teacher and the students discover a dynamic strategy for personalizing learning and improving comprehension.

Q: Hasn't writing always been in the social studies curriculum?

A: True, we have always had "writing to show." Students read, memorize facts, and take a test to show their rote learning. There is a place for this kind of writing, but it is not the same as writing to learn. Here is the difference: Writing to learn is exploratory writing that helps students create their own "webs of learning."

Q: How does writing to learn work?

A: Let's look at it this way. Students gain fluency from writing frequently. Writing in social studies allows them to think abstractly. Writing forms a link between new material and known information. Compared to speaking, writing is a slow, deliberate process. As students write words and capture thoughts, they sustain their thinking over a period of time. The slower pace frees the mind to explore, relate, and connect. With writing, students shape their perceptions. This is why we see writing as a unique learning strategy.

Q: How may teachers best introduce writing to learn?

A: Writing to learn is an informal writing activity. A quick, effective way to make writing informal is to ask for students' opinions. Following a reading, give students opportunities to make choices and to write rapid answers to open-ended questions like these:

- What stood out for you?
- What surprised or impressed you?
- What did you learn that you did not know before?
- What would you have done if you had been in charge?
- What other decisions were possible?
- Does this event remind you of anything similar today?
- How will this information affect your own life?
- Why did these people make the decision they chose?

Here are some small exploratory writing activities from Dr. Marian Davies Toth that focus upon the Christopher Columbus story.

Question Generation

Students create their own questions and use those questions in a discussion with a partner or in a whole class discussion.

① Why didn't Columbus take more ships and more supplies with him?

② I would like to know why Christopher Columbus was not afraid of falling off the end of the world as he knew it?

Free Write

Students write as fast as they can without worrying about spelling, punctuation, or grammar. The idea is to get words down quickly and make thinking visible. Students may use a Free Write as they respond to open-ended questions or a teacher-directed inquiry.

Wow! Christopher Columbus was such a brave man! I imagine sailing all alone to places uncharted in

The Journal Log

The journal log is a blank notebook or a separate section of a three-ring binder. It is a place for students to record their own ideas regarding the content in a social studies class. It takes from three to

Q: How does a writing activity like this help students learn social studies?

A: What I have observed is that students tend to become more independent learners. The questions encourage students to explore alternative interpretations of the historical story. Students see history in a different way — no longer simply as an account of what happened. When we imagine what might have happened if a different decision had been made, a subject has more relevance. We want students to have choices and freedom to express their own ideas in a non-intimidating environment. Another important consideration is this: We want to encourage students to contribute to their own learning.

Q: It's possible students will become more sensitive decision makers, too, don't you think?

A: Yes, that is true. Writing in itself is a decision-making activity when we allow students to choose topics and to decide what to include and what to exclude in the development of those topics.

Q: How do you grade "writing to learns"?

A: Usually teachers do not grade the writing to learns. They see this informal writing as an idea-generating activity. Writing to learn enhances personal learning and serves as a cognitive rehearsal for discussion. Also, it may become a beginning exploration for more demanding writing projects.

Q: What would you say are some of the most important benefits of writing to learn as a teaching strategy?

A: Research from cognitive psychology has taught us that all writing, even unfinished writing makes learning an active experience. Writing is thinking. Writing is learning. Writing is growing. I hope all social studies teachers will use it as a teaching strategy.

seven minutes of class time each day. Students write their spontaneous responses to a lesson, a lecture, or a class activity.

> *Today our class produced a Christopher Columbus play for the third grade. It was wonderful! I liked the sounds of the waves splashing and the realistic*

The "I Was There" Diary

Students imagine themselves to be a part of an historical event and record what happened by using the voice of a participant. In this way, students are better able to personalize history.

> *There I was standing on the hill with a wild turkey in one hand and a bow in the other when all of a sudden three ships*

Writing

helps personalize learning about people in time and place for ALL students.

From *Living in Families*, p. 124

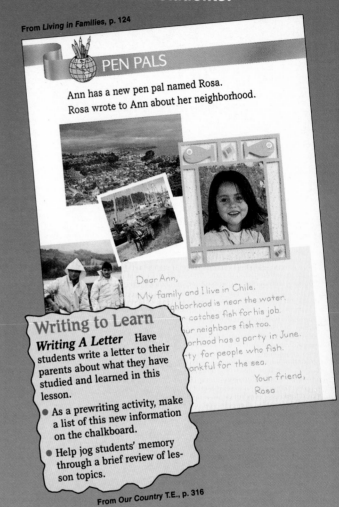

PEN PALS

Ann has a new pen pal named Rosa.
Rosa wrote to Ann about her neighborhood.

Dear Ann,
My family and I live in Chile.
...ghborhood is near the water.
...n catches fish for his job.
...ur neighbors fish too.
...orhood has a party in June.
...ty for people who fish.
...ankful for the sea.
Your friend,
Rosa

Writing to Learn

Writing A Letter Have students write a letter to their parents about what they have studied and learned in this lesson.

- As a prewriting activity, make a list of this new information on the chalkboard.
- Help jog students' memory through a brief review of lesson topics.

From *Our Country* T.E., p. 316

for more WRITING look for
- **Writing skills checks**
- **Skillbuilder**

and in the Teacher-to-Teacher Edition
- **Curriculum Connection**
- **Multidisciplinary Activity**

PE●PLE
in Time and Place

We bring it all together

Social Studies and LITERATURE: Powerful Partners

Incorporating appropriate selections of top-quality literature right into the social studies text can shed light on content and motivate students to a greater understanding and appreciation of literature.

Dr. Ben Smith, Dr. Jesse Palmer, and Dr. John C. Davis

As Carlos reached the end of the selection about New Amsterdam's leader, he raised his voice for emphasis.

'This New World is a mess!' Peter cried in distress. 'These animals need gates and fences. Take these birds to a cage!' Peter shouted in rage. 'Oh, good Dutchmen, let's come to our senses.'

Lively discussion followed. "Wow, I thought only *our* world was a mess," said Angela.

"Even three hundred years ago there was too much traffic — but too many animals instead of cars!" Carlos exclaimed. "No wonder they needed laws then, too!"

Through a selection from Arnold Lobel's *On the Day Peter Stuyvesant Sailed into Town,* these children have entered life in New Amsterdam, mid-1600s. The adjacent lively writing in their social studies textbook provides historical background and details, such as how Stuyvesant's bossiness led to the creation of the town's first government.

Literature Supports History as a Well-Told Story

Excerpts from top-quality literature *about* historical periods, such as Lobel's book, help students to identify with the emotions of others, to step into the shoes of people in time and place. Likewise, when literary excerpts *of* historical periods — such as quotes from **diaries** of pioneer women, **speeches** like Patrick Henry's, **letters** from Abagail Adams — are woven right into the text, it's as if people who actually lived in the past have stepped into your classroom to give students eyewitness views of events.

Literature Illuminates the Human Dimension of Social Studies

Relevant excerpts and selections, representing a wide range of literary genres and periods, encourage students to appreciate the diversity of humankind — the ordinary and the extraordinary, children and adults, representing many different cultures. Tales from the *Arabian Nights* and *The Anansi Tales,* for example, help provide multicultural perspectives. Literary works like *The Little Prince* provide students with an appreciation for the richness of geographic diversity.

Other Ways Social Studies and Literature Work Together

Just as literature stimulates interest in social studies content, prior knowledge of social studies content — of people, time, and place — increases students' understanding and appreciation of historical fiction, poetry, drama, myths, legends, fables, biography, and so on. For example, knowing about the history and geography of colonial New Amsterdam before reading *On the Day Peter Stuyvesant Sailed into Town* enabled the children to take greater delight, to be more actively engaged in reading and understanding the story.

Relating these two subjects can also encourage students to think critically. For instance, students will make comparisons, distinguish fact from fiction, and draw conclusions when they contrast an excerpt of a literary work — like Longfellow's "Paul Revere's Ride" — with historical accounts from their textbook.

In these and other ways, literary selections work for all grade levels, generating high interest in the fascinating world of people in time and place through the partnership of social studies and literature.

Dr. Ben A. Smith is Assistant Professor of Social Studies Education at Kansas State University, Manhattan, Kansas. Dr. John C. Davis is Professor of Elementary Education, University of Southern Mississippi, Hattiesburg, Mississippi. Dr. Jesse Palmer is Assistant Professor of Curriculum and Instruction, University of Southern Mississippi, Hattiesburg, Mississippi. Drs. Smith, Davis, and Palmer, all former classroom teachers, have collaborated on journal articles about the social studies-children's literature connection. They serve as the literature consultants for PEOPLE IN TIME AND PLACE.

PEOPLE IN TIME AND PLACE incorporates classic and contemporary literature to shed light on social studies content.

- **Short excerpts** from diaries, essays, poems, speeches, and other literary works, woven right into the text, provide quotes by and about historical people, places, and events

- **Read-Alouds** in Grades 1 and 2 and **Literature Selections** in Grades 3 through 7 provide longer literary excerpts that spark students' interest in learning about social studies and literature

- **Thinking About Literature** questions in the teacher edition help students articulate the social studies-literature connection by involving students in relating literary excerpts to social studies content

- **Annotated Bibliographies** in the teacher edition provide convenient references to literature for students and teachers

- **Multidisciplinary Activity** features and **Curriculum Connection** activities in the teacher edition provide a wide variety of ideas for involving students in extending the social studies-literature connection

---

Literature

illuminates the story of people in time and place for ALL students.

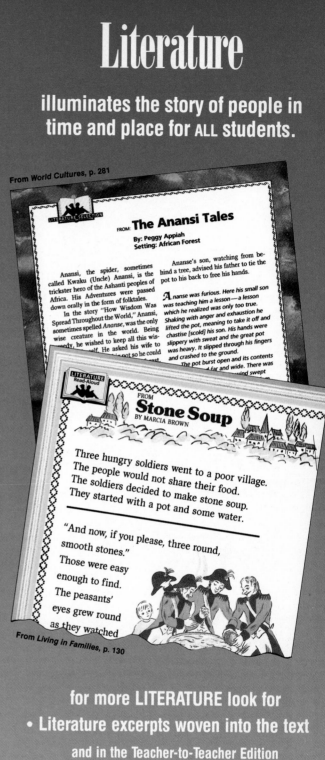

From World Cultures, p. 281

From Living in Families, p. 130

for more LITERATURE look for

- Literature excerpts woven into the text

  and in the Teacher-to-Teacher Edition

- **Thinking About Literature**
- **Annotated Bibliography**
- **Curriculum Connection**

PE PLE
in Time and Place

We bring it all together

Cooperative Learning & Social Studies: A Natural Combination

Here's how you can begin putting it to work in your social studies classroom

WANTED:

Proven teaching technique that will increase student learning, develop thinking skills, improve self-esteem, and offer opportunities to practice social skills. Must fit into busy social studies classroom routine and help to prepare students for a lifetime of active citizenship. Techniques that require extensive teacher training, cumbersome recordkeeping, and hours of planning time need not apply.

Research, as well as classroom experience, shows that cooperative learning is right for the job!

What is cooperative learning?

Cooperative learning is a technique through which small groups of two to six students of different levels of ability work together to learn or to review concepts. As a teaching technique, cooperative learning is uniquely effective when the learning tasks are open-ended and require problem solving and decision making. But if you've never used cooperative learning, beginning with simpler, more specific assignments gives you and your students a chance to grow in comfort level, familiarity, and skill.

How might you lay the foundation for a simple first-time cooperative learning lesson?

First, you might present a social studies lesson, using teacher-directed instruction. Next, you would lead a discussion of a social skill (perhaps the importance of one person talking at a time), letting students know that practicing this skill will be one of the objectives of the cooperative learning activity. With the social skill objective in place, you would then set the academic objective (perhaps that each group will demonstrate understanding of the content by answering one or more lesson review questions). Although you introduce the social skill and academic objectives separately, the groups work on both simultaneously.

How does the group work get started?

Once this foundation for the cooperative learning activity is completed, students join teacher– or student–selected groups, of two to six students. Having different levels of ability in each group facilitates learning and positive interdependence. Once the groups are selected, each group member is assigned an individual objective to help the group achieve its goal. That objective may relate to a specific part of the group's learning task (each member will be assigned a different question and share with the group his or her answer to that question),

or it may relate to the entire task (each group member will answer and share his or her answers to all the group's questions). In either case, all the members of a group participate to help their group achieve both its individual and group objectives.

You might then write on the chalkboard the heading "Remember to talk about" key vocabulary and list under it words, names, places and events to help guide the cooperative learning groups' work. No special furniture is needed, but group members should be able to see their work and hear each other when they talk quietly.

What is your role while the groups are working cooperatively?

As each group works together, you should circulate among the groups, recognizing when the social objective is being met (only one person is talking at a time) and facilitating the progress of a group toward mastery of the academic objective (demonstrate understanding of the content by answering the review questions). When a group needs your help, it can signal you by using two cups — one blue and one red — that have been taped together, bottom to bottom. When the blue cup is up, the group is proceeding independently; when the red cup is up, your help is needed.

What happens when the group work is completed?

Cooperative learning group work usually culminates in class discussion; each group shares its work and tells how well it used the social skill that was selected before the group work began. Each student usually demonstrates his or her individual learning as well. The vehicle might be a quiz in which each student answers one or more review questions. A bonus (perhaps having no written homework) given to the groups in which every member reaches a preset score (perhaps 80%) on the quiz reinforces positive interdependence.

What are the benefits of cooperative learning in the social studies classroom?

While cooperative learning is now enthusiastically used in all areas of the curriculum, it's a natural in social studies, where working interdependently teaches many social participation skills necessary for full and informed citizenship. Cooperative learning further supports citizenship by increasing retention of social studies information, promoting critical thinking, and increasing the self-esteem of ALL students.

Once you and your students gain facility in using cooperative learning, you will find that it lends itself to cross-curriculum activities, such as making a diorama (art) or reenacting a play (language arts). Cooperative learning also facilitates multidisciplinary activities, where the learning groups each explore a different content area tie-in simultaneously. Using cooperative learning in conjunction with cross-curriculum or multidisciplinary activities helps increase student motivation, while maximizing teaching time spent on social studies.

PEOPLE IN TIME AND PLACE
puts cooperative learning to work in your classroom.

- **Cooperative Learning** activities enable all students to practice social participation skills, think critically, experience positive interdependence, and grow in self-esteem

- A wide variety of **How To** projects and activities in the teacher edition allow you to vary your teaching approaches while sparking student motivation and increasing student retention

- **Multidisciplinary Activity** features in the teacher edition help you maximize teaching time spent on social studies through a rich menu of cooperative learning options that actively engage students in making connections between social studies and other curriculum areas

---

Cooperative Learning

increases interpersonal skills and self-esteem when ALL students work together to share discoveries.

From *Comparing Communities*, p. 317

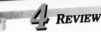

4 REVIEW

COOPERATIVE LEARNING

In this unit you learned about the past and present in several cities. In this activity you will work with four other classmates to make an exciting board game about the past and present in your own community. The object of the game will be to reach the square marked FUTURE by answering questions correctly.

REMEMBER TO:
- Give your ideas.
- Listen to other's ideas.
- Plan your work with the group.
- Present your project.
- Discuss how your group worked.

PROJECT
- With your group, choose a name for the board game.
- Two people should make question-and-answer cards about the past and present in your community. One side of an index card should have a question. The other side should have an answer. Below the answer, write *1, 2,* or *3* for the number of moves around the game board a correct answer is worth.
- Two people should make a game board of heavy posterboard or cardboard with colored squares drawn around the board. They should label the squares with names of special places in your community.
- One person should make game pieces that can be moved along the game board.

PRESENTATION AND REVIEW
- One person will explain your game.

Cooperative Learning

Plan a Community Divide the class into groups. Tell each group to pretend that they are going to form a new community. Ask them to decide the type of community they want and the kinds of things they will have in their community. Have each group report its decisions to the class.

From *Living in Communities* T.E., p. 51

---

for more COOPERATIVE LEARNING look for

- **Curriculum tie-ins**

and in the Teacher-to-Teacher Edition

- **Curriculum Connection**
- **How To**
- **Multidisciplinary Activity**

PE PLE
in Time and Place

We bring it all together

"Look sharp, sailor," says Captain Alex. "Do you see anything? We must be near now!"

"No, sir," answers Sailor Chris. "Not a thing. Maybe we've gone too far. Maybe we should turn back before it's too late."

"Nonsense," responds the captain. "I know we're near."

"Wait, Captain," breaks in First Mate Jesse. "Look over there. Land! Land ho!"

The captain seemed sure, though the sailors may have had their doubts — perhaps a typical situation in fifteenth- or sixteenth-century voyages of exploration. But in this case the explorers are twentieth-century elementary school children taking part in a role-playing activity.

Why are activities now playing such a vital role in social studies education?

For years, educators have acknowledged that social studies is one of the most important and relevant subjects taught in any classroom. Social studies is, after all, the study of people. Yet many of today's students reject the study of social studies as being too boring. What can be done to bring out the human interest in social studies? There is no single answer, of course. But one action that can help is to include a wide range of "hands-on/minds-on" activities in social studies instruction.

Activities provide the motivation and the direct experience essential to the development of concepts.

Compare, for instance, the prospect of memorizing state and country shapes with the prospect of participating in a classroom quiz show. Both teaching vehicles cover the same objective, but which promotes more student interest and understanding?

. . . What about learning latitude and longitude? Compare learning these concepts from a lecture with learning them through an activity that turns the entire classroom into a latitude and longitude game board!

. . . Consider the differences between reading about a historical debate and actively participating in one right in the classroom.

Activities bring vitality and variety to social studies.

Activities can be used to introduce, reinforce, or reteach concepts. They offer exciting alternative approaches and refreshing changes of pace. Activities can accommodate the learning styles of **ALL** students.

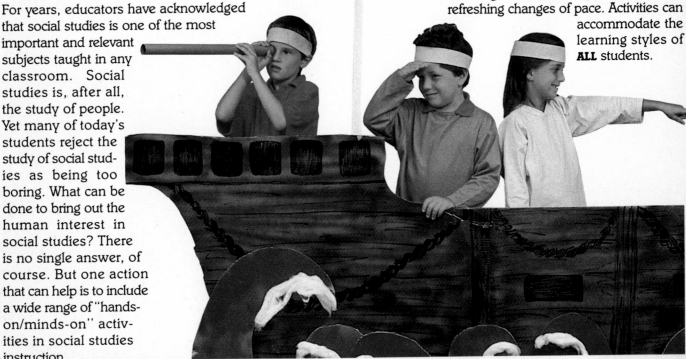

Multidisciplinary activities bring subject areas together.

There is no better way to help students see connections between social studies and other subjects they are learning than by doing activities that bring social studies together with math, language arts, science, art, and so forth. At the same time, such activities work toward our ultimate goal — helping students become active and informed citizens.

PEOPLE IN TIME AND PLACE gets students actively involved in "hands-on/minds-on" social studies.

- **Think About What You Know** activities help students connect prior knowledge with new learning

- **Curriculum tie-ins** help students integrate what they learn in social studies with what they learn in other subjects

- **Cooperative Learning** activities foster positive interdependence

- **Putting It All Together** chapter review activities, including graphic organizers, encourage thinking critically

- **Teacher-to-Teacher Edition** activities complement individual teaching and learning styles
  - **Meeting Individual Needs** activities provide alternative ways of helping students learn difficult concepts
  - **Motivation** activities help to tap prior knowledge
  - **Vocabulary** activities help to prepare students for reading
  - **Reteaching the Main Objective** activities offer alternatives for enhancing student understanding
  - **Current Events** activities increase student interest in history-in-the-making
  - **Multidisciplinary Activity** features bring basal subjects together, enhancing understanding
  - **How To** conduct projects and activities offer teachers easy-to-follow guidelines
  - **Optional Activities** involve students in role-playing, writing to learn, working with maps, interviewing, making curriculum connections, and skillbuilding

Activities
bring alive the story of people in time and place with "hands-on/ minds-on" experiences for ALL students.

From *Living in Families*, p. 185

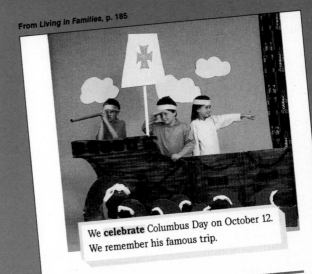

We **celebrate** Columbus Day on October 12. We remember his famous trip.

Lesson 1 —————— Review

Role-Playing
- Have the students pretend to be Christopher Columbus and his crew. Prepare a large piece of cardboard for a boat and make a flag.
- Have the students discuss how the crew prepared the ship for the trip. Have them role-play loading the ship.
- Then have the students imagine how it felt to leave the port, to sail on calm seas, to sail on rough seas, to be desperate to find land, and to find land.

From *Living in Families* T.E., p. 184

for more ACTIVITIES look for
- **Curriculum tie-ins**

  and in the Teacher-to-Teacher Edition
- **Meeting Individual Needs**
- **How To**
- **Multidisciplinary Activity**

PE●PLE in Time and Place

We bring it all together

Susan Grassmyer, Gr. 1

Janet Hogan, Gr. 1

Hazel Tseng Hsieh, Gr. 1

Charleen Kaaen, Gr. 1

Margaret Ricciardi, Gr. 1

Susan Barnes, Gr. 2

Gail Finger, Gr. 6/7

Linda Lucas, Gr. 6/7

Carol Gemmell, Gr. 6/7

Pamela Argo, Gr. 6/7

Eileen Lewis, Gr. 6/7

Teacher Tips for Successful Pacing

Making the most of time spent teaching social studies

Teacher-to-Teacher Edition Authors

PEOPLE IN TIME AND PLACE *proudly presents the teachers from across our nation who have been instrumental in bringing together everything you need to teach social studies to* **ALL** *students.*

We acknowledge the enthusiasm, conviction, and commitment they have displayed while participating in every stage of the development of this program, from critiquing every page of student text to authoring the Teacher-to-Teacher Edition.

We asked our Teacher-to-Teacher Edition authors to respond to the perennial question we are asked by elementary teachers: **Given everything that I have to teach, how can I realistically pace social studies instruction?**

We have collected their answers, based on insights gained from years of teaching experience. In summary, their suggestions fall into three categories: Be selective; Be flexible; Be good to yourself. We are pleased to share them.

Be selective.

One recurring recommendation is to be selective about the material that you teach. "A good starting point is your district's curriculum guide. Once you know what must be taught, you can look toward the textbook as one instructional tool at your disposal for meeting local goals and the needs of your students."

As you plan to use the textbook, don't feel that you have to "drag your students through the book, page by page, cover to cover," advises Susan Grassmyer.

Rather, use the textbook as "a resource that offers a smorgasbord of content and teaching ideas," adds Aldona Skrypa.

In deciding **what** to teach from the textbook, **with what emphasis,** and **when,** you may capitalize on timeliness to increase student interest. One way to do this is to "tie into the calendar," coordinating content with holidays, as Joyce Kemp does when she teaches patriotism in conjunction with Presidents' Day, or when she teaches the textbook material about American Indians' lifestyles, around Thanksgiving Day.

Another way to capitalize on timeliness is to use what's happening on the local, national, and international scene as a springboard into the text. Thus, in presidential election years, Marianne Geiger emphasizes chapters dealing with significant presidential elections.

Finally, although **you** are the professional decision maker, consider letting students participate in the content selection process by having them scan the table of contents at the start of the year. Don Smail suggests surveying students to find out what they're most interested in learning and then using that information as you prioritize content.

Susan Colford, Gr. 6/7

Sheila Allen, Gr. 6/7

Edward Graivier, Gr. 6/7

Lisa Johnson, Gr. 6/7

Don Smail, Gr. 6/7

Sharon Shelley, Gr. 6/7

Rhonda Allen, Gr. 2

Joyce Kemp, Gr. 2

Hortense Ward, Gr. 2

Mary Bosser Joyce, Gr. 3

Suzanne Peirsel, Gr. 3

Alfred Velasquez, Gr. 3

Be flexible.

One common thread in the suggestions about flexibility is "Don't feel that you are locked into presenting all social studies content in the same way." "Whatever you do, make sure you have a lot of student involvement," is the other.

Helping students become strategic readers in content-area materials is the key to flexibility for many teachers like Lisa Johnson, who feels that students' ability to read and acquire knowledge independently "opens the potential for a variety of instructional approaches."

One shared-learning alternative approach is cooperative learning. Rather than have the entire class reading the same lesson, let students take "group responsibility" for learning and sharing information, explains Mary Taylor, who believes it is important for students "to play an active role in the teaching/learning process." In this way, too, students who are more successful strategic readers can help those who are less successful.

Other alternative approaches include the use of "hands-on/minds-on" activities. Teachers like Beverley Wong Woo and Aldona Skrypa strongly advocate the use of unit multidisciplinary activities as a "time efficient" way to "tie into other subjects," while giving students an opportunity to use higher level thinking skills, such as synthesizing.

For other reading variations, students can learn the information from selected lessons or chapters by reading "just for pleasure," skimming, scanning, note-taking, or outlining.

Vardreane Elliot, Gr. 3

Beverley Wong Woo, Gr. 3

Be good to yourself.

Being "the jack-of-all-trades of the educational field," as Ed Graivier terms it, can make elementary teachers feel insecure about their expertise in social studies and other subject areas. Acknowledging that pressure, as well as the pressure that comes from feeling overwhelmed by the amount of material to be taught in the time allotted, our teacher authors offer this advice: "Be good to yourself."

"Be selective . . . relax and enjoy what you are teaching," says Eileen Lewis. "No one can do everything."

"Use community-parent resources. Invite guest speakers from different ethnic backgrounds. Bring in hands-on materials. Make social studies come alive in your classroom. Let your students enjoy what they are learning and let yourself enjoy teaching it!" Beverley Wong Woo advises.

"Have fun," says Alfred Velasquez. "By keeping track of what worked and what didn't, you'll have a head start on next year."

"Most important of all, teach from the heart," says Susan Grassmyer.

The final word is Marianne Geiger's. After hearing all the recommendations about "not covering the textbook," about "skipping around," about "picking and choosing," Marianne was concerned that first-year teachers might be getting the wrong message as they struggle for the first time with an entire primary curriculum. Here's her be-good-to-yourself advice: "Don't worry. You can save your social studies creativity for the second year of teaching. For the first year, you can trust Silver Burdett & Ginn. You can feel good about 'plowing ahead' in the student text and teacher edition."

Aldona Skrypa, Gr. 4

Gloria Ebbe, Gr. 4

Carolyn Hopp, Gr. 4

Joseph McGrath, Gr. 6/7

Mary Taylor, Gr. 5

Mary Jo Paniello, Gr. 5

Marianne Geiger, Gr. 5

Joan Atkinson, Gr. 5

Margaret Love, Gr. 4

Teacher-to-Teacher Edition

1 STARTING THE LESSON

- Identifies the main (★ starred) objective and other objectives

    (Optional activities for ★ Reteaching the Main Objective are found at the end of the lesson.)

- Provides a variety of before-reading activities that involves **ALL** students in

    - activating prior knowledge
    - studying vocabulary
    - establishing a reading purpose

LESSON **3**   PAGES 310–316

The New Government Begins

Objectives

★1. **Analyze** the problems the new government faced and how it coped with them.

2. **Identify** the following people and places: *John Adams, Abigail Adams, Washington, D.C.,* and *New York City.*

1 STARTING THE LESSON

Motivation Activity

- Before students learn about the specifics of our Bill of Rights, have them imagine what their life would be like without it.
- Ask them to imagine gathering to talk to friends outside the school, but being in danger of being fined.
- Question students as to whether they have ever complained about homework or a school policy. Tell them that without the Bill of Rights they might be arrested for such comments.

Think About What You Know

- Assign the THINK ABOUT WHAT YOU KNOW activity on p. 310.
- George Bush; answers should include the national debt, concerns over the environment, drugs, or world peace.

Study the Vocabulary

- Have students create their own word-search puzzle from the new vocabulary terms on this page. Definitions or clues should be given to help find the words in the puzzle.
- Then have students exchange papers and solve each other's puzzles.

310

LESSON **3**

The New Government

THINK ABOUT WHAT YOU KNOW
Who is the President of the United States? What are some problems that the President is trying to solve today?

STUDY THE VOCABULARY
inauguration   Cabinet
Bill of Rights   political party

FOCUS YOUR READING
How did the new government begin its work?

A. The Great Experiment Begins

On receiving the news of his election to the Presidency, George Washington climbed into his coach and left for New York City, the temporary capital of the United States, where his **inauguration** would be held. An inauguration is a ceremony to put someone into a government office. With him rode the hopes of the American people. As Washington's coach moved from one town to the next, crowds cheered their new President.

Finally on April 30, 1789, George Washington stood before thousands of fellow citizens in New York City. Placing his hand on a Bible, he promised to "preserve, protect, and defend the Constitution of the United States."

Soon after, Congress met and quickly acted to keep a promise. James Madison of Virginia wrote a number of amendments to the Constitution to protect the rights of the people. In 1791, ten of these amendments were ratified and added to the Constitution. They are known as the **Bill of Rights**. These rights were much the same as those listed in the different state constitutions.

George Washington is being rowed across New York Bay to prepare for his inauguration in New York City. Ships welcome him with a roar of cannons.
▶ What are the sailors on the left doing?

National Gallery of Art, Washington, D.C. Gift of Edgar William and Bernice Chrysler Garbisch

Making Comparisons

- Students may want to look in an encyclopedia to find out about how the President of the United States is guarded today. During George Washington's term, he took a three-month trip to visit the South. Very few people accompanied him, and he slept in inns along the way.
- Have students compare and contrast the presidency today to the presidency during Washington's time.
- Write the following headings on the chalkboard: *Alike* and *Different.* In a vertical column, write *Today* and *Yesterday.*
- Have students work together to complete the chart.

Optional Activities

Optional Activities

Here you will find an exciting menu of optional activities for all lessons, including:

- ## Graphic Organizers
- ## For Your Information
- ## Skillbuilder Review
- ## Cooperative Learning

A Teacher Edition Written *for* Teachers *by* Teachers

Uniquely *practical* and *professional*, built on years of classroom experience. Everything you need to teach social studies easily and effectively, right at your fingertips . . . starting with a 3-step basic lesson plan and lesson-extending optional activities.

WASHINGTON'S FIRST CABINET

Office	Official	Duties
Secretary of State	Thomas Jefferson	To conduct the relations of the United States with other nations
Secretary of the Treasury	Alexander Hamilton	To handle the government's finances
Secretary of War	Henry Knox	To take charge of all military matters
Attorney General	Edmund Randolph	To act as chief legal adviser to the executive branch
Postmaster General	Samuel Osgood	To run the post office and mail service

The office of Postmaster General did not become a Cabinet department until 1829.
▶ Which cabinet position do you think is the most important one?

The Bill of Rights protects such important personal freedoms as freedom of speech, freedom of worship, and freedom of the press.

Congress also created several departments to help the President. The State Department deals with foreign countries. The Treasury Department collects taxes, pays bills, and takes care of the government's money. The War Department was in charge of the country's defense.

The head of each department was called a *secretary*. President Washington often called upon these secretaries for advice. When the President met with his advisers, the group was called the **Cabinet.**

B. Disagreements Lead to Political Parties

President Washington chose Thomas Jefferson to head the State Department. He chose Alexander Hamilton to be the first secretary of the treasury. Jefferson and Hamilton were two of the ablest people ever to serve in government. But they disagreed on almost everything. At times, President Washington felt as though he

were driving a coach with horses pulling in opposite directions.

Hamilton wanted to encourage manufacturing to grow. He hoped the United States would soon have many large cities. He also favored an even stronger central government than the one that the new Constitution created.

Jefferson agreed that the country needed some manufacturing and trade. However, Jefferson did not want to see large cities grow. He wanted the United States to remain a nation of small farmers. As for the government itself, Jefferson wanted to keep it as small as possible.

The many disagreements between Hamilton and Jefferson led to the birth of **political parties**. A political party is a group of people who hold certain beliefs about how the government should be run and what it should do. These people join together to elect people who share their beliefs. In the 1790s, those Americans who favored Hamilton and his ideas were called *Federalists*. Supporters of Thomas Jefferson called themselves *Democratic-Republicans*.

311

---

2 DEVELOPING THE LESSON

Read and Think

Sections A and B

In order for students to comprehend the beginning of the Bill of Rights and the beginning of political parties, ask these questions:

1. **What types of freedoms are protected in the Bill of Rights?**
   (Freedom of speech, freedom of worship, and freedom of the press *pp. 310-311*)

2. **What were some of the beliefs held by Jefferson and Hamilton?**
   (Hamilton wanted to encourage manufacturing, the growth of large cities, and a strong central government; Jefferson did not want to see the growth of large cities, and favored small government and a nation of small farmers. *p. 311*)

Thinking Critically **How, do you think, would our lives be different without the freedom of speech?** (Analyze)
(Answers may include that we would have to be careful about what we said, we could be punished for saying certain things, and we would feel less free. *p. 311*)

Answers to Caption Questions
p. 310 ▶ Saluting or waving
p. 311 ▶ Answers should reflect independent thinking.

Identifying Areas of Responsibility

● Assist students in remembering the responsibilities of each of the departments created to help the President of the United States.

● Create a *Concentration*-style game on index cards, writing the name of each of the departments on one set of cards, and their responsibilities on another set.

● Number the cards on the back and tape them, in random order, to the chalkboard, number-side up.

● As students call two numbers, turn over the corresponding cards, looking for a match. Return any unmatched guesses to their original position.

Curriculum Connection

Art Have students make a bulletin-board display of the President's Cabinet.

● Have students find and display the names of the departments in the Cabinet today. (State, Treasury, Justice, Defense, Interior, Agriculture, Commerce, Labor, Education, Health and Human Services, Housing and Urban Development, Transportation, and Energy departments.)

● Have students find and identify newspaper pictures of each cabinet member.

● Then have them design pictures to illustrate each cabinet member's job, or symbols for each department.

311

Optional Activities

---

2 DEVELOPING THE LESSON

■ **Read and Think** questions, keyed to textbook sections, aid student comprehension through

- reading
- discussing
- thinking critically

■ Other lesson development features (shown on page 29) involve **ALL** students in

- reading and thinking about literature
- understanding difficult concepts by meeting their individual needs
- sharpening visual thinking skills
- building geography literacy

Optional Activities

- **Writing to Learn**
- **Current Events**
- **Curriculum Connection**
- **Reteaching Main Objective**

...and more

3 CLOSING THE LESSON

- ■ Provides answers to textbook questions to help you check students' comprehension

  - • Review questions
    (Annotations on the student text page indicates the thinking skill called for: recall, analyze, infer, synthesize, evaluate, hypothesize)
  - • Skills check questions
  - • Lesson focus question

- ■ Suggestions for additional practice help meet the needs of **ALL** students

  - • Lesson review master
  - • Workbook

---

3 CLOSING THE LESSON

Lesson 3 Review

Answers to Think and Write
A. The Bill of Rights, ratified in 1791, is a set of ten amendments to our Constitution designed to protect the rights of our people.
B. Many disagreements between Jefferson and Hamilton led to the birth of political parties. Those who favored Hamilton's views became Federalists, and supporters of Jefferson were called Democratic-Republicans.
C. The new government faced the problems of debt from the war, the Whiskey Rebellion (resulting from farmers' anger about taxes), and trouble with British seizure of American ships.
D. A decision John Adams faced was whether or not to avoid war with Britain because our country was not ready.
E. Maryland and Virginia each gave up some land for the District of Columbia.

Answer to Skills Check
Answers should reflect independent thinking.

Focus Your Reading
Ask the lesson focus question found at the beginning of the lesson: How did the new government begin its work?
(Congress met soon after Washington's inauguration. It ratified the Bill of Rights and created the State, War, and Treasury Departments to help the President. The new government had to deal with debt and angry farmers in the Whiskey Rebellion. There was trouble with British seizure of United States ships, but Washington and Adams avoided war.)

Additional Practice
You may wish to assign the ancillary materials listed below.
Understanding the Lesson p. 92
Workbook p. 83

— Answers to Caption Questions —
p. 316 ▶ No room had been completely finished, there was no firewood, the main stairway was unfinished, and there was no water.

316

James Hoban won $500 in a design contest for a plan for the President's house. His plan was used in building the White House.
▶ Name some new-house problems Mrs. Adams had.

Abigail Adams

The White House The President's Palace, later called the White House, was the first building ready for use. President Adams and his family were the first to live in it. When the Adamses arrived, not a single room had been completely finished. The plaster walls were still damp. There were fireplaces in each room to take the chill off the house, but no arrangement had been made to supply the house with firewood. The main stairway to the second floor was not finished. The President's wife, Abigail Adams, even used one of the unfinished rooms for hanging the family wash to dry. Servants carried water from a distance of five city blocks.

Still, Abigail Adams had a sense of history. She knew how far the young republic had already come. Like the new nation itself, the President's Palace was unfinished. Its rough edges would need smoothing out. In time the new house, like the new nation, would become great. "This House is built for ages to come," Abigail Adams wrote to her sister. And so it was.

LESSON 3 REVIEW

THINK AND WRITE
A. What is the Bill of Rights? (Recall)
B. How did political parties begin in the United States? (Synthesize)
C. What were some problems that the new government faced? (Analyze)
D. What was one major decision that John Adams made as President? (Infer)
E. How was the District of Columbia created? (Recall)

SKILLS CHECK
WRITING SKILL
Read the section on the Bill of Rights on pages 310–311. Select one of the rights listed. Write a paragraph telling why you think that right is important.

316

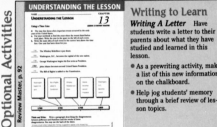

Writing to Learn

Writing A Letter Have students write a letter to their parents about what they have studied and learned in this lesson.

- ● As a prewriting activity, make a list of this new information on the chalkboard.
- ● Help jog students' memory through a brief review of lesson topics.

Optional Activities
Review Master, p. 92

Optional Activities

Review Master, p. 92

Here you will find:

- • Reduced lesson review master

Developing the Lesson Features

involve ALL students in...

reading and thinking about literature

Thinking About Literature

Use the information below to help students better understand the literature selection found on p. 266.

Selection Summary
The British soldiers were marching to Lexington and Concord to destroy the minutemen's supplies and to capture Sam Adams and John Hancock. These two leaders of the Sons of Liberty were troublemakers for the British. Paul Revere and William Dawes galloped on horseback, ahead of the British, warning the colonist that "The British are coming!"

Guided Reading
1. Where and when did "Paul Revere's Ride" take place?
   (Massachusetts, 1775)

2. What signal was Revere expecting?
   (Two lights in the church belfry)

3. What, do you think, was the author's attitude toward Paul Revere?
   (Answers may include that he was a hero.)

Literature-Social Studies Connection
1. From what you have learned in this lesson, why, do you think, did Henry Longfellow write that "the fate of a nation was riding that night"?
   (Answers may include that if the colonists had not been warned, General Gage's plan to destroy their supplies might have been successful, and the revolution might not have happened.)

VISUAL THINKING SKILL

Using a Photograph

- Tell students that the four men shown on p. 298 were important delegates to the Constitutional Convention.

- Ask students to decide which of the four they would like to interview the most. Students should then write five questions they would most like to ask that person.

sharpening visual thinking skills

GEOGRAPHY THEMES

 Location

- Direct students' attention to the map on p. 296 and have them work in pairs to do the following activity. Have one student in each pair name a territory, state, or body of water shown on the map. The other student should then orally describe its relative location. For example, if the first student names Virginia, that student's partner should respond: "north of North Carolina, south of Maryland, west of the Atlantic Ocean, and east of the Ohio River." Students should alternate between naming and describing.

building geography literacy

understanding difficult concepts by meeting their individual needs

Meeting Individual Needs

Concept: Understanding a Love of Freedom

It may be hard for students to comprehend why and how someone could feel strongly enough about freedom to risk their lives. Have students do the following activities to aid in this understanding.

◆ **EASY** Tell students to pretend they have the opportunity to have a "free day" at school to do whatever they wish, within reason.

Ask them to list what things they might be willing to give up in exchange for this freedom. Then ask, **What if you were told that you could not move to where you wanted or you had to feed soldiers in your home?**

Relate this to colonists who were willing to give up their lives to have the freedom we now enjoy.

Discuss the concept of sacrifice. Together, list those things (discussed in the lesson) the British did to anger the colonists enough to make them want to sacrifice their lives for freedom.

◀▷ **AVERAGE** Write two to three sentences from Patrick Henry's famous speech. These may include: "Is life so dear, or peace so sweet, as to be purchased at the price of chains and slavery?" and "I know not what course others may take; but as for me, give me liberty, or give me death!"

Have students rewrite these sentences in their own words, and discuss them aloud. Give gold "freedom stars" for every word out of his speech that students look up in the dictionary.

◀▮▶ **CHALLENGING** Have students do some "think like a Patriot" exercises and write their own speech to the Virginia House of Burgesses. What stirring remarks would they make to inspire their listeners to take up arms?

Multidisciplinary Activity

A Trip Across America

From Sea to Shining Sea!

Planning an imaginary cross-country trip will give students a good chance to "see" the United States. Have students start any place they wish on the east or the west coast and chart a journey to any place on the opposite coast. Ask students what kinds of geographical features they might come across, such as moutains, mesas, plains, valleys, rivers, and deltas.

SOCIAL STUDIES

Geography Have students trace a map of the United States that shows state boundaries and major geographic features.

■ Then have students draw at least one possible route across the entire country. They may also wish to hypothesize about which route might be easiest to travel, and which might be the most difficult.

History When students have finished plotting their journeys across the country, direct them to the stories of other Americans who made the same journeys.

■ Students could research the Lewis and Clark expedition, the Santa Fe Trail, the Oregon Trail, the trails blazed by the Mountain Men, and those used by the gold seekers in the 1850.

■ Ask students how our journey today would be different from the journeys listed above.

Economics As students study the journeys of their forebearers, ask them to consider the motivation. Ask students why they think the settlers made these journeys. In many cases, such as the Gold Rush, economics was the prime motivation. Have students list the reasons why they think various historical journeys were made. While discussing economics, students may wish to think about the cost of a transcontinental journey.

■ Have students contemplate the cost of a journey today versus the cost of a journey 100 to 150 years ago.

Global Awareness After the students have completed their imaginary journeys have them look at a physical map of the world and ask them to compare the major geographic features of the United States with the major geographic features of other countries around the world. Ask students to choose one country that interests them and answer the following comparison questions:

1. Does the country have mountains and rivers similar to those of the United States? How are our geographic features similar and how are they different?

MATHEMATICS

■ Using a road map of the United States, have students figure the mileage for each of their various journeys.

Have them estimate how may miles they could travel in a day, in a week, or even a month. You may wish to have students compare the mileage covered by following the road to that of going straight "as the crow flies."

LANGUAGE ARTS

■ After students have chosen their routes across the country, have them write a rationale for their choices. They should include some information about the physical features and attractions of their journey and should explain their reasons for selecting that specific route.

SCIENCE

■ Transportation has certainly improved over the last few hundred years. Ask students to answer the following questions:

1. What role has technology played in improving our transportation systems?

2. Have all the changes been for the better?

3. What are the advantages and disadvantages of each form of transportation? Did the horse have any advantage over the airplane? Does the airplane have any disadvantages?

ART

■ Draw students' attention to the various physical features of the United States by focusing their attention on the physical features they will pass on their journey.

■ Have students create visuals of each of these features and arrange them on a bulletin board. Students may also wish to make travel posters about some of the places to which their imaginary journeys will take them.

LITERATURE

■ Have students read about past journeys in order to appreciate the nature of the journey they have planned. *Oregon Trail*, by Francis Parkman Airmont, © 1964, ISBN 0-8049-0037), tells the story of a journey in the 1840 while Peter Jenkin's *Walk Across America* (Morrow © 1979, ISBN 0-688-03427-6) provides a more contemporary version.

U1-C

U1-D

Multidisciplinary Activity features provide an exciting way to bring subject area integration into your classroom.

For more resources, look for

• **Resource Center that identifies supplementary materials to be used with each lesson**

• **Annotated Bibliography of books, audiovisual materials, and computer software**

More ways to help you teach social studies easily and effectively

Study
Current Events

INSTRUCTIONS FOR THE TEACHER:

Why Should Current Events be Used in the Social Studies Classroom? It is difficult to walk into the middle of a movie and fully understand everything that is going on. It is also hard to pick up a novel in the middle and completely comprehend the story. In a very real way, our students are placed in a similar situation. They find themselves in a world that is an ongoing drama — a drama that is often not easy to understand. The goal of the Social Studies class is to provide students with the information they need to become thinking, caring, participating citizens. The introduction of current events is an important step in this process.

Unit 7 discusses the United States in a changing world. The previous chapters have established the students' knowledge base. Now the students can put that base to use, applying it to their world and its problems. When placed in this context, the study of current events helps students understand the relevance of social studies and provides them with valuable information about their world and their role in that world.

Obtaining Material A great number of events are continually happening in the world. Students need some structure when attempting to tackle the extensive subject of current events.

Selecting a Current-Events Topic First, help students focus their attention on one subject. Ask each student to select a topic for study that interests him or her, but make sure that the topic is broad enough to meet the students needs for this lesson.

After the student has picked a general topic, it may be necessary to narrow it down. Students that are interested in government elections or politics may select a topic such as "Politics in America." Since that topic is extremely broad, it will be necessary to help the student focus on a smaller portion of the related information. By narrowing the focus of their topic, students will find research data more manageable.

Researching the Topic Have students research their topics. Information on current events can be found in a wide variety of places. Students may wish to obtain information from one or more of the following sources:

— News Broadcasts (radio and television)
— Television specials
— Newspapers and magazines
— Primary Sources such as guest speakers

Have students take notes on their research. They may be able to obtain copies of any written articles that they use, but they will probably need to take notes while monitoring radio or television broadcasts.

Using the Material Resource materials can be used in a variety of ways. Students may wish to organize their information and present it to the class in the form of an oral report. Other students may wish to make a scrapbook and a written report. Materials could be gathered for a round-table discussion or for a class debate. Some students may wish to create an ongoing journal, keeping abreast of the situation as it changes. Other students may wish to create a bulletin board displaying their research.

ACTIVITY FOR THE STUDENTS:

Creating a Current-Events Fair Tell students that the class is going to spend the next week of class creating a current-events fair. This will be a chance for students to complete research about something going on in the world and then share that research with the class in display form. Each student will be given a station within the fair to create a display that showcases an issue.

Have the students turn in a list of topics they are interested in studying. After the topic has been approved, ask them to create a list of places they intend to check for information on their topic. Students need to research their topic and prepare information that would explain what is going on to a person who is not fully informed. This may be done in a variety of ways. The students may wish to share information through artwork, or with an audio tape, written information, graphic organizers, maps, or any combination of the above. They may also wish to create a current-events notebook or time line delineating information about their issue. They can provide background information on the topic as well as a personal guess as to what will happen next. Finally, all this information needs to be organized and presented in a display that can be set up within the amount of size allowed by the room. Have all the displays set up at the same time and allow time for students to visit each display and learn about the issues that their fellow classmates have researched.

Follow-Up Upon completion of the unit, the class may wish to hypothesize about the future. Ask the class to discuss and decide "Which of the materials we have been discussing will be included in history books of the future?"; "Which of these events will our children be studying?" and "What we will we tell them about this period of time?" Have the students discuss their feelings in a class discussion or in small groups.

How To projects provide valuable information for teachers and students to do a wide variety of activities to enhance learning.

- **Pacing Guide**
- **Bulletin Board Idea and related student activity**
- **Reduced reproductions of chapter review masters, vocabulary masters, place geography masters, test masters, and Teacher Edition of the Workbook**

CONTENT SUMMARY

Grade 1

Living in Families
Increases students' understanding of their family, school, and neighborhood, while developing citizenship, map and globe skills, and an increased awareness of children in other countries.

Grade 2

Living in Communities
Broadens students' knowledge of communities, past and present, and of ways people live in a variety of communities in our country and in other countries, while increasing their map and globe skills.

Grade 3

Comparing Communities
Deepens students' understanding of different kinds of communities by focusing on the geography, history, economy, and government of communities in our country and in other countries.

Grade 4

Comparing Regions
Encourages students to do an indepth study of the geography, culture, and economy of regions in the United States and to compare these regions with other regions in the world.

Grade 5

Our Country
Promotes citizenship and builds students' understanding of United States history, presented chronologically, by interweaving social, cultural, economic, and geography strands within a well-told story.

Grade 6/7

World Cultures
Engages students in the story of the development of civilization, presenting the geography, economy, government, and culture of the world's peoples, from the earliest times to the present.

Grade 6/7

Eastern Hemisphere
Focuses students' attention on the geography, history, economy, government, and culture of regions within the Eastern Hemisphere.

Grade 6/7

Western Hemisphere
Provides students with a knowledge base about the geography, history, government, economy, and culture of other countries within our hemisphere.

TEACHER SUPPORT SYSTEM

Our Gifts to You. Your Gifts to Them.

Everything you need to lead ALL students to new heights of creativity and understanding.

► Review Masters

► Test Masters

► Workbook Teacher Edition

► Outline Maps

► Wall Maps

► Transparencies

► SILVER WINGS WORKSHOP
a multisensory, multimedia package
- Workshop Guide
- Workshop Prop
- Audio Cassette
- Activity Cards
- Poster
- Trade Book

Yours *FREE!* when you adopt PEOPLE IN TIME AND PLACE
from SILVER BURDETT GINN

PROGRAM COMPONENTS

Student Texts, 1-7

Student Workbooks, 1-7

Teacher-to-Teacher Editions, 1-7

Teacher Support Systems, 1-7

► Review Masters

► Test Masters

► Workbook Teacher Editions

► Outline Maps

► Wall Maps

► Transparencies

► SILVER WINGS WORKSHOPS-
multimedia, multisensory packages

- Workshop Props
- Workshop Guides
- Audio Cassettes
- Activity Cards
- Posters
- Trade Books

Complete Poster Book Packages, K-2

► Poster Books

► Poster Book Teacher Manuals

► Poster Book Review Masters

► Poster Book Test Masters

Activity Kits, K-2

Videos, 1-7

Social Studies Libraries, 1-7

PE●PLE
in Time and Place

SILVER BURDETT GINN

Simon & Schuster   A Paramount Communications Company

ISBN 0-382-16892-5
04-92-203 (A137)

For information
1 (800) 848-95

PE❂PLE
in Time and Place

EASTERN HEMISPHERE

AUTHORS

Sheila Allen
Sixth-Grade Teacher, Mount Hebron School
Upper Montclair, NJ

Susan Colford
Sixth-Grade Teacher
Booker Arts Magnet Elementary School
Little Rock, AK

Edward Graivier
Sixth-Grade Teacher, Pleasant Ridge School
Glenview, IL

Lisa Johnson
Sixth-Grade Teacher, Conrad Ball Middle School
Loveland, CO

SERIES CONSULTANTS

Dr. James F. Baumann
Professor and Head of the Department of
Reading Education, College of Education
The University of Georgia
Athens, GA

Dr. Theodore Kaltsounis
Professor of Social Studies Education
University of Washington
Seattle, WA

LITERATURE CONSULTANTS

Dr. Ben A. Smith
Assistant Professor of Social Studies Education
Kansas State University
Manhattan, KS

Dr. Jesse Palmer
Assistant Professor, Department of Curriculum and Instruction
University of Southern Mississippi
Hattiesburg, MS

Dr. John C. Davis
Professor of Elementary Education
University of Southern Mississippi
Hattiesburg, MS

TEACHER EDITION

SILVER BURDETT GINN
MORRISTOWN, NJ • NEEDHAM, MA

Atlanta, GA • Dallas, TX • Deerfield, IL • Menlo Park, CA

PUPIL EDITION AUTHORS

Dr. W. Frank Ainsley
Professor of Geography
University of North Carolina
Wilmington, NC

Dr. Herbert J. Bass
Professor of History
Temple University
Philadelphia, PA

Dr. Kenneth S. Cooper
Professor of History, Emeritus
George Peabody College for Teachers
Vanderbilt University
Nashville, TN

Dr. Claudia Crump
Professor of Elementary Social Studies Education
Indiana University Southeast
New Albany, IN

Dr. Gary S. Elbow
Professor of Geography
Texas Tech University
Lubbock, TX

Roy Erickson
Program Specialist, K-12
Social Studies and Multicultural Education
San Juan Unified School District
Carmichael, CA

Dr. Daniel B. Fleming
Professor of Social Studies Education
Virginia Polytechnic Institute and State University
Blacksburg, VA

Dr. Gerald Michael Greenfield
Professor and Director, Center for International Studies
University of Wisconsin
Parkside
Kenosha, WI

Dr. Linda Greenow
Associate Professor of Geography
SUNY — The College at New Paltz
New Paltz, NY

Dr. William W. Joyce
Professor of Education
Michigan State University
East Lansing, MI

Dr. Gail S. Ludwig
Geographer-in-Residence
National Geographic Society
Geography Education Program
Washington, D.C.

Dr. Michael B. Petrovich
Professor Emeritus of History
University of Wisconsin
Madison, WI

Dr. Norman J.G. Pounds
Former University Professor of History and Geography
Indiana University
Bloomington, IN

Dr. Arthur D. Roberts
Professor of Education
University of Connecticut
Storrs, CT

Dr. Christine M. L. Roberts
Professor of Education
University of Connecticut
Storrs, CT

Parke Rouse, Jr.
Virginia Historian
and Retired Executive Director
of the Jamestown-Yorktown Foundation
Williamsburg, VA

Dr. Paul C. Slayton, Jr.
Distinguished Professor of Education
Mary Washington College
Fredericksburg, VA

Dr. Edgar A. Toppin
Professor of History
and Dean of the Graduate School
Virginia State University
Petersburg, VA

ACKNOWLEDGEMENTS

Page: 56: From *Gods, Graves, and Scholars* by C. W. Ceram. Translated by Edward B. Garside. Used courtesy of Alfred A. Knopf, Inc.

Page 73: From *The Children's Homer: The Adventures of Odysseus and the Tale of Troy* by Padraic Colum. Copyright 1918 by Macmillan Publishing Co. and renewed 1946 by Padraic Colum and Willy Pogany. Reprinted by permission of the publisher.

Page 117: "Good Samaritan" from the *New American Bible with Revised New Testament*, Copyright © 1986, 1970 by Confraternity of Christian Doctrine, Washington, D.C., is used with permission. All rights reserved.

Page 143: Copyright © 1984 by Leonard Everett Fisher. Reprinted by permission of Macmillan Publishing Co.

Page 240: From *The Diary of a Young Girl* by Anne Frank. © 1952 Otto H. Frank. © 1967 Doubleday & Co., Inc. Used by permission of the publisher.

Page 288: Copyright © 1968 by Esther Hautzig. Reprinted by permission of Harper & Row, Publishers, Inc.

Pages 294-295: Adapted from "Clever Manka" in the *Shepherd's Nosegay: Stories from Finland and Czechoslovakia* by Parker Fillmore, copyright 1950 and renewed 1986 by Harcourt Brace Jovanovich, Inc. Reprinted by permission of the publisher.

Page 367: From *Travellers Prelude: Autobiography 1893-1927*, by Freya Stark. Used by permission of John Murray (Publishers), Ltd.

Page 445: From *African Proverbs* by Charlotte & Wolf Leslau. Used by permission of Peter Pauper Press.

Page 456: From *Tales from an Ashanti Village* by Peggy Appiah, © 1966 Pantheon Books, a division of Random House, Inc. Used by permission of the publisher.

Page 524: From *The Travels of Marco Polo Book II.* Translated by Manuel Komroff. Used by permission of Liveright Publishing Corporation.

Page 551: *From Modern Japanese Haiku and Anthology* compiled and translated by Makoto Ueda. ©1976 University of Toronto Press. Reprinted by permission of the University of Toronto Press.

Pages 573-574: Copyright © 1984 by Elsie Roughsey. Reprinted by permission of Penguin Books, Australia, Ltd.

Page 583: From *Kon-Tiki* by Thor Heyerdahl. Used by permission of Simon & Schuster, Inc.

Contents

Unit 1

ANCIENT CIVILIZATIONS

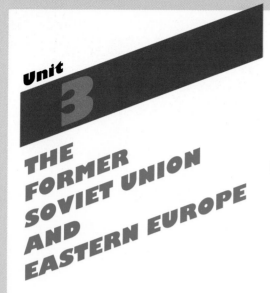

Unit

3

THE FORMER SOVIET UNION AND EASTERN EUROPE

Unit 4

THE MIDDLE EAST AND NORTH AFRICA

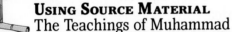

Unit

5

AFRICA
SOUTH OF
THE SAHARA

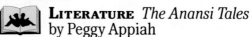

Unit 7

AUSTRALIA, NEW ZEALAND, AND THE PACIFIC ISLANDS

RESOURCE SECTION

TABLES

CHARTS

DIAGRAMS

SPECIAL FEATURES

USING SOURCE MATERIAL

LITERATURE

CITIZENSHIP AND AMERICAN VALUES

SOCIAL STUDIES

LANGUAGE ARTS

Skills are an integral part of any Social Studies program. Knowing where skills are introduced, practiced, and tested will enable you to incorporate the skills into your Social Studies lessons. To make the task easier for you, this **Teacher-to-Teacher Edition** includes a *Skill Trace Bar*. This bar tells you where key skills are introduced, practiced and tested in PEOPLE IN TIME AND PLACE. The bar will always appear in the marginalia where a skill is first introduced. A sample of a *Skill Trace Bar* is shown below. Listed are all the skills that are traced at this grade level.

SKILL TRACE: Understanding Symbols		
INTRODUCE	**PRACTICE**	**TEST**
PE pp. 16–17	**WB** p. 42, 88 **TE** p. 16	Unit 4 Test, TMB

MAP AND GLOBE SKILLS

SKILL	INTRODUCE	PRACTICE	TEST
Understanding the Globe	**PE** pp. 4-6	**PE** pp. 31-32; **RMB** p. 6; **TE** p. 9	Map Skills Post Test, **TMB**
Comparing Maps and the Globe	**PE** p. 19	**RMB** p. 6; **TE** p. 19	Map Skills Post Test, **TMB**
Understanding Symbols	**PE** pp. 16-17	**WB** pp. 42 and 88; **TE** p. 16	Unit 4 Test, **TMB**
Understanding the Legend (Key)	**PE** pp. 16-17	**WB** pp. 13, 17 and 42	Map Skills Post Test, **TMB**
Understanding Latitude and Longitude	**PE** pp. 8-10	**TE** pp. 8-9; **PE** pp. 293, 319; **RMB** p. 3; **WB** p. 33	Map Skills Post Test, **TMB**
Understanding Scale	**PE** pp. 12-13	**RMB** p. 4; **WB** pp. 14 and 125; **TE** p. 12	Map Skills Post Test, **TMB**
Using Scale to Measure Distance	**PE** p. 12	**PE** p. 219; **WB** pp. 14 and 33; **TE** pp.11-12	Ch. 14 Test, **TMB**
Understanding Coordinates (Grid System)	**PE** pp. 9-10	**PE** p. 383; **WB** p. 12; **TE** pp. 8-9	Map Skills Post Test, **TMB**
Understanding Elevation Tints	**PE** pp. 14-15	**PE** p. 307; **RMB** p. 4; **WB** p. 13; **TE** p. 14	Ch. 22 Test, **TMB**
Understanding Contour Lines	**PE** p. 15	**RMB** p. 4; **WB** p. 13; **TE** p. 14	Map Skills Post Test, **TMB**
Understanding Special-Purpose Maps	**PE** pp. 23-25	**TE** p. 24; **PE** p. 265; **RMB** p. 7; **WB** p. 17	Map Skills Post Test, **TMB**
Understanding Movements of the Earth	**PE** p. 4	**RMB** p. 2; **WB** pp. 11 and 55; **TE** pp. 4-5	Map Skills Post Test, **TMB**
Understanding Seasons	**PE** p. 5	**RMB** p. 2; **WB** pp. 11 and 74; **PE** p. 6; **TE** p. 5	Map Skills Post Test, **TMB**
Understanding Map Projections	**PE** pp. 19-21	**RMB** p. 6; **WB** p. 16; **TE** p. 19	Map Skills Post Test, **TMB**
Understanding Time Lines	**PE** pp. 28-29	**PE** p. 95; **TE** p. 28; **RMB** p. 8; **WB** p. 76	Map Skills Post Test, **TMB**

SOCIAL STUDIES SKILLS

SKILL	INTRODUCE	PRACTICE	TEST
Understanding Graphs	**PE** pp. 148-149	**TE** pp. 148-149; **PE** p. 265; **WB** pp. 45 and 77; **TE** p. 208	Unit 1 Test, **TMB**
Interpreting Information	**PE** pp. 276-277	**TE** pp. 276-277; **RMB** p. 86; **WB** pp. 77, 85 and 89; **TE** p. 306	Unit 2 Test, **TMB**
Understanding Times Zones	**PE** pp. 350-351	**TE** pp. 350-351; **PE** p. 289 and 585; **TE** p. 360	Unit 3 Test, **TMB**
Understanding Resource Maps	**PE** pp. 430-431	**TE** pp. 430-431; **RMB** p. 7; **WB** p. 88; **TE** p. 489	Unit 4 Test, **TMB**
Comparing Political Maps	**PE** pp. 498-499	**TE** pp. 498-499; **WB** p. 65; **TE** p. 536	Unit 5 Test, **TMB**
Budgeting and Banking	**PE** pp. 566-567	**TE** pp. 566-567; **TE** p. 584	Unit 6 Test, **TMB**
Summarizing Information	**PE** pp. 606-607	**TE** pp. 606-607; **WB** pp. 82-83	Unit 7 Test, **TMB**

LANGUAGE ARTS SKILLS

SKILL	INTRODUCE	PRACTICE	TEST
Characteristics of Various Text Types	**PE** pp. 150-151	**TE** pp. 150-151; **PE** p. 247; **WB** pp. 50-51; **TE** p. 240	Unit 2 Test, **TMB**
Understanding Main Ideas and Details	**PE** pp. 278-279	**TE** pp. 278-279; **TE** p. 282; **RMB** p. 2; **WB** pp. 20 and 35	Ch. 15 Test, **TMB**
Using Various Text Structures to Aid Comprehension	**PE** pp. 352-353	**TE** pp. 352-353, 379; **RMB** pp. 20 and 26; **WB** pp. 26 and 77	Unit 3 Test, **TMB**
Selecting and Using the Appropriate Resources	**PE** pp. 432-433	**TE** pp. 432-433; **WB** pp. 68 and 100; **PE** p. 538	Unit 4 Test, **TMB**
Skimming for Main Ideas	**PE** pp. 500-501	**TE** pp. 500-501, 545; **WB** pp. 56-57; **PE** p. 587	Unit 5 Test, **TMB**
Scanning for Specific Facts or Ideas	**PE** pp. 500-501	**TE** pp. 500-501, 545; **WB** pp. 42-43; **PE** p. 539	Unit 5 Test, **TMB**
Making and Verifying Predictions	**PE** pp. 568-569	**TE** pp. 568-569, 589; **WB** pp. 20 and 92	Unit 6 Test, **TMB**
Understanding an Author's Point of View	**PE** pp. 608-609	**TE** pp. 608-609; **WB** pp. 53 and 89	Unit 7 Test, **TMB**

KEY

PE — Pupil Edition   **TE** — Teacher Edition   **WB** — Workbook   **RMB** — Review Master Booklet   **TMB** — Test Master Booklet

UNIT ACTIVITIES

Multidisciplinary Activity

M*ultidisciplinary* ***A****ctivities* provide an exciting way to integrate Social Studies content into other curriculum areas. This special feature is found in every unit interleaf section. Below is a list of the *Multidisciplinary Activities* in this book.

How To

Activities

H*ow* ***T****o* activities provide not only student projects but also valuable information for the teacher on how to prepare for and execute the projects. *How To* activities can be found in every unit interleaf. Below is a list of the *How To* activities in this book.

Map Skills Handbook Resource Center

Map Skills Handbook
(pp. 2-31)

Handbook Theme: Maps and globes provide a wealth of information about people and the earth. To interpret maps, it is necessary to understand scale, symbols, latitude, longitude, and projections.

CHAPTER RESOURCES
Review Master Booklet
  Reviewing Chapter Vocabulary, p. 9
  Place Geography, p. 10
Summarizing the Chapter, p. 11
Map Skills Pre-Test
Map Skills Post-Test

LESSON *1* The Shape of the Earth
(pp. 4-6)
Theme: We have learned much about the earth since the days of Aristotle.

LESSON RESOURCES
Workbook, p. 11
Review Master Booklet
  Understanding the Lesson, p. 2

LESSON *2* Latitude and Longitude
(pp. 7-10)
Theme: Latitude and longitude help us locate places on maps.

LESSON RESOURCES
Workbook, p. 12
Review Master Booklet
  Understanding the Lesson, p. 3

LESSON *3* Scale and Elevation
(pp. 11-15)
Theme: There are many ways of measuring land and sea distances.

LESSON RESOURCES
Workbook, pp. 13-14
Review Master Booklet
  Understanding the Lesson, p. 4

LESSON *4* Taking a Bird's-eye View
(pp. 16-18)
Theme: Taking pictures of the earth has helped people make more accurate maps.

LESSON RESOURCES
Workbook, p. 15
Review Master Booklet
  Understanding the Lesson, p. 5

LESSON *5* Projection
(pp. 19-21)
Theme: Projections are a way of showing a drawing of the earth on a flat surface.

LESSON RESOURCES
Workbook, p. 16
Review Master Booklet
  Understanding the Lesson, p. 6

LESSON *6* Using an Atlas
(pp. 22-25)
Theme: Maps provide many different kinds of information.

LESSON RESOURCES
Workbook, p. 17
Review Master Booklet
  Understanding the Lesson, p. 7

LESSON *7* Dates and Time Lines
(pp. 26-29)
Theme: Dates and time lines help us learn about the past.

LESSON RESOURCES
Workbook, p. 18
Review Master Booklet
  Understanding the Lesson, p. 8

Review Masters

REVIEWING CHAPTER VOCABULARY

MAP SKILLS HANDBOOK

VOCABULARY MASTER

Review Study the terms in the box. Use your Glossary to find definitions of those you do not remember.

altitude	decade	isthmus	precipitation
anno Domini	distortion	latitude	Prime Meridian
atlas	elevation	longitude	projection
axis	grid	meridian	satellite
cartographer	hemisphere	odometer	scale
century	humidity	orbit	sphere
circa	International Date	parallel	time line
climate	Line	population density	
contour line			

Practice Complete the paragraphs using terms from the box above. You may change the forms of the terms to fit the meaning.

Passengers on flights from London to Australia often have wonderful views of many countries and oceans. However, they would not be flying at a high enough (1) _altitude_ to see that the earth is shaped like a (2) _sphere_ . Only pictures from spacecraft and (3) _satellites_ can give us this point of view. These pictures, unlike flat maps, show us how the earth looks without (4) _distortion_ .

Although the passengers may fly over Greenwich, England, they will not be able to see the (5) _Prime Meridian_ . They move from one day to the next as they cross the (6) _International Date Line_ , but they will not be able to see this line either. These imaginary lines are found only on maps. They make up part of the (7) _grid_ . used to help locate places.

What the airline passengers can see are some features of the landscape. For example, they observe changes in (8) _elevation_ as the plane flies over mountain ranges. The passengers might also see the narrow (9) _isthmus_ that connects the continents of Africa and Eurasia.

Write Choose ten terms from the box above. Use each term to write a sentence of your own. You may use the back of the sheet.

Sentences should show that students understand the meanings of the terms.

_____

_____

_____

LOCATING PLACES

MAP SKILLS HANDBOOK

PLACE GEOGRAPHY MASTER

✱ Knowing the latitude and longitude of any place on earth will enable you to find the place on a map. Use the Gazetteer in your textbook to find the latitude and longitude of each place listed below. Then locate each on the map.

	LAT.	LONG.
1. St. Petersburg, Russia	60°N	30°E
2. New Delhi, India	29°N	77°E
3. Rome, Italy	42°N	12°E
4. Paris, France	49°N	2°E
5. Cooperstown, New York	43°N	75°W
6. Lagos, Nigeria	6°N	3°E
7. Ankara, Turkey	41°N	33°E
8. Beijing, China	40°N	116°E
9. Jakarta, Indonesia	6°S	107°E
10. Melbourne, Australia	38°S	145°E

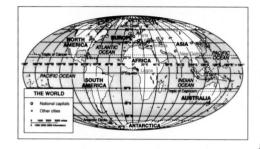

THE WORLD
○ National capitals
● Other cities

SUMMARIZING THE CHAPTER

MAP SKILLS HANDBOOK

GRAPHIC ORGANIZER MASTER

✱ Complete this graphic organizer. Under the main idea for each lesson, write two additional statements that support the main idea.

CHAPTER THEME Maps and globes provide a wealth of information about people and the earth. To interpret maps, it is necessary to understand scale, symbols, latitude, longitude, and projections.

LESSON 1
We have learned much about the earth since the days of Aristotle.
1. Shaped like sphere
2. Orbits around sun, rotates on axis
3. Revolves and tilts on axis, causing seasons

LESSON 2
Maps help us locate places.
1. Latitude lines
2. Longitude lines
3. Grid maps

LESSON 3
There are many ways of measuring land and sea distances.
1. Different scales
2. Elevation
3. Contour lines

LESSON 4
Taking pictures of the earth has helped people make more accurate maps.
1. Bird's-eye view
2. Aerial photographs
3. Photographs from space

LESSON 5
Projections are a way of showing a drawing of the earth on a flat surface.
1. Mercator's maps
2. Equal-distance projections
3. Distortion

LESSON 6
Maps provide many different kinds of information.
1. Political divisions
2. Physical features
3. Climate

LESSON 7
Dates and time lines help us learn about the past.
1. A.D. and B.C.
2. Century
3. Decade

MSH-B

Workbook Pages

UNDERSTANDING ROTATION AND REVOLUTION

Understanding Diagrams, Understanding Seasons

❋ The diagram below shows how the tilt of the earth's axis causes the seasons to change. Study the diagram and answer the questions.

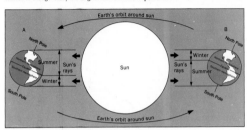

1. Which direction does the earth revolve around the sun, clockwise or counterclockwise? counterclockwise

2. When the North Pole is tilted toward the sun, in which hemisphere is it winter? the Southern Hemisphere

3. Which hemisphere is closer to the sun when it is summer in the Northern Hemisphere? the Northern Hemisphere

4. Why is it warmer in winter at a place near the Equator than in summer at the North Pole? Because the place near the Equator is closer to the sun

5. Which month of the year does globe A represent, June or December? June

6. Which month does globe B represent, June or December? December

7. When it is summer in the Southern Hemisphere, at which pole does the sun always shine? at the South Pole

Thinking Further: Write a paragraph explaining how the temperatures in winter and summer would change if the earth was tilted even more on its axis. Use a separate sheet.
Answers should mention that the summers would be hotter and the winters would be colder.

Map Skills Handbook, pages 4–6

11

IDENTIFYING CITIES BY GLOBAL ADDRESS

Understanding the Grid System, Understanding Latitude and Longitude

❋ The lines of latitude and longitude on the world map may be used to locate places, just as the signs at cross streets in a town help to locate addresses.
a. Locate and circle the following lines of latitude and longitude on the map below: 120°W, 80°W, 80°E, 120°E, 160°E, 60°N, 40°N, 20°S, 40°S.
b. Find each global address listed below on the world map. Write the name of the city located at that address in the blank.

1. 23°S/43°W   Rio de Janeiro, Brazil
2. 36°N/140°E   Tokyo, Japan
3. 60°N/6°E   Bergen, Norway
4. 12°S/131°E   Darwin, Australia
5. 33°S/19°E   Cape Town, South Africa
6. 33°N/8°W   Casablanca, Morocco
7. 38°N/122°W   San Francisco, California
8. 12°S/77°W   Lima, Peru

Thinking Further: Explain why the longitude lines on the map are curved.
Answers should mention that lines of longitude begin and end at the poles, but they curve around the earth.

12

Map Skills Handbook, pages 7–10

SHOWING THE HEIGHT OF THE LAND

Understanding Elevation Indicators, Understanding Contour Lines

❋ The map below uses contour lines to show the elevation of the land on two islands, Alpha and Beta.
a. Using colored pencils or markers, fill in each lettered box on the map key with a different color.
b. Color the islands, using the correct color for each elevation range.

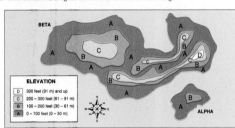

❋ Fill in each blank with the correct elevation range.

1. The elevation of land along the coast of Alpha and Beta: between 0 and 100 feet

2. The highest elevation in the western half of Beta: between 200 and 300 feet

3. The elevation of the valley on Beta: between 0 and 100 feet

4. The highest elevation on Beta: 300 feet and up

5. The highest elevation on Alpha: between 100 and 200 feet

6. The elevation found in only one area of Beta: 300 feet and up

Thinking Further: Write a paragraph describing some patterns you could use for your map key if you did not have color to show elevations.
Answers may mention dots, broken lines, dotted lines, or diagonal solid lines.

Map Skills Handbook, pages 11–15

13

FINDING DISTANCE ON A MAP

Using Scale to Measure Distance, Applying Information

❋ School bands from different states traveled to New York City to march in the Thanksgiving Day parade. Using the distance scale on the map below, estimate how far each band had to travel to reach New York.

City	Approximate Distance to New York	
	Miles	Kilometers
1. Omaha, Nebraska	1,200	1,900
2. Peoria, Illinois	850	1,350
3. Billings, Montana	1,750	2,800
4. Santa Monica, California	2,500	4,000
5. Dallas, Texas	1,450	2,300

Thinking Further: How big is the mainland United States? Use the distance scale to measure about how many miles it is across the United States from north to south and from east to west.
Answers should be around 2,900 miles east to west and 1,700 miles north to south.

14

Map Skills Handbook, pages 11–15

MSH-C

Workbook Pages

COMPARING A PHOTOGRAPH AND A MAP

Comparing Maps with Photographs, Understanding Perspective

✳ Cartographers often draw maps using photographs taken from above the earth. Mapmakers use symbols to represent features in the photograph. The map below was drawn from the aerial photograph shown on the right. Study the photograph and map carefully to see how they are alike and different. Then answer the questions that follow.

PLAYING FIELDS

- ♟ Buildings
- ▦ Parking lot
- ⬚ Playing fields
- ⊥ Streets
- ⬭ Track

| 0 | 200 | 400 | 600 feet |
| 0 | 60 | 120 | 180 meters |

1. How are the map and the photograph alike? _They both show the same area._

2. How are the map and the photograph different? _The photograph shows everything that is there, while the map shows only certain important features._

3. Which is more useful for finding a location? _the map_

4. List four things you can see on the photograph that do not appear on the map. _trees, small buildings, swimming pool, lines on playing fields_

5. Was the photograph taken from directly above the playing fields? _no_

Thinking Further: Trace one of the circles shown on the photograph onto another piece of paper. Explain why the circle is not really round. You may use a separate sheet. _Answers should mention that the photograph was taken from an angle, or that circles appear round only when viewed from directly above._

© Silver, Burdett & Ginn Inc.

Map Skills Handbook, pages 16–18 — 15

LEARNING ABOUT POLAR PROJECTIONS

Understanding Map Projections, Understanding Hemisphere

✳ The map below shows a polar projection of the earth. Study the map; then fill in the blanks in the paragraph.

This map shows a polar projection of the _Northern_ Hemisphere, with the _North_ Pole at its center. The outer boundary of this map is the _0°_ latitude line, or the _Equator_. While these maps show only 90° of latitude, they show _360°_ of longitude. The hemisphere shown on this map includes all of the continents of _North America_, _Asia_, and _Europe_, and about half of the continent of _Africa_. You can see that an airplane flying the most direct route from New York to Tokyo would cross the Arctic _Circle_ two times.

Thinking Further: Write a paragraph explaining which polar projection would show the part of the earth where most of the earth's people live. _Answers should mention a northern polar projection._

16 — Map Skills Handbook, pages 19–21

© Silver, Burdett & Ginn Inc.

LOOKING AT PRECIPITATION

Understanding Special-Purpose Maps, Drawing Conclusions

✳ The map below shows the average annual amount of precipitation in Australia. Almost all of the precipitation is rain. Study the map; then answer the questions.

AVERAGE YEARLY PRECIPITATION IN AUSTRALIA

- ◎ National capital
- ★ State and territorial capitals
- ● Other cities

Average Yearly Precipitation

Inches	Centimeters
Over 30	Over 75
20 to 30	50 to 75
10 to 20	25 to 50
5 to 10	13 to 25
Under 10	Under 25

1. Which areas of Australia receive most of the rainfall? _northern and eastern areas_

2. What pattern do you see in the amounts of precipitation in different areas of Australia? _Most of the precipitation falls in the areas near the sea._

3. Which city receives the most rainfall, Adelaide, Brisbane, or Kalgoorlie? _Brisbane_

4. What type of climate does the central region of Australia have? _desert_

5. Does most of Australia receive more than 20 inches or less than 20 inches of precipitation each year? _less than 20 inches_

6. On average, how much precipitation does Darwin receive? _more than 30 inches_

Thinking Further: Explain why most Australians live in the southeastern part of the country. _Answers should mention the amount of rainfall received by southeastern Australia compared to other parts of the country._

© Silver, Burdett & Ginn Inc.

Map Skills Handbook, pages 22–25 — 17

PLACING EVENTS ON A TIME LINE

Understanding Time Lines, Sequencing

✳ The time line below covers the period from 1000 B.C. to A.D. 2000. Put the letter of each event listed in the correct box on the time line.

| D | | B | E | | | C | | A | | H | | F | G |
| 1000 | 500 | B.C./A.D. | | 500 | 1000 | | 1500 | | | 2000 |

A. King John signs Magna Carta: A.D. 1215
B. Alexander the Great is born: 356 B.C.
C. Muslims invade Spain: A.D. 711
D. First Hindu states established in India: 1000 B.C.
E. Rome conquers Greece: 146 B.C.
F. America issues Declaration of Independence: A.D. 1776
G. United Nations established: A.D. 1945
H. Columbus lands in America: A.D. 1492

✳ Answer the following questions.

1. Number the four events below in the order they happened.

_4_ United Nations is established. _1_ Rome conquers Greece.

_2_ Muslims invade Spain. _3_ King John signs Magna Carta.

2. In which century did Columbus land in America? _the 15th century A.D._

3. How many years does the time line show? _3,000 years_

4. How many years after Alexander the Great was born did Greece fall to Rome? _210 years_

5. How many years after the first Hindu states were established in India did King John sign the Magna Carta? _2,215 years_

Thinking Further: Explain what the letters B.C. and A.D. on the time line stand for. _Answers should state that B.C. stands for before Christ and A.D. stands for Anno Domini, or after the birth of Christ._

18 — Map Skills Handbook, pages 26–29

© Silver, Burdett & Ginn Inc.

MSH-D

MAP SKILLS HANDBOOK

Knowing how to work with maps is a social studies skill that everyone must have. You can't learn history and geography without being able to read maps. Maps, however, have uses that go beyond what you are learning in school.

Watch the nightly news. How many times are maps used? The next time you are in the library, take a copy of a weekly newsmagazine and count the number of maps that accompany the articles. Are maps used in any advertisements in the magazine? Keep a record over a week of all the times you see or use a map.

As you study the Eastern Hemisphere this year, you will be using map skills that you already have. You will also be learning some new map skills. All the map skills you will need appear in this Map Skills Handbook. Study the lesson titles on these pages to see which skills you will learn.

LESSON *1*
The Shape of the Earth page 4

LESSON *2*
Latitude and Longitude page 7

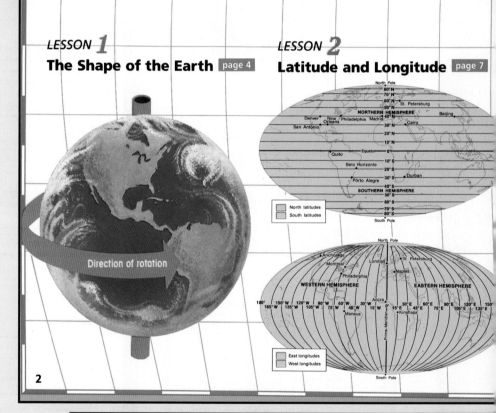

2

Optional Activities

Map Characteristics

- Point out to students that in the Map Skills Handbook they will learn how places are located on maps and how different maps are used for different purposes.

- Remind students that they already know a good deal about maps; ask them to summarize some of the characteristics, or features, that they would expect to find on most maps.

- Answers may include a title, a key, lines of latitude and longitude, a scale, some physical and political features, and perhaps some special symbols.

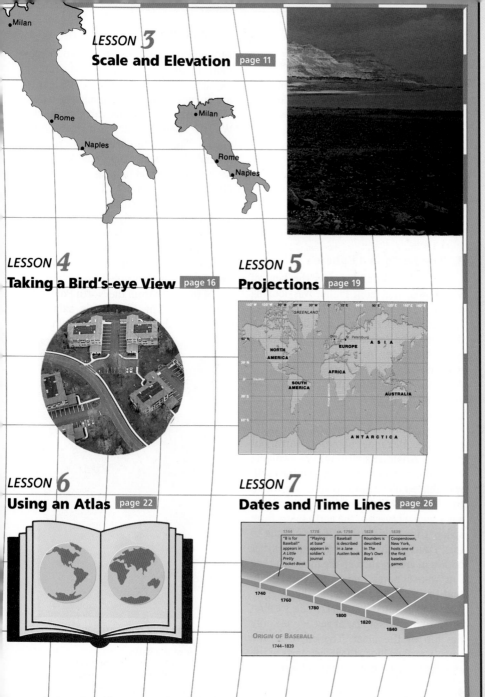

ORIGIN OF BASEBALL
1744–1839

| 1744 | 1778 | ca. 1798 | 1828 | 1839 |
| "B is for Baseball" appears in *A Little Pretty Pocket-Book* | "Playing at base" appears in soldier's journal | Baseball is described in a Jane Austen book | Rounders is described in *The Boy's Own Book* | Cooperstown, New York, hosts one of the first baseball games |

1740   1760   1780   1800   1820   1840

MAP SKILLS HANDBOOK

Using Maps and Graphs

- Ask students to think about how people use maps in their daily life.

- Answers may include that people use maps to show the locations of stores in shopping malls, to find exhibits in zoos and museums, and some people — pilots, drivers, weather forecasters, geographers, and others — use maps in their work.

Optional Activities

The Shape of the Earth

Objectives

★1. **Explain** the two ways in which the earth moves.

2. **Relate** the movement of the earth to the seasons.

3. **Evaluate** the accuracy of Aristotle's writings.

4. **Identify** the following person: *Aristotle*.

1 STARTING THE LESSON

Motivation Activity

■ Ask your students if they have ever had a ride on a tilt-a-whirl at an amusement park.

■ Ask those who have done so to describe how it works. (The tilt-a-whirl moves around a small circular platform that in turn moves around a larger platform).

■ Point out that such a double movement is similar to the way the earth moves around the sun, which they will learn about in this lesson.

Think About What You Know

■ Assign the THINK ABOUT WHAT YOU KNOW activity on p. 4.

■ Answers should reflect independent thinking, but might include that they literally see clouds, land, and water or might include the use of such imagery as "big blue marble" or "spaceship earth."

Study the Vocabulary

■ Have students look up each of the new words in the Glossary.

■ Students should locate an example of the vocabulary words *axis* and *hemisphere* in one of the diagrams on pp. 4–6.

SKILL TRACE: Understanding the Globe		
INTRODUCE PE pp. 4–6	**PRACTICE** PE pp. 31-32 RMB p. 6 TE p. 9	**TEST** Map Skills Post Test, TMB

The Shape of the Earth

THINK ABOUT WHAT YOU KNOW
Imagine that you are an astronaut looking down on the earth from space. Describe what you see.

STUDY THE VOCABULARY

sphere   axis
orbit   hemisphere

FOCUS YOUR READING
What is the shape of the earth?

A. The Earth Is a Sphere

Over 2,000 years ago in the land of Macedonia, the king, Philip, was looking for the best teacher in all of Greece for his 13-year-old son, Alexander. Philip thought that his friend Aristotle might be willing to teach Alexander. Aristotle, famous for his teaching and learning, agreed to become Alexander's teacher. He schooled Alexander in many subjects, including information about the earth.

We do not know exactly what Aristotle taught Alexander about the earth, but many of Aristotle's writings are available to us today. Aristotle wrote that the earth was shaped like a **sphere**, that is, a round ball. We know that this is true because we have seen pictures of the earth taken from space. How could Aristotle have come to this conclusion? He noted that other bodies in space, such as the moon and the sun, were spheres, and so it seemed likely that the earth had the same shape. Aristotle also pointed out that when we first catch sight of a ship far at sea, we see only the top of the mast. The curve of the earth's surface hides the lower parts of the ship from view until it comes closer.

4

B. What We Know About the Earth

Movement of the Earth Aristotle knew more about the earth than most people of his time did. Since then we have learned much more about our planet. Aristotle mistakenly thought the earth stood still. We now know that the earth moves in two ways. The earth **orbits**, or revolves around, the sun. Did you know that we are moving at almost 67,000 miles (107,803 km) an hour? This is the speed at which the earth revolves around the sun. The earth takes $365\frac{1}{4}$ days to make one revolution around the sun.

At the same time, the earth also rotates on its **axis**. The earth's axis is an imaginary line that runs through the middle of the earth from the North Pole to the South Pole. The tilt of this axis never changes as the earth orbits the sun.

THE EARTH'S AXIS
North Pole
Direction of rotation
South Pole   ← Axis

The earth spins on its axis, an imaginary line that goes through the center of the earth.
▶ Through which two points on the earth does the axis pass?

Curriculum Connection

Science This lesson is a good springboard to expand the discussion to the entire solar system and to discuss that all planets revolve around the sun.

● Have students discover the length of the orbit of each planet around the sun, which indicates the length of the year on that particular planet.

● Students could also find out how many planets rotate on an axis, then speculate about what they think happens on a planet that does not rotate on its axis. (They all rotate; if they did not, it might be very hot on one side and very cold on another. Gravity might also be affected.)

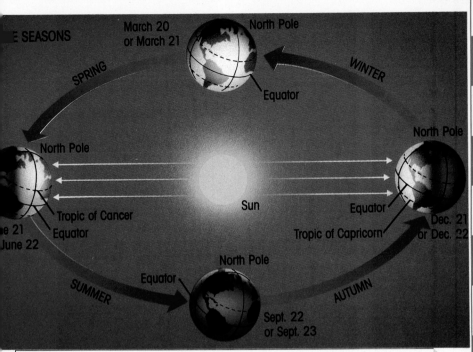

The tilt of the earth as it orbits, or travels around, the sun is the cause of our seasons.
► Which dates mark the start of winter in the Northern Hemisphere?

Change of Seasons The change of seasons is caused by both the revolving of the earth and the tilt of the earth's axis. Look at the diagram on this page. On June 21 or 22 the northern part of the earth is tilted toward the sun. This is the first day of summer and the longest day of the year for the area north of the Equator. The term *Equator* is used to name an imaginary line that circles the earth halfway between the North and South poles.

The Equator divides the earth into two equal halves. The Greek word for "half" is *hemi;* therefore, half the earth's sphere is called a **hemisphere**. The Equator divides the earth into two hemispheres,

called the Northern Hemisphere and the Southern Hemisphere.

For the Southern Hemisphere, June 21 or 22 is the first day of winter and the shortest day of the year. On this day, the southern part of the earth is tilted as far away from the sun as it ever gets. Half a year later, on December 21 or 22, summer begins in the Southern Hemisphere and winter begins in the Northern Hemisphere. During this half-revolution around the sun, the tilt of the earth causes a change in seasons from one extreme to the other.

Size and Shape Aristotle also thought that the earth was larger than it is in fact.

5

Read and Think
Sections A and B

Students will better understand the effects of the shape and movement of the earth after answering the following questions:

1. **What two factors led Aristotle to conclude that the earth was a sphere?** (Other bodies in space were spheres; the effect of the curve of the horizon on ships seen at a distance *p. 4*)

2. **In what two ways does the earth move?** (Orbits around the sun every $365\frac{1}{4}$ days and rotates on its axis, the tilt of which never changes. *p. 4*)

3. **What causes the change of seasons?** (The revolution of the earth and tilt of the earth's axis *p. 5*)

   Thinking Critically Why, do you think, did Aristotle have so many false beliefs about the earth? (Infer) (Answers might include that Aristotle often used logic and imagination, because actual observation was not available in his time. *pp. 4-6*)

SKILL TRACE:	Understanding Movements of the Earth	
INTRODUCE	**PRACTICE**	**TEST**
PE p. 4	RMB p. 2	Map Skills Post
	WB pp. 11, 55	Test, TMB
	TE pp. 4–5	

— Answers to Caption Questions —
p. 4 ► Through the North and South poles
p. 5 ► Winter starts on December 21 or 22 in the Northern Hemisphere.

For Your Information

The Earth's Size The first person to accurately measure the size of the earth was a Greek who was born and lived in Africa. Eratosthenes was an all-around scholar who was the librarian at Alexandria, Egypt. Using his knowledge that an imaginary line drawn all around the earth would form a complete circle, Eratosthenes applied geometry to estimate the distance around the earth. At noon on June 22 a straight pole at Aswan cast no shadow and a pole at Alexandria did. He measured the angle of the shadow at Alexandria. It came out to $\frac{1}{50}$ of a circle; therefore, he reasoned that the distance between the two cities was $\frac{1}{50}$ of the distance around the earth. He multiplied the actual distance between the cities by 50 and got 24,600 miles. He was only about 250 miles low!

Reteaching Main Objective

⭐ *Explain the two ways in which the earth moves.*

- Demonstrate this concept by using a tennis ball for the earth, a flashlight for the sun. Draw a black line on the tennis ball for the Equator.

- Tilt the ball accurately and rotate it as you move it around the sun.

- Have students write descriptions of the two ways they see the earth move.

Optional Activities

5

Lesson *1* Review

Answers to Think and Write

A. Aristotle was correct that the earth is a sphere.

B. Aristotle did not know that the earth orbits, or revolves around, the sun, and that it rotates on its axis. He did not know that the revolution of the earth and the tilt of the earth's axis cause the change of seasons. Aristotle did not know the size of the earth nor that it is not perfectly round.

Answer to Skills Check

March 20 or 21 is the first day of spring and June 20 or 21 is the first day of summer in the Northern Hemisphere.

Focus Your Reading

Ask the lesson focus question found at the beginning of the lesson: **What is the shape of the earth?**
(The earth is shaped like a sphere.)

Additional Practice

You may wish to assign the ancillary materials listed below.

Understanding the Lesson p. *2*
Workbook p. *11*

SKILL TRACE: Understanding Seasons		
INTRODUCE	**PRACTICE**	**TEST**
PE p. 5	RMB p. 2	Map Skills Post
	WB pp. 11, 74	Test, TMB
	PE p. 6	
	TE p. 5	

NORTHERN AND SOUTHERN HEMISPHERES

EASTERN AND WESTERN HEMISPHERES

North Pole

Equator

North Pole

South Pole

NORTHERN HEMISPHERE   **SOUTHERN HEMISPHERE**

North Pole — Prime Meridian

North Pole   **North Pole**

South Pole   **South Pole**

EASTERN HEMISPHERE   **WESTERN HEMISPHERE**

The Equator divides the earth into two hemispheres.
► What are the names of these two hemispheres?

The earth can also be divided into Eastern and Western Hemispheres.
► In which hemisphere can North America be found?

Today we know that the actual distance around the earth at the Equator is 24,902 miles (40,067 km), which is much smaller than many of the stars of our universe. We also know that the earth is not perfectly round, as Aristotle believed. The distance around the earth at the Equator is about 42 miles (68 km) greater than the distance around the poles.

Because of improvements in science and technology, we know more about the earth than Aristotle could have imagined. This year you will have an opportunity to learn more about the earth and its people.

LESSON *1* REVIEW

THINK AND WRITE

A. In what way was Aristotle correct in his ideas about the earth? (Recall)
B. What do we know about the earth that Aristotle did not know? (Recall)

SKILLS CHECK

THINKING SKILL

Look at the diagram on page 5. Which days of the year mark the first days of spring and summer in the Northern Hemisphere?

6

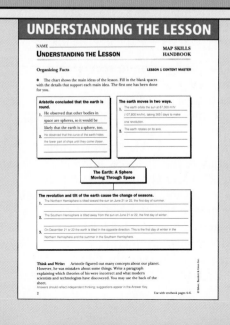

◄ Review Master Booklet, p. 2

6

THINK ABOUT WHAT YOU KNOW

Imagine that you and your family will be driving to Orlando, Florida for a visit. Discuss ways that your family could find out how to get from your home to Orlando.

STUDY THE VOCABULARY

grid	meridian
latitude	Prime Meridian
parallel	International
longitude	Date Line

FOCUS YOUR READING

How are lines of longitude and latitude used on a map?

A. A Geographical Mistake Leads Columbus to the Americas

The Greek scholar Claudius Ptolemy (KLAW dee us TAHL uh mee) did not believe that geography should include "chatter about people." Perhaps that is why we know so little about the author of one of the world's first geography books. We do know that Ptolemy lived in Egypt nearly 500 years after the time of Aristotle.

People were still studying Ptolemy's geography book more than 1,300 years later, when Christopher Columbus arrived in the Americas. In his book, Ptolemy explained that the earth is a sphere. But Ptolemy mistakenly thought that the earth was smaller than it is in fact. As a result of studying Ptolemy's book, Columbus believed the sailing distance from Europe west to the coast of Asia was much shorter. He did not realize that Asia actually lay more than halfway around the earth.

When Columbus set sail in 1492, he was not prepared for such a long trip. But, of course, he did not sail on to Asia. Instead, he reached another large mass of land that we now know as the Americas. So we can say that Ptolemy's error led to the voyage of Columbus. Few mistakes have ever had such far-reaching results.

B. Ptolemy Put a Grid on His Map

Ptolemy's Map Ptolemy wanted to give "a picture of the known world." By a "picture," he meant a map. As a matter of fact, Ptolemy might well have entitled his geography book "Instructions for Drawing Maps"! Even though Ptolemy made some mistakes in his book, we still follow some of his directions. For example, he located north at the top of the map, east on the right, south on the bottom, and west on the left. Most maps, including the ones found throughout this book, still show directions in this manner.

> This map of what is now Ireland, Great Britain, and northern France was drawn by Ptolemy.
> ▶ Do you think this map is accurate?

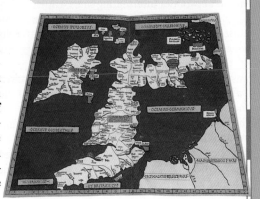

7

Writing to Learn

Writing for Contests Inform students that they have entered a writing contest. Their essays will be entitled "What Columbus Should Know Before His Trip to the Indies."

- Students should write to Columbus in 25 words or less giving him information that he did not possess and that they know. They must try to give as much information as 25 words will allow.

- Since concise writing is so important in this activity, students should exchange papers and function as editors or proofreaders for one another, making suggestions about how to get the most information in the 25 words while still maintaining proper grammar.

Optional Activities

Latitude and Longitude

Objectives

★ **1. Use** latitude and longitude to find locations on a map.

2. Explain Ptolemy's contributions to the study of geography.

3. Identify the following person and place: *Claudius Ptolemy* and *Greenwich, England*.

STARTING THE LESSON

Motivation Activity

- Blow up a large round balloon in front of the class. Use a magic marker to mark the balloon with a number of small *X*s.

- Ask students to tell the location of a particular *X* on the balloon. Students will find this difficult, for there are few ways to relate the *X*s to anything else.

- Ask students what might make it easier to locate a particular *X*. Lead students to conclude that lines on the balloon would help locate the *X*.

Think About What You Know

- Assign the THINK ABOUT WHAT YOU KNOW activity on p. 7.

- Answers should reflect independent thinking, but might include asking friends or using a map to find locations.

Study the Vocabulary

- Have students look up the new words in the Glossary.

- Then ask students to define *Prime Meridian* and *International Date Line*, using other vocabulary words from this lesson in their definitions.

┌─ Answers to Caption Questions ─┐

p. 6 *l.* ▶ Northern and Southern hemispheres

p. 6 *r.* ▶ Western Hemisphere

p. 7 ▶ Students will probably say that the map is not accurate. The shapes of the landforms and the scale are not correct.

2 DEVELOPING THE LESSON

Read and Think

Sections A, B, and C

The history and usage of latitude and longitude will be made clearer to students by answering the following questions:

1. **What were Ptolemy's contributions to the study of geography?**
(Ptolemy influenced Columbus regarding the shape and size of the earth and also introduced maps with north at the top and a grid system. *pp. 7-8*)

2. **Why are there 360 meridians?**
(One for each degree in a circle *pp. 8-9*)

3. **Which special meridians divide the world into Eastern and Western Hemispheres?**
(0° and 180° longitude, or the Prime Meridian and the International Date Line *p. 9*)

4. **When is it necessary to estimate the location of a place on a map?**
(When places are not found exactly on points where latitude and longitude lines cross *p. 10*)

Thinking Critically All degrees of longitude and most degrees of latitude are represented by lines. Which latitudes are not represented by lines? (Analyze)
(The North and South Poles, at 90°N and S latitude, are points, not lines. *pp. 8-10*)

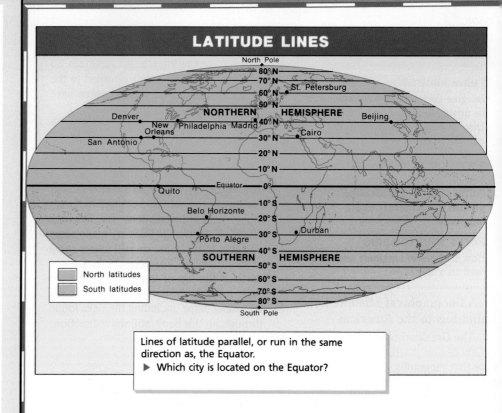

LATITUDE LINES

Lines of latitude parallel, or run in the same direction as, the Equator.
▶ Which city is located on the Equator?

Ptolemy instructed that maps should have a network of intersecting lines, called a **grid**, to locate places. He called the horizontal lines across the map **latitude**, which means "wide," because his map of the known world was wider than it was tall. Lines of latitude are also called **parallels** because they parallel, or run in the same direction as, the Equator. Like the Equator, these lines form whole circles around the earth. If you trace a parallel on a globe with your finger, your finger will always be the same distance from the Equator as it moves around the globe.

Measuring Distances The parallels measure distances in degrees from either side of the Equator toward the poles. The Equator is numbered 0° latitude. There are 90 degrees between the Equator and the North Pole, and 90 degrees between the Equator and the South Pole. We think of having a parallel for every degree. This is why we say there are 90 parallels north of the Equator and 90 parallels south of it. To make maps easier to read, mapmakers usually do not draw every parallel on maps.

The vertical lines on a map that run between the North and the South poles are lines of **longitude**, a word meaning "long." These lines are also called **meridians**. Each meridian crosses the Equator and all other lines of latitude. There are 360 meridians, or one for each degree in a circle. Meridians

8

Curriculum Connection

Math Questions about latitude and longitude make excellent math questions, especially when introducing graphing or absolute value.

● Sample questions follow:
1. Point A is 150°W and Point B is 30°W. How many degrees apart are the two points? (120°)
2. Point A is 150°W and Point C is 30°E. How many degrees apart are the two points? (180°)
3. If you were to go one-quarter of the way around the earth at the Equator, how many degrees of longitude have you traveled? (90°)

For Your Information

The Prime Meridian The Prime Meridian runs through Greenwich, England, because an observatory there was used to chart locations of the stars and the position of the earth. The Prime Meridian is an arbitrary line; that is, it could have been placed on any line drawn from the North to the South Pole. The decision was made by an international conference of astronomers meeting in Washington, D.C., in 1884. In addition to measuring longitude, the Prime Meridian is used to measure time zones for the world. Time around the world changes one hour every 15° from the Prime Meridian. The Equator differs from the Prime Meridian in that it could only have been located at one point — half way between the two poles where the earth's axis is located.

Optional Activities

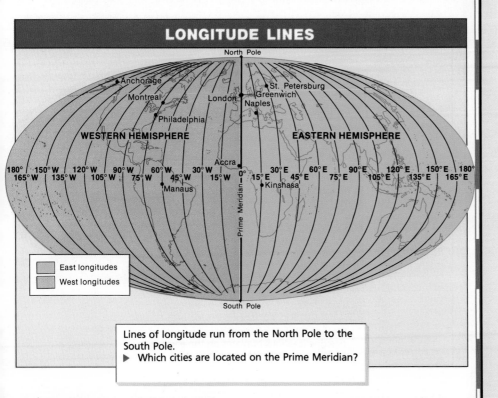

LONGITUDE LINES

North Pole

Anchorage
Montreal
London
St. Petersburg
Greenwich
Naples
Philadelphia

WESTERN HEMISPHERE

EASTERN HEMISPHERE

Accra

| 180° | 150° W | 120° W | 90° W | 60° W | 30° W | 0° | 30° E | 60° E | 90° E | 120° E | 150° E | 180° |
| 165° W | 135° W | 105° W | 75° W | 45° W | 15° W | | 15° E | 45° E | 75° E | 105° E | 135° E | 165° E |

Manaus
Kinshasa

Prime Meridian

South Pole

☐ East longitudes
☐ West longitudes

Lines of longitude run from the North Pole to the South Pole.
▶ Which cities are located on the Prime Meridian?

---

are numbered from the **Prime Meridian**. This imaginary line runs through Greenwich, England. Meridians are counted east and west from the Prime Meridian, which is numbered 0° longitude.

Exactly halfway around the world is the 180° meridian, or what is known as the **International Date Line**, the point at which each day begins. The Prime Meridian and the International Date Line divide the earth into two hemispheres, the Eastern and the Western hemispheres.

C. Using a Map Grid

People have learned much more about making maps since the time of Ptolemy. But today we make use of longitude and latitude lines for the same reason that he did — they make it easier to locate places! Knowing the longitude and latitude of any place on the earth will enable you to find that place on a map. For example, look at the map called Using Latitude and Longitude on page 10. To find St. Petersburg, formerly Leningrad, on that map, put one finger on the line of latitude marked 60°N. Put a finger of your other hand on the line of longitude marked 30°E. Now move your two fingers along those lines until your fingers meet. The city of St. Petersburg is located at the spot where the two lines cross each other. The short way to write these facts is 60°N/30°E. You do

9

◆ **Meeting Individual Needs**

Concept: Latitude and Longitude

Below are three activities that will aid in students' understanding of latitude and longitude.

◆ **EASY** Provide each student with a round balloon and a marker.

Have each student blow up the balloon and label it like a globe, showing the Equator, Prime Meridian, and International Date Line.

Have students label every 30° of north and south latitude and every 60° of east and west longitude.

◀▶ **AVERAGE** Have students practice finding locations on the map on p. 10 by answering the following questions:

1. **What city is located at 31°N/30°E?** (Alexandria)
2. **What city is located at 45°N/76°W?** (Ottawa)
3. **What city is located at 16°S/48°W?** (Brasília)
4. **Where is St. Petersburg located?** (60°N/30°E)
5. **Where is Bangkok located?** (14°N/101°E)

◀▮▶ **CHALLENGING** Ask students the following brainbuster: Why are parallels parallel and meridians not parallel?

Answers should reflect an understanding of the characteristics of the two terms. Parallels are properly named because the parallel lines never touch other parallel lines; each line is the same distance from the Equator. Meridians are not parallel to the Prime Meridian because they all meet at the North Pole and South Pole.

SKILL TRACE:	Understanding Latitude and Longitude	
INTRODUCE PE pp. 8–10	**PRACTICE** TE pp. 8–9 PE pp. 293, 319 RMB p. 3 WB p. 33	**TEST** Map Skills Post Test, TMB

— Answers to Caption Questions —
p. 8 ▶ Quito
p. 9 ▶ London and Accra

9

3 CLOSING THE LESSON

Lesson 2 Review

Answers to Think and Write

A. Ptolemy's mistake of thinking that the world is smaller than it is led Columbus to believe that the distance between Europe and Asia was shorter than it actually is. As a result of this belief, Columbus sailed west and reached the Americas.

B. The two kinds of lines that Ptolemy drew on his maps were lines of latitude, or parallels, and lines of longitude, or meridians.

C. Grids are placed on maps to make it easier to locate places.

Answer to Skills Check

Durban is at 30°S/31°E, New Orleans is at 30°N/90°W, Veracruz is at 19°N/96°W)

Focus Your Reading

Ask the lesson focus question found at the beginning of the lesson: **How are lines of latitude and longitude used on a map?** (Lines of latitude are used to measure distance in degrees north or south of the Equator; lines of longitude are used to measure distance in degrees east or west of the Prime Meridian. Where these lines intersect accurately pinpoints location on a map.)

Additional Practice

You may wish to assign the ancillary materials listed below.

Understanding the Lesson p. 3
Workbook p. 12

SKILL TRACE: Understanding Coordinates (Grid System)

INTRODUCE	PRACTICE	TEST
PE pp. 9–10	PE p. 383 WB p. 12 TE pp. 8–9	Map Skills Post Test, TMB

10

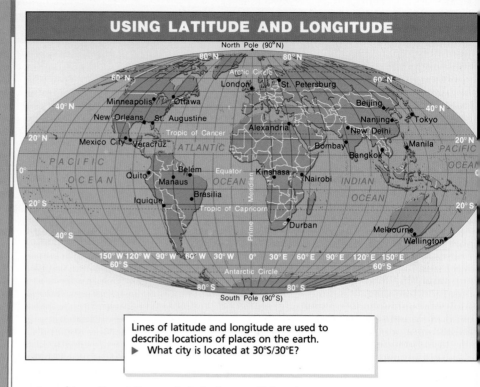

USING LATITUDE AND LONGITUDE

Lines of latitude and longitude are used to describe locations of places on the earth.
▶ What city is located at 30°S/30°E?

not need to write out the words *latitude* or *longitude*. That is because only latitude lines are counted north and south, and only longitude lines are counted east and west.

Sometimes the places you are looking for are not found exactly on points where lines of longitude and latitude cross. When this happens, you have to *estimate*, or figure generally, where those places are.

Using the map above, find the city of New Delhi (DEL ee), India. You will see that New Delhi is not exactly on any line of latitude or longitude. You have to estimate the latitude and longitude. New Delhi is between 20° and 30° north latitude and betwen 70° and 80° east longitude. What would you estimate New Delhi's latitude and longitude to be?

LESSON 2 REVIEW

THINK AND WRITE (Analyze)

A. How did Ptolemy's mistake lead Columbus to the Americas?

B. What are the two kinds of lines that form the grid that Ptolemy drew on his maps? **(Recall)**

C. Why are grids placed on maps? **(Recall)**

10

SKILLS CHECK

MAP SKILL

Look at the Using Latitude and Longitude map on this page. Find the latitude and longitude for the following cities: Durban, New Orleans, and Veracruz.

Optional Activities

UNDERSTANDING THE LESSON

NAME _____
UNDERSTANDING THE LESSON

MAP SKILLS
HANDBOOK

Comparing and Contrasting   LESSON 2 CONTENT MASTER

✳ The chart enables you to compare latitude and longitude. Write the missing information in the blanks. In the columns to the right and left, list information that is true *only* of latitude or longitude. In the center column, list information that is true of *both* latitude and longitude. One blank in each column has been done for you.

Latitude	Latitude and Longitude	Longitude
1. Horizontal lines	1. Lines on a map	1. Vertical lines
2. Also called parallels	2. Measured in degrees	2. Also called meridians
3. Run in the same direction as the Equator	3. Part of grid used to locate places on a map	3. Run from North to South poles
4. Always the same distance from the Equator	4. Form circles around earth	4. Each meridian crosses Equator and all other parallels
5. Equator is 0° latitude		5. One meridian for each degree in a circle—a total of 360
6. Ninety parallels north of the Equator and 90 parallels south of the Equator		6. Numbered east and west from Prime Meridian (0°)
		7. International Date Line is 180° meridian
		8. Prime Meridian and International Date Line divide earth into Eastern and Western hemispheres

Think and Write: Write a paragraph telling which of Ptolemy's map-making ideas are used today. How do these concepts make it easy to use maps? You may use the back of the sheet.
Answers should reflect independent thinking; suggestions appear in the Answer Key.

Use with textbook pages 7–10.   3

◀ **Review Master Booklet, p. 3**

THINK ABOUT WHAT YOU KNOW

What ways can you think of to measure the distance from your house to your school?

STUDY THE VOCABULARY

odometer   altitude
scale   contour line
elevation

FOCUS YOUR READING

How are scale and elevation shown on maps?

A. Measuring Distances Long Ago

Lack of Accurate Instruments In Ptolemy's time, people had no truly accurate way to measure long distances. They could measure a short distance, such as the size of a room, with a cord or rod, as we do with a tape measure or a yardstick. But they could not stretch a cord across a sea or from one city to another. The lack of accurate instruments was one reason for Ptolemy's mistake about the size of the earth.

Ptolemy knew that he could not depend on what sailors or overland travelers told him. If he asked a sailor how far he had come, the sailor would likely say the distance was a three-day sail. But how far could he sail in a day? It depended on the wind and the speed of the boat. Measuring land journeys was not much better. A merchant who had traveled with a caravan of camels or donkeys would also measure distance by days on the road. The merchant would say it was a five-day trip between cities. But animals do not always move at the same speed. Sometimes they get stubborn and do not move at all.

Marching armies provided a somewhat better way to measure distances on land. A troop of soldiers would usually march at about the same pace each day. A three-day march probably was a bit more accurate than a three-day camel caravan trip. But a day's march did not really give the distance unless the soldiers counted paces, and it is doubtful if troops ever counted each step.

A New Invention A Roman engineer invented a type of **odometer** (oh DAHM ut-ur). An odometer is an instrument that tells how far one has traveled. His invention used a wheel fastened to a frame that could be pushed like a wheelbarrow. On the frame he put a device that dropped a small ball into a box with each turn of the wheel. Afterward he would multiply the

This push odometer was invented by a Roman engineer.
▶ Do you think this was a good way of measuring distance?

11

LESSON 3   PAGES 11–15

Scale and Elevation
Objectives
★1. **Use** a map scale to find distance on a map.
2. **List** factors that once made measuring distance difficult.
3. **Determine** elevation by using contour lines and color bands.

1 STARTING THE LESSON

Motivation Activity

■ Have students take pencil and paper, but no measuring devices, to the playground.

■ Give each student five different distances to find (such as from home plate on the baseball diamond to the sixth-grade door). Ask each student to measure the distances.

■ When you return to the classroom, discuss the difficulty of measuring without the proper equipment. Ask what would be needed to make the task easier and more accurate.

Think About What You Know

■ Assign the THINK ABOUT WHAT YOU KNOW activity on p. 11.

■ Answers should reflect independent thinking, but might include distance in terms of length of time walking or riding the bus, or distance in miles or blocks.

Study the Vocabulary

■ Have students find the first usage of each vocabulary word (in boldface) and copy the contextual definition given.

■ Have students write a paragraph describing a hike in the mountains — imaginary or real — using all vocabulary words.

SKILL TRACE: Understanding Scale		
INTRODUCE	PRACTICE	TEST
PE pp. 12–13	RMB p. 4 WB pp. 14, 125 TE p. 12	Map Skills Post Test, TMB

Answers to Caption Questions
p. 10 ▶ Durban
p. 11 ▶ Students may respond that this odometer was not efficient or practical.

Writing to Learn

Writing Technical Directions Have students use any map in the Atlas section of this book. They should choose any two cities on the same map and measure the distance between each city, using the map scale. Students should describe how they used the map scale.

● Students should write and number step-by-step directions for using the map scale to find distance between two places.

● Directions should be concise and to the point, with each new direction beginning with a verb. Directions should contain information on how to find the answer both in miles and in kilometers.

Optional Activities

2 DEVELOPING THE LESSON

Read and Think

Sections A and B

Students can better compare measuring distance long ago with today by answering the following questions:

1. **What was one reason for Ptolemy's mistake about the size of the earth?** (Lack of accurate instruments *p. 11*)

2. **How did the Roman odometer work?** (Small balls dropped into a box every time the wheel turned; they were multiplied by the wheel size to find distance. *pp. 11-12*)

3. **What is the purpose of a map scale?** (Without a scale a person using a map would have no way of finding the real distance between two points. *p. 13*)

   Thinking Critically Why, do you think, is it inaccurate to measure distance by the amount of time it takes to get from place to place? (Hypothesize) (The amount of time depends on such variables as travel conditions, vehicles or animals used, and the person doing the traveling *p. 11*)

SKILL TRACE:	Using Scale to Measure Distance	
INTRODUCE PE p. 12	**PRACTICE** PE p. 219 WB pp. 14, 33 TE pp. 11-12	**TEST** Chapter 14 Test, TMB

Most cars have a speedometer to measure speed and an odometer to measure distance.
▶ How many miles has this car traveled?

distance around the wheel by the number of balls in the box to figure the distance the frame had been pushed. It is doubtful whether this push odometer was ever widely used.

B. Measuring Distances Today

Finding Distances Today it is much easier to find out how far you have traveled. For example, look on the dashboard of a car. Most cars today have both a speedometer and an odometer. The speedometer tells how fast you are going; the odometer tells you how far you have traveled. Odometers are but one of the instruments we have today to measure distances on the surface of the earth.

Another way to find the distance from one place to another is to use a map. When reading a map, you can estimate distances between places by using **scale**. Scale

---

THE METRIC SYSTEM OF MEASUREMENT

In this handbook you have learned that the distance around the earth is 24,902 miles, which is about the same as 40,067 kilometers. Kilometers and miles are both units of measure used to express distance or length. One kilometer and a little more than half a mile are about the same distance. A kilometer is a unit of measure in the metric system. The system is called metric because its standard unit of length is the meter.

The metric system is used for measuring distance. It is also used for measuring such things as weight, capacity, and temperature. The metric system is in use or is being introduced in the world's major countries except the United States.

We have used in this book both customary measurements that are in general use in the United States and metric measurements. When a customary measurement appears, it is followed in parentheses ( ) by the metric measurement that is about equal to it. Inches are changed to centimeters (cm), feet and yards to meters (m), miles to kilometers (km), and acres to hectares (ha). Pounds are changed to kilograms (kg), and quarts to liters (L). Degrees Fahrenheit (°F) changed to degrees Celsius (°C).

Understanding Scale

- Have your students trace their hands on a sheet of tracing paper.
- Cut up drawing paper and give each student a half sheet and a quarter sheet.
- On the half sheet, have students redraw their tracing on the scale of 1 inch = ½ inch. On the quarter sheet of paper, they should redraw their hand to the scale of 1 inch = ¼ inch.
- Discuss with students how this example relates to the scale on a map representing a number of miles or kilometers.

Estimating Distance

- Divide the class into teams of four or five students.
- Each team sends one member at a time to the front of the room. These panelists are given two cities and are asked to estimate in writing the distance between them without the use of a map scale.
- The remaining students on the team then use a map scale to find the actual distance between the two cities.
- The panelist whose estimate is closest to the distance given by his or her teammates scores a point for the team.
- The winning team should be awarded a certificate proclaiming them the "High Exalted Most Proficient Champion Map Scalers."

shows the relationship between distances on a map and real distances on the earth's surface. Without a scale a person using a map would have no way of knowing the real distance.

Using Scale A map can be drawn to many different scales. The scale line on a map shows how much an inch (or centimeter) on the map stands for in real distances on the earth. The two maps below show the country of Italy. But each map is drawn to a different scale. Put a ruler under the scale line of the map on the left. One inch stands for about 200 miles (322 km). Now measure

how many inches there are between the city of Milan and the city of Naples. There are about 2 inches. To find out how many actual miles (or km) there are between these two cities, multiply 2 × 200 (or 2 × 322). You will see that the distance between Milan and Naples is about 400 miles (644 km). Follow the same steps with the other map. The number of inches (or cm) is different from the number in the map on the left. However, when you use the scale for each map to figure the miles (or km) on the earth's surface, the distance between the two cities is the same.

ITALY: TWO DIFFERENT SCALES

Milan
Rome
Naples

Milan
Rome
Naples

| 0 | 100 | 200 miles |
| 0 | 100 | 200 kilometers |

| 0 | 200 | 400 miles |
| 0 | 200 | 400 kilometers |

Both these maps show the country of Italy, but each map is drawn to a different scale.
▶ What does one inch stand for on the map on the right?

13

Graphic Organizer

Use words and diagrams to show two ways to measure distance today and two ways to show elevation or altitude.

MEASURING

MEASURING DISTANCE	SHOWING ELEVATION
1. Odometers 2. Map scale	1. Contour lines 2. Color relief between contour lines

---

Concept:
How Odometers Work

The following three activities will help students comprehend how a common distance-measuring device, the odometer, works.

◆ **EASY** Review with students the information regarding odometers on pp. 11-12.

Have students draw and label a diagram of the early Roman odometer and write a brief paragraph explaining how it worked, also assessing its accuracy.

◀▶ **AVERAGE** Have students explain the difference in function between a *speedometer* and an *odometer*. (A speedometer tells how fast; an odometer tells how far.)

Have students use the description of a Roman odometer in the text to speculate in writing how the odometer on a car works. Any encyclopedia should explain the process in ample detail for those curious about the answer.

◀▮▶ **CHALLENGING** Have students attempt to build their own crude odometers that could be used for measurement in and around school.

Students may wish to attempt this in groups. They should not try to duplicate any existing methods.

GEOGRAPHY THEMES

Location

■ Use the maps on p. 13 to explain why the distance between two cities on earth does not change when different map scales are used.

■ Answers should reflect independent thinking, but should indicate that distance, map size, and map scale are relative to each other.

Answers to Caption Questions
p. 12 ▶ 20,426 miles
p. 13 ▶ 400 miles

Read and Think
Section C

Students will more fully comprehend how elevation is shown on maps by answering the following questions:

1. **How could people tell that they were climbing to higher elevations before it could be measured?**
(By realizing that the higher they climbed, the more difficult it was to breath *p. 15*)

2. **What is the difference between the highest and lowest elevations on the earth's surface?**
(More than 5 ¹/₂ miles (9 km) *p. 15*)

3. **In what two ways can elevation be shown on a map?**
(By contour lines and color. *p. 15*)

Thinking Critically If all elevation is measured from sea level, can you think of evidence that proves that sea level must be the same worldwide? (Synthesize)
(Answers should reflect independent thinking, but one possibility follows: All oceans are connected. A ship could travel around the world through all four oceans and never have to enter a lock. *p. 15*)

SKILL TRACE:	Understanding Elevation Tints	
INTRODUCE PE pp. 14–15	**PRACTICE** PE p.307 RMB p. 4 WB p. 13 TE p. 14	**TEST** Chapter 22 Test, TMB

C. Showing the Land's Elevation

Measuring Heights Maps can be used not only to measure distances on the earth's surface but also to measure the different heights of the land. As you know, the surface of the earth is uneven. Ptolemy showed mountains on his early map, but they are little more than drawings. You would never know from looking at Ptolemy's map that some mountains are two or three times taller than others. But Ptolemy is not to be blamed. In his time there were no ways to measure the height, called **elevation** or **altitude**, of places. There is

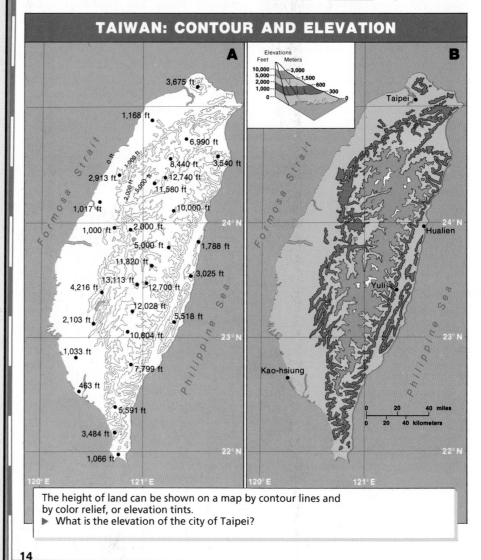

The height of land can be shown on a map by contour lines and by color relief, or elevation tints.
▶ What is the elevation of the city of Taipei?

14

Developing Scale and Elevation

- Have students work in pairs to create a map of an imaginary island on poster board. Each island map should have a scale and contour lines and/or color bands to show elevation.

- Students should develop a series of ten questions about their island that will require their classmates to measure distance and determine elevation.

- Remind students that the coast of their island is at sea level. They should also include several imaginary cities and natural landmarks for the purposes of measuring distance and elevation.

- Have students exchange maps and answer questions.

Reteaching Main Objective

⭐ *Use a map scale to find distance on a map.*

- Obtain a floor plan of your school, deleting the scale if one is included.

- Have students use the map and any measurement tool they need to determine the scale of the map.

- If students need a hint, have them start with the dimensions of your classroom and relate that to the floor plan, developing the scale from there.

- Finally, have students use their new-found scale to determine straight-line distances to the principal's office, to the playground equipment, and so on.

Optional Activities

The shore of the Dead Sea, more than 1,300 feet (396 m) below sea level, is covered with salt deposits.
▶ Where is the Dead Sea?

no doubt, though, that people knew there were differences between low hills and high mountains. People certainly must have known that the higher you climb over a mountain pass, the more difficult it becomes to breathe.

Today we measure elevation from the average height of the sea, or *sea level*. For example, if a mountain is 10,000 feet (3,048 m) high, the top of the mountain is

10,000 feet (3,048 m) above sea level. The elevation of the earth's land surface varies greatly. The highest mountain peaks are over 29,000 feet (8,839 m), but there are also places that are well below sea level. For example, the shore of the Dead Sea, between the countries of Israel and Jordan, is more than 1,300 feet (396 m) below the level of the sea. The difference between the highest and lowest elevations is more than 5 miles (8 km). Such differences are important facts about the earth and are shown on some maps.

Showing Elevation One good way to show the height of the land is to use **contour lines**. All points along one contour line are exactly the same distance above the level of the sea. Map A on page 14 shows the contour lines of the island country of Taiwan.

Another way to show the height of land is with a color relief map. Look at Map B of Taiwan on page 14. The different colors shown in the map key stand for different ranges of elevation. Light green shows land that is between sea level and 1,000 feet (300 m). Land that is between 1,000 feet and 2,000 feet (300 m and 600 m) above sea level is orange. Land shown in the same color may have hills, valleys, and mountains. But the elevation of all land shown in that color is within the range shown on the map key.

LESSON **3** REVIEW

THINK AND WRITE

A. Why was it difficult to get accurate measurements of land and sea distances during Ptolemy's time? (Infer)
B. How do maps show distance? (Recall)
C. What are two ways that land elevation is shown on a map? (Recall)

SKILLS CHECK

MAP SKILL

Look at the elevation map of Taiwan on page 14. What is the elevation of the city of Yuli?

15

◀ **Review Master Booklet, p. 4**

Optional Activities

---

3 CLOSING THE LESSON

Lesson **3** Review

Answers to Think and Write
A. Accurate measurements of land and sea distances were difficult to get during Ptolemy's time because people had no accurate instruments and because time approximations varied greatly according to who was traveling and how they traveled.

B. Maps show distance through the use of scale, which shows the relationship between distances on a map and real distances on the earth's surface.

C. Land elevation is shown on a map by contour lines and by color relief.

Answer to Skills Check
The elevation is 0-1000 ft (0-300m).

Focus Your Reading
Ask the lesson focus question found at the beginning of the lesson: **How are scale and elevation shown on maps?**
(Scale is shown on maps by the use of a scale line that shows how much an inch or centimeter on the map stands for in real distance on the earth. Elevation is shown by contour lines and/or by color.)

Additional Practice
You may wish to assign the ancillary materials listed below.

Understanding the Lesson p. 4
Workbook pp. 13-14

SKILL TRACE:	Understanding Contour Lines	
INTRODUCE	PRACTICE	TEST
PE p. 15	RMB p. 4	Map Skills Post Test, TMB
	WB p. 13	
	TE p. 14	

— Answers to Caption Questions —
p. 14 ▶ Between 0 and 1,000 feet (0 and 300m)
p. 15 ▶ Between Israel and Jordan

15

Taking a Bird's-eye View

Objectives

★1. **Recognize** the role of technology in the refinement of mapmaking.

2. **Describe** the relationship of an aerial photograph to a map.

3. **Identify** the following people: *Nadar* and *Gordon Cooper*.

1 STARTING THE LESSON

Motivation Activity

■ Have students tell about what they have seen while flying in an airplane, being on top of a mountain, or walking on a tall building's observation deck.

■ Ask: **What are the similarities and differences between looking down at the earth from such heights and looking at a map?**

Think About What You Know

■ Assign the THINK ABOUT WHAT YOU KNOW activity on p. 16.

■ Answers should reflect independent thinking, but should include streets and familiar landmarks—a school, the fire house, religious buildings, and the like.

Study the Vocabulary

■ Have students look up both of the new words in the Glossary.

■ Ask students if they know of any uses for satellites. (Most will probably identify transmission of telephone and television signals.)

■ Finally, have students guess how a *cartographer* might use a satellite. (If they need a hint, refer them to the map and photograph on p. 17.)

SKILL TRACE: Understanding Symbols		
INTRODUCE PE pp. 16–17	**PRACTICE** WB p. 42, 88 TE p. 16	**TEST** Unit 4 Test, TMB

16

Taking a Bird's-eye View

THINK ABOUT WHAT YOU KNOW
What would be included on a map of your neighborhood?

STUDY THE VOCABULARY
cartographer   satellite

FOCUS YOUR READING
How do pictures taken from above the earth help people make better maps of the earth's surface?

A. Taking Pictures of the Earth

New Mapmaking A Frenchman known simply as Nadar was famous for his photographs of people. But in 1858 he decided that he would photograph a much larger subject. He would take a picture of a whole village, not the people of the village but the village itself. To do this, he had to get well above his subject. Nadar packed his bulky camera into the basket of a hot-air balloon, ascended about 250 feet (76 m) over a village near Paris, and snapped the picture. This was the first step toward a new kind of mapmaking.

Mapmakers During World War I, airplane pilots acted as scouts and took pictures of battlefields from their airplanes. After the war, aerial photographs came into use in making maps. Using the photographs taken from an airplane flying directly above the surface of the earth enabled **cartographers**, or people who make maps, to make detailed maps of the earth's surface.

Compare the picture on page 17 with the map of the same place, shown on the bottom of page 17. You will notice that the

16

photograph and the map do not necessarily show all the same things. Can you find anything in the photograph that is not shown on the map? Maps also use symbols, and the key tells what each symbol stands for. Symbols stand for real places on the earth. Mapmakers pick out the most important features of a photograph and use symbols to show them. Can you find the buildings in the photograph? Try to find those same buildings on the map.

Cartographers must make careful measurements to ensure that their maps are accurate.
▶ What tools do you see here?

Optional Activities

Writing to Learn

Creative Writing Have students imagine the following situation as the basis for a brief writing activity.

● Students should pretend that they are aboard a satellite circling the earth, looking down at the entire continent of North America. Have them close their eyes for a minute to reflect on the experience.

● Next have students imagine they are in radio contact with the earth and that their parents are at NASA (National Aeronautics and Space Administration) mission control in Houston, Texas.

● Students should write the first things they would describe to their parents about this experience.

FROM PHOTOGRAPH TO MAP

Legend:
- Parking lots
- Buildings
- Roads
- Trees
- Pond
- River
- Other land

The photograph and the map show the same area, but the map shows the area differently. The map uses symbols to represent the most important features in the photograph.
▶ What do the orange symbols on the map represent in the photograph?

2 DEVELOPING THE LESSON

Read and Think
Sections A and B

The history and use of aerial photography can be understood by answering the following questions:

1. **When did cartographers start making maps from aerial photographs?**
(After World War I *p. 16*)

2. **How has the space program aided map-making?**
(By providing clear photographs of the earth's surface, which revealed new earth features. *p. 18*)

Thinking Critically What, do you think, might you learn from a photomosaic map of the United States that you could not learn from a traditional map? (Infer)
(Answers should reflect independent thinking, but might include the way the earth's surface really looks. *p. 18*)

SKILL TRACE:	Understanding the Legend (Key)	
INTRODUCE PE pp. 16–17	**PRACTICE** WB pp. 13, 17, 42	**TEST** Map Skills Post Test, TMB

Answers to Caption Questions
p. 16 ▶ Compass, pens and pencils, and a scale conversion wheel
p. 17 ▶ Buildings

Using Aerial Photography

- The city assessor's office will likely have aerial photographs available, as they use them to observe new construction for property taxes. Obtain a copy of a map showing the area around your school, if available.

- Have students study the photograph to try to pick out familiar landmarks.

- Have students do the work of a cartographer by making maps of areas bordering your school. The entire class should agree on using the same symbols and scale.

- Finally, take students' individual maps of each area and put the maps together to form a photomosaic, or picture map, of the area around your school. They should label their own homes, if possible.

Reteaching Main Objective

⭐ *Recognize the role of technology in the refinement of mapmaking.*

- Have each student write a paragraph describing what maps of the earth would be like had space travel never occurred.

- Students should include what new technology might have developed to take pictures of the earth's surface without having the ability to travel in space.

Optional Activities

3 CLOSING THE LESSON

Lesson 4 Review

Answers to Think and Write

A. Photographs taken from directly above the earth's surface help cartographers to make more accurate and detailed maps of the earth's surface.

B. Space exploration has helped mapmaking through detailed photographs that have revealed features of the earth unknown before, and through picture maps known as photomosaics.

Answer to Skills Check

Paragraphs should reflect independent thinking but might include that accuracy is necessary for navigation on the sea and in the air so that people are not misled by false information.

Focus Your Reading

Ask the lesson focus question found at the beginning of the lesson: **How do pictures taken from above the earth help people make better maps of the earth's surface?** (Pictures taken from above the earth allow for more detailed and accurate maps of the earth's surface and have revealed features of the surface that were previously unknown.)

Additional Practice

You may wish to assign the ancillary materials listed below.

Understanding the Lesson p. 5
Workbook p. 15

This picture of the United States was taken from a satellite. Satellite images help cartographers to make accurate maps.
▶ What color tells you where the bodies of water are in this picture?

B. A New View of the Earth

When astronauts went into space, they saw the earth as no one had ever seen it before. Through television and photographs, they have shared this view with us. In 1963, astronaut Gordon Cooper orbited the earth 22 times. He took many pictures of the earth's surface. His pictures of cloudless desert areas were remarkably clear and revealed features of the earth's surface that did not exist on the best maps at that time.

In the 1970s the United States launched unmanned **satellites** designed to send back to earth pictures of the earth's surface. A satellite is an object made to travel around the earth. By fitting 569 of these views together, it was possible to produce a picture map, or *photomosaic*, of the United States. Satellite photographs now help us make maps like one that Ptolemy asked for many centuries ago—"a picture of the known world."

LESSON 4 REVIEW

THINK AND WRITE

A. How do photographs taken from directly above the earth's surface help to make better maps?

B. How has exploration of space helped cartographers make better maps?

SKILLS CHECK

WRITING SKILL

Write a paragraph explaining why it is important for cartographers to be accurate when they make maps from photographs.

18

Optional Activities

UNDERSTANDING THE LESSON

NAME _____
UNDERSTANDING THE LESSON

MAP SKILLS
HANDBOOK

Putting Events in Order

LESSON 4 CONTENT MASTER

✷ The chart helps you describe how developments in aerial photography improved maps. The developments are listed below. Write the developments in the boxes in the order they occurred.

- Air photographs enable cartographers to make detailed maps.
- World War I pilots take pictures of battlefields from airplanes.
- Photomosaic map of the United States are produced.
- Astronaut Gordon Cooper takes pictures of earth from space.
- Nadar photographs a French village from a balloon.
- Unmanned satellites send back pictures of earth's surface.

| Nadar photographs a French village from a balloon. 1 | World War I pilots take pictures of battlefields from airplanes. 2 | Air photographs enable cartographers to make detailed maps. 3 |

| Astronaut Gordon Cooper takes pictures of earth from space. 4 | Unmanned satellites send back pictures of earth's surface. 5 | Photomosaic maps of the United States are produced. 6 |

Think and Write: Write a paragraph describing how cartographers draw a map from an aerial picture of an area. You may use the back of the sheet. Answers should reflect independent thinking; suggestions appear in the Answer Key.

Use with textbook pages 16–18.

5

◀ **Review Master Booklet, p. 5**

THINK ABOUT WHAT YOU KNOW

Take a look at a globe and a flat map of the world. Can you think of any instances when the flat map would be more useful to you than the globe?

STUDY THE VOCABULARY

projection   distortion

FOCUS YOUR READING

Why is projection important in map-making?

A. Drawing a Round Earth on a Flat Map

In 1492, Martin Behaim (BAY hym) of Nuremberg, Germany, made a globe that the people of his town called "Behaim's earthapple." It is the oldest existing globe. A globe is the best representation of the earth, but even a globe has some drawbacks. To show places on an easy-to-read scale, a globe would have to be quite large. Besides, how could you get a globe into a book? Because of these and other reasons, we also need flat maps of the earth.

Drawing the spherical earth on a flat sheet is an old problem for mapmakers. Throughout the years, mapmakers have tried to solve this problem by using different map **projections**. A projection is a way to show a drawing of the earth on a flat surface. No one kind of projection serves all purposes, so different projections have been developed to meet different needs.

B. A Map for Travelers and Sailors

Early Mapmaking One of the most famous map projections was invented over 400 years ago by a man named Gerardus

Mercator (juh RAHR dus   mur KAYT ur). Mercator used his knowledge of mathematics and geography and his skill as an engraver to become a mapmaker. At that time, mapmaking was a very popular business. With the exploration of the Americas, the demand for maps increased. Mercator printed the first map that carried the names of both the continents of North America and South America. He also made a map that showed that Asia and North America were separate continents.

Martin Behaim's "earthapple," completed in 1492, is the oldest globe in existence.
► Why was *earthapple* a good name for Behaim's globe?

19

Making Map Projections

- Challenge students to make their own flat map projections. They should attempt to create maps that have few distortions in shape and that show relative sizes of land masses.

- The following clue may help some students: One way to accomplish this task is to think in terms of cutting a globe apart and flattening the resulting pieces. Students might like to try to find examples of such a map.

- Students should be prepared to explain to the class how their projection works. The class should offer suggestions to improve each projection.

Optional Activities

Projection

Objectives

★ **1. Explain** why distortions exist when a flat map is drawn of the globe.

2. State one advantage and a distortion of the Mercator and equal-area projections.

3. Describe uses of each projection.

4. Identify the following person: *Gerhardus Mercator*.

1 STARTING THE LESSON

Motivation Activity

■ Draw a crude outline map of the seven continents on each of four grapefruits.

■ Instruct each of four groups of students to peel a grapefruit and reassemble its skin on a flat surface.

■ After all groups have completed this activity, discuss the difficulty of getting the round skin on a flat surface.

Think About What You Know

■ Assign the THINK ABOUT WHAT YOU KNOW activity on p. 19.

■ Answers should reflect independent thinking, but might include that a flat map is easier to carry than a globe and easier to work with because the entire world can be seen at once.

Study the Vocabulary

■ Have students check the meanings of the new words in the Glossary.

■ Ask if students can apply the words *projection* and *distortion* to the operation of a fun house mirror. (Your image is the projection; the way the mirror changes your image is the distortion.)

┌─ **Answers to Caption Questions** ─┐
p. 18 ► Blue-black
p. 19 ► Because the globe was round like an apple
└────────────────────────────────┘

Read and Think

Sections A, B, and C

Students will learn more about projection in mapmaking by answering the following questions:

1. **Why do we need flat maps of the earth as well as globes?**
(Globes might be too large to use if drawn to scale and could not be included in a book. *p.19*)

2. **Why are different map projections needed?**
(Because no one projection meets all needs *p. 19*)

3. **Compare the advantages of the Mercator and equal-area projections.**
(Mercator's projection shows directions clearly; equal-area projection shows land and water sizes accurately. *pp. 20-21*)

Thinking Critically Where do you think the distortion is greatest on equal-area maps? (Analyze)
(The distortion is greatest on equal-area maps the farther east and west of the Prime Meridian. *p. 21*)

SKILL TRACE: Comparing Maps and the Globe		
INTRODUCE PE p. 19	PRACTICE RMB p. 6 TE p. 19	TEST Map Skills Post Test, TMB

A New Projection Because of the growing interest in exploration and long journeys overseas, Mercator's maps had a new projection. On his maps, Mercator drew the parallels of latitude and the meridians of longitude as straight lines meeting at right angles. Look at the map below to see the Mercator projection.

Sailors found the Mercator projection useful because it showed directions clearly. On his maps, north and south were always up and down, and east and west were always right and left. This makes it easy to see that if you sailed straight west from Oslo, Norway, you would miss the coast of the United States.

The Mercator projection was, and still is, useful for figuring the course of a ship at sea, but like all projections, there is some **distortion**, or error, in the way the map shows the earth. To show longitude as straight lines, lands on either side of the Equator must be stretched in size. The greater the distance from the Equator, the greater the stretching must be. Greenland is a good example of this problem. On the Mercator projection, Greenland must be stretched so much that it appears as big as South America. Actually, South America is eight times as large as Greenland. Look at the map below and find Greenland and South America.

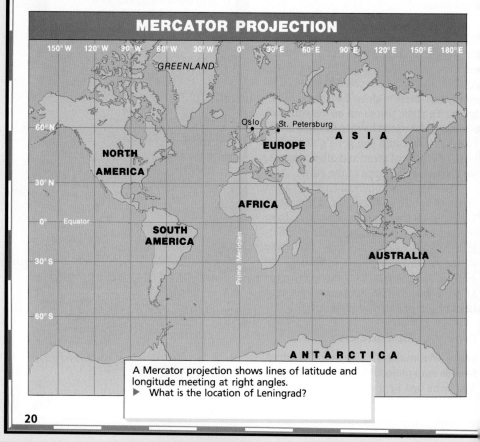

MERCATOR PROJECTION

A Mercator projection shows lines of latitude and longitude meeting at right angles.
▶ What is the location of Leningrad?

20

Designing Advertisements

- Have each student design a 30-second television or radio commercial for either the Mercator or equal-area projection map.

- Students should point out the features and advantages of each map, and perhaps criticize the shortcomings of the other map in their advertisements.

- Students should include as many uses for their type of projection as possible for an added sales feature.

- Radio and television commercials should be audio- or video- recorded for presentation as appropriate.

Reteaching Main Objective

⭐ *Explain why distortions exist when a flat map is drawn of the globe.*

- Show students a picture of the earth taken from outer space.

- Discuss with students why the entire earth is not visible at one time.

- Relate that understanding to the difficulty of making an accurate flat map of the earth.

AN EQUAL-AREA PROJECTION

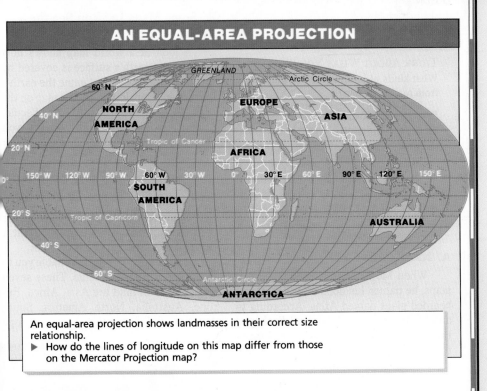

An equal-area projection shows landmasses in their correct size relationship.
▶ How do the lines of longitude on this map differ from those on the Mercator Projection map?

C. A Projection That Shows True Sizes of Land Areas

Most maps that are made today, including most maps used throughout this book, use equal-area projection. A map using equal-area projection shows land and water sizes accurately, but the shapes of the land are distorted. The lines of longitude are curved to show the curve of the earth's surface.

Equal-area projection maps serve most of our map-reading purposes better than maps using the Mercator projection. Although no one projection serves all purposes, maps are still very important tools in helping us learn about our world.

LESSON 5 REVIEW

THINK AND WRITE

A. Why do mapmakers have a problem making a flat map of the world? **(Analyze)**

B. What are the advantages and disadvantages of the Mercator projection? **(Recall)**

C. Why do most maps made today use equal-area projection? **(Recall)**

SKILLS CHECK

MAP SKILL

Look at the two maps on pages 20 and 21. Explain the differences between a map that uses the Mercator projection and a map that uses equal-area projection.

21

Optional Activities

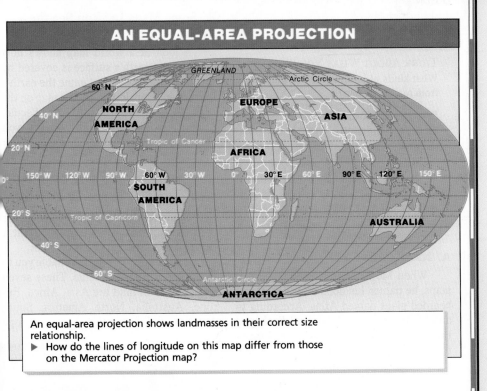

Lesson 5 Review

Answers to Think and Write

A. Since the world is round, mapmakers cannot make a flat map without distortions.

B. The Mercator projection shows direction well, but distorts the size of the land masses the further it goes from the equator.

C. Equal-area projections serve most of our map reading purposes better than the Mercator projection because equal-area projections show land and water sizes accurately but only distort shapes and are therefore used more frequently.

Answer to Skills Check

A Mercator projection shows straight lines of latitude and longitude meeting at right angles, therefore distorting size, especially farther away from the Equator. An equal-area projection shows longitude lines curved, showing size more accurately, but distorting land shapes.

Focus Your Reading

Ask the lesson focus question found at the beginning of the lesson: **Why is projection important in mapmaking?**
(Projection is important because different ways of drawing a round earth on a flat surface serve different purposes and cause different distortions; knowing these differences makes one a more effective map reader.)

Additional Practice

You may wish to assign the ancillary materials listed below.

Understanding the Lesson p. 6
Workbook p. 16

SKILL TRACE: Understanding Map Projections		
INTRODUCE PE pp. 19–21	**PRACTICE** RMB p. 6 WB pp. 16 TE p. 19	**TEST** Map Skills Post Test, TMB

Answers to Caption Questions

p. 20 ▶ 60°N/30°E
p. 21 ▶ Longitude lines appear curved

Using an Atlas

Objectives

★ 1. **Categorize** maps by their purpose.

2. **Review** the names of the oceans and continents.

3. **Explain** the uses of an atlas.

4. **Identify** the following person: *Atlas*.

1 STARTING THE LESSON

Motivation Activity

■ Bring to class as many kinds of maps as possible to show to students. Discuss with students the differences and similarities in the maps.

■ Mention to students that many people like to look at a map because it shows them interesting places they have visited, will visit, or would like to visit. Maps also show locations in relation to the rest of the world.

■ Ask your students for reasons they enjoy looking at maps.

Think About What You Know

■ Assign the Think About What You Know activity on p. 22.

■ Maps name the oceans and continents, show political boundaries and physical characteristics, and show weather and climate, vegetation, population density, and natural resources.

Study the Vocabulary

■ Have students look up the meanings of the new vocabulary words in the Glossary.

■ Ask them which of the words means a reference book that would contain maps that would show the other five words. (atlas)

■ Have students look through the Atlas of this book to find examples of maps that show the vocabulary words.

Using an Atlas

THINK ABOUT WHAT YOU KNOW

What kinds of information can you get from reading a map?

STUDY THE VOCABULARY

atlas	humidity
isthmus	precipitation
climate	population density

FOCUS YOUR READING

What is an atlas?

A. Named After a Mythical Giant

When Mercator published a book of maps, he named his book after a mythical bearded giant named Atlas. According to an old Greek myth, Atlas had disobeyed the gods. As punishment Atlas was made to stand and hold up the heavens. Some statues and pictures, like the one on this page show Atlas holding the sphere of heaven in his hands over the earth.

Mercator's Atlas became so well-known that people came to call any collection of maps an **atlas**. Today we still call a collection of maps an atlas. This book's Atlas can be found in the back of the book on pages 610–629.

Atlases, like dictionaries and encyclopedias, are reference books. We usually do not read a reference book all the way through from beginning to end. Instead, we turn to it when we want some specific information. You may find it interesting, and very helpful, to look through the Atlas in this book to discover the kinds of maps it contains. As you use this book throughout the year, you will find questions that refer to the Atlas.

B. Some Maps Let You See the Entire World

A look at a world map shows how much of the earth's surface is covered by the four oceans. Can you name the earth's four oceans from looking at the map on the next page? If you named the Pacific, Atlantic, Indian, and Arctic oceans, you are correct. The Pacific Ocean is by far the largest and deepest. It is nearly twice as large as the second largest ocean, the Atlantic. Ice covers much of the Arctic Ocean, which centers on the North Pole. No boundaries between the oceans appear on the map, because each ocean is but a part of one continuous body of water.

The world map will also enable you to locate the seven continents. These seven large bodies of land are Asia, Africa, Europe, Australia, North America, South America, and Antarctica. Locate Europe

This statue of Atlas stands in Rockefeller Center in New York.
▶ What is Atlas shown holding in this statue?

Writing to Learn

Writing an Introduction   Have students imagine that they have been selected to write an introduction to an atlas that will be used by sixth grade students all over the country.

● The introduction should explain the origins of the word *atlas*, tell the uses of an atlas, and describe the experiences students are likely to have when using an atlas.

● The conclusion to the introduction should contain a personal word from the author on his or her favorite way to use an atlas, perhaps including a fun map game or just a way to dream about faraway places.

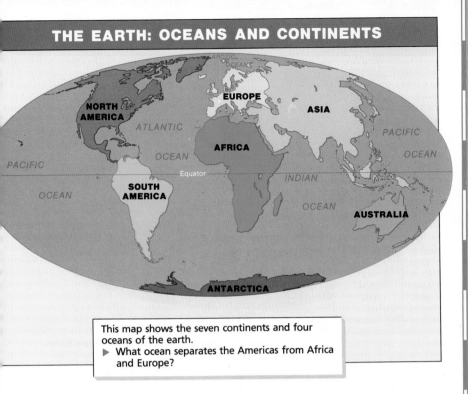

THE EARTH: OCEANS AND CONTINENTS

This map shows the seven continents and four oceans of the earth.
► What ocean separates the Americas from Africa and Europe?

and Asia on the map above. Notice that these two continents are one huge land mass. We sometimes call this land *Eurasia*, a combination of Europe and Asia.

Some continents are connected by a narrow strip of land, called an **isthmus** (IHS mus). Africa is attached to Eurasia by an isthmus, as North America is attached to South America. Australia and Antarctica are the only two continents wholly separated from the others.

C. Physical and Political Maps

In your Atlas you will find two maps for each continent. One is called a political map; the other is a physical map. Political maps show the nations, or countries, that have separate governments. Political

maps also usually give the locations of capitals and other important cities. Political maps of individual countries show the political divisions within those countries.

A physical map represents the natural features of the land. Important natural features are often labeled. Look at the physical map of North America on page 621. Find the Rocky Mountains on that map.

Sometimes, political and physical maps may be combined to make one map. Such a map makes clear the relationship between natural features and political boundaries. Look at the map of Australia and New Zealand on page 626. The Murray River serves as part of the political boundary between the Australian territories of Victoria and New South Wales.

23

Read and Think

Sections A, B, C, and D

Students will be better able to use an atlas by answering the following questions:

1. **How should an atlas be used?**
   (As a reference book to look up specific information *p. 22*)

2. **What kind of map shows the natural features of the land?**
   (Physical map *p. 23*)

3. **What is the difference between a weather map and a climate map?**
   (Weather maps show daily information and climate maps present average weather over a period of time. *p. 24*)

4. **What kind of map shows the locations of forests, grasslands, and deserts?**
   (Vegetation map *p. 24*)

Thinking Critically Refer to a world map to determine whether you think that Europe and Asia should be two continents or one continent, Eurasia. (Evaluate)
(Answers should reflect independent thinking but might include that Eurasia should be one continent because it is one large, connected land mass or that Europe and Asia should be separate continents because they are physically separated by the Ural Mountains. *pp. 22-23*)

Answers to Caption Questions
p. 22 ► The sphere of heaven
p. 23 ► The Atlantic Ocean

Cooperative Learning

Making a News Show Videotape a class news show in which maps play an important role.

● Have students work in groups of four or five, with two or three students writing copy, two students drawing maps, and all students participating in a 10-minute news broadcast.

● Suggested news areas and related maps follow.
  Weather: local and national weather maps
  National News: maps showing locations of stories
  World News: maps showing locations of stories
  Travel Special Feature: road map on how to get there
  Sports: U.S. map showing where teams are playing

Developing a Class Atlas

● Have students list all the types of maps mentioned in this lesson. (world, physical, political, weather, climate, vegetation, population density, resource maps)

● Students should look through the text and brainstorm to add other types of maps to the list. (agricultural products, time zones, historical maps, etc.) Make a list of all the maps on the chalkboard.

● Have the students develop a class atlas that includes an example of every type of map listed on the chalkboard. Students should locate the different types of maps, photocopies should be made, then students should label each and assemble their atlas.

Optional Activities

Meeting Individual Needs
Concept:
Using Maps

Below are three activities that will aid students in the use of map information.

◆ **EASY** Duplicate eleven copies of an outline map of the world.

On each map, shade in a different continent or ocean. Use these maps as flash cards for students still having difficulty identifying the four oceans and seven continents.

◀▮▶ **AVERAGE** Assemble a collection of many different types of maps. (If you made a class atlas in a previous activity, that would be ideal.)

Develop a game in which students challenge each other to see how fast they can name the different types of maps.

◀▮▶ **CHALLENGING** Explain briefly to students the idea of continental drift — the theory that all the earth's land once existed in a single mass and has moved apart over millions of years.

Provide students with an outline map of the seven continents. Have them cut out the continents and see if they can reassemble the landmasses in a single mass, like a giant puzzle. After they have tried, have them check an encyclopedia for possible arrangements.

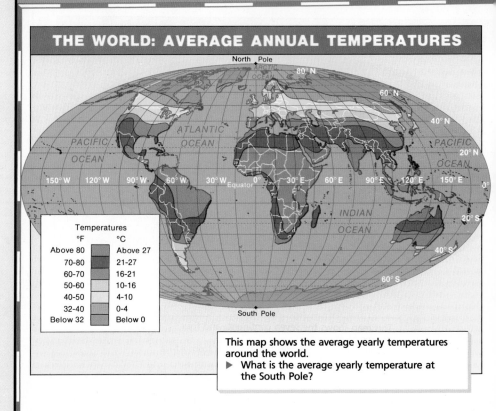

THE WORLD: AVERAGE ANNUAL TEMPERATURES

Temperatures	
°F	°C
Above 80	Above 27
70–80	21–27
60–70	16–21
50–60	10–16
40–50	4–10
32–40	0–4
Below 32	Below 0

This map shows the average yearly temperatures around the world.
▶ What is the average yearly temperature at the South Pole?

D. An Atlas Can Have Many Other Kinds of Maps

Weather Maps Can you imagine television weather reporters not using maps when they give weather reports? Newspapers, too, often print daily weather maps. Those who report the weather use maps because maps are the clearest and quickest way to present facts about the weather over a country or region.

Maps can also be used to show information about the **climate** of a place. Climate is the normal or usual pattern of weather for a place over a period of time. As you can see from the map above, some climate maps show temperatures. Like weather maps, climate maps may also

show the amount of dryness or dampness in the air, which is known as **humidity**, and the amount of **precipitation** a place gets. Precipitation is moisture that falls on the earth's surface in the form of rain, snow, sleet, or hail. Weather maps give you this information for a few particular days, whereas climate maps present average yearly statistics.

Other Maps There is almost no limit to the different types of facts that can be presented on maps. You can learn about the plant life of an area from a vegetation map. A vegetation map, such as the one shown on page 25, shows where there are forests, grasslands, and deserts. The Atlas at the

24

Optional Activities

Solving a Problem with Maps

- Suppose your family wanted to take a summer vacation to see the mountains in the western part of the United States. Have students write a paragraph describing how each of the following maps might be helpful.

- **Political** (Show cities and states to visit)
  Physical (Show where mountains are)
  Climate (Determine normal summer weather in area for packing necessary clothes and equipment.)
  Weather (Show likely weather for particular days.)
  Precipitation (Know what gear is needed)

- Finally, ask what kind of map not mentioned in this lesson might be most helpful of all. (Road map)

Reteaching Main Objective

⭐ *Categorize maps by their purpose.*

- Write on the chalkboard the names of the maps discussed in this lesson: political, physical, political-physical, climate, vegetation, population density, and resource maps.

- Have the students look through the Atlas in the back of the book and categorize each map by purpose.

- Also have students look through the entire book to find as many examples as possible of each type of map. Have them identify types of maps that do not fit the categories above as well.

THE WORLD: VEGETATION REGIONS

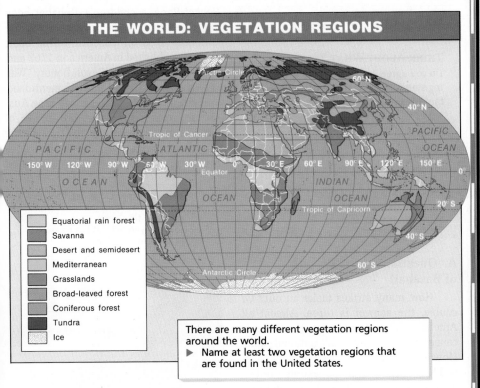

Legend:
- Equatorial rain forest
- Savanna
- Desert and semidesert
- Mediterranean
- Grasslands
- Broad-leaved forest
- Coniferous forest
- Tundra
- Ice

There are many different vegetation regions around the world.
▶ Name at least two vegetation regions that are found in the United States.

back of this book contains other types of maps. The **population density** map shows where the largest number of people live in the world. Population density is determined by the average number of people who live on a square mile (sq km) of land.

By looking at a resource map, you can quickly get facts about where there are mineral deposits such as coal, tin, and iron ore. Maybe Mercator was correct in thinking that holding a book of maps is like having the universe in your hands!

LESSON 6 REVIEW

THINK AND WRITE

A. Why is a collection of maps called an atlas? **(Recall)**

B. What are the names of the four oceans and seven continents? **(Recall)**

C. What is the difference between a political map and a physical map? **(Recall)**

D. What are some other kinds of maps that can be found in an atlas? **(Recall)**

SKILLS CHECK

MAP SKILL

Look at the temperature map on page 24. What is the average yearly temperature at 40°N/90°W?

25

◀ **Review Master Booklet, p. 7**

Lesson 6 Review

Answers to Think and Write

A. A collection of maps is called an atlas because they are named after Mercator's book of maps that he named after the mythical Atlas who, according to Greek myth, was forced to stand and hold up the heavens.

B. The four oceans are the Atlantic, Pacific, Indian, and Arctic. The seven continents are North America, South America, Africa, Asia, Europe, Australia, and Antarctica.

C. A political map shows countries and cities, and a physical map shows natural features of the earth.

D. Other kinds of maps found in an atlas include weather, climate, vegetation, population density, and resource maps.

Answer to Skills Check

The average yearly temperature at 40°N/90°W is 50°–60°F (10°–16°C).

Focus Your Reading

Ask the lesson focus question found at the beginning of the lesson: **What is an atlas?** (An atlas is a reference book made up of a collection of maps named after the Greek mythological character Atlas.)

Additional Practice

You may wish to assign the ancillary materials listed below.

Understanding the Lesson p. 7
Workbook p. 17

SKILL TRACE: Understanding Special-Purpose Maps		
INTRODUCE PE pp. 23–25	**PRACTICE** TE p. 24 PE p. 265 RMB p. 7 WB p. 17	**TEST** Map Skills Post Test, TMB

Answers to Caption Questions

p. 24 ▶ Below 32°F (below 0°C)
p. 25 ▶ Answers may include desert and semidesert, grasslands, broad-leaved forest, Mediterranean, or coniferous forest.

25

Dates and Time Lines

Objectives

★1. **Demonstrate** how to use a time line.

2. **Explain** how years are numbered on a time line.

3. **Define** common periods of time, such as a century and a decade.

4. **Identify** the following people: *Dionysius the Little* and *Jesus Christ.*

1 STARTING THE LESSON

Motivation Activity

■ If students have seen any of the popular *Back to the Future* movies, have them explain some of the difficulties the main character encountered functioning in a time different from his own.

■ Ask your students why they think it is important to know the year in which an event occurred. Ask why it is important to know which year we are living in and the years in which things are supposed to happen in the future. (Answers should reflect independent thinking, but might include that knowing our place in time is part of our identity.)

Think About What You Know

■ Assign the THINK ABOUT WHAT YOU KNOW activity on p. 26.

■ Answers should reflect independent thinking, but should recognize the link between learning dates as a way of organizing information about the past.

Study the Vocabulary

■ Have students look up the vocabulary words in the Glossary.

■ Draw a time line on the board from 200 B.C. to A.D. 200 at 100 year intervals.

■ Have students label *anno Domini, century, decade,* and *time line.* Have them locate a point *circa 100 B.C.*

Dates and Time Lines

THINK ABOUT WHAT YOU KNOW

Do you agree or disagree with the following statement: "Learning dates is important to learning about the past"?

STUDY THE VOCABULARY

anno Domini   circa
century   time line
decade

FOCUS YOUR READING

How are dates and time lines used to learn about the past?

A. Questioning the Origins of Baseball

How many strikes make an out? Of course, the answer is three. Almost all Americans can answer that question because baseball is America's national game. How long have people been playing baseball? The answer to that question is not so easy. In fact, it has been the subject of a great debate.

Many people believe that baseball grew out of an old English game called rounders. Among those who believed that baseball was started in America was A. G. Spalding, a businessman and former baseball player. He formed a special commission to investigate the origin of baseball. The commission reported that baseball was invented by a man named Abner Doubleday and that one of the first baseball games was played at Cooperstown, New York, in 1839.

Some people doubt the Doubleday story and point out that long before the year 1839 various writings mentioned baseball. For example, *A Little Pretty*

Pocket-Book, a children's alphabet book published in 1744 in England, used the sentence "B is for Baseball." This book was later published in America in 1762 and 1787. An American Revolutionary War soldier at Valley Forge in 1778 mentioned "playing at base" in his journal. Jane Austen, a famous English author, spoke of baseball in a book written about 1798. *The Boy's Own Book,* published in 1828, does not mention baseball, but the description

> The game of baseball has been a popular American pastime for over a hundred and fifty years.
> ▶ How can you tell this is a baseball game from long ago?

Optional Activities

Writing to Learn

Writing a Sports Column   Have students pretend that they are sports reporters for a newspaper of the 1840s.

● Have each student prepare a list of five questions that he or she would like to ask Abner Doubleday about his role in the origin of the game of baseball.

● Next, students should exchange questions with their classmates. They should attempt to answer the questions as best they can, pretending to be Abner Doubleday.

● Students should write sports columns based on the answers to their five questions and the information in the text.

of rounders sounds a great deal like a description of baseball.

The debate about the origin of baseball brings out the importance of dates. There is no doubt that Abner Doubleday was a real person or that he taught at a military school in Cooperstown, New York. The question is whether he invented a new game in 1839. The answer for that depends largely on dates. Dates, like maps, make it possible to have more exact knowledge about the people, lands, and events of the world. Maps tell us where; dates tell us when.

B. How Years Are Numbered

Numbering Years The year 1839 could have been numbered differently. We could say that the game at Cooperstown was played 63 years after the Declaration of Independence was signed in 1776. But for dates to be useful to us, they must be counted from the same point.

The point from which most dates are counted was first decided by a man who lived in Rome. He was named Dionysius (dye uh NISH us) the Little. We do not know much about this man, not even why he was called Dionysius the Little. We do know that he began the practice of numbering the years from the birth of Jesus Christ. Dionysius first began to do this in the year he called A.D. 525. The letters A.D. stand for the Latin term **anno Domini** (AH-noh DOH mee nee), which in the English language means "in the year of the Lord."

Dionysius' System Today most of the world uses the system Dionysius invented. When we write that the Cooperstown game was played in 1839, we mean that it was played one thousand eight hundred thirty-nine years after the birth of Christ. In practice we rarely use the letters A.D. when dating an event that occurred after Christ's birth.

The years before the birth of Christ are numbered backward from his birth. For example, the year before A.D. 1 was 1 B.C. The letters stand for "before Christ." The year before 1 B.C. was 2 B.C., and so on. When referring to dates before the birth of Christ, the higher the number, the earlier the year. For example, Aristotle lived from 384 B.C. to 322 B.C. The letters B.C. are always used with dates that show time before the birth of Christ.

27

Concept:
Making Time Lines

Below are three activities that will help students make accurate time lines.

◆ **EASY** Help students to understand the concept of scale as it applies to a time line. For example, on a time line of a student's life, if ½ inch stood for one year, the line would be 6 inches long for a 12-year old.

Ask students what kind of scale would be manageable for a time line showing 100 years. For 2,000 years? (Answers should reflect independent thinking but might include ½ inch = 10 years and ½ inch = 200 years respectively.) Discuss the advantages and disadvantages of smaller and larger scales.

◀▶ **AVERAGE** Have students develop comparative time lines, showing their lives next to their parents' lives.

Students should use the same scale on comparative time lines and note overlapping information.

◀▮▶ **CHALLENGING** Have students do comparative time lines showing themselves and events in the United States or world history.

Other students may prefer to develop time lines comparing the growth of professional sports, such as baseball, football, basketball, hockey, or soccer.

C. Other Ways to Date Events

One Hundred Years Sometimes we date events by a period of 100 years, called a **century**. We count centuries in the same way we count years—that is, before and after the birth of Christ. The years from 1 to 100 make up the first century A.D. We live in the 1900s, the twentieth century. The year 2000 will still be in the twentieth century, but when the year 2001 arrives, we will enter the twenty-first century. Centuries before the birth of Christ are numbered like years before the birth of Christ. For example, the years 1 B.C. to 100 B.C. are considered the first century B.C.

A CENTURY HAS 100 YEARS

Years	Centuries
2001 – 2100	21st century
1901 – 2000	20th century
1801 – 1900	19th century
1701 – 1800	18th century
1601 – 1700	17th century
1501 – 1600	16th century
1401 – 1500	15th century
1301 – 1400	14th century
1201 – 1300	13th century
1101 – 1200	12th century
1001 – 1100	11th century
901 – 1000	10th century
801 – 900	9th century
701 – 800	8th century
601 – 700	7th century
501 – 600	6th century
401 – 500	5th century
301 – 400	4th century
201 – 300	3rd century
101 – 200	2nd century
1 – 100	1st century

A century is a period of 100 years by which we sometimes date events.
► Which year will begin the 21st century?

It is especially useful, and often easier, to remember the century in which a person lived rather than to remember the years of his or her birth and death. For example, Aristotle lived in the fourth century B.C., while Mercator, who was born in 1512 and died in 1594, lived in the sixteenth century. In which century was the Cooperstown baseball game played?

Ten Years We can also speak of dates in ten-year periods of time, called **decades**. We often speak of a decade, such as the 1920s or the 1970s, when we refer to events that took place over a period of several years. For example, we can say that the first manned space flights occurred in the 1960s. It was during that decade that we first started to explore space. What decade are you living in now?

Sometimes it is impossible to know the exact year of an event, but we may know *about* when the event happened. For example, we do not know the exact year that Jane Austen wrote the book in which she mentioned baseball. In such a case we write the abbreviation *ca.* or *c.* before the date. These letters stand for the Latin word **circa**, which means "about." We know that Jane Austen's book was written about 1798, so we date the writing of the book as ca. 1798.

D. Using Time Lines

Just as we can show different places on a map, we can show a series of events on a **time line**. A time line, like a map, has a scale, but the scale represents years rather than distances.

Look at the time line on the next page. It lists some of the dates related to the possible origin of baseball. This time line has a scale that runs from left to right.

Analyzing Information

● Explain to students that as January 1, 1990, rolled around, there was a great deal of talk about beginning a new decade. As we approach the year 2000, there is anticipation of not only a new decade, but also a new century and a new millennium. Yet all of this talk is incorrect. Ask students to explain why.

● Answers may reflect independent thinking, but it goes back to the numbering system of Dionysius the Little. There is no 0 year; the first decade began at A.D. 1 and ended in A.D. 10. The first century began in 1 and ended at the end of A.D. 100. Therefore the new decade began in 1991, and the new century begins in 2001.

Reteaching Main Objective

⭐ *Demonstrate how to use a time line.*

● Have students turn to any time line in their textbooks and write five questions based on that time line.

● Students should exchange papers and see how many of each other's questions they can correctly answer in fifteen minutes.

● Pair students having difficulty answering questions with those students who have easily answered the questions. Have pairs of students attempt to solve the same problems together, explaining to each other how they arrived at the answers.

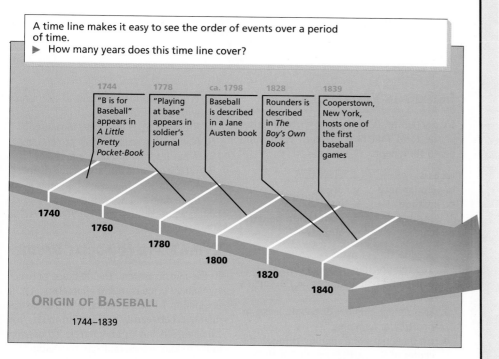

A time line makes it easy to see the order of events over a period of time.
► How many years does this time line cover?

1744	1778	ca. 1798	1828	1839
"B is for Baseball" appears in *A Little Pretty Pocket-Book*	"Playing at base" appears in soldier's journal	Baseball is described in a Jane Austen book	Rounders is described in *The Boy's Own Book*	Cooperstown, New York, hosts one of the first baseball games

1740
1760
1780
1800
1820
1840

ORIGIN OF BASEBALL
1744–1839

Each segment on this time line equals 20 years. The whole time line represents 100 years, from 1740 to 1840. Some events and their dates are named above the time line, and a black line leads to each event's date on the time line.

This time line makes it easy to see the order of events dealing with the origin of baseball. For example, you will notice by looking at the time line that the book *A Little Pretty Pocket-Book* was written many years before the game at Cooperstown was played. About how many years were there between the writing of Jane Austen's book and the Cooperstown game? Throughout this book, you will find time lines to help you understand when things happened.

LESSON 7 REVIEW

THINK AND WRITE

A. Why are dates important to the discussion of the origin of baseball? **(Analyze)**
B. Explain how we number years. **(Recall)**
C. What is the difference between a century and a decade? **(Recall)**
D. What kind of information can be shown on a time line? **(Recall)**

SKILLS CHECK

THINKING SKILL
Make a time line showing some important events in your life, such as the year you were born and the year you started school.

Lesson 7 Review

Answers to Think and Write

A. Dates are important to the discussion of the origin of baseball because there is disagreement about when baseball was first played.

B. All time is measured from the birth of Jesus Christ. Years after the birth of Christ are similar to positive numbers on a number line and are labeled *anno Domini* (A.D.); years before the birth of Christ are similar to negative numbers on a number line and are labeled Before Christ (B.C.).

C. A century is 100 years; a decade is 10 years.

D. The dates and the order in which important events happened are shown on a time line.

Answer to Skills Check

Time lines should reflect different individuals but should all begin at birth and end with the present and include a scale of years.

Focus Your Reading

Ask the lesson focus question found at the beginning of the lesson: **How are dates and time lines used to learn about the past?** (Dates help us know when certain things happened. Time lines are a way of organizing related events or a period of time to show what happened when.)

Additional Practice

You may wish to assign the ancillary materials listed below.

Understanding the Lesson p. 8
Workbook p. 18

SKILL TRACE: Understanding Time Lines		
INTRODUCE PE pp. 28–29	**PRACTICE** PE p. 95 TE p. 28 RMB p. 8 WB p. 76	**TEST** Map Skills Post Test, TMB

Answers to Caption Questions

p. **28** ► 2001
p. **29** ► 95 years

UNDERSTANDING THE LESSON

NAME _____
UNDERSTANDING THE LESSON
MAP SKILLS HANDBOOK

Recalling Facts LESSON 7 CONTENT MASTER

✳ Read each statement below. Write **True** if the statement is true and **False** if it is false. If the statement is false, cross out the part that is incorrect and write the correct words above it.

False   1. Our system for numbering dates was first used by Abner Doubleday in 1839.
False   2. Today we still use one system that marks dates before the birth of Christ as A.D., and those after the birth of Christ as B.C.
True   3. The date 1989 means one thousand nine hundred eighty-nine years after the birth of Christ.
True   4. For dates before the birth of Christ, the higher the number, the earlier the year.
False   5. Events can be dated by blocks of weeks called centuries and decades.
False   6. The twentieth century includes the years from 1900 to 1999.
True   7. The first manned space flights took place in the 1960s.
True   8. If we are not sure about the exact year of an event, we can write the letters ca. or c. before the date.
True   9. The scale of a time line is marked in years.
False   10. A time line makes it easy to see the reasons for events.

Think and Write: How might years be numbered if we did not use the birth of Christ as the starting point? Write a paragraph in which you choose two other events as starting points for numbering dates. Explain each starting point, and then renumber the present year using each new starting point. You may use the back of the sheet. Answers should reflect independent thinking; suggestions appear in the Answer Key.

8   Use with textbook pages 26–29.

◀ Review Master Booklet, p. 8

Optional Activities

Using the Vocabulary

1. g	6. d
2. e	7. j
3. i	8. b
4. a	9. f
5. h	10. c

Remembering What You Read

1. Orbits around the sun; rotates on its axis

2. Revolution and tilt of earth's axis

3. Because places are not always located on the intersection of the lines of latitude and longitude

4. You have no way of measuring actual distance.

5. Sea level

6. Mercator, equal-area

7. Symbols used on the map and their meanings

8. Pacific Ocean

9. Climate maps show usual pattern of weather over time; weather maps show atmospheric changes over brief periods of time.

10. Eighteenth century

MAP SKILLS HANDBOOK REVIEW

USING THE VOCABULARY

On a separate sheet of paper, write the letter of the term that best matches each numbered statement.

a. axis	f. elevation
b. hemisphere	g. atlas
c. latitude	h. isthmus
d. longitude	i. population density
e. scale	j. climate

1. A collection of maps
2. The relationship between distances on a map and real distances on the earth's surface
3. The average number of people living in a particular land area
4. An imaginary line running through the center of the earth from the North Pole to the South Pole
5. A narrow strip of land connecting two continents
6. Vertical lines on a map
7. A place's normal pattern of weather
8. Half the earth's sphere
9. The height of the land
10. Horizontal lines across a map

REMEMBERING WHAT YOU READ

On a separate sheet of paper, answer the following questions in complete sentences.

1. In what two ways does the earth move?
2. What causes the change of seasons?
3. Why is it sometimes necessary to estimate latitude and longitude?
4. Why would it be difficult to use a map without a scale?
5. From where is elevation measured?
6. Name two common map projections.
7. What information is in a map key?
8. Which ocean is the largest and deepest?
9. What is the difference between a climate map and a weather map?
10. In what century was 1789?

TYING MATH TO SOCIAL STUDIES

In the metric system, the distance between two places is measured in kilometers. A mile is equal to 1.61 kilometers. If you know the distance between two places in miles, you can figure it out in kilometers. To convert miles to kilometers, multiply the distance in miles by 1.61. Convert the distances between New York and these world cities to kilometers: Cairo—5,602 miles; Hong Kong —8,054 miles; Mexico City—2,094 miles.

THINKING CRITICALLY

On a separate sheet of paper, answer the following questions in complete sentences.

1. Which factor affects climate more— latitude or longitude?
2. How does climate affect people's lives?
3. Name five reasons why people use maps.
4. Compare the length of longitude lines on a Mercator projection with the length of those on an equal-area projection map.
5. Why do we need a standard system of time measurement?

30

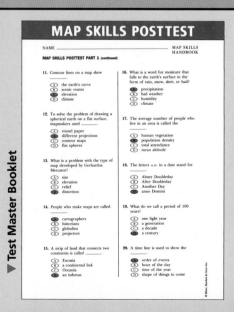

SUMMARIZING THE HANDBOOK

On a separate sheet of paper, copy the graphic organizer shown below. Beside the main idea of each lesson, write three statements that support the main idea.

HANDBOOK THEME
Maps and globes provide a wealth of information about people and the earth. To interpret maps, it is necessary to understand scale, symbols, latitude, longitude, and projections.

LESSON 1

We have learned much about the earth since the days of Aristotle.

1. Shaped like sphere   2. _____   3. _____

LESSON 2

Maps help us locate places.

1. Latitude lines   2. _____   3. _____

LESSON 3

There are many ways of measuring land and sea distances.

1. Different scales   2. _____   3. _____

LESSON 4

Taking pictures of the earth has helped people make more accurate maps.

1. Bird's-eye view   2. _____   3. _____

LESSON 5

Projections are a way of showing a drawing of the earth on a flat surface.

1. Mercator's maps   2. _____   3. _____

LESSON 6

Maps provide many different kinds of information.

1. Political divisions   2. _____   3. _____

LESSON 7

Dates and time lines help us learn about the past.

1. A.D. and B.C.   2. _____   3. _____

31

Thinking Critically

1. More by longitude, or distance from the Equator

2. Answers may include by requiring changes to clothing, shelter, or ability to produce food or use resources.

3. To find vegetation, climate, population density, distances, or natural resources

4. They appear longer on the Mercator projection map.

5. For dates to be useful, they must be counted from the same point.

Summarizing the Handbook

Lesson 1
2. Orbits around sun, rotates on axis
3. Revolves and tilts on axis, causing seasons

Lesson 2
2. Longitude lines
3. Grid maps

Lesson 3
2. Elevation
3. Contour lines

Lesson 4
2. Aerial photographs
3. Photographs from space

Lesson 5
2. Equal-distance projections
3. Distortion

Lesson 6
2. Physical features
3. Climate

Lesson 7
2. Century
3. Decade

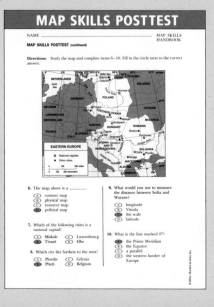

31

Interpreting a Chart

■ After students have studied the chart of countries of the Eastern Hemisphere on pp. 32-33, ask the following questions:

1. Which continents are not represented on the chart?
   (North America, South America, and Antarctica)

2. Which countries have crude oil, natural gas, or petroleum as their major export?
   (Afghanistan, Albania, Algeria, Angola, Bahrain, Brunei, Cameroon, and China)

3. Of the countries listed on this chart, which has the largest area?
   (China)

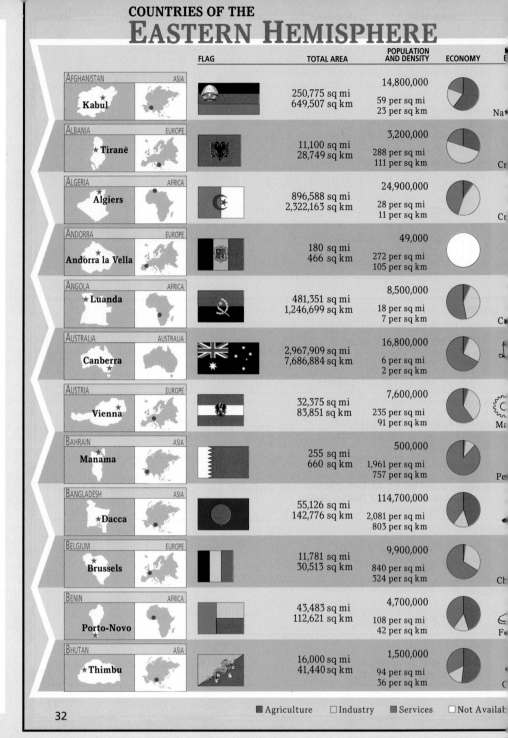

COUNTRIES OF THE
EASTERN HEMISPHERE

	FLAG	TOTAL AREA	POPULATION AND DENSITY	ECONOMY	
AFGHANISTAN ASIA ★Kabul		250,775 sq mi 649,507 sq km	14,800,000 59 per sq mi 23 per sq km		Na★
ALBANIA EUROPE ★Tiranë		11,100 sq mi 28,749 sq km	3,200,000 288 per sq mi 111 per sq km		Cr
ALGERIA AFRICA ★Algiers		896,588 sq mi 2,322,163 sq km	24,900,000 28 per sq mi 11 per sq km		Cr
ANDORRA EUROPE ★Andorra la Vella		180 sq mi 466 sq km	49,000 272 per sq mi 105 per sq km		
ANGOLA AFRICA ★Luanda		481,351 sq mi 1,246,699 sq km	8,500,000 18 per sq mi 7 per sq km		C
AUSTRALIA AUSTRALIA Canberra★		2,967,909 sq mi 7,686,884 sq km	16,800,000 6 per sq mi 2 per sq km		
AUSTRIA EUROPE ★Vienna		32,375 sq mi 83,851 sq km	7,600,000 235 per sq mi 91 per sq km		Ma
BAHRAIN ASIA ★Manama		255 sq mi 660 sq km	500,000 1,961 per sq mi 757 per sq km		Pe
BANGLADESH ASIA ★Dacca		55,126 sq mi 142,776 sq km	114,700,000 2,081 per sq mi 803 per sq km		
BELGIUM EUROPE ★Brussels		11,781 sq mi 30,513 sq km	9,900,000 840 per sq mi 324 per sq km		Ch
BENIN AFRICA ★Porto-Novo		43,483 sq mi 112,621 sq km	4,700,000 108 per sq mi 42 per sq km		F
BHUTAN ASIA ★Thimbu		16,000 sq mi 41,440 sq km	1,500,000 94 per sq mi 36 per sq km		C

■ Agriculture □ Industry ■ Services □ Not Availab

32

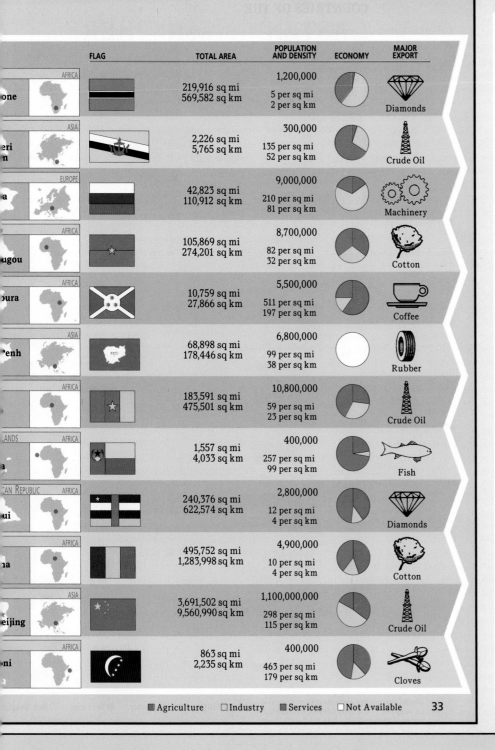

FLAG	TOTAL AREA	POPULATION AND DENSITY	ECONOMY	MAJOR EXPORT
AFRICA	219,916 sq mi / 569,582 sq km	1,200,000 / 5 per sq mi / 2 per sq km		Diamonds
ASIA	2,226 sq mi / 5,765 sq km	300,000 / 135 per sq mi / 52 per sq km		Crude Oil
EUROPE	42,823 sq mi / 110,912 sq km	9,000,000 / 210 per sq mi / 81 per sq km		Machinery
AFRICA	105,869 sq mi / 274,201 sq km	8,700,000 / 82 per sq mi / 32 per sq km		Cotton
AFRICA	10,759 sq mi / 27,866 sq km	5,500,000 / 511 per sq mi / 197 per sq km		Coffee
ASIA	68,898 sq mi / 178,446 sq km	6,800,000 / 99 per sq mi / 38 per sq km		Rubber
AFRICA	183,591 sq mi / 475,501 sq km	10,800,000 / 59 per sq mi / 23 per sq km		Crude Oil
AFRICA	1,557 sq mi / 4,033 sq km	400,000 / 257 per sq mi / 99 per sq km		Fish
AFRICA	240,376 sq mi / 622,574 sq km	2,800,000 / 12 per sq mi / 4 per sq km		Diamonds
AFRICA	495,752 sq mi / 1,283,998 sq km	4,900,000 / 10 per sq mi / 4 per sq km		Cotton
ASIA	3,691,502 sq mi / 9,560,990 sq km	1,100,000,000 / 298 per sq mi / 115 per sq km		Crude Oil
AFRICA	863 sq mi / 2,235 sq km	400,000 / 463 per sq mi / 179 per sq km		Cloves

■ Agriculture ▢ Industry ■ Services ▢ Not Available

33

Making a Graph

● Have students make a bar graph comparing the total area of each of the 24 countries on the chart on pp. 32-33.

● Have students arrange the countries from the largest area to the smallest area.

● Ask students to determine a scale and then graph the area of each country.

● Post completed graphs in your classroom for future reference.

Optional Activities

Analyzing a Chart

■ Have students study the chart of countries of the Eastern Hemisphere, which is continued on pp. 34-35. Ask the following questions to encourage analytical thinking.

1. **Which country and capital city share the same name?**
   (Djibouti)

2. **How many European nations are represented on pp. 34-35?**
   (Ten)

3. **Which countries export cocoa?**
   (Equatorial Guinea and Ghana)

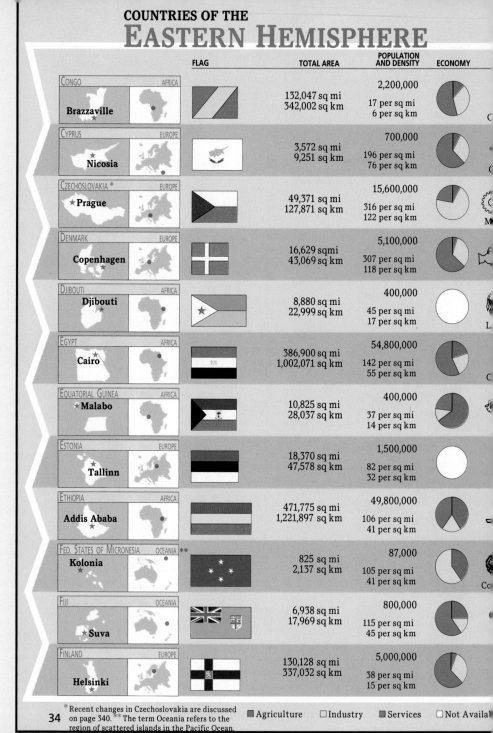

COUNTRIES OF THE
EASTERN HEMISPHERE

	FLAG	TOTAL AREA	POPULATION AND DENSITY	ECONOMY
CONGO — AFRICA — Brazzaville		132,047 sq mi 342,002 sq km	2,200,000 17 per sq mi 6 per sq km	
CYPRUS — EUROPE — Nicosia		3,572 sq mi 9,251 sq km	700,000 196 per sq mi 76 per sq km	
CZECHOSLOVAKIA * — EUROPE — ★Prague		49,371 sq mi 127,871 sq km	15,600,000 316 per sq mi 122 per sq km	
DENMARK — EUROPE — Copenhagen		16,629 sqmi 43,069 sq km	5,100,000 307 per sq mi 118 per sq km	
DJIBOUTI — AFRICA — Djibouti		8,880 sq mi 22,999 sq km	400,000 45 per sq mi 17 per sq km	
EGYPT — AFRICA — ★Cairo		386,900 sq mi 1,002,071 sq km	54,800,000 142 per sq mi 55 per sq km	
EQUATORIAL GUINEA — AFRICA — ★Malabo		10,825 sq mi 28,037 sq km	400,000 37 per sq mi 14 per sq km	
ESTONIA — EUROPE — ★Tallinn		18,370 sq mi 47,578 sq km	1,500,000 82 per sq mi 32 per sq km	
ETHIOPIA — AFRICA — Addis Ababa		471,775 sq mi 1,221,897 sq km	49,800,000 106 per sq mi 41 per sq km	
FED. STATES OF MICRONESIA — OCEANIA ** — Kolonia		825 sq mi 2,137 sq km	87,000 105 per sq mi 41 per sq km	
FIJI — OCEANIA — ★Suva		6,938 sq mi 17,969 sq km	800,000 115 per sq mi 45 per sq km	
FINLAND — EUROPE — Helsinki		130,128 sq mi 337,032 sq km	5,000,000 38 per sq mi 15 per sq km	

■ Agriculture □ Industry ■ Services □ Not Availa[ble]

34 * Recent changes in Czechoslovakia are discussed on page 340. ** The term Oceania refers to the region of scattered islands in the Pacific Ocean.

Optional Activities

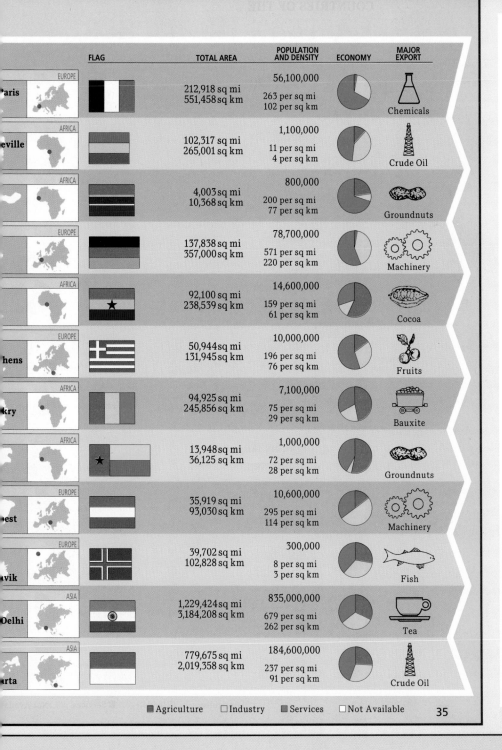

	FLAG	TOTAL AREA	POPULATION AND DENSITY	ECONOMY	MAJOR EXPORT
aris — EUROPE		212,918 sq mi / 551,458 sq km	56,100,000 / 263 per sq mi / 102 per sq km		Chemicals
eville — AFRICA		102,317 sq mi / 265,001 sq km	1,100,000 / 11 per sq mi / 4 per sq km		Crude Oil
AFRICA		4,003 sq mi / 10,368 sq km	800,000 / 200 per sq mi / 77 per sq km		Groundnuts
EUROPE		137,838 sq mi / 357,000 sq km	78,700,000 / 571 per sq mi / 220 per sq km		Machinery
AFRICA		92,100 sq mi / 238,539 sq km	14,600,000 / 159 per sq mi / 61 per sq km		Cocoa
hens — EUROPE		50,944 sq mi / 131,945 sq km	10,000,000 / 196 per sq mi / 76 per sq km		Fruits
kry — AFRICA		94,925 sq mi / 245,856 sq km	7,100,000 / 75 per sq mi / 29 per sq km		Bauxite
AFRICA		13,948 sq mi / 36,125 sq km	1,000,000 / 72 per sq mi / 28 per sq km		Groundnuts
est — EUROPE		35,919 sq mi / 93,030 sq km	10,600,000 / 295 per sq mi / 114 per sq km		Machinery
vik — EUROPE		39,702 sq mi / 102,828 sq km	300,000 / 8 per sq mi / 3 per sq km		Fish
Delhi — ASIA		1,229,424 sq mi / 3,184,208 sq km	835,000,000 / 679 per sq mi / 262 per sq km		Tea
rta — ASIA		779,675 sq mi / 2,019,358 sq km	184,600,000 / 237 per sq mi / 91 per sq km		Crude Oil

■ Agriculture □ Industry ■ Services □ Not Available 35

Making a Pie Graph

● Have students examine the economic data found on the pie graphs on pp. 34–35.

● Then, ask students to work together to make one comprehensive pie graph summarizing the contributions of agriculture, industry, and services to the total economy of the nations shown on these two pages.

● Ask students to follow up their visuals with a one-sentence statement summarizing their findings.

Optional Activities

VISUAL THINKING SKILL

Interpreting a Chart

■ Have students study the chart of countries of the Eastern Hemisphere on pp. 36-37 to answer the following questions.

1. **Which of the countries on this chart counts services as its chief export?**
(Lebanon)

2. **Which three countries on this chart have the highest population densities?**
(Maldives [1,739 per sq mi; 671 per sq km], Japan [858 per sq mi; 331 per sq km], and Lebanon [836 per sq mi; 323 per sq km].

3. **Which of these countries have machinery for their main export?**
(Ireland, Italy, Japan, and Liechtenstein have machinery for their main export.)

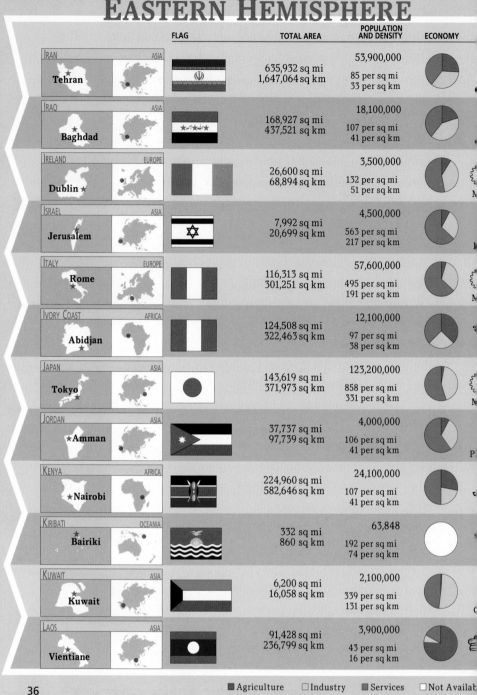

COUNTRIES OF THE
EASTERN HEMISPHERE

	FLAG	TOTAL AREA	POPULATION AND DENSITY	ECONOMY
IRAN ASIA Tehran		635,932 sq mi 1,647,064 sq km	53,900,000 85 per sq mi 33 per sq km	
IRAQ ASIA Baghdad		168,927 sq mi 437,521 sq km	18,100,000 107 per sq mi 41 per sq km	
IRELAND EUROPE Dublin ★		26,600 sq mi 68,894 sq km	3,500,000 132 per sq mi 51 per sq km	
ISRAEL ASIA Jerusalem		7,992 sq mi 20,699 sq km	4,500,000 563 per sq mi 217 per sq km	
ITALY EUROPE Rome		116,313 sq mi 301,251 sq km	57,600,000 495 per sq mi 191 per sq km	
IVORY COAST AFRICA Abidjan		124,508 sq mi 322,463 sq km	12,100,000 97 per sq mi 38 per sq km	
JAPAN ASIA Tokyo		143,619 sq mi 371,973 sq km	123,200,000 858 per sq mi 331 per sq km	
JORDAN ASIA ★Amman		37,737 sq mi 97,739 sq km	4,000,000 106 per sq mi 41 per sq km	
KENYA AFRICA ★Nairobi		224,960 sq mi 582,646 sq km	24,100,000 107 per sq mi 41 per sq km	
KIRIBATI OCEANIA ★ Bairiki		332 sq mi 860 sq km	63,848 192 per sq mi 74 per sq km	
KUWAIT ASIA ★Kuwait		6,200 sq mi 16,058 sq km	2,100,000 339 per sq mi 131 per sq km	
LAOS ASIA Vientiane		91,428 sq mi 236,799 sq km	3,900,000 43 per sq mi 16 per sq km	

36

■ Agriculture   □ Industry   ■ Services   □ Not Availab

Optional Activities

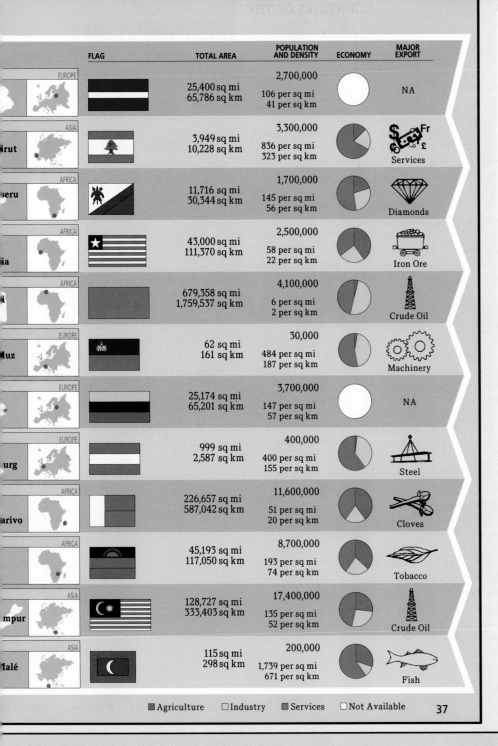

	FLAG	TOTAL AREA	POPULATION AND DENSITY	ECONOMY	MAJOR EXPORT
EUROPE		25,400 sq mi 65,786 sq km	2,700,000 106 per sq mi 41 per sq km		NA
ASIA ...irut		3,949 sq mi 10,228 sq km	3,300,000 836 per sq mi 323 per sq km		Services
AFRICA ...seru		11,716 sq mi 30,344 sq km	1,700,000 145 per sq mi 56 per sq km		Diamonds
AFRICA ...ia		43,000 sq mi 111,370 sq km	2,500,000 58 per sq mi 22 per sq km		Iron Ore
AFRICA		679,358 sq mi 1,759,537 sq km	4,100,000 6 per sq mi 2 per sq km		Crude Oil
EUROPE ...uz		62 sq mi 161 sq km	30,000 484 per sq mi 187 per sq km		Machinery
EUROPE		25,174 sq mi 65,201 sq km	3,700,000 147 per sq mi 57 per sq km		NA
EUROPE ...urg		999 sq mi 2,587 sq km	400,000 400 per sq mi 155 per sq km		Steel
AFRICA ...arivo		226,657 sq mi 587,042 sq km	11,600,000 51 per sq mi 20 per sq km		Cloves
AFRICA		45,193 sq mi 117,050 sq km	8,700,000 193 per sq mi 74 per sq km		Tobacco
ASIA ...mpur		128,727 sq mi 333,403 sq km	17,400,000 135 per sq mi 52 per sq km		Crude Oil
ASIA ...lalé		115 sq mi 298 sq km	200,000 1,739 per sq mi 671 per sq km		Fish

■ Agriculture □ Industry ■ Services □ Not Available 37

Ranking According to Size

Have students rank the countries shown on pp. 36–37
(from Iran to Maldives) according to their total areas.
(Libya is largest and Liechtenstein is smallest.)

- Then, have students infer how this relates to a country's
  population density.

- Answers should include that to calculate population
  density, one divides a country's total area into its
  population.

Interpreting a Chart

■ Use the following questions to prompt a class discussion and comparison of the countries found on the chart on pp. 38-39.

1. **What are the two largest countries on this chart?**
(Mongolia [604,247 sq mi; 1,565,000 sq km] and Niger [459,073 sq mi; 1,188,999 sq km])

2. **How many countries of Oceania are represented on this chart?**
(Five: The Marshall Islands, Nauru, New Zealand, Northern Marianas, and Papua New Guinea)

3. **Which country's main export is gold?**
(Papua New Guinea)

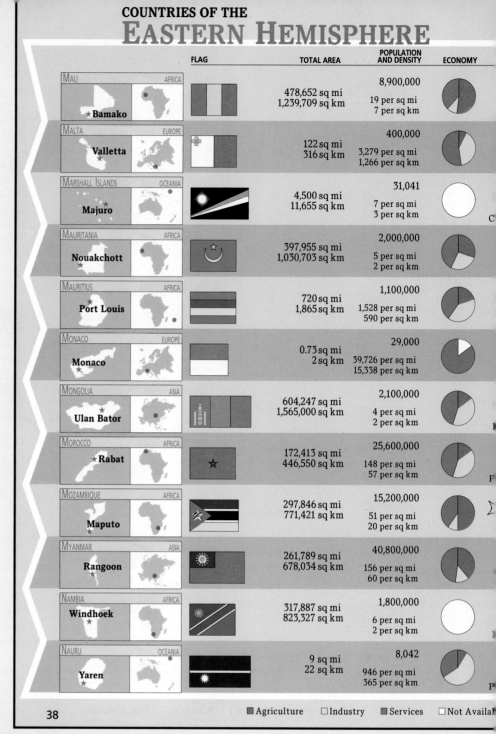

COUNTRIES OF THE
EASTERN HEMISPHERE

	FLAG	TOTAL AREA	POPULATION AND DENSITY	ECONOMY
MALI AFRICA ★Bamako		478,652 sq mi 1,239,709 sq km	8,900,000 19 per sq mi 7 per sq km	
MALTA EUROPE Valletta ★		122 sq mi 316 sq km	400,000 3,279 per sq mi 1,266 per sq km	
MARSHALL ISLANDS OCEANIA Majuro ★		4,500 sq mi 11,655 sq km	31,041 7 per sq mi 3 per sq km	
MAURITANIA AFRICA Nouakchott ★		397,955 sq mi 1,030,703 sq km	2,000,000 5 per sq mi 2 per sq km	
MAURITIUS AFRICA Port Louis ★		720 sq mi 1,865 sq km	1,100,000 1,528 per sq mi 590 per sq km	
MONACO EUROPE Monaco ★		0.73 sq mi 2 sq km	29,000 39,726 per sq mi 15,338 per sq km	
MONGOLIA ASIA Ulan Bator ★		604,247 sq mi 1,565,000 sq km	2,100,000 4 per sq mi 2 per sq km	
MOROCCO AFRICA ★Rabat		172,413 sq mi 446,550 sq km	25,600,000 148 per sq mi 57 per sq km	
MOZAMBIQUE AFRICA Maputo ★		297,846 sq mi 771,421 sq km	15,200,000 51 per sq mi 20 per sq km	
MYANMAR ASIA Rangoon ★		261,789 sq mi 678,034 sq km	40,800,000 156 per sq mi 60 per sq km	
NAMBIA AFRICA Windhoek ★		317,887 sq mi 823,327 sq km	1,800,000 6 per sq mi 2 per sq km	
NAURU OCEANIA Yaren ★		9 sq mi 22 sq km	8,042 946 per sq mi 365 per sq km	

■ Agriculture □ Industry ■ Services □ Not Availab[le]

38

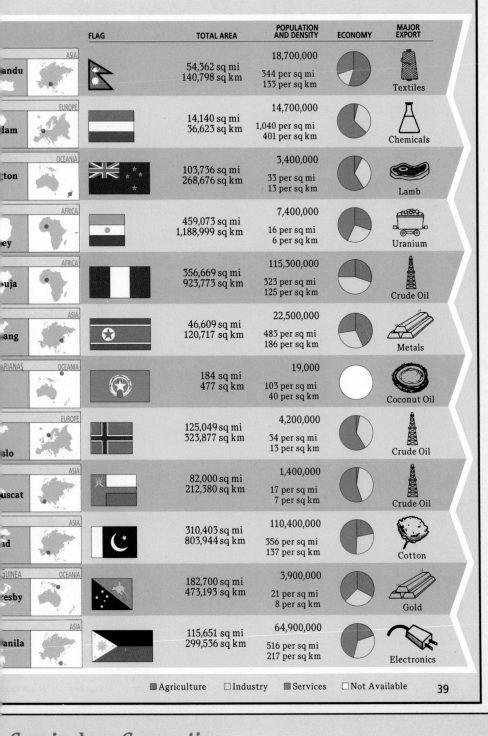

FLAG		TOTAL AREA	POPULATION AND DENSITY	ECONOMY	MAJOR EXPORT
...andu	ASIA	54,362 sq mi 140,798 sq km	18,700,000 344 per sq mi 133 per sq km		Textiles
...dam	EUROPE	14,140 sq mi 36,623 sq km	14,700,000 1,040 per sq mi 401 per sq km		Chemicals
...ton	OCEANIA	103,736 sq mi 268,676 sq km	3,400,000 33 per sq mi 13 per sq km		Lamb
...ey	AFRICA	459,073 sq mi 1,188,999 sq km	7,400,000 16 per sq mi 6 per sq km		Uranium
...uja	AFRICA	356,669 sq mi 923,773 sq km	115,300,000 323 per sq mi 125 per sq km		Crude Oil
...ang	ASIA	46,609 sq mi 120,717 sq km	22,500,000 483 per sq mi 186 per sq km		Metals
...RIANAS	OCEANIA	184 sq mi 477 sq km	19,000 103 per sq mi 40 per sq km		Coconut Oil
...slo	EUROPE	125,049 sq mi 323,877 sq km	4,200,000 34 per sq mi 13 per sq km		Crude Oil
...uscat	ASIA	82,000 sq mi 212,380 sq km	1,400,000 17 per sq mi 7 per sq km		Crude Oil
...ad	ASIA	310,403 sq mi 803,944 sq km	110,400,000 356 per sq mi 137 per sq km		Cotton
...GUINEA ...resby	OCEANIA	182,700 sq mi 473,193 sq km	3,900,000 21 per sq mi 8 per sq km		Gold
...anila	ASIA	115,651 sq mi 299,536 sq km	64,900,000 516 per sq mi 217 per sq km		Electronics

■ Agriculture ☐ Industry ■ Services ☐ Not Available

39

Curriculum Connection

Language Arts Have groups of students make up word search puzzles to help them learn to spell each of the 24 countries' names correctly.

- Have each group prepare an answer key along with their puzzle.
- Encourage students to exchange and solve each other's word search puzzles.

Optional Activities

Interpreting a Chart

■ Have students continue to interpret the data on the chart of the countries of the Eastern Hemisphere, focusing on pp. 40-41 as you ask the following questions:

1. **Which two countries have the same name as their capital cities?**
(San Marino and Singapore)

2. **Which country's major export is motor vehicles?**
(Spain)

3. **Which country's major export is diamonds?**
(Sierra Leone)

4. **After Singapore, which country has the highest population density?**
(South Korea; 1,134 per sq mi, or 438 per sq km)

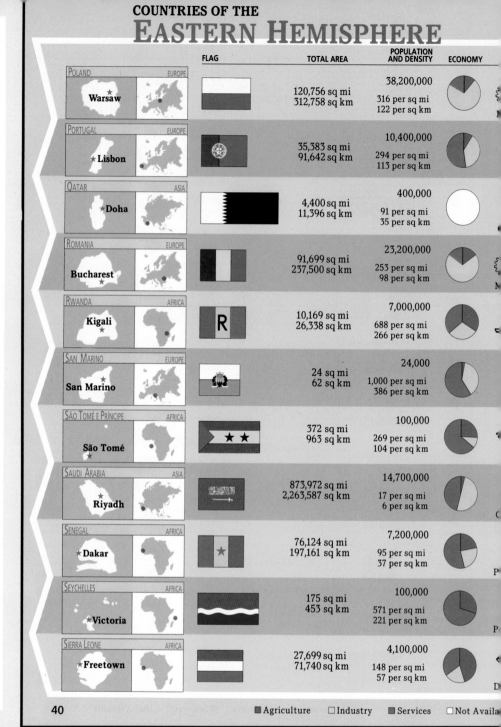

COUNTRIES OF THE
EASTERN HEMISPHERE

	FLAG	TOTAL AREA	POPULATION AND DENSITY	ECONOMY
POLAND EUROPE — Warsaw		120,756 sq mi 312,758 sq km	38,200,000 316 per sq mi 122 per sq km	
PORTUGAL EUROPE — ★Lisbon		35,383 sq mi 91,642 sq km	10,400,000 294 per sq mi 113 per sq km	
QATAR ASIA — ★Doha		4,400 sq mi 11,396 sq km	400,000 91 per sq mi 35 per sq km	
ROMANIA EUROPE — Bucharest ★		91,699 sq mi 237,500 sq km	23,200,000 253 per sq mi 98 per sq km	
RWANDA AFRICA — Kigali ★	R	10,169 sq mi 26,338 sq km	7,000,000 688 per sq mi 266 per sq km	
SAN MARINO EUROPE — San Marino ★		24 sq mi 62 sq km	24,000 1,000 per sq mi 386 per sq km	
SÃO TOMÉ E PRÍNCIPE AFRICA — São Tomé ★	★ ★	372 sq mi 963 sq km	100,000 269 per sq mi 104 per sq km	
SAUDI ARABIA ASIA — ★Riyadh		873,972 sq mi 2,263,587 sq km	14,700,000 17 per sq mi 6 per sq km	
SENEGAL AFRICA — ★Dakar	★	76,124 sq mi 197,161 sq km	7,200,000 95 per sq mi 37 per sq km	
SEYCHELLES AFRICA — ★Victoria		175 sq mi 453 sq km	100,000 571 per sq mi 221 per sq km	
SIERRA LEONE AFRICA — ★Freetown		27,699 sq mi 71,740 sq km	4,100,000 148 per sq mi 57 per sq km	

40

■ Agriculture □ Industry ■ Services □ Not Availa

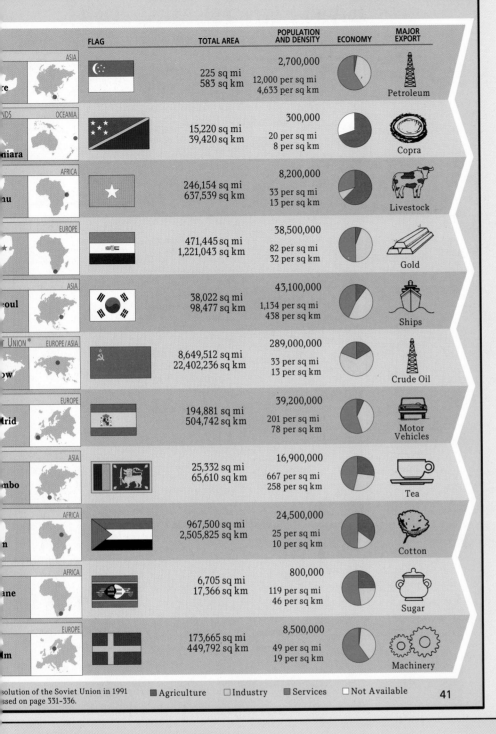

	FLAG	TOTAL AREA	POPULATION AND DENSITY	ECONOMY	MAJOR EXPORT
ASIA ...re		225 sq mi 583 sq km	2,700,000 12,000 per sq mi 4,633 per sq km		Petroleum
OCEANIA ...NDS ...niara		15,220 sq mi 39,420 sq km	300,000 20 per sq mi 8 per sq km		Copra
AFRICA ...nu		246,154 sq mi 637,539 sq km	8,200,000 33 per sq mi 13 per sq km		Livestock
EUROPE		471,445 sq mi 1,221,043 sq km	38,500,000 82 per sq mi 32 per sq km		Gold
ASIA ...oul		38,022 sq mi 98,477 sq km	43,100,000 1,134 per sq mi 438 per sq km		Ships
EUROPE/ASIA ...UNION* ...ow		8,649,512 sq mi 22,402,236 sq km	289,000,000 33 per sq mi 13 per sq km		Crude Oil
EUROPE ...drid		194,881 sq mi 504,742 sq km	39,200,000 201 per sq mi 78 per sq km		Motor Vehicles
ASIA ...mbo		25,332 sq mi 65,610 sq km	16,900,000 667 per sq mi 258 per sq km		Tea
AFRICA ...n		967,500 sq mi 2,505,825 sq km	24,500,000 25 per sq mi 10 per sq km		Cotton
AFRICA ...ane		6,705 sq mi 17,366 sq km	800,000 119 per sq mi 46 per sq km		Sugar
EUROPE ...lm		173,665 sq mi 449,792 sq km	8,500,000 49 per sq mi 19 per sq km		Machinery

...solution of the Soviet Union in 1991
...ssed on page 331-336.

■ Agriculture   □ Industry   ■ Services   □ Not Available

Curriculum Connection

Art   Have students focus on the flags of the nations on pp. 40-41.

● Ask students to draw and color the flag of their choice, then display their illustrations in the classroom during study of this unit.

● You may wish to have students research the symbols on their flags and orally present their findings to the class.

Optional Activities

VISUAL THINKING SKILL

Analyzing a Chart

■ Continue a class analysis of the countries of the Eastern Hemisphere as students turn their attention to the nations listed on the chart on pp. 42-43.

1. **Which two countries' major export is coffee?**
   (Tanzania and Uganda)

2. **What is the capital of Zaire?**
   (Kinshasa)

3. **Which countries on this chart have crude oil as their main export?**
   (Syria, Tunisia, United Arab Emirates, and the United Kingdom)

4. **Which countries have a picture of a crescent moon and a star on their flags?**
   (Turkey and Tunisia)

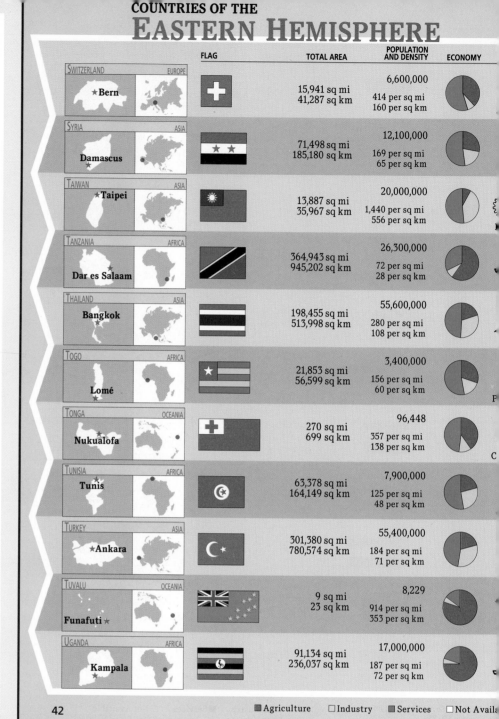

COUNTRIES OF THE
EASTERN HEMISPHERE

	FLAG	TOTAL AREA	POPULATION AND DENSITY	ECONOMY
SWITZERLAND EUROPE ★Bern		15,941 sq mi 41,287 sq km	6,600,000 414 per sq mi 160 per sq km	
SYRIA ASIA Damascus		71,498 sq mi 185,180 sq km	12,100,000 169 per sq mi 65 per sq km	
TAIWAN ASIA ★Taipei		13,887 sq mi 35,967 sq km	20,000,000 1,440 per sq mi 556 per sq km	
TANZANIA AFRICA Dar es Salaam ★		364,943 sq mi 945,202 sq km	26,300,000 72 per sq mi 28 per sq km	
THAILAND ASIA Bangkok ★		198,455 sq mi 513,998 sq km	55,600,000 280 per sq mi 108 per sq km	
TOGO AFRICA Lomé ★		21,853 sq mi 56,599 sq km	3,400,000 156 per sq mi 60 per sq km	
TONGA OCEANIA Nukualofa		270 sq mi 699 sq km	96,448 357 per sq mi 138 per sq km	
TUNISIA AFRICA Tunis ★		63,378 sq mi 164,149 sq km	7,900,000 125 per sq mi 48 per sq km	
TURKEY ASIA ★Ankara		301,380 sq mi 780,574 sq km	55,400,000 184 per sq mi 71 per sq km	
TUVALU OCEANIA Funafuti ★		9 sq mi 23 sq km	8,229 914 per sq mi 353 per sq km	
UGANDA AFRICA Kampala		91,134 sq mi 236,037 sq km	17,000,000 187 per sq mi 72 per sq km	

■ Agriculture   □ Industry   ■ Services   □ Not Availa

42

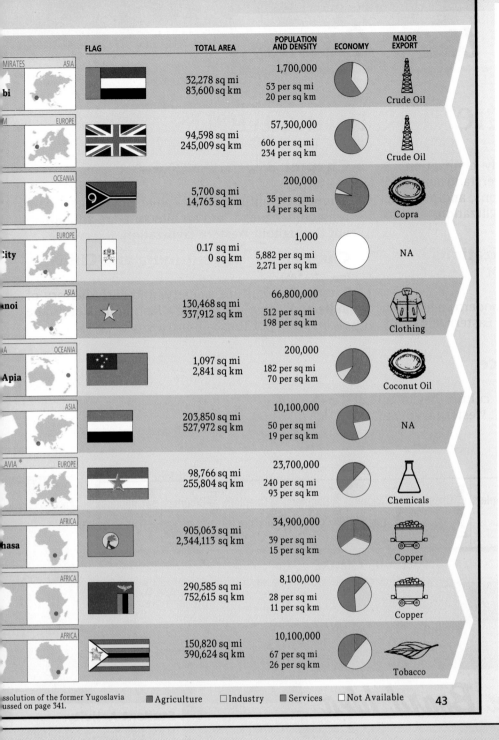

	FLAG	TOTAL AREA	POPULATION AND DENSITY	ECONOMY	MAJOR EXPORT
MIRATES ASIA bi		32,278 sq mi 83,600 sq km	1,700,000 53 per sq mi 20 per sq km		Crude Oil
M EUROPE		94,598 sq mi 245,009 sq km	57,300,000 606 per sq mi 234 per sq km		Crude Oil
OCEANIA		5,700 sq mi 14,763 sq km	200,000 35 per sq mi 14 per sq km		Copra
EUROPE City		0.17 sq mi 0 sq km	1,000 5,882 per sq mi 2,271 per sq km		NA
ASIA anoi		130,468 sq mi 337,912 sq km	66,800,000 512 per sq mi 198 per sq km		Clothing
A OCEANIA Apia		1,097 sq mi 2,841 sq km	200,000 182 per sq mi 70 per sq km		Coconut Oil
ASIA		203,850 sq mi 527,972 sq km	10,100,000 50 per sq mi 19 per sq km		NA
AVIA * EUROPE		98,766 sq mi 255,804 sq km	23,700,000 240 per sq mi 93 per sq km		Chemicals
AFRICA hasa		905,063 sq mi 2,344,113 sq km	34,900,000 39 per sq mi 15 per sq km		Copper
AFRICA		290,585 sq mi 752,615 sq km	8,100,000 28 per sq mi 11 per sq km		Copper
AFRICA		150,820 sq mi 390,624 sq km	10,100,000 67 per sq mi 26 per sq km		Tobacco

ssolution of the former Yugoslavia
ussed on page 341.

■ Agriculture □ Industry ■ Services □ Not Available   43

Making a Display

- Using the chart on pp. 42-43 as a starting point, have students make a list of the main exports of the countries shown.

- Ask students to use outside sources, such as an encyclopedia or other library reference book, to find out the relationship between the country's environment and its main export.

Ancient Civilizations

Unit Theme The study of early civilizations is important if we hope to better understand our world. Many of the discoveries, inventions, and other accomplishments of these early civilizations still influence us today.

Chapter 1 Ancient Civilizations in the Middle East and Egypt

(pp. 46-69)
Theme Many characteristics of modern civilization have their roots in ancient Middle Eastern and Egyptian civilizations.

Chapter 2 Ancient Greece

(pp. 70-97)
Theme Many things in modern culture began in ancient Greece. Under the Greeks, Western civilization made many advances.

Chapter 3 Ancient Rome

(pp. 98-125)
Theme The influences of Roman government, law, religion, language, and architecture are still apparent throughout Western civilization.

Chapter 4 Ancient India and China

(pp. 126-146)
Theme The culture, society, and early history of India and China have made a lasting impact on the civilizations of these countries.

September Chapters	October Chapters	November Chapters	December Chapters	January Chapters	February Chapters	March Chapters	April Chapters	May Chapters
MSH-1	2-4	5-7	8-9	10-12	13-14	15-17	18-20	21-23

PACING GUIDE

Bulletin Board Idea

Student Activity

Have five groups of students work together to make a class collage of the contributions of ancient civilizations to today's world. Each group should select and draw several items, each representing the civilization of ancient Egypt, Greece, Rome, China, or India. Have students arrange and display their artwork in a collage on the bulletin board. Then encourage students to identify and label the civilization each item represents.

Annotated Bibliography

Books for Teachers

Boardman, John, et al, eds. *The Oxford History of the Classical World.* New York: Oxford University Press, 1986. ISBN 0-19-872112-9. (Ch. 2) This stout, scholarly volume has been called "the best one-volume survey available" and should be of lasting value.

Burckhardt, Jacob. *The Age of Constantine.* Berkeley, CA: University of California Press, 1983. ISBN 0-520-0468-03. (Ch. 3) This scholarly book describes the era of Constantine the Great and the changes that he brought to the Roman Empire.

Kramer, Samuel Noah. *History Begins at Sumer: Thirty-nine "Firsts" in Man's Recorded History.* Philadelphia: University of Pennsylvania Press, 1981. ISBN 0-8122-1276-2. (Ch. 1) This popular work, by a leading authority on Ancient Mesopotamia, draws upon Sumerian clay tablets to give the earliest known examples of various institutions and practices, such as the first schools, first fables, and the first library catalogue.

Starr, Chester. *The Ancient Romans.* New York: Oxford University Press, 1971. ISBN 0-19-051455-3. (Ch. 3) A survey of Roman life and culture is presented through text, maps, and illustrations.

Books for Students

Corbishley, Mike. *The Roman World.* Danbury, CT: Warwick Press, 1986. ISBN 0-531-1-9018-8. (Ch. 3) The daily life of the average Roman citizen is described.

Colum, Padraic, trans. *The Children's Homer: The Adventures of Odysseus and the Tale of Troy.* New York: Macmillan Publishing, 1982. ISBN 0-02-042520-1. (Ch. 2) This is a classic, readable, literate retelling of Homer's heroic saga of Ancient Greece.

Gallant, Roy. *Lost Cities.* Danbury, CT: Franklin Watts, 1985. ISBN 0-531-04914-0. (Ch. 2) This text provides an explanation of how ancient cities were "lost" as well as supplying interesting facts about many ruins and archeological sites, including Crete, Mycenae, Troy, and Pompeii.

Hughes, Jill. *Imperial Rome.* Danbury, CT: Glouchester Press, 1985. ISBN 0-531-17003-9. (Ch. 3) Hughes describes life in the ancient Roman Empire from 28 B.C. to 138 A.D.

Kittredge, Mary. *Marc Anthony.* New York: Chelsea House, 1988. ISBN 0-8775-4505-7. (Ch. 3) This biography details the life of Marc Antony, the Roman general, orator, and statesman who ruled after the death of Julius Caesar.

Macaulay, David. *Pyramid.* Boston: Houghton Mifflin Co., 1975. ISBN 0-395-21407-6. (Ch. 3) With captivating sketches and an informative text, the method of building an Egyptian pyramid is explained.

Miquel, Pierre. *Life in Ancient Greece.* Morristown, NJ: Silver Burdett Press, 1986. ISBN 0-382-06887-4. (Ch. 2) The culture and legacy of Ancient Greece is briefly and concisely explained in this text.

Miquel, Pierre. *Life in Ancient Rome.* Morristown, NJ: Silver Burdett Press, 1980. ISBN 0-382-06473-9. (Ch. 3) Ancient Rome's influence on Europe is clarified in this slim, illustrated description of Roman life-styles, government, and agriculture.

Payne, Elizabeth. *The Pharaohs of Ancient Egypt.* New York: Random House, 1981. ISBN 0-394-84699-0. (Ch. 1) The stories of the early pharaohs, including Hatshepsut, are detailed, and readers are introduced to the archeologists who uncovered ancient history.

Rutland, Jonathan. *An Ancient Greek Town.* Danbury, CT: Franklin Watts, 1986. ISBN 0-531-19010-2. (Ch. 2) The daily habits, lifestyles, and experiences of a Greek citizen from the Golden Age of Greek antiquity are described.

Shakespeare, William, edited by Roger Burns. *Julius Caesar.* New York: Chelsea House, 1987. ISBN 0-8775-4516-6. (Ch. 3) Burns provides a thorough biography of this Roman general and statesman whose brilliant military leadership helped make Rome the center of a vast empire.

Ventura, Piero, and Gian P. Cesarani. *In Search of Tutankhamen,* Morristown, NJ: Silver Burdett Press, 1985. ISBN 0-382-09722-1. (Ch. 1) This oversized, heavily illustrated presentation on the archeologists who unsealed the hidden tomb of Tutankhamen also includes a discussion about everyday life in ancient Egypt.

Walworth, Nancy. *Augustus Caesar.* New York: Chelsea House, 1989. ISBN 1-5546-804-7. (Ch. 3) This is a biography of the first Roman emperor, under whom Rome achieved great glory.

Filmstrips and Videos

Medieval Women. Videocassette, 25 min. International Film Bureau, 1989. (Ch. 3) This video differentiates between the perceptions about women in the Middle Ages and the realities of their daily lives.

Comparing Ancient Civilizations and Their Cultures

How were ancient civilizations alike and different?

The people of the "B.C. years" often tend to be a blur to many students. Many important events and achievements came about during these years, yet few students really understand much about the period. Some students conclude that if certain civilizations existed in the same time period, they must have all been basically alike. While the civilizations of this unit were similar in many ways, they were also very diverse.

One way to help students appreciate this time period is to create a "Compare and Contrast Project." This project can be done in many ways, but the basic idea is to note the similarities and differences among these cultures. First, a master list of groups or civilizations should be created. Under this list needs to be a specific set of subheadings, such as

Art, Science, Political Science, Economics, Language Arts, and *Contributions.*

The basic goal is to create a thumbnail sketch of each civilization under its heading. The information will then be assembled into a master overview, report, or other vehicle for comparing these civilizations. Artwork could accompany each report and the report could be placed on a bulletin board or in the hall to be shared with other classes.

The work itself can be divided in several ways. The topics can be assigned according to subject (economics, for example), or by civilization (the Phoenicians, for example). The work can also be divided into more specific topics, such as Phoenician Economics. This work could be assigned to individuals, small groups, or as a cooperative learning project for the entire class. The following activities relate to this project.

SOCIAL STUDIES

Geography   Where were each of these civilizations located? Have students create a map of their assigned civilization. Then, create a master map plotting the location of each culture.

■ Many of these cultures existed next to an ocean, sea, or river. Ask students to describe in writing the importance of bodies of water to the various civilizations.

Political Science   What was the governmental system of each civilization? How was each ruled?

■ Have students write reports citing specific examples of each civilization's government, such as the dynasty system of China or Hammurabi's Code.

History Historically, each of these major civilizations experienced the cycle of nations — they rose from a small base, expanded, realized a great deal of power, and then declined.

■ Have students create a time line showing this pattern for each group. Then discuss with the class why each group eventually declined.

Economics Each of the civilizations had a thriving economic system. Have students create charts comparing and contrasting these systems.

■ Ask students to explain why economics is important to a civilization. Can a society build a great civilization without a successful economic system? Have students write reasons for their answers.

LANGUAGE ARTS

■ One mark of civilization is the development of the written word and the sharing of knowledge. This was a critical period for the development of the alphabet and writing.

■ Have students create a chart tracing the evolution of the letters that we use today. The Rosetta stone could be shown, as well as the evolution of Egyptian hieroglyphics into Sumerian cuneiform writing.

■ Ask students to write a paragraph explaining why writing is so important to civilizations.

MATHEMATICS

■ As in science, several important mathematical advances were made during this period. Have students list contributions of the ancient civilizations, such as the Egyptian solar calendar, the concept of zero, the 60-minute hour, the 360-degree circle, the Babylonian use of geometry, the Egyptian knotted rope triangles for constructing right angles, the Greek computation of the circumference of the planet, and so on.

■ Have students evaluate the importance of the items that they list.

SCIENCE

■ Each of these early civilizations achieved certain levels of scientific or technological advancement. Many of these advancements were extremely important, influencing how we live today. Some of the scientific advances may surprise students, such as the smelting of gold and silver, the beginnings of astronomy, the use of surgery, and the charting of planetary movements.

■ Have students write a short report about the scientific advancements of their assigned civilization and evaluate the importance of each.

ART

Along with the development of writing systems, came the evolution of material to write upon. Students may enjoy making their own early form of "writing paper."

■ Supply students with an old newspaper, water, instant starch, a square of window screening, a large bowl, a spoon, and an egg beater. Have them tear a page or less of newspaper into very small pieces and add it to approximately 1 cup of water in a large bowl. Let the mixture stand for about an hour, then have students beat it for 10 minutes, or until the paper is soft and mushy. Dissolve two heaping tablespoons of starch in a cup of water and add it to the mix in the bowl. Have students stir the pulp well.

■ Holding the screen in a horizontal position, dip it carefully into the bowl and lift it out, covered with as much pulp as possible. Place the pulp and screen on several thicknesses of newspaper, cover it with more newspaper and press down very firmly. Fold back the newspaper and let the pulp dry on the screen overnight. Peel the newly-made paper from the screen very carefully.

■ Invite students to create a design or write a few sentences to put on their home-made paper with crayons or markers. Display the "work of art" on the bulletin board for all to enjoy.

Hold a Class Election

INSTRUCTIONS FOR THE TEACHER:

Studying Democracy In this unit, students will learn about ancient civilizations. As they read about the Greeks, Romans, Chinese, and others, they may see similarities and differences and may want to compare all of these ancient civilizations. One aspect for comparison may be each group's form of government. Students will see aspects of each civilization that have been adapted, refined, and incorporated into our system of government today. One example of this would be the democratic form of government that the ancient Greeks used.

Background The ancient Greeks were the first people to use the concept of *democracy* in creating a system of government. The Greeks who adopted this new system passionately believed in it and fought hard to defend it against those who would have forced them to accept another form of government. From these early seeds grew the representative democracy system that so greatly influences the world today. The world owes a great deal to the efforts of the Greeks.

Although students will soon discover that the early Greeks' form of democracy was different from what we call democracy today (see "Focus On Citizenship: Direct vs. Indirect Democracy," p. 68), holding a class election will demonstrate this process and provide a "hands-on, minds-on" activity to begin this unit.

Why Tie Democratic Class Elections into This Unit? One reason lies in the fact that the word *democracy* came from the Greeks. Also, what better way for students to understand this vital Greek contribution than through participation in a class election? This activity is designed to help students gain an understanding and appreciation of the election process as well as help them comprehend how elections are important to them as citizens. The activity will help students appreciate the emotion, complexity, and vitality of the election process.

ACTIVITY FOR THE STUDENTS:

Identifying a Democracy Write the words *monarchy, democracy,* and *oligarchy* on the chalkboard and review their meanings. As you point to each form of government, have students describe it to you, and share whether citizens are allowed to vote (*monarchy:* a government headed by one ruler, usually a king or queen, *democracy:* a government in which power is held by the people, *oligarchy:* a government headed by a small group).

Discuss with students whether they would prefer electing students to represent them, or having you appoint one student — who perhaps is a younger brother or sister of a student who was in your class years ago. Relate this to a monarchy.

Students will likely express their preference for an election, at which time they may be asked to write nominations for a "class council" on slips of paper. Tell them that only those who meet the requirements on the chalkboard may vote:

Only "citizens" may vote. Citizens are those:

1. who are male.
2. whose parents were citizens.
3. whose parents were born in, and lived all of their lives in, _____ (insert name of community) _____ .

Tell the students that if their parents came from another community, they may not vote.

There may not be any students who qualify as "citizens." Students should discuss this, and these rules should be related to the democracy in Athens (p. 67). Only those who qualified as citizens were allowed to vote. Remind students that although they might see this as restrictive, it was considered to be the democracy at the time.

Students could then compare this system to democratic systems today. Students may demonstrate what a democracy is like today by 1) discussing voting requirements in the United States (age 18, residency, and citizenship), and 2) setting age and residency requirements for your class election. (Students who are at least nine years old and who have been in your class for at least one day can vote.)

Electing a Class Council Have students elect a class council that will exist for a set period of time, and will perform whatever function that you decide. You may wish to have the council plan class events or help plan community-service activities. The council should be re-elected often enough to allow many students to participate.

Allow nominations from the floor (limit to ten), and put the names of the nominees on the chalkboard. Ask each nominee to describe why he or she would be a good class council member and what he or she thinks the duties of the council should be.

Have the class vote for five members of the class council. Ask for volunteers to tally the votes, and announce the winners. Remind the class that there will be another election in four weeks.

Follow-up Encourage students to discuss the qualifications that they looked for when electing the class council. Remind them that the people they elect must work to represent the views of the class members. Have students discuss any local or national elections with which they are familiar. Ask them to compare those elections to the class election.

Unit Test

CONTENT TEST

Directions: Fill in the circle next to the correct answer.

1. Which of the following is *not* a characteristic of civilization?
- (A) organized government
- (B) different occupations
- (C) weapons ●
- (D) written records

2. Who developed a system of writing called cuneiform?
- (A) the Mesopotamians ●
- (B) Ralph Cunei
- (C) the Egyptians
- (D) Franklin P. Rosetta

3. Who discovered King Tut's tomb?
- (A) Jean-Francois Champollion
- (B) Howard Carter ●
- (C) Jean Fourier
- (D) Jean Paul Sartre

4. What important discovery enabled scholars to understand and translate hieroglyphics?
- (A) cuneiform
- (B) the Book of the Dead
- (C) papyrus
- (D) the Rosetta Stone ●

5. Who was the woman god-king that ruled Egypt between 1503 B.C. and 1482 B.C.?
- (A) Jean Fourier
- (B) Thutmose II
- (C) Thutmose III
- (D) Hatshepsut ●

6. What was King Solomon known for?
- (A) wisdom ●
- (B) beauty
- (C) mining
- (D) killing Goliath

7. The Athenians defeated Xerxes in the _____.
- (A) Peloponnesian War
- (B) Trojan War
- (C) Punic Wars
- (D) Battle of Salamis ●

8. What is a despot?
- (A) a person who rules with unlimited control ●
- (B) a place where trains stop
- (C) an ancient vase made in Greece
- (D) a long narrative poem that explains the past

9. What type of government did Athens have?
- (A) a democracy ●
- (B) a monarchy
- (C) a dictatorship
- (D) an oligarchy

10. The language, ideas, arts and general way of life of a people are their _____.
- (A) philosophy
- (B) mythology
- (C) culture ●
- (D) wisdom

© Silver, Burdett & Ginn Inc.

CONTENT TEST (continued)

11. Which of the following people was a philosopher?
- (A) Sappho
- (B) Plato ●
- (C) Zeppo
- (D) Hydrox

12. Which of the following people was a poet?
- (A) Thucydides
- (B) Pindar ●
- (C) Bucephalus
- (D) Hydrox

13. Who defeated Pompey's troops to become dictator of Rome?
- (A) Octavian
- (B) Romulus
- (C) Julius Caesar ●
- (D) Constantine

14. In A.D. 79, Mount Vesuvius erupted, burning the city of _____.
- (A) Pompeii ●
- (B) Rome
- (C) Troy
- (D) Carthage

15. Which Roman emperor became a Christian?
- (A) Constantine ●
- (B) Caesar Augustus
- (C) Pompey
- (D) Bucephalus

16. The first group of written Roman laws was called the _____.
- (A) Golden Rule
- (B) Ten Commandments
- (C) Twelve Tables ●
- (D) Fourteen Points

17. Tribes of people who moved about were called _____.
- (A) ascetics
- (B) Buddhists
- (C) Hindus
- (D) nomads ●

18. Aryans were divided into social classes called _____.
- (A) castes ●
- (B) ascetics
- (C) oracles
- (D) dialects

19. The Chinese model for official and personal behavior is _____.
- (A) Buddhism
- (B) Confucianism ●
- (C) Taoism
- (D) Hinduism

20. The Chinese model for behavior was developed by a philosopher named _____.
- (A) Shih Huang-ti
- (B) Confucius ●
- (C) Wang Chung
- (D) Xi'an Yao

© Silver, Burdett & Ginn Inc.

SKILLS TEST

Directions: Study the graph and complete items 1–6. Fill in the circle next to the correct answer.

CLIMOGRAPH: CAIRO, EGYPT
Location: 30°N/31°E

1. In Cairo, which month is the hottest?
- (A) June
- (B) July ●
- (C) August
- (D) September

2. In Cairo, which month is the coldest?
- (A) January ●
- (B) February
- (C) March
- (D) December

3. Which month has the greatest amount of rain?
- (A) April
- (B) July
- (C) January
- (D) May ●

4. There is usually no precipitation in _____.
- (A) January
- (B) May
- (C) June ●
- (D) April

5. Which season has the most precipitation?
- (A) winter
- (B) spring ●
- (C) summer
- (D) fall

6. In which month is Cairo's temperature about 25°C?
- (A) January
- (B) April
- (C) May ●
- (D) July

© Silver, Burdett & Ginn Inc.

SKILLS TEST (continued)

Directions: Read the selection and complete items 7–10. Fill in the circle next to the correct answer.

In ancient Rome, crowds often gathered at the Colosseum to watch men and animals fight to the death. Sometimes the animal killed the man. Other times the man survived. The Romans had a story about one fight that had a happy outcome for both the animal and the man.

Androcles, a slave, had run away from a cruel master and had hidden in a cave. While he was hiding, a fierce, wounded lion limped into the cave. Buried in the lion's swollen paw was a sharp thorn. Although he was afraid of the lion, Androcles removed the thorn. No longer in pain, the lion became quite friendly toward Androcles.

Later that day, Androcles wandered from the cave and was captured by Roman soldiers. Like other runaway slaves, he was sent to the Colosseum to fight a wild beast. As soon as Androcles was pushed into the arena, a cage was opened and a lion leaped forth. It rushed at Androcles, but instead of attacking, the lion licked his hand. It was the grateful lion Androcles had aided in the cave!

The crowd, surprised at this unusual turn of events, demanded that both Androcles and the lion be freed. According to one story, Androcles traveled through Rome showing his friendly lion in taverns.

7. The main idea of the story is that _____.
- (A) fighting with wild beasts can be dangerous
- (B) acts of kindness are often rewarded ●
- (C) a lion's growl is worse than its bite
- (D) fighting in the Colosseum was great fun

8. Androcles met the lion when he was _____.
- (A) hiding in a cave ●
- (B) visiting a tavern
- (C) working for his master
- (D) killing an animal

9. Why was Androcles sent to the Colosseum?
- (A) His master told him to take a message there.
- (B) He wanted to fight wild beasts.
- (C) He wanted to show his friendly lion to the crowd.
- (D) He was a captured runaway slave. ●

10. The crowd was surprised because _____.
- (A) Androcles was a good fighter
- (B) lions don't belong in caves
- (C) the lion did not attack ●
- (D) lions are not usually found in Italy

© Silver, Burdett & Ginn Inc.

Unit Test

ESSAY TEST

1

Directions: Write a response to items 1–4.

> **REMINDER:** Read and think about each item before you write your response. Be sure to think of the points you want to cover, details that support your response, and reasons for your opinions. Then, on the lines below, write your response in complete sentences.

1. What are the characteristics of a civilization?

A satisfactory response should include at least three of the following:

• development of cities

• specialized skills

• different occupations

• organized government

• organized religion

• development of trade

• written records

An excellent response might also

• mention at least five characteristics

• provide examples of specialized skills

• explain why writing is important to civilization.

2. Why were the writings of Herodotus important?

A satisfactory response should include the following statements:

• Herodotus was a historian.

• He wrote about the Persian Wars.

• His writings contain descriptions of the peoples and the lands ruled by the Persians.

• His writings provide a great deal of information about the Persian Empire.

An excellent response might also mention

• the location of the Persian Empire, which stretched from the Mediterranean to India

• the mythology included in his writings.

ESSAY TEST (continued)

3. What Roman achievements affect our lives today?

A satisfactory response should mention the Roman

• system of laws

• alphabet

• language and its influence

• architecture.

An excellent response might also mention the ways in which these achievements affect life today.

4. What was the caste system?

A satisfactory response should include the following statements:

• Aryan society was divided into four social classes called castes.

• The four castes included priests; warriors and rulers; farmers and merchants; and lowly workers and servants.

An excellent response might also include

• a definition of the term *Brahman*

• an explanation that a person's caste depended on birth

• an evaluative response that reflects independent thinking.

TEACHER NOTES

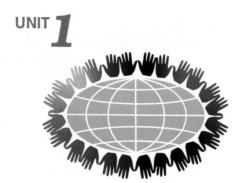

UNIT 1

MULTICULTURAL PERSPECTIVES

Ancient Mysteries *(pages 47–63)*

The Sahara is the world's largest desert, extending for some 3.5 million square miles (9,065,000 sq km) across North Africa. This is an area comparable in size to the United States.

There is evidence that the Sahara was once a fertile, green area. It was inhabited by people who hunted or tended elephants, wild buffaloes, and wild oxen. The rock paintings of the Sahara, which have withstood the ravages of time, depict hunters and are among the earliest known forms of African art.

Show students some pictures of the rock paintings. Then ask them to write a brief description of what Africa might have been like when the Sahara was not a desert.

- Who would have lived there?
- What might some of the natural resources have been?
- How might the course of history have been different if the Sahara had remained green?

Have students investigate and write reports about mysterious civilizations of the past. (Possibilities include Atlantis, Easter Island, and Stonehenge.) Then have them share their reports. Lead a discussion that gives students an opportunity to speculate about what happened to these mysterious civilizations and the people who lived there. Encourage students to let their imaginations run wild.

Point out to students that complex communities existed throughout the world at much earlier times than history books often indicate.

Source

Editors of *Reader's Digest. The World's Last Mysteries*. New York: Reader's Digest, 1976.

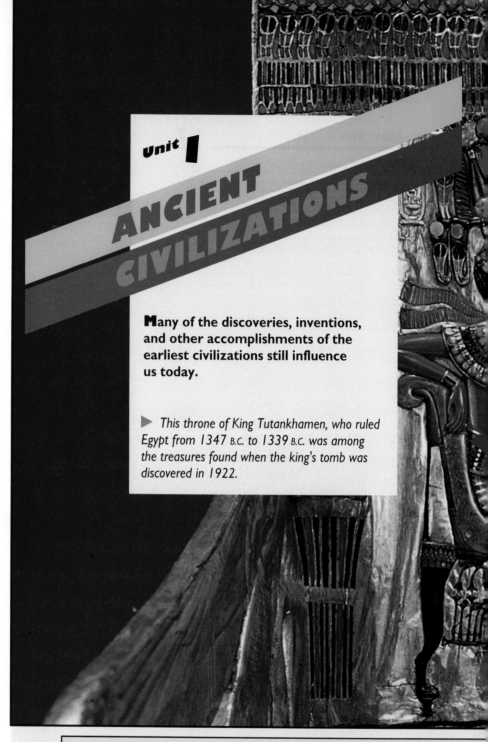

Unit 1

ANCIENT CIVILIZATIONS

Many of the discoveries, inventions, and other accomplishments of the earliest civilizations still influence us today.

▶ *This throne of King Tutankhamen, who ruled Egypt from 1347 B.C. to 1339 B.C. was among the treasures found when the king's tomb was discovered in 1922.*

Optional Activities

44

The Artist's Point of View
(pages 116–119)

Point out to students that no one actually knows what the historical Jesus of Nazareth looked like. There are only hints of descriptions in the Bible.

Obtain a copy of *The Faces of Jesus* by Frederick Buechner (New York: Harper & Row, 1989). This book contains pictures of paintings, carvings, and statues from around the world, showing the various ways in which different peoples have viewed and depicted Jesus.

Point out that in many of the pictures, Jesus looks like the people from the various cultures that depicted him. Asians drew Jesus to look Asian; Italians drew Jesus with European features.

Explain to students that people interpret history in much the same way that they have interpreted the faces of Jesus, each with a point of view that reflects the society from which the people have come.

For the most part, people in the United States have studied history from a European point of view. However, if we were to read history books written by Native Americans in the eighteenth and nineteenth centuries, we would have a different sense of American history. If we could study historical records of ancient sub-Saharan Africa, we would have a different impression of the African continent.

Ask students to plan an interview with a person from ancient times. The person may be from any continent. Have students draw up a list of questions about life in the time and place in which the person lived.

Students may enjoy role-playing the interview, taking turns playing the interviewer and the ancient citizen. Encourage them to stage the interview for the rest of the class. Then discuss the different points of view that students have expressed.

Optional Activities

Ancient Civilizations in the Middle East and Egypt
(pp. 46-69)

Chapter Theme: Many characteristics of modern civilization have their roots in ancient Middle Eastern and Egyptian civilizations.

CHAPTER RESOURCES
Review Master Booklet
  Reviewing Chapter Vocabulary, p. 16
  Place Geography, p. 17
  Summarizing the Chapter, p. 18
Chapter 1 Test

LESSON 1   The Origin of Civilization
(pp. 46-53)

Theme: As cities increased in number and grew in size, a system of laws, a written language, and walls for protection became a necessity.

 SOCIAL STUDIES LIBRARY: *City: A Study of Roman Planning and Construction*
Money

LESSON RESOURCES
Workbook, p. 19
Review Master Booklet
  Understanding the Lesson, p. 12

LESSON 2   Egypt — The Land of the Nile
(pp. 54-58)

Theme: The world's longest river, the Nile, helped Egyptian farmers grow crops and float barges with needed materials to build a stronger Egypt.

LESSON RESOURCES
Workbook, pp. 20-21
Review Master Booklet
  Understanding the Lesson, p. 13

LESSON 3   The Civilizations of the Egyptians
(pp. 59-63)

Theme: The development of a written language and Egyptian languages enabled the Egyptian civilization to expand.

LESSON RESOURCES
Review Master Booklet
  Understanding the Lesson, p. 14

LESSON 4   Ancient Israel
(pp. 64-67)

Theme: Abraham, David, and Moses were famous leaders whose stories are known to us because of the Bible.

SILVER WINGS WORKSHOP: The Courage of Your Convictions

LESSON RESOURCES
Workbook, pp. 22-24
Review Master Booklet
  Understanding the Lesson, p. 15

Review Masters

NAME _____
REVIEWING CHAPTER VOCABULARY

CHAPTER
1
VOCABULARY MASTER

Review Study the words in the box. Use your Glossary to find definitions of those you do not remember.

ancestor	delta	oasis	scribe
archaeologist	dike	papyrus	silt
civilization	hieroglyphics	pharaoh	ziggurat
Coptic	irrigate	pictograph	
cuneiform	mummy	pyramid	

Practice Complete the paragraphs using words from the box above. You may change the forms of the words to fit the meaning.

People often wonder what life was like long ago. Some important questions about how ancient people lived have been answered by the work of (1) _____archaeologists_____ Our knowledge of the ancient Egyptian (2) _____civilization_____, which grew up along the Nile River, came from the clues ancient people left behind.

We know, for example, that the ancient Egyptians built great (3) _____pyramids_____ Egyptian rulers were buried in these huge stone structures. The body of the (4) _____pharaoh_____ was laid to rest, along with many things the king could use in his next life. The discovery of these tombs, and the (5) _____mummies_____ found inside, tell us a great deal about the Egyptians and their beliefs.

Our knowledge of the ancient Egyptian people increased greatly after Jean Champollion solved the mystery of Egyptian writing. He discovered that the later Egyptians used (6) _____hieroglyphic_____ characters to stand for sounds. This was very different from the way their (7) _____ancestors_____ had used this form of writing. Once people could understand Egyptian writing, they were able to read the words the Egyptians wrote about themselves and their lives.

Write Choose ten words from the box above. Use each word to write a sentence of your own. You may use the back of the sheet.

Sentences should show that students understand the meanings of the words.

_____

_____

_____

_____

_____

16

© Silver, Burdett & Ginn Inc.

Use with Chapter 1, pages 47–67.

NAME _____
LOCATING PLACES

CHAPTER
1
PLACE GEOGRAPHY MASTER

✱ Listed below are ancient cities of Egypt and the Middle East. Use the Gazetteer in your textbook to find the latitude and longitude of each city. Then locate and label each on the map.

		LAT. ⊖	LONG. ⊕
1.	Babylon	33°N	44°E
2.	Thebes	26°N	33°E
3.	Cairo	30°N	31°E
4.	Rosetta	31°N	30°E
5.	Jerusalem	32°N	35°E

ANCIENT EGYPT AND THE MIDDLE EAST

© Silver, Burdett & Ginn Inc.

Use with Chapter 1, pages 47–67.

NAME _____
SUMMARIZING THE CHAPTER

CHAPTER
1
GRAPHIC ORGANIZER MASTER

✱ Complete this graphic organizer. Under the main idea for each lesson, write two additional key words or phrases that support the main idea.

CHAPTER THEME Many characteristics of modern civilization have their roots in ancient Middle Eastern and Egyptian civilizations.

LESSON 1
A civilization has specific characteristics.
1. Cities
2. Organized governments
3. Written records

LESSON 3
We have learned from writings about ancient Egypt.
1. Rosetta Stone
2. hieroglyphics
3. papyrus

LESSON 2
Egypt is called the land of the Nile.
1. Has fertile land
2. Sahara
3. floods

LESSON 4
Some famous leaders came from ancient Israel.
1. David
2. Abraham
3. Moses

18

© Silver, Burdett & Ginn Inc.

Use with Chapter 1, pages 47–67.

Workbook Pages

HAMMURABI'S CODE OF LAWS

Decoding a Message, Making Observations

✳ The following paragraph tells about the Code of Laws of King Hammurabi, who ruled Babylon from ca. 1792 B.C. to 1750 B.C. The coded messages below tell more about the law code.

a. In order to decode the messages, first fill in the key. Do this by writing the letter in the paragraph corresponding with each number. The first is done for you.

b. Referring to the key, decode the messages by writing the correct letter above each number.

The code of Hammurabi was made up of nearly three hundred legal listings. They were
3 11   1   7   1   10   9   14   3   5

based on Akkadian and Sumerian laws. The laws covered business, family life, government,
8   5   7   6   13   4   5   16

and witchcraft. There was one overriding principle for all laws.
17

KEY	A	D	E	F	G	H	I	K	L	N	O	R	S	T	U	V	W	Y
	1	2	3	4	5	6	7	8	9	10	11	12	13	14	15	16	17	18

The overriding principle for Hammurabi's laws was, "T h e   s t r o n g
14   6   3   13 14 12 11 10   5

s h a l l   n o t   h u r t   t h e   w e a k ."
13 6 1 9 9   10 11 14   6 15 12 14   14 6 3   17 3 1 8

The code provided for i n d i v i d u a l   r i g h t s
7 10 2 7 16 7 2 15 1 9   12 7 5 6 14 13

a n d   t h e   a u t h o r i t y   o f   t h e
1 10 2   14 6 3   1 15 14 6 11 12 7 14 18   11 4   14 6 3

s t a t e .
13 14 1 14 3

Thinking Further: What is the main principle underlying the laws of the United States? Give an example of the application of this principle.

This is a chance for students to think about the United States. Possibilities: equal rights for all; the majority should not

abuse a minority; equal opportunity and justice for all.

_____

_____

_____

LEARNING ABOUT THE EARLY EGYPTIANS

Understanding Main Ideas and Details, Hypothesizing

✳ Read the paragraphs below. Then circle the correct ending to complete the sentences that follow.

The Egyptians built many pyramids. The three largest and most famous are in the desert at Giza, near present-day Cairo. The largest is the Great Pyramid. Today it would cover nearly ten football fields. It is about 450 feet (137 m) high, but before some of the topmost stones were torn away, it rose to 482 feet (147 m).

Although the pyramids at Giza were built between about 2640 and 2500 B.C., scientists continue to make new discoveries about the individuals and the communities of workers involved in constructing them.

Earlier discoveries revealed much about the rulers of Egypt. More recent searches uncovered some information about the workers. A bakery site near the pyramids has been explored, and many clay pots and baking molds have been found. Scientists now believe workers labored in teams of 20 to 50 to drag the huge stones to the site of the pyramids. The stones were pulled with ropes up ramps from canal barges and from quarries. The workers' great pride in their accomplishments was recorded in pictures at the site.

1. Work on the pyramids began in about
   3100 B.C.   (2640 B.C.)   1500 B.C.   A.D. 250

2. The pyramids are at
   Cairo   Memphis   (Giza)   Athens

3. At present, the height of the Great Pyramid is about
   137 feet   482 feet   250 feet   (450 feet)

4. Early discoveries at the pyramids gave little information about
   (workers)   rulers   pharaohs   queens

5. More recent discoveries have been made at the site of a
   church   library   palace   (bakery)

6. At the recently excavated site, scientists have dug up
   crowns   jewels   wheels   (pots)

7. People building the large pyramids worked
   alone   (in teams)   in pairs   in huge groups

8. Workers dragged stones to the site with the aid of
   (ropes)   oxen   elephants   camels

Thinking Further: The Great Pyramid has lasted for some 4,500 years. Besides the pyramids, what large structures in the world today might last that long? Give a reason or two why you think the structure will be durable. Write your answer on a separate sheet.   Possibilities: Hoover Dam, Empire State Building, Taj Mahal. They might endure because of the strong materials (stone, steel, etc.) used and because of the high quality of the construction techniques.

20

EXAMINING THE COURSE OF THE NILE

Reading a Map for Details, Comparing and Contrasting, Making Inferences

✳ The Nile River is the world's longest river. It flows about 4,200 miles (about 6,800 km), from Burundi, in East Africa, to northern Egypt. It has several big waterfalls, called cataracts. In addition, the river has many tributaries, some of which are major rivers. Study the map below and answer the questions.

1. In which country is the greatest length of the Nile located?   Sudan
   Which country contains the second greatest length?   Egypt

2. Ruins of ancient Meroe exist today. About how many miles south of the Egyptian border are they?
   about 300 miles

3. What is the name of the largest lake in the Nile River System?   Lake Victoria
   What is the second largest lake?
   Lake Nasser

4. If you had the time and energy, could you row a small boat from Lake Victoria to Alexandria without taking it out of the water? Give a reason for your answer.
   No; the cataracts would make such a trip
   impossible.

5. Khartoum is a large, bustling city. Does its geographical location suggest one reason why it became important? Why?
   Yes; it grew in part because of its location where
   the White Nile and Blue Nile join.

Thinking Further: In what ways can a river link people living far apart?
Students may suggest that a river can link people by providing transportation for trade, leisurely travel, moving
armies, and so forth.

THE GEOGRAPHY OF ANCIENT ISRAEL

Gathering Information from a Map, Making Observations

✳ Study the map below of the kingdom of David and Solomon. Then fill in the blanks. Refer to a map in your textbook, if necessary.

1. The Mediterranean Sea, which formed part of the western boundary of the kingdom, is called the
   Great Sea   on this map.

2. Jerusalem was near what is now called the Dead Sea but was once called the
   Salt Sea

3. The kingdom of David and Solomon was made up of six territories named
   Edom, Moab, Ammon, Judah, Israel,
   Zobah

4. To the east of the kingdom was the
   Arabian Desert

5. Israel was bordered on the west by
   the Great Sea , and on the east by
   Zobah   and   Ammon

6. An independent kingdom located west of Judah was
   Philistia

7. The Salt Sea helped divide the territories of   Judah   and
   Moab

8. The territory located farthest north was called   Zobah

9. A major city in Ammon was
   Rabbath-ammon

10. A major city northwest of Ammon was
    Ramoth-gilead

Thinking Further: In ancient kingdoms a person might live in a community that was part of a larger political unit. The same is true today. To what two or three political units does your city or town belong?
Possibilities: county, state, country. My town is part of Marin County and the state of California.

22

C1-C

Left Page

NAME _____

THE LIFE OF KING SOLOMON

Understanding Stated Facts and Details, Identifying Value Positions, Interpreting Information

✻ A biography tells the story of a person's life. The author of a biography sometimes highlights a person's qualities. The admirable qualities are called strengths while others are considered weaknesses. Read this short biography about Israel's great King Solomon.

Soon after Solomon was made king of Israel, he became known for his great wisdom in judging people. To honor God for all his blessings, Solomon had a great temple built. He wrote wisely about life and observed and reported about the natural world around him. Solomon also wrote beautiful poetry about his love for God. In time Solomon became very wealthy, and with his great wealth he began to be wasteful. He built large ornamental war chariots and bought more and more horses for the huge stables he had constructed. Solomon had many wives, and he built idols to honor the gods of each wife. He taxed his people heavily and made slaves of the people he conquered to advance his building programs.

✻ On the lines that follow, write four strengths and four weaknesses of Solomon that are mentioned in the biography. One strength has been written in for you. Suggested answers are provided.

Strengths
1. Solomon wrote poetry.
2. Solomon wrote wisely about life.
3. Solomon made wise judgements about people.
4. Solomon honored God by building a great temple.

Weaknesses
1. Solomon was wasteful with his great wealth.
2. Solomon took slaves to help in his building programs.
3. Solomon taxed the people heavily.
4. Solomon spent too much money on chariots and horses.

Thinking Further: Choose someone whom you consider to be great and describe some of his or her strengths and weaknesses.
Answers should reflect independent thinking.

© Silver, Burdett & Ginn Inc.

Chapter 1, pages 64–67   23

Right Page

NAME _____

REMEMBERING PEOPLE

Recalling Details, Evaluating Information

✻ Fill in the blanks before the descriptions below with the names of the persons described. All possible names are in the box.

Gilgamesh	Tutankhamen	
David	Hatshepsut	Hammurabi
Saul	Belzoni	Joseph
Goliath	Champollion	

David	a shepherd who became a king
Belzoni	a treasure hunter who discovered the tomb of Seti I
Goliath	a giant who represented the Philistines
Gilgamesh	the hero of a popular work of Mesopotamian literature discovered in 1850
Joseph	a descendant of Abraham who became a high official of a pharaoh
Hammurabi	a king of Babylon who ordered that laws be carved on a pillar
Champollion	the solver of the puzzle of the Rosetta stone
Hatshepsut	the Egyptian god-king who wore a false beard
Tutankhamen	a boy-king who ruled Egypt in the middle of the twelfth century B.C.
Saul	the king who led the Israelites against the Philistines

Thinking Further: Which of the ten persons listed in the box above do you think was most important? Give two or three reasons to support your choice.
Answers should reflect independent thinking. Possibility: Champollion was most significant because his discovery enabled us to learn much about ancient civilizations.

© Silver, Burdett & Ginn Inc.

24   Chapter 1, pages 47–67

TEACHER NOTES

The Origin of Civilization

Objectives

★ **1. List** the characteristics of a civilization.

2. Explain why writing was important to the development of civilization.

3. Locate Mesopotamia on a map of Ancient Egypt and Mesopotamia.

4. Identify the following people and places: *Gilgamesh, Hammurabi, Mesopotamia, Uruk,* and *Babylon.*

1 STARTING THE LESSON

Motivation Activity

■ Explain to students that the earliest civilizations used symbols or pictures instead of an alphabet to write.

■ Have students write letters describing a day in their lives using only symbols or pictures.

■ Have students exchange letters and try to decipher one another's descriptions.

Think About What You Know

■ Assign the THINK ABOUT WHAT YOU KNOW activity on p. 47.

■ Student answers should reflect independent thinking but may include that they would have faster transportation and travel, or that they would have different farming equipment and housing, or that they would wear different clothing and have different kinds of jobs.

Study the Vocabulary

■ Have students look up the definition of each of the vocabulary words for this lesson in the Glossary.

■ Ask students to classify the words in a chart with the following headings: *Writing, Farming,* and *Religion.* Tell students that they will not use all the words.

CHAPTER *1* ANCIENT CIVILIZATIONS IN THE MIDDLE EAST AND EGYPT

History provides a pic of past cultures. The people of early civilizatio in the Middle East and Egypt left behind cities, ancient monuments, and rich cultures that still influence our lives.

Optional Activities

Making a Word-Search Puzzle

● Ask students to use the vocabulary words in this lesson to make word-search puzzles.

● Ask students to write an answer key for their puzzles.

● You may wish to show an example of a word-search puzzle on the chalkboard.

● Have students exchange and solve each other's puzzles.

The Origin of Civilization

THINK ABOUT WHAT YOU KNOW

Imagine that you have a machine that can bring ancient peoples into modern time. How do you think their lives today would differ from their lives in ancient times?

STUDY THE VOCABULARY

civilization   dike
archaeologist   irrigate
cuneiform   ziggurat
pictograph

FOCUS YOUR READING

What makes a civilization?

A. Civilizing a Wild Man

Long ago, people in Mesopotamia told a tale about a wild man named Enkidu who lived with the animals. Mesopotamia was the land between the Tigris and Euphrates rivers in the country now called Iraq. According to the story, Enkidu roamed the grasslands with herds of wild cattle and gazelles and came to the rivers only to drink. When a hunter dug pits to trap the animals, Enkidu filled them in. At first the hunter was puzzled, but one day he caught sight of the hairy man at a watering place. The hunter went to see his wise old father and asked for advice. His father told him to go to Uruk (OO ruk), the city ruled by the mighty Gilgamesh (GIHL-guh mesh), and ask for a beautiful woman. Such a woman would know how to deal with the wild man.

The hunter did as his father advised. He went to Gilgamesh's city and found a beautiful woman who went with him to the watering place, where they hid. After two days, Enkidu and the animals came to drink. As soon as the woman saw Enkidu, she stepped from her hiding place. The animals immediately fled, but Enkidu stood still and gazed at her. He was so struck by the woman's beauty that instead of running away, he walked up to her. She asked him, "Why do you live with the animals? You are a human being. You have a mind. Come with me."

The woman led Enkidu to a camp of shepherds who offered them bread. Enkidu did not know what the bread was, so the woman told him, "Eat the bread, Enkidu. This is food for humans." Enkidu tasted the bread and then continued to eat until he was full.

Enkidu and the woman stayed with the shepherds for a time. He kept watch over the flocks of sheep. Then the wild man who had protected the hunted animals became a hunter. He killed lions, wolves, and other wild animals that preyed on the sheep.

One day the woman said to Enkidu, "Let us both now go to Uruk, the city of King Gilgamesh, whose strength none can match."

Enkidu went with her but boasted, "I will challenge Gilgamesh to a fight, for I, too, am a strong one!" The woman warned, "Gilgamesh has greater strength than you, and he never rests."

When Enkidu met Gilgamesh in Uruk, the two strong men grappled in combat, smashing doors and shaking walls. Gilgamesh finally overcame Enkidu, but he then took Enkidu's hand and offered to be a friend. Never had the mighty Gilgamesh met another whose strength was nearly as great as his own. Gilgamesh and Enkidu became friends and shared many adventures. The story of those adventures is one of the oldest stories in the world.

47

Read and Think

Section A

To summarize the tale of Enkidu and Gilgamesh, ask the following questions:

1. **Where did the story of Enkidu take place?**
   (Mesopotamia *p. 47*)

2. **What is this area called today?**
   (Iraq *p. 47*)

   Thinking Critically Would you have befriended Enkidu, do you think, if you had been Gilgamesh?
   (Answers may include that their respect for Enkidu might also lead them to befriend him. *pp. 47-48*)

Storytelling

- Point out to students that many stories from the past are retold today by people all over the world. Some stories have morals, and others tell about specific people, events, or places.

- Have students share their favorite tales with their classmates.

- Encourage discussion about the point of the story, and why the story remains popular to this day.

For Your Information

The Epic of Gilgamesh The story of Enkidu and Gilgamesh is contained in a famous work known as the *Epic of Gilgamesh*. It chronicles the adventures and relationship of these two men. Near the end of the story, Enkidu dies and Gilgamesh desperately tries to bring his friend back to life. Gilgamesh miraculously finds a plant that can restore life, but a snake seizes the plant before he can give it to Enkidu. It is then that Gilgamesh comes to believe in and accept the permanence of death.

Optional Activities

Interpreting a Time Line

■ Direct students' attention to the time line on p. 48 to help them answer the following questions:

1. **In what year was Hatshepsut crowned god-king of Egypt?**
   (In 1503 B.C.)

2. **In what year did David become king of Israel?**
   (In 1000 B.C.)

3. **How many years passed between the time of the first Sumerian cities and Solomon's reign in Israel?**
   (2,539 years passed.)

B. Characteristics of Civilization

The story of Enkidu is, of course, only a story. It is not history. It is an imaginary tale about how a human being made a friend and became civilized, that is, how he learned to live in a **civilization**. A civilization is a way of living. The word *civilization* comes from the Latin word for *city*. But the development of cities was only one of the characteristics of a civilization. Another characteristic of a civilization is the development of specialized skills and different occupations. For example, as people became better farmers, it was not necessary for everyone in a community to cultivate the soil. Some people could work by making pots, jewelry, weapons, or tools. Other characteristics of a civilization include organized governments, religions, the development of trade, and the keeping of written records.

It is the exchange of ideas that makes writing so important for civilization. Writing makes it much easier for the ideas of one person to be passed on to another. Writing makes it possible to learn from people who are dead. Can you think of something you have read that was written by someone no longer living? The Constitution of the United States was written by persons who are no longer living.

C. A Book Buried Beneath Ruins

People in Mesopotamia told the story of Gilgamesh and Enkidu long before anyone wrote it down. We do not know exactly when it was first written, but we do know that there was a copy in a library

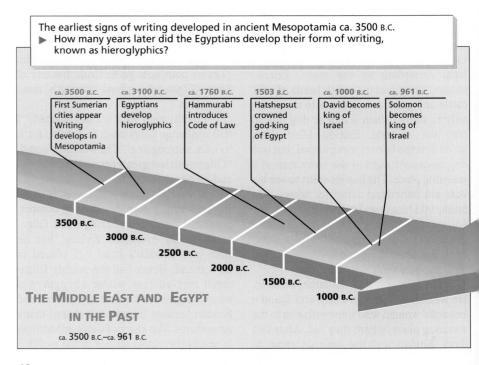

The earliest signs of writing developed in ancient Mesopotamia ca. 3500 B.C.
▶ How many years later did the Egyptians develop their form of writing, known as hieroglyphics?

ca. 3500 B.C.	ca. 3100 B.C.	ca. 1760 B.C.	1503 B.C.	ca. 1000 B.C.	ca. 961 B.C.
First Sumerian cities appear Writing develops in Mesopotamia	Egyptians develop hieroglyphics	Hammurabi introduces Code of Law	Hatshepsut crowned god-king of Egypt	David becomes king of Israel	Solomon becomes king of Israel

3500 B.C.
3000 B.C.
2500 B.C.
2000 B.C.
1500 B.C.
1000 B.C.

THE MIDDLE EAST AND EGYPT IN THE PAST
ca. 3500 B.C.–ca. 961 B.C.

48

Writing to Learn

Writing a Diary   Ask students to imagine that they were part of the 1850 archaeological team that uncovered the tablets that contained the story of Gilgamesh.

● Ask students to write a diary entry explaining how they feel about this great discovery.

Current Events

● Tell students that the people of Mesopotamia did not number their years as we do today. Instead, they associated each year with an important event that occurred during that year. For example, they might have referred to the year 3500 B.C. as the year Uruk was built.

● Ask students to think of a current event that would serve as a good reminder of each year in the decade of the 1980s.

● Then ask students to think of a current event that would serve as a good reminder of this year.

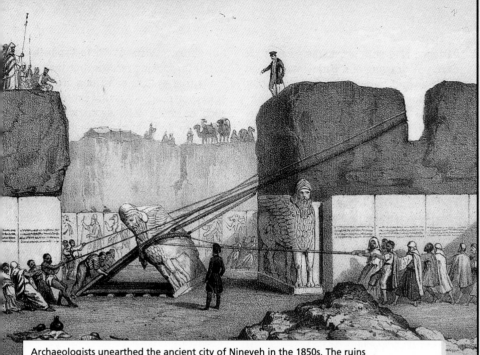

Archaeologists unearthed the ancient city of Nineveh in the 1850s. The ruins of this capital city are located in the present-day country of Iraq.
▶ How did the archaeologists move the stone statues?

destroyed in 612 B.C., more than 2,600 years ago.

The story of Gilgamesh was one of thousands of writings in a library at Nineveh (NIHN uh vuh) in northern Mesopotamia. In 612 B.C. an enemy army captured Nineveh and destroyed many buildings, including the library. Along with other writings, the story of Gilgamesh lay buried beneath the ruins until **archaeologists** dug them up in 1850. Archaeologists study ancient times and peoples by finding the remains of cities, tombs, buildings, and the like. How could a book lie buried so long and not have rotted away? It was not a book printed on paper. The story was written on 12 clay tablets. The words had been formed by marks on each clay tablet before it hardened. The marks, made by the tip of a wedge-shaped stick, are known as **cuneiform** (kyoo NEE uh form) characters. *Cuneiform* means "wedge-form."

D. The Development of Writing

Keeping Records The development of writing was important to the beginning of civilization in Mesopotamia. People needed to keep records. When one person borrowed barley from another, the lender wanted a record of how much he had lent. Barley is a grain used in making some cereals. Before a shepherd took sheep to graze on the grasslands, the owner wanted to have a record of how many sheep were in the flock.

The first records were very simple. A drawing of an ox head scratched on a bit of

49

Making a Rebus

● Ask students to define the word *rebus* (a puzzle in which pictures stand for sounds) and make up their own rebus puzzles about characteristics of the early civilizations that they are studying in this chapter.

● Have students guess the meaning of their classmates' puzzles.

Optional Activities

Read and Think
Sections B, C, and D

To focus students' attention on writing as a main factor of civilization, ask the following questions:

1. **What is a civilization?**
   (A way of living *p. 48*)

2. **List the characteristics of civilization.**
   (Cities; specialized skills and occupations; organized government and religion; trade; written records *pp. 48-49*)

3. **How was the story of Enkidu and Gilgamesh able to survive after being buried for thousands of years?**
   (It had been written on clay tablets. *p. 49*)

4. **How were ancient people able to write on clay?**
   (They formed marks on the clay before it hardened. *p. 49*)

5. **What can the remains of a city tell an archaeologist about the people who lived there?**
   (How they lived, the types of work they did, and their form of writing *p. 49*)

6. **Why was the development of writing important to the people of Mesopotamia?**
   (It enabled them to keep records. *p. 49*)

7. **Why did writing change from pictographs to cuneiform characters?**
   (In order to express sounds and actions instead of simply pictures *p. 50*)

Thinking Critically The people of Mesopotamia used clay tablets and sticks to write. What tools do we use today? (Analyze)
(Answers should reflect independent thinking but may include pens, pencils, paper, typewriters, and computers. *p. 50*)

Answers to Caption Questions

p. 48 ▶ 300 years
p. 49 ▶ They hoisted them with ropes in a tug-of-war formation.

49

Concept:
The Role of Laws in a Civilization

To better understand the difference between a civilized society and an uncivilized society, it is important to understand the role that laws play. The ancient civilizations of Sumer and Babylon both had codes of laws. Below are three activities that will help your students relate the concept of the role of laws to the laws in Section G on pp. 52-53.

◆ **EASY** Have students imagine that they are farmers in ancient Sumer.

Discuss with them why a farmer would need the protection of law. For example, a farmer would want to see his property claim protected so that others could not take his land from him.

Ask students to list three other concerns a farmer might have. Then have them write laws that would protect and address these concerns.

◀▶ **AVERAGE** A civilization's laws tell us a great deal about people's beliefs and attitudes. For example, the First Amendment to the Constitution shows that Americans think freedom of speech is a very important right of the people.

Have students reread Section G and write a paragraph explaining what the laws of Hammurabi tell us about the Babylonians.

◀▮▶ **CHALLENGING** Have students write a short essay entitled "An Uncivilized Society" in which they describe what life would be like if the United States had no laws.

Ask students to end their essays with a paragraph explaining why laws are important to our civilization.

flattened clay with six marks meant "six oxen." A drawing of a barley stalk stood for the word *barley*. A picture sign that stands for a word is called a **pictograph**.

The first pictographs looked somewhat like the things they represented. But as time went on, people did not bother to draw line pictures of oxen or barley. Instead they made marks simply by pressing the end of their wedge-shaped writing stick into the clay. This was the way that cuneiform writing began. As you can see by looking at the chart below, the cuneiform characters came to look less and less like pictures.

DEVELOPMENT OF EARLY WRITING

Meaning	Pictograph	Cuneiform Early	Cuneiform Later
Barley			
Fish			
Ox			
Bird			
Eat			
Walk/Stand			

Early writing began with the drawing of pictures that stood for objects.
▶ Why weren't pictographs a true system of writing?

Cuneiform Writing Pictographs were useful for making records, but they were not a true system of writing. To write a story, you need words that express action, such as *walk, talk, fight, hunt*. People began to make marks for actions rather than things. They made the cuneiform character for a thing connected with the action. For example, the character for foot meant "walk"; the character for mouth stood for "talk."

Writing was developed still more when characters came to be used for sounds. In time, the character for barley came to stand for the syllable *she* rather than for the grain. By using characters for syllables, people could write any word they could say. This type of cuneiform writing made it possible for the story of Gilgamesh to be written.

E. The Beginning of Cities

City Life Writing also made it possible for us to know many things about ancient civilizations. Mesopotamia did not have an ideal climate. Summers were very hot. Temperatures often climbed above 100°F (38°C) during the long summer, which lasted from early May through September. Almost no rain fell during the hot months. Some rains fell during the cooler winter and spring months, but the average yearly rainfall was less than 6 inches (15 cm).

Although summer was a time of drought in Mesopotamia, the Tigris and Euphrates rivers often flooded the land during the spring. Melting snow in the northern mountains sent waters rushing downstream, spreading over the lowland between the rivers.

Here is where city life began. A people we call the Sumerians built their cities in

Optional Activities

Curriculum Connection

Art Tell students that the Sumerians worshiped many gods and believed that the gods controlled natural events such as rainfall, harvests, health, and love. When the gods came to earth, they used the steps of the ziggurat as their ladder.

● Ask students to draw pictures of a Sumerian god coming to earth to influence some natural event.

● Have the class interpret individual drawings.

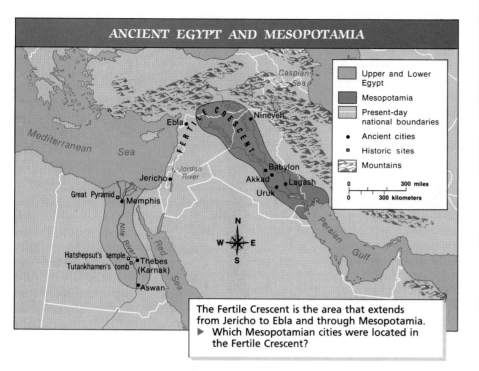

ANCIENT EGYPT AND MESOPOTAMIA

Upper and Lower Egypt

Mesopotamia

Present-day national boundaries

• Ancient cities

□ Historic sites

⌇⌇⌇ Mountains

300 miles

300 kilometers

The Fertile Crescent is the area that extends from Jericho to Ebla and through Mesopotamia.
▶ Which Mesopotamian cities were located in the Fertile Crescent?

Mesopotamia ca. 3500 B.C. Uruk, the city in the story of Gilgamesh, was a Sumerian city. It is certain that Gilgamesh was an early ruler, but it is doubtful that he had all the adventures described in the story.

Farming The Sumerians learned to make use of the spring floods. They built **dikes**, walls to hold back floodwater from their homes and fields. They dug canals and ditches to drain water into reservoirs, which were storage ponds. When the floodwater went down, the Sumerians used water from the reservoirs to **irrigate**, or bring water to, their fields during the summer months.

It took a lot of work to build dikes, ditches, and reservoirs, but the result was more food. By using the water during the dry summer, the Sumerians were able to grow two crops a year. Farmers not only had enough food for themselves and their families, but they produced a surplus, more than they needed.

Trading Since everyone did not have to work to raise food, some people could work at other jobs. These people erected buildings, made pottery, wove fine cloth, and worked at other crafts. A small number were overseers who directed the work of other workers.

People who spent their time doing one kind of work traded their products for other goods that they needed or wanted. The potter traded pots for the weaver's cloth, and both exchanged their products for food. In ancient times, as now, civilization depended on the exchange of goods as well as ideas.

51

Read and Think
Section E

To focus students' attention on the characteristics of early cities, ask the following questions:

1. **What was the climate of Mesopotamia?**
   (Long, hot summers; little rainfall *p. 50*)

2. **How were the Sumerians able to grow crops in their dry climate?**
   (They dug canals and ditches to catch water and used this water to irrigate their crops. *p. 51*)

Thinking Critically What types of businesses, do you think, were in the city of Uruk? (Infer)
(Answers may include pottery and weaving shops and a marketplace. *pp. 50-51*)

GEOGRAPHY THEMES

Location

■ Direct students' attention to the map on p. 51 to help them answer the following question: **What two rivers run through the Fertile Crescent?**
(The Euphrates and the Tigris)

┌─ **Answers to Caption Questions** ─
p. 50 ▶ They did not have any action words, only words for things.
p. 51 ▶ Nineveh, Babylon, Akkad, Uruk, and Lagash

Cooperative Learning

Creating the City of Uruk Divide the class into groups of five or six students, and assign to each group one of the following tasks: building a ziggurat; building houses and shops; building the city walls; building a marketplace; or building outlying farms and houses.

● Then have each group decide who will complete these assignments: (1) collect information and pictures of how the structure looked; (2) draw a rough sketch of the structure; (3) gather materials such as clay, papier mâché, or cardboard to build the structure; and (4) construct the building.

● Ask a member of each group to tell the class what their buildings tell us about life in Sumer.

For Your Information

The Contributions of the Sumerians The Sumerians did more than invent a system of writing. They knew how to make and use bronze and developed a way to measure time. They also had knowledge of mathematics, astronomy, and medicine. Education was important to the Sumerians, although only the sons of citizens in the highest classes were able to receive a formal education. Students studied many of the same subjects that today's students study, such as mathematics, history, reading, and foreign languages.

Optional Activities

51

Read and Think
Sections F and G

To focus students' attention on how the Sumerians solved disputes, ask the following questions:

1. **Why did the Sumerians surround their cities with thick walls?**
(For protection against enemies *p. 52*)

2. **How was the ziggurat used?**
(For religious services *p. 52*)

3. **Why did Hammurabi have the laws posted in a public place?**
(So that all would know them *pp. 52-53*)

Thinking Critically Why, do you think, did Hammurabi's "eye for an eye" rule apply only if the injured person was of the highest class? (Infer)
(Members of the highest class were considered to be more valuable members of society. *p. 53*)

GEOGRAPHY THEMES

Location

- Have students look at the map on p. 51 to help them answer the following question: **What historic sites shown in the key might people want to visit today?**
(Answers may include the Great Pyramid, the temple of Hatshepsut, and the tomb of Tutankhamen.)

F. Walls for Protection

The Sumerians surrounded their cities with thick walls to protect themselves from enemies. Warfare is as old as civilization, and fighting was very common in ancient times. In fact, for many centuries, cities in many parts of the world had walls for protection.

Houses and shops were closely packed together within the walls of a Sumerian city. In times of danger a city became very crowded. Farmers from villages flocked in for protection.

The largest structure in a city was a solid brick platform called a **ziggurat**. A temple for the god of the city stood on the ziggurat. Priests had charge of the temple and conducted services thought to please the god. The Sumerians believed that the

safety of a city depended on its god. Wars between cities were considered to be like wars between the gods.

G. The Need for Laws

Settling Disputes The Sumerians built the first cities in Mesopotamia. Other peoples followed their example. Cities increased in number and grew in size. As a result of wars, the rulers of some cities extended their power over others. Sargon the great of Akkad brought all of Sumer and the northern half of Mesopotamia under his rule ca. 2300 B.C. Later the rulers of Babylon conquered and ruled all of Mesopotamia. Babylon was famous for its wealth and entertainments. People still sometimes refer to a rich and pleasure-loving city as "a Babylon."

People living and working together closely needed ways of settling disputes. King Hammurabi, who ruled Babylon from ca. 1792 B.C. to 1750 B.C., ordered that laws be carved on a stone pillar. He had the

Stone statues of Sumerian worshipers (inset) were found in temples at the top of ziggurats.
► What did the Sumerians use to build their ziggurats?

The Oriental Institute Museum, University of Chicago

Optional Activities

Comparing Laws

- Have students work together to brainstorm what they know of the laws and cultures of the early settlers in the American West, and to compare these to the codes developed almost 4,000 years earlier to preserve law and order.

- Students can use old television shows, western movies, and cowboy folklore as a starting point for their comparisons (which might include cruel punishments for violent crimes; restrictions regarding the roles and rights of women; and the sheriff as mediator).

Reteaching Main Objective
⭐ *List the characteristics of a civilization.*

- Have students prepare a bulletin-board display to illustrate the characteristics of a civilization (cities, specialized skills and occupations, organized government and religion, trade, and written records).

- Tell them to divide the bulletin board into five sections and prepare titles for each section.

- Then have them use magazine illustrations or draw pictures to show each of the five characteristics.

- After they are done, have students write paragraphs explaining why each of these characteristics is important to civilization.

pillar placed in a public place so that all might know the laws of the city.

Hammurabi's Laws The laws of Hammurabi required that people be responsible for their actions. A person had to pay for any damages done to the property of others. If one man's boat ran into another's boat and sank it, he had to pay for both the boat and the goods it carried. If a man's ox killed another, he had to pay for the dead ox.

Some of Hammurabi's laws were based on the rule "An eye for an eye, a tooth for a tooth." According to this rule,

If a man puts out the eye of a noble, his eye shall be put out; if a man breaks the bone of a noble, his bone shall be broken; if he knocks out the tooth of a noble, his tooth shall be knocked out.

"An eye for an eye" is an old and harsh rule. It applied only if the injured person was of the highest, or noble, class. If the injured person belonged to a lower class, the penalty was the payment of silver. This practice is much more like the present-day practice of paying damages to the person who has been injured.

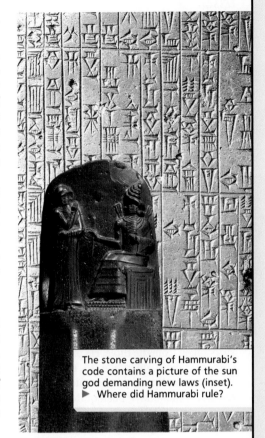

The stone carving of Hammurabi's code contains a picture of the sun god demanding new laws (inset).
▶ Where did Hammurabi rule?

Musee du Louvre, France

LESSON 1 REVIEW

THINK AND WRITE

A. How did the life of Enkidu change after he met the woman? **(Infer)**

B. Why was writing so important for the development of civilization? **(Recall)**

C. Why was the book with the story of Gilgamesh not destroyed in 612 B.C.? (all)

D. What kinds of characters were used in the development of writing? **(Recall)**

E. How were the Tigris and Euphrates rivers important to the building of cities? **(Infer)**

F. What was the purpose of building walls around a city? **(Recall)**

G. How were the laws of Hammurabi like or unlike those of today? **(Analyze)**

SKILLS CHECK

MAP SKILL

Look at the map of ancient Egypt and Mesopotamia on page 51. What two rivers were important bodies of water for the ancient cities of Mesopotamia?

53

Optional Activities

---

3 CLOSING THE LESSON

Lesson 1 Review

Answers to Think and Write

A. After Enkidu met the woman, he became civilized. He changed from a protector of animals to a hunter.

B. Writing was important to the development of civilization because it made the exchange of ideas easier.

C. The book was not destroyed because it was written on clay tablets.

D. Pictographs and cuneiform were used in the development of writing.

E. The rivers provided water for crops and people which enabled the population to thrive and build cities.

F. Walls were built to provide protection from enemies.

G. The laws of Hammurabi were like our laws because they required people to be responsible for their actions. Hammurabi's laws were unlike our laws in that they were based on the rule "An eye for an eye, a tooth for a tooth."

Answer to Skills Check

The Tigris and the Euphrates were important to the cities of ancient Mesopotamia.

Focus Your Reading

Ask the lesson focus question found at the beginning of the lesson: **What makes a civilization?**

(A civilization is characterized by the development of cities, the development of specialized skills and occupations, organized governments and religions, the development of trade, and the keeping of written records.)

Additional Practice

You may wish to assign the ancillary materials listed below.

Understanding the Lesson p. 12
Workbook p. 19

Answers to Caption Questions
p. 52 ▶ Solid brick
p. 53 ▶ In Babylon

53

Egypt–
The Land of the Nile

Objectives

★**1. Describe** the importance of the Nile to Egypt.

2. Describe the role of the pharaoh in ancient Egypt.

3. Identify the following people and places: *Belzoni, Seti, Menes, Carter, Tutankhamen, Egypt,* and *Thebes.*

1 STARTING THE LESSON

Motivation Activity

■ Explain to students that archaeologists study the items that they find and draw conclusions about life thousands of years ago.

■ Tell students to imagine that they are archaeologists who have found the following: a king's throne, baskets of fruit, statues of servants, items of gold, and wall paintings showing daily life in ancient Egypt.

■ Have students draw conclusions about ancient Egyptian civilization.

Think About What You Know

■ Assign the THINK ABOUT WHAT YOU KNOW activity on p. 54.

■ Student answers should reflect independent thinking but may include mummies, pyramids, King Tut, the Nile, and the desert.

Study the Vocabulary

■ Have students look up the definition of each of the vocabulary words for this lesson in the Glossary.

■ Using a *Wheel of Fortune*-style game, put blank spaces on the chalkboard to represent one of the vocabulary words.

■ Have students guess the word and the spelling. Students must correctly define the term to win.

THINK ABOUT WHAT YOU KNOW
What do you think of when someone mentions ancient Egypt?

STUDY THE VOCABULARY

mummy	delta
oasis	pharaoh
silt	pyramid

FOCUS YOUR READING
Why is Egypt called the land of the Nile?

A. Belzoni the Giant

A New Job About 180 years ago, Belzoni the Giant was amazing crowds at English fairs and circuses with feats of strength. Posters showed a tall, bearded man carrying 11 people perched on an iron harness. Belzoni also played Sampson in a famous story taken from the Bible. He pulled down scenery pillars on stage to show how Sampson destroyed his enemies in their temple. It must have been quite a show.

Giovanni Belzoni was an inventor as well as a strongman. He designed a machine for raising water from irrigation ditches. In 1815 he went to Egypt, hoping to interest the Egyptian ruler in his invention. Belzoni failed to do so, but he found a new job. People in Europe at that time had become interested in collecting ancient objects from such lands as Egypt. The British representative in Egypt hired Belzoni to collect things for the British Museum.

The representative knew that the head of a giant statue had fallen off and lay in the sand up the Nile River at Thebes. The statue was of Ramses II, an ancient ruler, but it was then mistakenly called "young Memnon." The representative

sent Belzoni to get the statue's head and ship it to England.

The head was large; it weighed over 7 tons (6,350 kg). Even a strongman could not lift such a weight. But Belzoni got it moved to a barge on the Nile River.

Discovering Treasures Securing the stone head aroused Belzoni's interest in ancient Egypt. He was probably more of a treasure hunter than an archaeologist. A true science of archaeology had not yet been developed, but Belzoni did make some important discoveries. He found the buried entrance to the tomb of Seti I, a ruler who died over 3,000 years ago. The tomb had been cut nearly 1,000 feet (305 m) through rock at the base of a mountain. Seti's body had long ago been removed, but much remained that told about life in ancient Egypt at the time Seti had lived. There were wooden statues, furniture, and marvelous wall paintings that showed people in ancient times.

detail, © 1991 The Metropolitan Museum of Art, Rogers Fund, (12.182.132c)

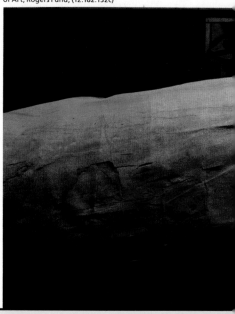

Optional Activities

Curriculum Connection

Math   Have students make a bar graph of the world's longest rivers.

● Put the following information on the chalkboard:
Nile, 4,160 miles (6,693 km); Amazon, 4,080 miles (6,565 km); Chang Jiang, 3,720 miles (5,985 km); Yenisei, 3,650 miles (5,873 km); Mississippi/Missouri, 3,740 miles (6,018 km).

● Have students locate the rivers on a map of the world.

When Belzoni returned to England, he opened an Egyptian exhibit. Crowds paid to see two rooms built to resemble Seti's tomb. They viewed statues, coins, ancient writings that no one could yet read, and a **mummy**. A mummy was a body treated for burial with preservatives and wrapped in airtight cloth bandages to keep it from decaying. The mummy probably attracted the most attention. Here were the remains of an Egyptian who had lived centuries ago.

B. Fertile Land Along the Nile

The Nile Egypt is a desert land crossed by the Nile River, the world's longest river. The narrow valley watered by the Nile has been called "one long, drawn-out **oasis**." An oasis is fertile land in a desert.

The Nile rises in the mountains and highlands of East Africa and flows north to

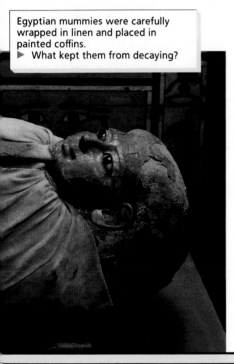

Egyptian mummies were carefully wrapped in linen and placed in painted coffins.
▶ What kept them from decaying?

the Mediterranean Sea. Melting snows and spring rains cause the river to rise in Egypt during the summer and spread over land along the river. Belzoni made use of the summer flood to float the barge on which he loaded the statue's head.

The flood brought tons of **silt** downstream, giving the water a muddy look. Silt is fine particles of soil carried in water. As the floodwater went down, it left a layer of fertile silt along the Nile Valley. The river also deposited silt where it emptied into the sea. Over the years the deposits built up the land at the river's mouth. The built-up land is called a **delta**, because it looks somewhat like the three-cornered Greek letter delta (Δ) turned upside down.

Farming The Egyptians took advantage of the yearly flood to grow crops in the desert. When the floodwater went down in late summer, farmers scattered grain on the damp land and drove herds of goats across the fields to push the seeds into the soil. By the time the fields dried, the grain was ready to harvest.

The Egyptians irrigated land that was not reached by the flood. They built dams to hold back the water and later let it out to irrigate fields of melons, cucumbers, onions, and other vegetables. Irrigating fields took much hard work, but the Egyptian farmers were able to grow two or even three crops a year. Like the farmers of Mesopotamia, Egyptian farmers produced a surplus of food.

C. Ruling the Land of the Nile

Many people had to work together to make the kind of life the ancient Egyptians had. It was the **pharaohs** (FAR ohz), or kings, and their many officials who ruled the land.

55

2 DEVELOPING THE LESSON

Read and Think
Sections A and B

To focus class discussion on early Egypt, ask the following questions:

1. **What important discovery did Giovanni Belzoni make?**
(He found the tomb of Seti I. *p. 54*)

2. **Why is the mouth of the Nile called a delta?**
(It looks like the three-cornered Greek letter delta turned upside down. *p. 55*)

3. **How did the farmers of Egypt plant their crops?**
(Scattered grain on the damp land and drove herds of goats across the fields to push the seeds into the soil *p. 55*)

4. **Compare the climate of ancient Egypt to that of Sumer.**
(Both had hot, dry climates, with heavy spring rains. *p. 55*)

Thinking Critically Some people believe that the objects taken from the ancient tombs should be returned to the Egyptians. Do you agree? (Analyze)
(Answers may include that the objects should be admired by everyone or that Egypt is the rightful owner. *pp. 54-55*)

— **Answers to Caption Questions** —
p. 55 ▶ They were treated with preservatives.

Using a Wall Map

● Using a wall map of the world, have students locate Egypt.

● Ask volunteers to name the continent in which Egypt lies and the countries that surround Egypt.

● Discuss with students how Egypt's geography affects its relationship with its neighbors.

For Your Information

Archaeology Archaeologists examine the remains that they find to help them explain how people lived in past times. There are three basic kinds of archaeological evidence: artifacts, features, and ecofacts. Artifacts are objects that were made by people. They include such objects as arrowheads, pots, beads, and sometimes clay tablets and other written records. Features consist of large structures such as houses, tombs, and canals built by people. Ecofacts are natural objects such seeds and animal bones. Ecofacts reveal how people responded to their surroundings.

Optional Activities

Meeting Individual Needs

Concept:
The Role of Government

To better understand the contributions of the Egyptians, it is important to think about the role the government played in helping the civilization to flourish. Below are three activities that will help your students relate the concept of the role of government to the greatness of ancient Egypt.

◆ **EASY** The pharaohs saw to it that disputes were settled and laws were enforced.

Ask students to write a paragraph describing what would happen if our traffic laws were not enforced.

◀▶ **AVERAGE** The pharaohs told the farmers when to expect the summer flood. Our government also gives advice and information.

Have students make a list of the information they can obtain through government agencies such as the Food and Drug Administration.

◀▮▶ **CHALLENGING** The pharaohs saw to it that surplus grain was stored until it was needed, which helped provide food for citizens in times of need.

Have students debate whether our government should have programs to help those in need or whether the federal government should not get involved in regional problems.

Howard Carter found the tomb of the pharaoh Tutankhamen. Hidden deep within the tomb were rooms filled with magnificent treasures (inset).
▶ What objects were found there?

The Egyptians served the pharaohs because they regarded them as gods. They believed that the rise and fall of the Nile depended on serving the god-kings. The pharaohs provided a government, which is necessary in any land where numbers of people live and work together. The pharaohs' officials settled disputes and enforced laws. They told farmers when to expect the summer flood. They saw to it that surplus grain was stored for later use.

Menes (MEE neez) was the first pharaoh whose name we know, although we do not know much more about him. The Egyptians said that he united the Nile Valley and the Nile Delta into one kingdom ca. 3100 B.C. The pharaohs ruled Egypt for 2,000 years after Menes. No other form of government has ever lasted so long.

56

D. The Tomb of King Tut Is Found

Nervously Carter lit a match, touched it to the candle, and held it toward the hole. As his head neared the opening— he was literally trembling with expectation and curiosity—the warm air escaping from the chamber beyond the door made the candle flare up. For a moment Carter, his eyes fixed to the hole and the candle burning within, could make out nothing. Then, as his eyes became gradually accustomed to the flickering light, he distinguished shapes, then their shadows, then the first colors. Not a sound escaped his lips; he had been stricken dumb. . . . Finally [he was asked] "Can you see anything?" Carter, slowly turning his head, said shakily: "Yes, wonderful things."

Optional Activities

Writing to Learn

Writing a Diary After students have read about Howard Carter's discovery of King Tut's tomb, ask them to imagine that they are on an archaeological dig and have just discovered an ancient pharaoh's tomb.

● Have students write entries in a diary that describe what they have found and how they feel.

Reteaching Main Objective

⭐ ***Describe the importance of the Nile to Egypt.***

● Have students trace the Nile River with their finger on a map of Ancient Egypt.

● Point out how the narrow valley watered by the Nile is a "long, drawn-out oasis."

● Then have students write a paragraph describing how the Nile River is important to Egypt.

● You may wish to allow students to review Section B before they write their paragraphs.

Carter found three layers of coffins in King Tut's tomb. The photographs above show Carter cleaning the coffins and separating them from one another.
▶ Of what material was Tut's coffin made?

The passage you just read on the previous page is from a book titled *Gods, Graves, and Scholars*. This book is about famous archaeological finds, such as the one made in 1922 by the British archaeologist Howard Carter. Carter had been searching for years to find the tombs of ancient Egyptian pharaohs.

What made Howard Carter's find so important is not the pharaoh who was buried in it but the contents of the tomb. Carter had discovered the tomb of a boy-king named Tutankhamen (too tahng-KAH mun), who ruled Egypt in the middle of the fourteenth century B.C. Today we commonly call this pharaoh King Tut. His rule was very short, only nine years, and he died before he was 20 years old. But he is best known of all the Egyptian pharaohs because of Howard Carter's discovery.

What were the "wonderful things" that Carter found in the tomb of King Tut? There was Tut's coffin made of solid gold. This coffin was neatly fitted into a second coffin, and the second coffin was carefully fitted into a third. There were also all sorts of things that the boy-king could use in his next life. For example, there was the king's throne, statues of servants to wait on him, and furniture for him to use. There was also a statue of King Tut that stands over 5 feet (1.5 m) tall. Even a toy box and painting set from his childhood had been placed in the tomb.

57

For Your Information

Carter's Search for Tutankhamen's Tomb   Howard Carter began his search for Tutankhamen's tomb in 1907 with the help of another Englishman, Lord Carnarvon. The problem in finding Tut's tomb was that earlier archaeologists had unknowingly covered the entrance to his tomb with rubble as they excavated other sites. After 15 years of searching, Carter discovered the tomb by accident. He was clearing away some rubble when he noticed a stone step that led downward. Within weeks of the discovery of the steps, one of the richest tombs of the pharaohs had been opened.

Optional Activities

Read and Think
Sections C and D

To focus students' attention on the Egyptian god-Kings, ask the following questions:

1. **Why did the Egyptians serve the pharaohs?**
   (Because they regarded them as gods *p. 56*)

2. **In what way was the government of the pharaohs unique?**
   (It lasted longer that any other government has lasted. *p. 56*)

3. **Who was Howard Carter?**
   (A British archaeologist who discovered the tomb of Tutankhamen *p. 57*)

4. **What did Carter find in King Tut's tomb?**
   (A coffin made of gold, things that could be used in his next life, and many items of gold and precious stones *p. 57*)

5. **Use your text and the map on p. 51 to locate the Great Pyramid. What ancient and modern cities is this most famous pyramid near?**
   (Giza-Memphis, near present-day Cairo *p. 58*)

   Thinking Critically Why, do you think, did it take Carter years of searching to find the tombs of some of the pharaohs? (Infer)
   (Answers should reflect independent thinking but may include that there were no written records indicating where they were, and that sandstorms may have hidden them from view. *pp. 56-58*)

VISUAL THINKING SKILL

Interpreting a Photograph

■ Direct students' attention to the photograph on p. 57 to help them answer the following question: **How did Carter separate the coffins?**
(With the use of ropes and pulleys)

— **Answers to Caption Questions** —
p. 56 ▶ Tut's coffin, throne, statues, furniture, a toy box, and painting set
p. 57 ▶ Solid gold

3 CLOSING THE LESSON

Lesson 2 Review

Answers to Think and Write

A. Belzoni brought back statues, coins, ancient writings, and a mummy.

B. The Nile River flooded each year, dampening the ground so that crops could be grown.

C. The government settled disputes, enforced laws, told farmers when to expect the summer flood, and stored surplus grain for times of need.

D. The discovery of Tut's tomb was important because the contents of the tomb revealed a great deal of information about the ancient Egyptians.

Answer to Skills Check

Answers should reflect independent thinking but include knowledge of typical artifacts found inside the tomb.

Focus Your Reading

Ask the lesson focus question found at the beginning of the lesson: **Why is Egypt called the land of the Nile?**
(Most of Egypt is a desert. In ancient times, only the land along the Nile was fertile. The Egyptian people depended on the Nile to grow their crops.)

Additional Practice

You may wish to assign the ancillary materials listed below.

Understanding the Lesson p. 13
Workbook pp. 20-21

The ruins of many pyramids stand near the Nile River. Each pyramid was constructed to protect the body of an Egyptian king. Thousands of workers built the pyramids without any machinery or iron tools.
► On what kind of land are these pyramids built?

The most famous of the pharaohs' tombs are the **pyramids** (PIHR uh mihdz). They are stone structures enclosing a small burial room, which once contained a pharaoh's mummy.

The Egyptians built a number of pyramids, but the three largest and most famous stand on the desert at Giza, near present-day Cairo. The largest is the Great Pyramid, built ca. 2500 B.C. Today it would cover nearly ten football fields. It is about 450 feet (137 m) high, but before some of the topmost stones were torn away, it rose to 482 feet (147 m).

LESSON 2 REVIEW

THINK AND WRITE

A. What kinds of things did Belzoni bring back to England from Egypt?   (Recall)
B. How did the Nile River help the farmers grow a surplus of crops?   (Recall)
C. What services did the government of the pharaohs provide to the Egyptians?   (Infer)
D. Why was the discovery of King Tut's tomb so important?   (Analyze)

SKILLS CHECK

WRITING SKILL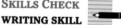

Pretend you are an archaeologist who discovered the tomb of an Egyptian pharaoh. Write a paragraph in which you describe what you saw inside the tomb, and how you felt as you made your discovery.

Optional Activities

UNDERSTANDING THE LESSON

NAME _____   CHAPTER

UNDERSTANDING THE LESSON   *1*

Recalling Facts   LESSON 2 CONTENT MASTER

✶ Read each statement below. Write **True** if the statement is true and **False** if it is false. If the statement is false, cross out the part that is incorrect and write the correct words above it.

False	1.	Archaeology had long been a true science when Giovanni Belzoni started working in Egypt in 1815.
False	2.	Belzoni was hired to collect ancient objects for the Egyptian Museum.
True	3.	Ancient Egyptian civilization grew up in the valley of the Nile River.
False	4.	Each year, the Nile flooded and left a layer of useless silt along the valley.
True	5.	The Egyptians could grow crops in the desert.
True	6.	Egyptian farmers irrigated land that was not reached when the Nile rose up.
False	7.	The Egyptians believed that their pharaohs were just like other people.
True	8.	Menes united the Nile Valley and the Nile Delta into one kingdom.
False	9.	The pharaohs ruled Egypt for more than 200 years, longer than any other form of government.
False	10.	The contents of King Tut's tomb included a coffin made of precious stones.

Think and Write: Write a paragraph explaining why the Nile River has been likened to "one long, drawn-out oasis." You may use the back of the sheet.
Answers should reflect independent thinking; suggestions appear in the Answer Key.

Use with textbook pages 40-44.   13

◄ **Review Master Booklet, p. 13**

The Civilization of the Egyptians

LESSON 3   PAGES 59–63

THINK ABOUT WHAT YOU KNOW

Imagine you discovered an ancient civilization. Explain how you would attempt to learn about the people.

STUDY THE VOCABULARY

Coptic   papyrus
hieroglyphics   scribe

FOCUS YOUR READING

What do we learn from writings about life in ancient Egypt?

A. Learning an Ancient Language

A few years before Belzoni was entertaining at fairs and circuses, a scientist, Jean Fourier (foor YAY), visited a school in Grenoble, France. Fourier had been in Egypt with the French army, and he told the students about the marvels he had seen in that land. One student, 11-year-old Jean-François Champollion (shahn paw-LYOHN), was fascinated by Fourier's remarks. Jean showed such interest that Fourier invited the boy to his home to see the collection of things he had brought back from Egypt.

Jean went to Fourier's house, where he carefully examined the various ancient objects. Some scraps of Egyptian writing especially interested him, and he asked, "Can anyone read them?" When Fourier answered that no one could, Jean announced, "I am going to do it. In a few years I will be able to, when I am grown."

Jean's boast was a bold one. Many great scholars had puzzled over the ancient Egyptian language without success. True, Jean was good at languages. He had

taught himself to read before he was 5, and a few years later he began to learn Latin and Greek. At the age of 13, Jean began to study **Coptic**, an Egyptian language no longer used except in the services of the Egyptian Christian Church. Some scholars thought that Coptic had come from the ancient language of the Egyptians. Jean thought that learning the Coptic language might provide a key to understanding this ancient language.

B. The Rosetta Stone

A piece of black stone about the size of a small coffee table provided the key to the language puzzle. Some French soldiers had found the stone, in 1799, buried near the city of Rosetta on the Nile Delta.

Three types of writing had been carved on the Rosetta Stone. One was

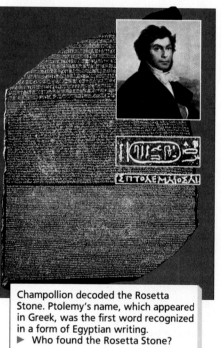

The British Museum

Champollion decoded the Rosetta Stone. Ptolemy's name, which appeared in Greek, was the first word recognized in a form of Egyptian writing.
► Who found the Rosetta Stone?

For Your Information

Egyptian Literature   The ancient Egyptians produced a body of written literature on many subjects. One book, *Instructions of the Vizier*, was written for his son by the chief minister of the pharaoh. It contains advice on how to succeed in the pharaoh's household. The Vizier suggests that the son not be overconfident but listen to the ignorant as well as the wise. He also urges his son to set an example of "blameless conduct" for others to follow, to be active and do more than he is asked to do, and to accept what his father teaches him.

Optional Activities

LESSON 3   PAGES 59–63

The Civilization of the Egyptians

Objectives

★1. **List** the contributions of the ancient Egyptians.

2. **Explain** how we have come to understand the meaning of Egyptian hieroglyphics.

3. **Identify** the following people and places: *Champollion, Hatshepsut, Thutmose III,* and *Rosetta.*

1 STARTING THE LESSON

Motivation Activity

■ Survey the class and make a list of all the foreign languages spoken by class members or their families.

■ Make a second column, allowing students to name other languages that they do not speak. If not mentioned, add Latin, Greek, and Coptic an Egyptian language to the list.

■ Point out that language is often the key that unlocks our knowledge of past civilizations.

Think About What You Know

■ Assign the THINK ABOUT WHAT YOU KNOW activity on p. 59.

■ Student answers may include studying the remains (such as buildings and artifacts), or trying to decipher its language.

Study the Vocabulary

■ Have students look up the definition of each of the vocabulary words in the Glossary.

■ Ask them to write a paragraph explaining how each of these words is related to the subject of language.

Answers to Caption Questions

p. 58 ► Desert land
p. 59 ► French soldiers

Read and Think

Sections A and B

To focus students' attention on major discoveries along the Nile, ask the following questions:

1. **Why did Champollion learn Coptic?**
   (He believed that it might provide him with a key to understanding the ancient Egyptian language. *p. 59*)

2. **What is the Rosetta Stone?**
   (A black stone found near the city of Rosetta in Egypt which had ancient Egyptian writing carved on it *p. 59*)

3. **Why was solving the writing on the Rosetta Stone so important?**
   (It enabled us to learn more about Egyptian civilization. *p. 60*)

Thinking Critically Was the discovery of King Tut's tomb more or less important than the discovery of the Rosetta Stone? (Hypothesize)
(Answers may include that the discovery of King Tut's tomb was more important because of what we have learned from the artifacts, or that the discovery of the Rosetta Stone was more important because we can now read about Egypt's ancient history. *pp. 59-60*)

VISUAL THINKING SKILL

Interpreting a Flowchart

■ Direct students' attention to the flowchart on p. 61 to help them answer the following question: **What did Egyptians do after they soaked the papyrus strips in water?**
(They crisscrossed two layers of strips and pounded them into paper.)

Greek, the other two were different types of Egyptian.

Scholars could read the Greek, but for more than 20 years, they had puzzled in vain over the Egyptian characters. They knew that one form of Egyptian writing, known as **hieroglyphics** (hye ur oh GLIHF-ihks), was that carved on many ancient buildings. They guessed that the hieroglyphic characters were pictographs, but they did not know the meaning of the marks, which looked like birds, snakes, feathers, and other objects.

Jean Champollion finally solved the puzzle. He discovered that although hieroglyphic characters had once been pictographs, they also stood for sounds in later times. This discovery provided the key to reading the ancient language. Scholars then worked out the meaning of the words carved on monuments and painted on tomb walls. The key to the language opened the way to learning much more about Egyptian civilization.

C. A Woman God-King

Being able to read the language made it possible for archaeologists to learn much more from the ruins they dug up. When they uncovered the tomb temple of Hatshepsut (hat SHEP soot), they learned about a remarkable woman who had ruled as a god-king.

Hatshepsut had been married to King Thutmose II (thoot MOH suh) who died young, leaving a small stepson Thutmose III. For a short time Hatshepsut ruled for the young boy, but she soon set him aside and ruled in her own name. Hatshepsut was crowned king, not queen. Some of her statues show her wearing a false beard. Like the god-kings before her, she was declared to be the child of a god.

Hatshepsut ruled the land from 1503 B.C. to 1482 B.C. She built temples and raised monuments that bore her name. Like earlier rulers, she began building her tomb temple while she was still alive. From the temple walls, scholars learned that Hatshepsut's ships brought back gold, ivory, perfumes, sweet-smelling trees, and live animals.

When Thutmose III grew up, he became ruler. We do not know how this came about, but we do know that he wanted to remove Hatshepsut's name from history. He had her name chiseled from temple

Hatshepsut ruled ancient Egypt as a king, not as a queen.
▶ Why, do you think, did Hatshepsut take the title of king?

Curriculum Connection

Art Have students illustrate the reign of Hatshepsut using hieroglyphic symbols.

● Tell students that their drawings should show how she came to power, what she accomplished during her reign, and who succeeded her as king.

Optional Activities

alls, and he had walls built to cover
rvings on her monuments. The walls
ter fell down, so that we are able to
ow at least part of this remarkable
oman's story.

. Paper from the Nile

aking Paper The Egyptians fortu-
tely did not have to do all their writing
stone. They also wrote on sheets of a
perlike material called **papyrus** (puh-
'E rus). Papyrus is a tall reed that grows
the Nile Valley. Egyptians dried stalks
papyrus and cut them into thin strips.
ey hammered the strips together to
rm a single sheet on which they wrote
ith brush and ink. They used a cursive
rm of writing, which was simpler than
e hieroglyphic characters.

ncient Writings Sheets of papyrus are
ot as durable as the clay tablets of the
esopotamians, but a surprisingly large
umber have survived. Among those writ-
gs that have survived is a schoolbook for
oung people learning to be **scribes**. Most
eople did not know how to write in an-
ent times. Scribes had the job of writing
tters and copying records.

The schoolbook for scribes was
the form of letters. These letters
ontained advice for both students
d their teachers. Students should "turn
eir hearts to books during the day and
ad during the night." Students who
iled to do so might end up working on an
rigation ditch rather than at a scribe's
esk. One letter stated that a student who
fused to study was like a lazy donkey and
ould be treated like one. The teacher
ould beat such a student.

Some surviving writings are more
ntertaining than the schoolbook. The

FROM PAPYRUS TO PAPER

1. Gather reeds.
2. Cut off outside bark.
3. Cut reed into strips.
4. Soak strips in water.
5. Crisscross two layers of strips.
6. Pound wet strips into paper.

Ancient Egyptians made an early
form of paper, called papyrus,
from a reed that grew along the
Nile River.
▶ What was used to make papyrus?

61

▬◆▬

Meeting Individual Needs

Concept:
The Importance of Written Records

To better study the history of Egypt, it is
important to understand the role written
records play in what we know about this
ancient civilization. Below are three activities that will help your students understand this concept.

◆ **EASY** Ask students to write a paragraph describing some things found in the
lesson that we might not know today if the
Book of the Dead had not been discovered.

◀▶ **AVERAGE** Have students discuss
why Thutmose III was unsuccessful in removing Hatshepsut's name from history.

Then have students write a paragraph
explaining how our knowledge of Egyptian civilization would be different if we
did not know about Hatshepsut.

◀▮▶ **CHALLENGING** Ask students to list
the written records that contain information about the American Revolution.

Next to each item, have students describe
the information found in these records.

Then ask students to explain why written
records are important.

┌─ **Answers to Caption Questions** ─┐
p. 60 ▶ Answers may reflect an understanding that women did not have the same rights
as men in ancient civilizations.
p. 61 ▶ A knife and mallet, or hammer, bowl,
water, and slab

Making Paper

- Students will need old newspaper, water, instant starch,
  a square of window screening, a large bowl, a spoon,
  and an egg beater.

- Tear a page of newspaper into tiny pieces and add to 1
  cup of water in the bowl.

- Let it stand for about an hour. Beat the mixture until the
  paper is soft and mushy.

- Dissolve 2 heaping tablespoons of starch in a cup of
  water and add to the mix in the bowl. Stir well.

- Holding the screen in a horizontal position, dip it into
  the bowl and lift it out covered with as much pulp as
  possible.

- Place the pulp and screen on several thicknesses of
  newspaper, cover with more newspaper, and press down
  very firmly. Fold back the newspaper and let the pulp
  dry on the screen overnight.

- Peel the newly-made paper from the screen very
  carefully.

Read and Think

Sections C, D, E, and F

To focus students' attention on some of the creations of the ancient Egyptians, ask the following questions:

1. **What was accomplished during the reign of Hatshepsut?**
   (Temples and monuments were built and trade was expanded. *p. 60*)

2. **How was papyrus made?**
   (Stalks of the reed were dried and cut into thin strips, then the strips were hammered together to form a single sheet. *p. 61*)

3. **What were the duties of a scribe?**
   (To write letters and copy records *p. 61*)

4. **According to the Book of the Dead, what kinds of behavior were wrong?**
   (Stealing, robbing, lying, and greediness *p. 62*)

5. **What is a solar year?**
   (The 365 ¼ days that it takes the earth to orbit around the sun *p. 63*)

Thinking Critically Why, do you think, was papyrus not as durable as clay tablets? (Infer)
(Answers may include that papyrus would be ruined by exposure to the sun or dampness while clay tablets would not. *p. 61*)

Egyptians, no doubt, told many stories that we can never know. But some of the stories written on papyrus have been found, and scholars can read them. For example, one story tells of a sailor who was shipwrecked and cast upon a desert island. Luckily he found fig trees on the island and was able to catch fish and fowls. He knew how to make fire by friction. He whirled a stick in a piece of dry wood until it smoldered. Have you ever read or heard of a story something like this?

E. "The Book of the Dead"

When the pyramids were built, the Egyptians believed that only the god-kings and those who served them lived after death. In later times they came to believe that life after death was for all people. They thought that the gods judged each person and decided whether he or she should be rewarded or punished.

To guide a person after death, scribes copied scrolls, which were placed in tombs. These scrolls are called The Book of the Dead, and a number of them have been found. The scrolls contain magic spells, advice on how to address the gods, and hymns, or songs, to the gods. Perhaps the most interesting part of The Book of the Dead reveals Egyptian ideas about the wrongs that a good person avoided. The Book of the Dead states that when a person faces the gods, he or she should be able to say truthfully,

> *I have not committed evil.*
> *I have not stolen.*
> *I have not robbed.*
> *I have not been covetous [greedy].*
> *I have not told lies.*

These ideas might seem familiar. Today we teach that stealing, lying, and greediness are wrong.

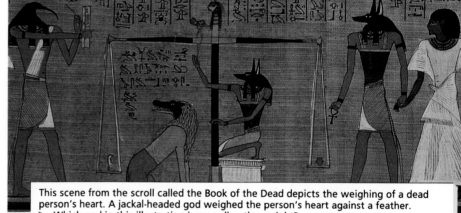

This scene from the scroll called the Book of the Dead depicts the weighing of a dead person's heart. A jackal-headed god weighed the person's heart against a feather.
► Which god in this illustration is recording the weight?

62

Optional Activities

Writing to Learn

Creative Writing Ask students to imagine that they are scribes writing entries into the Book of the Dead of an Egyptian pharaoh.

- Students may wish to write a hymn or song, or advice on how to address the gods.

Reteaching Main Objective

⭐ ***List the contributions of the ancient Egyptians.***

- Have students prepare a television special on the contributions of the ancient Egyptians.

- Tell students to begin by skimming the lesson and making a list of all the contributions mentioned in the lesson.

- Then have students write a brief description of one of the contributions.

- Have one student serve as the host of the program. The host will introduce students who would like to present their descriptions to the viewing audience.

Ancient peoples measured years by watching the moon. They based their calendar year on moon months. A moon month is the time from one new moon to another, a period of 29 1/2 days. Twelve moon months make a lunar year of 354 days. To keep the seasons and this short year together, the Mesopotamians added an extra month every two or three years.

The ancient Egyptians based their calendar year on the sun year, known as a solar year. As we now know, a solar year is the time it takes the earth to orbit, or move around, the sun. The Egyptians did not realize that the earth moved, but they were able to measure the solar year accurately by careful observation of the stars.

A solar year has 365 1/4 days. The Egyptian calendar year had 12 months of 30 days each and 5 extra holidays following the last month. This makes a year of 365 days, still 1/4 of a day less than the solar year. Today we base our calendar on the solar year, and we add an extra day every fourth year, which we call leap year. The Egyptians did not have a leap year, but they knew that their calendar year differed

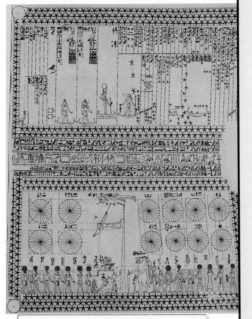

This Egyptian calendar, based on the sun, dates from about 1500 B.C.
► How many months did the Egyptian calendar year have?

from the solar year. Because of their careful observation of the stars, they knew what the difference was each year.

LESSON **3** REVIEW

THINK AND WRITE

A. What did Champollion decide to do when he was a schoolboy? (Infer)

B. Why was the Rosetta Stone a key to learning about ancient Egypt? (Analyze)

C. What was unusual about the god-king Hatshepsut? (Infer)

D. What sort of writings have been found on papyrus? (Recall)

E. What does The Book of the Dead reveal about Egyptian ideas concerning wrongdoing? (Recall)

F. How did the Egyptian way of measuring a year differ from that of the Mesopotamians? (Analyze)

SKILLS CHECK

THINKING SKILL

In the schoolbook for scribes it said, "A youth has a back and pays attention only when beaten, for the ears of the young are on their backs." What do you think this advice means?

63

◄ Review Master Booklet, p. 14

---

3 ▶ CLOSING THE LESSON

Lesson **3** Review

Answers to Think and Write

A. Champollion decided that he would figure out how to read ancient Egyptian writing.

B. The Rosetta Stone contained the key to the Egyptian language and opened the way to learning much more about Egyptian civilization.

C. Hatshepsut was a woman.

D. Schoolbooks and stories have been found on papyrus.

E. The Book of the Dead reveals that Egyptians regarded stealing, robbing, greediness, and lying as wrongs that a good person avoided.

F. The Egyptians measured their year by the sun, while the Mesopotamians measured their year by the moon.

Answer to Skills Check

Answers may include agreement with corporal punishment or disagreement, preferring positive reinforcement instead.

Focus Your Reading

Ask the lesson focus question found at the beginning of the lesson: **What do we learn from writings about life in ancient Egypt?** (We learn about Egyptian pharaohs, literature, education, religion, and values.)

Additional Practice

You may wish to assign the ancillary materials listed below.

Understanding the Lesson p. 14

┌─ **Answers to Caption Questions** ─┐
p. 62 ▶ The god with the bird's head
p. 63 ▶ 12 months

63

Ancient Israel

Objectives

★ 1. **Describe** the accomplishments of ancient Israel's great leaders.

2. **Explain** what is in the Old Testament.

3. **Identify** the following people and places: *David, Goliath, Saul, Solomon, Abraham, Moses, Israel,* and *Jerusalem.*

1 STARTING THE LESSON

Motivation Activity

- Ask students to imagine that they are judges hearing a case that involves two women who both claim to be the mother of an infant child.

- Tell them that there are no other witnesses who can give them information to determine who is telling the truth.

- Discuss with students how they would decide this case.

- Tell students they will be reading about a man who had to decide such a case.

Think About What You Know

- Assign the THINK ABOUT WHAT YOU KNOW activity on p. 64.

- Student answers should reflect independent thinking, but should include appropriate positive traits.

Study the Vocabulary

- Have students look up the definition of the vocabulary word for this lesson in the Glossary.

- Ask students to make a family tree, going back as many generations as they can.

- Explain that this tree shows them who their ancestors are.

THINK ABOUT WHAT YOU KNOW

If you were given the chance to be king of a country, what kind of ruler would you be?

STUDY THE VOCABULARY

ancestor

FOCUS YOUR READING

Who were some of the famous leaders of ancient Israel, and for what are they known?

A. A Battle with a Giant

Ancient histories tell about many wars and battles. One of the most famous battles was a combat between David, a shepherd boy, and Goliath, a man so big that he was called a giant. David was an Israelite; Goliath was a Philistine. About 3,000 years ago the Israelites and the Philistines were at war. David's older brothers had joined the Israelite army led by King Saul, but David was too young. David had remained at home, where he served as keeper of his father's sheep.

One day David's father told him to take some supplies to his brothers who were with King Saul. When David reached the Israelite camp, he found the two armies facing each other, ready for battle. The huge Goliath stood in front of the Philistines and dared the Israelites to send one man to fight him in single combat. "If he be able to fight with me, and to kill me, then we will be your servants: but if I prevail against him, then shall you be our servants."

When none of Saul's army stepped forward to meet Goliath, David said that

he would battle the huge Philistine. King Saul warned David that he was too young to fight such a large and experienced warrior. But David insisted that he was not afraid. Seeing that he was determined, Saul offered David his own sword and armor. David refused to take them, saying that the heavy armor would only hinder him. Instead David armed himself with only a sling and five small stones.

When Goliath saw David, he sneered that he would soon feed the boy to the birds. David said nothing. He stepped forward, whirled his sling, and let a stone fly. It hit Goliath right on the forehead and stunned him. He stumbled and fell to the ground. Then David rushed up and killed him with Goliath's own sword.

The story of David and Goliath is a famous biblical story.
► What scene from the story does this picture illustrate?

Optional Activities

Curriculum Connection

Art   Ask students to review the story of David and Goliath in Section A.

- Then ask students to illustrate the story.

- Remind students that they may want to choose a particular scene in the story to illustrate, such as David tending the sheep or David fighting the giant.

- Tell students to give their illustrations a title.

B. David, King of Israel

David became a hero to the Israelites. He became so popular that King Saul grew jealous and quarreled with him. At one time he had to flee to the hill country in order to escape. But after Saul's death, David became king. Saul was the first of Israel's kings, David the second, and his son Solomon was the third.

But King David is probably the best-known ruler of the ancient Middle East, yet his kingdom was not large. Israel was only about the size of Vermont. Much of the land is hilly, and summers are very dry.

David captured the city of Jerusalem and made it his capital, but it was not yet a great city. He built no great temples or tombs like those of the Egyptian pharaohs. Yet David's name is better known than those who built the Great Pyramids. David's fame has lasted because his story is told in a book — the Jewish Bible, which the Christians call the Old Testament.

C. Ancient Writings Tell of Israel's History

The Bible The Bible is a collection of writings that cover subjects, including law, history, and poetry. All these writings, or books, were written in ancient times. For Jews and Christians the books of the Bible are religious writings. But writers of other religious views also study them, just as they study other ancient writings.

Some books of the Bible give a history of Israel both before and after the time of David. They tell that Abraham, **ancestor** of the Israelites, had once lived in Mesopotamia. An ancestor is a person from whom a family or group is descended. According to the Bible, Abraham and his household moved west to the land that later would become Israel.

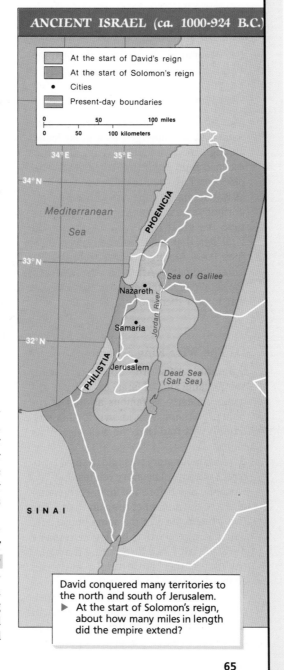

ANCIENT ISRAEL (ca. 1000-924 B.C.)

- At the start of David's reign
- At the start of Solomon's reign
- • Cities
- Present-day boundaries

0   50   100 miles
0   50   100 kilometers

Mediterranean Sea
PHOENICIA
Sea of Galilee
Nazareth
Jordan River
Samaria
Jerusalem
Dead Sea (Salt Sea)
PHILISTIA
SINAI

David conquered many territories to the north and south of Jerusalem.
▶ At the start of Solomon's reign, about how many miles in length did the empire extend?

65

2 DEVELOPING THE LESSON

Read and Think
Sections A and B

To discuss the story of David and Goliath and David's rule as King of Israel, ask the following questions:

1. **Why was David a hero?**
   (He saved his people from becoming servants of the Philistines. *p. 64*)

3. **Why has David's fame lasted so long?**
   (His story is in the Jewish Bible or Old Testament. *p. 65*)

   Thinking Critically **What personal characteristics were evident in David when he killed the giant?** (Infer)
   (Answers may include courage, intelligence, resourcefulness, and cleverness. *p. 64*)

GEOGRAPHY THEMES

Location

■ Direct students to the map on p. 65 to help them answer the following question: **What river connects the Dead Sea and the Sea of Galilee?**
(The Jordan River)

Answers to Caption Questions
p. 64 ▶ David shooting his slingshot at Goliath
p. 65 ▶ About 350 miles (about 563 km)

Writing a Giant Tale

- Have students reread the story of David and Goliath in the text.

- Discuss how courage and intellect prevail over strength and size.

- Then have students work in groups of three to write a contemporary tale sharing this theme, such as a rich person fighting a poor person or a small person fighting a neighborhood bully.

For Your Information

The Religion of the Israelites The Israelites were the first people of the ancient Middle East to worship only one god, whom they called Yahweh (YAH way). Many of their teachings dealt with values and behavior. The Israelites were also the first to believe that worship did not have to take place in sacred locations. Instead, they believed that worship could take place wherever people could come together. They called these meeting places *synagogues*.

Optional Activities

According to the Jewish Bible, G[od]
gave Moses and the Israelites a s[et]
of laws to live by.
▶ What are the laws called that
were given to Moses?

Meeting Individual Needs

Concept:
The Importance of Wise Leaders

To better understand the history of ancient Israel, it is important to understand the role that wise leaders played. These activities will help your students understand this concept.

◆ **EASY** Solomon was said to be "wiser than all men." Ask students to think of a famous American who would fit this description and have them explain their choice.

◀▶ **AVERAGE** Have students write a paragraph that explains how wise leadership, such as Solomon's, can help a leader stay in power for a long time.

◀▮▶ **CHALLENGING** Tell students that Solomon had to tax the people heavily to pay for the great buildings he constructed. Some people did not like this and they became discontented with his rule. Others believed him to be a very wise ruler.

Have students debate what attributes make a wise ruler.

Read and Think

Sections C and D

To focus a discussion on famous writings, ask the following questions:

1. **Who led the Israelites out of Egypt?**
(Moses *p. 66*)

2. **For what is King Solomon remembered?**
(Wisdom; building temples, palaces, and public buidings *pp. 66-67*)

3. **Where can we read Israel's ancient history?**
(In the Bible *p. 65*)

Thinking Critically How, do you think, did King Solomon know who the real mother was? (Evaluate)
(The real mother would rather lose her child than allow her baby to be harmed. *pp. 66-67*)

The Bible also relates that in a time of famine, some of Abraham's descendants went to Egypt, where one of them, Joseph, had become a high official of the pharaoh. For a time the Israelites lived freely in Egypt, until an unfriendly pharaoh enslaved them.

Moses After hundreds of years, a man named Moses emerged as a great leader among the Israelites. The Israelites escaped from Egypt under the leadership of Moses. For a number of years, they lived as wanderers in the desert. Those were important years in their history. During that time the great leader Moses taught the Israelites that their God had given them their laws. Among the laws were the Ten Commandments. After the time of Moses, the people of Israel settled in the land that was to bear their name.

D. The Wise King Solomon

Solomon's Wisdom Solomon, David's son, became king of Israel ca. 961 B.C. His name is nearly as famous as that of his father. Solomon was known for his wisdom. It was said that "he was wiser than all men."

A famous story was told to show Solomon's wisdom. The story relates that two women came before the king, each claiming to be the mother of the same baby. The two women lived in the same house, and both had given birth to babies on the same day. One baby had died during the night, and its mother arose and silently exchanged the dead baby for the living one. When the other mother awoke, she realized what had happened, but the mother of the dead baby claimed the living child as her own and refused to give it up.

When the two women and the baby came before King Solomon, he called for a sword. He said that since the women could not agree, he would have the baby cut in two so that each could have half. When the true mother heard the king's decision, she cried out, "Give her the living child, only do not kill him!" But the false mother said, "Let it be neither hers nor mine, so cut it in

66

Optional Activities

Reteaching Main Objective

⭐ *Describe the accomplishments of ancient Israel's great leaders.*

● Divide the class into groups of three students.

● Have one student in each group review David's accomplishments in the lesson, the second student review Moses's accomplishments, and the third student review Solomon's accomplishments.

● Have each student write an outline of the accomplishments of their assigned leader.

● When outlines are completed, have students exchange outlines and quiz each other orally.

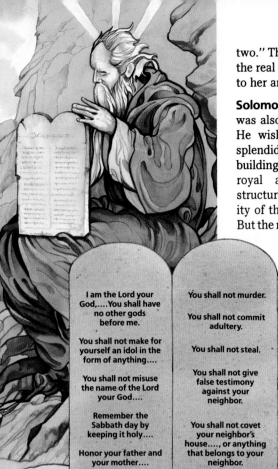

I am the Lord your God,....You shall have no other gods before me.

You shall not make for yourself an idol in the form of anything....

You shall not misuse the name of the Lord your God....

Remember the Sabbath day by keeping it holy....

Honor your father and your mother....

You shall not murder.

You shall not commit adultery.

You shall not steal.

You shall not give false testimony against your neighbor.

You shall not covet your neighbor's house...., or anything that belongs to your neighbor.

two." The wise king now knew which was the real mother, and he returned the child to her arms.

Solomon's Temple Solomon the Wise was also known as Solomon the Builder. He wished to make Jerusalem a truly splendid city. He erected great public buildings and a grand palace with fine royal apartments. These magnificent structures served to establish the authority of the laws and government of Israel. But the most important structure of all was the temple. Built of large stones and costly woods brought from other lands, the temple was a holy place for the people of Israel.

In later times, Israel's enemies captured Jerusalem and destroyed Solomon's temple. Not even the ruins of Solomon's temple remain. Yet we know quite a lot about the building, because the Bible contains a detailed description of it. In this case, ancient writings have proved more durable than stone.

LESSON 4 REVIEW

THINK AND WRITE

A. How was David able to overcome Goliath?
B. Why is David probably the best-known king of the ancient Middle East? (Infer)
C. What does the Bible tell about Abraham, Joseph, and Moses? (Recall)
D. How do you know that Solomon was wise? (Infer)

SKILLS CHECK

WRITING SKILL

Write two paragraphs in which you compare and contrast the following rulers: Hatshepsut, David, and Solomon.

67

UNDERSTANDING THE LESSON

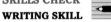

NAME _____ CHAPTER

UNDERSTANDING THE LESSON 1

Using a Time Line LESSON 4 CONTENT MASTER

❋ The time line is designed to show when important events in the history of ancient Israel took place.
a. Using your textbook, number the events in the order in which they took place.
b. Write the events in the correct boxes above and below the time line. The first one has been done for you.

5 David battles Goliath.   6 Temple at Jerusalem is built.
6 David becomes king of Israel.   4 Israelites wander in the desert.
3 Moses leads Israelites out of   1 Abraham moves west to Israel.
   Egypt.   2 Some of Abraham's descendants
7 Solomon becomes king of Israel.   move to Egypt.

| Abraham moves west to Israel. | Moses leads Israelites out of Egypt. | David battles Goliath | Solomon becomes king of Israel. |

| 2000 B.C. | 1500 B.C. | 1000 B.C. | 500 B.C. |

| Some of Abraham's descendants move to Egypt. | Israelites wander in the desert. | David becomes king of Israel. | Temple at Jerusalem is built. |

Think and Write: Write a short paragraph explaining why the years the Israelites spent wandering in the desert were important for them to them. You may use the back of the sheet.
Answers should reflect independent thinking; suggestions appear in the Answer Key.
Use with textbook pages 50–53.
15

◄ **Review Master Booklet, p. 15**

Optional Activities

---

3 CLOSING THE LESSON

Lesson 4 Review

Answers to Think and Write
A. David used a sling, stones, and a sword.
B. David's story is in the Bible.
C. It tells that Abraham was the ancestor of the Israelites, and that Joseph became a high official of the pharaoh in Egypt, and that Moses led the Israelites out of Egypt to escape a cruel pharaoh.
D. Solomon helped to solve his people's problems.

Answer to Skills Check
All three were intelligent, wise rulers who kept the well-being of their people in mind. They also built great buildings and monuments.

Focus Your Reading

Ask the lesson focus question found at the beginning of the lesson: **Who were some of the famous leaders of ancient Israel, and for what are they known?**
(David: killed Goliath; Solomon: wisdom, buildings; Abraham: Israelite ancestor; Moses: led Israelites out of Egypt)

Additional Practice

You may wish to assign the ancillary materials listed below.

Understanding the Lesson p. 15
Workbook pp. 22-24

┌─ **Answers to Caption Questions** ─┐
p. 66 ▶ The Ten Commandments
└─────────────────────────────────┘

67

Using the Vocabulary

1. ziggurat
2. delta
3. papyrus
4. mummy
5. ancestor
6. pictograph
7. civilization
8. archaeologist
9. pharaoh
10. hieroglyphics

Remembering What You Read

1. Cities, specialized skills and occupations, organized government and religion, trade, and written records
2. Cuneiform characters
3. They dug canals and ditches.
4. Laws carved on a stone pillar which was placed in a public place
5. Floods provided silt and water for crops.
6. The contents of the tomb revealed many things about ancient Egypt.
7. The Rosetta Stone
8. Scrolls which were placed in tombs to guide a person after death
9. Goliath, the giant
10. The Bible

USING THE VOCABULARY

civilization	delta
archaeologist	pharaoh
pictograph	hieroglyphics
ziggurat	papyrus
mummy	ancestor

On a separate sheet of paper, write the word from the list above that best completes each sentence.

1. A Sumerian temple stood on a solid brick platform called a _____.
2. Built-up land at the mouth of a river is a _____.
3. Egyptians made paper from reeds called _____.
4. A body treated for burial and wrapped in airtight cloth bandages is a _____.
5. An _____ is a person from whom a family or group is descended.
6. A picture sign that stands for a word is called a _____.
7. The word _____ comes from the Latin word for city.
8. An _____ studies ancient times and peoples by finding the remains of cities, tombs, and buildings.
9. A king of ancient Egypt was called a _____.
10. Egyptian pictographs carved on buildings are called _____.

REMEMBERING WHAT YOU READ

On a separate sheet of paper, answer the following questions in complete sentences.

1. What are five characteristics of a civilization?
2. What kinds of characters were used to write the story of Gilgamesh?
3. How did the Sumerians get water for the crops they planted?
4. What did King Hammurabi establish in Babylon?
5. How did the yearly floods help people who lived along the Nile River?
6. Why was archaeologist Howard Carter's discovery important?
7. What archaeological discovery provided the key to reading ancient Egyptian writing?
8. What is The Book of the Dead?
9. Whom did David fight against to become a hero?
10. What collection of writings tells about ancient Israel?

TYING LANGUAGE ARTS TO SOCIAL STUDIES

Imagine that you are a news reporter in the United States in the year 4300. Your task is to write about an archaeological discovery just made near where you live. Archaeologists have uncovered a city that they believe was an active city in the twentieth century. In your newspaper article, describe five items that have been dug up. Try to explain what the purpose of each item may have been way back in the twentieth century.

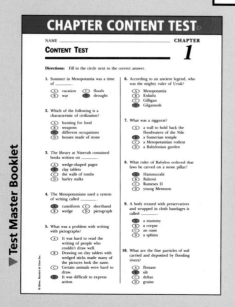

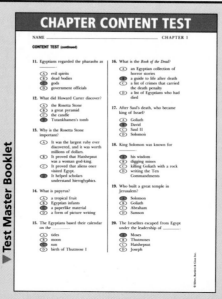

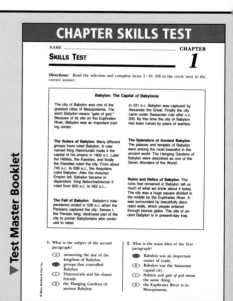

THINKING CRITICALLY

On a separate sheet of paper, answer the following in complete sentences.

1. Why, do you think, is it important to learn about ancient civilizations?
2. What reasons are there for having laws besides as ways of settling disputes?
3. Why would you have wanted or not wanted to help discover King Tut's tomb?
4. What kinds of symbols would you use to make up your own written language? Explain.
5. Why might people other than Christians and Jews study the Bible?

SUMMARIZING THE CHAPTER

Copy this graphic organizer on a separate sheet of paper. Under the main heading for each lesson, write three key words or phrases that support the main idea.

CHAPTER THEME

Many characteristics of modern civilization have their roots in ancient Middle Eastern and Egyptian civilizations.

LESSON 1

A civilization has specific characteristics.
1. Cities
2. _____
3. _____

LESSON 2

Egypt is called the land of the Nile.
1. Has fertile land
2. _____
3. _____

LESSON 3

We have learned from writings about ancient Egypt.
1. Rosetta Stone
2. _____
3. _____

LESSON 4

Some famous leaders came from ancient Israel.
1. David
2. _____
3. _____

69

Thinking Critically

1. Answers may include that we learn about the origins of humanity.
2. Answers may include that laws provide an orderly society.
3. Answers may include that they would because of the artifacts and treasures, or that they would not because tombs should be left alone.
4. Students may suggest stick figures, pictures, or other symbols.
5. To learn the history of ancient Israel

Summarizing the Chapter

Lesson 1
1. Cities
2. Organized governments
3. Written records

Lesson 2
1. Has fertile land
2. Sahara
3. floods

Lesson 3
1. Rosetta Stone
2. hieroglyphics
3. papyrus

Lesson 4
1. David
2. Abraham
3. Moses

Ancient Greece

(pp. 70-97)

Chapter Theme: Many things in modern culture began in ancient Greece. Under the Greeks, Western civilization made many advances.

CHAPTER RESOURCES

Review Master Booklet
  Reviewing Chapter Vocabulary, p. 23
  Place Geography, p. 24
  Summarizing the Chapter, p. 25
Chapter 2 Test

LESSON *1* Myths and History

(pp. 70-75)

Theme: Ancient Greek writings include myths, or stories that attempt to explain how things happen, and histories, or accounts of what actually happened.

LESSON RESOURCES

Workbook, p. 25
Review Master Booklet
  Understanding the Lesson, p. 19

LESSON *2* The Cities of Greece

(pp. 76-81)

Theme: Sparta and Athens, Greek city-states with differing ideologies, went to war when Sparta began to fear the growing power of Athens.

 SOCIAL STUDIES LIBRARY: *City: A Study of Roman Planning and Construction*

LESSON RESOURCES

Workbook, p. 26
Review Master Booklet
  Understanding the Lesson, p. 20

LESSON *3* Alexander the Great

(pp. 84-89)

Theme: Alexander the Great was a king and warrior who conquered a huge empire and spread Greek culture throughout his conquered lands.

 SOCIAL STUDIES LIBRARY: *Money*

LESSON RESOURCES

Workbook, p. 27
Review Master Booklet
  Understanding the Lesson, p. 21

LESSON *4* Greek Achievements

(pp. 90-95)

Theme: The ancient Greeks built a great culture — the influence of which survives today in philosophy, architecture, athletics, and the arts.

LESSON RESOURCES

Workbook, pp. 28-30
Review Master Booklet
  Understanding the Lesson, p. 22

Review Masters

REVIEWING CHAPTER VOCABULARY

Review Study the terms in the box. Use your Glossary to find definitions of those you do not remember.

alliance	culture	jury	philosophy
amphitheater	democracy	monarchy	strait
city-state	despot	myth	
colony	epic	oligarchy	

Practice Complete the paragraphs using terms from the box above. You may change the forms of the terms to fit the meaning.

Many of our modern ideas are not as new as they may seem. Some come from the great Greek civilization of the fourth and fifth centuries B.C. The (1) _culture_ developed by the Greeks produced writings such as Homer's (2) _epic_ poems. These poems are still widely read today. The Greeks also designed and constructed great buildings, such as the outdoor (3) _amphitheater_ in which people met and were entertained. You may have been to a similar kind of building to hear a concert or watch a sports event.

The Greeks were also interested in the study of knowledge and wisdom. These Greek ideas about (4) _philosophy_ play an important part in our modern lives. For example, our government is a (5) _democracy_ based on a belief in government by the people. This form of government was first used in ancient Greece. Also, a trial by (6) _jury_ determines whether a person is guilty or innocent in our courts. The Greeks dealt with lawbreakers in much the same way. Greek ideas about democratic government and justice are accepted by many countries around the world.

Write Choose ten terms from the box above. Use each term to write a sentence of your own. You may use the back of the sheet.

Sentences should show that students understand the meanings of the terms.

_____

_____

_____

_____

_____

LOCATING PLACES

✻ The places listed below were important in the history of ancient Greece. Use the Gazetteer in your textbook to find the latitude and longitude of each place. Then locate and label each on the map.

		LAT. ⊖	LONG. ⊙			LAT. ⊖	LONG. ⊙
1.	Athens	38°N	24°E	6.	Sparta	37°N	22°E
2.	Delphi	38°N	22°E	7.	Hellespont (Dardanelles)	40°N	26°E
3.	Thermopylae	39°N	22°E	8.	Thebes	38°N	23°E
4.	Salamis Island	38°N	23°E	9.	Olympia	38°N	22°E
5.	Mount Olympus	40°N	22°E	10.	Troy	40°N	26°E

SUMMARIZING THE CHAPTER

✻ Complete this graphic organizer. Under each main heading, write two additional statements that support it.

CHAPTER THEME Many things in modern culture began in ancient Greece. Under the Greeks, Western civilization made many advances.

LESSON 1

A myth is different from history.

1. Tells about gods

2. Is not totally accurate

3. May be based on history

LESSON 3

Alexander the Great was a famous leader with many major accomplishments to his credit.

1. Won a huge empire

2. Established many Greek colonies

3. Spread Greek culture throughout colonies

LESSON 2

There were many differences between the city-states of Sparta and Athens.

1. Athens: democracy, Sparta: military

2. Athens: learning, Sparta: simple life

3. Athens: citizens' government, Sparta: more slaves than citizens

LESSON 4

There were many great achievements in ancient Greek culture.

1. Established philosophy

2. Made great buildings

3. Wrote great poems and plays

Workbook Pages

Page 25

INTERPRETING A GREEK MYTH

Developing Reading Comprehension, Hypothesizing

✻ A myth is a story that explains some custom, belief, or happening in nature. It usually involves gods and goddesses, or other supernatural beings. Read this myth about the Greek goddess Athena. Then answer the questions that follow.

Athena, the goddess of war and wisdom, was the beautiful daughter of Zeus, ruler of the gods. She was generous and skilled, and she shared her knowledge with humans. She showed ordinary people how to make tools and musical instruments, and how to spin wool yarn and make woven cloth.

Athena was sometimes jealous of other gods or of humans who did something better than she. A young woman named Arachne (uh RAK nee) was an excellent weaver. Arachne was fast and neat and her designs were unusual and colorful. Neighboring people came to see the large tapestry (heavy cloth) that she had woven. The tapestry showed the gods Poseidon and

Prometheus and the goddess Aphrodite. All this attention made Arachne so proud that she boasted, "I am an even better weaver than Athena. She may have been the master teacher, but look at *my* beautiful work."

When Athena heard this, she went to see Arachne and the tapestry. She saw that it was indeed better than she could have done herself. This made Athena so jealous and angry that she ripped the tapestry apart.

Arachne was very frightened and ran into the woods to escape. However, Athena caught Arachne and transformed her into a spider, saying, "You can still weave, little one. But now your thread will be a thousand times finer and your work a thousand times more delicate."

1. Why do you think Athena shared her knowledge with humans? _Possible answers: Athena_
shared her knowledge to help people. She shared her knowledge to show how much she knew.

2. How did Arachne arouse Athena's anger? _Arachne aroused Athena's anger by bragging that Athena_
could not weave as well as she could.

3. Why was Athena so upset when she saw Arachne's tapestry? _Athena was upset because she saw_
that the tapestry was better than her own work. She became extremely jealous.

4. What Greek city is named in Athena's honor? _Athens_

Thinking Further: Do you think Athena had a right to be upset with Arachne?

Answers should reflect independent thinking. Possibilities: Athena had a right to be upset because Arachne boasted
too much. Athena did not have a right to be upset because she should have accepted someone more talented.

Page 26

COMPARING ATHENS AND SPARTA

Understanding Stated Facts and Details, Applying Information, Defending a Choice

✻ The statements below might have been written by citizens of either the city-state of Athens or the city-state of Sparta. On the line before each statement, enter the name of the city-state the writer probably lived in. The first has been done for you.

Sparta	1. "My son will be seven years old next month, and he will leave home to become a soldier."
Athens	2. "My brother has been called to serve on a jury next week. My uncle served on a jury last year."
Sparta	3. "I have just completed my military service. Now I may marry."
Athens	4. "I enjoyed learning about Pericles' ideas. He describes our government very well."
Athens	5. "Darius and his Persian soldiers attacked us recently. We achieved a great victory over the invaders at Marathon."
Athens	6. "When my friends and I were at the marketplace this morning, we heard many interesting ideas about equality before the law."
Sparta	7. "If I do not get married, I will be breaking the law."
Sparta	8. "My wife and I were relieved that our baby was born strong and healthy. Now he will be allowed to live."
Athens	9. "You do not have to be born into a wealthy family in order to get ahead. My parents are poor, but I own a successful business."
Athens	10. "I am very happy about Solon's reforms. He canceled my debts, and now I will be able to farm without having to worry about money I owe."

Thinking Further: In two or three sentences tell whether you would have preferred living in ancient Athens or in ancient Sparta. Support your choice with at least two specific reasons.

Answers should reflect independent thinking. Possibility: "I would have preferred to live in Athens. The citizens there
had more freedom. They had more contact with the rest of the world."

Page 27

ALEXANDER THE GREAT

Understanding Stated Facts and Details, Building Vocabulary

✻ This crossword puzzle is based on information in Lesson 3 of Chapter 2. Use the clues to complete the puzzle.

ACROSS

1. City where Alexander the Great died
2. Country Alexander fought to free Greek cities in Asia
4. Country in north Africa conquered by Alexander
7. Alexander's homeland
9. Person who taught Alexander
11. Alexander's age when he became king (write out number)
12. Alexander's father

DOWN

1. Name of Alexander the Great's horse
2. His house was the only one left standing when Thebes was destroyed by Alexander
3. Name given to many Greek cities in regions Alexander conquered
5. Macedonia was located in the _____ of Greece
6. Settlement of people living in new area while being ruled by government of another country
8. River at far eastern edge of Alexander's empire
10. City destroyed by Alexander to prove he was ready to be king

Thinking Further: What do you think is the most important fact about Alexander's career? Give two or three reasons for your choice.

Answers should reflect independent thinking. Possibility: Alexander's military conquests were most notable because
they enabled him to add more territory to Greece and to extend Greek influence to other parts of the world.

Page 28

THE GEOGRAPHY OF ANCIENT GREECE

Locating Places on a Map, Determining Significance of Geography

✻ On the facing page is a map of ancient Greece.
a. Locate the following places and geographical features on the map.
b. Write each number in the appropriate spot.
c. On the lines next to each place or geographical feature, give one or two important reasons why it was significant in ancient times. (You may wish to refer to a map in your textbook to help you with this exercise.)

Suggested answers are provided.

1. Mt. Olympus _highest mountain in Greece;_ _home of gods and goddesses_

2. Athens _strong city-state; leader of Delian_ _League; home of Socrates; site of Parthenon_

3. Sparta _strong city-state; winner of Trojan War;_ _winner of Peloponnesian War_

4. Troy _site of Trojan War_

5. Salamis _island where Athenians fled during_ _Persian Wars_

6. Thebes _city destroyed by Alexander the Great to_ _prove he was prepared to be king_

7. Macedonia _homeland of Alexander the Great_

8. Aegean Sea _part of the Mediterranean Sea, is_ _on the eastern coast of Greece_

Thinking Further: Identify and describe an important characteristic of the geography of Greece.

Possibilities: its many islands; its proximity to Asia Minor, Italy, and several seas.

C2-C

Workbook Pages

THE GEOGRAPHY OF ANCIENT GREECE *CONTINUED*

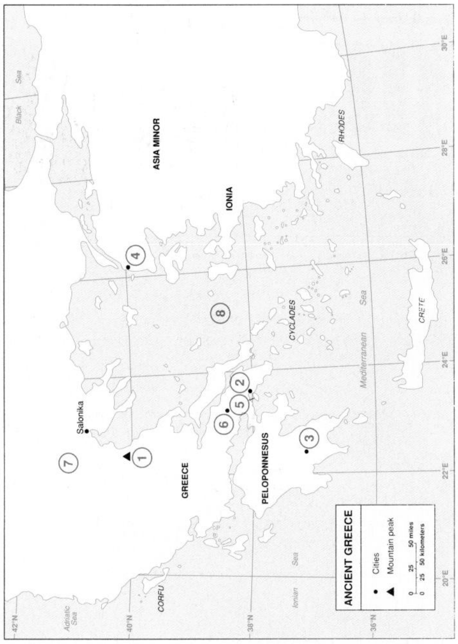

ANCIENT GREECE

- Cities
- ▲ Mountain peak

0 25 50 miles
0 25 50 kilometers

© Silver, Burdett & Ginn Inc.

Chapter 2, pages 71–95

29

COMPARING ANCIENT WARS

Identifying Relevant Detail; Comparing and Contrasting; Interpreting Facts

※ In Chapter 2 you read about several wars that were fought in and near ancient Greece. You may want to refer to your textbook as you fill in the chart below about the Trojan War, the Persian Wars, and the Peloponnesian War.

Suggested answers are provided.

	Trojan War	Persian Wars	Peloponnesian War
Who were the combatants?	Troy vs. Greece	Greece (mainly Athenians) vs. Persia	Athens vs. Sparta
What caused the war to start?	Paris of Troy kidnapped Helen, wife of the Greek king of Sparta.	Persians wanted to expand empire.	Sparta feared Athens was too powerful.
What was the main strategy or battle plan that led to victory in the war?	Wooden horse filled with soldiers brought into Trojan camp.	Athenians tricked Persian navy into battle in unfamiliar waters.	Spartans got Persian money to increase naval strength.
Why do you think this strategy was effective?	Horse was mysterious. Trojans let down their guard.	Persians were confused; didn't know bay.	Spartans became most powerful force on land and sea.
Who won the war?	Greece	Greece	Sparta

Thinking Further: How were the winning strategies similar in the Trojan War and the Persian Wars?

Possible answers: both strategies had element of surprise; both involved trickery.

_____

_____

© Silver, Burdett & Ginn Inc.

30

Chapter 2, pages 71–95

TEACHER NOTES

C2-D

Myths and History

Objectives

★**1. Explain** the difference between myth and history.

2. Describe the role of the gods and goddesses in Greek life.

3. Identify the following people and places: *Homer, Heinrich Schliemann, Herodotus, Troy,* and *Mt. Olympus.*

1 STARTING THE LESSON

Motivation Activity

■ Write the words *mythology* and *history* on the chalkboard.

■ List on the chalkboard everything that students can name which relates to these two words.

■ How are the descriptions similar? How are they different? Tell students that they will learn the difference between mythology and history in this lesson.

Think About What You Know

■ Assign the THINK ABOUT WHAT YOU KNOW activity on p. 71.

■ Student answers may include it enables us to learn how we have developed.

Study the Vocabulary

■ Have students look up the new vocabulary words in the Glossary.

■ Ask what events they would write about if they were to write an epic today. (You may suggest landing on the moon, tearing down the Berlin Wall, and so on.)

CHAPTER **2**

ANCIENT GREECE

The Greek civilizatio developed along the eastern Mediterranean ! Greek achievements in architecture, such as th Parthenon on the Acropolis, drama, and government enrich our lives today.

Optional Activities

Myths and History

THINK ABOUT WHAT YOU KNOW
Tell why studying history is important.

STUDY THE VOCABULARY
epic   myth

FOCUS YOUR READING
What is the difference between myth and history?

A. Greece and Troy at War

The story of the Trojan War was told by a blind poet named Homer. Homer was the greatest of the Greek poets. He described the Trojan War and the years that followed in two **epics**, the *Iliad* (IHL ee ud) and the *Odyssey* (AHD ih see). An epic is a long narrative poem about great heroes and their deeds. His epics tell of the role of the gods and goddesses during the war and in the years that followed.

Troy was a rich city on the Asian coast of the Aegean (ee JEE un) Sea, in the country now known as Turkey. At the time of the war, Greece was divided into a number of separate groups, each with its own government and laws.

The war began because of a quarrel over Helen, the beautiful wife of the Greek king of Sparta. Paris, the son of the Trojan king, had heard of Helen's beauty. Paris had visited the Spartan king and had carried off his host's wife. The angry king called upon other Greeks to join him in a war against the city of Troy. Many Greek warriors took to their ships and set sail for the coast of Asia.

The war was quickly begun but not quickly ended. For ten years the Greeks battled the Trojans on the plains before the walls of Troy. Many brave warriors fell in the bloody conflict, but the Greeks could not break through the walls of Troy. To learn more about Homer's tale, read the literature selection on page 73.

B. Greek Gods and Goddesses

According to Homer's account, gods and goddesses played a large part in the Trojan War. The Greeks believed that gods and goddesses never grew old and were more powerful than humans. The gods and goddesses took part in all sorts of human affairs. They had favorites whom they helped and protected. They sent misfortunes on those who displeased them or aroused their anger.

The most important gods and goddesses dwelt on Mount Olympus, the highest mountain in Greece. Each god or goddess had particular powers. For example, Zeus (zyoos) was supposed to rule the gods on Olympus. Zeus had two brothers — Poseidon (poh SYE dun), god of the sea, and Hades, god of the underworld. Hera, wife of Zeus, was the goddess of marriage, and Hestia, her sister, protected homes.

Aphrodite (af ruh DYT ee), the beautiful goddess of love, caused the quarrel between the Greeks and the Trojans. She helped Paris kidnap Helen and so aroused the Spartan king's demand for war. Athena (uh THEE nuh), goddess of both war and wisdom, aided the Greeks, as did Poseidon. Ares (AIR eez), god of battle, encouraged the Trojans.

C. Mixing Myth and History

History's Importance The story of the Trojan War as told by Homer and other poets is not totally accurate. We do not believe that gods took part in the war. The poets mixed **myths** into their accounts.

71

2 DEVELOPING THE LESSON

Read and Think
Sections A and B

To focus students' attention on the early myths presented in the reading, ask the following questions:

1. **Who was Homer and what did he do?**
   (The greatest Greek poet; he wrote *The Iliad* and *The Odyssey p. 71*)

2. **What beliefs did the Greeks have about their gods and goddesses?**
   (They never grew old, were very powerful, and each had particular powers. *p. 71*)

   Thinking Critically Why, do you think, did the Trojans build walls around their city? (Analyze)
   (Answers may include for protection from enemy armies. *p. 71*)

Role-Playing

● After you have read the literature excerpt on p. 73 aloud, have a group of students role-play Trojans who are discussing whether or not to bring the wooden horse inside their city walls.

● Choose one or two students to take a firm stand on each side and another three or four who are "undecided."

● Just before the group makes its final decision, stop the action and ask the students in the audience to vote on whether to let the horse inside the walls.

● Then have students from the audience take turns standing up to read aloud the final sentences of the literature excerpt and its epilogue.

Creating a Myth

● Explain that Greeks created myths, or stories, to explain natural events and the joys and tragedies of life. You may wish to read a Greek myth to the class.

● Have students create their own myths to explain a natural event such as why the sky darkens every night, what causes thunder and lightning, how the earth was formed, and so on.

● Give students an opportunity to tell these myths orally rather than to write them.

● You may find that students who have difficulty writing are creative oral storytellers.

Optional Activities

Distinguishing Mythology from History

In order to better recognize when information is historically accurate, it is important to understand the difference between mythology and history. Below are three activities that will help your students distinguish between mythology and history.

◆ **EASY** Have students who have difficulty distinguishing between mythology and history make a list of people mentioned in the lesson who are mythological and a list of people in the lesson who really lived.

◀▶ **AVERAGE** Write this question on the chalkboard: **Why did the Greeks win the war?**

Have students work in pairs to answer the question orally, with one student making up a myth and the other making up an answer that could be historically accurate.

◀▮▶ **CHALLENGING** Ask students who need a challenge to write a brief essay explaining what kind of evidence or information they would need to decide whether the Trojan Horse really existed.

Have them include whether it is possible to obtain this evidence.

Answers to Caption Questions

p. 72 ▶ Apollo

Greek gods and goddesses played an important role in ancient Greece. Each had a special function or job.
▶ Who was the god or goddess of music?

GREEK GODS AND GODDESSES

Myths are stories about the origins and doings of the gods. They attempt to explain how and why things happen. History is an account of what did happen. Myths may be interesting—sometimes more interesting than history—but they do not necessarily tell what really happened.

Myths may be based partly on history. Was there a city of Troy that was destroyed by attackers? This was the question Heinrich Schliemann (HYN rihk SHLEE mahn), a German boy, asked his father. Heinrich listened to his father tell of buried cities and ancient heroes, especially those of the Trojan War. The boy usually took the side of the Trojans, because he thought the Greeks had wronged

them. He once asked if any ruins of Troy remained, and he was disappointed when his father said that Troy had disappeared.

On Christmas in 1829, Heinrich received a history book with a picture showing the great walled city of Troy in flames. His father explained that the picture was based on the artist's imagination. When Heinrich asked if Troy might have had such great walls, his father said that it probably had. That was enough for Heinrich. He insisted, "If such walls once existed, vast ruins of them must remain, but they are hidden away beneath the dust of ages." His father thought this was doubtful, but Heinrich declared that some day he would dig up those walls.

72

For Your Information

Greek Mythology Twelve of the Greek's chief gods and goddesses, known as the Olympians, were Zeus (ruler of all gods), Hera (wife of Zeus), Apollo (god of music, poetry, and purity), Ares (god of battle), Athena (goddess of wisdom and war), Aphrodite (goddess of love), Hephaestus (blacksmith for the gods), Artemis (twin sister of Apollo and goddess of hunting), Hermes (messenger of the gods), Poseidon (god of earthquakes and the ocean), Demeter (goddess of agriculture), and Hestia (goddess of the home).

Writing to Learn

Writing a Journal Have students imagine that they are soldiers inside the Trojan Horse.

● Have them describe what it was like to wait for hours inside the horse until it was taken into Troy.

● Have them tell what happened when they left the horse and entered the city.

Optional Activities

FROM:

The Adventures of Odysseus and the Tale of Troy

By: Homer — translated by Padraic Colum
Setting: Ancient Troy

Homer was a blind poet who lived sometime between 800 B.C. and 700 B.C. His epics, the *Iliad* and *Odyssey*, describe the Trojan War and the travels of Odysseus. These epics, originally written in Greek, have been translated into many different languages. This excerpt is based on the story of the Trojan horse.

*A*nd then Odysseus devised the means by which we took Priam's [the Trojan king's] city at last. He made us build a great Wooden Horse. We built it and left it upon the plain of Troy and the Trojans wondered at it greatly. And Odysseus had counselled us to bring our ships down to the water . . . and to make it seem in every way that we were going to depart from Troy in weariness. This we did, and the Trojans saw the great host sail away from before their City. But they did not know that a company of the best of our warriors was within the hollow of the Wooden Horse, nor did they know that we had left a spy behind to make a signal for our return.

The Trojans wondered why the great Wooden Horse had been left behind. And there were some who considered that it had been left there as an offering to the goddess, Palla Athene, and they thought it should be brought within the city. Others were wiser and would have left the Wooden Horse alone. But those who considered that it should be brought within prevailed; and, as the Horse was too great to bring through the gate, they flung down part of the wall that they might bring it through. The Wooden Horse was brought within the walls and left upon the streets of the city and the darkness of the night fell.

73

Use the information below to help students better understand the literature selection found on p. 73.

Selection Summary
The Iliad is the oldest surviving Greek poem. Historians date it to the 700s B.C., and from it have learned much about life in Troy, and the feelings of people of long ago.

The Iliad, divided into 24 books covering a 54-day period, chronicles events of the last year of the Trojan War, fought for ten years, until Greece defeated Troy.

The passages shown here provide students with a vibrant description of the episode of the Wooden Horse.

Guided Reading
1. **Who devised the battle strategy using the Wooden Horse?**
   (Odysseus)

2. **Where were the Greek soldiers who were not hidden inside the horse?**
   (They were pretending to board their ships and retreat from weariness.)

3. **Where was Odysseus — on the ship or inside the horse?**
   (Inside the horse)

Literature–Social Studies Connection
1. **Why do you think *The Iliad* is important to Greek history?**
   (Answers may include that it contains historical events that might otherwise have been lost.)

Curriculum Connection

Literature   Explain to students that the ancient Greeks used the Trojan horse as a diversion so that they could carry out a suprise attack on Troy.

- Ask them to imagine that aliens from another planet are planning a suprise attack on a major city in the United States. In order to carry out their attack, the aliens want to distract the attention of the population of the city.

- Have students create, in writing, a contemporary diversionary tactic, explain the need for this diversion, and provide the directions for how it will be used.

Optional Activities

Read and Think
Sections C and D

To start a class discussion on myths and the writings of Herodotus, ask the following:

1. **Who found the site of Troy?**
   (Heinrich Schliemann *p. 74*)

2. **What was the main subject of Herodotus' history book?**
   (The Persian Wars *p. 75*)

   Thinking Critically **Why, do you think, did Herodotus record everything people told him even though he did not necessarily believe it was true?** (Infer)
   (Answers may include that he wasn't positive that the stories were false, that he thought they were interesting, or that the stories said something about those who told them. *pp. 74-75*)

■ Direct students' attention to the map of the Persian Empire on this page. Then ask students to think about and write a response to the following questions:

1. **What two bodies of water are joined by the Darius Canal?**
   (The Mediterranean and Red seas)

2. **What city was located between the Euphrates and Tigris rivers?**
   (Babylon)

Uncovering Troy It was many years before Heinrich Schliemann undertook his search for the city of Troy. He was 46 when he finally began exploring the Asian coast of the Aegean Sea. He was in his 50s when he excavated the site of an ancient fortified city. Schliemann mistakenly believed that he was excavating Homer's Troy. It was later learned that he had indeed found the site of Troy, but that he had dug through the ruins of Homer's Troy to those of still earlier times. Since Schliemann's excavation, the remains of Homer's Troy have been correctly identified and studied. We now know that there was a city of Troy and that it was destroyed by fire about the time of Homer's heroes. We also know that in those times the ancestors of the Greeks attacked cities on the coast of Asia. These are facts of history that Homer mixed with myths about the gods and goddesses.

D. Writing History

Long after the time of Homer, armies from Asia invaded Greece. Three times between 499 B.C. and 479 B.C., the Persians attacked the Greeks in Europe. The emperor of the Persians ruled the largest empire the world had yet known. The conquest of Greece would make it still larger.

Herodotus (hih RAHD uh tus) wrote the history of the Persian Wars. He was a Greek, but he was very fair to the Persians.

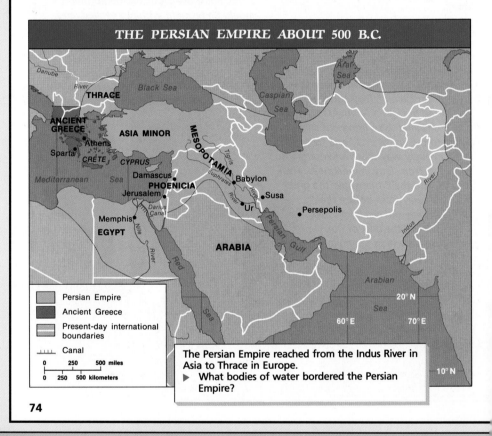

THE PERSIAN EMPIRE ABOUT 500 B.C.

Persian Empire
Ancient Greece
Present-day international boundaries
Canal

0   250   500 miles
0   250   500 kilometers

The Persian Empire reached from the Indus River in Asia to Thrace in Europe.
▶ What bodies of water bordered the Persian Empire?

74

He wrote to preserve the record of the "great and wonderful achievements of both our own [Greeks] and the Asian peoples."

The main subject of Herodotus' history was the Persian Wars, but he covered much more than the conflicts. He described most of the peoples and the lands ruled by the Persians. These lands reached from the Mediterranean Sea to India. Since this empire covered so much of the known world, Herodotus' book was almost a world history and geography.

Herodotus had traveled widely throughout the Persian Empire. His reports about what he had actually seen are believable. But Herodotus does tell some tall tales about faraway lands that he had not visited. He reports that in some places there are flying snakes, dog-headed men, and cattle that walk backward as they graze. They do so because they have long pointed horns that bend forward. Were they to walk forward as they nibbled grass, their horns would get stuck in the ground.

Such tales are hardly history, and Herodotus did not necessarily believe them. He admits, "I merely record the story without guaranteeing the truth of it." When he reports that the Persian magicians calmed a storm at sea by putting a spell on the wind, he adds, "Of course, it may be that

Herodotus was the first Greek historian.
▶ What was the main subject of his writings?

the wind just naturally dropped."

Homer mixed myth and history. Herodotus sometimes mixed history and fictional, fanciful tales. It is doubtful that he fooled many Greeks of his time. He certainly does not fool readers today. We have little trouble separating history from fancy in Herodotus' work. But the tall stories make the book more fun to read.

LESSON 1 REVIEW

THINK AND WRITE

A. According to Homer, what was the cause of the Trojan War? (Recall)

B. What were the powers of the major Greek gods and goddesses? (Recall)

C. Why do we think that Homer's account of the Trojan War was based partly on history? (Infer)

D. What different types of subjects did Herodotus write about? (Recall)

SKILLS CHECK

MAP SKILL

Compare the map of the Persian Empire on page 74 with that of the Eurasia political map in the Atlas. Make a list of at least five modern countries that are located within the land once ruled by the Persian emperor.

◀ Review Master
Booklet, p. 19

Optional Activities

Lesson 1 Review

Answers to Think and Write

A. Homer wrote that the Trojan War began when Paris, son of the Trojan king, abducted Helen, the Spartan king's daughter.

B. Each Greek god and goddess had special powers. Zeus was the ruler of the gods. Poseidon and Hades ruled the sea and the underworld. Hera was the goddess of marriage, and Hestia protected homes. Aphrodite was the goddess of love and Athena was the goddess of wisdom and war. Ares was the god of battle.

C. We believe Homer's account was based partly on history because there is evidence that Troy existed and was destroyed by fire. We also have evidence that the Greeks attacked cities in the region.

D. Herodotus wrote about the Persian Wars and the peoples and lands ruled by the Persians. He also described his own travels and the stories people told him.

Answer to Skills Check

Possible answers include Turkey, Syria, Lebanon, Israel, Jordan, Iran, and Iraq.

Focus Your Reading

Ask the lesson focus question found at the beginning of the lesson: **What is the difference between myth and history?**
(Myths are stories about the gods and goddesses. They attempt to explain how and why things happened. History is an account of what actually happened.)

Additional Practice

You may wish to assign the ancillary materials listed below.

Understanding the Lesson p. 19
Workbook p. 25

┌─ **Answers to Caption Questions** ─┐
p. 74 ▶ Persian Gulf, and Red, Mediterranean, Black, Caspian, Aral and Arabian seas
p. 75 ▶ The Persian wars
└──────────────────────────────┘

The Cities of Greece

Objectives

★1. **Compare** Athenian life with Spartan life.

2. **Define** "democracy," "oligarchy," and "monarchy."

3. **Identify** the following people and places: *Xerxes, Themistocles, Pericles, Sparta,* and *Athens.*

1 STARTING THE LESSON

Motivation Activity

- Have students look at the map of the Persian Empire on p. 74 in Lesson 1.

- Have them compare the size of Persia with the size of Greece. Ask them whether they think the Greeks would have any chance of winning a war against Persia and what strategies students might use to accomplish this if they were Greek leaders?

Think About What You Know

- Assign the THINK ABOUT WHAT YOU KNOW activity on p. 76.

- Answers may include that people would have less freedom.

Study the Vocabulary

- Have students look up the Greek prefixes and suffixes that form the words *democracy, oligarchy,* and *monarchy* in the dictionary. (*Demos-* means "people," *-cracy* means "form of government," *olig-* means "few," *-archy* means "rule," and *mono-* means "one.")

- Write the prefixes and suffixes on the chalkboard. Have students guess the definitions of the vocabulary words based on the prefixes and suffixes.

76

LESSON 2
The Cities of Greece

THINK ABOUT WHAT YOU KNOW

Think about what it would be like to live in a country where the people could not vote or participate in the government of the country. How, do you think, would life be different than it is in the United States?

STUDY THE VOCABULARY

despot	democracy
strait	monarchy
city-state	jury
oligarchy	alliance

FOCUS YOUR READING

What was the difference between the cities of Sparta and Athens, and why did they go to war?

A. Protection from a "Wooden Wall"

A Hidden Message "You shall be safe behind the wooden wall!" That was the oracle's message to the Athenians in the summer of 480 B.C. An oracle is a place or person that a god uses to reveal hidden knowledge. The Athenians, like all Greeks, believed that oracles gave messages from the gods. The Athenians had asked the oracles for advice because a great danger threatened their city. Xerxes (ZURK seez), the Persian emperor, had invaded Greece with a huge army and fleet. Efforts to stop the Persians at Thermopylae (ther MAHP-uh lee), a mountain pass, had failed. By land and sea, the Persians moved toward the city of Athens. They took Athens and burned it. All the men, women, and children of Athens escaped to the nearby island of Salamis.

76

The Athenians were puzzled over the oracle's words. That was the trouble with oracles; their messages were like riddles. What was the "wooden wall"? Some Athenians recalled that a wooden wall had at one time surrounded the Acropolis (uh-KRAHP uh lis), the high hill in the midst of the city. They said that the oracle meant for them to defend the city from the Acropolis. Themistocles (thuh MIHS tuh kleez), the boldest of the Athenian leaders, insisted, "The wooden wall is your ships." He persuaded the Athenians to abandon the city and withdraw to nearby islands. They would depend on their fleet of wooden ships for protection.

Battle of Salamis Themistocles realized that the Persians had far more ships than the Athenians. But he believed that the

A Greek army of 6,000 fought the Persians at Thermopylae.
▶ What weapons did these armies fight with in the battle of Thermopylae?

Optional Activities

Athenians would have a chance if they could fight in the narrow bay of Salamis, which they knew so well. To get the Persians to enter the bay and attack, Themistocles played a trick worthy of Odysseus. He sent a Greek posing as a deserter into the Persian camp. The Greek told the Persians that the Athenians planned to slip out of the bay of Salamis during the night. The Persians believed the Greek and sailed into the narrow waters.

Xerxes was sure that he would witness a great victory. He had a seat placed on a hill above the shore so he could watch. What he saw when the battle began did not please him. Confusion spread among the Persians as their ships crowded into the narrow, unfamiliar bay. They got in each other's way. Some Persian ships wrecked on the rocks as the Athenian ships skillfully darted between them. By the end of the battle, the Persians had lost the greater part of their fleet. Xerxes had witnessed a great victory, a victory of the Athenians!

Left without many ships, Xerxes returned to Asia, leaving an army in northern Greece. The next year the Greeks defeated the remaining Persian forces at the battle of Plataea. However, the battle in the bay of Salamis proved to be the turning point of the war.

B. Fighting the Persians

The Greeks were fighting to protect their country from the Persians. Persia was a foreign land ruled by one all-powerful person called a **despot** (DES put). A despot is a person who rules with total and unlimited control. The Greeks rightly feared such a ruler, because they knew that despots often abused their great powers. Herodotus tells of such an abuse in his history of the war.

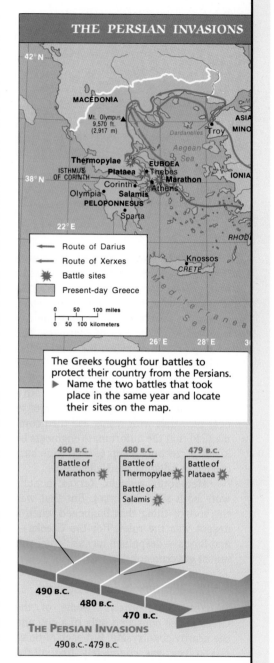

THE PERSIAN INVASIONS

Route of Darius
Route of Xerxes
Battle sites
Present-day Greece

0   50   100 miles
0   50   100 kilometers

The Greeks fought four battles to protect their country from the Persians.
▶ Name the two battles that took place in the same year and locate their sites on the map.

490 B.C. — Battle of Marathon
480 B.C. — Battle of Thermopylae, Battle of Salamis
479 B.C. — Battle of Plataea

THE PERSIAN INVASIONS
490 B.C.–479 B.C.

77

Read and Think

Section A

To focus students' attention on the battle of Salamis, ask the following questions:

1. **Why was the battle of Salamis important?**
   (It was the turning point of the war. *p. 77*)

   Thinking Critically How, do you think, were the battle of Salamis and the use of the Trojan Horse similar and how were they different? (Analyze)
   (Answers may include both relied on creativity to beat an enemy, but one is factual, the other is mythical. *pp. 76-77*)

GEOGRAPHY THEMES

Place

■ Direct students' attention to the map of the Persian Invasions on this page to help them answer the following question: **What body of water separated the Greeks from the Persians?**
(The Aegean Sea)

—— **Answers to Caption Questions** ——
p. 76 ▶ Bows and arrows, spears, shields, and swords
p. 77 ▶ Battle of Thermopylae, battle of Salamis, 480 B.C.

Curriculum Connection

Language Arts Many English words have Greek origins. Write some common Greek prefixes on the chalkboard: *geo-* (earth), *micro-* (small), *cosmo-* (universe), *bio-* (life), *phono-* (sound), *tele-* (distance).

● Then list some common suffixes: *-ology* (study of), *-gram* (drawn or written), *-phobia* (fear of), *-scope* (seeing).

● Have students look up the meanings of these Greek roots in the dictionary. Encourage them to make new combinations of the prefixes and suffixes in their list.

● How many familiar words can they make? How many new words can they make? Have them guess the meanings of any unfamiliar words that they make.

Writing to Learn

Writing a Speech Have students write a speech that Themistocles might have given to the Athenians to persuade them that the "wooden wall" of the oracle represented their ships.

Optional Activities

Read and Think
Sections B and C

The Greeks fought the Persians to protect themselves from the abuses of a despotic ruler. The Greek city-state of Sparta was proud of its freedom, but individual Spartans had little personal freedom. To discuss this theme, ask the following questions:

1. **What is a despot?**
(A ruler with total and unlimited control *p. 77*)

2. **What action of Xerxes did Herodotus describe as being both silly and cruel?**
(Xerxes ordered that the engineers who designed the bridge of boats across the Hellespont be killed when the bridge broke. *p. 78*)

3. **Name three types of government used in the Greek city-states and the differences among them.**
(*Oligarchy*, which means rule by a small group, *democracy*, which means rule by the people, and *monarchy*, which means government by one ruler *p. 78*)

4. **Why was a strong army important to the Spartans?**
(They feared a slave revolt. *p. 79*)

Thinking Critically Can an individual ruler with unlimited power, do you think, be counted on to be fair? (Hypothesize)
(Answers should reflect independent thinking but may include responses such as no, because no single person can understand the needs of all the members of a society, or yes because, it is possible for one person to be fair to everyone. *pp. 77-78*)

This drawing depicts the bridge of boats that Xerxes ordered to be built across the Hellespont.
▶ How were these boats used to build a bridge?

When Xerxes prepared to invade Greece, he ordered his engineers to build a bridge of boats across the Hellespont (HEL-us pahnt). The Hellespont was the **strait**, or narrow waterway, connecting the Aegean Sea and the Sea of Marmara. The Hellespont is now called the Dardanelles (dahr duh NELZ). A swift current flowed through the strait, and the first bridge of boats broke. The Persian despot fell into a violent rage. He ordered his servants to beat the strait with whips. He then commanded that the unfortunate engineers be killed. A second group of engineers succeeded in bridging the Hellespont.

Herodotus thought Xerxes' actions were both silly and cruel. But that was the sort of thing that happened when a despot was the ruler. For the Greeks—and for us—despotism means "cruel and unjust government."

C. The Military State of Sparta

Spartan Government Some of the Greek states consisted only of a city and the nearby countryside. But each of these **city-states** was completely free of the others. They had different types of governments. Some city-states were ruled by a small group. The Greeks called this type of government an **oligarchy** (AHL ih gahr-kee). In other city-states, such as Athens, government was by the people, which the Greeks called **democracy**. A king ruled Macedonia (mas uh DOH nee uh), in northern Greece. Government of a kingdom by one ruler was known as a **monarchy**. We still use these Greek words for forms of government. We call the government of the United States a democracy.

Military Life Sparta was a free city, but individual Spartans had little freedom to live as they liked. From the time a Spartan boy was seven, he trained to be a soldier. Boys lived together in military troops. Young men in charge of the troops taught the boys the skills that would make them strong, vigorous warriors. The boys learned to use spears and swords, and to live in the open in all kinds of weather.

When a man married, he continued to live with his fellow fighting men for another ten years. Only after that was he free to live with his family.

Spartan girls grew up in their own homes, but the city did not forget them. It was expected that they would become the wives and mothers of warriors, so they had to take part in vigorous sports that would make them strong. The girls also learned to manage household affairs.

Spartan laws discouraged everything that might take people's attention away from the military life. Sparta did not welcome visitors from other cities, and few Spartans were allowed to travel. The city's leaders feared that citizens might become interested in other ways of life.

For much the same reason, Spartans took no part in business. Outsiders carried

Cooperative Learning

Writing a TV Docudrama Divide students into three groups for TV-style documentaries on Life in Sparta, Life in Athens, and the Persian Wars.

● Encourage research to supplement the text, and costumes, maps, or posters to provide visual background.

● Select one student in each group to be the producer/director, one or two to be researchers, one or two to be scriptwriters, and one or two to be visual- aid, set, and prop people.

● Students will divide the roles of on-the-scene reporters and characters. Give each group three to five days to prepare a 10- to 15-minute drama.

The military was a large part of the life of a Spartan male.
▶ What did Spartan soldiers wear to protect themselves in combat?

D. Democracy in Athens

Pericles Pericles (PER uh kleez) was the leader of Athens for 30 years. He was neither a monarch nor a despot. The Athenians elected him year after year. Pericles proudly declared that Athens was a democracy. In Athens, power was "in the hands of the many rather than the few."

Pericles was right in calling Athens a democracy at that time. As compared with other ancient governments, the government of Athens *was* democratic. But it would not seem democratic today. When Pericles spoke of government by the people, he should have said government by the citizens. Not all of the people who lived in Athens were citizens. Being a citizen was like belonging to a family; it depended on birth. Only the child of a citizen could be a citizen. Children who were born in Athens and lived there all their lives were not considered citizens if their parents had come from other places.

on trade for the city. Not that there was much trade. The Spartans bought no fine clothing or rare foods. They prided themselves on their simple lives.

Even in sports the Spartans did not forget military training. The games they played were soldiers' games.

Why did the Spartans think it so important to have a strong army? They believed that they needed to have a strong army largely because they were afraid. The Spartans had a large number of slaves called *helots*, who worked their land. Since there were fewer Spartans than helots, the Spartans lived in fear of a slave revolt. It has been said that fear of their slaves enslaved the Spartans.

The Granger Collection

The Age of Pericles was the greatest period of ancient Athenian history.
▶ What type of government did Athens have under Pericles?

79

To focus a class discussion on the rivalry between Sparta and Athens, ask the following questions:

1. **What was citizenship based on in Athens?**
   (Birth; only children of citizens could be citizens *p. 79*)

2. **What is a jury?**
   (A group of people who have been chosen to settle a dispute *p. 80*)

3. **Why did some city-states try to leave the Delian League?**
   (Athens was too powerful. *p. 80*)

4. **Why did the Persians aid Sparta in the Peloponnesian War?**
   (They were glad that the Greeks were fighting among themselves. *p. 81*)

Thinking Critically If you had lived in Athens in the time of Pericles, how would you have felt about the exclusion of women in politics? (Evaluate) (Answers may include bad because women should have the same rights as any citizen, or pleased because women could be free to be involved in other areas of Athenian life.)

Citizens' Roles Athens seems undemocratic to us today because women had no voice in the city's affairs. Even women who were citizens could take no part in the government. Politics in Athenian democracy was for male citizens only.

Pericles said that all the citizens should take an active part in the politics of the city. But not all citizens could take part. If all 40,000 male citizens had shown up for the assembly, there would have been no room for them at the meeting place, which could seat only 6,000. Of course, that was quite a large group to discuss and decide matters anyway.

A citizen might also serve for a year on the Council of Five Hundred, which had charge of the city's day to day business. Members of the council were chosen by lot, that is, by drawing names, rather than by election. This was democratic in that every citizen had an equal chance to have his name drawn.

The Athenians selected their **juries** by lot, as we do. A jury is a group of people called into court to give a verdict, or decision, in a dispute. Athenian juries were much larger than ours. One jury would have hundreds of members. Since cases were decided by a majority of votes, the jurors did not all have to be in agreement as in American juries.

Slavery Perhaps the most undemocratic thing about Athens was slavery. Like the Spartans, the Athenians had slaves, though their slaves did not make up so large a part of the population. Slavery was common in ancient times. Some of the slaves were enemies who were captured rather than killed in battle. Other people were slaves by birth; their parents had been slaves.

80

E. Sparta and Athens Are Rivals

The Delian League Because the city-states were independent, they found it difficult to act together for any long period of time. After turning back the Persian invasion, Athens formed the Delian (DEE lee-un) League, an **alliance** with other Greek cities. An alliance is supposed to be a partnership, but in fact, the city-state of Athens soon ruled the league. Sparta, fearful of Athens' growing power, formed another league.

When some of the cities in the Delian League tried to withdraw, Athens forced them to stay a part of the league. These cities then complained that the alliance that they had formed had turned into an Athenian empire.

Graphic Organizer

Compare Athenian life with Spartan life.

- Have students compare life in Athens and Sparta by filling out the following Venn Diagram which lists characteristics of life in both places.

- The chart should have the following headings and contain the following information:

ATHENS	Women took no	SPARTA
Democracy	part in	Few freedoms
Citizens took	government	Military most important
part in government	Kept slaves	Took pride in simple lives
Trials by jury		

Rivalry between Sparta and Athens led to the Peloponnesian War.
▶ Why has this war been called a struggle of the elephant and the whale?

Peloponnesian War The growing power of Athens aroused Spartan fears. War broke out between Sparta and Athens in 431 B.C. In the struggle that followed, Sparta was more powerful on land, but Athens controlled the sea. The war, known as the Peloponnesian (pel uh puh NEE-shun) War, has been called a struggle of the elephant and the whale.

Both Athens and Sparta tried to get Persian support during the deadly Peloponnesian War. The Persians, happy to see the Greeks fighting among themselves, supplied the Spartans with money for ships. Once the Spartans had a fleet, they defeated the Athenians in 405 B.C.

The end of the Peloponnesian War did not mean a long period of peace in Greece. Quarrels continued among the cities for another half century.

A History Book Thucydides (thoo SIHD-ih deez) of Athens wrote a history of the Peloponnesian War. He started writing at the beginning of the war because he thought it would be a great war and worth writing about more than any war of earlier times. Although Thucydides was an Athenian, he was more interested in writing an accurate account than in defending Athens. Thucydides wanted to record exactly what happened during the Peloponnesian War. Unlike Herodotus, Thucydides did not mix history and fictional stories. His only aim was to tell what happened. Thucydides wrote one of the world's finest histories.

LESSON **2** *REVIEW*

THINK AND WRITE   (Recall)
A. What two opinions did the Athenians have about the meaning of the oracle?
B. Why did the Greeks dislike despotism?
C. What was the life of a Spartan like?
D. What was undemocratic about the government of Athens? (Recall)
E. What caused the Peloponnesian War? (Infer)

SKILLS CHECK

MAP SKILL

Look up *Athens* in the Gazetteer to find the latitude at which it is located. Turn to the map of North America in the Atlas. List cities in the United States that are near the same latitude.

UNDERSTANDING THE LESSON

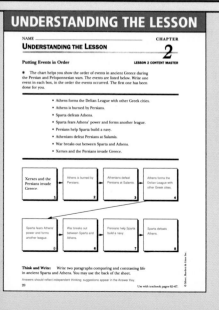

NAME _____ CHAPTER
UNDERSTANDING THE LESSON **2**

Putting Events in Order   LESSON 2 CONTENT MASTER

✦ The chart helps you show the order of events in ancient Greece during the Persian and Peloponnesian wars. The events are listed below. Write one event in each box, in the order the events occurred. The first one has been done for you.

• Athens forms the Delian League with other Greek cities.
• Athens is burned by Persians.
• Sparta defeats Athens.
• Sparta fears Athens' power and forms another league.
• Persians help Sparta build a navy.
• Athenians defeat Persians at Salamis.
• War breaks out between Sparta and Athens.
• Xerxes and the Persians invade Greece.

Think and Write: Write two paragraphs comparing and contrasting life in ancient Sparta and Athens. You may use the back of the sheet.

◀ **Review Master Booklet p. 20**

Optional Activities

---

3 CLOSING THE LESSON

Lesson 2 Review

Answers to Think and Write
A. Some thought the wooden wall referred to the Acropolis, but Themistocles thought it referred to the Athenians' ships.

B. The Greeks disliked despotism because they knew it meant "cruel and unjust government."

C. Spartans had little personal freedom. Boys and young men lived in military troops and devoted themselves to developing their physical strength. Women were also expected to be strong.

D. Only male citizens of Athens could vote. Women could not vote, and only people who were born to citizens could be citizens. The Athenians also kept slaves.

E. The Peloponnesian War was caused by the rivalry between Sparta and Athens.

Answer to Skills Check
Possible answers include San Francisco, St. Louis, and Washington, D.C.

Focus Your Reading
Ask the lesson focus question found at the beginning of the lesson: **What was the difference between Sparta and Athens and why did they go to war?**
(Sparta was a city-state devoted to military strength, governed by an oligarchy, in which citizens had little personal freedom. Athens was a democracy in which male citizens took an active role in government. The two city-states went to war because Sparta was alarmed by the growing power of Athens.)

Additional Practice
You may wish to assign the ancillary materials listed below.

**Understanding the Lesson p. 20
Workbook p. 26**

┌─ **Answers to Caption Questions** ─┐
p. 81 ▶Spartans were powerful on land so they were compared to a powerful land animal, and the Athenians were powerful at sea so they were compared to a powerful sea creature.
└──────────────────────────┘

81

CITIZENSHIP AND AMERICAN VALUES

Objectives

1. **Explain** the difference between direct and indirect democracy.

2. **Develop** an awareness of, and skills in, relating to public officials.

Guided Reading

1. **What did all the citizens of Athens do when they met in one place?**
   (Made laws and other important decisions)

2. **What is this form of democracy known as?**
   (Direct democracy, because all citizens participated directly in the making of decisions)

3. **Why would this form of democracy not work in the United States?**
   (Because there are so many people in the United States that it would be impossible for all of them to assemble in one place)

4. **What is our form of democracy known as?**
   (Indirect democracy, because citizens do not directly participate in the everyday workings of government)

5. **How do citizens in our country involve themselves in national decisions after they elect their representatives?**
   (By voting for people who will best represent their views, monitoring the work of these representatives, writing to their elected officials to let them know how they feel about certain issues, and by voting for new representatives in the next election)

DIRECT VS. INDIRECT DEMOCRACY

As you learned in the last lesson, the Greek city-state of Athens developed a democratic system of government. All the citizens of Athens met in one place to make laws and other important decisions. This form of democracy is known as direct democracy because the citizens participated directly in the making of decisions. The system worked well because Athens was a small community.

The United States also has a democratic form of government. But there are so many people in the United States that it would be impossible for all of them to assemble in one place. Therefore, our citizens elect representatives—the members of Congress—to make laws and important decisions. This system is called indirect democracy because citizens do not directly participate in the everyday workings of government.

Does this mean that citizens in our country are no longer involved in national decisions after they elect their representatives? Of course not. Citizens vote for people who will best represent their views. Good citizens have an obligation to monitor the work of these representatives. People can write to their elected officials to let them know how they feel about certain

President George Bush addresses the United States Congress in 1990.

Optional Activities

For Your Information

Participation in Politics Widespread participation in politics is necessary for a successful democracy. All adult citizens have the duty to vote in local, state, and national elections as well as serve on juries. They may run for public office if they are qualified. Speaking out on important issues is one way that citizens can shape public opinion. One of the best guarantees against corrupt government is an active population.

issues. When citizens are unhappy with the way in which they are being represented, they can vote for new representatives in the next election. In this way, elected officials are responsible for listening to the concerns of the public.

Thinking for Yourself

Answer the following questions on a separate sheet of paper.

1. What do you think are the benefits and problems of an indirect democracy?
2. Why is it important that elected representatives listen to the concerns of the people they represent?
3. What are some ways to let your representatives know your point of view on certain issues?
4. Write a letter to your local or state representative. Express your concerns about an issue that interests you or choose one of the following issues: pollution, hunger, or homelessness.

Thinking for Yourself

1. Answers may include that the benefits of indirect democracy are a more stable and efficient type of government and the problems may be that it is less responsive and slower to change.

2. Answers may include that it is important that elected representatives listen to the concerns of the people they represent because the people are trusting them to do so, and if they do not listen, they most likely will not be reelected.

3. You can let your representatives know your point of view on an issue by writing to them or by voting for or against them.

4. Students' letters should clearly express a point of view and use correct letter-writing style.

Current Events

● Bring in newspapers and news magazines.

● Distribute to students articles that discuss relationships between elected officials and special interest groups and citizens' lobbies.

● Ask students to put a checkmark in the margin of the newspaper or magazine article when they find a paragraph that describes the workings of indirect (or representative) democracy.

Optional Activities

Alexander the Great

Objectives

★ 1. **Describe** the achievements of Alexander the Great.

2. **Locate** the boundaries of Alexander's empire on a map.

3. **Identify** the following people and places: *King Philip II, Alexander the Great,* and *Macedonia.*

1 STARTING THE LESSON

Motivation Activity

■ Have the students look at the map of Alexander's conquests on p. 87.

■ Explain that by using the scale (³/₄″ equals 500 miles [804 km]), we can get an idea of the distance that Alexander covered. The east-to-west distance alone is equal to approximately 3,500 miles (5,631 km [5 ¹/₄″ if we measure in a straight, horizontal line from the easternmost point to the westernmost point]).

■ To put this in perspective, show students a map of the United States and tell them that the distance between the east and west coasts is approximately 3,200 miles (5,149 km). Ask students how they would feel about walking this distance.

Think About What You Know

■ Assign the THINK ABOUT WHAT YOU KNOW activity on p. 84.

■ Student answers should reflect independent thinking but may include leadership, intelligence, understanding, compassion, and determination.

Study the Vocabulary

■ Have students look up the definitions of each of the new vocabulary words for this lesson in the Glossary.

■ Ask them to use each word in a sentence.

LESSON 3

Alexander the Great

THINK ABOUT WHAT YOU KNOW

What characteristics, do you think, make a ruler great?

STUDY THE VOCABULARY

colony   culture

FOCUS YOUR READING

Who was Alexander the Great, and what did he accomplish?

A. The Value of Observation

It happened one day when Alexander's father, King Philip II of Macedonia, was offered the opportunity to buy a horse called Bucephalus (byoo SEF uh lus). The name means "bull-headed." Philip decided to take a look at the horse, and Alexander went along. Bucephalus appeared to be easily frightened. As soon as anyone approached, he kicked up a fuss. Not even the most experienced riders could get on him. Philip was angry at the trader for trying to sell him an unruly animal. But Alexander shook his head and sighed, "What a fine horse you are losing, just because your men do not know how to handle him."

The king, not pleased at all by his son's remark, burst out, "I suppose you could handle him better than your elders!"

"I certainly could."

Irked by his son's boldness, Philip offered to make a bet. If Alexander could ride Bucephalus, he could have the horse. If he failed, he would have to pay an amount equal to the price of the horse. Alexander readily took the bet.

Philip did not know that Alexander was applying a lesson learned from his teacher, Aristotle. When Alexander was

young, Aristotle had taught him the importance of observing, that is, paying careful attention to what you see. But Aristotle probably never guessed that his teaching would help Alexander win a horse.

Young Alexander had observed that Bucephalus had been frightened by his own shadow. When Alexander approached the horse, he spoke softly, took hold of the bridle, and gently turned Bucephalus toward the sun so that he could not see his shadow. As soon as the horse calmed down a bit, Alexander leaped lightly upon his back, taking care not to pull the rein too hard. Bucephalus took off at full gallop. Those who watched thought the king's son would surely be killed. But Bucephalus seemed to sense that he had met his master. After a run across the field,

Alexander and his horse Bucephalus saw many a battle together.

▶ Why, do you think, was Bucephalus Alexander's favorite horse?

Optional Activities

Curriculum Connection

Art   Have students make a storyboard illustrating parts of Alexander's life, for example, the episode where Alexander rides Bucephalus for the first time.

● Tell students to choose a series of events that is described in the text, or events that they can imagine, based on Alexander's characteristics.

Alexander turned the horse about and trotted back to the starting point.

Bucephalus became Alexander's favorite horse. In later years, he carried Alexander through battles in far-off lands. At least a dozen times, Alexander owed his life to the strength and spirit of his horse. It was quite an unexpected result from Aristotle's teaching.

B. Greece Controlled by a Macedonian King

Although the city of Macedonia was in northern Greece, many Greeks considered the Macedonian people backward farmers and shepherds.

Philip took advantage of the quarrels among the Greek city-states. He formed a well-trained and powerful army. Backed

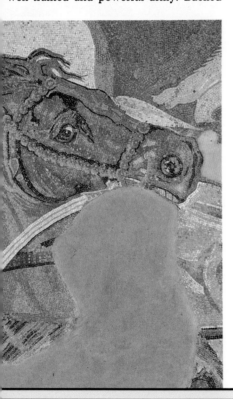

by his army, he extended his power over them. By 338 B.C. the king of Macedonia controlled all of Greece.

Philip planned to invade Asia, which was still ruled by the Persian emperor. The Greeks had long talked about invading the Persian Empire. Such a war would pay back the Persians for Xerxes' invasion of Greece so many years before. But Philip never led an army into Asia. He was murdered in 336 B.C. before he could do so.

Alexander became king when he was only 20 years old. The Greeks, who had opposed Philip, thought they could now throw off Macedonian rule, since the new king was "a mere boy." But Alexander was well prepared and proved them wrong by capturing the city of Thebes (theebz). As a warning to others, Alexander destroyed Thebes. He left only one house standing— that of the poet Pindar. By his treatment of Thebes, Alexander wished to show that he was both a powerful military leader and a lover of Greek poetry.

C. Alexander's Conquests

Building an Empire After making sure that the Greeks accepted his leadership, Alexander launched the long-discussed war against Persia. He crossed the Hellespont, where Xerxes had long ago built a bridge of boats. He reminded the Greeks that their ancestors had once fought on the Asian coast at Troy. Alexander led his troops to the site of ancient Troy and camped on the plain where Homer's warriors had fought.

Alexander freed the Greek cities in Asia from Persian rule, but he did not stop there. He moved east and defeated the Persian army, even though they outnumbered the Greeks. Alexander moved down the east coast of the Mediterranean into

Read and Think

Sections A and B

To focus a class discussion on Alexander the Great, ask the following questions:

1. **Who was Alexander's teacher?**
   (Aristotle *p. 84*)

2. **What skill helped Alexander win the bet with his father?**
   (Observation *pp. 84-85*)

3. **How did Alexander's father, Philip, gain control of Greece?**
   (Fighting among the city-states allowed him to conquer them. *p. 85*)

4. **How did Alexander show his power after he became king?**
   (By capturing the city of Thebes and destroying everything except the poet Pindar's house *p. 85*)

--- **Answers to Caption Questions** ---
p. 84 ▶ Answers should reflect independent thinking but may include that Alexander believed he owed his life to Bucephalus, and the unique way Alexander obtained the horse.

For Your Information

Alexander's Birth and Death According to Plutarch, author of *Lives of the Noble Greeks*, Alexander's mother, Olympias, dreamed, just before her marriage, that she was struck by lightning. After their marriage, his father dreamed that his wife's body was sealed with the mark of a lion. They were told that these dreams meant that Olympias would give birth to a boy who would prove to be "as stout and courageous as a lion."

Alexander died of malaria. There were no medicines against the disease at that time, and he was weakened from the stress of continual fighting.

Optional Activities

Read and Think

Section C

To discuss the conquests and far-flung empire of Alexander, ask the following questions:

1. **Why was Alexander known as "the Great"?**
(He conquered the largest empire the world had ever known. *p. 86*)

2. **What did Alexander do after he conquered a region?**
(Started Greek colonies *p. 86*)

Thinking Critically Do you think Alexander would have been a good ruler if he had lived longer? (Evaluate)
(Answers should reflect independent thinking *p. 85-86*)

Meeting Individual Needs

Concept: Greatness

In order to better understand the concept of greatness, it is important to analyze the meaning of this term in our culture. Below are three activities that will help your students relate Alexander's accomplishments and reputation to modern times.

◆ **EASY** Have students find words used in the text to describe Alexander.

Make a list of these words and discuss their definitions. How do they relate to greatness?

◀▶ **AVERAGE** Have students write stories about Alexander's career and his accomplishments.

Remind them that some things that occurred after his death could still be considered his "accomplishments." Put the students' work on a bulletin board.

◀▮▶ **CHALLENGING** Ask students who need a challenge to choose a person who has accomplished great things in a non-military area, such as the arts, science, or social reform.

Have them research this person's life and achievements and then write a position paper arguing why this person should have "the Great" added to his or her name.

Alexander the Great was one of the greatest military geniuses of the ancient world.
▶ How had Alexander won his place in history as Alexander the Great?

Egypt. He went on to conquer the lands of the Middle East. Not content to stop, he led his army east to the Indus River, in what is now Pakistan. He wanted to go still further, but his weary troops refused. Alexander yielded and marched back to Babylon. It is easy to understand why. They had conquered the largest empire the world had ever known. Even though he was not yet 30, Alexander had won his place in history as Alexander the Great.

Alexander did more than conquer. He also planted Greek **colonies** in Egypt and the Middle East. A colony is a settlement of people living in a new territory while being ruled by the government of another country. These colonies were ruled by

Greece. The colonies took the form of Greek cities, many named Alexandria. The most famous Alexandria was in Egypt, on the delta of the Nile River. This city still bears its founder's name.

Bucephalus Captured Bucephalus accompanied Alexander on the invasion of Asia. Once near the Caspian Sea, a band of horse thieves captured the conqueror's favorite horse. Alexander was so upset that he sent out messengers who announced that unless Bucephalus was returned unharmed, the Greeks would destroy every village in the region. The thieves hurriedly returned Bucephalus to his master. The horse had not been harmed, but he was

Optional Activities

Writing to Learn

Writing a Diary Entry Have students pretend to be a citizen of a town in Arabia or Persia that has recently been conquered by Alexander.

● Have students write about their feelings concerning Alexander's takeover of their city.

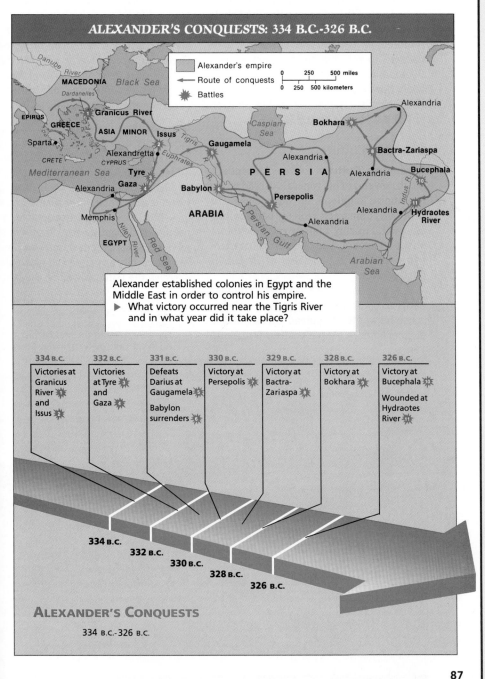

ALEXANDER'S CONQUESTS: 334 B.C.-326 B.C.

Alexander's empire
→ Route of conquests
✸ Battles

0   250   500 miles
0   250   500 kilometers

Alexander established colonies in Egypt and the Middle East in order to control his empire.
▶ What victory occurred near the Tigris River and in what year did it take place?

334 B.C.	332 B.C.	331 B.C.	330 B.C.	329 B.C.	328 B.C.	326 B.C.
Victories at Granicus River and Issus ✸	Victories at Tyre and Gaza ✸	Defeats Darius at Gaugamela ✸ Babylon surrenders ✸	Victory at Persepolis ✸	Victory at Bactra-Zariaspa ✸	Victory at Bokhara ✸	Victory at Bucephala ✸ Wounded at Hydraotes River ✸

334 B.C.
332 B.C.
330 B.C.
328 B.C.
326 B.C.

ALEXANDER'S CONQUESTS
334 B.C.-326 B.C.

87

Place

■ Direct students' attention to the map and time line of Alexander's conquests on this page. Ask students to think about and write a response to the following questions:

1. **Where was Alexander's first victory and in what year did it take place?**
   (Granicus River, 334 B.C.)

2. **What two victories occurred near the Persian Gulf?**
   (Babylon and Persepolis)

3. **When Alexander was at the southernmost part of his travels, he was near what large body of water?**
   (The Arabian Sea)

4. **Name the three cities that Alexander passed through twice.**
   (Babylon, Persepolis, and Gaza)

— **Answers to Caption Questions** —
p. 86 ▶ Alexander conquered the largest empire the world had ever seen at the time.
p. 87 ▶ Gaugamela, 331 B.C.

Creating a Crossword Puzzle

● Have students use as many names of physical features and territories as possible to create a crossword puzzle based on Alexander's conquests.

● Students should make an answer key for their own puzzles.

● Have students exchange and try to solve each other's puzzles.

Creating a Time Line

● Have students create a time line that shows all of the wars and battles described in this chapter.

● Students should first skim through the text to make a list of all the battles.

● Have students include the year that each war or battle occurred.

● Suggest that they do the time line in the form of a bulletin board.

Optional Activities

Read and Think

Section D

To discuss the material on Greek culture, ask the following questions:

1. **What were two reasons why Alexander started colonies?**
(To control his empire and to spread Greek culture *p. 88*)

2. **What activities took place in the Greek gymnasiums?**
(Athletic training, reading, and discussion *p. 88*)

Thinking Critically **Why, do you think, did Alexander want to spread Greek culture?** (Analyze)
(Answers should reflect independent thinking but may include that he thought that Greek culture would improve the lives of people who imitated it. *p. 89*)

---

growing old. When he died, Alexander named one of the colonial cities Bucephala in honor of his horse. Alexander never returned to Greece. He seems to have planned to rule his empire from ancient Babylon, in Mesopotamia. We will never know how well the conqueror would have ruled, because Alexander died in Babylon in 323 B.C., at the age of 32.

D. Greek Culture

Spreading Culture After Alexander's death, several of his generals carved out of his empire kingdoms for themselves. His boyhood companion Ptolemy became king of Egypt. Ptolemy's family ruled Egypt for about 300 years. The famous queen Cleopatra was the last member of Ptolemy's family to rule.

Alexander had planted colonies partly to control the empire and partly because he wanted to spread Greek **culture** in other lands. A people's culture is made up

of their language, ideas, arts, and ge~~neral~~ way of life.

The Greek kings who ruled after A~~lex~~ander continued his plan of sprea~~ding~~ Greek culture in Egypt and the Mi~~ddle~~ East. Government officials used the G~~reek~~ language, as did many of the busi~~ness~~ people in the cities.

Gymnasiums Much life in the G~~reek~~ cities was centered in the gymnasi~~ums.~~ Today we use that word to mean a pla~~ce for~~ athletic exercises and playing such g~~ames~~ as basketball and volleyball. The G~~reek~~ gymnasiums were places for athletic t~~rain~~ing, but they were also places w~~here~~ people could gather for discussions ~~and~~ reading. Some gymnasiums had libra~~ries.~~ In a Greek city a gymnasium was a pla~~ce to~~ exercise the mind as well as the body~~.~~

The ruins of Persepolis, an ancient capital of Persia, prove that Greek culture spread to the Middle East.
▶ What can you learn about Greek architecture from these ruins?

Researching a Library

- The library at Alexandria (in Egypt) housed many volumes of fascinating works. Ask students to work in small groups to find facts about the library, such as what types of works it contained (scholarly works), what materials were used instead of books (scrolls made of papyrus), how many scrolls it contained (400,000), and when it was founded (330 B.C.).

- Provide students with encyclopedias and other appropriate reference materials.

- Have students write the answers to these questions and hold an oral question-and-answer session.

Reteaching Main Objective

⭐ *Describe the achievements of Alexander the Great.*

- Imagine that through the miracle of time travel, Alexander the Great is coming to your city or town to give a speech.

- Have students design posters that give information about Alexander's achievements and will make people want to come to the speech.

The Museum Artists and writers in the Greek cities copied Greek models. Buildings were made in the Greek style. The Ptolemys established a center for Greek culture at Alexandria in Egypt. They called it the Museum, which means "place of the muses." The muses were Greek goddesses of art and learning. For example, Calliope (kuh LYE uh pee) was a muse of poetry; Terpsichore (turp SIHK uh ree), of dance; and Clio (KLYE oh), of history. At the Museum, people studied these and other subjects. There was a great library, the largest in the ancient world. The Museum was somewhat like a modern university.

The spread of Greek culture had been Alexander's dream. He shared the belief of his teacher Aristotle that Greek culture was the best in the world. He thought that by spreading it to others, he offered them a great gift.

The Museum in Alexandria, Egypt, was a learning center of Greek culture.
▶ How does the Museum resemble a library of today?

LESSON **3** REVIEW

THINK AND WRITE

A. Why was Alexander able to ride Bucephalus? (Infer)
B. How were Philip II and Alexander able to control all of Greece? (Recall)
C. What lands did Alexander conquer?
D. How and why was Greek culture spread?

SKILLS CHECK

WRITING SKILL

Alexander the Great was a great leader. Choose someone who you think is a great leader today and write a paragraph explaining why you chose that person. (Infer)

89

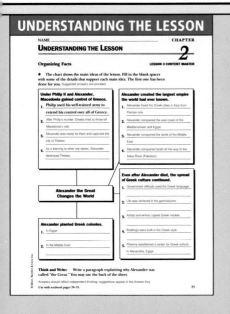
Optional Activities

Lesson **3** Review

Answers to Think and Write

A. Alexander was able to ride Bucephalus because he understood that the horse was afraid of its own shadow and was careful to turn the horse so that it faced the sun.

B. Philip II and Alexander were able to control all of Greece because internal fighting among the Greek city-states left them vulnerable to conquest.

C. Alexander conquered Greece, the Persian Empire, and land east of the Indus River.

D. Alexander believed that Greek culture was the best in the world and he spread it by establishing Greek colonies throughout his empire.

Answer to Skills Check

Answers should reflect independent thinking but may include that leader's achievements and accomplishments.

Focus Your Reading

Ask the lesson focus question found at the beginning of the lesson: **Who was Alexander the Great, and what did he accomplish?**

(Alexander the Great was a Macedonian ruler who united Greece and conquered most of the known world, including the Persian empire and the lands beyond it. He established colonies that spread Greek culture throughout his empire.)

Additional Practice

You may wish to assign the ancillary materials listed below.

Understanding the Lesson p. 21
Workbook p. 27

┌─ **Answers to Caption Questions** ─┐

p. 88 ▶ Greeks built their structures using columns or pillars.

p. 89 ▶ It has bookshelves, a ladder that librarians use to reach high shelves, and table and chairs for reading.

89

Greek Achievements

Objectives

★1. **Describe** major Greek achievements in the fields of knowledge, art, and sports.

2. **Name** the ways that Greek achievements influence our lives today.

3. **Identify** the following people and places: *Socrates, Plato, Aristotle, Pindar, Sappho,* and *the Parthenon.*

1 STARTING THE LESSON

Motivation Activity

■ Tell students that they will learn about a man called "the wisest of the Greeks."

■ Ask them how they would feel and what they would do if they were told that they were the wisest person in the country.

Think About What You Know

■ Assign the THINK ABOUT WHAT YOU KNOW activity on p. 90.

■ Student answers should reflect independent thinking but may include track and field, swimming, gymnastics, hockey, skiing, and other Olympic events.

Study the Vocabulary

■ Have students look up the definitions of each of the new vocabulary words for this lesson in the Glossary, and add these words to their list of Greek-derived words.

■ Also have them look up the prefix *amphi-* (both), and see what new combinations they can form by combining this new prefix with the suffixes in their list.

90

THINK ABOUT WHAT YOU KNOW

The first Olympic Games were held in Greece. How many sports can you name that are played in the Olympic Games today?

STUDY THE VOCABULARY

philosophy   amphitheater

FOCUS YOUR READING

What were some important Greek achievements?

Socrates, a Greek philosopher, is one of the most admired people in history.
▶ For what work was Socrates admired?

A. The Search for a Wise Man

Socrates (SAHK ruh teez) of Athens was a philosopher. That was not his business, for **philosophy** is not a business or trade. Philosophy is "the love of wisdom."

Socrates had a great desire to understand things. He spent much time talking to people and asking them questions. He was one of the world's great teachers.

A friend of Socrates once asked the oracle at Delphi, "Who is the wisest of the Greeks?" The oracle answered that it was Socrates. When Socrates heard of the oracle's answer, he was deeply puzzled. He knew that he was not wise. What did the oracle mean? Socrates decided to search for someone wiser and then go to the oracle and say, "Here is one wiser than I."

Socrates first sought out a politician who was thought to be wise by many, a view that the politician himself fully shared. As Socrates listened to the politician, he soon decided that this was by no means a wise man.

Socrates questioned other politicians and found them no wiser. He then visited some poets. He asked them to explain passages from their own poems. He learned that although the poets could say many fine things, they did not truly understand their meaning.

At last, Socrates questioned skilled craftworkers. They certainly knew a great deal about their crafts, but they made the same mistake as the poets. "Because they were good workers, they thought they also understood every other subject."

Socrates admitted that his questioning had not made him a popular man, but he kept on. As a true lover of wisdom, he must find out the meaning of the oracle. In the end, he concluded that what the oracle meant was this: If you would be wise, be like Socrates, who knows that he knows nothing.

Socrates did not stop his questioning with his search for the wise man. He spent many hours asking people about matters that they thought they understood. He led his students to examine their beliefs and ideas. He told them, "The unexamined life is not worth living."

90

Optional Activities

Writing to Learn

Writing a Letter of Application   Have students write letters of application to study with either Socrates, Plato, or Aristotle.

● Have them describe what appeals to them about the teacher they choose and make an argument that might persuade that teacher to accept them into his school.

Some Athenians thought Socrates' questions upset the beliefs of his students. When some of the students took part in the overthrow of the Athenian government, they said that Socrates was to blame. After the old government was restored, Socrates was brought to trial before a large Athenian jury. The majority voted him guilty and condemned him to death. He died in 399 B.C. after drinking hemlock poison.

B. The Search for Knowledge and Wisdom

Socrates did not write about his teachings. We know of them from dialogues written by Plato, his most famous student. Plato's dialogues are like plays in which Socrates and others have speaking parts.

Some years after Socrates' death, in 387 B.C., Plato started a school near Athens, called the Academy. In time, the name of Plato's school was used by many schools and centers of learning.

Among those who came to Plato's Academy was a young man from Macedonia named Aristotle. He remained in Athens until Plato's death. As you have already read, he later returned to Macedonia to become Alexander's teacher. Aristotle started teaching in a grove known as the Lyceum (lye SEE um). He had the habit of walking up and down the paths of the Lyceum while teaching, so his followers were nicknamed "the walkers."

Aristotle told the students who walked about with him, "All men by nature desire to know."

Plato (center left) and Aristotle (center right) are shown in the *School of Athens*, by Raphael.
▶ How can you tell that the painting shows a center for learning?

DEVELOPING THE LESSON

Read and Think
Sections A and B

To focus a discussion on the achievements of Socrates, ask the following questions:

1. **What did Socrates finally decide that the oracle meant?**
   (It meant that the truly wise realize how little they know. *p. 90*)

2. **What style did Plato's dialogues follow?**
   (They were like plays, in which Socrates and others have speaking parts *p. 91*)

3. **What were some of the subjects studied and written about by Aristotle?**
   (Politics, poetry, philosophy, and the sciences *pp. 91-92*)

   Thinking Critically How, do you think, might Socrates' search have been different if he were to look for a wise man today? (Evaluate)
   (Answers may include that he might have asked people from other fields that did not exist when Socrates was alive, such as the field of computer technology. *pp. 90-91*)

┌─ **Answers to Caption Questions** ─┐
p. 90 ▶ For being a teacher
p. 91 ▶ People are reading and writing.

For Your Information

Greek Architecture While it is true that many public buildings in Washington, D.C., and elsewhere are modeled after structures built by the ancient Greeks, they differ in one important respect. When the Greeks first built their buildings, they painted them bright colors. Time has worn the paint away and we have modeled our classically inspired buildings on the white, unpainted ruins.

Optional Activities

Read and Think

Sections C and D

To help students understand early Greek achievements in architecture and sporting events, ask the following questions:

1. **According to Pericles, what was the goal of the Athenians** as they rebuild their city?
   ("To cheer the heart and delight the eye" *p. 92*)

2. **What is the name of the temple of Athena that stands on the Acropolis?**
   (The Parthenon *p. 92*)

3. **Why did the ancient Greeks hold sporting events?**
   (To honor the gods *p. 93*)

4. **What kind of events were featured in the Olympian Games?**
   (Track and field events, wrestling, and chariot and horse races *p. 93*)

   Thinking Critically **Why, do you think, did the Greeks not play any team sports at the Olympian Games?** (Hypothesize)
   (Answers may include that team sports simply did not exist or that the purpose of the Olympian games was to honor the gods, not a group of team members. *p. 93*)

VISUAL THINKING SKILL

Interpreting a Photograph

■ Have students study the photographs on p. 92 and then answer the following question: **How does the art of the Greeks compare with the art of Egyptians?** (Greek figures are more lifelike and less rigid.)

92

Even if this is not true of everyone, it was certainly true of Aristotle. He studied and wrote about politics, poetry, and philosophy. Later, Aristotle became known as the philosopher. He was called "the master of them that know."

Royal Ontario Museum, Ontario

C. Built to Delight the Eye

The Parthenon When the Athe— returned after the battle of Salamis, found their city in ruins. Scarcely a ing or house was left standing. The nians set about rebuilding the city stronger walls and finer buildings. cles, the leader of the democracy, suaded the people to build a city "to the heart and delight the eye."

One of the greatest works of arch ture was the Parthenon (PAHR thuh na the temple of Athena, goddess of the The Parthenon stood on the Acropo high rocky hill, so it could be seen fr parts of the city. The Parthenon is o the best-known buildings of all Thousands of people each year climb Acropolis to see the ruins that are there. People from all over the w

The ruins of the Parthenon attract many visitors each year. This statue of Athena stands in Toronto, Canada.
▶ Of what materials is the statue made?

92

Oral Reports

● Have students prepare oral reports describing one event of the Greek Olympian Games.

● Each student should tell how the event was played; whether or not the event is part of today's Olympic Games; and if the event is still played, what the Olympic records are.

● Encourage students to find or create visuals to include in their reports.

recognize the columned structure, shown below on page 92.

Phidias (FIHD ee us), the greatest of Greek sculptors, was in charge of carving the statues that decorated the outside of the Parthenon. He also made the statue of Athena that stood inside the temple. This was no ordinary statue of stone. It was made of gold and ivory, and it stood 38 feet (11 m) tall. The Greeks had no electric spotlights such as we would use today. Instead, Phidias had a shallow pool of water placed in front of the statue to reflect light that came through the thin tiles of the roof. All of that gold and ivory must have made a dazzling sight.

Greek Columns Greek builders made use of many stone columns. They designed the three styles shown in the drawing. It is easy to identify each of these styles by their capitals, the top part of the columns. The capital of the Doric columns, used on the Parthenon, is quite plain. The Ionic column has a capital with scrolls, and the Corinthian capital has carved stone leaves. We still use these styles. In Washington, D.C., the Lincoln Memorial has Doric columns. The Jefferson Memorial has Ionic columns, and the columns on the Supreme Court Building are Corinthian.

D. Gods Honored Through Sports

Ancient Olympics The Greeks took sports seriously. It was a saying of the Greeks that a person should have "a sound mind in a sound body." By *sound* they meant "healthy."

Greek sporting events were part of religious festivals. Athletes believed that they honored the gods by taking part in the games. According to an old myth, Zeus,

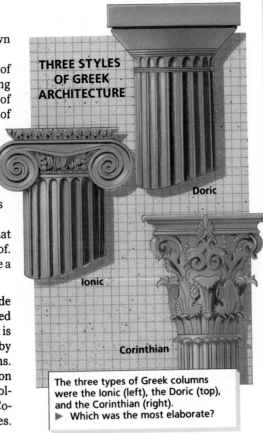

THREE STYLES OF GREEK ARCHITECTURE

Doric

Ionic

Corinthian

The three types of Greek columns were the Ionic (left), the Doric (top), and the Corinthian (right).
▶ Which was the most elaborate?

the greatest of the gods, had established the Olympic Games in his own honor. A temple to Zeus stood at Olympia, where the games took place every four years. In ancient times the Olympic Games were called the Olympian Games.

Athletes at the Olympian Games did not play team sports, such as football or basketball. Many of the contests were what we call track and field events. Athletes ran races, took part in jumping contests, and threw the discus and javelin. They also competed in wrestling matches. Wrestling was a popular sport. Both Plato and Aristotle mention it in their writings.

Read and Think
Section E

To begin a class discussion on early Greek poetry and plays, ask the following questions:

1. **What did Pindar mean when he wrote "Unsung the noblest deed will die."?**
(He meant that people remember deeds only when storytellers, historians, and poets tell about them. *p. 94*)

2. **Describe a Greek amphitheater.**
(An open-air, semicircular structure with ascending rows of seats set into a hillside *p. 95*)

Thinking Critically Why, do you think, have plays been a popular form of entertainment over the centuries? (Infer)

(Answers should reflect independent thinking but may include that people enjoy seeing their favorite stories represented on the stage. *p. 95*)

The ancient Greeks participated in many events during their Olympian Games.
▶ What event is pictured here?

The Olympian Games also had chariot and horse races. Chariot racing was dangerous, but crowds loved it. Horse races aroused great excitement. It was the ambition of many wealthy people to have their horse win at Olympia. It was said that 356 B.C. was a lucky year for King Philip II of Macedonia. In that year he won an important battle, his son Alexander was born, and his horse won the Olympian race.

Modern Olympics The modern Olympic Games have never been held at Olympia. The first modern games were at Athens in 1896. Since then they have been held in cities all over the world. The games have taken place every four years since 1896 except during World Wars I and II.

The Olympic Flame that is lighted at the opening ceremony of the modern games comes from ancient Olympia in Greece. Thousands of runners in cross-country relays bring the lighted torch to the host country. The last runner carries the torch into the stadium, circles the stadium, and then lights the Olympic Flame. The flame burns until the end of the games.

The modern games have no connection with religion. Their purpose is to encourage understanding and friendship among the different nations.

E. Important Events Live on Through Poems and Plays

Pindar Pindar was the poet whose house Alexander left standing at Thebes. Pindar described the purpose of his poems when he wrote, "Unsung the noblest deed will die." By this Pindar meant that people remember great deeds only when storytellers, historians, and poets tell about them. Pindar composed poems in praise of great achievements. One group of poems praised athletes who won glory at the games. Many of Pindar's poems have been

94

Writing to Learn

Writing a Poem One group of Pindar's poems praised athletes.

● Have students write a short poem about their favorite team or their favorite athlete.

● Students do not need to choose someone famous, nor does the poem have to rhyme, but it should praise the athlete's or the team's achievement.

Reteaching Main Objective

⭐ *Describe major Greek achievements in the fields of knowledge, art, and sports.*

● Write the three headings above on the chalkboard (*knowledge, art,* and *sports*).

● Ask students to reread the lesson and take notes when they find descriptions of these areas of achievement.

● After students have finished, have them write a paragraph about achievements in these categories. Student paragraphs may contain the following: Greek philosophers began the tradition of self-examination and started schools; Greek buildings; the Olympic Games; Greek plays and poems.

lost. He may well have praised others, but the memories of their deeds have died.

Even the poems that have survived have an important part missing. Pindar's poems were composed to be sung, but the music is lost. We can only guess what they were like when Pindar sang them. But we at least have some wise sayings that he put in the poems and that do not need music. One of these sayings reads: "Not every truth is better for showing its face and often silence is the wisest thing for a man to heed."

Sappho We know only a little about another great poet, Sappho of Lesbos. She seems to have taught music and poetry to girls. Plato declared that Sappho wrote like a goddess. Unfortunately, only a few fragments of her poems survive. From these fragments we know that she wrote about friendship, love, and nature. One fragment reads: "The stars about the lovely moon hide their shining forms when it lights up the earth at its fullest." How could this idea be expressed differently?

Plays The ancient Greeks liked plays. Every Greek city had its theater, and plays were a part of religious festivals. The stories were well-known to the audiences.

The Greeks performed their plays in amphitheaters.
▶ For what events today do we use arenas similar to amphitheaters?

People came to the **amphitheaters** (AM fuh thee ut urz), or large open-air theaters, not for the stories but to hear the fine speeches of the characters in the plays. An amphitheater is a semicircular structure with ascending rows of stone seats set into a hillside. Some of these Greek plays have survived over thousands of years and are presented today.

LESSON 4 REVIEW

THINK AND WRITE

A. How did Socrates solve the riddle of the oracle's reply? (Recall)

B. How did Plato and Aristotle continue the work that Socrates started? (Recall)

C. What would you have seen if you had visited the Parthenon when it was first built? (Recall)

D. What sports were included in the Olympian Games? (Recall)

E. Who were Pindar and Sappho? (Recall)

SKILLS CHECK

THINKING SKILL

Make a time line for the period from 500 B.C. to 300 B.C., using a scale of one inch (5 cm) for each 25 years. Show the following events on the time line: Battle of Salamis (480 B.C.); Alexander becomes king (336 B.C.); Death of Socrates (399 B.C.); Peloponnesian War begins (431 B.C.); Plato establishes the Academy (388 B.C.).

UNDERSTANDING THE LESSON

NAME _____ CHAPTER
UNDERSTANDING THE LESSON 2

Organizing Facts   LESSON 4 CONTENT MASTER

* The chart below can help you describe some of the achievements of the early Greeks. Fill in the blank spaces with several examples or descriptions of each achievement. The first one has been done for you.
Suggested answers are provided.

Philosophy
1. Socrates searched for wisdom by asking questions.
2. Plato wrote dialogues containing Socrates' teachings.
3. Plato started a school called the Academy.
4. Aristotle studied and wrote about many subjects.

Art and Architecture
1. The Parthenon is one of the best known buildings of all times.
2. Phidias' gold and ivory statue of the goddess Athena stood 38 feet (11 m) tall.
3. A pool in front of the statue reflected the light.
4. Builders used Doric, Ionic, and Corinthian columns.

↓
Greek Achievements
↓

Literature
1. Pindar's poems praised great achievements.
2. Sappho wrote about friendship, love, and nature; only a few of her poems survive.
3. Greek plays were a part of their religious festivals.

Sports
1. Greeks believed a person should have a sound mind in a sound body.
2. The Olympic Games were established to honor the Greek gods.
3. Athletes competed in running, jumping, chariot races, and horse races.

Think and Write: Write a paragraph explaining some ways the ancient Greeks still influence us. Use examples from art, architecture, and athletics. You may use the back of the sheet.
Answers should reflect independent thinking; suggestions appear in the Answer Key.

Use with textbook pages 76-91.

◀ **Review Master Booklet, p. 22**

Lesson 4 Review

Answers to Think and Write

A. Socrates solved the riddle of the oracle's reply by questioning men whom he thought to be wiser than himself. He concluded that the oracle considered him the wisest because he was the only one who knew how little he knew.

B. Plato continued Socrates's work by writing his teachings in the form of dialogues. Plato and Aristotle both continued Socrates's work by teaching.

C. Students would have seen a huge, columned structure atop the Acropolis, a hill above Athens. Inside, there was a 38-ft. statue of Athena made of gold and ivory.

D. The ancient Olympian Games included track and field events, wrestling, and chariot and horse racing.

E. Pindar and Sappho were poets. Pindar composed poems set to music that honored great achievements. Sappho wrote about friendship, love, and nature.

Answer to Skills Check

Student answers should reflect events occurring between 500 B.C. and 300 B.C.

Focus Your Reading

Ask the lesson focus question found at the beginning of the lesson: **What were some important Greek achievements?**
(Important achievements of Greek culture include the thoughts and teachings of Socrates, Plato, and Aristotle; the development of the column and other architectural features; and great works of literature.)

Additional Practice

You may wish to assign the ancillary materials listed below.

Understanding the Lesson p. 22
Workbook pp. 28-30

--- **Answers to Caption Questions** ---
p. 94 ▶ Chariot racing
p. 95 ▶ Answers may include concerts and sporting events.

Using the Vocabulary

1. philosophy
2. jury
3. city-state
4. colony
5. culture
6. amphitheater
7. democracy
8. myth
9. monarchy
10. alliance

Remembering What You Read

1. The *Iliad* and the *Odyssey*

2. Zeus, ruled the gods; Poseidon, god of the sea; Hades, god of the underworld; Hera, goddess of marriage; Hestia, protector of homes

3. Remains of the city have been found.

4. Men, women, and children had to put the military above all other considerations, and few people were allowed to travel

5. Only citizens could participate in government, and the only way to become a citizen was to be the child of a citizen; women had no voice in government, and the Athenians kept slaves.

6. He built the largest empire in history until that time, and he spread Greek culture and learning in all of the new colonies.

7. Several of his generals divided the empire, became kings, and continued to spread Greek culture throughout their new kingdoms.

8. Socrates, Plato, and Aristotle

9. To honor the gods and to build their own bodies

10. Poems and plays

USING THE VOCABULARY

myth	alliance
city-state	colony
democracy	culture
monarchy	philosophy
jury	amphitheater

Each of the following sentences contains the wrong vocabulary word. On a separate sheet of paper, rewrite each sentence with the correct vocabulary word from above.

1. To the ancient Greeks, monarchy was the love of wisdom.
2. A myth is a group of people called into court to give a verdict in a dispute.
3. A Greek philosophy consisted of a city and the nearby countryside.
4. People who live in an amphitheater live in a new territory but are ruled by the government of another country.
5. A people's democracy is made up of their language, ideas, arts, and general way of life.
6. A large open-air theater is a city-state.
7. The Greeks called government by the people a monarchy.
8. A culture is a story about the origins and doings of the gods.
9. The government of a kingdom by one ruler was known as an alliance.
10. A jury is a partnership.

REMEMBERING WHAT YOU READ

On a separate sheet of paper, answer the following questions in complete sentences.

1. What poems written by Homer tell about the Trojan War?
2. What were the names and powers of five gods or goddesses?
3. What evidence is there that the city of Troy really existed?
4. In what ways did the people of Sparta have little freedom?
5. How was democracy in the city-state of Athens limited?
6. What were the accomplishments of Alexander the Great?
7. In what ways did Greek culture continue to spread after Alexander died?
8. Who were three famous ancient Greek philosophers?
9. Why did the Greeks participate in sporting events?
10. From what types of literature can we learn about the ancient Greeks?

TYING MATH TO SOCIAL STUDIES

A marathon is a 26.2-mile race. How many marathons would you have to run to cover 131 miles? If you completed only one half of a marathon, how many miles would you have run? To train for a marathon, you might run 7 miles on Monday, 15 miles on Tuesday, 9 miles on Wednesday, 5 miles on Thursday, 4 miles on Friday, and 2 miles on Saturday. What is the average number of miles you would run on those days?

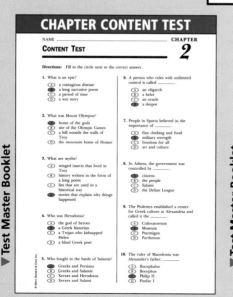

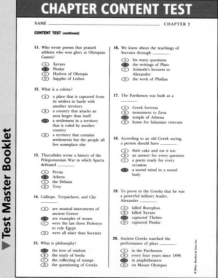

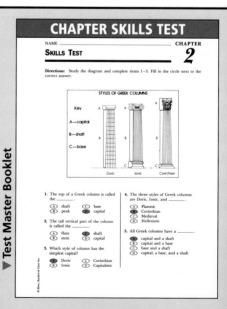

THINKING CRITICALLY

On a separate sheet of paper, answer the following in complete sentences.

1. How are myths related to history?
2. Which government is best—a monarchy, an oligarchy, or a democracy? Explain.
3. Where would you have preferred to live, Sparta or Athens? Explain why.
4. What characteristic of Greek culture do you think was most valuable? Explain why.
5. How were the Olympian Games different from the modern Olympic Games?

SUMMARIZING THE CHAPTER

On a separate sheet of paper, draw a graphic organizer that is like the one shown here. Copy the information from this graphic organizer to the one you have drawn. Under each main heading write three statements that support it.

CHAPTER THEME — Many things in modern culture began in ancient Greece. Under the Greeks, Western civilization made many advances.

LESSON 1

A myth is different from history.

1. Tells about gods
2.
3.

LESSON 3

Alexander the Great was a famous leader with many major accomplishments to his credit.

1. Won a huge empire
2.
3.

LESSON 2

There were many differences between the city-states of Sparta and Athens.

1. Athens: democracy, Sparta: military
2.
3.

LESSON 4

There were many great achievements in ancient Greek culture.

1. Established philosophy
2.
3.

Thinking Critically

1. Myths are imaginative stories about the past, and history is the record of what actually happened.

2. Answers may include that democracy is best because it allows all to participate, while in an oligarchy only a few rule, and in a monarchy only a king or queen rule.

3. Answers may include Athens, because it was a democracy, or Sparta, because it was a very organized society.

4. Answers may include philosophy, because it developed people's minds; literature or architecture, because they are still appreciated today; or sports, because they developed people's bodies.

5. There were no team sports, and they were played to honor the gods.

Summarizing the Chapter

Lesson 1
2. Is not totally accurate
3. May be based on history

Lesson 2
2. Athens: learning; Sparta: simple life
3. Athens: citizens' government; Sparta: more slaves than citizens

Lesson 3
2. Established many Greek colonies
3. Spread Greek culture throughout colonies

Lesson 4
2. Made great buildings
3. Wrote great poems and plays

▶ Test Master Booklet

CHAPTER SKILLS TEST

NAME _____ CHAPTER 2

SKILLS TEST (continued)

Directions: Study the list and complete items 6–10. Fill in the circle next to the correct answer.

Roots from Greek

agora	= a gathering place	cosmos	= an organized universe
anthropos	= human being	cracy	= rule or form of government
aristos	= best	demos	= the people
auto	= self (oneself)	geo	= earth
bios	= life	logy	= study (science) of
phobia	= fear	morph	= form

6. The word *agoraphobia* means the "_____"
   Ⓐ study of gathering places
   Ⓑ government by humans
   Ⓒ desire to attend meetings
   Ⓓ fear of public places

7. The study of the universe is called _____.
   Ⓐ cosmophobia
   Ⓑ cosmocracy
   Ⓒ cosmology
   Ⓓ cosmopolitanism

8. The word *biology* means "_____."
   Ⓐ the study of life
   Ⓑ government by life
   Ⓒ the study of the earth
   Ⓓ fear of living things

9. An autocracy is _____.
   Ⓐ the class of nobles who study government
   Ⓑ a government vehicle
   Ⓒ the study of the self
   Ⓓ a government in which one person rules

10. Geology means "_____."
    Ⓐ the study of the earth
    Ⓑ a government of the earth
    Ⓒ the study of the form of the universe
    Ⓓ the fear of dirt and minerals

▶ Test Master Booklet

CHAPTER WRITING TEST

NAME _____ CHAPTER 2

ESSAY TEST

Directions: Write a response to items 1–4.

REMINDER: Read and think about each item before you write your response. Be sure to think of the points you want to cover, details that support your response, and reasons for your opinions. Then, on the lines below, write your response in complete sentences.

1. Who was Homer?
   A satisfactory response should include the following statements.
   • Homer was a blind Greek poet.
   • He described the Trojan War and the years that followed in the Iliad and the Odyssey.
   • Homer's work blended history with myths.
   An excellent response might also include
   • specific examples of events or characters from Homer's work.
   • the terms epic, myth, or narrative.
   • a discussion of the excavation of Troy.

2. Describe the battle of Salamis.
   A satisfactory response should include the following statements.
   • The Persians burned Athens, forcing the citizens to flee to nearby islands.
   • The Persian fleet pursued the Athenians into the narrow bay of Salamis.
   • There the Greek ships destroyed most of the Persian fleet.
   • The loss of ships forced the Persians to return to Asia.
   An excellent response might also
   • mention Themistocles, Xerxes, Thermopylae, and oracle.
   • explain how Salamis was the turning point of the war against Persia.

▶ Test Master Booklet

CHAPTER WRITING TEST

NAME _____ CHAPTER 2

ESSAY TEST (continued)

3. What was Greek democracy?
   A satisfactory response should include the following statements.
   • Democracy was a form of government developed and practiced by Greek city-states.
   • It is a form of government in which the people rule.
   • Greek citizens met in assemblies to make political decisions.
   An excellent response might also include
   • the terms majority, citizenship, juries, Council of Five Hundred, and Pericles.
   • a comparison between a democracy and other forms of government.
   • a discussion of the limitations of Greek democracy.

4. Who was Socrates?
   A satisfactory response should include the following statements.
   • Socrates was a Greek philosopher.
   • Socrates taught people by questioning them about matters that they thought they understood.
   • Socrates was sentenced to death because many Athenians thought his teachings upset the beliefs of his students.
   An excellent response might also
   • explain that we learned about Socrates's teachings through the writing of Plato.
   • describe the incident with the oracle at Delphi.
   • provide specific quotes or examples.

Ancient Rome

(pp. 98-125)

Chapter Theme: The influences of Roman government, law, religion, language, and architecture are still apparent throughout Western civilization.

CHAPTER RESOURCES
Review Master Booklet
    Reviewing Chapter Vocabulary, p. 31
    Place Geography, p. 32
    Summarizing the Chapter, p. 33
Chapter 3 Test

LESSON *1* The Republic

(pp. 98-105)

Theme: Rome became a republic when it overthrew its corrupt king; it became ruler of the Mediterranean when it defeated Carthage.

LESSON RESOURCES
Workbook, pp. 31-32
Review Master Booklet
    Understanding the Lesson, p. 26

LESSON *2* The Empire

(pp. 106-111)

Theme: After the murder of Julius Caesar, Rome became a monarchy to better control its far-flung empire.

LESSON RESOURCES
Workbook, p. 33
Review Master Booklet
    Understanding the Lesson, p. 27

 SOCIAL STUDIES LIBRARY: *City: A Study of Roman Planning and Construction*
Money

LESSON *3* Life in a Roman City

(pp. 112-115)

Theme: The volcanic ashes that covered Pompeii preserved many objects which tell us about the lifestyle of this ancient people.

LESSON RESOURCES
Workbook, pp. 34-35
Review Master Booklet
    Understanding the Lesson, p. 28

LESSON *4* The Beginning of Christianity

(pp. 116-119)

Theme: Over time, Christianity went from being an illegal religion to the official religion of the Roman Empire.

LESSON RESOURCES
Workbook, p. 36
Review Master Booklet
    Understanding the Lesson, p. 29

LESSON *5* Roman Achievements

(pp. 120-123)

Theme: The Romans developed laws, an alphabet, a language, and buildings that continue to influence our lives today.

LESSON RESOURCES
Workbook, p. 37
Review Master Booklet
    Understanding the Lesson, p. 30

Review Masters

REVIEWING CHAPTER VOCABULARY

CHAPTER 3

VOCABULARY MASTER

Review Study the terms in the box. Use your Glossary to find definitions of those you do not remember.

aqueduct	emperor	parable	republic
assassination	ex post facto law	patrician	Romance language
civil war	gladiator	peninsula	Senate
consul	historical source	plebeian	volcano
dictator	legend	province	

Practice Complete the paragraphs using terms from the box above. You may change the forms of the terms to fit the meaning.

Many forms of entertainment were popular in ancient Rome. People often went to outdoor amphitheaters, where they watched chariots race around a huge oval track. Fights between armed (1) _gladiators_ were also popular events. Often the ruler of the Roman Empire, the (2) _emperor_, also attended these races and fights.

Many myths and (3) _legends_ about Rome and its rulers have been handed down from earlier times. One describes how the Roman ruler Nero played his violin during the great fire of Rome. Some written records from Roman times also exist. From these (4) _historical sources_ we can piece together what Roman life was like.

The first Romans were indeed a warlike people. They fought many wars and conquered whole populations during the history of the Roman Empire. However, we also know that the Romans established a form of government called a (5) _republic_. In this government, some citizens could become members of the (6) _Senate_. The Romans were also interested in making just laws for people all over the Roman Empire. For example, no (7) _ex post facto laws_ could be passed. All of this information is part of our picture of the Romans.

Write Choose ten terms from the box above. Use each term to write a sentence of your own. You may use the back of the sheet.

Sentences should show that students understand the meanings of the terms.

_____

_____

_____

_____

_____

_____

LOCATING PLACES

CHAPTER 3

PLACE GEOGRAPHY MASTER

✱ Ancient Rome expanded and ruled the lands around the Mediterranean Sea. Listed below are ancient cities that were under Roman rule. Use the Gazetteer in your textbook to find the latitude and longitude of each place. Then locate and label each on the map.

	LAT.	LONG.		LAT.	LONG.
1. Alexandria	31°N	30°E	6. Pompeii	41°N	15°E
2. Athens	38°N	24°E	7. Pergamum	39°N	27°E
3. Jerusalem	32°N	35°E	8. Cordoba	38°N	5°W
4. Constantinople	41°N	29°E	9. Carthage	37°N	10°E
5. Rome	42°N	13°E	10. Timgad	35°N	6°E

THE ROMAN EMPIRE

SUMMARIZING THE CHAPTER

CHAPTER 3

GRAPHIC ORGANIZER MASTER

✱ Complete this graphic organizer. Next to the five questions, fill in each blank with an answer.

CHAPTER THEME	The influences of Roman government, law, religion, language, and architecture are still apparent throughout Western civilization.

LESSON 1	What were some characteristics of the Roman Republic?	1. Representative government
		2. City-state
		3. Patricians and plebeians

LESSON 2	What were some characteristics of the Roman Empire?	1. Rule by emperors
		2. Rule by dictator
		3. Adoption of Christianity

LESSON 3	What can we learn from the ruins of Pompeii?	1. Buildings
		2. Markets
		3. Entertainment

LESSON 4	How did Christianity in the Roman Empire change over the course of time?	1. Against the law
		2. Tolerated
		3. The official religion

LESSON 5	What were some of the achievements of the Romans?	1. Law
		2. Alphabet
		3. Building

C3-B

Workbook Pages

COMPARING GOVERNMENTS

Comparing and Contrasting, Inferring Unstated Ideas, Drawing Conclusions

❋ The United States is a republic. In a republic citizens choose representatives to run the country. The government of the United States resembles and differs from that of the ancient Roman Republic. In the chart below, basic information about the two governments is listed in categories. Fill in the missing information.

	Roman Republic	United States Today
Equality of citizens	Citizens were divided into two unequal groups, patricians and plebeians.	With few exceptions, such as some convicted criminals, all citizens are equal.
Voting rights	Only male citizens could vote.	With few exceptions, all citizens 18 years old and older can vote.
Qualifications for senator	Only patricians could become senators.	With few exceptions, any citizen, 30 years or older, can become a senator.
Title of chief executive and length of term	Consul; one year	President; four years
Number of chief executives at one time	Two consuls served at a time.	One President serves at a time.
Government during major emergency	During an emergency, a dictator could be appointed for six months.	The President continues to lead during emergencies, no matter how serious.

Thinking Further: Did average citizens play a larger role in the government of the ancient Roman Republic, compared to citizens in the United States today? Support your answer with specific reasons.

Average citizens play a larger role in the United States. More citizens can vote, and they can become a chief execu-

tive or a senator or hold many other high government positions.

© Silver, Burdett & Ginn Inc.

Chapter 3, pages 99–105   31

ROMULUS AND REMUS

Understanding Sequence, Hypothesizing

❋ Historians know little about the founding of the city of Rome. According to myth, the city was founded by twin brothers, Romulus and Remus. The passage below tells one version of their story. (A myth explains something about the world, usually by referring to gods or other supernatural beings.)

According to myth, twin boys were born to a priestess named Rhea Silvia. The father of the babies was Mars, the Roman god of war. When the king of the region heard of the babies' birth, he ordered them thrown into the Tiber River because he feared the god Mars. The babies were put into a basket and thrown into the river. However, the basket was washed ashore and became tangled in the roots of a large tree on a riverbank. Mars sent a wolf to care for the twins. A poor herdsman found the babies in the wolf's den and took them home to raise. He named them Romulus and Remus.

Many years later, the twins, now grown, were reunited with their grandfather, a king named Numitor. After living with Numitor for several years, Romulus and Remus yearned for power. They set out to establish a new settlement on the banks of the Tiber River where they had been found by the wolf. After working together to start the new city, the twins began to fight about which of them should rule. The strife ended when Romulus flew into a rage and killed his brother. The people of the new city accepted Romulus as their king. The city came to be called Rome after its ruler.

❋ Rank the following events according to the order in which they take place in the myth. (Use the numbers 1 to 8.)

1 ___ Twin sons are born to Rhea Silvia.

5 ___ Romulus and Remus are reunited with their grandfather.

8 ___ A city is named Rome after its leader.

3 ___ Mars sends a wolf to care for the babies.

6 ___ Romulus and Remus set off to start a new city.

4 ___ A herdsman finds the babies in a wolf's den.

7 ___ Remus is killed by his brother.

2 ___ The babies are thrown into the Tiber River.

Thinking Further: You have just read a myth about the founding of Rome. Describe a more realistic way in which Rome might have been founded.

Students might say that Rome could have started as a farming or trading center. It could also have started as a

military outpost.

32   Chapter 3, pages 99–105

© Silver, Burdett & Ginn Inc.

INTERPRETING A MAP OF ANCIENT BRITAIN

Identifying Places on a Map; Understanding Compass Directions, Map Scale, Latitude and Longitude

❋ In 55 B.C., the Roman conqueror Julius Caesar landed in Britain to prevent the British from helping the Gauls, who were at war with Rome. Caesar returned to Britain the following year, but he never conquered it. A century later, portions of the island were seized by the Roman emperor Claudius I. By A.D. 85, Rome possessed most of Britain. The map shows Britain in A.D. 85. Study the map, and then answer each question by writing the letter of the correct choice in the blank.

c ___ **1.** Which of the cities below is farthest west?
  a. Eburacum **c.** Isca
  b. Lindum **d.** Deva

a ___ **2.** In which direction should you travel to get from Londinium to the Wall of Hadrian?
  a. north **c.** south
  b. east **d.** west

a ___ **3.** Where is the Wall of Antoninus?
  a. north of Deva **c.** west of Isca
  b. west of Ireland **d.** east of Lindum

c ___ **4.** Which of the following cities is closest to the North Sea?
  a. Isca **c.** Eburacum
  b. Deva **d.** Cassiterides

b ___ **5.** About how far is it from Camulodunum to Eburacum?
  a. 100 miles **c.** 225 miles
  b. 175 miles **d.** 300 miles

c ___ **6.** Which ancient British town is nearest Ireland?
  a. Cassiterides **c.** Deva
  b. Lindum **d.** Eburacum

ANCIENT BRITAIN

c ___ **7.** Which ancient British town is closest to the Prime Meridian (0° longitude)?
  a. Isca **c.** Londinium
  b. Deva **d.** Eburacum

Thinking Further: Discuss at least two major differences in geography between ancient Britain and modern Great Britain.

Possible answers include that names differ, there were far fewer towns in ancient Britain, and some things (like Wall

of Hadrian) are no longer important.

© Silver, Burdett & Ginn Inc.

Chapter 3, Pages 106–111   33

THE ROMAN FORUM

Understanding Diagrams, Inferring Unstated Ideas, Comparing

❋ On the facing page is an illustration of part of the Roman Forum in early times. The following paragraphs give some background information. Use the illustration and the paragraphs to answer the questions below.

The Roman Forum was the main center of public life. People met friends at the forum and kept up with the news. They bought and sold goods at the open-air marketplace, and they held meetings there. The buildings around the marketplace included basilicas and temples. A basilica was a large hall used for public meetings and law courts.

The Romans worshiped many gods. They even made gods of their dead heroes. Each god had his or her own temple, and many of these temples were clustered around the forum. A forum also included other structures that related to public life, such as arches and statues built to commemorate heroes and great events.

1. What is a basilica? a large building used for public meetings and law courts

2. Name two basilicas in the Roman Forum. Basilica Julia and Basilica Aemilia

3. From where would a politician address an outdoor meeting? the rostra, or speaker's platform

4. Name three types of activities that took place at a forum. possible answers: meetings, buying and selling, worshiping, court hearings

5. Where did the Roman senate meet? the curia, or senate house

6. Do you think there were forums in the towns the Romans built in Britain and other provinces? Explain your answer. Yes, because forums were central to Roman social life and government.

Thinking Further: Think of a major government or religious building in your community. In what specific ways is its appearance similar to, or different from, a comparable building in a Roman forum?

Some modern buildings reflect Roman architecture. Most differ in height, ornamentation, and basic lines, however.

34   Chapter 3, pages 112–115

© Silver, Burdett & Ginn Inc.

Workbook Pages

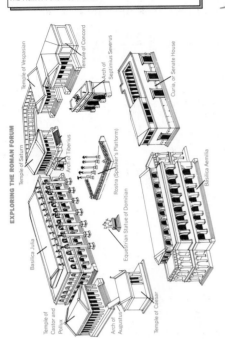

EXPLORING THE ROMAN FORUM

Temple of Vespasian
Temple of Concord
Arch of Septimius Severus
Curia, or Senate House
Temple of Saturn
Arch of Tiberius
Rostra (Speaker's Platform)
Basilica Aemilia
Equestrian Statue of Domitian
Basilica Julia
Temple of Castor and Pollux
Arch of Augustus
Temple of Caesar

Chapter 3, pages 112–115

THE SAYINGS OF JESUS

Understanding Main Ideas, Drawing Conclusions

✴ The Gospels include many sayings of Jesus. (A saying is a statement of wisdom or truth.) These sayings are noted for their beauty and their understanding of human nature. Read the following sayings. Then tell in your own words the main idea of each. Do not write more than two sentences for each. The sayings are taken from Chapter 6 of the Gospel According to Luke.

Suggested answers are provided.

1. "Blest are you who hunger; you shall be filled. Blest are you who are weeping; you shall laugh."

   You may be suffering now, but conditions will improve in the future, perhaps in an afterlife.

2. "When someone slaps you on one cheek, turn and give him the other; when someone takes your coat, let him have your shirt as well."

   Do not fight back against wrongdoers; give a thief more than he or she asks for.

3. "Do to others what you would have them do to you."

   Treat others in the same way that you would want them to treat you.

4. "Do not judge, and you will not be judged. Do not condemn, and you will not be condemned. Pardon, and you shall be pardoned."

   Accept the shortcomings of others, because you also have shortcomings. Similar to saying 3, above.

Thinking Further: Tell which of the above sayings is your favorite and explain why.

Answers should reflect independent thinking.

36
Chapter 3, pages 116–119

LATIN INFLUENCE ON ENGLISH

Understanding Etymology, Using Context Clues, Recognizing Roots and Affixes

✴ Each sentence below contains one Latin word, printed in italic type. On the line, write an English word that comes from the Latin word. The English word should make sense in the sentence.

school	1. Not all children living in ancient Rome attended a *schola*.
inexcusable	2. Marc thought Julia's rude behavior was *inexcusabilis*.
add	3. After you *addera* the numerals, write down the total.
elegance	4. Many buildings in the Roman Forum were known for their *elegantia*.
Music	5. *Musica* and theater were important to the Romans.
survive	6. Hannibal was able to *supervivere* in the Alps because he came well prepared.
comfort	7. A pat on the back can be a *comfortare* when you're feeling sad.
captive; prisoner	8. A Roman *captivus* found his cell was dark and often damp.

Thinking Further: Many English prefixes come from Latin. (A prefix is a syllable or word placed at the beginning of another word or root to change its meaning or to create a new word.) Below are three English prefixes that come from Latin. The meaning of each prefix is in parentheses. Write two English words that begin with each prefix. Write a sentence for each word.

Suggested answers are provided.

bi- (two)

bicycle   A bicycle has two wheels.

binoculars   Binoculars have two sets of lenses.

in- (not)

incomplete   The student's assignment was incomplete as it was only half finished.

indefinite   The coach was indefinite about when the first practice would be held.

re- (again)

reappear   The sun will reappear when the storm passes.

redraw   The picture was messy, so the artist decided to redraw it.

Chapter 3, Pages 120–123
37

C3-D

CHAPTER **3**

ANCIENT ROME

*A*ncient Rome was a leader in cultural development. Rome gave us great art, literature, and architecture, such as the Colosseum, whose ruins still stand in the city of Rome today.

The Republic

Objectives

★ **1. Describe** the government of the Roman republic.

2. Explain why the Romans formed a republic.

3. Discuss the cause and outcome of the Punic Wars.

4. Identify the following people and places in this lesson: *Virgil, Aeneas, Cincinnatus, Horatius, Hannibal, Rome, Carthage, Sicily,* and *Troy.*

1 STARTING THE LESSON

Motivation Activity

■ Ask students to imagine that a world power such as the Soviet Union felt that it was in its interest to control Canada.

■ Discuss with students whether this would pose a threat to the United States and why.

■ Tell them that Rome found itself in a similar situation in the third century B.C. In this lesson they will read about the course of action that the Romans pursued.

Think About What You Know

■ Assign the THINK ABOUT WHAT YOU KNOW activity on p. 99.

■ Student answers may include no right to vote or little or no say in decisions made about our country.

Study the Vocabulary

■ Have students look up the definition of each of the vocabulary words for this lesson in the Glossary.

■ Ask students to write a fictional story in which they correctly use each of the new vocabulary terms at least once.

■ You may wish to have some volunteers read their stories to the class.

Optional Activities

Making a Crossword Puzzle

● Ask students to make crossword puzzles using the vocabulary words for this lesson.

● You may wish to show samples of crossword puzzles from a newspaper or book.

● Have students create answer keys for their puzzles using the definitions of the vocabulary terms found in the Glossary.

● Then have students exchange and solve each other's puzzles.

The Republic

THINK ABOUT WHAT YOU KNOW

Imagine our country is ruled by a king. The king's powers are unlimited. How would your life be different than it is with our type of government?

STUDY THE VOCABULARY

republic	consul
patrician	dictator
plebeian	peninsula
Senate	legend

FOCUS YOUR READING

Why did the Roman city-state become a republic and the ruler of the western Mediterranean?

A. Greek Myths Borrowed by a Roman Poet

The Roman poet Virgil wrote about the ancestors of the Romans in the *Aeneid* (ee NEE ihd). Virgil based his long poem on myths borrowed from the Greeks. Gods and goddesses play important parts in the *Aeneid*. They are the gods and goddesses of the Greeks, although Virgil uses their Roman names. The chief of the gods is known as Jupiter rather than Zeus, and his wife is called Juno rather than Hera.

The *Aeneid* is a continuation of Homer's *Iliad*. Virgil recounts the adventures of Aeneas (ee NEE us), a prince of Troy. When the Greeks inside the wooden horse open the gates to Troy, Aeneas prepares to fight to his last breath. A goddess tells him to take his family and escape rather than remain and face certain death. Aeneas does as the goddess orders. He escapes to the hills, taking his small son and carrying his aged father on his back.

On the slopes of Mount Ida, Aeneas joins other Trojans who have fled the burning city. Aeneas wishes to remain on the mountain until they can return and build a new Troy on the site of the old. But his father advises the Trojans to leave the place that has such unhappy memories. He tells them to build ships and sail in search of a new homeland.

The Trojans follow the old man's advice. They cut timbers from a forest and build ships. When the ships are completed, the Trojans set sail without knowing where they are going. Aeneas receives a message in a dream from the god Apollo, who tells him to seek a new home in Italy.

In the course of their journey, the Trojans encounter a monster with the body of a large bird and the head of a woman. She warns the Trojans that they will face great hardships. They will not reach their new homeland until they are so hungry that "they will eat their tables."

The goddess Juno continues to cause trouble for the Trojans. After they set sail from Sicily, she sends a terrible storm that blows them away from Italy. But Neptune, god of the sea, calms the storm. Aeneas and the remaining Trojans make their way to the coast of North Africa.

In North Africa, Aeneas meets the beautiful Dido, queen of Carthage, and they fall in love. Aeneas remains with Dido for a year, delaying his search for the new Troy. Jupiter grows impatient and sends a messenger to remind Aeneas of his duty. When Dido discovers that Aeneas is leaving, she pleads with him to stay. He is touched by her love but tells her that when the gods command, people must obey. As Aeneas sails away, Dido kills herself.

The Trojans set sail again and this time reach the land of the Latins, in central

Read and Think

Section A

To help students understand this famous piece of literature, ask the following questions:

1. **What story is told in Virgil's *Aeneid*?**
   (How the Trojans came to settle in Italy and why the language of Rome was Latin *p. 99*)

   Thinking Critically What parts of the *Aeneid*, do you think, might be true? (Evaluate)
   (Aeneas, Dido, and the king of the Latins may have been real people. The Trojans fled Troy, they had a rough journey that included going to North Africa, and they ended up in Italy. *p. 99*)

Illustrating the *Aeneid*

- Ask students to select one episode from the *Aeneid* that is described in this section and illustrate it on a piece of paper.

- Collect student illustrations for display on a bulletin board entitled "The Journey of Aeneas."

- Before putting the illustrations up, ask students to help you arrange them in correct chronological order.

Learning About Oral History

- A discussion of the epics of Homer is a good opportunity to introduce the idea of oral history. *Oral history* refers to stories, poems, songs, events, and so on, that are passed orally through successive generations.

- Perhaps students can recall stories told by their parents or grandparents about important events.

- Help students understand the value of oral history.

- Remind them that events transmitted orally are not always totally accurate, but that they do give an indication of cultural and social changes through generations.

Optional Activities

Read and Think

Section B

To help students understand the history of Rome, ask the following questions:

1. **Where is Rome located?**
   (On the Tiber River *p. 101*)

2. **What were the first Romans like?**
   (They were a warlike, quarrelsome people who were called "ignorant" and "uncivilized" by at least one historian. *p. 101*)

3. **Why was Tarquin the Proud driven from the throne?**
   (He abused his powers and killed those who objected. *p. 101*)

   Thinking Critically How, do you think, did the Trojans hold positions of power in Rome? (Infer)
   (The first king of Rome was a descendant of Aeneas, a Trojan. *p. 101*)

VISUAL THINKING SKILL

Interpreting a Photograph

■ Direct students' attention to the photograph on the next page to help them answer the following question: **How would you describe the architecture of this bridge that crossed the Tiber River in Rome?**
(It is arched and it appears to be made of stone.)

Italy. They leave their ships and gather in a grove of trees to eat. They do not bother to set up tables with platters on them. Instead they place meat on large slabs of bread. After gobbling the meat, they hungrily eat the slabs of bread. The son of Aeneas jokes, "We were so hungry we even ate our tables!" Then Aeneas remembers what the monster had said. He hugs his son and happily declares, "Now I know we have reached the right place!"

It is true the Trojans have reached the right place, but they have not yet reached the end of their troubles. The king of the Latins wishes to marry his daughter to Aeneas, but the other Latins oppose mixing with newcomers. A war breaks out in which many brave warriors lose their lives.

Jupiter asks Juno why she continues to trouble Aeneas. Juno sighs and agrees that she will no longer keep the Trojans from their new home in Rome. But she begs Jupiter not to let the Latins lose their name and language and become Trojans. She said "Let Rome rule the world, but let Troy perish forever." Jupiter agrees. "The Trojans will mingle with the Latins to become one people and all will be called Latins." By this myth, Virgil explained why the language of Rome was Latin.

Virgil, the greatest Roman poet, is shown in this mosaic with the spirits who inspired him.
▶ What is Virgil holding?

This bridge stretches across the Tiber River in Rome.
► How did Rome's location help to make it a prosperous city-state?

B. Rule by Kings Overthrown

Rome began as a city-state on the Tiber River. Its size was about the same as that of the Greek city-states. According to an old story, the first king was Romulus (RAHM yuh lus), a descendant of Aeneas.

The first Romans were a warlike people who fought fiercely against their enemies in war but quarreled among themselves in time of peace. Numa, the second king, realized that the Romans must learn peaceful ways. He told the Romans that the gods punished those who wronged their neighbors. To persuade people to respect the rules he gave them, Numa invented a story. He told the people that a goddess spoke to him. A Roman historian in later years excused Numa's story about the goddess. It was, the historian wrote, the only way he could rule "an ignorant and yet uncivilized people."

The Romans remembered Numa as a good and wise king, but later kings were neither good nor wise. Tarquin the Proud abused his powers and killed those who objected. The Romans finally drove Tarquin from the throne in 510 B.C.

C. Roman Republic Established

Citizens of Rome To take the place of the Roman king, the Romans established a **republic**. The Latin word means a government that is the "people's affair." A republic is a government in which citizens choose representatives to run the country. But not all of the people had an equal voice in the republic. Only male citizens could take any part in Roman government, and they were divided into two classes, **patricians** and **plebians** (plee BEE unz). Most of the patricians in Rome were upper-class landowners. The plebeians were the common people who made up about 90 percent of the Roman population. Being a citizen in the early Roman Republic was a matter of birth.

101

For Your Information

The Founding of Rome According to ancient Roman legend, Romulus and Remus were the twin grandsons of a king who had been overthrown by his brother. The king's brother ordered the twins to be drowned, but the men charged with executing the order left the twins on a riverbank. The twins were discovered by a female wolf who fed and cared for them. When they grew up, Romulus and Remus killed the cruel king and returned their grandfather to his throne. The brothers, however, quarreled and Romulus killed Remus. Thus, Romulus became the first king of Rome and gave his name to the city.

Optional Activities

Read and Think
Section C

To help students understand the establishment of the republic, ask the following questions:

1. **Why did the Romans establish a republic?**
   (To take the place of the king *p. 101*)

2. **How was the Roman government organized?**
   (Leaders were elected by an assembly made up of patricians and plebeians. Among those leaders were 300 senators. Two senators were elected by the citizens to serve as consuls, or top officials, of the republic. *pp. 101-102*)

3. **Which citizens could attend the assembly?**
   (Male citizens of the plebeian and patrician classes *p. 102*)

4. **Why did each consul in the Senate have as much power as the other?**
   (So they could keep watch over and check each other *p. 102*)

5. **Why did the Romans have dictators?**
   (To act quickly in a state of emergency *p. 102*)

   Thinking Critically Do you agree or disagree with the idea that only male citizens should participate in the government? (Evaluate)
   (Answers may include agree because many male citizens have more experience in government affairs, or disagree because female citizens are as capable as males. *pp. 101-102*)

Answers to Caption Questions
p. 100 ► A book, probably the *Aeneid*
p. 101 ► Rome was located near water, which would increase trade.

Read and Think

Section D

To help students understand the growth of the Republic, ask the following questions:

1. **What was one of the duties of every male citizen in the Roman Republic?**
   (Service in the army *p. 103*)

2. **What was expected of Roman soldiers?**
   (Discipline, skill, and bravery *p. 103*)

3. **How did Rome gain control of the Italian peninsula?**
   (By winning wars against the other Italian states *pp. 102-103*)

4. **How did the Romans take over the Italian peninsula?**
   (Roman soldiers defeated other states in Italy and won control of the whole peninsula. *p. 103*)

Thinking Critically **How, do you think, are the Roman republic and the republic of the United States different?**
(Analyze)
(Answers may include that all adult citizens can vote and hold office in the United States. In Rome, only male citizens could vote and only patricians could be senators and consuls. *pp. 102-103*)

A Roman political leader named Cicero is shown addressing the Roman Senate.
▶ Who were the members who made up the Roman Senate?

Both patricians and plebeians could attend the large assembly, a group that elected leaders. But, the patricians controlled the assembly. Only patricians served as members of the council of elders. The Romans called this council the **Senate**. It was a body of 300 older men from which the citizens elected two **consuls** every year. A consul was one of the top officials in the republic. Having overthrown a king, the Romans did not want a single leader who ruled for life. Each consul held office for one year. Each consul had as much power as the other, so they could keep watch over and check each other.

Cincinnatus   In time of emergency the Senate might choose a single leader, called a **dictator**. A dictator takes complete charge of a government. A dictator held power for six months or until the emergency had passed. The word *dictator* has an unfavorable meaning today. We think of dictators as being unjust or unreasonable. But the Romans remembered Cincinnatus, a very different kind of dictator.

Cincinnatus was plowing his field one day when several senators came to his farm and told him that the Senate had chosen him dictator. Rome needed a single leader because an enemy army threatened the city. Cincinnatus left his plow and took command of the republic. He called all the citizens to arms. He led them into battle and won a quick victory. After having done his duty, Cincinnatus returned to his farm.

Many different governments have been called republics since the time of Cincinnatus. The United States is a republic. Indeed, it can more correctly be called a "people's affair" than the ancient Roman Republic. In the United States today, all adult citizens have an equal right to vote and hold office.

D. Taking Over the Italian Peninsula

Rome was only one of a number of city-states and kingdoms on the Italian **peninsula**. A peninsula is a piece of land surrounded by water on three sides and

Optional Activities

Comparing Governments

● Extend the discussion of the limitations on political participation in the Roman Republic (only male citizens could participate in government and only patricians served in the Senate) by comparing it with any limitations that exist in the United States.

● Ask students if limitations such as race, religion, sex, or national origin prevent Americans from participating in the political process.

● Discuss the limitations that do exist, such as age and citizenship.

● Then have students discuss orally which government allows greater political participation among its people.

Writing to Learn

Writing a Newspaper Article   Have students write a newspaper article describing how Horatius saved Rome.

● Remind students that their articles should answer the questions who, what, when, where, why, and how, and that their headlines should contain a verb.

connected to a larger piece of land. Wars between the small states were as common as wars between the cities of Greece.

Service in the army was the duty of every male citizen in the Roman Republic. Each man furnished his own weapons and equipment. Discipline was very strict. Cowards could be punished by death.

The story of Horatius (hoh RAY shus) described the ideal citizen soldier. According to the story, Horatius and two companions held back an enemy army at a bridge across the Tiber until the Romans could destroy it. As the timbers began to crack, Horatius ordered his two companions to go back. He fought alone until he heard the bridge crash into the river. He then leaped, fully armed, into the rushing river and swam safely to the other side. Horatius' bravery saved the city of Rome.

Here Horatius is shown bravely fighting the enemy to save Rome.
► Where did Horatius defeat the enemy army?

Every Roman citizen was in the army.
► What weapons is this Roman soldier holding?

The story of Horatius may only be a **legend** rather than true history. A legend is a story handed down from earlier times that may be no more than partly true. But whether legend or history, the story of Horatius at the bridge tells what Romans expected of their soldiers.

Roman soldiers may not all have been as brave and skillful as Horatius, but they did win wars. Rome defeated other states in Italy and won control of the whole peninsula. The city-state on the Tiber now ruled a whole country.

E. The Punic Wars

Carthage Rome controlled Italy, but the North African city of Carthage controlled the western Mediterranean lands. In myths, Carthage was the city of Queen Dido. In fact, Carthage was a city established by the Phoenicians (fih NIHSH unz), who came from what today is known as

103

For Your Information

Gaining Control of the Peninsula In order to gain control of the Italian peninsula, the Romans had to defeat a number of enemies. To the north were the Etruscans, whom the Romans defeated in 396 B.C. The Romans also held back an invading European army of Gauls in 334 B.C., forcing them to live in only the northernmost part of Italy. In central Italy, the Romans defeated the Samnites in 290 B.C. By 266 B.C., the Romans had conquered the Greek city-states in the south. This period of nearly a century and a half of warfare was a testament to the strength, courage, and persistence of the Roman army.

Read and Think

Section E

To help students understand the three Punic Wars, ask the following questions:

1. **What was the cause of the Punic Wars?**
(Both Carthage and Rome had interests in Sicily. This rivalry led to the wars. *p. 104*)

2. **What territory did Rome rule at the end of the third Punic War?**
(Rome now ruled both Italy and the western Mediterranean. *p. 105*)

Thinking Critically Was Cato correct, do you think, to call for the destruction of Carthage? (Evaluate)
(Answers may include yes, because he feared that the Carthaginians might regain their former strength, or no, because both Carthage and Rome should have been able to coexist. *pp. 104-105*)

VISUAL THINKING SKILL

Reading a Time Line

■ Direct students' attention to the time line on p. 105 to help them answer the following question: **How many years passed from the time the city of Rome was founded until the end of the Roman Empire in the west?**
(1,276 years passed.)

Lebanon. Carthage became a prosperous and powerful city that ruled the coasts of North Africa and Spain.

Both Carthage and Rome had interests in Sicily, the large island off the tip of the Italian peninsula. The Carthaginians (kahr thuh JIHN ee unz) thought that the Romans in Sicily threatened their control of the western Mediterranean. The Romans thought the Carthaginians threatened their control of Italy. The rivalry in Sicily lead to three wars, which the Roman people called the Punic Wars. *Punic* means "Phoenician."

First Punic War In the First Punic War, between 264 B.C. and 241 B.C., the Romans forced the Carthaginians out of Sicily. But this did not end the struggle. In the years that followed, the Carthaginian general Hannibal prepared to fight again. He trained an army in Spain, which Carthage ruled. Hannibal led his troops over the

Pyrenees mountain range, through southern France, and across the Alps, the most rugged mountains in western Europe. Hannibal's forces included not only men and horses but elephants as well. Using elephants in war was an idea that Alexander's army had brought back from India. The large animals frightened troops not familiar with them, but they sometimes turned and trampled their own handlers. It was difficult to move such an army over the snow-covered Alps, but Hannibal finally reached Italy.

Second Punic War In the Second Punic War, Hannibal defeated the Roman army, but he failed to take the walled city. After their defeat the Romans wisely showed patience. They waited until they were strong enough to send a force to attack Carthage. The Carthaginians called their best general back home, but this time Hannibal was defeated.

Hannibal crossed the Rhone River to attack the Romans.
▶ Why, do you think, did he and his men use elephants?

The Granger Collection

Optional Activities

Role-Playing

● Divide the class into pairs and have them participate in a *Meet the Press*-type interview with the Carthaginian general Hannibal.

● Have each "interviewer" draw up a list of three questions and have the "subject" prepare for the session by reviewing the material on Hannibal in the lesson.

Reteaching Main Objective

⭐ *Describe the government of the Roman republic.*

● Have students work in small groups to create an organizational chart that shows how the Roman government was organized.

● Tell students to begin by placing the most powerful figure(s) at the top of the chart. For example, the dictator or consuls should go at the top and senators and members of the assembly should go below.

● After students have created the chart, have them write brief descriptions of the powers or responsibilities of each body or office of the Roman government.

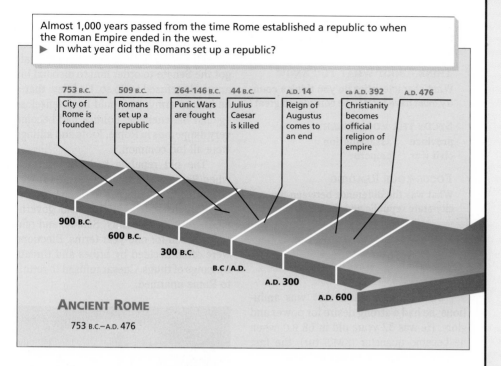

Almost 1,000 years passed from the time Rome established a republic to when the Roman Empire ended in the west.
▶ In what year did the Romans set up a republic?

753 B.C. | City of Rome is founded
509 B.C. | Romans set up a republic
264-146 B.C. | Punic Wars are fought
44 B.C. | Julius Caesar is killed
A.D. 14 | Reign of Augustus comes to an end
ca A.D. 392 | Christianity becomes official religion of empire
A.D. 476

900 B.C.
600 B.C.
300 B.C.
B.C / A.D.
A.D. 300
A.D. 600

ANCIENT ROME
753 B.C.–A.D. 476

Third Punic War Even after its defeat, Carthage continued to be a prosperous trading city. Cato, a Roman senator, feared that Carthage would grow strong and try to avenge Hannibal's defeat. Cato ended every speech in the Senate with the cry, "Carthage must be destroyed!" Rome waged the Third Punic War from 149 B.C. to 146 B.C. and again defeated Carthage. Cato was dead by then, but he got his way: Carthage was totally destroyed. Rome now ruled both Italy and the western Mediterranean. The map on page 110 shows the land Rome controlled after the Punic Wars.

LESSON *1* REVIEW

THINK AND WRITE (Infer)

A. What was the connection between the story of Aeneas and the Trojan War?
B. Why did the Romans overthrow rule by kings? (Infer)
C. Why wasn't the Roman Republic a government by all of the people? (Recall)
D. What can we learn from the legend of Horatius at the bridge? (Recall)

E. What was the outcome of each of the three Punic Wars? (Recall)

SKILLS CHECK
WRITING SKILL
Write two paragraphs in which you compare and contrast a patrician and a plebeian.

105

Optional Activities

Lesson *1* Review

Answers to Think and Write

A. The story of Aeneas explains how some Trojans came to settle in Italy; they left Troy during the Trojan War.

B. The Romans overthrew rule by kings because some of the kings were abusive.

C. The Roman Republic was not a government by all of the people because women had no role in it and plebeians were excluded from positions of power.

D. The legend of Horatius tells us that Romans expected their soldiers to be brave and fearless.

E. The Romans won the first and third Punic wars, but lost the second.

Answer to Skills Check

Paragraphs should include that patricians were the upper class who could hold positions of power in Roman government, and plebeians were common people who could attend the assembly.

Focus Your Reading

Ask the lesson focus question found at the beginning of the lesson: **Why did the Roman city-state become a republic and the ruler of the western Mediterranean?**
(The Roman city-state became a republic because many of the kings had been cruel and unwise. Rome became the ruler of the western Mediterranean in order to protect its interest in Sicily.)

Additional Practice

You may wish to assign the ancillary materials listed below.
Understanding the Lesson p. 26
Workbook pp. 31-32

Answers to Caption Questions
p. **104** ▶ Their size frightened the enemy.
p. **105** ▶ 509 B.C.

The Empire

Objectives

★1. **Identify** the builders of the Roman Empire and name their accomplishments.

2. **Describe** the Byzantine Empire.

3. **Identify** the following people and places: *Julius Caesar, Pompey, Brutus, Augustus, Constantine, Gaul,* and *Constantinople.*

1 STARTING THE LESSON

Motivation Activity

■ Ask students to describe the characteristics of great leaders and those of weak leaders. Write student responses on the chalkboard.

■ Tell students to keep these characteristics in mind when determining whether the Roman leaders in this lesson were great.

Think About What You Know

■ Assign the THINK ABOUT WHAT YOU KNOW activity on p. 106.

■ Student answers should reflect independent thinking but may include responses such as wealth, advanced technology, education, and military strength.

Study the Vocabulary

■ Have students look up the definition of each of the vocabulary words for this lesson in the Glossary.

■ Then, present the class with misuses of the words and ask students to tell you why the vocabulary words are being used incorrectly. For example, "The United States is a province of North America." (It is a nation, not a province.)

LESSON *2*

The Empire

THINK ABOUT WHAT YOU KNOW
What characteristics do you think a country must have for it to be considered great?

STUDY THE VOCABULARY
province   assassination
civil war   emperor

FOCUS YOUR READING
What was the difference between the city-state republic and the empire?

A. Julius Caesar and the Roman Empire

Julius Caesar (SEE zur) was ambitious; he had a strong desire for power and glory. He was 32 years old in 68 B.C. when he became quaestor (KWES tur), the first step up the political ladder in Rome.

By the time Caesar was 41, he became consul, one of the two top officials in the republic. After a one-year term, Caesar became governor of the **province** of Gaul, a region ruled by Rome. A province is a division of a country. Gaul consisted of northern Italy and part of southern France.

Rising politicians sought to become governors of provinces because they had command of armed forces. An army enabled an ambitious politician to win both glory and wealth. The glory came from conquering new lands for Rome; the wealth came from looting the conquered.

Caesar spent nine years as governor of Gaul. He enlarged the province by conquering all of what is now France along with Belgium and Switzerland. Caesar crossed to Britain twice, but he did not add the islands to the empire.

B. Caesar—Dictator for Life

Dangerous Politics When Caesar finished his years in Gaul, his political rivals got the Senate to order him to disband his army. He refused to do so. He knew that if he had no army, he would be defenseless against his enemies. Politics had become very dangerous in Rome. Riots and killings were all too common.

The old republic had been formed when Rome was a small city-state. It was not suited to govern a far-flung empire. Yet the Romans still kept their old government, with its assembly, Senate, and officials chosen for one-year terms. Elections were often decided by bribes and threats by gangs of thugs. Caesar refused to return to Rome unarmed.

Julius Caesar was a talented, strong leader who had ambitious goals.
► How did Caesar enlarge the Roman Empire?

Optional Activities

Writing to Learn

Writing a Letter   Ask students to imagine that they are Julius Caesar and that they have just learned of an assassination plot against them.

● Have students write a letter to a friend explaining why they are either afraid or not afraid of the plot.

Many Romans believed Caesar ruled wisely, but some feared his power. This painting depicts the assassination of Caesar.
▶ Do you think this painting is accurate?

As Caesar led his army to Rome, his enemies, led by Pompey, fled to Greece. Pompey and Caesar had once been political partners, but they were now on opposite sides in a **civil war**, that is, a war between groups within the same city or country. This conflict between two groups of Romans divided families. Brother sometimes fought against brother.

Caesar as Dictator   After making sure that he controlled Italy, Caesar led his army to Greece. In a bloody battle on August 9, 48 B.C., Caesar's troops defeated the forces that backed Pompey. Caesar went on to overcome his opponents throughout the empire. In 44 B.C. the Romans made Caesar dictator for life. They hoped that a strong leader would bring peace to Rome. One month of the year was renamed *July*, "the month of Julius," in his honor. Many people probably thought rule by a dictator was better than civil war.

Caesar had plans for a number of reforms, but he had time to carry out only a few of them. One was an improved calendar much like the one we still use. The three regular years have 365 days, but the fourth year, called a leap year, has 366.

Death of Caesar   Meanwhile, Caesar's enemies whispered to others that the dictator intended to become king. They reminded the Romans that their ancestors had long ago driven a king from Rome and created the republic. Anyone wishing to become a king was an enemy. Patriotic Romans should kill a would-be king as readily as an enemy on the battlefield. On March 15, 44 B.C., the **assassination** of Caesar occurred when 60 of his enemies stabbed him to death in the Senate house. An assassination is murder by a secret or sudden attack. To learn more about the assassination of Caesar, read the literature selection on the next page.

107

Thinking About Literature

Use the information below to help students better understand the literature selection found on this page.

Selection Summary

The central character of this play is Brutus, a Roman general and Caesar's best friend. As the remainder of the play unfolds, Brutus unwisely allows Marc Antony to deliver a funeral speech over Caesar's body. Antony gradually turns the crowd into a mob ready to burn and kill in order to avenge Caesar's death. In the end, the assassination plotters are forced to flee Rome and are defeated in battle by a Roman army led by Marc Antony.

Guided Reading

1. **Who is speaking in this literature selection?**
   (Brutus)

2. **What reason did Brutus give for killing Caesar?**
   (He loved Rome more)

3. **According to Brutus, what would have happened to all Romans if Caesar continued to rule the Empire?**
   (All Romans would have become like slaves.)

Literature-Social Studies Connection

1. **Based on what you have read in this lesson about Caesar and about politics in Rome during his time, do you think that Brutus's decision to kill Caesar was a wise one?**
   (Answers may include that it was wise because it kept Caesar from becoming king and Rome from regressing, or unwise because Caesar could have made great positive changes in Rome if he had lived.)

LITERATURE SELECTION

FROM:

Julius Caesar

By: William Shakespeare
Setting: Roman Senate

The English writer William Shakespeare is one of the greatest playwrights of all time. In 1599, William Shakespeare wrote a play called *Julius Caesar*. The play takes place in ancient Rome and describes events before and after the assassination of Caesar. Brutus, a Roman general who was a friend of Caesar's, is one of the men who plots Caesar's murder. Brutus and his group of conspirators stab Caesar to death as he enters the Roman Senate.

Although Brutus believes that Caesar's death is necessary to ensure the safety of Rome, he is torn between his friendship for Caesar and his sense of duty. In this literature selection, Brutus explains to the Roman Senate why he betrayed Caesar.

*R*omans, countrymen, and lovers! hear me for my cause, and be silent, that you may hear: believe me for mine honour, and have respect to mine honour, that you may believe: censure [condemn] me in your wisdom, and awake your senses, that you may better judge. If there be any in this assembly, any dear friend of Caesar's, to him I say, that Brutus' love to Caesar was no less than his. If then that friend demand why Brutus rose against Caesar, this is my answer:—Not that I loved Caesar less, but that I loved Rome more. Had you

rather Caesar were living and die all slaves, than that Caesar were dead, to live all free men? As Caesar loved me, I weep for him; as he was fortunate, I rejoice at it; as he was valiant [brave], I honour him: but, as he was ambitious, I slew [killed] him. There is tears for his love; joy for his fortune; honour for his valour; and death for his ambition. Who is here so base that would be a bondman [slave]? If any, speak; for him have I offended. Who is here so rude that would not be a Roman? If any, speak; for him have I offended. Who is here so vile that will not love his country? If any, speak; for him have I offended. I pause for a reply.

Optional Activities

Curriculum Connection

Literature Ask students to reread Brutus's speech in the literature selection on p. 108.

● Ask students to paraphrase the speech.

● Then, have them write a brief character sketch of Brutus.

C. Rome and the Emperor Augustus

Octavian Apollonia (ap uh LOH nee uh) was a Greek city on the coast of what is now Albania. It was a port and a sort of university town. Among the students there in 44 B.C. was Octavian (ahk TAY vee un), the 18-year-old grandnephew of Caesar.

When news of Caesar's death reached Apollonia, Octavian's friends urged him to flee to northern Greece and seek protection from troops loyal to Caesar. Octavian was not only Caesar's grandnephew but also his adopted son and heir. An heir is a person who is entitled to inherit property or to succeed to an office. Caesar's friends feared that those who had killed Caesar would also kill his heir.

Octavian did not take his friends' advice. Instead he returned to Rome and plunged into the struggle for power. The peace that Caesar had established was broken by another civil war. Some politicians supported Octavian because they thought he was "a mere boy" whom they could either control or set aside. However, they were quite wrong. Octavian proved to be the most able leader in the dangerous struggle, and by the year 31 B.C. he alone controlled Rome.

Ruling Rome Octavian avoided the title of king, but he was in fact a monarch. He spoke of his position as princeps, which meant "first citizen." Octavian was also the first Roman ruler to be called **emperor**, a Roman title meaning "commander." An emperor is the supreme ruler of an empire. Octavian did not do away with the old Senate, but he made sure that he controlled it. The Senate named him *Augustus*, that is, "honored." It is as the Emperor Augustus that Octavian is known in history. That name survives on our calendar along

Emperor Augustus brought order to Rome and made many improvements there for which he is remembered.
▶ What do we use today that his name appears on?

with that of Julius Caesar. The Romans named the eighth month of the year *August*, "the month of Augustus."

Emperor Augustus ruled the Roman Empire for over 40 years. Within the empire it was a time of peace. People, no doubt, welcomed peace after the civil wars. Some of the great Roman writers praised Augustus. Virgil was one of them. Virgil wrote the poem the *Aeneid* at the emperor's request.

Augustus' Accomplishments Augustus made Rome a grander city. He built large public buildings and erected monuments. Toward the end of his life, he proudly declared that he had found Rome a city of brick and had left it a city of marble.

109

Read and Think
Section C

To help students understand the man who gained control of the Roman empire after Julius Caesar, ask the following questions:

1. **In what ways was Octavian a monarch?**
   (He described his position as being the "first citizen" of Rome, he was called emperor, and he controlled the Senate. *p. 109*)

2. **What did Augustus do to improve life in the Roman Empire?**
   (He brought peace, made Rome a grander city, and improved the government of the provinces. *p. 109*)

Thinking Critically Which part of Augustus's life, do you think, would be interesting material for a play? (Evaluate)
   (Answers may include his struggle to gain control of Rome or specific incidents during his rule. *pp. 109–110*)

┌─ **Answers to Caption Questions** ─┐
p. 109 ▶ The calendar

Writing a Play

● Ask students to write a play about the life of Emperor Augustus.

● Have them first determine the cast of characters who will have parts in the play.

● Then have them decide how many acts the play will have.

● Finally, have them decide the events that will take place in each act and develop the dialogue for each act.

For Your Information

The Roman Calendar Julius Caesar realized that the calendar of the Egyptians was better than the one used by the Romans of earlier times. However, he also thought that the Egyptian calendar could be improved. Caesar asked a Greek scholar to work out a calendar year that would be the same as the solar year. The scholar suggested a plan that Caesar adopted for the Roman calendar. The improved calendar was almost the same as our modern calendar. In fact, it is even responsible for our current concept of leap year. According to the Roman Calendar, an extra day was to be added to the month of February every fourth year.

Optional Activities

Read and Think

Section D

To discuss what happened after Augustus's reign, ask the following questions:

1. **What changes did Constantine make?**
   (Built new capital, erected fine buildings, and adopted Christianity *pp. 110-111*)

   Thinking Critically **Why, do you think, did the Roman Empire break apart?** (Evaluate)
   (Answers may include that it was too large and had bad rulers. *pp. 106-111*)

Meeting Individual Needs

Concept:
Imperial Rule

These activities will help students better understand the strengths and weaknesses of an imperial monarchy.

◆**EASY** Have students write some of the strengths and weaknesses of a government that places all power in the hands of one person.

◀▶ **AVERAGE** Ask students to list benefits and drawbacks of living under an emperor in the United States. Have them write paragraphs explaining their preference of governments.

◀▮▶ **CHALLENGING** Have students write an essay in which they agree or disagree with this statement: "Power tends to corrupt and absolute power corrupts absolutely."

GEOGRAPHY THEMES

Location

■ Direct students' attention to the map on this page to help them answer the following question: **What country is roughly in the center of the Roman Empire?** (Italy)

110

Augustus improved the government of the provinces. Officials treated people under Rome's rule more fairly. But Augustus did not make any of his reforms quickly. His favorite saying was, "Make haste slowly." How can you say that in a different way?

D. A "New Rome" in the East

Emperors Rule Rome remained a monarchy after the death of Augustus in A.D. 14. For the next four centuries, emperors ruled the empire. Some ruled well; some ruled badly. The Romans never found a way to make sure that only able and just men became monarchs. In fact, some seemingly good men became bad rulers once they secured power.

The emperors ruled a great variety of peoples and lands. The map below shows the Roman Empire when it was at its largest. As you can see from the map, Rome ruled all of the lands surrounding the Mediterranean Sea.

Constantine Emperor Constantine ruled from A.D. 306 to 337. He built a new capital in the eastern part of the empire, which had the largest population. Constantine located the "New Rome" on the site of an

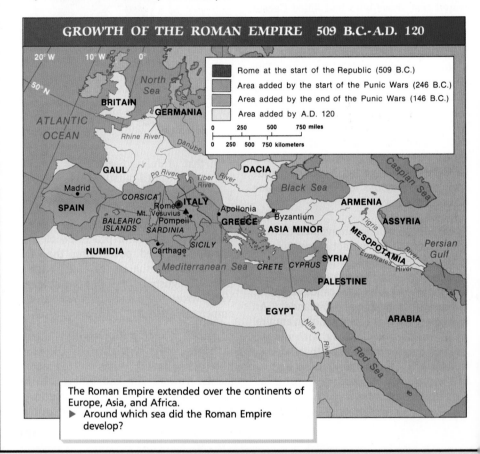

GROWTH OF THE ROMAN EMPIRE 509 B.C.-A.D. 120

- Rome at the start of the Republic (509 B.C.)
- Area added by the start of the Punic Wars (246 B.C.)
- Area added by the end of the Punic Wars (146 B.C.)
- Area added by A.D. 120

The Roman Empire extended over the continents of Europe, Asia, and Africa.
▶ Around which sea did the Roman Empire develop?

Reteaching Main Objective

⭐ *Identify the builders of the Roman Empire and name their accomplishments.*

● Pair students who understand the objective with students who need reinforcement.

● Have pairs of students review the lesson and have them write the accomplishments of Julius Caesar, Caesar Augustus, and Constantine.

● You may wish to have students write down the information in graph form. For example, *Builders of the Roman Empire* could be the heading, and the names of the three emperors could be subheads.

Constantine built the Hagia Sophia as a Christian church, but since 1935 it has been a museum.
▶ Where is the Hagia Sophia?

ancient Greek city called Byzantium (buh-ZAN shee um). The new city was called Constantinople (kahn stan tuh NOH pul) —"the city of Constantine." Today it is known as Istanbul.

Constantine erected fine palaces and public buildings in the new capital. He had statues and monuments moved from the old Rome to the new. Unlike old Rome, there were no temples honoring the old Roman gods in the new capital. Constantine had adopted the Christian religion; he was the first Roman emperor to do so. Constantine also built a large Christian church called Hagia Sophia, which means "Church of Holy Wisdom."

Byzantine Empire In time the Roman Empire broke apart. The emperors at Constantinople ruled less and less of what had been the empire. Finally all that was left of the empire was the city of Constantinople and a part of Greece. Historians call the empire of later times the Byzantine Empire. The name comes from the original Greek city on the Bosporus strait. The Byzantine Empire grew out of the old Roman Empire, but it existed for about a thousand years after the fall of the Roman Empire in western Europe.

LESSON *2* REVIEW

THINK AND WRITE

A. What positions in the Roman government did Caesar hold? (Recall)
B. How did Caesar become dictator? (Recall)
C. What position did Octavian come to hold? (Recall)
D. What was the advantage of the site Constantine chose for the new capital? (Infer)

SKILLS CHECK

MAP SKILL

Using the map on page 110, name the areas Rome had added to its empire by the end of the Punic Wars.

111

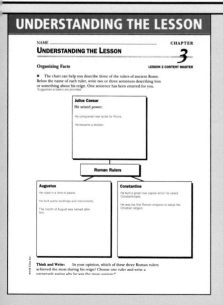

UNDERSTANDING THE LESSON

NAME _____ CHAPTER
UNDERSTANDING THE LESSON *3*

Organizing Facts LESSON 2 CONTENT MASTER

✶ The chart can help you describe three of the rulers of ancient Rome. Below the name of each ruler, write two or three sentences describing him or something about his reign. One sentence has been entered for you.
Suggested answers are provided.

Julius Caesar
He seized power.

He conquered new lands for Rome.

He became a dictator.

Roman Rulers

Augustus
He ruled in a time of peace.

He built public buildings and monuments.

The month of August was named after him.

Constantine
He built a great new capital which he called Constantinople.

He was the first Roman emperor to adopt the Christian religion.

Think and Write: In your opinion, which of these three Roman rulers achieved the most during his reign? Choose one ruler and write a paragraph saying why he was the most outstanding.

◀ Review Master Booklet, p. 27

Optional Activities

---

3 CLOSING THE LESSON

Lesson *2* Review

Answers to Think and Write

A. Caesar held the positions of quaestor, consul, governor of Gaul, and dictator in the Roman government.

B. Caesar became dictator by marching his army to Rome, gaining control of Italy, and defeating Pompey and other opponents throughout the empire.

C. Octavian became emperor.

D. Constantine chose the site because it would give him direct control over the largest population in the empire.

Answer to Skills Check

The areas that Rome had added by the end of the Punic Wars were Spain, Corsica, Sardinia, Sicily, Balearic Islands, Carthage, portions of Greece, and the land northwest of Greece.

Focus Your Reading

Ask the lesson focus question found at the beginning of the lesson: **What was the difference between the city-state republic and the empire?**
(In the city-state republic, people were ruled by two elected consuls who had equal power and served for only one year. In the empire, the people were ruled by emperors who had absolute power and served until their death.)

Additional Practice

You may wish to assign the ancillary materials listed below.

Understanding the Lesson p. 27
Workbook p. 33

┌─ **Answers to Caption Questions** ─┐
p. 110 ▶ The Mediterranean Sea
p. 111 ▶ In Istanbul
└───────────────────────────────────┘

Life in a Roman City

Objectives

★1. **Describe** what life was like in a Roman city.

2. **Explain** how Pompeii was destroyed.

3. **Identify** the following people and places: *Pliny the Elder, Pliny the Younger, Mount Vesuvius,* and *Pompeii.*

1 STARTING THE LESSON

Motivation Activity

■ Have students look at the photographs in this lesson and close their books.

■ Then ask them to write a paragraph describing what life was like in a Roman city. Tell students to save their descriptions until they have read the lesson.

■ After they read the lesson, have students compare their paragraphs to the lesson material to see how accurate their descriptions were.

Think About What You Know

■ Assign the THINK ABOUT WHAT YOU KNOW activity on p. 112.

■ Student answers may include artifacts, written records, and ruined buildings.

Study the Vocabulary

■ Discuss with students the new vocabulary words in this lesson by asking them if they have heard any of these words used before.

■ Then, ask them if they think they know the definition of any of the words.

■ Finally, ask the students to look up each of the words in the Glossary to see if they were using the correct definitions.

112

THINK ABOUT WHAT YOU KNOW

Imagine that you are an archaeologist digging up ruins of an ancient Roman city. What remains of the city might you expect to find?

STUDY THE VOCABULARY

volcano   gladiator

aqueduct

FOCUS YOUR READING

What can we learn from the ruins of Pompeii?

A. The Day the Mountain Erupted

Pliny the Elder, friend of the emperor, commanded the Roman fleet. From his house on the Bay of Naples, he could look across the water toward Mount Vesuvius (vuh SOO vee us). Shortly after lunch on an August day in A.D. 79, Pliny's sister drew his attention to a strange cloud rising from Mount Vesuvius. His nephew, known as Pliny the Younger, wrote that the cloud looked "like an umbrella pine tree," with a trunk rising high in the sky and then spreading out like branches. What they were seeing was the eruption of a **volcano**, which is an opening in the earth from which melted rock, stone, and ashes are thrown out.

Pliny the Elder had a great curiosity about things in nature, so he decided he wanted to take a closer look. He ordered that a small boat be made ready so that he could sail closer to the mountain. Just as he was preparing to leave, he received a message that people living on the lower slopes of the mountain were trapped and had no way to escape except by sea. Pliny ordered a ship so that he might rescue those fleeing from the volcano.

Pliny's ship reached the shore where the people waited, but he could not sail away because the wind was blowing in the wrong direction. To reassure people, Pliny went to a nearby house where he calmly ate supper and then lay down to sleep. During the night the fall of ashes became so heavy that it was feared the house might fall in. Pliny told people it would be better to wait in the open. He advised them to tie pillows on their heads to protect them from falling stones and heavy ashes. Pliny himself lay down on the beach, where he was later found dead. He was not buried in ashes nor hit by a falling rock. Pliny the Younger thought that his uncle had been killed by gas from the volcano. Modern writers think it more likely that he died of a heart attack.

112

Curriculum Connection

Art Ask students to draw a picture of Mount Vesuvius.

● Have students include (and label) the core, the mountain, the lava, and the crater of the volcano.

● You may wish to have students research volcanoes in the encyclopedia before drawing their pictures.

In this photograph you can see the ruins of Pompeii after Mount Vesuvius, shown in the background on the left, erupted in the year A.D. 79. The mosaic (inset) shows a painting that once decorated a wall in a Pompeian home.
▶ What can you tell about Pompeii from these ruins?

B. A City Beneath Ashes

The ashes and rocks thrown up by Vesuvius on that August day buried the city of Pompeii (pahm PAY ee). A layer from 19 to 20 feet (6 to 7 m) deep covered what had been a city of 20,000 people. Most Pompeians had fled in time, but some had not. Their bodies lay beneath the ashes.

Little was done after the eruption to uncover Pompeii. Not until 1748 did treasure hunters dig tunnels into the mound. They were seeking marble statues and other objects for wealthy buyers. Archaeologists did not begin excavating until after 1860. Since then, a large part of the city has been uncovered.

The disaster that destroyed the living city preserved the ruins of homes, baths, temples, and shops. These ruins tell a great deal about how people lived in a Roman city more than 19 centuries ago.

C. Old Ruins and Public Baths

Crowded Living Few things are as interesting to visitors to Pompeii as the ruins of houses and public baths. Pompeii had no large apartment buildings such as those in Rome, yet people had to live close together within this walled city. Houses were crowded along narrow streets that were not much wider than broad sidewalks.

Shopkeepers and their families usually lived in a room or two at the back of their shops. The houses of wealthier people had more rooms, but they, too, lived close to their neighbors. Houses did not have windows on the outside walls. Pictures of outdoor scenes were painted on the walls to make them seem larger. Rooms opened on an inner courtyard, which was only partly covered by a roof. Some of the largest homes had enclosed gardens with rooms along the sides.

113

To study life in Rome, it is important to compare it to other civilizations. The activities below will help your students understand this concept.

◆ **EASY** Have pairs of students skim the lesson to compare the way people lived in Pompeii to the way we live today.

Tell students to summarize their answers in a chart. You may wish to help students start by writing these headings on the chalkboard: *Conveniences, Industries,* and *Jobs.*

◀▶ **AVERAGE** Have students list similarities and differences between life in Rome and life in Greece.

Then have them identify the place where they would have prefered to lived.

◀▮▶ **CHALLENGING** Have students compare a modern civilization, other than our own, with Rome's.

Tell students to write a paragraph identifying these similarities and differences. You may wish to allow students to use the encyclopedia.

Read and Think

Sections C and D

To help students understand what life was like in ancient Rome, ask these questions:

1. **What was one of the similarities between the homes and the public baths of Pompeii?**
   (Many had running water. *p. 114*)

2. **What was Pompeii's largest industry?**
   (Making cloth *p. 114*)

3. **What crops did farmers of Pompeii grow?**
   (Grapes, olives, other fruits and vegetables, wheat, and barley *p. 114*)

Thinking Critically **Do you think having criminals fight as gladiators was fair?** (Evaluate)
(Answers will reflect independent thinking but should show some compassion for other human beings. *p. 115*)

114

City Water Some of the homes had running water. Other people could get water from flowing fountains in the streets. A water channel such as an **aqueduct**, or a stone canal, brought water to the city from a stream about 15 miles (24 km) outside the walls. Lead pipes under the street carried water to the houses and fountains.

Roman Baths The baths in a Roman city were more than places to wash up. A bath was somewhat like an athletic or health club where people met and exercised. They could relax in the steam room, take warm and hot baths, and then refresh themselves with a plunge in a cold bath.

Roman baths were where people went to socialize. Signs such as the one here advertised the baths.
▶ What purpose did the holes in the ceiling and the wall serve?

D. Making a Living in Pompeii

Farms A number of well-to-do families who lived in Pompeii owned land outside the city. They did not work on the land themselves, but they depended on their estates for their living. Farmers living in villages outside the city of Pompeii actually cared for the owner's vineyards and olive groves. Slaves also did much of the work on the land. The Romans, like the Greeks, had slaves.

Markets Farmers brought fresh fruits and vegetables to the city and sold them in the open marketplace. People who fished for a living also brought their fresh catch to the market.

Many Pompeians kept shops along the streets of the crowded city. Among other things, they sold olive oil, wine, leather goods, perfume, meat, and a fish sauce that most people liked.

Bakeries Much of the bread to supply the 20,000 inhabitants of Pompeii came from establishments which combined milling and baking. Pompeii had at least 40 bakery shops. Wheat and barley were brought directly to the bakery, where the grain was ground into flour. The large stone wheels in the bakery mills were turned by donkeys or slaves. Bakers made the flour into loaves and baked them. The bakery shops turned out at least ten different kinds of bread, not counting dog biscuits.

Making Cloth Pompeii's largest industry was making cloth. Country people spun and wove wool into rough cloth that they brought to the cloth finishing shops in the city. There workers bleached the cloth, that is, made it lighter. Then they would dye it. Judging by the size of the cloth finishers' hall, Pompeii must have had a number of people employed in this business.

Reteaching Main Objective

⭐ *Describe what life was like in a Roman City.*

● Have each student make a booklet showing what life was like in Pompeii.

● Each booklet should include drawings of the city's marketplace, peoples' homes, the baths, and Pompeian entertainment.

● You may wish to allow students to review the lesson before beginning this activity.

E. Roman Entertainment

The largest place of amusement in Pompeii was the amphitheater. An overhead awning provided shade for at least part of the audience. People could see plays at the theater or watch variety shows with clowns, jugglers, and acrobats. People enjoyed stage shows, but they did not consider acting a respectable occupation.

The amphitheater at Pompeii could hold almost the entire population. The fact that it was so large suggests that Pompeians liked the cruel, bloody sports that took place there. Most people in the Roman world did.

The amphitheater was a place for fights between wild animals. For example, bears were forced into fighting tigers. Lions were matched against wild bulls. The animals usually fought until one had killed the other.

Gladiators also fought in the amphitheater. Gladiators were usually slaves or condemned criminals who were trained to fight with swords and other weapons to entertain the crowds. Gladiators sometimes fought wild animals; sometimes they fought each other. The fight in the arena

Gladiators fought wild beasts to amuse the crowds.
▶ What weapons did the gladiator use to defend himself?

gave the gladiators a chance to escape their fate. A skillful gladiator might win his freedom by defeating his opponent. However, the loser all too often lost his life. Such sports were one of the least attractive parts of life in a Roman city.

LESSON 3 REVIEW

THINK AND WRITE

A. From what danger was Pliny the Elder trying to rescue people? **(Recall)**

B. Why have ruins of Pompeii been so well preserved? **(Recall)**

C. Describe a house and a public bath in Pompeii. **(Recall)**

D. What are some ways that people in Pompeii made a living? **(Recall)**

E. What were some of the entertainments in Pompeii? **(Recall)**

SKILLS CHECK

THINKING SKILL

Find *Mount Vesuvius* in the Gazetteer. What makes this volcano unique to Europe's mainland?

115

Writing to Learn

Writing an Editorial

Explain that an editorial has appeared in *The Roman Times* stating that "It is wrong for Romans to hold games in which people are killed for sport or amusement."

● Have students write letters to the paper either attacking or defending the editor's statement.

Optional Activities

---

3 CLOSING THE LESSON

Lesson 3 Review

Answers to Think and Write

A. Pliny was trying to rescue people from the volcanic eruption of Mount Vesuvius.

B. The ruins of Pompeii have been so well preserved because the city was buried under a deep layer of ashes and rock from the eruption of Mount Vesuvius.

C. Houses were small, had few rooms, and were built very close together. They did not have outside windows. Instead, they opened onto an inner courtyard. Roman baths were like modern-day health clubs. They included a steam room and cold baths.

D. People in Pompeii made a living by farming, fishing, retailing, baking, and making cloth.

E. Pompeian entertainments included: watching plays, variety shows, and stage shows; fights between wild animals and gladiators, and the public baths.

Answer to Skills Check

Mount Vesuvius is the only active volcano on Europe's mainland.

Focus Your Reading

Ask the lesson focus question found at the beginning of the lesson: **What can we learn from the ruins of Pompeii?**

(We can learn about the homes, the livelihoods, the foods, the industries, and the entertainments of the ancient Romans.)

Additional Practice

You may wish to assign the ancillary materials listed below.

Understanding the Lesson p. 28
Workbook pp. 34–35

┌─ **Answers to Caption Questions** ─┐
p. 114 ▶ To let light in and let sun warm the bathwater
p. 115 ▶ Shield and sword

115

The Beginning of Christianity

Objectives

★1. **Explain** why Christianity was against the law in the early Roman Empire.

2. **Discuss** what is contained in the Gospels.

3. **Name** the emperors who helped Christianity spread within the empire.

4. **Identify** the following people and places in this lesson: *Jesus, Pontius Pilate, Emperor Constantine, Emperor Theodosius the Great, Jerusalem,* and *Constantinople.*

1 STARTING THE LESSON

Motivation Activity

■ Ask students to list what comes to mind when you say the word "Christianity."

■ Share students' lists with the whole class by making a master list on the chalkboard. Add to the list until new additions have been exhausted.

■ Tell students that in this lesson they will learn about the beginnings of Christianity and its spread within the Roman Empire.

Think About What You Know

■ Assign the THINK ABOUT WHAT YOU KNOW activity on p. 116.

■ We gain information about the past through archaeological digs, written records, artifacts, buildings that still stand, primary and secondary sources, and oral history.

Study the Vocabulary

■ Have students look up the definitions of the vocabulary words for this lesson in the Glossary.

■ Ask students to think of examples of historical sources and parables. Write student answers on the chalkboard.

116

The Beginning of Christianity

THINK ABOUT WHAT YOU KNOW

Name ways in which we get some information from the past.

STUDY THE VOCABULARY

historical source   parable

FOCUS YOUR READING

How did Christianity in the Roman Empire change over the course of time?

A. Pliny the Younger and the Christians

Pliny the Younger was 17 when his uncle died on the beach near Vesuvius. He inherited his uncle's property and, following his example, became a Roman official.

Pliny the Younger wrote many letters that have been published. These letters are valuable **historical sources**. Historical sources are writings that provide information about the past.

In A.D. 110 the emperor sent Pliny to a province on the south shore of the Black Sea. This region is now part of Turkey. Pliny wrote a number of letters to the emperor, describing conditions in the province. In one letter, Pliny tells how he dealt with persons who were accused of being Christians. Christianity was one of the few religions that was against the law in the empire. The Romans allowed people to worship a wide variety of gods and goddesses so long as they also worshiped the

> The Sermon on the Mount is one of the most famous speeches of Jesus.
> ▶ How do we learn about the life and teachings of Jesus?

---

official gods of Rome. They considered that praying to the official gods showed loyalty to Rome. Since the Christians refused to worship the Roman gods, the emperors considered them dangerous.

Pliny wrote that when he questioned people charged with being Christians, he gave them three chances to deny it. If they did, he made them prove their loyalty by praying to the Roman gods. Pliny knew that no real Christian would do so.

The emperor replied that Pliny was doing the right thing. People had to be given a chance to prove that they were not Christians. Of course, if they refused, they had to be punished.

B. Writings About Jesus

The Christians, who were brought before Roman officials like Pliny, were followers of Jesus. Jesus had lived in the land of the Jews, which was part of the Roman Empire. Jesus wrote no books. What historians know about him comes mostly from

Optional Activities

Writing a Modern Parable

● Ask students to review the parable of the Good Samaritan in Section B.

● Then ask students to write a modern version of the parable.

● You may wish to have students brainstorm modern themes, such as helping a runaway teenager, helping a hurt animal, or helping a fellow classmate, before they write their parables.

Many of the teachings of Jesus were in the form of parables.
▶ How did the Good Samaritan help the man left to die?

Read and Think

Sections A, B, C, and D

To help students understand how Christianity began, ask the following questions:

1. **Why was Christianity against the law in the Roman Empire?**
   (Christians would not worship Roman gods, so the Roman government considered them to be dangerous. *p. 116*)

2. **What information is contained in the Gospels?**
   (Jesus's life and teachings *pp. 116-117*)

3. **What is the significance of Paul of Tarsus?**
   (He helped spread the teachings of Christianity through his writings. *pp. 118-119*)

4. **How did Constantine help spread Christianity?**
   (He forbade the erection of temples to the old gods; he gave Christianity a favored place in Constantinople. *p. 119*)

Thinking Critically Why, do you think, did Jesus use parables to explain his teachings? (Infer)
(Answers may include to help people understand the teachings by relating them to things that they knew. *p. 117*)

— **Answers to Caption Questions** —
p. 116 ▶ Through the Gospels and parables
p. 117 ▶ He put the man on his horse, brought him to an inn, and cared for him.

the writings of his followers. The most important sources about his life and teachings are four books that Christians call the Gospels. The Gospels are included in the Christian New Testament, a part of the Christian Bible.

According to the Gospels, Jesus did not teach in a school. Jesus talked to people wherever he found them. The Gospels tell of his teaching people on a mountainside and on the shore of a lake. Jesus often spoke of the Jewish laws and prophets in his teachings. All of his early followers were Jews. Jesus often explained his teachings by telling stories called **parables**. A parable is the teaching of Jesus in story form. One of the best-known parables, printed on this page, is the story of the Good Samaritan.

A man fell victim to robbers as he went down from Jerusalem to Jericho. They stripped and beat him and went off leaving him half-dead. A priest happened to be going down that road, but when he saw him, he passed by on the opposite side.

Likewise a Levite came to the place, and when he saw him, he passed by on the opposite side. But a Samaritan traveler who came upon him was moved with compassion at the sight. He approached the victim, poured oil and wine over his wounds and bandaged them. Then he lifted him up on his own animal, took him to an inn and cared for him. The next day he took out silver coins and gave them to the innkeeper with the instruction, "Take care of him. If you spend more than what I have given you, I shall repay you on my way back."

117

Curriculum Connection

Art Ask students to illustrate a scene in the life of Jesus.

● Have students review Section B to help them choose a scene to illustrate.

● You may wish to display students' illustrations in the classroom.

For Your Information

Paul of Tarsus Paul was a Jew from Tarsus (a city in present-day Turkey) who did much to spread Christianity throughout the Roman Empire. He not only became a Christian, but he also believed that the teachings of Jesus were for all people. Paul traveled throughout Asia Minor and to the cities of Greece spreading the Christian message.

Optional Activities

Meeting Individual Needs

Concept:
Religious Intolerance

To better study the history of Christianity, it is important to understand that freedom of religion was not practiced in ancient Rome. Below are three activities that will help your students understand this concept.

◆ **EASY** Ask students to find evidence in the lesson to support the statement, "The Romans did not allow freedom of religion," and discuss the importance of religious freedom.

◀▶ **AVERAGE** Ask students to write a defense or rebuttal to the following statement: "After the reign of Emperor Theodosius, Romans practiced religious freedom."

◀▮▶ **CHALLENGING** Have students research and compare religious intolerance in ancient Rome with that in Puritan Massachusetts.

Discuss what both societies did to prevent other religions from being practiced and to punish observers of other faiths. Then, have students debate which society was more intolerant.

GEOGRAPHY THEMES

 Location

■ Direct students' attention to the map on this page to help them respond to the following question: **Christianity spread to the islands of Crete and Cyprus in the first century. Where are these islands located?**
(In the Mediterranean Sea)

Jesus spoke to his followers about the "kingdom of Heaven." Some people took this to mean that he planned to overthrow the Romans and set up a government. These people had Jesus brought before Pontius Pilate, the Roman official at Jerusalem. Jesus was tried, condemned, and put to death by being nailed to a cross. The followers of Jesus believe that he rose from the dead three days later.

C. Paul of Tarsus

A man named Paul was one of the most important early Christian leaders. Paul was a Jew from Tarsus, a city which is located in present-day Turkey. Paul left his home to go to Jerusalem to study the Jewish law.

Paul at first strongly opposed the Christians, but he had a complete change of heart. Paul of Tarsus became a Christian and traveled from city to city to spread the Christian religion. Paul went to Athens, Greece, a city where people liked to hear about new things. The book of Acts in the New Testament of the Christian Bible contains an account of what Paul said to the Athenians.

Paul kept in touch with Christians in different cities by writing letters. These

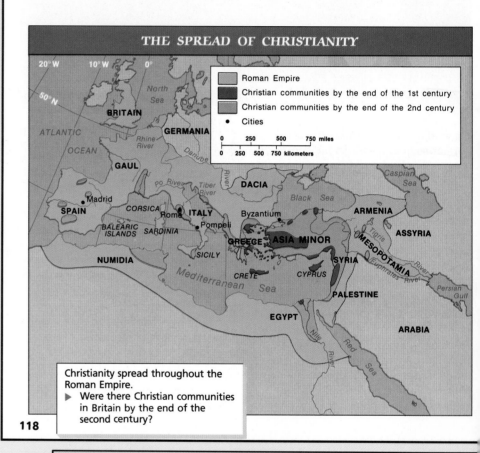

THE SPREAD OF CHRISTIANITY

Roman Empire
Christian communities by the end of the 1st century
Christian communities by the end of the 2nd century
• Cities

Christianity spread throughout the Roman Empire.
▶ Were there Christian communities in Britain by the end of the second century?

118

Reteaching Main Objective

⭐ **Describe the spread of Christianity throughout the Roman Empire.**

● Write these names on the chalkboard: *Pliny the Younger, Jesus, Paul of Tarsus, Constantine,* and *Theodosius.*

● Have students search the lesson for details about these people. Students should then write a short explanation of how each of these people helped or did not help the spread of Christianity.

letters, called epistles, are also a part of the New Testament. They are among the sources that historians use in tracing the history of Christianity.

D. The Official Religion of the Empire

Roman laws against the Christians did not keep their religion from spreading within the empire. As you have read, Emperor Constantine became a Christian ca. 312. What caused Constantine to accept the Christian religion? The emperor himself gave a reason to the Roman historian Eusebius (yoo SEE bee us).

According to Constantine's account, in the year 312 he was preparing for a battle in which his troops were greatly outnumbered. Before the battle, Constantine believed that he had a vision in which he saw a flaming cross against the sun and a message written across the sky that said, "By this sign you will conquer." Constantine's army won the battle and, in gratitude, Constantine proclaimed religious freedom throughout the Roman Empire.

Constantine did not try to do away with all other religions, but he did give Christianity a favored place in the new capital at Constantinople. However, he did

Constantine was the first Roman emperor to convert to Christianity.
▶ What event does this painting depict?

The Granger Collection

not permit the erection of temples to the old gods. Later, ca. 392, Emperor Theodosius the Great made Christianity the official religion of the empire.

LESSON **4** REVIEW

THINK AND WRITE   (Recall)
A. How could people brought before Pliny prove that they were not Christians?
B. What source do historians have for the life and teachings of Jesus? (Recall)
C. How did Paul of Tarsus spread Christianity? (Recall)

D. How did the position of Christians change between the times of Constantine and Theodosius? (Recall)

SKILLS CHECK

THINKING SKILL
You have read the parable about the Good Samaritan. What do you think Jesus was trying to teach in this parable?

119

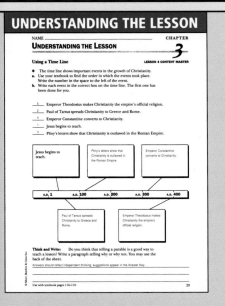

◀ Review Master Booklet, p. 29

Optional Activities

---

3 CLOSING THE LESSON

Lesson **4** Review

Answers to Think and Write
A. They could prove that they were not Christians by praying to the Roman gods.
B. Historians have the writings of the New Testament as a source.
C. He traveled throughout the Roman empire and Greece spreading the religion.
D. When Constantine ruled, Christians were merely allowed to practice their religion. By the time of Emperor Theodosius, Christianity was the official religion of the empire.

Answer to Skills Check
A good Christian is one who helps others.

Focus Your Reading

Ask the lesson focus question found at the beginning of the lesson: **How did Christianity in the Roman Empire change over the course of time?**
(At first, the Romans forbade the practice of the religion. Later, they allowed it. Finally, it became the empire's official religion.)

Additional Practice

You may wish to assign the ancillary materials listed below.

Understanding the Lesson p. 29
Workbook p. 36

┌─ **Answers to Caption Questions** ─
p. 118 ▶ No, there were not.
p. 119 ▶ Constantine's conversion to Christianity

Roman Achievements

Objectives

★**1. List** Roman contributions in law, language, and architecture.

2. Explain why the Romans felt it was necessary to write down their laws.

3. Identify the following places: *Rome,* and *Latin America.*

1 STARTING THE LESSON

Motivation Activity

■ Ask students to list ways that they could communicate without using the written alphabet.

■ Tell students that they will learn in this lesson that the Romans gave us our alphabet, as well as many other parts of our culture.

Think About What You Know

■ Assign the THINK ABOUT WHAT YOU KNOW activity on p. 120.

■ Student answers may include that people would be less safe.

Study the Vocabulary

■ Have students make a list of all the *Romance languages* (Spanish, Portuguese, French, Italian, and Romanian).

■ Ask them to try to identify a word from each language. You may wish to supply a list of words on the chalkboard.

LESSON **5**

Roman Achievements

THINK ABOUT WHAT YOU KNOW

Imagine that your city or town has no written laws. How would this affect the way you live?

STUDY THE VOCABULARY

ex post facto   Romance language
  law

FOCUS YOUR READING

What were some of the achievements of the Romans, and how do they influence our lives today?

A. A Need to Write Laws Down

In the days when Rome was a small city-state, a quarrel broke out between the patricians and the plebeians. It was a quarrel about laws. Rome at this time had no written laws. When a dispute arose between people, the law was whatever the judge said it was. Since only patricians could be judges, the plebeians complained that they were not treated fairly.

The quarrel between patricians and plebeians grew so bitter that it threatened to destroy the republic. To keep this from happening, ten leading men were chosen in 451 B.C. to collect and write down the laws. After working a year, the ten men called the citizens together and showed them ten wooden tables, or tablets, on

which they had written laws. The people were partly satisfied with the ten tables, but it was pointed out that they were not complete. Some laws had not been included. Two more tables were drawn up, making twelve in all.

Some laws of the Twelve Tables, such as one declaring that a patrician could not marry a plebeian, seem unfair to us today. But the Twelve Tables were only the beginning of Roman law. The Romans in later times created different and fairer laws.

B. Just Laws for an Empire

The Twelve Tables could not serve as the laws for Rome's large empire. The empire included so many different peoples, each with their own laws and customs. To govern these different groups, the Romans had to develop a system of laws that all of the groups would accept.

Some Roman philosophers observed that all peoples wanted laws to do the

Quarrels often arose between the patricians and plebeians, the two classes of Romans, about the fairness of their laws.
▶ What did the Romans do to make the laws clear?

Optional Activities

Writing to Learn

A Letter to the Editor Ask students to imagine that they are either Roman plebeians or patricians.

● Tell them to write a letter to the editor of their newspaper which supports or opposes putting Roman laws in writing.

same thing — provide justice. But what is justice? The philosophers said that justice is giving each person what he or she deserves. How can we know what each person deserves when people come from so many different groups? The philosophers pointed out that although people differed, they all had reason and the ability to think. A just law would be one that seemed reasonable to thinking people, whatever their group. For example, it would seem reasonable that people accused of a crime should have a chance to face their accusers and defend themselves.

Some Roman laws that are based on reason have lasted longer than their empire. The Constitution of the United States contains this rule: "No **ex post facto law** shall be passed." The Latin words *ex post facto* mean that no law can be used to punish a person for something done before the law was made. This rule seemed reasonable to both the ancient Romans and the Americans who wrote the Constitution. It still seems reasonable today.

C. The Roman Alphabet

Good ideas get passed around, and an alphabet is a good idea. Each letter of an alphabet stands for one of the sounds from which words are formed. It is far easier to learn an alphabet than to memorize the hundreds of signs used in either cuneiform or ancient Egyptian writing.

The Romans borrowed the idea of an alphabet from their Italian neighbors, the Etruscans (ee TRUS kunz). But the Etruscans had not invented the alphabet; they borrowed it from the Greeks. The Greeks in turn had borrowed the alphabet from the Phoenicians.

The Phoenicians were the ones who had established Hannibal's city of Carthage,

DEVELOPMENT OF THE ROMAN ALPHABET			
Phoenician	Greek	Etruscan	Roman
ⴹ	A	A	A
Ⴒ	B		B
ⴼ	Γ	⟩	C
ⴺ	Δ	△	D
ⴸ	E	ⴺ	E

This chart shows how each civilization that borrowed this alphabet changed it.
▶ Which letters of the Greek alphabet did the Romans change?

in North Africa. Their homeland was the land now called Lebanon, but they traded throughout the Mediterranean. It was from Phoenician traders that the Greeks learned the advantage of writing with an alphabet. The chart on this page shows the different ways in which the Phoenicians, Greeks, Etruscans, and Romans wrote *A B C D E*. Notice that the Etruscans did not have letters for *B* and *D*.

In time the Roman alphabet was used to write other languages. Today the languages of western Europe are written in the Roman alphabet. The words you are reading on this page are printed in that alphabet. It is the most widely used alphabet in the world.

121

Read and Think

Sections A, B, C, and D

To help students understand why so much of our culture is taken from the Romans, ask the following questions:

1. **What caused the Romans to write down their laws?**
(Without written laws, patrician judges were free to create or change laws at will. *p. 120*)

2. **Why weren't the Twelve Tables good laws for the empire?**
(They were not broad enough, some were unfair, and others were too severe. *pp. 120-121*)

3. **Why is an alphabet superior to cuneiform and ancient Egyptian writing?**
(Because the letters stand for sounds from which words are formed, and there are fewer letters than signs. *p. 121*)

4. **Why are Central and South America referred to as Latin America?**
(Their main languages developed from Latin. *p. 122*)

Thinking Critically Why, do you think, are Roman laws and the Roman alphabet such important contributions? (Evaluate)
(Answers may include that both are still used today by other nations such as our own. *pp. 120-121*)

┌─ **Answers to Caption Questions** ─┐
p. 120 ▶ They wrote them down.
p. 121 ▶ The C and D

Curriculum Connection

American Government Tell students that one Roman law stated, "It is better for a crime to be left unpunished than for an innocent person to be punished."

● Ask students if they agree with this law.

● Then ask them if our system of justice has adopted a similar rule. Have them identify what this rule is. (A person is innocent until proven guilty.)

For Your Information

The Roman Alphabet The entire alphabet was made up of only capital letters for hundreds of years. However, scribes who copied books often used rounded letters called uncials, which were easier to form than some capitals. True lowercase letters were developed later, when scribes, in order to save space, used smaller letters.

Optional Activities

121

Read and Think
Section E

To help students understand the Romans' building skills, ask the following questions:

1. **At what kinds of construction did the Romans excel?**
   (Road and bridge building, aqueducts, and concrete structures *pp. 122-123*)

Thinking Critically **Which Roman building achievement, do you think, was the most important?** (Hypothesize)
(Answers may include the Cloaca Maxima, the aqueduct at Pompeii, or the Pantheon, and should include details to support each choice. *pp. 122-123*)

D. The Language of the Romans

The alphabet was not the only thing western Europeans borrowed from the Romans. A number of them also borrowed the Latin language. As with the alphabet, the borrowers changed what they had borrowed. Spanish, Portuguese, French, Italian, and Romanian are different languages, but they all grew out of Latin. They are called **Romance languages** because they developed from the Roman tongue. Note that two of the Romance languages are the main languages of Central and South America. For that reason, those regions are known as Latin America.

English is not a Romance language, but it includes many words that come from Latin. For example, the following words used for parts of this book come from Latin words: *table, contents, unit, index.*

The Granger Collection

E. The Romans as Builders

Roads and Bridges The Romans were practical people. Their engineers did their best work when building useful structures such as roads, bridges, and aqueducts. One of the oldest structures in Rome is the Cloaca Maxima, the great sewer. It was built more than 2,500 years ago, and it still drains into the Tiber River.

Roman road builders knit the empire together with more than 2,500 miles (4,023 km) of roads. Many were simply dirt or graveled roads, but important highways were paved with flat stones. Engineers built beautiful arched stone bridges across streams and deep valleys. In some places, they tunneled through mountains.

The network of roads made it possible for the Romans to move armies quickly throughout the empire. Officials could

The Pont du Gard is a Roman aqueduct in southern France.
▶ What purpose did aqueducts serve for the Romans?

travel or send messages from one part of the empire to another. The fastest travelers went on horseback or in light carriages and could cover from 40 to 50 miles (64 to 80 km) a day. That seems slow now, but it was fast for that time. People did not travel faster overland until the invention of the steam locomotive centuries later.

Roman Buildings Aqueducts, such as that at Pompeii, carried water great distances from springs and streams to cities. In some places, aqueducts ran through tunnels. In others they were supported by stone bridges, as shown on page 122.

The Romans were master builders in concrete. The great dome on the Pantheon shows their skill. It rises 71 feet (22 m) from its base and is 142 feet (43 m) across. It has stood for nearly 19 centuries. The Pantheon is used as a model for modern buildings constructed today.

The Colosseum (kahl uh SEE um) was a huge stadium that covered 6 acres (2 ha) of land and could seat about 45,000 spectators. The Romans used the Colosseum as the site of mock naval battles, fights between gladiators, struggles between men and wild animals, and other forms of public entertainment. Ruins of the Colosseum still stand in Rome today.

The Pantheon, built ca. 126, served as a temple to the Roman gods.
▶ What building in the United States has a shape similar to that of the Pantheon?

LESSON 5 REVIEW

THINK AND WRITE   (Recall)

A. Why did the plebeians want written laws?

B. According to Roman philosophers, what kind of laws would different peoples accept? (Recall)

C. What different alphabets led to the one used in printing this book? (Recall)

D. Which languages are Romance languages? (Recall)

E. What are some types of structures built by the Romans? (Recall)

SKILLS CHECK

WRITING SKILL

Choose one of the Roman achievements mentioned in this lesson. Write a paragraph or two describing what your life would be like without that achievement.

123

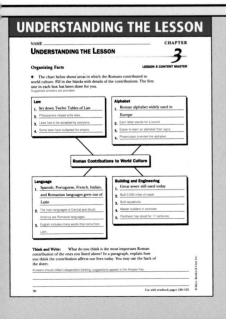
Optional Activities

Lesson 5 Review

Answers to Think and Write

A. Without written laws, the judges decided what the law was. Since only patricians could be judges, the plebeians felt that they were treated unfairly.

B. Different peoples would accept laws that provided justice and were reasonable.

C. The Phoenician, Greek, and Etruscan alphabets led to the one used in this book.

D. Spanish, French, Portuguese, Italian, and Romanian are Romance languages.

E. Roads, bridges, aqueducts, and concrete structures were built by the Romans.

Answer to Skills Check

Students' paragraphs should show an understanding of how life would be without the heritage of Roman achievements (laws, language, architecture, and alphabet).

Focus Your Reading

Ask the lesson focus question found at the beginning of the lesson: **What were some of the achievements of the Romans, and how do they influence our lives today?**
(The Romans developed written laws, an alphabet, and a language and built useful structures. Roman laws are found in our Constitution, we use the Roman alphabet, the Roman language led to the Romance languages, and Roman building know-how is still used today.)

Additional Practice

You may wish to assign the ancillary materials listed below.

Understanding the Lesson p. 30
Workbook p. 37

Answers to Caption Questions
p. 122 ▶ Aqueducts carried water great distances from springs and streams to cities.
p. 123 ▶ The Capitol in Washington, D.C.

Using the Vocabulary

1. dictator
2. emperor
3. historical source
4. patrician
5. republic
6. ex post facto
7. civil war
8. gladiators
9. aqueducts
10. Senate

Remembering What You Read

1. Patricians and plebeians
2. Romans and Carthaginians
3. He planned to become king and his enemies disagreed.
4. Augustus
5. Constantine
6. By farming, fishing, running shops and bakeries, and making cloth
7. Theater, variety shows, sports, fights
8. The Gospels
9. Spanish, French, Italian
10. Roads, bridges, buildings, and aqueducts

USING THE VOCABULARY

republic	civil war
patrician	aqueducts
Senate	gladiators
dictator	historical source
emperor	ex post facto

On a separate sheet of paper, write the word or words from above that best complete the sentences.

1. A person who takes complete charge of a government is called a _____.
2. Octavian was the supreme ruler, or _____, of the entire Roman Empire.
3. Writings that provide information about the past are called _____.
4. Roman landowners who had the most power, property, and money were called the _____ class.
5. Rome changed its form of government from a monarchy to a _____, in which people elect representatives to rule.
6. The Latin words _____ mean that no law can be used to punish a person for something done before the law was made.
7. Fighting between groups within the same city or country is called a _____.
8. Roman professional fighters, called _____, fought one another at public games.
9. Water was brought to the city through _____, or stone canals.
10. The wealthy kept their voice in government by serving in the _____.

REMEMBERING WHAT YOU READ

On a separate sheet of paper, answer the following questions in complete sentences.

1. The male citizens of Rome were divided into what two classes?
2. What two armies battled during the Punic Wars?
3. Why was Caesar assassinated?
4. What name did the Roman Senate give to Octavian?
5. Who was the first Roman emperor to adopt Christianity?
6. How did the people make a living in Pompeii?
7. Name some types of Roman entertainment.
8. From what writings have Christians learned about Jesus?
9. Name three Romance languages.
10. What types of structures did the Romans build?

TYING MATH TO SOCIAL STUDIES

The Romans used letters to represent numbers. These are the Roman numerals and their values:

I = 1	L = 50	M = 1,000
V = 5	C = 100	
X = 10	D = 500	

Write the numerical value for the following: XXX, XII, MMCCLV, LXV. Write Roman numerals for the following: 35, 58, 221, 553.

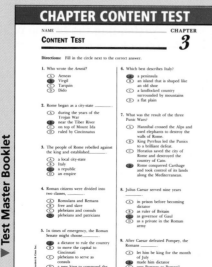

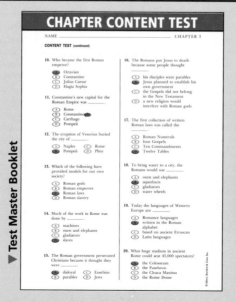

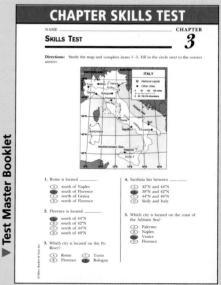

THINKING CRITICALLY

On a separate sheet of paper, answer the following questions in complete sentences.

1. The eruption of Mount Vesuvius destroyed Pompeii. What other natural occurrences can cause such destruction?
2. How was the government of ancient Rome like our government?
3. Compare the Romans' public games at the Colosseum with a modern-day sporting event.
4. What kind of a leader do you think Julius Caesar was?
5. What do you consider to be the greatest accomplishment of the ancient Romans?

SUMMARIZING THE CHAPTER

Copy this graphic organizer on a separate sheet of paper.
Beside the five questions, fill in each blank with an answer.

CHAPTER THEME	The influences of Roman government, law, religion, language, and architecture are still apparent throughout Western civilization.

LESSON 1	What were some characteristics of the Roman Republic?	1. _____ 2. _____ 3. _____
LESSON 2	What were some characteristics of the Roman Empire?	1. _____ 2. _____ 3. _____
LESSON 3	What can we learn from the ruins of Pompeii?	1. _____ 2. _____ 3. _____
LESSON 4	How did Christianity in the Roman Empire change over the course of time?	1. _____ 2. _____ 3. _____
LESSON 5	What were some of the achievements of the Romans?	1. _____ 2. _____ 3. _____

125

Thinking Critically

1. Earthquakes, hurricanes, tornadoes, and monsoons
2. The people had representation in government.
3. Roman public games were much more cruel to humans and animals than sporting events today (except for bullfights and cockfights).
4. Answers may include strong and courageous.
5. Answers may include government, alphabet, literature, architecture, science, or mathematics.

Summarizing the Chapter

Lesson 1
1. Representative government
2. City-state
3. Patricians and plebeians

Lesson 2
1. Rule by emperors
2. Rule by dictator
3. Adoption of Christianity

Lesson 3
1. Buildings
2. Markets
3. Entertainment

Lesson 4
1. Against the law
2. Tolerated
3. The official religion

Lesson 5
1. Law
2. Alphabet
3. Building

▼ Test Master Booklet

CHAPTER SKILLS TEST

NAME _____ CHAPTER 3

SKILLS TEST (continued)

Directions: Study the entries and complete items 6–10. Fill in the circle next to the correct answer.

Alps (alps). Mountain system extending in an arc from the Mediterranean coast between Italy and France through Switzerland and Austria and into the northwestern coast of the former Yugoslavia. The highest peak is Mont Blanc, with an elevation of 15,771 feet (4,807 m). p. 157.

Carthage (KAHR thihj). Ancient city and nation once located on coast of North Africa near the present-day city of Tunis, Tunisia. (37°N/10°E). p. 110.

Mediterranean Sea. (med ih tuh RAY nee un see). Large body of water surrounded

by Europe, Africa, and Asia. It is the largest sea in the world. p. 157.

Pompeii (pahm PAY ee). Ancient Roman city at the base of Mount Vesuvius. Destroyed in A.D. 79 by an eruption of Mount Vesuvius. (41°N/15°E). p. 110.

Rome (rohm). Capital and most populated city in Italy. Located on the Tiber River. Most important city in the Roman Empire. (42°N/12°E). p. 110.

Tiber River (TYE bur RIHV ur). River in Italy. p. 110.

6. The ancient city of Carthage was located near the present-day city of
   Ⓐ Tunis
   Ⓑ North Africa
   Ⓒ Tunisia
   Ⓓ Pompeii

7. Rome is located at
   Ⓐ 42°N/12°E   Ⓒ 42°E/13°W
   Ⓑ 38°N/42°E   Ⓓ 44°N/46°E

8. The highest point in the Alps is
   Ⓐ Mount Vesuvius
   Ⓑ Mount Everest
   Ⓒ Monte Albán
   Ⓓ Mont Blanc

9. If you wanted to see a map that contained Rome, you would
   Ⓐ go to Italy
   Ⓑ turn to page 92
   Ⓒ turn to page 110
   Ⓓ do what Romans do

10. Which is the largest sea in the world?
    Ⓐ the Pacific
    Ⓑ Mont Blanc
    Ⓒ the Mediterranean
    Ⓓ the Sea of Tranquility

© Silver, Burdett & Ginn Inc.

▼ Test Master Booklet

CHAPTER WRITING TEST

NAME _____ CHAPTER **3**
ESSAY TEST

Directions: Write a response to items 1–4.

> **REMINDER:** Read and think about each item before you write your response. Be sure to think of the points you want to cover, details that support your response, and reasons for your opinions. Then, on the lines below, write your response in complete sentences.

1. Describe two levels of society in the Roman Republic.
   A satisfactory response might include the following statements.
   • Patricians were landowners who held most of the wealth and power.
   • Plebeians were workers, artisans, merchants, and soldiers who could not hold public office and who had little voice in government.
   An excellent response might also
   • provide specific examples
   • mention that Rome also used slaves, who had no rights and were bought and sold like property.

2. How did Julius Caesar gain power in Rome?
   A satisfactory response might include the following statements.
   • Caesar served as consul and then became governor of the province of Gaul.
   • He conquered all of what is now France, Belgium, and Switzerland in the Gallic Wars.
   • Caesar's rivals gained power in Rome and ordered him to disband his army.
   • Caesar refused and led his army to Rome.
   • He defeated Pompey and his other rivals in a civil war.
   • Romans made him dictator for life.
   An excellent response might also mention the problems that led to Caesar's rule or provide specific examples.

© Silver, Burdett & Ginn Inc.

▼ Test Master Booklet

CHAPTER WRITING TEST

NAME _____ CHAPTER 3
ESSAY TEST (continued)

3. Why was Pompeii important to historians?
   A satisfactory response might include the following statements.
   • The volcanic eruption of Mount Vesuvius buried the Roman city of Pompeii in A.D. 79.
   • The city remained buried until the mid-eighteenth century.
   • Since then archaeologists have uncovered much of the ancient city.
   • The preserved ruins of homes, baths, temples, and shops tell historians a great deal about how people lived.
   An excellent response might also
   • provide examples of the discoveries in Pompeii
   • mention Pliny the Elder and Pliny the Younger
   • describe the disaster that buried the city.

4. Why did the Roman government persecute Christians, and why did it stop?
   A satisfactory response might include the following statements.
   • Romans allowed people to worship many gods as long as they prayed to the official gods too.
   • Christians refused to pray to the official gods.
   • Romans believed that Christians were disloyal.
   • The Roman Emperor Constantine became a Christian.
   • Later, Emperor Theodosius made Christianity the official religion.
   An excellent response might also
   • provide specific examples
   • explain why Christianity flourished in spite of persecutions
   • describe the conversion of Constantine.

125

Ancient India and China
(pp. 126-146)

Chapter Theme: The culture, society, and early history of India and China have made a lasting impact on each of the countries' civilizations.

LESSON 1 Cities on the Indus River
(pp. 126-130)

Theme: During this century, archaeologists have unearthed ancient cities that have taught us much about the history of the South Asian subcontinent.

 SOCIAL STUDIES LIBRARY: *Money*

LESSON 2 Buddhism and Hinduism
(pp. 131-134)

Theme: Buddhism teaches that the only way to a satisfying life is to forget yourself; Hinduism teaches respect for all living creatures.

 SOCIAL STUDIES LIBRARY: *The Cat Who Went to Heaven*

LESSON 3 The Beginnings of Civilization in China
(pp. 135-144)

Theme: The early history of China is marked by the reigns of wise rulers and the development of a Chinese system of writing and code of ethics.

SILVER WINGS WORKSHOP: The Walls Came Tumbling Down

 SOCIAL STUDIES LIBRARY: *Young Fu of the Upper Yangtze*

Review Masters

REVIEWING CHAPTER VOCABULARY

4

VOCABULARY MASTER

Review   Study the words in the box. Use your Glossary to find definitions of those you do not remember.

ascetic	caste	dialect	Pinyin
Brahman	Confucianism	nomad	subcontinent

Practice   Complete the paragraphs using words from the box above. You may change the forms of the words to fit the meaning.

The teachings of two men greatly influenced the people of Asia. The first was Siddhartha Gautama, whose family ruled part of the South Asian (1) _subcontinent_. The second was Confucius, who lived in a city-state in northern China.

Both men were interested in the way people lived. At first, Gautama tried to live the difficult life of an (2) _ascetic_. Later, he believed the way to live a satisfying life was to forget yourself. Gautama's teachings, which became the religion of Buddhism, taught people to live peaceful lives. Confucius's followers were taught to respect their superiors and be kind to other people. People who followed (3) _Confucianism_ also learned that it was better to get along with others than to argue.

The teachings of these two important people spread across their countries. Each man had followers who told others what they had learned. Long after Gautama and Confucius had died, people who lived in many different places and spoke many different languages and (4) _dialects_ heard about their teachings.

Write   Write a sentence of your own for each word in the box above. You may use the back of the sheet.

Sentences should show that students understand the meanings of the words.

_____

_____

_____

_____

_____

_____

_____

_____

_____

_____

LOCATING PLACES

4

PLACE GEOGRAPHY MASTER

✳   The South Asian subcontinent is set off from the rest of Asia by the Hindu Kush and Himalayan Mountains. Listed below are places of importance to modern and ancient civilizations of this region. Use the Gazetteer in your textbook to find the latitude and longitude of each place. Then locate and label each on the map.

		LAT. ⊖	LONG. ⦶
1.	Harappa	31°N	73°E
2.	Mohenjo-Daro	28°N	69°E
3.	Khyber Pass	34°N	71°E
4.	New Delhi	29°N	77°E
5.	Dacca	24°N	90°E

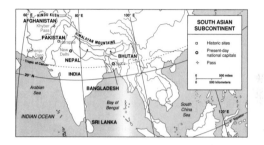

SUMMARIZING THE CHAPTER

4

GRAPHIC ORGANIZER MASTER

✳   Complete this graphic organizer. In both columns of the chart, fill in each box with an answer. Some boxes may have more than one answer.

CHAPTER THEME	The culture, society, and early history of India and China have made a lasting impact on each country's civilization.

ANCIENT CIVILIZATIONS	INDIA	CHINA
LEADERS	Asoka	Confucius, Shih Huang-ti
LANGUAGES	Indus script	Written characters
RELIGIONS	Buddhism, Hinduism	No organized religion
ARCHAEOLOGICAL DISCOVERIES	Mohenjo-Daro, Harappa	Oracle shells and bones, clay army
RIVERS	Ganges, Indus	Chang Jiang, Xi Jiang, Huang He

C4-B

Workbook Pages

THINKING LIKE AN ARCHAEOLOGIST

Classifying and Evaluating Information

✳ Archaeology is the scientific study of the materials of ancient civilizations. Such materials include buildings, pottery, and tools. An archaeologist is one who searches for and studies the materials to determine what life was like in the past. Archaeologists at the Harappa and Mohenjo-Daro sites uncovered a great deal of information about life in ancient India and Pakistan.

Imagine it is the year A.D. 3020. A team of archaeologists is conducting a "dig" in the remains of the community where you lived. What types of items might the archaeologists uncover to help them understand what life was like in the 1990s? Remember that an item must be very hard and strong to last for more than 1,000 years. For example, wood and cloth made in 1990 would probably disintegrate long before 3020. On the other hand, most metals and bricks can last for many centuries. Write at least two examples next to each type of item in the list below. Two items have already been listed for you.

Suggested answers are provided.

Type of Item	Examples
Home life	Microwave oven, dish, lawnmower, fork
Clothing	Shoe, brass button, zipper
Transportation	Automobile, train car, airplane, bicycle
Communications	Television set, radio, telephone, FAX machine
Art	Statue, mural
Recreation	Skateboard, baseball, soccer ball, computer game

Thinking Further: Archaeologists study the ancient past. Their work has little direct connection with our day-to-day life. Do you think archaeology nevertheless is important for all of us? Support your answer with two or three specific reasons.

Answers should reflect independent thinking; look for supporting reasons. Some students may say that by learning

about the past we understand the present better. Others may say the distant past is irrelevant to our present lives.

COMPARING THE BUDDHA AND ASOKA

Understanding Main Ideas and Details, Making and Supporting a Value Judgment

✳ Each statement below describes either the Buddha or Emperor Asoka. Write either **B**, for the Buddha, or **A**, for Emperor Asoka, in the blanks on the left.

B	1. His name means "the enlightened one."
A	2. He was a powerful ruler who decided that war and suffering were wrong.
B	3. He lived in caves to try to find a more satisfying way of life.
A	4. He erected stone pillars with Buddhist teachings carved on them.
A	5. He sent religious teachers to Alexandria and perhaps to China.
B	6. When he was growing up, he was not allowed to see or hear anything unpleasant.
A	7. He planted trees and dug wells to make travel in his kingdom more comfortable.
B	8. He was the son of a king who ruled part of what is now India and Nepal.
B	9. He believed that a truly wise person is an unselfish person.
A	10. He lived in the third century B.C.
B	11. He got his name from his students.
A	12. According to legend, his children planted a bo tree in Sri Lanka.
B	13. He was influenced by the sight of an ascetic.

100 % Blue

Thinking Further: According to legend, Siddhartha Gautama's life might have taken him in either of two directions. He could have become a powerful king or a great teacher of wisdom. He took the second direction and eventually became the Buddha. Tell whether you think Siddhartha took the right course. Give two or three reasons to support your opinion.

Many students will say he took the right course because his ideas

had great influence. Other students may say Siddhartha could have

built a great empire like Asoka.

EARLY CHINESE CIVILIZATION

Understanding Main Ideas and Details, Relating Information to Prior Knowledge, Evaluating Ideas

✳ The following statements might have been spoken by great figures in ancient China. Write the name of the likely speaker in the blank following each statement. A speaker may have uttered more than one statement.

1. "I showed the Chinese people the advantage of trade." Good Emperor Shen-nung

2. "I taught the Chinese people to respect all religions." Confucius

3. "I made sure that all Chinese used the same kind of money." Shihuangdi

4. "I was alive at the same time as the Buddha." Confucius

5. "I had the people build an army of clay soldiers to protect my tomb." Shihuangdi

Thinking Further: Here are some sayings that probably originated with Confucius and his followers. On the lines following each saying tell *in your own words* what the saying means. Then tell whether you agree or disagree with the saying. Do not write more than three sentences for any saying.

Suggested answers are provided.

1. "When you have faults, do not fear to abandon them." Possible restatement: do not remain wedded to faulty ways.

2. "To go beyond is as wrong as to fall short." Possible restatement: everything should be done in moderation. Many students probably will disagree with this saying.

3. "The superior man is modest in his speech, but surpasses in his actions." Possible restatement: an admirable person speaks modestly about his ability and accomplishes much more in practice.

4. "What you do not want done to yourself, do not do to others." Many students will recognize the similarity of this saying to the Golden Rule; see Matthew 7:12.

CHINESE CULTURE

Understanding Stated Facts and Details, Interpreting Information

✳ Read the following paragraph about the importance of writing in China since ancient times. Then complete each sentence in Column 2 below by writing in the correct word(s) from Column 1.

Writing and painting have been a part of Chinese life for many centuries. Many Chinese consider fine writing to be a part of painting. The same brush is used for both, and a painting and a poem are often prepared as one piece of art. The Chinese expect all writing to be expressed in beautiful language. This writing includes works about science, history, religion, and politics as well as poetry. The people chosen for government service have been highly honored in China. Government officers have long had to pass tests to obtain a post. The most important parts of these tests require candidates to demonstrate their ability to compose poetry or prose.

Column 1	Column 2
government service	1. To become government officials Chinese people have to show their ability to compose poetry and prose
write and paint	2. Writing and painting have been important in China for many centuries
many centuries	3. Writing and painting are often prepared together as one piece of art
test	4. People in China have been highly honored when chosen for government service
beautiful language	5. Writers of science and history are expected to use beautiful language
compose poetry and prose	6. Besides poetry, subjects of good writing are science, history, religion, and politics
one piece of art	7. One brush is used to write and paint
science, history, religion, and politics	8. To obtain a government post the Chinese have to pass a test

Thinking Further: Do you think poetry and painting are similar to one another, or are they quite different? Give specific reasons for your answer. Write your answer on a separate sheet. Answers should reflect independent thinking. Some students may feel that a poem and a painting both try to capture a moment in a beautiful way.

C4-C

Workbook Pages

INTERPRETING A MAP

Understanding Physical and Product Maps, Hypothesizing Based on Information

✳ Below are products and symbols to represent them and a map of part of the Indian subcontinent. The map depicts the upper Indus River System of modern Pakistan. Refer to the products list and map to answer the questions.

Barley Cotton Sheep
Rice Wheat

THE INDUS RIVER SYSTEM
○ National capitals
★ Provincial capital

1. In which area on the map do you think large numbers of people might have settled long ago? Give a reason for your answer. People might have settled in the fertile plain because conditions there would support agriculture.

2. Why would people be less likely to settle in the area south of the fertile plain? Settlement would be less likely because the area is a desert.

3. How might people reach Islamabad by land from Kabul? They might travel via the Khyber Pass.

4. In which direction does the Indus River System probably flow? It flows southwest, away from the mountains.

5. Name two reasons why a river system can be important to a region such as the fertile plain. A river system can supply water for drinking and crops and can be used for transport.

6. According to the maps, which of the products listed above are raised in the fertile plain? All—barley, cotton, sheep, rice, and wheat—are raised in the fertile plain.

Thinking Further: A limited number of items are produced in the fertile plain. What basic products would people of the region need to import, or bring in? In two or three sentences name a few imports and tell why they would be needed. Possible answers include: Metals are needed to make tools for farming; building materials are needed to construct houses; chemicals are needed to nourish crops and to kill insects.

42

Chapter 4, pages 127–144

© Silver, Burdett & Ginn Inc.

UNDERSTANDING KEY FACTS ABOUT BELIEFS

Interpreting Information in a Table

✳ Use the information in the table to help answer the questions below. (Islam is not included in the table because it was founded much later than the belief systems listed.)

Early Religions and Philosophies

Belief System	Region Where Founded	Time Founded	Traditional Founder	Major Holy Writings
Judaism	Middle East	ca. 1700 B.C.	Abraham	Torah
Hinduism	India	ca. 1500 B.C.	[no single founder]	Vedas
Buddhism	India	ca. 500 B.C.	Siddhartha Gautama	Tripitika
Confucianism	China	ca. 500 B.C.	Confucius	Five Classics
Christianity	Middle East	ca. A.D. 30	Jesus	Bible

1. In what order do the belief systems appear on the table? chronological

2. In what other logical order might the table be arranged? alphabetical

3. What does the abbreviation ca. stand for? circa What does this word mean? about, approximately

4. Over approximately how many years were the five belief systems founded? 1,730

5. In which regions were two beliefs founded? India, Middle East

6. Which belief system has no single founder? Hinduism

7. For which belief system are Five Classics the major holy writings? Confucianism

8. Which of the belief systems shown was founded earliest? Judaism

9. Which system's founder lived most recently? Christianity

10. Which two belief systems were founded at approximately the same time? Buddhism, Confucianism

Thinking Further: On which of the belief systems are the dates in the table based? How do you know? The dates are based on Christianity. The birth of Jesus marks the division between B.C. and A.D. dates.

© Silver, Burdett & Ginn Inc.

Chapter 4, pages 127–144

43

TEACHER NOTES

C4-D

Cities on the Indus River

Objectives

★ **1. List** three facts archaeologists have learned about the Indus people by studying the ruins of ancient Indus cities.

2. Describe what is known about early Aryan settlers on the South Asian subcontinent.

3. Identify the following people and places: *H. G. Wells, Mohenjo-Daro, Harappa, South Asian subcontinent, Indus River, Hindu Kush, Himalayas,* and *Ganges River.*

1 STARTING THE LESSON

Motivation Activity

■ Have students imagine that a time machine has carried them back to a city in Asia some four thousand years ago.

■ What would they expect to find? Ask them to write a short description of the scene.

Think About What You Know

■ Assign the THINK ABOUT WHAT YOU KNOW activity on p. 127.

■ Student answers may include the ease of trade and travel, availability of fish, a natural barrier against hostile armies, and a source of fresh water.

Study the Vocabulary

■ Have students look up the definition of each of the new vocabulary words for this lesson in the Glossary.

■ As a class, make a list on the chalkboard of words that use the prefix *sub.* (Possible words include *suburban, submarine, substitute, subway, subscribe,* and *subject.*) Ask what *sub* means (under, less than, secondary to, part of). Discuss which meaning of *sub* is used in *subcontinent.*

CHAPTER **4**

ANCIENT INDIA AND CHINA

The ancient civilization of India and China have dominated Asia for thousands of years. Their cultures thrived with powerful rulers, kingdoms, and religious beliefs.

Optional Activities

THINK ABOUT WHAT YOU KNOW
Why do you think a group of people would choose to develop a civilization near water?

STUDY THE VOCABULARY
subcontinent   nomad

FOCUS YOUR READING
How have we learned about the history of the South Asian subcontinent?

A. Cities the World Forgot

Could a book prevent war? An English writer, H. G. Wells, thought so. Wells believed that wars began because of the ways people think. He also believed that the ways people think depend on the kind of history they have learned. Wells noted that in 1919 most people knew little history except that of their own country. Wells thought that people needed to have a new kind of history. He set to work to write a book that would "tell truly and clearly the whole story of mankind so far as it is known."

Wells turned out a volume of about half a million words, which he called *The Outline of History.* He wrote of early civilizations in Mesopotamia, Egypt, Greece, Rome, and China. But his account of civilization along the Indus River in the country now called Pakistan consisted of only three short paragraphs.

Wells failed to mention the Indus cities because he could write history only "so far as it is known." In 1919, historians knew nothing of the Indus cities. Their history lay hidden beneath mounds on the plain of the Indus River.

It is true that British railroad builders had dug into one mound some years earlier. But they were not searching for an ancient city. They only wanted crumbling bricks and rubble on which to lay railroad tracks. Workers found a few carved stones, but no one had any idea that what they had dug into was the ruins of the ancient city Harappa (huh RAP uh).

B. Archaeologists Uncover Lost Cities

Shortly after Wells wrote *The Outline of History,* archaeologists started digging into a mound known as Mohenjo-Daro (moh hen joh DAHR oh). This name means "hill of the dead," but we have no idea what the place was called by the people who lived there 4,000 years ago.

The archaeologists discovered that the "hill of the dead" covered what must have been a city that existed from ca. 2300 B.C. to 1750 B.C. Archaeologists also discovered that Harappa, where the railroad builders had dug for rubble, had been a city of perhaps as many as 35,000 people ca. 2300 B.C.

Both Harappa and Mohenjo-Daro stood on river plains frequently covered by floods. Both cities had been erected on built-up platforms of earth and brick so as to be above the floods.

Since the 1920s, archaeologists have discovered the remains of a number of ancient towns and villages in Pakistan and parts of western India. These countries are located on the large peninsula that extends from southern Asia into the Indian Ocean. The peninsula is so large that it is called the South Asian **subcontinent**. It is called a subcontinent because although it is a large landmass, it is still smaller than a continent.

Read and Think
Sections A and B

To summarize the main points in this reading about Harappa and Mohenjo-Daro, the cities that lay hidden on the plain of the Indus River, ask the following questions:

1. **Why did H. G. Wells write *The Outline of History?***
(He thought that if people knew about the history of all nations, they would be less likely to go to war. *p. 127*)

2. **What does Mohenjo-Daro mean?**
(Hill of the dead *p. 127*)

3. **What was the population of Harappa?**
(Perhaps 35,000 *p. 127*)

Thinking Critically Why, do you think, did Wells believe that teaching people about history could prevent war? (Evaluate)
(Answers should reflect independent thinking but may include that knowledge of the history of other countries might increase mutual understanding, or that people could learn from other peoples' mistakes. *p. 127*)

Writing to Learn

Writing a Book Summary   Ask students to pretend that they work for H. G. Wells's publishers in 1919.

- They have been asked to write a one- or two-paragraph blurb to appear on the inside jacket of *The Outline of History.*

- Tell students that the purpose of the copy found on book-jacket flaps is to motivate the reader to open the book and read.

- Their goal will be to convince people to buy Wells's interesting and important book.

Curriculum Connection

Science   When archaeologists find pottery and ceramic objects they learn more about a culture than just its artistic style and taste.

- Ask students what other things pottery can tell us about a culture. (People acquired some technical and scientific knowledge as well as artistic skills.)

- Ask students to discuss the kinds of scientific and technical knowledge needed to create pottery. (Answers may include the kind of material or clay to use, how much water to add, which plants and minerals can be ground up to make colors, how to make ovens, how long to bake objects, and baking temperature.)

Optional Activities

Read and Think

Sections C, D, and E

Ask students to think about what they have learned about Mohenjo-Daro, Harappa, and the Aryans. Use the questions below to discuss this material:

1. **How do we know that Mohenjo-Daro was a planned city?**
   (Main streets formed a grid; houses were much alike; each bathroom had a drain connected to a sewer *p. 128*)

2. **What makes scholars believe that the Indus people knew how to write?**
   (Stone seals carved with script *p. 129*)

3. **Why are there no ruins to tell archaeologists about the early Aryans?**
   (They did not build cities. *pp. 129-130*)

Thinking Critically What, do you think, do the findings of archaeologists tell us about how rich or poor Mohenjo-Daro and its inhabitants were? (Analyze)
(Answers may include that luxuries such as jewelry, and the buildings for storing extra grain show that they were wealthy. *pp. 128-129*)

GEOGRAPHY THEMES

Human-Environment Interactions

■ Have students look at the map of Ancient India on p. 129 and ask this question: **If you were an archaeologist looking for ancient cities, which regions on this map would you excavate first and why?**
(Answers may include river valleys, because most ancient cities were built near rivers.)

C. Ruins Tell a Story

A City Plan Many ancient cities grew haphazardly, that is, without any plan. But the ruins of Mohenjo-Daro tell a different story. The main streets were laid out in straight lines, forming a grid. People lived in brick houses that were much alike. Each had a bathroom with a drain in the floor. The drains connected with sewers that ran along the streets. It seems clear that someone planned and directed the building of this city. It could hardly have grown in such a regular pattern on its own.

Ancient Findings Various objects found by the archaeologists tell about games and toys of the Indus people. They had dice and stone marbles. The spots on the dice are arranged in exactly the same pattern that appears today. Among the toys there were a clay monkey that could be made to slide down a string and a clay bull that wiggled its head. A little clay cart must have looked much like a real one.

Jewelry from the ruins shows that the Indus people traded for goods from other lands. There are beads of turquoise, jade,

Artifacts discovered in the ruins of the ancient city of Harappa provided clues about the lives of the Indus people.
▶ What ancient artifacts are shown here?

Optional Activities

Cooperative Learning

Role-Playing Divide the class into groups of four or five and allow one class period for this activity.

● Have each group make up a brief skit about a meeting between 12-year-olds in Mohenjo-Daro and children in your class.

● Assign one or two students in each group the responsibility of writing about the similarities between the two groups of children, and have one or two others write about the differences between the two groups. Assign one student the role of constructing or finding appropriate props for the skit. Students should then work as a group to put the skit together. Have the groups take turns presenting their skits to the rest of the class.

nd jasper. These stones are not found ear the Indus plain, so the Indus people ust have traded for the stones.

The ruins of the city give proof of what as grown on the land. The largest struc- res were granaries, buildings for storing rain. Traces of cotton fibers on a silver ox show that the Indus people were the rst to grow cotton.

. Mysteries Still Remain

eligion The remains in the mounds have evealed much, yet mysteries remain. We now little about the religion of the Indus eople. It is not clear what role religion layed in the Indus civilization. However, number of clay images have led histo- ans to think that these people may have orshiped a mother goddess. The bodies f the dead were buried with their heads to he north. Was this related to their reli- ous beliefs? We do not know.

anguage The greatest unsolved mys- ry is the language that the Indus people poke. Historians do not know what it as. If they knew, perhaps they could find ut more about the Indus people, such as here they came from and what happened them. It appears that they had some sort f writing. Archaeologists have found tone seals with a type of script carved on em, but no one knows how to read it. No ne has found a Rosetta stone for the dus script.

Historians are not sure what hap- ened to the Indus cities. The cities seem have been abandoned ca. 1700 B.C. It is ossible that future discoveries will help to olve this mystery. Historians may some- ay be able to write much more about the dus cities that H. G. Wells did not even now existed.

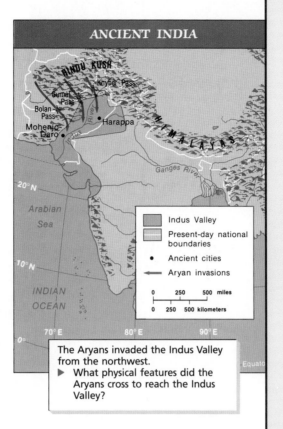

ANCIENT INDIA

- ▨ Indus Valley
- ▢ Present-day national boundaries
- • Ancient cities
- ← Aryan invasions

0   250   500 miles
0 250 500 kilometers

The Aryans invaded the Indus Valley from the northwest.
▶ What physical features did the Aryans cross to reach the Indus Valley?

E. The Aryans on the Subcontinent

The subcontinent is set off from the rest of Asia by a mountain wall formed by the Hindu Kush and the Himalayas. Passes in the northwestern part of the Hindu Kush have served as gateways through which peoples have moved from time to time. It was through these gate- ways that the Aryans (ar EE unz) entered the subcontinent between 1500 B.C. and 1000 B.C.

The early Aryans were **nomads**, tribes of people who moved about with herds of goats, sheep, and cattle. Since

129

◆ **Meeting Individual Needs**
Concept:
Using Artifacts to Draw Conclusions

It is important to understand how scholars use artifacts to draw conclusions. Below are three activities that will help your students understand this concept.

◆ **EASY** Have students work in pairs to make a list of artifacts found at Mohenjo-Daro.

Have them group artifacts under the headings *Food*, *Shelter*, *Work*, and *Play* which describe different aspects of life in Mohenjo-Daro.

◀▶ **AVERAGE** Have students make a list of the artifacts of Mohenjo-Daro and group them under *Food*, *Shelter*, *Work*, and *Play*.

Then have them write a paragraph de- scribing their criteria for the groups.

◀▮▶ **CHALLENGING** Have students make a list of objects that they would include in a time capsule to be opened in A.D. 6000.

Have them exchange their lists with one another. Based on their partner's list, have students write a paragraph about the society from which the artifacts came.

┌─ **Answers to Caption Questions** ─┐
p. 128 ▶ Pottery, stone seal with script, and a toy horse
p. 129 ▶ The Hindu Kush and the Indus River

Reteaching Main Objective

List three facts archaeologists have learned about the Indus people by studying the ruins of ancient Indus cities.

- Ask students to think about the artifacts that archaeologists found in the Indus River Valley.

- Then draw the graphic organizer to the right on the chalkboard and have students supply answers for the three subheadings. Ask students to come to the chalkboard and list an artifact under the statement that the artifact proves.

- Have the class decide whether or not each artifact is categorized under the correct heading and write each one under the appropriate heading on a sheet of paper.

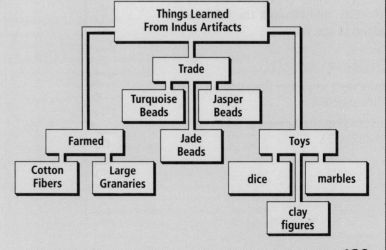

Things Learned From Indus Artifacts
- Trade
  - Turquoise Beads
  - Jasper Beads
- Farmed
  - Cotton Fibers
  - Large Granaries
- Jade Beads
- Toys
  - dice
  - marbles
  - clay figures

Optional Activities

129

3 CLOSING THE LESSON

Lesson 1 Review

Answers to Think and Write

A. According to H. G. Wells, by learning history, people might realize that they have a lot in common with other nations and might be less likely to go to war against them.

B. Indus cities were built on platforms of brick and earth to protect them from floods.

C. Archaeologists learned that Mohenjo-Daro was a planned city, the Indus people played with toys, traded with people from other regions, and grew grains and cotton.

D. The language and religion of the Indus people and why they abandoned their cities are still mysteries to us.

E. We know about the early Aryans through hymns and chants that were eventually written down in books called Vedas.

Answer to Skills Check

Student letters may include that Mohenjo-Daro and Harappa were planned cities erected on platforms on a flood plain. The houses were much the same; each had a bathroom with a drain in the floor. The residents traded for jewelry and grew grains and cotton.

Focus Your Reading

Ask the lesson focus question found at the beginning of the lesson: **How have we learned about the history of the South Asian subcontinent?**
(We have learned about the history of the South Asian subcontinent by studying ruins of cities that have been excavated by archaeologists, and through the information contained in the Vedas.)

Additional Practice

You may wish to assign the ancillary materials listed below.

Understanding the Lesson p. 34
Workbook p. 38

130

The warlike Aryans settled on the lands they conquered.
▶ What form of transportation did the Aryans use?

they built no cities, they left no ruins to tell their story to archaeologists. They had no written language, so they left no written sources for historians.

Most of what we know about the early Aryans comes from hymns and chants. These were not written down until much later. They were preserved in the memories of priests. In much later times the hymns were put into books called Vedas, a name that means "knowledge." The language of the Vedas is Sanskrit (SAN-skriht). Some modern languages spoken in India come from Sanskrit.

When the Aryans came through the mountain passes, they were a warlike people. They drove horse-drawn chariots into battle. The sight of galloping horses pulling armed warriors in chariots must have struck fear in the hearts of lightly armed foot soldiers.

After entering the subcontinent, the Aryans settled on the lands that they had conquered. In time, herders took up farming. Later many of the Aryans moved eastward into the plain of the Ganges River. The descendants of the Aryans became the rulers of many kingdoms in the subcontinent.

LESSON 1 REVIEW

THINK AND WRITE

A. In what ways could history that people have learned influence the ways they think? (Analyze)

B. How were the Indus cities protected from floods? (Recall)

C. What facts did archaeologists learn from what they found in the ruins? (Recall)

D. What mysteries about the Indus people remain? (Recall)

E. How do we know about the early Aryans? (Recall)

130

SKILLS CHECK

WRITING SKILL

Pretend you were one of the archaeologists who uncovered the ancient cities of Mohenjo-Daro and Harappa. Then imagine that H. G. Wells asked you to send him a report on your findings so he could continue his book *The Outline of History*. Write him a letter describing your discoveries.

Optional Activities

UNDERSTANDING THE LESSON

NAME _____
UNDERSTANDING THE LESSON

CHAPTER **4**

Recalling Facts
LESSON 1 CONTENT MASTER

✳ Read each statement below. Write **True** if the statement is true and **False** if it is false. If the statement is false, cross out the part that is incorrect and write the correct words above it.

True	1. Before 1919, historians knew nothing about early Indus people.
False	2. Harappa and Mohenjo-Daro were early Indus burial grounds.
False	3. Both Harappa and Mohenjo-Daro were built far from rivers to protect them from flooding.
False	4. The way the streets of Mohenjo-Daro were laid out shows that the city's growth was haphazard.
True	5. Evidence shows that Indus River people grew grain and cotton.
False	6. Historians would know more about these people if samples of their writing were found.
True	7. The Indus cities seem to have been abandoned about 1700 B.C.
False	8. The Aryans came to the subcontinent through passes in the Himalayas.
False	9. The early Aryans were farmers who left no ruins to tell their story.
True	10. Most of what we know about the early Aryans comes from hymns or chants handed down from the priests to their students.
True	11. Many Aryan hymns were written down in books called Vedas.
True	12. The descendants of the Aryans ruled many kingdoms on the subcontinent.

Think and Write: What sort of information would we learn about the Indus people if we knew their language? Write a paragraph giving some examples. You may use the back of the sheet.

Answers should reflect independent thinking; suggestions appear in the Answer Key.

◀ **Review Master Booklet, p. 34**

LESSON 2

Buddhism and Hinduism

THINK ABOUT WHAT YOU KNOW

If you were asked to name five things in your life that make you the happiest, what would they be?

STUDY THE VOCABULARY

ascetic   caste
Brahman

FOCUS YOUR READING

What were some teachings of the Buddha and of Hinduism?

A. The Suffering of a Prince

Siddhartha Gautama (sihd DAHR tuh GOUT uh muh) was the son of a king who ruled a land that included part of what is now India and Nepal. Many stories and legends have been told about Siddhartha. At the time of Siddhartha's birth, ca. 563 B.C., a priest said that Siddhartha would become either a great king or a great teacher of wisdom. If he remained in his father's palace, he would become a king. But if he learned of the suffering outside the palace and its gardens, he would become a teacher.

The king wished above all else that his son would become a great king. To keep him satisfied with life at the royal court, the king built his son several palaces. The king even tried to keep Siddhartha from seeing or hearing anything unpleasant. Gardeners even picked the flowers once they had bloomed so that the prince never saw a fading or dead blossom.

One day as he rode in his chariot, Siddhartha happened to see a weak old man. He asked his driver what had happened to the man. The driver replied,

"Such is life, he has grown old as everyone must." On another day, Siddhartha saw a man suffering from a painful illness. The prince asked his driver if others suffered from illness. Again the driver answered, "Such is life, many are ill." On a third day, Siddhartha saw the body of a dead man. When he asked if others died, the driver said, "Such is life, all must die."

B. Siddhartha's Search

Finding Contentment Prince Siddhartha thought much about what he had learned. He no longer found life within the palace rewarding. He wanted to find a

This statue of the Buddha stands in India. Buddha is the name Siddhartha's followers gave him.
▶ Of what is the statue made?

131

Creating a Documentary

- Divide students into three groups. Assign each group a portion of Siddhartha's life (in the palace, as an ascetic in the forest cave, and under the bo tree, where he received enlightenment).

- Students in each group should work together to write the copy for an "on-air" presentation. The three segments will fit together to form a television documentary that summarizes the life of Siddhartha.

- You may wish to have them include interviews with characters such as Siddhartha's chariot driver or Siddhartha's father. Choose a reporter from each group to read that group's portion of the documentary to the rest of the class.

Optional Activities

LESSON 2   PAGES 131–134

Buddhism and Hinduism

Objectives

★1. **List** teachings of Buddhism and Hinduism.

2. **Describe** the origins of Hinduism and Buddhism.

3. **Identify** the following people and places: *Siddhartha Gautama, Buddha, Asoka, Brahmans, India, Nepal,* and *Sri Lanka.*

1 STARTING THE LESSON

Motivation Activity

- Tell students that in this lesson they will learn about a rich young man who had wealth and lived in beautiful surroundings, yet found his life unsatisfying.

- Ask students to guess what they think was missing in his life. (Answers may include a sense of purpose, development of a skill, satisfaction gained by helping others, and so on.)

Think About What You Know

- Assign the THINK ABOUT WHAT YOU KNOW activity on p. 131.

- Student answers should reflect independent thinking but may include family, friends, religion, money, food, sports, and other things that make them happy.

Study the Vocabulary

- Have students look up the definition of each of the new vocabulary words in the Glossary.

- Have students skim the lesson to find how the vocabulary terms are used in context (*ascetic:* a holy man; *Brahman:* ancient Hindu priest; *caste:* social class in early Aryan society).

Answers to Caption Questions

p. 130 ▶ Horse-drawn chariots
p. 131 ▶ Carved stone or rock

131

Read and Think

Sections A, B, C, and D

Discuss Buddhism and Hinduism by asking the following questions:

1. **What prediction did the priest make about Siddhartha Gautama?**
(He would become either a great king or a great teacher of wisdom. *p. 131*)

2. **What did Siddhartha realize when he received enlightenment?**
(He realized that he had been thinking only of himself and the way to a satisfying life is to forget yourself. *p. 132*)

3. **Who was Asoka, and what did he do?**
(The most powerful ruler of the subcontinent in 269 B.C. who helped spread Buddhism *p. 133*)

4. **Why do many Hindus eat only grain and vegetables?**
(Because they believe it is wrong to kill animals *p. 134*)

Thinking Critically **Why, do you think, does Buddhism urge its followers to respect the religious beliefs of others?** (Hypothesize)
(Answers may include that the Buddha never intended for Buddhism to replace other religions. *p. 134*)

VISUAL THINKING SKILL

Using a Time Line

■ Direct students' attention to the time line on this page. Ask the following question: **When did cities begin to develop in the Indus Valley?**
(Ca. 2500 B.C.)

more satisfying way of life. As he was thinking, he saw an **ascetic**, a holy man who had given up all comforts and pleasures. The ascetic had no possessions, ate very little, and seemed not to notice pain. Perhaps, Siddhartha thought, this is the satisfying way of life. One night he slipped out of the palace and joined a group of ascetics living in forest caves. He adopted their way of life. He prayed, recited chants, and fasted, that is, ate very little food. He fasted so strictly that he nearly died. The other ascetics admired Siddhartha's spirit, but he was not yet content. He still had not found a satisfying way of life.

Siddhartha left the ascetics. One day he seated himself under a bo tree and vowed that he would not arise until he understood why he had failed to find a satisfying way of life. It was under the bo tree that Siddhartha received enlightenment, or understanding. He realized that in the palace and in the forest cave, he had been thinking only of himself. The way to a satisfying life is to forget yourself.

Buddha Other people came to learn from Siddhartha. He told them, "A man is not learned because he talks much; he who is patient, free from hatred and fear, is called learned." A wise person understands that "the fault of another is easily seen, but the fault of oneself is hard to see."

Siddhartha spent the rest of his long life teaching others what he had discovered. Those whom he taught called him the *Buddha,* which means "the enlightened one." His followers are called Buddhists.

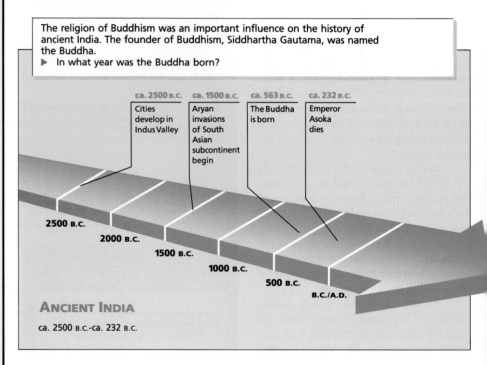

The religion of Buddhism was an important influence on the history of ancient India. The founder of Buddhism, Siddhartha Gautama, was named the Buddha.

▶ In what year was the Buddha born?

ca. 2500 B.C.	ca. 1500 B.C.	ca. 563 B.C.	ca. 232 B.C.
Cities develop in Indus Valley	Aryan invasions of South Asian subcontinent begin	The Buddha is born	Emperor Asoka dies

2500 B.C.

2000 B.C.

1500 B.C.

1000 B.C.

500 B.C.

B.C./A.D.

ANCIENT INDIA
ca. 2500 B.C.–ca. 232 B.C.

Optional Activities

Writing a Personal Essay

● Discuss the concept of enlightenment with students.

● Tell them that it means more than learning something new. It means finding a whole new spiritual or ethical way of seeing oneself and the world.

● After defining the words *spiritual* and *ethical* for your students, ask them to write a brief essay about a person or an event that has given them new understanding of the way that they feel they should live.

● Students who feel that they have never had such an experience might write about why they would or would not like to have this happen.

C. Asoka Spreads Buddhism

The Buddha chose to be a great teacher rather than a great king. But it was a ruler who did much to spread Buddhism in later times. Emperor Asoka (uh SOH-kuh) was the most powerful ruler on the subcontinent ca. 261 B.C. In his early years he was a warlike king who attacked and conquered a neighboring kingdom. But the death and suffering caused by the war greatly troubled Asoka. He declared that he would never again go to war.

Asoka turned to the teachings of the Buddha. He decided to relieve suffering rather than cause it. He had trees planted along roads to shade hot, weary travelers. Asoka ordered that wells be dug so that travelers could refresh themselves. He also built hospitals to care for people and for animals.

Asoka believed that his duty to his people came before everything else. He instructed his officials to keep him informed about the affairs of his people. If necessary, the officials were told to interrupt him if he was busy and awaken him if he was sleeping.

Asoka wished his people to learn of the Buddha's teachings. He built stone pillars with Buddhist teachings carved on them. Some of Asoka's pillars still stand. One pillar has the following message.

> Father and mother must be listened to; the teacher must be respected by the pupil; and courtesy must be shown to friends, relatives, and servants.

Asoka sent Buddhist teachers to other lands. Some went west to Alexandria in Egypt and perhaps to other Mediterranean lands. Asoka's son and daughter went to Sri Lanka, the island off the southern tip of the subcontinent. According to a

Asoka built stone pillars and had Buddhist teachings carved on them.
▶ What is carved on top of Asoka's pillar?

Lesson 2 Review

Answers to Think and Write

A. Siddhartha's father tried to keep him from learning about suffering because he wanted his son to be a king, and the priest had predicted that Siddhartha would be a teacher if he learned about suffering.

B. Siddhartha decided that in both the palace and the cave he had thought only of himself, and that he had to forget himself if he wanted a truly satisfying life.

C. Asoka taught others about Buddhism by making an example of himself, by carving the teachings of Buddha on pillars for people to read, and by sending teachers to carry Buddha's message to other countries.

D. Hinduism accepts the worship of all gods and goddesses and teaches respect for all living creatures.

Answer to Skills Check

Student answers may include that the mouth of the body was used to represent the Brahmans because they spoke to the people about religion; the feet were used to represent the workers because they did the lowly manual labor that was needed to carry the society.

Focus Your Reading

Ask the lesson focus question found at the beginning of the lesson: **What were some teachings of the Buddha and of Hinduism?** (The Buddha taught that the key to a satisfying life was overcoming selfishness. He urged his followers to relieve suffering, to show respect to parents and teachers, to be courteous to friends and servants, and to respect other religions. Hinduism accepted the worship of many different gods and taught respect for all living creatures.)

Additional Practice

You may wish to assign the ancillary materials listed below.

Understanding the Lesson p. 35
Workbook p. 39

---

legend, they carried with them a root from the bo tree under which the Buddha had sat. They planted the tree in Sri Lanka, where some say it still grows.

D. A Religion of Many Beliefs

Hinduism Asoka did not intend that Buddhism replace other religions. Buddhism did not, in fact, become the religion of the subcontinent. The religion of most peoples in this land is called Hinduism.

Hinduism grew partly out of the religion of the early Aryans as it is described in the Vedas. The early Aryans believed in a number of gods. Like the Greeks, the Aryans thought that the gods and goddesses were like human beings except that they had greater powers and did not die.

Caste System The early Aryans were divided into four social classes: priests, called **Brahmans**; warriors and rulers; farmers and merchants; and lowly workers. These classes have been called **castes**. A person's caste depended upon birth. Each caste had its special duties.

Hinduism accepts the worship of all gods and goddesses, although some of them are considered more important than others. Hinduism teaches respect for all living creatures. Many Hindus eat only

The Aryan god Indra is shown holding symbols of his power in his many hands.
▶ On what is Indra riding?

grain and vegetables because they believe it is wrong to kill animals.

Hinduism remains the religion of most people in India, which is the largest country on the subcontinent today. When people moved from India to other lands, they took the Hindu religion with them.

LESSON 2 REVIEW

THINK AND WRITE

A. Why did Siddhartha's father try to keep him from learning about suffering? (Recall)
B. Why did Siddhartha decide that he had failed to find a satisfying way of life in either the palace or the forest cave? (Recall)
C. How did Asoka teach others about Buddhism? (Recall)
D. What are the beliefs of Hinduism? (Recall)

SKILLS CHECK

THINKING SKILL

One of the Vedas compares the castes with parts of the body. For example, the Brahmans are the mouth, and the workers are the feet. How would you explain this comparison?

Optional Activities

UNDERSTANDING THE LESSON

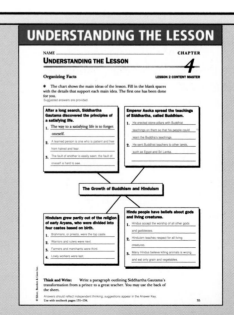

◀ Review Master Booklet, p. 35

The Beginnings of Early Civilization in China

Try to write a sentence using only symbols to stand for your words.

STUDY THE VOCABULARY
dialect **Confucianism**
Pinyin

FOCUS YOUR READING
What does the early history of China tell about Chinese ideals, writing, and government?

A. Chinese Legends

Shen-nung The Chinese in ancient times told legends about the "Good Emperors" of still earlier times. The legends did not explain exactly what happened in those times, so they were not history. The legends sought to explain the development of Chinese ideals, or goals for ways to live.

According to the legends, the Good Emperors invented civilization—better ways of living—in China. Emperor Shen-nung taught people how to use hoes and plows to cultivate crops. He also showed them the advantage of trade. As told in an old Chinese history, he had the people gather together "so they could part with goods they did not want in order to obtain goods they needed." As a result, "everyone was better off."

Huang-ti A second Good Emperor, Huang-ti (hwahng dee), was much admired for his mind. It was said that he could speak when he was only 2 months old. By the time he was 15 years old, he had mastered every subject.

Huang-ti invented boats and taught people to harness horses and oxen. He showed his people how to make bows and arrows "so they would be feared by those who intended to harm them."

Yao The legends say that a third Good Emperor, Yao, was truly a good man. He lived simply, dressing in the same rough clothing used by his subjects. He ate only plain food from a clay spoon. Yao's reign set an example of ideal harmony, that is, people living together in peace and friendship. Harmony was an ideal much praised by the Chinese teachers of later times. The legends told that Yao first brought harmony to his family and then to his kingdom. Afterward he encouraged harmony among all peoples.

The Wellcome Institute, London

In this ivory carving, two of the Good Emperors discuss a book.
▶ According to legends, what did the Good Emperors invent?

Creating a Skit

● Divide the class into groups of five or six. Have each group choose one of the Good Emperors as the subject of their skit.

● The skits should be approximately five minutes in length.

● Have the groups take turns performing their skits.

● If there is more than one group representing the rule of the same Good Emperor, discuss any differences after the skits have been presented.

Optional Activities

The Beginnings of Early Civilization in China

Objectives

★ **1. Describe** the beliefs of Confucianism.

2. Explain how the Chinese character system of writing works.

3. Evaluate the rule of Shih Huang-ti according to Confucian ideals.

4. Identify the following people and places: *Good Emperors, Confucius, Shih Huang-ti, Ch'in, Chang Jiang, Xi Chiang, Huang He, China,* and *the Great Wall.*

1 STARTING THE LESSON

Motivation Activity

■ Tell students that in this lesson they will learn about Confucius, a man who was born in China just twelve years after Siddhartha was born in India.

■ Explain that Confucius also devoted himself to improving life for others, but he thought the way to do this was by training good leaders.

Think About What You Know

■ Assign the THINK ABOUT WHAT YOU KNOW activity on p. 135.

■ Answers should include only symbols.

Study the Vocabulary

■ Have students look up each of the new vocabulary words in the Glossary.

■ Have the class create symbols that could stand for each of these words and tell something about their meaning.

■ Which word is easiest to create symbols for? Which is hardest? Talk about the advantages and disadvantages of using symbols instead of letters for writing.

┌─ **Answers to Caption Questions** ─┐
p. 134 ▶ An elephant
p. 135 ▶ Civilization—better ways of living in China

Read and Think

Section A

Use the questions below to help students understand the ideals that are expressed in the legends of the Good Emperors.

1. **Who were the "Good Emperors"?**
(Shen-nung, Huang-Ti, and Yao, rulers who, according to legends, invented better ways of living in China *p. 135*)

2. **What did the Good Emperors teach?**
(How to farm, trade, build boats, and live in peace and friendship *p. 135*)

Thinking Critically Why, do you think, were the legends of the Good Emperors told and retold? (Evaluate)
(Answers may include that they taught ideals and gave people pride. *pp. 135-136*)

When Yao grew old, he decided to find the best person in the kingdom to take his place. After much searching, he heard of Shun, who showed ideal loyalty to his family. Shun's family was by no means an ideal family. His father was wicked and unfair, his stepmother was stingy and mean, and his half-brother was spoiled, lazy, and nasty. The family was so bad that it tried to kill Shun so that the half-brother would get all the family's property.

One day while Shun was painting the top of the barn, his father set fire to the building. Shun jumped, using two wide-brimmed straw hats as a parachute, and landed safely. You might think that Shun would have had nothing to do with his

wicked family after that. But according the legend, he continued to be patient a act rightly, even toward those who h wronged him. Yao decided that Shun w just the man to rule the kingdom. course, this is only a legend. But althou it does not give us history, it does tell about ancient Chinese ideals.

B. Writing on Shells and Bones

Like the Greeks, the ancient Chin believed in oracles. You have read that o cles were supposed to give messages fr the gods. The Chinese wrote questions

This illustrates the legend of Shun, who showed ideal loyalty to his family.
▶ What was Shun's parachute?

Curriculum Connection

Art Invite an art teacher or someone from your community who is familiar with Chinese calligraphy to demonstrate the art to the class.

● Ask your guest to bring or identify materials to have on hand so that students can try the techniques.

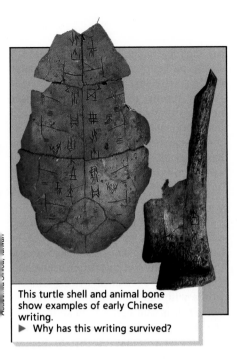

This turtle shell and animal bone show examples of early Chinese writing.
▶ Why has this writing survived?

C. Chinese Writing

Early Pictographs The Chinese system of writing grew from the written characters scratched on the oracle shells and bones. Like cuneiform or Egyptian writing, the earliest Chinese characters were pictographs. The chart on this page shows the pictographs for *turtle*. As you can see, the earliest pictographs looked somewhat like a turtle. But the later ways of writing these characters changed so much that they no longer looked like pictures.

A character that stood for the name of one thing could be combined with other characters to form new words. Two characters for a tree meant "forest." The characters for dog and mouth meant "bark." The characters for the sun and moon together stood for "bright." Some characters stood for sounds rather than things.

the oracle on turtle shells and animal bones. Scratched on one shell was the question, "Should the king go to war this spring?" Another read, "Will Lady Hao be in good health after she has a baby?" There is one bone with the question "Will it rain tomorrow?" The shell or bone bearing a question was heated until it cracked. Priests then could supposedly tell the answer to the question by the way the shell or bone cracked.

Questions scratched on oracle shells and bones may not seem to be important sources of history, but they prove a significant fact. The Chinese had a written language as early as 1500 B.C. The oracle shells and bones are the oldest surviving Chinese writings. Archaeologists believe that the ancient Chinese probably also wrote on strips of wood and bamboo. But wood and bamboo rot, so such writings would have disappeared long ago.

DEVELOPMENT OF CHINESE WRITING

1 2 3 4

The earliest Chinese characters were pictographs.
▶ Which character most resembles a turtle?

137

Using Community Resources

● If someone in your community speaks or writes Chinese, invite them to visit the classroom to talk about the differences between English and Chinese.

● If there is a Chinese restaurant in town, check to see if the menu is written in Chinese as well as English.

● Ask the proprietor if it is possible to get literal translations of the characters so that students can see how Chinese characters stand for ideas rather than just sounds.

Optional Activities

Read and Think
Section B

Ask students the following questions to summarize the information in the reading about oracle shells and bones.

1. **What are the oldest examples of Chinese writing that we know about?**
(Shells and bones with oracle questions scratched on them *p. 137*)

2. **How were shells and bones used to predict the future?**
(Shells and bones with questions scratched on them were heated and priests could supposedly tell the answers to the questions by the way the bones cracked. *p. 137*)

Thinking Critically Why, do you think, did the Chinese write on shells, bones, wood, and bamboo instead of paper? (Hypothesize)
(Answers should reflect independent thinking but may include that they didn't know how to make paper yet, or that shells, bones, wood, and bamboo were more readily available to them. *pp. 136-137*)

VISUAL THINKING SKILL

Using a Photograph

■ Direct students' attention to the photograph of the ancient Chinese writing done on a turtle shell on this page. Ask students to choose one of the characters and ask the following question: **What do you think the character represents?**
(Answers may include a person, a mountain, a stream, or a house.)

Answers to Caption Questions
p. 136 ▶ Two wide-brimmed straw hats
p. 137 *t.* ▶ Shells and bones do not rot.
p. 137 *b.* ▶ The first character (top left)

Section C

Use the questions below to help students summarize the characteristics of the Chinese system of writing and spelling.

1. **How was early Chinese writing similar to the writing of the ancient Egyptians?**
(Both used pictographs *p. 137*)

2. **What is a dialect?**
(A variety of the same language *p. 138*)

3. **Why is a system of writing that is based on pictures and concepts instead of sounds an advantage for the Chinese?**
(It allows people in different parts of the country to communicate even though they pronounce words differently. *p. 138*)

Thinking Critically **Why, do you think, is it easier for modern scholars to read ancient Chinese writing than the writing found in the ruins of the ancient Indus River cities?** (Infer)
(Answers should reflect independent thinking but may include that modern scholars can interpret the pictographs without having to know the words that the ancient Chinese used. *p. 138*)

Chinese Characters The many different kinds of characters made up the Chinese system of writing. To read and write, a person had to memorize a great many characters. Altogether there are nearly 50,000 characters, but most are rarely used today. However, a person must learn about 1,000 characters to read even simple material. Newspapers use between 2,000 and 3,000 characters. A dictionary for college students will have about 14,000 characters. In comparison, how many letters must you learn to read English?

Although the Chinese writing system is indeed hard to learn, it has had one advantage. People in different parts of China speak in different **dialects**, but they all use the same written characters. A dialect is a variety of the same language. Some people

The writing on this wall shows some ancient Chinese characters, many of which are still used.
▶ Why do you think Chinese is a difficult language to learn?

say *shan* for "mountain," while others say *si*. But all people can recognize the same written character.

In recent years the Chinese have made writing somewhat simpler. Characters can now be written in fewer lines, so they are easier to learn. The government has tried to have all Chinese speak the same national language.

D. Chinese Spelling

People writing in English have used different ways to spell Chinese names. The Chinese government now encourages them to use the **Pinyin** system of spelling. Pinyin is one system of writing Chinese words with our alphabet, the Roman alphabet. It is said that Pinyin shows quite accurately how the Chinese pronounce the words. For example, the Pinyin spelling for the name of one of China's great rivers is *Chang Jiang* (chahng jee AHNG). In the past it was usually spelled *Yangtze* (yang-SEE). The Pinyin spelling for the Hsi Chiang (see jee AHNG), another great river, is *Xi Jiang* (shee jee AHNG). *Huang He* (hwahng hih) is the Pinyin name for the Yellow River. It is called the Yellow River because its waters carry so much yellow soil.

Pinyin spelling is used in this book for most Chinese names. You will see as you use the book that whenever we have used the Pinyin term, we have often mentioned its older English spelling.

E. The Teachings of Confucius

The most famous person of ancient China was a man known by the name Confucius (kun FYOO shus). Confucius was a sage, a very wise man, whose greatest wish was to advise kings. He was born in

Creating a Pictograph System

● Have students develop a system of pictograph communication to be used among themselves.

● Divide students into groups of three or four and ask each group to come up with a list of five commonly used words.

● Make sure there is no overlap between lists, and have students develop pictograph characters for each of their words.

● The words and their pictographs can be posted in the class, and students can try writing a few sentences with them.

Writing to Learn

Writing a Letter Have students write a letter that Confucius, were he alive today, might have written to the President of the United States.

● Have them express Confucius's ideas about good government and explain why the President should follow these ideas.

In this etching, Confucius spreads his ideas for an orderly society to his followers in ancient China.
▶ Where is Confucius seated?

551 B.C., just a few years after Prince Siddhartha, but the lives of these two began very differently. Prince Siddhartha grew up in a palace. Confucius was an orphan who worked as a boy. Siddhartha left the palace because he did not want to be a king. Confucius spent years seeking to become the adviser of a king. Siddhartha sought a satisfying way of life. Confucius sought to create a good government.

Confucius was deeply troubled by conditions in China. The land was divided into a number of kingdoms. The kings fought each other and oppressed the people they ruled. Confucius believed that there could be peace and justice under a good government. But he knew there could be good government only when good people governed. Confucius searched for a king who would put his teachings into practice. He never found one, so he spent his time teaching young

men. Perhaps they would be advisers to kings in the future.

Once when Confucius and some of his students were traveling through a wild region, they came upon an old woman weeping beside a grave. Confucius asked her why she wept. She replied that a tiger had killed her only son, just as another tiger had once killed her husband. "Why do you live in this place?" asked Confucius. "Because there is no oppressive [cruel] government here," she replied. Confucius turned to his students and told them, "Remember this woman; oppressive government is worse than a tiger."

Confucius carefully observed all religious ceremonies. He taught that all should respect the gods and the "will of heaven." But Confucius did not establish a religion. He once said that he did not expect his followers to be saints, that is, holy persons. He would be satisfied if they were

139

Making a Filmstrip

- Have students collaborate to make a filmstrip on the career of Confucius.
- As a class, decide which scenes will be illustrated, and make a list of these scenes on the chalkboard.
- Decide how many frames are to be created, and divide the class into small groups.
- Assign specific frames to each group, making sure each group is responsible for an equal number of frames. Have each group draw their frames on posterboard or construction paper and write appropriate captions for each frame. Have each group present their portion of the filmstrip, taking turns reading the captions. Have each group walk "off stage" when they have finished.

Optional Activities

Thinking About Source Material

Background Information

It was not until after Confucius's death (551 B.C.-479 B.C. that Confucius's followers recorded his beliefs in a book called the *Analects*, which emphasizes a person's need to develop character and act responsibly.

Guided Reading

1. **Why is the *Analects* a primary source?**
   (Because it is from sources directly attributed to Confucius)

2. **What, do you think, does the first saying in this selection mean?**
   (Answers may include it means that a wise person knows their abilities and limitations.)

3. **What, do you think, does the third saying in this selection mean?**
   (Answers may include it means that a wise person knows his or her abilities and limitations.)

Understanding Source Material

1. Answers should reflect independent thinking.

2. Answers should reflect independent thinking.

USING SOURCE MATERIAL

ANALECTS: SAYINGS OF CONFUCIUS

Confucius, who is shown below teaching his students, used his teaching as a tool for making changes in the world around him. The goal that Confucius had for his students was that they be able to act effectively in the world. For that reason, he taught his followers how to get along with others.

The *Analects* contains the teachings of Confucius and his followers. Below are some of the sayings of Confucius taken from this book.

> To know what you know and know what you don't know is the characteristic of one who knows.
>
> Learning prevents one from being narrow-minded.
>
> A gentleman blames himself, while a common man blames others.
>
> A man who committed a mistake and doesn't correct it is committing another mistake.
>
> When asked, what do you think of repaying evil with kindness, Confucius replied: Then what are you going to repay kindness with? Repay kindness with kindness but repay evil with justice.
>
> A man who does not think and plan long ahead will find troubles right at his door.
>
> Don't criticize other people's faults, criticize your own.
>
> A man who brags without shame will find great difficulty in living up to his bragging.

Understanding Source Material

1. Which saying do you most agree with?
2. Which saying do you least agree with?

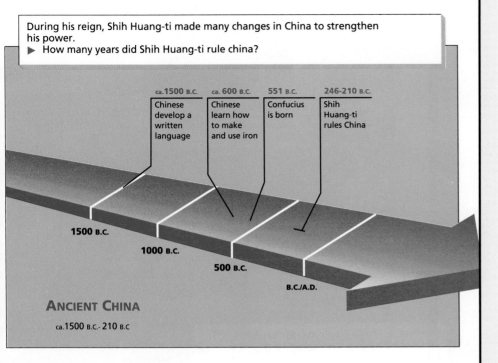

During his reign, Shih Huang-ti made many changes in China to strengthen his power.
▶ How many years did Shih Huang-ti rule china?

ca.1500 B.C. Chinese develop a written language

ca. 600 B.C. Chinese learn how to make and use iron

551 B.C. Confucius is born

246-210 B.C. Shih Huang-ti rules China

1500 B.C.

1000 B.C.

500 B.C.

B.C./A.D.

ANCIENT CHINA
ca.1500 B.C.- 210 B.C

gentlemen, that is, men who were honest, fair, and courteous. A true gentleman followed the rule, "What you do not want done to yourself, do not do to others."

Confucius and his followers probably invented the legends about the Good Emperors. They hoped that the real rulers would follow the good examples of the legendary Yao and Shun. Although Confucius never found such a king, his teachings were not forgotten. Over the years the sage had more influence than any king. For more than 2,000 years, Chinese students studied his teachings concerning the ideal gentleman. These teachings, known as **Confucianism**, became the Chinese model for official and personal behavior.

F. A Clay Army

In 1974, workers digging a well near the city of Xi'an, once known as Hsien-yang (shee en YAHNG), discovered an army—an army of clay soldiers. These were not toy soldiers but life-sized statues of men and horses that lay buried in a large underground chamber. At one time thousands of the soldiers stood four abreast along the corridors of the chamber, but the stout timbers that held up the earth-covered ceiling had collapsed long ago. Most of the statues lay in pieces when the workers uncovered them.

As archaeologists began putting the figures together, they could see how carefully the figures had been made. Even

141

Optional Activities

141

Concept: Understanding How Beliefs Affect Behavior

In order to better understand ancient China, it is important to understand how beliefs affect behavior. Below are three activities that will help your students understand how beliefs influence the lives of individuals and how they affect a culture.

◆ **EASY** In order to make this abstract concept more accessible, have students relate it to their own lives.

Have them list two or three beliefs that they have. Then have students write a paragraph describing how one of these beliefs has affected their daily life.

◀▶ **AVERAGE** Have students write essays evaluating the administration of Shih Huang-ti by their standards.

Ask: Shih Huang-ti accomplished much, but do you think he was a good ruler? Why or why not? (Have students answer this question in their essay.)

◀❚▶ **CHALLENGING** Have students who need a challenge write a persuasive paper.

They can argue either that good government is the best way to improve people's lives or that teaching people to overcome selfishness is more effective.

Have students support their answers with examples from the lesson.

VISUAL THINKING SKILL

Interpreting a Photograph

■ Direct students' attention to the photograph on this page. Ask them to write a paragraph in which they describe the findings of the archaeologists in Xi'an and how those archaeologists must have felt when they uncovered the statues.

Shih Huang-ti had a life-sized clay army made. It is said that each figure was modeled after a real soldier.
▶ Besides soldiers, what is pictured here?

more astonishing than the size and numbers of the clay figures was the fact that they were all different; no two soldiers and no two horses looked alike. Some of the soldiers wore armor and some belted robes. Some warriors had braided hair, some had hair pulled into a knot on top of their heads. Even the expressions on their faces were different.

The clay army had been armed with real weapons. The soldiers had held swords, spears, bows, and crossbows. The wooden parts of the weapons had rotted away long ago, but the bronze arrowheads, swords, and crossbow fittings lay in the ruins. The chamber also held full-sized

chariots, each hitched to four life-sized horses. Each chariot had a clay charioteer and guard.

Since 1974, two more underground chambers containing clay figures have been discovered. Altogether the three chambers contain between 7,000 and 8,000 figures of men and horses. It would have taken the labor of many people to make these figures and construct the underground chambers. Why did they do it? They were forced to work by a powerful ruler. The clay army was supposed to protect, in some magical way, the tomb of Shih Huang-ti (SHEE hwahng dee), an emperor who died over 2,300 years ago.

Optional Activities

Drawing Political Cartoons

● Have students draw political cartoons depicting an aspect of Shih Huang-ti's rule.

● Explain to them that the purpose of political cartoons is to make a point about a leader, a government, a law, or a situation by using symbols and other visuals.

● Have them write captions to accompany their drawings if they wish.

● Have volunteers share their cartoons with the class, or create a classroom display.

G. Burning Books and Building Walls

Shih Huang-ti Shih Huang-ti was king of Ch'in, a warlike kingdom in northwestern China. Shih Huang-ti brought the whole land under his rule by conquering the other kingdoms. We still call the country he conquered *China*, which means "land of the Ch'in." Shih Huang-ti ruled China from 246 B.C. to 210 B.C.

Shih Huang-ti was by no means Confucius's ideal gentleman. In fact, he strongly opposed the sage's teachings, which he thought dangerous. Since many books contained Confucius's sayings, Shih Huang-ti ordered that all books be burned except those about useful subjects. By "useful" Shih Huang-ti meant books on farming and medicine. Fortunately, some students hid their books. Others knew their books so well that they later wrote them down from memory.

Thousands of Chinese people built the Great Wall of China.
▶ What were some of the steps involved in building the wall?

Among Shih Huang-ti's most important projects was the building of the Grand Canal in China.
▶ What else did he have built?

Great Wall The burning of the books was only one of the steps Shih Huang-ti took to strengthen his power. He forced thousands to build projects, including his tomb. He also sent many people to work on the Great Wall. Earlier kings had built walls to protect parts of the land from the raids of horse-raiding tribes. Shih Huang-ti connected these shorter walls to form the Great Wall. Below is how Leonard Everett Fisher, in his book *The Great Wall of China*, tells how Shih Huang-ti may have described his plans for the Great Wall.

> *I shall build a new and mightier wall and shall join all the walls together. I shall have one long wall across the top of China. . . . It will be six horses wide at the top, eight at the bottom, and five men high. I shall build it at the edge of our steepest mountains. No Mongol . . . will be able to go around it, over it, under it, or through it. It will be the Great Wall!*

143

To summarize the rule of Shih Huang-ti, ask the following questions:

1. **What does *China* mean?**
   (Land of the Ch'in *p. 143*)

2. **What is the Great Wall?**
   (A wall stretching 1,500 miles [2,413 km] across northern China, said to be the largest structure ever built *p. 143*)

Thinking Critically Why, do you think, would Shih Huang-ti consider the teachings of Confucius to be dangerous? (Analyze)
(Answers may include that if people found out that Shih Huang-ti was not following the example of an "ideal gentleman" he might lose the faith of the people and lose power. *p.143*)

GEOGRAPHY THEMES

Human-Environment Interactions

■ Have students refer to the map on p. 144 and ask the following question: **Why, do you think, was the Great Wall not built in the west as well as the north?**
(Answers may include the Chinese probably felt the mountain range in the west would serve as a deterrent to invaders.)

Answers to Caption Questions
p. 142 ▶ Horses
p. 143 *l.* ▶ The Great Wall
p. 143 *r.* ▶ Lifting stones, laying them next to one another

Writing to Learn

Writing a Journal Have students write an entry in their journals from the perspective of one of the workers who was digging a well near the city of Xi'an in 1974.

● Have students describe their reactions as they discover the clay army that was supposed to protect the tomb of Shih Huang-ti.

Reteaching Main Objective

★ *Describe the beliefs of Confucianism.*

● Divide the class into teams. Have each team use the information in the text to develop *Jeopardy*-style answers that require questions about the beliefs of Confucianism.

● For example, "What you do not want done to yourself, do not do to others" would be an answer for the question, "What is the Confucian idea of a true gentleman?" Then have students exchange answers and questions.

3 CLOSING THE LESSON

Lesson 3 Review

Answers to Think and Write

A. The legends of the Good Emperors taught people to live in harmony.

B. The people of ancient China wrote questions to the oracles on shells and bones to receive information from the gods.

C. Character writing allows people to communicate, no matter how they pronounce words, but it is hard to learn.

D. The Chinese government encourages foreigners to use the pinyin spelling because it conveys correct pronunciation.

E. Confucius taught his followers to be honest, fair, courteous, and considerate.

F. Shih Huang-ti's underground army of clay soldiers and horses was supposed to protect his tomb.

G. Shih Huang-ti took the following steps to strengthen his power: conquered neighboring kingdoms, ordered books he considered dangerous to be burned, forced thousands to labor on building projects, built the Great Wall, and ordered everyone to use the same system of writing.

Answer to Skills Check

The Huang He flows into the Yellow Sea; the Chang Jiang flows into the East China Sea.

Focus Your Reading

Ask the lesson focus question found at the beginning of the lesson: **What does the early history of China tell about Chinese ideals, writing, and government?**
(Answers should reflect understanding of the ideals, writing, and government of ancient China.)

Additional Practice

You may wish to assign the ancillary materials listed below.

Understanding the Lesson p. 36
Workbook p. 40

Answers to Caption Questions
p. 144 ▶ The northern border

144

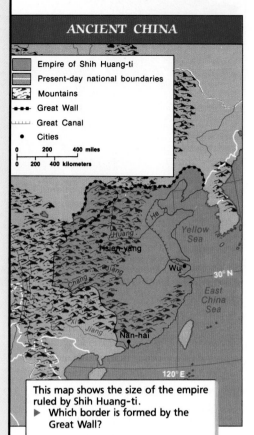

ANCIENT CHINA

- Empire of Shih Huang-ti
- Present-day national boundaries
- Mountains
- Great Wall
- Great Canal
- Cities

0   200   400 miles
0   200   400 kilometers

He
Huang·
Hsien-yang
Yellow Sea
Jiang
Chang
Wu
30° N
East China Sea
Xi Jiang
Nan-hai
120° E

This map shows the size of the empire ruled by Shih Huang-ti.
▶ Which border is formed by the Great Wall?

In later times other emperors made the wall stronger and larger. The Great Wall stretches 1,500 miles (2,413 km) across northern China, as shown by the map on this page. If such a wall were built in the United States, it would reach halfway across the country. The Great Wall is said to be the largest structure ever built. In fact, the Great Wall is the only structure made by humans that can be seen from outer space.

A Powerful Ruler Some things Shih Huang-ti did to make himself powerful probably benefited China. He directed that all should write characters in the same way so that there would be only one system of writing throughout the empire. He even ruled that wheels on carts must be placed the same distance apart. The unpaved roads were little more than cart tracks. It was easier for animals to pull carts when all followed the same tracks.

Shih Huang-ti was a very powerful ruler, but in the end there were things he could not do. He forced thousands of people to build his tomb, but the underground army of clay soldiers failed to protect it. Shortly after his death, thieves entered the tomb and robbed it.

LESSON 3 REVIEW

THINK AND WRITE

A. What ideals were taught in the legends of the Good Emperors? (Recall)

B. What was the purpose of the writings on shells and bones? (Infer)

C. How was character writing useful yet difficult? (Infer)

D. Why does the Chinese government encourage foreign writers to use Pinyin spelling? (Infer)

E. What did Confucius teach? (Recall)

F. What was the purpose of Shih Huang-ti's underground army? (Recall)

G. What steps did Shih Huang-ti take to strengthen his power? (Recall)

SKILLS CHECK

MAP SKILL

Look at the map of ancient China on this page. Which two rivers cross the Grand Canal? Tell what body of water each of these rivers flows into.

144

Optional Activities

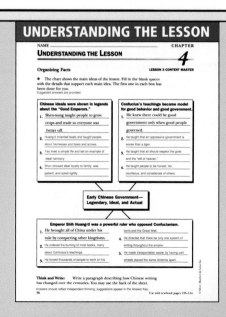

UNDERSTANDING THE LESSON

NAME
UNDERSTANDING THE LESSON   CHAPTER
                                            4
Organizing Facts   LESSON 3 CONTENT MASTER

✱ The chart shows the main ideas of the lesson. Fill in the blank spaces with the details that support each main idea. The first one in each box has been done for you.
Suggested answers are provided.

Chinese ideals were shown in legends about the "Good Emperors."	Confucius's teachings became model for good behavior and good government.
1. Shen-nung taught people to grow crops and trade so everyone was better off.	1. He knew there could be good government only when good people governed.
2. Huang-ti invented boats and taught people about harnesses and bows and arrows.	2. He taught that an oppressive government is worse than a tiger.
3. Yao lived a simple life and set an example of ideal harmony.	3. He taught that all should respect the gods and the "will of heaven."
4. Shun showed ideal loyalty to family, was patient, and acted rightly.	4. He taught people to be honest, fair, courteous, and considerate of others.

Early Chinese Government—
Legendary, Ideal, and Actual

Emperor Shih Huang-ti was a powerful ruler who opposed Confucianism.
1. He brought all of China under his rule by conquering other kingdoms.
2. He ordered the burning of most books about Confucius's teachings.
3. He forced thousands of people to work on his
tomb and the Great Wall.
4. He directed that there be only one system of writing throughout the empire.
5. He made transportation easier by having cart wheels placed the same distance apart.

Think and Write: Write a paragraph describing how Chinese writing has changed over the centuries. You may use the back of the sheet.
Answers should reflect independent thinking; suggestions appear in the Answer Key.
36   Use with textbook pages 135–144.

◀ **Review Master Booklet, p. 36**

USING THE VOCABULARY

On a separate sheet of paper, write the letter of the term that best matches each numbered statement.

a. subcontinent
b. nomads
c. castes
d. dialect
e. Pinyin

1. A variety of a particular language
2. Social classes of the people of India
3. A large landmass that is smaller than a continent
4. A system of writing Chinese words with the Roman alphabet
5. Tribes of people who move about with herds of goats, sheep, and cattle

REMEMBERING WHAT YOU READ

On a separate sheet of paper, answer the following questions in complete sentences.

1. What two Indus cities were uncovered by archaeologists after Wells wrote *The Outline of History*?
2. What ancient objects did archaeologists find in the ruins of Mohenjo-Daro?
3. What are the Vedas?
4. In what language are the Vedas written?
5. For what was Siddhartha searching?

6. What are the followers of Buddha called?
7. What is the religion of most of the people on the subcontinent?
8. What ruler helped to spread Buddhism?
9. Into what four classes were the early Aryans divided?
10. On what are the oldest surviving Chinese writings found?
11. What are the names of China's three great rivers?
12. What teachings have become the Chinese model for official and personal behavior?
13. Whose tomb was the clay army supposed to protect?
14. How did Shih Huang-ti strengthen his power?
15. What in China is the largest structure in the world?

TYING ART TO SOCIAL STUDIES

The caste system developed as a result of the practices of Aryan society. People were divided into four major groups. As a class, make a mural that shows people from each of the four castes. Divide into groups, with each group responsible for drawing the members of one of the castes. Decide how your mural will be organized and how you will label each of the castes. Your class can display the mural when it is completed.

Using the Vocabulary

1. dialect
2. castes
3. subcontinent
4. Pinyin
5. nomads

Remembering What You Read

1. Mohenjo-Daro and Harappa
2. Games, toys, jewelry
3. Books containing hymns about the Aryans
4. Sanskirt
5. A more satisfying way of life
6. Buddhists
7. Hinduism
8. Asoka
9. Priests called *Brahmans*; warriors and rulers; farmers and merchants; and workers
10. Shells and bones
11. Chang Jiang, Xi Jiang, and Huang He
12. Confucianism
13. Shih Huang-ti
14. Conquered neighboring kingdoms, burned books that he thought were dangerous, forced thousands to labor on building projects, built the Great Wall, and ordered everyone to use the same system of writing.
15. The Great Wall

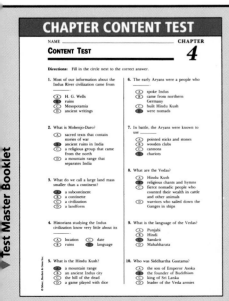

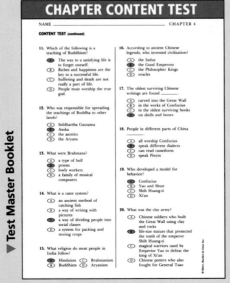

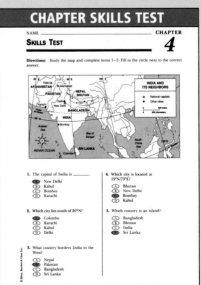

Thinking Critically

1. Answers may include that it helps us appreciate our heritage, or that it helps us avoid the mistakes of the past.

2. Answers should reflect facts from individuals' neighborhoods.

3. Answers may include that it is bad because it limits people's possibilities based on birth, or that it is good because everyone in society is given a role

4. Answers may include that advantages would be being able to see mistakes and avoid them before they happen and being able to utilize tomorrow's advances today; disadvantages might include that people would change their lives because of information from the future.

5. Answers may include that it tells us that the Chinese believed that life after death would be much like life as we know it.

Summarizing the Chapter

India: Leaders–Asoka; Languages–Indus script; Religions–Buddhism, Hinduism; Archaeological discoveries–Monhenjo-Daro, Harappa; Rivers–Ganges, Indus.

China: Leaders–Confucius, Shih Huang-ti; Languages–written characters; Religions–no organized religion; Archaeological discoveries–oracle shells and bones, clay army; Rivers–Chang Jiang, Xi Jiang, Huang He.

THINKING CRITICALLY

On a separate sheet of paper, answer the following in complete sentences.

1. H. G. Wells wanted his book to "tell truly and clearly the whole story of mankind. . . ." Why is it important for us to have a clear record of the past?

2. How might historians describe your neighborhood if they discovered it in the year 4000?

3. What is your opinion of the caste system?

4. The ancient Chinese people were interested in knowing the future. They believed that oracles could predict the future. If people could see into the future, what would be some possible advantages and disadvantages for humanity?

5. What does the discovery of the clay army at Xi'an tell us about ancient Chinese beliefs in life and death?

SUMMARIZING THE CHAPTER

Copy this graphic organizer on a separate sheet of paper. In both columns of the chart, fill in each box with an answer. Some boxes may have more than one answer.

CHAPTER THEME	The culture, society, and early history of India and China have made a lasting impact on each country's civilization.	
ANCIENT CIVILIZATIONS	**INDIA**	**CHINA**
LEADERS		
LANGUAGES	Indus Script	
RELIGIONS		No organized religion
ARCHAEOLOGICAL DISCOVERIES		
RIVERS		Chang Jiang

146

COOPERATIVE LEARNING

When travelers prepare for a visit to a foreign country, they may read guidebooks. Guidebooks describe the geography and interesting places of various regions and also describe customs of people who live in those regions. How would you go about writing a guidebook?

PROJECT

Work with a group of classmates to plan and write a guidebook for time travelers. In it, you will describe one of the ancient civilizations you studied in Unit 1. Your group's guidebook might include information on ancient sporting events, temples and monuments, religious practices, languages, land features, or climate. Use your imaginations. Ask yourselves, "What would a time traveler need to know?"

Hold a group meeting to decide what information your guidebook will include. Be sure to share ideas and record group members' suggestions. Use the information in your textbook. You may also want to visit a library to gather more information.

Divide tasks among group members. Depending on the number of students in the group and the information your guidebook will include,

REMEMBER TO:
- Give your ideas.
- Listen to others' ideas.
- Plan your work with the group.
- Present your project.
- Discuss how your group worked.

your group might divide tasks as follows:

- One group member could write about the important temples and monuments in the civilization.
- Another group member could write about religious practices.
- A third group member could draw pictures to illustrate what has been written for the guidebook.
- One group member could draw a map of the region and label where the important monuments and temples were built.
- Another group member could prepare a cover, title page, and table of contents for the guidebook.

PRESENTATION AND REVIEW

After your group members have met to put all your information together, present your guidebook to the rest of your class. Work together to answer any questions the other students may have about the ancient civilization your guidebook describes.

After your group has made its presentation, meet again to evaluate your project. How well did your group members work together? How could your guidebook have been improved?

147

You may wish to refer to the article on Cooperative Learning found in the front of your Teacher's Edition.

Objectives

★1. **Describe** the uses of a pie graph, bar graph, line graph, and pictograph.

2. **Interpret** information presented on different forms of graphs.

Why Do I Need This Skill?

To help students better understand the importance of graphs ask the following question: **Is it easier to remember how a soccer game is played by reading about it in a book or by watching an actual soccer game being played?**

(Answers should include that it is easier to remember how a soccer game is played by watching the game because of the visual relationships that are formed when you watch or observe something.)

Then tell students that the same is true with graphs. Graphs make information easier to remember because they present the information visually, as opposed to just listing the information.

Learning the Skill

To check the students' comprehension of the different types of graphs, ask the following questions:

1. **What are the most common graphs?**
   (Pie graphs, bar graphs, line graphs, and pictographs)

2. **What are the purposes of a pie graph?**
   (To show and compare percentages, or parts of the whole)

3. **What is the purpose of a bar graph?**
   (To compare facts)

4. **What do line graphs show?**
   (Changes over time)

5. **What does a pictograph use and what is its purpose?**
   (A pictograph uses pictures and it is used to show amounts.)

148

A. WHY DO I NEED THIS SKILL?

Graphs are a visual way of organizing information. They present facts in ways that are clear and easy to read. When facts are organized in a graph, it is much easier to understand the facts and to see the relationships between them.

B. LEARNING THE SKILL

There are different kinds of graphs. The most common are pie graphs, bar graphs, line graphs, and pictographs.

A pie graph is used to show and compare percentages, or parts of a whole. Each "slice" of the "pie" represents a certain percentage—a part of the whole pie.

The pie graph below shows how much of the world's total land area each of the seven continents occupies. The whole circle stands for the world's total land area, or 100 percent. Each slice stands for a continent and how much of the total land area it occupies. The pie graph also shows how the continents compare with each other in size.

A bar graph can also be used to show and compare facts. The bar graph below shows the land area of each continent in the world. The left side of the graph is divided into segments that each represent 2 million square miles. The right side of the graph has segments that each represent 5 million square kilometers.

Each bar that extends from the bottom of the graph shows the land area of a continent. For example, the land area of Asia is about 17 million square miles (44 million sq km), and the land area of Europe is about 4 million square miles (10 million sq km). By

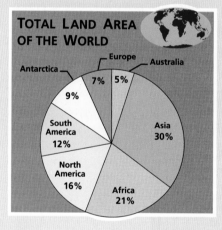

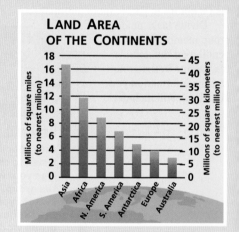

148

Optional Activities

Homework Activity

- Ask students to use the chart of countries of the Eastern Hemisphere found on pp. 32-43 to complete the following graphs:

- Make a bar graph showing the population of the following countries: China, France, Australia, and Greece.

- Make a pictograph showing the population of the following cities: London, England; Moscow, Soviet Union; and Tokyo, Japan.

looking at the bars for these two continents, you can visualize about how many times larger Asia is than Europe.

Line graphs are used to show changes over time. The line graph on this page shows how world population has changed since the year 2000 B.C. and includes projections to the year A.D. 2000.

On left side of the graph, there are segments that represent the number of people, in billions. Along the bottom of the graph, there are segments that represent 1,000 years each.

A pictograph—a graph that uses picture-symbols—is used to show amounts, such as population figures. To see an example of a pictograph, turn to page 541 in Chapter 21. The graph on that page shows population figures for the most populated countries in the world.

C. PRACTICING THE SKILL

1. On the pie graph, what percentage of the world's land area is occupied by Asia?
2. According to the bar graph, what is the land area of the North American continent?
3. What is the land area of Antarctica?
4. How many years does each segment on the bottom line of the line graph represent?
5. What was the approximate world population in the year A.D. 1800?

D. APPLYING THE SKILL

Take a survey to find out which ice-cream flavor each student in your class likes best. Then organize your results in a pie graph.

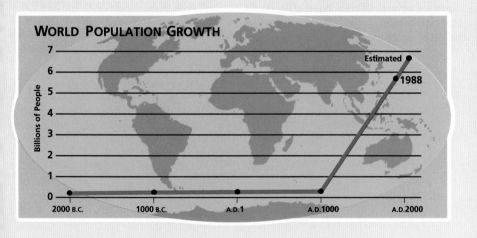

WORLD POPULATION GROWTH

Billions of People

Estimated
1988

2000 B.C. 1000 B.C. A.D.1 A.D.1000 A.D.2000

Practicing the Skill

1. 30 percent
2. Approximately 9 million square miles (23 million sq km)
3. Approximately 5 million square miles (13 million sq km)
4. 1,000 years
5. Approximately 5 billion people

Applying the Skill

Since the answers for this activity could vary greatly, you may wish to find out the top five flavors of ice cream in the class. Then ask one or two students to draw a pie graph showing this information on the chalkboard.

SKILL TRACE: Understanding Graphs		
INTRODUCE PE pp. 148–149	**PRACTICE** TE pp. 148–149 PE p. 265 WB pp. 45, 77 TE p. 208	**TEST** Unit 1 Test, TMB

149

Reteaching Activity

- Have students who are still having difficulty with the concept of graphs complete one or more of the following activities:
- Count the total number of students in the class, then find out how many are boys and how many are girls. Find out what percent of the class is boys and what percent is girls. Create a pie graph showing this information.
- Use the school library to find out the population of your town in 1960, 1970, 1980, and 1990. Create a line graph showing this information.

Optional Activities

Objectives

1. **Describe** the *pretend, imagine,* and *visualize* reading strategies.

2. **List** the different types of literature that relate to history.

Why Do I Need This Skill?

To help students understand the importance of literature, ask the following question: **Which do you remember more clearly, the *Adventures of Odysseus and the Tale of Troy* (with the wooden horse inside) or the length of the Trojan War?** (Most students will probably remember the story of the wooden horse better.)

Explain to students that this poem is one example of literature that relates to history, and that literature can enhance our understanding and enjoyment of history.

Learning the Skill

To check students' comprehension of the *pretend, imagine,* and *visualize* reading strategies as well as the different types of literature that relate to history, ask the following questions:

1. **List the types of literature that relate to history.**
   (Historical fiction, biographies, poetry, drama, myths, legends, fables, diaries, and journals)

2. **Describe the *pretend* strategy.**
   (*Pretend* that you are the character and try to feel what she or he must have felt.)

SKILL TRACE:	Understanding the Characteristics of Various Text Type	
INTRODUCE PE pp. 150–151	**PRACTICE** TE pp. 150–151 PE p. 247 WB pp. 50–51 TE p. 240	**TEST** Unit 2 Test, TMB

150

A. Why Do I Need This Skill?

This social studies textbook tells about people, places, and events of the past and present. The book presents facts — accepted or verified information — about the history of peoples of the Eastern Hemisphere.

People besides textbook authors write about historical events. These other authors might write stories, myths, poems, or plays that tell something about history. We call these writings literature, and their purpose is not so much to present facts but to entertain, excite, or inspire readers. Reading literature that deals with historical events can give you insight into the feelings, attitudes, and daily lives of the people who lived at different times in history.

B. Learning the Skill

There are several different types of literature that can relate to history. The table found on page 151 describes some of the more common types.

On page 73 of Chapter 2, you read an excerpt from *The Adventures of Odysseus and the Tale of Troy*, which tells about the fall of Troy to the Greeks. This is a modern version of the *Iliad*, which was written thousands of years ago by the Greek poet Homer.

This literature excerpt gives you a firsthand, real-life feeling for what it would have been like to be at Troy as the Greeks hid inside the wooden horse and tricked the Trojans.

You can use the following reading strategies to increase your understanding and enjoyment of literature.

- **Pretend** you are the main character in the selection; try to feel the excitement or fear she or he must have felt. For example, how would you have felt if you had been Odysseus?

- **Imagine** that you are an observer watching what is going on. For example, what would you have thought if you had been a Trojan citizen watching the Greeks deliver a huge wooden horse to your city?

- **Visualize** the event; think of the sights, the smells, and the sounds that you would have experienced. For example, what might you have seen, smelled, or heard if you had been inside the Trojan horse?

C. Practicing the Skill

Select one of the strategies for reading literature and use it as you reread the excerpt about the Trojan horse. See if the piece of

150

Optional Activities

Homework Activity

- As a homework activity, ask students to use the *pretend, imagine,* or *visualize* strategy as they read an article in a newspaper or magazine.

- Have students write two or three sentences about the news story, and tell whether the reading strategy helped them understand or appreciate the story better.

- Ask them if the strategy influenced their opinion. For example, if the story was about a court case or a politician, did they feel more sympathy for the person?

- You may wish to have students bring in their articles and discuss their findings.

literature and the actual historical event "come alive" for you. Then use the **pretend**, **imagine**, or **visualize** strategy that you have just learned about as you reread the selection from *Julius Caesar*, on page 108 in Chapter 3. How do you feel as you explain your actions to the Roman Senate?

D. APPLYING THE SKILL

Use a **pretend**, **imagine**, or **visualize** strategy as you read the other literature excerpts in this book. Perhaps you will become so interested that you will find the source of the literature and read the entire piece.

Practicing the Skill

Discuss with the class whether or not the strategy that they selected for reading literature helped them to understand or appreciate either the excerpt from the *Arabian Nights* or the Anansi tale.

For students who are still having difficulty with the *pretend, imagine,* or *visualize* strategies, you may wish to use the reteaching activity listed below.

Applying the Skill

As you read the excerpts of literature listed in the table on this page, you may wish to have students use one of the reading strategies that they have learned.

LITERATURE THAT RELATES TO HISTORY		
Type of Literature	**Characteristics**	**Example**
Historical fiction	Stories set in the past; based on real, historical events but with much information made up by the author	*Ivanhoe* p. 176
Poetry	Rhythmical writings that may or may not rhyme; makes reader imagine and understand various feelings and events	*The Adventures of Odysseus and the Tale of Troy,* p. 73
Drama	Stories intended to be performed by actors; helps audience or reader picture and be affected by events	*Julius Caesar,* p. 108
Myths, legends, and fables	Stories intended to teach a moral lesson or explain the origins of things; sometimes based on historical events but featuring fantasy or exaggeration	Anansi Tale: "How Wisdom Was Spread Throughout the World," p. 456
Diaries, journals, and biographies	Writings about real people and their experiences; written by the people themselves (diaries, journals) or by someone else (biographies)	*The Diary of a Young Girl,* p. 240

151

Reteaching Activity

● For students who are still having difficulty with the *pretend, imagine,* and *visualize* reading strategies have them complete the following activity:

● Bring to class an excerpt of literature that relates to history (such as *The Grapes of Wrath* or *Gone With the Wind*) and have students read the excerpt using one of the three reading strategies that they have learned.

● Divide students into three groups and assign each group one of the reading strategies.

● After students have read the excerpt, discuss it as a class. Ask the class whether it thinks one strategy worked better than another with this excerpt.

Optional Activities

Western Europe

Unit Theme Since the earliest times in Western Europe, dramatic changes have taken place throughout the region. Many of these changes were the result of the Renaissance, the Reformation, several important revolutions, and two world wars.

Chapter 5 Geography of Western Europe

(pp. 154-171)

Theme The blend of physical features, natural resources, and different peoples in Western Europe make it a unique region.

Chapter 6 History of Western Europe

(pp. 172-199)

Theme The way of life that developed in Western Europe during the Middle Ages changed with the growth of trade, the influences of the Renaissance and the Reformation, and the rise of national rulers.

Chapter 7 Three Revolutions

(pp. 200-221)

Theme Revolutions in science, industry, and politics changed the ways people thought, worked, and lived, and the types of governments in Western Europe.

Chapter 8 Nationalism and Two World Wars

(pp. 222-245)

Theme Nationalism and two world wars resulted in great changes in Western Europe.

Chapter 9 Western Europe Today

(pp. 246-272)

Theme The physical features, resources, economies, and governments blend together to make the countries of Western Europe what they are today.

September	Chapters MSH-1	October	Chapters 2-4	November	Chapters 5-7	December	Chapters 8-9	January	Chapters 10-12	February	Chapters 13-14	March	Chapters 15-17	April	Chapters 18-20	May	Chapters 21-23

PACING GUIDE

Bulletin Board Idea

Student Activity

Have students make a time line spanning the changes in Western Europe discussed in Unit 2. Ask students to identify and illustrate key people and events as they read about them. At the end of the unit, have students write a summary paragraph entitled, Western Europe Yesterday and Today.

Annotated Bibliography

Books for Teachers

Bernier, Oliver. *Louis XIV.* New York: Doubleday, 1987. ISBN 0-385-19785-3. (Ch. 7) The life of the Sun King is described and his effects on society are examined in this concise work.

Barzina, Luigi. *The Europeans.* New York: Simon & Schuster, 1983. ISBN 0-1400-7150-4. (Ch. 7) Descriptive chapters on each of the principal European nations are provided by a journalist who has written for American and Italian newspapers.

Doyle, William. *The Oxford Illustrated History of the French Revolution.* New York: Oxford University Press, 1989. ISBN 0-19-82278-17. (Ch. 7) This is an excellent one-volume guide to the French Revolution.

Oxford University Press, eds. *The Oxford Illustrated History of Medieval Europe.* New York: Oxford University Press, 1988. ISBN 0-19-82007-30. (Ch. 6) This summary of Europe during the Middle Ages stresses the historical significance of many of the events of that time.

Schama, Simon. *Citizens: A Chronicle of the French Revolution.* New York: Random House, 1989. ISBN 0-394-55948-7. (Ch. 7) Schama provides an interesting examination of the influence of the common man in revolutionary events.

Books for Students

Bains, Rae. *Europe.* Mahwah, NJ: Troll Associates, 1985. ISBN 0-8167-0305-1. (Ch. 9) This colorful guide to life in modern Europe emphasizes life in Western European countries more than life in their less-developed Eastern counterparts.

Balerdi, Susan. *France: The Crossroads of Europe.* Minneapolis, MN: Dillon Press, 1984. ISBN 0-87518-248-8. (Ch. 5) The culture, history, and geography of France are presented and enhanced by color photographs and an appendix of facts in this volume in the Discovering Our Heritage series.

Cairns, Trevor. *The Birth of Modern Europe.* Minneapolis, MN: Lerner Publications, 1975. ISBN 0-8225-0806-0. (Ch. 7) This history of modern Europe spans from the Renaissance to the Reformation and the English Revolution, with maps, illustrations, and photographs.

Cairns, Trevor. *The Old Regime and the Revolution.* Minneapolis, MN: Lerner Publications, 1990. ISBN 0-8225-0807-9. (Ch. 7) The downfall of the French monarchy under Louis XVI and the impact of the French Revolution on Europe is explored in this up-to-date text.

Cameron, Fiona. *We Live in Switzerland.* New York: Bookwright Press, 1987. ISBN 0-531-18090-5. (Ch. 9) The author describes daily life in today's Switzerland through brief text and photographs.

Frank, Anne. *Anne Frank: The Diary of a Young Girl.* New York: Doubleday, 1967. ISBN 0-385-04019-9. (Ch. 8) A young Jewish girl and her family go into hiding to escape Nazi persecution during World War II.

Miquel, Pierre. *The Age of Discovery.* Morristown, NJ: Silver Burdett Press, 1980. ISBN 0-382-06477-7. (Ch. 7) This is an oversized, colorful presentation on Europe at the end of the Middle Ages and the changes that came about during the age of discovery.

_____. *The Age of Steam.* Morristown, NJ: Silver Burdett Press, 1985. ISBN 0-382-06644-8. (Ch. 7) The author describes the age of steam and how it lead to the Industrial Revolution, which changed Europe's history.

Riordan, James. *Eastern Europe.* Morristown, NJ: Silver Burdett Press, 1987. ISBN 0-382-09468-9. (Ch. 5) This brief introduction to life in Eastern Europe in the mid-1980s is well-illustrated with maps and photographs.

Scott, Sir Walter. *Ivanhoe.* New York: Dodd, Mead, and Co., 1979. (Ch. 6) This classic novel details the conflict between the Normans and the Saxons in the days of chivalry.

Snyder, Louis. *World War II.* Danbury, CT: Franklin Watts, 1981. ISBN 0-531-0433-9. (Ch. 8) This introduction to the important people and events of World War II includes photographs and maps.

Filmstrips and Videos

My Brother's Keeper: The Holocaust Through the Eyes of an Artist. Filmstrip. Society for Visual Education, 1988. (Ch. 8) German expressionistic art conveys the powerful visualization of the Holocaust by German painter Israel Bernbaum.

On This Rock: A Look Inside the Vatican. Videocassette. Centre Productions, 1987. (Ch. 6) This video takes a look at the history of the Catholic Church in Europe and the role of the Vatican as its seat of government.

Western Europe Today. Filmstrip. United Learning, 1988. (Ch. 9) This well-organized program mixes maps, historic artwork, and photos, and includes reproducible handouts and maps.

Life in Medieval Europe

What was life like long ago?

The United States has gone through several cycles in its history — depression, prosperity, war, and peace. Medieval Europe, or the period of time between ancient and modern times (about A.D. 500–A.D. 1500) in Western Europe, also went through these cycles. Some of the times in Medieval Europe were very good, and often great strides were made. But during one period in the Middle Ages, things ground to a halt in much of Europe. Conditions worsened, plagues swept the continent, and the overall standard of living was poor. These years have come to be known as the Dark Ages. The following activities center around this period of time in Europe.

SOCIAL STUDIES

Economics The economic system of Europe evolved from feudalism to capitalism during the Middle Ages. However, for most of the years known as the Dark Ages, the barter system was the most widely used economic system.

■ To help students appreciate the complexity and awkwardness of the barter system, set up a scenario where they have the opportunity to barter with each other for specific objects.

■ Give students objects such as pens, pencils, erasers, notepads, or stickers and let them see what exchanges they can make with classmates.

■ To further illustrate the system, you may wish to dictate the terms of some deals. For instance, you

may tell the student with the pen that he or she must end up with the pencil, but the student cannot directly trade the pen for the pencil.

Political Science When the Roman Empire fell, no new, single entity rose to replace it. Instead, Europe divided into several smaller fiefdoms.

■ Have students research the politics of feudalism and create a graphic organizer that shows the power structure of Medieval Europe.

History History was very important to the people of the Middle Ages, but there were few books and the vast majority of people could not read. Therefore, one source of information was the traveling troubadour.

■ Ask students to research how the troubadour shared both ancient tales and current events.

■ Students may wish to role-play a troubadour who is bringing news of current events to the students of the class.

Anthropology An interesting misconception about Medieval life is that the rich enjoyed a high standard of living.

■ Ask students to research the actual standard of living enjoyed by the upper classes. Have them center on issues such as heat and water, food production and preparation, and overall comfort of life.

■ It is interesting to note that neither the rich nor the poor had glass in their windows; the castles were extremely drafty, damp, and smoky, and few people in any class had furniture. Students may be surprised to learn that they probably would not have enjoyed living in a castle as much as they think they would.

Global Awareness The Dark Ages were very intense times in Europe, but it is important to remember that the Dark Ages were not experienced by the entire world. Ask students to hypothesize about the following questions:

1. Why did the Dark Ages happen in Europe?
2. Which areas did not experience the Dark Ages?
3. Why did the Dark Ages not spread from Europe throughout the world?

■ Have students research and write a short report about what was happening in another part of the world (such as Japan, China, or North America) during the Dark Ages.

SCIENCE

■ One of the most puzzling issues for many students is the state of Medieval medicine in Europe. For instance, in approximately 500 B.C., the Indian surgeon Susrate performed cataract operations, the Greek physician Alcmaeon discovered the ear's eustachian tubes, as well as the differences between veins and arteries. He is also credited with discovering the connection between the brain and the sense organs. Yet as late as one thousand years later, European doctors were attributing disease to evil spirits floating in the blood. Their favorite remedy was to force these spirits from the body by bleeding the patient.

■ Ask students to research the state of Dark Ages medicine, making sure to study the causes and effects of the plagues. After their research is finished, have students answer the following questions in a written report.

1. Would this situation have come about if people had had great medical knowledge? Why or why not?
2. How is knowledge lost in a society?
3. Could a period such as the Dark Ages happen to us today?

ART

■ Students may wish to research the form and structure of European castles and then build a model of one.

■ Other students may wish to create illustrations of a castle. One excellent source of information about castles is David MacCaulay's *Castle* (Boston: Houghton Mifflin, 1977. ISBN 0-395-25784-0).

LANGUAGE ARTS

■ People's ways of life in the Middle Ages depended largely on who they were. The lives of the peasants, or the poor who worked the land, were very different from the lives of the rich, or nobles, who owned the land. The lives of townspeople were different from those of both the peasants and the nobles.

■ Have students research the different life styles of the Middle Ages and compose journal entries from the point of view of one or two of the following people:

1. a serf's wife
2. a lord's daughter or son
3. a city dweller
4. a knight
5. a king

Have a Guest Speaker

INSTRUCTIONS FOR THE TEACHER:

Why Have a Guest Speaker? Most teachers agree that primary sources are very important to the teaching of Social Studies. However, many teachers overlook one very important primary source — guest speakers. Not only can these speakers "bring history alive" for students, but they also provide a change of pace, allowing students to evaluate primary source material, just like real historians.

Choosing a Guest Speaker for This Unit This unit covers the history of the lands and peoples of Western Europe. Such a broad topic lends itself to many opportunities for guest speakers.Discuss with students the types of people who would be good resources for this unit. Most can be found right in your own community. Try to elicit the following suggestions:

1. World War II veterans who served in Western Europe
2. Immigrants from Western Europe
3. Those who have visited or lived in Western Europe
4. Local college or university professors who teach a course in the history or geography of the region

Many of these specialists will enjoy volunteering their time for a presentation to your class and are often equipped with wonderful slides and other audiovisual aids that are interesting to students. You may even find someone in your own school building who would make an excellent speaker.

What If I Can't Find People Who Lived During That Time Period? There are many resources for guest speakers besides people who lived through the time period being studied. Experts in a relevant field can also provide entertaining and informative presentations for your students. For example, students could compare the role of the military in Europe during World War II with the role of the military today by listening to a guest speaker who currently serves in the armed forces.

ACTIVITY FOR THE STUDENTS:

Preparation for the Guest Speaker The guest speaker is most effective when students have been properly prepared for his or her visit. The following tips would help accomplish this.

■ Students need to have as much background on the subject as possible. If the speaker is talking about life in France, students should know as much about the country as possible. Therefore, it is advisable to invite guest speakers after the students have studied a unit or chapter that relates to the subject matter. This will allow students to build a broad knowledge base from which they can draw good questions.

■ Have students prepare a list of questions that they would like to ask the guest. This could be done individually or in groups.

■ You may wish to have students create a K-W-L chart on the chalkboard before the guest speaker arrives. First, write the speaker's topic on the board.

Next, have students

1. write under the K all that they currently *know* about the topic.
2. write under the W all that they *want* to know about that topic.
3. write under the L all that they *learned* from the speaker (as a follow-up activity after the speaker has left).

Extension Students might also enjoy the following activities:

■ Writing a news report about the guest speaker's presentation for a class newsletter or school newspaper

■ Preparing invitations or thank-you notes for the guest, citing the exciting things that they expect to learn, or things that they did learn

■ Interviewing the guest speaker before or after the presentation for a class or schoolwide video news program (The interview could also be adapted to the school's public-address system, or it could be conducted live in front of other sixth graders.)

Unit Test

Content Test

Directions: Fill in the circle next to the correct answer.

1. The Ural Mountains form the dividing line between _____.

- (A) Europe and Asia
- (B) Asia and Africa
- (C) Africa and Europe
- (D) Western Europe and Africa

2. What effect does the North Atlantic Drift have on Europe?

- (A) It is moving the continent closer to the Americas.
- (B) It is moving the continent closer to Asia.
- (C) It makes Europe cooler in the winter.
- (D) It makes Europe warmer in the winter.

3. Population density is a measure of _____.

- (A) how many people live in an area
- (B) the average rainfall a place receives
- (C) the number of people moving to a place
- (D) how many people can read

4. Which European language is spoken by the most people?

- (A) English
- (B) German
- (C) Spanish
- (D) French

5. An association of townspeople in the same business was called a _____.

- (A) fief
- (B) guild
- (C) manor
- (D) monastery

6. The document that guaranteed the rights of English nobles was the _____.

- (A) Magna Carta
- (B) Runnymede
- (C) common law
- (D) Crusades

7. The effort to free the Holy Land from Muslim control was called the _____.

- (A) War of the Roses
- (B) Crusades
- (C) Hundred Years' War
- (D) Viking raid

8. The reformer who believed that the Bible was the most important authority in Christianity was _____.

- (A) King John
- (B) Martin Luther
- (C) Leonardo da Vinci
- (D) Johann Gutenberg

9. Who discovered that the earth moves around the sun?

- (A) Pope Urban II
- (B) Anton Van Leeuwenhoek
- (C) Nicolaus Copernicus
- (D) Eli Whitney

10. Gabriel Fahrenheit invented a _____.

- (A) cotton gin
- (B) telescope
- (C) steam engine
- (D) thermometer

CONTENT TEST (continued)

11. The change in how people work brought about by inventions during the 1700s was called the _____.

- (A) Middle Ages
- (B) Industrial Revolution
- (C) Renaissance
- (D) Inquisition

12. Radicals began a "reign of terror" following the revolution in _____.

- (A) the United States
- (B) Britain
- (C) France
- (D) Waterloo

13. The belief in loyalty and devotion to one's country is called _____.

- (A) unification
- (B) nationalism
- (C) genocide
- (D) Fascism

14. Which leader helped bring about a united Germany in 1871?

- (A) Otto von Bismarck
- (B) Giuseppe Mazzini
- (C) Carl Schurz
- (D) Adolf Hitler

15. Which is a landlocked country?

- (A) Germany
- (B) Sweden
- (C) Switzerland
- (D) France

16. Which was a result of World War I?

- (A) the division of Germany among the Allies
- (B) the creation of the United Nations
- (C) the payment of damages by Germany
- (D) the unification of Italy

17. World War II began when Germany refused to halt its attack on _____.

- (A) Britain
- (B) Poland
- (C) Bosnia
- (D) Japan

18. The association of nations that once made up the British Empire is called the _____.

- (A) Commonwealth of Nations
- (B) European Community
- (C) United Kingdom
- (D) League of Nations

19. Which country's name means "low lands"?

- (A) the Netherlands
- (B) Liechtenstein
- (C) Luxembourg
- (D) Ireland

20. Which country is located on the Iberian Peninsula?

- (A) Malta
- (B) Belgium
- (C) San Marino
- (D) Spain

Skills Test

Directions: Read the biography and complete items 1–6. Fill in the circle next to the correct answer.

Bertha von Suttner (1843–1914)

When Bertha Kinsky was a young girl in Austria, she read *Uncle Tom's Cabin* by the American writer Harriet Beecher Stowe. The book told of suffering caused by slavery. Years later, Bertha wrote a book that was compared to *Uncle Tom's Cabin*. Bertha's book, *Lay Down Your Arms*, told of the suffering caused by wars.

Bertha had taken a job as a governess in the Vienna home of Baron von Suttner where she fell in love with the Suttner's son, Arthur. The baron did not approve, so Bertha went to Paris to work for Alfred Nobel, the inventor of dynamite.

Bertha was in Paris for only one week. Arthur followed her there and persuaded her to marry him. They then went to live in Russia for nine years. Returning to Vienna, Bertha began

to think seriously about wars. "Day by day," she wrote, "it became a fixed idea with me that wars must cease . . ."

Bertha began to work on *Lay Down Your Arms*. She read about wars, visited battlefields, and talked to eye-witnesses. *Lay Down Your Arms* appeared in 1889 and was a huge success. The Russian writer Leo Tolstoy said of the book, "What *Uncle Tom's Cabin* did against slavery in America, your book should do for peace."

Bertha convinced Alfred Nobel to leave part of his fortune for a peace prize. The first Nobel Peace Prize was awarded in 1901. And in 1905 Bertha von Suttner was the first woman to win it.

Bertha von Suttner died on June 20, 1914. Less than two months later, World War I began.

1. The baron probably disapproved of the relationship between Bertha and his son because Bertha was _____.

- (A) a governess
- (B) a woman
- (C) against slavery
- (D) not very intelligent

2. The eye-witnesses with whom Bertha talked probably _____.

- (A) knew her husband
- (B) wrote history books
- (C) had been slaves
- (D) had lived through a war

3. Bertha's main reason for writing *Lay Down Your Arms* was to _____.

- (A) show that war is wrong
- (B) tell of her experiences in Russia
- (C) pay homage to Alfred Nobel
- (D) tell about the life of Harriet Beecher Stowe

4. Leo Tolstoy said that he hoped von Suttner's book would _____.

- (A) become very popular
- (B) end slavery
- (C) make people proud
- (D) help to bring peace

5. Both *Lay Down Your Arms* and *Uncle Tom's Cabin* are about _____.

- (A) war
- (B) slavery
- (C) suffering
- (D) Russia

6. Which statement about Bertha von Suttner is true?

- (A) Her death led to World War I.
- (B) Her ideas became known to many people.
- (C) She won the first Nobel Prize.
- (D) She dedicated her life to nursing.

SKILLS TEST (continued)

Directions: Study the table and complete items 7–10. Fill in the circle next to the correct answer.

Using SQR			
Survey	• Look at headings, questions, vocabulary words, and visuals.	• Think about what you already know about the topic.	• Make predictions about the lesson topic.
Question	• Think about the questions already in the lesson.	• Use vocabulary words, headings, and other lesson features to prepare your own questions.	• Make predictions about the lesson content.
Read	• Read to answer your questions.	• Write down the answers or say them to yourself.	• Ask and answer any other questions that come to mind as you read.

7. You should use the SQR plan when you want to _____.

- (A) read for enjoyment
- (B) waste your time
- (C) don't really want to read the whole book
- (D) understand and remember ideas in a textbook

8. In which step do you make predictions about content?

- (A) Survey
- (B) Question
- (C) Read
- (D) Write

9. In which step do you look at vocabulary words and visuals?

- (A) Survey
- (B) Question
- (C) Read
- (D) Write

10. Which step gives you a general idea of what the lesson is about?

- (A) Survey
- (B) Question
- (C) Read
- (D) Write

Unit Test

ESSAY TEST

Directions: Write a response to items 1–4.

> **REMINDER:** Read and think about each item before you write your response. Be sure to think of the points you want to cover, details that support your response, and reasons for your opinions. Then, on the lines below, write your response in complete sentences.

1. What was a manor?

A satisfactory response should include the following statements:

- A manor was a large farm or estate in the Middle Ages.
- A noble was the lord of each manor and ran it.
- The economy of the manor was based on farming, in which peasants—most of them serfs—worked for the lord.

An excellent response might also mention that

- serfs differed from free peasants in that they owed their labor to the lord and could not leave the manor without his permission
- nobles lived in large houses on their manors, and the most powerful nobles lived in castles
- each manor had a village in which the peasants lived.

2. What is Parliament?

A satisfactory response should explain that Parliament is the law-making body in Britain.

An excellent response might also describe the British Parliament as

- made up of two houses—the House of Lords and the House of Commons
- the center of the dispute that led to the bloodless revolution in 1688
- part of the system of constitutional monarchy.

ESSAY TEST (continued)

3. How did nationalism help lead to World War I?

A satisfactory response will explain that the war began after Serbian nationalists from Bosnia assassinated the archduke of Austria as part of their campaign for freedom from the Austro-Hungarian Empire.

An excellent response might add that other nations were quickly drawn into the conflict between Serbia and Austria because of the complicated system of alliances between European countries.

4. Describe the governments of Western Europe.

A satisfactory response will state that the countries of Western Europe have democratic governments.

An excellent response might explain that different countries have different governing arrangements and give some examples:

- *democratic republics:*   Germany, Austria, France, Italy, San Marino, Portugal, Cyprus
- *principalities:* Liechtenstein, Andorra
- *democratic monarchies:* United Kingdom, Norway, Sweden, Denmark, Belgium, Spain
- *grand duchy:* Luxembourg.

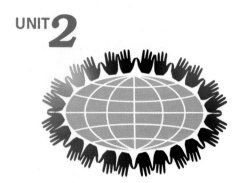

MULTICULTURAL PERSPECTIVES

English as Another Language
(pages 167–168)

Several countries in Europe have more than one official language. Ask your students to write a one-page essay that addresses whether or not the United States should have more than one official language. What would that language or languages be?

Ask students to look at the graph on page 168, which depicts major European languages around the world. Ask students to speculate on why English, Spanish, and Russian are the three European languages spoken by the greatest number of people in the world. (Answers may include that Great Britain and Spain were leaders in exploration and colonization throughout the world. Russia has a very large population and takes up a significant geographical area.)

Time Sequence *(pages 174-183)*

Ask students to list the dates of events of the medieval period, as outlined in Chapter 6. Remind the students that the medieval period, or the Middle Ages, occurred approximately between the years A.D. 500 and A.D. 1500.

Divide the class into three teams, assigning to each team one region—Asia, Africa, or the Americas. Instruct each team to select five dates for events that happened in their region between the years 500 and 1500. For their research, the students should refer to other chapters in the text and use encyclopedias and other library resources.

Then have each team of students create a time line for its region on a sheet of oaktag. Suggest that the teams make their time lines more interesting by finding pictures that highlight the time period in their region.

Optional Activities

Making Inferences

● Have students infer, from analyzing the visuals and reading the descriptions on pp. 152-153, three things that they will study in this unit.

● Student answers may include architecture (for the castle and Big Ben and the British parliament), machinery or inventions (for the spinning frame), and military leaders or history (for Otto von Bismarck).

unit 2
WESTERN EUROPE

For centuries, Western Europe has been a center of dramatic changes that have had far-reaching effects on other parts of the world.

▶ *Hundreds of years ago, powerful lords in Western Europe built castles that provided protection during attacks. Bodiam Castle, complete with a moat, still stands in Sussex, England.*

Three Revolutions *(pages 201–219)*
The French Revolution began in 1789, not very long after the American Revolution ended. In 1791, more than 100,000 African slaves initiated a revolution in Haiti. Ask students to read about the reasons for each of these revolts. What were the similarities between the three revolutions? (Answers should focus on the issue of liberty.)

The Effects of War *(pages 235–243)*
Studies have shown that young people today worry about the effects of nuclear war, pollution, and disease, and about other humanistic concerns.

The atomic bombs that the United States dropped on Hiroshima and Nagasaki, Japan, in 1945 changed the course of history. Never before had such total destruction taken place so quickly. The people of Japan spent years recovering from the effects of radiation.

You may want to share with students some firsthand accounts of the bombings. A possible source is John Hershey's *Hiroshima* (New York: Random House, 1989). However, some students may find the information and this type of discussion very disturbing.

Discuss with students their ideas about what steps people in today's world should take to help to ensure world peace.

Optional Activities

Geography of Western Europe
(pp. 154-171)

Chapter Theme: The blend of physical features, natural resources, and different peoples in Western Europe make it a unique region.

LESSON *1* The Continent and Its Climate
(pp. 154-162)

Theme: Western Europe's geography features rivers, seas, mountains, islands, and plains.

LESSON *2* A Variety of Peoples on a Small Continent
(pp. 163-169)

Theme: Europe is a small continent with a large and varied population.

Review Masters

REVIEWING CHAPTER VOCABULARY

VOCABULARY MASTER

Review Study the terms in the box. Use your Glossary to find definitions of those you do not remember.

climograph	deciduous	metropolitan area	rural
coniferous	forestry	natural resource	urban
current	Gulf Stream	North Atlantic Drift	

Practice Complete the paragraphs using terms from the box above. You may change the forms of the terms to fit the meaning.

The climate in the north of the former Soviet Union is so harsh that few people can live there. A (1) __climograph__ for that area would show that temperatures drop very low in the winter. Because so few people live there, the region is still covered with forests. The (2) __coniferous__ forests, green all year, are an important (3) __natural resource__ for the former Soviet Union. Loggers brave the cold winters to fell the trees used to make paper and other products.

In the past, much of Western Europe was covered with forests. However, because the soil was rich, people used the land in other ways. First, the forests were cleared for farmland. Then, as time passed and factories were built, many people moved from (4) __rural__ areas into the developing towns and cities. Today, most people live in (5) __urban__ areas, and some cities have grown into huge (6) __metropolitan areas__. However, some of the old forests, such as the Black Forest in Germany, still exist and attract many tourists each year.

Write Write a sentence of your own for each term in the box above. You may use the back of the sheet.

Sentences should show that students understand the meanings of the terms.

_____
_____
_____
_____
_____
_____
_____
_____
_____

© Silver, Burdett & Ginn Inc.

LOCATING PLACES

PLACE GEOGRAPHY MASTER

✱ In the eighteenth century, wealthy young Englishmen were often sent on a "Grand Tour" of Europe visiting places they had studied. Listed below are European cities that were often a part of this trip. Use the Gazetteer in your textbook to find the latitude and longitude of each place. Then locate and label each on the map.

	LAT.	LONG.			LAT.	LONG.
1. Dover, England	51°N	1°E	6. Milan, Italy		45°N	9°E
2. London, England	52°N	0°	7. Berlin, Germany		53°N	13°E
3. Florence, Italy	44°N	11°E	8. Paris, France		49°N	2°E
4. Rome, Italy	42°N	12°E	9. Athens, Greece		38°N	24°E
5. Venice, Italy	46°N	12°E	10. Bern, Switzerland		47°N	7°E

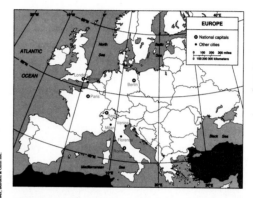

© Silver, Burdett & Ginn Inc.

SUMMARIZING THE CHAPTER

GRAPHIC ORGANIZER MASTER

✱ Complete this graphic organizer. Under the heading, fill in each blank with an answer to support it.

CHAPTER THEME The blend of physical features, natural resources, and different peoples in Western Europe make it a unique region.

Land of Western Europe

Mountains
1. Alps
2. Pyrenees
3. Apennines

Rivers
1. Rhine
2. Rhone
3. Po

Seas
1. Mediterranean
2. Adriatic
3. Aegean

Natural Resources
1. Good soil
2. Plentiful rainfall
3. Trees

People of Western Europe

Densely Populated Countries
1. France
2. West Germany
3. The Netherlands

European Languages
1. French
2. Italian
3. English

Democratic Freedoms
1. Freedom of speech
2. Freedom of the press
3. Freedom of worship

© Silver, Burdett & Ginn Inc.

C5-B

Workbook Pages

KEY FACTS OF EUROPEAN GEOGRAPHY

Identifying Landforms and Bodies of Water; Understanding Compass Directions

✳ Below are six categories of information about the land, waters, and natural resources of Europe. Fill in the blanks, referring to a map in your textbook when necessary.
Possible answers are provided.

PENINSULAS

A peninsula is a land area almost surrounded by water. The word *peninsula* comes from a Latin term meaning "almost island." Name seven countries in Western Europe that form peninsulas by themselves or with one other country.

1. Italy
2. Spain and 3. Portugal
4. Greece
5. Norway and 6. Sweden
7. Denmark

ISLANDS

Name three Western European countries that are islands.

1. Great Britain (United Kingdom)
2. Ireland
3. Iceland

EUROPEAN INDUSTRY

Name three ways in which Western Europeans use their natural resources to make a living.

1. Fishing
2. Manufacturing goods
3. Forestry, etc.

BODIES OF WATER

Name seven large bodies of water of Europe.

1. Adriatic Sea
2. Aegean Sea
3. Atlantic Ocean
4. Baltic Sea
5. Black Sea
6. Mediterranean Sea
7. North Sea, etc.

INTERIOR WATERWAYS

Name the rivers on which the following European cities are located.

1. Bonn, Germany — Rhine River
2. Paris, France — Seine River
3. London, Great Britain — Thames River
4. Rome, Italy — Tiber River

COMPASS DIRECTION

1. Which island countries lie west of Belgium and the Netherlands?

   Great Britain; Ireland

2. Switzerland lies — northeast — of Spain.
3. Denmark lies — north — of Germany.

Thinking Further: Europe is made up of many independent countries, whereas North America is divided into very few. On a separate sheet of paper, describe three or more ways an American tourist might notice the different countries of Europe. The differences might include languages, laws, customs, clothing, or money.

      © Silver, Burdett & Ginn Inc.

CREATING A PICTOGRAPH

Understanding Graphs, Applying Information

✳ Using information in the table, complete the pictograph showing the populations of six major European cities.

a. Write the names of the cities on the lines to the left of the graph. The city with the most people—Madrid—has been written on the top line for you. Put the second largest city on the second line, and so forth.

b. Look at the picture above the graph. The whole picture represents 500,000 people. You can use up to one picture per square on the graph. Use only part of a picture to indicate a number of less than 500,000. For example, draw two fifths of a picture to indicate 200,000 people. That was done to indicate 200,000 people in the line for Madrid. Draw only as many pictures or parts of pictures as needed.

City	Population (estimate)
Athens, Greece	890,000
Bonn, Germany	290,000
Madrid, Spain	3,200,000
Paris, France	2,200,000
Rome, Italy	2,800,000
Stockholm, Sweden	660,000

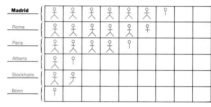 = 500,000 people

Thinking Further: The same information is presented in two forms on this page. Describe one advantage and one disadvantage of each form, as shown on the page.

Advantages: table shows exact numbers; pictograph makes it easy to compare cities. Disadvantages: on table, comparisons are difficult; pictograph provides inexact numbers.

© Silver, Burdett & Ginn Inc.

IDENTIFYING COUNTRIES ON A MAP

Using Latitude and Longitude, Making Observations

✳ The map on the facing page shows outlines of countries in Europe, including part of Russia. The table below lists some of the countries and the latitude and longitude coordinates of a location in each country. For each country, use the coordinates to identify its location on the map. Then write the name of the country on the map. A few have been done for you.

Country	Location in Country	Country	Location in Country
Albania	41°N/20°E	Ireland	53°N/8°W
Austria	47°N/15°E	Italy	45°N/10°E
Belgium	51°N/5°E	Luxembourg	50°N/8°E
Bulgaria	43°N/25°E	Netherlands	52°N/5°E
Czechoslovakia	50°N/15°E	Norway	60°N/10°E
Denmark	57°N/10°E	Poland	52°N/20°E
Finland	62°N/25°E	Portugal	40°N/8°W
France	45°N/5°E	Romania	45°N/25°E
Germany	50°N/10°E	Russia	55°N/40°E
Great Britain	52°N/0°	Spain	40°N/5°W
Greece	40°N/22°E	Sweden	60°N/15°E
Hungary	47°N/20°E	Switzerland	47°N/8°E

      © Silver, Burdett & Ginn Inc.

IDENTIFYING COUNTRIES ON A MAP *CONTINUED*

Thinking Further: Name the countries in Europe that are landlocked and explain why being landlocked could be a problem.

Students should list Czechoslovakia, Luxembourg, Austria, Hungary, Switzerland, and Macedonia, and may mention that landlocked countries can be denied access to the sea if they are not on friendly terms with neighboring countries.

© Silver, Burdett & Ginn Inc.

Workbook Pages

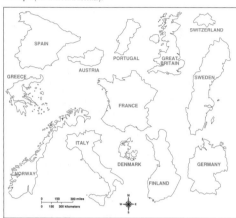

TEACHER NOTES

The Continent and Its Climate

Objectives

★**1. Describe** the physical characteristics of Western Europe.

2. Explain how the term *Western Europe* developed.

3. List the resources of Western Europe.

4. Identify the following people and places: *Michael Paccard, British Isles, Eurasia, Balkan Peninsula, Italian Peninsula, Iberian Peninsula,* and *Jutland.*

1 STARTING THE LESSON

Motivation Activity

■ Ask students to name some things that come to mind when they hear the word *Europe*.

■ If students need help, you may want to mention specific countries in Europe or start them off with sights such as the Eiffel Tower, Buckingham Palace, and the Leaning Tower of Pisa.

■ Write their answers on the chalkboard. Then, tell students that they will read about this interesting continent in this lesson.

Think About What You Know

■ Assign the THINK ABOUT WHAT YOU KNOW activity on p. 155.

■ Student answers may include Mount Olympus, Thermopylae, Bay of Salamis, Hellespont, Aegean Sea, Tiber River, the Alps, or Mount Vesuvius.

Study the Vocabulary

■ Have students look up in their Glossary the definition of each of the new vocabulary words for this lesson.

■ Then, ask students to categorize the words by placing those related to the land in one column and those related to climate in another.

CHAPTER 5

GEOGRAPHY OF WESTERN EUROPE

*T*he physical landscape of Western Europe include majestic mountains, rivers and peninsulas. The moderate climate, good soil, and valuable natural resources make Western Europe a favorable region

Optional Activities

Writing to Learn

Writing a Letter   Tell students to imagine that they are being sent on a Grand Tour of Europe.

● Have them use the photographs in this chapter and the information in this lesson to write a letter home.

● Letters should describe where they have been, what they have seen, and what they have learned about Europe.

The Continent and Its Climate

THINK ABOUT WHAT YOU KNOW

The region of Western Europe includes many countries with many different physical characteristics. What are some physical features in Greece and Italy that you have already studied?

STUDY THE VOCABULARY

natural resource   current
deciduous   Gulf Stream
coniferous   North Atlantic
forestry   Drift
climograph

FOCUS YOUR READING

What are some of the physical characteristics of Western Europe?

A. The Grand Tour

The Grand Tour was a trip through Western Europe taken by a young Englishman and his tutor, or teacher. In the eighteenth century, wealthy English families often sent their sons on the Grand Tour after they had finished school. The eighteenth century, you remember, was the hundred years between 1701 and 1800.

It was thought that the Grand Tour completed a young gentleman's education. It was supposed to improve his manners and develop his mind. There were probably good reasons for attempting to do both. The manners of some young men were compared to those of wild bears, so their tutors were called bearkeepers. As for developing their minds, this task must have been difficult in some cases. One young fellow journeyed through Italy scarcely looking out the window of his coach. He was more interested in his dog and her puppies than in enjoying the beautiful Italian countryside.

The Grand Tour began with crossing the English Channel. This is the arm of the Atlantic Ocean that connects with the North Sea and separates the British Isles from the European continent. The British Isles are a large group of islands located off the west coast of Europe. The two largest islands are Great Britain and Ireland. The travelers gathered at Dover or one of the other channel ports to board a sailboat. Sometimes they had to wait several days for a favorable wind. This was before there were steamships.

The English Channel is narrow, but its waters can be rough. Some of the young tourists became so seasick that they thought they would die. Of course, they didn't, but seasickness can make a person feel miserable.

Once on shore, the students and their tutors traveled either in horse-drawn coaches or in barges called water carriages. Travel by water was much smoother than travel by coach over rough roads, and Western Europe had a number of rivers and canals. In later chapters you will read about some important waterways that are still used for shipping.

Few of the eighteenth-century tourists were interested in Western Europe's mountains. Most travelers regarded the Alps in Switzerland as a barrier to cross rather than a natural wonder to be visited. Of course, travel across the Alps was difficult 200 years ago. There were no good roads or tunnels, only steep and dangerous trails over the high passes. A coach could not be driven over these trails. Instead it had to be taken apart and loaded on the backs of pack animals, such as donkeys. A

2 DEVELOPING THE LESSON

Read and Think

Section A

To summarize what the Grand Tour was like for young men in the eighteenth century, ask the following questions:

1. **What was the Grand Tour supposed to do for young English gentlemen?**
(Complete their education, improve their manners, and develop their minds *p. 155*)

2. **Why was the Grand Tour a difficult trip to make 200 years ago?**
(There were no steamships to make the channel crossing quick and smooth, roads were rough, and mountains were difficult to cross. *p. 155*)

Thinking Critically What, do you think, can a person learn by traveling to another country? (Infer)
(Answers should reflect independent thinking, but may include that one can learn about other ways of life, history, art, architecture, and languages. *p. 155*)

For Your Information

The English Channel   The English Channel is an arm of the Atlantic Ocean extending between Britain and France to the North Sea. Noted for its rough seas and bad weather, the channel is about 350 miles (563 km) long, with a maximum width of about 150 miles (241 km). Its narrowest part is 21 miles (34 km), between Dover and Cap Gris-Nez. It is believed that the channel was once a gulf and that Britain was joined to the continent.

Optional Activities

Read and Think
Sections B and C

Begin a discussion of the countries and land of Western Europe with the following questions:

1. **What separates Europe from Asia?**
(The Ural Mountains *p. 156*)

2. **Why does Europe have such a long coastline?**
(Because of its shape—Europe has several small peninsulas that extend into the sea *p. 156*)

3. **Name the peninsulas of Europe.**
(Italian, Iberian, Balkan, Jutland, and Scandinavian *p. 156*)

4. **Which Western European countries are not located on the European mainland?**
(Great Britain, Ireland, Iceland, Malta, and Cyprus *p. 156*)

5. **How did the term *Western Europe* develop?**
(After World War II the countries of Europe were divided into two groups. Those in Eastern Europe fell under the control of the Soviet Union. Those in Western Europe remained free of Soviet control. *pp. 156-158*)

Thinking Critically Keeping the location of Europe in mind, what, do you think, can you infer about how some Europeans make their living?
(Infer)
(Answers should reflect independent thinking but may include by fishing, shipping, and boatbuilding. *pp. 156-158*)

People endured difficulties as they climbed Mont Blanc in the 1850s.
▶ Are these tourists well equipped for mountain climbing?

traveler unable to make the climb on foot could arrange to be carried on a seat hanging between two poles. But it took a team of six strong people to carry a person of average size over a steep pass. A heavier person required eight, and a truly hefty tourist needed a team of ten people.

Because of the difficulty of crossing the Alps, some tourists avoided the mountains altogether. They took a boat in southern France and sailed along the Mediterranean coast to Italy.

Europe has changed greatly since the young English gentlemen took the Grand Tour, but the rivers, seas, mountains, and plains are still there. In this chapter you will learn about them by taking your own Grand Tour through reading.

B. Europe: A Part of Eurasia

Europe and Asia are both called continents, although they are both located on the same great landmass. These two continents are separated by the Ural Mountains. The landmass is called Eurasia, which is a combination of *Europe* and *Asia*. Europe is a peninsula of Eurasia, as the map on pages 618–619 shows.

Even though Europe is a small continent, it has a long coastline because of its shape. Several smaller peninsulas extend into the seas from the larger peninsula of Europe. Italy is the boot-shaped peninsula of southern Europe. Spain and Portugal are on the Iberian Peninsula, which has the Atlantic Ocean on one side and the Mediterranean Sea on the other. The Balkan Peninsula of southeastern Europe is divided into six countries. Greece forms the tip. The other countries are Albania, Bulgaria, Romania, European Turkey, and Yugoslavia. In northern Europe the Arctic Circle crosses the Scandinavian peninsula, which is divided into Norway and Sweden. Jutland is a smaller peninsula in the north. Denmark is located on Jutland.

C. The Land and Water of Western Europe

Most of the lands that make up Western Europe are located on the western part of the European mainland, but some are not. Some are islands. Great Britain, Ireland, and Iceland are islands in the Atlantic Ocean. Malta and Cyprus are islands in the Mediterranean Sea. Greece is located on the continent, but it is in the southeastern part rather than the western part.

The term *Western Europe* grew out of history rather than geography. After World War II the countries of Europe were divided into two different groups. In

Optional Activities

Building a Model

● Have students use an opaque projector to enlarge an outline map of Western Europe. Have them trace the map on posterboard.

● Students can then build a three-dimensional model of Western European physical features on the posterboard.

● Tell students to include features such as boundaries, mountains, rivers, and seas.

WESTERN EUROPE: PHYSICAL

The Alps

The lands of Western Europe include high mountain ranges and fertile valleys.
► In which mountain range can Mont Blanc be found?

Elevations
Meters
3,000
1,500
600
300
0

● Cities
▲ Mountain peak
▦ Canals

0   200   400 miles
0   200   400 kilometers

Interpreting a Painting

■ Direct students' attention to the painting on p. 156. Have students compare this painting of the top-hatted mountain climbers with our current view of rugged mountaineers.

GEOGRAPHY THEMES

Location

■ Direct students' attention to the map on p. 157. Ask them to think about and write a response to the following question: **Locate and name the mountain ranges that Hannibal crossed when he left Spain to invade and defeat Rome.**
(The Pyrenees, the Alps, and the Apennines)

Answers to Caption Questions

p. 156 ► No, they appear to be inappropriately dressed.
p. 157 ► The Alps

Playing a Geography Game

● Prepare flashcards for all the countries of Europe as shown on the map on p. 157.

● Divide the class into four teams. Tell students that they will be playing a geography game in which you will hold up a flashcard of a European country and they will have to identify on which peninsula of Europe that country is located.

● Remind students that some European countries are not located on peninsulas.

● Give a point to the first team to provide each correct answer. The team with the most points at the end of the game wins.

For Your Information

The Rock of Gibraltar   The Rock of Gibraltar is a huge limestone mass that lies at the southern tip of the Iberian Peninsula. It rises nearly 1,400 feet (427 m) above the sea. The rock stands on the European side of the Strait of Gibraltar while a similar rocky ridge stands on the African side.

The ancient Greeks called these two rocks the Pillars of Hercules. According to an old myth, the opening to the Mediterranean had once been much wider. Hercules, the strong son of a god, pulled the two pillars closer together to keep the Atlantic Ocean's sea monsters from entering the Mediterranean.

Optional Activities

Read and Think

Section D

Begin a discussion of the mountains of Western Europe and the first mountaineers with the following questions:

1. **Name the mountain ranges of Western Europe.**
   (Alps, Pyrenees, and Apennines *pp. 158-160*)

2. **What was the great accomplishment of Paccard and Balmat?**
   (They were the first people to reach the top of Mont Blanc, the highest peak in the Alps. *p. 158*)

   Thinking Critically Which mountain range, do you think, would be most difficult for mountaineering? (Evaluate)
   (Answers should reflect independent thinking, but may include either the Alps, because they have the tallest mountains, or the Pyrenees, because they are so rugged. *pp. 159-160*)

VISUAL THINKING SKILL

Appreciating a Photograph

■ Direct students' attention to the photograph of Mont Blanc on p. 159. After students have read the description of Mont Blanc written by Mark Twain, ask them to write a descriptive paragraph of the mountain based on what they see in the photograph.

Eastern Europe the Soviet Union established its government in a number of countries. The countries of Western Europe remained free of Soviet control. You will read about this division of Europe and its end in later chapters.

Because of the continent's shape, no place in Western Europe is more than 300 miles (481 km) from the sea. Ships enter the Mediterranean Sea from the Atlantic Ocean through the Strait of Gibraltar. Here only about three fourths of a mile (1 km) separates Europe from Africa. The Adriatic and Aegean seas are arms of the Mediterranean. Ships can sail from the Aegean

This fancy dress and stockings were considered fashionable for women mountain climbers in the 1870s.
► Was this outfit practical?

through the Dardanelles and Bosporus (BAHS puh rus) into the Black Sea. The North and Baltic seas provide routes to northern Europe. A look at the map on page 157 suggests why many Europeans became sailors or fishers. It has been easy to go to sea from much of Western Europe.

D. Mountains of Western Europe

Mont Blanc Dr. Michael Paccard (pak-kar) was a village physician, but he was not seeing patients on the day of August 8, 1786. Instead, he and a companion named Balmat were slowly making their way over snow and slippery ice to the top of Mont Blanc (mohn blahn) in France. No one had ever climbed Mont Blanc, the highest peak in the Alps.

In the village below the mountain, a man watched the slow progress of the climbers through his telescope. When the climbers finally reached the top of the peak, Dr. Paccard tied a handkerchief on his climbing stick and waved it so the watcher would know that Mont Blanc had been conquered.

On that August day over 200 years ago, Paccard and Balmat climbed Mont Blanc just for the thrill of doing it. Their climb is said to have marked the birth of mountaineering, mountain climbing as a sport. Many men and women took up the sport in the years that followed. The picture on this page shows what the fashionable woman of 1870 was supposed to wear when she went mountaineering.

Almost a century after Paccard and Balmat had reached the peak, Mark Twain saw Mont Blanc while touring Europe. He later wrote a travel book about his tour. The following is an excerpt from Twain's book *A Tramp Abroad*, describing Mont Blanc.

Writing to Learn

Writing a Newspaper Article Ask students to imagine that they are journalists writing newspaper articles about Paccard and Balmat's climb to the top of Mont Blanc in 1786.

● Remind them to include the five *w*'s (who, what, when, where, and why) in the article.

● Display the articles on a bulletin board.

Curriculum Connection

Art Have students collect travel posters and magazine photographs that show the physical features of Western Europe.

● Ask them to put the photographs and posters on a bulletin-board display entitled "The Land of Western Europe."

● Tell students to put a label underneath each picture so that observers will know what part of Western Europe they are viewing.

Mont Blanc, the highest peak in the Alps, was called the "monarch of the Alps" by Mark Twain. This photograph shows Mont Blanc rising above Chamonix Valley in France.
▶ Why, do you think, did Mark Twain refer to this mountain as the "monarch of the Alps"?

About half an hour before we reached the village . . . a vast dome of snow with the sun blazing on it drifted into view and framed itself in a strong V-shaped gateway of the mountains, and we recognized Mont Blanc, "the monarch of the Alps." With every step after that this stately dome rose higher and higher into the blue sky and at last seemed to occupy the zenith [peak.] . . . We . . . saw exquisite prismatic colors [rainbow colors] playing about some white clouds which were so delicate as to almost resemble gossamer [threadlike] webs. . . . We sat down to study and enjoy this singular spectacle.

The Alps The Alps are the largest group of mountains in Western Europe. The Alps form parts of France, Switzerland, Italy, Germany, Austria, as well as the former Yugoslavia. Waters from the Alps flow into four of Europe's major rivers: the Rhine River, the Rhone River, the Po River, and the Danube River. If you locate these rivers on the physical map on page 157, you will discover that the four rivers flow in quite different directions. The Rhone flows south to the Mediterranean Sea; the Rhine flows north to the North Sea; the Po flows into the Adriatic Sea; and the Danube follows its long route eastward to the Black Sea.

159

Curriculum Connection

Literature After students have finished reading the excerpt from *A Tramp Abroad,* found on p. 159, ask the following questions:

● **How do you know that Twain's first glimpse of Mont Blanc was in the daytime?**
(He mentions that the sun was blazing on the mountain and that the sky was blue.)

● **Can you tell what time of year it is in the excerpt?**
(No; he does not mention the temperature. Although the mountain has snow on its dome, a mountain as tall as Mont Blanc would probably have snow on it all year round.)

Optional Activities

Meeting Individual Needs

Concept: The Importance of Natural Resources

To better understand why Western Europe is considered to be a "fortunate" place, it is important to see the role that natural resources play in the economies of Western European countries. Use the following activities to help students relate the presence of natural resources to Western European economies.

◆ **EASY** Have students make a list of products that can be made from trees.

Then ask them to write a paragraph explaining why West Germany is fortunate to have the Black Forest region.

◀▶ **AVERAGE** Tell students that France's richest natural resource is its soil. About 90 percent of the land is fertile enough to grow crops. Rich land allows the French to raise food for their own people as well as for export.

Discuss why France would want to export food.

Then have students describe, in writing, how life in France would be different if the country did not have this resource.

◀▮▶ **CHALLENGING** Tell students that some wealthy nations have only one natural resource. For example, Saudi Arabia's wealth comes primarily from oil.

Other rich nations have many resources. West Germany, for instance, has timber, lead, and iron.

Have students explain, in writing, the risks that a nation runs when it depends on only one resource for its wealth.

Read and Think

Section E

Western Europe possesses many valuable resources. Discuss these resources, asking the questions below:

1. **List the natural resources of Western Europe.**
   (Good soil, plentiful rainfall, trees, coal, iron, lead, zinc, copper, salt, limestone, and oil *pp. 160-161*)

2. **Why is limestone an important mineral?**
   (It is necessary for making concrete, which is used in building. *p. 161*)

   Thinking Critically Why, do you think, is forestry an important science for our world today? (Hypothesize)
   (Answers should reflect independent thinking but may include that to preserve forests for future generations, it is important never to cut more wood than the new growth can replace. *p. 160*)

VISUAL THINKING SKILL

Interpreting Climographs

■ Direct students' attention to the climographs found on p. 161. Then ask the following questions:

1. **In which month does Minneapolis recieve the most precipitation?**
   (June)

2. **Which three months are the coldest in London?**
   (January, February, December)

The Pyrenees The Pyrenees (PIHR uh-neez) form a mountain wall between the Iberian Peninsula and the rest of Europe. Though its peaks are not as high as those of the Alps, the Pyrenees are rugged mountains. A third range, the Apennines, has been described as the spine or backbone of the Italian peninsula. A look at the map on page 157 will show you why.

There is little chance for mountaineering on the North European Plain. This lowland area stretches from the coast of France eastward into the Soviet Union.

This wooded mountain region in Germany is called the Black Forest.
▶ What types of trees grow in this region?

160

E. Natural Resources of Western Europe

Forests The North European Plain has an abundance of good soil, only one of Europe's valuable **natural resources**. A natural resource is any material provided by nature that people use. Natural resources are not evenly distributed over the earth. Western Europe is one of the fortunate places. This region has good soil and plentiful rainfall.

At one time, forests covered most of Western Europe. Much of the forestland has been cleared for farms and cities, but there are still great forests, especially in northern Europe. Forests cover most of the Scandinavian peninsula and Finland. Even countries with large populations, such as France and Germany, have preserved some forestland. **Deciduous** (dee-SIHJ oo us) trees can be found in most of these forests. *Deciduous* comes from a Latin word that means "to fall off." The leaves of deciduous trees fall every year. Oaks, elms, and maples are examples of deciduous trees.

The Black Forest is the name given to an entire region in Germany that is a **coniferous** (koh NIHF ur us) forest. *Conifer* means "cone-bearing." Trees in coniferous forests bear cones. Evergreen trees, such as pines, firs, and spruces, are conifers. The Germans have been among the world's leaders in **forestry**, which is the science of caring for forests. Trees are grown and harvested as crops, but the amount of wood cut is never greater than the new growth.

Minerals Western Europe has deposits of various minerals, including coal, iron, lead, zinc, copper, salt, and limestone. Limestone is not a rare mineral, but it is an

Optional Activities

Curriculum Connection

Language Arts Tell students that there is another word that sounds the same as *lead* but is spelled differently and has a different meaning.

● That word is *led*, which means "guided" or "directed."

● Write both words on the chalkboard and tell students that these words are called *homonyms*.

● Ask students to find other homonyms in Section E (wood/would; new/knew; sea/see).

Current Events

● Tell students that according to the United Nations Food and Agricultural Organization, half of the world's forests have disappeared since 1950. If this trend continues, only two giant forests will remain in the year 2000—one in Brazil, the other in Central Africa.

● Discuss with students what kinds of problems the deforestation of our planet presents to people and to wildlife.

important one. Limestone is necessary for making concrete, which is widely used in building. Oil is also a valuable mineral. Western Europe became an important oil producer when oil was discovered offshore in the North Sea.

F. Ocean Streams and Altitude

Climate   London, England, is farther north than Minneapolis, Minnesota, yet London has a milder climate. London winters are warmer and summers are cooler than those in the middle of North America. Remember that latitude measures distance from the Equator. London is 51° north of the Equator; Minneapolis is 45° north of the Equator.

The **climographs** on this page show the differences between the climates of the two cities. A climograph is a graph that shows both the average temperature and the average precipitation for a certain place. The line shows the average temperature for each month. An average temperature is halfway between the high and low temperatures. For example, if the high was 60°F (16°C) and the low was 40°F (4°C), the average temperature would be 50°F (10°C). Note that the temperature scale is on the left side of the climograph.

The bars on the climograph show the average rainfall for each month of the year. By comparing the climographs, you can see that the rainfall is more evenly distributed throughout the year in London than in Minneapolis.

A comparison of the curves of the temperature lines shows that temperatures vary more in Minneapolis than in London. Temperatures rise much higher in the summer and fall much lower in the winter in Minneapolis.

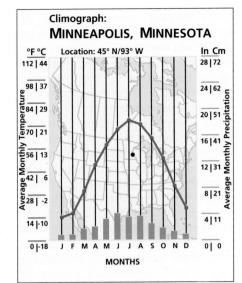

Climograph:
MINNEAPOLIS, MINNESOTA
Location: 45° N/93° W

MONTHS

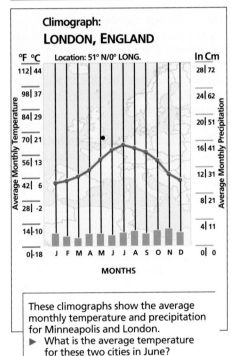

Climograph:
LONDON, ENGLAND
Location: 51° N/0° LONG.

MONTHS

These climographs show the average monthly temperature and precipitation for Minneapolis and London.
▶ What is the average temperature for these two cities in June?

161

Read and Think
Section F
Use the questions below to discuss the climate of Western Europe:

1. **What is a climograph?**
   (A graph that shows both the average temperature and the average precipitation for a certain place *p. 161*)

2. **What is the climate of Western Europe like?**
   (Mild winters, cool summers *p. 162*)

Thinking Critically   **Based on what you have learned in this lesson, which region of the United States, do you think, has the milder climate—the Midwest or the West Coast?** (Infer)
(Answers should reflect independent thinking but may include the West Coast, because ocean currents from the Pacific Ocean keep the weather milder. *p. 162*)

GEOGRAPHY THEMES

Place

■ Have students look at the map on p. 162 to help them answer the following question: **What helps keep ice from forming along the coast of Western Europe?** (North Atlantic Drift)

Reteaching Main Objective
Describe the physical characteristics of Western Europe.

● Have students divide a sheet of paper into five columns. Tell them to list the major geographical and climatic features of Europe in these columns. The headings for the columns should be *Peninsulas, Mountains, Rivers, Seas,* and *Climatic Influences.*

● Have five groups of students separately skim the text and list the features of individual sections.

● After all groups complete their lists, have a student spokesperson summarize his or her group's findings for the class.

Optional Activities

3 CLOSING THE LESSON

Lesson 1 Review

Answers to Think and Write

A. Young English gentlemen were sent on the Grand Tour to complete their education, improve their manners, and develop their minds.

B. Europe is a peninsula of the landmass Eurasia, and also has a number of peninsulas.

C. Before the breakup of the U.S.S.R., any country in Europe that was free of Soviet control was considered to be part of Western Europe, regardless of its location on the continent.

D. The Alps, the Pyrenees, and the Apennines are three important groups of mountains in Western Europe.

E. Western Europe possesses many valuable resources.

F. Ocean currents keep Western Europe's climate mild in spite of its northern location.

Answer to Skills Check

Norway is the farthest north; Iceland is the farthest west; Cyprus is the farthest east; and Greece and Cyprus are the farthest south.

Focus Your Reading

Ask the lesson focus question found at the beginning of the lesson: **What are some of the physical characteristics of Western Europe?**

(Western Europe is a lowland plain with three major mountain ranges, the Alps, the Pyrenees, and the Apennines. Western Europe has a long coastline because it has several peninsulas.)

Additional Practice

You may wish to assign the ancillary materials listed below.

Understanding the Lesson p. 40
Workbook p. 44

Ocean Streams Ocean **currents** make the difference between the climates of Minneapolis and London. Currents are streams that flow in the oceans. Minneapolis is in the middle of the North American continent, which is far from any ocean. London is on an island in the Atlantic Ocean. Currents in the Atlantic affect the climate of London and much of Western Europe. The **Gulf Stream** flows north and east from the warm waters of the Gulf of Mexico into the North Atlantic. There it merges with other warm currents to form the **North Atlantic Drift**. This very large stream moves toward the coast of Western Europe. Air blowing over Western Europe from off the North Atlantic Drift usually keeps winter temperatures warmer. In summer, ocean breezes cool those parts of Western Europe near the coast.

Ocean currents have less effect on places farther from the coast. Berlin, a city in Germany, is located at about the same latitude as London, but Berlin is farther from the ocean. As a result, Berlin winters are somewhat cooler.

Altitude also affects climate. Places at high elevations, such as mountains like the Alps, are cooler than are places at low elevations, like those nearer sea level. Average temperatures in the Alps generally decrease 2°F (1°C) with every 650-foot (198-m) rise in altitude.

NORTH ATLANTIC DRIFT

The Gulf Stream combines with the warm currents in the Atlantic Ocean to form the North Atlantic Drift.
▶ In which direction does the North Atlantic Drift flow?

LESSON 1 REVIEW

THINK AND WRITE

A. Why were young English gentlemen sent on the Grand Tour? (Recall)

B. Why may Europe be called "a peninsula with peninsulas"? (Infer)

C. Why are some European countries not located on the western part of the continent still called Western European countries? (Infer)

D. What are three important groups of mountains in Western Europe? (Recall)

E. Why can it be said that nature has been generous to Western Europe? (Infer)

F. Why does Western Europe have a mild climate in spite of its location? (Recall)

SKILLS CHECK

MAP SKILL

By looking at the physical map on page 157, you can see that Western Europe is a large region. Which four countries in the region lie the farthest north, south, east, and west?

162

Optional Activities

UNDERSTANDING THE LESSON

NAME
UNDERSTANDING THE LESSON   CHAPTER **5**

Organizing Facts   LESSON 1 CONTENT MASTER

* The chart can help you describe the features of Western Europe. Fill in the blank spaces with the names of specific features.

Five peninsulas are part of Western Europe.	Western Europe includes five islands.	
1. Italy	1. Great Britain	**Western Europe contains three mountain ranges.**
2. Iberian	2. Ireland	1. Alps
3. Balkan	3. Iceland	2. Pyrenees
4. Scandinavian	4. Malta	3. Apennines
5. Jutland	5. Cyprus	

Features of Western Europe

Eight bodies of water make up the coastline of Western Europe.	Western Europe has many important natural resources.	Western Europe has many rivers.
1. English Channel	1. Good soil	1. Rhine
2. Atlantic Ocean	2. Plentiful rainfall	2. Rhone
3. Mediterranean Sea	3. Forests	3. Po
4. Strait of Gibraltar	4. Coal, iron, lead	4. Danube
5. Adriatic Sea	5. Zinc, copper, salt	
6. Aegean Sea	6. Limestone	
7. Baltic Sea	7. Oil	
8. North Sea		

Think and Write: Write a paragraph describing two things that affect the climate of Western Europe. You may use the back of the sheet.
Answers should reflect independent thinking; suggestions appear in the Answer Key.
40   Use with textbook pages 155–162.

◀ Review Master Booklet, p. 40

A Variety of Peoples on a Small Continent

THINK ABOUT WHAT YOU KNOW
While on the Grand Tour, students traveled through Italy. What are some of the ancient ruins of Rome that the students may have visited?

STUDY THE VOCABULARY
rural   metropolitan
urban   area

FOCUS YOUR READING
How do you think the resources of Europe contributed to its population?

A. Students on the Grand Tour

The main purpose of the Grand Tour in the eighteenth century was to let students see the peoples and cities they had studied. Students may not have known as much as their tutors had hoped. One student wrote that his tutor "taught me a number of hard names yesterday which I tried hard to remember, but I forgot everything in ten minutes."

Those people who took the Grand Tour in the eighteenth century visited many of the places that tourists visit today. Students and tutors went to the Cathedral of Notre Dame (noh truh DAHM) in Paris. They climbed the bell tower and looked out at the size of the city. There they could try to compare the size of Paris with the size of London.

When English students visited the Palace of Versailles (vur SYE), outside Paris, they sometimes caught sight of the king. France still had a king at that time. One of the attractions of Versailles was the chance to see the king dine in public. What

did students learn from this visit? One of them noted that the king held his fork in his left hand, as is the English custom.

Tourists visiting the German city of Berlin saw King Frederick II, who came to be known as Frederick the Great, reviewing his well-drilled troops. Some of the English students journeyed to Switzerland to see the estate of Voltaire (vahl TER), a famous French writer. A few managed to meet Voltaire. Those less fortunate stared through the gate, hoping to catch a glimpse of the famous man.

A visit to Italy was the high point of the Grand Tour. Students in the eighteenth century spent much time studying Latin. Tutors probably hoped that a visit to Rome would remind students of Julius Caesar

Students on the Grand Tour visited the Palace of Versailles, just as many tourists do today.
► Where is Versailles located?

Cooperative Learning

Reporting   Divide the class into groups of five students.

● Tell the groups to prepare a short television special entitled "Close-up on Europe." Assign each group one of the following Western European countries: France, Germany, Italy, the Netherlands, Sweden, and England.

● Tell students to use the maps, graphs, and information in this lesson, as well as in the Index, for reference. One person in each group should report on the country's population, one should report on its language, one should report on its government, one should provide visuals to accompany each report, and one should serve as the program narrator.

● Have each group present its special to the class.

Optional Activities

A Variety of Peoples on a Small Continent

Objectives

★**1. List** ways in which the resources of Western Europe have contributed to its population.

2. Name the continents where European languages have spread.

3. Describe the governments of Western European countries.

4. Identify the following places: *Paris, Berlin, Rome, London, Athens, Italy, Germany, France, Switzerland, the Netherlands, Great Britain, Norway, Sweden, Belgium,* and *Luxembourg.*

1 STARTING THE LESSON

Motivation Activity

■ List on the chalkboard the word for *goodbye* in German (auf Wiedersehen) and Portuguese (adeus).

■ Ask students if they know the word for *goodbye* in Spanish (adiós), French (au revoir), or Italian (arrivaderci). Point out that while the languages of Western European countries may be different from one another, the people of the continent have much in common.

Think About What You Know

■ Assign the THINK ABOUT WHAT YOU KNOW activity on p. 163.

■ Answers should reflect independent thinking but may include the remains of bridges, aqueducts, roads, baths, the Pantheon, and the Colosseum.

Study the Vocabulary

■ Challenge students to use all the vocabulary words in one sentence that expresses the relationship of the terms.

— Answers to Caption Questions —
p. 162 ► Northeast
p. 163 ► Outside Paris

2 DEVELOPING THE LESSON

Read and Think

Sections A and B

Use the following questions to review the Grand Tour and to help students understand the concept of population density:

1. **What cities did people visit while on the Grand Tour in the eighteenth century?**
(Paris, Berlin, Rome, Milan, Florence, and Venice *pp. 163-164*)

2. **How is the population density of a country determined?**
(By dividing the number of people by the total land area *p. 165*)

3. **How does Europe compare to other continents in terms of size and population?**
(Only Australia is smaller, and only Asia has more people. *p. 167*)

Thinking Critically If you were a student on the Grand Tour, which place, do you think, would you most like to visit? (Evaluate)
(Answers should reflect independent thinking but may include Notre Dame, because students climbed the bell tower of the cathedral, or Versailles, because students sometimes glimpsed the king at the palace. *pp. 163-164*)

and Cicero. Some students did find Rome interesting, but others were struck by its shabbiness. Many of the poorer Romans lived in shacks built amid ancient ruins. The area inside the Colosseum, where gladiators had once fought, was a crowded slum neighborhood. The great circus, where chariots had once raced, was used as a cow pasture.

Tourists in the eighteenth century, like those today, bought souvenirs to take home. Italy was the favored place to look for souvenirs. Tourists bought gold jewelry and scented soaps in Milan (muh-LAHN) and paintings in Florence. Some paintings were copies of famous works.

Others were portraits of the tourists themselves. In Venice they found all sorts of glassware, including glass models of a full-rigged ship. Venice was famous for its ships as well as its glassblowers. It was very stylish to buy ancient relics or keepsakes in Rome. Pieces of ancient statuary were preferred.

The young gentlemen who took the Grand Tour may not have learned as much as their parents and tutors had hoped. But the young men surely must have learned something about the peoples and lands of Western Europe. Otherwise, parents would hardly have continued to send their sons on the Grand Tour.

Eighteenth-century tourists often visited the city of Venice, in Italy. Venice was well known for its ships and for its glassware.
▶ What takes the place of streets in Venice?

164

Optional Activities

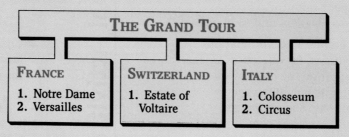

Graphic Organizer

You may wish to use this graphic organizer to help students recall the sights seen by the young eighteenth-century gentlemen who took the Grand Tour.

THE GRAND TOUR		
FRANCE	**SWITZERLAND**	**ITALY**
1. Notre Dame	1. Estate of	1. Colosseum
2. Versailles	Voltaire	2. Circus

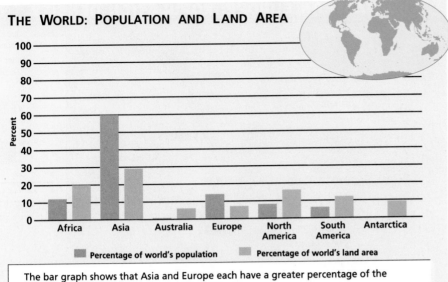

THE WORLD: POPULATION AND LAND AREA

(bar graph with vertical axis labeled "Percent" from 0 to 100, horizontal axis showing: Africa, Asia, Australia, Europe, North America, South America, Antarctica)

■ Percentage of world's population   ■ Percentage of world's land area

The bar graph shows that Asia and Europe each have a greater percentage of the world's population than of the world's land area.
► How do the two continents compare in population and in land area?

B. A Small Continent with Many Faces

Ever since the eighteenth century, people have toured Europe to learn about its people and history. Such trips have been called grand tours even in later times. In 1891 a 15-year-old girl from Nashville, Tennessee, made a trip to Europe with seven other girls. She kept a diary of her trip, which she later stored in an old trunk. It was found by her grandson nearly 90 years later. It was published and given the title *A Young Nashvillian's Grand Tour: Europe in 1891.*

Europe is a small continent. Only Australia is a smaller continent. Yet Europe today has many people. Only Asia has more. The bar graph on this page shows important facts about the size of Europe and its population. The pink bars

on this graph show what percentage of the world's population lives on each continent. The blue bars show the percentage of the world's land area for each continent. By comparing the set of bars for Europe, you can see that Europe's percentage of population is greater than its percentage of land area.

We measure how many people live in an area by population density. This is the average number of people living in a square mile or square kilometer. We find the population density of a country by dividing the number of people by the total land area.

The population density of the larger Western European countries is fairly high. France has a population density of 263 persons per square mile (102 per sq km). Germany has a population density of 571 persons per square mile (220 per sq km).

165

Calculating Population Density

● Tell students that Spain's population is 39,200,000 people and its land area is 194,881 square miles (504,742 sq km).

Have students figure out the population density of Spain (39,200,000 ÷ 194,881 = 201.1 people per square mile) (39,200,000 ÷ 504,742 = 77.6 people per sq km).

Optional Activities

Read and Think

Section C

Ask students to think about what they have learned about the people of Western Europe. To continue this line of thought, ask the following questions:

1. In what kind of area do most Western Europeans live?
(Urban areas *p. 167*)

2. In most Western European countries, what cities are usually the largest?
(The capital cities *p. 167*)

Thinking Critically Why, do you think, do most Western Europeans live in urban areas? (Hypothesize)
(Answers should reflect independent thinking but may include that work opportunities are greater in urban areas. *p. 167*)

GEOGRAPHY THEMES

Regions

■ Have students look at the map on this page to help them answer the following question: What countries in Western Europe have areas with a population density of 500 persons per square mile (200 per sq km)?
(Portugal, Spain, Italy, France, Germany, Belgium, the Netherlands, and the United Kingdom)

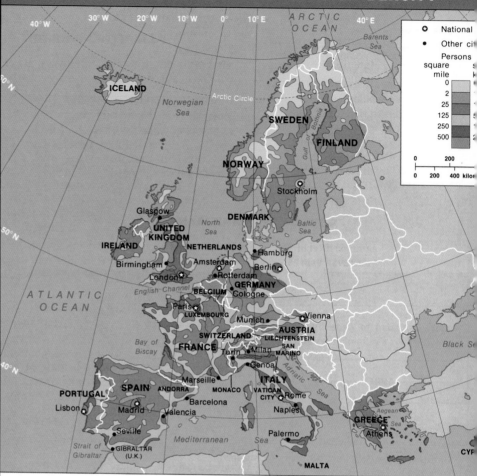

WESTERN EUROPE: POPULATION DENSITY

	National
	Other ci
	Persons
	square s
	mile k
	0
	2
	25
	125
	250
	500

THE 25 LARGEST CITIES OF WESTERN EUROPE

London (U.K.)	6,755,000	Milan (Italy)	1,515,000	Birmingham (U.K.)	920,000	Palermo (Italy)	
Madrid (Spain)	3,200,000	Vienna (Austria)	1,512,000	Athens (Greece)	886,000	Amsterdam (Netherlands)	
Berlin (Germany)	3,056,000	Munich (Germany)	1,267,000	Marseille (France)	874,000	Seville (Spain)	
Rome (Italy)	2,826,000	Naples (Italy)	1,206,000	Lisbon (Portugal)	818,000	Stockholm (Sweden)	
Paris (France)	2,176,000	Turin (Italy)	1,035,000	Valencia (Spain)	785,000	
Barcelona (Spain)	1,770,000	Rotterdam (Netherlands)	1,025,000	Glasgow (U.K.)	762,000	
Hamburg (Germany)	1,592,000	Cologne (Germany)	922,000	Genoa (Italy)	736,000	

About one half of the 25 largest cities of Western Europe have a population of more than 1 million.
▶ Which of the 25 largest cities are national capitals with a population greater than 1 million?

166

Optional Activities

Curriculum Connection

Language Arts Ask students what the singular form of the word *cities* is. Then write *city* on the chalkboard.

● Ask students if they can tell you what the rule is when making a plural from an English word whose last two letters are a consonant and "y". (Change the "y" to "i" and add "es".)

● Have students skim the first paragraph of Section C and write down the singular and plural forms of other words that follow this rule (country/countries; territory/territories; density/densities).

The small country of the Netherlands has the highest population density, with 1,040 persons per square mile (401 per sq km). Compare these figures with the figure for the United States, which has a population density of 69 persons per square mile (27 per sq km).

C. Western Europe's Population

The population of a country is never spread evenly over its territory. Cities have more people per square mile or kilometer than rural, or country, areas. Paris, the capital city of France, has a population density of 19,893 persons per square mile (7,715 per sq km), but there are parts of France with less than 125 persons per square mile (48 per sq km). The map on page 166 shows how the population density varies within the many countries of Western Europe.

Most Western Europeans live in urban areas, that is, in cities and towns. Over 92 percent of the British population is urban. France's city-dwellers make up 77 percent of its population. Even in the country of Sweden, which has a low population density of 49 persons per square mile (19 per sq km), 85 percent of the people live in cities.

In most Western European countries, the capital cities are also the largest cities. Rome is the largest city in Italy, Paris is the largest in France, and London the largest in England. About 30 percent of the Greek population lives in the metropolitan area of Athens. A metropolitan area is made up of a large city and the city's suburbs, or surrounding towns.

Western Europe still has many productive farms. But today most people live in cities. You will read more about farms in Europe in later chapters.

D. European Languages Around the Globe

Dozens of different languages are spoken in Europe. Most countries have one single national language. The French speak French, the Italians speak Italian, and so on. But several small countries have more than one official language because they use the languages of their bordering countries. Belgium has two languages, Luxembourg has three, and Switzerland has four. Because of the location and size of their countries, people in Western Europe find it useful to speak more than their own language.

All Western European countries have close neighbors. France's boundaries touch those of six other countries, and only about 20 miles (32 km) of the English

People shopping in the country of Belgium often will encounter more than one language written on storefront signs.
▶ What is sold in this store?

Reading a Bar Graph

- Have a volunteer read the title of the bar graph on this page. Point out that the title tells what the bar graph shows.

- Then ask students to list in order from least to greatest the European languages shown on the graph that are spoken around the world.

Read and Think
Section E

Use the questions below to discuss democracy in Western Europe.

Why is it important to be literate in order to enjoy the full benefits of democratic freedoms?
(People who can read have more freedom to get information. They do not have to depend on what others choose to tell them. *p. 169*)

Thinking Critically   In the African nation of Zaire, only 40 percent of males and 15 percent of females are literate. What, do you think, does this tell you about education in Zaire? (Infer)

(Answers should reflect independent thinking but may include that information is passed orally, that formal education is probably not universal, or that it is not customary for women to get an education.)

Channel separates France and England. Switzerland borders four countries, each with its own official language. Students in European schools spend more time studying foreign languages than American students do. For example, Swedish students begin to study a foreign language when they are in the third grade.

The use of European languages has spread far outside Europe. Nine of the 20 most widely spoken languages in the world are European. This book was written in a European language — English. Almost all of the people of North America and South America speak either English, Spanish, Portuguese, or French. English is also the language of the Australians and many others in Asia and Africa. Indeed, English is the second most widely spoken language in the world. The first is Chinese, with over a billion speakers.

E. Democratic Governments and the European Community

The Western European countries are democracies. Some, such as Italy, Germany, and France, are democratic republics. Others, such as Norway, Great Britain, and the Netherlands, have monarchs as heads of state. But the monarchs do not actually govern. The people elect representatives to make laws and govern in the monarchies as well as in the republics.

Western Europeans enjoy many democratic freedoms, such as freedom of speech, the press, and worship. Some countries have official religions, but people are free to follow other religions.

All Western European countries today have universal education, that is, schooling for all children. Almost everyone is literate, or able to read. To enjoy the full

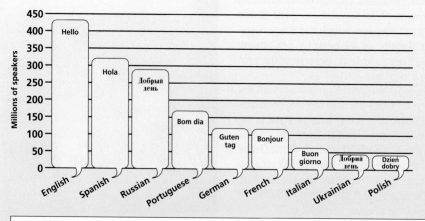

MAJOR EUROPEAN LANGUAGES SPOKEN AROUND THE WORLD

Almost half of the 20 most widely spoken languages in the world are European.
► About how many people speak English?

168

Curriculum Connection

Economics   Tell students that in a number of European countries the government owns many businesses such as banks, television stations, railway systems, and airlines.

- Have students discuss the advantages and disadvantages of government ownership of one of the businesses mentioned above.

Reteaching Main Objective

⭐ *List ways in which the resources of Western Europe have contributed to its population.*

- Divide the class into groups of five students. Tell the groups that they will be preparing a list of facts about the ways that resources have affected the lives of Western Europeans.

- Tell students to give their lists a heading such as *Western Europe: The Effects of Resources on Population.* Have them skim the lesson and write at least three relevant facts under this heading. (For example: The location and size of each country have prompted many Western Europeans to learn more than one language.)

- Then, have the groups share their lists with the class.

Young students in Switzerland listen to their teacher during a mathematics class. Education is extremely important in Western European countries.
▶ How is this classroom similar to your classroom?

benefits of democratic freedoms, people must be educated.

Belgium, Denmark, France, Germany, Greece, Ireland, Italy, Luxembourg, the Netherlands, Portugal, Spain, and the United Kingdom have joined the European Community (EC), with the intention of becoming a single "home" market. Eventually the countries of the EC will have a common currency, probably called the *ecu*. EC members are working toward greater cooperation on many other issues.

LESSON *2* REVIEW

THINK AND WRITE

A. In what ways was the Grand Tour in the eighteenth century like a tourist trip today? **(Analyze)**

B. How is population density figured? **(Recall)**

C. How does a population density map tell more about where people live than a population density figure for the whole country? **(Synthesize)**

D. Why do Europeans generally spend more time studying foreign languages than American students do? **(Infer)**

E. Explain the connection between democratic freedoms enjoyed by Western Europeans and the ability to read. **(Infer)**

SKILLS CHECK
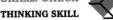

THINKING SKILL

Refer to the bar graph on page 165 to do this activity. Rank the continents of the world according to the percentage of the world's land area each has. The continent with the largest land area should be ranked number 1. Then rank the continents according to percentage of population.

169

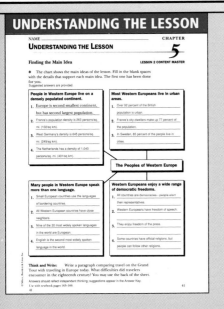
◀ **Review Master Booklet, p. 41**

Optional Activities

3 CLOSING THE LESSON

Lesson *2* Review

Answers to Think and Write

A. Those who took the Grand Tour in the eighteenth century visited many of the places that tourists visit today.

B. Population density is figured by dividing the number of people by the total land area.

C. A population density map shows the population density in each area of the country. A population density figure for the whole country does not tell anything about where within that country people live.

D. Europeans generally spend more time studying foreign languages than American students do because all Western European countries have close neighbors with whom they wish to communicate.

E. Western Europeans' ability to read enables them to get the information needed to enjoy the freedoms of democracy.

Answer to Skills Check

Land Area: 1. Asia 2. Africa 3. North America 4. South America 5. Antarctica 6. Europe 7. Australia; *Population:* 1. Asia 2. Europe 3. Africa 4. North America 5. South America 6. Australia 7. Antarctica

Focus Your Reading

Ask the lesson focus question found at the beginning of the lesson: **How do you think the resources of Europe contributed to its population?**
(Resources such as good soil and plentiful rainfall have enabled European countries to feed a large number of people, which has caused the population to grow.)

Additional Practice

You may wish to assign the ancillary materials listed below.

Understanding the Lesson p. 41
Workbook pp. 45-48

--- **Answers to Caption Questions** ---
p. 168 ▶ About 440 million
p. 169 ▶ Answers will vary but should note the similarities between the classroom in the photograph and the students' classroom.

169

Using The Vocabulary

1. climograph
2. current
3. urban
4. Gulf Stream
5. deciduous
6. natural resource
7. North Atlantic Drift
8. forestry
9. metropolitan area
10. coniferous

Remembering What You Read

1. The Grand Tour was a trip through Western Europe taken by a young Englishman and his tutor.

2. Eurasia is the name of the landmass that combines Europe and Asia.

3. The five peninsulas that extend into the ocean from Europe are the Balkan, Italian, Iberian, Scandinavian and Jutland peninsulas.

4. Paccard and Balmat climbed to the top of Mont Blanc.

5. The largest group of mountains in Western Europe is the Alps.

6. The Pyrenees form a wall between the Iberian Peninsula and the rest of Europe.

7. Australia is smaller than Europe.

8. Population density is the average number of people living in a square mile or square kilometer.

9. The second most widely spoken language in the world is English.

10. The Western European countries have democratic governments.

Thinking Critically

1. It gave students exposure to other cultures, languages, art, and history.

2. Forestry ensures that we will not use up our supply of trees.

Using the Vocabulary

On a separate sheet of paper, write the word or words that best complete each sentence.

natural resource	Gulf Stream
deciduous	North Atlantic
coniferous	Drift
forestry	urban
climograph	metropolitan area
current	

1. A graph that shows both the average temperature and the average precipitation for a certain place is called a _____.

2. A stream that flows in the oceans is called a _____.

3. Cities and towns make up _____ areas.

4. The _____ flows north and east from the warm waters of the Gulf of Mexico into the North Atlantic.

5. The Latin word _____ means to "fall off."

6. Any material provided by nature that people use is called a _____.

7. The Gulf Stream merges with other warm currents to form the _____.

8. The science of caring for forests is called _____.

9. A large city and its suburbs, or surrounding towns, makes up a _____.

10. Trees in _____ forests bear cones.

Remembering What You Read

On a separate sheet of paper, answer the following questions in complete sentences.

1. What was the Grand Tour?

2. What is the name of the landmass that combines Europe and Asia?

3. Name the five peninsulas that extend into the ocean from Europe.

4. Paccard and Balmat climbed to the top of what mountain peak?

5. What is the largest group of mountains in Western Europe?

6. What mountains form a wall between the Iberian Peninsula and the rest of mainland Europe?

7. What continent is smaller than Europe?

8. What is population density?

9. What is the second most widely spoken language in the world?

10. What kind of government do the Western European countries have?

Tying Language Arts to Social Studies

Imagine that your class is planning a Grand Tour through Western Europe. Choose a place in Western Europe you have read about or seen a picture of that you would be interested in visiting. Write a few paragraphs explaining why you think the place you have chosen should be part of the class's Grand Tour. If possible, add a picture or drawing to your paper to visualize the place you are describing. Then combine your paper with those of your classmates to make a travel brochure. With your classmates, add a title page and a table of contents to complete the brochure.

170

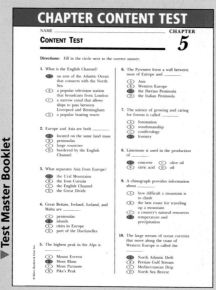

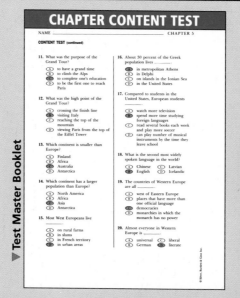

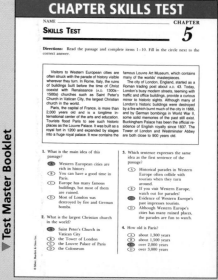

THINKING CRITICALLY

On a separate sheet of paper, answer the following questions in complete sentences.

1. Why do you think going on the Grand Tour was a good learning experience for students?
2. Why do you think forestry is important?
3. Why, do you think, do urban areas have a higher population density than rural areas?
4. Why is it useful to speak more than one language in Europe?
5. Why is it important for a country to educate all its people?

SUMMARIZING THE CHAPTER

On a separate sheet of paper, copy the graphic organizer shown below. Beside each heading write three answers to support it.

CHAPTER THEME — The blend of physical features, natural resources, and different peoples in Western Europe make it a unique region.

LAND OF WESTERN EUROPE		PEOPLE OF WESTERN EUROPE	
Mountains	1. ____	Densely Populated Countries	1. ____
	2. ____		2. ____
	3. ____		3. ____
Rivers	1. ____	European Languages	1. ____
	2. ____		2. ____
	3. ____		3. ____
Seas	1. ____	Democratic Freedoms	1. ____
	2. ____		2. ____
	3. ____		3. ____
Natural Resources	1. ____		
	2. ____		
	3. ____		

3. Urban areas offer more employment opportunities.
4. It is useful for Europeans to speak more than one language in order to communicate with their neighbors.
5. An educated population helps the country achieve economic prosperity and protects democratic freedoms.

Summarizing the Chapter

Land of Western Europe

Mountains:
1. Alps
2. Pyrenees
3. Apennines

Rivers:
1. Rhine
2. Rhone
3. Po

Seas:
1. Mediterranean
2. Adriatic
3. Aegean

Natural Resources:
1. Good soil
2. Plentiful rainfall
3. Trees

People of Western Europe

Densely Populated Countries:
1. France
2. Germany
3. The Netherlands

European Languages:
1. French
2. Italian
3. English

Democratic Freedoms:
1. Freedom of speech
2. Freedom of the press
3. Freedom of worship

▶ Test Master Booklet

CHAPTER SKILLS TEST

NAME ____________ CHAPTER 5

SKILLS TEST (continued)

5. The word *Renaissance* refers to ____.
   - (A) an Italian artist who lived from 1300 to 1500 and painted a magnificent scene of Rome on the ceiling of Saint Peter's Church
   - (B) the coexistence of Christ
   - (C) a time between the fourteenth and sixteenth centuries
   - (D) the last 200 years of the Roman Empire
6. Westminster Abbey ____.
   - (A) stands next door to the Tower of London
   - (B) is the official residence of English royalty
   - (C) has been providing mirrors since 1837
   - (D) was built about 900 years ago
7. Tourists in Paris ____.
   - (A) go to see its historic floods
   - (B) can see many of the world's masterpieces
   - (C) cause severe floods around the Louvre
   - (D) are required to speak French only
8. Many of London's oldest buildings ____.
   - (A) can be seen only with a curious mirror
   - (B) provide convex and concave mirrors to interest tourists
   - (C) were ruined by bombs and fire
   - (D) are curious reflections of solid memories
9. This passage describes ____.
   - (A) the history of European architecture from the time of Christ to World War II
   - (B) historic places in London, Paris, and Rome
   - (C) the damp climate of Paris and the slums of Rome
   - (D) how such disasters as floods, fires, and bombings have created historic ruins
10. Which of the following is a Renaissance building?
    - (A) Saint Peter's Church
    - (B) the Tower of London
    - (C) Buckingham Palace
    - (D) a ruin built before the time of Christ

▶ Test Master Booklet

CHAPTER WRITING TEST

NAME ____________ CHAPTER 5

ESSAY TEST

Directions: Write a response to items 1–4.

> **REMINDER:** Read and think about each item before you write your response. Be sure to think of the points you want to cover, details that support your response, and reasons for your opinions. Then, on the lines below, write your response in complete sentences.

1. What was the Grand Tour?

   A satisfactory response should include the following statements:
   - The Grand Tour was a trip through Western Europe taken by wealthy young Englishmen and their tutors.
   - Its purpose was to complete a young man's education.
   - It was supposed to improve his manners and develop his mind.

   An excellent response might also include
   - examples of a possible itinerary
   - a description of Europe in the eighteenth century.

2. What is the difference between deciduous and coniferous trees?

   A satisfactory response should include the following statements:
   - Deciduous trees shed their leaves every year.
   - Coniferous, or cone-bearing, trees remain green throughout the year.

   An excellent response might also include
   - examples of deciduous trees (oak, elm, maple)
   - examples of coniferous trees (pine, fir, spruce).

▶ Test Master Booklet

CHAPTER WRITING TEST

NAME ____________ CHAPTER 5

ESSAY TEST (continued)

3. What is a climograph?

   A satisfactory response should include the following statements:
   - A climograph is a graph that shows the average temperature and average precipitation of a certain place.
   - The line on a climograph indicates average monthly termperature.
   - The bars on a climograph show average monthly rainfall.

   An excellent response might also include
   - possible uses for a climograph.

4. What is population density, and how is it determined?

   A satisfactory response should include the following statements:
   - Population density is the average number of people living in a square mile or square kilometer.
   - It is determined by dividing the total number of people by the total land area.

   An excellent response might also
   - explain the difference between high and low density
   - provide specific examples.

History of Western Europe
(pp. 172-199)

Chapter Theme: The way of life that developed in Western Europe during the Middle Ages changed with the growth of trade, the influences of the Renaissance and the Reformation, and the rise of national rulers.

CHAPTER RESOURCES
Review Master Booklet
   Reviewing Chapter Vocabulary, p. 49
   Place Geography, p. 50
   Summarizing the Chapter, p. 51
Chapter 6 Test

LESSON *1*   Feudal Lords and Serfs
(pp. 172-178)

Theme: During the age of feudalism, nobles were obligated to protect their serfs, and serfs had to provide labor for their lord.

SILVER WINGS WORKSHOP: The Courage of Your Convictions
The Walls Came Tumbling Down

LESSON RESOURCES
Review Master Booklet
   Understanding the Lesson, p. 45

LESSON *2*   The People of the Towns and the Church
(pp. 179-183)

Theme: Structure in the Middle Ages was provided by the church and the guilds.

SOCIAL STUDIES LIBRARY: *Money*

LESSON RESOURCES
Workbook, p. 49
Review Master Booklet
   Understanding the Lesson, p. 46

LESSON *3*   A Time of "Rebirth"
(pp. 184-190)

Theme: The Renaissance produced great men of many talents.

SOCIAL STUDIES LIBRARY: *Ferdinand Magellan*
The Mayas

LESSON RESOURCES
Workbook, pp. 50-52
Review Master Booklet
   Understanding the Lesson, p. 47

LESSON *4*   Changes in Church and Government
(pp. 191-195)

Theme: During the Renaissance, reformers lead the way to changes in the Catholic Church and in national governments.

SILVER WINGS WORKSHOP: The Courage of Your Convictions

LESSON RESOURCES
Workbook, pp. 53-54
Review Master Booklet
   Understanding the Lesson, p. 48

Sheet 1 (page 49)

NAME _____

REVIEWING CHAPTER VOCABULARY

CHAPTER 6

VOCABULARY MASTER

Review Study the terms in the box. Use your Glossary to find definitions of those you do not remember.

apprentice	explorer	knight	Reformation
convent	feudalism	manor	Renaissance
Crusade	fief	monastery	serf
divine right	guild	monopoly	tax
economy			

Practice Complete the paragraphs using terms from the box above. You may change the forms of the terms to fit the meaning.

In England during the Middle Ages, people had little freedom to decide how they would live their lives. Only the monarchs, who believed that they ruled by (1) _divine right_, could do as they chose. The monarchs were free to give land and power to certain people. They could also force those who had land to pay higher (2) _taxes_. When a king granted a (3) _fief_, the vassal who was given the land had to provide the king with (4) _knights_. These trained warriors would fight in the king's army. For the (5) _serfs_ who worked the land for the vassals, life was particularly difficult. They had to work hard and were not free to leave the vassal's land without permission.

Other people also had to follow strict rules and regulations. The long training of craftworkers was controlled by rules made by (6) _guilds_. These rules allowed master craftworkers to decide who could learn a trade. Priests and people who spent their lives in (7) _monasteries_ also lived according to strict rules. These were the rules of the Roman Catholic Church.

Write Choose ten terms from the box above. Use each term to write a sentence of your own. You may use the back of the sheet.

Sentences should show that students understand the meanings of the terms.

_____

_____

_____

_____

_____

_____

_____

© Silver, Burdett & Ginn Inc.

Use with Chapter 6, pages 173–195.

49

Sheet 2 (page 50)

NAME _____

LOCATING PLACES

CHAPTER 6

PLACE GEOGRAPHY MASTER

✱ Places that were important during the Renaissance and Reformation are listed below. Use the Gazetteer in your textbook to find the latitude and longitude of each place. Then locate and label each on the map.

	LAT. ⊝	LONG. ⊙
1. Florence, Italy	44°N	11°E
2. Rome, Italy	42°N	12°E
3. Milan, Italy	45°N	9°E
4. Rotterdam, Netherlands	52°N	4°E
5. Geneva, Switzerland	46°N	6°E

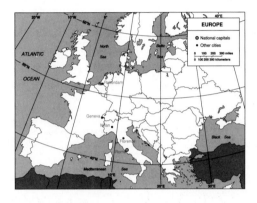

EUROPE
- ⊙ National capitals
- • Other cities

0 100 200 300 miles
0 100 200 300 kilometers

50

Use with Chapter 6, pages 173–195.

© Silver, Burdett & Ginn Inc.

Sheet 3 (page 51)

NAME _____

SUMMARIZING THE CHAPTER

CHAPTER 6

GRAPHIC ORGANIZER MASTER

✱ Complete this graphic organizer. Under the main idea for each lesson, write four statements that support the main idea.

CHAPTER THEME → The way of life that developed in Western Europe during the Middle Ages changed the growth of trade, the influences of the Renaissance and the Reformation, and the rise of national rulers.

The Middle Ages—GUIDE	The Renaissance—GUIDE
LESSON 1 **Feudal nobles and serfs had obligations.** 1. Lords governed their manors. 2. Serfs owed their labor to their lords. 3. Serfs had to give gifts to their lords. 4. Crusades	**LESSON 3** **The period after the Middle Ages is called a time of rebirth.** 1. Artists and writers expressed new ideas. 2. Students found a new interest in ancient writings. 3. People made new discoveries. 4. Explorers searched for new sea routes and lands.
LESSON 2 **The people of the town and Church had specific functions.** 1. They led lives of prayer and labor. 2. Monks and nuns helped people. 3. Priests performed religious services. 4. Townspeople sometimes paid taxes.	**LESSON 4** **Changes were brought about in the Church and government.** 1. The Bible was translated into the common language. 2. The Reformation divided Christians. 3. Many Protestant churches were created. 4. National rulers replaced feudal rulers.

© Silver, Burdett & Ginn Inc.

Use with Chapter 6, pages 173–195.

51

Workbook Pages

CHAPTER **6**

LIFE IN THE MIDDLE AGES

Understanding Sequence, Distinguishing Fact from Opinion, Hypothesizing

✷ To become a tradesman in the Middle Ages, a person went through several steps. The people described below are at various steps in the process of becoming tradesmen. Place the people in the ascending order by writing a number **1** in front of the first step, **2** in front of the second step, and so on. On the line following each description, write the title given to the person at that level of training. You will use the same title more than once. The first one is done for you.

2 This person has been with an experienced craftsman for three years. He is learning the more difficult skills of a craft. _____Apprentice_____

5 This person belongs to a craft guild. He is teaching several young people his craft. _____Master_____

1 This person receives no pay but gets food and clothing. He does odd jobs and learns the basic skills of a trade. _____Apprentice_____

3 This person has just started a job in which he is paid for each day's work. _____Journeyman_____

4 This person wants to produce a masterpiece, a product that meets his guild's highest standards. _____Journeyman_____

✷ Read each statement below. If it's a fact, write **Fact** on the line. If it's an opinion, write **Opinion** on the line.

Fact **1.** Saint Benedict established the Abbey of Monte Cassino.

Opinion **2.** Life in a monastery was too hard.

Fact **3.** Monks spent a lot of time in prayer.

Opinion **4.** Some of the finest buildings erected in the Middle Ages were cathedrals.

Fact **5.** Nuns often did the tasks that teachers and nurses do today.

Thinking Further: Imagine that you are a journeyman silversmith. (A silversmith is a person who uses silver to make fine things, like teapots, candlesticks, and jewelry.) What item would you make as your masterpiece? Write a description of it. Include several details. If you wish, draw a small sketch of the item. Make sure the item chosen can be made of silver and that the details given are relevant to the item.

Example: I would make a necklace with a thick, 20-inch-long chain and a pendant shaped like a star.

CHAPTER **6**

ENJOYING SHAKESPEAREAN DRAMA

Understanding Stated Facts and Details, Evaluating Ideas

✷ One of the best-known figures of the Renaissance was the English playwright and poet William Shakespeare (1564–1616). Many people consider him to be the greatest writer of all time. Shakespeare wrote many plays that are still popular. These plays include _Romeo and Juliet, Julius Caesar, Hamlet,_ and _Macbeth._ The following is a famous passage from Shakespeare's play _As You Like It._ The passage describes seven phases in the life of a man.

The Seven Ages of Man

All the world's a stage,
And all the men and women merely players;
They have their exits and their
    entrances;
And one man in his time plays many parts,
His acts being seven ages. At first the
    infant,
Mewling [crying] and puking in the
    nurse's arms.
And then the whining school-boy, with his
    satchel [school bag],
And shining morning face, creeping like
    snail
Unwillingly to school. And then the
    lover,
Sighing like furnace, with a woful ballad
Made to his mistress' [girlfriend's]
    eyebrow. Then a soldier,
Full of strange oaths, and bearded like
    the pard [leopard],
Jealous in honor, sudden and quick in
    quarrel,
Seeking the bubble reputation
Even in the cannon's mouth. And then the
    justice,

In fair round belly with good capon
    [chicken] lined,
With eyes severe and beard of formal cut,
Full of wise saws [sayings] and modern
    instances [examples];
And so he plays his part. The sixth age
    shifts
Into the lean and slippered pantaloon
    [old man],
With spectacles on nose and pouch on
    side,
His youthful hose [stockings] well saved,
    a world too wide
For his shrunk shank [leg]; and his big
    manly voice,
Turning again toward childish treble,
    pipes
And whistles in his sound. Last scene of
    all,
That ends this strange eventful history,
Is second childishness, and mere
    oblivion,
Sans [without] teeth, sans eyes, sans
    taste, sans everything.

ENJOYING SHAKESPEAREAN DRAMA _CONTINUED_

✷ List each of the seven phases in a man's life, as described by Shakespeare. Give two or three details of each phase. The first one has been done for you.
Suggested answers are provided.

1. _infant_
   details
   cries, spits up in nurse's arms

2. _schoolboy_
   details
   carries satchel, walks slowly to school, has
   shining face

3. _lover_
   details
   sighs, sings songs to girlfriend

WILLIAM SHAKESPEARE

4. _soldier_
   details
   has unkempt beard, jealous, quarrelsome,
   seeks fame

5. _justice_
   details
   portly, eats well, has neat beard, severe glance,
   many opinions

6. _pantaloon (old man)_
   details
   wears eyeglasses, has thin legs, voice is high-
   pitched

7. _second childhood_
   details
   no teeth, can't see, can't taste

Thinking Further: Do you think Shakespeare's description of a man's lifetime is basically correct? Give two or three reasons to support your answer.
Answers should reflect independent thinking. Many students probably will say Shakespeare is basically correct.

CHAPTER **6**

EARLY EXPLORERS AND CARTOGRAPHERS

Understanding a Chart, Drawing Conclusions, Hypothesizing

✷ The charts below list important facts about early explorers and cartographers of the Western Hemisphere. Use the charts to determine whether the following statements are true or false. Write **True** in the blank before each statement that is true. Write **False** in the blank before each statement that is false.

Explorers			
Year	Explorer	Nationality	Sailing paid by	Area of Exploration
1492	Christopher Columbus	Italian	Spain	San Salvador; Hispaniola
1497	John Cabot	Italian	England	Newfoundland
1499	Amerigo Vespucci	Italian	Spain	West Indies; Amazon River
1500	Pedro Álvares Cabral	Portuguese	Portugal	Brazil
1501	Rodrigo de Bastidas	Spanish	Spain	Central America
1524	Giovanni da Verrazano	Italian	France	New York Harbor
1534	Jacques Cartier	French	France	Gulf of St. Lawrence

Cartographers		
Year	Cartographer	Nationality	Achievement
1507	Martin Waldseemüller	German	gave the name America to the New World
1538	Gerardus Mercator	Flemish	showed North America with more accuracy than Waldseemüller had

True **1.** The maps of Gerardus Mercator could have included all the explorations shown on this chart.

False **2.** The expedition to Newfoundland led almost immediately to the exploration of the Gulf of St. Lawrence.

False **3.** John Cabot was one of the early English explorers who sailed under his own country's flag.

True **4.** Martin Waldseemüller could not have included an accurate drawing of New York Harbor on his map of the New World.

False **5.** Amerigo Vespucci gave his own name to South America but not to North America.

True **6.** Neither cartographer was of the same nationality as any of the explorers.

True **7.** Christopher Columbus set sail on his voyages of exploration about seven years earlier than Amerigo Vespucci did.

Thinking Further: How do you think the achievements of the explorers affected educated Europeans of the time? Be specific. Write on a separate sheet. _Possible effects: Europeans learned about new peoples, new areas, new foods, and so forth. Their horizons were extended in many ways._

C6-C

Workbook Pages

LUTHER AND CHARLES V

Understanding Stated Facts and Unstated Ideas, Hypothesizing

❋ The Protestant Reformation began in 1517, when Martin Luther, a German monk, wrote 95 statements protesting what he saw as abuses in the Catholic Church. Holy Roman Emperor Charles V and other leaders called for Luther to take back his criticisms of the Church. After Luther replied to these leaders, Charles made a statement about Luther. Read Luther's reply and Charles's statement. Then answer the questions.

Luther's Reply

Since Your Imperial Majesty and Your Highnesses insist upon a simple reply, I shall give you one—brief and simple but deprived neither of teeth nor horns. Unless I am convicted of error by the testimony of the Bible (for I place no faith in the mere authority of the Pope, or of councils, which have often been wrong, recognizing, as I do, no other guide but the Bible), I cannot and will not retract [take back] my statements, for we must never act against our conscience.

Statement by Charles V

A single monk, led astray by private judgment, has set himself against the faith upheld by all Christians for more than a thousand years. He believes that all Christians up to now have been wrong. I am now sorry that I have so long delayed moving against him and his false doctrines. I have made up my mind never again to listen to him. He is forbidden to preach and to win over men with his evil beliefs and incite them to rebellion.

1. Does Luther agree to take back his criticisms? no

2. What would cause Luther to change his views? if the Bible shows he is incorrect

3. Why does Luther have no confidence in decisions made by the Pope or councils of church leaders? because they have often been wrong

4. How does Charles describe Luther's beliefs? He calls them "false doctrines" and "evil beliefs."

5. What does Charles do to move against Luther? He forbids Luther from preaching or winning converts to his beliefs.

6. Do you think either Luther or Charles V is likely to change his views? The statements suggest that both have strong opinions and will not change their views.

Thinking Further: Why do you think people often hold so strongly to their opinions about religion?
Possible answer: Religion often forms the foundation of a person's overall beliefs. Since a change in religious beliefs might force a person to reexamine his or her other beliefs, people usually cling to their religious ideas.

© Silver, Burdett & Ginn Inc.

REVIEWING EVENTS IN EUROPE

Understanding Facts and Details, Making and Defending a Choice

❋ Read the following statements about Western Europe. Circle the correct word or words in parentheses to complete each statement.

1. (Windsor Castle/Runnymede) was the site of the signing of the Magna Carta.

2. Taxes are monies paid (to/by) a king or emperor to help run the government.

3. Magna Carta is (Latin/French) for Great Charter.

4. The Middle Ages was the period in history between about (A.D. 500 and 1500/100 B.C. and A.D. 500).

5. A vassal was a person who owned a (fief/kind of ship).

6. (Feudalism/Monarchy) is the name given to the form of government that developed in Western Europe in the Middle Ages.

7. Castles were built with thick stone walls so that they would be (cool in the summer/safe from attack).

8. Serfs were expected to give gifts to the (king of the country/lord of their manor) several times a year.

9. (Richard the Lionhearted/Pope Urban II) was the person responsible for starting the Crusades.

10. John Calvin led the reform movement in (Germany/Switzerland).

❋ On the line to the left of each description, write the term that is described.

monastery	1. a place where religious men live, work, and pray
guild	2. during the Middle Ages, an association of people in the same business
apprentice	3. a person who worked for another at no pay to learn a skill or trade
Da Vinci	4. Renaissance artist who was also an engineer
printing	5. a process made easier and faster by Johann Gutenberg
Genoa	6. city where Christopher Columbus was born
protest	7. root word of the term Protestant
German	8. the language into which Martin Luther translated the Bible
Elizabeth I	9. Queen of England in the late sixteenth century

Thinking Further: What do you think was the most important event (or closely related series of events) in Europe between about 1200 and 1600? Support your answer with specific reasons.
Some possibilities: drawing up of Magna Carta; a Crusade; Renaissance; voyages of exploration; Reformation; development of printing.

© Silver, Burdett & Ginn Inc.

TEACHER NOTES

C6-D

Feudal Lords and Serfs

Objectives

★**1. Describe** the feudal system.

2. Explain the significance of the Magna Carta.

3. List the reasons for the Crusades.

4. Identify the following people and places: *King John, Pope Urban II,* and *the Holy Land.*

1 STARTING THE LESSON

Motivation Activity

■ Supply the class with several pictures of castles. Point out features such as thick walls, small windows, moats, draw-bridges, and battlements (low walls with open spaces for shooting).

■ Ask students to discuss the reasons for including these features in a building.

Think About What You Know

■ Assign the THINK ABOUT WHAT YOU KNOW activity on p. 173.

■ Answers should reflect independent associations with the word *castle*, such as kings, queens, knights, and fairy tales.

Study the Vocabulary

■ Have students look up the definition of each of the new vocabulary words for this lesson in the Glossary.

■ Have students create crossword puzzles using all of the vocabulary words. Have them use the definitions as clues.

■ Ask students to exchange papers and solve each other's puzzles.

CHAPTER **6**

HISTORY OF WESTERN EUROPE

*S*trong rulers, new la[w] and the development o[f] cities like Carcassone h[as a] great impact on Europe[an] system of loyalties and protection developed i[n] a distinctive system of government.

Optional Activities

Writing to Learn

Writing a Diary   Have students write a diary entry for June 15, 1215, the day of the signing of the Magna Carta.

● Students can choose to write from the perspective of one of the nobles or from the perspective of King John.

Feudal Lords and Serfs

THINK ABOUT WHAT YOU KNOW
What things do you think of when you hear the term *castle*?

STUDY THE VOCABULARY
tax   manor
fief   economy
knight   serf
feudalism   Crusade

FOCUS YOUR READING
What were the obligations, or responsibilities, of feudal nobles and serfs during the Middle Ages?

A. King John Goes to Runnymede

King John's Reign The king was probably not in a good mood that Monday morning in 1215. It was a pleasant June day, and King John was on his way to Runnymede (RUN ih meed), a meadow along the south bank of the Thames (temz) River. But this was no royal pleasure trip. John was on his way to make peace with the nobles, who had threatened to drive him from the throne. Nobles were the people to whom the king had given land.

King John had ruled England for 16 years. His reign, or rule, had been filled with troubles—many of his own making. From the start some people had questioned his right to the throne. They believed that his nephew, Arthur, had a better claim. The question was settled when Arthur mysteriously disappeared. Some said that John had had him murdered. To this day no one knows for sure.

John's Opponents Throughout the years, John had his share of quarrels. He quarreled with the king of France, with his own nobles, and with the pope in Rome, the head of the Roman Catholic Church. Troubles with the nobles began because John had insisted that, as king, he had the power to do whatever he wished. He paid no attention to the old customs and laws of England. He forced the nobles to pay higher **taxes**. A tax is money paid to a ruler or government in return for government services. John sometimes seized the nobles' land without just cause. He also limited their right to hunt, and hunting was their main amusement.

Finally the nobles had had enough. They banded together and declared that they would make war against the king unless he accepted limits on his power. At first, John angrily refused to give in to the nobles. But he soon discovered that he had little support. He finally agreed to accept the nobles' demands. That was the reason for King John's trip to Runnymede on June 15, 1215.

B. King John Accepts the Magna Carta

When King John reached Runnymede, he entered a tent and seated himself on a throne. The nobles presented the king with a list of their demands. John gloomily put his seal on the list, showing that he accepted the demands. This list became the basis of the Great Charter, which is known by its Latin name *Magna Carta* (MAG nuh KAHR tuh).

The Magna Carta's real significance went beyond the dispute between John and his nobles. For the first time, a king of England was bound by the law. He could not do as he pleased. The king could not have unlimited power. The Magna Carta set forth rules that the king and his

173

2 # DEVELOPING THE LESSON

Read and Think

Sections A and B
Use the questions below to help students understand the importance of the Magna Carta:

1. **Why did King John have so many problems with the nobles during his reign?**
   (He ignored the old customs and laws of England and said that he could do whatever he pleased because he was king. *p. 173*)

2. **What does the term *Magna Carta* mean?**
   (Great Charter *p. 173*)

3. **What was the real significance of the Magna Carta?**
   (For the first time, a king of England and his officials were bound by the law. *p. 173*)

   Thinking Critically Why, do you think, did the nobles band together to oppose John? (Infer)
   (Answers should reflect independent thinking but may include that no one person had enough power to oppose him. *p. 173*)

Making a Students' Bill of Rights
● Have students work in groups to make a list of rights that they would like to see upheld in their school or classroom.

● Students should, of course, be reminded that a teacher will limit himself or herself only to realistic restrictions.

Optional Activities

Read and Think

Section C

To help students understand the concept of feudalism, ask the following questions:

1. **To what period of European history does the term *Middle Ages* refer?**
   (The period between ancient and modern times, approximately between the years 500 and 1500 *p. 174*)

2. **What did kings receive in exchange for land during the Middle Ages?**
   (Loyalty and military service *p. 174*)

3. **What system of government was used in Western Europe during the Middle Ages?**
   (Feudalism *p. 174*)

4. **How was a lord also a vassal?**
   (Vassals who gave parts of their land to others, especially knights, became lords. *p. 174*)

Thinking Critically Why, do you think, did feudal governments not provide schools, hospitals, and other services that governments provide today?
(Hypothesize)
(Answers may include that people in the Middle Ages did not have enough power to demand these services from the government since they did not elect their rulers. *p. 174*)

---

officials had to follow. For example, the king could not collect taxes unless the great council of the kingdom agreed to them. Royal officials could not take a freeman's horse or wagon without the owner's permission. The Magna Carta stated that the people were guaranteed a trial by jury. The king promised in the charter "to no one will we deny or delay justice." The Magna Carta was the root of many rights and liberties, and was the basic beginning of twentieth-century democracy.

John did not keep the promises made in the Magna Carta. It is doubtful that he ever intended to do so. Within a very short time, he was at war with the nobles. Fortunately the war did not last long, because the king became deathly ill. John died 16 months after putting his seal on the Magna Carta.

Mounted warriors served to protect the kings during the Middle Ages.
▶ What did the knight and his horse wear for their protection?

174

C. Land Granted for Services

Vassals and Knights King John had lived in a time of a medieval civilization, which historians call the *Middle Ages*. It was so named because it was the period of European history between ancient and modern times, approximately between the years 500 and 1500.

Kings during the Middle Ages did not command a strong central government like that of the Roman emperors. Instead, kings granted land, or **fiefs** (feefs), in exchange for loyalty and military service. Those who received a fief were called *vassals*. Each vassal who was given land by the king had to agree to give the king a certain number of armed men each year for his service. These men were called **knights**. A knight was a trained warrior who fought on horseback with swords and lances during the Middle Ages. To read more about knights, turn to page 176.

Government A vassal who promised knights to the king got the knights by giving them parts of his own fief. When a vassal gave land to others, he became a *lord*. The person who received the land became his vassal. These vassals, in turn, would grant parts of their fiefs to still others. Thus many of the king's vassals became lords of their own vassals. This form of government that developed in Western Europe during the Middle Ages is called **feudalism** (FYOOD ul ihz um). It was a system of government, a way of life, and a distinctive kind of society.

Feudal governments provided a way to settle disputes. Aside from that and providing some military protection, they did little else. They did not provide schools, hospitals, fire protection, or other services that governments provide today.

Optional Activities

Graphic Organizer

To help students better understand the relationships among kings, lords or nobles, knights, freemen, and serfs on a feudal manor, you may wish to use the graphic organizer.

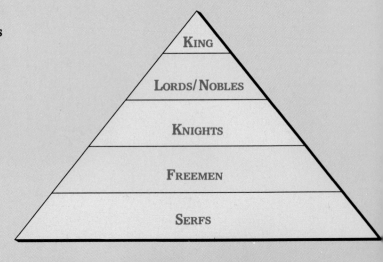

KING
LORDS/NOBLES
KNIGHTS
FREEMEN
SERFS

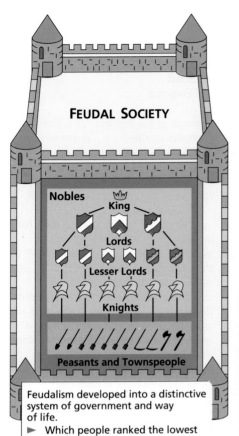

FEUDAL SOCIETY

Nobles
King
Lords
Lesser Lords
Knights
Peasants and Townspeople

Feudalism developed into a distinctive system of government and way of life.
► Which people ranked the lowest in feudal society?

D. Life on a Manor

Lords and Peasants Most nobles lived on **manors**, which were large farms or estates on their fiefs. The noble became the lord of his manor. He was responsible for governing it. The manor was the source of the noble's wealth.

The **economy** of the feudal manor was based on agriculture. Economy is the way in which natural resources and workers are used to produce goods and services. The peasants, or farm workers, were the backbone and muscle of agriculture, which was the economic foundation of feudalism. All peasants were either freemen or **serfs**. Most of them were serfs. The serf owed his labor to his lord. Serfs were not free to leave the manor without the lord's permission, but they could not be sold like slaves. The other peasants were freemen who owned or rented land from a lord. Freemen owed few, if any, obligations to a lord.

Castles and Villages The lord lived in the most important house on the manor. Powerful lords lived in castles. Perhaps you think living in a castle would be pleasant, but castles were designed for protection, not comfort. These castles were

This fifteenth-century painting shows serfs working in the fields.
► What is in the background of this feudal manor?

Optional Activities

Interviewing

● Ask students to imagine that they have the opportunity to interview one of the following people on a feudal manor:
  a. a serf's wife
  b. a lord's daughter
  c. a knight
  d. a king
  e. a freeman

● Have each student choose one of these characters and write one or two questions that they would like to ask him or her.

● You may wish to conclude this activity by asking some students to read their questions to the class.

Use the information below to help students better understand the literature selection found on p. 176.

Selection Summary

Ivanhoe, published in 1819, is Sir Walter Scott's historical romantic novel about knighthood. Like many of Scott's works, it depicts the struggle between different cultures — Normans and Saxons. Ivanhoe is a young knight who has returned from war to pit his wits, skills, and strength against a villainous knight. In the passage on p. 176, Scott describes a battle tournament between two groups of knights.

Guided Reading

1. **What types of weapons were used in the battle described in this passage?**
   (Lances [spears] and swords)

2. **How did the knights do battle?**
   (Mounted on horseback and on foot, in hand-to-hand combat)

Literature—Social Studies Connection

What, do you think, supports calling *Ivanhoe* a "historical romantic novel"?
(Answers should reflect independent thinking but may include specific references to knights' armor and descriptions of medieval England in the form of a novel.)

FROM:

Ivanhoe

By: Sir Walter Scott
Setting: Medieval England

Sir Walter Scott was born in Scotland in 1771. As an adult, he had a remarkable career as a poet, novelist, historian, and biographer. But the great success of his first narrative poem encouraged Scott to dedicate himself to literature. In fact, Scott invented a new type of literature: the historical novel.

Ivanhoe, published in 1819, is Scott's historical romantic novel about knighthood. The character Ivanhoe is a young knight who has returned from war to pit his wits, skills, and strength against a villainous knight.

In this passage, Scott describes a battle tournament between two groups of knights.

*T*he knights held their long lances upright, their bright points glancing to the sun, and the streamers with which they were decorated fluttering over the plumage of the helmets. . . . The trumpets sounded . . . the spears of the champions were at once lowered . . . the spurs were dashed into the flanks of the horses, and the two [groups of knights] rushed upon each other in full gallop.

. . . When the fight became visible, half the knights on each side were dismounted, some by the dexterity [skill] of their adversary's [opponent's] lance, — some by the superior weight and strength of opponents, which had borne [brought] down both horse and man, — some lay stretched on earth as if never more to rise, — some had already gained their feet, and were closing hand to hand with those of their antagonists [opponents] who were in the same predicament, — and several on both sides, who had received wounds by which they were disabled, were stopping their blood with their scarfs.

Curriculum Connection

Literature Ask students to review the literature selection on p. 176 and list on a sheet of paper three words whose meaning they do not know.

- Have students use a dictionary to find the meanings of the words on their lists.
- Ask them to record the definitions.
- Have volunteers read aloud one word and its definition until all the words that students listed have been presented.

Designing Castles and Crests

- Have students design their own castle or have them design their own crest that would be displayed on a flag and painted on the doors of their castle. (You may wish to have students look for examples of medieval crests in the library.)
- Tell students to draw their castles and crests on construction paper.
- Display the students' castles and crests around the classroom.

drafty, dirty, damp, and dim. They were usually built in hard-to-reach places. The first castles were made of wood. Later in the Middle Ages, they had thick stone walls, which were hard to attack but which kept the inside of the castles cold and damp. Small windows served well as look-outs, but they let in little sunlight. A moat, a water-filled ditch that surrounded the castle, and a heavy metal gate that protected the massive wooden door kept attackers away from the walls.

A manor also had a village, where the peasants lived. Most of the people who lived on the manor were peasants. A typical manor might have between 50 and 500 peasants. In addition to the peasant huts, a village usually had a church, a shed that served as a blacksmith shop, a mill for grinding grain, and farm fields.

Serfdom The life of a serf was a hard one. Women and girls worked in the fields with the men and boys. The serfs planted and harvested the crops. They cut hay in the summer and cut wood in the winter.

Serfs owed their lord more than work. They had to present him with gifts at certain times of the year. Nobles feasted during the holidays on the gifts from the serfs.

The lord of a manor controlled the village grain mill, bake oven, and wine or cider press. After a serf had the grain ground into meal, the lord received a share of it. When serfs baked loaves of rye bread, they gave a loaf for the lord's household.

The Magna Carta meant very little to the serfs. The king promised to respect the rights of his great vassals and certain freemen. But the charter said nothing about the serfs, who were not free.

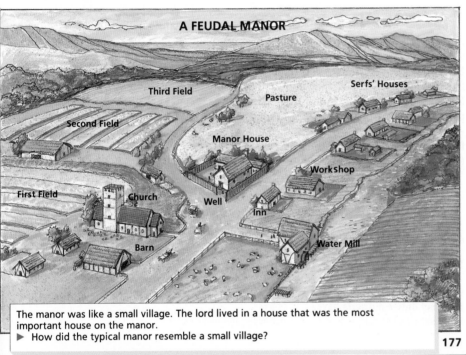

A FEUDAL MANOR

Third Field
Pasture
Serfs' Houses
Second Field
Manor House
First Field
Church
Workshop
Well
Inn
Barn
Water Mill

The manor was like a small village. The lord lived in a house that was the most important house on the manor.
▶ How did the typical manor resemble a small village?

177

Reteaching Main Objective
Describe the feudal system.

● Have students role-play the different kinds of people on a typical feudal manor.

● Divide the class into small groups and assign each group different parts to role-play. Have one group represent serfs, another freemen, another knights, another lords, and another the king and his family.

● Have students describe where they live, a typical day, and what they like and do not like about the feudal system.

Optional Activities

Life was far from comfortable for anyone during the Middle Ages. Peasants lived in huts, while those who enjoyed the most wealth lived in cold, damp castles. Knights were commandeered to fight in the long Crusades. Use the questions that follow to help students understand daily life and religious obligations in the Middle Ages:

1. **What were the two types of peasants on a feudal manor and how did they differ?**
(Serfs owed labor to their lord; freemen rented land from a lord or owned land and had few obligations to the lord. *p. 175*)

2. **Describe a typical village on a feudal manor.**
(A typical village held between 50 and 500 peasants, had peasant huts, a church, a blacksmith's shed, a mill for grinding grain, and farm fields. *p. 177*)

3. **List three reasons Pope Urban II gave for fighting the first Crusade.**
(It was a religious duty; it was better to fight the Muslims in the Middle East than in Europe; and there were great riches to be won. *p. 178*)

4. **What was the Holy Land for which Pope Urban II asked the nobles to fight?**
(The part of the Middle East where Jesus had lived *p. 178*)

Thinking Critically Do you think it was fair that the lord of a manor took a share of whatever the serfs made when they used his mill, oven, and wine or cider press? (Evaluate)
(Answers should reflect independent thinking but may include yes, it was fair since the lord owned these things and deserved something for allowing the serfs to use them; or no, it was not fair since the lord already received the labor of the serfs as well as gifts from the serfs at certain times of the year. *p. 177*)

┌─ **Answers to Caption Questions** ─
p. 177 ▶ It contained houses, a church, an inn, a barn, a workshop, and a mill.
└───────────────────────────────

CLOSING THE LESSON

Lesson *1* Review

Answers to Think and Write

A. The nobles threatened to rebel against King John in 1215 because he ignored the old customs and laws.

B. The purpose of the Magna Carta was to limit the king's power.

C. In the feudal system, a king gave land to vassals in exchange for a vow of loyalty and military service. Each vassal gave the king a certain number of knights each year. A vassal got knights by giving them parts of his own fief.

D. Serfs performed farm work and gave gifts to the lord at certain times of year. They had to give the lord a share of anything that they made using the lord's grain mill, oven, and wine or cider press.

E. The purpose of the Crusades was to free the Holy Land from Muslim control.

Answer to Skills Check

Answers should reflect independent thinking but may include that one would have greater freedom and independence on an American farm.

Focus Your Reading

Ask the lesson focus question found at the beginning of the lesson: **What were the obligations, or responsibilities, of feudal nobles and serfs during the Middle Ages?** (Nobles owed loyalty and military service or knights, to their king or lord and were responsible for governing their manors. Serfs owed labor and gifts to their lord and could not leave the manor without the lord's permission.)

Additional Practice

You may wish to assign the ancillary materials listed below.

Understanding the Lesson p. 45

After Richard I became king, he went off to fight in the Third Crusade.
► How can you tell from the engraving which man is King Richard?

E. Feudal Lords Fought "Wars for the Cross"

Feudal nobles and knights were warriors, and they had many opportunities to use their fighting skills. In 1095, Pope Urban II called upon nobles and knights to fight for the Holy Land, that part of the Middle East where Jesus had lived. The pope asked them to take part in a **Crusade** —a "war for the cross"—to free the land from Muslim control. Muslims followed the religion of Islam.

The pope told the knights that going on the Crusade was a religious duty. He also told them that it would be far better for Christian knights to fight Muslims in the Middle East than to fight each other in Europe. He also noted that there were great riches to be won in the Middle East.

The Crusade Pope Urban called for was the first in a series of Crusades during the Middle Ages. King John's brother, Richard the Lion-Hearted, led the Third Crusade in 1189. The Crusades affected both the Middle East and Western Europe.

LESSON *1* REVIEW

THINK AND WRITE (Recall)

A. Why did the nobles threaten to rebel against King John in 1215?

B. What was the purpose of the Magna Carta? (Infer) (Analyze)

C. Explain how the feudal system worked.

D. What duties did serfs have? (Recall)

E. What was the purpose of the Crusades? (Recall)

SKILLS CHECK

WRITING SKILL

Think about what it might be like to live on an American farm today. Then write a paragraph comparing this way of life with the life of a serf in the Middle Ages.

(Recall)

Optional Activities

UNDERSTANDING THE LESSON

NAME _____ CHAPTER
UNDERSTANDING THE LESSON ***6***

RecallingFacts LESSON 1 CONTENT MASTER

★ Read each statement below. Write **True** if the statement is true and **False** if it is false. If the statement is false, cross out the part that is incorrect and write the correct words above it.

False	1. In 1215, the English nobles were ~~pleased~~ with the rule of King John.
True	2. The nobles forced King John to sign the Magna Carta, which limited the king's powers.
False	3. The Magna Carta was important because for the first time a king of England ~~had to pay taxes.~~
False	4. The Middle Ages is the period of European history between the years ~~1000 and 1800.~~
True	5. During the Middle Ages, the government, economy, and society of Western Europe was based on a system called feudalism.
False	6. In the feudal system, kings granted land to ~~peasants~~ in return for loyalty and military service.
False	7. The economic foundation of feudalism was ~~commerce.~~
True	8. Serfs were peasants who worked on their lord's land, while freemen owned or rented their own land.
False	9. In the Magna Carta, the king promised to respect the rights of ~~vassals and serfs.~~
False	10. Those who fought in the Crusades wanted to ~~open new trade routes.~~

Think and Write: Write a paragraph comparing the lives of a lord and a serf during the Middle Ages. You may use the back of the sheet.

Use with textbook pages 175-178. 45

◄ **Review Master Booklet, p. 45**

The People of the Towns and the Church

THINK ABOUT WHAT YOU KNOW

Why, do you think, do people live in towns?

STUDY THE VOCABULARY

monastery	monopoly
convent	apprentice
guild	

FOCUS YOUR READING

What were the functions of the people of the church and the town?

A. Life in a Monastery During the Middle Ages

Saint Benedict During the early Middle Ages, a man later known as Saint Benedict began to live in a lonely cliffside cave near Rome. He lived there for three years, eating little else but bread that a friend lowered on a rope to his cave.

Benedict came to believe that a worthwhile life could be lived by men who lived together and worked hard. So Benedict established a **monastery**, a dwelling for monks, religious men who devote their lives to prayer and labor. For 1,400 years men went to the monastery seeking to live peaceful lives of prayer. The monastery, known as the Abbey of Monte Cassino, was the most famous one in Western Europe. The Abbey of Monte Cassino still stands today.

Caring for the sick was one of the duties of a monk during the Middle Ages.
▶ What, do you think, is in the box the monk is holding?

Daily Routine By today's standards, life in a monastery was hard. The monks got up during the night to pray. They worked long hours in the fields where they grew their own food. At certain times during the day, the monks went to church to sing and pray. Parts of each day were set aside for reading and study.

Usually the monks ate only one full meal a day. But during the summer and at times of plowing and harvest, they would have a second meal. The monks ate simply. Only the sick had meat or eggs. The monks went to bed early. At sundown it was time for evening prayers and for bed.

Nuns also lived lives full of prayer and work. They made the same kinds of

179

For Your Information

Benedictines Monks who follow the teachings of Saint Benedict today are known as Benedictines. They pledge themselves to obedience to their superiors, celibacy, a spare diet, poverty, and hard work. They must also abstain from laughter. Known as the "Black Monks," they are renowned for their learning.

Optional Activities

The People of the Towns and the Church

Objectives

★ **1. Explain** the functions of townspeople and church people during the Middle Ages.

2. Compare life in a town with life on a manor in the Middle Ages.

3. Identify the following people and places: *Saint Benedict* and *Abbey of Monte Cassino.*

---

1 STARTING THE LESSON

Motivation Activity

■ Explain that not everyone in the Middle Ages lived on a manor. Some people lived in towns.

■ Have students write a short paragraph in which they describe what they think a town in the Middle Ages was like.

■ After students have read the lesson, have them check their predictions.

Think About What You Know

■ Assign the THINK ABOUT WHAT YOU KNOW activity on p. 179.

■ Answers may include that people live in towns for safety, for companionship, and for convenience.

Study the Vocabulary

■ Have students look up in the Glossary each of the new vocabulary words for this lesson.

■ Then, divide the class into small groups to play "What am I?".

■ Have students take turns giving clues to vocabulary words in the form of definitions. Students must guess the vocabulary word that matches the clue.

Answers to Caption Questions

p. 178▶ The man wearing the crown
p. 179▶ Probably bandages and medicine or first-aid materials

---

179

Read and Think

Sections A and B

Help students understand the role of monks, nuns, and village priests in the Middle Ages by asking the following questions:

1. **How did monks and nuns help people?**
   (Fed the poor, sheltered travelers, taught children, cared for the sick *p. 180*)

2. **Describe a typical day in a monk's life.**
   (Work in the fields, sing and pray in the church, read, study, eat simply, go to bed early, get up in the night to pray *pp. 179-180*)

3. **What person of the church would the people on a feudal manor have been most likely to know?**
   (The village priest *p. 180*)

   Thinking Critically Why, do you think, were monks and nuns required to give up everything they owned and never marry? (Infer)
   (Answers may include that they could better focus on helping other people if they were not distracted by possessions or busy with their own family. *pp. 179-180*)

VISUAL THINKING SKILL

Interpreting a Photograph

- Tell students that the photograph on p. 180 shows a cathedral.

- After students have finished reading Section B, ask them to trace the outline of the pictured cathedral on a piece of notebook paper.

- Have them list inside the outline the activities that took place in cathedrals during the Middle Ages. (Learning, worshiping)

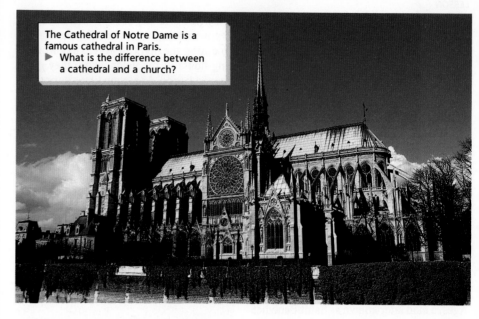

The Cathedral of Notre Dame is a famous cathedral in Paris.
► What is the difference between a cathedral and a church?

promises that monks made. They gave up everything they owned and never married. Nuns lived in houses called **convents**.

Helping people was part of the work in both monasteries and convents. The monks and nuns fed the poor. They gave travelers shelter for the night. They taught children, and they cared for the sick. It was a way of life very different from that of kings, queens, and knights.

B. Duties of a Village Priest

Priest's Duties The village priest was the person of the church best known to people on the manor. The priest held services in the village church, baptized babies, and taught children their religious duties. He performed marriages for the villagers in the church and conducted the services when they were buried in the churchyard.

Here is how one book described an ideal, or model, priest. He should teach children "to read, spell, and sing." He should even teach them that "their play should be honest and merry, without great noise." Of course, the book described the *ideal*, the way it should be. Actually most village children did not learn to read, and one doubts that many learned to play without great noise.

Bishop's Duties From time to time a high-ranking church official, the bishop, would visit the village church. A bishop was in charge of all the churches within a certain area.

As towns began to grow and prosper, people had more time for learning, literature, and the arts. Many young men who wanted to be priests entered schools run by bishops. The schools were located in large churches called *cathedrals*, which were often located in towns. Some of the finest and largest buildings erected in the Middle Ages were cathedrals.

Optional Activities

Writing to Learn

Writing a Journal Ask students to imagine that they are monks living in a monastery or nuns living in a convent in the Middle Ages.

- Have them write a paragraph in their journals describing their activities on a typical day.

C. Town Air Makes a Man Free

Travelers journeying to a town during the Middle Ages did well to arrive before sundown. If they failed to do so, they might be locked out. Many towns had walls, and the gates were closed at night. Towns built walls and gates for the same reason that feudal nobles had castles. Walls gave protection from bandits and even armies.

Houses were crowded close together within the walls of the towns. Sunlight shone only for brief periods on the narrow streets, which were only 6 to 10 feet (2 to 3 m) wide. Yet townspeople had one big advantage over people who lived on the rural manors. They did not have to labor for a lord, although the townspeople sometimes had to pay yearly taxes to a great lord. Nobles had such a need for money that they sometimes encouraged the establishment of towns by granting townspeople greater freedom. In some cases, if a serf lived for a year and a day in a town, he became free. It was said in those towns that "town air makes a man free."

This mural, entitled *The Effects of Good Government,* shows how wooden houses were crammed in next to each other so they might fit within the stone walls that encircled the town for protection.
▶ What kinds of activities took place in medieval towns?

181

Read and Think
Section C

Not everyone lived on a manor or in a monastery during the Middle Ages. As the period progressed, more and more people lived in towns, but the towns of the Middle Ages were quite different from towns today. Discuss town life with students, using the questions below:

1. **What advantage did townspeople have over people who lived on rural manors in the Middle Ages?**
   (They did not have to labor for a lord. *p.181*)

   Thinking Critically What, do you think, would be the hardest thing about town life during the Middle Ages? (Infer)
   (Answers may include that people in towns were crowded closely together inside the town walls. *p. 181*)

— **Answers to Caption Questions** —
p. 180 ▶ Cathedrals were larger and more elaborate.
p. 181 ▶ Shopping, street performing, parading, working in a guild

Public Speaking

● Ask students to recall an episode in which they learned a skill from another person, as the apprentices did in the Middle Ages.

● Have students share their experiences orally with the class.

For Your Information

Surnames Many last names of people of European descent come from the old crafts and skills of the Middle Ages. For example, a townsman who made bread might be known as Mr. Baker, and a man who beat metal into tools and pots might be called Mr. Smith (short for Blacksmith).

Other examples of names derived from crafts are Carpenter, Barber, Potter, Mason (a bricklayer), and Weaver.

Optional Activities

Meeting Individual Needs
Concept: Monopolies

The activities below will help students relate the organization of craftworkers into guilds to the concept of monopolies.

Read and Think
Sections D and E

To help students understand guilds, ask the following questions:

1. **Name some standards that all members of the same craft guild had to follow.**
   (Using the same materials and selling their goods at the same price *p. 182*)

2. **How did an apprentice become a craftworker?**
   (Worked without pay for four or more years, learning the skills of a trade until able to turn out a piece of work according to guild standards *p. 182*)

Thinking Critically **How do you think customers benefited from craft guilds?** (Hypothesize)
(Answers may include that customers were assured that every product met the same high-quality standards. *p. 182*)

182

D. Guilds Controlled the Town Markets

The Magna Carta stated that "all merchants shall be safe and secure in going out from England, coming into England, and going through England." However, a merchant could sell goods in a town only with the consent of its merchant **guild**. A guild was an association of people in the same business. The guild of merchants set the rules for the town market. The basic purpose of the merchant guilds was to promote the business and the personal well-being of their members.

Craft guilds were made up of people in the same trade or craft. Tailors, shoemakers, hatters, and metalsmiths all had

This etching below shows members of a craft guild busily making coins during the Middle Ages.
▶ Of what guild are these workers members?

182

their guilds. Each guild controlled the making and selling of its product within the town. This kind of control over the production of goods by one group is called a **monopoly**. All members of the guild had to follow the same standards. They had to use the same materials and sell their goods for the same price. The guilds did not want a free market—one in which sellers compete.

E. Guilds Controlled the Training of Workers

Pupils of Trade A young person wishing to take up a trade became an **apprentice** (uh PREN tihs), a pupil. An apprentice agreed to live and work with a master craftworker who belonged to the craft guild. An apprentice was not paid, but the master agreed to provide food and clothing as well as teach the apprentice the skills of the trade. Apprentices often lived with the master's family, above the shop. Sometimes apprentices slept in the attic.

An apprentice served four or more years, depending on the trade. A new apprentice did odd jobs requiring little skill. As time went on, more difficult skills had to be learned so that the apprentice could turn out a piece of work according to certain guild standards.

Going to Work When the period of training was completed, the apprentice became a *journeyman*. The name comes from the French word *jour*, meaning "day." A journeyman was paid for each day's work. A journeyman who wished to become a master in a guild would work for a number of years striving to produce a masterpiece. The masterpiece had to be a product made according to the very highest guild standards. A journeyman shoemaker, for example, would have to produce a very fine pair of shoes or boots.

Wives commonly worked alongside their husbands in their trades, and daughters were apprenticed in the same way as their brothers. If a husband died, a woman carried on his business and craft. Many women became guild members, even members of traditional male trades. Such women were highly respected in the community. If a woman worked for a wage, however, she often received less than a man for the same work.

Guild rules for training apprentices served two purposes. The rules produced skilled workers, and they gave master craftworkers control of who could learn a trade. The masters made sure that there would not be too many workers in their line of business. This made it easier to keep prices high.

Most towns developed a town council made up of representatives of the various guilds. This council carried out many of the duties of a modern city government. Modern life as we know it today was beginning to develop.

An apprentice learned a trade such as masonry, the building with stone, brick, or concrete.
▶ What materials and equipment did members of this trade guild use?

LESSON 2 REVIEW

THINK AND WRITE   (Evaluate)
A. What might the life of a monk be like?
B. What were the duties of a village priest?
C. What was the difference between the positions of a townsperson and a serf?
D. How did the guilds limit freedom?   (Infer)
E. What were the purposes of the apprentice system?   (Infer)

SKILLS CHECK

THINKING SKILL

Skim through the lesson to find five types of people who worked in towns or churches during the Middle Ages and find one characteristic for each of them. Make a chart using this information.

183

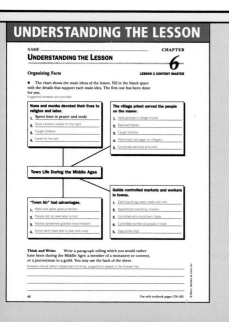
Optional Activities

3 CLOSING THE LESSON

Lesson 2 Review

Answers to Think and Write
A. Monks grew their own food. Each day they would go to church services, pray, read, and study. They helped the poor, the sick, and travelers.

B. The duties of a village priest were to perform church services, baptize babies, provide religious instruction, and conduct ceremonies for marriages and funerals.

C. A townsperson, unlike a serf, did not owe his or her labor to a lord in exchange for land.

D. Guilds limited freedom by controlling the production and pricing of crafts.

E. The apprentice system trained young people in a craft and let master craftworkers decide who could learn a skill.

Answer to Skills Check
Charts may include monks (religious), nuns (selfless), priests (instructive), townspeople (free), apprentices (young), and master craftworkers (skilled).

Focus Your Reading
Ask the lesson focus question found at the beginning of the lesson: **What were the functions of the people of the church and the town?**
(People of the church helped the poor and the sick, taught children, and conducted church services, marriages, and funerals. Townspeople crafted and sold goods.)

Additional Practice
You may wish to assign the ancillary materials listed below.

Understanding the Lesson p. 46
Workbook p. 49

┌─ **Answers to Caption Questions** ─
│ p. 182 ▶ The metalsmith guild
│ p. 183 ▶ Stones, bricks, ladders

183

A Time of "Rebirth"

Objectives

★ 1. **Explain** why the period of time following the Middle Ages is called the Renaissance.

2. **Identify** three artists of the Renaissance.

3. **Explain** the importance of Gutenberg's invention of the printing press.

4. **Identify** the following people and places: *Leonardo da Vinci, Michelangelo, Raphael, Johann Gutenberg, Christopher Columbus, Florence,* and *Sistine Chapel.*

1 STARTING THE LESSON

Motivation Activity

■ Have students look in their books and compare a picture from the Middle Ages with a picture from the Renaissance.

■ Encourage discussion of the differences between the two pictures.

■ Then explain that the period you are about to study ushered in a new approach to art as well as a whole new way of thinking.

Think About What You Know

■ Assign the THINK ABOUT WHAT YOU KNOW activity on p. 184.

■ Answers should reflect independent thinking but may include a new planet, a cure for cancer, or other places and discoveries.

Study the Vocabulary

■ Ask each student to skim through the lesson and make a list of words or terms that they feel might prove difficult for other students.

■ Collect the lists of terms and make a master list of the terms most commonly mentioned. Make sure that the vocabulary words for this lesson are included in the list.

184

A Time of "Rebirth"

THINK ABOUT WHAT YOU KNOW

Tell about some thing or place that you would like to discover.

STUDY THE VOCABULARY

Renaissance   **explorer**

FOCUS YOUR READING

Why is the period of time after the Middle Ages called a time of rebirth?

A. A Rediscovery of Old Ideas

The change from the Middle Ages, or medieval history, into modern history took place gradually over many years and involved many events and developments in the arts and literature. One change was the rediscovery of the cultural heritages of ancient Greece and ancient Rome, which had become lost or forgotten during the Middle Ages. This interest in learning about the Romans and Greeks led to a birth of interest in newer types of learning. Old ideas led to new ones. Historians have used the term **Renaissance** (REN uh sahns), a French word meaning "rebirth," for this period of time following the Middle Ages.

The Renaissance started as early as the fourteenth century in Italy and then spread throughout most of Europe. The Renaissance gave Europeans new and different ideas about themselves and about the world. These ideas were expressed by writers and artists. The three best-known Renaissance artists were Leonardo da Vinci, Michelangelo, and Raphael (rah-fah EL). All three of these men advanced the Renaissance style of showing nature and depicting the feelings of people.

184

B. Da Vinci Has New Ideas

Artist and Engineer Leonardo da Vinci was born in 1452 in the Italian village of Vinci. The *da Vinci* in his name means "of Vinci." As a boy, Leonardo showed such an unusual ability to draw that his father took him to Florence and placed him as an apprentice in the shop of an artist.

Da Vinci was very sure of his own abilities as an artist. "I can carry out sculpture in marble, bronze, or clay, and I can do in painting whatever may be done, as well as any other [can], be he whom he may." Clearly, Da Vinci was not a modest man, yet he was not boasting. He could in fact do all these things and a great many more.

Da Vinci was an engineer as well as an artist. In 1482 he wrote to the duke of Milan, looking for a job. Leonardo said he could make devices that would be useful in war. He had an idea for a lightweight bridge that an army could easily move. He knew how to make a variety of cannons,

Da Vinci was one of the greatest painters of the Renaissance.
▶ Besides painting, what other talents did Da Vinci have?

Optional Activities

Comparing Past and Present

● Review with students the process by which learning about old ideas gave birth to new ones during the Renaissance (*p. 184*). Explain that a similar process occurs even today. (For example, knowledge of how government works enables citizens to make improvements in government; the invention of tape recorders led to the development of videotape recorders.)

● Encourage students to think of other ideas or inventions that have led to new ones.

● As students name inventions, pair them with new inventions that these inspired and write them side-by-side on the chalkboard.

efforts to restore *The Last Supper* since Da Vinci's day.

Da Vinci later painted *Mona Lisa*, which has been called the most famous portrait in the world. But no one knows for sure just whose portrait it is.

The duke of Milan gave Da Vinci the job of making a huge bronze statue of a horse and rider. It would stand 23 feet (7 m) tall and would require 79 tons (72 t) of bronze. Da Vinci made a clay model, but he never cast the statue because the bronze was needed for making cannons.

Da Vinci's pen-and-ink drawings show his covered chariot.
▶ Why, do you think, did he draw his ideas?

including one that "could fling small stones almost like a storm." Perhaps his most unusual plan was for a cannon-firing tank, which he called a "covered chariot."

Da Vinci's Great Works Da Vinci was about 30 when he wrote his letter to the duke of Milan. The duke offered him the position of official engineer and artist. During his years in Milan, Da Vinci designed a canal and painted *The Last Supper*. He was always eager to try new things, so he used a new method of applying paint on a plaster wall for this famous painting. Unfortunately the new method did not work. The paint soon began to fade and flake off. There have been a number of

Leonardo da Vinci's *Mona Lisa* is probably the most famous portrait ever painted.
▶ How did Da Vinci portray her?

185

Interpreting a Photograph

- Ask students to look at the photograph of Michelangelo's *Pieta* on this page.

- Then ask the following question: **What emotion do you think Michelangelo wanted to convey with this sculpture?** (Answers may include sadness, beauty, love, and devotion to God.)

Meeting Individual Needs

Concept:
Defining the Renaissance

Many of the art forms, inventions, and innovations of the Renaissance grew from advances that were made in ancient Greece and Rome but were lost or forgotten in the Middle Ages. The activities below will help students relate the changes of the Renaissance to the earlier advances from which they grew.

◆ **EASY** Tell students to use the information in this lesson to make an outline of the developments that occurred during the Renaissance.

Have them use the headings *Art, Writing, Printing,* and *Exploring.*

◀▶ **AVERAGE** Tell students to make a list of the developments that occurred during the Renaissance.

Ask them to write a paragraph that tells which things on their list are discoveries and which are rediscoveries of ideas from the past.

◀▮▶ **CHALLENGING** Ask students to write an essay in which they defend or attack the following statement: *The Renaissance is an appropriate name for the period of time following the Middle Ages because it was a time of "rebirth" of old ideas.*

Have them support their answers with examples from the text.

Michelangelo's famous *Pietà*, found in St. Peter's Church in Rome, is a marble sculpture of Mary holding the dead body of Christ on her lap.
▶ How does Christ's body appear?

C. A Man of Many Talents

Michelangelo was another man of many talents. He became a great painter, architect, and poet, though he was mainly interested in sculpture. In 1504, he sculpted the biblical hero David, who was the second king of Israel. The statue still stands in Florence, Italy.

Among Michelangelo's most famous paintings are those he painted on the ceiling of the Sistine Chapel in the Vatican. The Sistine Chapel is a famous chapel in Rome where the chief ceremonies involving the pope take place. Michelangelo lay on his back on a high scaffold, or movable platform, and covered the ceiling of the Sistine Chapel with more than 300 massive figures that show scenes from the Bible. It took four years to finish the task.

D. Raphael Saves Ancient Ruins

Raphael had come to Florence as a young man to study the works of the city's great artists, especially those of Da Vinci and Michelangelo. Raphael's paintings include a number of famous Madonnas, pictures of Mary the mother of Jesus.

In 1515, Raphael was appointed Keeper of the Remains of Rome. It was his job to save what could be saved of the remains of ancient buildings and monuments. During the Middle Ages, Rome had greatly shrunk in size. People freely used stones taken from ancient ruins to erect other buildings.

By Raphael's time, people took a very different view of the old Roman remains. They regarded the ancient Roman statues and buildings as models to be copied. Architects studied the ruins so that they could erect churches and palaces in the Roman style. Fragments of antique statues dug up from time to time became valuable. They served as models for sculptors to copy.

E. Ancient Writings Spark New Interest

Studying Latin Students during the Renaissance found a new interest in the ancient Latin writings of the Romans. There was nothing new about studying Latin. Priests and monks had done so throughout the Middle Ages. Latin was the language of the church services and the Bible in Western Europe. But some of the students during the Renaissance did not study Latin in order to become priests. They planned to become government employees or merchants. They were more interested in politics and philosophy, the love of wisdom, than religion. Students wanted to read ancient authors because some of the authors,

Optional Activities

Writing to Learn

Writing a Diary Ask students to imagine that they are Raphael living in Rome in the year 1515.

● Have students write diary entries describing a day on the job as Keeper of the Remains of Rome.

such as Cicero (SIHS ur oh), had had the same interests they did. They also found much in the history of Greece and Rome that reminded them of the recent history of the Italian cities. Such discoveries made the ancient writings seem new.

Like the architects, students tried to copy ancient styles. They wrote letters and speeches like those of Cicero. A few students tried to write histories and biographies like those by the ancient writers.

Studying Greek Some students wanted to study the Greek language as well as Latin. After all, the Roman writers often referred to the beauty and wisdom found in Homer, Plato, and other Greek authors. If students knew Greek, they could read those works themselves.

When the city of Florence hired a Greek professor, students jumped at the chance to study with him. One of those students described his excitement at that time. He and his fellow students believed that "all knowledge comes from the Greeks." By learning Greek, they could "speak with Homer and Plato." The student said that he studied so hard during the day that he dreamed in Greek at night. It must have pleased the professor to have had a student like that.

F. Printing Makes Books Cheaper

Handwritten Books The interest in ancient writings led students to search for books that might have been forgotten. They searched in monasteries, and they visited libraries in the eastern Mediterranean lands. In the monasteries they found some dusty books that no one had read for years. In the eastern cities they found works not known in Western Europe.

Many students were eager to read the books that had been found, but only a few could do so. There were only a few copies

In this illuminated manuscript a scholar is shown teaching students Greek during the Renaissance.
▶ How are the students learning?

Read and Think
Sections C, D, and E

Use the following questions to discuss the outpouring of interest in art and scholarship that occurred during the Renaissance:

1. **Name two of Leonardo da Vinci's most famous works of art.**
(*The Last Supper* and the *Mona Lisa* p. 185)

2. **Where are some of Michelangelo's most famous paintings located?**
(On the ceiling of the Sistine Chapel in the Vatican in Rome p. 186)

3. **Why were Renaissance students eager to study Latin?**
(They wanted to become government employees or merchants, and wanted to read the works of ancient authors who had the same interests in politics and philosophy that they did. pp. 186-187)

Thinking Critically Based on what you have learned about Michelangelo, what, do you think, is meant by the term "Renaissance Man"? (Infer)
(Answers should reflect independent thinking but may include one who has wide interests and is an expert in several different areas. p. 186)

┌─ **Answers to Caption Questions** ─
p. 186 ▶ Limp and lifeless
p. 187 ▶ From a book

For Your Information
Niccolo Machiavelli Niccolo Machiavelli (1469-1527) wrote *The Prince*, one of history's most influential books of political theory. Unlike Plato or St. Augustine, who combined discussions of political behavior with ethics, morals, and theology, Machiavelli described how those in power *actually* behave instead of describing how they *should* behave.

The Prince has been called "a handbook for dictators," and Napoleon, Hitler, and Stalin are all said to have followed its advice. Today, *Machiavellian* means ruthless and deceitful. Ironically, Machiavelli was a devoted civil servant in the Florentine Republic who was arrested and tortured by Medici conquerors.

Optional Activities

As Renaissance students discovered new ideas in old books, the demand for books increased dramatically. A German printer developed an invention that made books cheaper and more available. While some people searched for ancient books, others searched for sea routes to Asia. Ask the following questions to discuss these developments:

1. **How were books made before Gutenberg's invention?**
   (They were copied by hand, and they were printed from carved wooden blocks. *pp. 187-188*)

2. **Name three explorers who searched for new lands during the Renaissance.**
   (Christopher Columbus, Vasco da Gama, and Ferdinand Magellan *p. 190*)

   Thinking Critically **If you could have lived during the Renaissance, would you have chosen to be an artist, an inventor, or an explorer?** (Evaluate)
   (Answers should reflect independent thinking but should show an understanding of the role of each person during the Renaissance. *pp. 184-186; 188-189*)

Johann Gutenberg used a printing press to print the first page of the Bible in his workshop in Mainz, Germany.
▶ How did the printing press increase learning?

of most books. The only way to make more was to copy them by hand. As a result, books were very costly. Only rulers and the rich could afford to have libraries.

Printed Cards Books did not become more plentiful until after the development of printing. The first printing was done from carved wooden blocks. The blocks were used chiefly for printing playing cards, since only 52 blocks were needed. To print an entire book by this method would require carving a separate block for each page.

Printed Books By the 1450s a German printer named Johann Gutenberg (YOH-hahn GOOT un burg) had developed a better method of printing. Gutenberg made separate metal blocks, called type, for each letter. He could spell out the words for each page with letter type and fasten them in a frame. After printing one page, the movable type could be used to set another page. Since the type was made of metal, it could be used over and over without wearing out.

The printing of books made them much cheaper, so many more people could have books. Since Gutenberg's time, millions of books have been printed. Today most schools have far more books than even the richest person could have had before Gutenberg invented movable type. You can see from the pictures on page 189 how printing has changed over time.

Writing an Oral Report

● Have students prepare oral reports that compare Western Europe during the Middle Ages and during the Renaissance by focusing on one of the following topics:

1. etiquette
2. food
3. clothing
4. technology
5. the role of women
6. the role of the church
7. art

● Ask volunteers to read their reports to the rest of the class.

Printing: THEN AND NOW

1 The Chinese invented block printing around the second century A.D.

2 Scribes hand copied books throughout the Middle Ages.

3 Gutenberg first used movable type in Europe by about 1455.

4 Web-fed printing presses are commonly used today.

Printing is one of our most important means of mass communication. Advances in printing have made it possible for more people to obtain more knowledge faster and more cheaply than ever before.
▶ What invention changed the method of printing?

189

Making a Time Line

● Have students make a time line in which they show the discoveries and developments that occurred during the Renaissance in art, printing, and exploring.

● First, have students go through the lesson and make a list of the discoveries and developments, noting the year for each one. Next, have them divide the list into the categories of *Art, Printing,* and *Exploring.* Ask them to use a different color of ink for each category.

● After students have made their time lines showing the events in chronological order, have them make a key to show which color goes with each area.

Reteaching Main Objective

★ *Explain why the period of time following the Middle Ages is called the Renaissance.*

● Write the word *Renaissance* on the chalkboard vertically (the letter R should appear at the top and the second E at the bottom.)

● Ask students to think of a word, phrase, person, or development associated with the Renaissance for each letter. Write the words and phrases on the board to the right of each letter. For example:

  Raphael
  Explorers
  New ideas

Lesson 3 Review

Answers to Think and Write

A. The period after the Middle Ages is known as the Renaissance because renewed interest in the ideas of the ancient Greeks and Romans led to a birth of interest in newer types of learning.

B. Da Vinci's new ideas included a lightweight, portable bridge; several types of cannons; a canal; and a method of applying paint directly to plaster.

C. Michelangelo was a talented painter, architect, poet, and sculptor.

D. Raphael was appointed Keeper of the Remains of Rome so that the ancient ruins could be studied and copied.

E. Students of the Renaissance who wanted to be government employees or merchants found that ancient writers shared many of their interests in politics and philosophy.

F. Johann Gutenberg's invention made more books available to more people.

G. The Renaissance was a time of rebirth as well as discovery because as people rediscovered old things, they were inspired to discover new things.

Answer to Skills Check

Genoa is a port city.

Focus Your Reading

Ask the lesson focus question found at the beginning of the lesson: **Why is the period of time after the Middle Ages called a time of rebirth?**
(This period is called a time of rebirth because the renewal of interest in the teachings and ideas of ancient Greece and Rome led to innovations in almost every area of life and society.)

Additional Practice

You may wish to assign the ancillary materials listed below.

Understanding the Lesson p. 47
Workbook pp. 50-52

Christopher Columbus arrived in the New World on October 12, 1492.
▶ How can you tell from this engraving that Columbus and his crew have seen land?

G. A Time of New Discoveries

While some people searched for ancient books, others searched for sea routes to Asia. Christopher Columbus is perhaps the most famous **explorer** of the Renaissance. An explorer is a person who searches for new things and places. Columbus was only one of the great explorers of this period. At the same time, Vasco da Gama and Ferdinand Magellan were also making great voyages of exploration.

Much was happening during the Renaissance, and not all of it can be described as "rebirth." It was a time when people had new ideas and made new discoveries. Leonardo da Vinci had ideas for new inventions. Gutenberg produced a new way to make books that changed the world. Columbus reached land that Europeans did not know existed. After his voyage, Europeans began to explore the Americas, which they called the New World.

LESSON 3 REVIEW

THINK AND WRITE

A. Why is the period after the Middle Ages known as the Renaissance? **(Infer)**

B. What were Da Vinci's new ideas? **(Recall)**

C. What were Michelangelo's talents? **(Recall)**

D. Why was Raphael appointed Keeper of the Remains of Rome? **(Recall)**

E. Why did ancient writings spark new interest in students during the time of the Renaissance? **(Recall)**

F. Explain the importance of Johann Gutenberg's invention. **(Analyze)**

G. Why was the Renaissance a time of discovery and rebirth? **(Infer)**

SKILLS CHECK

THINKING SKILL

Look up the following cities in your Gazetteer: *Florence, Milan, Genoa.* Which city is a port city?

Optional Activities

UNDERSTANDING THE LESSON

NAME _____

UNDERSTANDING THE LESSON   CHAPTER **6**

Recalling Facts   LESSON 3 CONTENT MASTER

✶ Fill in the blanks with the word or words that correctly complete the statement.

1. One change that marked the end of the Middle Ages was a new interest in the cultural heritages of ancient ___Greece___ and ___Rome___

2. The period that followed the Middle Ages is known as the ___Renaissance___

3. Although the Renaissance spread throughout Europe, it began in ___Italy___

4. Three of the best-known Renaissance artists were ___Leonardo da Vinci___ ___Michelangelo___ and ___Raphael___

5. Besides being an artist and sculptor, Leonardo da Vinci was also an ___engineer___

6. Michelangelo's great works include a statue of ___David___ and the paintings on the ceiling of the ___Sistine Chapel___

7. After Raphael was appointed ___Keeper of the Remains of Rome___ he tried to preserve the ruins of ancient buildings and monuments.

8. During the Renaissance, architects studied ancient ruins so they could build churches and palaces in the ___Roman___ style.

9. ___Latin___ was the language of the church during the Middle Ages.

10. During the Renaissance, people studied Latin to learn about ___politics___ and ___philosophy___

11. In 1492, a German named ___Johann Gutenberg___ developed a better method of printing.

12. Instead of using carved wooden blocks for printing, printers could now use ___movable type___ made of metal.

13. Gutenberg's invention made books much ___cheaper___ so more people could have them.

14. Perhaps the most famous explorer during the Renaissance was ___Christopher Columbus___

15. Two other important Renaissance explorers were ___Vasco da Gama___ and ___Ferdinand Magellan___

Think and Write: Write a paragraph explaining how one inventor or explorer during the Renaissance changed life for people since that time. You may use the back of the sheet.
Answers should reflect independent thinking; suggestions appear in the Answer Key.
Use with textbook pages 184–190.

47

◀ **Review Master Booklet, p. 47**

Changes in Church and Government

Changes in Church and Government

Objectives

★ **1. List** the changes in church and government brought about through the Protestant Reformation.

2. Identify the following people and places: *Thomas More, Martin Luther, John Calvin, King Henry VIII, Queen Elizabeth I, Germany,* and *England.*

THINK ABOUT WHAT YOU KNOW

Choose one thing about your school that you would change if you had the chance. What would you have to do to accomplish this change?

STUDY THE VOCABULARY

Reformation   divine right

FOCUS YOUR READING

How were changes brought about in the church and in government?

A. A Traveler Makes Plans for a Book

Planning One Book It was a slow trip across the Alps on horseback in 1509. Desiderius Erasmus (des uh DIHR ee us ih-RAZ mus) decided that he would not waste his time trading stories with his fellow travelers. Instead, he busied his mind with plans for a little book he would write as soon as he had a chance.

Erasmus was on his way back to England after spending many years in Italy, where he studied Greek. England, however, was not his home. Erasmus was born in Rotterdam, a city in the Netherlands. He sometimes signed his name "Erasmus of Rotterdam." But he had spent little time in his native land since he first left to study.

When Erasmus reached England, he lived for a time in the house of his friend Thomas More. It was in More's house that Erasmus wrote the book he had planned while traveling. The book is entitled *The Praise of Folly.*

Erasmus' Bible Erasmus wanted very much for people to know more about the teachings of Christianity. He believed that students should use their learning to help people discover Christian teachings. He wanted students to learn Greek so that they could read the Christian New Testament in the language in which it had been written. Toward this end, he published the first printed Greek New Testament. Erasmus realized that only a few students would be able to read Greek. Since he wanted all people to read the Bible, he favored the translation of the Bible into the languages used by the commoners, or people who were not nobles.

Erasmus was a Dutch priest and a scholar in the early 1500s.
▶ How can you tell from this portrait that Erasmus must have been a wealthy man?

---

1 STARTING THE LESSON

Motivation Activity

■ Write the word *Protestant* on the chalkboard. Ask students to explain its meaning.

■ Then erase the last three letters of the word and ask someone to pronounce and define the new word that has been created. Ask students to speculate about what this word tells them about the roots of the Protestant Church.

Think About What You Know

■ Assign the THINK ABOUT WHAT YOU KNOW activity on p. 191.

■ Answers will vary and should indicate a procedure for accomplishing the change, such as petitioning the school board.

Study the Vocabulary

■ Have students look up in the Glossary the definition of the new vocabulary words for this lesson. Ask each student to use the definitions to write a sentence predicting the subject of this lesson.

■ After students have read the lesson, have them go back and read their predictions.

— Answers to Caption Questions —

p. 190 ▶ They are rejoicing, pointing toward land, and looking at the land.
p. 191 ▶ His clothing is elaborate and expensive-looking.

Translating

● Review with students Erasmus' task of translating the Bible into the common language (p. 191). Then, involve students in a similar task.

● Write on the chalkboard one or two quotations in an archaic, formal language (You may wish to use the Declaration of Independence or the works of Shakespeare or Chaucer as a source.)

● Ask students to translate the sentences into the language of ordinary American people today.

● Have volunteers read their translations aloud.

Optional Activities

Read and Think

Sections A and B

The Renaissance spirit of inquiry gave rise to the Protestant Reformation. Use the questions that follow to discuss this movement for Church reform:

1. **Name the leader of the Reformation in Germany.**
(Martin Luther *p. 192*)

2. **Explain who the Protestants were.**
(People who protested against certain practices of the Roman Catholic Church *p. 192*)

Thinking Critically How do you think translating the Bible into German spread the Protestant Reformation? (Infer)
(Answers may include that as more people could read the Bible themselves, there was less need for church officials to interpret it for them. *p. 192*)

In 1517, Martin Luther wrote 95 theses, or statements, protesting abuses by the Roman Catholic Church.
► How did Luther display his protests?

B. Luther Protests Against Church Authority

The Bible's Authority Among those who made use of Erasmus' Greek New Testament was a German monk and teacher, Martin Luther. Luther's study of the Bible had led him to question some teachings of the Roman Catholic Church. People of the Church pointed out that popes had long ago condemned the ideas that Luther had adopted. Luther answered that these ideas came from the Bible and that even a pope could not condemn them.

Luther did not believe that the pope in Rome was head of the Church. Luther followed only the Bible. He insisted that the Bible provided all the guidance people needed to live a Christian life. His opponents agreed that the Bible was a book of authority, but they believed that its meaning needed to be explained.

Luther wanted the Bible to be available to all people. Only priests and students could read the Latin translation that had been used during the Middle Ages. Luther therefore translated the Bible into German, a language of the common people.

A Movement for Reform In 1521, Luther was excommunicated, or excluded, from the Roman Catholic Church. He was declared an outlaw when he would not retract, or take back, his teachings. He had become a leader of the **Reformation**, a movement to reform the Roman Catholic Church. The movement led eventually to the establishment of new churches. Followers of Luther's ideas became known as Protestants. The Protestant revolt against the authority of the pope soon spread through many parts of Europe.

192

Cooperative Learning

Working with Maps Divide the class into groups of five and have them look at the maps on pp. 193 and 614.

● Have students work together to make a larger version of the map on p. 193 that shows the places where the following people lived: John Calvin (Switzerland), Martin Luther (Germany), Erasmus (Netherlands, Italy, England), Thomas More (England), and Henry VIII (England).

● Have one student develop the scale for the map. Have two students draw the map. Have one student make a key with a different color or symbol to represent each person. Have one student label the countries and the places where the people from the Reformation lived.

Curriculum Connection

Music Martin Luther was not only a monk, a teacher, and a religious leader but was also a composer. Many of the hymns he wrote or adapted are still sung in Protestant churches today. The most famous is "Ein feste Burg ist unser Gott" (A Mighty Fortress Is Our God).

● Bring in a recording of this or another hymn that Luther wrote and play it for the class. Have students share their reactions to the hymn.

Optional Activities

C. The Reformation Divides Christians

Protestant Churches John Calvin led the Reformation in Switzerland. Like Luther, he believed in the authority of the Bible. Calvin wished to discard any church practice that was not based on the Bible.

There were a number of other Protestant leaders. They all disagreed with the Roman Catholic Church, but they also disagreed among themselves. So instead of there being one Protestant Church, there were many.

Church of England In England the Protestants won the support of King Henry VIII. The king broke away from the pope's authority and set up a Protestant church, the Church of England. Although it still

MAJOR RELIGIOUS DIVISIONS ABOUT 1600

Roman Catholic
Lutheran
Calvinist
Anglican
Orthodox
Muslim

0   200   400 miles
0   200   400 kilometers

Many Christians broke away from the Roman Catholic Church during the Protestant Reformation. One group of Christians set up the Anglican Church.
▶ In what country did most Anglicans live?

193

Writing to Learn

Writing a News Article Have students choose a person from this lesson who was involved in the Protestant Reformation.

● Tell each student to write a news article that describes the role that the person played in the Reformation.

● Remind students that a news article answers the five "w's" and one "h" about its subject (who, what, where, when, why, and how).

Optional Activities

Read and Think
Sections C and D

To help students understand the changes in church and government that occured during the Reformation, ask the following questions:

1. **Why did King Henry VIII have Thomas More beheaded?**
   (Moore refused to swear loyalty to the Church of England. *p. 194*)

2. **How did national rulers at the time of the Reformation obtain armies and officials?**
   (They hired them with taxes that they collected. *p. 194*)

3. **In what way did the function of monarchs change as feudalism ended?**
   (Monarchs were rulers of nations rather than just chief feudal lords. *p. 195*)

4. **Explain why the rule of Queen Elizabeth was known as the Golden Age.**
   (Because it was a time of great achievement during which great works of literature and art were produced *p. 195*)

   Thinking Critically **How was the rule of Queen Elizabeth I different from that of King James I?** (Infer)
   (Answers may include that Queen Elizabeth sought the support of all the people whereas King James believed that he could ignore the people's will. *p. 195*)

had its own bishops and archbishops, the Church of England, or Anglican Church, no longer accepted the authority of the pope in Rome. But some of the English disagreed with King Henry's actions. Erasmus' friend Thomas More refused to swear loyalty to the Church of England. More's refusal cost him his life. King Henry had him beheaded.

Churches Agree Quarrels between Protestants and Roman Catholics sometimes led to wars. But after many years of fighting, there remained many devoted Roman Catholics and many equally devoted Protestants in Western Europe. Both sides finally decided to live together in peace. They still did not agree about religion; they simply agreed to disagree. How would you explain what that means?

D. National Rulers Replaced Feudal Rulers

Feudalism Ends The governments of most Western European countries at the time of the Reformation differed from those of the Middle Ages. Kings no longer depended upon the services of their vassals. They paid for people to join their armies instead of calling for the knights promised by the vassals. Nobles still held high positions, but they held them "at the king's pleasure," meaning that the king could remove them whenever he wished. Rulers hired a number of officials who were commoners.

To pay for hired armies and officials, rulers collected taxes. The need for money was usually greater than the amount raised from taxes, so rulers were often in

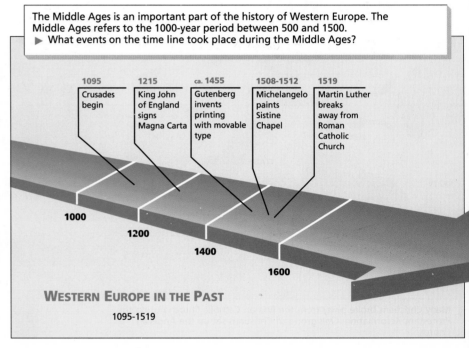

The Middle Ages is an important part of the history of Western Europe. The Middle Ages refers to the 1000-year period between 500 and 1500.
▶ What events on the time line took place during the Middle Ages?

1095	1215	ca. 1455	1508-1512	1519
Crusades begin	King John of England signs Magna Carta	Gutenberg invents printing with movable type	Michelangelo paints Sistine Chapel	Martin Luther breaks away from Roman Catholic Church

1000
1200
1400
1600

WESTERN EUROPE IN THE PAST
1095-1519

194

Optional Activities

Reteaching Main Objective

⭐ *List the changes in church and government brought about through the Protestant Reformation.*

- As a class activity, make an outline on the chalkboard for the events of the Protestant Reformation.

- Begin by writing *I. The Protestant Reformation* on the chalkboard. Then, indented under it, write *A. Erasmus* and under that write the numbers *1, 2,* and *3*.

- Ask students to help complete the outline by filling in an event next to one of the numbers.

- Continue the process using *B. Luther, C. Calvin,* and *D. Henry VIII*.

debt. Bankers who lent money became as important to governments as nobles were.

Queen Elizabeth I Monarchs were no longer just the chief feudal lords. A king or queen was the ruler of a nation. When Elizabeth I became queen of England in 1558, she realized that she needed the support of all the people. She often toured England to see her people and to be seen by them. The queen made the tours for much the same reason that political leaders today appear on television.

Elizabeth's reign became known as the Golden Age or Elizabethan Age because it was a time of great achievement in England. Writers and poets produced great works of art. English literature thrived during this period. One poet and playwright of this era, William Shakespeare, wrote some of the finest literature the world has known. You read an excerpt from his play *Julius Caesar* in Chapter 3.

King James I Although wise monarchs like Elizabeth sought the support of the people, they did not believe that the people could choose their rulers. King James I, who became king after Elizabeth's death, insisted that he ruled by **divine right**. By this he meant that his powers came from

Elizabeth I, who ruled for 45 years, saw England emerge as a world power.
▶ What do you think the artist tried to show about the queen?

God, not from the people. It was not until later times that the people won the right to elect their governments. You will read that story in the next chapter.

LESSON 4 REVIEW

THINK AND WRITE

A. Why did Erasmus publish a Greek New Testament? **(Recall)**
B. What led Martin Luther to break away from the Roman Catholic Church? **(Infer)**
C. What were some results of the Reformation? **(Infer)**
D. How did the position of a national ruler differ from that of a feudal ruler? **(Analyze)**

SKILLS CHECK

MAP SKILL

Look at the map on page 193 to answer the following questions: In which countries did Roman Catholics live? In which countries did Lutherans live? What was the religion of the people who lived in Scotland?

195

UNDERSTANDING THE LESSON

◀ **Review Master Booklet, p. 48**

NAME _____
UNDERSTANDING THE LESSON | CHAPTER 6

Recalling Facts | LESSON 4 CONTENT MASTER

● Place a check mark in the box next to the correct answer for each item.

1. Desiderius Erasmus published a Greek New Testament so that people could
   ☐ a. learn Greek. ☐ c. not understand the Bible.
   ☐ b. read the Bible in the language ☐ d. have a variety of Bibles.
   in which it had been written.

2. Martin Luther believed that Christians could receive all the guidance they needed from
   ☐ a. the pope. ☐ c. the Bible.
   ☐ b. monks. ☐ d. local priests.

3. Luther's opponents claimed that the teachings of the Bible had to be
   ☐ a. translated into English. ☐ c. explained to the people.
   ☐ b. spoken aloud. ☐ d. available to everyone.

4. When King Henry VIII of England became a Protestant, the country
   ☐ a. broke away from the authority ☐ c. recognized the authority of the pope.
   of the pope. ☐ d. became less religious.
   ☐ b. threw out its bishops.

5. When Thomas More refused to swear loyalty to the Church of England, he was
   ☐ a. knighted. ☐ c. congratulated.
   ☐ b. beheaded. ☐ d. promoted.

6. To help pay for hired armies and officials, kings and queens often borrowed money from
   ☐ a. commoners ☐ c. bankers.
   ☐ b. reformers. ☐ d. priests.

7. Monarchs at the time of the Reformation were different from monarchs during the Middle Ages because they were
   ☐ a. rulers of nations. ☐ c. chosen by their people.
   ☐ b. chief feudal lords. ☐ d. less democratic.

Think and Write: Write a paragraph discussing the advantages and disadvantages of a monarch ruling by divine right. You may use the back of the sheet.

Answers should reflect independent thinking; suggestions appear in the Answer Key.

48 | Use with textbook pages 191–195.

Optional Activities

Lesson 4 Review

Answers to Think and Write

A. Erasmus published a Greek New Testament so that people could read it in the original language.

B. Martin Luther broke with the Roman Catholic Church because he believed that the Bible, not the pope, provided all the guidance Christians needed.

C. Some results of the Reformation were that Christians were divided into many churches and Henry VIII broke away from the pope's authority.

D. A national ruler was not just lord of his vassals; he or she ruled a whole nation. Instead of relying on vassals and serfs for services and gifts, they collected taxes and hired people to work for them.

Answer to Skills Check

Roman Catholics lived in Ireland, Spain, Portugal, France, Switzerland, Italy, Corsica, Sardinia, Sicily, Holy Roman Empire, Ottoman Empire, and Poland. Lutherans lived in Norway, Sweden, Denmark, and the Holy Roman Empire. The people who lived in Scotland were Calvinists.

Focus Your Reading

Ask the question found at the beginning of the lesson: **How were changes brought about in the church and in government?** (Changes in the church were caused by the Reformation, when large numbers of people broke away from the Roman Catholic Church. Changes in government were caused by the rise of national rulers, who no longer depended on their vassals but hired armies and officials with the money that they collected in taxes.)

Additional Practice

You may wish to assign the ancillary materials listed below.

Understanding the Lesson p. 48
Workbook pp. 53-54

--- **Answers to Caption Questions** ---
p. 194 ▶ The Crusades began, King John signed the Magna Carta, and Gutenberg invented printing with movable type.
p. 195 ▶ Answers will vary but might include that she looks regal, remote, and authoritative.

195

CITIZENSHIP AND AMERICAN VALUES

WHY IS FREEDOM OF RELIGION IMPORTANT?

The First Amendment to the United States states that "Congress shall make no law respecting an establishment of religion, or prohibiting the free exercise thereof. . . . " This means the United States government cannot declare any religion to be an official religion that all citizens must follow. It also means that the people are free to choose what religion they want to practice or to choose to practice no religion at all.

In Lesson 3 of this chapter, you read about some changes in how people practiced their religions in the sixteenth century. Martin Luther was one of many people who thought that the Bible should be translated into different languages so that everyone would be able to read it. The common people began to demand that they be free to study and understand what had only been available to priests, students, and nobles.

Martin Luther and others involved in the Protestant Reformation helped to establish a number of new Christian churches including the Lutheran Church, the Calvinist Church, and the Church of England. The members of these churches believed in the same God but chose to worship in different ways. The people who broke away from the Roman Catholic Church because they did not agree with all of its teachings were exercising their own right to freedom of religion.

Some countries still required all of their citizens to belong to official state religions. Members of various religious groups left their home in Europe and looked for a new place to live

because their freedom of religion was being denied. The new place that these groups of people came to was what is now the United States.

Today, people all around the world—people from all different religious backgrounds—want to have the right to worship as they choose, openly and freely. We can all become better world citizens by respecting the beliefs of other people. If all people can peacefully "agree to disagree" about religion, perhaps we can learn tolerance, improve communication, and make the world a better place to live.

Objectives

1. **Explain** the meaning of freedom of religion.

2. **Describe** how the Protestant Reformation exercised the right to religious freedom.

3. **Summarize** the reasons freedom of religion is of worldwide importance.

Guided Reading

1. **How does the First Amendment to the United States Constitution guarantee freedom of religion?**
   (It prohibits the government from making an official religion and allows people to practice the religion of their choice or none at all.)

2. **Why was the Bible translated into different languages?**
   (So that the common people could study and understand it)

3. **How did Martin Luther and others involved in the Protestant Reformation exercise the right to religious freedom?**
   (They broke away from the Roman Catholic Church and established new Christian churches.)

4. **How would you be personally affected if the right to freedom of religion were taken away?**
   (Answers should reflect independent thinking but may include not being able to go to the church of one's choice or having to accept a religion with which one did not agree.)

5. **How do you think respecting freedom of religion can improve the world?**
   (Answers should reflect independent thinking but may include that it teaches people tolerance, better communication, and how to work with others to make the world a better place.)

Optional Activities

For Your Information

Religion in Russia   Before the Communists came to power, the official religion of Russia was the Russian Orthodox Church. The Communists, however, were atheists (people who believe that there is no God) and destroyed many churches and arrested or killed church leaders who refused to follow Communism. Nonetheless, religious worship survived, and persecution gradually decreased.

Although the Communists did all they could to discourage religion, many Soviet citizens continued to worship in secret as well as in public. The Russian Orthodox Church has from 20 million to 45 million followers.

Thinking For Yourself

On a separate sheet of paper, answer the following questions in complete sentences.

1. Imagine that you are a member of a group of government officials who are writing a constitution for a new country. How would you convince the rest of the group that freedom of religion is a right that should be included in the constitution?
2. What right besides freedom of religion did Protestants exercise during the Reformation?
3. Do you think there are any people today who would give up their lives rather than give up religious freedom? Explain.
4. How do you think respecting the beliefs of other people can make you a better world citizen?
5. What do you think it would be like to live in a country where there was no freedom of religion?

Thinking For Yourself

1. Answers should reflect independent thinking but may include mention that citizens often leave a country where freedom of religion is not allowed.
2. Answers should reflect independent thinking but may include freedom of speech.
3. Answers should reflect independent thinking but may include mention of recent religious conflicts in Iran, Ireland, and Lebanon.
4. Answers should reflect independent thinking but may include learning tolerance, communicating better, and being able to work with others to improve the world.
5. Answers should reflect independent thinking but may include that it would be oppressive and possibly dangerous if people decided to practice their own choice of religion secretly.

197

Current Events

● Point out to students that improved communication has made the world smaller, and now, more than ever, people must learn to tolerate the beliefs of people from many different nations.

● Ask students to write a short essay beginning as follows: "The people who wrote our Constitution believed that tolerance was important if people were to live peacefully and happily with one another. Without tolerance . . ."

● Remind students to use topic sentences in each paragraph and support every statement with sound reasoning.

Optional Activities

Using the Vocabulary

1. Renaissance
2. crusade
3. guild
4. knight
5. serf
6. monastery
7. monopoly
8. Reformation
9. feudalism
10. apprentice

Remembering What You Read

1. The Great Charter, which bound a king of England by the law for the first time

2. To plant and harvest the crops, give their lord a share of their food and drink, and present their lord with gifts at certain times of the year

3. By telling them that going on the Crusade was a religious duty and that there were great riches to be won in the Middle East

4. Because they saw him most often — the village priest held services in the village church, baptized babies, taught children their religious duties, and performed marriages and conducted funerals for the villagers

5. People in the same trade or craft; for example, tailors, shoemakers, hatters, and metalsmiths

6. By working with a master craftworker

7. Leonardo da Vinci, Michelangelo, and Raphael

8. Because some of the ancient authors had the same interests as they did

9. Martin Luther and John Calvin

10. Monarchs were no longer just chief feudal lords but the rulers of nations.

USING THE VOCABULARY

knight	guild
feudalism	monopoly
serf	apprentice
Crusade	Renaissance
monastery	Reformation

From the list above, choose a vocabulary word that could be used in place of the underlined word or words in each sentence. Rewrite the sentences on a separate sheet of paper.

1. Michelangelo was an artist during the period after the Middle Ages.
2. The pope asked nobles and knights to take part in a war for the cross.
3. The association of merchants set the rules for the town markets.
4. A trained warrior fought on horseback with swords and lances.
5. A peasant bound to the land owed labor to the lord of the manor.
6. The Abbey of Monte Cassino was a dwelling for monks.
7. Each craft guild had a control over the making and selling of goods.
8. Martin Luther was a strong leader in the movement for reform in the Christian religion.
9. Vassals became lords of their own vassals under the form of government during the Middle Ages.
10. A new pupil working for a master in a guild would start by doing odd jobs.

198

REMEMBERING WHAT YOU READ

On a separate sheet of paper, answer the following questions in complete sentences.

1. What was the Magna Carta?
2. What were a serf's duties on a manor?
3. How did Pope Urban II convince nobles and knights to participate in a Crusade?
4. Why was the village priest the person of the church best known to people on a manor?
5. Who were the people who belonged to a craft guild?
6. How did an apprentice learn a trade?
7. Who were three important artists of the Renaissance?
8. Why did students during the Renaissance want to read the works of ancient authors?
9. Who were two important leaders of the Reformation?
10. How did the governments of most Western European countries change about the time of the Reformation?

TYING LANGUAGE ARTS TO SOCIAL STUDIES

The tournaments between knights during the Middle Ages were exciting events. Find out more about them in your school library. Working with other members of your class, write a play in which characters such as lords, ladies, and knights explain how they prepare for a tournament.

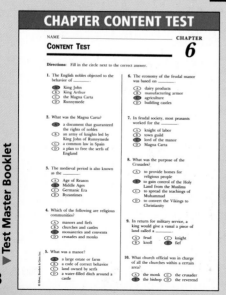

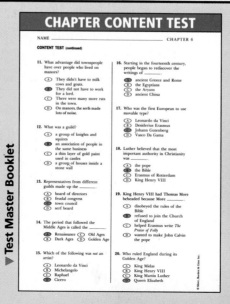

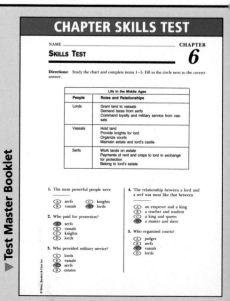

THINKING CRITICALLY

On a separate sheet of paper, answer the following in complete sentences.

1. Would you have wanted to live in a castle during the Middle Ages? Explain.
2. To what kind of job would you want to be an apprentice?
3. What person living today could be called a man or woman of many talents? Explain why.
4. Why, do you think, did people like Columbus want to discover new lands?
5. How might a government raise the money it needs without collecting taxes or getting loans from banks?

SUMMARIZING THE CHAPTER

On a separate sheet of paper, draw a graphic organizer that is like the one shown here. Copy the information from this graphic organizer to the one you have drawn. Under the main idea for each lesson, write four statements that support the main idea.

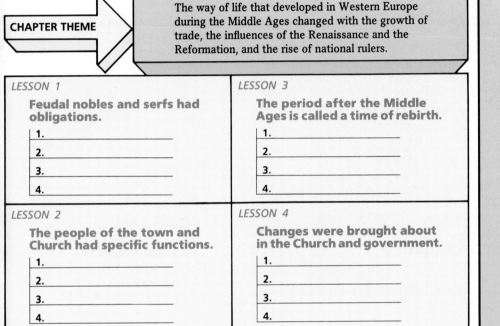

CHAPTER THEME The way of life that developed in Western Europe during the Middle Ages changed with the growth of trade, the influences of the Renaissance and the Reformation, and the rise of national rulers.

LESSON 1
Feudal nobles and serfs had obligations.
1. _____
2. _____
3. _____
4. _____

LESSON 3
The period after the Middle Ages is called a time of rebirth.
1. _____
2. _____
3. _____
4. _____

LESSON 2
The people of the town and Church had specific functions.
1. _____
2. _____
3. _____
4. _____

LESSON 4
Changes were brought about in the Church and government.
1. _____
2. _____
3. _____
4. _____

199

Thinking Critically

1. Answers may include no, because castles were drafty, dirty, damp, and dim.
2. Answers may include shoemaker, hatter or metalsmith.
3. Answers may include Jesse Jackson; he is a minister and a political leader.
4. Answers may include that the Renaissance spirit of inquiry led people like Columbus to search for new lands.
5. Answers may include by producing and selling goods such as food or airplanes.

Summarizing the Chapter

Lesson 1
1. Lords governed their manors.
2. Serfs owed their labor to their lords.
3. Serfs had to give gifts to their lords.
4. Crusades.

Lesson 2
1. They led lives of prayer and labor.
2. Monks and nuns helped people.
3. Priests performed religious services.
4. Townspeople sometimes paid taxes.

Lesson 3
1. Artists and writers expressed new ideas.
2. Students found a new interest in ancient writings.
3. People made new discoveries.
4. Explorers searched for new sea routes and lands.

Lesson 4
1. The Bible was translated into the common language.
2. The Reformation divided Christians.
3. Many Protestant churches were created.
4. National rulers replaced feudal rulers.

Three Revolutions

(pp. 200-221)

Chapter Theme: Revolutions in science, industry, and politics changed the ways people thought, worked, and lived, and had a great effect on the types of governments in Western Europe.

CHAPTER RESOURCES
Review Master Booklet
   Reviewing Chapter Vocabulary, p. 55
   Place Geography, p. 56
   Summarizing the Chapter, p. 57
Chapter 7 Test

LESSON 1   **A Revolution in Science**

(pp. 200-205)

Theme: Scientists' new ideas and new instruments led to a revolution in astronomy.

SILVER WINGS WORKSHOP: The Courage of Your Convictions

LESSON RESOURCES
Workbook, pp. 55-57
Review Master Booklet
   Understanding the Lesson, p. 52

LESSON 2   **The Industrial Revolution**

(pp. 206-211)

Theme: The Industrial Revolution increased economic output and greatly changed the way people lived.

CITIZENSHIP AND AMERICAN VALUES VIDEO LIBRARY: Clean Up Your Act!

SOCIAL STUDIES LIBRARY: A Chance Child
                           Money

LESSON RESOURCES
Workbook, p. 58
Review Master Booklet
   Understanding the Lesson, p. 53

LESSON 3   **Political Revolutions**

(pp. 212-219)

Theme: Disagreements over the importance of royal power led to revolutions in England and France, which resulted in more political power for the people.

SILVER WINGS WORKSHOP: The Courage of Your Convictions

LESSON RESOURCES
Workbook, pp. 59-60
Review Master Booklet
   Understanding the Lesson, p. 54

Review Masters

REVIEWING CHAPTER VOCABULARY

CHAPTER

7

VOCABULARY MASTER

Review Study the terms in the box. Use your Glossary to find definitions of those you do not remember.

astronomy	factory	Industrial	profit
capital	free enterprise	Revolution	revolution
constitutional	guillotine	Inquisition	standard of living
monarchy		Parliament	

Practice Complete the paragraphs using terms from the box above.
You may change the forms of the terms to fit the meaning.

Many dramatic changes took place in Europe during the 1600s and 1700s. Advances in science, especially in (1) ___astronomy___, gave people new ways to think about the world and their lives. Fresh ideas led to new inventions, and soon the people of Europe were living in a changed world. Instead of working at home or on the land, many were now operating machines in factories. Because of this (2) ___Industrial Revolution___ more people could afford to buy more goods. Although these changes raised the (3) ___standard of living___, the industrial cities were often crowded and dirty.

New ideas also brought about changes in the way some European countries were governed. In England, the people finally were able to limit royal power. Before William and Mary could begin their reign, they had to agree to rule according to a basic law. This change to a (4) ___constitutional monarchy___ was called the bloodless (5) ___revolution___, because there was no fighting. In France, instead of limiting royal power, the French people abolished the monarchy, and King Louis XVI was put to death on the (6) ___guillotine___. These actions helped produce the forms of government that still exists in England and France today.

Write Write a sentence of your own for each term in the box above.
You may use the back of the sheet.

Sentences should show that students understand the meanings of the terms.

_____
_____
_____
_____
_____
_____

LOCATING PLACES

CHAPTER

7

PLACE GEOGRAPHY MASTER

✽ Inventors from Poland, Italy, Germany, the Netherlands, and England played important roles in the scientific and industrial revolutions. Listed below are present-day cities in each of these countries. Use the Gazetteer in your textbook to find the latitude and longitude of each place. Then locate and label each on the map.

	LAT.	LONG.
1. Manchester, England	54°N	2°W
2. Amsterdam, Netherlands	52°N	5°E
3. Pisa, Italy	44°N	10°E
4. Hamburg, Germany	54°N	10°E
5. Warsaw, Poland	52°N	21°E

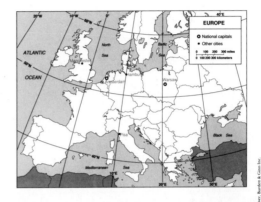

SUMMARIZING THE CHAPTER

CHAPTER

7

GRAPHIC ORGANIZER MASTER

✽ Complete this graphic organizer. In the blanks next to the main idea for each lesson, write four statements that support the main idea.

CHAPTER THEME → Revolutions in science, industry, and politics changed the ways people thought, worked, and lived, and the types of governments in Western Europe.

LESSON 1
Copernicus, Galileo, and other scientists affected the way people thought.

1. Copernicus showed the sun as the center about which the earth and planets revolve.
2. Van Leeuwenhoek invented a powerful microscope.
3. Galileo discovered features of the moon, the Milky Way, and Jupiter.
4. Fahrenheit invented the thermometer.

LESSON 2
Many changes resulted from the Industrial Revolution.

1. Creation of factories
2. Growth of cities and towns
3. Rise in the standard of living
4. Development of free-enterprise economy

LESSON 3
Revolutions in England and France resulted in political changes.

1. Establishment of a constitutional monarchy in England
2. Limitation of the king of France's powers
3. Loss of nobles' privileges in France
4. Abolition of serfdom in France

Workbook Pages

Page 55

NAME _____ CHAPTER **7**

A REVOLUTION IN SCIENCE

Understanding Sequence, Understanding Movements of the Earth, Hypothesizing

✳ Study the events in the box. Decide which came first, second, third, fourth, and fifth. Then write the events in order on the lines below the box.

- Galileo uses a telescope to discover four of Jupiter's moons.
- *On the Revolutions of the Heavenly Bodies* is printed.
- Ptolemy says the sun, moon, and planets revolve around the earth.
- Leeuwenhoek's microscope enables people to study microorganisms.
- Copernicus is convinced the earth and planets revolve around the sun.

1. Ptolemy says the sun, moon, and planets revolve around the earth.
2. Copernicus is convinced the earth and planets revolve around the sun.
3. On the Revolutions of the Heavenly Bodies is printed.
4. Galileo uses a telescope to discover four of Jupiter's moons.
5. Leeuwenhoek's microscope enables people to study microorganisms.

✳ Copy the group of words that correctly completes each of the following sentences.

1. Copernicus did not want to publish his book because he was afraid that
   people would scorn him

   a. people would scorn him **b.** he was wrong **c.** it was not well-written

2. Galileo learned about pendulums and falling objects by _____
   observing them

   a. talking with Copernicus **b.** observing them **c.** studying Aristotle

3. The invention of the telescope enabled scientists to _____
   study distant objects

   a. study distant objects **b.** become famous **c.** work with sea captains

4. Observation and experiments brought about a change in
   people's thinking

   a. people's thinking **b.** the nature of the earth **c.** lens grinding

Thinking Further: Why do you think people in the 1500s found it so difficult to change their beliefs from Ptolemy's view of the universe to Copernicus's?
Possibilities: the unmoving earth at center of the universe can give us a feeling of security; the earth moving around
sun can bring insecurity.

© Silver, Burdett & Ginn Inc.

Chapter 7, pages 201–205

55

Page 56

NAME _____ CHAPTER **7**

ANALYZING VIEWS OF OUR SOLAR SYSTEM

Understanding Diagrams, Interpreting Information

✳ The paragraphs below describe three scientists who made important discoveries about our solar system. On the facing page are two illustrations. One shows the place of the earth in the universe according to a theory, or set of ideas, devised in the first century A.D. The second shows a major revision of the theory during the Renaissance. Read the paragraphs and study the illustrations. Then answer the questions.

You have probably studied the solar system in school. Our solar system consists of the sun, the nine major planets and their moons, and a belt of asteroids, or minor planets. All these bodies, including the earth, revolve around the sun.

For many centuries, however, people thought that the sun, other stars, and the planets revolved around the earth. One man who believed this was Ptolemy, an Egyptian astronomer who lived from about A.D. 100 to 165. Ptolemy spent many years trying to figure out how the stars and planets moved around the earth. Scientists later gave his name to this theory. They called it the Ptolemaic Theory.

Around 1512 a Polish astronomer,

Nicolaus Copernicus, decided that this ancient view of the universe was wrong. He was the first to observe that the sun is the center of our solar system and that the earth and other planets move around it. This theory is called the Copernican Theory.

About 1609, Johannes Kepler, a German astronomer, made another important discovery. He observed that the planets do not move around the sun in circular orbits. Rather, they move in paths shaped like ellipses or ovals.

The discoveries of the Renaissance scientists Copernicus and Kepler made possible much of what we know today about our solar system.

1. Identify and describe briefly the three astronomers mentioned in the paragraphs.
   a. Ptolemy was an Egyptian astronomer who lived from about A.D. 100 to 165.

   b. Copernicus was a Polish astronomer of the early sixteenth century.

   c. Kepler was a German astronomer of the early seventeenth century.

2. What did Ptolemy think was at the center of the universe? He thought the earth was at the center of the universe.

3. Who first observed that the planets revolve around the sun? Copernicus first made this observation.

© Silver, Burdett & Ginn Inc.

56

Chapter 7, pages 201–205

Page 57

NAME _____

ANALYZING VIEWS OF OUR SOLAR SYSTEM *CONTINUED*

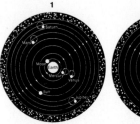

1 **2**

Ptolemaic Theory Ptolemy thought that the earth was the center of the universe and that the sun and the planets circled the earth. Ptolemy also believed the planets moved in smaller circles, called epicycles.

Copernican Theory Copernicus was the first astronomer to observe that the earth, moon, and planets orbit the sun.

4. What did Kepler add to the Copernican Theory? Kepler showed that the planets travel in elliptical, or oval, orbits—not in circular orbits.

5. What is the main difference in how the earth is shown between illustrations 1 and 2 above? In illustration 1 the earth is at the center of the solar system. In illustration 2 the sun is at the center.

6. Describe two ways in which illustrations 1 and 2 are alike. Both show that the planets travel in circles and that the moon orbits the earth.

Thinking Further: For centuries people have observed the solar system and stars. How did improvements in the telescope by Galileo (1564–1642) and others make observing the universe easier?
Answers should reflect independent thinking. The telescope enables astronomers to see things in space more
clearly and in more detail. Improved telescopes allow them to see things that are farther away from the earth.

© Silver, Burdett & Ginn Inc.

Chapter 7, pages 201–205

57

Page 58

NAME _____ CHAPTER **7**

WORKING AS A CHILD

Evaluating Child Labor, Identifying Details that Support Main Ideas

✳ Imagine that you are a young worker in a cotton factory in Manchester, England, in the early nineteenth century. Complete the paragraphs below to tell about your work. Use the words in parentheses under each answer line to guide your writing. For many blanks there is more than one correct answer, so don't worry if a classmate writes in different information.
Suggested answers are provided.

"What a long and weary day I have! I must be in my place at the factory at

six in the morning (time of day) , because that is the time when the steam engine (kind of machine) starts

running. Then I must work until eight (time of day) at night.

"The machines in this mill spin and weave cotton (kind of cloth) . Before the machines

were invented, people did this work by hand (method) . It took

many years (length of time) to learn to be a skillful weaver. But a boy or girl only

11 or 12 (age) years old can quickly learn how to tend a machine. And the factory

owners do not have to pay children as much as they pay adults (other workers) ."

Thinking Further: In England today—and in many other countries as well—there are laws that say children cannot work in factories. In some other countries, it is legal for employers to hire children as factory workers. The table below lists reasons supporting each idea.

Why Children *Should Not* Work in Factories	Why Children *Should* Work in Factories
1. The work is too dangerous for them.	1. Many families need the extra income.
2. Children need time for school.	2. Employers should be able to hire anyone.
3. Children need time for play.	3. Children learn skills.

Think about the information presented in the table. Then, in two or three sentences, tell whether children should or should not be allowed to work in factories. Support your answer with at least two reasons. The reasons need not be from the table.
Answers should reflect independent thinking. Reasons should be germane to the issue. A possibility: children should
not work in factories because they are not strong enough, and because they need a lot of time for school and play.

© Silver, Burdett & Ginn Inc.

58

Chapter 7, pages 206–211

Workbook Pages

IDENTIFYING FAMOUS PEOPLE

Understanding Stated and Unstated Information, Evaluating and Responding to Information

✻ Study the information and clues in each paragraph. Then decide who the famous speaker is and write his or her name on the line at the start of the paragraph.

1. _____James I_____: "Almost 400 years before I became king of England, King John had agreed to the Magna Carta, which allowed nobles to control the monarch in some ways. However, I continued to believe that a monarch's powers came from God. My son Charles I and my grandsons, Charles II and James II, believed the same thing!"

2. _____Oliver Cromwell_____: "I was a leader in a civil war to overcome the tyranny of Charles I. Then I ruled England as a dictator. After my death, the English Parliament set up a monarchy again."

3. _____James II_____: "I believed that the king had the power to set aside any law passed by Parliament. When my advisors and soldiers began to desert me, I fled England, taking with me the Great Seal of the Kingdom. That way, I thought, no one could issue orders in my place."

4. _____Mary_____: "My father, the king of England, was so high-handed in his use of power that even I turned against him! My husband William and I later ruled England together. Because we accepted Parliament's Bill of Rights without fighting about it, we were part of a bloodless revolution."

5. _____Marie Antoinette_____: "My husband and I were young when we assumed the throne of France. It was such a burden to think about France's problems! We were more interested in wearing fine clothes and attending parties."

6. _____Napoleon Bonaparte_____: "During France's revolution, I became so famous as a soldier that I eventually became emperor. I met my downfall when my armies suffered terrible losses during the harsh Russian winter. After that, my weakened troops could not fight off France's other enemies."

Thinking Further: Which of the above people do you think is the most important? In two or three sentences identify the person and tell why he or she is important. Support your answer with two reasons.

Answers should reflect independent thinking. A possibility: Mary was the most important because she did not support

a tyrannical ruler and because she helped all people by accepting the Bill of Rights.

© Silver, Burdett & Ginn Inc.

RECALLING KEY INFORMATION

Recalling Details, Analyzing Information

✻ First, read the clues and write the appropriate word in the blanks. (A few blanks have been filled in for you.) Then write the circled letters in the blanks in the box below.

1. A person who wants to make extreme, or very great, changes in a short time:
   r a d i c a l

2. Science dealing with the study of the stars, planets, and other bodies in space:
   a s t r o n o m y

3. General, later emperor, of France:
   N a p o l e o n   B o n a p a r t e

4. Italian mathematician and astronomer:
   G a l i l e o

5. Careful study of something:
   o b s e r v a t i o n

6. A turning around or a complete change:
   r e v o l u t i o n

7. Late seventeenth-century law limiting royal power in England:
   B i l l   o f   R i g h t s

8. Wealth in the form of goods or money used for making more goods:
   c a p i t a l

9. Last name of person who developed the microscope to see microorganisms:
   L e e u w e n h o e k

10. Royal prison-fortress in Paris attacked in 1789:
    B a s t i l l e

C	o	p	e	r	n	i	c	u	s
1	2	3	4	5	6	7	8	9	10

Thinking Further: Identify the person whose name is spelled out in the box above. Then, in two or three sentences, tell how his ideas amounted to a revolution in science. **Write on a separate sheet.** Possible answer: Copernicus (1473–1543), a Polish astronomer, was revolutionary in saying that the earth and planets revolve around the sun. This was very different from the view that the sun and planets revolve around the earth.

© Silver, Burdett & Ginn Inc.

TEACHER NOTES

C7-D

A Revolution in Science

Objectives

★ **1. Explain** how Copernicus, Galileo, Fahrenheit, and other scientists affected the way people thought.

2. Identify the following people and places: *Copernicus, Ptolemy, Rheticus, Galileo, Aristotle, Fahrenheit, Van Leeuwenhoek, Italy,* and *the Netherlands.*

1 STARTING THE LESSON

Motivation Activity

■ Ask students the following question: **What would you say if I told you that the stars and sun revolve around the earth?**

■ Accept all answers, but help students understand that scientific observation can disprove this statement.

■ Tell students that they will read about a man who used scientific observation to disprove this false idea about the earth, sun, and stars.

Think About What You Know

■ Assign the THINK ABOUT WHAT YOU KNOW activity on p. 201.

■ Student answers should reflect independent thinking but may include planets, stars, asteroids, moons, and satellites.

Study the Vocabulary

■ Have students look up in the Glossary the definition of each of the new vocabulary words in this lesson.

■ Then have them use the vocabulary terms to write headlines for news articles about scientific discoveries.

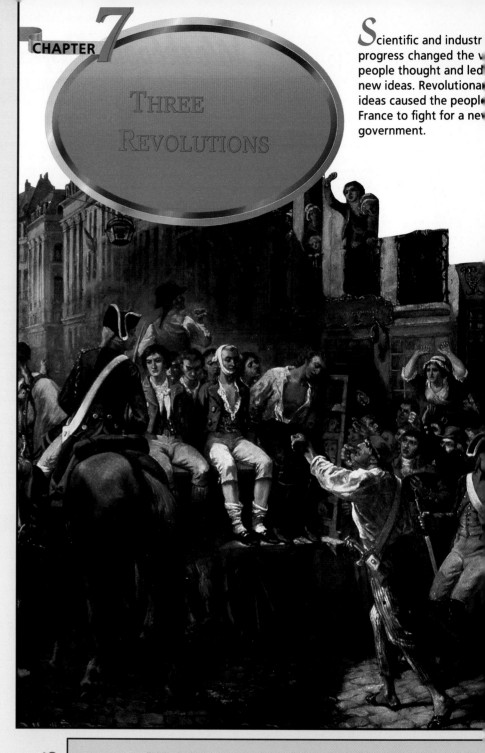

CHAPTER **7**

THREE REVOLUTIONS

*S*cientific and industr progress changed the v people thought and led new ideas. Revolutionar ideas caused the people France to fight for a ne government.

Optional Activities

Writing a Character Sketch

● Have students write a brief character sketch about Nicolaus Copernicus.

● First, have students skim Section A and write down statements from the text that illustrate different aspects of Copernicus's personality.

● Then, have students use these statements to help them write a paragraph describing Copernicus.

● You may wish to have volunteers read their character sketch to the rest of the class.

THINK ABOUT WHAT YOU KNOW
Imagine that you are traveling in a rocket through space. Tell what kinds of things you might see.

STUDY THE VOCABULARY
revolution   Inquisition
astronomy

FOCUS YOUR READING
What did Copernicus, Galileo, and other scientists do to affect the way people thought?

A. Copernicus Turns Astronomy Upside Down

Studying Space Nicolaus Copernicus lived a quiet life. He seems to have been a rather shy person who did not like to upset things. Yet upset things he did when he wrote the book *On the Revolutions of the Heavenly Bodies.*

The word **revolution** has at least two meanings. It may mean either "turning round" or "a complete change." Copernicus intended the first meaning in the title of his book. It is about the "turning round" of the earth and other planets. But the book also brought about a revolution, "a complete change," in the way people thought about the universe.

In 1497, Copernicus left Poland to study law, medicine, mathematics, Greek, and **astronomy** in Italy. Astronomy is a science that deals with the study of the stars, planets, sun, moon, and other bodies in space. In the fifteenth century, astronomy was still based on the teachings of Claudius Ptolemy (TAHL uh mee), one of the greatest astronomers and geographers

of ancient times. Ptolemy believed that the earth stood still. According to him, the sun, moon, and planets revolved around the earth. However, some people did not agree with Ptolemy, and Copernicus was one of them.

Copernicus's Book After many years of observing the positions of stars and planets from a tower, Copernicus was convinced that Ptolemy was wrong. Copernicus noted that even some ancient thinkers had believed that the earth moved, rather than stood still as Ptolemy said. Copernicus spent many hours working on a book that showed that the sun is the center about which the earth and planets revolve. The book also showed that the moon moves about the earth, which constantly revolves on its axis.

Copernicus spent many years studying the stars and planets.
▶ How did Copernicus revolutionize astronomy?

The Granger Collection

201

Read and Think

Section A
To help students understand the life of Copernicus, ask the following questions:

1. **What were the beliefs that Copernicus wrote about in his book?**
   (Copernicus believed that the sun is the center about which the earth and planets revolve. *p. 201*)

2. **Why was Copernicus reluctant to have his findings made public?**
   (He was afraid that his ideas would be scorned. *p. 202*)

   Thinking Critically What other scientists and inventors, do you think, were ridiculed for their early ideas? (Hypothesize)
   (Answers should reflect independent thinking, but may include Henry Ford and his ideas about automation or the Wright brothers and their plans for air travel. *p. 202*)

— **Answers to Caption Questions** —
p. 201 ▶ He wrote a book stating that the planets moved around the sun, and that the earth was not stationary.

Curriculum Connection

Science Ask students to list the planets that revolve around the sun in our solar system. (Mercury, Venus, Earth, Mars, Jupiter, Saturn, Uranus, Neptune, and Pluto)

● Explain to students that any heavenly body that orbits around a planet is known as a "satellite."

● Then ask them to identify any satellites that revolve around the earth (the moon).

Optional Activities

Concept:
How Knowledge Grows

To better understand the scientific revolution, it is important to understand how knowledge grows. Knowledge grows when people act upon the discoveries of others. Below are three activities that will help students understand this concept.

◆ **EASY** Have students answer the following question in writing: *In what way was Copernicus responsible for the discoveries made by Galileo?*

◀▶ **AVERAGE** Have students answer the following question in writing: *Who, do you think, influenced the works of Fahrenheit and Van Leeuwenhoek more, Copernicus or Galileo?*

Students should defend their choices with information from the text.

◀▮▶ **CHALLENGING** Have students research the discoveries made by a scientist such as Thomas Edison, Alexander Bell, Albert Einstein, or Jonas Salk.

Ask them to write a short essay identifying which people or discoveries influenced the person that they are researching.

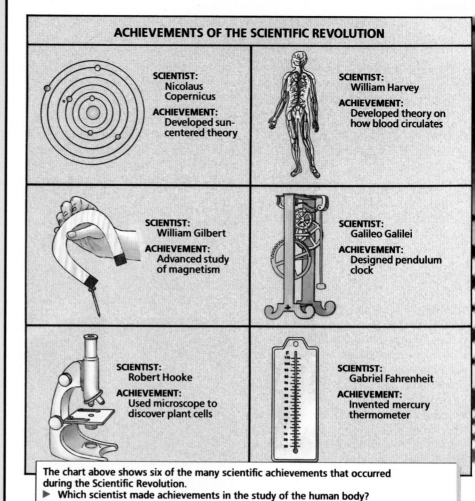

ACHIEVEMENTS OF THE SCIENTIFIC REVOLUTION

SCIENTIST: Nicolaus Copernicus
ACHIEVEMENT: Developed sun-centered theory

SCIENTIST: William Harvey
ACHIEVEMENT: Developed theory on how blood circulates

SCIENTIST: William Gilbert
ACHIEVEMENT: Advanced study of magnetism

SCIENTIST: Galileo Galilei
ACHIEVEMENT: Designed pendulum clock

SCIENTIST: Robert Hooke
ACHIEVEMENT: Used microscope to discover plant cells

SCIENTIST: Gabriel Fahrenheit
ACHIEVEMENT: Invented mercury thermometer

The chart above shows six of the many scientific achievements that occurred during the Scientific Revolution.
▶ Which scientist made achievements in the study of the human body?

After finishing his book, Copernicus put it away. Why did he not publish it? He later said that he feared "the scorn which my new opinion would bring on me." It was some time before Copernicus's friends persuaded him to write a brief summary of his ideas. He finally did so, but he would not let it be printed. Only handwritten copies were passed about.

His Ideas Spread In spite of Copernicus's effort to keep quiet, word about his ideas spread. As the shy man feared, people did make fun of him. One man scoffed, "This fool will turn the whole science of astronomy upside down." But some people who heard of Copernicus's ideas wanted to learn more, including the pope and some other Church officials.

202

Writing to Learn

Writing a Letter Ask students to imagine that they are Rheticus, the German professor who strongly believed that Copernicus should make his ideas public.

Tell students to write a letter from Rheticus to Copernicus in which Rheticus tries to persuade Copernicus to publish his book.

Making Inferences

● Many people in the Church were opposed to Copernicus's ideas.

● Ask students why they think this was so.

● List student responses on the chalkboard and discuss their answers.

● If students do not come up with the actual answer, explain that the Church opposed Copernicus's theory because it meant that human beings were no longer at the center of the universe.

It was a young German professor named Rheticus (RE tih kus) who finally got Copernicus to make his ideas public. After much discussion, Rheticus was allowed to publish a short summary of the book, provided he did not mention Copernicus by name.

Rheticus went to see Copernicus months later. This time Rheticus managed to get permission to publish Copernicus's book. *On the Revolutions of the Heavenly Bodies* was printed in the spring of 1543. By that time, however, Copernicus was very ill. A copy of the printed book was shown to him just before he died.

B. Galileo Tries Out His Ideas

Studying Pendulums Among those who accepted Copernicus's ideas was Galileo Galilei (gal uh LEE oh galuh LAY ee). Galileo was born in Pisa, Italy, 21 years after the publication of *On the Revolutions of the Heavenly Bodies*. As a young man he studied medicine, science, and mathematics. He went on to become a great mathematician and a famous astronomer.

Galileo's restless mind could be set working by quite ordinary incidents. For example, one day in church he noticed a lamp swinging back and forth like a pendulum. A pendulum is a weight hung so that it swings freely back and forth. He started to time each swing by counting his pulse. He discovered that regardless of how far the lamp swung, the time of each swing was the same. Galileo later discovered that the swings of a pendulum take equal time regardless of their width.

Galileo Experiments Galileo learned about pendulums by observation, or careful study, and experimentation. He tried out an idea and observed how it worked.

Aristotle, an ancient philosopher, had once said that if two objects of different weights were dropped at the same time, the heavier one would fall faster than the lighter one. Galileo tested the idea and observed that the objects of different weights reached the ground at the same time.

C. Galileo Points a Telescope Skyward

Looking at the Sky In 1609, Galileo heard that a Dutch inventor had built an instrument that made distant objects appear near. The instrument was, of course, the telescope. The government of the

Many people, such as the English poet John Milton, visited Galileo in his observatory in Italy.
▶ What instrument is used in an observatory?

203

Read and Think
Sections B and C

Galileo's restless mind led him to accept Copernicus's ideas and to develop many of his own. To help students understand some of Galileo's ideas and how he developed them, ask the following questions:

1. **How did Galileo test his ideas?**
   (Through observation and experimentation *p. 203*)

2. **What discoveries did Galileo make about the universe?**
   (The moon has mountains and valleys; the Milky Way is made up of countless stars; Jupiter has four moons; and the universe is sun-centered. *p. 203*)

3. **Why did the Church of Rome want Galileo to stop writing that the earth moved?**
   (They thought that the information was dangerous and false. *p. 204*)

Thinking Critically Did Galileo, do you think, do the right thing at the Inquisition? (Evaluate)
(Answers may include yes, because it allowed him to continue his work, or no, because he was not being true to his beliefs. *p. 204*)

Role-Playing

● Have students role-play the trial of Galileo in a two-act skit.

● Ask for volunteers to play the roles of Galileo, his defense lawyers, the Church's lawyers, and the Church officials deciding the case.

● In the first act, tell students to act out the part of the trial when Galileo is charged with spreading ideas that go against Church belief.

● In the second act, ask students to role-play what might have happened to Galileo and the scientific revolution if Galileo had refused to admit that he was wrong.

Optional Activities

─ **Answers to Caption Questions** ─
p. 202 ▶ William Harvey
p. 203 ▶ A telescope

Interpreting a Painting

■ Direct students' attention to the painting on this page. Ask students to write a short newspaper article with a headline reporting on the Inquisition of Galileo.

Read and Think

Section D

To summarize some improvements that resulted from the scientific revolution, ask the following questions:

1. **What scientific instrument did Fahrenheit invent?**
(The thermometer *p. 205*)

2. **How did Van Leeuwenhoek improve the microscope?**
(He developed a lens powerful enough to make microorganisms visible. *p. 205*)

Thinking Critically In what ways, do you think, are we experiencing a revolution in the field of science today?
(Hypothesize)
(Answers should reflect independent thinking but may include advances in computers, medicine, and space technology. *p. 205*)

Netherlands bought telescopes to be used by sea captains and military leaders. But Galileo quickly realized that telescopes could have other uses, so he made several, each more powerful than the other.

When Galileo pointed his most powerful telescope toward the sky, he saw sights that no one had ever seen before. He discovered that there were mountains and deep valleys on the moon. He saw that the Milky Way was not simply a broad band of faint light; it was made up of countless separate stars. Through the telescope he could see that the planet Jupiter had four moons that revolved around it.

Supporting Copernicus Galileo had no doubt that what he saw through the telescope provided more support for Copernicus's ideas, but not everyone trusted such observations. Some still held to the ideas of Aristotle and Ptolemy. They refused to believe that these great thinkers of ancient times could have been wrong. Some people who defended the ancient ideas held high positions in the Church at Rome. They thought Copernicus's book contained dangerous ideas, and 73 years after its publication, they finally succeeded in having it condemned as false.

To stop the spread of Copernicus's ideas, Galileo was ordered to stop writing that the earth moved. But he disregarded this order in one of his writings and was brought before the **Inquisition**, a special Church court. Threatened with severe punishments, Galileo finally swore that it was an error to say that the earth moved. There is a legend that as the old man left the court, he muttered, "But it does move." It is doubtful that he actually said this, although he may well have thought it.

This painting depicts Galileo being condemned for his writings on astronomy before the Inquisition, a special Church court.
▶ How does this courtroom compare with and differ from a courtroom of today?

204

For Your Information

Anton van Leeuwenhoek Anton van Leeuwenhoek (1632–1723) was born in Delft, Netherlands. After brief schooling, he was apprenticed to a cloth merchant and became a bookkeeper.

Van Leeuwenhoek began grinding lenses as a hobby. He used them to study small objects, especially tiny organisms. Using single, small, double-convex lenses mounted so that they could be held close to the eye, Van Leeuwenhoek was able to magnify images with more power than early compound microscopes.

The development of his microscope allowed him to observe such things as the muscle fibers, hairs, and nerves of various animals.

204

Reteaching Main Objective

⭐ ***Explain how Copernicus, Galileo, Fahrenheit, and Van Leeuwenhoek affected the way people thought.***

● To help students remember the contributions of the great scientists of the scientific revolution, construct a game.

● Write the name of each scientist on a small piece of posterboard. Tape these to a wall or a bulletin board.

● Then, write the contributions of each scientist on separate pieces of posterboard.

● Have students match the contributions to the correct scientists.

D. New Instruments Improve Observation

Taking Measurements Galileo timed the swinging lamp by counting his pulse. His experiments with pendulums led to the development of more accurate clocks and watches. These instruments provided a more precise way to time an observation.

Scientific experiments required other types of accurate measurements. A German scientist, Gabriel Fahrenheit (FER-un hyt), invented a thermometer to measure temperatures. Fahrenheit put mercury into a glass tube with marked spaces. Each marked space represented a degree of temperature. One could tell if the temperature was getting warmer or colder by noting the rise or fall of the mercury.

Lenses for Seeing More Glass lenses in telescopes made it possible to observe distant planets. Lenses were also used to see objects too small for the naked eye to see. By 1674 a lens grinder in the Netherlands named Anton van Leeuwenhoek (LAY vun-hook) had a microscope so powerful that he could see microorganisms, or "little animals," in rainwater. A microorganism is any living thing too tiny to be seen without the use of a microscope.

The invention and improvement of scientific instruments were an important

Leeuwenhoek developed hundreds of lenses with powerful magnifying power.
▶ What two scientific instruments did his lenses improve?

part of the revolution in science. The use of instruments made it possible for more accurate observations and experiments. And observations and experiments were important in bringing about the revolution in science that changed the ways that people thought.

LESSON 1 REVIEW

THINK AND WRITE

A. How did Copernicus's idea of the universe differ from that of Aristotle and Ptolemy? (Infer)

B. According to Galileo, what was the best way to learn? (Infer)

C. What facts about the universe did Galileo discover by using a telescope? (Recall)

D. Why were new instruments important for the development of the sciences? (Recall)

SKILLS CHECK

THINKING SKILL

On one side of a sheet of paper, list the ways in which Galileo and Copernicus were alike. On the other side, list the ways in which these two scientists were different.

205

◀ **Review Master Booklet, p. 52**

Optional Activities

---

3 CLOSING THE LESSON

Lesson 1 Review

Answers to Think and Write

A. Copernicus believed that the sun was the center about which the earth and planets revolved, whereas Aristotle and Ptolemy believed that the earth was the center of the universe.

B. Galileo believed that the best way to learn was through observation and experimentation.

C. By using a telescope, Galileo discovered that there were mountains and valleys on the moon, that the Milky Way was made of countless stars, and that four moons revolved around Jupiter.

D. New instruments brought greater accuracy to observations and experiments. These observations and experiments brought about the revolution in science.

Answer to Skills Check

Galileo and Copernicus were alike in that both believed that the sun was the center about which the earth and planets revolved. Both men were careful observers. Both men were criticized for their ideas. The two men were different in that Copernicus was reluctant to have his findings published whereas Galileo was not.

Focus Your Reading

Ask the lesson focus question found at the beginning of the lesson: **What did Copernicus, Galileo, and other scientists do to affect the way people thought?**
(They used observation, experimentation, and precise instruments to expand people's knowledge.)

Additional Practice

You may wish to assign the ancillary materials listed below.

Understanding the Lesson p. 52
Workbook pp. 55–57

Answers to Caption Questions

p. 204 ▶ There is no jury and there is more than one judge; Galileo is testifying, and there are court spectators.
p. 205 ▶ Telescopes and microscopes

205

The Industrial Revolution

Objectives

★ 1. **Explain** how the Industrial Revolution changed where people worked and how they lived.

2. **Describe** what it was like to work in a factory.

3. **Examine** the role that capitalists played in the Industrial Revolution.

4. **Identify** the following people and places: *James Watt, Matthew Boulton,* and *Manchester.*

1 STARTING THE LESSON

Motivation Activity

■ Tell students to imagine that they are going to open a car wash in their driveway.

■ Ask students what expenses they might have (soap, towels, hoses).

■ Point out that with such expenses, they would actually lose money before they opened their business.

■ Ask students why they would want to do that. (They would hopefully make money when their business opened.)

■ Explain to the class that they will read about people who took similar risks during the Industrial Revolution.

Think About What You Know

■ Assign the THINK ABOUT WHAT YOU KNOW activity on p. 206.

■ Student answers should reflect independent thinking but may include that it would take longer to do household chores, such as washing dishes and cooking foods.

Study the Vocabulary

■ Have students use the vocabulary words for this lesson to construct word-search puzzles that can be exchanged and solved by classmates.

206

THINK ABOUT WHAT YOU KNOW

Think about the kinds of machines that you have in your home. How would your life be different if you did not have these machines?

STUDY THE VOCABULARY

Industrial Revolution	capital
factory	profit
standard of living	free enterprise

FOCUS YOUR READING

What changes resulted from the Industrial Revolution?

A. James Watt Puts Steam to Work

A Curious Boy Some of the best-known stories about famous people are hard to prove. One such story has been often told about James Watt who was born in Scotland in 1736. According to the story, one afternoon when James was a small boy, he sat in the kitchen watching a boiling teakettle. He discovered that when he put a spoon on the spout and stopped the steam, the steam would lift the lid. His aunt, busy with her work, paused just long enough to scold him.

"I never saw such an idle boy! For the last hour you have done nothing but watch that kettle. Go read a book or do something useful!"

We do not know whether or not James Watt did go read a book as his aunt had suggested to him. But if the story is true, that may have been the first time that James had observed the pressure of steam.

206

Watt Uses His Ideas When James Watt grew older, he went to London and served as an apprentice to an instrument maker. Later he returned to Scotland and took a job making and repairing equipment for science classes. One day Watt was given a model steam engine to repair. He fixed the engine, but he saw that it was not an efficient machine. He noticed that steam engines of this type worked slowly and wasted a lot of energy. He was sure that it was possible to make a much better steam engine. Watt continued to experiment until, by 1776, he was making and selling a more efficient steam engine.

The young James Watt was fascinated by steam. As an adult, he invented an improved steam engine.
▶ What sparked Watt's interest in steam?

Optional Activities

For Your Information

The Cat and the Cotton Gin Eli Whitney's inspiration for the cotton gin came from a most unlikely source — a cat! While pondering the problem of how to separate the seeds from the fibers, he watched a cat poised by a fence waiting to snatch a passing chicken. The cat's paw lunged out and missed the chicken, but got a pawful of feathers. Whitney applied this principle of friction and separation in developing the cotton gin. A cylinder with spikes clawed the cotton, leaving the seeds behind the cylinder and allowing the pure cotton to emerge. While it had taken a slave one day to process one pound of cotton, one person could now produce 50 pounds, using a power-driven version of the machine.

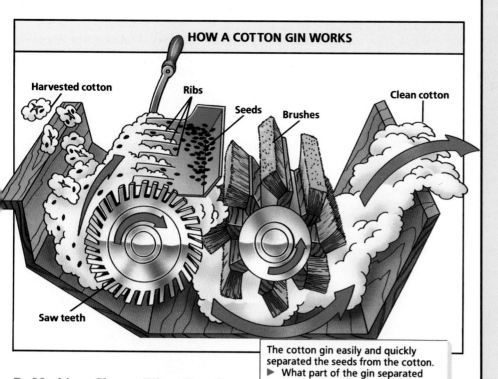

HOW A COTTON GIN WORKS

Harvested cotton

Ribs

Seeds

Brushes

Clean cotton

Saw teeth

The cotton gin easily and quickly separated the seeds from the cotton.
▶ What part of the gin separated the seeds from the cotton?

B. Machines Change Where People Work

Revolutionary Inventions Watt's steam engine was just one of the inventions that greatly changed the ways people worked. These changes brought about a revolution —the **Industrial Revolution.**

The first machines were powered by the muscles of the workers. Spinning wheels were turned by hand or foot pedal. One of the first inventions of the Industrial Revolution was a spinning machine called the spinning jenny. It increased the amount of thread that could be spun, but it was still worked by the spinner. It was not until 1769 that water power was used to work spinning machines. Water power was not used for weaving cloth until 16 years later.

The Cotton Gin As the methods for producing cloth improved, the demand increased for better ways to process the raw cotton before it went to **factories,** or buildings in which goods are manufactured. An American, Eli Whitney, visited a cotton plantation in Georgia and invented the cotton gin in 1793. This machine could clean 50 pounds (23 kg) of cotton fiber a day by separating the newly picked cotton from the seeds. This invention created a dramatic increase in the production of raw cotton for British factories.

Growth of Factories As long as people worked with hand tools or simple machines, such as a spinning wheel, they

207

2 DEVELOPING THE LESSON

Read and Think
Sections A and B

Use the following questions to discuss James Watt's invention and the effect that machines had on where people work:

1. **How did Watt improve the steam engine?**
   (He made it more efficient. *p. 206*)

2. **What caused the Industrial Revolution?**
   (The invention of machines, which caused great changes in how people worked *p. 207*)

3. **Why did the workplace move from the home to the factory?**
   (The use of water-powered machines meant that the workplace had to be located near waterfalls or by dams or streams. *pp. 207-208*)

Thinking Critically What, do you think, was ironic about the story of what James Watt's aunt said? (Evaluate)
(Answers should reflect independent thinking but may include that James was not being idle since his observation of steam was time well spent. *p. 206*)

┌─ **Answers to Caption Questions** ─┐
p. 206 ▶ A boiling teakettle
p. 207 ▶ The ribs

Debating

● Divide the class into two teams to debate the following issue: *The Industrial Revolution did more harm than good.*

● Tell students to refer to the material in this lesson for factual information to support their arguments.

● Assign three people to act as judges to decide which side was more persuasive.

Optional Activities

207

Read and Think
Section C

Use the following questions to discuss with students how machines changed working conditions:

1. **Why did many factory owners hire children?**
   (Because children did not have to be paid as much as adults *p. 208*)

2. **How long was the work day for factory workers?**
   (Fourteen hours long *pp. 208-209*)

3. **How do you know that the air in most factory towns was probably very polluted?**
   (According to the excerpt from *Hard Times*, serpents of smoke endlessly poured out into the air from factory chimneys. *p. 209*)

Thinking Critically Why, do you think, were most factory towns unattractive places in which to live?
(Evaluate)
(Answers should reflect independent thinking but may include that workers had almost no free time to spend on beautifying their homes and towns and the factories themselves were unattractive buildings. *pp. 208-209*)

would work in their own homes or small shops. However, the use of water-powered machines changed the places where people worked. The water wheels that supplied power for the machines had to be located near waterfalls or by dams on streams. As a result, factories replaced some home workshops.

When steam engines took the place of water wheels, factories no longer needed to be near waterfalls or dams. But workers did not go back to working in their homes or small workshops. Machines had to be connected by wheels and belts to the steam engine that made them go, so the workers still had to come to the factory.

C. Machines Set the Pace

Factory Workers The cotton facto[ ] Manchester, England, employed [ ] children. Factories hired children bec[ ] they did not have to be paid as muc[ ] adults. A girl or boy of 11 or 12 could d[ ] job as well as a skilled hand weaver. [ ] not take a lot of skill to tend a machi[ ]

Tending machines in a factory [ ] quite different from working with too[ ] hand-powered machines in a shop. [ ] workers in the cotton factory in Man[ ] ter had to follow a strict schedule. [ ] steam engine started running at six o'[ ] in the morning. All workers had to [ ] their places by that time. At eight o'[ ]

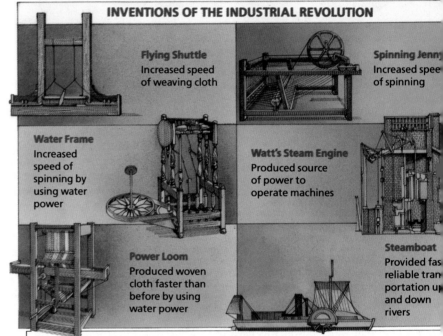

INVENTIONS OF THE INDUSTRIAL REVOLUTION

Flying Shuttle
Increased speed of weaving cloth

Spinning Jenny
Increased spee[ ] of spinning

Water Frame
Increased speed of spinning by using water power

Watt's Steam Engine
Produced source of power to operate machines

Power Loom
Produced woven cloth faster than before by using water power

Steamboat
Provided fas[ ] reliable tran[ ] portation u[ ] and down rivers

The table above shows some of the machines that were invented during the time of the Industrial Revolution.
▶ Which two inventions had to be used in a factory that was located near a waterfall or dam?

Optional Activities

Curriculum Connection

Math Have students calculate the savings that a capitalist could realize by consolidating many home-based operations into a single factory.

● Tell students that a small textile factory could house 72 spindles and it would only need one supervisor and nine children to operate. Weekly wages for these 10 workers would cost the factory owner only about $5.00.

● If the factory did not exist, the work would be done by 72 skilled women, each working out of her own home and making about $1.00 per week.

● Ask students how much the factory owner saved by bringing the spindles under one roof. ($67.00 per week)

SKILLBUILDER REVIEW

Understanding Graphs On pp. 148-149 students learned to identify and use different kinds of graphs.

● Provide students with the factual information presented in the Curriculum Connection at the left.

● Ask students to determine which kind of graph would best compare factory-based work and home-based operations in these categories: employees and wages.

● Have students graph their comparisons and display them as you complete this lesson.

Sheffield, England, grew rapidly during the Industrial Revolution.
▶ How can you tell that Sheffield was an industrial city?

To help students summarize how machines raised the standard of living, ask the following questions:

1. **How did machines bring about a higher standard of living?**
   (Machines produced far more goods than people working by hand, so more goods were available for more people. *p. 210*)

   Thinking Critically If you were a factory worker in Manchester, in what ways do you think your life would be better after the Industrial Revolution? (Infer)
   (Answers may include that there would be more goods available, free public parks, and free public libraries. *p. 210*)

VISUAL THINKING SKILL

Interpreting a Picture

■ Ask students to suggest ways in which the picture on this page and the passage from *Hard Times* go together. (For example: the photograph shows tall, smoking chimneys, which are described in the passage, and the photograph shows the same bleak atmosphere that the passage describes.)

■ Then, have students draw a scene of their choice and describe it in writing.

---

the machines were stopped while the workers ate breakfast. Half an hour later, the wheels started turning again and ran until noon. Workers could not leave their machines while the steam engine was running, so they surely must have welcomed the sound of the noon whistle.

The machines started again at one o'clock and ran until four. Workers could then take a half hour rest. Then they went back to the machines and worked until eight, when the steam engine stopped. Workers hurried to their nearby homes, because in ten hours they would have to be back in their places at the factory.

Factory Towns Workers had to live near the factories where they worked. So the growing use of steam brought with it the growth of towns and cities. Most of these towns were not attractive. The following passage is how Charles Dickens described a fictitious town during the Industrial Revolution in his novel *Hard Times*.

It was a town of machinery and tall chimneys, out of which interminable [endless] serpents of smoke trailed themselves for ever and ever, and never got uncoiled. . . . It contained several large streets all very like one another, and many small streets still more like one another, inhabited by people equally like one another, who all went in and out at the same hours, with the same sound upon the same pavements, to do the same work, and to whom every day was the same as yesterday and to-morrow, and every year the counterpart of the last and the next.

D. Machines Raise the Standard of Living

How People Lived The factory workers of Manchester lived in a crowded, smoky city, but so did people in other places. London was known for its smoky air during the Middle Ages, long before there were any factory steam engines. The city

209

Cooperative Learning

● Have groups of five to six students hold mock government hearings, which might have taken place in England in the 1700s, to decide whether working conditions in factories need to be improved.

● In each group, one student should represent the factory owners; one, the workers; one, the capitalists; and one, the interests of children. The remaining group members will serve as government representatives.

● Have representatives make up several questions to ask each witness, while witnesses prepare statements of their views.

● Have representatives present their decision.

┌─ **Answers to Caption Questions** ─┐
p. 208 ▶ The water frame and power loom
p. 209 ▶ Smoking chimneys and dark atmosphere from factories

Concept:
Economic Freedom

The following activities will help students understand the economic effects of the Industrial Revolution:

◆ **EASY** Tell students that in a planned economy, the government decides what will be produced, for whom it will be produced, and who will produce it. Ask students to identify who makes these decisions in a free-enterprise economy like ours.

◀▶ **AVERAGE** Have students list advantages and disadvantages of guild-controlled economy and free-enterprise economy.

◀▮▶ **CHALLENGING** Have students imagine that they want to start a fast-food business in a guild-controlled economy and identify in writing the problems they might face in starting their business.

Read and Think
Section E

To summarize how capitalists helped Western Europe industrialize, ask the following questions:

1. **Why can Boulton be called a capitalist?** (He financed Watt's experiments. *pp. 210-211*)

Thinking Critically Which American do you think could be called a capitalist today? (Hypothesize) (Answers may include Donald Trump.)

of Edinburgh in Scotland did not have factories like Manchester, but it was known as "Auld Reekie," that is, "Old Smoky."

People had to work long hours in the factories, but so did those who worked as farmers or in home workshops. Living in an industrial city did have some advantages, though. Manchester was one of the first cities in England to provide free public parks and a free public library. Businesspeople in Manchester were quicker to try new ways of living than many people who lived in old-fashioned villages and towns. Perhaps this was because they were accustomed to seeing new inventions work in the factories.

More Goods The Industrial Revolution changed how people worked and brought about a higher **standard of living**, or a measure of how well people live.

A standard of living depends on the amount of goods that makes life more comfortable and pleasant. People working in factories with machines produced far more goods than people working with tools or hand-powered machines. Commoners, those who were not nobles, could buy goods that had once been luxuries. More goods for more people was the great result of the Industrial Revolution.

E. Business People Take Risks

Money for Businesses Watt needed more than an idea to make a better steam engine. He also needed money to pay for trying out his ideas and making engines. Watt formed a partnership with Matthew Boulton, a successful businessman, who provided the **capital**. Capital can be simply defined as wealth in the form of goods or money used for making more goods.

During the Industrial Revolution some cities established parks, such as Regent's Park in Brighton, England, for people to enjoy.
▶ How are these people enjoying themselves?

210

Writing to Learn

Writing a Letter Ask students to imagine that they are a frustrated James Watt with a way to make a better steam engine but without the necessary capital to do it.

● Tell them to write a letter to Matthew Boulton, trying to convince him to invest in your idea.

Reteaching Main Objective

⭐ *Explain how the Industrial Revolution changed where people worked and how they lived.*

● Ask students to do before-and-after illustrations of life in Western Europe during the Industrial Revolution.

● The first illustration should show where and how people *worked* before the Industrial Revolution and where and how they worked after the Industrial Revolution began.

● The second illustration should show how people *lived* before the Industrial Revolution started and how they lived after the Industrial Revolution began.

● Display student illustrations on a bulletin board entitled *Changing Times: The Industrial Revolution.*

It was a risky business venture. Watt and Boulton experimented with making and selling engines for 18 years before they made any **profit** on the engines that they sold. A profit is the financial gain after paying the costs of workers and materials to produce something.

A person who provides the capital for a business is known as a *capitalist*. It required the money of capitalists to build the factories of Manchester. Before a single yard of cloth could be produced, a capitalist had to pay for a building, buy the machines, and pay the engineers who installed them.

Risks and Opportunities Capitalists took risks, the chance of losing their money. Factories and other businesses sometimes failed to make profits. New inventions did not always work well enough to make a profit. Boulton had to wait years before he began to get his money back from Watt's invention.

Freedom to take risks was part of the new way to do business. It was quite different from the Middle Ages when guilds controlled the making and selling of goods. The masters of a guild decided who could make a product, how it was made, and its price. People now had choices about how

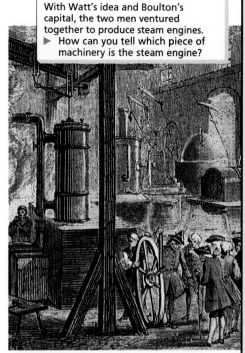

With Watt's idea and Boulton's capital, the two men ventured together to produce steam engines.
▶ How can you tell which piece of machinery is the steam engine?

The Granger Collection

to make and spend their money. This type of economy is called **free enterprise**. People could start businesses if they were willing to risk their money for capital. This greater economic freedom made the Industrial Revolution possible in Western European countries.

LESSON 2 REVIEW

THINK AND WRITE

A. What did James Watt learn from experiments that failed? **(Infer)**

B. Why did the use of machines change the places where people worked? **(Recall)**

C. Describe an average day for a factory worker. **(Recall)**

D. What was the benefit of the Industrial Revolution? **(Infer)**

E. Why did providing capital have its risks? **(Recall)**

SKILLS CHECK
WRITING SKILL

Would you like to have lived during the time of the Industrial Revolution? Write a short essay discussing the reasons for your decision.

211

◀ **Review Master Booklet, p. 53**

Optional Activities

Lesson 2 Review

Answers to Think and Write

A. Watt learned that it was possible to make a more efficient steam engine.

B. Machines at first were water-powered, so people had to leave their small shops and go to work in factories located near a water source.

C. A typical factory worker would work from 6 A.M. until 8 P.M. with half-hour breaks for breakfast and dinner and a one-hour lunch break.

D. The Industrial Revolution raised the standard of living, providing more goods for more people.

E. Providing capital was risky because capitalists could lose their money.

Answer to Skills Check

Answers should reflect independent thinking but may include no, because students would not want to work 14-hour days.

Focus Your Reading

Ask the lesson focus question found at the beginning of the lesson: **What changes resulted from the Industrial Revolution?** (Factories became the main place of employment, children were put to work, the standard of living rose, and free enterprise replaced the guild-controlled economy.)

Additional Practice

You may wish to assign the ancillary material listed below.

Understanding the Lesson p. 53
Workbook p. 58

┌─ **Answers to Caption Questions** ─┐
p. 210 ▶ Riding in carriages in the park
p. 211 ▶ The machine on the left with steam coming out of it

Political Revolutions

Objectives

★ **1. List** the causes and results of the English and French revolutions.

2. Compare the outcome of the Glorious Revolution with the outcome of the French Revolution.

3. Identify the following people and places: *Charles I, Oliver Cromwell, Charles II, James II, William and Mary, Louis XIV, Marie Antoinette, Napoleon Bonaparte, Bastille, Russia,* and *Waterloo.*

1 STARTING THE LESSON

Motivation Activity

■ Ask students to identify the one freedom that they consider to be the most important. List student responses on the chalkboard.

■ Then, ask students what they would do if they found themselves living in a country where these freedoms did not exist.

■ Tell students that they will be reading about people who found themselves in this type of situation.

Think About What You Know

■ Assign the THINK ABOUT WHAT YOU KNOW activity on p. 212.

■ Student answers may include the United States and Vietnam.

Study the Vocabulary

■ Ask students to write a newspaper headline using as many of the vocabulary words as they can.

■ Encourage them to look up the words in the Glossary.

THINK ABOUT WHAT YOU KNOW
What countries can you think of that have fought civil wars?

STUDY THE VOCABULARY
Parliament   guillotine
constitutional
    monarchy

FOCUS YOUR READING
What brought about revolutions in England and France, and what were the results of each of these revolutions?

A. Disputes Lead to Civil War in England

Power Disputes Revolutions, or great changes, have taken place in governments from time to time. One such revolution in England was the result of the old dispute about the powers of the king. This dispute had not ended when King John granted the Magna Carta. Nearly 400 years later, King James I believed that a king received his powers from God, not from the people he ruled. Many of James's subjects disagreed. They held that a monarch, or king or queen, was bound by the ancient laws and customs, such as those included in the Magna Carta.

During the reign of James's son, King Charles I, the dispute about power led to a civil war. Charles I lost the war, and both his sons, Charles and James, fled the country. The king's foes led by Oliver Cromwell beheaded the king in 1649. Oliver Cromwell and his army ruled England after the king's death. Cromwell, called Lord Protector, exercised the powers of a dictator.

212

A Law-Making Body Most English people decided that rule by a king was better than rule by a dictator. After Cromwell's death, **Parliament** met in 1660 and invited Charles, son of the executed king, to return to England. Parliament is a law-making body made up of two groups of people. The nobles and bishops, or leaders of the Church, met as the House of Lords. Representatives of the commoners formed the House of Commons. King Charles II said that he would respect the laws of England, but he did his best to be free from Parliament's control. The dispute about royal power had not yet been settled.

When Charles II died, his brother James came to the throne. King James II insisted that the king had the power to suspend, or set aside, any law that Parliament passed. However, James's actions

In 1653, Cromwell dismissed Parliament and ruled as a dictator.
▶ How did the artist depict Cromwell in the drawing?

Optional Activities

Writing to Learn

Writing a Petition Ask students to imagine that they are English citizens and it is the year 1687, before the bloodless revolution has taken place.

● Tell them to draw up a petition demanding changes in the government.

● Remind students to be respectful in their words and demands, as the revolution has not yet begun.

became high-handed, and he lost the support of many people who had strongly favored bringing back the rule of a king in 1660. James even lost the support of his daughter Mary, who was the wife of the Dutch ruler William of Orange.

B. A Bloodless Revolution Ends the Dispute

James Flees England In 1688 a group of English leaders decided that they could no longer put up with a king who thought he was above the law. So they invited William of Orange to come to England with an army to protect the people of England from their own king.

By now, most of King James's advisors had deserted him. He also found that he could not even count on the loyalty of his soldiers. James, remembering all too well what had happened to his father, Charles I, decided to flee the kingdom. So on a dark December night, he slipped out of the palace by a secret passageway. He took with him the Great Seal of the Kingdom. Impressions of the Great Seal were placed on all royal orders to show that they were official. James seemed to have thought that by taking the seal he would make it difficult for anyone to issue orders in his place.

James got into a small boat and started across the Thames River. Halfway across, the king dropped the Great Seal into the river. Word spread quickly that the king had fled and several watchful fishermen soon captured the king.

William and his English supporters were not pleased to learn of James's capture. William knew that it would be far better if James fled the country. He feared that holding James prisoner would cause people to sympathize with him. The

In 1689, Parliament offered the throne of England to William and Mary.
▶ How did the artist show this event in the etching?

leaders of the revolution gave James a second chance to flee. This time they made sure that no one prevented his escape.

A New Monarchy After the king had fled, Parliament declared the throne vacant. Mary was next in line for the throne, but she would accept a crown only if William was made king. Parliament finally agreed that William and Mary would be king and queen.

The Parliament that offered William and Mary their crowns also passed a Bill of Rights. This was a law setting limits on the royal power. The government of England became a **constitutional monarchy**. In a constitutional monarchy, monarchs rule according to a constitution, or basic law.

213

2 DEVELOPING THE LESSON

Read and Think
Sections A and B

Discuss the Glorious Revolution and its effects on England by asking the following questions:

1. **What caused a civil war to break out in England during the reign of Charles I?**
(A dispute over the king's power *p. 212*)

2. **Why were most English people dissatisfied with their government after Charles I?**
(Cromwell ruled like a dictator. *p. 212*)

3. **How was a constitutional monarchy finally established in England?**
(Parliament passed a Bill of Rights that set limits on the royal power and made England a constitutional monarchy *p. 213*)

Thinking Critically Why, do you think, did monarchs like Charles I and James II resist giving up some of the powers when the people so clearly wanted the government to change? (Hypothesize)
(Answers may include that the monarchs believed in the divine right of kings and felt the people were wrong. *pp. 212-213*)

┌─ **Answers to Caption Questions** ─
p. 212 ▶ As a strong, forceful ruler
p. 213 ▶ As a greatly ceremonial affair, with William and Mary being offered the crown

Comparing Governments

- Ask students to review the information in Sections A and B in order to compare the government of the United States with that of England.

- Make a chart on the chalkboard, beginning with the headings *American Government* and *English Government*.

- In the *American Government* column, list the following: *House of Representatives, Senate, Congress, President,* and *Constitution.*

- Have students use their books to find the English equivalents to these parts of government (House of Commons, House of Lords, Parliament, monarch, and Bill of Rights.)

For Your Information

The Interregnum The period of Cromwell's rule is called the Interregnum, which means "between reigns" in Latin. Cromwell ruled with a heavy hand for 11 years. As a Puritan, he saw to it that theaters and taverns were closed, and he tried to make the people live by strict standards of behavior. When Parliament disagreed with his actions, he simply dissolved it.

During his rule, Cromwell imposed heavy taxes on the people and took away the property of those who had supported the king. He also was responsible for the massacre of thousands of people when his army put down a rebellion in Ireland in 1649.

Optional Activities

Concept:
Changing a Government

Below are three activities that will help your students better understand the political revolutions in England and France.

◆ **EASY** Ask students to list methods by which American citizens can change their government. Students should mention such methods as voting, circulating petitions, and running for office.

Then ask students why these methods did not work in seventeenth-century England. (For example: The dispute between monarchs and people about royal power had not been settled. James II insisted that the king had the power to suspend any law that Parliament passed.)

◀▶ **AVERAGE** Ask students to make a chart comparing the causes of the French and English revolutions.

Then, ask them to predict, in writing, which country was most likely to undergo further political change.

◀▮▶ **CHALLENGING** Ask students to imagine that the Glorious Revolution failed and James II remained on England's throne.

Have them write the next "chapter" of English history. Ask them to decide whether a bloodless or a bloody revolution would have occurred.

The Bill of Rights The Bill of Rights was seen as a part of England's basic law. It said that the monarchs could not suspend laws passed by Parliament. Neither could they collect taxes nor keep an army without the consent of Parliament. The election of members of Parliament would be free, and they would enjoy freedom of debate. Parts of the Bill of Rights applied to all people in the kingdom. Anyone accused of a crime had the right to a trial by jury.

In accepting the throne, William and Mary accepted the Bill of Rights. There was no longer any question about the monarchs being above the law. The long dispute had been settled by a revolution without fighting. The English have called it the Glorious Revolution because it was a bloodless revolution.

Perhaps you wonder what happened to the Great Seal that James dropped in the river. Some time later a fisherman accidently caught it in his net and brought it to the surface. Even James's last act as king was a failure.

C. France Faces Problems

France's Monarchs Unlike the Glorious Revolution, the French Revolution was not bloodless. Perhaps if the French king Louis XVI had been a better leader, things may have been different.

Louis had never wanted to be king. He was only 19 years old and his wife, Marie Antoinette (an twuh NET), was about 18 when they came to the throne in 1774. He thought himself too young for the position, which frightened him. He complained to a

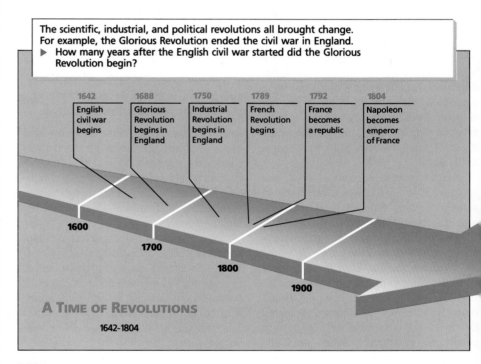

The scientific, industrial, and political revolutions all brought change. For example, the Glorious Revolution ended the civil war in England.
▶ How many years after the English civil war started did the Glorious Revolution begin?

1642	1688	1750	1789	1792	1804
English civil war begins	Glorious Revolution begins in England	Industrial Revolution begins in England	French Revolution begins	France becomes a republic	Napoleon becomes emperor of France

1600   1700   1800   1900

A TIME OF REVOLUTIONS
1642-1804

214

Curriculum Connection

Literature In order to give students a feel for life in France and England around the time of the French Revolution, ask them to read a portion or all of Charles Dickens's *A Tale of Two Cities* (New York: Putnam, 1948. ISBN: 0-448-06023-X).

Comparing Rights

Tell students that the French set forth the ideas of their revolution in a document called the *Declaration of the Rights of Man and the Citizen*. This document stated that the natural rights of every citizen included liberty, property, security, and the resistance to cruelty and injustice.

● Ask students how these natural rights compare with those contained in our *Declaration of Independence*.

● Discuss what might account for these differences.

Louis XVI and Marie Antoinette ruled for 18 years, although neither had an interest in the monarchy.
▶ How do the paintings depict them as royalty?

friend, "What a burden! It seems that the universe will fall upon me!"

Marie Antoinette was not any more suited to be a queen than Louis was fit to be a king. As a young queen, she enjoyed fine clothes and going to parties. She was bored by court life, uninterested in serious matters, and lacked a good education. One of her teachers said that she was intelligent but rather lazy. "She would learn only so long as she was being amused."

Unfair Laws and Debt Louis XVI was not responsible for all the problems that France faced in 1789. But neither the king nor his people had much confidence in his ability to deal with the problems. They

arose partly because of the special privileges of the nobles and the Church.

The French were not equal before the law. There were different sets of laws for the nobles and the common people. Nobles held most of the best land in France, yet they paid no taxes. Nobles held the high positions in the government. Officers in the army were nobles. Many young noble officers knew far less about warfare than the men they commanded.

Nobles also held most of the high positions in the Church. The Church owned large amounts of land, and it had its own courts and laws. The Church collected taxes from the peasants, but it paid no taxes to the king.

215

For Your Information

France's Debts The United States was largely responsible for France's debts in the late 1700s. France's support of the patriots in the Revolutionary War was great and the United States was slow in repaying its debt, so France was on the verge of bankruptcy.

Optional Activities

Read and Think
Section C

To help students understand the context of the French Revolution, ask the questions below:

1. **What problems led to the French Revolution?**
   (A king and a people who had no confidence in his abilities, the common people's resentment of the special privileges given to nobles and the Church, and government debt *pp. 214-216*)

2. **How did changes in the American government affect the way that the common people in France felt about the problems with their government in 1789?**
   (When the French people heard of the changes in the American government, they knew that it was possible to change their own government. *p. 216*)

3. **What special privileges did nobles have in France before the revolution?**
   (They had the best land, paid no taxes, and held the highest positions in government and the army. *p. 215*)

Thinking Critically How might French history have been different, do you think, if Louis XVI had been a stronger, more confident leader? (Hypothesize)
(Answers may include that France might have avoided a revolution because he would have made needed changes. *p. 216*)

VISUAL THINKING SKILL

Using a Painting

■ Ask students how the painting of Marie Antoinette on p. 215 is the same as and different from the description in the text. (She is wearing fine clothes and appears to be reading a document. The text says that she enjoyed fine clothes but was uninterested in serious matters.)

┌─ **Answers to Caption Questions** ─┐
p. 214 ▶ 46 years
p. 215 ▶ Elaborate clothing, regal looking, proud

215

Read and Think

Section D

Summarize the changes that resulted from the French Revolution by asking the following questions:

1. **What effort did the king make to solve the problems that faced France in 1789?**
   (He called representatives of the nobles and commoners together to consider new taxes. *p. 216*)

2. **What event started the French Revolution?**
   (The attack on the Bastille *pp. 216-217*)

3. **What did the king's official mean when he said that the attack on the Bastille signified a revolution, rather than a revolt?**
   (He meant that the people of France were no longer demanding changes in the monarchy but were rebelling against the monarchy itself. *pp. 216-217*)

4. **Who controlled the French government after the monarchy was abolished?**
   (Radicals *p. 217*)

5. **Why were the radicals overthrown?**
   (Because they began a "reign of terror" against those suspected of opposing them, which threatened many people *p. 217*)

Thinking Critically **How do you think the French Revolution differed from the Glorious Revolution?** (Recall)
(The French Revolution was a violent revolution, while the Glorious Revolution was bloodless. The French Revolution did not bring political stability, while the Glorious Revolution did. *pp. 216-217*)

The storming of the Bastille marked the start of the French Revolution.
▶ What United States holiday is similar to Bastille Day?

The common people of France paid for the government, but they did not pay as much as the government spent. As a result, the king's government was deeply in debt. That was one of the most pressing problems that faced the king in 1789.

A Time for Change The special privileges of the nobles and the Church had existed since the Middle Ages. But by 1789, people were getting new ideas. A growing number had come to believe that it was time for a change. They knew that changes were possible because governments had been changed in other lands. The English had limited the powers of the king. The Americans had become independent and had set up a republic. And the American Declaration of Independence had stated that all people are created equal. If such things could happen in England and America, why not in France?

D. The Revolution Brings Changes

Violence Begins Changes came rapidly in 1789 and the years that followed. The king called representatives of the nobles and commoners together to consider new taxes. The representatives of the commoners insisted that France have a constitution that would limit royal powers.

However, some people were not willing to wait for a constitution. In Paris, many poor citizens focused their anger toward the government on the Bastille (bas TEEL), a prison-fortress within the city, where they believed hundreds of French citizens had been unjustly imprisoned. On July 14, 1789, a crowd of people in Paris took up arms and attacked the Bastille. The mob released the prisoners and destroyed the Bastille. King Louis XVI was shocked when told of what had happened. "Why, it's a revolt!" he told the official who brought

Optional Activities

Curriculum Connection

Music Have students listen to a recording of the *1812 Overture* by Tchaikovsky.

- Tell them that the music was written by Tchaikovsky as a memorial to Napoleon's defeat in Russia.

- Tell them that the music begins with the battle at Borodino, where the Russians were badly defeated by the French, and culminates with Napoleon's flight from Moscow.

- Ask students to listen for the mood of the music and to imagine themselves as Russians in Moscow at that time.

- Have them express their feelings in a descriptive paragraph, a poem, or a picture.

him the news. The official answered, "No sire, it's a revolution."

The Monarchy Ends The attack on the Bastille was the beginning of a revolution. Great changes followed. The king's powers were limited; the nobles lost privileges; the Church lost most of its lands; and serfdom was finally abolished.

Rulers in other countries grew alarmed by the changes in France. They feared that revolution would spread, so they declared war against France. Because King Louis and Marie Antoinette were suspected of secretly favoring the foreign enemies, the monarchy was abolished. France became a republic in 1792. King Louis was tried as a traitor and put to death on the **guillotine** (GIHL uh teen), a device for beheading people. Marie Antoinette went to the guillotine the following year.

Terror Reigns Radicals now controlled the French republic. Radicals are people who want to make extreme, or very great, changes in a short amount of time. The radicals began a "reign of terror" against those suspected of opposing them. A great many people were imprisoned. More than 20,000 people were put to death by the guillotine. Finally the rule of the radicals threatened so many people that the radicals were overthrown. Their leaders, who had sent so many to the guillotine, were sent there themselves.

E. A General Becomes Emperor

A Young Dictator The overthrow of the radicals did not end changes in France. General Napoleon Bonaparte (nuh POH lee-un BOH nuh pahrt) seized control of the government in 1799.

The painting below shows King Louis XVI approaching his execution by guillotine on January 21, 1793.
▶ Where is the guillotine in this painting?

217

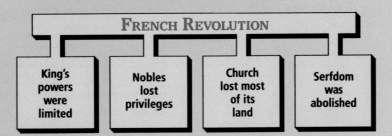

Read and Think

Section E

Use the following questions to discuss Napoleon's reign:

1. **How successful was Napoleon in defeating France's enemies?**
(He defeated all of France's enemies on the mainland except for the Russians. His retreat from Russia enabled France's enemies to reunite against him and defeat him at Waterloo. *pp. 218-219*)

Thinking Critically Harsh winters protected the Russians from defeat. What other natural barriers, do you think, can protect a people from invasion? (Hypothesize)
(Answers should reflect independent thinking but may include deserts, jungles, oceans, and mountains. *p. 219*)

GEOGRAPHY THEMES

Regions

■ Have students look at the map on this page to help them answer the following question: **What territories were allied with Napoleon?**
(Norway, Denmark, Prussia, and the Austrian Empire)

Bonaparte had risen rapidly in the army during the revolution. He was a general by the time he was 24 years old. He was only 30 when he seized control. For a few years, Bonaparte continued to call the government a republic, but he was really a dictator. In 1804 the dictator crowned himself Emperor Napoleon. France once again had a monarch.

Napoleon kept many of the changes made during the revolution. He did not bring back serfdom or give land back to the Church. All people were equal before the laws drawn up by Napoleon's order.

Napoleon's Mistake Napoleon was a very successful military leader. He defeated France's enemies on the mainland,

Napoleon met his final defeat at the battle of Waterloo in 1815.
▶ In which empire did the battle of Waterloo take place?

Expressing a Point of View

● Tell students that, after the battle of Waterloo, Napoleon abdicated his throne and was exiled to St. Helena, a British island in the South Atlantic.

● Ask students why they think France's enemies felt it necessary to send Napoleon so far from his home.

● Then, ask students if they feel that this was just punishment for the French emperor.

Reteaching Main Objective

★ *List the causes and results of the English and French revolutions.*

● Divide the class into two groups.

● Have one group prepare a "You Are There" television program about the Glorious Revolution in England. Have the other group prepare a similar program about the French Revolution.

● Tell students that their programs should explain the causes and results of each revolution either by live coverage of the events as they take place or by interviews with the key people or groups responsible for the revolution.

Musée d'Orsay, France

Napoleon's troops, weakened by hunger and cold, were forced to retreat from Russia. This defeat was the beginning of Napoleon's decline.
▶ Do you think that Napoleon's invasion of Russia was a good idea?

although he did not conquer Great Britain. British sea power kept him from crossing the English Channel. However, Napoleon made a great mistake in 1812 when he invaded Russia. He reached and occupied Moscow, but he could not force the Russians to surrender. The French were not prepared to spend the winter in Moscow, so Napoleon had to retreat. His armies suffered terrible losses as a result of the harsh Russian winter.

France's enemies saw their opportunity. They once again united to make war against Napoleon. He met his final defeat in 1815 at Waterloo, in the country we now call Belgium. He died six years later.

LESSON 3 REVIEW

THINK AND WRITE

A. What was the cause and the result of the civil war in England? (Analyze)

B. What did the Glorious Revolution accomplish? (Infer)

C. What problems did France face in 1789? (Recall)

D. What changes did the revolution make in France? (Recall)

E. How did Napoleon become an emperor? (Recall)

SKILLS CHECK

MAP SKILL

After Napoleon and his troops retreated from Moscow, they marched back home to Paris, France. How many miles (km) was their trip? Use the mileage scale on the map on page 218 to estimate the distance between the two cities.

UNDERSTANDING THE LESSON

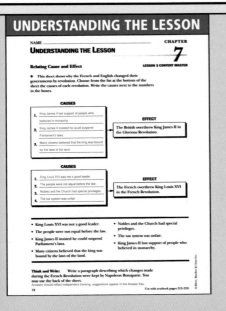

◀ **Review Master Booklet, p. 54**

---

3 CLOSING THE LESSON

Lesson 3 Review

Answers to Think and Write

A. The English civil war was caused by a quarrel between Charles I and his subjects over the power of the monarch. Charles I lost the war, and his foes, led by Oliver Cromwell, took control.

B. It made England a constitutional monarchy and made the Bill of Rights a basic part of English law.

C. France was led by a weak king; the common people resented the special privileges given to nobles and the Church; and the government was in debt.

D. The revolution led to limitations on the king's power; the loss of privileges by the nobles; the loss of most Church lands; and the abolition of serfdom.

E. Napoleon seized control of the French government and crowned himself emperor.

Answer to Skills Check

Their trip was about 1,500 miles (2,414 km).

Focus Your Reading

Ask the lesson focus question found at the beginning of the lesson: **What brought about revolutions in England and France, and what were the results of each of these revolutions?**

(England's revolution was caused by disagreement over the extent of a monarch's power. It led to a constitutional monarchy and a Bill of Rights. France's revolution was caused by weak leadership, unequal treatment of people, and high taxes. It resulted in more rights for the common people and restrictions on the nobility and the Church.)

Additional Practice

You may wish to assign the ancillary materials listed below.

Understanding the Lesson p. 54
Workbook pp. 59-60

┌─ **Answers to Caption Questions** ─┐
p. 218 ▶ In the French Empire
p. 219 ▶ No, because he suffered one of the worst retreats in military history
└─────────────────────────────┘

Using The Vocabulary

1. Inquisition
2. capital
3. constitutional monarchy
4. astronomy
5. standard of living
6. Parliament
7. free enterprise
8. Industrial Revolution
9. revolution
10. profit

Remembering What You Read

1. Ptolemy believed that the sun, moon, and planets revolved around the earth. Copernicus believed that the earth and planets revolved around the sun.

2. That there were mountains and deep valleys on the moon, that the Milky Way was made up of countless separate stars, and that Jupiter had four moons

3. He developed a microscope that made microorganisms visible.

4. Workers had to live near the factories where they worked, which led to the growth of cities and towns.

5. More goods available to more people

6. They risked losing their money

7. Monarchs could not suspend laws passed by Parliament and could not collect taxes or keep an army without the consent of Parliament.

8. Nobles had the best land, paid no taxes, and held the highest positions in government and the Church. The Church had its own courts and laws, and collected taxes from the peasants but paid no taxes to the king.

9. A crowd of people in Paris attacked the Bastille, marking the beginning of the French Revolution.

10. His armies had been weakened by trying to conquer Russia.

USING THE VOCABULARY

revolution	capital
astronomy	profit
Inquisition	free enterprise
Industrial Revolution	Parliament
constitutional monarchy	standard of living

On a separate sheet of paper, write the word or words from above that best complete the sentences.

1. Galileo was brought before the _____, a special Church court, because of the things he wrote.

2. Matthew Boulton provided the _____, or money or goods, so that James Watt could build and sell steam engines.

3. In a _____ a monarch rules according to a basic law.

4. In Italy, Copernicus studied _____, a science that deals with space.

5. A measure of how well people live is called a _____.

6. _____ is made up of the House of Lords and the House of Commons.

7. In a _____ economy, people have a choice about how to make and spend money.

8. The great changes in the ways people worked brought about the _____.

9. Copernicus wrote a book about the _____, or turning round, of the earth and other planets.

10. It took 18 years for Watt and Boulton to make any _____, or financial gain, on the steam engines they sold.

220

REMEMBERING WHAT YOU READ

On a separate sheet of paper, answer the following questions in complete sentences.

1. How did Copernicus's beliefs about space differ from Ptolemy's?

2. What did Galileo discover when he looked at the sky through a powerful telescope?

3. What was Leeuwenhoek's contribution to the Scientific Revolution?

4. Why did the invention of machines affect the growth of cities and towns?

5. How did the Industrial Revolution raise the standard of living?

6. What risks did capitalists take in providing money for businesses?

7. What were three limits set on monarchs according to the English Bill of Rights?

8. What special privileges did nobles and the Church have in France before the revolution?

9. What happened in Paris on July 14, 1789?

10. Why were Napoleon's enemies able to defeat him at the battle of Waterloo?

TYING SCIENCE TO SOCIAL STUDIES

Make a map to show the nine planets of our solar system in their orbits, or circular paths, around the sun. First look up the following planets in a science book or another reference book to find out their order from the sun: Earth, Jupiter, Mars, Mercury, Neptune, Pluto, Saturn, Uranus, Venus. Then draw the sun and the planets in their correct order in nine orbits around the sun. Be sure to label each planet.

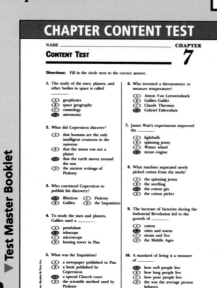

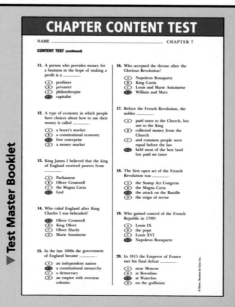

THINKING CRITICALLY

On a separate sheet of paper, answer the following questions in complete sentences.

1. How do you think the discovery of new facts about space might change the way people think?
2. What similarities are there between the revolution in science and the revolution in industry?
3. If you had been Matthew Boulton, would you have formed a partnership with James Watt? Explain.
4. Why, do you think, was the English Parliament made up of two separate groups of people?
5. Which problems facing France in 1789 might King Louis XVI have been able to solve? Explain how.

SUMMARIZING THE CHAPTER

On a separate sheet of paper, copy the graphic organizer shown below. Beside the main idea for each lesson, write four statements that support the main idea.

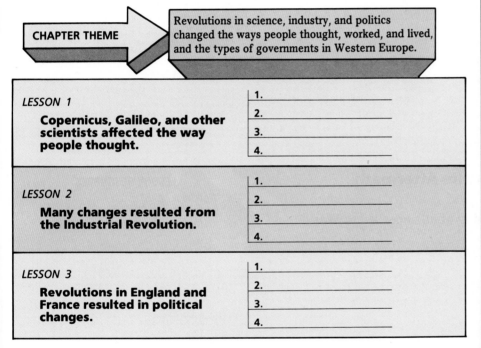

CHAPTER THEME → Revolutions in science, industry, and politics changed the ways people thought, worked, and lived, and the types of governments in Western Europe.

LESSON 1
Copernicus, Galileo, and other scientists affected the way people thought.
1. _____
2. _____
3. _____
4. _____

LESSON 2
Many changes resulted from the Industrial Revolution.
1. _____
2. _____
3. _____
4. _____

LESSON 3
Revolutions in England and France resulted in political changes.
1. _____
2. _____
3. _____
4. _____

221

Thinking Critically

1. Answers may include that people might come to believe that aliens do exist.
2. Both brought complete changes in the ways that people viewed things.
3. Answers may include yes, because Watt already experimented in making a more efficient steam engine.
4. Answers may include that Parliament was formed long before people supported the idea that all men were equal.
5. Answers may include that he could have eliminated privileges enjoyed by the nobles and the Church and he could have cutback on his own expenses.

Summarizing the Chapter

Lesson 1

1. Copernicus showed the sun as the center about which the earth and planets revolve.
2. Van Leeuwenhoek invented a powerful microscope.
3. Galileo discovered features of the moon, the Milky Way, and Jupiter.
4. Fahrenheit invented the thermometer.

Lesson 2

1. Creation of factories
2. Growth of cities and towns
3. Rise in the standard of living
4. Development of a free-enterprise economy

Lesson 3

1. Establishment of a constitutional monarchy in England
2. Limitation of the king of France's powers
3. Loss of nobles' privileges in France
4. Abolition of serfdom in France

Nationalism and Two World Wars

(pp. 222-245)

Chapter Theme: Nationalism and two world wars resulted in great changes in Western Europe.

LESSON *1* New Nations Appear on the Map

(pp. 222-226)

Theme: Through the use of war and skillful politics, Italy and Germany experienced unification in the 1800s.

SILVER WINGS WORKSHOP: The Courage of Your Convictions

LESSON *2* World War I and Its Aftermath

(pp. 227-234)

Theme: An assassination and a string of alliances led to World War I.

 SOCIAL STUDIES LIBRARY: *Friedrich*

LESSON *3* World War II and What Followed

(pp. 235-243)

Theme: Germany and Japan had many victories during World War II, but in the end, they were defeated by the Allies.

SILVER WINGS WORKSHOP: The Courage of Your Convictions

SOCIAL STUDIES LIBRARY: *Friedrich*
 Listen for the Singing

Review Masters

REVIEWING CHAPTER VOCABULARY

Review   Study the terms in the box. Use your Glossary to find definitions of those you do not remember.

armistice	Fascist	League of	prime minister
Axis	genocide	Nations	unification
Blitzkrieg	Holocaust	nationalism	United Nations
depression			

Practice   Complete the paragraphs using terms from the box above. You may change the forms of the terms to fit the meaning.

After the (1) ___unification___ of Italy, the people of the different regions began to think of themselves as Italians. In fact, in many countries all across Europe feelings of (2) ___nationalism___ were strong. The spread of these beliefs led to the shooting of Archduke Ferdinand and the outbreak of World War I. When the war ended with the signing of an (3) ___armistice___, people began to look for ways to prevent such a tragedy from happening again.

Unfortunately, the efforts to keep the peace were not successful. In 1939, the German (4) ___Blitzkrieg___ attacks across Europe led to the outbreak of World War II. In 1941, the United States joined the Allied effort to defeat the (5) ___Axis___ countries. After the war ended in 1945, people began to search for a more successful way to avoid war. The result was the (6) ___United Nations___. Today, this organization continues to promote peace and friendly relations among all nations.

Write   Write a sentence of your own for each term in the box above. You may use the back of the sheet.

Sentences should show that students understand the meanings of the terms.

_____

_____

_____

_____

_____

_____

_____

_____

© Silver, Burdett & Ginn Inc.

Use with Chapter 8, pages 223–243.   61

LOCATING PLACES

✽   Critical events of World War I and World War II happened at the places listed below. Use the Gazetteer in your textbook to find the latitude and longitude of each place. Then locate and label each on the map.

	LAT. ⊖	LONG. ⊕			LAT. ⊖	LONG. ⊕
1. Sarajevo	44°N	18°E	6. Paris		49°N	2°E
2. Vienna	48°N	16°E	7. Warsaw		52°N	21°E
3. Auschwitz	50°N	19°E	8. Rome		42°N	12°E
4. Moscow	56°N	38°E	9. London		52°N	0°
5. Amsterdam	52°N	5°E	10. Prague		50°N	14°E

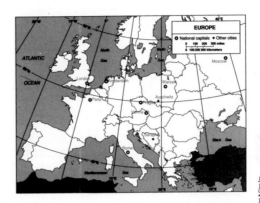

© Silver, Burdett & Ginn Inc.

62   Use with Chapter 8, pages 223–243.

SUMMARIZING THE CHAPTER

✽   Complete this graphic organizer. Under the main idea for each lesson, write three statements that support the main idea.

CHAPTER THEME → Nationalism and two world wars resulted in great changes in Western Europe.

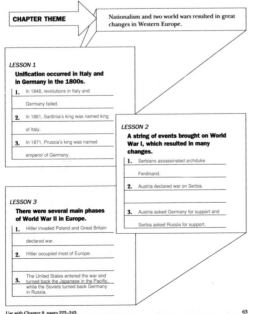

LESSON 1
Unification occurred in Italy and in Germany in the 1800s.
1. In 1848, revolutions in Italy and Germany failed.
2. In 1861, Sardinia's king was named king of Italy.
3. In 1871, Prussia's king was named emperor of Germany.

LESSON 2
A string of events brought on World War I, which resulted in many changes.
1. Serbians assassinated archduke Ferdinand.
2. Austria declared war on Serbia.
3. Austria asked Germany for support and Serbia asked Russia for support.

LESSON 3
There were several main phases of World War II in Europe.
1. Hitler invaded Poland and Great Britain declared war.
2. Hitler occupied most of Europe.
3. The United States entered the war and turned back the Japanese in the Pacific, while the Soviets turned back Germany in Russia.

© Silver, Burdett & Ginn Inc.

Use with Chapter 8, pages 223–243.   63

C8-B

Workbook Pages

Page 61

ANALYZING WORLD WAR I

Classifying and Interpreting Information, Understanding Diagrams

✳ Fill in diagrams **A** and **B** to show the main countries involved in World War I. Choose the names of countries from the countries box. You will use some names more than once. The first name is filled in for you.

Countries

Austria	Germany	Japan	Turkey
Bosnia	Great Britain	Russia	United States
France	Italy	Serbia	

A.

1. Austria — had an alliance with → 2. Germany
ruled ↓ which wanted to unite with →
3. Bosnia → 4. Serbia
which had an alliance with ↓
5. Russia
which had an alliance with ↓
6. France

B.

The Allies,
7. Russia
8. France, and — fought the →
9. Great Britain
were joined by ↓
12. Japan
13. Italy, and
14. United States

Central Powers,
10. Germany and
11. Austria

The Central Powers were joined by
15. Turkey

Thinking Further: The war of 1914 to 1918 was fought almost entirely in *Europe*. Nevertheless, it is called a *world* war. Why is this so?

The war is known as a world war because people from many countries outside Europe fought in it.

Page 62

THE REGIONS OF ITALY

Gathering Information from a Map, Interpreting Information

✳ On the facing page is a map of Italy in the 1990s. The map shows the country's 20 regions, which are political units similar to states in the United States. The capitals of the regions are also shown. Study the map, and then answer the following questions.

1. Name the 13 regions located north of Molise. Abruzzi, Latium, Marches, Umbria, Tuscany, Emilia-Romagna, Liguria, Piedmont, Lombardy, Veneto, Friuli-Venezia Giulia, Valle d'Aosta, and Trentino-Alto Adige

2. Name the two regions that are made up wholly of islands. Sardinia and Sicily

3. Name the seven regions that border on the Adriatic Sea. Apulia, Molise, Abruzzi, Marches, Emilia-Romagna, Veneto, and Friuli-Venezia Giulia

4. Name the two regions that border on the Ligurian Sea. Tuscany and Liguria

5. Name the seven regions that border on the Tyrrhenian Sea. Sicily, Calabria, Basilicata, Campania, Latium, Sardinia, and Tuscany

6. On the lines provided, write in the capital of each of Italy's regions. One region has two capitals.

Abruzzi	L'Aquila	Marches	Ancona
Apulia	Bari	Molise	Campobasso
Basilicata	Potenza	Piedmont	Turin
Calabria	Catanzaro	Sardinia	Cagliari
Campania	Naples	Sicily	Palermo
Emilia-Romagna	Bologna	Trentino-Alto Adige	Bolzano, Trento
Friuli-Venezia Giulia	Trieste	Tuscany	Florence
Latium	Rome	Umbria	Perugia
Liguria	Genoa	Valle D'Aosta	Aosta
Lombardy	Milan	Veneto	Venice

Thinking Further: Identify an important feature of the geography of Italy and tell why it is significant.

Students may note that almost all the country is near the sea, that much of the mainland is a boot-shaped peninsula, or that the country includes two large islands.

Page 63

THE REGIONS OF ITALY *continued*

REGIONS OF ITALY
★ Regional capitals

Page 64

UNDERSTANDING WORLD WAR II

Identifying Details, Evaluating Information

✳ Below is a box with words relating to World War II. In the blank before each statement, write the word or words from the box that the statement describes.

Blitzkrieg	Japan, Germany, Italy	Britain and France	1945
United Nations	September 3, 1939	December 7, 1941	Poland
Austria	genocide	Joseph Stalin	Soviet Union

Austria — This country was taken over by Germany in 1938.

Joseph Stalin — This Soviet leader made an agreement with Adolf Hitler to divide Poland.

Britain and France — These nations declared that they would defend Polish independence.

Poland — In 1939, the German army invaded this nation.

September 3, 1939 — On this day, the British entered into war with Germany.

Blitzkrieg — This "lightning war" enabled Germany to conquer Denmark, Norway, the Netherlands, Belgium, and France.

Soviet Union — The Germans invaded this country in 1941, and were driven from it in 1944.

genocide — Through this policy, the Nazis carried out the killing of 6 million Jews.

Japan, Germany, Italy — These nations formed an alliance called the Axis.

December 7, 1941 — On this date, the Japanese attacked American bases in Hawaii and the Philippine Islands.

Thinking Further: What do you find most significant about World War II? Give two or three reasons for your choice.

Answers should reflect independent thinking. The reasons should be relevant to the choice. A possibility: The most significant aspect of World War II was the great number of people who were killed. There was tremendous suffering and millions of families were torn apart.

C8-C

TEACHER NOTES

New Nations Appear on the Map

Objectives

★**1. Explain** how nationalism was involved in the unification of Italy and Germany.

2. Describe how Italy and Germany were united.

3. Identify the following people and places: *Giuseppe Mazzini, Count Camillo di Cavour, Carl Schurz, Otto von Bismarck, Italy, Germany,* and *Prussia.*

1 STARTING THE LESSON

Motivation Activity

■ Write the word *nationalism* on the chalkboard and ask students to define the word. If no one can, cover up the last part of the word so that only *nation* is visible. Now ask students to guess what the word means. (Loyalty and devotion to a nation)

■ Explain that in this lesson students will read about how two different groups of states were united to form Italy and Germany. Have students brainstorm how nationalism might be involved.

Think About What You Know

■ Assign the THINK ABOUT WHAT YOU KNOW activity on p. 223.

■ Student answers may include that the states would have different governments, laws, and types of money; there would be more potential for wars between states; and it would be easier for another country to take over other states.

Study the Vocabulary

■ Have students look up the definition of each of the new vocabulary words for this lesson in the Glossary.

■ Then, ask students to use a dictionary or a thesaurus to find as many synonyms as they can for each of the words.

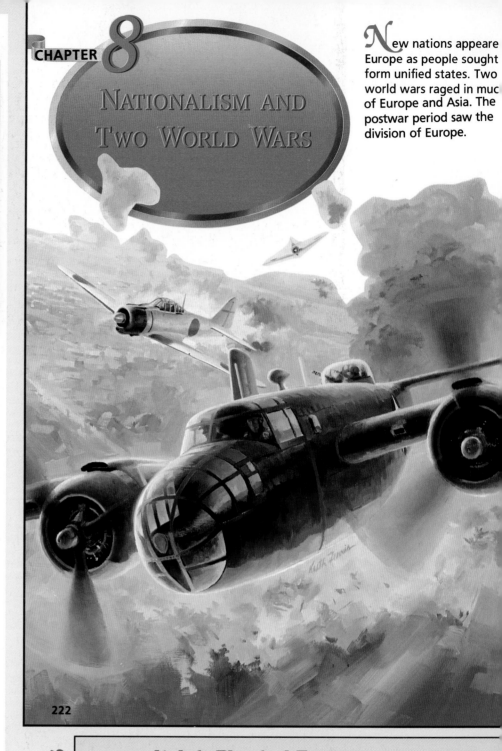

CHAPTER 8

NATIONALISM AND TWO WORLD WARS

New nations appear Europe as people sought form unified states. Two world wars raged in muc of Europe and Asia. The postwar period saw the division of Europe.

222

Optional Activities

Italy's Physical Features

● Have students research what Italy looks like today. List different cities and regions on the chalkboard for students to choose from (Rome, Florence, Venice, Sicily, the Italian Alps, the Italian Riviera, and so on).

● Tell students to look in tour guides (such as Frommer's, Fodor's, or Michelin's) for pictures of some of the tourist attractions in the city or region that they are researching. Encourage students to bring the pictures they find to class to share with other students.

● Ask students to write a paragraph describing their impressions of their city or region. Ask for volunteers to read their paragraphs to the rest of the class.

Imagine that each state in the United States is independent of the others. What kinds of problems or difficulties could this cause?

nationalism   **prime minister**
unification

How did unification occur in Italy and in Germany?

A. Giuseppe Mazzini Discovers His Duty

In 1821, when Giuseppe Mazzini (joo-ZEP pe maht TSEE nee) was 16, he met a tall, black-bearded man asking for money on the streets of Genoa, Italy. Young Mazzini could see at a glance that the tall man did not look like an ordinary beggar. He was one of the rebel soldiers who crowded into Genoa after an unsuccessful revolt against the royal government of Sardinia. Sardinia was one of the states on the Italian peninsula. Italy did not appear as a country on the map of Europe in 1821. Italy was only the name of the peninsula, which was divided into seven major states.

Loyalty and devotion to one's country is called **nationalism**. Most of the people of Italy did not have any nationalism. They did not think of themselves as Italians. They thought of themselves as belonging to a particular city or region. For example, people of Genoa called themselves Genoese; and people of Venice, Venetians.

Mazzini was troubled by his meeting with the unfortunate rebel soldier. He asked himself, did he, too, not have a duty to help to free Italy? Did he not have a duty to work for Italy's **unification**? Unification is the uniting of separate regions and cities into one nation. Mazzini realized that such a unified republic could be created only if there was a revolution.

B. Mazzini Becomes a Revolutionist

Getting Organized Mazzini decided to help unite Italy. He wrote articles for newspapers and joined a revolutionary group. The government had him exiled, or forced to leave the country, so he went to France. While in exile, he formed a group that he called Young Italy. He believed that the young people of Italy could

Giuseppe Mazzini worked for the unification of Italy.
▶ What actions did he take to help to unify his country?

2 DEVELOPING THE LESSON

Read and Think

Sections A, B, and C

Use the following questions to discuss the unification of Italy:

1. **Were people in Italy nationalistic in 1821?**
(No, people thought of themselves as being from the city or region that they lived in rather than being from Italy. *p. 223*)

2. **What did Mazzini want to teach the young people of Italy?**
(To think of themselves as Italians with a duty to unite Italy *p. 223*)

3. **How was Cavour's approach to unifying Italy different from Mazzini's?**
(Mazzini thought that it would take a revolution to unify Italy. Cavour thought that skillful politics were more effective. *p. 224*)

   Thinking Critically Why, do you think, did Cavour succeed in unifying Italy while Mazzini failed? (Infer)
(Answers may include that Cavour had more power and influence since he was both a noble and a government official. *p. 224*)

--- **Answers to Caption Questions** ---

p. 223 ▶ He wrote articles for newspapers about unifying Italy, formed a group called Young Italy, and established a school in England for poor Italian boys.

Writing to Learn

Writing a Diary Have students imagine that they are Giuseppe Mazzini. Tell them to write an entry in their diary based on one of the following days:

1. The day in 1821 when Mazzini sees the rebel soldier in Genoa

2. The day Mazzini was forced to leave Italy and go to France

Read and Think
Sections D and E

Use the following questions to discuss the unification of Germany:

1. **What kind of government did Carl Schurz envision for Germany?**
(A republic in which Germans could speak freely and elect their government *p. 225*)

2. **How did Bismarck unite Germany?**
(Through wars and skillful politics *p. 226*)

Thinking Critically Do you agree with Otto von Bismarck's idea that power depends upon "blood and iron" (military strength)? (Evaluate)
(Answers should reflect independent thinking but may include yes, a government needs military strength to protect itself from its enemies and stay in power, or no, a government needs the support of the people to remain in power. *p. 226*)

GEOGRAPHY THEMES

Location

■ Have students look at the map on this page and the map on p. 226 to answer the following questions:

1. **List the nations that bordered Italy in 1866.**
(France, Switzerland, and Austria-Hungary)

2. **Why, do you think, did Rome finally become part of Italy in 1870?**
(Answers may include that it was surrounded on three sides by Italy so it finally became part of that nation.)

3. **In 1871, what nations bordered Germany to the west?**
(The Netherlands, Belgium, and Luxembourg)

4. **Which empire extended farther north, Germany or Italy?**
(Germany)

---

unite their homeland if they were organized. Mazzini wrote that the members of Young Italy must teach people to think of themselves as Italians rather than Venetians or Genoese. Again and again, Mazzini told young people that they had a duty to unite Italy.

Encouraging Pride Mazzini moved to England, where he continued to work for the unification of Italy. There he established a school for poor Italian boys in London. Most of the boys worked at odd jobs. Mazzini taught the boys to read and write, and—just as important—he taught them to be proud of being Italian. Every week he spoke to them about Italy's great men and its history.

When revolution broke out in Italy in 1848, Mazzini hurried home, but the uprising failed. Mazzini could stir the hearts of the Italian people, but it took a different kind of leader to put a unified Italy on the map of Europe.

C. Cavour Puts Italy on the Map

Different Ideas Count Camillo Benso di Cavour (kah MEEL loh BAYN soh dee kah VOOR) also wanted the unification of Italy, but his ideas differed from those of Mazzini. Indeed, the two men disliked and distrusted each other. Mazzini was an exile who spent years planning unsuccessful revolutions. Cavour was an aristocrat, a member of the noble class, who made a fortune managing his family's estates. Mazzini dreamed of establishing an ideal democratic republic. Cavour thought a limited monarchy, like that of Great Britain, would be much more practical. Mazzini insisted that it would take a revolution to free Italy. Cavour believed that far more could be done through skillful politics.

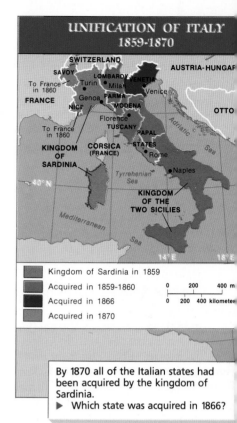

UNIFICATION OF ITALY 1859-1870

SWITZERLAND
SAVOY
To France in 1860
FRANCE
Turin Milan
Genoa PARMA
NICE MODENA
Florence
To France in 1860 TUSCANY
KINGDOM OF SARDINIA
CORSICA (FRANCE)
Tyrrhenian Sea
KINGDOM OF THE TWO SICILIES
Mediterranean Sea
AUSTRIA-HUNGARY
LOMBARDY VENETIA
Venice
PAPAL STATES
Rome
Naples
Adriatic Sea
OTTO

- Kingdom of Sardinia in 1859
- Acquired in 1859-1860
- Acquired in 1866
- Acquired in 1870

0 200 400 m
0 200 400 kilometers

By 1870 all of the Italian states had been acquired by the kingdom of Sardinia.
▶ Which state was acquired in 1866?

United Italy In 1852, Count di Cavour became the **prime minister**, or chief official, of Sardinia. He wanted to combine Italy with Sardinia. Find the kingdom of Sardinia on the map above. Through wars and politics, Cavour enlarged the kingdom. One after another the Italian states united with Sardinia. Because of Cavour and Mazzini, by 1861 the king of Sardinia was declared king of Italy. The new kingdom did not yet include Venice or Rome, but they would be added within nine years. Mazzini had dreamed of a united Italy; Cavour's skill put it on the map.

Writing to Learn

Writing a Letter Have students imagine that they are living in Germany in 1848, before their country has become unified.

● Ask students to write a letter to either Carl Schurz or Otto von Bismarck.

● Have students express their views about unification and tell what they like and what they do not like about Schurz's or Bismarck's approach to unification.

Carl Schurz dreamed of a free and united Germany.
▶ Why was Schurz unhappy with life in Germany?

D. A Revolution Fails in Germany

A Student's Ideas Italy was not the only country that struggled to become united. One morning in February 1848, a young German student, Carl Schurz (shurts), sat writing in his room. Schurz, a student at the university at Bonn, was writing a play about a German hero of earlier times. He hoped that his play would make the Germans proud of their history. Perhaps if they were proud of being Germans, their country could be united.

At the time Schurz wrote, Germany was even more divided than Italy into a number of independent states ruled by kings and nobles. Prussia was by far the largest state, but Schurz did not want a united Germany to be like Prussia. The kings of Prussia had ruled their kingdom as if it were an army. People were supposed to obey orders. Anyone who talked about freedom or democracy was viewed with suspicion. The government controlled what the newspapers printed. There were spies in the schools to report teachers or students who spoke against the ideas of the authorities.

Students like Schurz wanted Germany to be free as well as united. They dreamed of a republic in which the Germans could think and speak freely and elect their own government.

France's Example Schurz's thoughts that February morning were suddenly interrupted when a friend burst into the room. "Don't you know what has happened? The French have established a new republic!" In 1848 the Second Republic in France had been formed.

The ideas of the French quickly spread in Germany in 1848 as they had already spread in Italy. Some people said the Germans should follow the French example. The Germans should overthrow the rulers of the separate states and form a German republic.

The Granger Collection

Germans stormed the arsenal at Berlin in 1848. They wanted democracy and unification.
▶ How are they breaking the door?

Lesson *1* Review

Answers to Think and Write
A. Italy was divided into seven separate states.

B. To further his dreams for Italy, Mazzini wrote newspaper articles, joined a revolutionary organization, formed a group in France called Young Italy, and started a school for poor Italian boys in England.

C. Cavour united the Italian states into one kingdom.

D. Schurz's dream for Germany, like Mazzini's dream for Italy, was to form an ideal democratic republic.

E. Bismarck united other German states with Prussia to form a united Germany.

Answer to Skills Check
Sardinia and Sicily are part of Italy. Corsica is part of France.

Focus Your Reading
Ask the lesson focus question found at the beginning of the lesson: **How did unification occur in Italy and in Germany?** (Although revolutionaries in each country dreamed of creating democratic republics, both countries were finally united through wars and skillful politics by the prime ministers of powerful kingdoms.)

Additional Practice
You may wish to assign the ancillary materials listed below.

Understanding the Lesson p. 58
Workbook pp. 62-63

226

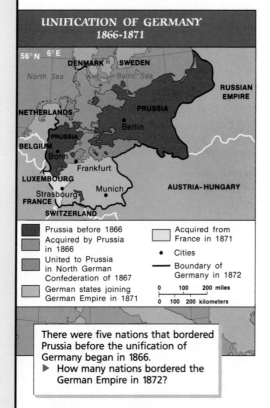

UNIFICATION OF GERMANY
1866-1871

56°N 6°E

DENMARK SWEDEN
North Sea Baltic Sea
NETHERLANDS
PRUSSIA
Berlin
RUSSIAN EMPIRE
BELGIUM PRUSSIA
Bonn
Frankfurt
LUXEMBOURG
Munich
Strasbourg AUSTRIA-HUNGARY
FRANCE
SWITZERLAND

- Prussia before 1866
- Acquired by Prussia in 1866
- United to Prussia in North German Confederation of 1867
- German states joining German Empire in 1871
- Acquired from France in 1871
- Cities
- Boundary of Germany in 1872

0   100   200 miles
0   100   200 kilometers

There were five nations that bordered Prussia before the unification of Germany began in 1866.
▶ How many nations bordered the German Empire in 1872?

broken out in Berlin, the capital of Prussia. The situation grew so serious that the Prussian king agreed to give the people a voice in the government. Other German rulers followed the Prussian king's example. However, in the months that followed, the rulers did little to carry out their promises.

E. Bismarck Puts Germany on the Map

Otto von Bismarck became chancellor to the Prussian king in 1862. A chancellor has duties similar to those of a prime minister. Bismarck was an aristocrat who had little regard for democratic republics—at least for Germany. He scoffed at governments conducted "by speeches and majority votes." Power, Bismarck declared, depended on "blood and iron," that is, on military strength. Yet, Bismarck did not oppose all changes in Germany—as long as Prussia controlled the changes.

Like Cavour in Italy, Bismarck used wars and skillful politics to unite the other German states with Prussia. Bismarck wanted a unified Germany under Prussian control to be the most powerful European nation. In 1871 the king of Prussia became emperor of a united Germany.

A few days later the news reached the city of Bonn—an uprising had taken place in other parts of Germany. Fighting had

---

LESSON *1* REVIEW

THINK AND WRITE
A. What was the political situation in Italy prior to 1821? (Recall)
B. What did Mazzini do to further his dreams for Italy? (Infer) (Recall)
C. What was Cavour's accomplishment?
D. How was Carl Schurz's dream for Germany like Mazzini's dream for Italy? (Analyze)

E. What was Bismarck's accomplishment?

SKILLS CHECK

MAP SKILL
Locate the islands of Sardinia, Sicily, and Corsica on a map of present-day Europe in the Atlas. Which two are part of Italy?

226

UNDERSTANDING THE LESSON

NAME
UNDERSTANDING THE LESSON
CHAPTER
8

Recalling Facts
LESSON 1 CONTENT MASTER

* Place a check mark in the box next to the correct answer for each item.

1. In 1821, the name *Italy* referred to a
   □ a. kingdom.   □ c. peninsula.
   □ b. city.   □ d. state.

2. Giuseppe Mazzini believed that Italy could be united only by
   □ a. a revolution.   □ c. the royal government.
   □ b. an outside power.   □ d. a vote of the people.

3. Mazzini wanted Italy to become
   □ a. a dictatorship.   □ c. an ideal democratic republic.
   □ b. a monarchy.   □ d. a Communist state.

4. Camillo di Cavour, an Italian aristocrat, thought it would be more practical for Italy to become a
   □ a. dictatorship.   □ c. republic.
   □ b. limited monarchy.   □ d. socialist state.

5. By 1861, the king of Sardinia was declared king of
   □ a. Great Britain.   □ c. Venice.
   □ b. Rome.   □ d. Italy.

6. In 1848, Germany was made up of
   □ a. one state.   □ c. one large and one small state.
   □ b. many independent states. □ d. Prussia.

7. The uprisings of 1848 caused the Prussian king and other German rulers to
   □ a. wipe out the revolutionaries.   □ c. leave their countries.
   □ b. give the people a voice in   □ d. build up their armies.
      government.

8. The man who combined Prussia and the other German states into a united Germany was
   □ a. Carl Schurz.   □ c. Giuseppe Mazzini.
   □ b. Camillo di Cavour. □ d. Otto von Bismarck.

Think and Write: Why do you suppose that Germany and Italy did not have more democratic governments after they were united? Write a paragraph discussing your answer. You may use the back of this sheet. Answers should reflect independent thinking; suggestions appear in the Answer Key.

58
Use with textbook pages 223-226.

◀ Review Master Booklet, p. 58

The Germans thought it was wrong to blame them for a war into which countries had been drawn by their alliances. Disputes about the payments for damages continued years after the war ended.

Terms of the Treaties The peace treaties of 1919 changed the map of Europe. You can see these changes by comparing the map below with the map on page 228. Austria and Hungary were made into separate countries. Serbia was combined with large parts of the old Austro-Hungarian Empire, including Bosnia, to form Yugoslavia. Czechoslovakia was also created from lands of the Austro-Hungarian Empire. Part of the empire also went to Poland, which received territory from Germany and Russia as well.

The peace treaties of World War I created a new international organization called the **League of Nations**. Its purpose was to provide a peaceful way to settle disputes and to prevent future wars.

D. A Dictator Takes Power in Italy

Problems in Italy Italy was on the winning side in World War I, but the Italians faced difficulties in 1919. Many returning soldiers could not find jobs. Prices kept rising, so money became worthless. The government was deeply in debt but

EUROPE AFTER WORLD WAR I

New countries
Cities

0   200   miles
0   200   kilometers

World War I ended in November 1918. The peace treaty that was signed greatly changed Europe.
► How many new countries were established in Europe after the war?

Writing to Learn

Writing a Journal Have students imagine that they are Italians living in Rome in 1922.

● Ask students to write a journal entry describing their impressions of the "march on Rome" staged by the Black Shirts.

Optional Activities

In 1914, a local quarrel between Austria and Serbia turned into a world war. Other nations who had alliances with these two countries were drawn into their conflict. Many Germans felt that the peace treaties of 1919 were unfair, since Germany was drawn into the war by its alliance with Austria. Below are three activities to help students better understand how alliances were involved in World War I.

◆ **EASY** Have students make a chart to show the alliances between nations in 1914.

Ask students to make columns with the following headings: *Austria*, *Serbia*, *Germany*, *Russia*, and *France*.

Tell students to fill in the alliance(s) that each country had in 1914.

◀▶ **AVERAGE** Have students write a paragraph describing why they think it was fair or unfair to punish Germany for a war that it was brought into because of its alliance with Austria.

◀❙▶ **CHALLENGING** Have students imagine that the United States is being dragged into a war — not because of national interests, but because of a mutual-protection alliance.

Ask students to write a paragraph describing how this would make them feel.

Read and Think

Sections D and E

Tell students that the conditions of peace that were established after World War I actually set the stage for another war. Help them understand how a treaty planted the seeds of war by asking these questions:

1. **What ideas do Fascists support?**
   (A political system supporting a single party with a single ruler and total governmental control of all political, economic, cultural, and religious activities *p. 232*)

2. **Who was Benito Mussolini?**
   (An ambitious politician who made himself dictator of Italy *p. 232*)

3. **Who were the Black Shirts, and what did they do in 1922?**
   (Private military squads organized by Mussolini; they staged a "march on Rome" in 1922 *p. 232*)

4. **How did most Germans feel about the peace treaty that ended World War I?**
   (Most believed that the treaty was unfair, since it forced them to give up German territory and pay for the losses of the war. *p. 232*)

5. **What promises did Adolf Hitler make to the German people?**
   (That the Nazi party would do away with the peace treaties and make Germany rich and powerful again *p. 233*)

Thinking Critically How, do you think, did the Fascists take advantage of the problems caused by the post war depression? (Synthesize)
(Answers may include that the post war depression made the governments who were in power unstable, which helped the Fascist effort, and the people who could not find work during the depression were more likely to believe the answers that the Fascists offered. *pp. 231-232*)

232

---

seemed unable to collect taxes. Many people no longer trusted their government.

An ambitious politician, a man named Benito Mussolini, took advantage of these troubled times. In 1919, Mussolini formed the first political group to be called the **Fascists**. Fascists believe in a political system that supports a single party and a single ruler, and involves total government control of political, economic, cultural, and religious activities. Mussolini organized Fascists into private military squads, called Black Shirts because of the color of their uniforms.

The New Leader Mussolini declared that Italy needed a strong leader. He spoke

> The front page of this Italian newspaper shows Hitler and Mussolini together.
> ▶ How were these men alike?

LA TRIBUNA ILLUSTRATA

LA STORICA VISITA DEL DUCE AL FÜHRER
I due Condottieri acclamati dal grande popolo tedesco

232

---

much about the need for action. Mussolini convinced a large number of people that he was the strong leader who could save Italy from disorder. Thousands of Black Shirts staged a "march on Rome" in 1922. The Italian king was so alarmed that he offered to make Mussolini the prime minister. However, Mussolini went on to make himself dictator, even though Italy still had a king. The Fascists called Mussolini "Il Duce" (il DOO che), which simply means "the leader."

E. Adolf Hitler and the Nazis Take Power in Germany

A German Republic After their defeat in 1918, the Germans set up a republic with leaders elected by the people. The new government had to sign the peace treaty with the victorious Allies. Most Germans honestly believed that the peace treaty was unfair because it forced them to give up German territory and pay for the losses of the war.

Some Germans, including a man named Adolf Hitler, opposed the republic from the start. Hitler was born in 1889 in Austria. At 16, he quit high school. In 1907, Hitler went to Vienna to become an art student, but he twice failed the entrance examination to the Academy of Fine Arts in Vienna. He stayed in Vienna and took odd jobs until 1914, when he volunteered in the German army and fought in World War I.

The Nazis Like many German-speaking Austrians, Hitler considered himself German. After World War I he joined a nationalist group. Hitler became the leader of this group; its members were known as *Nazis* (NAHT seez).

In 1923, Hitler and the Nazi party attempted unsuccessfully to overthrow the

---

Adolf Hitler was a charismatic leader who successfully used public rallies to promote Nazism and to gain the support of the German people. By 1933 he controlled the government of Germany.

▶ In what ways did Hitler try to appeal to the German people?

German government. Hitler was sent to prison for nine months. In prison he wrote a book titled *Mein Kampf* (myn kahmpf), which means "my battle." In this book he set forth his views about future German conquests. There were not many people outside Germany who knew about Adolf Hitler in 1924.

Hitler developed a speaking style that was truly impressive. He was an exciting speaker who talked for hours in taverns and at political meetings. He told all who listened that the German army had not lost the war. Traitors at home had betrayed the fighting men at the front. Hitler repeated over and over that Germany had lost the war because of a "stab in the back."

Hitler Gains Support Hitler had very few followers until the beginning of the world depression in 1929. A depression is a time when business is bad and many people are out of work. Hitler shrewdly took advantage of the bad times. He said over and over that Germany's troubles were caused by the unfair peace treaties. He promised that the Nazis would do away with the treaties and make Germany once again rich and powerful.

The Nazis and other foes of the republic created much disorder within Germany. Some Germans decided that the Nazis could bring order if they were given power. In January 1933, Hitler headed the government of Germany.

233

VISUAL THINKING SKILL

Interpreting a Visual

■ Ask students to look at the photograph on p. 233 to answer the following question: **How can you tell that Hitler was an effective speaker?**
(He has the undivided attention of a huge crowd of people at a rally.)

Read and Think
Section F

Ask students the following questions to start a class discussion about how Adolf Hitler and the Nazi party ruled Germany in the 1930s:

1. **How did Hitler justify Nazi attacks on the Jews?**
(He blamed the Jews for the defeat of Germany in World War I and for the country's other difficulties and said that Jews could not be true Germans. *p. 234*)

Thinking Critically **If you were an 11-year-old Jewish boy or girl living in Germany in 1938, how, do you think, would you feel about Hitler and the Nazis?** (Evaluate)
(Answers may include feelings such as fear, anger, sorrow, and loss. *p. 234*)

─ **Answers to Caption Questions** ─

p. 232 ▶ They were both strong political leaders who formed their own political groups; both went on to become dictators.
p. 233 ▶ Hitler appealed to the German people by making them believe that the Nazis could make Germany rich and powerful again.

Writing to Learn

Writing a Diary Have students write an entry in their diary from the perspective of a Jewish boy or girl living in Germany while Hitler and the Nazis were in power. Ask students to imagine and write about one of the following situations:

● Their father can no longer be a doctor.

● Their older brother or sister cannot go to college.

● Their family's store has just been vandalized.

Reteaching Main Objective

★ *List the causes of World War I.*

● Have each student go through the lesson and make a time line of the events leading to World War I.

● After students have finished, make a time line on the chalkboard.

● Ask volunteers to take turns going up to the chalkboard to write one of the events that led to the war.

Optional Activities

233

3 CLOSING THE LESSON

Lesson 2 Review

Answers to Think and Write

A. The Serbs saw the assassination as a way of protesting Austrian rule.

B. As a result of the assassination of the archduke, World War I began.

C. The peace treaties broke up the Austro-Hungarian Empire, took land from Germany, and made the defeated countries pay damages to the countries that had suffered great losses in the war.

D. Mussolini convinced people that he was a strong leader who could save Italy from its many economic and social problems.

E. German resentment about the unfair terms of the peace treaty and the world depression in 1929 helped the Nazis gain power.

F. Hitler's Nazi party outlawed all other political parties, killed its opponents, took citizenship away from German Jews, and directed the organized persecution and murder of Jews.

Answer to Skills Check

Answers should indicate an understanding of how Benito Mussolini and Adolf Hitler each came to power and what each leader did once he was in power.

Focus Your Reading

Ask the lesson focus question found at the beginning of the lesson: **What brought on World War I, and what were the results of the war?**

(The war was brought on by the assassination of the Austrian archduke by Serbs, and the alliances that Austria-Hungary and Serbia had with other countries. The war resulted in a restructuring of Europe and the creation of the League of Nations.)

Additional Practice

You may wish to assign the ancillary materials listed below.

Understanding the Lesson p. 59
Workbook p. 61

F. Hitler Becomes Germany's Dictator

Hitler Controls Germany Hitler acted quickly against all who opposed him. The Nazis outlawed all other political parties, and so Germany became a one-party state. The Nazis did not hesitate to murder their opponents. Hitler even approved the murder of Nazi party members whom he thought might cause him trouble.

Attacks on Jews Hitler attacked one whole group of Germans, the Jews. He blamed them for Germany's defeat in World War I as well as for the country's other difficulties. Hitler insisted that Jews could not be true Germans, even though their families had lived in Germany for generations. The Nazis changed the laws so that Jews were no longer citizens; they were even forbidden to fly the German flag. Universities did not accept Jews. No longer could Jewish doctors and dentists practice their professions. Many Jews lost their businesses.

On a November night in 1938, gangs directed by the Nazis attacked and burned synagogues (SIHN uh gahgz), Jewish houses of worship, and vandalized thousands of Jewish stores. Nearly a hundred Jews were murdered, and thousands were thrown into prison. Unfortunately, this was only the beginning. Far more Jews were to be imprisoned and killed in the next few years.

> Hitler often spoke to the German people, promising them victory.
> ▶ Who, do you think, are the men in the foreground of the photo?

LESSON 2 REVIEW

THINK AND WRITE (Recall)

A. Why did the young Bosnian Serbs plan the death of the Austrian archduke?

B. What was the result of the assassination of the archduke? (Infer)

C. What did the peace treaties do to the Austro-Hungarian Empire and to Germany? (Recall) (Infer)

D. Why was Mussolini able to take power? (Infer)

E. What helped the Nazis rise to power? (Infer)

F. What did Hitler do after he became Germany's dictator? (Recall)

SKILLS CHECK

THINKING SKILL

Use the information you have learned in this lesson to make a chart comparing and contrasting two leaders of World War I, Benito Mussolini and Adolf Hitler.

234

World War II and What Followed

THINK ABOUT WHAT YOU KNOW

Have a discussion about something you have read, heard, or seen in movies or on television about World War II.

STUDY THE VOCABULARY

Blitzkrieg   Axis
genocide   United Nations
Holocaust

FOCUS YOUR READING

What were the main phases of World War II in Europe?

A. World War II Begins

At War with Germany People all over Britain watched the clock on Sunday morning, September 3, 1939. They saw the hands move slowly to 11 o'clock and then past. They waited, listening to their radios for an announcement. Finally, at 11:15 A.M. they heard the prime minister, Neville Chamberlain, tell them, "This country is at war with Germany."

The war began that day because Germany had refused to stop its invasion of Poland. The attack on Poland was the latest of Hitler's moves to make Germany the most powerful country in Europe.

Hitler's Power Grows Ever since becoming dictator in 1933, Hitler had brushed aside the peace treaties of 1919. The treaties had limited the size of Germany's armed forces. Hitler began building up the army as soon as he came to power. He knew that France, with its strong military power, could stop Germany from building up its own army. If the French had threatened to march, Germany

would have had to back down. But the French did not march, so Hitler continued to assemble his military forces.

Having succeeded, Hitler paid no attention to other parts of the treaties. He sent troops into the region between the Rhine River and the French border. This, too, was against the treaties, but again the French did not act.

Germany took over Austria in 1938 to create what Hitler called Greater Germany. Germany next took over Czechoslovakia. By the spring of 1939, it was clear that Hitler wanted to do more than set aside the peace treaties of 1919; he wanted Germany to control all of Europe.

The Granger Collection

The New York Times.

GERMAN ARMY ATTACKS POLAND;
CITIES BOMBED, PORT BLOCKADED;
DANZIG IS ACCEPTED INTO REICH

On September 1, 1939, Nazi troops invaded Poland.
▶ What event occurred as a result of this invasion?

Making Maps

- Ask students to make "before" and "after" maps that show the political boundaries of Europe before and after World War II.

- Tell students to draw their "before" maps first, then trace current, or "after," maps on tracing paper and lay them over the "before" maps to compare boundaries.

- Students may compare these maps with the maps that they made (in the previous lesson) of Europe before and after World War I. Ask the following question: **Which war had the biggest impact on boundaries? (WW I)**

Optional Activities

World War II and What Followed

Objectives

★ **1. List** the events that started World War II.

2. Describe the results of World War II.

3. Discuss the terror spread by the Nazis and the horror of the Holocaust.

4. Identify the following people and places: *Joseph Stalin, Anne Frank, Poland, West Germany, East Germany, the Soviet Union, Japan,* and *Hawaii.*

1 STARTING THE LESSON

Motivation Activity

■ Read aloud the excerpt from *The Diary of a Young Girl* on p. 240.

■ Ask students what this entry tells them about the war. Have them think of words that describe the war.

Think About What You Know

■ Assign the THINK ABOUT WHAT YOU KNOW activity on p. 235.

■ Allow students to discuss what they know about World War II. Be sure that they are referring to the right war and correct any erroneous information that they offer.

Study the Vocabulary

■ Have students look up the new vocabulary words for this lesson in the Glossary.

■ Write the word *genocide* on the chalkboard. Have students look up the meaning of the prefix *geno-* (race) and the suffix *-cide* (killing) in a dictionary.

■ Ask students if they can think of any other words that contain the suffix *-cide* and discuss what these words have in common. (Killing something)

┌─ **Answers to Caption Questions** ─
p. **234** ▶ Probably Nazis
p. **235** ▶ World War II

2 DEVELOPING THE LESSON

Read and Think

Sections A and B

When Germany refused to pull its troops out of Poland, Great Britain declared war; thus began World War II. Ask the following questions to help students understand these events:

1. **Name two ways that Hitler violated the treaties of 1919 before his troops invaded Austria.**
   (He built up the army and sent troops into the region between the French border and the Rhine River. *p. 235*)

2. **Why did Hitler invade Poland, knowing that Britain and France would defend Polish independence?**
   (He knew that neither Britain nor France could send troops quickly enough to Poland to protect it from invasion. *p. 236*)

3. **To what does the term *Blitzkrieg* refer?**
   (The "lightning war," or the German attack characterized by the use of fast-moving tanks and other motorized equipment *p. 236*)

4. **Describe what happened when German armies tried to conquer the Soviet Union.**
   (They advanced rapidly at first, but found it difficult during the winter months and were driven back by Soviet armies. *p. 238*)

Thinking Critically Why, do you think, did the rest of Europe sit back and let Hitler take over surrounding territories? (Hypothesize)
(Answers may include that they thought Hitler would stop once he had recaptured the territory that Germany lost in World War I. *pp. 235-236*)

The German air force launched a vicious attack on Great Britain.
▶ Was the German attack against Great Britain successful?

Germany Invades Poland It looked as if Poland would be Hitler's next victim. Britain and France now realized that Germany had to be stopped. Both countries declared that they would defend Polish independence. They tried to get the Soviet Union to join them. But instead the Soviet leader, Joseph Stalin, made an agreement with Hitler to divide Poland.

Hitler knew in 1939 that neither Britain nor France could send troops quickly enough to Poland to protect it from German invasion. On Friday, September 1, German troops crossed the Polish border. The British sent word on Saturday that unless the Germans agreed to stop their attack by 11 o'clock Sunday morning, Britain would declare war. The Germans did not reply, so on that September morning, World War II began.

B. German Armies Invade Europe

A Lightning War German armies rapidly overran Poland. The Germans called their attack a **Blitzkrieg** (blihts KREEG)—"lightning war." The troops had fast-moving tanks and other motorized equipment. They conquered Poland in less than three weeks.

The Blitzkrieg swept over Denmark, Norway, the Netherlands, Belgium, and France in the spring of 1940. In less than a year, Germany had defeated all its foes—except Great Britain.

Hitler considered an invasion of the British Isles. To win control over Britain, the Germans launched an air attack. The British air force battled wave after wave of German planes. If the British had lost the air battle, Hitler would have been able to send the Blitzkrieg across the English Channel. But the British air force did not lose, so Hitler gave up the idea of invading Britain at that time.

Optional Activities

Curriculum Connection

Math Write on the chalkboard the dates and events listed below that occurred in the life of Adolf Hitler. Then, ask the questions that follow:

> 1889 Hitler is born in Braunau, Austria.
> 1914-1918 Hitler serves in the German army.
> 1924 Hitler writes *Mein Kampf* while in prison.
> 1933 Hitler becomes dictator of Germany.
> 1939 Hitler invades Poland; World War II begins.
> 1945 Hitler commits suicide in Berlin.

1. **How old was Hitler when he became an author?** (35)

2. **For how many years did Hitler rule Germany?** (12)

3. **What important event occurred when Hitler was half a century old?** (World War II began.)

Military Airplanes: THEN AND NOW

1 The German **Fokker DR-1 Triplane** was used during the last part of World War I.

2 The British **Spitfire Supermarine** fighter was used in World War II.

3 The American **B-52** bomber was used during the Vietnam War.

4 The American **F-14 Tomcat** fighter was developed in 1970.

Improvements in military airplanes have increased their speed and ability to maneuver. For example, after World War II, the increased technology of jet engines dramatically improved the speed of military airplanes.
▶ How did military airplanes change between World War I and World War II?

For Your Information

Adolf Hitler Hitler was one of the most destructive men in history. He was responsible for the Holocaust and, through the war he started, caused the deaths of 35 million people and the injury and displacement of millions more.

Judging by Hitler's ability to move people to action, he may also have been one of the greatest orators in history. Still, Hitler did not accomplish all he aimed to do. He wanted to expand Germany, eliminate the Jews, and wipe out communism. Instead, in the aftermath of the war, Germany was diminished, Israel was established, and communism's influence increased.

Optional Activities

237

Meeting Individual Needs

Concept:
The Horrors of Nazism

To better understand the horror of World War II and the Holocaust, it is important to understand what Hitler did to the Jews and to the European population in general. The activities below will help students better comprehend these events.

◆ **EASY** Have students work in pairs to make a list of all the crimes committed by Hitler.

Ask one student to skim Lesson 2 and one student to skim Lesson 3 to put together the list.

◀▶ **AVERAGE** Have students work in pairs to list the horrible crimes committed by Hitler.

Ask each student to select two crimes from their list and write a paragraph explaining why we consider these actions to be criminal.

◀▮▶ **CHALLENGING** Ask students who need a challenge to write an essay in which they argue whether or not a leader like Hitler could ever come to power again.

Ask students to include at least three facts from this lesson to support their position.

Attacking the Soviets Although Germany and the Soviet Union had divided Poland, neither nation's government trusted the other. So Hitler went on to invade the Soviet Union in 1941. At first the Germans advanced rapidly. They got within 20 miles (32 km) of Moscow, the Soviet capital. But the Soviets did not surrender. Hitler discovered, as Napoleon had, that it was easier to invade this large country than to defeat it. The Germans found it difficult to operate against the Soviets in the cold weather. An old Russian ruler once said that Russia had two great generals, General January and General February. These generals were on the Soviet side during the three winters of World War II. By 1944 the Soviet armies were driving the Germans from Soviet lands.

C. Nazis Spread Terror in Europe

More Attacks on Jews The Nazis persecuted the Jews in Germany before World War II. But the plight of the Jews became even worse when German armies extended Nazi power over other parts of Europe. You can read about a Jewish girl living in Nazi Europe in the literature special feature on page 240.

A large number of Jewish people fell into Nazi hands when the Germans occupied Poland and the western parts of the Soviet Union. Before attacking the Soviet Union, Hitler had told his generals that they must not only defeat the enemy but also destroy them. The Germans created special death squads to carry out this terrible task of destruction. Jews in particular were marked for death.

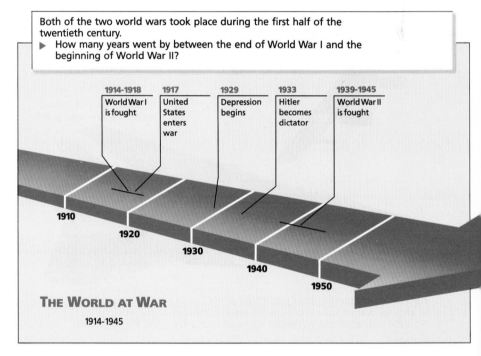

Both of the two world wars took place during the first half of the twentieth century.

▶ How many years went by between the end of World War I and the beginning of World War II?

1914–1918	1917	1929	1933	1939–1945
World War I is fought	United States enters war	Depression begins	Hitler becomes dictator	World War II is fought

1910
1920
1930
1940
1950

THE WORLD AT WAR
1914–1945

238

Writing to Learn

Writing a Journal Tell students that there were many concentration camps in Germany that were similar to Auschwitz in Poland. For example, Dachau was a concentration camp that was built (in 1933) 10 miles (16 km) from the city of Munich.

● Have students imagine that they are German citizens living near Dachau. As a prewriting activity, ask students what they would see on a typical day (Nazi soldiers bringing many people into the camp, no one but soldiers ever leaving the camp).

● Have students write an entry in their journal which describes their feelings.

Making a Chart

● Have students research the United States' military casualties from World War I and World War II.

● Ask students to make a chart comparing the United States' military casualties from these two world wars.

● Tell students to use the following headings: *Killed, Wounded, Prisoners or Missing,* and *Total Casualties.* (World War I: 116,516 killed; 204,002 wounded; 4,500 prisoners or missing; 325,018 total casualties. World War II: 405,399 killed; 670,846 wounded; 139,709 prisoners or missing; 1,215,954 total casualties.

238

Millions of Jews were tortured and killed in Nazi concentration camps.
► Why are photographs like this important today?

Read and Think
Section C

Use the questions below to help students understand how the Nazis terrorized Europe:

1. **What were the death camps?** (Places where the Nazis killed millions of people in gas chambers *p. 239*)

2. **About how many Jews were killed in the Holocaust?** (About 6 million *p. 239*)

   Thinking Critically Why, do you think, did Hitler tell his generals to not only defeat, but also destroy the enemy? (Hypothesize)
   (Answers may include that Hitler wanted to prevent the enemy from attempting to overthrow the Nazis at a later time. *p. 238*)

The Death Camps The Nazis adopted a policy of **genocide**, that is, the planned killing of a whole group of people because of their race, religion, or nationality. To carry out this policy, the Nazis established special death camps with gas chambers for mass killings. The camp at Auschwitz (OUSH vihts), Poland, had a gas chamber in which 2,000 people could be killed at the same time.

Jews from all parts of Europe were taken to Auschwitz and other death camps. Altogether about 6 million Jews perished in the mass killings known as the **Holocaust**. Millions of other non-Jewish men, women, and children also were destroyed in the death camps.

Many able-bodied captives were forced to work as slave laborers. One of the captives who survived said that the Germans took far better care of their machines than of the slave laborers. The Germans cleaned and oiled the machines regularly. But a slave laborer was treated "like a piece of sandpaper which, rubbed once or twice, becomes useless and is thrown away to be burned with the waste."

D. The United States Enters World War II

At the beginning of World War II, many Americans hoped that the United States could stay out of the struggle. But when Germany overran Europe and threatened Britain, the United States sent supplies to the British.

Meanwhile, Japan had joined Germany and Italy in an alliance called the

239

Researching a Historic Site

● Have students go to the library to find photographs and information about the Anne Frank House in Amsterdam. This house, where Anne Frank lived while writing her diary, is a museum today.

● Ask students to write a brief description of what it would have been like to be Anne Frank, living in that house.

● Students should include at least one visual aid in their reports, such as a drawing of the museum itself or a drawing of an object in the museum.

Optional Activities

Use the information below to help students better understand the literature selection found on p. 240.

Selection Summary

The Diary of a Young Girl is the daily account of a young German Jewish girl's life while hiding from the Nazis. Anne Frank was born in Frankfurt, Germany. She and her family escaped the Nazi persecution of the Jews by moving to the Netherlands, where, in 1942, they hid in an attic in an Amsterdam office building. It was during this time that Anne described in her diary her experiences and the horrors of the Holocaust.

Guided Reading

1. **Who was Anne Frank?**
   (A German Jewish girl who fled to the Netherlands with her family to escape Nazi persecution in Germany)

2. **Why, do you think, did Anne's father have her diary published after the war?**
   (Answers may include that he wanted to keep her memory alive or that he wanted people to understand the horrors of the persecution of the Jews.)

Literature-Social Studies Connection

1. **How is *The Diary of a Young Girl* a historical account?**
   (Answers may include that it tells what was happening in the world at that time by describing the Holocaust's effects on people's lives.)

LITERATURE SELECTION

FROM: **The Diary of a Young Girl**

By: Anne Frank
Setting: Amsterdam

A young girl, Anne Frank, and her family had moved to the Netherlands in 1933 to escape the Nazis in Germany. However, in 1942 the spread of Nazi terror throughout Europe forced Anne and her family to go into hiding in Amsterdam, the capital of the Netherlands.

It was during that time in hiding that Anne described in her diary, which she called Kitty, what daily life was like for her family and other Jews. The following passage is an excerpt from her diary, which was published as a book, *The Diary of a Young Girl.*

Wednesday,
13 January, 1943

𝘿*ear Kitty,*
Everything has upset me again this morning, so I wasn't able to finish a single thing properly.

It is terrible outside. Day and night more of those poor people are being dragged off, with nothing but a rucksack [knapsack] and a little money. On the way they are deprived even of these possessions. Families are torn apart, the men, women, and children all being separated. Children coming home from school find that their parents have disappeared. Women return from shopping to find their homes shut up and their families gone.

The Dutch people are anxious too, their sons are being sent to Germany. Everyone is afraid.

And every night hundreds of planes fly over Holland [the Netherlands] and go to German towns, where the earth is so plowed up by their bombs, and every hour hundreds and thousands of people are killed in Russia and Africa. No one is able to keep out of it, the whole globe is waging war and although it is going better for the Allies, the end is not yet in sight.

. . . There is nothing we can do but wait as calmly as we can till the misery comes to an end. Jews and Christians wait, the whole earth waits; and there are many who wait for death.

Yours, Anne

Anne and her family remained in hiding until August 4, 1944, when their hiding place was discovered. Anne and the other occupants of the hiding place were arrested and sent to death camps. Anne's diary was published in 1947, two years after her death.

Curriculum Connection

Literature Have students read *The Diary of a Young Girl* by Anne Frank (New York: Doubleday, 1967, ISBN 0-385-04019-9) in its entirety and write a brief character analysis of Anne Frank.

Skillbuilder Review

Appreciating Literature On pp. 150-151, students completed a Language Arts Skillbuilder activity on appreciating literature.

● Have students review this skill by using the *pretend* strategy to describe Anne Frank.

● Discuss if, and how, this reading strategy helped them better understand Anne Frank.

Optional Activities

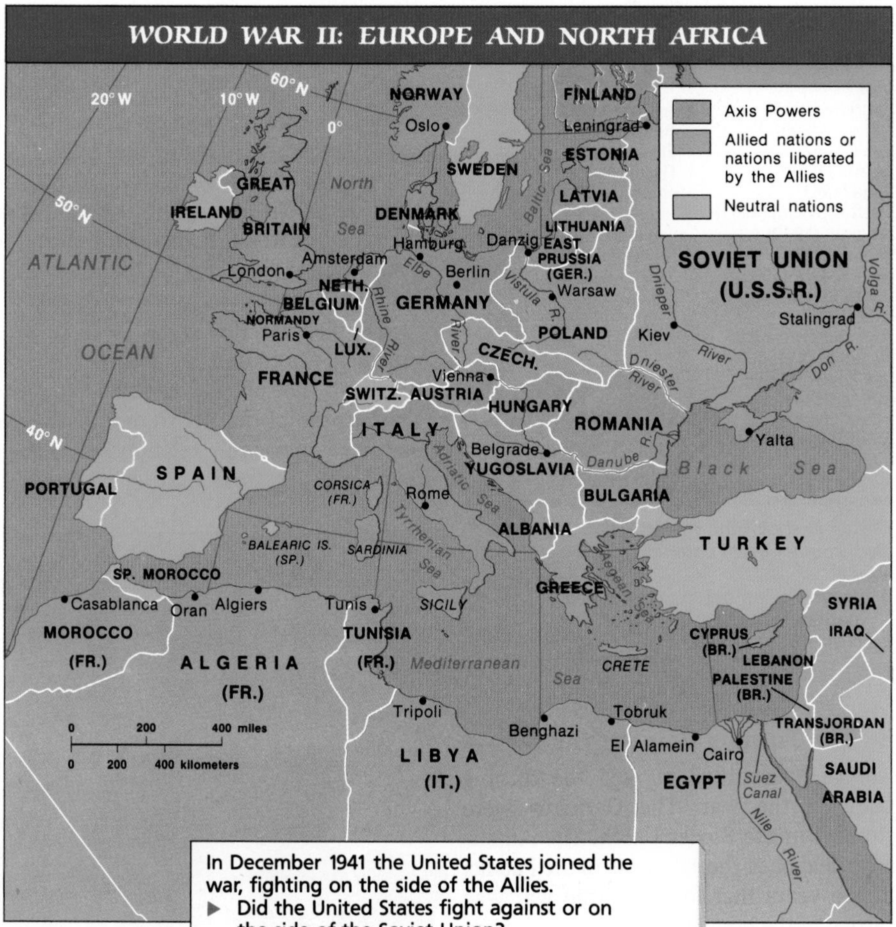

WORLD WAR II: EUROPE AND NORTH AFRICA

▨	Axis Powers
▨	Allied nations or nations liberated by the Allies
▨	Neutral nations

Map labels: 20°W, 10°W, 0°, 60°N, NORWAY, Oslo, FINLAND, Leningrad, ESTONIA, SWEDEN, LATVIA, North Sea, Baltic Sea, 50°N, GREAT IRELAND BRITAIN, DENMARK, Hamburg, Danzig, LITHUANIA, EAST PRUSSIA (GER.), SOVIET UNION (U.S.S.R.), London, Amsterdam, Elbe, Berlin, Warsaw, Volga R., ATLANTIC OCEAN, NETH. BELGIUM, GERMANY, POLAND, Kiev, Dnieper River, Stalingrad, NORMANDY, Paris, LUX., Rhine River, CZECH., Dniester River, Don R., FRANCE, Vienna, SWITZ. AUSTRIA, HUNGARY, ROMANIA, Yalta, 40°N, ITALY, Belgrade, YUGOSLAVIA, Danube, Black Sea, SPAIN, CORSICA (FR.), Rome, BULGARIA, Adriatic Sea, PORTUGAL, ALBANIA, TURKEY, BALEARIC IS. (SP.), SARDINIA, Tyrrhenian Sea, GREECE, SYRIA, SP. MOROCCO, Casablanca, Oran, Algiers, Tunis, SICILY, IRAQ, CYPRUS (BR.), LEBANON, MOROCCO (FR.), TUNISIA (FR.), Mediterranean Sea, CRETE, PALESTINE (BR.), ALGERIA (FR.), Tripoli, Tobruk, TRANSJORDAN (BR.), Benghazi, El Alamein, Cairo, SAUDI ARABIA, LIBYA (IT.), EGYPT, Suez Canal, Nile River

0   200   400 miles
0   200   400 kilometers

In December 1941 the United States joined the war, fighting on the side of the Allies.
▶ Did the United States fight against or on the side of the Soviet Union?

Axis countries. When Germany defeated France, Japan took over the French colonies in Southeast Asia. The United States opposed the Japanese actions and threatened to cut off Japan's oil supplies. The Japanese launched a surprise attack against the American fleet at Pearl Harbor in Hawaii and on American bases in the Philippine Islands on December 7, 1941.

The next day the United States declared war on Japan. By doing this the United States joined the war on the side of the countries known as the Allies: France, Great Britain, and the Soviet Union. Three days later, Japan's Axis partners, Germany and Italy, declared war on the United States. During the remaining years of World War II, American forces fought both in the Pacific and in Europe.

241

Using Eyewitness Accounts

● Have students use *The Readers' Guide to Periodical Literature* (New York: H.W. Wilson Co.) to locate eyewitness accounts of the attack on Pearl Harbor.

● Ask students to make a list of ten descriptive details (visual, auditory, or tactile) mentioned in these accounts.

● Then have students write a diary entry describing the attack.

● They should include the descriptive details they have gathered as a basis for their diary entries.

Optional Activities

Read and Think
Section D

Tell students that after the Japanese attack on Pearl Harbor, the United States joined the Allies. The infusion of fresh troops brought about a turning point in the war. Help students understand these events by asking the following questions:

1. **Why did the Japanese attack Hawaii?**
(The United States had threatened to cut off Japan's oil supplies after the Japanese takeover of the French colonies. *p. 241*)

2. **What were the major Axis countries and the major Allied countries?**
(Axis: Germany, Italy, and Japan; Allied: France, Great Britain, the Soviet Union, and the United States *pp. 239-241*)

Thinking Critically Do you think that the United States would have joined World War II if Japan had not attacked Pearl Harbor? (Hypothesize)
(Answers may include that yes, the United States would have joined the war because of the atrocities that were being committed against the Jews, or no, the United States would not have joined the war because it did not want to risk the lives of young Americans on foreign soil. *p. 241*)

GEOGRAPHY THEMES

Regions

■ Have students look at the map on p. 241 to help them answer the following question: **How does this map help you understand that World War II was also fought in Africa?**
(It shows that Morocco, Algeria, and Tunisia were French colonies and that Libya was an Italian colony, which helps explain why the war was also fought in Africa.)

Interpreting a Chart

■ Have students look at the chart on p. 242 to answer the following question: **How many nations entered World War II in 1939?**
(8 nations)

Read and Think
Sections E and F

Ask students to think about the final days of World War II and its aftermath. Use the following questions to help them better understand the effects of the war:

1. **Why did the Axis nations surrender?**
(The Allies invaded Italy and Germany, and atomic bombs were dropped on Japan. *p. 242*)

2. **What happened to Germany after the war?**
(It was divided and eventually became two nations, the German Federal Republic, or West Germany, and the German Democratic Republic, or East Germany. *p. 243*)

Thinking Critically Why, do you think, did the Allies divide Germany after the war? (Infer)
(Answers may include as punishment, as prizes to the victors, or to keep Germany from becoming powerful enough to invade other nations again. *p. 243*)

THE WARRING NATIONS IN WORLD WAR II

Major Allied Nations	The Axis Nations
Australia (1939)	Albania (1940)
Belgium (1940)	Bulgaria (1941)
Brazil (1942)	Finland (1941)
Canada (1939)	Germany (1939)
China (1941)	Hungary (1941)
Czechoslovakia (1941)	Italy (1940)
Denmark (1940)	Japan (1941)
France (1939)	Romania (1941)
Great Britain (1939)	Thailand (1942)
Greece (1940)	
India (1939)	
Luxembourg (1940)	
Netherlands (1940)	
New Zealand (1939)	
Norway (1940)	
Poland (1939)	
Soviet Union (1941)	
United States (1941)	
Yugoslavia (1941)	

This table shows the year in which each country listed entered World War II.
► In which year did the most Allied nations enter the war?

E. The Turning Point of the War

The year 1942 marked the turning point in the war. The Germans were stopped in the Soviet Union. The Americans held back the Japanese in the Pacific. In the years that followed, the war was carried to the homelands of the Axis countries in Europe. Italy and Germany were invaded. Hitler killed himself on April 30, 1945, and Germany surrendered eight days later. The Japanese continued the war for a short time. They surrendered after the United States dropped atomic bombs on two Japanese cities, Hiroshima and Nagasaki, on August 6 and 9, 1945.

World War II was more a *world* war than World War I. World War II was fought by forces from all over the world, and it was fought in Asia, Africa, and Europe.

242

F. The Effects of World War II

A New Organization Even before the end of World War II, the leaders of the victorious nations began to think about a peace settlement. Plans were made for a new international organization to be called the **United Nations** (UN). It was hoped that the UN would be more successful in avoiding war than was the old League of Nations.

A plan for the United Nations was drawn up at a conference in San Francisco, California. The plan stated that it would be the purpose of the UN to promote peace and develop friendly relations among the nations of the world.

On D-Day, June 6, 1944, Allied troops invaded Normandy.
► How did the Allied troops arrive at Normandy?

For Your Information

The Nuremberg Trials From 1945 to 1946, in Nuremberg, Germany, the first international war-crimes trial was held. Representatives from the United States, Great Britain, France, and Russia conducted the trial. In later trials at Nuremberg, defendants included Nazi industrialists, diplomats, judges, and doctors who had conducted cruel and deadly medical experiments in the concentration camps.

It is significant that these trials were held in Nuremberg, since it was here that the Nuremberg Laws were passed by the Nazis. These laws deprived German Jews of civil rights and forbade intermarriage between Jews and Aryans.

242

Reteaching Main Objective

★ *List the events that started World War II.*
● Have students trace the outlines of Germany and the surrounding countries from the map of World War II on page 241.
● Then, have them review this lesson and list in chronological order the events that led to the British declaration of war.
● Ask students to write the number of each event in their list on the country in which the event occurred. For example, students should have "Germany builds up its army" as the first event in their list. They should then write the number "1" inside the outline of Germany on their map.

The United Nations is headquartered in New York City.
► Why was the United Nations established?

Occupied Countries World War II caused other political changes. After the war the Soviet Union occupied most of the countries of Eastern Europe including Bulgaria, Romania, and Hungary, which had surrendered, and Poland and Czechoslovakia, which the Soviets had freed from Nazi control. After Germany's surrender the Soviet Union also occupied eastern Germany. The rest of Germany was divided among the United States, Britain, and France.

In 1949 the United States and the countries of Britain and France formed the nation called the German Federal Republic, or West Germany. Eastern Germany remained under Soviet control and became the German Democratic Republic, or East Germany, in that same year.

World War II caused the role of Western Europe to change. The many losses and damages in Western Europe had weakened the countries there. World affairs then were put into the hands of two superpowers, the United States and the Soviet Union. Unfortunately, the United States and the Soviet Union had different postwar aims. The Soviet Union was interested in spreading its control throughout the world. The United States, on the other hand, was determined to stop the control of the Soviet Union.

The UN had 51 members in 1945 when it started. It now has more than three times that many members. The UN has lasted longer than the old League of Nations. The United Nations has played an important part in world affairs since World War II. But it has not prevented all wars.

LESSON 3 REVIEW

THINK AND WRITE

A. What events led to the start of World War II in 1939? (Analyze) (Recall)

B. What countries did Germany invade?

C. How did the Nazis spread terror in Europe? (Recall)

D. Why did the United States enter the war? (Recall)

E. Why was 1942 the turning point of the war? (Infer)

F. What were the effects of World War II? (Analyze)

SKILLS CHECK

WRITING SKILL

Pretend you had kept a diary during World War II. What might a page from it say?

243

Optional Activities

---

3 CLOSING THE LESSON

Lesson 3 Review

Answers to Think and Write

A. Hitler built up the German army, sent troops into the area between France and the Rhine River, took over Austria and Czechoslovakia, and invaded Poland.

B. Germany invaded Poland, Denmark, Norway, the Netherlands, Belgium, France, and the Soviet Union. (Students may also include Austria and Czechoslovakia from Lesson 1.)

C. The Nazis spread terror by enslaving and killing Jews and others.

D. The United States entered the war after Japan attacked Hawaii and American bases in the Philippines.

E. In 1942, Soviet armies stopped the German advance into the Soviet Union and the Americans kept the Japanese from gaining ground in the Pacific.

F. The effects of World War II were the formation of the United Nations, the division of Germany, the Soviet occupation of most of Eastern Europe, and the rise of the United States and the Soviet Union as dominant world powers.

Answer to Skills Check

Student answers should include information about World War II supported by the text.

Focus Your Reading

Ask the lesson focus question found at the beginning of the lesson: **What were the main phases of World War II in Europe?** (The main phases were Britain's declaration of war, the German occupation of most of Europe, the United States' entry into the war, turning back German troops in Russia, the Allied invasion of Germany and Italy, and the German surrender.)

Additional Practice

You may wish to assign the ancillary materials listed below.

Understanding the Lesson p. 60
Workbook p. 64

┌─ **Answers to Caption Questions** ─
p. 242 *l.* ►1939
p. 242 *r.* ► By boat
p. 243 ►To try to prevent more wars
└─

243

Using the Vocabulary

1.	d	6.	a
2.	j	7.	i
3.	h	8.	e
4.	c	9.	b
5.	g	10.	f

Remembering What You Read

1. Wrote newspaper articles, joined a revolutionary organization, formed a group in France called Young Italy, and started a school for poor Italian boys in England

2. Count Camillo di Cavour

3. For Prussia to control a unified Germany

4. Austria charged that Serbia had encouraged the assassination; soon both countries' alliances became involved.

5. Austria, Serbia, Germany, Russia, and France

6. The League of Nations

7. Mussolini in Italy and Hitler in Germany

8. Hitler wanted Germany to control Europe.

9. The Japanese attack on Hawaii and American bases in the Philippine Islands

10. Germany became two countries, the Soviet Union occupied most of Eastern Europe, and the United States and the Soviet Union dominated as world powers.

USING THE VOCABULARY

On a separate sheet of paper, write the letter of the term that best matches each numbered statement.

a. nationalism
b. unification
c. prime minister
d. alliance
e. armistice
f. Fascist
g. Blitzkrieg
h. genocide
i. Axis
j. United Nations

1. An agreement between nations to act together
2. An international organization formed after World War II
3. The planned killing of a whole group of people because of their race, religion, or nationality
4. A chief official
5. The Germans' "lightning war"
6. Loyalty and devotion to one's country
7. The German, Italian, and Japanese alliance during World War II
8. An agreement to stop fighting
9. The uniting of separate regions and cities into one nation
10. One who believes in a single party, a single ruler, and total governmental control of political, economic, cultural, and religious activities

REMEMBERING WHAT YOU READ

On a separate sheet of paper, answer the following questions in complete sentences.

1. What did Giuseppe Mazzini do to help work toward the unification of Italy?
2. Who was the aristocratic politician who became prime minister of Sardinia?
3. What was Otto von Bismarck's goal for Germany?
4. How did the assassination of Archduke Franz Ferdinand lead to World War I?
5. Which five countries were initially involved in World War I?
6. What international organization was created by the peace treaties after World War I?
7. What dictators came to power in Italy and Germany in the period between the two world wars?
8. Why did Adolf Hitler want Germany to invade other European countries?
9. What event led the United States to enter World War II?
10. What political changes resulted from World War II?

TYING LANGUAGE ARTS TO SOCIAL STUDIES

Pretend that you are either an Italian or a German journalist covering the national movement in your country. The unification has just been completed, and you are interviewing people at a festival celebrating the event. Write a paragraph that describes people's feelings about the unification, including what advantages there will be to living in a united country.

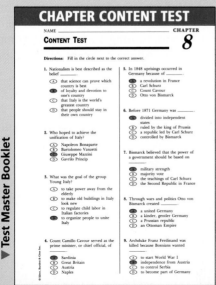

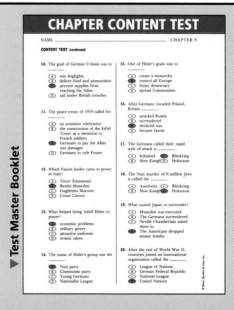

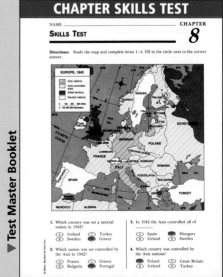

THINKING CRITICALLY

On a separate sheet of paper, answer the following questions in complete sentences.

1. Why, do you think, was Count di Cavour more successful than Giuseppe Mazzini in his efforts to unite Italy?
2. How, do you think, might World War I have been prevented?
3. What similarities are there in the ways that Benito Mussolini and Adolf Hitler came to power?
4. Do you think something like the Holocaust could happen in our world today? Explain why or why not.
5. What do you think an international organization like the United Nations does to try to prevent wars?

SUMMARIZING THE CHAPTER

On a separate sheet of paper, draw a graphic organizer like the one shown here. Copy the information from this graphic organizer to the one you have drawn. Under the main idea for each lesson, write three statements that support the main idea.

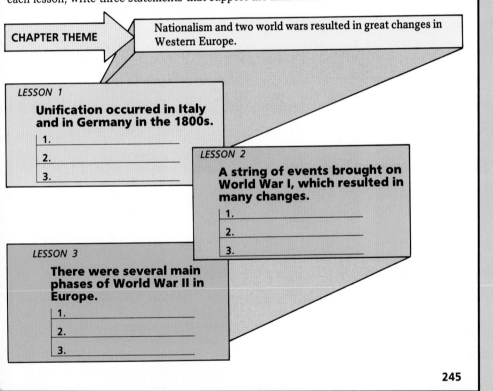

CHAPTER THEME → Nationalism and two world wars resulted in great changes in Western Europe.

LESSON 1
Unification occurred in Italy and in Germany in the 1800s.
1. _____
2. _____
3. _____

LESSON 2
A string of events brought on World War I, which resulted in many changes.
1. _____
2. _____
3. _____

LESSON 3
There were several main phases of World War II in Europe.
1. _____
2. _____
3. _____

245

Thinking Critically

1. Cavour was an aristocrat and a government official.
2. An international organization could have settled the dispute between Austria and Serbia.
3. Both took advantage of the world depression in their rise to power.
4. Answers may include no, since we have learned from history, or yes, because prejudice still exists.
5. It provides a setting where countries may work out their disputes.

Summarizing the Chapter

Lesson 1

1. In 1848, revolutions in Italy and Germany failed.
2. In 1861, Sardinia's king was named king of Italy.
3. In 1871, Prussia's king was named emperor of Germany.

Lesson 2

1. Serbians assassinated Archduke Franz Ferdinand.
2. Austria declared war on Serbia.
3. Austria asked Germany for support and Serbia asked Russia for support.

Lesson 3

1. Hitler invaded Poland, and Great Britain declared war.
2. Hitler occupied most of Europe.
3. The United States entered the war and turned back the Japanese in the Pacific, while the Soviets turned back Germany in Russia.

Western Europe Today

(pp. 246–274)

Chapter Theme: The physical features, resources, economies, and governments blend together to make the countries of Western Europe what they are today.

CHAPTER RESOURCES
Review Master Booklet
  Reviewing Chapter Vocabulary, p. 68
  Place Geography, p. 69
  Summarizing the Chapter, p. 70
Chapter 9 Test

LESSON **1** **Switzerland, Austria, and Germany**

(pp. 246–254)

Theme: Among the resources of Austria, Germany, and Switzerland are tourism, farmland, and forests.

CITIZENSHIP AND AMERICAN VALUES VIDEO LIBRARY: *Clean Up Your Act!*

SILVER WINGS WORKSHOP: *The Walls Came Tumbling Down*

LESSON RESOURCES
Workbook, p. 65
Review Master Booklet
  Understanding the Lesson, p. 64

LESSON **2** **British Isles and Nordic Lands**

(pp. 255–262)

Theme: The British Isles and Nordic Lands enjoy green landscapes and a democratic heritage.

SOCIAL STUDIES LIBRARY: *Money*

LESSON RESOURCES
Workbook, p. 66
Review Master Booklet
  Understanding the Lesson, p. 65

LESSON **3** **France and the Low Countries**

(pp. 263–267)

Theme: France has hills, rolling plains, and a high plateau, and the Low Countries have a high population density and fertile soil.

LESSON RESOURCES
Workbook, p. 67
Review Master Booklet
  Understanding the Lesson, p. 66

LESSON **4** **Countries of Southern Europe**

(pp. 268–272)

Theme: The people of Southern Europe make good use of their agricultural resources.

CITIZENSHIP AND AMERICAN VALUES VIDEO LIBRARY: *Clean Up Your Act!*

LESSON RESOURCES
Workbook, p. 68
Review Master Booklet
  Understanding the Lesson, p. 67

Review Masters

Review Study the terms in the box. Use your Glossary to find definitions of those you do not remember.

acid rain	export	maritime climate	pollution
bilingual	fjord	Mediterranean	principality
Commonwealth	geyser	climate	raw material
of Nations	landlocked	plateau	service industry

Practice Complete the paragraphs using terms from the box above. You may change the forms of the terms to fit the meaning.

The country of Norway is well known for its beautiful scenery. Many visitors to the area view the towering cliffs and beautiful forests by taking a cruise along one of the many (1) _____fjords_____. These tourists, the forests they visit, and the sea on which they cruise are all important to Norway's economy.

Norway's forests provide (2) __raw materials__ for its major industries. These industries include the production of wood pulp, paper, and manufactured goods. Norway also (3) __exports__ lumber to other countries in Europe and around the world.

Today, the forests of Norway, along with other forests in Europe, are threatened by air (4) __pollution__ from large cities and industrial areas. The fumes released into the air are carried by the wind into the forested areas. When these fumes fall back to earth as (5) __acid rain__, they damage and kill trees. The governments of European countries are working hard to find ways to save the trees, rivers, and even the buildings that are endangered by acid rain.

Write Choose ten terms from the box above. Use each term to write a sentence of your own. You may use the back of the sheet.

Sentences should show that students understand the meaning of the terms.

_____
_____
_____
_____
_____
_____
_____
_____

✳ Great Britain is divided into four regions: England, Wales, Scotland, and Northern Ireland and is officially called the United Kingdom of Great Britain and Northern Ireland. Ireland, too, had been a part of Great Britain but became independent in 1922. Listed below are cities within Great Britain and Ireland. Use the Gazetteer in your textbook to find the latitude and longitude of each place. Then locate and label each on the map.

	LAT. ⊖	LONG. ⊙
1. Edinburgh, Scotland	56°N	3°W
2. London, England	52°N	0°
3. Belfast, Northern Ireland	54°N	5°W
4. Dublin, Ireland	53°N	6°W
5. Cardiff, Wales	51°N	3°W

GREAT BRITAIN AND IRELAND
⊙ National capitals
● Other cities

✳ Complete this graphic organizer. Under each main idea, write three statements that support it.

CHAPTER THEME

Physical features, resources, economies, and governments blend together to make the countries of Western Europe what they are today.

LESSON 1
Many resources are found in Switzerland, Austria, and Germany.
1. Mountains and forests
2. Lakes and streams
3. Rivers, farms, and gardens

LESSON 3
France and the Low Countries have distinctive physical features.
1. Plateau and rugged mountains
2. Sand dunes
3. Low, flat land

LESSON 2
The British Isles and the Nordic countries have various geographic features.
1. Long coastline and mountains
2. Hills and pastures
3. Glaciers, forests, and fjords

LESSON 4
The people of the countries of southern Europe make good use of their resources.
1. Tourists
2. Exports
3. Ancient ruins

Workbook Pages

A DIVIDED COUNTRY

Gathering Information from a Map, Writing a Caption, Evaluating Information

✳ Study the questions under each map. Then write a caption for each map by answering the questions. Write the captions on the fill-in lines provided.

POSTWAR GERMANY
○ National capitals

POSTWAR BERLIN

1. According to the map, what were the two parts of Postwar Germany?

2. When was Germany divided in this way?

3. Where was the city of Berlin?

1. The two parts of Germany were East Germany and West Germany.   2. Germany was divided after World War II.   3. The city of Berlin was located in East Germany.

1. What were the two parts of Berlin?

2. Which four countries divided Berlin after World War II?

3. Which of the four countries controlled East Berlin?

1. The two parts of Berlin were West Berlin and East Berlin.   2. France, Great Britain, the Soviet Union, and the United States divided Berlin.   3. The Soviet Union controlled East Berlin.

Thinking Further: In 1990 East Germany and West Germany were united to form one country. Do you think this was a good idea?

Possible answers might include that it was a good idea because East Germany and West Germany had once been united and should be that way again. Another view might be that, because of Germany's role in World War II, the two Germanies should not have been united.

© Silver, Burdett & Ginn Inc.

Chapter 9, pages 247–254   65

MAKING A PICTOGRAPH

Using a Pictograph, Following Directions

✳ The chart below shows the populations of major cities in Scotland, Wales, and Northern Ireland. Complete the pictograph of the populations of these cities.
a. Write the names of the cities in the blanks next to the chart. Put the cities in the order of their populations, with the most populous city at the top.
b. Draw a stick figure of a person in the box in the key.
c. Draw the correct number of stick figures beside each city name to represent its population. Use part of a figure to represent numbers less than 100,000. The first one has been done for you.

Aberdeen, Scotland	215,000
Belfast, Northern Ireland	322,000
Cardiff, Wales	274,000
Edinburgh, Scotland	493,000
Glasgow, Scotland	733,000

POPULATION OF MAJOR CITIES

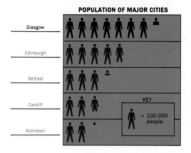

Glasgow

Edinburgh

Belfast

Cardiff

Aberdeen

KEY

= 100,000 people

Thinking Further: London, England, has a population of almost 7 million people. About how many times larger is London's population than the total population of the cities on the pictograph? Write your answer on a separate sheet.

Answers should state that London is about 3 1/2 times larger than the total of the cities on the chart.

66   Chapter 9, pages 253–260

© Silver, Burdett & Ginn Inc.

COMPARING COUNTRIES AND U.S. STATES

Comparing and Contrasting, Gathering and Evaluating Information

✳ Europe consists of several countries of varying sizes. The largest country in the world, Russia, is partially in Europe. Some European countries are the approximate size of some states in the United States. The following table lists areas of some European countries and of some states in our country. Use the information in the table to answer the questions below.

Selected European Countries	Area (sq. mi.)	Selected U.S. States	Area (sq. mi.)
Austria	32,375	California	158,706
Denmark	16,629	Connecticut	5,018
France	212,918	Florida	58,664
Germany	137,838	Georgia	58,910
Ireland	26,600	Indiana	36,185
Italy	116,313	Maine	33,265
Netherlands	14,140	Massachusetts	8,284
Norway	125,049	New Hampshire	9,279
Portugal	35,383	New York	49,108
Spain	194,881	Ohio	41,330
Switzerland	15,941	Rhode Island	1,212
United Kingdom	94,598	Utah	84,899

1. Which of the countries shown has the largest area? France

2. Which of the countries shown has the smallest area? Netherlands

3. Which country shown is about the size of Maine? Austria

4. Which country is about the size of Georgia and Florida combined? Italy

5. Which country is slightly smaller than Indiana? Portugal

6. The area of Ireland and Switzerland combined is about the same as the area of which state? Ohio

7. The area of California and Indiana combined is almost the same as the area of which country? Spain

Thinking Further: If you knew only the size of a country or U.S. state, could you tell much else about it?

Size alone does not tell you much about a country. For instance, Austria and Maine are about the same size but differ very much culturally, economically, and politically.

© Silver, Burdett & Ginn Inc.

Chapter 9, pages 263–267   67

EXPLORING LANGUAGE

Understanding Etymology, Using a Dictionary, Interpreting Information

✳ The English language consists of many words from Western European languages. Use a dictionary to find the meaning of each word in the column on the left. Write the word's meaning in the middle column. In the third column, write the name of the language from which the word came.
Suggested answers are provided.

Word	Meaning	Language from Which Word Came
1. banshee	spirit that wails	Irish
2. blouse	loose shirt reaching to the waist	French
3. buffalo	bison of North America	Italian
4. cozy	warm and comfortable	Scottish or Norwegian
5. dodo	large clumsy bird, now extinct	Portuguese
6. gull (bird)	water bird with long wings	Celtic
7. mesa	high plateau with steep sides	Spanish
8. penguin	short-legged sea bird	Welsh
9. picnic	meal in the open air	French
10. ranch	large farm where animals graze	Spanish
11. slim	slender; thin	Dutch
12. snorkel	breathing tube for swimmers	German

✳ Look in a dictionary to find a word that comes from Spanish. On the lines below identify the word and tell what it means.

Possibilities: cargo (freight); savanna (treeless plain); avocado (thick-skinned fruit); mesa (small plateau with steep sides).

Thinking Further: The English word *spaghetti* is taken from Italian. Does this fact tell you anything about where spaghetti probably was invented?

Students should figure out that Italians probably invented spaghetti, and that the English-speaking world learned about it from them.

68   Chapter 9, pages 247–272

© Silver, Burdett & Ginn Inc.

C9-C

Switzerland, Austria, and Germany

Objectives

★1. **List** the important industries of Switzerland, Austria, and Germany.

2. **Explain** why the rivers of Germany have become polluted.

3. **Describe** the governments and languages of Germany, Austria, and Switzerland.

4. **Identify** the following person and places: *William Tell, Switzerland, Austria, Germany,* and *Liechtenstein.*

1 STARTING THE LESSON

Motivation Activity

■ Ask students what words or descriptions come to mind when you say the names of the following countries: Germany, Austria, and Switzerland.

■ Put students' answers on the chalkboard.

■ Then, have students look at a wall map of Western Europe and ask them if any additional words come to mind.

Think About What You Know

■ Assign the THINK ABOUT WHAT YOU KNOW activity on p. 247.

■ Answers may include that people in industrialized countries are concerned about the long-term effects pollution will have on people's health and on the environment.

Study the Vocabulary

■ Have students look up in the Glossary the definition of each vocabulary word in this lesson.

■ Then have them use the words to construct word-search puzzles that can be exchanged and solved by other students.

CHAPTER **9**

WESTERN EUROPE TODAY

*L*anguage, customs, a architecture are as varie Western Europe as the landscape. Many old towns have grown into modern cities, but histo monuments and tourist attractions, such as the Eiffel Tower, have been preserved.

Optional Activities

Reenacting a Legend

● Have students role-play the legend of William Tell in two acts.

● In the first act, have students recreate the events of the legend up to the point where Tell is about to shoot an arrow at the apple on his son's head.

● In the second act, tell students to make up a different ending to the story.

● Have them continue role-playing with this new twist to the legend, acting out what they think might have happened next.

Switzerland, Austria, and Germany

THINK ABOUT WHAT YOU KNOW

Why is pollution a concern in many industrialized countries?

STUDY THE VOCABULARY

landlocked   raw material
plateau   principality
pollution

FOCUS YOUR READING

Describe the relationship between government, industry, and the environment in Switzerland, Austria, or Germany.

A. The Legend of William Tell

According to a legend, William Tell was a brave man who stood up for Swiss freedom during the Middle Ages. An old story relates that the emperor who ruled Austria and Switzerland once sent a cruel governor named Gessler to Altdorf, Switzerland. Gessler believed that the Swiss did not show him the proper respect, so he decided to teach them a lesson. The governor put his hat on a pole in the village and ordered each person passing by to bow to it. William Tell was too proud to bow to a hat, so he paid no attention.

When Gessler learned that Tell paid no attention to his order, he decided to make an example of him. He ordered Tell to shoot an apple off the head of Tell's own son. Gessler, no doubt, thought that the nervous father would kill his son, a dreadful punishment indeed! William Tell protested against the cruel order, but it did no good. So Tell picked up two arrows, placed one in his crossbow, and let it fly. His aim was perfect; the arrow split the apple in two. The disappointed Gessler asked Tell why he had picked up two arrows. The Swiss coolly replied that if he had hit his son, he would have sent the second arrow straight into Gessler's heart.

Angered by this bold reply, Gessler had Tell arrested. But the brave man soon escaped, seeking revenge on the cruel governor. Tell's opportunity for revenge came while a peasant woman pleaded with Gessler to release her imprisoned husband.

"Mercy, dear Governor!" she cried. "At last I can speak to you. . . ."

"What right have you to come to me so rudely, without asking for audience? Out of my way!" Desperately she seized his [horse's] reins. . . . "Let go of my reins or I will ride you down."

"Do so then!" She threw herself and her children on the ground before him. Gessler kicked his horse. The animal reared—and Gessler fell under its hoof, an arrow in his chest. A figure appeared on the rock above him and cried in a terrible voice: "You know the archer, Gessler! . . . You could not escape my arrow."

Gessler struggled to his feet. "William Tell . . . murderer!" he whispered harshly. "Catch him, men, that I can see him die before me." He clutched at the arrow to pull it out, but it had reached his heart. Blood came to his mouth and he fell back.

Most historians agree that the story of William Tell's shooting the apple is a legend. But it tells something important about the people who have kept the story alive. According to the legend, Tell's act led to a revolt that helped to free Switzerland. The statue of William Tell and his young son in Switzerland shows how much the Swiss have valued their freedom.

247

Read and Think

Section A

To summarize the legend of William Tell, ask the following questions:

1. **Who was William Tell?**
   (A brave man from Switzerland who stood up for Swiss freedom during the Middle Ages *p. 247*)

2. **According to the legend, why did Tell pick up two arrows when he was ordered to shoot an apple off his son's head?**
   (If he had hit his son, he was going to use the second arrow on Governor Gessler. *p. 247*)

   Thinking Critically Why, do you think, are legends such as that of William Tell important to a country? (Infer)
   (Answers may include that legends preserve the values of the people in a country. *p. 247*)

Curriculum Connection

Art Ask students to design book covers for the legend of William Tell.

- Have students review Section A to get ideas for their covers.
- Remind them to include the important elements of the story in their artwork.
- Display the book covers on a bulletin board or on the walls of the classroom.

Writing to Learn

Writing an Obituary Ask students to imagine that they are Swiss newspaper reporters of the Middle Ages.

- Have each student write an obituary for either Governor Gessler or William Tell.
- Remind them that obituaries usually contain short biographical sketches of the person's life, including the cause of death, and often contain comments from people who knew the person.
- You may wish to display the students' work around the classroom.

Optional Activities

Read and Think
Sections B and C

Use the questions below to help students summarize information about the resources and industries of Switzerland, Austria, and Germany.

1. **Why do many people visit Switzerland?**
   (Its mountains are beautiful and offer fine skiing. *p. 248*)

2. **What do Austria and Switzerland have in common?**
   (Both are small landlocked countries with mountains that attract large numbers of tourists. *pp. 248–250.*)

3. **How have the German people made use of their forests without destroying them?**
   (They replace mature trees with new growth. *p. 251*)

4. **What are some major industries in Switzerland, Austria, and Germany?**
   (All three countries tourism; Switzerland time-keeping devices, business machines, scientific instruments, banking; Germany industries that produce steel, ships, vehicles, machinery, chemicals. *pp. 248–251*)

Thinking Critically What kinds of jobs do you think most Swiss people have? (Infer) (They have jobs related to tourism, such as jobs in restaurants, hotels, and ski resorts. *p. 248*)

VISUAL THINKING SKILL

Interpreting a Photograph

■ Direct students' attention to the photograph of the Swiss Alps on p. 248 to help them answer this question: **What can you infer about the weather in the Swiss Alps?**
(It is cold and there is much precipitation in the form of snow.)

B. Tourism and Industry

Switzerland Though thousands of tourists have seen the William Tell statue, it is certainly not the main reason that they went to Switzerland. Switzerland, a small **landlocked** country is bordered by five countries. Landlocked means "having no seacoasts." Locate Switzerland on the map on the opposite page. What countries border on Switzerland?

More than half of Switzerland is covered with mountains. Most of Switzerland's 6.6 million people live on a **plateau** (pla TOH) that stretches across the middle of the country, between the mountains.

A plateau is sometimes called a tableland; it is a plain that is elevated above the surrounding land.

It is the mountains, however, that make tourism such an important industry in Switzerland. The Swiss Alps offer tourists some of the finest skiing and mountain scenery in the world. The Matterhorn is one of the most famous peaks in the Alps. It has an elevation of 14,690 feet (4,478 m). The peak, which is located on the border between Switzerland and Italy, is shown in the photograph at the bottom of this page.

Tourism is not the only important industry in Switzerland. The Swiss people

Switzerland is famous for its spectacular mountains, such as the Matterhorn (left), and for the skill and precision of its watchmakers (inset).
▶ What recreational activity are these tourists doing?

Optional Activities

Curriculum Connection

Geography Have students look at a wall map of the world or the world map in the Atlas to locate other landlocked countries.

● Ask students to make a list of these countries on the chalkboard.

● Have students discuss some of the problems that landlocked countries might face.

WESTERN EUROPE: POLITICAL

Cities less than 100,000
Kopavogur (Iceland)............ A-1
Luxembourg (Luxembourg)..... C-4
Reykjavik (Iceland)............. A-1
Segovia (Spain)................ C-3
Valletta (Malta)................ D-5

Cities 100,000 to 499,999
Bern (Switzerland)............. C-4
Bonn (Germany)............... B-4
Bordeaux (France)............. C-3
Cork (Ireland)................. B-3
Florence (Italy)................ C-5
Ghent (Belgium)............... B-4
Göteborg (Sweden)............ B-5
Helsinki (Finland)............. A-6
Nice (France)................. C-4
Nicosia (Cyprus)............... D-7
Oslo (Norway)................. B-5
Salonika (Greece)............. C-6
The Hague (Netherlands)...... B-4
Vienna (Austria)............... C-5
Zurich (Switzerland)........... C-4

Cities 500,000 to 999,999
Amsterdam (Netherlands)....... B-4
Athens (Greece)............... D-6
Dublin (Ireland)............... B-3
Lisbon (Portugal).............. D-3
Marseille (France)............. C-4
Rotterdam (Netherlands)....... B-4
Stockholm (Sweden)........... B-5

Cities 1,000,000 or more
Barcelona (Spain).............. C-4
Berlin (Germany)............... B-5
Birmingham (U.K.)............. B-3
Brussels (Belgium)............. B-4
Copenhagen (Denmark)........ B-5
Hamburg (Germany).......... B-5
London (U.K.)................. B-3
Madrid (Spain)................ C-3
Milan (Italy).................. C-4
Paris (France)................. C-4
Rome (Italy).................. C-5

Western Europe extends from about 80° north latitude to about 30° north latitude.
▶ Through which Western European countries does the Arctic Circle pass?

have developed industries that require great skill. They became famous for making watches and clocks. They still make fine time-keeping devices, but they also produce such products as business machines and scientific instruments.

Switzerland has become an international business center. People and companies from many other countries do business with Swiss banks. A number of international companies have headquarters in Switzerland.

249

Current Events
- Ask students to skim newspapers and magazines for articles about the countries covered in this lesson (Switzerland, Austria, and Germany).
- Tell students to cut out the articles they find and write a brief summary of the contents of each article.
- Then have them present their summaries orally to the class.
- Use the summaries as a springboard to a class discussion of current events.

Optional Activities

Munich, which was founded in 1158 by Duke Henry the Lion, is one of Germany's largest cities.
▶ What are some reasons that people like to visit cities?

Austria Austria is another small landlocked country located in Central Europe. There are about 7.6 million people living in Austria. Although most people live in cities and towns, they enjoy recreation in their country's many forests, lakes, and mountains. The mountain scenery in Austria draws large numbers of tourists from all over the world. There are more than 500 places to go skiing in Austria.

Germany Germany lies north of Switzerland and Austria. Germany has about twelve times more people and nearly nine times more land than does Switzerland. Unlike Switzerland and Austria, Germany is not landlocked; it has coasts on the North and Baltic seas.

Germany is one of the world's leading industrial countries. Its major products are steel, ships, vehicles, machinery, and chemicals. The country is one of the largest exporters in the world.

Tourism is important in Germany as well. Germans as well as foreigners visit cities such as Berlin, Munich, and Hamburg. The villages of the Black Forest, the castles overlooking the Rhine River, and the recreation areas of the Bavarian Alps are some other popular tourist destinations.

C. Natural Resources

Germany has many farms and gardens that supply a large part of the nation's food. Forests and woodlands cover large areas of the country. For many years the people of western Germany have been able to make use of the forests without destroying them. Trees are cut as they mature. The removal of mature trees allows space and sunlight for the growth of young trees and reduces the danger of forest fires. Unfortunately, **pollution** in the air from industries and automobiles has destroyed some of the forests, especially in eastern Germany. Pollution is the unclean condition of the earth's soil, air, and water.

The forested mountains of Austria provide industries with **raw materials.** Raw materials are natural materials that can be processed into finished products.

Some rivers are important waterways for shipping. The Rhine River is a waterway for Germany and its neighbors. Great efforts have been required to clean up rivers such as the Rhine, which have been polluted by industry.

D. Governments and Languages

Germany Divided As you have learned, after World War II the victorious Allies occupied Germany and divided it into four zones. In 1949 the United States, Britain, and France combined the three zones they occupied to form West Germany. The zone under Soviet control became East Germany. West Germany was more than twice

Hamburg is the most important industrial center in Germany.
▶ For what do you think these ships are used?

251

Read and Think
Section D

Use these questions to begin a class discussion about the fall of the Berlin Wall and the uniting of East Germany and West Germany.

1. **How did Germany come to be divided?**
(The victorious Allies occupied Germany at the end of World War II and divided it into four zones. *pp. 251–252*)

2. **What was the Berlin Wall?**
(It was a concrete wall with barbed wire that the East German government built to divide the city of Berlin. *p. 252*)

3. **How were East Germany and West Germany alike, and how were they different?**
(Both countries were industrialized, but West Germany had a higher standard of living as well as far more freedom. *pp. 252–253*)

4. **Why was the opening of the border between East Germany and West Germany an important event?**
(It allowed East Germans to visit West Germany. It led to the Communists' losing control of the East German government and to the unification of East Germany and West Germany. *p. 253*)

Thinking Critically How do you think you would have felt if you had been living in East Berlin in 1961 when construction on the Berlin Wall was begun? (Infer)
(Answers should reflect independent thinking but may include afraid, angry, sad, depressed, and helpless. *p. 252*)

Writing to Learn

Writing a Journal Have students write two journal entries from one of the following perspectives:

● (1.) An East Berliner who works in West Berlin and decides to stay there, just as construction of the Wall begins

● (2.) An East Berliner who is separated and then reunited with the rest of his or her family in West Berlin in November, 1989, when people were once again allowed to freely cross between East and West Berlin

● Journal entries should focus on how the wall influenced the lives of the people.

Optional Activities

as large as East Germany. In addition, West Germany had almost four times as many people as East Germany.

Berlin, the old German capital, lay within East Germany, but it, too, was divided. West Germany held one section of the city. East Berlin became the capital of East Germany. However, Bonn, located in West Germany on the Rhine, was chosen as the capital of West Germany.

On a Sunday morning in 1961, people in Berlin awakened to the sounds of workers putting up a tall barbed-wire fence. By the end of the day a barricade 26 miles (42 km) long divided the eastern and western sections of the city. Armed East German police stood along the fence to make sure that no one tried to cut the wire or sneak through it. A concrete wall was built later to reinforce the fence through Berlin.

The Communist government of East Germany was trying to stop the movement of millions of people leaving East Germany for West Germany, especially through Berlin. But in spite of the wall and its guards, some East Germans still managed to escape to the West. Others lost their lives in the attempt. Why did people keep trying to cross to the West, even after the wall was built? One answer is for freedom. Although East Germany's formal name was the German Democratic Republic, it was *not* democratic. The Communist party ruled the country and did not allow free elections. The government owned or controlled most industries and large businesses. People had to be careful about what they said or wrote because the government did not permit free expression. When an uprising broke out during the 1950s, it was put down with the help of Soviet troops, which still occupied the country.

In West Germany, people could vote and express their ideas freely. Farmers could own the land they worked. Businesses could be owned by private individuals and companies. Freedom to do business enabled the West Germans, with the help of the United States, to rebuild their country rapidly after World War II.

Both East and West Germany became important industrial countries, but West Germany had a far higher standard of living. You may remember that the standard of living is a measure of how well people live. The standard of living in a country depends on the availability of goods that make living more comfortable and pleasant. People in West Germany had more

For nearly 30 years, East Germans were imprisoned within their country.
▶ What barriers prohibited travel in and out of East Germany?

Cooperative Learning

Reenacting the Fall of the Berlin Wall Divide students into four groups (East Berliners, West Germans, East German Communist party officials, and Soviet officials) to dramatize the November 1989 fall of the Berlin Wall.

- Give students one class period to research roles and put together a play; then allow them another class period to act it out.

- In Act I, West Germany decides to open its embassy and refugees stream to Czechoslovakia.

- In Act II, East Germany opens its borders and the people celebrate.

automobiles, telephones, TV sets, and other goods. Many people, especially the young, [fl]ed East Germany for a better standard of [li]ving as well as for more freedom.

[G]ermany United Germany was divided [fo]r 28 years. But television and radio [b]roadcasts made the East Germans aware [o]f West Germany's higher standard of liv[in]g and of the freedoms that people [e]njoyed there. People in East Germany [g]rew increasingly discontented with con[d]itions in their own country. In the late [1]980s, increasing dissatisfaction led to [la]rge demonstrations and brought about [im]portant changes.

On November 9, 1989, the border [b]etween the two Germanies was opened.

Thousands of cheering people passed through the wall that had divided Berlin. The East German police, who had once shot at those trying to escape, only stood and watched the celebrating crowd. In places, the crowd knocked holes in the graffiti-covered wall that had kept families apart.

Other changes quickly followed. The Communists lost control of the government of East Germany. A free election was held in 1990. Later that year the two Germanies were united to form a single country. Berlin once again became the capital of Germany, the most populous country in Western Europe.

Unification has presented many challenges to the German government. In the

Germans rejoiced when the Berlin Wall opened in 1989. East Germans traveled freely to the West for the first time since the wall had been built.
▶ What did the opening of the Berlin Wall represent?

253

3 CLOSING THE LESSON

Lesson 1 Review

Answers to Think and Write

A. It suggests that the Swiss people value their freedom.

B. Switzerland's industries are tourism; the manufacture of time-keeping devices, business machines, and scientific instruments; and banking. Austria's main industry is tourism. Germany's industries produce steel, ships, vehicles, machinery, and chemicals.

C. Germany—rivers, good soil, forests; Austria—forests, mountains

D. Germany is a democracy; the people speak German. Austria is a democratic republic; most Austrians speak German. Switzerland has four official languages. Liechtenstein is a principality; the people speak German.

Answer to Skills Check

Germany: rivers, good soil, forests; democracy; automobiles, agriculture, and forest products; *Austria:* forests, mountains; democratic republic; tourism, forest products, and electric energy; *Switzerland:* mountains; democratic confederation; tourism, banking, manufacture of fine time-keeping devices, business machines, and scientific instruments.

Focus Your Reading

Ask the lesson focus question, found at the beginning of the lesson: **Describe the relationship between government, industry, and the environment in Switzerland, Austria, or Germany.** (The environment of much of Switzerland, Austria, and Germany has helped create tourism industries. Germany is highly industrialized. Its government is working to solve the resulting pollution problem, especially in what was East Germany.)

Additional Practice

You may wish to assign the ancillary materials listed below.

Understanding the Lessson p. 64
Workbook p. 65

east, businesses must be converted to private ownership, and the standard of living must be raised. Saving the environment is a priority of the German people. Cleaning up pollution, especially in the east, is a huge task for the German government.

Austria Before World War I, Austria was part of a large empire with a monarchy and with people of many different nationalities. Today, Austria is a democratic republic made up almost entirely of German-speaking Austrians.

Switzerland Switzerland has four official languages: German, French, Italian, and Romansch (roh MAHNSH). German is by far the most commonly spoken language. Only about 1 percent of the Swiss people speak Romansch, a language that comes from the Latin of the ancient Romans. Many Swiss also speak English.

Liechtenstein Tucked between Austria and Switzerland is the tiny **Principality** of Liechtenstein (LIHK tun styn). A principality is a territory or country ruled by a prince. The whole country of Liechtenstein is smaller than Washington, D.C. Liechtenstein has a prince and a democratically elected assembly of 15 members.

This castle is typical of the many ancient buildings that still stand in Liechtenstein today.
▶ What kind of people might have lived here?

This small country has not had an army for over a century and has managed to stay out of all wars during this time. The official language of Liechtenstein is German.

LESSON *1* REVIEW

THINK AND WRITE

A. What does the William Tell legend suggest to us about the Swiss? (Recall)

B. What are the important industries in Switzerland, Austria, and Germany? (Recall)

C. What are some of the natural resources in Germany and Austria? (Recall)

D. What governments and languages exist in Germany, Austria, Switzerland, and Liechtenstein? (Recall)

SKILLS CHECK

THINKING SKILL

Divide a sheet of paper into three columns. Write one of these country names at the top of each column: *Germany, Austria, Switzerland.* Along the side of the paper, write the following topics: *Natural Resources, Government, Industry.* Make a chart by filling in the information.

Optional Activities

UNDERSTANDING THE LESSON

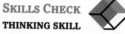

NAME _____

UNDERSTANDING THE LESSON

CHAPTER **9**

Organizing Facts

LESSON 1 CONTENT MASTER

✻ The chart shows the main ideas of the lesson. Fill in the blank spaces with the details that support each main idea. The first one has been done for you.
Suggested answers are provided.

Tourism, machinery, and business are important in Switzerland and Austria.

1. The Swiss Alps offer some of the world's finest skiing and scenery.

2. The Swiss make watches, clocks, machines, and scientific instruments.

3. Switzerland has become an international business center.

4. Austria's scenery and skiing draw tourists from all over the world.

Germany is one of the world's major industrial nations.

1. East Germany and West Germany were united in 1990.

2. Germany has used its resources as raw materials for its industries.

3. Its major products are steel, ships, vehicles, machinery, and chemicals.

Germany, Austria, and Switzerland

Germany and Austria make use of their natural resources.

1. Germany's farms and gardens supply much of the nation's food.

2. The Germans have learned to use forests without destroying them.

3. Austria's forest-covered mountains provide raw materials for industries.

These nations are democracies and have a variety of languages.

1. Germany is a democracy.

2. Austria is a democratic republic in which German is the official language.

3. Switzerland has four official languages.

Think and Write Do you think that all the people of a country should be required to speak the same language? Write a paragraph giving your opinion and supporting it with reasons. You may use the back of the sheet.
Answers should reflect independent thinking; suggestions appear in the Answer Key.

64

Use with textbook pages 247-254.

◀ **Review Master Booklet, p. 64**

The British Isles and Nordic Lands

THINK ABOUT WHAT YOU KNOW

Most countries are represented by national symbols. What symbols can you think of that represent the United States?

STUDY THE VOCABULARY

maritime climate
export
service industry

Commonwealth
of Nations
fjord
geyser

FOCUS YOUR READING

What are the geographic features of the lands of the British Isles and of the Nordic countries?

A. Four Regions in One Kingdom

Great Britain The ancient Romans called Great Britain *Britannia* when it was part of their empire. Great Britain is the largest island of the British Isles. One Roman historian wrote that Britannia was shaped like a double-headed ax. Look at the map on this page. Perhaps if you have a good imagination, you may be able to see an ax in the shape of Great Britain.

The official name of the country today is the United Kingdom of Great Britain and Northern Ireland. But the name is often shortened to Great Britain or the United Kingdom. However, the official name tells something about the history of the country. It is called the *United* Kingdom because it unites four regions. England, Wales, and Scotland make up the island of Great Britain. Wales was united with England during the Middle Ages. Scotland became part of the United Kingdom nearly 300 years ago. At one time the United

Kingdom included all of Ireland, but now only Northern Ireland is included. The term *British Isles* refers to the group of islands that includes Great Britain, Ireland, and some smaller islands.

England England is the largest region of the United Kingdom, and it has far more people than does Scotland, Wales, or

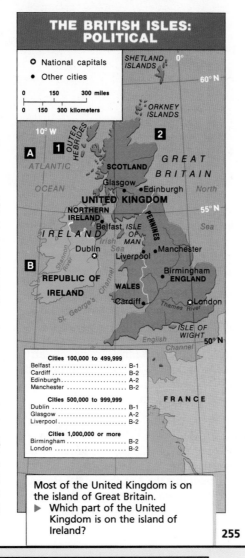

THE BRITISH ISLES: POLITICAL

⊘ National capitals
• Other cities

Cities 100,000 to 499,999	
Belfast	B-1
Cardiff	B-2
Edinburgh	A-2
Manchester	B-2

Cities 500,000 to 999,999	
Dublin	B-1
Glasgow	A-2
Liverpool	B-2

Cities 1,000,000 or more	
Birmingham	B-2
London	B-2

Most of the United Kingdom is on the island of Great Britain.
▶ Which part of the United Kingdom is on the island of Ireland?

255

Curriculum Connection

Math Have students figure out the population density of the United Kingdom per square mile and per square kilometer.

● Remind students that to figure out the density they should divide the total population by the area.

● Tell them that the total population is 57,300,000 and the land area is 94,598 square miles (245,009 sq km). (The correct answer is 605.72 people per square mile and 233.86 per square kilometer.)

Optional Activities

The British Isles and Nordic Lands

Objectives

★1. **Describe** the geographic features of the British Isles and of the Nordic countries.

2. **Compare** the resources of the British Isles with those of the Nordic lands.

3. **Name** the types of government found in the British Isles and Nordic lands.

4. **Identify** the following people and places: *Elizabeth II, British Isles, Norway, Sweden, Denmark, Finland,* and *Iceland.*

1 STARTING THE LESSON

Motivation Activity

■ Ask students the following question: **Which Western European nation once ruled the largest empire the world has ever known?** (The United Kingdom)

■ Tell students that they will be reading about this and other Western European nations in this lesson.

Think About What You Know

■ Assign the THINK ABOUT WHAT YOU KNOW activity on p. 255.

■ Answers may include Uncle Sam, the American eagle, and the American flag.

Study the Vocabulary

■ After students have looked up the vocabulary words in the Glossary, ask them to categorize the words under these headings: *Physical Geography, Political Geography,* and *Economics.*

--- **Answers to Caption Questions** ---
p. 254 ▶ Answers may include a prince, a king, a queen, or other noble.
p. 255 ▶ Northern Ireland

255

2 DEVELOPING THE LESSON

Read and Think
Sections A, B, and C

Discuss with students the land, climate, resources, and industries of the British Isles by asking the following questions:

1. **What regions make up the island of Great Britain?**
   (Wales, England, and Scotland *p. 255*)

2. **Describe the climate of the British Isles.**
   (It is a maritime climate, influenced by winds blowing off the North Atlantic. Winters tend to be warmer than would be expected that far north, and rain falls throughout the year. *p. 256*)

3. **For what is most of the land of the British Isles used?**
   (Crops and pastures *p. 257*)

4. **What has enabled Great Britain to become an exporter of oil?**
   (The discovery that there are large deposits of oil under the North Sea *p. 257*)

5. **Most people of the British Isles work in what kinds of industries?**
   (Service industries *p. 257*)

   Thinking Critically Why, do you think, is the Pennine Chain called "the backbone of England"? (Infer)
   (Because it runs in a north-south direction on the western side of the country, the side that does not "face" the continent of Europe *p. 256*)

GEOGRAPHY THEMES

Location

■ Have students look at the map on p. 255 to help them answer the following question: **In which country are the largest cities of the United Kingdom located?** (England)

The majority of land in the British Isles is used for crops or pastures.
▶ How is this land being used?

Northern Ireland. However, England has its fine open spaces, such as the hills in the northwest and along the Pennine Chain, mountains that are sometimes called "the backbone of England."

English Channel The English Channel separates England from the European continent. In 1986 the British and French governments approved a plan to construct a tunnel under the channel. Trains will carry cars and trucks 32 miles (51 km) through this underwater tunnel. The tunnel is scheduled for completion by 1993.

B. A Green and Pleasant Land

Climate The Roman historian who thought Great Britain was shaped like an ax did not like the British climate. He was used to the sunny Mediterranean lands, and he complained that in Britannia "the

256

sky is hidden by continual rain clouds." Actually, southeastern England does not receive much rainfall. The average yearly rainfall in London is less than it is in Rome. But in London, rain falls throughout the year; Rome usually has dry summers.

The British Isles have what is known as a **maritime climate**. *Maritime* means "having to do with the sea." A maritime climate is a climate influenced by winds blowing off the sea. Since the North Atlantic has warm currents, winters tend to be warmer than would be expected so far north. Even the Roman historian admitted that Britannia did not have extremely cold weather. He also reported that the "extreme moistness of the land" made it possible to grow most crops known to the Romans except olives. An English poet later described his homeland as "a green and pleasant land."

Interpreting Quotes

● Tell students that in 1900, when the British ruled an empire that included colonies on every continent, a popular saying of the time was "The sun never sets on the British Empire."

● Ask students to explain what the statement meant. (Answers may include that the British Empire was in so many parts of the world that the sun was shining on some part of it at all times.)

Land Use In Roman times forests covered most of the British Isles, but today about 80 percent of the land is used for crops or pastures. Although only a very small part of the population works on the land, the British produce about half of their country's food.

C. Working in Industries

Manufacturing Today many more British people work in industry than work on farms. As you know, the Industrial Revolution began in Great Britain. The country possessed large deposits of coal and iron ore for making steel, from which machines were constructed. Coal provided the principal source of energy in the days when steam engines turned factory wheels.

The United Kingdom still has deposits of coal, iron, tin, and other ores. Some mines have been worked for many years. As the mines became deeper, the costs of mining coal and ore increased.

Great Britain's sources of energy today include not only coal but also oil and natural gas. At one time the United Kingdom imported most of its oil. This changed with the discovery of large oil and natural gas deposits under the North Sea. The United Kingdom now **exports**, or sends to other countries, its oil.

Service Although the United Kingdom is still a manufacturing country, the number of people working in mines and manufacturing industries has been declining. Far more people work in **service industries**, or businesses that provide some kind of useful work for another business or person. Service industries provide services rather than make goods. People who fly airplanes provide service, as do those people who provide health care. Many people are employed in the tourism industry.

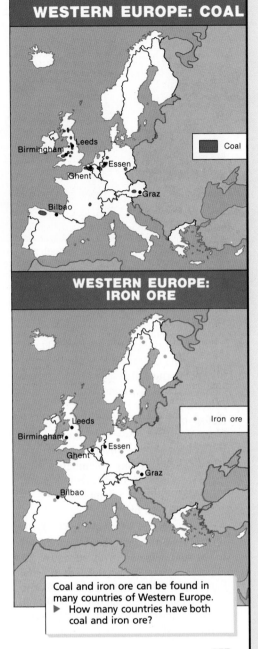

WESTERN EUROPE: COAL

Coal

WESTERN EUROPE: IRON ORE

Iron ore

Coal and iron ore can be found in many countries of Western Europe.
▶ How many countries have both coal and iron ore?

257

GEOGRAPHY THEMES

Human-Environment Interactions

■ Have students look at the maps on p. 257 to help them answer these questions:

1. **Which cities, do you think, may have developed because of their close proximity to coal?**
   (Birmingham, Leeds, Ghent, and Essen)

2. **Which cities, do you think, may have developed because of their close proximity to iron ore?**
   (Bilbao, Graz, and Birmingham)

VISUAL THINKING SKILL

Interpreting a Visual

■ Direct students' attention to the visual on p. 256 to help them respond to the following question: **How would you describe the terrain in this photograph?**
(Answers may include rolling hills surrounded by a mountainous area, green pastures.)

— **Answers to Caption Questions** —
p. 256 ▶ For pasture
p. 257 ▶ Five countries

For Your Information

London The United Kingdom's capital, London, is the largest city in Western Europe. It is located on the banks of the Thames River, about 40 miles (64 km) from the North Sea. Although London is not located on the coast, it is one of the world's busiest ocean ports. London is also home to many popular tourist attractions. Sights such as the Tower of London, Westminster Abbey, St. Paul's Cathedral, Buckingham Palace, and Big Ben bring hundreds of thousands of tourists to London each year.

Optional Activities

257

Read and Think
Sections D and E

Review the structure of the British government by asking the following questions:

1. **Describe the British government.**
   (It has a two-part lawmaking body which is elected by the voters, and it has a monarch, the queen. *p. 258*)

2. **What are the duties of the monarch of the United Kingdom?**
   (To receive foreign visitors and to address Parliament at the opening of each session *p. 258*)

3. **Why is Ireland referred to as the Emerald Isle?**
   (Ireland receives abundant moisture so it has lush, green vegetation. *p. 259*)

4. **How did Ireland become a divided island?**
   (When Ireland became independent of the United Kingdom in 1922, the Protestant majority in Northern Ireland chose to remain a part of the United Kingdom. *p. 259*)

   Thinking Critically Why, do you think, did the United Kingdom lose its large empire? (Infer)
   (Answers may include that the empire was too diverse and too spread out to control. *pp. 258–259*)

VISUAL THINKING SKILL

Describing a Photograph

■ Draw students' attention to the photograph of Queen Elizabeth II on this page to help them perform the following activity. Write a paragraph describing what Queen Elizabeth is wearing. Ask students if this picture confirms their ideas of how queens should dress.
(Paragraphs should include descriptions of Queen Elizabeth's attire and will indicate that the Queen is indeed very regal in her fancy dress, jewelry, and tiara.)

The Parliament and Queen Elizabeth II (inset) represent the democratic monarchy of the United Kingdom. The photograph shows the Houses of Parliament and Big Ben, the great clock in the tower, on the Thames River.
▶ What is the role of the queen in the British government?

D. A Democratic Monarchy

The Glorious Revolution of 300 years ago limited the powers of the monarch. Since then the British government has become increasingly democratic. Parliament has two parts, the House of Lords and the House of Commons, but the House of Lords has little power over the making of laws. The power to govern rests with the House of Commons. Members of this house are elected by the voters, so the United Kingdom is a democracy — a government chosen by the people.

Although it is a democracy, the United Kingdom has a monarch. Elizabeth II has been queen since 1952. She receives important foreign visitors and addresses Parliament at the opening of each session. The monarch now serves as the living symbol of the country. The British national anthem is "God Save the Queen."

The United Kingdom once ruled a very large empire; it was the largest the world has ever known. It included lands on every inhabited continent. Today almost all the lands of the old empire are independent. Many have chosen to belong to the **Commonwealth of Nations**, an association of countries that were once a part of the British Empire. The Commonwealth includes such countries as Canada in North America, Kenya in Africa, India in Asia, and Australia. The monarch serves as the living symbol of the Commonwealth as well as of the United Kingdom.

E. An Island Divided

Climate If you were to cross the Atlantic Ocean from the United States to Europe by the shortest route, Ireland would be the first land you would see. Ireland, like the rest of the British Isles, enjoys a maritime

---

Cooperative Learning

Making a Visual Display Divide the class into groups of five students. Have each group choose one of the countries covered in this lesson and make a visual display about it.

● Four members of each group should prepare visuals that illustrate the following: the climate, the land, the industries, and the government.

● The fifth member of the group should organize the visuals into an attractive and easy-to-understand display with a title.

climate, even though the cities of Dublin and Belfast are farther north than most Canadian cities.

A travel guidebook warns tourists going to Ireland to be prepared for some wet weather, whatever the season. Ireland receives more moisture than does most of Great Britain. The abundant moisture gives the island its nickname—the Emerald Isle, or the green island. The pastures and fields of Ireland make it a good land for raising livestock and crops. At one time the majority of the Irish people worked on the land, but today far more work in manufacturing and service occupations.

Political Differences The island is divided between the independent Republic of Ireland and Northern Ireland, which is part of the United Kingdom. The reason for the division goes far back in history. English kings conquered Ireland during the Middle Ages. Revolts broke out from time to time, so the English monarch sent a number of English and Scottish settlers to northern Ireland. Most of the settlers were of the Protestant religion, while most of the Irish were Roman Catholics.

Even though settlement in Northern Ireland took place long ago, differences between the two groups of Irish have lasted throughout the years. The Catholic Irish revolted against British rule and Ireland became independent in 1922. However, the Protestant majority in Northern Ireland chose to remain a part of the United Kingdom. Today, Northern Ireland includes a Catholic minority who want a united Ireland. Disputes about the division of Ireland continue to trouble the island.

The conflict between Catholics and Protestants in Northern Ireland has often resulted in violence.
▶ What has happened here?

259

Read and Think
Section F

To summarize the information about the Nordic countries, ask the following questions:

1. **What are the Nordic countries?**
   (Norway, Sweden, Finland, Denmark, and Iceland *p. 260*)

2. **How are the Nordic countries alike?**
   (All are located in the northern part of Western Europe and all are democracies. *p. 260*)

   Thinking Critically Do you think that "land which was forest must always be forest"? (Analyze)
   (Answers should reflect independent thinking but might include that forests should always be preserved to protect the environment or that forests should be cleared sometimes to provide housing or other buildings that people need.)

GEOGRAPHY THEMES

Location

■ Have students look at the map on this page to help them answer the following question: **On which peninsula is Denmark located?**
(Jutland Peninsula)

F. The Nordic Countries

Norway, Sweden, and Finland, along with Denmark and Iceland, are known as the Nordic countries. The word *nordic* means "north." Norway, Sweden, and Finland all extend above the Arctic Circle. Find these three countries and the Arctic Circle on the map below. Norway extends farther north than any other country of Western Europe.

Sweden is the largest and most populous Nordic country. Most Swedes live in towns and cities located in the southern part of the country. Stockholm, the capital, is its largest city. It grew around an island fortress built during the Middle Ages.

Denmark is the smallest of the Nordic countries, but it is second only to Sweden in population. Denmark consists of the Jutland Peninsula and about 500 islands. Copenhagen, the capital, is located on the second largest island.

All the Nordic countries are democracies. Like the United Kingdom, the countries of Norway, Sweden, and Denmark are monarchies as well as democracies. The monarchs are heads of state, but elected representatives govern these countries.

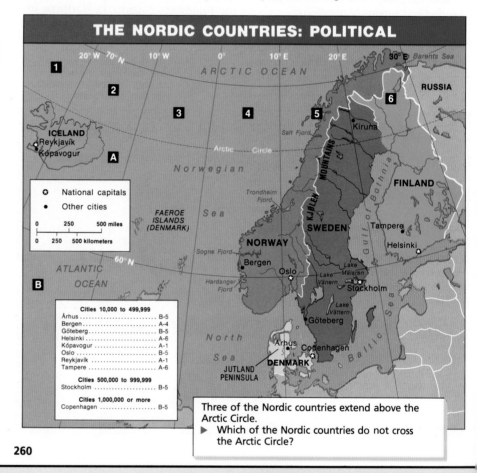

THE NORDIC COUNTRIES: POLITICAL

⊕ National capitals
• Other cities

0   250   500 miles
0   250   500 kilometers

Cities 10,000 to 499,999	
Árhus	B-5
Bergen	A-4
Göteberg	B-5
Helsinki	A-6
Kópavogur	A-1
Oslo	B-5
Reykjavík	A-1
Tampere	A-6

Cities 500,000 to 999,999	
Stockholm	B-5

Cities 1,000,000 or more	
Copenhagen	B-5

Three of the Nordic countries extend above the Arctic Circle.
▶ Which of the Nordic countries do not cross the Arctic Circle?

Optional Activities

Planning a Trip Itinerary

● Have students use tourist guides, travel brochures, and their textbook to plan the itinerary of a trip to the British Isles and Nordic countries.

● Tell students to list the cities, countries, and places of interest that they will visit on their imaginary ten-day ocean cruise.

● For each stop, have students describe some of the major points of interest

Curriculum Connection

Art Have students draw pictures of what a Viking raid might have looked like.

● Tell students that the Vikings began raiding the coasts of Europe around 800 A.D. and quickly gained a reputation for being ruthless and destructive. They frequently looted the towns and settlements that they raided and then left the area in ruins.

● Display the students' artwork on a bulletin board or around the classroom.

G. Natural Resources of the Nordic Lands

Forests Denmark does not have a lot of natural resources, but the Danes make good use of the ones that they have. Denmark has laws protecting its forests. In 1805 a law was made stating that "land which was forest must always be forest." Later laws required that a new tree must be planted for every old one cut down.

Norway, Sweden, and Finland also have large forests. Sweden's forests cover half the land. All three countries export timber. Finland's forests are the basis for its major industries exporting lumber, wood pulp, and paper along with other manufactured goods.

The Seas Although there is a limited amount of farmland in Norway, there is an abundance of marvelous scenery. It is a land of rocky mountains, glaciers, forests, and the great **fjords** (fyords). The fjords are narrow arms of the sea lying between narrow cliffs. The western coast of Norway is indented with hundreds of fjords.

The sea has been very important in Norway's history. The ancestors of the Norwegians were Vikings who raided the coasts of Europe during the Middle Ages. In later times, Norwegians made their living from the sea as fishers and sailors. The discovery of oil under the floor of the North Sea has provided Norway with additional wealth from the ocean.

The Danes also make good use of their country's location between the North and Baltic seas. Danish fishers provide large amounts of food from the seas for both home use and export.

Minerals The countries of Norway, Finland, and Sweden have important mineral deposits. Sweden's high-grade iron ore

Fjords such as this one make Norway's coast one of the most jagged in the world.
▶ What types of land surround the fjords?

deposits provide raw material for high-grade steel, which is used in making such products as tools and machines.

Iceland's Resources Contrary to its name, Iceland consists of more than just ice. This island has active volcanoes, fast-flowing rivers, and some grassy valleys. Cattle and sheep pasture on the grasslands. Sheep supply wool for clothing, particularly the sweaters that Iceland exports. Crops such as potatoes and turnips are grown in Iceland. Iceland's main resource is fish. Fishing is the main industry.

261

Reteaching Main Objective

Describe the geographic features of the British Isles and of the Nordic countries.

● Put the names of the countries located in the British Isles and Nordic lands along the top of the chalkboard.

● Then, have student volunteers write the geographic features of each country below the appropriate headings.

● Finally, have each student write a short paragraph in which they describe the geography of each country.

Optional Activities

Ask the students what they think the major resources of the Nordic countries might be. Use the questions below to compare students' responses with the actual resources:

1. **What resource do Denmark, Norway, Sweden, and Finland have in common?** (Forests *p. 261*)

2. **How has the sea been important in Norway's history?** (The Vikings raided the coasts of Europe during the Middle Ages, Norwegians made their living from the sea as fishers and sailors, and oil has been discovered under the floor of the North Sea. *p. 261*)

3. **What is Iceland's main resource?** (Fish *p. 261*)

4. **How is the water from the hot springs used?** (To heat buildings *p. 262*)

Thinking Critically What, do you think, would be a more appropriate name for the country of Iceland? (Hypothesize) (Answers may include Fishland, Geyserland, or Sheepland. *pp. 261–262*)

─ **Answers to Caption Questions** ─
p. 260 ▶ Iceland and Denmark
p. 261 ▶ Rocks, cliffs, and mountains

261

3 CLOSING THE LESSON

Lesson 2 Review

Answers to Think and Write

A. The four regions are England, Scotland, Wales, and Northern Ireland.

B. Great Britain's climate is mild and wet, which makes the land pleasant and green.

C. They work in manufacturing, mining, and service industries.

D. She meets important foreign visitors and addresses the first session of Parliament.

E. Ireland divided because of differences between Irish Catholics and Protestants.

F. They are in the northern part of Europe.

G. Resources found in the Nordic countries include forests, oil, iron, fish, good soil, fast-flowing rivers, and beautiful scenery.

Answer to Skills Check

The North Sea and the English Channel separate Great Britain from Europe. St. George's Channel and the Irish Sea separate Britain from Ireland. London has more than 1 million people. It is in southeastern England on the Thames River.

Focus Your Reading

Ask the lesson focus question found at the beginning of the lesson: **What are the geographic features of the lands of the British Isles and of the Nordic countries?**
(The geographic features of the British Isles include hills, mountains, coastlines, maritime climate, and green pastures, while the Nordic countries have rocky mountains, glaciers fjords, active volcanoes, and grassy valleys.)

Additional Practice

You may wish to assign the ancillary materials listed below.

Understanding the Lesson p. 65
Workbook p. 66

Despite its name, Iceland has more geysers (left) and hot springs (right) than any other country in the world.
▶ What is one way that the people of Iceland use these hot springs?

Iceland has hot springs and **geysers** (GYE zurz), which are fountains of steam and water that have been heated by hot volcanic rocks. When the water becomes extremely hot, it is released as steam. Water from some of the springs is used to heat buildings such as greenhouses near the Arctic Circle, where flowers, tomatoes, and other vegetables are grown. You may wonder if this country has any ice at all. Yes, glaciers cover the mountains in the southeastern part of the island.

LESSON 2 REVIEW

THINK AND WRITE

A. Which four regions make up the United Kingdom? (Recall)

B. Why can Great Britain be described as a green and pleasant land? (Infer)

C. In what industries do the people in the United Kingdom work? (Recall)

D. What is the queen's role in governing the United Kingdom? (Recall)

E. Why is Ireland a divided island? (Recall)

F. Why are the countries Norway, Sweden, Finland, Denmark, and Iceland known as the Nordic countries? (Infer)

G. What are some of the resources that can be found in Nordic countries? (Recall)

SKILLS CHECK

MAP SKILL

Look at the map of the British Isles on page 255. What two bodies of water separate Great Britain from mainland Europe? What bodies of water separate Great Britain from Ireland? Which capital city has a million or more people? Describe its location.

Optional Activities

UNDERSTANDING THE LESSON

NAME _____

UNDERSTANDING THE LESSON

Recalling Facts

CHAPTER **9**

LESSON 2 CONTENT MASTER

✽ Read each question and write the correct answer on the blank that follows. Use complete sentences.

1. What is the United Kingdom? The United Kingdom is a union of England, Scotland, Wales, and Northern Ireland.

2. What is most of the land in the British Isles used for? Most of the land, about 80 percent, is used for crops or pasture.

3. Besides coal, what are two of Great Britain's major sources of energy? Where are they found? The other sources are oil and natural gas, found under the North Sea.

4. In what kind of industry are most people of the United Kingdom employed? They are employed in service industries.

5. How is the island of Ireland divided? It is divided into Northern Ireland, which is part of the United Kingdom, and the Republic of Ireland, an independent country.

6. Why do violent disputes trouble Northern Ireland today? The Catholic minority of Northern Ireland wants to have a united Ireland. The Protestant majority wants to remain part of the United Kingdom.

7. Which countries make up the Nordic countries of Europe? The Nordic countries include Norway, Sweden, Finland, Denmark, and Iceland.

8. What kind of government do the Nordic countries have? They are all democracies, and Norway, Sweden, and Denmark are also monarchies.

9. Which two natural resources are important to Norway, Sweden, and Finland? Forests and mineral deposits are important to Norway, Sweden, and Finland.

10. In what way do the people of Iceland use geysers? They use steam and hot water from geysers to heat their buildings and greenhouses.

Think and Write: Where would you rather live—in the British Isles or in one of the Nordic countries? Write a paragraph explaining your decision. You may use the back of the sheet.
Answers should reflect independent thinking; suggestions appear in the Answer Key.

Use with textbook pages 253–260.   65

◀ **Review Master Booklet p. 65**

THINK ABOUT WHAT YOU KNOW
What different languages can you name?

STUDY THE VOCABULARY
Mediterranean climate   bilingual

FOCUS YOUR READING
What distinctive physical features would travelers see if they visited France and the Low Countries?

A. Mark Twain in France

Years before Mark Twain wrote the books *The Adventures of Tom Sawyer* and *Adventures of Huckleberry Finn*, he wrote the book *The Innocents Abroad*. The book was about a trip to France with a group of tourists in 1867. In this book, Twain describes the countryside through which they traveled.

> We have come five hundred miles by rail through the heart of France. What a bewitching land it is!—What a garden! Surely the leagues of bright green lawns are swept and brushed and watered every day and their grasses trimmed by the barber. . . . There are no unsightly stone walls, and never a fence of any kind. There is no dirt, no decay, no rubbish anywhere—nothing that even hints at untidiness—nothing that ever suggests neglect. All is orderly and beautiful—every thing is charming to the eye.

In Paris the tourists visited many of the most famous sites. Mark Twain went to the Louvre (loovr) museum, where he "looked at miles of its paintings." The Louvre has one of the world's great art

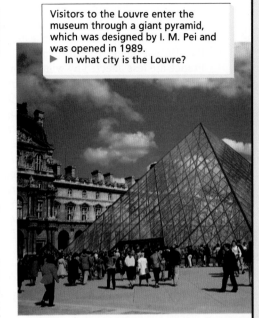

Visitors to the Louvre enter the museum through a giant pyramid, which was designed by I. M. Pei and was opened in 1989.
▶ In what city is the Louvre?

collections, and contains more than a million works of art. He went on to the city of Versailles, expecting to be disappointed. He was sure that artists' paintings of the great palace and its gardens showed them "more beautiful than it was possible for any place in the world to be." But Mark Twain's doubts vanished when he saw Versailles with his own eyes. He decided that "no painter would represent Versailles on canvas as beautiful as it is in reality."

B. A Land with Variety

Climates France, the largest country of Western Europe, is a country with variety. It has hills, rolling plains, a high plateau, and rugged mountains. Both the Alps and the Pyrenees are located partly in France. The island of Corsica, in the Mediterranean, is part of France.

263

Curriculum Connection

Geography   Tell students that the area of France is 212,918 square miles (551,458 sq km).

- Have them look at a wall map of the United States and tell them only two states are larger than the country of France.
- Ask them to figure out which two states these might be. (Alaska and Texas)
- Then have students compare the area of their own state with that of France.

Optional Activities

France and the Low Countries

Objectives

★ **1. List** the similarities and differences between the resources found in France and the Low Countries.

2. Describe the lands of France and the Low Countries.

3. Name the types of government found in France and the Low Countries.

4. Identify the following people and places: *Mark Twain, France, Monaco, Belgium, Luxembourg,* and *the Netherlands.*

1 STARTING THE LESSON

Motivation Activity

■ Bring a number of items to class that were made in France and the Low Countries (perfume, clothing, cheese, cookware).

■ Ideally, these items should be each labeled with the name of the country of origin. Do not say anything about the similar origins of these items.

■ Ask the students to examine the items to consider what they have in common.

Think About What You Know

■ Assign the THINK ABOUT WHAT YOU KNOW activity on p. 263.

■ Answers may include languages such as English, Spanish, French, German, Italian, Japanese, and others.

Study the Vocabulary

■ Ask students if they think they know the definition of either of the new vocabulary words.

■ Then ask the students to look up each of the words in their Glossary to see if they were using the correct definitions.

> **Answers to Caption Questions**
> **p. 262 ▶** To heat buildings
> **p. 263 ▶** Paris

263

Read and Think

Sections A and B

Mark Twain was impressed by the beauty of France. Others have remarked on the variety of the land, climate, and resources. Discuss these characteristics with your students by asking the following questions:

1. **What did Mark Twain mean when he said that "no painter would represent Versailles on canvas as beautiful as it is in reality"?**
(The palace was more beautiful than any painting of it could be. *p. 263*)

2. **Why is France called a land with variety?**
(France has many different landforms and a variety of climates and resources. It has also had a variety of governments. *pp. 263–266*)

3. **What are France's natural resources?**
(Good soil, minerals, and streams *p. 264*)

4. **What is France's present government called?**
(The Fifth Republic *p. 266*)

Thinking Critically Why, do you think, has France had so many governments? (Evaluate)
(Answers may include because of bad rulers or governments that did not represent the will of the people. *pp. 264–266*)

France has a variety of climates. The regions along the Atlantic coast have a maritime climate, somewhat like that of the British Isles. Central and eastern France are less affected by winds blowing off the ocean currents. As a result, winters are colder and summers warmer in inland Paris than in coastal Cherbourg (SHER-boorg), even though both cities are located near the same latitude. The beaches of southern France attract many vacationers because of their **Mediterranean climate**. A Mediterranean climate has cool, rainy winters and hot, dry summers. Palm, orange, and lemon trees grow in Nice (nees), a seaport located on the section of the Mediterranean coast known as the French Riviera.

The rich soil of the Rhone Valley in France is ideal for growing wine grapes.
▶ What is in the background?

Nine miles east of Nice lies the country of Monaco, with an area of 0.73 square miles (2 sq km). The en country of Monaco is smaller than m American farms. It is mainly a tourist res

Natural Resources France has a var of natural resources, including good s valuable mineral deposits, and strea used to generate electrical energy. cause of its good soil, France is abl export more food than any other West European country. Northern France duces vegetables, grains, and more su beets and wheat than any country in W ern Europe. Southern France has m vineyards, making the region famous its wines.

Choropleth Maps The map on the n page shows the distribution of whea the countries of Western Europe. This t of map is called a *choropleth map*. It u different colors to show the distributio a product within a region. The colors a show how much of the product is produ by the countries in the region.

The key on the choropleth map i cates the amount of a product that e color on the map represents. For exam on this choropleth map you can see t red means a country produces 15, thousands of tons or more of wheat. yellow means a country produces 0 1,900 thousands of tons of wheat. T choropleth map allows you to find wh Western European countries produce largest and smallest amounts of whe and which countries rank in between.

Governments The climates and natu resources are not the only aspects France that vary. France has had a vari of governments since the establishmen the First Republic after the Revolution

Writing to Learn

Writing a Letter Ask students to imagine that they are on a trip through France.

● Have them write a letter to a friend at home describing the sights that they have seen.

● Review proper greetings and closings for personal letters, taking care to ensure that students know how to properly address envelopes.

● Have students "mail" their letters to students in their class or in another social studies class in their school.

Making a Resource Map

● Provide students with outline maps of France.

● Tell students to review the material in Section B in order to make resource maps of France.

● When location information is provided, students should put the symbols for the resources in the appropriate region of the country.

● Remind students to include a map key and map title.

● Display the maps on a bulletin board or on classroom walls.

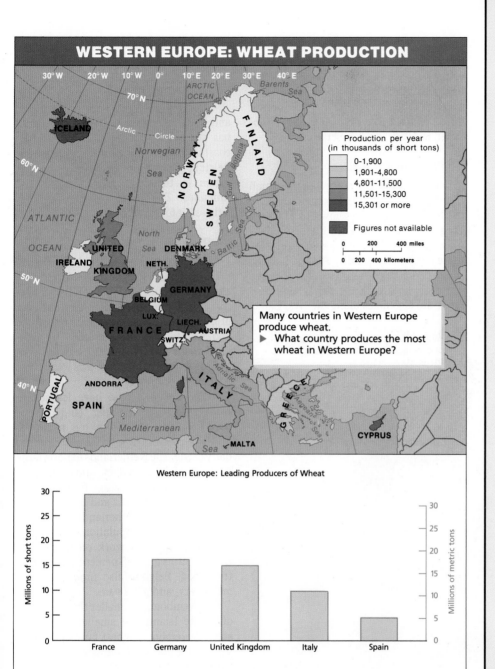

WESTERN EUROPE: WHEAT PRODUCTION

Production per year (in thousands of short tons)
- 0–1,900
- 1,901–4,800
- 4,801–11,500
- 11,501–15,300
- 15,301 or more

Figures not available

0   200   400 miles
0   200   400 kilometers

Many countries in Western Europe produce wheat.
▶ What country produces the most wheat in Western Europe?

Western Europe: Leading Producers of Wheat

(bar graph showing Millions of short tons / Millions of metric tons for France, Germany, United Kingdom, Italy, Spain)

Graphic Organizer

To help students know which products come from France and the Low Countries, you may wish to use this graphic organizer.

FRANCE AND THE LOW COUNTRIES

COUNTRY	PRODUCTS
France	food, wine, perfume, steel, autos, machinery
The Netherlands	tulips, dairy products, diamonds, oil
Belgium	steel, machinery, glassware
Luxembourg	steel, food

Optional Activities

Meeting Individual Needs

Concept: The Importance of Being Bilingual

To better understand why the people of the Low Countries speak more than one language, it is important to understand how being bilingual can help people. Below are three activities that will help your students understand this concept.

◆ **EASY** Have students imagine that they are German-speaking owners of restaurant in Belgium.

Since they speak only one language, have them identify the problems that they might encounter in operating their business as speakers of only one language.

◀▶ **AVERAGE** Ask students to plan to start a daily newspaper in Luxembourg.

Have them write a paragraph explaining in which language or languages they will print their newspaper and why.

◀▮▶ **CHALLENGING** Tell students that some people feel American students should be required to learn a second language in school.

Have students debate the following issue: *American students should be required to learn a second language.*

GEOGRAPHY THEMES

Place

■ Direct students' attention to the map on this page to help them answer the following question: **Which countries in Western Europe produce 0 to 1,900,000 short tons of wheat per year?**
(Norway, Sweden, Finland, Ireland, Belgium, the Netherlands, Luxembourg, Switzerland, Austria, and Portugal)

Answers to Caption Questions
p. 264 ▶ A castle
p. 265 ▶ France

Read and Think
Sections C, D, and E

To summarize the information about the land, governments, resources, and languages of the Low Countries, ask the following questions:

1. **What are the Low Countries?**
   (Belgium, Luxembourg, and the Netherlands *p. 266*)

2. **Why are they called the Low Countries?**
   (Because much of the land of these countries lies below sea level *p. 266*)

3. **What products are exported from the Netherlands?**
   (Dairy products, electric razors, tulip bulbs, cut diamonds *p. 266*)

4. **What product do both Belgium and Luxembourg produce?**
   (Steel *p. 266*)

5. **What kind of government do all three of the Low Countries have?**
   (Democratic monarchies *p. 267*)

6. **Belgium is a nation of what three languages?**
   (French, German, and Flemish *p. 267*)

Thinking Critically Why, do you think, do the people of Luxembourg and Belgium speak so many languages? (Infer)
(Answers should reflect independent thinking but may include that they are small countries dependent upon their neighbors for trade, therefore, they speak many languages to improve relations with their neighbors. *p. 267*)

1789. As you have read, Napoleon did away with the republic and made himself emperor. Since the revolution, the French have had three kings, another emperor, and five republics, including the present Fifth Republic. The Fifth Republic, established in 1958, is a democracy.

C. The Low Countries

Just north of France lie the small countries of Belgium, Luxembourg, and the Netherlands, also known as Holland. These countries are called the Low Countries. The Netherlands is well named — its name means "low lands." Almost half the country lies below sea level. Sand dunes and dikes hold back the sea at high tide. There are also dikes along the river banks

> Canals used as drainage ditches run through this grassland area in the Netherlands.
> ▶ For what is this land being used?

266

that flow across the Netherlands into the North Sea. No people have done so much as the Dutch, as Netherlanders are called, in pushing back the sea.

Located between France, Germany, and the Netherlands is Belgium. Belgium has some low, flat land that forms the coastland along the North Sea. However, Belgium also includes a hilly forested region in the southeast known as the Ardennes. The Ardennes extends from Belgium into Luxembourg.

D. Resources of the Low Countries

Land is precious in the Netherlands, because it has the highest population density of any country in Western Europe. Yet this crowded, small country has quite a lot of open space. There are green pastures and well-tended fields crossed by tree-lined roads and canals. The canals serve both as drainage ditches and as waterways for boats.

The Dutch people have learned to make good use of their land. Grass-covered dikes, and fields too moist for growing crops, are used as pastures for dairy cattle. The Netherlands exports large amounts of dairy products and a variety of other products, ranging from electric razors to cut diamonds and tulip bulbs.

Just as the Netherlands does, Belgium has a dense population. Only 3 percent of the people work on farms. Yet Belgian farms grow 85 percent of the country's food. Belgium also produces steel, machinery, and glassware.

Luxembourg is smaller than the state of Rhode Island, the smallest American state. Luxembourg's best farmland lies in the south. Its steel industry and other manufacturing industries produce goods for export through Belgium.

Optional Activities

Reteaching Main Objective

⭐ *List the similarities and differences between the resources found in France and the Low Countries.*

- Write *France* and the names of the Low Countries on the chalkboard and ask students to skim the lesson and locate the resources of each of these countries.

- Put their answers under the appropriate countries.

- Have students reorganize this information by making a new chart with the headings *Similarities* and *Differences*, and list the resources under the appropriate headings.

E. Governments and Languages

Luxembourg The Low Countries are democratic monarchies. Luxembourg's official name is Grand Duchy of Luxembourg. The term *duchy* means "a territory ruled by a duke or duchess." Like the other monarchs of Western Europe, the grand duke of Luxembourg is head of state, but the government is elected by the voters.

The people of Luxembourg have their own national language, called Letzeburgesch (LET se boor gush), but French and German are also official languages. The country's name can be spelled correctly as Luxembourg or Luxemburg. The first spelling is French; the second, German.

The Netherlands The law requires that the people of the Netherlands vote for members of parliament. Amsterdam, the largest city of the Netherlands, is the capital, but the city known as The Hague (hayg), is the seat of government. The queen lives at The Hague and the parliament meets there. The people of the Netherlands are called Dutch, since that is the language they speak.

Belgium Like the Netherlands, Belgium is a monarchy with an elected parliament. Belgium is a nation with three languages:

This magnificent building is the Peace Palace, located in The Hague.
▶ What kind of flower shown here is symbolic of the Netherlands?

French, German, and Flemish, a form of Dutch. Flemish is the primary language of over half of the population. The capital, Brussels, is officially **bilingual**, that is, having two languages. Flemish and French are the official languages. Students are taught in the language of their region and later study the second language.

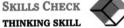

THINK AND WRITE   (Recall)

A. How did Mark Twain describe France?
B. Why is France called a land with variety?
C. Why is the term *Low Countries* a good name to describe the Netherlands, Belgium, and Luxembourg?   (Recall)
D. What are some of the resources in the Low Countries?   (Recall)
E. What governments and languages do the Low Countries have?   (Recall)

SKILLS CHECK

THINKING SKILL

Look at the graph on page 265. About how many times more tons of wheat does France produce than the United Kingdom? About how many times more tons of wheat does France produce than Germany? What two countries together produce about the same amount of wheat as the United Kingdom?

◀ Review Master Booklet, p. 66

Optional Activities

Lesson 3 Review

Answers to Think and Write

A. Twain described France as an orderly and beautiful garden.

B. France has many different landforms, climates, and natural resources.

C. The term *Low Countries* is a good description of the Netherlands, Belgium, and Luxembourg because much of the land of these countries lies below sea level.

D. Some of the resources of the Low Countries include land in the Netherlands that is used for grazing dairy cattle and farmland in Belgium and Luxembourg.

E. All three Low Countries have democratic monarchies. In the Netherlands, the people speak Dutch. In Belgium, the people speak Flemish, French, and German. The languages of Luxembourg are Letzeburgesch, French, and German.

Answer to Skills Check

France produces about twice as much wheat as the United Kingdom. France produces almost twice as much wheat as Germany. Spain and Italy together produce about the same amount of wheat as the United Kingdom.

Focus Your Reading

Ask the lesson focus question found at the beginning of the lesson: **What distinctive physical features would travelers see if they visited France and the Low Countries?**
(In France, they would see the Alps, the Pyrenees, rolling plains, hills, and a high plateau. In the Low Countries, they would see sand dunes, dikes, and windmills.)

Additional Practice

You may wish to assign the ancillary materials listed below.

Understanding the Lesson p. 66
Workbook p. 67

Answers to Caption Questions

p. 266 ▶ Pasture Land
p. 267 ▶ Tulips

267

Countries of Southern Europe

Objectives

★ **1. List** the industries and forms of government of the countries of southern Europe.

2. Describe the land and climate of the countries of southern Europe.

3. Explain how acid rain is threatening some of southern Europe's tourist attractions.

4. Identify the following people and places: *Francisco Franco, San Marino, Vatican City, Iberian Peninsula, Cyprus,* and *Malta.*

1 STARTING THE LESSON

Motivation Activity

■ Ask students to think of the names of some of the great empires of the past. Put these names on the chalkboard.

■ Tell students that they will be reading about the centers of these once-great empires in this lesson.

Think About What You Know

■ Assign the THINK ABOUT WHAT YOU KNOW activity on p. 268.

■ Answers may include the Colosseum, the Parthenon, and the Acropolis.

Study the Vocabulary

■ Have students look up the definition of acid rain in the Glossary.

■ Ask them if *acid rain* is a problem in this country. Have students give examples of buildings or areas that have been affected by acid rain.

LESSON **4**

Countries of Southern Europe

THINK ABOUT WHAT YOU KNOW

You have already learned about Greece and Rome in ancient times. What sights from those times do you think tourists would be interested in visiting today?

STUDY THE VOCABULARY

acid rain

FOCUS YOUR READING

How do the peoples of the countries of southern Europe make use of their resources?

A. The Value of Ruins

Touring Italy Italy is the boot-shaped peninsula that extends from the Alps mountains into the Mediterranean Sea. The country also includes the two islands of Sicily and Sardinia.

When Mark Twain reached Italy, he tried to take in all the famous sights. He went to Milan to see Leonardo da Vinci's famous painting *The Last Supper.* He went to Venice, where canals took the place of streets and where people traveled in boats called gondolas rather than in carriages and streetcars. He noted that traveling in a gondola was a lot smoother than riding in a carriage over bumpy streets. Mark Twain went on to Rome and tried to see all the famous ruins as well as the modern city. He admired the Colosseum. He observed that lizards sunned themselves on the stone seats where ancient emperors had sat watching gladiators.

Mark Twain visited Italy more than a hundred years ago, and people still go there today, partly to see the same sights.

Ruins, museums, and historic churches are among Italy's valuable resources, making tourism an important industry.

Industry and Farming Yet it would be a mistake to think that tourism is Italy's only industry. Italy has become an important industrial country since World War II. Modern Italy has skilled workers and factories that make machinery, automobiles, shoes, and clothing. The Italians export these products all over the world. Much of the industry is located in the northern part of the country.

Besides prosperous industry, northern Italy has the most productive farmland

Italy has many skilled craftspeople who work in factories to produce some of Italy's finest products.
► In what type of factory is this woman working?

Making a Bar Graph

● Have students make a bar graph of the population of the countries covered in this lesson.

● Provide the following population figures: Italy, 57,600,000; Spain, 39,200,000; Portugal, 10,400,000; Greece, 10,000,000; Cyprus, 700,000; Malta, 400,000; Andorra, 49,000; San Marino, 24,000; Vatican City, 1,000.

● Make sure that students properly label each section of their bar graph.

in the broad valley of the Po, Italy's longest river. The Po rises in the Alps and flows eastward to the Adriatic Sea. The Adriatic is an arm of the Mediterranean. Southern Italy is mostly an agricultural region, with little industry. Southern Italians grow grain, grapes, and olives, much as the ancient Romans did.

Government   Many things remind us of the ancient Romans. Even Italy's government has been restored from the days of ancient Rome. Remember that the word *republic* was originally used for the government of ancient Rome. Italy, now a democratic republic, was a monarchy when it was united in the 1860s. It remained officially a monarchy until 1946, although the dictator Benito Mussolini actually ruled the country from 1925 until 1943. After World War II the Italians voted whether to keep the monarchy or establish a republic. Even the king had the right to vote in the election, but the monarchy lost.

San Marino   San Marino is a very small country in the Apennines mountains of Italy. Covering only 24 square miles (62 sq km), it is even smaller than the country of Andorra. San Marino is the world's oldest existing republic. It can be well described as a "postage stamp country." It not only is very small but also receives considerable income from the sale of postage stamps.

Vatican City   Vatican City is even smaller than San Marino. Vatican City is the smallest independent state in the world. It is located within the city of Rome. The pope, head of the Roman Catholic Church, is in charge of Vatican City. The Italian government agreed to the independence of Vatican City because the Roman Catholic Church is not just an Italian church.

The Rock of Gibraltar is the site of a large British military base.
▶ Why is this a good location for a military base?

B. Spain, on the Iberian Peninsula

Gibraltar   At the southern tip of the Iberian Peninsula is a limestone mass known as the Rock of Gibraltar. The Iberian Peninsula is located between the Mediterranean and the Atlantic Ocean. The coast of Africa is about 14 miles (23 km) from the Rock, across the Strait of Gibraltar.

Because of its location at the narrow entrance to the Mediterranean Sea, Gibraltar has great military worth. The British acquired Gibraltar in 1704. Later they turned it into a large fort and established a military base there, which still exists.

Land and Climate   Spain, Portugal, and Andorra are the countries on the Iberian Peninsula. The Pyrenees separate these countries from the rest of Europe.

Spain is the largest country on the Iberian Peninsula and the second largest in Western Europe. The greater part of

269

Read and Think
Sections C, D, and E

Review with students Spain's neighbors on the Iberian Peninsula and Greece's neighbors in the Mediterranean Sea by asking the following questions:

1. **Why have the Portuguese always been a seagoing people?**
   (Because Portugal has its coast on the Atlantic Ocean *p. 270*)

2. **When did Portugal become a republic with an elected government?**
   (1974 *p. 271*)

3. **What two countries rule Andorra?**
   (It is a principality ruled jointly by France and Spain. *p. 271*)

4. **Why is Greece considered to be a Western European nation?**
   (Because it remained free from control by the Soviet Union after World War II *p. 271*)

5. **How is acid rain hurting some of Greece's ancient ruins?**
   (It is eating away at the surface of ancient statues and carvings. *p. 271*)

6. **Why is farming difficult in Greece?**
   (Most of the land is too rugged and rocky for farming. *p. 271*)

7. **What caused Cyprus to become a divided nation?**
   (Disputes between the Greek majority and Turkish minority led the Turkish government to send troops to the island in 1974. The Turks captured a large part of northeastern Cyprus, dividing the nation. *p. 272*)

8. **Why are many nations interested in Malta as a military base?**
   (It is located in the middle of the narrowest passage in the Mediterranean. *p. 272*)

Thinking Critically **Why, do you think, did Britain want control of Cyprus and Malta in the past?** (Infer)
(Answers may include that Britain wanted them in order to better protect its colonies in North Africa and the Middle East. *p. 272*)

Spain is a high plateau. Madrid, the capital, is located in the middle of the central plateau. Spain has coasts on both the Atlantic Ocean and the Mediterranean Sea.

The combination of mountains, plateau, and seacoasts gives Spain a variety of climates. Snow covers the peaks in the Pyrenees. On the central plateau, summers are quite hot and dry, but in the winter, cold winds sweep across the land. The Atlantic coast has a maritime climate, so the winters are warmer and the summers are cooler than in the interior. However, Barcelona, on the Mediterranean coast, has a Mediterranean climate.

Farming and Industry The Spaniards raise wheat and other grains on the plateau. There are also large areas used as pasture, particularly for sheep, which are Spain's most important domestic animals. Oranges, lemons, limes, and olives are grown in the warmer south. Spain leads the world in the production of olives. Almonds are also an important crop.

Not so long ago many Spaniards worked on the land, but today fewer than 5 percent work in agriculture. Industry has developed rapidly in Spain. Over half the workers in Spain are employed in service industries, such as education, health care, and the military. Another important industry is manufacturing. Spain ranks among the world's leading makers of automobiles. Machinery, steel, iron, and clothing are some other important manufactured products in Spain.

Government In 1931, Spain became a democratic republic after years of being ruled by a monarch. King Alfonso XIII fled Spain in that year due to an overwhelming vote for republican government officials in the city elections. After the Spanish Civil

The dictator Francisco Franco ruled Spain from 1939 to 1975.
▶ After what war did Franco come into power?

The Granger Collection

War ended in 1939, Francisco Franco, a dictator, ruled Spain until 1975. After Franco's death, Spain established a democratic monarchy. King Juan Carlos I was made the head of state.

C. Spain's Neighbors on the Peninsula

Portugal Portugal, the second largest country on the peninsula, has its coast on the Atlantic Ocean. Lisbon, the capital of Portugal, is located farther west than any other port on the European mainland. The Portuguese have always been a seagoing people. Portuguese sailors discovered the sea route around Africa to Asia about the time that Columbus reached America.

At one time this seagoing nation ruled a large overseas empire that included lands in the continents of Africa, Asia, and South America. The Portuguese no longer rule this large empire, but their influence is

Optional Activities

Writing to Learn

Writing a Letter to the Editor Have students write a letter to the editor of your local newspaper about the acid-rain problem or another type of pollution that is affecting your community.

● Tell students to explain why pollution poses a threat to the community, and ask them to include some suggestions regarding what the community can do to solve this problem.

still felt overseas. For example, Portuguese is the official language of Brazil, the largest country in South America.

The last Portuguese king was driven from his throne in 1910, and for many years a dictator ruled the country until he was overthrown by military officers in 1974. Portugal is now a republic with an elected government.

Andorra Tucked away in the Pyrenees is Andorra, one of Western Europe's smallest countries. The country covers 180 square miles (466 sq km), which is less than half the area of New York City, with only about 49,000 people living there. Andorra is a principality, jointly ruled by France and Spain.

D. Ancient Ruins and Modern Pollution

Tourism The term *Western Europe* comes from history rather than from geography. The countries that remained free from control by the Soviet Union after World War II have been called Western countries. Greece is located in Eastern Europe, but like Finland, it is considered a Western European country.

Like many other Western European countries, Greece has an important tourist industry. People are attracted by its scenery and ancient ruins. Probably no ancient structure is so famous as the Parthenon on the Acropolis at Athens.

Pollution Athens is more than a city of ruins and museums. It is the capital of modern Greece and the country's largest city. There are many industries in the Athens area. There are also many people and automobiles. When fumes from industrial plants and automobiles mix with moisture in the air, they form **acid rain**. This is a form of air pollution that contains

These statues on the Acropolis are copies of the originals, which are now in the Acropolis Museum.
▶ Why, do you think, were the originals put into the museum?

certain chemicals that can damage trees and plants and even stone structures. Chemicals in the rain have been eating away the surface of ancient statues and carvings on stone. The Greek authorities have removed ancient statues from the Acropolis to protect them.

Farming Greece consists of a mountainous peninsula and more than 2,000 islands, of which only about 169 are inhabited. Much of Greece is not suitable for farming; it is too rugged and rocky. Yet Greek farmers still produce wheat, olives, and grapes. The modern Greeks, like ancient Greeks, are a seagoing people.

Government Greece has had many different forms of government since ancient times. Today, Greece is a republic in which people elect those who govern and make the laws.

271

3 CLOSING THE LESSON

Lesson 4 Review

Answers to Think and Write

A. The ancient ruins bring many tourists to Italy, making tourism a major industry.

B. Spain has a high plateau, mountains, coastlines, and a variety of climates. Snow covers the mountains. The central plateau has hot, dry summers and cold winters. The Atlantic coast has a maritime climate, and the Mediterranean coast has a Mediterranean climate.

C. Portugal and Andorra are Spain's neighbors on the Iberian Peninsula.

D. The pollution generated by industries and autos in Athens produces acid rain which eats away at the surfaces of ancient ruins.

E. Cyprus attracts tourists and grows citrus fruits. Malta's location has made many nations interested in it as a military base.

Answer to Skills Check

Paragraphs may include the countries of the Iberian Peninsula because of their variety of climate and ancient ruins, or Greece because of its ancient ruins, or Cyprus and Malta for their sandy beaches and sunny weather.

Focus Your Reading

Ask the lesson focus question found at the beginning of the lesson: **How do the peoples of the countries of southern Europe make use of their resources?**
(They use their agricultural resources to feed their own people and for export. They use their industrial resources to produce goods for their own people and for export. They use their ruins and natural beauty to attract tourists.)

Additional Practice

You may wish to assign the ancillary materials listed below.

Understanding the Lesson p. 67
Workbook p. 68

Answers to Caption Questions
p. 272 ▶ Lemons

272

E. Island Nations

Cyprus The island of Cyprus is located in the eastern Mediterranean. A large majority of Cypriots are Greeks; the minority are Turks. Disputes between the Greek majority and the Turkish minority have troubled Cyprus in recent times. Cyprus was a British colony before World War II. It became an independent republic in 1960.

In 1974 a dispute caused the Turkish government to send troops to northern Cyprus to support Turkish Cypriots. The Turks captured a large part of northeastern Cyprus, and thousands of Greek Cypriots fled to the southwestern part of the country. Since that time the island has been divided; most Greeks live in the southwest, and most Turks live in the northeast.

Farming, mining, and tourism are major industries in Cyprus. About half of the Cypriots are farmers who grow mainly citrus fruits, such as lemons and oranges. Asbestos is an important mineral on the island. Cyprus had rich deposits of copper, but the mines are now almost empty. In fact, the name *Cyprus* comes from the Greek word for "copper." Cyprus also has sandy beaches and sunny weather for tourists to enjoy.

These workers are harvesting a citrus crop in Cyprus.
▶ What fruit are these citrus farmers harvesting?

Malta Malta is another island nation, but it is much smaller than Cyprus. Malta is located in the middle of a narrow passage in the Mediterranean. As a result, many nations are interested in Malta as a military base. For many years the British controlled Malta because of its location, but in 1964, Malta became an independent republic. Today Malta is a member of the Commonwealth of Nations.

LESSON 4 REVIEW

THINK AND WRITE

A. Why can Italy's ancient ruins be considered a valuable resource? (Infer)

B. Describe the climates and lands of Spain. (Recall)

C. Which countries are Spain's neighbors on the Iberian Peninsula? (Recall)

D. How have modern developments threatened ancient ruins in Athens? (Analyze)

E. Why are Cyprus and Malta important island nations? (Analyze)

SKILLS CHECK

WRITING SKILL
Pretend you are a travel agent. Which of the countries that you have just read about would you recommend to a tourist? Write a descriptive paragraph or two telling the reasons for your recommendation.

272

UNDERSTANDING THE LESSON

NAME _____
UNDERSTANDING THE LESSON   CHAPTER
                                              9
Making Comparisons   LESSON 4 CONTENT MASTER

● The chart helps you to compare the characteristics of three European countries—Spain, Italy, and Greece. Write the missing information in each blank on the chart. A few have been done for you.

	Spain	Italy	Greece
Location	Largest country of Iberian Peninsula	Boot-shaped peninsula in Mediterranean Sea	Peninsula in Mediterranean Sea
Capital	Madrid	Rome	Athens
Geographical Features	High plateau, coasts on Atlantic and Mediterranean, Pyrenees Mountains on northern border	Alps, Apennine Mountains, coasts on Adriatic and Mediterranean, peninsula plus islands of Sicily and Sardinia	Mountainous peninsula, eastern coast on Aegean Sea, 2,000 islands, rugged and rocky
Industry	Service industries, automobiles, machinery, steel, iron, clothing	Machinery, automobiles, shoes, clothing, tourism	Tourism, shipping
Farm Products	Wheat, grains, sheep, oranges, lemons, limes, olives, almonds	Grain, grapes, olives	Wheat, olives, grapes

Think and Write: Write a paragraph comparing the locations and governments of the island nations of Cyprus and Malta. You may use the back of the sheet.
Answers should reflect independent thinking; suggestions appear in the Answer Key.
Use with textbook pages 268–272.

67

◀ Review Master Booklet, p. 67

9 PUTTING IT ALL TOGETHER

USING THE VOCABULARY

landlocked
plateau
pollution
raw materials
exports
Commonwealth of
Nations

fjord
Mediterranean
climates
bilingual
acid rain

From the list above, choose a term that could be used in place of the underlined word or words in each sentence. Rewrite the sentences on a separate sheet of paper.

1. The Netherlands sends to other countries goods such as tulip bulbs and dairy products.
2. Forests produce trees that can be processed into products such as paper and lumber.
3. The group of countries that were once a part of the British Empire includes countries such as Canada and Kenya.
4. A tableland is a plain elevated above the surrounding land.
5. Narrow arms of the sea lying between narrow cliffs are found all along the western coast of Norway.
6. France and most of Italy have cool, rainy winters and hot, dry summers.
7. The unclean condition of some of Germany's rivers has made the North Sea one of the dirtiest bodies of water in the world.
8. Students in Belgium learn to be well-spoken in two languages.
9. Fumes from automobiles mix with moisture in the air to form air pollution.
10. Austria and Switzerland are countries that are surrounded entirely by land.

REMEMBERING WHAT YOU READ

On a separate sheet of paper, answer the following questions in complete sentences.

1. Name three industries in Switzerland.
2. What important event in German history took place in 1990?
3. What four regions make up the United Kingdom?
4. What are the duties of the monarch of the United Kingdom?
5. Why is Ireland a divided island?
6. What countries are known as the Nordic countries?
7. What countries are known as the Low Countries?
8. What type of government do the Low Countries have?
9. Name the three countries on the Iberian Peninsula.
10. What are the two island nations in the Mediterranean Sea?

TYING HEALTH TO SOCIAL STUDIES

In many parts of the world, but especially in industrialized countries, pollution affects people's health. Pretend your class has been asked to participate in Health Awareness Week. You and your classmates have been chosen to create projects promoting the theme "Stop the Pollution." Choose a way that will allow you to best express the theme. You may make a poster, write an essay, make a speech, or choose your own idea. Dedicate the week as Health Awareness Week and share your project with the rest of the class.

273

Using The Vocabulary

1. exports
2. raw materials
3. Commonwealth of Nations
4. plateau
5. fjords
6. Mediterranean climates
7. pollution
8. bilingual
9. acid rain
10. landlocked

Remembering What You Read

1. Three industries in Switzerland are tourism, manufacturing fine time keeping devices, and banking.
2. In 1990, East and West Germany were united to form one country.
3. England, Wales, Scotland, and Northern Ireland make up the United Kingdom.
4. Duties of the monarchy include receiving important foreign visitors and addressing the opening session of Parliament.
5. Protestants in Northern Ireland chose to remain a part of the United Kingdom in 1922.
6. Norway, Sweden, Finland, Denmark, and Iceland are known as the Nordic countries.
7. The Netherlands, Belgium, and Luxembourg are known as the Low Countries.
8. All have democratic monarchies.
9. Spain, Portugal, and Andorra lie on the Iberian Peninsula.
10. Cyprus and Malta are two island nations in the Mediterranean.

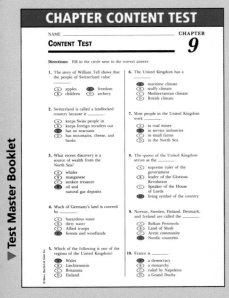

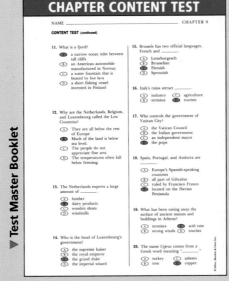

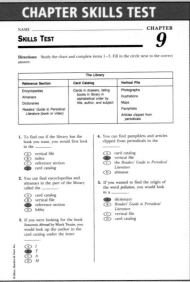

Thinking Critically

1. Possible answers include by not dumping wastes into the rivers, and by finding nontoxic chemicals to use in industry.
2. Answers may include to promote good relations and for convenience when traveling.
3. Possible answers include airline pilots, doctors, travel agents, lawyers, police officers.
4. Answers should reflect independent thinking.
5. Many tourists are interested in traveling to countries that have ancient ruins.

Summarizing The Chapter

Lesson 1
1. Mountains and forests
2. Lakes
3. Rivers, farms, and gardens

Lesson 2
1. Mountains
2. Hills and pastures
3. Glaciers, forests, and fjords

Lesson 3
1. Plateau and rugged mountains
2. Sand dunes
3. Low, flat land

Lesson 4
1. Tourists
2. Exports
3. Ancient ruins

THINKING CRITICALLY

On a separate sheet of paper, answer the following questions in complete sentences.

1. What are some ways that people in industrialized countries can help to eliminate their pollution problem?
2. Why, do you think, is knowing more than one language important for people who live in Western European countries?
3. Many workers in the United Kingdom are employed in service industries. Name at least five service industries in the United States.
4. Denmark has a law requiring that a new tree be planted for every one cut down. Do you think this is a good law? Explain.
5. Explain the connection between ancient history and tourism.

SUMMARIZING THE CHAPTER

On a separate sheet of paper, draw a graphic organizer that is like the one shown here. Copy the information from this graphic organizer to the one you have drawn. Under each main idea, write three statements that support it.

CHAPTER THEME

Physical features, resources, economies, and governments blend together to make the countries of Western Europe what they are today.

LESSON 1
Many resources are found in Switzerland, Austria, and Germany.
1. _____
2. _____
3. _____

LESSON 3
France and the Low Countries have distinctive physical features.
1. _____
2. _____
3. _____

LESSON 2
The British Isles and the Nordic countries have various geographic features.
1. _____
2. _____
3. _____

LESSON 4
The people of the countries of southern Europe make good use of their resources.
1. _____
2. _____
3. _____

274

COOPERATIVE LEARNING

You may wish to refer to the article on Cooperative Learning found in the front of your Teacher's Edition.

As you learned in Unit 2, new ideas and inventions can change society. For example, the invention of the printing press put more information in the hands of more people than ever before. This made modern democracy possible. In addition, developments in agriculture, transportation, and manufacturing have altered the way people live.

Every day, new inventions change our lives. Inventors develop machines that help us do things more efficiently. Many inventors work with others. By sharing ideas, they can solve problems creatively. Similarly, you can share ideas with other students to solve a problem.

PROJECT

Work with a group of classmates to think of an invention for the future. The purpose of the invention will be to solve a problem that exists in today's society or to make people's lives easier.

The first step in the project will be brainstorming. Hold a group meeting to talk about possible inventions. Try to come up with at least ten ideas. Choose one group member to write down all your group's ideas. When you are finished

brainstorming, that person should read the list aloud and ask group members to vote on what they think is the best idea. The winner will be your group's invention.

Next, brainstorm again to discuss ways that your invention would change society. Talk about how your invention would affect people's lives. Choose one group member to take notes on your group's ideas.

Another group member should use the notes to write a short explanation of your invention and a summary of how it would affect society. Someone else in the group should draw a picture to illustrate the invention.

PRESENTATION AND REVIEW

Choose one group member to present your group's invention to the class. Then your group can answer any questions that come up and discuss with the rest of the students how your invention would improve people's lives.

Finally, hold another group meeting to evaluate your project. Did everyone in your group have a job to do? Did the group work well together? Did the class think your invention was a good one?

REMEMBER TO:
- Give your ideas.
- Listen to others' ideas.
- Plan your work with the group.
- Present your project.
- Discuss how your group worked.

275

Objectives

1. **Explain** what *interpreting information* means.

2. **Interpret** information from a paragraph.

Why Do I Need This Skill?

To help students better understand the importance of interpreting information, ask the following question: **If you met a friend in the hallway and he or she frowned at you and said that he or she needed to talk to you after school, how would you interpret that information?**
(Answers may include that the friend is angry or needs your help.)
Explain to students that when they are given some information, often their own knowledge will help them draw certain conclusions.

Learning the Skill

Castles were designed for protection, not comfort. The walls were made of thick stone to make them hard to attack. The windows were small to serve as lookouts. The moat kept attackers away from the walls.

A. WHY DO I NEED THIS SKILL?

The first subheading you read in Chapter 7 said "Copernicus Turns Astronomy Upside Down." This phrase conveys a piece of information, but what does it really mean? How can astronomy be turned upside down?

Copernicus disagreed with the ideas of Ptolemy, the ancient astronomer who believed that the sun, moon, and planets revolve around the earth. Thus, he "turned astronomy upside down" by advancing an idea that was the opposite of what people had believed for centuries.

As you can see, there can be a great deal of meaning behind a simple five-word phrase. But the meaning may not be obvious from the words alone. Often we must seek other facts so that we can better **interpret**, or better understand, information. Knowing how to interpret information is an important skill to learn.

B. LEARNING THE SKILL

This textbook presents a lot of information for you to interpret. One way to get the full meaning behind information is to pose questions and try to think of logical answers based on facts. You might ask yourself questions like these: Why did a particular event occur? What was the result? What picture does some information create in my mind?

In Chapter 6 you read some information about castles built during the Middle Ages. Suppose a typical medieval castle was described to you like this.

Medieval castles were usually found in hard-to-reach places. The first castles were made of wood, but later in the Middle Ages they had thick stone walls. These walls kept the inside of the castles cold and damp. The windows were very small, letting in little sunlight. A moat, a water-filled ditch, circled the castle walls on the outside. The water in the moat looked dirty.

By asking and trying to answer questions about the statements presented, you can interpret the information to discover its full meaning. For example, why were the castles built in hard-to-reach places? Why were the walls thick and made of stone? Why weren't the windows made larger to allow more sunlight to come in and reduce the dampness? What is the function of the moat around the castle? Turn back to pages 175 and 177 and reread the section about castles to find answers to these questions.

By asking questions and probing deeper into the information your social studies textbook presents, you can gain a better understanding of the facts.

C. PRACTICING THE SKILL

The following statements are from Lesson 3 of Chapter 6. Use the questioning strategy and the information in the lesson, which begins on page 184, to interpret each statement. Find facts to support the statements and write your interpretations on a separate sheet of paper.

Optional Activities

Reteaching Activity

● Have students skim Chapter 9, Lesson 4, and develop interpretations about the information presented.

● Have them write down the facts that were presented and develop an interpretation for each.

● Student answers should approximate the following: (Fact) The countries of southern Europe have many resources. (Interpretation) They all make use of their resources to create income. Many use their ancient ruins and beautiful countryside as tourist attractions that bring in revenue. Others export their natural and manufactured products.

1. This interest in learning about the Romans and Greeks led to a birth of interest in newer types of learning.
2. The Renaissance gave Europeans new and different ideas about themselves and about the world.
3. By learning Greek, they [the students] could "speak with Homer and Plato."
4. Many students were eager to read the books that had been found, but only a few could do so.
5. Much was happening during the Renaissance, and not all of it can be described as "rebirth."

The following statements are from Lesson 2 of Chapter 8, which starts on page 227. Again, use the questioning strategy that you learned about on page 276 to help you interpret the statements below. Then find facts in the lesson to support these statements and write your interpretations on a separate sheet of paper.

1. People had good reason to call this a *world war*.
2. The peace treaties of 1919 changed the map of Europe.
3. Italy was on the winning side in World War I, but the Italians faced difficulties in 1919.
4. The Italian king was so alarmed that he offered to make Mussolini the prime minister.
5. Hitler repeated over and over that Germany had lost the war because of a "stab in the back."

D. APPLYING THE SKILL

To get the most out of your social studies textbook—and all books that you read—you will need to interpret information. Think about what questions you need to raise to interpret what you read. What is the meaning behind each statement? How are the presented facts related to each other? What additional information do you need to better understand statements? Use this skill to interpret as you read this textbook.

277

 Optional Activities

Homework Activity
- Have students complete a diagram that shows information presented in Chapter 9, Lesson 4; questions raised by the information; and their interpretations.
- Information could include: The countries of southern Europe use their resources to create revenue, and the lands and climates of these countries vary.
- Questions could include: How do resources create revenue? How do land and climate affect industry?
- Interpretations could include: Southern European countries use their natural geography and ancient ruins to attract tourism, which brings in revenue. Some countries export oil, coal, and manufactured products.

Practicing the Skill
1. Old ideas and rediscovery of cultural heritages led to new ideas.
2. Europeans changed their views about themselves and the universe.
3. Students were able to read and understand great Greek writers and philosophers.
4. Very few copies of the ancient works were available.
5. New ideas and new discoveries occurred as well as a "Renaissance" or "rebirth."

For students who are having difficulty with the concept of interpreting information, you may wish to use the reteaching activity shown below.

Applying the Skill
Encourage students to use this skill in all of their readings.

SKILL TRACE: Interpreting Information		
INTRODUCE PE pp. 276–277	**PRACTICE** TE pp. 276–277 RMB p. 86 WB pp. 77, 85, 89 TE p. 306	**TEST** Unit 2 Test, TMB

277

Objectives
★**1. Define** *SQR*.

2. Describe Each step in the SQR study-reading strategy.

Why Do I Need This Skill?

To help students better understand the importance of SQR when organizing and remembering important information from any reading material, ask students to brainstorm how they could possibly remember all the information in their textbook. Answers should reflect an understanding that trying to remember *all* that they read is not practical. Students will need to devise some way to summarize information to remember the most important points. Tell students that SQR—Survey, Question, Read—is just such a strategy. Not only will it help students with social studies, but they can also apply this skill to any other subjects that they read.

Learning the Skill

To check students' comprehension of SQR, ask the following questions:

1. **What is the reason for surveying the lesson before you read?**
(It will give you a good idea of the topic.)

2. **What steps are involved in surveying any text?**
(First scan the heading, questions, and vocabulary words, then look at the visuals to get an overview.)

3. **What section of your social studies book helps you with the second step of SQR?**
(The "Focus Your Reading" questions provide a built-in focus question.)

SKILL TRACE:	Understanding Main Ideas and Details	
INTRODUCE PE pp. 278–279	**PRACTICE** TE pp. 278–279 TE p. 282 RMB p. 2 WB pp. 20, 35	**TEST** Chapter 15 Test, TMB

A. WHY DO I NEED THIS SKILL?

Your social studies textbook contains a great deal of information about people, places, and events. You will find many ideas to learn and understand. Using a study-reading strategy such as **SQR** will help you identify, organize, and remember main ideas and important information.

B. LEARNING THE SKILL

SQR stands for **Survey**, **Question**, and **Read**.

Survey—When you survey, or skim over, the lesson, you will get a general idea of what the lesson is about. Begin surveying by scanning the headings, questions, and vocabulary words. Look at any pictures, maps, tables, or charts you find in the lesson. Doing this will give you a good idea of the topic of the lesson. Think about what you already know about this topic. Then see if you can make some predictions, or guesses, about what will be in the lesson.

Question—The next step is preparing a list of questions about the lesson. The FOCUS YOUR READING questions in this book will help you concentrate on the main idea of each lesson. Take another look at the vocabulary list, headings, and picture captions, and compose questions that you think deal with important ideas. You should be able to answer your questions as you read. Write your questions on a sheet of paper or make a mental list of them.

Read—The last step is reading the lesson to find the answers to your questions. Write down the answers as you find them. Other questions may come to mind as you read. Add them to your list and try to answer them, too.

C. PRACTICING THE SKILL

Turn to page 179. You can practice **SQR** on Lesson 2 in Chapter 6, "The People of the Towns and the Church." Refer to the **USING SQR** table to help you remember the steps.

Survey the lesson, following the directions given above. Think about what you might already know about the people in the Middle Ages. Try to make predictions about the lesson.

Now make a list of questions about the lesson and write them on a sheet of paper. Leave some space after each question so you can write the answer later. You might begin by writing down the FOCUS YOUR READING question. This question is very valuable because it helps you understand the main idea of the lesson. Take another look at the vocabulary list. Make up a question for each unfamiliar word. For instance, you might write *What is a monastery?* The lesson headings can also be turned into questions. You

278

Homework Activity

● To illustrate to students the effectiveness of good reading skills, have students practice the SQR reading strategy at home with sources other than textbooks.

● Ask students to select an appropriate reading of their choosing. You may wish to help students select the materials, suggesting perhaps a newspaper or magazine article, a book for another class or subject, or a book for pleasure reading.

● Have students follow the SQR strategies to complete the reading.

● Ask student volunteers to describe what they read, explain the process they followed, and the questions asked and answers given.

could ask, "What was life in a monastery like during the Middle Ages?" See if you can think of five questions about this lesson.

Now you are ready to read the lesson and answer your questions. Write the answers on your paper. If you think of any more questions as you read, write those questions on your paper and look for the answers.

SQR will be especially helpful when you study for a test. Save your **SQR** questions and answers so you can use them to review the chapter.

Use **SQR** as you read the next chapter, which is about the geography of the Soviet Union and Eastern Europe. See if using **SQR** helps you to understand and remember the important ideas in that chapter. See if it is any easier to complete the Chapter Review.

D. APPLYING THE SKILL

You can use **SQR** steps to learn and understand the material in almost any subject. The **USING SQR** table will help you.

USING SQR

Survey	• Look at headings, questions, vocabulary words, and visuals.	• Think about what you already know about the topic.	• Make predictions about the lesson topic.
Question	• Think about the questions already in the lesson.	• Use vocabulary words, headings, and other lesson features to prepare your own questions.	• Make predictions about the lesson content.
Read	• Read to answer your questions.	• Write down the answers or say them to yourself.	• Ask and answer any other questions that come to mind as you read.

279

4. **Why might writing down questions be preferable to remembering them?**
(Answers may include that there is so much to remember, that it would be handier to have a written list than to trust all your questions to memory.)

5. **Why, do you think, is "Read" the last step of SQR instead of the first step?**
(Answers may include that by using the first two prereading strategies, information and questions are organized and focused, allowing the reader to concentrate on the key information.)

Practicing the Skill
Answers should reflect independent thinking but should reflect appropriate SQR reading strategies and corresponding questions and answers. You may wish to review the chart at the bottom of p. 279 with students who are having difficulty implementing the concept independently.

Applying the Skill
Encourage students to use SQR with future lessons. You may wish to have student volunteers make a poster of the chart on p. 279 in order to provide visual support throughout the year.

Reteaching Activity

● Select a reading selection of approximately one page in length and copy it for each student who demonstrates difficulty in implementing the SQR reading strategy independently.

● Guide students through a review of the chart on p. 279, pausing to ask questions to ensure students' comprehension of each step.

● Guide students through implementation of the first step of SQR (surveying), helping students scan the passage for important information.

● Continue with the remaining steps of the process.

● Reinforce the SQR strategy with follow-up assignments.

Optional Activities

The Former Soviet Union and Eastern Europe

Unit Theme The region of the former Soviet Union and Eastern Europe is unique because of its history, geography, and diverse peoples.

Chapter 10 Geography of the Former Soviet Union and Eastern Europe

(pp. 282–301)

Theme The former Soviet Union and the countries of Eastern Europe are lands of great diversity, in both geography and the people who live there.

Chapter 11 History of Russia and Eastern Europe

(pp. 302–321)

Theme Many changes occurred in Russia and Eastern Europe during the period from the Middle Ages to 1917.

Chapter 12 The Former Soviet Union and Eastern Europe Today

(pp. 322–348)

Theme Events that began in the 1980s have resulted in great changes in the former Soviet Union and in the countries of Eastern Europe.

September	October	November	December	January	February	March	April	May
Chapters MSH-1	Chapters 2-4	Chapters 5-7	Chapters 8-9	Chapters 10-12	Chapters 13-14	Chapters 15-17	Chapters 18-20	Chapters 21-23

PACING GUIDE

Bulletin Board Idea

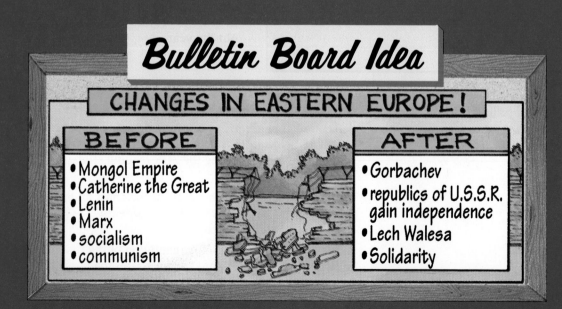

CHANGES IN EASTERN EUROPE!

BEFORE
- Mongol Empire
- Catherine the Great
- Lenin
- Marx
- socialism
- communism

AFTER
- Gorbachev
- republics of U.S.S.R. gain independence
- Lech Walesa
- Solidarity

Student Activity
Encourage students to be aware of current events in the region of the former Soviet Union and Eastern Europe. Ask students to present oral reports on media coverage of current events in this region and to bring in newspaper and magazine articles about the events.

Annotated Bibliography

Books for Teachers

Massie, Suzanne. *Land of the Firebird.* New York: Simon & Schuster, 1982. ISBN 0-671-46059-0-5. (Ch. 11) This easily read history of Russia from the Middle Ages to the Revolution treats arts, dance, and music, as well as the leading political figures.

Shipler, David K. *Russia: Broken Idols, Solomn Dreams.* New York: Viking Penguin, 1984. ISBN 0-1400-7408-2. (Ch. 12) This is a lively description of Soviet life by an American journalist who served as a correspondent for an American newspaper in the Soviet Union.

Time-Life Books, eds. *Library of Nations: Soviet Union.* Alexandria, VA: Time-Life Books, 1985. ISBN 0-8094-5327-4. (Ch. 12) One volume in a series of books dealing with individual countries and published by Time-Life, this presents in text and pictures the geography, historical background, and contemporary life in the Soviet Union.

Books for Students

Donica, Ewa and Tim Sharman. *We Live in Poland.* Danbury, CT: Franklin Watts, 1985. ISBN 0-531-03879-X. (Ch. 12) A portrait of Poland is presented through the eyes of Polish citizens from a variety of backgrounds and experiences, and includes color photographs.

Carren, Betty. *Romania.* Chicago: Children's Press, 1988. ISBN 0-516-02703-4. (Ch. 12) This is a well-illustrated guide to one of Eastern Europe's most ardently Communist countries prior to the revolutions of 1989.

Gibson, Michael. *The Knights.* New York: Arco Publishing, 1979. ISBN 0-668-04785-2. (Ch. 14) Gibson describes the lifestyle, training, dress, and skills required of the brave knights of old.

Hautzig, Esther. *The Endless Steppe: Growing up in Siberia.* New York: Thomas Crowell Publishers, 1960. ISBN 0-690-26371-6. (Ch. 11) This true story of the author's girlhood in Siberia, where she and her parents were sent in 1939, captures not only the political reasons for deportation but the physical and social realities of the Siberian climate.

Lye, Keith. *Take a Trip to Eastern Europe.* Danbury, CT: Franklin Watts, 1987. ISBN 0-531-10287-4. (Ch. 10) A look inside the daily life of Eastern Europe is given through this brief, yet thorough, book.

Lye, Keith. *Take a Trip to Trip to Czechoslovakia.* Danbury, CT: Franklin Watts, 1986. ISBN 0-531-10195-9. (Ch. 10) The history, culture, and geography of Czechoslovakia are presented along with numerous photographs and maps.

Lye, Keith. *Take a Trip to Romania.* Danbury, CT: Franklin Watts, 1988. ISBN 0-531-10468-0. (Ch. 10) Excellent illustrations add to the effectiveness of the text in covering life in Romania during the mid-1980s.

Lye, Keith. *Take a Trip to Yugoslavia.* Danbury, CT: Franklin Watts, 1988. ISBN 0-531-10289-0. (Ch. 10) Another in the "Take a Trip" series, this title presents the life of average citizens who live and work in Yugoslavia.

Resnick, Abraham. *Russia: A History to 1917.* Children's Press, 1983. ISBN 0-516-02785-9. (Ch. 11) This colorful history of the Russian empire, its czars and serfs, is presented with photographs and maps.

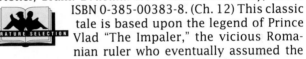

Stoker, Bram. *Dracula.* New York: Doubleday, 1973. ISBN 0-385-00383-8. (Ch. 12) This classic tale is based upon the legend of Prince Vlad "The Impaler," the vicious Romanian ruler who eventually assumed the name "Dracula," meaning "son of the devil."

Tucker, Ernest E. *The Story of Knights in Armor.* New York: Lothrop, Lee, and Shepard, 1961. (Ch. 14) Tucker describes the romantic, yet arduous life of the knight in armor.

Filmstrips and Videos

Children of the Soviet Union. 16mm or videocassette. Coronet Film & Video, 1988. (Ch. 12) This video profiles the daily life of children in the Soviet Union.

A Day in the Life of The Soviet Union. Videocassette. AIMS Media, 1988. (Ch. 12) This fascinating documentary follows the photojournalists who set out to record the vast array of lifestyles, regions, and cultures in the world's largest country.

Eastern Europe: An Introduction. Videocassette. Phoenix/BFA Film & Video, 1987. (Ch. 12) The history, culture, and customs of Eastern European countries are shown in a positive light.

Mountain People. Videocassette, 50 min. Landmark Films, 1989. (Ch. 11) This video looks at life in a mountain village in the Soviet state of Georgia, which retains much of its culture from the 19th century.

Soviet Union: Changing Times. 16mm or videocassette. Churchill Films, 1989. (Ch. 12) This video looks at life in the Soviet Union in the late 1980s and the changes being brought about by the policy of perestroika.

The Russian Revolutions

Why did the Russian revolutions occur?

The Russian revolutions of the 20th century changed the history of Russia and the world. Like the American Revolution before them, the Russian revolutions were felt far beyond the borders of the country where they occurred. The effects of the revolutions were felt for years by millions of people. The following activities center on these revolutions, their causes, effects, and ramifications.

SOCIAL STUDIES

Economics Like the American Revolution, the Russian revolutions were influenced by the economic conditions of the day.

■ Have students research the economic conditions at the time of the Russian revolutions. Make sure that they differentiate among the nobles, clergy, middle class, and peasants.

■ Ask students to explain the impact economics had on the revolutions.

■ Other students may wish to create a chart paralleling the American Revolution of 1776 with the Russian Revolution of 1917. Have them list the differences and similarities.

Political Science The people of Russia objected to the autocratic power of the czar. In 1917, the people demanded more power. When it was denied, the people revolted.

■ Have students look up the word autocracy. Ask the students to think about the nature of an autocracy.

■ Students may want to role-play or debate the following topics:

1. What are some advantages and disadvantages of autocracy?

2. Should the United States turn to autocracy to solve its problems? Why or why not?

History The Russian revolutions of 1905 and 1917 were not isolated events. They were part of an ongoing process. Some people trace these events back to the French Revolution.

■ Review the definitions of cause and effect with the students and then ask them to examine Russia's history.

■ Have students list the events that caused the Russian revolutions and place these events on a time line. Events may include the Crimean War (1853), the assassination of Czar Alexander II (1881), the reign of Czar Nicholas II (1894-1917), Bloody Sunday (1905), Lenin's seizure of power (1917), and World War I (1914-1917).

Global Awareness The Russian revolutions affected more than just the people of Russia. Have students create a chart showing the countries that were directly affected by the revolutions and have them briefly describe how they were affected. (For example, after 1917, many European countries sent troops to Russia to prevent the spread of Communism.

■ Students may wish to locate (on a world map) the countries that were affected or they may wish to practice their critical thinking by answering the following question in a written report: How might the world be different if the Russian revolutions had not occurred?

LANGUAGE ARTS

■ After students have learned about the events that lead to the Russian Revolution of 1917, have them imagine that they were alive in Russia during these years. Ask them to write a journal entry that reflects the events of the day.

ART

■ Many of the peasants who took part in the revolutions were uneducated or illiterate. People often communicated through political cartoons and drawings.

■ Have students create a picture, cartoon, or poster designed to convey information about the revolutions or the causes of the revolutions.

MATHEMATICS

■ Part of the problem with the ruling of Russia in the late 19th and early 20th century was the size of the country (in terms of area and population). It is estimated **that** 10% of the world's people lived in Russia in 1900.

■ Have students use an atlas, almanac, or encyclopedia to research the population of the world in 1900, and then have students compute the population of Russia at that time.

■ Have students research the following questions and put the answers in graph form:

1. What is the current population of Russia?

2. What is the current population of the world?

3. Which country has the most people today?

4. What percentage of the world's population lives in Russia today?

MUSIC

■ A popular form of classical music, known as "nationalistic music," flourished in Russia during the time of the revolutions. The leading Russian nationalistic composer of the time, Sergei Prokofiev (1891–1953), expressed the feelings of the Russian people in his works by including elements of folk songs and folk dances.

■ Borrow one of Prokofiev's works from a local library and play it for the class. (Students may already be familiar with his *Peter and the Wolf* or enjoy his *Classical Symphony*.)

■ Ask students to share what feelings the music evokes in them and suggest how Prokofiev's experience living in Russia during the time of the revolutions might have influenced his music.

Do Current Events

INSTRUCTIONS FOR THE TEACHER:

Using Current Events With This Unit In this unit, students will be learning about the lands, people, and history of Eastern Europe and the former Soviet Union. In light of the history-making changes that have recently taken place in this region, this seems the perfect place to use current events in your social studies curriculum.

Defining *Current Events* Direct students' attention to the chalkboard as you write the word *current*. Discuss what this word means, and look it up in the dictionary. Do the same with the word *event*. Now, ask students what *current events* are, and have them give examples of *current events*. (Students may respond by giving you recent news stories.) Now ask: *Where can we find out about current events in our community, our state, our nation, and our world? Let's name at least five places.* (Responses may include newspapers, magazines, television news broadcasts or specialty news shows, radio news, radio and television talk shows, pamphlets, and so on.)

Why Study Current Events? Share with students that the answer to the above question is probably the same as the answer to the question *Why study history?* We study history to learn about our past. This helps us to understand why things are the way they are today. We can learn from our mistakes. Studying history makes studying current events more meaningful, and studying current events enhances the study of history.

An Example to Share You may wish to explain the importance of studying current events by using the following example: It would be hard for students to understand why many Soviet people were happy when the Soviet Union collapsed in 1991 if they did not know something about the history of the Soviet Union. A knowledge of the many nationalities that made up the Soviet Union and the fact that many of these groups were forced to become part of the U.S.S.R. contributes to an understanding of the significance of the collapse of the Soviet Union. Students should note that current events are the continuation or next chapter of the story concerning many of the things that they are reading in their history book today. The following activities should help them see current events as such.

ACTIVITIES FOR THE STUDENTS:

Current Events Bulletin Board Have the class work together to write a synopsis of one lesson or chapter from this unit on a large index card. Post the card on the bulletin board. The card should end with the words *TO BE CONTINUED...* Students should then find some type of media coverage (newspaper or magazine article, written summary of a radio or television newscast), that deals with the topic today. The article or summary should be added to the bulletin board. (An example would be a summary of the lesson about the collapse of the Soviet Union, followed by an article or summary of a newscast featuring an interview with someone who has recently visited the former Soviet Union.)

Current Events Scrapbook Students can build a class scrapbook of current events by bringing relevant articles to class as they study a particular topic. The articles can be pasted in the scrapbook, accompanied by a short, written summary. This can be an individual activity or a small-group activity.

Sharing In Class As students share their current events with the class, award one extra-credit point for each current event that is somehow related to the lesson or chapter being studied. Students may wish to share their current events through a five-minute "news broadcast" at the beginning of class each day.

Current Events Game Have students bring current-events articles about Eastern Europe or the former Soviet Union to class. After these have been posted on a bulletin board, a game can be played. Show students sentence strips on which you have written a one-sentence summary of each article. Students can then match each summary to the corresponding headline or article.

Using video In light of how fast history-making changes are occurring in the Eastern Hemisphere, your students may wish to evaluate these current events via videotape. This can be done by recording excerpts of news broadcasts that relate to this unit (events in any of the countries in the region of the former Soviet Union and Eastern Europe). These videotapes can be brought to school (by you or students) and watched by the class. Video equipment might be in your school or school library, or can be rented inexpensively in your community. Students may follow up the video presentation with a discussion or by answering questions that you provide.

Unit Test

CONTENT TEST

Directions: Fill in the circle next to the correct answer.

1. Which of the following is the definition of *tributary*?
   - Ⓐ a country that must give money to an empire
   - Ⓑ a river that flows into the sea
   - Ⓒ a small stream that flows into a larger stream
   - Ⓓ an official in a Soviet assembly

2. The Ural Mountains form part of the boundary that separates Europe _____.
   - Ⓐ from Asia Minor
   - Ⓑ into the east and the west
   - Ⓒ from Asia
   - Ⓓ from the Communist world

3. In which of the following places would you find permafrost?
   - Ⓐ at the frozen source of the Volga River
   - Ⓑ under the surface of the magnetic North Pole
   - Ⓒ several feet below the topsoil in the tundra
   - Ⓓ in the northernmost steppe

4. The treeless arctic plain is called the _____.
   - Ⓐ steppes
   - Ⓑ ice cap
   - Ⓒ taiga
   - Ⓓ tundra

5. Where is the source of the Danube River?
   - Ⓐ the Red Sea
   - Ⓑ the Black Forest
   - Ⓒ the Black Sea
   - Ⓓ the White Nile

6. Which of the following provides an outlet for the Black Sea?
   - Ⓐ the Volga
   - Ⓑ the Bosporous
   - Ⓒ the Urals
   - Ⓓ the Vistula

7. Which of these rivers flows through the most countries?
   - Ⓐ Po River
   - Ⓑ Danube River
   - Ⓒ Volga River
   - Ⓓ Rhone River

8. What is a folk tale?
   - Ⓐ a story handed down from one generation to another
   - Ⓑ a falsehood shared by a culture to confuse outsiders
   - Ⓒ a German plan for social equality developed by Carl Schurz
   - Ⓓ a type of traditional music played on banjo and guitar

9. The process that divided the Roman Catholic Church and the Eastern Orthodox Church was called the _____.
   - Ⓐ Vatican Council
   - Ⓑ reformation
   - Ⓒ partition
   - Ⓓ schism

10. Which leader gained undisputed control of the steppes in 1206?
   - Ⓐ Ali Akbar Khan
   - Ⓑ Kublai Khan
   - Ⓒ Peter Kropotkin
   - Ⓓ Genghis Khan

© Silver, Burdett & Ginn Inc.

CONTENT TEST (continued)

11. The Russian state of Muscovy was forced to pay tribute to _____.
    - Ⓐ Ivan the Terrible
    - Ⓑ Nicholas I
    - Ⓒ the Golden Horde
    - Ⓓ Napoleon Bonaparte

12. What is the Russian word for *Caesar*?
    - Ⓐ czar
    - Ⓑ Kezar
    - Ⓒ Kaiser
    - Ⓓ Chekhov

13. Which Russian ruler was interested in shipbuilding?
    - Ⓐ Catherine the Great
    - Ⓑ Peter the Great
    - Ⓒ Ivan III
    - Ⓓ Alexander II

14. Which Russian ruler abdicated and was later executed?
    - Ⓐ Nicholas II
    - Ⓑ Nicholas III
    - Ⓒ Ivan IV
    - Ⓓ Alexander Herzen

15. Which leader is regarded as the founder of the Soviet Union?
    - Ⓐ Marx
    - Ⓑ Lenin
    - Ⓒ Stalin
    - Ⓓ Bakunin

16. In which year did the Russian Revolution take place?
    - Ⓐ 1776
    - Ⓑ 1850
    - Ⓒ 1789
    - Ⓓ 1917

17. Joseph Stalin enforced a plan to _____.
    - Ⓐ kill the czar and his family
    - Ⓑ form collective farms
    - Ⓒ introduce *perestroika*
    - Ⓓ make Kropotkin ruler of Russia

18. Who defended Nikita Khrushchev's attack on Joseph Stalin?
    - Ⓐ Mikhail Gorbachev
    - Ⓑ Peter Kropotkin
    - Ⓒ Alexander Kerensky
    - Ⓓ Vaslav Nijinsky

19. Which event signaled the unification of East and West Germany?
    - Ⓐ the election that put Solidarity in control of the Parliament
    - Ⓑ the election of Vaclav Havel as the country's first non-communist president
    - Ⓒ the opening of the wall that separated East and West Berlin
    - Ⓓ the execution of Nikolae Ceausescu

20. By 1990, which of the following countries had not experienced democratic reforms?
    - Ⓐ Czechoslovakia
    - Ⓑ Romania
    - Ⓒ Albania
    - Ⓓ Poland

© Silver, Burdett & Ginn Inc.

SKILLS TEST

Directions: Read the paragraphs and complete items 1–5. Fill in the circle next to the correct answer.

By the 1960s, there were three kinds of farms in the Soviet Union. About half of the farmland was in state farms, and a little less in collective farms. Only a small percentage of the land was privately owned.

The state farms were completely owned by the state. The farmers got a salary from the government and were treated like any other worker. A typical state farm was very large. It might have about 600 workers. These were the best equipped farms in the Soviet Union. They were also the most specialized. Many were dairy farms or cattle ranches. Some of them were huge vegetable farms near large cities.

The collective farms were half as large as the state farms. They were less well equipped and less specialized. On the collective farms, the harvests of all the farmers were combined and sold at a set price. From the money earned, each farmer was paid according to the amount of time he or she worked. Few people wanted to work on the collectives.

The private farms were not true farms. They were small plots that were worked by the owners in their spare time. They worked hard on their private plots because they were allowed to sell their produce for a profit. They specialized in such things as vegetables and eggs, which could be sold for high prices. These private plots produced 30 percent of the food in the Soviet Union, even though they took up only 3 percent of the farmland.

1. The main purpose of these paragraphs is to compare _____.
   - Ⓐ the importance of crops and dairy products in the Soviet Union
   - Ⓑ Soviet farm and factories
   - Ⓒ state, collective, and private farms in the Soviet Union
   - Ⓓ publicly and privately owned businesses in the Soviet Union

2. Which statement is true?
   - Ⓐ Collective farms used the least land.
   - Ⓑ State farms employed the fewest workers.
   - Ⓒ Private farms produced about one third of the food grown in the Soviet Union.
   - Ⓓ Collective farms were the most specialized.

3. One difference between private and state farms was that on private farms the farmers _____.
   - Ⓐ earned money
   - Ⓑ owned the land
   - Ⓒ specialized in certain products
   - Ⓓ sometimes raised vegetables

4. Compared to state farms, collective farms were _____.
   - Ⓐ larger
   - Ⓑ less well equipped
   - Ⓒ more specialized
   - Ⓓ more popular

5. Which farms were most alike?
   - Ⓐ private and collective
   - Ⓑ collective and state
   - Ⓒ state and private
   - Ⓓ collective and specialized

© Silver, Burdett & Ginn Inc.

SKILLS TEST (continued)

Directions: Study the map and complete items 6–10. Fill in the circle next to the correct answer.

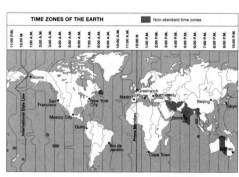

TIME ZONES OF THE EARTH   ▓ Non-standard time zones

6. At 2:00 P.M. in San Francisco, what time is it in Rio de Janeiro?
   - Ⓐ 7:00 P.M.
   - Ⓑ 9:00 A.M.
   - Ⓒ 9:00 P.M.
   - Ⓓ 4:00 A.M.

7. If you are in New York and want to call a friend in Mexico City shortly before 8:00 A.M., her time, when should you call?
   - Ⓐ 6:30 A.M.
   - Ⓑ 8:30 A.M.
   - Ⓒ 7:30 A.M.
   - Ⓓ 9:30 A.M.

8. What is the time difference between Nome and Cape Town?
   - Ⓐ 4 hours
   - Ⓑ 7 hours
   - Ⓒ 10 hours
   - Ⓓ 12 hours

9. When it is 1:00 P.M. in Bucharest, Romania, the time in New York is _____.
   - Ⓐ 12 hours later
   - Ⓑ 6 hours earlier
   - Ⓒ 9 hours later
   - Ⓓ 7 hours earlier

10. When it is 3:00 P.M. on April 21 in Bucharest, what is the time and date in Tokyo, Japan?
    - Ⓐ 5:00 A.M., April 22
    - Ⓑ 11:00 P.M., April 20
    - Ⓒ 10:00 P.M., April 21
    - Ⓓ 10:00 A.M., April 21

© Silver, Burdett & Ginn Inc.

NAME _____   U N I T

ESSAY TEST   **3**

Directions: Write a response to items 1–4.

> **REMINDER:** Read and think about each item before you
> write your response. Be sure to think of the points you want to
> cover, details that support your response, and reasons for your
> opinions. Then, on the lines below, write your response in
> complete sentences.

1. What straits allow ocean traffic to and from the Black Sea?

A satisfactory response should include the following statements:

• The straits, the Dardanelles and the Bosporus, provide the only outlets from the Black Sea.

• Both straits control access from the Black Sea to the Mediterranean Sea.

• The straits are important for trade and transportation for these countries and for all the lands on the Danube.

An excellent response might also

• mention that the straits divide Europe from Asia

• explain that the Bosporus leads to the Sea of Marmara, and the Dardanelles leads to the Aegean Sea.

_____

_____

_____

_____

2. What was the Golden Horde?

A satisfactory response should include the following statements:

• The Golden Horde consisted of people from Mongolia who gained control of all the nomadic people living on the steppes.

• Armies led by these Mongols conquered most of Asia and eastern Europe.

• The Mongols created a huge empire, and they demanded money and laborers from the lands they conquered.

An excellent response might also

• include information about the Golden Horde's invasion of Russia and their eventual defeat

• identify Genghis Khan and Batu Khan.

_____

_____

© Silver, Burdett & Ginn Inc.

NAME _____   UNIT 3

ESSAY TEST (continued)

3. How did Communists gain control of the Russian revolution?

A satisfactory response should include the following statements:

• After revolution broke out in Russia, different groups argued about what kind of government the new Russia should have.

• Lenin and his followers, who believed in Communism, took control of Petrograd and Moscow and claimed to be the official government.

• After two years of civil war, the communists controlled all of Russia.

An excellent response might also

• mention the influence of Karl Marx

• define communism and socialism

• describe Lenin's career before the revolution

• explain the results of the communist takeover.

_____

_____

_____

_____

4. What Soviet leader brought reform to the Soviet Union and influenced change throughout Eastern Europe?

A satisfactory response should identify Mikhail Gorbachev, mention his policies of *glasnost* and *perestroika*, and explain his influence on change during the 1980s and 1990s.

An excellent response might also

• include specific examples

• reflect independent thinking

• compare Soviet policy under Gorbachev with that of his predecessors.

_____

_____

_____

_____

_____

_____

_____

_____

© Silver, Burdett & Ginn Inc.

Midterm Test

CONTENT TEST

Directions: Fill in the circle next to the correct answer.

1. In a civilization, people always _____.

- (A) have different occupations
- (B) hunt animals for food
- (C) use weapons to kill their enemies
- (D) travel in boats

2. The Rosetta Stone helped scholars understand _____.

- (A) the Code of Hammurabi
- (B) hieroglyphics
- (C) Rosettan civilization
- (D) Babylonian writings

3. Who controlled the government of ancient Athens?

- (A) all the people of Athens
- (B) Socrates
- (C) male Athenian citizens
- (D) the Acropolis

4. Plat's writings tell about the teachings of _____.

- (A) Bucephalus
- (B) Aristotle
- (C) Xerxes
- (D) Socrates

5. Rome defeated Carthage in the _____.

- (A) Battle of Salamis
- (B) Battle of Marathon
- (C) Peloponnesian Wars
- (D) Punic Wars

6. In Rome citizens were divided into two classes, _____.

- (A) Caesars and Italians
- (B) masters and slaves
- (C) plebeians and patricians
- (D) consuls and consoles

7. One of the oldest ruins in India is _____.

- (A) the Hindu Kush
- (B) Mohenjo-Daro
- (C) Mojo Asoka
- (D) the Taj Mahal

8. What are dialects?

- (A) different forms of a language
- (B) the sayings of Confucius
- (C) life-size soldiers made of clay
- (D) characters used in Chinese writing

9. What kind of information do you find on a climograph?

- (A) temperature and precipitation
- (B) climate and altitude
- (C) height and weight
- (D) news and weather

10. A group of angry nobles forced King John to _____.

- (A) swim the English Channel
- (B) sign the Magna Carta
- (C) have Thomas More beheaded
- (D) become a serf

Use after the completion of Chapter 12.

© Silver, Burdett & Ginn Inc.

CONTENT TEST (continued)

11. What was the purpose of the Reformation?

- (A) to win control of the Holy Land
- (B) to make Martin Luther king of Germany
- (C) to reform the Catholic Church
- (D) to renew interest in art and science

12. The growth of cities was caused by the increase of _____.

- (A) buildings
- (B) farms
- (C) industrial serfs
- (D) factories

13. What leader became emperor of France?

- (A) Louis XVII
- (B) Oliver Cromwell
- (C) Napoleon Bonaparte
- (D) Giuseppe Mazzini

14. Who was responsible for uniting Germany?

- (A) Carl Schurz
- (B) Otto von Bismarck
- (C) Count Cavour
- (D) Archduke Franz Ferdinand

15. Who is the living symbol of the United Kingdom?

- (A) the queen
- (B) Winston Churchill
- (C) the pope
- (D) the bald eagle

16. Which river flows into the Black Sea?

- (A) the Danube
- (B) the Volga
- (C) the Rhine
- (D) the Mississippi

17. Which of the following best describes the Golden Horde?

- (A) wildebeests
- (B) Mongols
- (C) the czar's treasury
- (D) Lenin and his followers

18. What do we call the belief in the common ownership of land and industry by all the people of a country?

- (A) capitalism
- (B) fascism
- (C) communism
- (D) industrialism

19. During the 1930s Stalin forced Soviet farmers to combine their land into _____.

- (A) labor camps
- (B) collective farms
- (C) socialist republics
- (D) farm teams

20. Which leader introduced the policy of *glasnost* in the Soviet Union during the 1980s?

- (A) Mikhail Gorbachev
- (B) Nikita Khrushchev
- (C) Carl Schurz
- (D) Joseph Stalin

Use after the completion of Chapter 12.

© Silver, Burdett & Ginn Inc.

ESSAY TEST

Directions: Write a response to items 1–4.

> **REMINDER:** Read and think about each item before you write your response. Be sure to think of the points you want to cover, details that support your response, and reasons for your opinions. Then, on the lines below, write your response in complete sentences.

1. What are the *Iliad* and the *Odyssey*?

A satisfactory response should include the following statements:

- The *Iliad* and the *Odyssey* are epic poems.
- They were written by Homer, a blind Greek poet.
- They tell about the Trojan War and the years that followed.

An excellent response might also include

- an explanation of how Homer combined myth and history
- specific incidents or characters from the works
- the terms *epic*, *myth*, and *narrative*.

2. How did the Roman government treat Christians?

A satisfactory response should include the following statements:

- At first the Roman government persecuted Christians because they refused to worship the official gods of Rome.
- Then, when the Roman emperor Constantine became a Christian, the Christian religion was encouraged.
- Later, Emperor Theodosius made Christianity the official Roman religion.

An excellent response might also

- explain that although the Romans had always allowed people to practice other religions, they required people to worship Roman gods too
- provide examples of persecution
- mention that the two Roman capitals, Constantinople and Rome, became the centers of Christianity.

Use after the completion of Chapter 12.

© Silver, Burdett & Ginn Inc.

ESSAY TEST (continued)

3. How did World War I help cause World War II?

A satisfactory response should include the following statements:

- Bitter feelings remained on both sides after World War I.
- Germany was forced to make harsh reparations payments to the Allies.
- These payments caused severe economic problems.
- People turned to Fascist leaders to solve the problems created by the aftermath of World War I.

An excellent response might also

- mention the terms *Treaty of Versailles, inflation, Nazis, Hitler*.
- provide specific examples.
- reflect independent thinking.

4. How has the government of the Soviet Union changed since World War II?

A satisfactory response should

- compare the repressive policies of the Stalin era with the policy of *glasnost* introduced by Gorbachev in the 1980s.
- discuss the factors and events that led to the dissolution of the Soviet Union in 1991.

An excellent response might also

- include the terms *collectivism, perestroika,* and *glasnost*.
- provide specific examples of leaders and events.
- reflect independent thinking.

Use after the completion of Chapter 12.

© Silver, Burdett & Ginn Inc.

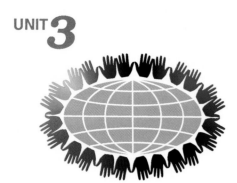

MULTICULTURAL PERSPECTIVES

Northern Peoples *(pages 283–289)*

Eskimos are native inhabitants of coastal areas of the Arctic and sub-Arctic regions of North America and northeastern Siberia. Eskimos reside in four countries: the United States, Canada, Greenland, and Russia. Direct students' attention to a world map or globe and ask them to locate each of these countries.

Eskimos refer to themselves by words that mean people. In Canada they use the word *Inuit*. In Alaska they use the words *Inupiat* and *Yupik*. In Russia they use the word *Yuit*.

Ask students to research the cultures of these northern peoples. Students should analyze how each group has adapted to the environment in which it lives. You might ask some students to compare how the lifestyles of these northern peoples have varied, according to the country in which they live.

A History of Persecution
(pages 294–299)

People of many nationalities and religions live in Eastern Europe and the former Soviet Union. These include Jews who have often been victims of persecution. During the late 1800s and early 1900s many Jewish families were killed or forced from their villages in Russia.

In *The Night Journey* Kathryn Lasky tells the story of one family's escape from persecution. You may want to have students read this book to learn more about this period in Russian history.

Source

Lasky, Kathryn. *The Night Journey*. New York: Puffin Books, Penguin USA, 1986.

Optional Activities

Unit **3**

THE FORMER SOVIET UNION AND EASTERN EUROPE

The vast area of the former Soviet Union and Eastern Europe, which extends from Europe into Asia, has great diversity in its geography and in the many ethnic groups who live in the countries that make up this region.

▶ *The colorful domes of St. Basil's Cathedral are one of the most recognized landmarks of Moscow, Russia.*

Yugoslavia: Past and Present

(page 341)

The area that later became Yugoslavia has been inhabited for at least 100,000 years. During the seventh century B.C., the Greeks established colonies along the Adriatic Sea. Later the Romans invaded the region. In A.D. 395 the Roman Empire was divided into two parts. The Western Roman Empire included what is now Croatia, Slovenia, and part of Bosnia. The Eastern Roman, or Byzantine, Empire included what is now Macedonia, Montenegro, and Serbia. People in the Western Roman Empire became Roman Catholics and used the Roman alphabet. People in the Byzantine Empire adopted the Eastern Orthodox faith and the Cyrillic alphabet.

In the sixth century A.D., groups of southern Slavs began to move into the area. Each Slavic group formed its own independent state. By 1400, foreign powers had gained control of nearly all the lands of the southern Slavs.

The movement for Slavic unity began in the early 1800s. While under French rule, Slovenia and Croatia were united briefly. Later, Serbia, which had gained independence from Turkey in 1878, sought union with Slovenia and Croatia. But Austria-Hungary, which now ruled them, refused to grant them independence. It also extended its control of the area by gaining Bosnia and Hercegovina.

After Austria-Hungary was defeated in World War I, the southern Slavs founded a new nation. It consisted of Bosnia and Hercegovina, Croatia, Dalmatia, Montenegro, Serbia, and Slovenia.

During World War II, when Axis troops occupied Yugoslavia, the Yugoslavs organized resistance groups, including the Partisans, led by Josip Broz Tito. After the war, Tito ruled Yugoslavia for many years. In the 1990s, conflicts between ethnic groups led to the breakup of the old federal government.

Discuss with students problems that a nation with many ethnic groups might face. Even after the dissolution of the former Yugoslavia, problems remain. Ask students to read newspapers and watch television newscasts for reports about any of the nations created from the former Yugoslavia. Have students bring in for a bulletin-board display any relevant clippings they find or report on any television news stories they have seen.

Chapter 10 Resource Center

Geography of the Former Soviet Union and Eastern Europe

(pp. 282-301)

Chapter Theme: The former Soviet Union and the countries of Eastern Europe are lands of great diversity, in both geography and the people who live there.

CHAPTER RESOURCES
Review Master Booklet
 Reviewing Chapter Vocabulary, p. 74
 Place Geography, p. 75
 Summarizing the Chapter, p. 76
Chapter 10 Test

LESSON 1 Visiting a Vast Empire

(pp. 282-289)

Theme: The former Soviet Union is a vast empire that has long rivers, mountains, forests, grasslands, and a variety of climates.

LESSON RESOURCES
Workbook, p. 69
Review Master Booklet
 Understanding the Lesson, p. 71

LESSON 2 The Lands of Eastern Europe

(pp. 290-293)

Theme: Traveling down the Danube, Vistula, and Oder rivers, one would see plains, mountains, and many cities.

LESSON RESOURCES
Workbook, p. 70
Review Master Booklet
 Understanding the Lesson, p. 72

LESSON 3 More Nationalities than Countries

(pp. 294-299)

Theme: Eastern Europe is an area of diverse nationalities, languages, and cultures.

LESSON RESOURCES
Workbook, p. 71
Review Master Booklet
 Understanding the Lesson, p. 73

Review Masters

REVIEWING CHAPTER VOCABULARY

Review Study the terms in the box. Use your Glossary to find definitions of those you do not remember.

continental climate	gorge	sanctuary	time zone
crest	permafrost	steppe	tributary
folk tale	proverb	taiga	tundra

Practice Complete the paragraphs using terms from the box above. You may change the forms of the terms to fit the meaning.

The former Soviet Union is so large that it has many different types of climates. The coldest part of this area is the arctic region. Here, the sun never thaws the

(1) _permafrost_ . Few people, animals, or even plants can live in this cold, treeless

(2) _tundra_ region.

South of the tundra lies one of the largest forested areas in the world. Children often learn about these dark, mysterious forests when they hear old Russian

(3) _folk tales_ from their parents or grandparents. These forests are able to withstand the extreme changes in temperature found in regions with a

(4) _continental climate_ . Because these forests are far away from cities and towns, they

are (5) _sanctuaries_ for many different species of animals. The former Soviet Union also has large areas where the climate is suitable for farming, and even for growing citrus fruits.

Write Write a sentence of your own for each term in the box above. You may use the back of the sheet.

Sentences should show that students understand the meanings of the terms.

_____
_____
_____
_____
_____
_____
_____
_____
_____
_____

Use with Chapter 10, pages 283–299.

© Silver, Burdett & Ginn Inc.

LOCATING PLACES

✱ Listed below are some cities in the former Soviet Union and Eastern Europe. Use the Gazetteer in your textbook to find the latitude and longitude of each. Then locate and label each on the map.

	LAT.	LONG.			LAT.	LONG.
1. Belgrade	45°N	21°E	6. Moscow		56°N	38°E
2. Bucharest	44°N	26°E	7. Prague		50°N	14°E
3. Budapest	48°N	19°E	8. Sofia		43°N	23°E
4. Gdańsk	54°N	19°E	9. Tiranë		41°N	20°E
5. St. Petersburg	60°N	30°E	10. Warsaw		52°N	21°E

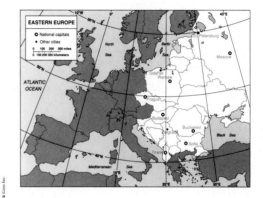

© Silver, Burdett & Ginn Inc.

SUMMARIZING THE CHAPTER

✱ Complete this graphic organizer. Next to the main idea for each lesson, write three key words or phrases that support the main idea.

CHAPTER THEME → The former Soviet Union and the countries of Eastern Europe are lands of great diversity in both geography and the people who live there.

LESSON 1

The former Soviet Union has various geographic characteristics.

1. Long rivers and inland seas
2. Rugged mountain ranges
3. Deserts, tundra, beaches, forests, and steppes

LESSON 2

The Danube, Vistula, and Oder rivers flow through the different types of lands in Eastern Europe.

1. The Danube flows through plains, mountains, a gorge, and a delta.
2. The Vistula flows from mountains to lowlands.
3. The Oder flows from mountains into Germany and Poland.

LESSON 3

In the former Soviet Union and each country of Eastern Europe, there are many different nationalities.

1. About half of the people in the former Soviet Union are Russian.
2. Czechoslovakia is a country of both Czechs and Slovaks.
3. The former Yugoslavia has a number of nationalities.

Use with Chapter 10, pages 283–299.

© Silver, Burdett & Ginn Inc.

Workbook Pages

Worksheet 1 (page 69)

THE WORK OF GEOLOGISTS

Understanding Stated Facts and Details, Applying Information

✳ Geology has branched out into many special fields since Alexander von Humboldt visited Russia in 1829. The chart below names and describes some of these fields. Study the chart. Then read the sentences below it. Write the special branch of geology that each sentence tells about.

Field of Geology	Definition
Geophysics	Study of the structure of the earth, and the effect on the earth of weather, tides, earthquakes, and so on
Petrology	Study of the structure and history of rocks
Mineralogy	Study of minerals, such as diamonds
Economic geology	Study of how industry can use coal, iron ore, and other minerals
Environmental geology	Use of ideas and information from geology to study problems caused by use of the environment

1. Some scientists study the structure of the earth in the former Soviet Union. Their field is ____geophysics____.

2. Humboldt was eager to learn about the minerals in different parts of Russia. He was studying the field of ____mineralogy____.

3. Based on Humboldt's findings, other geologists were able to explore the Urals and find minerals that could be used in Russian industry. These scientists specialized in ____economic geology____.

4. Some geologists study how waste from industry affects the environment in the former Soviet Union. Their field is ____environmental geology____.

5. Some experts specialize in determining the history of rocks in the Urals. Their field is called ____petrology____.

Thinking Further: Imagine that you have been invited to take part in a geology field trip to the former Soviet Union. Choose one of the fields of geology on the chart as your specialty. Write a paragraph describing one or two specific problems or subjects your geology team might study. Be sure to include where your team might go in the former Soviet Union to study the problem.

Answers should reflect independent thinking. Make sure the problems to be studied are relevant to the field of geology. A student specializing in petrology might want to study rocks of the Caucasus.

Worksheet 2 (page 70)

TRAVELING THE DANUBE

Gathering Information from a Map, Making Observations

✳ The map shows the course of the Danube River. The river flows through many countries before emptying into the Black Sea. Study the map. Then supply the necessary information below.

1. Area where the Danube begins: ____Black Forest____

2. Western European nations through which the Danube passes: ____Germany and Austria____

3. Two countries of Eastern Europe through which the Danube flows just after it leaves Western Europe: ____Czechoslovakia and Hungary____

4. Hungarian city on the Danube: ____Budapest____

5. Czechoslovakian city through which the Danube flows: ____Bratislava____

6. Site of a wildlife sanctuary: ____Danube Delta____

THE DANUBE
◎ National capitals   • Other cities
▦ Wildlife sanctuary   ⟩ Gorge
0   100   200   300 miles
0   100 200 300 kilometers

7. The Danube forms a small part of the boundary between Germany and Austria. It also forms parts of the boundaries between ____Czechoslovakia____ and ____Hungary____, between ____Romania____ and ____Yugoslavia____, between ____Romania____ and ____Bulgaria____, and between ____Romania____ and ____Ukraine____.

Thinking Further: Many composers have written music about rivers and oceans. For instance, the Viennese composer Johann Strauss, Jr. (1825–1899), wrote a favorite waltz called "By the Beautiful Blue Danube." Why do you think composers are inspired by bodies of water?

Students might note the beauty of bodies of water or the musical sounds of waves lapping on a beach or river water splashing against rocks.

Worksheet 3 (page 71)

REMEMBERING KEY WORDS

Understanding Word Meanings, Using Context Clues, Evaluating Information

✳ Use the definitions to complete the puzzle. Many words in the puzzle refer specifically to the former Soviet Union or Eastern Europe.

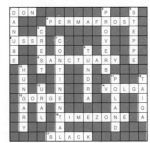

ACROSS
1. River flowing south into Black Sea
4. Layer of permanently frozen earth
6. Abbreviation of the former Union of Soviet Socialist Republics
9. Place where animals (birds) are protected
14. Longest river in Europe
15. Narrow pass between land
16. Another name for a time division (two words)
17. Name of a forest and a sea

DOWN
1. River that flows from the Black Forest to the Black Sea
2. Short saying
3. Treeless plain in the former U.S.S.R.
5. Highest point of a mountain
7. Climate of most of the former U.S.S.R.
8. Treeless arctic plain
10. This country's capital is Budapest
11. This country's capital is Warsaw
12. Northern forests of the former U.S.S.R.
13. Mountains visited by Humboldt

Thinking Further: What do you consider to be the most remarkable feature of the geography of the former Soviet Union? Give one or two reasons for your choice.

Possibilities: the most remarkable geographic feature of the former Soviet Union is its huge size; the Urals and Caucasus mountain ranges; the huge Caspian Sea.

C10-C

TEACHER NOTES

LESSON *1*   PAGES 283–289

Visiting a Vast Empire

Objectives

★**1. Identify** the major geographic features of the former Soviet Union.

2. Describe the climate of the former Soviet Union.

3. List the six different vegetation regions in the former Soviet Union.

4. Identify the following people and places: *Alexander von Humboldt, the former Soviet Union, Siberia, St. Petersburg,* and *Moscow.*

1   STARTING THE LESSON

Motivation Activity

■ Tell students to imagine that they are taking a trip to the former Soviet Union.

■ Ask students what clothes they will pack and list their responses on the chalkboard.

■ Tell students that the former Soviet Union has many different climates and what they pack should depend on what area of the former Soviet Union they are going to visit.

Think About What You Know

■ Assign the THINK ABOUT WHAT YOU KNOW activity on p. 283.

■ Answers may include by using a network of trusted messengers and governors or by using electronic communications.

Study the Vocabulary

■ Ask students to look up the definitions of each of the new vocabulary words for this lesson in the Glossary.

■ Next, have students make a word-search puzzle using all of the new words for this lesson.

■ Ask students to trade puzzles with another student and then solve each other's puzzles.

CHAPTER *10*

GEOGRAPHY OF THE FORMER SOVIET UNION AND EASTERN EUROPE

The former Soviet Union and Eastern Europe stretch from the Baltic Sea to the Pacific Ocean. Much of the region is an extension of the North European Plain, interrupted by mountains that serve as a boundary between Europe and Asia.

Optional Activities

SKILLBUILDER REVIEW

Using SQR   On pp. 278–279, students learned to use *SQR* to help them organize and remember important information.

● Ask students to apply this skill to Lesson 1, *Visiting a Vast Empire.*

● Students should *survey* the lesson before reading, write down *questions* to focus reading, then *read* for information.

● Reinforce the *SQR* strategy in later chapters.

Visiting a Vast Empire

THINK ABOUT WHAT YOU KNOW
Imagine that you are the ruler of an empire so large that you could never visit all of the lands you rule. How would you find out what is happening in the outer reaches of your empire?

STUDY THE VOCABULARY
tributary	continental climate
crest	taiga
tundra	steppe
permafrost	time zone

FOCUS YOUR READING
What are the geographic characteristics of the former Soviet Union?

A. Humboldt Visits Russia

A Smart Man When Alexander von Humboldt visited the Russian empire in 1829, he told the wife of the Russian ruler that diamonds would be found in the Ural Mountains. Sure enough, a short time later a 14-year-old boy working in a Urals gold mine found a diamond. It was the first time a diamond had ever been found in this region of the world.

How did Humboldt know that there would be diamonds in the Urals? It was not just a guess. Humboldt was a scientist and explorer who based his remark on his knowledge of geology, the science that deals with the earth's crust. Humboldt was known for his great learning in many fields. People said that he was "a man who knew everything." That was the reason a poor peasant stopped Humboldt one day and asked where he could find his stolen horse. The peasant thought surely a man who knew everything would know *that*.

The Vast Empire When Alexander Humboldt visited Russia in 1829, its empire consisted of lands in Asia and the eastern part of Europe. These lands came to be known as the Union of Soviet Socialist Republics; the name was often shortened to U.S.S.R. or Soviet Union. (As you read this chapter, you will find references to the former Soviet Union. Late in 1991 the 15 republics that made up the Union of Soviet Socialist Republics became 15 independent nations. In Chapter 12 you will learn how the collapse of the U.S.S.R. came about. The largest of these new nations is Russia, which has the largest area of any nation in the world. Russia was also the name of the empire that Alexander von Humboldt visited in 1829.)

The ruler of the Russian empire had invited Humboldt to visit the empire and to report about minerals that might be found in the Ural Mountains. Humboldt had a great curiosity and he was eager to learn all he could about the earth. He welcomed a chance to visit the vast Russian empire, which occupied such a large part of the earth's surface.

Travel across the huge empire was difficult in 1829, even for official guests. The empire stretched from the Baltic Sea across Siberia to East Asia. Since there were no railroads, Humboldt traveled in horse-drawn carriages or on river barges.

B. Large Bodies of Water

Long Rivers Humboldt traveled for three days on a sailing barge down the Volga River. Unfortunately, the wind blew from the wrong direction, so sailors had to row the boat along. Otherwise the barge would have traveled no faster than the slow-moving river current.

283

---

2 DEVELOPING THE LESSON

Read and Think

Section A
Although much has changed in the former Soviet Union since Humboldt's visit in 1829, the geology and climate have remained the same. Use the following questions to begin discussing the geography of the former Soviet Union.

1. **How did Humboldt know that diamonds could be found in the Ural Mountains?**
(Through his knowledge of geology *p. 283*)

2. **Why was Humboldt eager to visit Russia?**
(He wanted to learn as much as he could about the earth. *p. 283*)

Thinking Critically What other reasons, do you think, might the ruler of the Russian empire have had for inviting Humboldt to visit, other than to find out about the minerals in the Ural Mountains? (Hypothesize)
(Answers should reflect independent thinking but may include that he might have wanted to establish better relations with Germany or he might have wanted to meet Humboldt in person. *p. 283*)

Optional Activities

Read and Think
Sections B and C

The former Soviet Union has some of the world's longest rivers, largest inland seas, and tallest mountains. Discuss the most prominent physical features of the former Soviet Union, using the questions below:

1. **Compare the Volga River and the Danube River.**

   (The Volga River is longer than the Danube River, but the Danube carries more water than the Volga. *p. 284*)

2. **Explain why the Aral Sea is becoming saltier.**

   (Much of the water that once flowed into the Aral Sea is now used for irrigation, so as the sea decreases in size, the proportion of salt increases. *p. 284*)

3. **Describe the Ural Mountains and their importance to the former Soviet Union.**

   (The Ural Mountains extend from north to south through much of the former Soviet Union. They are part of the boundary between Europe and Asia, and because of the presence of minerals, are one of the most important industrial regions in the former Soviet Union. *pp. 284, 286*)

4. **Describe the Caucasus Mountains.**

   (The Caucasus Mountains stretch from the Black Sea to the Caspian Sea, serve as a boundary between Europe and Asia, are about three times as high as the Urals, and are higher than the Alps. *p. 286*)

   Thinking Critically If you were a mountain climber, which mountain ranges in the former Soviet Union would appeal to you most? (Analyze)

   (Answers should reflect independent thinking but may include the mountain ranges along the border between Afghanistan and China, since these have the highest peaks in the former Soviet Union. Accept any answer that is based on students' understanding of geography. *pp. 284, 286*)

284

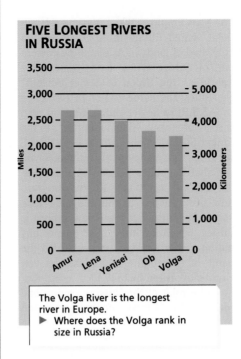

FIVE LONGEST RIVERS IN RUSSIA

The Volga River is the longest river in Europe.
► Where does the Volga rank in size in Russia?

The Volga is the longest river in Europe. However, it does not carry as much water as Europe's second longest river, the Danube (DAN yoob). The Volga flows about 2,200 miles (3,500 km) in a southeasterly direction from an area northwest of Moscow to the Caspian (KAS pee-un) Sea. Find the Volga River on the map on the opposite page.

Humboldt did not travel on two other important Russian rivers, the Don and the Dnieper (NEE pur). These two rivers flow south into the Black Sea. Today a canal connects the Volga and the Don. Another system of waterways connects the upper Volga with the Baltic Sea. The rivers and canals are important parts of the transportation system of the former Soviet Union, but they cannot be used during the cold winter months because they freeze.

284

The Yenisei (yen uh SAY) River and the Ob River are two of the largest Siberian rivers. They flow northward and empty into the Arctic Ocean.

Inland Seas The Caspian Sea, into which the Volga flows, has shores in both Europe and Asia. The Caspian is the largest inland body of water in the world. It is more than four times as large as Lake Superior, one of the Great Lakes of North America. And unlike the Great Lakes, the Caspian has no outlet to the sea, and its waters are salty.

The Aral Sea, east of the Caspian, is another saltwater sea. In fact, it is becoming saltier. Much of the water that once flowed into the Aral Sea is now used for irrigation. As a result, the sea has greatly decreased in size. In turn, the proportion of salt has increased. The waters of the Aral Sea have become so salty that many fish can no longer live in it. This is destroying the fishing industry in the area.

Lake Baikal (bye KAWL), in eastern Siberia, is a freshwater lake with an outlet through a **tributary** of the Yenisei River. A tributary is a small stream that flows into a larger stream. Lake Baikal is more than a mile deep; it is the world's deepest lake.

C. Mountains That Separate Continents

The Urals The Ural Mountains, where Humboldt correctly said there would be diamonds, extend from north to south through much of the former Soviet Union. When Humboldt reached the Urals, he tramped about for days, collecting rock samples. What he found convinced him that the Urals were rich in minerals, including iron, copper, gold, and platinum. Because of the presence of minerals, the

Writing to Learn

Writing a Letter Have students imagine that they live near the Aral Sea and that they make their living by fishing.

- Ask students to write a letter to a government official expressing their concern about the increasing salinity of the Aral Sea.

- As a prewriting activity, brainstorm the consequences of fish not being able to survive in the Aral Sea. (People who fish for a living would lose their jobs and a source of food would be gone for both people and animals such as birds.)

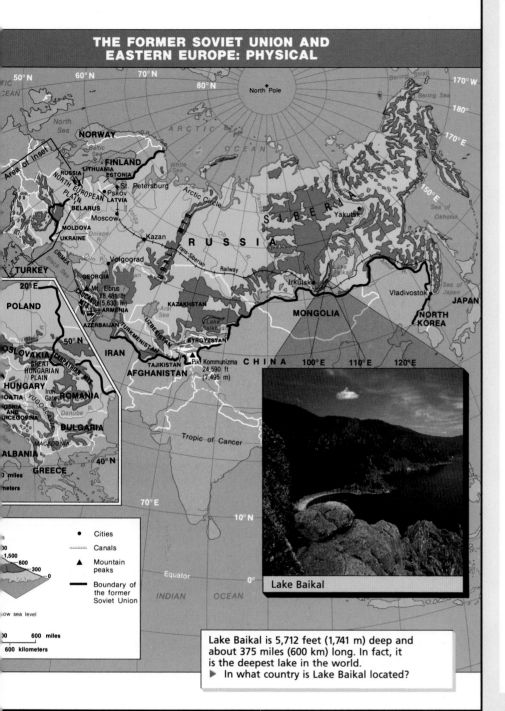

THE FORMER SOVIET UNION AND EASTERN EUROPE: PHYSICAL

Map labels

North Pole

ARCTIC OCEAN

Bering Strait
Bering Sea

NORWAY
Baltic Sea
FINLAND
LITHUANIA
ESTONIA
RUSSIA
St. Petersburg
Pskov
LATVIA
Moscow
BELARUS
MOLDOVA
UKRAINE
Dnieper R.
Kazan
Volgograd
TURKEY
GEORGIA
Mt. Elbrus
18,481 ft
(5,633 m)
CAUCASUS MTS.
ARMENIA
AZERBAIJAN
TURKMENISTAN
UZBEKISTAN
KYRGYZSTAN
TAJIKISTAN
Pik Kommunizma
24,590 ft
(7,495 m)
AFGHANISTAN
IRAN
Aral Sea
Lake Balkash
KAZAKHSTAN
SIBERIA
Yakutsk
Irkutsk
Lake Baikal
Vladivostok
MONGOLIA
CHINA
NORTH KOREA
JAPAN
Sea of Okhotsk
Sea of Japan
Trans-Siberian Railway
North Sea
White Sea
Arctic Circle
Volga R.
Don R.
Black Sea
Amur R.
Ob R.
Lena R.

POLAND
CZECHOSLOVAKIA
CARPATHIAN MTS.
GREAT HUNGARIAN PLAIN
HUNGARY
CROATIA
YUGOSLAVIA
BOSNIA AND HERCEGOVINA
Iron Gate
ROMANIA
Danube R.
BULGARIA
MACEDONIA
ALBANIA
GREECE
Vistula R.

50°N 60°N 70°N 80°N
170°W 180° 170°E 150°E 120°E 110°E 100°E
20°E 50°N 40°N 70°E 10°N 0° Equator
Tropic of Cancer
NORTH EUROPEAN PLAIN
Area of Inset

Legend

- • Cities
- ⌇⌇⌇ Canals
- ▲ Mountain peaks
- ━ Boundary of the former Soviet Union

1,500
600
300
0
below sea level

600 miles
600 kilometers

Lake Baikal is 5,712 feet (1,741 m) deep and about 375 miles (600 km) long. In fact, it is the deepest lake in the world.
▶ In what country is Lake Baikal located?

Lake Baikal

GEOGRAPHY THEMES

Human-Environment Interactions

■ Have students look at the physical map of the former Soviet Union and Eastern Europe on p. 285 to answer the following question: **What information on the physical map could help explain why the area west of the Ural Mountains and south of the Arctic Circle is the most densely populated area of the former Soviet Union?** (The area seems flat enough for farming and transportation and has many rivers to provide water and transportation.)

VISUAL THINKING SKILL

Interpreting a Graph

■ Ask students to look at the graph on p. 284 to answer the following question: **Which two rivers in Russia are the same length?** (The Amur and Lena rivers)

Answers to Caption Questions

p. 284 ▶ It is the fifth longest river in Russia.
p. 285 ▶ Lake Baikal is located in Russia.

Curriculum Connection

Math Have students look up the height of the highest peak in each of the following mountain ranges:

Urals: (Mt. Narodnaya 6,184 ft [1,905 m])
Caucasus: (Mt. Elbrus 18,510 ft [5,642 m])
Carpathians: (Mt. Gerlachovka 8,737 ft [2,663 m])
Alps: (Mt. Blanc 15,771 ft [4,807 m])
Rockies: (Mt. Elbert 14,433 ft [4,399 m])
Appalachians: (Mt. Mitchell 6,684 ft [2,037 m])
Himalayas: (Mt. Everest 29,028 ft [8,848 m])

- Ask students to make a bar graph to illustrate the relative heights of these mountains.

Creating Tourist Brochures

- Bring in examples of tourist brochures. Divide the class into three groups. Have the groups design brochures featuring the geography of the former Soviet Union.
- Assign one group the rivers, another group the seas, and the third group the mountains of the former Soviet Union.
- Allow students 20 minutes to illustrate and describe the geographic features in a way that would attract tourists.
- Have one or two students in each group work on each page of the brochure, focusing on a particular river, sea, mountain range, or mountain.
- Put the finished pages together to create three different brochures. Post them on a bulletin board.

Optional Activities

Read and Think

Sections D and E

Discuss the many climates and vegetation zones in the former Soviet Union by asking the following questions:

1. **Why is much of the land in the former Soviet Union of limited use?**
   (Large areas are either too cold or too dry for growing crops. *p. 286*)

2. **How does the climate of most of the former Soviet Union differ from the climate of much of Western Europe?**
   (The continental climate of the former Soviet Union is not greatly affected by ocean currents, therefore, it is not as moderate as the maritime climate of Western Europe. *p. 287*)

3. **Describe the steppes.**
   (Treeless, grassy plains that offer an unbroken view of the horizon *p. 288*)

   Thinking Critically **Where, do you think, would you go for vacation in the former Soviet Union?** (Evaluate)
   (Answers may include the Crimean peninsula or the east coast of the Black Sea because of their mild climates. *p. 288*)

Urals today are one of the most important industrial regions in the former Soviet Union.

The Urals are the first mountains a traveler sees when journeying eastward from the Baltic Sea. They are part of the boundary between Europe and Asia. But the Urals are not a high and rugged range like the Alps or the Pyrenees. When travelers cross the **crest**, or highest point, of the Ural Mountains, they see little to suggest that they are crossing from one continent to another.

The Caucasus   It is easier to see that the rugged Caucasus (KAW kuh sus) Mountains form a natural boundary. The Caucasus, which stretch from the Black Sea to the Caspian Sea, serve as a boundary between Europe and Asia in the south. The peaks of the Caucasus are about three times as high as the highest point of the Urals. The Caucasus are also higher than the Alps.

Mount Elbrus, the tallest Caucasus peak, is the highest mountain in Europe. But the Pamir mountains in the central Asian republic of Tajikistan, between Afghanistan and China, are even higher than the Caucasus. The highest peak in this republic is more than a mile higher than Mount Elbrus.

D. The Climates of a Vast Land

Hot and Cold   The former Soviet Union occupied one sixth of the earth's land surface, but much of this land has only limited use. Large areas are either too cold or too dry for growing crops. If you look at the map on page 287, you will see that much of the land of the former Soviet Union lies north of the Arctic Circle. You will also see that a large area of land north and east of

286

The Caucasus Mountains are rich in many minerals.
► For which two continents do these mountains serve as a boundary?

the Caspian Sea is a desert region. What other regions are shown on the vegetation map on page 287?

The arctic region is a treeless area called the **tundra**, where only mosses and low bushes can grow. The tundra receives little precipitation—usually less than 10 inches (25 cm) a year. Winters are cold and long in the arctic, but the long summer days can be quite warm or even hot. Yet the sun on long summer days thaws only the top layer of the frozen soil. A few feet below the surface, the earth remains frozen. This layer of permanently frozen earth is called **permafrost**.

Writing a Report

- Ask students to write a report about one of the six vegetation regions of the former Soviet Union.

- Have students use information in their books and then go to the library to do extra research. Information may include the high and low temperatures in different seasons, rainfall, types of plants found in the region, the location of the region, and the way the land is used.

- Tell students to include at least one illustration in their reports.

Discussing Permafrost

- Tell students that only 11% of the land in the former Soviet Union is suitable for farming compared to 21% in the United States.

- Tell students that about half of the land in the former Soviet Union has permafrost under its surface.

- Brainstorm the effects of permafrost. (Limits mining and farming)

- Ask students: **What would happen if the climate changed and caused the permafrost to disappear?** (More land could be used for farming and mining, but this would take time as the land initially would be too wet for planting.)

THE FORMER SOVIET UNION: VEGETATION

Tundra	Desert
Taiga	Mountain vegetation
Steppe	Hardwood forest

...e six vegetation regions of the former Soviet ...n, the northern forests, known as the taiga, ... the largest land area. ... which region is the Aral Sea found?

Most lands in the former Soviet Union have what is called a **continental climate**, in which winters are cold and summers are hot. Unlike the maritime climate of much of Western Europe, the climate of the former Soviet Union is not greatly affected by ocean currents. Even land near the Baltic Sea is too far from the Atlantic Ocean to be much affected by its currents. St. Petersburg, a major Russian port on the Baltic, has colder winters than Oslo, Norway. Both ports are located at the same latitude, but the climate is more moderate in Oslo because it is close to the Atlantic

Ocean. Moscow, which is farther south but also farther away from the Atlantic Ocean, has even colder winters than St. Petersburg has.

Most of Siberia has great variations between summer and winter temperatures. When Humboldt traveled east of the Urals in July and August, he suffered from the heat. His discomfort was increased by having to wear a leather mask to protect his face from hordes of mosquitoes. If Humboldt had visited the same areas in January, he would have experienced very cold weather. In places where temperatures

287

Playing a Geographic-Recall Game

- Divide the class into four groups. Assign each group a different category relating to the geography of the former Soviet Union, such as *Mountains, Bodies of Water, Vegetation Regions,* and *Climate.*

- Have each group make a list of ten Jeopardy-style questions and answers for their category. (Example: "The highest mountain in Europe" would be answered by "What is Mt. Elbrus?")

- When students have completed their lists, start the game by reading the questions from the first group's list. Only students in the other three groups can respond. When a student responds correctly, award a point to his or her team. The team with the most points wins.

Meeting Individual Needs

Concept:
Classifying Physical Features

To better understand the vastness of the former Soviet Union, it is important to understand the variety of its climates and regions. The activities below will help students comprehend the geography of the former Soviet Union.

◆ **EASY** Ask students to label the major rivers, bodies of water, cities, and mountain ranges on an outline map of the former Soviet Union.

◀▶ **AVERAGE** Have students make a chart with the following headings: *Rivers, Seas, Mountains,* and *Vegetation.*

Ask students to review Lesson 1 and list the rivers, seas, mountains, and types of vegetation in the former Soviet Union under the appropriate heading.

◀▮▶ **CHALLENGING** Have students complete a chart with the following headings: *Region, Characteristics,* and *Occupation.*

Ask students to list each of the six vegetation regions of the former Soviet Union and the characteristics of each.

Tell students to include a column in which they predict the ways that people in each region would earn a living.

GEOGRAPHY THEMES

Regions

■ Have students look at the map of the vegetation regions of the former Soviet Union on p. 287 and answer the following questions:

1. **Which vegetation region extends farthest east?**
   (Tundra)

2. **Where is most of the desert land in the former Soviet Union?**
   (East of the Caspian Sea)

Answers to Caption Questions
p. 286 ▶ Europe and Asia
p. 287 ▶ The desert region

Read and Think
Section F

Use a globe or map to point out the eleven time zones of the former Soviet Union and the six time zones of the United States (including Alaska and Hawaii). Ask the following questions to help students understand the concept of time zones:

1. **Why are there more time zones in the former Soviet Union than in any country in the world?**
(It covers a wider region of the globe than any nation in the world. *p. 289*)

Thinking Critically Why, do you think, are time zones more important today than they were in Humboldt's era? (Hypothesize)
(Answers should reflect independent thinking but may include that today there is faster travel by plane and instantaneous communication through telephones and technology. *p. 289*)

VISUAL THINKING SKILL

Comparing Photographs

■ Direct students' attention to the photographs on pp. 288 and 289. Then ask them to write a short paragraph in which they compare the photograph of the taiga to the photograph of the steppes. (Taiga — forested, tree-covered, rolling plains; steppes — treeless plains, completely flat)

---

may reach 90°F (32°C) or higher in July, they can fall as low as −50°F (−46°C) in January.

Milder Climates The Crimean (kry MEE un) peninsula, or Crimea, extends into the Black Sea. Crimea has a milder climate than most parts of the former Soviet Union. There is a lot of sunny weather in summer. Some people called the beaches of Crimea the Riviera on the Black Sea. The name suggests the French Riviera, a famous beach resort on the Mediterranean coast. However, winters in Crimea are decidedly colder than on the French Riviera.

The east coast of the Black Sea is protected by the Caucasus Mountains. It has a more truly Mediterranean climate. Citrus fruit can even be grown in this area.

The taiga, a huge forest zone, sweeps across 5,000 miles of the former Soviet Union.
▶ What kinds of trees can be found in the taiga?

288

E. The Forests and the Steppes

Great Forests Although the former Soviet Union has high mountains, most of it is flat or rolling plains. It is part of the North European Plain, which extends eastward from France. Forests cover much of the land, as shown by the map on page 287. The northern forests are known as the **taiga** (TYE guh). These forests have coniferous trees, or trees with cones, such as pines. South of the taiga are the hardwood forests of trees such as maples and oaks.

As in North America, much forest land in the former Soviet Union has been cleared for farms and cities. But there are still great forests.

Treeless Steppes South of the forests stretch the treeless plains that are called the **steppes** (steps). Humboldt compared his carriage crossing the steppes to a boat crossing a calm sea with an unbroken view of the sky. In the book *The Endless Steppe: Growing Up in Siberia*, author Esther Hautzig describes what she thought when she first saw the steppes.

The flatness of this land was awesome. There wasn't a hill in sight; it was an enormous, unrippled sea of parched and lifeless grass.

"[Father], why is the earth so flat here?"

"These must be steppes, Esther."

"Steppes? But steppes are in Siberia."

"This is Siberia," he said quietly.

If I had been told that I had been transported to the moon, I could not have been more stunned.

"Siberia?" My voice trembled. "But Siberia is full of snow."

"It will be," my father said.

Reteaching Main Objective

★ ***Identify the major geographic features of the former Soviet Union.***

● Provide students with outline maps of the former Soviet Union that include unlabeled major bodies of water.

● On the chalkboard, list words that include proper names (cities, rivers, mountains); adjectives describing the landforms and climate (flat, mountainous, dry, warm); types of vegetation (grasses, coniferous trees, mosses); and words from the vocabulary list for this lesson.

● Have students write each word from the list in its correct location on the map. Then have each student exchange maps with another student and complete the other student's map.

A vast area of treeless plains, known as the steppes, has some of the area's richest soil.
▶ What crops are grown here?

In the former Soviet Union, wheat and other grains can be grown on the parts of the grassy steppes that receive sufficient precipitation. The dry parts of the steppes are used for grazing.

F. A Land That Had Eleven Time Zones

We measure the hours of the day by the turning of the earth. The time of day at any particular moment depends on where you are. When it is noon in London, England, it is two o'clock in the afternoon in Moscow, Russia.

Time changes with the longitude as the earth turns. Therefore the earth is divided into 24 standard **time zones,** one for each hour of the day. Some time zone boundaries zigzag so that people living in the same region or country can have the same time.

Some countries are so large that they are divided into more than one time zone. In the United States, for example, when it is noon in New York, it is 9:00 A.M. in San Francisco and 7:00 A.M. in Honolulu. The former Soviet Union was so large that it covered 11 time zones. When it was noon in Moscow, it was 11:00 P.M. on the Pacific coast of the Bering Strait, which was the easternmost territory of the Soviet Union. You will learn more about time zones when you read pages 350–351.

LESSON 1 REVIEW

THINK AND WRITE

A. What can we learn about the former Soviet Union from Humboldt's visit to the Russian empire? **(Infer)**

B. What are the important bodies of water in the former Soviet Union? **(Recall)**

C. Which two mountain ranges mark the boundary between Europe and Asia? **(Recall)**

D. Describe the climate of the former Soviet Union. **(Recall)**

E. What types of land cover the former Soviet Union? **(Recall)**

F. How is the earth divided into time zones? **(Recall)**

SKILLS CHECK

MAP SKILL

Use the map on page 287 to answer these questions: Which vegetation region of the former Soviet Union covers the largest land area? What type of vegetation region surrounds the Aral Sea?

289

UNDERSTANDING THE LESSON

NAME _____ CHAPTER

UNDERSTANDING THE LESSON **10**

Recalling Facts LESSON 1 CONTENT MASTER

✱ Read each statement below. Write **True** if the statement is true and **False** if it is false. If the statement is false, cross out the part that is incorrect and write the correct words above it.

False 1. Europe's longest river is the ~~Danube~~. *Volga*

True 2. The Aral Sea decreased in size because water that once flowed into it is used for irrigation.

False 3. The Ural Mountains and the Caucasus Mountains form the boundary between ~~China~~ and the ~~Soviet Union~~. *Europe Asia*

True 4. Rich mineral deposits make the Urals an important industrial region.

False 5. Most of the land in the Soviet Union has a ~~Mediterranean~~ climate. *continental*

False 6. Siberia has ~~little~~ variations between its summer and winter temperatures. *great*

True 7. Most of the land in the Soviet Union is flat or rolling plains.

True 8. Although most of the forests in the Soviet Union have been cleared for farms and cities, trees are still an important natural resource.

False 9. The grassy steppes in the Soviet Union are used for grazing and for growing ~~vegetables~~. *wheat and other grains*

True 10. The earth is divided into 24 time zones, one for each hour of the day.

False 11. The Soviet Union is so large that it covers ~~15~~ time zones. *11*

Think and Write: Write a paragraph telling what challenges the geography and climate of the Soviet Union might present to the Soviet government. You may use the back of the sheet.

Answers should reflect independent thinking; suggestions appear in the Answer Key.

Use with textbook pages 281–287. 71

◀ **Review Master Booklet, p. 71**

Optional Activities

---

3 CLOSING THE LESSON

Lesson 1 Review

Answers to Think and Write

A. Humboldt's visit to the Russian empire revealed its huge size, its wealth of natural resources, and the variety of its lands and climates.

B. The important bodies of water in the Soviet Union are the Volga, Don, Dnieper, Yenisei, and Ob rivers; the Black, Baltic, Caspian, and Aral seas; and Lake Baikal.

C. The Ural and the Caucasus mountain ranges mark the boundary between Europe and Asia.

D. Most of the former Soviet Union has a continental climate, which means that it is cold in the winter and hot in the summer.

E. The former Soviet Union has six types of land: mountains, taiga, hardwood forest, desert, tundra, and steppes.

F. The earth is divided into 24 standard time zones, one for each hour of the day.

Answer to Skills Check

The taiga covers the largest land area. Desert surrounds the Aral Sea.

Focus Your Reading

Ask the lesson focus question found at the beginning of the lesson: **What are the geographic characteristics of the former Soviet Union?**

(The geographic characteristics of the former Soviet Union include its huge size; extreme climate; some of the largest rivers, seas, and mountains in the world; and vast areas of cold, dry, inhospitable plains.)

Additional Practice

You may wish to assign the ancillary materials listed below.

Understanding the Lesson p. 71
Workbook p. 69

┌─ **Answers to Caption Questions** ─┐
p. 288 ▶ Coniferous trees
p. 289 ▶ Wheat and other grains
└────────────────────────┘

289

Other Lands of Eastern Europe

Objectives

★ 1. **Describe** the main geographic features of eastern Europe.

2. **Trace** the course of the Danube, Vistula, and Oder Rivers on a map.

3. **Identify** the following places: *Black Forest, Black Sea, Baltic Sea, Bosporus, Dardanelles, Budapest,* and *Great Hungarian Plain.*

1 STARTING THE LESSON

Motivation Activity

■ Play a recording of the Johann Strauss waltz "The Beautiful Blue Danube" (An den schonen blauen Donau) for students.

■ After the music ends, ask students what it makes them think of or how it makes them feel. Tell them the title of the piece and explain that they will be learning more about the river for which this work was named.

Think About What You Know

■ Assign the THINK ABOUT WHAT YOU KNOW activity on p. 290.

■ Answers may include that the countries have plains, mountains, rivers, and other similar characteristics.

Study the Vocabulary

■ Have students look up the definitions of the new vocabulary words for this lesson in the Glossary.

■ Ask students to write a descriptive paragraph that uses the new vocabulary words.

290

LESSON 2

The Lands of Eastern Europe

THINK ABOUT WHAT YOU KNOW
Find the countries of Eastern Europe on the inset map on page 285. What physical characteristics do you think these countries may have in common?

STUDY THE VOCABULARY
gorge   sanctuary

FOCUS YOUR READING
What kinds of lands could be seen on a trip down the Danube, Vistula, and Oder rivers?

A. One Continent, Two Regions

Europe As you learned in earlier chapters, the continent of Europe was divided into Western Europe and Eastern Europe as a result of World War II. This political division between Western and Eastern Europe continued until 1989. In that year the Soviet government lost control of Eastern Europe, and new governments not tied to the Soviet Union came to power.

Because of these political changes, the distinction between Eastern and Western Europe will no longer exist someday. But for now, it is still convenient to consider the countries of Europe as part of these two regions.

The Trip Begins It is easy to remember where the Danube River begins and ends. It flows from the Black Forest to the Black Sea. The Black Forest is in Germany. To travel from the Danube's source to its mouth—that is, from its beginning to its end—you would start out in Western Europe. But after passing through Germany

290

and Austria, you would travel between two countries of Eastern Europe, Czechoslovakia (chek uh sloh VAH kee uh) and Hungary. At the "elbow" of the Danube, you would turn sharply south as the river carried you through Hungary to its capital city of Budapest (BOOD uh pest).

Across Plains Below Budapest you would follow the Danube across the Great Hungarian Plain. This gently rolling land is about the size of the state of Virginia. The Great Hungarian Plain extends from Hungary into the former Yugoslavia and Romania.

While traveling in Hungary, you might want to take a side trip to see Hungary's "Far West." It is here you could see longhorn cattle, cow ponies, and cowhands. As with American cowhands, pictures of the Hungarian cowhands usually

This Hungarian cowhand entertains tourists on the cattle range.
▶ How is this cowhand similar to an American cowhand?

Curriculum Connection

Art Have students make a copy of a flag of one of the Eastern European countries.

● Students may either paint the flags, draw the flags with colored pencils or markers, or cut and glue different colors of construction paper to create the patterns.

● For examples of these flags, refer students to the Table of Countries found on pages 32–43.

● You may wish to have students do extra research and write a paragraph about the history and symbolism of the flag that they have chosen.

The Iron Gate between Serbia and Romania is the deepest gorge in Europe.
► What river flows through it?

show them wearing broad-brimmed hats and very colorful clothing. Actually, one is more likely to see this sort of dress at horse shows staged for tourists rather than on the cattle range.

Once back on the Danube, you would go downstream to Belgrade, Serbia. The Danube flows through the area that was once Yugoslavia. Some of this area is part of the Great Hungarian Plain, but much of the area is mountainous. Along the Adriatic coast mountains and beaches attract many tourists.

Through Mountains Farther down the Danube the river forms the boundary between Serbia and Romania. Here you would come to the Iron Gate, a deep **gorge,** or a narrow passage through land. The Iron Gate is probably the most scenic section of the river. Here the Danube rushes through the gorge between the Carpathian (kahr PAY thee un) and Balkan mountains. This is the deepest gorge in Europe. At one time it was difficult to

move boats through the Iron Gate. Now, dams and locks make it much easier.

Below the Iron Gate you would follow another national boundary. North of the river is Romania; to the south is Bulgaria.

The Trip Ends The Danube makes still more turns before it finally reaches its delta on the Black Sea. Recall that a delta is the built-up land at the mouth of a river. Just before its final turn toward the sea, the Danube touches the boundary of the former Soviet Union. As you can see from the map on page 285, a trip down the Danube would take you to many countries, several of them in Eastern Europe.

If you are interested in birds and animals, you would probably want to take a trip onto the Danube Delta. It is one of Europe's great wildlife **sanctuaries.** A sanctuary is a place where birds and animals are protected from hunters and others who would disturb them. More than 300 species of birds and many kinds of animals are found on the Danube Delta.

291

② DEVELOPING THE LESSON

Read and Think
Sections A, B, and C

Discuss the geography of eastern Europe, using the following questions:

1. **What are some of the sights that you could see if you took a boat trip on the Danube River?**
   (Black Forest, Great Hungarian Plain, mountains, the Iron Gate, Black Sea, as well as a number of cities *pp. 290-291*)

2. **Name the two straits that are located along the narrow outlet of the Black Sea.**
   (The Bosporus and the Dardanelles *p. 292*)

3. **How do winters in eastern Europe compare to winters in western Europe and winters in the former Soviet Union?**
   (They are milder than in most of the former Soviet Union but colder than in western Europe. *p. 293*)

   Thinking Critically Why, do you think, are maritime climates more moderate than continental climates? (Synthesize)
   (Answers may include that the ocean currents warm the air in winter and cool the air in summer, making the climate of coastal areas more moderate in summer and winter. *p. 293*)

   ┌─ **Answers to Caption Questions** ─
   p. 290 ► He has some of the same skills in handling horses.
   p. 291 ► Danube

Graphic Organizer

The graphic organizer on this page will help students better understand two important physical features found along the Danube River.

PHYSICAL FEATURES ALONG DANUBE RIVER

IRON GATE	DANUBE DELTA
A deep gorge, or narrow passage, through land Located between the Carpathian and Balkan Mountains The deepest gorge in Europe Dams and locks have made the gorge navigable	A build-up of land at the mouth of the Danube River Located where the Danube River reaches the Black Sea A great wildlife sanctuary located here Home for over 300 species of birds and many animals

Optional Activities

B. Travel to the Black Sea and the Baltic Sea

The Black Sea The Danube, Dnieper, and Don are among the Eastern European rivers that flow into the Black Sea. But the Black Sea has only one narrow outlet. This outlet passes through two straits, the Bosporus and the Dardanelles. The Bosporus links the Black Sea with the Sea of Marmara. The Dardanelles, called the Hellespont in ancient times, connects the Sea of Marmara with the Aegean Sea, which is an arm of the Mediterranean Sea. The straits serve as a narrow gateway not only to the countries located on the Black Sea but also to all the lands on the Danube.

The straits divide Europe from Asia, although it is now easy to cross back and forth between the two continents. A bridge spans the Bosporus, which is less than a half mile (1 km) wide at this point. The Turkish city of Istanbul, formerly Constantinople, stands on both sides of the Bosporus. Most of the city is in Europe, but part of it is in Asia.

The Baltic If you were to travel down the Vistula River, you would start in the Carpathian Mountains that stretch along Poland's southern border. On your journey to the river's mouth, you would never leave Poland. The Vistula is Poland's own river. It is also the longest river flowing into the Baltic Sea.

The Vistula begins as a rushing mountain stream, but it becomes a slow-moving lowland river as it makes its way to the sea. Although Poland is mountainous in the south, most of it is part of the North European Plain.

A trip down the Vistula would take you to Warsaw, Poland's capital, and several of the country's largest cities. The port

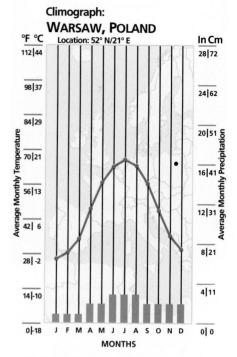

Climograph: WARSAW, POLAND
Location: 52° N/21° E

This climograph is for Warsaw, which has a continental climate.
▶ About how cold is it in Warsaw during the month of February?

of Gdańsk (guh DAHNSK) is located at the mouth of the Vistula River. Gdańsk was once known as Danzig.

The Oder River is the second longest river flowing to the Baltic. Unlike the Vistula, the Oder is an international river. Its source is in the mountains of Czechoslovakia, but farther downstream the Oder River serves as the boundary between Germany and Poland. Canals connect the Oder and Vistula, so these rivers form part of a network of waterways in Germany and Poland.

292

292

Climograph:
BERGEN, NORWAY
Location: 60° N/5° E

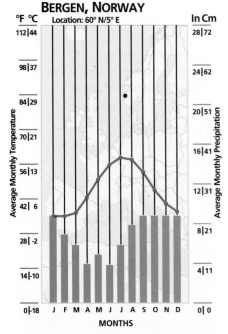

°F °C

112|44

98|37

84|29

70|21

56|13

42| 6

28| -2

14|-10

0|-18

In Cm

28|72

24|62

20|51

16|41

12|31

8|21

4|11

0| 0

Average Monthly Temperature

Average Monthly Precipitation

J F M A M J J A S O N D

MONTHS

This climograph is for Bergen, which has a maritime climate.
► About how cold is it in Bergen during the month of February?

C. Eastern Europe's Continental Climate

If you want to take a trip down the Danube or Vistula, plan to go in the summer. Parts of the rivers freeze during the winter. Most places in Eastern Europe have a continental climate. Winters here are milder than in most of the former Soviet Union but colder than in Western Europe, which has a maritime climate.

The differences between maritime and continental climates can be seen by comparing average summer and winter temperatures of cities in Western Europe and Eastern Europe. Warsaw, on the Vistula, has colder winters than Bergen, Norway, even though Bergen is located much farther north. On the other hand, a July day in Warsaw will likely be warmer than one in Bergen. Warsaw also has much colder winters than London, although these cities are located at about the same latitude. Remember that Warsaw and London are both farther from the Equator than is northern Maine or North Dakota.

Places on the Baltic coast of Poland are somewhat warmer than inland cities, such as Warsaw. But these coastal cities still have cooler winters than cities of comparable latitudes on the Atlantic coast.

LESSON **2** *REVIEW*

THINK AND WRITE

A. What geographic features of Eastern Europe could you see on a trip down the Danube? **(Recall)**

B. What rivers could you travel down to reach the Black Sea and the Baltic Sea? (call)

C. Why do Budapest and Warsaw have colder winters than Brussels and London?

(Analyze)

SKILLS CHECK

THINKING SKILL

Turn to the Atlas map on pages 616–617 and estimate the latitude of each of these cities: Budapest, Brussels, Warsaw, and London. Check your estimates by looking up the latitudes for these cities in the Gazetteer.

293

◄ **Review Master Booklet, p. 72**

Optional Activities

---

3 CLOSING THE LESSON

Lesson *2* Review

Answers to Think and Write

A. On a trip down the Danube, you could see the Great Hungarian Plain, the Iron Gate, the Carpathian and Balkan mountains, the Danube Delta, and the Black Sea.

B. You could travel down the Danube River, the Dnieper River, or the Don River to reach the Black Sea. You could reach the Baltic Sea by traveling down the Vistula River or the Oder River.

C. They have colder winters than both Bergen and London because Budapest and Warsaw have continental climates that are not influenced by the ocean, while Bergen and London both have maritime climates that are influenced by the ocean.

Answer to Skills Check

Estimates will vary; the latitude of Budapest is 48° N, Brussels is 50° N, Warsaw is 52° N, and London is 52° N.

Focus Your Reading

Ask the lesson focus question found at the beginning of the lesson: **What kinds of lands could be seen on a trip down the Danube, Vistula, and Oder rivers?**
(On a trip down the Danube, Vistula, and Oder rivers, one would see plains, mountains, and a gorge.)

Additional Practice

You may wish to assign the ancillary materials listed below.

Understanding the Lesson p. 72
Workbook p. 70

--- Answers to Caption Questions ---
p. 292 ► About 29° F (-2° C)
p. 293 ► About 34° F (1° C)

More Nationalities Than Countries
Objectives

★**1. Describe** the concept of a nationality.

2. List the major nationalities of the former Soviet Union and Eastern Europe.

3. Identify the following places: *Ukraine, Armenia, Estonia, Latvia,* and *Lithuania.*

1 STARTING THE LESSON

Motivation Activity

■ Read aloud the folk tale about Manka in Section A.

■ Ask students to describe Manka. (Smart, a loving wife, hates injustice) Ask why Manka is an appealing character.

■ Ask why people would pass such a story from generation to generation. (Manka portrays qualities that they admire.)

Think About What You Know

■ Assign the THINK ABOUT WHAT YOU KNOW activity on p. 294.

■ Answers may include a common language, the Constitution, the Bill of Rights, foods, music (jazz, rock, folk), and shared attitudes (hopeful, friendly).

Study the Vocabulary

■ Have students look up the definition of each of the new vocabulary terms for this lesson in the Glossary.

■ Ask students to locate in the text other examples (besides the story of Manka) of folk tales and proverbs.

■ Discuss the difference between folk tales and proverbs. (Both are passed down from generation to generation and reflect the nationality from which they come, but folk tales are stories that reflect ideas and traditions while proverbs are short statements that reveal a truth or fact.)

More Nationalities Than Countries

THINK ABOUT WHAT YOU KNOW
In the United States there are many citizens who originally came from other countries. What things can you think of that unite the citizens of the United States?

STUDY THE VOCABULARY
folk tale　　　proverb

FOCUS YOUR READING
What is the difference between country and nationality?

A. An Old Tale About a Clever Woman

Eastern Europe has a variety of nationalities. Indeed, some countries have more than one nationality. For example, the former Soviet Union was a country of diverse nationalities. Each of these nationalities valued its language, literature, beliefs, and traditions that had been handed down from generation to generation.

Folk tales, or stories handed down from one generation to another, often reflect ideas and traditions that a nationality values. Czechoslovakians have a folk tale about a woman named Manka.

According to the folk tale, Manka was the beautiful and clever daughter of a shepherd. She married a village judge. The judge loved his wife, but he warned her, "My dear Manka, you are not to use that cleverness of yours at my expense. I won't have you interfering in any of my cases. In fact, if ever you give advice to anyone who comes to me for judgment, I'll turn you out

of my house at once and send you home to your father."

For a time, Manka was careful not to interfere with her husband's cases. But one day he made a very unjust decision, and Manka secretly told the man how to get her husband to change his mind. The judge found out and angrily ordered her to go back to her father's house. But he added, "You may take with you the one thing you like best in my house, for I won't have people saying I treated you shabbily."

Manka did not weep or beg her husband to change his mind. Instead she asked to stay until after supper. "We have been very happy together, and I should like to eat one last meal with you."

The story of Manka, in this Czechoslovakian folk tale, has been handed down through many generations.
▶ In what way was Manka clever?

Optional Activities

Curriculum Connection

Music Bring to class music from some of the different nationalities of Eastern Europe.

● The following suggestions are available in Silver Burdett & Ginn's *World of Music* (Grade 6): "Waters Ripple and Flow" (a Slovakian folk song); "Stodola Pumpa" and "Dancing" (both, Czech folk songs); and "The Peddler" and "Russian Slumber Song" (both, Russian folk songs).

The judge agreed, and Manka prepared a fine supper of all the dishes she knew he liked best. The judge ate heartily and drank so much that he became drowsy and fell sound asleep in his chair. Manka had the servants carry him quietly to a wagon and drove to her father's house.

When the judge awoke in the morning, he rubbed his eyes in surprise and burst out, "What does this mean?" Manka smiled and answered sweetly, "You know you told me I might take with me the one thing I liked best in your house, so of course I took you!" The judge could not help but laugh, and he told his wife, "Manka, you're too clever for me. Come on, my dear, let's go home."

B. Other Parts of Nationality

Proverbs and History A **proverb** (PRAHV urb) is a short saying that expresses some truth or fact. Like folk tales, proverbs are handed down from one generation to another and reflect valued ideas. Almost every nationality has its own proverbs. Those given here are Russian.

> *A small hole can sink a big ship.*
> *Yesterday's storm causes no damage today.*
> *It does not help the mouse to say "meow" to the cat.*
> *Just because the child has lice, you need not cut off its head.*

Folk tales and proverbs that people have in common are not the only things that unite people as a nationality. Knowledge of history is usually very important in causing a group of people to feel that they are a nationality. Hungarians are said to remember the battle of Mohacs that cost Hungary its freedom, even though it took place more than 400 years ago. The Hungarians have a saying whenever things go wrong: "No matter, more was lost at Mohacs Field!"

Language Language is an important bond between people who belong to a nationality. A common language is a very strong tie between people. Most nationalities in the former Soviet Union and Eastern Europe have their own languages. A nationality is sometimes thought of as a group of people who share the same language.

Related languages are said to belong to the same family of languages. You read earlier about the Romance languages, which grew out of Latin, the language of the Romans. Most languages of Eastern Europe belong to the Slavic family of

Read and Think
Sections A and B

Spoken language, stories, and sayings are all things that tie people of the same nationality together. Use these questions to discuss the role of language, folk tales, and proverbs in national identity:

1. **What does the story of Manka say about the ideas and traditions valued by the people of Czechoslovakia?**
   (They value marriage, justice, cleverness, and humor. *pp. 294–295*)

2. **To what family of languages do most of the languages of Eastern Europe belong?**
   (The Slavic family of languages *p. 296*)

   Thinking Critically Why, do you think, do attempts to change or limit the use of a language often lead to strong feelings and sometimes violence? (Analyze)
   (Answers may include that language is such an important part of national identity that efforts to change or limit its use are felt as an attack on the people themselves. *pp. 295–296*)

--- **Answers to Caption Questions** ---
p. 294 ▶ She got her husband to change his mind about sending her back to her father's house.

Writing to Learn

Writing a Folk Tale Ask students to write a folk tale.

- Students may start with a story about something they did as a baby or a story about their parents, grandparents, friends, or neighbors.

- Explain that in folk tales the heroes and heroines are usually "beautiful and clever" or "handsome and good." Typically, there is some problem that their virtue (loyalty, patience, or honesty) enables them to overcome.

- Encourage students to make things up or use exaggeration to make the story work. Have fun!

Making Pirog(i)s

Pirogs, or pirogis, are a popular Russian food. Have students try this recipe at home or use the school kitchen to make it as a class:

- Mix 1 beaten egg with 1/4 cup flour and a pinch of salt.

- Add 1/2 cup water.

- Roll the dough into thin sheets. Cut into 2" - 3" squares.

- Put a tablespoon of filling (mashed potatoes and either grated cheese or sauerkraut) on each square. Fold to form triangles and pinch edges.

- Boil in lightly salted water for 5 minutes.

- Brown with onions and butter. Serve with sour cream.

Optional Activities

Meeting Individual Needs

Concept:
Comparing Nations and Nationalities

To better understand the concept of nationality, it is important to understand that nations and nationalities are not the same. The activities below will help students better comprehend the relationship between nations and nationalities.

◆ **EASY** Have students work in pairs, asking each pair to make a chart with the former Soviet Union and the countries of Eastern Europe as headings.

Ask students to skim the lesson and list under each heading the different nationalities that live in that country.

◀▶ **AVERAGE** Have students work independently to make a chart like the one described above.

Ask students to write a paragraph describing the pros and cons of having a nation made up of many different nationalities. (Pros include diversity and tolerance; cons include difficulty in communication, possible tension, and violence.)

◀▮▶ **CHALLENGING** Ask students who need a challenge to write an essay arguing that nationalities either unite or divide people.

Students may use either the United States or Eastern Europe to support their arguments.

GEOGRAPHY THEMES

Human-Environment Interactions

■ Have students look at the map on this page to answer the following question: **What language is spoken in Kiev and Kharkov?**
(Ukrainian)

Russian
Ukrainian
Byelorussian
Latvian, Lithuanian
Armenian
Georgian
Moldavian
Tajik
Azerbaijani, Bashkir, Chuvash, Kazakh, Kirghiz, Tatar, Turkmen, Uzbek, Yakut
Estonian, Finnish, Karelian, Komi, Mari, Mordvin, Udmurt
Other languages

There are over 90 nationalities in the former Soviet Union; most of the nationalities have their own language. The map shows where the major languages of the former Soviet Union are spoken.
▶ What is the major language spoken in Moscow?

languages. They are related, although they differ from each other. The people who speak one of the Slavic languages as their native tongue are called *Slavs*.

C. Nationalities and Languages in the Former Soviet Union

The map above shows the many languages that are spoken in the former Soviet Union. The people do not use the same alphabet as that used for Western European languages. Instead they have an alphabet based on one invented during the Middle Ages by a Christian monk named Cyril. This alphabet is known as the Cyrillic (suh-RIHL ihk) alphabet.

When the Soviet Union existed, about half of the people who lived in that country were Russians. The Russians are the largest Slavic nationality. Two other groups of Slavs, the Ukrainians and Belorussians, make up one fifth of the population of the former Soviet Union.

Not all the people in the former Soviet Union are Slavs. Other nationalities include the Armenians and Georgians, who live south of the Caucasus Mountains, and the Uzbeks, of Central Asia. Three nationalities living on the Baltic Coast—the Estonians, the Latvians, and the Lithuanians—had their own countries before they were taken over by the Soviet Union at the beginning of World War II.

All of the nationalities mentioned in this section became independent nations in 1991. Find these nations on the map above. Some names have changed slightly.

296

Optional Activities

Cooperative Learning

Making Posters Divide the class into groups of four or five students. Have each group choose a different nationality of Eastern Europe or of the former Soviet Union.

● Ask each group to make a poster that displays information about the food, dress, history, nationalities, languages, folk tales, and proverbs of the country that they have chosen. Have each student in each group research one of the above categories. Information may be presented in the form of drawings, photos, recipes, lists of facts, brief stories, proverbs, or anecdotes.

● Allow one class period for gathering information and one class period for making the posters. Display the finished posters.

The lands of the former Soviet Union are home to many different nationalities. Most of the nationalities have their own language, culture, and way of life.
▶ What problems might arise from so many different nationalities?

VISUAL THINKING SKILL

Interpreting a Photograph

■ Direct students' attention to this photographic collage of ethnic groups in the former Soviet Union. Then ask students to choose one of the ethnic group members pictured and write a short monologue of introduction. Students should name the person they chose, and describe the dress or custom shown in the photograph.

┌─ **Answers to Caption Questions** ─┐
p. 296 ▶ Russian is spoken.
p. 297 ▶ Problems of communication and conflict of cultures

297

For Your Information

Armenia Today   Armenia became a sovereign nation in 1991 after it declared its independence from the U.S.S.R. This small country is located on the Turkish border. A 1915 conflict with the Turks drove many Armenians out of the country to begin new lives in other parts of the world.

Today, young Armenians are especially interested in preserving and rejuvenating their culture. These children are exploring their artistic talents as they paint, draw, and sculpt themes from Armenian life and history. A large collection of such works is located at the Children's Art Center in Yerevan. The success of the collection has drawn other countries to contribute to the exhibit. Today, the center houses art designed by children living in over 90 countries around the world.

Optional Activities

Read and Think
Sections C and D

The borders of countries in Central and eastern Europe are the results of wars, conquests, and treaties. Help students understand the relationship between nations and nationalities in these regions by asking the following questions:

1. **What percentage of the people in the former Soviet Union are Russian?**
(Fifty percent are Russian. *p. 296*)

2. **Compare the language of the Serbs and the Croatians.**
(They speak the same language but use different alphabets when writing: the Serbs use an alphabet based on the Cyrillic, or Russian alphabet, and the Croatians use the Roman alphabet, which is the same as the English alphabet. *p. 299*)

Thinking Critically How, do you think, did the Latvians, Estonians, and Lithuanians, feel about their countries being taken over by the Soviet Union? (Analyze)
(Answers should reflect independent thinking, but may include that most were probably angry and afraid and wanted to gain their independence from the Soviet Union. *p. 296*)

GEOGRAPHY THEMES

Location

■ Have students look at the population density map on p. 298. Ask the following questions:

1. **What is the approximate latitude and longitude of the largest city in the former Soviet Union?**
(Moscow at 56° N latitude and 38° E longitude)

2. **What city is located at approximately 55° N latitude and 73° E longitude?**
(Omsk)

298

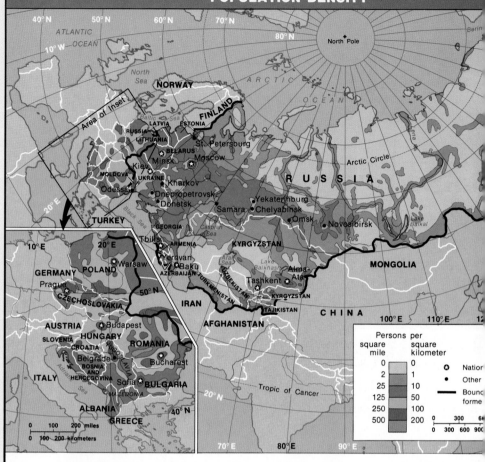

THE FORMER SOVIET UNION AND EASTERN EUROPE: POPULATION DENSITY

Persons per square mile	square kilometer	
0	0	✪ Nation
2	1	• Other
25	10	— Bound
125	50	forme
250	100	
500	200	

THE 24 LARGEST CITIES OF THE FORMER SOVIET UNION AND EASTERN EUROPE

Moscow (Russia) 8,527,000	Minsk (Belarus) 1,510,000	Dnepropetrovsk (Ukraine) 1,166
St. Petersburg (Russia) 4,359,000	Belgrade 1,470,000	Yerevan (Armenia) 1,164
Kiev (Ukraine) 2,495,000	Novosibirsk (Russia) 1,405,000	Odessa (Ukraine) 1,132
Budapest (Hungary) 2,080,000	Yekaterinburg (Russia) 1,315,000	Omsk (Russia) 1,122
Tashkent (Uzbekistan) 2,077,000	Samara (Russia) 1,267,000	Baku (Azerbaijan) 1,114
Bucharest (Romania) 1,976,000	Prague (Czechoslovakia) 1,194,000	Chelyabinsk (Russia) 1,107
Warsaw (Poland) 1,659,000	Sofia (Bulgaria) 1,183,000	Alma-Ata (Kazakhstan) 1,088
Kharkov (Ukraine) 1,567,000	Tbilisi (Georgia) 1,174,000	Donetsk (Ukraine) 1,081

Many cities in the former Soviet Union have over a million people.
▶ How many cities in Russia have more than one million people?

Reteaching Main Objective
⭐ *Describe the concept of a nationality.*

● Make an outline on the chalkboard of the different characteristics of a nationality. (*Shared language, history, folk tales,* and *proverbs*)

● Under each item in the outline, have students list examples that unite the people of the United States. (The English language, slang words, humor; the American Revolution, other examples of recent history; examples of folk tales; proverbs such as "A penny saved is a penny earned." and "The early bird always catches the worm.")

● Discuss how the items in the list help unite the people in the United States.

D. Nationalities in Other Eastern European Countries

Czechoslovakia, as the name suggests, is the country of both Czechs and Slovaks. Both speak a Slavic language, so both Czech and Slovak are official languages. Fortunately, the differences between these languages are not great, so a person who knows one of the languages can usually understand the other.

The former Yugoslavia, like the former Soviet Union, was made up of several nationalities. The Serbs were the largest single group. There were also Croatians (kroh AY shuns), Slovenians, Albanians, and other national groups. The Serbs and Croatians speak the same language, but they use different alphabets when writing. The Serbs, like the Russian people, use an alphabet based on the Cyrillic alphabet. The Croatians use the Roman alphabet, which is the alphabet we use.

Three Eastern European nations do not have a Slavic language. The language of most Hungarians is Magyar, which was brought to Europe by Asian conquerors during the Middle Ages. Romanian, as you have read, comes from the language of the Romans. The origins of Albanian, the language of mountainous Albania as well as parts of the former Yugoslavia, has long puzzled historians. It does not seem to be

People cross the Charles Bridge towards the historic center of Prague, in Czechoslovakia.
► How can you tell that this section of the city is old?

related to any other European language. But like the other languages spoken in Eastern Europe and the former Soviet Union, Albanian is an important part of a nationality. Together, the nationalities of Eastern Europe and the countries that were once part of the Soviet Union help to make this region of the world a land of great diversity.

LESSON 3 REVIEW

THINK AND WRITE

A. How are folk tales related to the study of nationalities? **(Infer)**

B. Besides folk tales, what things do people of the same nationality have in common? **(Recall)**

C. What are some of the nationality groups who live in the former Soviet Union? **(Recall)**

D. How do the languages of Hungary, Romania, and Albania differ from those of other Eastern European nations? **(Analyze)**

SKILLS CHECK

WRITING SKILL

Using the information in this lesson, describe the characteristics of a nationality.

299

◄ **Review Master Booklet, p. 73**

Optional Activities

Lesson 3 Review

Answers to Think and Write

A. Folk tales are related to the study of nationalities because they reflect the ideas and traditions that a nationality values.

B. In addition to folk tales, people of the same nationality also have proverbs, history, and language in common.

C. Nationalities in the former Soviet Union include Russians, Ukrainians, Belorussians, Armenians, Georgians, Uzbeks, Estonians, Latvians, and Lithuanians.

D. Hungary, Romania, and Albania do not have Slavic languages. Hungarians speak Magyar; the Romanian language comes from the language of the Romans; the Albanian language does not seem related to any other European language.

Answer to Skills Check

The characteristics of a nationality are a shared language and history and a shared tradition of folk tales and proverbs.

Focus Your Reading

Ask the lesson focus question found at the beginning of the lesson: **What is the difference between country and nationality?**
(A country is a political entity that is shown on a map; a nationality is a group of people who share a language, history, and tradition. People of the same nationality may live in different countries, just as people who live in the same country may be of different nationalities.)

Additional Practice

You may wish to assign the ancillary materials listed below.

Understanding the Lesson p. 73
Workbook p. 71

┌─── **Answers to Caption Questions** ───
p. 298 ► Albania
p. 299 ► The buildings are old, not modern-looking.

Using the Vocabulary

1. gorge
2. continental climate
3. folk tale
4. tundra
5. sanctuary
6. permafrost
7. steppe
8. proverb
9. time zone
10. taiga

Remembering What You Read

1. Alexander von Humboldt was invited to Russia to report on minerals that might be found in the Ural Mountains.

2. The Volga River is the longest river in Europe.

3. Lake Baikal is the world's deepest lake.

4. The Ural Mountains and the Caucasus Mountains form a boundary between Europe and Asia.

5. The beaches of Crimea have a climate that is more moderate than most other areas of the former Soviet Union, so they are sometimes called the Riviera on the Black Sea.

6. There were 11 time zones in the former Soviet Union.

7. The Danube River flows through six Eastern European countries—Czechoslovakia, Hungary, Croatia, the new Yugoslavia (Serbia), Romania, and Bulgaria.

8. The Bosporus and Dardanelles serve as a gateway to countries located on the coast of the Black Sea.

9. Most places in eastern Europe have a continental climate, which means that they have hot summers and cold winters.

10. Most eastern European languages belong to the Slavic family of languages.

USING THE VOCABULARY

On a separate sheet of paper, write the letter of the term that best matches each numbered statement.

a. tundra
b. permafrost
c. continental climate
d. taiga
e. steppe
f. time zone
g. gorge
h. sanctuary
i. folk tale
j. proverb

1. A narrow passage through land
2. Climate in which winters are cold and summers are hot
3. A story handed down from one generation to another
4. The treeless arctic region of the former Soviet Union
5. A place where birds and animals are protected
6. A layer of permanently frozen earth
7. A name for a treeless plain in the former Soviet Union
8. A short saying that expresses some truth or fact
9. One of 24 standard divisions of the earth
10. The northern coniferous forests of the former Soviet Union

REMEMBERING WHAT YOU READ

On a separate sheet of paper, answer the following questions in complete sentences.

1. Why was Alexander von Humboldt invited to Russia?
2. What river in the former Soviet Union is the longest river in Europe?
3. What is the name of the world's deepest lake?
4. What two mountain ranges form a boundary between Europe and Asia?
5. Why have the beaches of Crimea been called the Riviera on the Black Sea?
6. How many time zones were there in the former Soviet Union?
7. Through how many Eastern European countries does the Danube River flow?
8. What two straits serve as a gateway to countries located on the coast of the Black Sea?
9. What kind of climate do most places in Eastern Europe have?
10. To what family of languages do most Eastern European languages belong?

TYING LANGUAGE ARTS TO SOCIAL STUDIES

Try to write your own folk tale to describe a characteristic of your nationality. First think of an idea or a tradition that you feel is specific to your nationality. Then make up a story to try to explain how that idea or tradition developed.

300

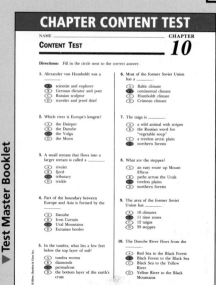

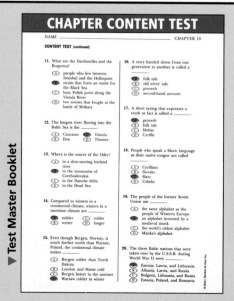

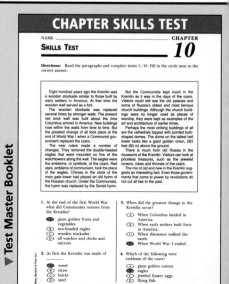

THINKING CRITICALLY

On a separate sheet of paper, answer the questions below in complete sentences.

1. Would you have wanted to travel around the Russian empire with Alexander von Humboldt? Explain.
2. Why are wildlife sanctuaries important?
3. How accurate, do you think, are stories that are handed down from one generation to another?
4. What does the proverb "Yesterday's storm causes no damage today" mean?
5. Do you think every country should be divided into smaller countries on the basis of nationality alone?

SUMMARIZING THE CHAPTER

Copy this graphic organizer on a separate sheet of paper. Beside the main heading for each lesson, write three key words or phrases that support the main idea.

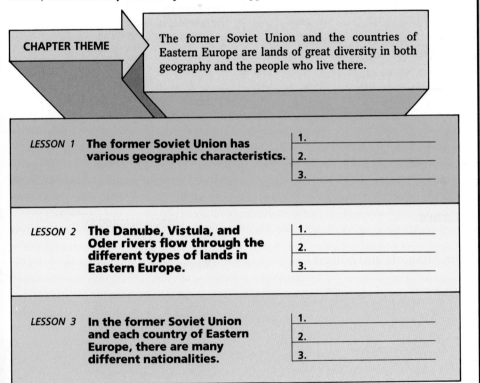

CHAPTER THEME — The former Soviet Union and the countries of Eastern Europe are lands of great diversity in both geography and the people who live there.

LESSON 1 The former Soviet Union has various geographic characteristics.
1. _____
2. _____
3. _____

LESSON 2 The Danube, Vistula, and Oder rivers flow through the different types of lands in Eastern Europe.
1. _____
2. _____
3. _____

LESSON 3 In the former Soviet Union and each country of Eastern Europe, there are many different nationalities.
1. _____
2. _____
3. _____

301

Thinking Critically

1. Answers may include no, the trip would have been too hot, too far, and too uncomfortable; or yes, it would have been unforgettable to see the Russian empire.
2. They help preserve species from extinction.
3. Answers may include that they are not very accurate because they may change with each retelling.
4. It means that one should forget about past worries and focus on the present.
5. Answers may include no, it would be too confusing; or yes, it is better to divide a country because of nationality rather than politics.

Summarizing the Chapter

Lesson 1
1. Long rivers and inland seas
2. Rugged mountain ranges
3. Deserts, tundra, beaches, forests, and steppes

Lesson 2
1. The Danube flows through plains, mountains, a gorge, and a delta.
2. The Vistula flows from mountains to lowlands.
3. The Oder flows from mountains into Germany and Poland.

Lesson 3
1. In the former Soviet Union, only 50 percent of the people are Russian.
2. Czechoslovakia is a country of both Czechs and Slovaks.
3. The former Yugoslavia was made up of Serbs, Croatians, and other nationalities.

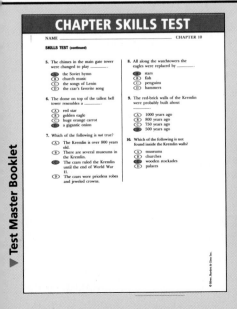

CHAPTER SKILLS TEST

NAME _____ CHAPTER 10

SKILLS TEST (continued)

5. The chimes in the main gate tower were changed to play _____.
   Ⓐ the Soviet hymn
   Ⓑ church music
   Ⓒ the songs of Lenin
   Ⓓ the czar's favorite song

6. The dome on top of the tallest bell tower resembles a _____.
   Ⓐ red star
   Ⓑ golden eagle
   Ⓒ huge orange carrot
   Ⓓ a gigantic onion

7. Which of the following is not true?
   Ⓐ The Kremlin is over 800 years old.
   Ⓑ There are several museums in the Kremlin.
   Ⓒ The czars ruled the Kremlin until the end of World War II.
   Ⓓ The czars wore priceless robes and jeweled crowns.

8. All along the watchtowers the eagles were replaced by _____.
   Ⓐ stars
   Ⓑ fish
   Ⓒ penguins
   Ⓓ hammers

9. The red-brick walls of the Kremlin were probably built about _____.
   Ⓐ 1000 years ago
   Ⓑ 800 years ago
   Ⓒ 750 years ago
   Ⓓ 500 years ago

10. Which of the following is not found inside the Kremlin walls?
   Ⓐ museums
   Ⓑ churches
   Ⓒ wooden stockades
   Ⓓ palaces

▶ Test Master Booklet

CHAPTER WRITING TEST

NAME _____ CHAPTER 10

ESSAY TEST

Directions: Write a response to items 1–4.

REMINDER: Read and think about each item before you write your response. Be sure to think of the points you want to cover, details that support your response, and reasons for your opinions. Then, on the lines below, write your response in complete sentences.

1. Why are the Dardanelles and the Bosporus important to countries on the Black Sea?
A satisfactory response should include the following statements:
- These straits provide the only narrow outlet from the Black Sea.
- Both straits control access from the Black Sea to the Mediterranean Sea.
- The straits are important for trade and transportation for these countries and for all the lands on the Danube.
An excellent response might also:
- explain that the Bosporus leads to the Sea of Marmara, and the Dardanelles leads to the Aegean Sea.
- mention that the straits divide Europe from Asia.

2. What are the Urals, and why are they important to industry in the former Soviet Union?
A satisfactory response should include the following statements:
- The Urals are a mountain range that extends from north to south through much of the former Soviet Union.
- They are part of the boundary that separates Europe from Asia.
- Because the mountains are an important source of minerals, they are one of the most important industrial regions in the former Soviet Union.
An excellent response might also include examples of the minerals found in the Urals, such as iron, copper, gold, and platinum.

▶ Test Master Booklet

CHAPTER WRITING TEST

NAME _____ CHAPTER 10

ESSAY TEST (continued)

3. What is the Iron Gate?
A satisfactory response should include the following statements:
- The Iron Gate is a deep gorge between the Carpathian and Balkan mountains.
- The Danube River flows through the Iron Gate.
- Dams and locks make boat passage through the gorge easier.
An excellent response might also:
- identify the location of the Iron Gate (on the border between Yugoslavia and Romania).
- mention that the Iron Gate is the deepest gorge in Europe.

4. What can you learn about a country by studying its folk tales?
A satisfactory response should explain that folk tales:
- reflect a country's traditions
- can give the reader a sense of national ideals and values
- help one understand a country's culture
An excellent response might also include:
- a definition of a folk tale
- references to or examples of folk tales.

▶ Test Master Booklet

301

Chapter 11 Resource Center

History of Russia and Eastern Europe

(pp. 302-321)

Chapter Theme: Many changes occurred in Russia and Eastern Europe during the period from the Middle Ages to 1917.

CHAPTER RESOURCES

Review Master Booklet
- Reviewing Chapter Vocabulary, p. 80
- Place Geography, p. 81
- Summarizing the Chapter, p. 82

Chapter 11 Test

LESSON 1 The Middle Ages in Russia and Eastern Europe

(pp. 302-307)

Theme: Two hundred years after Russia imported Christianity from Constantinople, Russia was conquered by the Mongols.

LESSON RESOURCES

Workbook, p. 72
Review Master Booklet
- Understanding the Lesson, p. 77

LESSON 2 In the Time of the Czars

(pp. 308-314)

Theme: Three Russian czars defeated the Mongols and helped to build and modernize Russia.

LESSON RESOURCES

Workbook, pp. 73-74
Review Master Booklet
- Understanding the Lesson, p. 78

LESSON 3 The Russian Revolution

(pp. 315-319)

Theme: The Russian Revolution completely changed life in Russia.

SILVER WINGS WORKSHOP: The Courage of Your Convictions

LESSON RESOURCES

Workbook, p. 75
Review Master Booklet
- Understanding the Lesson, p. 79

Review Masters

REVIEWING CHAPTER VOCABULARY

Review Study the words in the box. Use your Glossary to find definitions of those you do not remember.

abdicate	communism	czar	socialism
anarchy	coronation	schism	

Practice Complete the paragraphs using words from the box above. You may change the forms of the words to fit the meaning.

The first rulers to be called emperors were in ancient Rome. Later, when Constantinople was the center of the Roman Empire, Byzantine rulers also took the title of emperor. In time, Constantinople fell and Moscow took its place as the most important Christian city. During this time, Russian rulers were called (1) _____czars_____, the Russian word for *caesar*, or *emperor*.

These Russian rulers were among the richest people in the world at that time. They had beautiful palaces, and the (2) _____coronation_____ of each new ruler was a splendid occasion. However, while the rulers had great wealth, most of the Russian people were poor serfs leading hard lives.

The life of the Russian emperors was very different from the lives of Russian leaders after the 1917 revolution. During that revolution, the people forced czar Nicholas II to (3) _____abdicate_____, and they hoped their lives would improve. The party that took power in Russia believed in (4) _____communism_____. Lenin, the leader of the party, promised the people control over the land, industry, and wealth of the country. In the years after the revolution, however, the party's policies failed to provide either freedom or economic security for the country's people.

Write Write a sentence of your own for each word in the box above. You may use the back of the sheet.

Sentences should show that students understand the meanings of the words.

_____
_____
_____
_____
_____
_____
_____

Use with Chapter 11, pages 303–319.

LOCATING PLACES

✱ Listed below are places of importance during the time of the Golden Horde and during later years in Russia and Eastern Europe. Use the Gazetteer in your textbook to find the latitude and longitude of each place. Then locate and label each on the map.

		LAT. ⊖	LONG. ↺			LAT. ⊖	LONG. ↺
1.	Kiev	50°N	31°E	7.	Constantinople (Istanbul)	41°N	29°E
2.	Pskov	58°N	28°E				
3.	Moscow	56°N	38°E	8.	Iron Gate	45°N	23°E
4.	Astrakhan	46°N	48°E	9.	Pik Kommunizma	39°N	72°E
5.	Samarkand	40°N	67°E				
6.	St. Petersburg	60°N	30°E	10.	Sofia	43°N	23°E

THE GOLDEN HORDE
● Cities
≋ Dam
▲ Mountain peak

Use with Chapter 11, pages 303–319.

SUMMARIZING THE CHAPTER

✱ Complete this graphic organizer. In the boxes next to the main idea for each lesson, fill in each missing cause and effect. The first one has been done for you.

CHAPTER THEME — Many changes occurred in Russia and eastern Europe during the period from the Middle Ages to 1917.

	CAUSE	EFFECT
LESSON 1 Constantinople and the Mongol Empire affected Russia and eastern Europe during the Middle Ages.	Vladimir, the ruler of Kiev, was curious about different religions.	Christianity was accepted in Kiev in A.D. 988.
	There were important differences between the Christian Church in eastern Europe and that in western Europe.	The Church split into the Roman Catholic Church in the west and the Eastern Orthodox Church in the east.
	The Mongols conquered much of Russia and eastern Europe.	The Russian people had to pay money and send laborers to the Golden Horde.
LESSON 2 Important rulers changed Russia in the time of the czars.	Ivan the Great forced the Golden Horde out of Muscovy and enlarged Muscovy's territory.	Russia became a large and powerful empire.
	Peter I greatly admired the culture of western Europe.	Peter ordered young nobles to learn a western European language and ordered Russian men to shave their beards.
	After serfdom ended, the nobles still held the land and large estates.	Most serfs still lived in villages and worked as servants.
LESSON 3 The revolution of 1917 affected Russia.	A demonstration by the people of Petrograd turned into a riot.	There was anarchy in the capital, and the czar was forced to abdicate.
	Vladimir Ulyanov's brother was hung for his part in a failed plot to kill the czar. The czar's police suspected that Vladimir might also pose a threat.	Vladimir Ulyanov adopted the name Nikolai Lenin and fled to western Europe.
	Lenin controlled the Communist party, and the party controlled the government.	The Communists were in total control of the government.

Use with Chapter 11, pages 303–319.

C11-B

Workbook Pages

NAME _____

THE GOLDEN HORDE

CHAPTER **11**

Using Scale to Measure Distance, Interpreting Information

✳ The map below shows the area controlled by the Mongols, or the Golden Horde. Study the map. Then answer the questions that follow.

THE GOLDEN HORDE
- ☐ Area controlled by the Golden Horde
- Boundaries of the former Soviet Union and Mongolia
- ● Present-day cities

(Map showing ATLANTIC OCEAN, ARCTIC OCEAN, FORMER SOVIET UNION, MONGOLIA, PACIFIC OCEAN, cities Kiev, Moscow, Istanbul, Volgograd)

0 500 1000 miles
0 500 1000 kilometers

1. Over how many miles did Golden Horde control extend from east to west? about 2,800 miles

2. The capital city of the Golden Horde was near present-day Volgograd. About how many kilometers was their capital from Moscow? about 925 kilometers

3. What river would members of the Golden Horde have crossed on a trip from Moscow to Constantinople (present-day Istanbul)? the Dnieper River

4. How many miles from the Arctic Circle was the closest boundary of Golden Horde territory? about 750 miles

5. By what two ways could a person have crossed Golden Horde territory by water? by way of the Caspian Sea and the Volga River or the Black Sea and the Dnieper River

6. Which river empties into the Caspian Sea? the Volga

Thinking Further: Why might the Golden Horde not have wanted to control land farther north? Answers may mention the cold climate, short growing season, or small population.

72   Chapter 11, pages 303–307

NAME _____

RUSSIAN RULERS

CHAPTER **11**

Understanding Time Lines, Understanding Sequence

✳ Study the time line of Russian rulers and the table of important events in American and world history below.

(Time line 1400–1900: Ivan III, Ivan IV, Michael Romanov, Peter I, Catherine II, Alexander II)

SELECTED MAJOR EVENTS
- The American Revolution—1776–1781
- Sir Francis Drake circumnavigates the earth—1577–1580
- Columbus arrives in America—1492
- The Emancipation Proclamation—1863
- The Pilgrims land at Massachusetts—1620

✳ Decide if each of the following statements is correct or incorrect. If the statement is incorrect, change the name of the ruler to make the statement correct.

1. The Russian czar who was in power when Sir Francis Drake sailed around the world was ~~Ivan III~~. Ivan IV

2. News of the discovery of the New World might have reached ~~Ivan I~~. Ivan III

3. Alexander II freed the serfs in Russia before Abraham Lincoln issued the Emancipation Proclamation in the United States.

4. The Pilgrims' first Thanksgiving took place during the reign of ~~Peter I~~. Michael Romanov

5. ~~Peter I~~ was probably aware of the American fight for independence. Catherine II

6. Ivan III and Peter I ruled the same number of years. Ivan III and Peter I

7. ~~Ivan III and Catherine II~~ each ruled during two different centuries.

Thinking Further: What are some reasons that news of events in America might not have reached Russia until long after the events occurred? Answers may mention that news traveled slowly, since it had to be carried over land by people on foot or horseback, and by ship between Europe and America.

Chapter 11, pages 308–314   73

NAME _____

WINTERING IN RUSSIA

CHAPTER **11**

Using Context Clues to Understand Word Meanings, Understanding Seasons

✳ In 1588, a poet named Giles Fletcher traveled to Russia. The passage below, in the spelling of his time, is Fletcher's description of the harsh winter he experienced. Read the passage. Then answer the questions that follow.

. . . The whole Countrey in the Winter lyeth under Snow, which falleth continually, and is sometimes of a yard or two thicke, but greater towards the North. The Rivers and other waters are all frozen up, a yard or more thicke, how swift or broad soever they bee: and this continueth commonly five moneths . . . from the beginning of November, till towards the end of March, what time the Snow beginneth to melt. . . . The sharpenesse of the ayre [air] you may judge of by this: for the water dropped downe or cast up into the ayre, congealeth into Ice before it come to the ground. In the extremitie of Winter, if you hold a Pewter dish or pot in your hand, or any other metall (except in some chamber where their warme Stoves bee) your fingers will freeze fast unto it, and draw off the skinne at the parting. . . . Divers not only that travell abroad, but in the very Markets, and streets of their Townes, are mortally pinched and killed withall; so that you shall see many drop downe in the Streets, many Travellers brought into the Townes sitting dead and stiffe in their Sleds. . . . Many times (when the winter is very hard and extreame) the Beares and Wolves issue by troupes out of the woods driven by hunger, and enter the Villages, tearing and ravening all they can finde: so that the Inhabitants are faine to flee for safeguard of their lives.

1. What does the word *congealeth* in column 1, line 13 mean? to harden

2. According to Fletcher, how long does the Russian winter usually last? about five months, from the beginning of November till the end of March

3. According to the poet, what will happen if a person in an unheated place in winter allows a metal object to touch his or her skin? The object will stick to the person's skin, and when pulled away, it will pull some of the skin with it.

4. In column 2, line 4, what does *Divers* mean: jumpers, hardly anyone, or various people? various people

5. What does the poet say drives wild animals into the towns in extremely cold winters? hunger

6. What does *ravening* in column 2, line 14 mean? eating, or eating greedily, or prowling for food

Thinking Further: What do you think is the most dangerous part of an extremely cold winter? Write your answer on a separate sheet. Answers may include ice storms, blizzards, lack of heat, running out of food, or illness.

74   Chapter 11, pages 303–314

NAME _____

READING ABOUT ALEXANDER KERENSKY

CHAPTER **11**

Understanding Stated Facts, Hypothesizing

✳ Read the following paragraphs. Then put a check in the box before each word or phrase that correctly completes the statements below. One or more endings may be correct.

Alexander Kerensky (1881–1970) is one of the great might-have-beens of world history. Born in the same town as Lenin, Kerensky became a leader of the provisional government that ruled Russia for about eight months in 1917. Given the chance to help bring democracy to his country, Kerensky saw his dreams collapse and the government turn into a Communist dictatorship when Lenin and his followers seized power in November 1917.

As a young man, Kerensky was a well-known lawyer. He supported a democratic revolution in Russia. Although he favored Russian involvement in World War I, he thought that Czar Nicholas II conducted the war effort badly. Therefore, Kerensky became a leader in the movement to overthrow the czar. After the czar was replaced by a provisional government, Russians looked to Kerensky to solve the country's problems.

Kerensky was popular for a short time. A brilliant speaker, he initiated important reforms. All Russians were given the right to vote. Kerensky also supported equal rights for women and freedom of the press and of worship. Kerensky did not, however, bring peace, and as World War I continued support for him faded. Using the peace issue, the Communists campaigned tirelessly against Kerensky. When the Communists seized power, Kerensky could do no more than flee to Western Europe. He later settled in the United States.

1. Kerensky was a prominent
   - ☐ Communist.
   - ☑ lawyer.
   - ☑ revolutionary.

2. Kerensky stayed in office for
   - ☐ one year.
   - ☑ several months.
   - ☐ seven years.

3. Kerensky supported
   - ☑ equal rights for women.
   - ☑ freedom of the press.
   - ☑ the overthrow of the czar.

4. Russian involvement in World War I
   - ☐ brought much success.
   - ☑ was a major problem for Kerensky.
   - ☐ ended in 1916.

5. Kerensky failed to
   - ☑ keep Lenin from seizing power.
   - ☐ make any worthwhile reforms.
   - ☐ stick to his own principles.

6. Kerensky fled to
   - ☐ Russia.
   - ☐ Argentina.
   - ☑ Western Europe.

Thinking Further: On a separate sheet, explain why you think Kerensky was popular with American and Western European leaders. Possible answer: Kerensky wanted to make Russia more like the United States and Western Europe. He wanted to make democratic reforms.

Chapter 11, pages 315–319   75

C11-C

The Middle Ages in Russia and Eastern Europe

Objectives

★ **1. Explain** how the Mongols gained control of Russia and eastern Europe.

2. List the differences between the Christian Church in eastern Europe and the one in western Europe.

3. Identify the following people and places: *Vladimir, Genghis Khan, Batu Khan, Russia, Kiev, Dnieper River, Constantinople, Rome, Mongolia,* and *Volga River.*

1 STARTING THE LESSON

Motivation Activity

■ Ask students to make a list of what they know about different religions. Write students' answers on the chalkboard.

■ Explain that in this lesson students will read the legendary tale of how Prince Vladimir used a similar method to find the best religion for the people of Kiev.

Think About What You Know

■ Assign the THINK ABOUT WHAT YOU KNOW activity on p. 303.

■ Answers should reflect independent thinking but may include that nuns and monks fed the poor, gave travelers shelter, taught children, and cared for the sick; village priests held services and taught children.

Study the Vocabulary

■ Have students look up the definition of *schism* in the Glossary.

■ Ask students to think of synonyms for this term (split, separation).

CHAPTER 11 HISTORY OF RUSSIA AND EASTERN EUROPE

Outside influences shaped the history of region, which was one part of large empires. the result of a revoluti 1917, the Russian emp was reorganized. Sma independent countries replaced old empires i Eastern Europe.

Optional Activities

Writing to Learn

Writing a Letter   Tell students to imagine that they are citizens of Kiev in the year 988. Prince Vladimir has just ordered all pictures of their god burned. Next, he has ordered the baptism of all citizens.

● Ask students to write a letter to a friend in Moscow telling him or her of these events and how they feel about them.

The Middle Ages in Russia and Eastern Europe

THINK ABOUT WHAT YOU KNOW

In Chapter 6 you read about some things that happened in western Europe during the Middle Ages. How did religion affect life in western Europe at that time?

STUDY THE VOCABULARY

schism

FOCUS YOUR READING

How did Constantinople and the Mongol Empire affect Russia and eastern Europe during the Middle Ages?

A. The Tale of Bygone Years

Princess Olga Nearly 900 years ago, Christian monks prepared the earliest written history of the Eastern Slavs, *The Tale of Bygone Years*. This work can be called a tale because it combines legend and history. As you know, we learn about people from their legends as well as from their history.

Among the stories told in *The Tale of Bygone Years* is that of Princess Olga, who lived more than a thousand years ago. Olga was the wife of a prince of Kiev (kee EV), a city located on the Dnieper River. When Olga's husband was killed in battle, she took over the city and led it to victory over its enemies.

Olga later journeyed to Constantinople, the gateway to the Black Sea and the capital of the Byzantine Empire. That empire had become far smaller by the time Olga went on her journey, but Constantinople was still the largest and richest city in Europe.

When Olga met the Byzantine emperor, he was struck by her beauty and her wisdom. In fact, he proposed marriage. Olga did not give him an answer; instead she asked to be taught about his religion, Christianity. People from Kiev were not Christians at that time. They worshiped a variety of gods and goddesses.

The emperor, eager to win Olga's hand, asked the patriarch to teach her. The patriarch was the head of the church at Constantinople. According to *The Tale of Bygone Years*, Olga took in the patriarch's teachings "like a sponge absorbing water." She accepted the Christian religion but turned down the emperor's offer of marriage. She returned to Kiev, where she tried without success to introduce the Christian religion among her people.

Vladimir of Kiev Olga's grandson Vladimir (VLAD uh mihr) became ruler of Kiev in A.D. 980. At first he supported the old religion, so the people could continue to worship the old gods and goddesses. Yet Vladimir was curious about other religions. When he questioned travelers who came to Kiev about the religions of their homelands, they each said that their religion was the best.

Vladimir asked his nobles what they thought about the different views. The nobles told Vladimir that if he wanted to learn about different religions, he should send "ten good and true men" to visit other lands and observe how people there worshiped. Vladimir did as the nobles suggested. When the ten advisers returned, they reported that Christian services in the city of Constantinople were by far the most beautiful.

Vladimir of Kiev became a Christian in the year 988. He directed that all statues

---

Read and Think

Section A

The story of how Christianity came to Russia is contained in a book called *The Tale of Bygone Years*. Discuss this story with your students by asking the following questions:

1. **What is *The Tale of Bygone Years*?** (A history of the Russian empire that combines legend and history *p. 303*)

2. **According to *The Tale of Bygone Years*, how did Vladimir decide to become a Christian?** (He sent ten men to visit other lands and observe how people worshiped. The men said that Christian services were by far the most beautiful. *p. 303*)

Thinking Critically Why, do you think, is it not surprising that *The Tale of Bygone Years* says that Russians accepted Christianity gladly? (Analyze) (Answers should reflect independent thinking but may include that the book was written by Christian monks. *p. 303*)

For Your Information

The Introduction of Writing in Russia With the Christian religion came the Bible, but the Bible needed to be written in a language that the Russians could understand. This task was actually accomplished about 100 years before the Russians became Christians.

Two monks, Cyril and his brother Methodius, invented a way to write the spoken language of the Slavs. Cyril worked out an alphabet of 43 letters to represent the sounds used by the Slavs when speaking. The letters he used came from the Greek and Hebrew alphabets. This alphabet, known as the Cyrillic alphabet, is the basis of the modern Russian alphabet, although the Russian alphabet today has only 32 letters.

Optional Activities

Read and Think

Section B

Differences between the Christian Church in Rome and the Christian Church in Constantinople developed into a split between the two churches. Review the causes of this split by asking the following questions:

1. **What were the major differences between the eastern and western branches of the Christian Church?**
   (Roman Catholics followed the teachings of the church at Rome, accepted the pope as head of the church, and had services in Latin, while the Eastern Orthodox Church was headed by the patriarch and the services were held in Greek. *p. 304*)

   Thinking Critically **Why, do you think, were the eastern and western churches unable to resolve their differences?** (Infer)
   Answers should reflect independent thinking but may include that their differences centered on who was the head of the church, which meant that it was a power struggle. *p. 304*)

VISUAL THINKING SKILL

Interpreting a Picture

■ Direct students' attention to the picture on the lower-right portion of this page. Then ask: **How would you compare St. Basil's Church to churches you've seen in your town?**
(Distinctively shaped domes, quite ornate)

Grand Prince Vladimir of Kiev brought the Christian religion to his people in the year 988.
▶ How did the artist portray Vladimir in this drawing?

and pictures of the old gods and goddesses be cut into pieces and burned. Vladimir ordered all the people in Kiev to come to the Dnieper River to be baptized as Christians. *The Tale of Bygone Years* would have us believe that the people of Kiev accepted Christianity gladly. Perhaps this is true, but one wonders if the monks' tale tells the full story.

B. The Christian Churches of Eastern Europe and Russia

Church Divisions Vladimir's advisers had observed Christian services in Germany as well as in Constantinople. There were important differences between the Christian Church in eastern Europe and that in western Europe. Christians in Germany, as in most of the western European

304

countries, followed the teachings of the church at Rome and accepted the pope as head of the church. The church at Constantinople was headed by the patriarch. The Bible and services of the Roman church were in Latin. The Bible and services of the church at Constantinople were in Greek.

Other differences between the church at Rome and at Constantinople led in time to a **schism** (SIHZ um), or division, between the eastern and western branches of the Christian Church. The western branch was called Roman Catholic; the eastern was known as Eastern Orthodox. The word *orthodox* means "having the right views," and the word *catholic* means "general" or "universal."

Orthodox Church The Eastern Orthodox Church spread Christianity throughout several eastern European countries as

This cathedral was built as a place of worship for Russian Christians.
▶ How would you describe the domes of this church?

---

well as Russia. In time the church in Russia had its own patriarch and was known as the Russian Orthodox Church. A number of other eastern European nations also came to have their own churches, among them the Serbian Orthodox Church and the Romanian Orthodox Church.

The Christian Church, however, was not the only thing to affect Russia and eastern Europe during the Middle Ages. More than 200 years after Vladimir of Kiev accepted Christianity, conquerors from the steppes would invade Russia and eastern Europe, and bring much of this large territory under their control.

C. Conquerors from the Steppes

The Nomads The steppes that stretch from the Black Sea into central Asia were the home of nomadic tribes during the Middle Ages. These nomads had learned to live on the dry grasslands. They kept herds of horses, cattle, sheep, and goats. The nomads lived in tents so that they could easily pack up and move with their herds to better pastures. The animals provided milk and meat for food, as well as hides and wool for clothing.

Sometimes the nomads traded for certain goods; other times they raided settled areas and took what they wanted. The nomads looked down on anyone who sought safety behind town walls. The nomadic warriors were fierce fighters, and their small, tough, fast horses enabled them to cover long distances and catch their victims by surprise. Those victims even included other tribes of nomads until the people of the steppes were united under the leadership of the Mongols.

The Mongols lived in the land that is still called Mongolia. The chief of the Mongol tribe had a son who would come to be

Genghis Khan became ruler of the Mongols, who were known as marvelous horsemen and fierce fighters.
► What does Genghis Khan's name mean?

known as Genghis Khan (GENG gihs kahn). When the boy was 13 years old, his father died, leaving him at the mercy of his rivals. In spite of his youth, the boy outwitted those rivals and took his father's place as leader of the Mongol tribe. In the years that followed, Genghis Khan brought other tribes under his rule and thus earned his name, which means "mighty leader." By the year 1206, Genghis Khan was widely known as the undisputed master of the steppes.

Mongol Conquests Armies led by the Mongols began a rapid conquest of neighboring lands. They swept across Eurasia from China to eastern Europe. By 1240 the army of Batu Khan, grandson of Genghis Khan, reached Kiev. Batu sent word to the

305

Writing to Learn

Writing a News Story Have students write a newspaper article describing the fall of Kiev to the Mongols.

● Tell students to include quotes from the surviving citizens of Kiev describing how they feel about what has happened to their city.

● Be sure to remind students to answer the five "W"s and one "H" of newspaper reporting (who, what, where, when, why, and how).

Optional Activities

Meeting Individual Needs

Concept: Comparing Life Under Different Rulers

To better understand the influence of the Mongols on eastern Europe and Russia, it is important to see how their rule affected life in these regions. Below are three activities that will help your students understand this concept.

◆ **EASY** Ask students to imagine that the Mongols had all the Russian princes killed, replacing them with Mongol rulers.

Have students write a paragraph describing how life in Russia would have been different.

◀▶ **AVERAGE** Tell students to compare Prince Vladimir's rule of Kiev with the Mongols' rule of Russia by listing any similarities and differences.

Then, have students write a paragraph explaining which ruler would have affected daily life in Russia more.

◀▮▶ **CHALLENGING** Ask students who need a challenge to imagine that they are Russian peasants.

Have students write a letter to a friend in western Europe describing how life under the Mongols' rule is different from life under Prince Vladimir's rule.

VISUAL THINKING SKILL

Analyzing an Illustration

■ Have students study the illustration on this page in order to answer the following question: **How did the artist depict Genghis Khan?**
(As a fighter and an expert horseman)

Answers to Caption Questions
p. 304 *l.* ► As a regal ruler, opulently dressed
p. 304 *r.* ► Gold onion-shaped domes
p. 305 ► "Mighty leader"

305

Read and Think
Sections C and D

Much of eastern Europe and Russia was conquered by the Mongols. Review with students the extent of the Mongols' conquest and the nature of their rule by asking these questions:

1. **Who was Genghis Khan, and what does his name mean?**
(He was a famous chief of the Mongol tribe who brought other tribes under his rule, thus earning his name, which means "mighty leader." *p. 305*)

2. **What parts of eastern Europe were conquered by the Mongols?**
(Much of Russia and eastern Europe, including Kiev, Poland, and lands in the Great Hungarian Plain *p. 306*)

3. **How did the Mongols govern the lands they conquered in Russia?**
(The Mongols allowed the Russian princes to govern their own states. However, they had to pay the Mongols and provide them with laborers. *p. 307*)

Thinking Critically Do you think the Mongols were wise to control Russia as they did? (Evaluate)
(Answers should reflect independent thinking but may include no, because the Russian princes profited from the arrangement, or yes, because the Mongols made money without having to govern. *p. 307*)

prince of Kiev, "Give me one tenth of everything—one man in ten, and the tenth part of your wealth." To this demand the prince answered, "We will give you nothing: when we are dead, then you can have it all!"

These were brave words indeed, but words did not stop the Mongols. They broke down the gates of the city with a battering ram and launched a fierce attack. Kiev fell in five days, and a terrible slaughter followed. According to one famous account, "No eye was left open to weep for the dead."

The Mongols did not stop at Kiev. They pressed farther west, into Poland, where they defeated an army of heavily armed knights. The Mongols advanced south across the Great Hungarian Plain and crossed the Danube. They destroyed towns and villages throughout much of Russia and eastern Europe. People in western Europe shuddered fearfully when they heard about the Mongols and worried that these fierce warriors from the steppes would come farther west. Fortunately for the western Europeans, Batu Khan turned back to central Asia. When he later returned west, he made his empire's permanent capital on the lower Volga River.

The fast-riding Mongols conquered towns and villages throughout much of Russia and eastern Europe.
▶ What weapons did the Mongol forces use?

306

Optional Activities

Interpreting Information On pp. 276–277, students learned to interpret information in order to get the full meaning.

- Have them review this skill by analyzing the statement on this page which describes the slaughter that followed the Mongols' attack on Kiev. The statement relates that "No eye was left open to weep for the dead."

Reteaching Main Objective

⭐ *Explain how the Mongols gained control of Russia and eastern Europe.*

- Have students create a classroom television special on the Mongol conquest of Russia and eastern Europe.

- Ask students to role-play reporters, newscasters, and important people of this period in history.

- Reporters should describe some of the battles, and newscasters may interview important people such as Genghis Khan and Batu Khan regarding their strategies and goals.

D. Paying the Golden Horde

The Mongols conquered a huge territory, creating the Mongol Empire—the largest empire the world has ever known. The Russians called the Mongols the Golden Horde. Gold was the color of Batu's tent. *Horde* comes from a Mongol word meaning "camp."

The Golden Horde did not directly govern the lands they conquered in Russia. They only wanted the conquered people to pay them money and to send laborers to serve them. The Mongols were quite willing to let the Russian princes continue governing their states as long as they paid money on demand. The princes in turn had to collect the money from their own people. Some princes collected more than they had to pay the Golden Horde, so they profited from the arrangement. It was the large number of peasants who carried the heavy burden. The Golden Horde would continue to control Russia in this way for many years.

A Russian prince is shown visiting the Mongol headquarters of Batu Khan. The Russians called the Mongols the Golden Horde.
▶ What decorated the Mongol headquarters?

LESSON **1** *REVIEW*

THINK AND WRITE (Recall)

A. According to *The Tale of Bygone Years*, how was Christianity brought to Kiev?

B. What were the results of the schism between the eastern and western branches of the Christian Church? (Recall)

C. Describe what areas the Mongol armies conquered. (Recall)

D. What did the Golden Horde want from the Russians? (Recall)

SKILLS CHECK

MAP SKILL

Locate Mongolia on the political map of Eurasia on Atlas pages 616–617. Then locate Mongolia on the physical map on pages 618–619. How does the land elevation of Mongolia differ from that of the area along the northern coast of the Caspian Sea?

307

Optional Activities

---

3 CLOSING THE LESSON

Lesson *1* Review

Answers to Think and Write

A. According to the tale, Princess Olga brought Christianity to Kiev after learning about the religion in Constantinople.

B. The schism led to the two branches practicing their own forms of Christianity.

C. The Mongol armies conquered much of Russia and eastern Europe, including Kiev, Poland, and the lands of the Great Hungarian Plain.

D. The Golden Horde wanted money and laborers.

Answer to Skills Check

The elevation of Mongolia is much higher than the area along the northern coast of the Caspian Sea.

Focus Your Reading

Ask the lesson focus question found at the beginning of the lesson: **How did Constantinople and the Mongol Empire affect Russia and eastern Europe during the Middle Ages?**

(Constantinople introduced Christianity to eastern Europe and Russia. The Mongols gained control of Russia and eastern Europe for a long period during the Middle Ages.)

Additional Practice

You may wish to assign the ancillary materials listed below.

Understanding the Lesson p. 77
Workbook p. 72

Answers to Caption Questions
p. 306 ▶ Spears and bows and arrows
p. 307 ▶ Statues

In the Time of the Czars

Objectives

★1. **List** the contributions of the czars of Russia.

2. **Explain** why the Russian rulers were called czars.

3. **Describe** what the life of a serf was like in Russia.

4. **Identify** the following people and places: *Ivan Kalita, Ivan the Great, Ivan the Terrible, Peter I, Sophia, Catherine the Great, Muscovy, Moscow, St. Petersburg, Leningrad, Neva River,* and *Baltic Sea.*

1 STARTING THE LESSON

Motivation Activity

■ List the following names on the chalkboard: *Ivan Kalita, Ivan the Great,* and *Ivan the Terrible.*

■ Ask students to think of possible reasons why these three rulers of Russia were given these titles.

■ Have students check their answers as they read about these and other Russian rulers in this lesson.

Think About What You Know

■ Assign the THINK ABOUT WHAT YOU KNOW activity on p. 308.

■ Answers should reflect independent thinking but may include setting up a system of loyal, educated adults to help you.

Study the Vocabulary

■ Have students look up in the Glossary the definition of each new vocabulary word in this lesson.

■ Then, ask students to use the words in one sentence and to read their sentences to the class.

LESSON 2

In the Time of the Czars

THINK ABOUT WHAT YOU KNOW

Imagine that you will become the ruler of a nation on your thirteenth birthday. What methods will you use to govern your nation?

STUDY THE VOCABULARY

czar   coronation

FOCUS YOUR READING

How did important rulers change Russia in the time of the czars?

A. The Story of Three Ivans

Ivan I and Ivan III Three rulers named Ivan played parts in creating the Russian empire. Ivan I, later called Ivan Kalita, was the prince of Muscovy from 1328 to 1341. Muscovy was the Russian state ruled from Moscow. Ivan believed it was better to work for the Golden Horde than to oppose it. He collected money for the Mongols not only from the people in Muscovy but also from other Russian princes. This expanded the area that Ivan controlled. Also, in return for his services, the Mongols let Ivan keep a share of what he collected. He was an efficient collector and also very thrifty, so he did well through this arrangement. That was why people gave him the name Kalita, which means "moneybags."

Like Ivan I, later rulers gained more land for the state of Muscovy. But it was not until the reign of Ivan III that the Golden Horde lost its hold on Muscovy. Ivan III ruled Muscovy from 1462 to 1505. He was called Ivan the Great because he enlarged Muscovy's territory so that it was the largest Russian state at that time. The map on page 309 shows how much land

Ivan the Great gained control of during his reign. He eventually became so powerful that he simply refused to pay any money to the Golden Horde.

Ivan the Terrible Ivan IV took full control of the government in 1547 and ruled until 1584. He is known as Ivan the Terrible. That name tells something about him and his reign. Ivan the Terrible believed that people respected a ruler only when they feared that ruler. He inspired fear by such acts as having the tongue torn out of a man who had criticized him.

Ivan IV was born in 1530. Both of his parents were dead by the time he was eight years old. Ivan feared that the nobles who

Ivan IV, known as Ivan the Terrible, expanded Russia's territory and made Moscow his capital.
▶ What is shown in the background?

Optional Activities

Reading a Newspaper

● Have students skim the newspaper for one week to locate any articles pertaining to the Soviet Union's current leader.

● Tell students to read the articles and compare the current leader and government of the Soviet Union to the czars and their government.

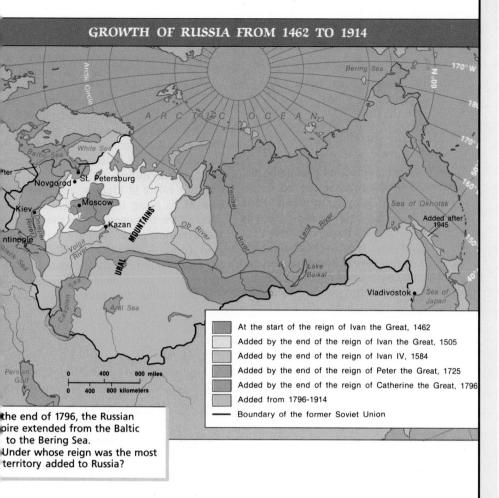

GROWTH OF RUSSIA FROM 1462 TO 1914

At the start of the reign of Ivan the Great, 1462
Added by the end of the reign of Ivan the Great, 1505
Added by the end of the reign of Ivan IV, 1584
Added by the end of the reign of Peter the Great, 1725
Added by the end of the reign of Catherine the Great, 1796
Added from 1796-1914
— Boundary of the former Soviet Union

the end of 1796, the Russian
pire extended from the Baltic
to the Bering Sea.
Under whose reign was the most
territory added to Russia?

had taken control of the government would kill him before he could take power. When Ivan was 13, he decided to act first. He had his servants kill the leading noble. The other nobles, caught by surprise, were now afraid of the boy who had succeeded in issuing such an order. Thus, Ivan IV discovered the power of fear. It was a lesson he never forgot.

Ivan the Terrible has long puzzled historians. He was a harsh ruler, but he did

accomplish some great things. He defeated the Mongols in the lands along the Volga River. Russia was now an empire that extended to the Caspian Sea. He celebrated his victory over the Mongols by building the cathedral of St. Basil in Moscow, which is shown on pages 280–281.

Along with having a terrible temper, Ivan had a good mind. He read many more books than most rulers of his time. He had books imported from other lands and

309

2 DEVELOPING THE LESSON

Read and Think

Section A

Discuss with your students the reigns of the three Ivans by asking the following questions:

1. **How did Ivan Kalita become wealthy?** (He collected money for the Mongols. For his services, they let him keep a share of what he collected. *p. 308*)

2. **Under which ruler did the Golden Horde lose its hold on Muscovy?** (Ivan the Great *p. 308*)

Thinking Critically Why, do you think, did Ivan IV become such a terrible ruler? (Infer) (Answers may include that, as an orphan, he learned to be distrustful of others and bitter. *pp. 308–309*)

GEOGRAPHY THEMES

Regions

■ Ask students to refer to the map on this page to answer the following question: **Under whose reign did Russia first reach the shores of the Black Sea?** (Under the reign of Catherine the Great)

— **Answers to Caption Questions** —
p. 308 ▶ The cathedral of St. Basil
p. 309 ▶ Under the reign of Peter the Great

Graphic Organizer

To help students better understand the differences among the czars named Ivan, you may wish to use the graphic organizer shown below.

	IVAN I	IVAN III	IVAN IV
NICKNAME	Ivan Kalita	Ivan the Great	Ivan the Terrible
DATE OF RULE	1328-1341	1462-1505	1547-1584
KNOWN FOR	thrift, money collection	enlarged territory, didn't pay Golden Horde	made people fear him, built cathedral of St. Basil

Optional Activities

Read and Think

Section B

Discuss the origin and history of the word *czar* with your students by asking the following questions:

1. **How did Russian rulers come to regard Moscow as the third Rome?**
   (After Constantinople, the second Rome, fell in 1453, some Russians said that Moscow had replaced Constantinople as the greatest of Christian cities. *p. 310*)

2. **Why did Russian rulers begin to call themselves *czars*?**
   (Russian rulers adopted the title once held by the Roman and Byzantine emperors because they believed that Moscow was the third Rome. *p. 310*)

   Thinking Critically **What, do you think, happened to end czarist rule in 1917?** (Hypothesize)
   (Answers should reflect independent thinking but may include a revolution or a takeover by another country. *p. 310*)

---

brought the first printing press to Russia. Ivan had a great love of music and recommended that schools all over the land teach music. Perhaps if Ivan the Terrible had not learned about the power of fear as a boy, he might have been known as another Ivan the Great.

B. Why the Russian Rulers Were Called Czars

The Roman emperor Constantine had made Constantinople the second Rome. For that reason, later Byzantine emperors claimed that they held the same office as the rulers of ancient Rome. For more than a thousand years, they were called caesar, the title of the ancient Roman emperors.

Turkish Muslims conquered Constantinople and killed the last of the Byzantine emperors in 1453. Christian Constantinople was now ruled by people who followed another religion. You will read more about the Turkish Muslims and their conquests in a later chapter.

After the fall of Constantinople, some Russians said that Moscow had taken the place of Constantinople as the greatest of Christian cities. Constantinople had been the second Rome; Moscow, they argued, was the third Rome.

The rulers at Moscow accepted the idea of its being the third Rome. They adopted the title once held by the Roman and Byzantine emperors. They were called **czar** (zahr) — sometimes spelled *tsar* — the Russian form of the title *caesar*. Russia had a czarist government, or was ruled by emperors called czars, until 1917.

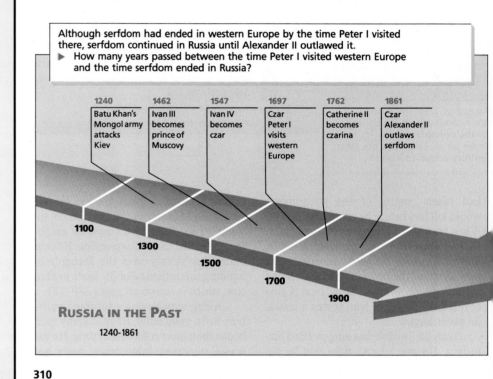

Although serfdom had ended in western Europe by the time Peter I visited there, serfdom continued in Russia until Alexander II outlawed it.
▶ How many years passed between the time Peter I visited western Europe and the time serfdom ended in Russia?

1240	1462	1547	1697	1762	1861
Batu Khan's Mongol army attacks Kiev	Ivan III becomes prince of Muscovy	Ivan IV becomes czar	Czar Peter I visits western Europe	Catherine II becomes czarina	Czar Alexander II outlaws serfdom

1100   1300   1500   1700   1900

RUSSIA IN THE PAST
1240-1861

310

Writing to Learn

Writing a Diary Tell students to imagine that they are Peter the Great on his journey through western Europe.

- Have students write five diary entries that Peter might have made about his travels.

- Ask individual students to read their entries and identify what they think might interest Peter.

Constructing a Time Line

- Have students skim the lesson and make a time line of important dates in the reigns of the czars.

- Ask for volunteers to share their time lines with the class.

310

Peter the Great visited a shipyard in western Europe.
▶ What are some of the tools used to build the ships?

C. Czar Peter I Learns About Western Europe

Two Czars at Once Peter I and his half brother Ivan V were both declared czars in 1682. At their **coronation**, or crowning ceremony, the two czars sat on a double throne. Concealed by a curtain behind the throne, their sister Sophia sat telling them what to say. Sophia had to prompt her brothers during the long ceremony because 16-year-old Ivan was sickly and Peter was only 10 years old.

In truth, Sophia ruled Russia for the next seven years. Ivan was not able to rule, and Peter was still thought to be too young. This left Peter free to follow his own interests.

What Peter Learned For the most part, Peter learned only what he wanted to learn. He never became a good speller, but he knew quite a lot of geography because he liked to look at a large globe that stood taller than a man. He also learned a great deal about army affairs by playing war games with a group of companions. They had uniforms, lived in barracks, and even spent a year building an earth and timber fort, which they bombarded with a cannon.

Peter's great curiosity led him to spend time talking with western Europeans who lived in one section of Moscow. He made friends with a Dutch merchant named Franz Timmerman. One day they found an old boat in a storage building on a royal estate. It was unlike any of the flat-bottomed riverboats that Peter had seen. Timmerman said it was a common western European boat that could sail against the wind as well as with it.

Peter insisted that the old boat be repaired and fitted with sails. Once he saw

311

311

Read and Think
Sections D and E

Peter the Great and Catherine the Great worked hard to make Russia a modern and strong nation. Still, serfdom remained an important element of the Russian economy. Help students to understand these concepts by asking the following questions:

1. **How did Peter try to modernize Russia?**
   (He reformed the army, created a navy, had canals built, and attempted to establish modern industries. He also ordered young nobles to learn a western European language, and he ordered Russian men to make their appearance more western by shaving. *pp. 312–313*)

2. **Why did Peter want to build a modern city on the Baltic Sea?**
   (To give Russia an outlet to the sea and a "window on Europe" *p. 313*)

3. **What did Catherine do for Russia?**
   (She added a large amount of territory to the Russian empire, including lands north of the Black Sea and a large part of Poland. *p. 313*)

4. **Why did most of Catherine's subjects have little freedom?**
   (More than half of her subjects were serfs who were much like slaves. *p. 314*)

5. **Why did the serfs know little about the world around them?**
   (Most could not read, and they could not leave their villages without their master's permission. *p. 314*)

6. **How did freedom affect the lives of the serfs?**
   (They could no longer be sold, but their way of life did not change much. *p. 314*)

Thinking Critically Why, do you think, did Czar Alexander end serfdom? (Hypothesize)
(Answers should reflect independent thinking but may include that the serfs were starting to agitate for more rights and the government wanted to prevent a violent uprising. *p. 314*)

---

the boat sail a zigzag course against the wind, he decided that someday the people of Russia would learn how to build and sail such boats. Peter later called the small boat "the grandfather of the Russian navy." Today it is a prize exhibit in a Soviet naval museum.

When Peter was 17 years old, he sent Sophia away from Moscow and took the government into his own hands. Ivan lived for another seven years, but Peter was in fact the sole ruler of Russia.

Peter's Travels Peter strongly believed that Russia could learn a lot more than shipbuilding from the West. He decided to see for himself how western Europeans lived. In the spring of 1697, Czar Peter I and a party of 270 set out for western Europe. Peter did not travel as the czar. He posed as a sailor named Peter Mikhailov, but the disguise fooled no one.

Peter the Great studied shipbuilding and made this model of a ship.
► Why is Peter dressed in a sailor's clothing?

When the party reached the Netherlands, Peter went to work in a shipyard. This excerpt from the book *Peter, the Revolutionary Tsar*, written by Peter Brooks Putnam, describes what the experience was like for Peter.

> Peter had come to Europe to learn, and the next few months were a period of intensive learning. At the simplest level, he studied shipbuilding. He and ten companions worked under the master shipwright Gerrit Claes Pool. Peter enjoyed the physical labor and the experience of being treated as a workman.

After several months, Peter received a certificate stating that he was a qualified shipwright. He was quite proud of it.

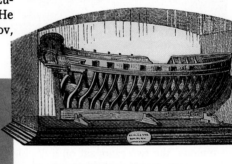

D. Great Rulers Made Some Major Changes

Peter the Great Peter I wanted to make Russia a modern nation. He firmly believed that his empire was held back by its clinging to old customs. Peter had his greatest success in reforming the army and creating a navy. He also had canals built to connect some of the rivers. He attempted to establish modern industries like those he had seen in western Europe.

Peter insisted that the Russians change their ways of thinking and living. He ordered nobles to learn a western

---

Designing an Advertisement

- Have students create advertisements to attract workers to help build St. Petersburg.
- Tell students that the advertisement should not mention the job's difficult working conditions. Instead, it should entice workers to apply for employment.
- To help students, ask them to list working conditions that might have attracted the people of this time period.
- Illustrate the advertisements and display them on a bulletin board when students are finished.

Peter outlawed the traditional long coats and beards worn by many Russian men.
▶ Why is Peter cutting the sleeves of the man in this picture?

The Granger Collection

European language so that they could read the books of other nations. The czar thought that changing the appearance of his subjects would change their way of thinking. Peter ordered Russian men to shave their beards, since they were no longer the fashion in western Europe, and to change the way they dressed.

Peter built a new capital to take the place of Moscow. The capital was to be a modern city with buildings like those in western Europe. Peter believed that it was of greatest importance that Russia have an outlet to the sea and a "window on Europe," so the capital was built where the Neva River empties into the Baltic Sea. The city was called St. Petersburg to honor the saint for whom Peter was named. It would be renamed Petrograd at the beginning of World War I.

Peter tried to make many changes in Russia, but much remained unchanged. Russia was a large land, and even the most energetic czar could only do so much. But Peter did enough to be remembered as Peter the Great.

Catherine the Great Peter the Great died in 1725, and in the next 75 years, half of the Russian rulers were women. These empresses were called czarinas. Catherine II, the czarina from 1762 to 1796, came to be known as Catherine the Great.

Catherine added a large amount of territory to the Russian empire. Her armies conquered the Turks on lands north of the Black Sea. With the gain of these lands, Russia had outlets on both the Baltic Sea and the Black Sea. Catherine also added a large part of Poland to her empire. In North America the earliest Russian settlements in what is now Alaska were established during Catherine's reign.

Like Peter the Great, Catherine admired western Europe and wanted to make changes in Russia, but she did not intend to change its form of government. She believed, as Peter the Great had believed, that the power to rule must belong to the monarch alone.

313

Lesson 2 Review

Answers to Think and Write

A. Ivan Kalita, which means "moneybags," collected money for the Mongols and kept some for himself, Ivan the Great enlarged Muscovy's territory, and Ivan the Terrible treated people brutally.

B. When Russian rulers believed that Moscow was the third Rome, they adopted the title "caesar" ("czar" in Russian).

C. Peter the Great went to western Europe to learn shipbuilding and to see how western Europeans lived.

D. Peter the Great reformed the army, created a navy, built canals, and tried to establish modern industries. Catherine the Great added territory to the empire and tried to get her subjects to improve themselves.

E. Serfdom was much like slavery. Serfs had little freedom, they could be punished, and they were sold like livestock.

Answer to Skills Check

Answers should reflect independent thinking but should be backed with the facts from the lesson.

Focus Your Reading

Ask the lesson focus question found at the beginning of the lesson: **How did important rulers change Russia in the time of the czars?**

(Ivan the Great enlarged Muscovy's territory, Ivan the Terrible extended Russia's empire to the Caspian Sea, Peter and Catherine tried to modernize Russia, and Alexander II ended serfdom.)

Additional Practice

You may wish to assign the ancillary materials listed below.

Understanding the Lesson p. 78
Workbook pp. 73-74

Answers to Caption Questions
p. 314 ▶ He is portrayed in military attire.

Alexander II, known as "the reforming czar," abolished serfdom in Russia and freed peasants from the personal control of the nobles.
▶ How is Alexander portrayed?

1796. But in Russia, serfs still worked the land of the nobles and czars.

Most serfs knew little about the world outside their own village. Few could read, and serfs could not leave their village without their master's permission. Some serfs on large estates worked as household servants. They served as cooks, maids, butlers, and carpenters. Great nobles took pride in having everything done by the people on their own estate. A wealthy master might have a personal tailor, cobbler, or piano tuner.

Serfdom in Russia was much like slavery. Masters could punish their serfs or sell them as if they were livestock. Serfdom in Russia lasted about as long as slavery in the United States. Czar Alexander II issued a law ending serfdom in 1861. That was four years before African-American slaves in the United States gained their freedom at the end of the Civil War.

Alexander's law gave the serfs their freedom. They could no longer be sold. But the serfs did not receive all the land to which they felt they were entitled. The nobles still held large estates, so freedom did not greatly change the ways the former serfs lived. Most were still poor and uneducated. They still lived in villages and worked as servants or on the land.

E. How Serfs Lived in the Time of the Czars

Most of Catherine's subjects had very little freedom. More than half of the people were serfs. You learned in Chapter 6 that serfs were people bound to the land they worked. Serfdom had disappeared in most of Europe by the time Catherine died in

---

LESSON 2 REVIEW

THINK AND WRITE (Recall)

A. Why was one Ivan called "Kalita," one called "the Great," and another called "the Terrible"? (Recall)

B. Why were the Russian rulers called czars?

C. Why did Peter I visit western Europe? (Infer)

D. What changes did Peter the Great and Catherine the Great make in Russia? (Recall)

E. What was the life of a serf like? (Evalua...

SKILLS CHECK

WRITING SKILL

Which Russian ruler that you read about in this lesson was the best ruler? Write a paragraph explaining why you think he or she was the best.

314

UNDERSTANDING THE LESSON

NAME _____
UNDERSTANDING THE LESSON

CHAPTER
11

LESSON 2 CONTENT MASTER

Organizing Facts

❋ The chart shows the main ideas of the lesson. Fill in the blank spaces with the details that support each main idea. The first one has been done for you.
Suggested answers are provided.

Czars expanded Russian Empire.
1. Ivan III made Muscovy largest Russian state.
2. Ivan the Terrible expanded empire to the Caspian Sea.
3. Catherine the Great gained outlets on Black Sea; added large part of Poland to empire; planted settlements in Alaska.

Peter the Great made many changes.
1. Reformed the army, created a navy, and built canals to connect some rivers.
2. Attempted to establish modern industry.
3. Ordered nobles to learn western European languages.
4. Built modern capital, with buildings like those in western Europe.

Russia During the Time of the Czars

Catherine the Great added territory to the Russian Empire.
1. Conquered the Turks on lands north of the Black Sea.
2. Added a large part of Poland.
3. Settlements in what is now Alaska were established during Catherine's reign.

Life of serfs did not change much under czars.
1. At the time of Catherine's death, serfs still worked lands of nobles and czars.
2. Most serfs could not read and could not leave land without lord's permission.
3. Before 1861, serfs were treated like slaves; could be punished and bought and sold.
4. Alexander II freed serfs in 1861, but little changed.

Think and Write: Why didn't the changes made by Peter the Great, Catherine the Great, and Alexander II affect all Russians? Why did life remain the same for so many people? Write a paragraph discussing these questions. You may use the back of the sheet.
Answers should reflect independent thinking; suggestions appear in the Answer Key.
78
Use with textbook pages 300–312.

◀ **Review Master Booklet, p. 78**

The Russian Revolution

THINK ABOUT WHAT YOU KNOW

If you had been a Russian peasant after serfdom ended in 1861, what kinds of changes would you have wanted to occur in Russia?

STUDY THE VOCABULARY

anarchy   socialism
abdicate   communism

FOCUS YOUR READING

How did the revolution of 1917 affect Russia?

A. The Last of the Czars

Riots Begin On a cold March evening in 1917, a train pulled into Pskov (puh-KOF), a city southwest of Petrograd. The train carried Czar Nicholas II. He had been at the Russian army headquarters near where the battles of World War I were being fought. Now the czar was trying to get back to Petrograd because he had heard alarming news from the capital city.

There had been crowds marching in the streets of Petrograd, shouting "Bread, bread, give us bread!" Then the demonstrations had turned into riots. Worst of all, troops called out to control the crowds had joined them. Shop windows were smashed, prisons were broken open, buildings were set on fire. When firefighters tried to put out the flames, crowds of rioters stopped them. An official had telegraphed the czar with the warning, "There is **anarchy** in the capital." Anarchy is a complete lack of government and law.

Nicholas Gives Up When Nicholas's train got within 100 miles (161 km) of Petrograd, he learned that armed men were blocking the route into the city. The czar then ordered the train to Pskov, where there was an army headquarters. There Nicholas received more bad news. The uprising had gone too far: it was now a revolution. Messages from Nicholas's army generals advised him to **abdicate**, or give up power. Nicholas realized that if the generals no longer supported him, he could not hope to put down the revolution. Thus on March 15, 1917, Nicholas II abdicated, and czarist rule in Russia came to an end.

Nicholas hoped that he and his family would be allowed to continue living in Russia or, if that was not possible, to go to England. But the revolutionary government arrested the former czar and his family. They were later sent to a town in the Ural Mountains, where they were killed in July 1918.

Czar Nicholas II abdicated the throne of Russia. Later he and his family were killed.
▶ Why did the czar abdicate?

Writing to Learn

Writing a Journal Tell students to imagine that they are Czar Nicholas II on the train to Petrograd. They have just learned about the rioting in Petrograd and they have also learned that their generals do not support them.

● Ask students to write journal entries that Nicholas might have made.

● Tell students to answer these questions as they describe their concerns and fears: What has caused the rioting? How can the rioting be stopped? Should they abdicate? What will happen to them and to their country if they abdicate?

Optional Activities

The Russian Revolution

Objectives

★1. **Describe** the methods the Communists used to control Russia.

2. **List** the events that led to the end of czarist rule in Russia.

3. **Explain** how Lenin came to power.

4. **Identify** the following people and places: *Nicholas II, Karl Marx, Nikolai Lenin, Pskov, Petrograd, Moscow,* and *Leningrad.*

1 STARTING THE LESSON

Motivation Activity

■ Ask students to write down everything they know about communism.

■ Explain that students will soon read about the introduction of communism to Russia.

■ At the end of the lesson, have students compare their initial impressions of communism with what they have learned.

Think About What You Know

■ Assign the THINK ABOUT WHAT YOU KNOW activity on p. 315.

■ Answers should reflect independent thinking but may include giving land to the peasants and providing the peasants with free public education.

Study the Vocabulary

■ Have students look up the definition of each of the new vocabulary words in the Glossary.

■ Ask students to use the terms in a short newspaper article with the headline "Revolution in Russia!"

— Answers to Caption Questions —
p. 315▶ He knew that he could not put down the revolution without the support of the generals.

315

Read and Think

Sections A and B

In March 1917, a revolution shook Russia, ending czarist rule forever. After the czar abdicated, the government of Russia was in turmoil, but within eight months of the revolution, a clever politician named Nikolai Lenin had seized power. Review this period of history with students by asking the following questions:

1. **Why was Czar Nicholas II headed for Petrograd?**
   (He had heard that there was rioting in the city. *p. 315*)

2. **Why did Nicholas abdicate?**
   (His army generals advised him to abdicate, and he realized that if the generals no longer supported him, he could not hope to put down the revolution. *p. 315*)

3. **What kinds of governments were the Russians considering in 1917, after the revolution?**
   (A limited monarchy, a democratic republic, and a socialist government *p. 316*)

4. **What did Karl Marx and Nikolai Lenin have in common?**
   (Both favored socialism. *p. 316*)

5. **How did Lenin come to power in Russia?**
   (He and his Communist-led groups took part in a bloody struggle for control of the capital. By November 1917, Lenin and the Communists had seized power and declared that they were the true government of Russia. *p. 317*)

Thinking Critically Why, do you think, did it take two years for the Communists to control all of Russia? (Infer) (Answers should reflect independent thinking but may include that support for the Communists was not widespread or that because Russia is such a vast land, it took time to gain control of the whole country. *p. 317*)

B. Taking Control of the Russian Revolution

Different Ideas The uprising in the city of Petrograd was indeed the beginning of a revolution. For years many Russians had discussed the need for a major change in their country. But those who agreed that a change was needed had very different ideas about what the change should be.

Some Russians wanted a government like that of Great Britain. They wanted a limited monarchy, in which the monarch serves as head of state but does not govern. Other Russians wanted to follow the example of France or the United States. They wanted a democratic republic, in which the people elect those who make the laws and govern.

There were other Russians who believed that a revolution ought to change much more than the type of government. They wanted a revolution that would do away with the private ownership of land and industry. Some of these people favored **socialism**, a system in which the government not only rules but also owns all the land and industry. Some socialists followed the ideas of Karl Marx, a German writer who had died in 1883. Marx argued that the struggle between the rich and the poor would not end until a revolution brought about socialism.

Lenin's Ideas Vladimir Lenin was a Marxist, that is, he accepted the ideas of Karl Marx. Lenin's original name had been Vladimir Ulyanov (VLAD uh mihr ool YAHnuf). His older brother had taken part in a plot to kill the czar. The plot failed, and the plotters were hanged. The czar's police suspected that Vladimir might also pose a threat. Their suspicions were right.

Vladimir had joined a group that was working to overthrow the czarist government. He was arrested and sent to Siberia for three years. It was after his release from exile that Vladimir Ulyanov adopted the name Nikolai Lenin to confuse the czar's police. However, the police were not fooled, so Lenin fled to western Europe.

Lenin was living in Switzerland at the time of the uprising in Petrograd. A new government had been formed by the time he returned to Russia. Lenin came not to support the new government but to overthrow it. He believed that only his small Marxist party could lead a true revolution. Lenin called his party the Communists because they believed in **communism**, the

Karl Marx believed that socialism could end the struggle between the rich and the poor.
▶ What were his followers called?

For Your Information

A Weak Czarist Government One of the reasons why riots broke out in March 1917 was that the Russian government was being poorly managed. With Czar Nicholas away supervising the Russian army during World War I, the government was left in the hands of Czarina Alexandra and her court.

The czarina was a frail and susceptible woman who easily fell under the influence of a strange adventurer from Siberia named Rasputin. Rasputin eventually gained a great deal of power over the government, which aroused jealousy and fear among the nobles. They despised Rasputin so much that a group of nobles murdered him in 1916. However, his murder did nothing to improve the management of the government.

The Communists engaged in a bloody battle against government troops in 1918.
► Where did the battle take place?

common ownership of land and industry by the people as a group.

Lenin was a skillful leader willing to do anything to get power. He declared that the Communists alone acted for the soldiers and workers of Petrograd. Communist-led groups took part in a bloody struggle for control of the capital. By November 1917, Lenin and the Communists had seized power in Petrograd and declared that they were the true government of all Russia. Later they took control of Moscow and made it the capital.

Even though the Communists held Petrograd and Moscow, they did not yet control the whole country. It took two years of civil war before the Communists controlled all of Russia. The civil war caused much suffering. Many people were killed, and many more starved to death. The Russian people paid a heavy price for the revolution.

C. The Communist Control of Russia

Government Lenin did not believe in democracy as it is understood in western Europe and the United States. He claimed that most people did not know what was

317

Read and Think

Section C

The Communist government that Lenin established not only took control of politics and the press, but it also took control of the church, the land, and industry. Review these takeovers with students by asking the following questions:

1. **How did Lenin prevent opponents from challenging his government?**
   (He outlawed other political parties, he did not permit people to speak out or print anything against the government, and he created a secret police force to spy on suspected opponents. *p. 318*)

2. **How did Lenin feel about religion?**
   (He strongly opposed religion, took over all church property, and tried to discourage all religious beliefs. *p. 318*)

   Thinking Critically Why, do you think, did Lenin initially support the peasant and worker takeovers of large estates and factories? (Hypothesize)
   (Answers should reflect independent thinking but may include that, in order to gain power, Lenin wanted the people to believe that he supported their ownership of the land and industry. *p. 319*)

good for them and that the Communists acted for the good of the people. Lenin's way of thinking was much like that of the czars. They, too, said that they ruled for the good of the people.

Lenin controlled the Communist party, and the party controlled the government. Only Communist party members held positions of authority. Other political parties were outlawed. No one was allowed to speak out or print anything against the government. Indeed, control of the press was even tighter than it had been under the czars. The Communists created a secret police force that spied on anyone suspected of opposing Communist rule.

Other Takeovers Lenin strongly o[pposed] posed religion, particularly the Russi[an] Orthodox Church. The Communist go[v]ernment took over all church property a[nd] tried to discourage all religious belie[fs] particularly among young people. At t[he] time of the revolution, there were 4[ ] churches in Moscow. Twenty years lat[er] only 25 were still used for religious se[r]vices. Some of the others had been d[e]stroyed or allowed to decay. Some we[re] put to use as museums and other secul[ar,] or nonreligious, public places.

In the confused months after the f[all] of the czar, peasants began taking over t[he] large estates. Groups of workers seiz[ed]

This painting shows Lenin speaking to a group of workers in 1917.
▶ Does Lenin seem to have the support of his audience?

This monument in Moscow contains Lenin's tomb.
▶ Where are there monuments to honor American political leaders?

control of a number of factories. The Communists at first supported these takeovers. The Communists declared that the land belonged to the peasants, and that the factories belonged to the workers. The Communists issued an order that the local revolutionary governments could take over private homes, particularly those of rich people. But after the Communists were firmly in control of the country, they declared that all of the land and factories belonged to the state rather than to groups of people.

Lenin became seriously ill in 1922 and died two years later. But by that time those who held his views had a firm grip on the government. The Communists made Lenin the country's official hero. Lenin's picture became as common in schools and public places as those of the czars had been in earlier times. Lenin's body was preserved and put on display in a tomb in Moscow's Red Square. The city of Petrograd was renamed Leningrad in his honor. Today the city of Leningrad is called St. Petersburg.

LESSON 3 REVIEW

THINK AND WRITE

A. What events led to the end of czarist rule in Russia? (Analyze)

B. What kind of revolution did Lenin lead in Russia? (Infer)

C. What methods did the Communists use to control Russia? (Analyze)

SKILLS CHECK

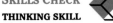

THINKING SKILL

Look up *Constantinople, Moscow*, and *Leningrad* in the Gazetteer to find the latitude and longitude for each city. Then make a table to show this information for the cities.

319

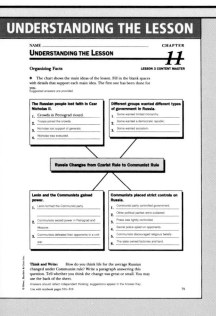
Optional Activities

Lesson 3 Review

Answers to Think and Write

A. A riot broke out among the people in Petrograd in March of 1917. Troops who were called out to control the crowds joined in. Armed men blocked the route of the czar's train into the city. At the advisement of his own generals, Nicholas abdicated and czarist rule ended.

B. Lenin led a Communist revolution in Russia.

C. The Communists controlled Russia by outlawing all political parties, by placing only Communist party members in positions of authority, by forbidding anyone to speak out or print anything against the government, and by creating a secret police force that spied on anyone suspected of opposing Communist rule.

Answer to Skills Check

The latitude and longitude for the following cities is: Constantinople: 41° N/29° E; Leningrad: 60° N/30° E.

Focus Your Reading

Ask the lesson focus question found at the beginning of the lesson: **How did the revolution of 1917 affect Russia?**
(It brought an end to czarist rule and established a Communist government.)

Additional Practice

You may wish to assign the ancillary materials listed below.

Understanding the Lesson p. 79
Workbook p. 75

┌─ **Answers to Caption Questions** ─
p. 318 ▶ Lenin seems to have the complete attention of his audience.
p. 319 ▶ Monuments to American political leaders can be found in every state and in Washington, D.C.

Using the Vocabulary

1. communism
2. abdicate
3. anarchy
4. czar
5. socialism

Remembering What You Read

1. *The Tale of Bygone Years* tells the story of Princess Olga and Vladimir of Kiev.

2. The name of the eastern branch was Eastern Orthodox.

3. Batu Khan and his armies destroyed towns and villages throughout Russia and eastern Europe.

4. Because he enlarged Muscovy's territory into the largest Russian state at that time

5. Ivan the Terrible loved books and music, but was a cruel ruler.

6. Peter I reformed the army, created a navy, had canals built, tried to establish modern industries, ordered young nobles to learn a western European language, ordered Russian men to shave their beards, and built a new capital, St. Petersburg.

7. Catherine the Great, like Peter the Great, admired western Europe and wanted to make changes in Russia. They both believed that the power to rule belonged to the monarchs alone.

8. Czar Nicholas abdicated because he lost the support of the people and his army generals.

9. Nikolai Lenin wanted Russia to have a government controlled by the Communist party.

10. The Communists hung Lenin's picture in schools and public places and his body was preserved and displayed in a tomb in the center of Moscow.

320

USING THE VOCABULARY

czar   socialism
anarchy   communism
abdicate

On a separate sheet of paper, write the word from above that best completes each of the sentences below.

1. The common ownership of land and industry by the people as a group is known as _____.
2. To give up power is to _____.
3. A complete lack of government and law is called _____.
4. The Russian form of the title *caesar* is _____.
5. A system in which the government not only rules but also owns all land and industry is called _____.

REMEMBERING WHAT YOU READ

On a separate sheet of paper, answer the following questions in complete sentences.

1. What book tells the story of Princess Olga and Vladimir of Kiev?
2. What was the name of the eastern branch of the Christian Church?
3. What did Batu Khan and his armies do in Russia and eastern Europe?
4. Why was Ivan III called Ivan the Great?
5. What were some good characteristics of Ivan the Terrible?
6. What changes did Peter the Great make in Russia?

320

7. How was Catherine the Great similar to Peter the Great?
8. Why did Czar Nicholas II abdicate?
9. What kind of government did Nikolai Lenin want Russia to have?
10. How did the Communists honor Lenin after his death?

TYING ART TO SOCIAL STUDIES

You have learned that many peasants in Russia had to work for nobles and czars on large estates. Draw a picture of what you think one of these large estates might have looked like. You may want to include the workers in your drawing.

THINKING CRITICALLY

On a separate sheet of paper, answer the following questions in complete sentences.

1. What reasons might the Mongol armies have had for not advancing into western Europe?
2. Do you think Ivan Kalita was right to work for the Golden Horde rather than to oppose it? Explain.
3. How much do you think changing people's appearance changes their way of thinking?
4. What do you think would have happened in Russia if Nicholas II had not abdicated on March 15, 1917?
5. What advantages might there be to communism, or the common ownership of land and industry by the people as a group?

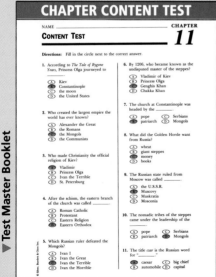

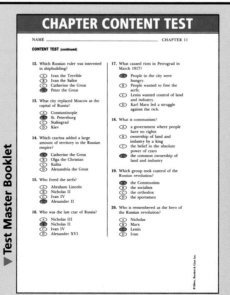

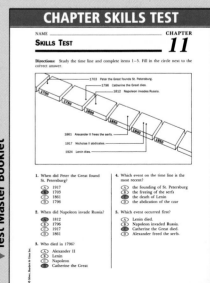

Summarizing the Chapter

On a separate sheet of paper, copy the graphic organizer shown below. Beside the main idea for each lesson, fill in each missing cause and effect. The first one has been done for you.

CHAPTER THEME Many changes occurred in Russia and eastern Europe during the period from the Middle Ages to 1917.

	CAUSE	EFFECT
LESSON 1 Constantinople and the Mongol Empire affected Russia and eastern Europe during the Middle Ages.	Vladimir, the ruler of Kiev, was curious about different religions.	Christianity was accepted in Kiev in A.D. 988.
	There were important differences between the Christian Church in eastern Europe and that in western Europe.	
		The Russian people had to pay money and send laborers to the Golden Horde.
LESSON 2 Important rulers changed Russia in the time of the czars.		Russia became a large and powerful empire.
	Peter I greatly admired the culture of western Europe.	
	After serfdom ended, the nobles still held the land and large estates.	
LESSON 3 The revolution of 1917 affected Russia.		There was anarchy in the capital, and the czar was forced to abdicate.
		Vladimir Ulyanov adopted the name Nikolai Lenin and fled to western Europe.
	Lenin controlled the Communist party, and the party controlled the government.	

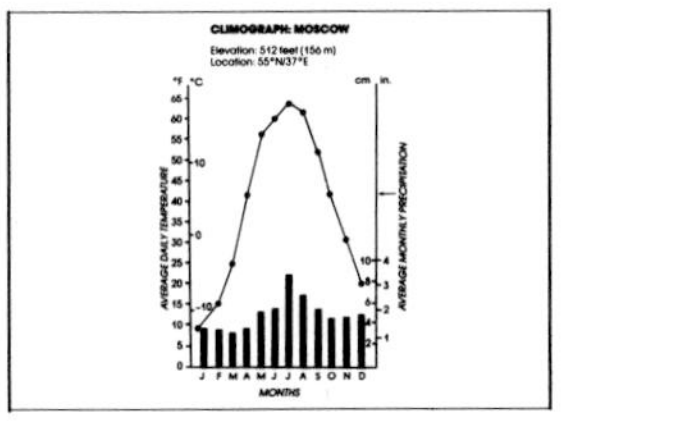

Thinking Critically

1. The Mongols may have feared the large armies of western Europe or the geographic obstacles that stood in their way.
2. Answers should reflect independent thinking.
3. Answers should reflect independent thinking.
4. The Russian people might have continued to riot until the government changed. Democratic reforms might have been adopted to avoid the revolution.
5. Answers may include that there might be no poor, homeless, or hungry people.

Summarizing the Chapter

2. Effect: The Church split into the Roman Catholic Church in the west and the Eastern Orthodox Church in the east.
3. Cause: The Mongols conquered much of Russia and eastern Europe.
4. Cause: Ivan the Great forced the Golden Horde out of Muscovy and enlarged Muscovy's territory.
5. Effect: Peter ordered young nobles to learn a western European language and ordered Russian men to shave their beards.
6. Effect: Most serfs still lived in villages and worked as servants.
7. Cause: A demonstration by the people of Petrograd turned into a riot.
8. Cause: Vladimir Ulyanov's brother was hung for his part in a failed plot to kill the czar. The czar's police suspected that Vladimir might also pose a threat.
9. Effect: The Communists were in total control of the government.

▶ Test Master Booklet

CHAPTER SKILLS TEST

NAME ____________ CHAPTER 11

SKILLS TEST (continued)

Directions: Study the graph and complete items 6–10. Fill in the circle next to the correct answer.

6. Which month has the least precipitation?
   (A) January (B) February (C) March (D) April
7. When is it coldest in Moscow?
   (A) January (B) February (C) March (D) April
8. The average temperature for April is ______.
   (A) 14° (B) 32° (C) 24° (D) 42°
9. How many months have an average daily temperature above 40°F?
   (A) 5 (B) 7 (C) 9 (D) 11
10. What is the warmest month in Moscow?
    (A) May (B) June (C) July (D) August

▶ Test Master Booklet

CHAPTER WRITING TEST

NAME ____________ CHAPTER 11

ESSAY TEST

Directions: Write a response to items 1–4.

REMINDER: Read and think about each item before you write your response. Be sure to think of the points you want to cover, details that support your response, and reasons for your opinions. Then, on the lines below, write your response in complete sentences.

1. What was the schism between the two branches of the Christian church?

An excellent response should include the following statements:
- There were important differences between the churches of eastern Europe and those of the west.
- Most people in western Europe followed the church in Rome. They accepted the pope as head of the church and Latin as the church language.
- Those in the east followed the church in Constantinople, which was headed by a patriarch and used the Greek language.
- These differences and others caused the groups to divide.
- They split into the Roman Catholic Church and the Eastern Orthodox Church.

An excellent response might also include
- the definitions of *catholic* and *orthodox*
- other divisions within the Orthodox Church.

2. How did Peter the Great make Russia a modern nation?

A satisfactory response should include the following statements.
- Peter the Great tried to change old customs.
- He encouraged people to learn the languages and cultures of other nations.
- He tried to establish modern industries.
- He modernized Russia's army and navy.
- He built a new capital near the sea.

An excellent response might also
- provide specific examples
- describe Russian society before the time of Peter.

▶ Test Master Booklet

CHAPTER WRITING TEST

NAME ____________ CHAPTER 11

ESSAY TEST (continued)

3. Who were the Mongols?

An excellent response should include the following statements:
- The Mongols were people from Mongolia who gained control of all the nomadic people living on the steppes.
- Armies led by the Mongols conquered most of Asia and eastern Europe.
- The Mongols created a huge empire, and they demanded money and laborers from the lands they conquered.

An excellent response might also include
- information about the Mongols' experiences in Russia and their eventual defeat
- the term *Golden Horde*
- information about Genghis Khan and Batu Khan.

4. Who gained control of the Russian revolution?

A satisfactory response should include the following statements:
- After the revolution, different groups argued about what kind of government Russia should have.
- Lenin and his followers, the Communists, took control of Petrograd and Moscow and claimed to be the official government.
- After two years of civil war, the Communists controlled all of Russia.

An excellent response might also
- define communism and socialism
- describe Lenin's career before the revolution
- explain the results of the Communist takeover
- mention the teachings of Karl Marx.

Chapter 12 Resource Center

The Former Soviet Union and Eastern Europe Today
(pp. 322-348)

Chapter Theme: From the end of World War II until the collapse of the Soviet Union in 1991, communism was the strongest force in the Soviet Union and in Eastern Europe.

LESSON 1   Communist Rule in the Soviet Union
(pp. 322-327)

Theme: After the 1917 revolution, the Soviet government took control of the country's agriculture and industries.

LESSON 2   The Collapse of Soviet Communism and the U.S.S.R.
(pp. 328-336)

Theme: The 1980s were a time of great change in the Soviet Union culminating in 1991, with the collapse of Soviet communism and the Soviet Union itself.

SILVER WINGS WORKSHOP: The Walls Came Tumbling Down

CITIZENSHIP AND AMERICAN VALUES VIDEO LIBRARY: *Clean Up Your Act!*

SILVER WINGS WORKSHOP: The Courage of Your Convictions

LESSON 3   Poland and Czechoslovakia
(pp. 337-340)

Theme: The Soviet Union exerted a strong influence on Poland and Czechoslovakia in the period after World War II, but by the 1980s both countries had set up their own independent governments.

LESSON 4

Theme: The amount of control that communism exercised on the people of southeastern Europe varied from country to country.

Review Masters

REVIEWING CHAPTER VOCABULARY

Review Study the terms in the box. Use your Glossary to find definitions of those you do not remember.

arable	collective farm	ethnic group	perestroika
atheism	collectivism	glasnost	Solidarity
central planning	consumer goods	market economy	

Practice Complete the paragraphs using terms from the box above. You may change the forms of the terms to fit the meaning.

For more than 70 years Communist control of the Soviet Union greatly affected the way the Soviet people lived and worked. In the years directly preceding the dissolution of the Soviet Union in 1991, President Mikhail Gorbachev tried to bring about major changes in the Soviet Union. Because of Gorbachev's policy of (1) _glasnost_, Soviet newspapers gained the freedom to print full accounts of events in the Soviet Union and the world.

For years the government of the Soviet Union had controlled the nation's economy through (2) _central planning_. This control resulted in food shortages and a lack of (3) _consumer goods_ for people to buy and use. The economy of the Soviet Union lagged behind the economies of other industrialized countries. To improve the Soviet economy, Gorbachev called for reforms in Soviet industry and agriculture. These reforms were called (4) _perestroika_. The reforms reduced government control of industry and encouraged competition. These were important steps toward building a (5) _market economy_. Changes also affected Soviet farmers who were now allowed to work the land as individuals rather than as workers on (6) _collective farms_.

Write Write a sentence of your own for each term in the box above. You may use the back of the sheet.

Sentences should show that students understand the meanings of the terms.

_____

_____

_____

_____

LOCATING PLACES

* Fifteen countries were created from the former Soviet Union. Listed below are major cities from five of these countries. Use the Gazetteer in your textbook to find the latitude and longitude of each place. Also list the country in which each city is found. Then locate and label each city and country on the map.

		COUNTRY	LAT. ⊖	LONG. ①
1.	Moscow	Russia	56°N	38°E
2.	Kiev	Ukraine	50°N	31°E
3.	Tashkent	Uzbekistan	41°N	69°E
4.	Baku	Azerbaijan	40°N	50°E
5.	Vilnius	Lithuania	55°N	25°E
6.	St. Petersburg	Russia	60°N	30°E

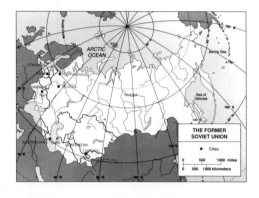

THE FORMER SOVIET UNION

● Cities

0   500   1000 miles
0   500   1000 kilometers

SUMMARIZING THE CHAPTER

* Complete this graphic organizer. Next to each question, write four answers from the chapter.

> Tremendous changes occurred in the governments and economies of the Soviet Union and the countries of Eastern Europe.

LESSON 1

What changes in agriculture and industry took place in the Soviet Union after the 1917 revolution?

1. Government took over ownership of land.
2. State and collective farms were started.
3. Government took control of factories and mills.
4. Central planning policy was begun.

LESSON 2

What factors led to the collapse of the Soviet Union?

1. Policy of _glasnost_ permitted discussion of discontent.
2. _Perestroika_ did not improve the standard of living.
3. The Soviet Union had many nationalities.
4. "Freedom fever" erupted in the Soviet Union.

LESSON 3

What are some examples of the growth of freedom in Poland between 1980 and 1990?

1. In 1980 workers went on strike to demand more freedom.
2. Solidarity was legalized in 1989.
3. Free elections were allowed for the first time in 1989.
4. Lech Walesa was elected president of Poland in 1990.

LESSON 4

How did Soviet influence vary among the countries of southeastern Europe?

1. Yugoslavia and Hungary had less Soviet control.
2. Soviet influence on Albania varied over the years.
3. Romania's government was installed by the Soviet army.
4. Soviet Union had a strong influence on Bulgaria.

C12-B

Workbook Pages

LEARNING ABOUT SOVIET LEADERS

Understanding Time Lines, Making Observations

✳ Generally, the head of the Soviet Communist party was the most powerful leader in the Soviet Union. In the box is a list of the major leaders of the Soviet Union from 1917 to 1991. The list also includes the year each leader became head of the Communist party.

a. Place the letter before each Soviet leader in its proper box on the time line.

b. Referring to the time line, answer the questions below. The time line shows when some Presidents of the United States took office.

> A. Nikita Khrushchev, 1953
> B. Mikhail Gorbachev, 1985
> C. Nikolai Lenin, 1917
> D. Leonid Brezhnev, 1964
> E. Joseph Stalin, 1922

1. Which Communist Party leader listed had the shortest term? _Lenin_

2. Which Soviet leader listed had the longest term? _Stalin_

3. Which Soviet leader took office the year Eisenhower became President of the United States? _Khrushchev_

4. How long was Khrushchev's term as party leader? _eleven years_

5. How long was Lenin's term? _five years_

6. Who was President of the United States when Gorbachev took office? _Reagan_

George Bush
Ronald Reagan
Jimmy Carter
Gerald Ford
Richard Nixon
Lyndon Johnson
John Kennedy
Dwight Eisenhower
Harry Truman
Franklin Roosevelt
Herbert Hoover
Calvin Coolidge
Warren Harding
Woodrow Wilson

(Time line: 1990, B; 1980; 1970, D; 1960; 1950, A; 1940; 1930; 1920, E, C; 1910)

Thinking Further: Do you think it is a good idea for leaders of a country to hold office for more than ten years? Support your answer with specific reasons.

Possible answers: It is a good idea because leaders gain experience and wisdom over the years. It is a bad idea because over many years a leader can become unresponsive to people or dictatorial.

© Silver, Burdett & Ginn Inc.

THE CHANGING SOVIET UNION

Understanding Graphs, Comparing and Contrasting, Interpreting Information

✳ Graphs A and B show the population of the Soviet Union by age in 1983 and 1989. Graphs C and D show the types of jobs held by this country's workers in 1983 and 1989. Refer to the graphs to complete the sentences below by underlining the correct item or items.

1. Graphs (A, B, C, D) tell about the age breakdown of the Soviet Union.

2. Graphs A and B (show, do not show) that the total population of the Soviet Union grew from 1983 to 1989.

3. The percentage of people in the 20–59 age group (increased, decreased, remained about the same) from 1983 to 1989.

4. The percentage of people aged 60+ (increased, decreased, remained about the same) from 1983 to 1989.

5. Graphs (A, B, C, D) tell about the major divisions of the labor force in the Soviet Union.

6. In 1989 the largest percentage of Soviet workers was employed in (agriculture, manufacturing, services).

7. The percentage of people working in agriculture (increased, decreased, remained the same) from 1983 to 1989.

8. The percentage of people working in manufacturing (increased, decreased, remained the same) from 1983 to 1989.

A. Soviet Population by Age, 1983
Age 60+ 13%, Age 0-19 37%, Age 20-59 50%

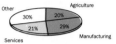

B. Soviet Population by Age, 1989
Age 60+ 13%, Age 0-19 25%, Age 20-59 62%

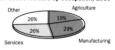

C. Soviet Workers by Occupation, 1983
Other 30%, Agriculture 20%, Manufacturing 29%, Services 21%

D. Soviet Workers by Occupation, 1989
Other 26%, Agriculture 19%, Manufacturing 29%, Services 26%

Thinking Further: How do graphs A and B suggest that the population of the Soviet Union as a whole became older between 1983 and 1989?

The fact that the 0–19 age group decreased while the 20–59 age group increased indicates that the Soviet population became older.

© Silver, Burdett & Ginn Inc.

RECOGNIZING COUNTRIES

Identifying Shapes, Hypothesizing

✳ Below are outlines of the countries of Eastern Europe and Russia. The countries are drawn to scale. Write the name of the country on each outline. One has been written in for you. (You may want to look at a map in the textbook.)

(Map labels: FORMER YUGOSLAVIA, CZECHOSLOVAKIA, HUNGARY, ALBANIA, ROMANIA, POLAND, RUSSIA, BULGARIA)

Thinking Further: Describe one or two ways it can be helpful to know the shape and size of a country.

Possible answers: By knowing the shape of a country, you can recognize it quickly on a map. By knowing the shape and size of a country, you can easily estimate how long it will take to travel across the country while on a trip.

© Silver, Burdett & Ginn Inc.

FARMING IN SOUTHEASTERN EUROPE

Understanding Bar Graphs, Hypothesizing

✳ Farming makes up at least 20 percent of the economy of each of the countries of southeastern Europe shown on the bar graph below. Each country raises many farm animals, such as dairy cows, beef cattle, and hogs. Note that the graph has two scales. The scale at the top shows the percentage of the economy from farming. The one at the bottom shows the number of farm animals in millions. Use the graph to complete the statements.

Farming in Southeastern Europe

Percentage of Economy from Farming (0, 10, 20, 30, 40, 50)

Albania, Bulgaria, Hungary, Romania, Former Yugoslavia

Farm Animals (Millions) (0, 5, 10, 15, 20, 25, 30, 35, 40, 45, 50)

▨ = percentage of economy from farming ▨ = number of farm animals

1. _Romania_ raises the most farm animals.

2. _Albania_ raises the fewest farm animals.

3. _Romania_ raises about twice as many farm animals as the former Yugoslavia.

4. About 22 percent of the economy of _Bulgaria_ comes from farming.

5. _Hungary_ derives the smallest percentage of its economy from farming.

6. _Albania_ raises just under 2 million farm animals.

7. About 27 percent of _Romania's_ economy comes from farming.

Thinking Further: Briefly describe two or three major farm products. What is each used for?

Major farm products include grain, vegetables, milk, and meat. Uses include the following: Grain is used to make flour. Vegetables are used as human food, often with little or no processing. Milk is used directly as human food or, indirectly, as the chief ingredient in cheese, cream, and other products. Meat is used as human food.

© Silver, Burdett & Ginn Inc.

C12-C

Communist Rule in the Soviet Union

Objectives

★**1. Explain** the difference between central planning and a market economy.

2. Summarize the changes in the Soviet economy under communism.

3. Discuss the natural resources of the U.S.S.R. and the ways that they were used.

4. Identify the following person and places: *Joseph Stalin, the U.S.S.R., Afghanistan.*

STARTING THE LESSON

Motivation Activity

■ Ask students to imagine that they are the leaders of the largest country on earth. Tell them that their country has millions of people and many resources, but the citizens are not wealthy.

■ How might they improve the standard of living for the people? Explain that in this lesson they will learn what Soviet leaders did to try to improve the standard of living in the U.S.S.R.

Think About What You Know

■ Assign the THINK ABOUT WHAT YOU KNOW activity on p. 323.

■ Students' answers may include that the U.S.S.R. did not fit the definition of a *republic* (a government in which citizens choose representatives to run the country).

Study the Vocabulary

■ Have students look up the definitions of the new vocabulary words in the Glossary.

■ Have students identify the sentences in the lesson that define the vocabulary terms. Ask students to hypothesize about whether collective farms and central planning were successful in the U.S.S.R.

THE FORMER SOVIET UNION AND EASTERN EUROPE TODAY

The former Soviet Un and the countries of Ea Europe have undergone many political and econ changes since the end o 1980s. The dismantling Lenin's statue symboliz the collapse of commu

Optional Activities

Writing to Learn

Writing a Diary   Have each student write a diary entry either from the perspective of the 12-year-old boy who denounced his father in the show trial of 1928 or from the perspective of the boy's father.

● As a prewriting activity, have students make two lists of adjectives — those that could describe the feelings of the boy and those that could describe the feelings of his father.

● Write the two lists on the chalkboard.

● Have students make the diary entries for the day in 1928 when the boy's letter was read in court.

Communist Rule in the Soviet Union

THINK ABOUT WHAT YOU KNOW
Look up the term *republic* in the Glossary. Using what you have already learned about the former Soviet Union, discuss whether you think the country fit the definition of *republic*.

STUDY THE VOCABULARY
collectivism central planning
collective farm market economy

FOCUS YOUR READING
How did the Communist government reorganize industry and agriculture in the Soviet Union?

A. A Show Trial

This letter, written in 1928 by a 12-year-old boy living in the Soviet Union, appeared in *Pravda,* the official Communist party newspaper.

I denounce [speak against] my father as a whole-hearted traitor and enemy of the working class. I demand for him the severest punishment. I reject him and the name he bears. Hereafter I shall no longer call myself by his name.

The boy's father was one of 53 mining engineers on trial before a court in the Soviet Union. The Soviet engineers were charged with trying to harm the country by wrecking the coal mines. They supposedly had broken machines, set fires, and flooded the mines.

The boy's letter was read in court, even though it offered no proof of guilt. In fact, no real proof was ever produced in court, since the trial was not an effort to decide if the charges were true. It was a "show trial," designed to show what would happen to anyone suspected of opposing Communist rule. In the end, five of the mining engineers were executed; the others were sent to prison.

The trial of 1928 was only one of the show trials staged by the Communist government during the years that Joseph Stalin ruled the Soviet Union. Stalin had gained control of the Communist party when Lenin died, in 1924, and control of the party guaranteed control of the government. Stalin's dictatorship lasted until his death, in 1953.

The Communists had renamed the Russian empire in 1922, calling it the Union of Soviet Socialist Republics. The name was usually shortened to Soviet Union or U.S.S.R. It was a huge area, about one sixth of the earth's land surface.

B. Revolutions in Agriculture and Industry

After the revolution of 1917, most Russian peasants believed they would finally be allowed to own the land they worked. After the Communists took power, however, the peasants discovered that their new rulers had very different plans.

The Communist party believed in ownership by all the people together, or **collectivism.** In practice this meant ownership by the state, or the central government, which Stalin controlled. The state forced peasants to combine their small farms to form large **collective farms.** Stalin thought that fewer people would now be needed to work the land, leaving more people free to work in mines and factories.

323

---

2 DEVELOPING THE LESSON

Read and Think
Section A
The show trials were one method that Stalin used to dominate people. Use the following questions to help students understand show trials and their purpose:

1. **What is a "show trial"?**
   (A trial designed to warn people of what will happen to them if they disobey authorities *p. 323*)

2. **Who was Joseph Stalin?**
   (He was a dictator who ruled the Soviet Union from 1924 to 1953. *p. 323*)

   Thinking Critically **Why, do you think, did the engineer's son denounce his father?** (Infer)
   (Answers may include that he was pressured by authorities, that he was angry with his father and wanted revenge, or that he truly believed his father was a traitor. *p. 323*)

Writing to Learn

Writing a Diary Have each student write a diary entry from the perspective of a Russian revolutionary in 1917.

- Ask students: **Why was this person fighting? What hopes did he or she have for the newly created nation?**
- Then have students write another entry from the perspective of the same person 15 years later, in 1932.
- Ask: **What was the result of the revolution? How did the former revolutionary feel about the government?**
- Ask volunteers to read their entries aloud and follow up with a class discussion.

Curriculum Connection

Language Arts Have each student write a short story about a family living in Russia in 1917, when the Communists took power after the revolution.

- The family in their stories could have owned a mill, mine, or factory, and then had it taken over by the Communist government.
- As a prewriting activity, have students brainstorm how it would make them feel to have something they owned taken away from them by the government.
- Make a list of these adjectives on the chalkboard for the students to refer to as they write.

Optional Activities

Read and Think
Sections B and C

The Soviet government tried several ways of harnessing resources to feed its people and develop its industries. Discuss the successes and failures of central planning with the following:

1. **Explain why peasants were not allowed to own the land on which they worked after the revolution of 1917.**

   (After the revolution, the land was collectively owned by all the people, but in practice this meant that it was controlled by the central government. *p. 323*)

2. **What did collective farms and state farms have in common?**

   (Both types of farms had production goals set by the central planners. *pp. 323–324*)

3. **By the 1980s, how did the Soviet Union compare with other industrialized countries?**

   (The Soviet Union was lagging behind other industrialized countries. Its factories were inefficient; its equipment was out-of-date and wasteful; and its plants often had more workers than were needed. *p. 325*)

4. **What did the Soviet Union do to gain influence around the world?**

   (It worked to make sure that the Communist party won control of the countries in Eastern Europe. It provided arms and other support for revolutionary movements in Cuba, Central America, Vietnam, and elsewhere. It also sent troops to Afghanistan. *p. 327*)

   Thinking Critically Why, do you think, did peasants resist collectivization, even though they knew it could mean arrest and even death? (Evaluate)

   (Answers may include that the peasants did not want to give up their property after having fought for freedom, that they did not want to abandon a familiar way of life, or that they felt that they knew how to run their farms better than the new government did. *pp. 323–324*)

324

A collective farm sold everything it produced to the government.
► What crop is being harvested on this collective farm?

Members of a collective farm worked as a group. Some had specialized jobs, such as tractor mechanics; others did less skilled work in the fields. A collective farm rented the land from the Soviet government but owned its farm equipment and livestock.

A collective farm had to sell everything it produced to the government, so the farm had little control over the prices it received. Members of the collective farm were paid wages according to the kind of work they did. All these farm workers received a share of the profit from the sale of farm products.

State Farms The Communist government also formed state farms. An average

324

state farm covered about 175 squar (453 sq km)—about ten times the s collective farm. State farms were o like factories. The land and produc owned by the government, and the v were paid wages. But state farm v did not share in a farm's profits, as tive farm workers did.

Small Plots The large collectiv state farms produced most of the Union's potatoes, cotton, wheat, an beets. But an important part of the food supply was grown on small p sections of land. The government ted people to grow vegetables and fr plots of land up to 1 acre (0.4 ha) People who held these small plots sell their crops in city markets. Pr those "free" city markets were wl the buyers were willing to pay.

Most peasants opposed collec But Stalin insisted that there woul "revolution in agriculture," whether the peasants wanted it. Many pe who refused to give up their farm arrested. Some were killed, and mai ers were sent to labor camps, wher numbers of peasants died. In fact, S revolution in agriculture cost milli peasants their lives.

Natural Resources and Ind Before the 1917 revolution, Russ largely an agricultural country, had most of the natural resources for modern industries. Forests th ered Russia and the rest of the L made up a fourth of the world's reserves. The area was—and still i in many minerals, including coal, ir copper, and bauxite. The area also and still has—large amounts of natural gas. The Communists d

Optional Activities

For Your Information

Stalin's Five-Year Plans Five-Year Plans started in 1928 as a method of strengthening the Soviet Union industrially and defensively. The Five-Year Plans set specific production goals in industry and agriculture to bring the Soviet Union up to the standards of modern nations surrounding it. Between 1928 and 1949, the Soviet Union made impressive gains: steel production quadrupled, oil production tripled, and the Soviet Union became Europe's second-largest producer of iron and steel. The quality of goods was often poor, however. Some projects were only showpieces for foreign journalists. Workers who failed to meet quotas were punished for laziness.

at all of these resources belonged to the ate. The government also took over the nks, mills, and factories. The former vners received nothing for the property at the government took away from em.

During the years of Communist rule, e Soviet Union grew into an industrial untry. It became one of the world's leadg producers of steel, oil, gold, and elecicity. No longer were most of the people asants, working the land. Instead, two irds of the people lived and worked in ban areas.

Although the Soviet Union became an dustrial country, it was lagging behind her countries by the 1980s. Soviet factoes were inefficient as compared with ose in Western Europe, the United ates, and Japan. Equipment was out of te and wasteful. Many plants employed ore workers than were needed.

LEADING STEEL-PRODUCING COUNTRIES

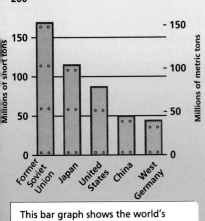

This bar graph shows the world's leading steel-producing countries.
▶ About how many short tons of steel does the former Soviet Union produce?

Planners Set Goals The Communists established **central planning** for the state-owned industries. This meant that a government committee set production goals for each industry. For example, the central planners would tell a garment factory manager that the factory should produce a

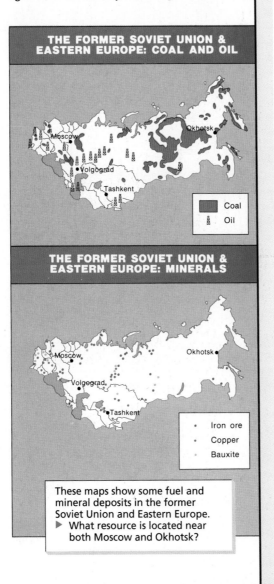

THE FORMER SOVIET UNION & EASTERN EUROPE: COAL AND OIL

Moscow
Okhotsk
Volgograd
Tashkent

Coal
Oil

THE FORMER SOVIET UNION & EASTERN EUROPE: MINERALS

Moscow
Okhotsk
Volgograd
Tashkent

· Iron ore
· Copper
· Bauxite

These maps show some fuel and mineral deposits in the former Soviet Union and Eastern Europe.
▶ What resource is located near both Moscow and Okhotsk?

Meeting Individual Needs

Concept: Comparing a Market Economy to a Planned Economy

Below are three activities that will help students comprehend the differences between a market economy and a centrally planned economy.

◆ **EASY** Have students make a chart with two columns, one labeled "Market Economy" and one labeled "Planned Economy."

Ask students to find facts about each system from the lesson, write them in the appropriate column, and discuss the similarities and differences.

◀▶ **AVERAGE** Ask students to list factors that central planners might consider when making decisions about what goods will be produced. Then have students list factors that might be considered in deciding what goods will be produced in a market economy.

◀▮▶ **CHALLENGING** Ask students who need a challenge to list the pros and cons of both a market economy and a centrally planned economy and then write a one-page description of what they consider to be the ideal system.

GEOGRAPHY THEMES

Human-Environment Interactions

■ Direct students' attention to the political map of the former Soviet Union and Eastern Europe on this page. Ask which countries have two cities with populations of more than 1,000,000. (Ukraine and Russia)

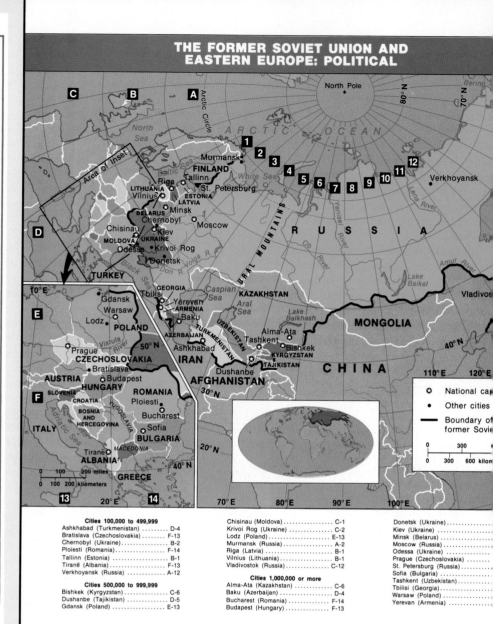

THE FORMER SOVIET UNION AND EASTERN EUROPE: POLITICAL

Legend:
- ✪ National capital
- • Other cities
- — Boundary of former Soviet...

Cities 100,000 to 499,999
Ashkhabad (Turkmenistan) D-4
Bratislava (Czechoslovakia) F-13
Chernobyl (Ukraine) B-2
Ploiesti (Romania) F-14
Tallinn (Estonia) B-1
Tiranë (Albania) F-13
Verkhoyansk (Russia) A-12

Cities 500,000 to 999,999
Bishkek (Kyrgyzstan) C-6
Dushanbe (Tajikistan) D-5
Gdansk (Poland) E-13

Cities 1,000,000 or more
Alma-Ata (Kazakhstan) C-6
Baku (Azerbaijan) D-4
Bucharest (Romania) F-14
Budapest (Hungary) F-13

Chisinau (Moldova) C-1
Krivoi Rog (Ukraine) C-2
Lodz (Poland) E-13
Murmansk (Russia) A-2
Riga (Latvia) B-1
Vilnius (Lithuania) B-1
Vladivostok (Russia) C-12

Donetsk (Ukraine) ....
Kiev (Ukraine) ....
Minsk (Belarus) ....
Moscow (Russia) ....
Odessa (Ukraine) ....
Prague (Czechoslovakia) ....
St. Petersburg (Russia) ....
Sofia (Bulgaria) ....
Tashkent (Uzbekistan) ....
Tbilisi (Georgia) ....
Warsaw (Poland) ....
Yerevan (Armenia) ....

This map shows the boundaries of the former Soviet Union and the 15 independent countries that were Soviet republics until the U.S.S.R. was dissolved in 1991.
▶ How large is the population of the capital of Ukraine?

Optional Activities

Reteaching Main Objective
★ *Explain the difference between central planning and a market economy.*

● Have students draw storyboards (sequential frames with explanatory sentences beneath the pictures) that show how one item is produced (grown or manufactured) under central planning. The storyboards should illustrate each step of production from the time the decision is made to produce it until it is sold and used.

● Then have students make storyboards that show how the same item is produced in a market economy.

● Display the finished storyboards in the classroom.

certain number of garments during the year. The manager would then tell each worker how much he or she must do to receive full pay. Because the goal—the number of garments produced—was the most important part to the planners, neither the manager nor the workers would pay much attention to the quality of the products.

Buyers' Choices The central planners based their decisions on what products they thought people should have, not on what people might actually want. The planned economy system in the U.S.S.R. differed greatly from the **market economy** that exists in the United States and Western Europe. In a market economy the buyers largely decide what items will be produced. The owners and managers of businesses try to find out what people want to buy and then produce the items. The goal is to make what will sell.

C. Soviet Influence Around the World

Soviet Communists believed that socialism would spread throughout the world. That is what a Soviet leader meant when he told an American president, "History is on our side. We will bury you."

Following World War II the Soviet Union worked to make sure that the Communist party won control of the countries

For about ten years, Soviet troops fought in Afghanistan.
▶ How do you think these troops felt as they left Afghanistan?

in Eastern Europe. The Soviet Union also provided arms and other support for revolutionary movements in Cuba, Central America, Vietnam, Africa, and elsewhere.

In 1979 a Soviet-backed government in the neighboring country of Afghanistan (af GAN ih stan) was threatened. The government had come to power by a revolution, but it was opposed by many Afghans. The Soviet Union sent an army into Afghanistan, and a long, bitter war followed. Not until May 1988 did the Soviet Union begin to withdraw its troops. By February 1989 more than 100,000 Soviet soldiers had left Afghanistan.

LESSON 1 REVIEW

THINK AND WRITE
A. What was the purpose of the show trial of 1928? (Recall)
B. How does a planned economy differ from a market economy? (Recall)
C. Why did the Soviet Union provide arms and other support to various countries? (Infer)

SKILLS CHECK
WRITING SKILL
Look up the word *revolution* in the Glossary. Write a paragraph explaining why the Communist revolution was more than a change of governments.

Optional Activities

Lesson 1 Review

Answers to Think and Write
A. The show trial of 1928 was meant to show what would happen to anyone suspected of opposing Communist rule.

B. In a planned economy, central planners decide what will be produced based on what they think people should have. In a market economy, owners and managers of businesses try to find out what people want to buy, and then produce it.

C. The Soviet Union provided arms, soldiers, and other support to different countries to gain influence around the world and to promote the spread of its form of government.

Answer to Skills Check
Answers will vary but should show an understanding of how the Communist revolution resulted in changes that affected people's lives in many ways.

Focus Your Reading
Ask the lesson focus question found at the beginning of the lesson: **How did the Communist government reorganize industry and agriculture in the Soviet Union?** (When the Communists took power after the revolution, the government took control of industry and agriculture. Central planners made decisions about what and how much would be produced. In agriculture, the state established collective farms and state farms.)

Additional Practice
You may wish to assign the ancillary materials listed below.

Understanding the Lesson p. 83
Workbook p. 76

┌─ **Answers to Caption Questions** ─
p. 326 ▶ 1,000,000 or more
p. 327 ▶ Answers may include happy and relieved.
└─

The Collapse of Soviet Communism and the U.S.S.R.

Objectives

★**1. Describe** the factors and events that led to the collapse of both Soviet communism and the U.S.S.R.

2. Explain the significance of the criticisms of Stalin by Khrushchev and Gorbachev.

3. Explain the reforms that took place in the Soviet Union under the leadership of Mikhail Gorbachev.

4. Identify the following people and place: *Nikita Khrushchev, Mikhail Gorbachev, Boris Yeltsin, Chernobyl.*

1 STARTING THE LESSON

Motivation Activity

■ Ask students if they think it is disloyal to criticize one's country or leaders.

■ Ask students if it is possible to love one's country and still be critical of some of its government's policies. Have students defend their positions.

Think About What You Know

■ Assign the THINK ABOUT WHAT YOU KNOW activity on p. 328.

■ Answers may include that, as the Soviet people became more aware of how people in other countries lived, they may have wanted more freedom, more choice in how they lived their lives, and a higher standard of living.

Study the Vocabulary

■ Have students look up the definitions of the new vocabulary words in the Glossary.

■ Ask students to name the characteristics of the type of leader who they think would introduce the ideas of *glasnost.*

328

LESSON **2**

The Collapse of Soviet Communism and the U.S.S.R.

THINK ABOUT WHAT YOU KNOW
Why, do you think, did people in the Soviet Union become discontented with Communist rule?

STUDY THE VOCABULARY
glasnost   perestroika

FOCUS YOUR READING
What changes took place in the Soviet Union during and after the mid-1980s?

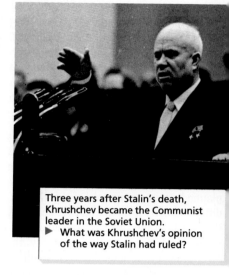

Three years after Stalin's death, Khrushchev became the Communist leader in the Soviet Union.
▶ What was Khrushchev's opinion of the way Stalin had ruled?

A. A Critical Look at Stalin

A Leader Speaks Out For many years loyal Soviet Communists never dared to criticize Stalin. He was praised as a great leader who did what was necessary to make the Soviet Union a socialist state. The Soviet silence about Stalin's dictatorship was not broken until 1956, three years after his death. By that time, Nikita Khrushchev (nih KEE tah KROO shawf) had become the leader of the Communist party in the Soviet Union. Khrushchev shocked many Communists with a speech condemning the wrongs committed during Stalin's rule.

Although he criticized Stalin, Khrushchev did not criticize socialism. Indeed, he boasted that the Soviet Union would become the model for the world in the future. It was he who had boasted to an American President, "History is on our side. We will bury you."

Not all the Communist party members approved of Khrushchev's attack on Stalin. They feared that the criticisms would weaken the Communist party. Finally, in 1964, Khrushchev's opponents forced him to retire from office.

Later Criticisms It was not until more than 20 years later that a Soviet leader spoke out in defense of Khrushchev and what he had said. In 1985, Mikhail Gorbachev (mee kah EEL GOR buh chawf) became the leader of the Soviet Communist party. He said that Khrushchev had shown courage in speaking out about Stalin's "enormous and unforgivable crimes." Gorbachev also said that the Soviet people should be proud of their socialistic society but that it was sometimes necessary to "examine our history with a critical eye."

Some Soviet writers went on to publish accounts admitting that millions of Soviet people had been killed under Stalin's rule. The secret police finally revealed that 787,000 people had been shot as "enemies of the state" during Stalin's rule.

328

Optional Activities

For Your Information

Joseph Stalin Stalin, or "Man of Steel," was the pseudonym of Iosif Vissarionovich Dzugashvili. Stalin's show trials and purges affected not only enemies of the Communist state but also a high proportion of the men who had been leaders during the revolution and under Lenin. If Thomas Jefferson had rounded up all the signers of the Declaration of Independence and the Constitution, forced them to confess to treason in public trials, and had them executed, it would have been similar to Stalin's horrifying tactics. It has been estimated that through forced labor, purges, and the systematic starvation of peasants who resisted collectivization, Stalin was responsible for the deaths of about 20 million people.

This was not news to historians out-[side] the Soviet Union. But it was the first [time] that these facts were printed openly [i]n the Soviet Union.

Reforming the Government

Need for Openness Mikhail Gor-[bach]ev was born 14 years after the Russian [Revo]lution, so he had grown up under [com]munism. However, he believed that [som]e important changes were needed. [Gorb]achev called for **glasnost** (GLAHS-[nost], which means "openness." Glasnost [woul]d result in less secrecy about public [affai]rs.

The Communist policy had always [been] to keep secret any unfavorable news [abou]t the government, such as disagree-[men]ts among the leaders. Newspapers did [not p]rint full accounts of natural disasters or accidents, such as the nuclear power plant accident in 1986. A nuclear plant in Chernobyl (chur NOH bul), a town in the Soviet Union, caught fire and melted down. Over 30 people were killed immedi-ately, and radiation from the nuclear fuel in the plant leaked into the atmosphere. The Soviet government did not announce the accident until days later. This policy of secrecy allowed officials to hide their mis-takes and flaws.

Under glasnost, the Soviet people were finally allowed to read books that had once been banned by the government. Television broadcasts showed Communist party conferences in which delegates were disagreeing. The Soviet government granted the Russian Orthodox Church per-mission to build the first new church in Moscow since the revolution.

[As] part of his political reform, Mikhail [Go]rbachev allowed free elections in the Soviet [Un]ion in 1989.
How is Gorbachev voting?

Read and Think

Section A

Use these questions to help students understand the significance of the criti-cisms of Stalin by Khrushchev and Gorbachev:

1. **What did Khrushchev mean when he said "We will bury you"?**
(That socialism would spread through-out the world *p. 328*)

2. **Why did Khrushchev's 1956 speech about Stalin shock many Communists?**
(In his speech, Khrushchev condemned the wrongs committed during Stalin's rule. Before that, Soviet Communists had never dared to criticize Stalin. *p. 328*)

3. **Why did some Communist party mem-bers disapprove of Khrushchev's attack on Stalin?**
(They feared that the criticisms would weaken the Communist party. *p. 328*)

4. **What did Gorbachev think about Khrushchev's criticism of Stalin?**
(He praised Khrushchev's courage in speaking out against Stalin and said that it was sometimes necessary to examine the country's history with a critical eye. *p. 328*)

Thinking Critically Why, do you think, did Khrushchev feel that the United States and the Soviet Union were enemies? (Evaluate)
(Answers may include that Khrushchev, like many Communists of his time, believed that socialism would spread throughout the world and that the United States stood in the way because it was a major democratic world power. *p. 328*)

Read and Think
Section B

Use the questions below to start a discussion of glasnost:

1. **Give an example of how glasnost changed life in the Soviet Union.**
   (Answers may include that Soviet citizens were finally allowed to read books that had once been banned, disagreements among politicians were no longer hidden, and the government allowed a new church to be built in Moscow. *p. 329*)

2. **What was the result of Gorbachev's saying the people of the Soviet Union should have more voice in their government?**
   (The Communist party was weakened; more than one party member was allowed to compete in an election for a position. Later, other political parties were allowed. *p. 329*)

Thinking Critically Imagine that you are a 12-year-old Russian living in Moscow in 1988. Describe the feelings that you have as you witness some of the first results of glasnost. (Infer)
(Answers may include feelings such as wonder, joy, skepticism, and hope. *p. 329*)

330

End of One-Party Rule Along with promoting glasnost, Gorbachev spoke of the need for **perestroika** (per es TROI kuh), the reform of the government and economy. This was the most striking—and revolutionary—of Gorbachev's reforms. Gorbachev proposed that the Soviet people should have a voice in how their country was governed. To make this happen, he gradually introduced a number of changes.

These changes weakened the position of the Communist party, which had ruled the Soviet Union for so many years. In 1988, Gorbachev introduced a measure that allowed more than one Communist party member to compete in an election for a position. Two years later a more important change took away the Communist position as the only legal political party. Other parties could now be formed and could offer candidates in elections. This change was an important step toward giving people a real choice in elections, a right that is necessary for a democracy.

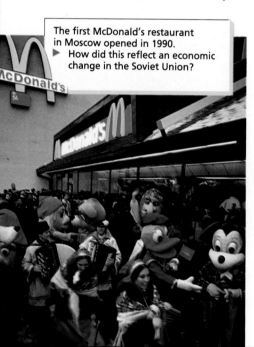

The first McDonald's restaurant in Moscow opened in 1990.
▶ How did this reflect an economic change in the Soviet Union?

C. Reforming Industry and Agriculture

Less Central Planning Because Soviet economy was lagging behind economies of other industrial countri Gorbachev called for changes in indus and agriculture. He told the Communi that the country needed to encourage b ter work. Reforms were needed that wo allow people to make profits. Socialis Gorbachev insisted, should not preve one individual from making more mor than another. Perestroika must inclu reforms in the ways factories, farms, a mines were operated.

The first reforms reduced the amou of central planning and attempted encourage competition in the Soviet eco omy. Industries would still belong to t government, but they must compe against each other in selling their good The managers of factories would try make profits rather than to fulfill goa handed down by central planners.

The reforms would also allow son individuals to rent space in governmen owned buildings so that they could esta lish their own businesses. Forei companies would also be encouraged set up enterprises within the Soviet Unio

Making Room for Competitio Perestroika also included reforms for agr culture. The land would still belong to th state, but individuals could lease farm from the government for periods of 5 years. Farmers could work the land as ind viduals rather than as members of larg collective groups. Like the holders of sma plots, the individual farmers could gro crops for sale in the free markets.

Gorbachev introduced the reform because he believed that complete stat

Making a Word Search Puzzle
- Have students make a word search puzzle using the vocabulary words and other words from this lesson that describe various aspects of the Soviet Union.
- Then have students exchange papers and find the words in each other's puzzles.
- You may wish to have students supply answer keys for their puzzles.

ownership had destroyed the people's willingness to work hard. In order to improve the economy, he said, the country must make room for competition."

Many of the Soviet people agreed with Gorbachev at first. They supported reforms that gave the people a greater choice in government. They agreed that something had to be done to make the economy more productive. But, unfortunately, the economic reforms introduced by Gorbachev did not produce immediate benefits for most people. Indeed, daily life for many became worse rather than better. All too often, shelves in the stores were bare. People stood in long lines waiting to buy food and other necessities. Food prices in the free markets rose rapidly.

The first years of perestroika did not give people a higher standard of living, but glasnost made it possible for them to express their discontent. People who had supported Gorbachev at first began to criticize him. Some complained that his

Soviet people often had to wait in long lines to buy goods.
▶ What is the cause of these lines?

These women are selling produce in a free market in the Soviet Union.
▶ What type of reform does this indicate?

reforms did not go far enough. Some reformers wanted the country to move more rapidly to establish a market economy. A market economy is one in which choices about what is produced depend upon what people will buy. Goods are produced in order to make profits. In 1991 the Soviet government passed a law allowing the sale of state-owned businesses to private individuals and companies.

D. The Soviet Union Collapses

The Republics of the Soviet Union The old Russian empire extended from the Baltic Sea to the Pacific Ocean. When the Communists seized control of this vast land, they divided it into separate republics. Even though they were called republics,

331

Help students understand the importance of perestroika in the Soviet Union with these questions:

1. **What were some of the reforms in industry that were brought about by *perestroika*?**
   (There were reforms in the ways factories and mines were run. The amount of central planning was reduced. Individuals could start their own businesses. Competition and foreign investment were encouraged. *p. 330*)

2. **How was agriculture in the Soviet Union affected by perestroika?**
   (Individuals could lease land themselves and could work the land and sell their produce in the free markets. *p. 330*)

3. **Why did Gorbachev institute the reforms in agriculture?**
   (He believed that complete state ownership had destroyed the people's willingness to work hard and that competition would help to improve the country's economy. *pp. 330–331*)

4. **Why were many people unhappy with Gorbachev's reforms?**
   (The reforms did not produce a higher standard of living for many people. Shelves were often bare. People often had to wait in long lines. Prices rose rapidly. Some people felt the reforms did not go far enough. *p. 331*)

Thinking Critically **What do you think was the most important reform that resulted from perestroika?** (Analyze)
(Answers might include less central planning, more competition, foreign investment, more opportunities for individuals. *pp. 330–331*)

331

Read and Think

Section D

Use the questions below to start a discussion of the recent drastic changes in the Soviet Union:

1. **How were different nationalities distributed throughout the republics of the Soviet Union?**
   (Each republic contained more than one nationality. Some republics had a nationality that was in the majority—for example, Latvians in Latvia. *p. 333*)

2. **What effect did reducing the powers of the central government have on the republics of the Soviet Union?**
   (The republics wanted their independence. *p. 334*)

3. **Describe the events that led to the breakup of the Soviet Union.**
   (After Lithuania declared its independence, other republics began to declare independence. After a coup attempt failed in August of 1991, Boris Yeltsin became the leader of the reform movement and demanded more reforms. Before the end of 1991 the Soviet Union had been dissolved and Gorbachev had resigned. *pp. 335–336*)

Thinking Critically Do you think the Soviet Union would have collapsed if Gorbachev's reforms had been more successful? Why? (Hypothesize)
(Some students may conclude that the Soviet Union might have remained intact if the reforms had resulted in a higher standard of living. Other students may conclude that many people were ready for independence because the reforms had not brought the changes they had hoped for. They also had more loyalty to their nationality group than to the U.S.S.R., and they resented the power of the central government. *pp. 331–335*)

332

these divisions were not independent. The Communist party controlled all of them, and Communists in all parts of the U.S.S.R. followed orders from authorities in Moscow.

The Soviet Union was made up of 15 republics. As you can see on the map below, Russia was by far the largest republic. It contained over half of the Soviet population and three fourths of the territory. The Ukraine was the most thickly populated republic. It had a much small area than Russia, but its black soil be supplied most of the Soviet Union's whea

Three republics—Estonia, Latvi and Lithuania—were located on the Balti Sea. They had been part of the old Russia empire, but they became independen after World War I. They remained free unt World War II, when they were occupie and made part of the Soviet Union.

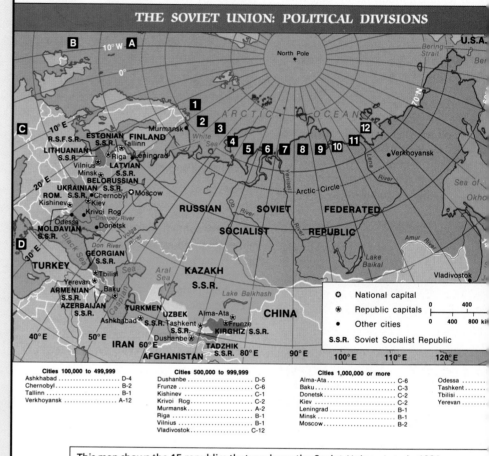

THE SOVIET UNION: POLITICAL DIVISIONS

Cities 100,000 to 499,999		Cities 500,000 to 999,999		Cities 1,000,000 or more		
Ashkhabad	D-4	Dushanbe	D-5	Alma-Ata	C-6	Odessa
Chernobyl	B-2	Frunze	C-6	Baku	C-3	Tashkent
Tallinn	B-1	Kishinev	C-1	Donetsk	C-2	Tbilisi
Verkhoyansk	A-12	Krivoi Rog	C-2	Kiev	C-2	Yerevan
		Murmansk	A-2	Leningrad	B-1	
		Riga	B-1	Minsk	B-1	
		Vilnius	B-1	Moscow	B-2	
		Vladivostok	C-12			

This map shows the 15 republics that made up the Soviet Union. Late in 1991 the Soviet Union was dissolved and these republics became independent nations.
▶ Which republic had Tbilisi as its capital city?

332

For Your Information

In 1939, Nazi Germany and the Soviet Union reached an agreement that gave the Soviets control of the Baltic area, including Lithuania. One year later, the Soviets occupied Lithuania and established a Communist government. Then the country passed back and forth between Germany and the Soviet Union during World War II.

Lithuanian guerrillas fought the Soviet Union from 1944 to 1952. Thousands of Lithuanians were killed in the fighting. About 35,000 Lithuanians were sent to labor camps in Siberia as punishment for their political beliefs or for resisting the Soviet government.

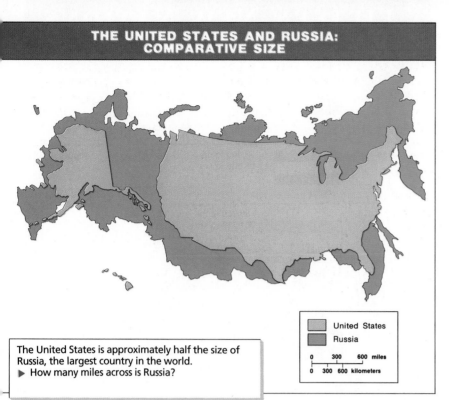

THE UNITED STATES AND RUSSIA: COMPARATIVE SIZE

United States

Russia

0   300   600 miles
0   300 600 kilometers

The United States is approximately half the size of Russia, the largest country in the world.
▶ How many miles across is Russia?

■ Direct students' attention to the map on p. 332. Ask them to name and locate five cities in the Soviet Union that had populations of 1,000,000 or more.
(Answers may include Donetsk, Kiev, Leningrad, Minsk, Moscow, Odessa, Tashkent, Tbilisi, and Yerevan.)

There were two other Soviet republics in Europe and five more in Central Asia. In addition, three Transcaucasian republics were located across the Caucasus Mountains, between the Black and Caspian Seas.

Many Nationalities, Many Languages

Only about half of the people in the former Soviet Union were Russians. This huge country had more than a hundred different nationalities. Each republic contained more than one nationality. For example, the large Russian republic included areas inhabited largely by the Tatars. Tatars are descendants of the Mongols, who once swept across Europe from Asia. Not all Russians lived in Russia. About half of the people in the Central Asian republic of Kazakhstan were Russians or Ukrainians. Even small republics usually had more than one nationality. Only half of Latvia's residents in 1990 were Latvians; a third of its people were Russians. The U.S.S.R. had been compared to a wooden doll that has within it dolls within other dolls.

Some of the different nationalities had their own languages. The Communist government did not try to prevent the use of these languages. But Russian was the official language of the central government

333

Optional Activities

333

Interpreting a Table

■ The table on pp. 334–335 lists the countries that were created from the former Soviet Union. Have students study the chart to answer the following questions:

1. **What country has the largest area and the largest population?**
(Russia)

2. **Which country was formerly called Byelorussia?**
(Belarus)

3. **Which country was the first to declare independence? Which was the last to declare independence?**
(Lithuania; Kazakhstan)

4. **Which three countries use the crescent and the star on their flags?**
(Azerbaijan, Turkmenistan, and Uzbekistan)

5. **Which country has the greatest population density? Which has the smallest population density?**
(Moldava; Kazakhstan)

FIFTEEN NEW NATIONS

These nations once belonged to the Union of Soviet Socialist Republics.

	FLAG/CAPITAL	TOTAL AREA	POPULATION AND DENSITY	INDEPENDENCE DECLARED
ARMENIA	★Yerevan	11,306 sq mi 29,283 sq km	3,300,000 292 per sq mi 113 per sq km	September 21, 1991
AZERBAIJAN	★Baku	33,400 sq mi 86,506 sq km	7,000,000 210 per sq mi 81 per sq km	August 30, 1991
BELARUS [1]	★Minsk	80,200 sq mi 207,718 sq km	10,200,000 127 per sq mi 49 per sq km	August 25, 1991
ESTONIA	★Tallinn	17,413 sq mi 45,100 sq km	1,600,000 92 per sq mi 35 per sq km	August 20, 1991
GEORGIA	★Tbilisi	26,911 sq mi 69,699 sq km	5,500,000 204 per sq mi 79 per sq km	April 9, 1991
KAZAKHSTAN	★Alma-Ata	1,049,200 sq mi 2,717,428 sq km	16,500,000 16 per sq mi 6 per sq km	December 16, 1991
KYRGYZSTAN [2]	★Bishkek	76,642 sq mi 198,503 sq km	4,300,000 56 per sq mi 22 per sq km	August 31, 1991

[1] Formerly Byelorussia   [2] Formerly Kirghizia

and the language of the largest nationality. The authorities encouraged people to learn Russian as a second language. Many people belonging to other nationalities found it to their advantage to do so.

Independence for the Republics
Glasnost and perestroika brought some changes that Gorbachev did not expect or want. He expected that openness and reform would provide for greater freedom *within* the Soviet Union. But the republics came to demand freedom *from* the Soviet Union. They wanted independence.

When the reforms reduced the power of the central government, "freedom fever" erupted in the U.S.S.R. Conflict broke out between the Transcaucasian republics of Armenia and Azerbaijan. In the Baltic republics a growing number of people

Current Events

● Have students make a list of the 15 nations that were once republics of the Soviet Union. For the names of these nations, refer students to the table on pp. 334–335.

● Have students look in newspapers and newsmagazines for reports on events and changes in these nations.

● Have students clip out the articles, bring them to class, and summarize them in their own words.

	FLAG/CAPITAL	TOTAL AREA	POPULATION AND DENSITY	INDEPENDENCE DECLARED
LATVIA	★Riga	24,695 sq mi 63,960 sq km	2,700,000 109 per sq mi 42 per sq km	August 21, 1991
LITHUANIA	★Vilnius	26,173 sq mi 67,788 sq km	3,700,000 141 per sq mi 55 per sq km	March 11, 1990
MOLDOVA [3]	★Chisinau	13,012 sq mi 33,701 sq km	4,300,000 330 per sq mi 128 per sq km	August 27, 1991
RUSSIA	★Moscow	6,592,800 sq mi 17,075,352 sq km	147,400,000 22 per sq mi 9 per sq km	December 8, 1991
TAJIKISTAN [4]	★Dushanbe	54,019 sq mi 139,909 sq km	5,100,000 94 per sq mi 36 per sq km	September 9, 1991
TURKMENISTAN [5]	★Ashkhabad	188,417 sq mi 488,000 sq km	3,500,000 19 per sq mi 7 per sq km	October 27, 1991
UKRAINE	★Kiev	233,100 sq mi 603,729 sq km	51,700,000 222 per sq mi 86 per sq km	August 31, 1991
UZBEKISTAN	★Tashkent	172,700 sq mi 447,293 sq km	19,900,000 115 per sq mi 44 per sq km	August 31, 1991

[3] Formerly Moldovia   [4] Formerly Tadzhikistan   [5] Formerly Turkmenia

began to openly speak out against Soviet control. They wanted to regain the freedom they had had before being taken over by the Soviet army. Early in 1990 the Lithuanians voted to withdraw from the Soviet Union. Gorbachev opposed Lithuania's effort to break away, but he failed to stop the movement for independence. The other two Baltic republics, Estonia and Latvia, voted to follow Lithuania's example. Other republics, including Ukraine, also declared their independence. Russia, the largest of the republics, took over functions that had belonged to the central government. As symbols of their independence, republics replaced the red Soviet flag with their own national flags. Russia brought back the old white, blue, and red flag used before the 1917 revolution. The Soviet Union was breaking apart.

335

335

Lesson 2 Review

Answers to Think and Write

A. Their views altered the Soviets' views of Stalin and his rule.

B. There was less secrecy about public affairs. Disagreement on public issues was allowed. Soviets could read books that had previously been banned. A new church was built in Moscow.

C. There were reforms in the ways factories, farms, and mines were run.

D. Gorbachev's economic reforms did not produce immediate benefits. As the power of the central government was reduced, republics began to demand their independence. In August of 1991, an attempted coup resulted in the emergence of Boris Yeltsin as the leader of the reform movement. By the end of 1991, the U.S.S.R. had been dissolved and Gorbachev had resigned.

Answer to Skills Check

Russia was the largest republic; part of the Russian S.F.S.R., Georgian S.S.R., Armenian S.S.R., Azerbaijan S.S.R., Kazakh S.S.R., Turkmen S.S.R., Uzbek S.S.R., Kirghiz S.S.R., Tadzhik S.S.R.

Focus Your Reading

Ask the lesson focus question found at the beginning of the lesson: **What changes took place in the Soviet Union during and after the mid-1980s?**
(Gorbachev's policy of glasnost resulted in less secrecy about public affairs. His policy of perestroika called for reform of the government and the economy. In 1991 there was an attempted coup. That same year the U.S.S.R. was dissolved, and the 15 republics became independent nations.

Additional Practice

You may wish to assign the ancillary materials listed below.

Understanding the Lesson p. 84
Workbook p. 77

Gorbachev tried to persuade the republics to form a federation of equal states. In the federation each republic would be free to run its own affairs, but the central government would control foreign affairs and certain other matters. Gorbachev faced two very different groups of opponents. One group of Communist leaders charged that his reforms were destroying the country. Another group was led by Boris Yeltsin (BOR ihs YELT sihn), president of the Russian Republic. Yeltsin declared that Gorbachev's reforms did not go far enough.

While Gorbachev was away from Moscow on vacation in August 1991, a group of Communist leaders who opposed the reforms attempted to take over the government. Yeltsin and his supporters opposed this attempt to seize power. Yeltsin was backed by large crowds of people who took to the streets in Moscow. Faced with such strong opposition, the attempt to take over the government failed. Gorbachev returned to Moscow, but Boris Yeltsin was now the leader of the reform movement.

On Christmas Day in 1991, Gorbachev resigned as president of the Soviet Union, which had already been dissolved.

This crowd assembled in Moscow to protest an attempted takeover in the Soviet Union in August 1991.
▶ Why, do you think, has a hole been cut in the Soviet flag?

The breakup of the Soviet Union was only one of the great changes taking place at that time. You are living in a time of many changes, and the future, no doubt, will bring still more changes—some expected, some not. In order to keep learning about the world and its peoples, you will need to follow the history of your times. You will find that history in newspapers, news magazines, and television and radio broadcasts.

LESSON 2 REVIEW

THINK AND WRITE
A. What was the importance of Khrushchev's and Gorbachev's views of Soviet history? (Infer)
B. What changes did glasnost bring about in the Soviet government? (Recall)
C. What changes did perestroika produce in Soviet industry and agriculture? (Recall)
D. What factors contributed to the collapse of the Soviet Union? (Infer)

SKILLS CHECK

MAP SKILL
The map on page 332 shows the republics of the former Soviet Union. Which was the largest republic? Which other republics were located south of 50°N latitude and east of 40°E longitude?

336

UNDERSTANDING THE LESSON

NAME _____
CHAPTER
UNDERSTANDING THE LESSON
12

Recalling Facts
LESSON 2 CONTENT MASTER

Read each statement below. Write **True** if the statement is true and **False** if it is false. If the statement is false, cross out the part that is incorrect and write the correct words above it.

_____ False _____ 1. Stalin died in 1953, but no loyal Soviet Communists dared to
criticize his dictatorship until after Mikhail Gorbachev took power.

_____ True _____ 2. Khrushchev's opponents thought his criticisms of Stalin would
weaken the Communist party, so they forced Khrushchev to retire.

_____ True _____ 3. Although Mikhail Gorbachev was a prominent member of the
Communist party, he felt that major changes were needed in the
Soviet government.

_____ True _____ 4. Under glasnost, Gorbachev allowed newspapers to print news
about accidents, natural disasters, and political conflicts.

_____ False _____ 5. Gorbachev worked to reform the government and economy, a policy
called openness.

_____ False _____ 6. As a result of perestroika, daily life became better for many people in
the Soviet Union.

_____ False _____ 7. One result of the attempted coup in August of 1991 was that Nikita
Khrushchev became the leader of the reform movement.

_____ True _____ 8. By the end of 1991 the republics of the Soviet Union had become
independent nations.

Think and Write: Write a paragraph telling how you think glasnost
affected relations between the United States and the Soviet Union.
Support your ideas with facts or reasons. You may use the back of the
sheet.
Answers should reflect independent thinking; suggestions appear in the Answer Key.
84
Use with textbook pages 328–336.

◀ **Review Master Booklet, p. 84**

THINK ABOUT WHAT YOU KNOW
If you had a choice between owning your own farm and working on a collective farm owned by the government, which one would you choose? Explain your reasons.

STUDY THE VOCABULARY
Solidarity   consumer goods

FOCUS YOUR READING
What are some major changes that have taken place in Poland and Czechoslovakia in recent years?

A. Communist Rule in Poland

Early Rule After World War II ended the Soviet Union took over about 70,000 square miles (181,300 sq km) of eastern Poland. To make up in part for this loss, Poland was given about 40,000 square miles (103,600 sq km) of German territory. Ten million people, both Polish and German, were told they had to leave their homes. They were forced to relocate within the new boundaries.

The Soviet Union not only took a thick slice of Polish territory but also made sure that the Polish government was controlled by Communists. In the early years of Communist rule in Poland, the government followed Stalin's example. No open opposition to the government was allowed.

Demands for Freedom In 1980, after years of Communist rule, shipyard workers led by a man named Lech Walesa (lekh vah WEN sah) went on strike. The workers demanded more freedom, particularly the freedom to form a union not controlled by

the government. So many Poles supported the shipyard workers that the government agreed to their demand for a free union. No other Communist country allowed such freedom at that time.

Other Polish workers joined with the shipyard workers to form a large free union called **Solidarity**. The name means "strongly united." As the union grew, its leaders demanded that the Polish people be allowed to vote on whether the Communists should rule. The Communist leaders decided that the union had gone too far in demanding free elections. In 1981 the military took control of the country, and Solidarity was outlawed. Many union members, including Walesa, were arrested. Walesa was not released from jail until about a year later.

Polish Solidarity leader Lech Walesa helped to bring about free elections in Poland.
▶ How do you think these people feel about Walesa?

Optional Activities

Poland and Czechoslovakia

Objectives

★1. **Identify** the similarities and differences between Poland and Czechoslovakia.

2. **Explain** the reasons for increased political and economic freedom in Poland and Czechoslovakia.

3. **Identify** the following people and places: *Lech Walesa, Pope John Paul II, Poland,* and *Czechoslovakia.*

1 STARTING THE LESSON

Motivation Activity

■ Ask students what they think of when they hear the term *solidarity*.

■ After students have expressed their ideas, read them this definition of *solidarity:* "complete unity, as of opinion, purpose, interest, feeling."

Think About What You Know

■ Assign the THINK ABOUT WHAT YOU KNOW activity on p. 337.

■ Answers may include their own farm because they would be able to make their own decisions and reap the profits, or a collective farm because they would not have the burden of responsibility for the farm's success or failure.

Study the Vocabulary

■ Have students look up the definitions of the new vocabulary terms in the Glossary.

■ Have them write copy for a poster, urging workers to join Solidarity.

┌─ **Answers to Caption Questions** ─┐
p. 336 ▶ The area that has been removed from the flag contained the hammer and sickle, the emblem of the Communist party. Removing the emblem was probably a protest against Communist rule.
p. 337 ▶ Answers may include supportive, inspired, and respectful.

337

Read and Think

Sections A, B, and C

Use these questions to prompt a discussion of the changes that have taken place in Poland in recent years.

1. **Summarize the history of Solidarity in Poland.**
   (Solidarity began when shipyard workers went on strike in 1980 and demanded the freedom to form a union not controlled by the government, was outlawed in 1981, and then was legalized in 1989. *pp. 337–338*)

2. **When the Communists came to power in Poland, what did their central plan call for?**
   (It called for producing such things as steel, chemicals, and ships, and less attention was given to consumer goods. *pp. 338–339*)

3. **What is the strongest non-Communist force in Poland?**
   (The Roman Catholic Church *p. 339*)

Thinking Critically **What personal qualities, do you think, did Lech Walesa need to be able to stand up to the Soviet Union?** (Infer)
(Answers should reflect independent thinking but may include courage, unselfishness, and a willingness to sacrifice his own safety for the good of his country. *p. 337*)

Reduced Controls Within a few years, however, the Polish government greatly reduced its controls over the nation. In April 1989, Solidarity was legalized. In June the government allowed a free election. For the first time in over 40 years, Poles could vote for candidates not chosen by the Communist party. Candidates representing Solidarity won a sweeping victory and went on to help elect a non-Communist prime minister for Poland. Solidarity's victory marked the beginning of the political revolution in Eastern Europe. In 1990, Lech Walesa, the Solidarity leader, was elected president of Poland by an overwhelming majority.

B. Farming and Industry in Poland

Economy Before World War II, Poland was largely an agricultural country. After the war, the Polish Communists tried to form collective farms but had little success. Today about 85 percent of the farmland is privately owned, and the farmers are free to sell what they grow. Poland ranks among the world's leading producers of potatoes. Other important crops grown in Poland include sugar beets and wheat. However, more people in Poland work in industry than in farming.

When the Communists came to power in Poland, they laid down a central plan for

THE FORMER SOVIET UNION AND EASTERN EUROPE: POTATO PRODUCTION

Production per year (in thousands of short tons)
- 0–500
- 501–3,900
- 3,901–10,900
- 10,901–43,000
- 43,001 or more

—— Boundary of the former Soviet Union

0   400   800 miles
0   400   800 kilometers

Farms in the former Soviet Union and in all countries of Eastern Europe produce potatoes.
▶ Which country is the second largest producer of potatoes in this region?

Optional Activities

Making Children's Books
- Divide the class into small groups.
- Have each group choose one of the two countries presented in this lesson (Poland and Czechoslovakia).
- Tell students to write and illustrate a children's book, to be entitled *How Greater Freedom Came to [name of country]*.
- Have them include the events that led up to the greater freedom won by the people of that country.
- Make a classroom display with the finished books.

industry. This plan called for producing such things as steel, chemicals, and ships. Less attention was given to **consumer goods**, the products that people use in their daily lives.

Today there is a move toward a Western-style market economy. The Solidarity government hopes this will provide Poland with the economic growth that it did not achieve under communism.

A Polluted Land   In building large industries, the planners seem to have thought very little about pollution. But after Solidarity came to power, the government began to report that Poland was suffering from enormous environmental problems. For years, Poland's steel, chemical, and power plants used coal for power. But there were no regulations about how much coal smoke could be released. As a result, trees are dying from acid rain, and the air is heavy with coal dust.

C. Religion in Communist Poland

The Polish Communist government at first tried to discourage religious practices, but these efforts also failed. About 92 percent of all Poles are Roman Catholics, and the Church became the strongest non-Communist force in the country. In fact, Church holy days are national holidays on which even government offices are closed.

The Roman Catholic Church had chosen a Polish churchman as pope in 1978. Pope John Paul II was welcomed by huge, cheering crowds whenever he visited his homeland of Poland. During a visit in 1987, the pope spoke openly in favor of Solidarity, even though it had been outlawed by the Polish government.

Poland had been home to more than 3 million Jews before World War II. The

Friendly crowds greet Pope John Paul II when he visits Poland.
▶ What reasons can you give to explain why the pope is so popular in Poland?

Nazis killed a very large number of these people during the German occupation. The Nazis also transported Jews from other lands to the terrible death camps they built in Poland. Today there are very few Jews in Poland — perhaps only about 5,000.

D. Land of the Czechs and Slovaks

In 1948, Soviet-backed Communists took over the government of Czechoslovakia. Twenty years later these Communists tried to reform their socialist country to allow greater freedom. However, the Soviet Union sent an army into

339

Reteaching Main Objective

★ *Identify the similarities and differences between Poland and Czechoslovakia.*

● Write on the chalkboard the following headings for an outline of the similarities and differences between the countries (for students to fill in).

  I **Similarities**
   A. (Both are industrialized.)
   B. (Both came under Soviet control after World War II.)
   C. (Both won some freedom from the U.S.S.R.)
  II **Differences**
   A. (Poland was the first to gain some independence.)
   B. (Holy days are national holidays in Poland.)

CLOSING THE LESSON

Lesson 3 Review

Answers to Think and Write

A. The Solidarity movement was important because its victory marked the beginning of the political revolution in Eastern Europe. Polish workers were able to get the government to agree to a free union, and eventually, to allow free elections.

B. Following World War II, Polish Communists made a central plan for industry that emphasized production of steel, chemicals, and ships. Efforts to collectivize farms failed.

C. Efforts to discourage religious practices failed; church holy days are national holidays.

D. In 1948, Soviet-backed Communists took over the government of Czechoslovakia. In 1989, people demonstrated against communism, and the Soviet Union did not send in tanks to stop the demonstrations. By the end of 1989, the Communist party was out of power, and a new government, under Vaclav Havel, was in power. In 1992, Havel resigned after a vote in the Slovak Parliament made it probable that Czechoslovakia would be divided into two nations.

Answer to Skills Check

Both Prague and Warsaw are capital cities, and both are located on rivers.

Focus Your Reading

Ask the lesson focus question found at the beginning of the lesson: **What are some major changes that have taken place in Poland and Czechoslovakia in recent years?**

(The Solidarity movement in Poland resulted in a free union and free elections. In 1989, people in Czechoslovakia demonstrated against communism, and by the end of the year, the Communist party was out of power.)

Additional Practice

You may wish to assign the ancillary materials listed below.

Understanding the Lesson p. 85

340

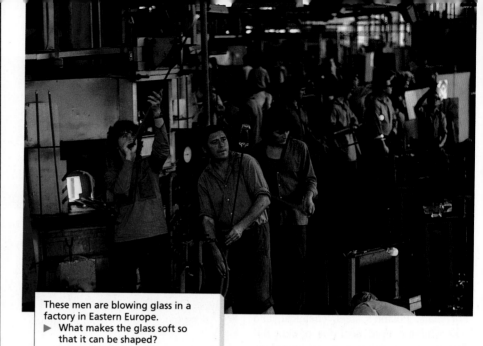

These men are blowing glass in a factory in Eastern Europe.
▶ What makes the glass soft so that it can be shaped?

Czechoslovakia, sent in new Communist leaders, and put an end to the reforms.

In 1989, however, Soviet tanks did not enter Prague when people demonstrated for an end to communism. By year's end, the Communist party was out of power. The new government was headed by Vaclav Havel. At one time he had been jailed for asking for a democratic government; now he was the head of one.

Havel remained in office until 1992. He resigned after a vote in the Slovak Parliament made it probable that Czechoslovakia would be divided into two nations. One would be a Czech republic, the other a Slovak republic.

LESSON 3 REVIEW

THINK AND WRITE

A. Why was the Solidarity movement important? (Infer)

B. What policies did the Polish Communists follow for farming and industry after World War II? (Recall)

C. What was the Communist position on religion in Poland? (Recall)

D. Why are 1948, 1989, and 1992 important dates in the history of Czechoslovakia? (Infer)

SKILLS CHECK

THINKING SKILL

In the Gazetteer, find the entries for Prague and Warsaw. What do these two cities have in common?

UNDERSTANDING THE LESSON

NAME _____

UNDERSTANDING THE LESSON   CHAPTER **12**

Recalling Facts   LESSON 3 CONTENT MASTER

❋ Read each question and write the correct answer on the blank that follows. Use complete sentences.

1. What event symbolized the rapid change in Eastern Europe in 1989? The opening of the Berlin Wall on November 9, 1989, symbolized the changes in Eastern Europe.

2. After East Germany held free elections in 1990, talks began for what political change? East Germany and West Germany began talks on reuniting.

3. What industrial products does East Germany produce? The East Germans produce high quality steel, machinery, and electrical devices.

4. How did Poland come to have a Communist government? After World War II, the Soviet Union made sure that Communists controlled the Polish government.

5. What did the Polish shipyard workers demand in 1980? They demanded the freedom to form a union not controlled by the government.

6. How did the Polish political scene change in 1989? A partly free election was held, in which Solidarity candidates won a sweeping victory.

7. What is agriculture in Poland like today? About 85 percent of the farmland is privately owned, and farmers are free to sell what they grow.

8. How successful have attempts by the Polish Communists to ban religion been? The Polish government has been unable to ban religion.

9. What happened in 1968 when the Communists in Czechoslovakia tried to reform their country to allow greater freedom? The Soviet Union sent in an army, brought in new leaders, and ended the reforms.

10. Why do some Czechoslovakians complain about industry in their nation? They claim that their factories have not kept up to date and their country has fallen behind other industrial nations.

Think and Write How do you think the Soviet Union's policies of *glasnost* and *perestroika* have affected the Communist countries of Eastern Europe? Write a paragraph explaining your answer. You may use the back of the sheet. Answers should reflect independent thinking; suggestions appear in the Answer Key.

Use with textbook pages 335–340.   85

◀ Review Master Booklet, p. 85

THINK ABOUT WHAT YOU KNOW

You have learned that the former Soviet Union was made up of different nationality groups. How do you think people of different nationalities might feel if they were forced to join together to form a new country?

STUDY THE VOCABULARY

ethnic group   arable
atheism

FOCUS YOUR READING

What are some ways in which changes in the governments of the countries of southeastern Europe were brought about?

A. Yugoslavia: Past and Present

Under Communist Rule Yugoslavia was created after World War I when several **ethnic groups** were joined together in one country. An ethnic group is a nationality with its own special characteristics, such as language, customs, and religion. The ethnic groups in the new country spoke Slavic languages. The name Yugoslavia means "land of the South Slavs."

Communists led by Jospip Broz Tito (YOH seep brohz TEE toh) took over Yugoslavia at the end of World War II. Tito had worked with the Soviet Communists before the war, but he refused to let the U.S.S.R. control his country.

Breakup of Yugoslavia Under Tito's rule, Yugoslavia had a federal government made up of six republics: Serbia, Croatia, Slovenia, Bosnia and Hercegovina, Macedonia, and Montenegro. Each republic had its own government as well as representatives in the central government. Each major ethnic group had its own republic, although individuals might live anywhere within the country.

In the 1990s conflicts arose between some ethnic groups which led to the breakup of the old federal government. Declarations of independence by Slovenia, Croatia, Bosnia and Hercegovina, and Macedonia set off a destructive civil war. At first Serbia supported the Serbs in the other republics, but in 1992 Serbia established a New Federal Republic of Yugoslavia. The new republic consisted of Serbia and Montenegro. It was only about half as large as the old Federal Republic.

THE NEW BALKAN STATES
(As of August 1992)

The new Balkan states were once part of the former Yugoslavia.
▶ Which of these Balkan states is bordered by Austria, Italy, Hungary, and Croatia?

341

For Your Information

Tito Josip Broz Tito established a Communist government in Yugoslavia after World War II. Tito was born in 1892 in Croatia, which was then a part of Austria-Hungary. As a soldier in World War I, he was captured and jailed by the tsar's government in Russia. When released by the Communists after the revolution in 1917, he joined the Communist party and later helped to organize the party in Yugoslavia. When he became leader of Yugoslavia in 1945, Tito resisted Soviet efforts to control his country. He became the first leader of an independent Communist country. In 1971, Tito became the chairman of the collective presidency of Yugoslavia.

Optional Activities

★1. **Describe** the relationship that each nation in southeastern Europe had with the Soviet Union.

2. **Compare** the economies of southeastern Europe with the economy that the Soviet Union had.

3. **Identify** the following person and places: *Josip Broz Tito, Yugoslavia, Albania, Hungary, Romania,* and *Bulgaria.*

1 STARTING THE LESSON

Motivation Activity

■ Ask students what they think of when they hear the term "Iron Curtain."

■ Explain that this term described the barrier to the free exchange of information and goods between the countries of Eastern Europe and Western Europe.

■ Point our that there were also physical barriers, such as barbed wire and the Berlin Wall, that marked much of the boundary between Eastern Europe and Western Europe.

Think About What You Know

■ Assign the THINK ABOUT WHAT YOU KNOW activity on page 341.

■ Answers may include anger, resentment, apprehension, fear.

Study the Vocabulary

■ Have students look up the definitions of the new vocabulary words in the Glossary.

■ Ask each student to write two true-or-false questions for each word and then exchange their papers with another student and answer each other's questions.

┌─ **Answers to Caption Questions** ─┐
p. 340 ▶ Heat
p. 341 ▶ Slovenia

Read and Think

Sections A, B, and C

Southeastern European nations had different relationships with the Soviet Union. Use these questions to discuss these countries:

1. **Who was Tito?**
(The Yugoslavian leader from 1945 to 1980 who kept the Soviets from taking control. *p. 341*)

2. **What is the role of religion in Albania?**
(It has no role; Albania is an atheistic state. *p. 342*)

3. **How did life in Hungary differ from life in the Soviet Union before glasnost and perestroika?**
(Hungarians had more freedom of expression and more freedom to own their own businesses. *p. 343*)

Thinking Critically In which of these countries, do you think, would citizens have the fewest civil rights? (Evaluate)
(Answers may include Albania because of its lack of religious freedom. *pp. 341–346*)

In 1967, Albania outlawed religious groups and seized their property, for example, this Orthodox church.
▶ How can you tell that this building is a church?

B. Albania: A Country in Isolation

Land and Language Only the narrow Adriatic Sea separates Albania from Italy, and Albania's borders touch Yugoslavia and Greece. But in spite of this closeness to other countries, Albania has long been isolated from both Eastern Europe and Western Europe.

Albania is a rugged, mountainous land. It has no navigable rivers and had few good roads or railroads until recent times. Even language sets Albania apart from other nations. As you know, Albanians speak an ancient tongue not closely related to any other.

342

Communist Policy The Albanian Communist party ruled the country for years after World War II. The Albanian party quarreled with both Communist Yugoslavia and the Soviet Union, so Albania was cut off even from other Communist countries.

The Albanian Communist party strongly opposed religion and instead supported **atheism** (AY thee ihz um). Atheism is the belief that there is no God. The government declared Albania to be the first atheistic state in the world.

In 1990, changes in the rest of Eastern Europe affected Albania too. Its Communist rulers opened relations with the Soviet Union. They also allowed some religious observances. Other changes followed the next year. Demonstrations against the government forced the Communists to permit other political parties and to share power with them.

Economy Albania is a poor country—the poorest in Europe—but it does have some valuable resources. The mountains contain a variety of minerals, and mining is an important industry. The mountain streams are being used to produce electricity both for use in Albania and for sale to neighboring countries.

C. Changes in Hungary

Early Communism Communists supported by the Soviet Union took over Hungary in 1947. Large numbers of people who fought against the takeover were arrested, and some were executed. Nine years later an anti-Communist revolt broke out, but it was put down by the Soviet army. Many more Hungarians lost their lives, and more than 50,000 fled the country.

Graphic Organizer

To help students understand the factors that isolate Albania, you may wish to use the graphic organizer shown.

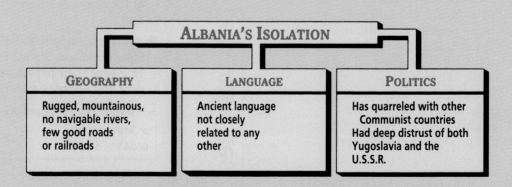

ALBANIA'S ISOLATION

GEOGRAPHY	LANGUAGE	POLITICS
Rugged, mountainous, no navigable rivers, few good roads or railroads	Ancient language not closely related to any other	Has quarreled with other Communist countries. Had deep distrust of both Yugoslavia and the U.S.S.R.

Freedom Increases The Communists continued to rule Hungary, but in 1968 they began to make some changes. The Hungarian government reduced the amount of central control. Industries and collective farms were allowed to make profits in which workers and farm members would share. Hungarians could own small businesses and also were encouraged to grow and sell crops from their own small plots of land.

More than half the land in Hungary is **arable**, that is, suitable for growing crops. Farmers there raise enough food to export to other lands. Factories turn out a variety of goods, many of which are exported. Mines produce coal and bauxite, the ore from which aluminum is obtained.

Along with the freedom to make profits, the Hungarians were allowed more freedom to speak out and express themselves than people in the Soviet Union were. In fact, by the late 1980s, Hungary was being described as the most reform-minded Communist country in Eastern Europe. Thus it was no surprise that Hungary was one of the first Eastern European countries to allow democratic elections in 1990. The elected Hungarian prime minister, Jozsef Antall, pledged that his democratic government would represent all of the Hungarian people. The non-Communist Hungarian Democratic Forum, the party that won the elections, also has called for quicker movement to a market economy.

Although some changes were made in the economy in 1968, the government of Hungary today continues to strive for a market economy.
▶ What kinds of produce is this man selling in the sidewalk market?

343

Read and Think

Sections D and E

Use these questions to guide your discussion of Romania and Bulgaria:

1. **How do people in Romania make a living?**
   (Some Romanians are employed in industries such as petroleum production; others raise crops such as corn, wheat, potatoes, and sugar beets; and others make a living from tourism. *p. 344*)

2. **What was the relationship between the government of Bulgaria and the Soviet Union?**
   (The government of Bulgaria closely followed the leadership of the Soviet Union. *p. 346*)

   Thinking Critically **If you had a choice of living for one year in Bulgaria or in Romania, where would you live and why?** (Evaluate)
   (Answers should reflect independent thinking but may include Bulgaria, because it would be interesting to live in a country that had had close ties to the Soviet Union, or Romania, since it would probably be easier to learn the language. *pp. 344, 346*)

GEOGRAPHY THEMES

Human-Environment Interactions

- Have students look at the map on this page and answer this question: **Which part of the former Soviet Union produces wheat, cotton, and sugar beets?** (The northwest)

D. Romania's Ancient History

Outside Influences Romanians say that a Roman emperor began the conquest of their land in A.D. 101 and that the descendants of the Romans inhabited their country throughout the Middle Ages. It is for this reason that the land is called Romania, "land of the Romans." As you

THE FORMER SOVIET UNION & EASTERN EUROPE: WHEAT & COTTON

- Wheat
- Cotton

THE FORMER SOVIET UNION & EASTERN EUROPE: SUGAR BEETS

- Sugar beets

Wheat, cotton, and sugar beets are grown in parts of the former Soviet Union and Eastern Europe.
▶ Which of these crops are grown in the area near Kiev?

---

have already learned, the Romanian language comes from Latin and is written with the Roman alphabet.

The Soviet army helped to put a Communist government in power in Romania after World War II. Later differences between the Romanians and the Soviet Union did not result in more freedom for the Romanian people. The Romanian Communist government kept strict control over the Romanian people.

Romania, too, saw changes in its government. Unlike the other Eastern European countries, however, a bloody revolution was required to overthrow the Communist ruler, Nicolae Ceausescu (chou SHES koo). Thousands died as supporters of the government fired on unarmed citizens protesting Ceausescu's rule. Finally the army joined with the civilians and helped overthrow Ceausescu. A new government was elected in May 1990.

Economy Romania has good soil that produces crops of corn, wheat, potatoes, and sugar beets. However, more Romanians today are employed in industry than in farming. Romania produces petroleum and is a leading oil producer in Europe.

The Romanian government encourages tourists to come and spend money at resorts on the Black Sea coast. The government has also developed other tourist attractions, including an old castle restored as Dracula's castle. You can read a literature selection from Bram Stoker's famous novel *Dracula* on the next page.

E. Bulgaria's Ties with Other Nations

In the Past In Sofia, the capital city of Bulgaria, there is a church named after a Russian hero, Alexander Nevsky. The

---

Optional Activities

Curriculum Connection

Literature Read aloud the excerpt from Bram Stoker's *Dracula*, omitting the introductory and concluding material.

- Ask students to write a continuation of the story.
- Ask volunteers to share their conclusions with the rest of the class.
- How did most people end the story?
- You may wish to have students draw pictures of Count Dracula based on the description in this selection, and make a classroom display of the drawings.

FROM:

Dracula

By: Bram Stoker

Setting: Romania and England in the 1800s

Bram Stoker was born in Dublin, Ireland, in 1847. Stoker wrote stories in his spare time. *Dracula*, his most famous work, was first published in 1897 and is still a bestseller, more than 75 years after Stoker's death.

In *Dracula*, Stoker uses remote settings, an eerie atmosphere, and extraordinary events to tell a tale of horror. The novel is written in the form of the journals, diaries, and letters of characters whose lives are touched by Count Dracula—a vampire in human form.

The story begins in the Carpathian Mountains of Transylvania, a region in Romania. Jonathan Harker, a law clerk, has traveled to the count's castle to complete a business deal. The excerpt below is from an entry in Harker's journal.

$\mathcal{A}$s I leaned from the window my eye was caught by something moving a storey below me, and somewhat to my left, where I imagined, from the order of the rooms, that the windows of the Count's own room would look out. The window at which I stood was tall and deep. . . . I drew back behind the stonework, and looked out.

What I saw was the Count's head coming out from the window. . . . I was at first interested and somewhat amused, for it is wonderful how small a matter will interest and amuse a man when he is a prisoner. But my very feelings changed to repulsion and terror when I saw the whole man slowly emerge from the window and begin to crawl down the castle wall over that dreadful abyss [cliff], face down with his cloak spreading out around him like great wings. At first I could not believe my eyes. I thought it was some trick of moonlight, some weird effect of shadow; but I kept looking, and it could be no delusion. I saw the fingers and toes grasp the corners of the stones, worn clear of the mortar by the stress of years, and by thus using every projection and inequality move downwards with considerable speed, just as a lizard moves along a wall.

What manner of man is this, or what manner of creature in the semblance [appearance] of man? I feel the dread of this horrible place overpowering me; I am in fear—in awful fear—and there is no escape for me. . . .

Thinking About Literature

Use the information below to help students better understand the literature selection found on p. 345.

Selection Summary

Count Dracula is the main character of this novel, which is the most famous vampire story of all time. By day, Dracula is a wicked nobleman; by night he is a vampire—a corpse that returns to life at night, attacks innocent people, and sucks their blood. As the story progresses, Dracula is traced, hunted down, and destroyed when a stake is driven through his heart.

Guided Reading

1. **Who is speaking in this selection?** (Harker)

2. **What does Harker see from his window?** (Dracula crawling down the castle wall)

3. **What emotions does Harker feel?** (Fear, repulsion, terror, and dread)

Literature-Social Studies Connection

1. **Why might Bram Stoker have chosen Romania as the setting for a horror novel?** (Answers may include that its remoteness in relation to western Europe and the mountains of Transylvania lent themselves to creating an eerie atmosphere.)

—— **Answers to Caption Questions** ——
p. 344 ▶ Wheat and sugar beets

Current Events

- Have students find an article (or articles) in current editions of newspapers or newsmagazines about one of the countries in this lesson.

- Ask them to glue their article on construction paper and write an accompanying statement giving background information from the lesson that allows them to better understand the current events in that country.

- Display the articles on a bulletin board.

Reteaching Main Objective

⭐ *Describe the relationship that each nation in southeastern Europe had with the Soviet Union.*

- Have students create five wide columns with the name of one of the countries in this lesson written across the top of each column.

- Then, have them reskim the text and list phrases that describe each country's historical relationship with the Soviet Union in the appropriate column.

- After students complete this activity, lead a class discussion about which countries had the strongest ties to the Soviet Union and which were most independent.

Optional Activities

Lesson 4 Review

Answers to Think and Write

A. In 1991, Croatia and Slovenia declared their independence, and a civil war broke out. The war began the breakup of the country.

B. Albania is isolated by its terrain, lack of transportation networks, and language.

C. Hungary's government reduced central control, encouraged profits in farms and factories, allowed private ownership of small businesses and farms.

D. The name recalls Romania's conquest by Romans, whose Latin language was the foundation for modern Romanian.

E. Ties include similar languages, alphabets, and religions; Russia helped free Bulgaria from the Ottoman Empire; Soviet Communist party supported formation of Bulgaria's government; for years the Bulgarian government closely followed the U.S.S.R.'s leadership.

Answers to Skills Check

The capitals are Tiranë (Albania), Budapest (Hungary), Bucharest (Romania), and Sofia (Bulgaria).

Focus Your Reading

Ask the lesson focus question found at the beginning of the lesson: **What are some ways in which changes in the governments of the countries of southeastern Europe were brought about?**

(Conflicts between ethnic groups in Yugoslavia resulted in the breakup of the old federal government and a civil war. In Albania, demonstrations forced the Communists to permit other political parties. By 1990, Hungary and Bulgaria had free elections and permitted non-Communist parties to compete. A bloody revolution in Romania overthrew the Communist ruler.

Additional Practice

You may wish to assign the ancillary materials listed below.

Understanding the Lesson p. 86
Workbook pp. 78–79

Answers to Caption Questions
p. 346 ▶ Perfume

Bulgarians built the church more than a hundred years ago to show their thanks to the Russians for help in a war against the Turks. Bulgaria had been part of the Ottoman Empire for nearly five centuries. The armies of the Russian empire had helped Bulgaria win its freedom.

There were other ties between the Bulgarians and the Russians. Both groups of people spoke related Slavic languages and used the Cyrillic alphabet. The two nations also shared a religion. Most Bulgarians belonged to the Eastern Orthodox Church, as did the Russians.

In Recent Times Bulgaria's ties with its large neighbor have continued in more recent times. The Soviet Union supported the creation of the Bulgarian Communist government after World War II. For years the Bulgarian government closely followed the leadership of the Soviet Union.

Bulgaria also made many changes during the years 1989 and 1990. The ruling Communist party renamed itself the Bulgarian Socialist party. It also allowed free elections in June 1990. Even non-Communist parties were allowed to compete.

Economy About one third of Bulgaria is mountainous, but there is also level farm-

More than half of Bulgaria's land is used for raising livestock and for growing crops such as roses.
▶ What product is made from roses?

land. Bulgarians grow grain, vegetables, fruits, and tobacco. Roses are another important crop. The blossoms are pressed to make an oil used in perfume.

Like Romania, Bulgaria has fine Black Sea beaches. There are also mountains in the central and southern parts of Bulgaria. These beaches and mountains are the basis for the country's tourist industry.

LESSON 4 REVIEW

THINK AND WRITE

A. What major events took place in Yugoslavia in 1991? (Recall)

B. Why is Albania isolated? (Recall)

C. What changes were introduced in Hungary after 1968? (Recall)

D. What does the name *Romania* tell you about that country's history and its language? (Recall)

E. What ties did Bulgaria have with the Soviet Union and the earlier Russian empire? (Recall)

SKILLS CHECK

MAP SKILL

Look at the Atlas map on page 614. List the national capitals of the following countries: Albania, Hungary, Romania, Bulgaria.

UNDERSTANDING THE LESSON

NAME _____
UNDERSTANDING THE LESSON

CHAPTER
12

Making Comparisons   LESSON 4 CONTENT MASTER

* This chart helps you compare the southeastern European countries discussed in the lesson. Write the missing information in each blank on the chart. Some have been done for you.

Country	Government	Natural Resources/ Farm Products	Industries
Yugoslavia	Six socialist republics	Good soil, minerals, forests	Tourism, wood products, processed food, automobiles
Albania	Communist	Mountain streams, minerals	Electricity, mining
Hungary	Communist	Good soil, coal, bauxite	Factory goods, food for export, mining
Romania	Communist	Good soil, oil, corn, wheat, potatoes, sunflowers	Petroleum, tourism
Bulgaria	Communist	Grain, vegetables, fruits, tobacco, roses	Perfume oils, tourism

Think and Write: Choose one of the five southeastern European countries and write a paragraph describing what you think it would be like to live there. Give specific details in your answer. You may use the back of the sheet.

Answers should reflect independent thinking; suggestions appear in the Answer Key.
86   Use with textbook pages 341–346.

◀ **Review Master Booklet, p. 86**

USING THE VOCABULARY

On a separate sheet of paper, write the letter of the term that best matches each numbered definition.

a. collectivism
b. glasnost
c. perestroika
d. collective farm
e. central planning
f. market economy
g. Solidarity
h. consumer goods
i. ethnic group
j. atheism

1. The Polish free union whose name means "strongly united"
2. A farm worked by members who share in the profits, but owned and controlled by the government
3. The products that people use in their daily lives.
4. The openness that Mikhail Gorbachev wanted in the Soviet Union
5. An economy in which the choices of buyers decide what is produced
6. Ownership by all the people together
7. A system in which the government decides what industries should produce
8. The belief that there is no God
9. A nationality with its own special characteristics
10. Gorbachev's proposed reforms for the Soviet government and economy

REMEMBERING WHAT YOU READ

On a separate sheet of paper, answer the following questions in complete sentences.

1. Which Soviet leader wanted collective farms as part of his revolution in agriculture?
2. Why were accounts of accidents or natural disasters not printed in Soviet newspapers before glasnost?
3. Why did the Soviet Union lag behind other industrial countries by the 1980s?
4. On what basis did central planners in the Soviet Union set production goals?
5. How did Boris Yeltsin become the leader of the reform movement in the Soviet Union?
6. Compare the demonstrations of 1948 and 1989 in Czechoslovakia.
7. What did Solidarity achieve in 1989?
8. In what ways is Albania isolated from other countries?
9. How did Hungary change between 1968 and 1990?
10. What tourist attraction do Romania and Bulgaria have in common?

TYING MATH TO SOCIAL STUDIES

Over eight years the former Soviet Union produced these amounts of potatoes, rounded to the nearest million tons: 100 million, 74 million, 79 million, 86 million, 91 million, 94 million, 80 million, and 96 million. What was the total amount of potatoes produced in the eight years? What was the average number of tons produced each year?

347

Using The Vocabulary

1. g	4. b	7. e	10. c
2. d	5. f	8. j	
3. h	6. a	9. i	

Remembering What You Read

1. Stalin wanted collective farms.
2. Officials feared that bad news would suggest they were doing a bad job.
3. Soviet factories were inefficient and often had more workers than needed.
4. By what they thought people should have
5. Yeltsin became the reform leader after he opposed the coup in August of 1991.
6. In 1948 the Soviet Union sent an army into Czechoslovakia to put down demonstrations. In 1989 it did not.
7. Solidarity was legalized in 1989. Its candidates won in free elections.
8. Albania has a rugged terrain, lacks a transportation network, and has a language not related to its neighbors.
9. Hungary reduced central control and let workers share in the profits. In 1990 non-Communists won the election.
10. Both have fine Black Sea beaches.

Thinking Critically

1. Answers may include that if a leader criticizes the government, people may lose respect for the government, thereby making it weaker, or no, if freedom of expression exists, it shows the strength of that government.
2. Improving their standard of living motivates people because they can reap the benefits of their work.

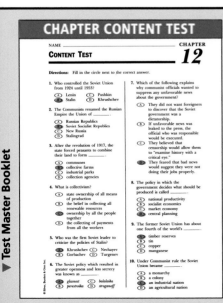

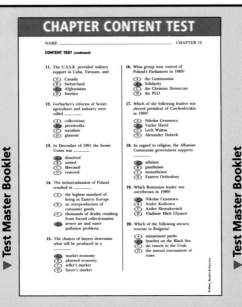

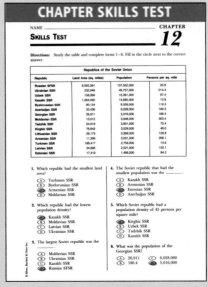

3. Answers may include cleaning products, dress clothes, and other consumer goods.

4. The right to vote, freedom of religion, the right to join independent unions, and the right to leave the country

5. Answers may include because countries have different leaders and histories.

Summarizing the Chapter

Lesson 1
1. Forced peasants to organize collective farms
2. Formed state farms
3. Took over resources and industries
4. Established central planning

Lesson 2
1. Glasnost
2. Perestroika
3. Attempted coup in August of 1991
4. Collapse of Soviet communism and of the Soviet Union

Lesson 3
1. Solidarity formed in Poland
2. Free elections in Poland in 1989
3. Demonstrations in Czechoslovakia in 1989
4. Vote to divide Czechoslovakia into two separate republics

Lesson 4
1. Civil war between ethnic groups
2. Demonstrations against the government
3. Revolution and gradual reform by the government
4. Revolution against dictator

THINKING CRITICALLY

On a separate sheet of paper, answer the following questions in complete sentences.

1. Do you think a government is weakened when one of its leaders openly criticizes that government? Explain.
2. How does competition and the chance to make a profit encourage people to work harder and produce better products?
3. What consumer goods, or products used in daily life, would you be willing to give up? Explain.
4. What freedoms gained recently in the former Soviet Union and Eastern Europe are freedoms that we have in our country?
5. Why, do you think, was communism not exactly the same in all the countries of Eastern Europe?

SUMMARIZING THE CHAPTER

On a separate sheet of paper, copy the information from this graphic organizer. Next to each question, write four answers from the chapter.

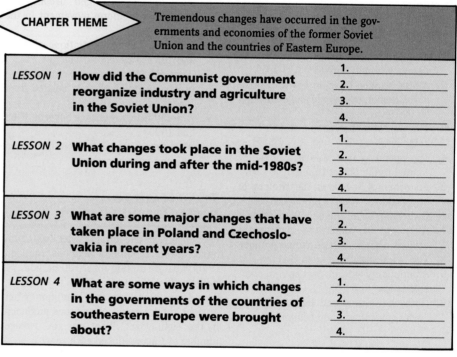

CHAPTER THEME — Tremendous changes have occurred in the governments and economies of the former Soviet Union and the countries of Eastern Europe.

LESSON 1 **How did the Communist government reorganize industry and agriculture in the Soviet Union?**
1. ____
2. ____
3. ____
4. ____

LESSON 2 **What changes took place in the Soviet Union during and after the mid-1980s?**
1. ____
2. ____
3. ____
4. ____

LESSON 3 **What are some major changes that have taken place in Poland and Czechoslovakia in recent years?**
1. ____
2. ____
3. ____
4. ____

LESSON 4 **What are some ways in which changes in the governments of the countries of southeastern Europe were brought about?**
1. ____
2. ____
3. ____
4. ____

348

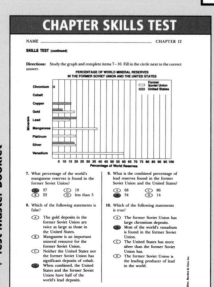

▶ **Test Master Booklet**

CHAPTER SKILLS TEST

NAME _____ CHAPTER 12

SKILLS TEST (continued)

Directions: Study the graph and complete items 7–10. Fill in the circle next to the correct answer.

PERCENTAGE OF WORLD MINERAL RESERVES IN THE FORMER SOVIET UNION AND THE UNITED STATES

7. What percentage of the world's manganese reserves is found in the former Soviet Union?
   Ⓐ 37   Ⓒ 18
   Ⓑ 22   Ⓓ less than 5

8. Which of the following statements is false?
   Ⓐ The gold deposits in the former Soviet Union are twice as large as those in the United States.
   Ⓑ Manganese is an important mineral resource for the former Soviet Union.
   Ⓒ Neither the United States nor the former Soviet Union has significant deposits of cobalt.
   Ⓓ When combined, the United States and the former Soviet Union have half of the world's lead deposits.

9. What is the combined percentage of lead reserves found in the former Soviet Union and the United States?
   Ⓐ 68   Ⓒ 86
   Ⓑ 54   Ⓓ 14

10. Which of the following statements is true?
   Ⓐ The former Soviet Union has large chromium deposits.
   Ⓑ Most of the world's vanadium is found in the former Soviet Union.
   Ⓒ The United States has more silver than the former Soviet Union has.
   Ⓓ The former Soviet Union is the leading producer of lead in the world.

▶ **Test Master Booklet**

CHAPTER WRITING TEST

NAME _____ CHAPTER 12

ESSAY TEST

Directions: Write a response to items 1–4.

REMINDER: Read and think about each item before you write your response. Be sure to think of the points you want to cover, details that support your response, and reasons for your opinions. Then, on the lines below, write your response in complete sentences.

1. How did Joseph Stalin change Soviet agriculture?
A satisfactory response should include the following statements:
- Instead of giving more land to the peasants, Stalin made peasants combine their small holdings into collective farms.
- Stalin believed that this method of farming would require fewer workers, leaving more people free to work in factories and mines.
- Many peasants opposed collectivism, but the policy was forced on them.
An excellent response might also:
- include specific dates and examples.
- discuss methods used to punish those who resisted collectivism.
- mention later criticisms of Stalin's rule.

2. Discuss the influence that Mikhail Gorbachev had on the Soviet Union and Eastern Europe.
A satisfactory response should include the following statements:
- Gorbachev introduced the policies of glasnost and perestroika, which brought new freedoms and reforms to the Soviet Union.
- Changes in the Soviet Union led to demands for change in other Communist countries in Eastern Europe.
- Democratic reforms were introduced in Poland, Czechoslovakia, Hungary, and Romania.
An excellent response might also:
- include specific examples of changes.
- discuss how the changes initiated by Gorbachev contributed to the eventual dissolution of the Soviet Union in 1991.

▶ **Test Master Booklet**

CHAPTER WRITING TEST

NAME _____ CHAPTER 12

ESSAY TEST (continued)

3. What is Solidarity?
A satisfactory response should include the following statements:
- Solidarity is a Polish labor union.
- It began when other workers joined with striking shipyard workers in demanding greater freedom.
- After several years of struggle, the Polish government allowed a free election.
- Candidates representing Solidarity won control of the national parliament.
An excellent response might also:
- identify Lech Walesa as a leader of Solidarity.
- reflect independent thinking.

4. What were some of the factors and events that led to the dissolution of the Soviet Union?
A satisfactory response should include the following statements:
- The Soviet Union had many nationalities.
- Gorbachev's reforms did not improve the Soviet standard of living significantly.
- Republics had a growing desire for independence.
An excellent response might also:
- use the terms glasnost and perestroika.
- that glasnost resulted in more open discussion of dissatisfaction with the government.
- the failed attempt to take over the government in August of 1991.
- the emergence of Boris Yeltsin as reform leader.

COOPERATIVE LEARNING

In the 1980s and early 1990s tremendous changes took place in the Soviet Union and Eastern Europe. During that time, people in this region worked for social reform, freedom, and independence. Some accomplished their goals through political means and legislation. Some used peaceful demonstrations and others resorted to bloody revolutions.

Who are some of the people who changed the course of history in the former Soviet Union and Eastern Europe? What methods did these people use to try to make reforms? Were the methods successful? You and a group of classmates can use information in Unit 3 to create a television talk show that answers these questions about the individuals who have made an impact on the former Soviet Union and Eastern Europe.

PROJECT

Meet as a group and decide which guests your talk show will feature. Everyone in the group should have a role to play on the show, including one person who will serve as the host. Choose the appropriate number of guests from among the following: Nikolai Lenin, Peter the Great, Catherine the Great, Nikita Khrushchev, Lech Walesa, Mikhail Gorbachev, and Boris Yeltsin.

REMEMBER TO:
- Give your ideas.
- Listen to others' ideas.
- Plan your work with the group.
- Present your project.
- Discuss how your group worked.

Next select a host and decide which guest role each group member will play. Then discuss the questions the host will ask and the answers the guests will give. Your program should cover reasons for change, methods used, and the successes and failures of the individuals involved.

Each group member should write down the questions and answers that apply to the role he or she will play. Those of you who will be guests may need to do research to find answers to some of the host's questions.

PRESENTATION AND REVIEW

Your group should rehearse your talk show. Once you are sure all group members are prepared to play their roles, present the talk show to the class. The host might want to open the discussion to include questions and comments from the audience.

After the presentation, your group should meet to evaluate your talk show. Was each group member prepared? Did you teach your audience anything new about the leaders of the former Soviet Union and Eastern Europe? How might your project have been improved?

349

Objectives

1. **Describe** the system of time zones.

2. **Interpret** information presented on a time-zone map.

Why Do I Need This Skill?

Ask students to imagine that they have a relative living in Europe who is celebrating a birthday. Tell them that they have forgotten to send a card and have decided to call the relative to wish them a happy birthday. Ask them: **How can you be sure not to wake up your relative in the middle of the night?** (Students should say they would find out what time it was in Europe before calling.) Tell students that by understanding time zones, they can know what time it is in any part of the world.

Learning the Skill

To check students' comprehension on time zones, ask the following questions:

1. **Why do time zones zigzag in places?** (So that people living in the same region can have the same clock time)

2. **What is the *Prime Meridian?*** (It is the line of longitude that passes through Greenwich, England, and is the point from which time is measured around the world.)

3. **What does A.M. represent?** (A.M. stands for *ante meridian,* which means "before noon.")

SKILL TRACE:	Understanding Time Zones	
INTRODUCE PE pp. 350–351	**PRACTICE** TE pp. 350–351 PE p. 301 PE pp. 289, 585 TE p. 360	**TEST** Unit 3 Test, TMB

A. WHY DO I NEED THIS SKILL?

As you know, the earth is constantly moving. It rotates on its axis from west to east. Because of this movement, the direct rays of the sun do not hit everywhere on the earth at the same time. While it is night in some parts of the world, it is daytime in other parts. In order to know the time it will be when you travel to a distant part of the world, you need to understand the world's time zones.

B. LEARNING THE SKILL

The earth is divided into 24 standard time zones, one for each hour of the day. The earth makes a complete 360° revolution in those 24 hours. Since 360 divided by 24 equals 15, each time zone is 15° wide.

Notice on the map below that the time zones zigzag in several places. This has been done so that people living in the same region or country can have the same clock time.

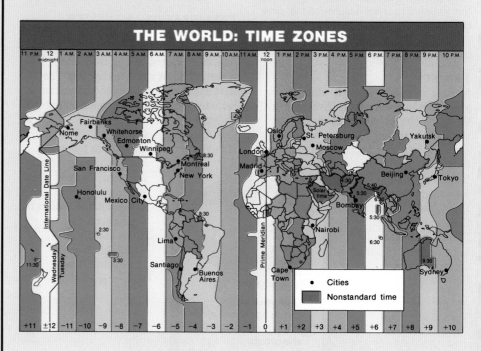

THE WORLD: TIME ZONES

Homework Activity

● As a homework activity, have students make up word problems using the time-zone map.

● Students should provide answer keys to accompany their problems.

● Have students bring their word problems to class, exchange papers, and solve each other's problems.

● Students should exchange papers again to check the answers against the answer key.

Lines of longitude are sometimes called *meridians.* There are two meridians that are very important for understanding time zones. One is the *Prime Meridian.* It passes through Greenwich, England. By international agreement, time around the world is measured against the time in Greenwich.

As you can see on the map on the previous page, if it is 12:00 noon in Greenwich, the time in other zones is different, depending on how far east or west of the Prime Meridian they are. The time in the zone immediately to the east of the Prime Meridian time zone is 1:00 P.M. The time in the zone immediately to the west is 11:00 A.M.

The other important meridian is the *International Date Line.* It is exactly halfway around the world from the Prime Meridian. It is at the International Dateline that the day changes. For example, when it is Sunday east of the line, west of the line is Monday. If it is Sunday west of the line, it is Saturday east of the line.

What do A.M. and P.M. represent? A.M. stands for the Latin term *ante meridiem,* which means "before noon." P.M. stands for *post meridiem,* which means "after noon."

C. PRACTICING THE SKILL

1. Why are there different time zones?
2. How many time zones are there?
3. Which country has the most time zones?
4. If you are traveling from east to west on a Thursday, what day is it when you cross the Date Line?
5. What time is it in your town or city when it is noon in Greenwich, England?
6. When it is 3:00 P.M. in Moscow, what time is it in Mexico City?
7. If it is 2:00 P.M. in Greenwich, what time is it in Nairobi, Kenya?

D. APPLYING THE SKILL

Pick three places in the world that you would like to visit. Using the time zone map, figure out what time it would be in each of these places if it is 8:00 P.M. in Greenwich.

Suppose you were going to fly across the United States from New York City to San Francisco. If your plane left the airport in New York at 3:00 P.M. and the flight took five hours, what time would it be when you arrived in San Francisco?

Practicing the Skill

1. There are different time zones because the sun does not shine on all parts of the earth at the same time.

2. There are 24 time zones.

3. The former Soviet Union has the most time zones.

4. Friday

5. Answers will depend on the location of your town.

6. 6:00 A.M.

7. 5:00 P.M.

For students who are still having difficulty with the concept of time zones, you may wish to use the reteaching activity listed below.

Applying the Skill

Since the answers for this activity culd vary greatly, you may wish to find out the top five places that students have chosen. Then ask individual students to tell what time it would be in each of these places if it is 8:00 P.M. in Greenwich.

It would be 5:00 P.M. when the flight arrived in San Francisco.

351

Reteaching Activity

- Write the following problems on the chalkboard, and have students solve them by using the time-zone map.

    1. When it is 1:00 P.M. in Madrid, Spain, what time is it in Tokyo, Japan? (9:00 P.M.)

    2. When it is 11:00 A.M. in Santiago, Chile, what time is it in Lima, Peru? (10:00 A.M.)

    3. If you left Edmonton, Canada, at 7:00 A.M., and took a four-hour flight to Montreal, what time would it be when you landed? (1:00 P.M.)

- Then have individual students to to the chalkboard to solve the problems.

Optional Activities

Objectives

1. **Describe** the importance of making comparisons.

2. **Demonstrate** the ability to make comparisons.

Why Do I Need This Skill?

Ask students to pretend that they are at a shoe store trying to decide which pair of athletic shoes to buy. Ask: **What would you do to make your decision easier?**
(Students should answer that they would make comparisons between the two pairs of shoes.) One pair might be more comfortable than the other, the design of one might be more visually appealing or more suited to the sport that they are interested in, and so on. Tell students that understanding comparisons is also an important key to reading comprehension.

Learning the Skill

To check students' understanding of comparisons, ask the following questions:

1. **What do comparisons tell readers?**
   (How things are alike and different)

2. **How does the skill of recognizing and making comparisons help readers?**
   (By making it easier for them to understand what they read)

SKILL TRACE:	Using Various Text Structures to Aid Comprehension	
INTRODUCE PE pp. 352–353	**PRACTICE** TE pp. 352–353, 379 **RMB** pp. 20, 26 **WB** p. 26, 77	**TEST** Unit 3 Test, TMB

A. WHY DO I NEED THIS SKILL?

Writers sometimes organize ideas by making comparisons. Comparisons tell the reader how things are alike and different. If you are able to recognize and make comparisons, it will be easier for you to understand what you read.

B. LEARNING THE SKILL

Comparisons help us make sense of our world. For example, on page 286 in Chapter 10, you read that the peaks of the Caucasus Mountains are about three times as high as the Urals and are higher than the Alps. What if the author of this book told you only that the Caucasus peaks are high? This information would be correct, but by comparing the Caucasus with the Urals and the Alps, the author helps you better understand *how high* the Caucasus Mountains are. You will find many comparisons like this in your social studies textbook.

Sometimes comparisons are not stated directly. But by reading carefully, you will be able to make comparisons yourself. For instance, on page 288 you learned that the steppes have no trees. Earlier in the chapter, you read about another treeless region of the former Soviet Union, the tundra. Howev you also learned that these two regions different in that crops can be grown on t steppes but not on the tundra.

C. PRACTICING THE SKILL

One way for you to organize information a make your own comparisons is to mak comparison table like the one on page 3 The subjects that are to be compared listed in the left-hand column; specific ch acteristics are listed in a row across the t of the table.

Each box in the table is to be filled with a plus (+) or a minus (−). A plus used when the subject has a particular ch acteristic; a minus is used when the subj does not have the characteristic. Once all t boxes have been filled in, you can look at t comparison table to see how the subjects alike and different.

Copy this comparison table on a sep rate sheet of paper. Use the information Chapter 10 to add more characteristics the table and then fill in the rest of t boxes. Finally, review the table and n how the tundra, taiga, and steppes are ali and different.

Optional Activities

Homework Activity

Making Comparisons   Have students practice this skill by reviewing Lesson 4 and comparing facts about the countries discussed (the former Yugoslavia, Albania, Hungary, Romania, and Bulgaria).

• For example, students could compare how closely related each country was to the Soviet Union (the former Yugoslavia, not close; Albania, distant; Hungary, not close; Romania, not close; Bulgaria, very close).

COMPARING REGIONS OF THE FORMER SOVIET UNION					
	Grasses and low-growing plants	Farming	Permafrost		
Tundra	+	−			
Taiga	−	+			
Steppes	+	+			

D. APPLYING THE SKILL

Look for comparisons as you read the next chapter, which is about the geography of the Middle East and North Africa. Using the table above as a model, make some of your own comparison tables to show how the peoples and lands of these areas are alike and different.

Use this skill to compare peoples and lands of different regions of the Eastern Hemisphere that you will read about during the year. Remember, if you are able to recognize and make comparisons, it will be easier for you to understand what you read. Knowing how to make comparisons is an important skill to learn and to apply to all your reading.

353

Practicing the Skill

Students' charts should contain the following information: *Permafrost*: Tundra +; Taiga −; Steppes −. Additional categories might include *Rivers* and *Coniferous Trees*, under which the following information would be placed: *Rivers*: Tundra +; Taiga +; Steppes +; *Coniferous Trees*: Tundra −; Taiga +; Steppes −.

For students who are still having difficulty with the concept of making comparisons, you may wish to assign the reteaching activity below.

Applying the Skill

Students' comparison charts should follow the same format and contain the types of information presented in the chart on this page.

SKILL TRACE:	Using Various Text Structures to Aid Comprehension	
INTRODUCE PE pp. 352–353	PRACTICE TE pp. 352–353, 379 RMB pp. 20, 26 WB p. 26, 77	TEST Unit 3 Test, TMB

Reteaching Activity

● Have students practice the skill by making comparison charts of their own which compare information about the countries discussed in this chapter.

● Have students find information in the text concerning the countries' economies, governments, and resources.

● Ask students to write the information in chart form and present their charts to the class.

● Ask students to be prepared to show the portions of the text that support the information presented in their charts.

Optional Activities

353

The Middle East and North Africa

Unit Theme Perhaps more than any other region, the region of the Middle East and North Africa has been significantly influenced by religion. The unique geography of this region has also had a major impact on the people who live there.

Chapter 13 Geography of the Middle East and North Africa

(pp. 356-375)

Theme The people of the Middle East and North Africa have learned to use the gifts of nature to survive in their unique geographic environment.

Chapter 14 History of the Middle East and North Africa

(pp. 376-401)

Theme The Middle East has had an important place in the world's history not only because of the universal contributions its people have made but also because it was the birthplace of world religions, such as Islam and Christianity.

Chapter 15 The Middle East and North Africa Today

(pp. 402-428)

Theme Geography, resources, religions, and political policies and conflicts continue to have a strong influence on daily life in the Middle East and North Africa today.

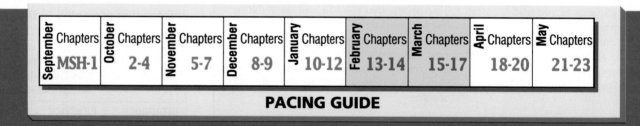

September Chapters	October Chapters	November Chapters	December Chapters	January Chapters	February Chapters	March Chapters	April Chapters	May Chapters
MSH-1	2-4	5-7	8-9	10-12	13-14	15-17	18-20	21-23

PACING GUIDE

Bulletin Board Idea

Student Activity

To help students identify and locate the many countries of the Middle East and North Africa, use an opaque projector to draw them. Then, position an outline map of this area on a bulletin board. On sentence strips, write the name of each country. You may wish to use other sentence strips to identify geographic features, resources, or items of interest as students read Unit 4.

Annotated Bibliography

Books for Teachers

Bill, James A. *The Eagle and the Lion: The Tragedy of American-Iranian Relations.* New Haven, CT: Yale University Press, 1988. ISBN 0-300-04097-0. (Ch. 15) The ideologies and emotions involved in the political rift between the United States and Iran are examined.

Billings, Malcolm. *The Cross and the Crescent: A History of the Crusades.* New York: Sterling Publishing Co., 1988. ISBN 0-8069-6094-0. (Ch. 14) This self-contained overview of the Crusades can also be used as an accompaniment to the BBC radio series of the same name, first broadcast in 1987.

Carter, Jimmy. *The Blood of Abraham.* Boston: Houghton Mifflin, 1985. ISBN 0-395-41498-9. (Ch. 14) The historical background and current issues of the Middle East are presented from the viewpoint of the former President.

Books for Students

Abdallah, Maureen. *Middle East.* Morristown, NJ: Silver Burdett Press, 1986. ISBN 0-382-06417-8. (Ch. 13) A summary of the geography and people of this important region of the world is concisely presented.

Alotaibi, Muhammad. *Bedouin: The Nomads of the Desert.* Vero Beach, FL: Rourke Publications, 1989. ISBN 0-86625-265-7. (Ch. 13) The lives of these desert nomads are introduced and their lifestyles are explained.

Asimov, Isaac. *How Did We Find out About Oil?* New York: Walker & Co., 1980. ISBN 0-8027-6381-2. (Ch. 13) The formation of oil, its recovery from the earth, and its impact on the world and the future are discussed in this book from the "How Did We Find Out" series.

Charing, Douglas. *The Jewish World.* Morristown, NJ: Silver Burdett Press, 1983. ISBN 0-382-06930-7. (Ch. 15) The story of the Jewish people is clearly presented in this slim, oversized book filled with photographs, drawings, and graphs.

Evans, Michael. *The Gulf Crisis.* Danbury, CT: Franklin Watts, 1983. ISBN 0-531-04543-9. (Ch. 15) The recent Gulf war between Iran and Iraq and other tensions between nations in the Middle East are explained thoroughly for students.

James, R.S. *The West Bank and the Gaza Strip.* New York: Chelsea House, 1988. ISBN 1-55546-782-2. (Ch. 14) The importance of the West Bank area to Jews and Arabs in Israel is explained, and the possible future of this region is explored.

Lang, Andrew, trans. *Arabian Nights.* Minneola, NY: Dover Books, 1969. ISBN 0-486-22289-6. (Ch. 13) This great collection of stories of the Islamic world is edited for younger readers.

Lengyel, Emil. *Iran.* Danbury, CT: Franklin Watts, 1981. ISBN 0-531-02242-0. (Ch. 14) The history, geography, lifestyles, religion, and culture of Iran are presented with photographs and maps.

Mason, Anthony. *Middle East.* Morristown, NJ: Silver Burdett Press, 1988. ISBN 0-382-09514-6. (Ch. 13) An examination of the history, geography, and customs of those who live in the Middle East is given.

Shapiro, William. *Lebanon.* Danbury, CT: Franklin Watts, 1984. ISBN 0-531-04854-3. (Ch. 15) Shapiro gives an overview of the people and culture of this country torn by years of civil war.

Time-Life Books, eds. *Arabian Peninsula.* Alexandria, VA: Time-Life Books, 1985. ISBN 0-8094-5312-6. (Ch. 13) The rich geographic resources of the Arabian Peninsula are presented to students through excellent illustrations.

Filmstrips and Videos

Friends in the Holy Land. Videocassette. Films for the Humanities & Sciences, 1988. (Ch. 15) Two teens from the United States travel to Israel where they meet an Israeli girl and a Bruse boy and find that, though their new friends' country has problems, they are not much different from the Americans.

Introduction to the Arab World. Videocassette. AMID-EAST, 1989. (Ch. 14) Ancient traditions persisting within modern culture are illuminated in this concise study of the Arab World.

Israel: The Other Reality. Videocassette. Wombat Film & Video, 1989. (Ch. 15) Viewers pay a visit to a village where Jews and Arabs live in harmony with one another.

Jerusalem, Shining Still. Videocassette. Caedmon, 1988. (Ch. 14) Music and excellent photography add much to the story of the historic city of Jerusalem.

Computer Software

MECC Dataquest: The Middle East and North Africa. MECC, 1989. Apple compatible. (Ch. 13) Information about 25 Middle East countries is presented to students through questions and answers, and an excellent teacher's guide is included.

The Crusades

How did the Crusades affect the world?

During the twelfth and thirteenth centuries, thousands of Europeans flowed into the Middle East to fight a series of wars known as the Crusades. The wars did little to settle things, little geography changed hands, and, in military terms, the wars would have to be considered failures. But, in many other ways, these wars were extremely important. They helped change the histories of the Middle East and Europe, and, therefore, the entire world. The following activities center around these wars and their effects on the world.

SOCIAL STUDIES

Economics   The Crusades greatly influenced the economic systems of both the Middle East and Europe.

■ Have students list the ways in which the Crusades influenced the European economic system and compare them to the ways in which the Middle Eastern economic system was influenced.

Geography   Have students draw a map of the Middle East, the Mediterranean, and Europe. (You may wish to refer students to the map on p. 404 of their textbook.) Then, have them place this map on a large piece of cardboard or on a bulletin board.

■ Using pieces of string or yarn of one color, students will trace the paths of the major Crusades.

■ Then using string or yarn of a different color, they will trace the path of economic growth that spread between the two cultures.

■ If space permits, you may wish to have students expand the yarn path to include the Orient, showing the path of the Silk Road.

Global Awareness   The Crusades led to major economic trading efforts between the Europeans and the people of the Middle East. Not all the products obtained by the Europeans were from the Middle East. Europeans craved things such as silks from China, spices such as pepper, nutmeg, allspice, and cinnamon from the Indies, as well as dyed fabrics from the Middle East.

■ Have students find these places on a world map in the Atlas and explain how the Crusades helped the Europeans learn about cultures beyond those of the Middle East.

History   The lands around Jerusalem were important to the people of the Middle East and Europe.

■ Have students research and write a short report about why this particular area was important to both Muslims and Christians.

LANGUAGE ARTS

■ Have students practice persuasive writing. Using the research about why both Muslims and Christians wanted Jerusalem, have students select one side or the other and write a persuasive article convincing a reader that their side should own the territory.

■ Ask volunteers to share their articles with the class.

■ Students who need a challenge may wish to write reports comparing the wars over Jerusalem during the Crusades to the problems in the Middle East today.

SCIENCE

■ The invaders from Europe soon learned that the culture of the Muslim world was far different from their own. One of the major differences between the two was the state of scientific information. Although the Europeans had historically been interested in science, the field saw few advances after the fall of the Roman Empire.

■ Have students create a bulletin board display showing the differences between the state of scientific knowledge in the Middle East and in Europe. Students may wish to start by examining the fields of astronomy and medicine.

ART

■ The art created in the Middle East during these years was very different from the art created in Europe or the Orient.

■ Have students research these differences and create their own work of Middle Eastern–style art. They may wish to create a mosaic. Students may make their mosaics from paper or tile, or they may wish to draw them with ink, paint, or markers.

MATHEMATICS

■ People in the Middle East were as interested in mathematics as they were in science. Have students research Arabic contributions to mathematics and decide how much influence the people of the Middle East had on modern mathematics.

■ Students may wish to examine the Arabic influence on the concept of zero and on the fields of trigonometry and geometry.

LITERATURE

■ The main armies sent by Pope Urban II during the Crusades consisted chiefly of well-trained French and Norman knights. These men in armor were well-equipped and trained to fight on horseback. Becoming a knight grew to become a mark of honor and distinction.

■ Students may enjoy reading or listening to excerpts from the following books that discuss the romantic yet arduous life of knights in armor.

The Story of Knights in Armor by Ernest E. Tucker. (New York: Lothrop, Lee, and Shepard, 1961.)

The Knights by Michael Gibson. (New York: Arco Publishing, 1979. ISBN 0-668-04785-2.)

■ Have students write their own tale of a knight in armor who joins one of the Crusades. Encourage them to include details about why the knight believes in the Crusade's cause and what he hopes the wars will achieve.

Teach the Writing Process

INSTRUCTIONS FOR THE TEACHER:

Why Teach Writing with Social Studies? Research has taught us that writing improves reading comprehension and enhances learning in every subject — especially social studies. Teachers now realize that writing sharpens critical thinking skills, stimulates the processing of information, and fosters creative thinking. Students also learn to connect facts in different ways, binding new information to what they already know.

Why Use the Writing Process? In the past, teachers have merely assigned writing. Now, teachers can teach it as a process, through a series of five simple steps: Prewriting, Writing, Revising, Proofreading, and Publishing.

This process helps teachers teach students to write better and with less difficulty. This process also gives students a concrete tool that helps answer questions such as:

1. What can I write about?
2. How do I start my report?
3. How can I see my mistakes?
4. What is a fun way to share what I've written?

Using the Writing Process No matter what the content area or your reason for having students write, the writing process can always be used. Here are the steps for you and your students to follow.

1. Prewriting (Getting ready to write)
2. Writing (Putting your ideas on paper)
3. Revising (Making changes to improve your writing)
4. Proofreading (Looking for and fixing errors)
5. Publishing (Sharing your writing with others)

ACTIVITY FOR THE STUDENTS:

STEP ONE (Prewriting) Before students begin to write, they should do the following exercise.

■ *Choosing a Topic* Have students choose a topic from this unit about the Middle East and North Africa. Make sure students realize that to write a good report, they must choose the right topic. First, they should choose a topic that is narrow enough to cover in their short report.

(a) *Think About It:* Have students make a list of possible topics. Ask them: Which topic makes you most curious? Make sure they narrow their topic. Instead of writing about "The Birthplace of Three Religions" they may want to write about the beginning of one religion.

(b) *Talk About It:* Have students find out what topics their classmates chose. They should ask how classmates made their choices. Working with a partner often helps individuals come up with more ideas.

■ *Choosing Their Strategy* Have students choose a fact-finding strategy. The following is just one choice:

Take Notes: Students should take notes on what they discover as they do their research. They should make a note card for each main idea. Each card should include supporting details. Tell students to put the ideas in their own words.

STEP TWO (Writing) Have students arrange their prewriting notes in the order in which they plan to use them. They should state their topic in the first paragraph. They might want to begin with a dramatic, attention-getting fact. They should end with a summary paragraph, which might contain a prediction for the future, based on facts from their report.

STEP THREE (Revising) Have students look at their first draft with the intention of making it clearer or more interesting. They may want to try the following.

■ *Reading the Report to Themselves* They should ask themselves these questions.

1. Did I accomplish my purpose?
2. Will my audience find my report interesting and understandable?

■ *Reading the Report to a Partner* The partner will want to tell the reader what parts are unclear, especially interesting, and so on. Students will then want to take a different colored pen and make revision marks on their papers to show any changes that they wish to make.

STEP FOUR (Proofreading) In order to be courteous to those who are reading their writing, students should make sure that their report is correct and neat. Students can use a ruler under each line of their report as they read for mistakes. They may want to ask themselves:

1. Did I spell words correctly?;
2. Did I indent paragraphs?
3. Did I use capital letters correctly?

STEP FIVE (Publishing) Students will need to make a bibliography for their reports, listing all sources in alphabetical order according to the authors' last names. Students may want to read their reports aloud, asking classmates to note facts and tell what interested them, or you may wish to paste the reports in a scrapbook entitled *Interesting Facts About The Middle East and Africa,* to be displayed in the school library.

Unit Test

CONTENT TEST

Directions: Fill in the circle next to the correct answer.

1. What has given the Middle East a variety of peoples?
   - Ⓐ the hot, dry climate
   - Ⓑ centuries of migration
   - Ⓒ the discovery of oil
   - Ⓓ the Crusades

2. Which group gets its name from the Arabic term for "desert dwellers"?
   - Ⓐ Israelis   Ⓒ Oasians
   - Ⓑ Bedouins   Ⓓ Nomads

3. Which language is used throughout the Middle East and North Africa?
   - Ⓐ Arabic   Ⓒ Bedouinese
   - Ⓑ Hebrew   Ⓓ Latin

4. A dry stream bed is called a
   - Ⓐ wadi
   - Ⓑ dead sea
   - Ⓒ gulch
   - Ⓓ parched oasis

5. The Dead Sea has the _____.
   - Ⓐ driest water on earth
   - Ⓑ lowest elevation on earth
   - Ⓒ world's highest population of salted fish
   - Ⓓ Suez Canal as an outlet to the Mediterranean

6. Ships entering and leaving the Persian Gulf must pass through the
   - Ⓐ Nile River
   - Ⓑ Strait of Hormuz
   - Ⓒ Panama Canal
   - Ⓓ Tigris River

7. How does a nation determine its per capita income?
   - Ⓐ by eliminating its trade imbalance and budget deficit
   - Ⓑ by multiplying the minimum wage by the amount of people in the work force
   - Ⓒ by dividing its total income by its total population
   - Ⓓ by subtracting the total salaries of all workers from the gross national product

8. Because much of the Middle East is dry and mountainous,
   - Ⓐ millions of tourists visit the region each year
   - Ⓑ few crops are grown
   - Ⓒ camels are the main form of transportation
   - Ⓓ the land is used for oil fields

9. Allah's messages to Muhammad were written in the _____.
   - Ⓐ Koran   Ⓒ Hegira
   - Ⓑ Kaaba   Ⓓ Bible

10. All faithful Muslims are required to
   - Ⓐ make a pilgrimage to Mecca
   - Ⓑ memorize the Kaaba
   - Ⓒ shave their heads
   - Ⓓ change their names

11. Which of the following is a landlocked country?
   - Ⓐ Lebanon   Ⓒ Algeria
   - Ⓑ Israel   Ⓓ Afghanistan

CONTENT TEST (continued)

12. Which group conquered the Anatolian peninsula, which became known as Turkey?
   - Ⓐ the Iranians
   - Ⓑ the Armenians
   - Ⓒ the Seljuks
   - Ⓓ the Turkeys

13. What leader encouraged people to begin the Crusades?
   - Ⓐ the Caliph of Baghdad
   - Ⓑ Omar Khayyam
   - Ⓒ King Louis XVI
   - Ⓓ Pope Urban II

14. What was the purpose of the Crusades?
   - Ⓐ to convert unbelievers to Islam
   - Ⓑ to convert Muslims to Christianity
   - Ⓒ to create a home for Jews in Palestine
   - Ⓓ to drive the Muslims out of Jerusalem

15. Which leader of Iran was overthrown by followers of Ayatollah Khomeini?
   - Ⓐ Reza Khan
   - Ⓑ Muhammad Reza Pahlavi
   - Ⓒ Muammar al-Qaddafi
   - Ⓓ Golda Meir

16. Israel was created from the country of _____.
   - Ⓐ Iraq   Ⓒ Jordan
   - Ⓑ Palestine   Ⓓ Syria

17. Which leader of Turkey led the modernization of his country?
   - Ⓐ Mustafa Kemal
   - Ⓑ Omar Khayyám
   - Ⓒ Atilla
   - Ⓓ Seljuk

18. Which of the following is an important industry in Turkey?
   - Ⓐ diamond cutting
   - Ⓑ camel ranching
   - Ⓒ coal mining
   - Ⓓ fez knitting

19. In which country did religious differences lead to civil war?
   - Ⓐ Lebanon
   - Ⓑ Saudi Arabia
   - Ⓒ Yemen
   - Ⓓ Syria

20. Which country has gained wealth from its oil deposits?
   - Ⓐ Israel
   - Ⓑ Turkey
   - Ⓒ Tunisia
   - Ⓓ Saudi Arabia

SKILLS TEST

Directions: Study the map and complete items 1–5. Fill in the circle next to the correct answer.

NORTH AFRICA: MINERAL RESOURCES

1. Which country has phosphate deposits in the most locations?
   - Ⓐ Morocco   Ⓒ Algeria
   - Ⓑ Tunisia   Ⓓ Egypt

2. Which country has the greatest variety of mineral resources?
   - Ⓐ Algeria   Ⓒ Libya
   - Ⓑ Morocco   Ⓓ Tunisia

3. Phosphates in Algeria are located entirely in the _____.
   - Ⓐ north   Ⓒ northwest
   - Ⓑ west   Ⓓ southeast

4. Which countries have petroleum resources?
   - Ⓐ Libya, Morocco, and Egypt
   - Ⓑ Tunisia, Algeria, and Morocco
   - Ⓒ Algeria, Libya, and Egypt
   - Ⓓ Morocco, Tunisia, and Libya

5. The resources located between 10°W and 0° are _____.
   - Ⓐ phosphates and petroleum
   - Ⓑ coal and phosphates
   - Ⓒ petroleum and coal
   - Ⓓ only phosphates

SKILLS TEST (continued)

Directions: Read the definitions and complete items 6–10. Fill in the circle next to the correct answer.

Dictionary: a book that lists words in alphabetical order, tells where they came from, explains their meanings, shows how to pronounce them, and tells how to use them.

Encyclopedia: a book or set of books containing articles that give factual information about many different subjects—people, places, events, and things. The articles are arranged in alphabetical order according to main subject.

Almanac: a book that lists or briefly states facts about every country, including its population, area, geography, type of government, religions, industries, and currency. An almanac may also include many other kinds of information. Almanacs are published every year so that the information is kept up-to-date.

Atlas: a collection of maps.

Gazetteer: a geographical dictionary containing the names and locations of countries, cities, rivers, lakes, mountains, deserts, and other places.

6. The best source of information on the life of Muhammad is _____.
   - Ⓐ a dictionary
   - Ⓑ an encyclopedia
   - Ⓒ a gazetteer
   - Ⓓ an atlas

7. To find the distance between Giza and Cairo, you would look in
   - Ⓐ a gazetteer   Ⓒ a dictionary
   - Ⓑ an almanac   Ⓓ an atlas

8. If you wanted to read about the Suez Canal, you would look in an encyclopedia under _____.
   - Ⓐ S   Ⓒ M
   - Ⓑ C   Ⓓ T

9. In a gazetteer, you could find out
   - Ⓐ the population of Libya
   - Ⓑ who Ferdinand de Lesseps was
   - Ⓒ where the Anatolian peninsula was located
   - Ⓓ how to pronounce *calligraphy*

10. If you wanted to quickly compare the current populations of Israel, Turkey, Iran, and Afghanistan, the best place to look would be
   - Ⓐ an encyclopedia
   - Ⓑ a gazetteer
   - Ⓒ a dictionary
   - Ⓓ an almanac

ESSAY TEST

Directions: Write a response to items 1–4.

> **REMINDER:** Read and think about each item before you write your response. Be sure to think of the points you want to cover, details that support your response, and reasons for your opinions. Then, on the lines below, write your response in complete sentences.

1. Why was the Suez Canal built?

A satisfactory response should include the following statements:

• The Suez Canal connects the Red Sea and the Mediterranean Sea.

• The canal became an important link in trade between Europe, the Middle East, and Asia.

An excellent response might also discuss the building of the canal by Ferdinand de Lesseps

2. What is Islam?

A satisfactory response should include the following statements:

• Islam is a major religion founded by the prophet Muhammad.

• Muhammad received the teachings of Allah, which were written in the Koran.

• Muhammad and his followers spread Islam throughout the Middle East and North Africa.

An excellent response might also include specific examples from the life of Muhammad, the practices and teachings of Muslims, or Islamic culture.

ESSAY TEST (continued)

3. What did European crusaders hope to achieve?

A satisfactory response should include the following statements:

• People joined the Crusades to win control of Jerusalem from the Muslims.

• European knights believed that they could win glory and riches by fighting Muslims.

• Pope Urban II encouraged people to fight for religious reasons.

An excellent response might also include

• specific examples

• the results of specific Crusades

• statements that reflect independent thinking.

4. What were the goals of Iran's Islamic revolution?

A satisfactory response should include the following statements:

• People in Iran believed that the shah's policy of modernization was weakening their religion.

• They also objected to political oppression.

• The Iranian people forced the shah from power and established the Islamic Republic of Iran.

• Although the Islamic republic has an elected president and legislature, final authority rests with the chief religious leader.

An excellent response might also

• provide specific examples of Iranian society before or after the revolution

• include the terms *mullah, ayatollah,* and *shah*

• identify Reza Pahlavi, Ruhollah Khomeini, Hashemi Rafsanjani.

TEACHER NOTES

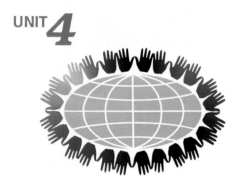

MULTICULTURAL PERSPECTIVES

The Quest for Knowledge

(pages 395–399)

With the rise of Islam came an increase in the level of scientific discovery. African Islamic patrons and scholars founded the first universities in Cairo, Egypt; Granada, Seville, and Córdoba, in Spain; and Carthage, in present-day Tunisia.

One of the most famous of the learning centers was Dar el-Hikma, "The House of Wisdom," built in Cairo, Egypt, around A.D. 1005. The academic contributions that came from this center continued a 4,000-year Egyptian tradition and were later studied by the scientists of the European Renaissance.

The cities of Gao and Jenné in the West African kingdom of Mali were prominent learning centers. Doctors at Jenné became famous for their surgical skills.

The Muslims are credited with founding these institutions, and Arabic was the dominant language of learning in much the same way that English is today. However, scientists were of many other religions as well, including Judaism, Christianity, and Hinduism.

Point out to students that scientists and scientific discoveries today come from many cultures, just as they did in ancient times. Have students look through magazines and newspapers to find issues and concerns that are of importance to scientists today.

You or your students may want to write to the corporate communications or public relations departments of large pharmaceutical or technology-oriented companies. These companies often have biographical material that is of interest to teachers and students.

Optional Activities

THE MIDDLE EAST AND NORTH AFRICA

The history of the Middle East and North Africa has been significantly influenced by religion. The unique geography of this region has also had a major impact on the people who live here.

▶ *The Sahara, the world's largest desert, is about the size of the United States and is nearly as large as the entire continent of Europe.*

A Mingling of Cultures
(pages 409–410)

Bring in a series of news articles about the Arab-Israeli conflict in the Middle East. Read the headlines to the class.

Lead a discussion about the conflict between Arabs and Jews in the Middle East. Ask students how they think the conflict started and what they feel might be some possible solutions to the problem. How do they feel about the continuing hostilities between these peoples? What is being gained? What is being lost?

In spite of the conflict between Arabs and Jews, these two peoples possess many cultural similarities. They have lived together and interacted for more than 13 centuries.

Islam, like Christianity, grew out of Judaism. Thus the Koran has numerous references to biblical characters and stories that have been handed down through oral tradition. According to David Shipler, author of *Arab and Jew: Wounded Spirits in a Promised Land* (New York: Random House, 1986), the Old Testament of the Bible describes customs that are still very much a part of Arab life today.

Obtain a copy of *Arab and Jew: Wounded Spirits in a Promised Land*. Share with your students some of the interesting information found in Chapter 13, "A Mingling of Cultures."

Have students write essays entitled "One Day We'll Get Together," predicting what the Middle East and the world might be like if the Arabs and Jews were at peace.

Geography of the Middle East and North Africa

(pp. 356-375)

Chapter Theme: The people of the Middle East and North Africa have learned to use the gifts of nature to survive in their unique geographic environment.

CHAPTER RESOURCES
Review Master Booklet
  Reviewing Chapter Vocabulary, p. 93
  Place Geography, p. 94
  Summarizing the Chapter, p. 95
Chapter 13 Test

LESSON **1** **The Peoples of the Middle East and North Africa**

(pp. 356-362)

Theme: The history of North Africa has been closely linked with that of the Middle East because they both lie in the middle of a great land mass formed by Asia, Europe, and Africa.

LESSON RESOURCES
Workbook, p. 80
Review Master Booklet
  Understanding the Lesson, p. 90

LESSON **2** **The Lands of the Middle East and North Africa**

(pp. 363-366)

Theme: The lands of the Middle East and North Africa include deserts, plateaus, mountains, great rivers, and the Dead Sea, which is the lowest place on the Earth's surface.

LESSON RESOURCES
Workbook, p. 81
Review Master Booklet
  Understanding the Lesson, p. 91

LESSON **3** **Resources of the Middle East and North Africa**

(pp. 367-373)

Theme: The resources of the Middle East and North Africa include oil, water, dry-land animals such as camels and donkeys, and a good location for trade.

LESSON RESOURCES
Workbook, pp. 82-83
Review Master Booklet
  Understanding the Lesson, p. 92

 SOCIAL STUDIES LIBRARY: *Money*

Review Masters

Review Study the terms in the box. Use your Glossary to find definitions of those you do not remember.

Bedouin	labor force	per capita income	wadi
ground water	migration	petroleum	

Practice Complete the paragraphs using terms from the box above. You may change the forms of the terms to fit the meaning.

Some countries in the Middle East have large reserves of oil, while others do not. In oil-rich countries such as Saudi Arabia and Kuwait, the (1) _____ per capita income _____ is very high. Using income from the sale of oil, the governments of these countries now provide better services for their people.

In countries without large oil reserves, most of the people in the (2) _____ labor force _____ work in agriculture. Because much of the land in the Middle East is desert, farmers have learned to make use of (3) _____ ground water _____ rather than rain to grow their crops. A few people raise animals in this dry region. The (4) _____ Bedouins _____ find water and pasture for their animals at oases. Here, the animals graze until no food is left, and then they are moved to a new location.

Write Write a sentence of your own for each term in the box above. You may use the back of the sheet.

Sentences should show that students understand the meanings of the terms.

_____

_____

_____

_____

_____

_____

_____

_____

_____

_____

_____

✻ The Middle East and North Africa lie in the middle of a great land mass formed by three continents—Asia, Europe, and Africa. Listed below are cities in some of the countries that make up this region. Use the Gazetteer in your textbook to find the latitude and longitude of each place. Then locate and label each on the map.

	LAT. ⊖	LONG. ⊕			LAT. ⊖	LONG. ⊕
1. Algiers, Algeria	37°N	3°E	6. Jerusalem, Israel		32°N	35°E
2. Baghdad, Iraq	33°N	44°E	7. Rabat, Morocco		34°N	7°W
3. Cairo, Egypt	30°N	31°E	8. Tehran, Iran		36°N	51°E
4. Damascus, Syria	34°N	36°E	9. Tripoli, Libya		33°N	13°E
5. Istanbul, Turkey	41°N	29°E	10. Tunis, Tunisia		37°N	10°E

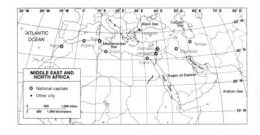

MIDDLE EAST AND NORTH AFRICA
◉ National capitals
• Other city

✻ Complete this graphic organizer. Next to each main idea write three statements that support it.

CHAPTER THEME The people of the Middle East and North Africa have learned to use the gifts of nature to survive in their unique geographic environment.

LESSON 1 **The peoples of the Middle East and North Africa are alike and different.**	1. They do similar work. 2. They use the same alphabet. 3. Different dialects and languages
LESSON 2 **The Middle East and North Africa have many geographical features.**	1. Deserts make up a large part of the region. 2. Abundance of sea water around the region 3. Mountain ranges rise from the Anatolian and Iranian plateaus.
LESSON 3 **The Middle East and North Africa have many resources.**	1. A large part of the world's petroleum supply comes from the region. 2. Water is an important resource. 3. Donkeys, camels, sheep, and goats help people make use of the dry lands.

C13-B

Workbook Pages

Page 80

POPULATION CHANGES IN THE MIDDLE EAST

Understanding Pictographs, Recognizing Cause and Effect

✳ Study the pictograph of population in Middle East countries. Then complete the statements.

Population of Middle East countries in 1984 and 1989.

Algeria	1984	🧍🧍🧍🧍
	1989	🧍🧍🧍🧍
Egypt	1984	🧍🧍🧍🧍🧍🧍🧍🧍🧍
	1989	🧍🧍🧍🧍🧍🧍🧍🧍🧍🧍
Saudi Arabia	1984	🧍🧍🧍
	1989	🧍🧍🧍
Iran	1984	🧍🧍🧍🧍🧍🧍🧍🧍🧍
	1989	🧍🧍🧍🧍🧍🧍🧍🧍🧍🧍
Libya	1984	🧍
	1989	🧍

= 5 million people

1. Each of the large figures on the pictograph stands for ____5 million people____

2. The period of time covered by the pictograph is ____5 years, from 1984 to 1989____

3. The Middle East country shown with the largest population in 1984 was ____Egypt____

4. The country shown with the smallest population is ____Libya____, which had fewer than ____5 million____ in both 1984 and 1989.

5. ____Saudi Arabia____ and ____Libya____ had the smallest growth in population of the countries shown from 1984 to 1989.

6. ____Iran____ had a population growth of about 10 million in the 5 years shown.

7. ____All the countries____ had a population increase in the five-year period shown.

Thinking Further: What impact do you think the increase in population has on the economy of a country?

Possible answer: A country needs a greater supply of food, water, housing, clothing, and jobs to meet the needs of a growing population.

© Silver, Burdett & Ginn Inc.

Page 81

THE VASTNESS OF THE DESERTS

Analyzing a Bar Graph, Recognizing Relative Size, Identifying a Problem

✳ The bar graph below shows how much land in some countries of North Africa and the Middle East is desert. Study the graph, and then answer the questions.

Desert Land in North Africa and the Middle East

Countries: Algeria, Egypt, Iran, Libya, Saudi Arabia

Sq. Miles in Thousands (100–1,000)

☐ Desert ▨ Other Land Area

1. Which of the countries shown has the largest total land area? ____Algeria____

2. Which of the countries shown contains the largest area of desert? ____Saudi Arabia____

3. Which country has the smallest total land area? ____Egypt____

4. Which country has the smallest desert area? ____Iran____

5. Which two countries have the smallest areas of non-desert land? ____Libya and Saudi Arabia____

✳ How do the land areas in these countries compare to sizes of American states? Draw a line from each area on the left to the state closest to it in size. One state is used twice.

Desert area of Algeria ——— Indiana, 36,185 square miles

Total land area of Egypt ——— California, 158,706 square miles

Total land area of Iran ——— Alaska, 586,412 square miles

Non-desert land of Algeria ——— Texas, 266,807 square miles

Desert land of Iran

Thinking Further: What part of a country's economy is most affected if large areas of the country are desert? Give a reason for your answer.

Answers may mention agriculture, because crops cannot be grown in desert land without irrigation.

© Silver, Burdett & Ginn Inc.

Page 82

TRACING THE PATHS OF TRADE

Making and Analyzing a Table, Summarizing Information

✳ Read the article below about import and export trade by nations in North Africa and the Middle East. Use the information in the article to complete the table on the facing page.

Trade has long been important to nations of North Africa and the Middle East. It is a major part of the economy of most countries. Algeria exports a total of over $8 billion worth of goods. Its major trading partners are the United States, France, Germany, and Spain. Algeria imports nearly $8 billion in goods. Major sources of imports are France, Belgium, Italy, the Netherlands, Germany, Canada, and the United States.

Egypt exports over $3 billion worth of goods to the United States, Japan, Italy, Germany, France, the United Kingdom, and Israel. Egypt's imports amount to over $11 billion. Most of these goods come from the United States, Germany, France, Japan, the Netherlands, the United Kingdom, and Italy.

Saudi Arabia's exports amount to over $26 billion. Major buyers are the United States and Japan. Imports amount to over $24 billion, with the United States, Japan, and Germany as major trading partners.

✳ Use the information on the table to answer the questions below.

1. Which countries on the table are major trading partners of the United States? ____Algeria, Egypt, Saudi Arabia____

2. Which country on the table has no major trade with Japan? ____Algeria____

3. Which country's imports exceed its exports by $8 billion? ____Egypt____

4. Which country's exports exceed its imports by about $2 billion? ____Saudi Arabia____

5. Which of the countries that Algeria trades with do not receive many of Algeria's exports? ____Belgium, Italy, Netherlands, Canada____

Thinking Further: Which total, imports or exports, is probably the greatest when a country has a strong economy? Give a reason for your answer.

Possible answer: A nation with a strong economy has more exports than imports because the country has more to sell than it needs to buy.

© Silver, Burdett & Ginn Inc.

Page 83

TRACING THE PATHS OF TRADE CONTINUED

Country	Exports to:	Value of Exports (dollars)	Imports From:	Value of Imports (dollars)
Algeria	United States France Germany Spain	$8 billion	France Belgium Italy Netherlands Germany Canada United States	$8 billion
Egypt	United States Japan Italy Germany France United Kingdom Israel	$3 billion	United States Germany France Japan Netherlands United Kingdom Italy	$11 billion
Saudi Arabia	United States Japan	$26 billion	United States Japan Germany	$24 billion

© Silver, Burdett & Ginn Inc.

C13-C

TEACHER NOTES

The Peoples of the Middle East and North Africa

Objectives

★ 1. **Explain** what the Middle East and North Africa have in common.

2. **Describe** where these people live and what kind of work they do.

3. **List** the similarities between the Roman alphabet and the Arabic alphabet.

4. **Identify** the following people and places: *Scheherazade, Bedouins, Arabs, Middle East, North Africa,* and the *Arabian Peninsula.*

1 STARTING THE LESSON

Motivation Activity

■ Ask students to what area of the world they think the term *Middle East* refers.

■ Have students write down five things that they think of when they hear this term.

■ Give students an opportunity to share their lists with their classmates.

Think About What You Know

■ Assign the THINK ABOUT WHAT YOU KNOW activity on p. 357

■ Student answers should reflect independent thinking but may include Sumerians, Egyptians, Israelites, Philistines, and Carthaginians.

Study the Vocabulary

■ Ask students if they know the definitions of any of the lesson's new vocabulary words.

■ Have the students look up each of the words in the Glossary to see if they were using the correct definitions.

356

CHAPTER 13

GEOGRAPHY OF THE MIDDLE EAST AND NORTH AFRICA

Much of the region of the Middle East and North Africa is desert. The Sahara, which is nearly as large as the entire continent of Europe, extends across North Africa from the Atlantic coast to the Red Sea.

356

Optional Activities

Current Events

● Have students start current-events notebooks, to be kept during the study of this unit.

● Tell students to collect articles about the Middle East and North Africa from newspapers and magazines and to write summaries of them.

● At the end of each week, set aside some class time to review and discuss with students important events in the region.

The Peoples of the Middle East and North Africa

THINK ABOUT WHAT YOU KNOW

In earlier chapters you learned about the ancient civilizations in the Middle East and North Africa. What peoples can you think of who were in these lands during ancient times?

STUDY THE VOCABULARY

migration   Bedouin
labor force

FOCUS YOUR READING

How are the peoples of the Middle East and North Africa alike, and how are they different?

A. Tales from Many Lands

The tales in *Arabian Nights* are among the world's best-known stories. These tales are supposed to be ones told by Scheherazade (shuh her uh ZAH duh), the clever wife of a cruel king. Scheherazade was by no means the first of the king's wives. He had had many wives, and he had distrusted them all. Every day he chose another wife and then had her head chopped off the following morning.

Scheherazade wished to escape the fate of the other wives, so she thought of a plan. On the night after her marriage, she started telling the king a story. The king became very interested in her marvelous tale, but just when she reached the most interesting part of the story, the sun came up. Scheherazade said that she would continue the story that night if the king would allow her to live. The king, eager to know how the story ended, let her live another day so that she could finish the tale.

That night, Scheherazade finished the first story and then began to tell an even more wonderful tale. But once again, dawn came before she finished, and the clever young woman said she would finish the story that night if the king let her live. Again the king said, "I will not kill her until I have heard the rest of this truly remarkable tale!" And so it went on, night after night. Finally the king realized that a wife who knew such stories was a true treasure. He never again threatened to take her life.

Some of the stories told by Scheherazade are very famous. You can read an excerpt from "The Voyages of Sinbad" on page 358. Not all the stories in *Arabian Nights* are Arabian. The book is, instead, a collection of

Scheherazade told her husband, the king, marvelous stories.
▶ In what book can we find some of these wonderful tales?

357

2 DEVELOPING THE LESSON

Read and Think
Section A

Review the role of Scheherazade in *Arabian Nights* by asking students the following questions:

1. **Why is Scheherazade described as a clever woman?**
   (She avoided being killed by her husband by telling him stories each night and leaving them unfinished. *p. 357*)

2. **What is *Arabian Nights*?**
   (A collection of tales told by Scheherazade that include stories from different lands and peoples in the Middle East and North Africa *pp. 357-359*)

   Thinking Critically Why, do you think, did some of the stories told by Scheherazade become very famous? (Hypothesize)
   (Answers should reflect independent thinking but may include that they are very exciting and full of suspense. *pp. 357-359*)

┌─ **Answers to Caption Questions** ─
p. 357 ▶ The *Arabian Nights*

For Your Information

A Thousand and One Nights   Experts believe that the stories of the *Arabian Nights* were originally folk tales from many different lands, including India, Egypt, and Greece. The stories were first collected and then given the framework of the tale of Scheherazade. Originally, there were perhaps only a few hundred stories, and the title was only meant to show a large number. Later, however, more stories were added to bring the total up to 1,001.

Optional Activities

357

Use the information below to help students better understand the literature selection found on p. 358.

Selection Summary

In the tale of Sinbad the Sailor, Sinbad, a wealthy merchant from the city of Baghdad, entertains his friends with the story of how he found, lost, and regained vast riches during his seven exciting sea voyages. In addition to encountering the cannibal giant described in the excerpt, Sinbad confronts a roc—a legendary bird so big that it can hold an elephant in its claws—and a whale. Sinbad and his shipmates escape from the cannibal by blinding him and then hiding from him.

Guided Reading

1. **Why was Sinbad horrified by what he saw?**

   (The pile of human bones and the roasting spit indicated that the creature ate humans.)

2. **What did the creature look like?**

   (He was very tall, with one eye in the middle of his forehead. He had long, sharp teeth, ears like an elephant, and nails like the claws of a fierce bird.)

Literature–Social Studies Connection

1. **Why, do you think, did the author choose Baghdad as Sinbad's home town?**

   (Answers should reflect independent thinking but may include that Baghdad was the richest city of the time and that the author wanted Sinbad to seem very rich.)

358

FROM: **Arabian Nights**

Translated by: Andrew Lang
Setting: A strange island

The *Arabian Nights*, or *The Thousand and One Nights*, is a collection of stories from many parts of the East. There were people long ago whose profession it was to amuse others by telling tales. At last, a storyteller wrote down the tales, which have since been translated into many languages.

Sinbad the Sailor, a famous character from an *Arabian Nights* tale, journeyed to unknown seas and adventures. He was shipwrecked seven times during his many voyages. In the passage below he describes an encounter with a creature during his third voyage.

Pushing back the heavy ebony doors we entered the courtyard, but upon the threshold of the great hall beyond it we paused, frozen with horror, at the sight which greeted us. On one side lay a huge pile of bones—human bones, and on the other numberless spits for roasting! Overcome with despair we sank trembling to the ground, and lay there without speech or motion. The sun was setting when a loud noise aroused us, the door of the hall was violently burst open and a horrible giant entered. He was as tall as a palm tree, . . . and had one eye, which flamed like a burning coal in the middle of his forehead. His teeth were long and sharp and grinned horribly, while his lower lip hung down upon his chest, and he had ears like [an] elephant's ears, which covered his shoulders, and nails like the claws of some fierce bird.

At this terrible sight our senses left us and we lay like dead men. . . . we lay shivering with horror the whole night through, and when day broke he awoke and went out, leaving us in the castle.

Curriculum Connection

Literature Ask students to complete the story of Sinbad's third voyage.

- Have each student write three additional paragraphs that could be added to the Literature Selection on p. 358.

- Tell students to describe how Sinbad escaped from the creature and the land where the creature resided.

- When students have finished writing, ask for volunteers to read their story endings to the class.

THE MIDDLE EAST AND NORTH AFRICA: PHYSICAL

Nile River

The world's largest desert, the Sahara, and the world's longest river, the Nile, are both found in North Africa.
▶ What Egyptian city lies along the Nile?

Map labels: 20°W, 10°W, 0°, 10°E, 20°E, 30°E, 40°E, 50°E, 60°E, 70°E, 80°E
ATLANTIC OCEAN, Strait of Gibraltar, MOROCCO, WESTERN SAHARA (MOROCCO), MAURITANIA, MALI, ALGERIA, TUNISIA, ATLAS MTS., LIBYA, SAHARA, AHAGGAR MTS., Tropic of Cancer, Equator, Mediterranean Sea, Aegean Sea, Black Sea, BULGARIA, GREECE, Istanbul, TURKEY, ANATOLIAN PLATEAU, Mt. Ararat 16,945 ft (5,165 m), Caspian Sea, Aral Sea, UZBEKISTAN, TAJIKISTAN, TURKMENISTAN, 40°N, Mt. Damāvand 18,934 ft (5,771 m), ZAGROS MTS., ELBURZ MTS., IRAN, IRANIAN PLATEAU, AFGHANISTAN, SYRIA, LEBANON, ISRAEL, Baghdad, IRAQ, JORDAN, Gulf of Sidra, Suez Canal, Cairo, EGYPT, LIBYAN DESERT, Red Sea, Persian Gulf, KUWAIT, BAHRAIN, QATAR, U.A.E., SAUDI ARABIA, ARABIAN PENINSULA, OMAN, Arabian Sea, YEMEN, Gulf of Aden, 30°, 20°, 10°
U.A.E. -UNITED ARAB EMIRATES

• Cities
▲ Mountain peaks

Elevations
Feet / Meters
10,000 — 3,000
5,000 — 1,500
2,000 — 600
1,000 — 300
0 — 0
Land below sea level

0   300   600 miles
0   300   600 kilometers

---

tales from different lands and peoples. The word *Arabian* in the title refers to the Arabic language, the language in which the collected stories are written. The book was created about a thousand years ago.

B. Linking the Middle East with North Africa

Naming the Region The lands from which the *Arabian Nights* stories came are located in the Middle East and North

Africa. The term *Middle East* was invented by western Europeans as a name for southwestern Asia. The Middle East and North Africa lie in the middle of a great land mass formed by three continents—Asia, Europe, and Africa. The region is called the Middle East to distinguish it from the Far East, a region that contains the lands of East Asia.

The history of the Middle East has been closely linked with that of North

359

Read and Think
Sections C and D

Discuss the population and languages of the Middle East and North Africa with your students by asking the following questions:

1. **Where does the greater part of the population of the Middle East and North Africa live?**
(In urban areas *p. 360*)

2. **Describe the life of the Bedouins.**
(They are nomadic herders who live in tents and move about on the desert and dry grasslands in search of water and pasture for their animals. *p. 360*)

3. **What is the language of most of the countries in the Middle East and North Africa?**
(Arabic *p. 361*)

4. **How are the Arabic and Roman alphabets similar?**
(Both are used to write a variety of languages. *p. 362*)

Thinking Critically Imagine that you are a Bedouin. What, do you think, would you like and dislike about this lifestyle? (Evaluate)
(Answers should reflect independent thinking but may include liking the exposure to different places and different people and disliking the instability of the lifestyle. *p. 360*)

Africa. These lands have similar climates, even though they stretch across two continents. The map on page 359 shows the two areas, which extend from Morocco in the west to Afghanistan in the east. Turkey is the northernmost country, and Yemen is the country farthest south.

The Region's History The Middle East and North Africa have a very long history. You have already read about the beginnings of civilization in Egypt and in Mesopotamia, which is now Iraq. You have also read that much of the Middle East and North Africa had been a part of the empires of the Roman emperors and of Alexander the Great. The land of Persia, which Alexander conquered, is now known as Iran. Some of the descendants of the ancient peoples still live in the region.

Like Europe, North Africa and the Middle East is a region with a variety of peoples and more than 20 nations. Over the centuries there has been a **migration** of peoples to this middle region from other parts of Asia, Europe, and Africa. Migration is the movement from one place to another. Some of the descendants of the peoples who migrated also make up part of the present-day population.

C. Where People Live and Work

City Dwellers At one time most people of the Middle East and North Africa were farmers or herders. Today the greater part of the population is urban. There are 17 cities that have a million or more people. Cairo in Egypt, Tehran in Iran, and Istanbul in Turkey rank among the world's largest cities. As you can see by looking at the population density map on the next page, some of the large cities in this region are very crowded.

Farmers Even though there are more city dwellers, many people still live in rural villages and work on the land, as did their ancestors. In Egypt, 40 percent of the **labor force**, the working population, works in agriculture. Farmers are a large part of the labor force in a number of countries in the region.

Nomads A very small part of the population are still nomadic herders. The nomads of the Middle East and North Africa are usually known as **Bedouins** (BED oo-ihnz), an Arabic term meaning "desert dwellers." The Bedouins live in tents so that they can easily move about on the desert and dry grasslands in the endless search for water and pasture for their herds of sheep, goats, and camels.

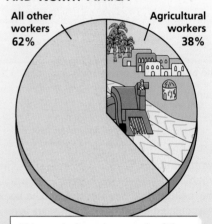

WORKERS IN THE MIDDLE EAST AND NORTH AFRICA

All other workers 62%   Agricultural workers 38%

This graph shows how much of the labor force in the Middle East and North Africa works in agriculture.
► What percentage of workers do not work in agriculture?

Identifying Mountain Ranges

- Have students refer to the map on p. 359 to complete the following activities.
- Have them identify the highest point in the Middle East and North Africa (Mt. Ararat).
- Have them identify the major mountain ranges of these regions (Atlas Mountains, Ahaggar Mountains, Agros Mountains, and Elburz Mountains).
- You may wish to conclude this activity by asking students to generalize about the land of North Africa and the Middle East. (It is mostly desert with some mountains.)

SKILLBUILDER REVIEW

- Have students practice this skill by using the population density map on p. 361 and the time zone map on p. 350 to answer these questions.

1. **If a telegram were sent from Casablanca at 8:00 A.M., at what time would it be received in Damascus?**
(10:00 A.M.)

2. **If a telephone call were placed to you from Cairo at midnight, at what time would you receive the call at home?**
(Answers should reflect students' time zones.)

THE MIDDLE EAST AND NORTH AFRICA: POPULATION DENSITY

Map showing the Middle East and North Africa with population density, national capitals, and other cities.

Labels visible on map: ANTIC, OCEAN, Strait of Gibraltar, Casablanca, Rabat, Oran, Algiers, Tunis, MOROCCO, TUNISIA, ALGERIA, Tripoli, LIBYA, MALI, MAURITANIA, ERN ARA (CCO), NIGER, CHAD, SUDAN, EGYPT, Alexandria, Giza, Cairo, ISRAEL, JORDAN, Amman, Tropic of Cancer, Riyadh, SAUDI ARABIA, Jidda, YEMEN, Gulf of Aden, OMAN, QATAR, U.A.E., BAHRAIN, KUWAIT, Strait of Hormuz, Gulf of Oman, Arabian Sea, PAKISTAN, IRAN, Isfahan, Baghdad, IRAQ, Tehran, Mashhad, Kabul, AFGHANISTAN, Tabriz, SYRIA, Damascus, Beirut, Aleppo, LEBANON, Adana, Ankara, Izmir, TURKEY, ARMENIA, AZERBAIJAN, GEORGIA, Istanbul, Black Sea, BULGARIA, GREECE, Aegean Sea, Mediterranean Sea, UZBEKISTAN, TURKMENISTAN, TAJIKISTAN, Caspian Sea, Aral Sea, Red Sea, Gulf.

Legend:
Persons per
0 square 1 kilometer
1
10
50
100
200

◇ National capitals
● Other cities

0   400   800 miles
0   400   800 kilometers

THE 25 LARGEST CITIES OF THE MIDDLE EAST AND NORTH AFRICA

City	Population
...t)	6,205,000
...)	5,752,000
...rkey)	5,495,000
...aq)	4,649,000
...Egypt)	2,821,000
...key)	2,252,000
...(Morocco)	2,139,000
Algiers (Algeria)	1,722,000
Giza (Egypt)	1,608,000
Beirut (Lebanon)	1,500,000
İzmir (Turkey)	1,490,000
Jidda (Saudi Arabia)	1,308,000
Damascus (Syria)	1,259,000
Aleppo (Syria)	1,173,000
Isfahan (Iran)	1,121,000
Mashhad (Iran)	1,103,000
Kabul (Afghanistan)	1,036,000
Riyadh (Saudi Arabia)	1,000,000
Tabrîz (Iran)	929,000
Tripoli (Libya)	859,000
Amman (Jordan)	800,000
Adana (Turkey)	776,000
Oran (Algeria)	664,000
Tunis (Tunisia)	597,000
Rabat (Morocco)	519,000

The area of highest population density in the Middle East and North Africa is found in Egypt.
► Along which river in Egypt is the population highest?

D. The Arabic Language and Alphabet

Arabic Alphabet Arabic is the language of most countries in the Middle East and North Africa. Arabic-speaking people are often called Arabs, even though most of them do not live on the Arabian Peninsula.

Arabic is written with an alphabet of 28 letters, which differ from those of the Roman alphabet. In Arabic the first line of a paragraph is indented on the right rather than on the left. This is because Arabic is written from right to left rather than from left to right, as are the words on this page.

361

Reteaching Main Objective

Explain what the Middle East and North Africa have in common.

● Have each student divide a sheet of paper into three vertical columns.

● Tell students to label their columns with the following headings: *Land, People,* and *Language.*

● Then ask students to complete the chart by showing how the Middle East and North Africa are similar.

● Compare responses and create a summary chart on the chalkboard for students to copy.

Optional Activities

---

3 CLOSING THE LESSON

Lesson 1 Review

Answers to Think and Write
A. Scheherazade would tell him part of a story one night and then would complete the story the next night.

B. Migration has produced variety.

C. Most people in the Middle East and North Africa live in cities, but many live and work on farms, and some are still nomadic herders.

D. The Arabic alphabet is used in the Middle East and North Africa, and Arabic, Persian, and Hebrew are among the languages spoken there.

Answer to Skills Check
Rabat: 519,000 people, 125 to 250 people per sq mi; Alexandria: 2,821,000 people, 500 or more people per sq. mi; Tripoli: 859,000 people, 25 to 125 people per sq mi; Isfahan: 1,121,000 people, 25 to 125 people per sq mi.

Focus Your Reading
Ask the lesson focus question found at the beginning of the lesson: **How are the peoples of the Middle East and North Africa alike, and how are they different?**
(They use the same alphabet, do similar work, and live in cities and rural villages, but they speak different dialects and different languages.)

Additional Practice
You may wish to assign the ancillary materials listed below.

Understanding the Lesson p. 90

This writing shows how Arabic letters differ from the letters in the Roman alphabet.
▶ Why is the first line of this paragraph indented on the right?

As you have learned, an alphabet can be used to write more than one language. The Roman alphabet is used to write a variety of European languages, such as Spanish and Italian. The Arabic alphabet, too, is used for writing different languages. It is the second most widely used alphabet in the world. Both Persian and the language of Afghanistan are written with Arabic letters.

Arabic Language Written Arabic is much the same in all Arab countries, but the dialects, or forms of the same language, differ from one country to another. Some Arabic dialects differ so greatly that people who speak one dialect can hardly understand people who speak another. An English woman who had learned to read Arabic discovered that when she first visited an Arab country and listened to people talk, she "understood about one word in a hundred."

Not all peoples of the Middle East and North Africa speak Arabic. Hebrew is the language of the people of Israel. The Iranians speak Persian, and the people of Afghanistan speak a language closely related to Persian. The people of Turkey also have their own distinctive language. The Middle East and North Africa make up a large region that has a variety of languages, histories, as well as lands and resources, which you will read about later in this chapter.

LESSON **1** REVIEW

THINK AND WRITE
A. How did Scheherazade prevent the king from killing her? **(Recall)**
B. Why is there a variety of peoples in the Middle East and North Africa? **(Recall)**
C. Where do people live and work today in the Middle East and North Africa? **(Recall)**
D. What alphabet and languages are used in the Middle East and North Africa?
(Recall)

SKILLS CHECK

MAP SKILL

Look at the population density map on page 361. What are the population and population density for the following cities: Rabat, Morroco; Alexandria, Egypt; Tripoli, Libya; Isfahan, Iran?

Optional Activities

UNDERSTANDING THE LESSON

NAME _____ CHAPTER
UNDERSTANDING THE LESSON **13**

Organizing Facts LESSON 1 CONTENT MASTER

✱ The chart shows the main ideas of the lesson. Fill in the blank spaces with the details that support each main idea. Some have been done for you.

Different peoples contributed to stories in the *Arabian Nights.*	Four countries mark the boundaries of the Middle East and North Africa.
1. Arabs	1. Morocco in the west
2. Iranians	2. Afghanistan in the east
3. Turks	3. Turkey in the north
4. Egyptians	4. The two Yemens in the south

The Middle East and North Africa: A Large, Diverse Region

In the Middle East and North Africa, people live in cities and rural areas.	The region's peoples speak various languages.
1. Most of population is urban.	1. Most people speak Arabic.
2. Seventeen cities have over 1 million people	2. Hebrew is the language of Israel.
3. Many people still live in villages.	3. Iranians speak Persian
4. Some people are still nomadic herders.	4. Afghan language is close to Persian
	5. Turks speak Turkish

Think and Write: Do you know a language other than English? Do you know someone who does? In a paragraph, describe this other language—what it sounds like, what it looks like when written. You may use the back of the sheet.
Answers should reflect independent thinking; suggestions appear in the Answer Key.

90 Use with textbook pages 557–562.

◀ **Review Master Booklet, p. 90**

The Lands of the Middle East and North Africa

The Lands of the Middle East and North Africa

THINK ABOUT WHAT YOU KNOW
Imagine that you are standing in the middle of a desert. What five adjectives would you use to describe the desert?

STUDY THE VOCABULARY
wadi

FOCUS YOUR READING
What are the main geographical features of the region of the Middle East and North Africa?

A. From Deserts to Seas

Deserts Perhaps you think of a desert as a sandy wasteland where winds blow the sand into shifting dunes. Some deserts are like that, but less than a third of the world's deserts are sandy wastelands. Though many deserts are bare and rocky, some deserts have hardy plants that need little moisture.

Deserts are lands that average less than 10 inches (25 cm) of precipitation a year. Although precipitation is rare in deserts, rainstorms sometimes do occur. During one of these rare downpours, waters may rise rapidly in dry stream beds called **wadis** (WAH deez). Travelers who have carelessly camped in a dry wadi have been known to drown in the desert. Water can also be found in the desert in an oasis, which is a place where there is water from wells or springs.

Deserts make up a large part of the Middle East and North Africa. The Sahara, the world's largest desert, extends across North Africa from the Atlantic coast to the Red Sea. The Sahara is nearly as large as the entire continent of Europe. The Arabian Peninsula is not much more than the

These people are harvesting squash in the Sinai desert in Israel.
► How can farming be accomplished in a desert?

For Your Information

Deserts of the Middle East and North Africa

People often think of deserts as land covered with sand dunes where no plants grow. However, dunes make up only about one third of the Sahara and one third of the Arabian Peninsula. The rest of the land is covered with rocks, stones or gravel, and plants that need little moisture.

Temperatures tend to be extreme in these deserts. At Riyadh, in the center of the Arabian Peninsula, temperatures rise to 100° F (38° C) on most days from March through September. The dry desert air, however, cools very quickly after the sun goes down. On an average January day, the high temperature is about 70° F (21° C) and the low temperature is about 46° F (8° C).

The Lands of the Middle East and North Africa

Objectives

★1. **Describe** the main geographical features of the Middle East and North Africa.

2. **Explain** how elevation affects the climate of Middle East lands.

3. **Identify** the following places: *Sahara, Arabian Desert, Mediterranean Sea, Black Sea, Caspian Sea, Arabian Sea, Red Sea, Zagros Mountains, and Elburz Mountains.*

1 STARTING THE LESSON

Motivation Activity

■ Tell students that they will be reading about the world's largest desert, the Sahara, in this lesson.

■ Tell them that, much like the rest of the world's deserts, only about 30 percent of the Sahara is covered by sand.

■ Have students volunteer suggestions of what they think the other 70 percent of the Sahara looks like.

Think About What You Know

■ Assign the THINK ABOUT WHAT YOU KNOW activity on p. 363.

■ Student answers should reflect independent thinking but may include hot, dry, dusty, treeless, and endless.

Study the Vocabulary

■ Have students look up the definition of *wadi* in the Glossary.

■ Ask students to write a short, fictional story in which they correctly use the new vocabulary term.

Answers to Caption Questions

p. 362 ► Because Arabic is written from right to left
p. 363 ► With irrigation

Read and Think
Sections A, B, and C

The land, climate, and elevation of the Middle East and North Africa are quite varied. Discuss this with your students by asking the following questions:

1. **Why is it accurate to say that the climate of North Africa and the Middle East is varied?**
(It ranges from a Mediterranean climate along the coastal lands of the Mediterranean to a more severe climate on the high central plateaus. *pp. 364-365*)

2. **What do the Anatolian and Iranian plateaus have in common?**
(Both are rugged or barren lands from which rise hills and mountains. *pp. 364-365*)

3. **What is the lowest place on the surface of the earth?**
(The Dead Sea *p. 366*)

Thinking Critically How do you think the elevation of the Dead Sea affects temperatures in the area around the sea? (Hypothesize)
(Answers should reflect independent thinking but may include that it keeps temperatures high. *p. 366*)

Arabian Desert. Although the Arabian Desert is not as large as the Sahara, it is more than four times the size of France.

Five Seas Just as there is an abundance of desert land within the Middle East and North Africa, there is an abundance of sea water around the region. This region is set among five seas: the Mediterranean, Black, Caspian, Arabian, and Red seas. All the countries in the region except Afghanistan have outlets to the sea.

Climate The coastal lands along the Mediterranean have a climate somewhat like that of the Mediterranean lands of Europe. Winters are cool and rainy; summers are hot and dry. The average January and July temperatures in Algiers, Algeria, in

North Africa, are about the same as those in Athens, Greece. The beaches of Israel and Lebanon are much like the Mediterranean beaches of southern Europe.

B. The Anatolian and Iranian Plateaus

Anatolian Plateau The Anatolian (an uh-TOH lee un) peninsula is located between the Black and Mediterranean seas. It is also called Asia Minor. Look at the physical map on page 359. Notice that the Anatolian peninsula includes the country of Turkey and a small tip of southeastern Europe, where Istanbul is located.

Most of the Anatolian peninsula is a rugged plateau, from which rise hills and mountains. The highest part of the plateau

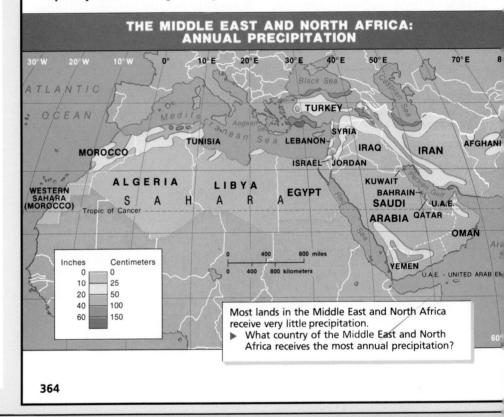

THE MIDDLE EAST AND NORTH AFRICA: ANNUAL PRECIPITATION

Inches	Centimeters
0	0
10	25
20	50
40	100
60	150

Most lands in the Middle East and North Africa receive very little precipitation.
▶ What country of the Middle East and North Africa receives the most annual precipitation?

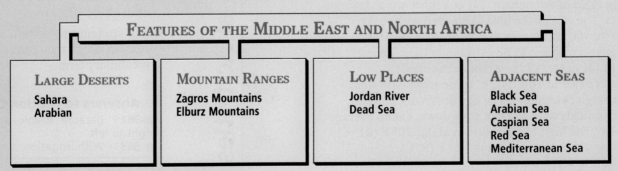

Graphic Organizer

To help students better understand the geography of the Middle East and North Africa, you may wish to use the graphic organizer shown below.

FEATURES OF THE MIDDLE EAST AND NORTH AFRICA

LARGE DESERTS	MOUNTAIN RANGES	LOW PLACES	ADJACENT SEAS
Sahara	Zagros Mountains	Jordan River	Black Sea
Arabian	Elburz Mountains	Dead Sea	Arabian Sea
			Caspian Sea
			Red Sea
			Mediterranean Sea

Optional Activities

Mount Damāvand, located in Iran, is the highest peak in the Elburz Mountains.
▶ How can you tell that the elevation has affected the climate on Mount Damāvand?

is in eastern Turkey. Mount Ararat is located on Turkey's eastern border. The Tigris and Euphrates rivers, the two great rivers of ancient Mesopotamia, rise from sources on the Anatolian plateau.

The lands along the western and southern coasts of the Anatolian peninsula have a climate greatly affected by elevation. Like southern Europe, these lands have a Mediterranean climate. The Black Sea coast is cool, but its climate is mild when compared with that of the high central plateau. Winters are cold and summers hot on the plateau. The land is dry although not dry enough to be called a desert.

Iranian Plateau Mountain ranges rise along the edges of the Iranian plateau, located south of the Caspian Sea. The Zagros (ZAG rus) Mountains separate the plateau

from the plain of the Tigris and Euphrates rivers to the west. The Elburz (el BOORZ) Mountains form a wall between the plateau and the narrow coastland along the Caspian Sea. Find these mountain ranges on the map on page 359.

The climb from the Caspian coast to the plateau is steep. The Caspian is an inland sea about 92 feet (28 m) below sea level. From its low-lying coast one can look up to Mount Damāvand (DAM uh-vand), which rises 18,934 feet (5,771 m) above sea level. Mount Damāvand is higher than Mont Blanc, the highest peak in the Alps.

Elevation greatly affects climate in the lands south of the Caspian Sea. The coast has very heavy summer rainfall, and much of the land is forested. The high plateau has very dry summers, and much of the land is barren desert.

365

Reteaching Main Objective

Describe the main geographical features of the Middle East and North Africa.

● Have students make up riddles about one of the main geographical features of the Middle East and North Africa. For example, "I am located on the Arabian Peninsula and I am four times the size of France. What am I?" (Arabian Desert)

● Have students take turns reading their riddles aloud.

● Tell students that the information in this lesson will help them solve other students' riddles.

Optional Activities

Lesson 2 Review

Answers to Think and Write

A. The important deserts are the Sahara and Arabian deserts. The important seas are the Arabian, Black, Caspian, Mediterranean, and Red seas.

B. The high elevations of these plateaus cause extremely cold winters and very hot summers.

C. The hot desert sun evaporates the water in the Dead Sea, leaving behind large deposits of salt and other minerals.

Answer to Skills Check

The Mediterranean is the largest sea in the world. The Caspian Sea is the largest inland body of water in the world.

Focus Your Reading

Ask the lesson focus question found at the beginning of the lesson: **What are the main geographical features of the Middle East and North Africa?**
(The main features are the deserts, the five seas, the two plateaus, and the Dead Sea, which is the lowest place on earth.)

Additional Practice

You may wish to assign the ancillary materials listed below.

Understanding the Lesson p. 91
Workbook p. 81

366

The mountains and deserts of Afghanistan are located east of the Iranian plateau. The mountains in this rugged land are the highest in the Middle East.

C. The Lowest Place on the Earth's Surface

The Jordan River has the lowest elevation of all the world's rivers. It begins at the foot of a mountain in Syria, but it flows down through a valley that is below sea level. The Jordan empties into the Dead Sea, located between Israel and Jordan. The Dead Sea lies nearly one fourth of a mile (402 m) below sea level. It is the lowest place on the surface of the earth.

Because its elevation is so low, no water can drain out of the Dead Sea. But the hot desert sun evaporates the water about as fast as it flows in from the river. Evaporation leaves behind large deposits of salt and other minerals. The Dead Sea is about seven times saltier than are the oceans. If you completely evaporate a cup of Dead Sea water, you will have about one-fourth cup of dry salt left. People can easily float on the surface of this salty sea, but when they get out they have a salty crust left on their skin. The Dead Sea is so salty that fish cannot live in it. That is the reason for the name Dead Sea.

The photograph above shows salt columns in the Dead Sea, the saltiest body of water in the world.
▶ Why is there so much salt in the Dead Sea?

LESSON 2 REVIEW

THINK AND WRITE

A. What are the important deserts and seas (Recall) of the Middle East and North Africa?
B. How does elevation affect the climates (Infer) of the Anatolian and Iranian plateaus?
C. Why is the Dead Sea so salty?   (Recall)

SKILLS CHECK

THINKING SKILL
The Middle East and North Africa are set among five important seas: the Arabian, Black, Caspian, Mediterranean, and Red seas. Look in the Gazetteer to find out which of these seas is the largest in the world and which is the largest inland body of water in the world.

366

Optional Activities

UNDERSTANDING THE LESSON

NAME _____
UNDERSTANDING THE LESSON   CHAPTER
                                                      13
Recalling Facts   LESSON 2 CONTENT MASTER

✱ Place a check mark in the box next to the correct answer for each item.

1. The Sahara is so large that it would almost completely cover
   ☐ **a.** France.   ☐ **c.** Europe.
   ☐ **b.** Asia.   ☐ **d.** North America.

2. Besides the Sahara, the other major desert area of the Middle East and North Africa is located in
   ☐ **a.** the Arabian peninsula.   ☐ **c.** Afghanistan.
   ☐ **b.** the Anatolian peninsula. ☐ **d.** Iran.

3. The best way to describe the Anatolian peninsula is to say it is
   ☐ **a.** a rugged plateau.   ☐ **c.** mostly desert.
   ☐ **b.** low and flat.   ☐ **d.** a tropical rain forest.

4. The climate of lands along the western and southern Anatolian coasts is
   ☐ **a.** continental.   ☐ **c.** maritime.
   ☐ **b.** tropical.   ☐ **d.** Mediterranean.

5. The Iranian plateau is separated from the plain of the Tigris and Euphrates rivers by
   ☐ **a.** the Caspian Sea.   ☐ **c.** Mount Damavand.
   ☐ **b.** the Elburz Mountains. ☐ **d.** the Zagros Mountains.

6. Much of the coastal area south of the Caspian Sea is forested because
   ☐ **a.** the plateau has dry summers.   ☐ **c.** there are no rivers in the region.
   ☐ **b.** it gets heavy summer rainfall. ☐ **d.** the Caspian is an inland sea.

7. The river that has the lowest elevation of all the world's rivers is the
   ☐ **a.** Jordan.   ☐ **c.** Tigris.
   ☐ **b.** Nile.   ☐ **d.** Euphrates.

8. The Dead Sea is salty because
   ☐ **a.** the land around it is salty.   ☐ **c.** many rivers flow out of it.
   ☐ **b.** water evaporates, leaving salt.   ☐ **d.** there are so many fish in it.

Think and Write: What is the land like in the Middle East and North Africa? How does that affect where people live? Write your answers in a paragraph. You may use the back of the sheet.
Answers should reflect independent thinking; suggestions appear in the Answer Key.

Use with textbook pages 363–366.   91

◀ **Review Master Booklet, p. 91**

Resources of the Middle East and North Africa

THINK ABOUT WHAT YOU KNOW

Recall what you have learned about the natural resources of other countries. Can you name any natural resources that are found in the area where you live?

STUDY THE VOCABULARY

petroleum   ground water
per capita
    income

FOCUS YOUR READING

What are the resources of the Middle East and North Africa?

A. In the Neighborhood of Oil

When Freya Stark, an English girl, was nine years old, her aunt gave her a copy of the *Arabian Nights*. For Freya the gift inspired a lifelong interest in the Middle East. She wanted to live and travel in the Middle East because, she explained,

§ *I thought the most interesting things in the*
§ *world were likely to happen in the neigh-*
§ *borhood of oil.*

When Freya Stark began her studies of Arabic in 1921, the Middle East produced only about 2 percent of the world's **petroleum**, or oil. She was not a geographer or a scientist, but she correctly guessed that the amount of oil discovered in the Middle East would increase greatly. She was exactly right. Today a large part of the world's petroleum supply comes from the Arabic-speaking lands of the Middle East and North Africa.

As Freya Stark guessed, the growing importance of oil caused interesting things

to happen. Countries that had been poor desert lands in 1921 were rich by the 1970s. The **per capita incomes** in Saudi Arabia, Kuwait, and Bahrain were among the highest in the world. Per capita income is the amount of money that each person in the country would have if the country's total income were divided equally among all of its people.

Although petroleum has been found in a number of Middle Eastern and North African countries, it has not been found in every land. The resource map on page 369 shows where the oil fields are located.

The main source of the wealth in Saudi Arabia comes from the oil industry.
▶ Where in Saudi Arabia is this oil rig drilling for petroleum?

367

Curriculum Connection

Economics   Have students compare and analyze the per capita incomes of several Middle Eastern and North African countries.

● Give students the following per capita income figures: Morocco: $750; Kuwait: $18,180; Tunisia: $1,100; Qatar: $27,000.

● Have them graph the information using a bar graph.

● Ask students to draw conclusions about the resources and standard of living in each of these nations.

Optional Activities

Resources of the Middle East and North Africa

Objectives

★ **1. List** the resources of the Middle East and North Africa.

2. Explain why the forests of the Middle East and North Africa have disappeared.

3. Identify the following people and places: *Freya Stark, Ferdinand de Lesseps, Said Pasha, Kuwait, Persian Gulf, Suez Canal,* and *Bosporus.*

1 STARTING THE LESSON

Motivation Activity

■ Discuss with students what they know about camels.

■ Then, help students see how well-adapted these animals are to life in the desert by asking students to hypothesize why camels have three eyelids (to keep out sand) and why they have large, cushioned feet (to walk across sand without sinking into it).

Think About What You Know

■ Assign the THINK ABOUT WHAT YOU KNOW activity on p. 367.

■ Student answers should reflect independent thinking and should point out local resources.

Study the Vocabulary

■ Have students look up the definitions of the new vocabulary terms in this lesson.

■ Ask students to calculate the per capita income of a country with a total income of $50,000 and a total population of 1,250 people. ($50,000 divided by 1,250 people equals $40 per person.)

── Answers to Caption Questions ──
p. 366 ▶ The sun quickly evaporates the water, leaving the salt deposits behind.
p. 367 ▶ In the desert

DEVELOPING THE LESSON

Read and Think

Sections A and B

Important resources of the Middle East and North Africa include oil and water. Review how these resources have helped people by asking students the following questions:

1. **How has the discovery of oil changed countries such as Bahrain and Kuwait?** (These poor desert lands have become rich and per capita income has risen. *p. 367*)

2. **Why is water such an important resource in the Middle East and North Africa?** (Because it is so scarce *p. 368*)

3. **How do people in the Middle East and North Africa grow crops in dry lands and deserts?** (They use irrigation and ground water to grow crops. *pp. 368-369*)

4. **How has the rapid population growth in the Middle East and North Africa affected the water supply of the area?** (Water in some areas has become more scarce and more polluted. *p. 369*)

Thinking Critically **What, do you think, can the people of the Middle East and North Africa do to protect their sources and supplies of water?** (Hypothesize)
(Answers may include penalizing people who pollute or waste it. *pp. 369-370*)

VISUAL THINKING SKILL

Interpreting a Chart

■ Ask students to look at the chart on p. 368 and think about which products of the date palm tree are, in their opinion, most and least important.

■ Then, have students list in order, from most to least important, products of the date palm tree.

■ Ask volunteers to share their lists with the class, and discuss why students ranked the products of the date palm tree in the order that they did.

PRODUCTS OF THE DATE PALM TREE

Date Palm Fruit — Sugar — String and Rope — Cooking Oil — Bowls — Animal Food — Baskets and Mats — Medicine — Animal Food — Sandals

The date palm tree supplies many products to the people of the Middle East and North Africa.
▶ What are the food products that come from the date palm tree?

B. Making Use of the Dry Lands

Irrigating the Land Oil is not the only important resource of the Middle East and North Africa. Water is perhaps even more important in dry lands, which make up so large a part of this region. Kuwait, a small country on the Persian Gulf, has a lot of oil but almost no sources of fresh water. At one time, Kuwait imported river water from the nearby country of Iraq. Today Kuwait gets water from the world's largest factory for turning salty sea water into fresh water.

Much of the land in the Middle East and North Africa is too dry and too mountainous for growing crops. In some countries less than 5 percent of the land is arable, that is, suitable for cultivation.

Other countries have more arable land, but none have as much as do the Western European countries. Yet this dry part of the world is where people first learned to grow wheat, barley, peas, onions, and a variety of melons. Here people first cultivated fig and date trees. The chart above shows some products of the date palm tree. The largest part of the world's date supply still comes from the Middle East. Almonds were probably first raised in this region. English walnuts are probably more accurately called Persian walnuts, since the nuts were first cultivated in Persia.

People are able to grow crops in dry lands and deserts if they have water for irrigation. As you have read, the ancient Egyptians drew water from the Nile River

368

Curriculum Connection

Science Tell students that some people who live in the desert collect small amounts of water from the air, using a bowl, an animal skin, and a pebble.

● Have students simulate this, using a bowl or a glass covered with plastic wrap. Tell students to secure the wrap with a rubber band and to place a pebble in the middle of the wrap.

● Then have them put the bowl or glass in a refrigerator overnight to parallel the nighttime drop in temperature in the desert.

● Have students check on the bowl in the morning. They should find that water has condensed on the plastic.

irrigate the desert. Modern Egyptians do the same. The resource map below shows areas of irrigated agriculture. Note that the two largest areas lie along the Nile and the Tigris and Euphrates rivers. You will also see that the map shows small areas of irrigated lands scattered across the Sahara and Arabian deserts. These are places where people have learned to use **ground water** to grow crops. Ground water is water that has seeped below the ground during the occasional rains and has collected in layers of soil, sand, and rock. People tap this underground water by digging or drilling wells. In some lands, tunnels are dug to carry underground water from the highlands to lower valleys. In the

past the digging of wells and the lifting of water was done by human muscle and by animals. Today machines and pumps are used for these tasks.

A Need for Water The population of the Middle East and North Africa has grown rapidly in recent years. As the number of people has increased, so has the need for water. In some places, ground water is being used more rapidly than it is being replaced. Consequently, the precious waters of the region's great rivers have become more and more polluted.

It has been difficult to make plans for the use of the rivers in the region, because the major streams run through more than

GEOGRAPHY THEMES

Place

■ Direct the students' attention to the map on this page. Then ask which countries in this region have deposits of coal. (Morocco, Algeria, Turkey, and Iran)

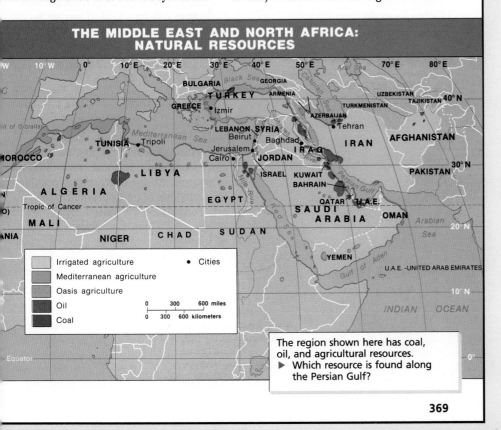

THE MIDDLE EAST AND NORTH AFRICA: NATURAL RESOURCES

Legend:
- Irrigated agriculture
- Mediterranean agriculture
- Oasis agriculture
- Oil
- Coal
- Cities

0   300   600 miles
0   300   600 kilometers

The region shown here has coal, oil, and agricultural resources.
▶ Which resource is found along the Persian Gulf?

369

Communicating Visually

● Have students illustrate the water problems of the Middle East and North Africa.

● First, review with students why the Middle East and North Africa have water problems. (The growing population and demand for water are outstripping the supply; the rivers are polluted; and the nations that share a water supply are not working together to conserve and protect the water source.)

● Then, tell students to design and create posters that illustrate these problems.

For Your Information

Camels Camels are not the most friendly or cooperative animals. They are quick to bite if they are angry, and they also kick and spit.

Camels don't like to work or to obey. They moan and groan a great deal. However, they are an important source of transportation in desert lands. Camels can carry a load of goods weighing 500 pounds (227 kg).

Optional Activities

369

Read and Think

Sections C and D

Some resources, such as animals that survive in dry lands, have served the people of this region for thousands of years. Other resources, such as forests, have disappeared. Discuss these resources with students by asking the following questions:

1. **Why were camels once useful forms of transportation, and how are they used today?**
(They can go without water and food for long periods, which enables them to easily travel through a desert; today, they are raised for food and leather. *p. 370*)

2. **Why have the forests of the Middle East and North Africa disappeared?**
(Partly because the people needed the wood for shelter and fuel and never replaced the trees that they cut down; partly because of sheep and goats that eat young trees and shrubs *p. 371*)

Thinking Critically **How do you think the land of the Middle East and North Africa would be different if the forests had been replanted?** (Infer)
(Answers should reflect independent thinking but may include that there would be less dry, unusable land. *p. 371*)

one country. Although the source of the Jordan River is in Syria, it receives water from other rivers in Lebanon. The Jordan River flows to both the country of Israel and the country of Jordan. The Euphrates River rises in Turkey and crosses Syria before it finally reaches Iraq. All of the countries along these rivers depend on the water from them.

C. Animals for Dry Lands

Donkeys Long ago in the Middle East and North Africa, people domesticated, or tamed, animals for use in dry lands. The sturdy donkey was perhaps the first animal trained to carry loads. Donkeys are hearty

Camels are among the most useful animals in hot, dry lands, such as the Middle East and North Africa.
▶ What kind of camel is shown in the photograph below?

creatures able to survive in regions where vegetation and water are too scarce for most large animals to survive.

Camels It is believed that camels were also first used in the Middle East. Dromedary camels, those with one hump, were probably domesticated in the Arabian Peninsula. Bactrian camels, camels with two humps, were most likely first used in Bactria, a land now known as Afghanistan. Both of these camels are found mainly in central Asia.

Camels are very useful in dry lands. They can go without water for long periods of time. A camel may drink 15 to 25 gallons (57 to 95 L) of water at one time, and then not drink again for several days or longer. If a camel can find food, it can go for 20 days without water. Camels will eat various sorts of desert plants. They store the energy that they get from food in their humps, which are piles of fat under the skin. The stored energy makes it possible for camels to go without food for days.

Since camels can go without water and food for long periods, they can easily travel through a desert. Camels are able to carry loads and riders and can pull plows or wagons. At one time, camels provided the main form of transportation in the desert. Today they are raised for food and leather. Camel herds provide milk, meat, and hides. Camels are well suited to the Middle East and North Africa because they can be raised on land where cattle would starve.

Sheep and Goats Raising sheep and goats is also another way to make use of dry lands. Like camels, these animals can feed on desert plants. Since the plants are sparse in the desert, herds must travel over large areas in search of more plant life.

Taking an Opinion Poll

- Ask students to prepare an opinion poll on whether we have an obligation to conserve our resources.

- Have students develop questions for the poll. Start them off with an example such as this: *Should we require all paper to be recycled in order to save trees?*

- Write all suggested questions on the chalkboard; then have students narrow the list to five questions.

- Have each student poll five people outside of class. Then have students calculate the percentage of positive and negative responses that they received.

- Discuss the results of the poll in class.

Long ago the mountainsides of Lebanon were covered with cedar forests.
▶ After looking at the photograph above, how would you describe the mountainsides of today?

D. The Lost Forests

Once, forests covered many of the hills and mountains throughout the Middle East and North Africa. The cedar forests of Lebanon were famous in ancient times. The Egyptian pharaohs imported cedar wood to make coffins for tombs. Solomon, king of ancient Israel, imported cedar wood from Lebanon to build a temple at Jerusalem. Today there are small remains of Lebanon's ancient forests. But like nine tenths of the forests in the Middle East and North Africa, the cedar forests were destroyed and never replaced. Trees grow slowly in the dry climate, and the forests were cut faster than they could grow.

Part of the reason the forests disappeared is that wood is such a useful resource. People used wood for buildings, furniture, and tools. Wood is also excellent fuel, so trees were cut to heat homes and cook meals.

People's need for wood was not the only reason for the destruction of forests. Herds of sheep and goats also did their part in destroying the forests. Since these animals eat such a wide variety of plants, they have stripped the ground of shrubs and young trees.

E. The Suez Canal Opens New Trade Routes

Difficult Trade Routes Because of its location the Middle East has had the advantage of being on major trade routes between three continents. In ancient times, traders brought silk from China by way of the long "Silk Road" across Asia. This

371

Read and Think

Section E

To help students summarize how the Suez Canal came to be built and why it has been beneficial to the Middle East and North Africa, ask the following questions:

1. **Who was responsible for building the Suez Canal?**
   (Ferdinand de Lesseps and Said Pasha of Egypt *pp. 372-373*)

2. **How did the canal help the Middle East and North Africa?**
   (It put the region on one of the world's most important sea routes. *p. 373*)

Thinking Critically **If you had the opportunity to interview Ferdinand de Lesseps or Said Pasha, which one would you choose, and what questions would you ask?** (Hypothesize)
(Answers should reflect independent thinking but may include Lesseps, because he had the idea for the Suez Canal, or Said, because he was the ruler of Egypt. *pp. 372-373*)

high-priced cloth was then carried by ship from ports on the Mediterranean to Rome. Ships from East Africa and South Asia brought goods to ports on the Persian Gulf and Red Sea. From there camel caravans carried the goods to Mediterranean ports, where they could be reloaded onto ships bound for southern Europe.

Ships from East Africa and South Asia could not sail directly to Europe because the Isthmus of Suez blocked the way. The isthmus separates the Red Sea and the Mediterranean by a narrow strip of land that connects Africa and Asia.

The Suez Canal A canal across the Isthmus of Suez was not completed until 1869. The building of the canal at that time was partly the result of a friendship between Ferdinand de Lesseps, a French

official, and a young Egyptian who liked macaroni. The friendship began when Lesseps was serving as the French representative in Egypt. At that time the Egyptian ruler had a teenage son named Said, who was somewhat overweight. Said's father decided that his son must do vigorous exercises and go on a strict diet.

Almost every day after doing his exercises, Said was very hungry, and he would go to the house of his French friend. There he would have the cook make him a large dish of macaroni, which was one of Said's favorite foods. The macaroni did not reduce Said's weight, but it strengthened his friendship with Lesseps.

Lesseps left Egypt in 1837. Seventeen years later, Said, now called Said Pasha, became the ruler of Egypt. He remembered his old friend and invited him to

The Suez Canal opened for use in November 1869.
► How has the Suez Canal served as an important resource for the Middle East and North Africa?

372

Optional Activities

Cooperative Learning

Dramatizing Divide the class into groups of four students to dramatize the story of the Suez Canal.

- Have each group decide who will be responsible for the following roles: Said's father, Said Pasha, Ferdinand de Lesseps, and the narrator.

- Then have the play's characters write their dialogue, working with other members of their group to make the play interesting, factual, and informative.

- Give each group the opportunity to rehearse.

- Then have the groups perform their plays for the class.

Reteaching Main Objective

⭐ ***List the resources of the Middle East and North Africa.***

- Ask students to imagine that they are in charge of an art exhibit organized to teach the public about the resources of the Middle East and North Africa.

- Tell the students that they will be responsible for drawing pictures and maps and making models that will illustrate the resources of this region.

- Before students begin, have them make a list of the resources that they wish to include in the exhibit.

visit. Lesseps jumped at the chance to return to Egypt. He wanted to tell Said Pasha about a project he had in mind, the building of a modern ship canal across the Isthmus of Suez. A canal connecting the Mediterranean and Red seas would greatly shorten the route between Europe and Asia. When Lesseps explained his plan to Said Pasha, the ruler assured his friend, "I am convinced. You can count on me."

Improved Trade Routes Work on the Suez Canal began in 1859 and was completed ten years later. The completion of the canal put the Middle East and North Africa on one of the world's most important sea routes. Ships traveling from western Europe to East Africa or to South and East Asia could now go through the point where Africa and Asia met.

Other trade routes, which pass through the Middle East, have opened up between Europe and Asia. In 1973 a bridge was built across the Bosporus at Istanbul. A second bridge was completed in 1988. The bridges make it possible for large trucks to carry goods from Europe to cities in the Middle East. Now, as in ancient times, trade routes still pass through the Middle East and North Africa.

This bridge is one of two bridges that link the Asiatic and European sections of Istanbul.
▶ How have the bridges helped to increase trade?

LESSON 3 REVIEW

THINK AND WRITE

A. How did the demand for oil affect the Middle East and North Africa? **(Infer)**

B. In what ways have people made use of land in the Middle East and North Africa?

C. Why are donkeys, camels, sheep, and goats useful in the Middle East and North Africa? **(Recall)**

D. What happened to most of the forests in the Middle East and North Africa? **(Recall)**

E. What changes in the Middle East and North Africa have resulted from the completion of the Suez Canal? **(Infer)**

SKILLS CHECK

WRITING SKILL

Imagine that you are riding a camel across the Sahara. Write a short descriptive essay about your journey.

373

◀ **Review Master Booklet, p. 92**

Optional Activities

3 CLOSING THE LESSON

Lesson 3 Review

Answers to Think and Write

A. Countries that had been poor desert lands in 1921 became rich by the 1970s as a result of the growing demand for oil.

B. They have made use of the land by irrigating, using ground water and water from rivers.

C. Donkeys, camels, sheep, and goats are useful in the Middle East and North Africa because they are able to survive where vegetation and water are scarce.

D. Most of the forests were destroyed by people and grazing animals.

E. The Suez Canal put the Middle East and North Africa on one of the world's most important sea routes.

Answer to Skills Check

Answers should reflect independent thinking but may include descriptions of sights such as oases and areas where people have learned to use ground water to grow crops, or may tell why the donkey is a good means of transportation (able to survive in regions where vegetation and water are scarce).

Focus Your Reading

Ask the lesson focus question found at the beginning of the lesson: **What are the resources of the Middle East and North Africa?**

(The resources of the Middle East and North Africa include oil, land, water, animals that can survive on dry land, and trade routes.)

Additional Practice

You may wish to assign the ancillary materials listed below.

Understanding the Lesson p. 92
Workbook pp. 80, 82–83

┌─ **Answers to Caption Questions** ─┐
p. 372 ▶ It put the Middle East and North Africa on one of the world's most important sea routes.
p. 373 ▶ Large trucks can carry goods from Europe to cities in the Middle East.
└────────────────────────┘

373

Using the Vocabulary

1. wadi
2. migration
3. petroleum
4. ground water
5. labor force

Remembering What You Read

1. Scheherazade
2. Asia, Europe, and Africa
3. Desert dwellers
4. Arabic
5. The Sahara
6. The Mediterranean, Black, Caspian, Arabian, and Red seas
7. Because it is too salty
8. They can go without food and water for long periods of time.
9. The Isthmus of Suez
10. The Suez Canal

Thinking Critically

1. Answers should reflect independent thinking but may include that a people can sometimes find better work by migrating to a different country, but that migrating can also cause a people to lose its distinct identity.
2. Both the Arabic and Roman alphabets are used to write different languages, however, the two alphabets are written with different letters, and Arabic is written from right to left, whereas Roman is written from left to right.

USING THE VOCABULARY

migration   petroleum
labor force   ground water
wadi

From the list above, choose a vocabulary term that could be used in place of the underlined word or words in each sentence. Rewrite the sentences on a separate sheet of paper.

1. During a rainstorm, water can rise quickly in a <u>dry stream bed</u> in a desert.
2. Over the centuries there has been a <u>movement</u> of people into the Middle East.
3. A large part of the world's <u>oil</u> is found in some of the countries in the Middle East and North Africa.
4. <u>Water that has seeped below the ground during the occasional rains and has collected in layers of soil, sand, and rock</u> is used to grow crops.
5. Much of the <u>working population</u> in Egypt works in agriculture.

REMEMBERING WHAT YOU READ

On a separate sheet of paper, answer the following questions in complete sentences.

1. Who tells the tales in the *Arabian Nights*?

2. The Middle East and North Africa lie in the middle of a landmass formed by what three continents?
3. What does the Arabic term *Bedouin* mean?
4. What is the language that most people of the Middle East and North Africa speak?
5. What is the world's largest desert?
6. Name the five seas that surround the Middle East and North Africa.
7. Explain why fish cannot live in the Dead Sea.
8. Why are camels useful animals in the desert?
9. What strip of land blocked the way for ships from Africa and South Asia to sail directly to Europe?
10. What improved trade routes for the Middle East and North Africa after 1869?

TYING MATH TO SOCIAL STUDIES

Figure out the per capita income of the fictitious countries of Northland and Southland, using the following information: Northland has a total income of $5,000,000 and a population of 10,000. Southland has a total income of $4,000,000 and a population of 20,000. What would be the per capita income if these two countries united?

374

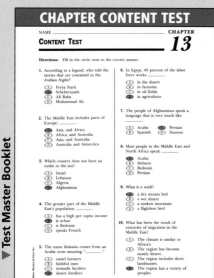

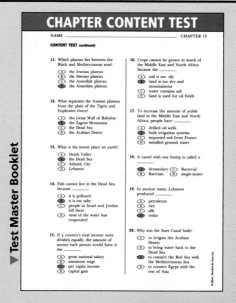

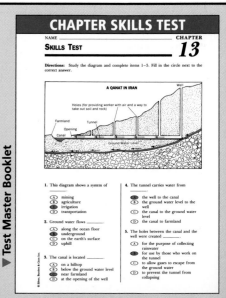

THINKING CRITICALLY

On a separate sheet of paper, answer the following in complete sentences.

1. What are the advantages and disadvantages of people migrating to different countries?
2. Compare and contrast the Arabic alphabet and the Roman alphabet.

3. Why, do you think, do some countries in the Middle East, such as Saudi Arabia and Qatar, have among the highest per capita incomes in the world?
4. How do you think the Middle East and North Africa can conserve their ground water?
5. How would the economy of the Middle East and North Africa have been affected if the Suez Canal had not been built?

SUMMARIZING THE CHAPTER

On a separate sheet of paper, copy the graphic organizer shown below. Beside each main idea, write three statements that support the idea.

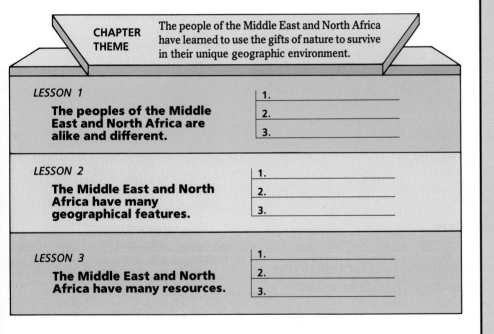

CHAPTER THEME
The people of the Middle East and North Africa have learned to use the gifts of nature to survive in their unique geographic environment.

LESSON 1
The peoples of the Middle East and North Africa are alike and different.
1. ___
2. ___
3. ___

LESSON 2
The Middle East and North Africa have many geographical features.
1. ___
2. ___
3. ___

LESSON 3
The Middle East and North Africa have many resources.
1. ___
2. ___
3. ___

3. Answers may include that some countries in the Middle East have the highest per capita incomes in the world because they produce a large part of the world's petroleum.
4. Answers may include that the Middle East and North Africa can conserve their ground water by developing and enforcing laws that regulate digging and drilling wells.
5. Answers may include that the economy of the Middle East and North Africa would have been adversely affected if the Suez Canal had not provided an easy way for goods to be shipped through the region.

Summarizing the Chapter

Lesson 1
1. They do similar work.
2. They use the same alphabet.
3. Different dialects and languages

Lesson 2
1. Deserts make up a large part of the region.
2. Abundance of sea water around the region
3. Mountain ranges rise from the Anatolian and Iranian plateaus.

Lesson 3
1. A large part of the world's petroleum supply comes from the region.
2. Water is an important resource.
3. Donkeys, camels, sheep, and goats help people make use of the dry lands.

CHAPTER SKILLS TEST

NAME _____ CHAPTER 13

SKILLS TEST (continued)

Directions: Read the paragraphs and complete items 6–10. Fill in the circle next to the correct answer.

Ferdinand de Lesseps (1805–1894)

The building of the Suez Canal was partly the result of a friendship between Ferdinand de Lesseps, a young French official, and an Egyptian prince who loved to eat macaroni. The friendship began in 1832 when Ferdinand, then 27 years old, was sent to Egypt to serve as France's official representative.

At that time, the Egyptian Prince, Said (sah EED), was in his teens and overweight. His father decided that Said must exercise vigorously and start a diet.

Poor Said was exhausted by the exercise, and he was also very hungry. He often went to Lesseps's house where he had the cook make him macaroni. The macaroni did nothing to reduce Said's weight, but it did strengthen his friendship with Lesseps.

Lesseps left Egypt in 1837 when he was sent to represent France in another country. Seventeen years later, Said succeeded his

father as ruler of Egypt and invited Lesseps back for a visit.

Lesseps jumped at the chance to return to Egypt and see his old friend. He also wanted to tell Said about a project he had in mind—the building of a modern canal between the Mediterranean Sea and the port of Suez on the Red Sea. Lesseps knew that such a canal would greatly shorten sea voyages between Europe and India.

Lesseps explained his plan to Said. The new ruler assured his friend, "I am convinced. You can count on me."

For several years, Lesseps worked hard to raise money and make arrangements to build the canal. Work began in 1859 and was completed ten years later. Thousands of Egyptian workers were drafted to dig. They had none of today's huge earth-moving machinery. They dug the long ditch with nothing but their picks and shovels.

6. Ferdinand de Lesseps was a citizen of—
   Ⓐ Spain Ⓒ Egypt
   Ⓑ France Ⓓ India

7. Lesseps first came to Egypt to work as—
   Ⓐ an architectural engineer
   Ⓑ a chef
   Ⓒ his country's representative
   Ⓓ an army officer

8. The prince's response to Lesseps's plan for building the canal was—
   Ⓐ enthusiastic Ⓒ amused
   Ⓑ timid Ⓓ distrustful

9. The canal was dug with picks and shovels because—
   Ⓐ the prince wanted to supply thousands of workers with jobs
   Ⓑ Egypt could not afford bulldozers and steam shovels
   Ⓒ the workers were uneducated slaves
   Ⓓ machines for this purpose had not been invented

10. The canal was completed in—
    Ⓐ 1859
    Ⓑ 1857
    Ⓒ 1869
    Ⓓ 1827

▼ **Test Master Booklet**

CHAPTER WRITING TEST

NAME _____ **CHAPTER 13**

ESSAY TEST

Directions: Write a response to items 1–4.

REMINDER: Read and think about each item before you write your response. Be sure to think of the points you want to cover, details that support your response, and reasons for your opinions. Then, on the lines below, write your response in complete sentences.

1. Describe the Dead Sea.
   A satisfactory response should include the following statements:
   • The Dead Sea is located between Jordan and Israel.
   • It has the lowest elevation of any place on earth.
   • The Dead Sea is extremely salty—too salty for fish to live in it.
   An excellent response might also:
   • explain that the deposits of salt and minerals are caused by evaporation
   • mention that the Jordan River flows into the Dead Sea
   • cite the Dead Sea's elevation (nearly one-fourth of a mile below sea level)

2. How has migration influenced the development of the Middle East?
   A satisfactory response will include the following statements:
   • Because of its location, the Middle East has attracted people from other parts of Asia, Africa, and Europe.
   • Over the centuries, people from different cultures migrated to the region, and
   descendants of these people make up its population today.
   • As a result, the region has a variety of peoples.
   An excellent response might also:
   • provide specific examples
   • reflect independent thinking

▼ **Test Master Booklet**

CHAPTER WRITING TEST

NAME _____ CHAPTER 15

ESSAY TEST (continued)

3. How has oil affected life in the Middle East and North Africa?
   A satisfactory response should include the following statements:
   • Today a large part of the world's oil supply comes from the Middle East and North Africa.
   • As a result, some countries that had been poor desert lands became rich.
   • The per capita incomes of some of these countries are among the highest in the world.
   An excellent response might include:
   • examples of countries where petroleum has been found
   • an explanation of how oil has made these countries wealthy

4. What happened to Lebanon's forests?
   A satisfactory response should include the following statements:
   • In ancient times, the forests of Lebanon were famous for producing cedar.
   • However, trees grow slowly in the dry climate, and the forests were cut faster than they could grow.
   • Herds of sheep and goats also helped destroy the forests by stripping the ground of shrubs and young trees.
   An excellent response might include:
   • examples of the uses of cedar
   • countries that once imported cedar from Lebanon
   • a statement that stresses the importance of conservation

▼ **Test Master Booklet**

History of the Middle East and North Africa

(pp. 376-401)

Chapter Theme: The Middle East has had an important place in the world's history not only because of the universal contributions its people have made but also because it was the birthplace of world religions, such as Islam and Christianity.

CHAPTER RESOURCES
Review Master Booklet
  Reviewing Chapter Vocabulary, p. 99
  Place Geography, p. 100
  Summarizing the Chapter, p. 101
Chapter 14 Test

LESSON *1*   Origins of the Muslim Religion

(pp. 376-383)

Theme: The Muslim religion was started by a merchant named Muhammad.

SILVER WINGS WORKSHOP: The Courage of Your Convictions

LESSON RESOURCES
Workbook, p. 84
Review Master Booklet
  Understanding the Lesson, p. 96

LESSON *2*   Caliphs and Crusaders

(pp. 386-394)

Theme: The Crusades began when Pope Urban called for help to take Jerusalem back from the Muslims, and as a result, trade increased between the Middle East and Europe.

LESSON RESOURCES
Workbook, pp. 85-86
Review Master Booklet
  Understanding the Lesson, p. 97

LESSON *3*   Art and Learning in the Muslim Lands

(pp. 395-399)

Theme: North Africa and the Middle East made many contributions to art, mathematics, science, and writing.

LESSON RESOURCES
Workbook, p. 87
Review Master Booklet
  Understanding the Lesson, p. 98

Review Masters

REVIEWING CHAPTER VOCABULARY

Review Study the words in the box. Use your Glossary to find definitions of those you do not remember.

caliph	minaret	pilgrimage	shrine
calligraphy	mosque	prophet	sultan

Practice Complete the paragraphs using words from the box above. You may change the forms of the words to fit the meaning.

Islam, one of the world's largest religions, has over 500 million followers. Most Muslims, or followers of Islam, live in the Middle East and North Africa, but today Muslims live in many countries. People who follow Islam believe that Muhammad, who was born in Mecca about A.D. 570, was the last (1) __prophet__ sent by God.

Muslims, like people of other religions, have certain duties they must perform. One of these duties is praying five times a day while facing Mecca. These prayers take place at daybreak, noon, mid-afternoon, after sunset, and early in the night. The prayers may be performed alone, with others, or in a place of worship. In addition, men are expected to go to the (2) __mosque__ to pray together at noon on Fridays. Muslims are called to prayer by people called muezzins. Muezzins may be heard calling from towers called (3) __minarets__ in cities and towns throughout the Muslim world.

Because Mecca was the birthplace of Muhammad, it is an important city to the followers of Islam. Muslims believe it is their duty to make a (4) __pilgrimage__ to this holy city at least once during their lives. Pilgrims from all over the world travel to Mecca to visit the (5) __shrine__ of the Kaaba and to kiss the black stone that stands inside.

Write Write a sentence of your own for each word in the box above. You may use the back of the sheet.

Sentences should show that students understand the meanings of the words.

_____
_____
_____
_____
_____
_____
_____

© Silver, Burdett & Ginn Inc.

LOCATING PLACES

✳ The cities listed below were centers of Muslim culture and learning. Use the Gazetteer in your textbook to find the latitude and longitude of each city. Then locate and label each on the map. (The names of modern countries are given in parentheses.)

	LAT.	LONG.
1. Damascus (Syria)	34°N	36°E
2. Baghdad (Iraq)	33°N	44°E
3. Córdoba (Spain)	38°N	5°W
4. Cairo (Egypt)	30°N	31°E
5. Istanbul (Turkey)	41°N	29°E

ATLANTIC OCEAN

MUSLIM CULTURAL CENTERS
⊙ Present-day national capitals
● Other cities

0   200   400   600   800 miles
0   200   400   600   800 kilometers

© Silver, Burdett & Ginn Inc.

SUMMARIZING THE CHAPTER

✳ Complete this graphic organizer. Under each main idea write three statements that support it.

CHAPTER THEME → The Middle East has had an important place in the world's history not only because of the universal contributions its people have made but also because it was the birthplace of world religions, such as Islam and Christianity.

LESSON 1
The Muslim religion began about 1400 years ago.
1. Muhammad _____
2. The Kaaba _____
3. The Koran _____

LESSON 2
The Crusades brought about many results.
1. The Holy Land _____
2. Jerusalem _____
3. Trade _____

LESSON 3
The people of the Middle East and North Africa made many contributions.
1. Arabic numbers _____
2. Algebra _____
3. Chemistry _____

© Silver, Burdett & Ginn Inc.

C14-B

Workbook Pages

CHANGES IN RELIGIOUS MEMBERSHIP

Understanding a Bar Graph, Hypothesizing

✳ The bar graph shows the change in the membership of four major religions from 1980 to 1988. Study the bar graph, and then circle the correct answer to each question below.

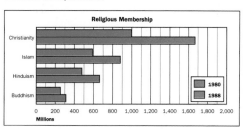

Religious Membership

Christianity, Islam, Hinduism, Buddhism — Millions: 0, 200, 400, 600, 800, 1,000, 1,200, 1,400, 1,600, 1,800, 2,000 — 1980, 1988

1. How did the number of people in each of the religions change between 1980 and 1988?
   Stayed the same   Decreased   (Increased)   Doubled

2. Which religion had more than 1 billion members in 1988?
   Hinduism   Islam   (Christianity)   Buddhism

3. Which religious group had a membership of about 900 million in 1988?
   Buddhism   (Islam)   Hinduism   Christianity

4. Which two groups had memberships under 500 million members in 1980?
   Buddhism and Islam   (Buddhism and Hinduism)
   Christianity and Buddhism   Hinduism and Christianity

5. Which group grew by about 300 million from 1980 to 1988?
   (Islam)   Christianity   Hinduism   Buddhism

6. Which group grew the most in the eight-year period shown on the graph?
   (Christianity)   Islam   Hinduism   Buddhism

Thinking Further: The world population is about 5 billion people. Why does the combined memberships of the four religions not equal 5 billion? Write your answer on a separate sheet. Students should mention that some people follow other religions or do not belong to any religion.

84   Chapter 14, pages 377–383

THE CRUSADES

Understanding Stated Facts and Details, Interpreting Information

✳ Read about the Crusades below. Then answer the questions.

> **1095–1099: First Crusade**—Crusaders capture Jerusalem and form four states in Holy Land.
> **1147–1148: Second Crusade**—Crusaders, led by the kings of Germany and France, are defeated by Muslims.
> **1189–1192: Third Crusade**—After Saladin and the Muslims recapture Jerusalem, the Third Crusade forms. It fails, but Richard I of England persuades Saladin to let Christian pilgrims enter Jerusalem.
> **1201–1204: Fourth Crusade**—Crusaders become involved in wars in Europe and never reach the Holy Land.
> **1212: Children's Crusade** leaves Europe for the Holy Land, but most of the children are taken to North Africa as slaves.
> **1218–1221: Fifth Crusade**—After seriously threatening the Muslims, the crusaders are forced to retreat because of a flood.
> **1227–1229: Sixth Crusade**—Frederick II, the leader of the crusade, signs a treaty with the Muslims, giving Jerusalem to the crusaders for ten years.
> **1248–1254: Seventh Crusade**—King Louis IX of France leads an attack on the Muslims. The Muslims capture the king and his nobles and hold them until a ransom is paid.
> **1270: Eighth Crusade**—Louis IX leads his second Crusade. He dies at Carthage and his army returns to France.

1. In which Crusade did most of the crusaders become slaves? Children's Crusade

2. In which Crusade did Richard I of England fight? Third Crusade

3. Which king led two Crusades? Louis IX of France

4. In which Crusade was Jerusalem given up without a battle? Sixth Crusade

5. Which Crusade never reached the Holy Land because of European wars? Fourth Crusade

6. In which Crusade were the leaders captured and held for ransom? Seventh Crusade

7. Which two Crusades were the most successful? Why? The First and Sixth were the most successful because they gained control of Jerusalem.

Thinking Further: People today support many different causes, such as peace, human rights, or cleaning up the environment. Choose one cause and explain why people support it. Write your answer on a separate sheet. Students may explain that people support human rights because they believe all people should have the freedom to live their lives however they wish.

Chapter 14, pages 386–394   85

LOCATING IMPORTANT MUSLIM PLACES

Gathering Information from a Map, Making Observations

✳ The map shows places that are important to Muslims. Study the map, and then answer the questions that follow.

1. In which direction did Muhammad travel on the Hegira from Mecca to Medina? north

2. When Muslims today retrace the Hegira, how far do they travel? about 200 miles (320 km)

3. What four geographic features may Muslims on pilgrimages to Mecca pass? An Nafud, Rub' Al Khali, Tuwayq Mountains, Red Sea

4. When Muslims in the United Arab Emirates pray facing Mecca, in which direction do they face? west

5. The Kaaba shrine in Mecca is located in which country? Saudi Arabia

6. How far is the mosque in Medina from the Red Sea? about 100 miles (160 km)

7. Which two cities on the map are northwest of Mecca? Yanbu and Jidda

Thinking Further: If a map showed your community and other major places within 100 miles, what would it show? Include in your description physical features such as mountains and lakes. Write your answer on a separate sheet. Answers will reflect independent thinking, but students should mention nearby towns, bodies of water, and land features.

86   Chapter 14, pages 377–394

MUSLIM HOUSES OF WORSHIP

Reading for Details, Making Observations

✳ Read the following description of Muslim houses of worship. Then complete the statements below.

The Muslim houses of worship, called mosques, are among the most beautiful examples of architecture in the world. Every mosque has a tall, slender tower, or minaret, that can be seen from afar. Another prominent part of a mosque is the mihrah, or gate. The gate is often decorated with intricate designs, and stands out from the plain front wall facing the street. A court is inside the gate and in front of the main building. Many mosques have great domed roofs. A pulpit, or mimbar, made of wood or stone, is the only furniture inside.

1. A Muslim house of worship is called a mosque

2. The gate of a mosque is called a mihrah

3. The only furniture inside a Muslim house of worship is a pulpit, or mimbar

4. Front walls of Muslim houses of worship are often plain

5. Gates of Muslim houses of worship are often decorated with designs

6. From far away, people can see the minaret

7. Some Muslim houses of worship have a large rounded dome

8. Inside the gate and in front of the main building of a Muslim house of worship is a court

Thinking Further: Describe an important building in your community. Describe the building's features and what it is used for. Answers will reflect independent thinking, but students should mention the building's features and use.

Chapter 14, pages 395–399   87

TEACHER NOTES

Origins of the Muslim Religion

Objectives

★1. **Describe** the role of Muhammad in establishing the Muslim religion.

2. **Discuss** the early history and some of the important beliefs of the Muslim religion.

3. **Identify** the following people and places: *Muhammad, Mecca,* and *Medina.*

1 STARTING THE LESSON

Motivation Activity

■ Ask students to talk about what they know about the Muslim religion.

■ Ask questions such as these: **Where is it practiced? How is it similar to or different from Christianity and Judaism? About how many followers do you think the religion has?**

■ Write students' comments and impressions on the chalkboard and explain that in this lesson students will learn about the history and beliefs of the Islamic world.

Think About What You Know

■ Assign the THINK ABOUT WHAT YOU KNOW activity on p. 377.

■ Student answers may include Jesus Christ, who is important to Christians, and Buddha, who is important to Buddhists.

Study the Vocabulary

■ Have students look up the definitions of the vocabulary words in the Glossary.

■ Write the following sentence on the board and ask students to fill in the blanks: Both Christians and Muslims might make a (1.)_____ to a (2.)_____ or study the teachings of a (3.)_____ .
(1. pilgrimage, 2. shrine, 3. prophet)

CHAPTER **14** HISTORY OF THE MIDDLE EAST AND NORTH AFRICA

*T*he religion of Islam developed in the Middle East. Its culture has had a strong impact on many parts of the world. Beautiful houses of prayer, such as this one in Cairo, Egypt, are part of that Islamic culture.

Optional Activities

For Your Information

Muhammad   Muhammad helped the unorganized Bedouin tribesmen who followed him reach a level of civilization that was comparable to that of the Christians and Jews of the time. When Muhammad first began to preach, Arabia was a wild, lawless land. As a community leader, Muhammad made his religious message law. He ended the custom of killing unwanted baby girls, and he limited polygamy, or the taking of several wives. He regulated slavery and encouraged people to eschew violence except for self-defense and for the cause of Islam. He replaced tribal loyalty with a new tie of equality and allegiance among all Muslims.

LESSON 1

Origins of the Muslim Religion

THINK ABOUT WHAT YOU KNOW

You have learned about the importance of religion in different cultures. Name some religious leaders that you have studied about in earlier chapters and tell to whom they were important.

STUDY THE VOCABULARY

shrine   pilgrimage
prophet

FOCUS YOUR READING

How did the Muslim religion begin?

A. How Muhammad Settled a Dispute

Rebuilding the Kaaba   The Kaaba (KAH-buh) is a building in Mecca, a city located in the Arabian Desert. It is a simple stone structure built in the shape of a cube. In fact, the name *Kaaba* comes from the Arabic word for cube. Set in the wall at one corner of the Kaaba is a black stone encased in silver.

For centuries the Kaaba has been a religious **shrine**, a place considered holy. At one time, people came to the Kaaba to worship the images of gods and goddesses and to touch the black stone, which was considered sacred, or holy.

About 1,400 years ago one of the rare thunderstorms in the desert flooded Mecca. Rushing waters destroyed the walls of the Kaaba so that it had to be rebuilt. Men from all of the city's leading families took part in rebuilding the important shrine. At last all the stones were in place, except for the sacred black stone that the leaders of the four major families claimed the honor of putting back in the Kaaba. Since they could not decide who would replace the sacred stone, it was agreed upon to settle the dispute by chance. It was decided that the first man who walked through the gate would

People from all over the world journey to Mecca to pray at the Kaaba.
▶ What is the Kaaba?

---

2 DEVELOPING THE LESSON

Read and Think

Section A

The ancient Kaaba at Mecca had religious significance for the people of the Middle East even before the time of Muhammad. Use the questions below to discuss the rebuilding of this important shrine:

1. **Why did people travel to the Kaaba more than 1,400 years ago (before the flood)?**
   (People went to the Kaaba to worship images of gods and goddesses and to touch the sacred black stone. *p. 377*)

2. **What dispute did Muhammad settle during the rebuilding of the Kaaba?**
   (The dispute over which of the four major families would replace the sacred black stone in the Kaaba *p. 377*)

   Thinking Critically   What qualities do you think were shown by Muhammad in the story about the rebuilding of the Kaaba? (Analyze)
   (Answers should reflect independent thinking but may include wisdom, a desire for peace, and respect for people's feelings. *p. 378*)

Answers to Caption Questions
p. 377 ▶ A religious shrine

Mnemonic Devices

- Students will encounter many unfamiliar Arabic words in this lesson. These may include *Kaaba, Allah, Koran, Islam, Muslim,* and *Hegira.*
- Have them skim the lesson, list unfamiliar words, and read the words in context to learn each meaning.
- After explaining what mnemonic devices are, have students create mnemonic devices to help them remember the new words and their meanings.
- For example, "Karen always ate big apples" may help students remember the term *Kaaba.*

Cooperative Learning

Creating a No-lose Game   Review Muhammad's solution to the dispute over the black stone and explain that it was a solution which allowed everyone to win.

- Divide students into groups of four or five and give each group 20 or 30 minutes to create a game (to play in class) in which everyone wins.
- Have one or two students in each group write down the rules of their group's game.
- Another student should make the game board.
- Have another student make the playing pieces.
- Finally, have one student explain the game to the class.

Optional Activities

Read and Think

Section B

To summarize the early life of Muhammad and his founding of the Islamic religion, ask the following questions:

1. **What was Muhammad's occupation before he became a religious leader?**
(A merchant *p. 378*)

2. **What religions influenced Muhammad during his caravan trips with his uncle?**
(The Christian and Jewish religions *p. 378*)

3. **What Arabic word did Muhammad use that means "the God"?**
(Allah *p. 379*)

4. **How was the Koran, the holy book of the Islamic religion, written?**
(Followers of Muhammad memorized his teachings, wrote them down, and gathered them together into the Koran. *p. 379*)

Thinking Critically Why, do you think, is the Muslim religion also called **Islam?** (Hypothesize)
(Answers should reflect independent thinking but may include that *Islam* is an Arabic word meaning "surrender to God" which is very close to the meaning of the word *Muslim* meaning "one who has surrendered to God." *p. 379*)

VISUAL THINKING SKILL

Reading a Time Line

■ Have students look at the time line on p. 378 to help them answer the following questions:

1. **When was Muhammad born?**
(In the year 570)

2. **Did Constantinople fall before or after the Crusades?**
(After the Crusades)

3. **How long did Suleiman the Magnificent rule?**
(46 years)

378

---

choose the person to place the black stone in the wall.

Muhammad Enters As it happened, the first man through the gate was a respected merchant named Muhammad. When the dispute was explained to him, he asked for a large cloth. He spread the cloth on the ground and placed the black stone in the center. He then had the leading men from the four families each take hold of a corner of the cloth. He told them to lift the cloth and carry the stone to its place in the wall. The men did as the merchant directed. When they had raised the stone to the proper height, Muhammad pushed it into place. Muhammad's wise decision satisfied all four families. All had shared equally in the honor of restoring the black stone.

B. The Messages of Muhammad

A Young Boy The merchant later became the founder of the religion of the Muslims. Muhammad was born about A.D. 570 in Mecca. Muhammad's father had died before he was born. His mother died when he was about 6 years old, leaving his grandfather and an uncle to raise him.

The uncle was a merchant who took trading caravans to cities on the edge of the desert. When Muhammad was 12 years old, he persuaded his uncle to take him on a caravan trip to Syria. While on the trips, Muhammad met many different people. He talked with a Christian monk, who taught him about Jesus and Christianity, and with Jews, who taught him about the laws of Judaism.

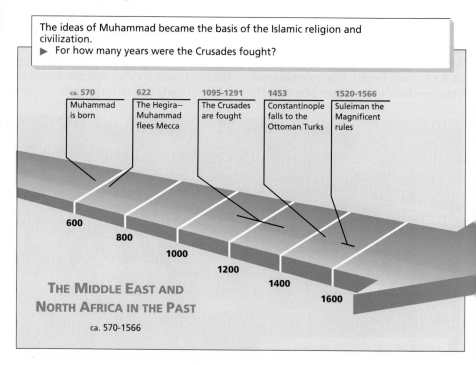

The ideas of Muhammad became the basis of the Islamic religion and civilization.
▶ For how many years were the Crusades fought?

ca. 570 Muhammad is born

622 The Hegira-- Muhammad flees Mecca

1095-1291 The Crusades are fought

1453 Constantinople falls to the Ottoman Turks

1520-1566 Suleiman the Magnificent rules

600 800 1000 1200 1400 1600

THE MIDDLE EAST AND NORTH AFRICA IN THE PAST
ca. 570-1566

378

Comparing Religions

● Have students work in small groups to make a chart comparing and contrasting Islam, Judaism, Christianity, Buddhism, and Hinduism.

● Have them skim any previous chapters that are appropriate and do additional research in the library, if necessary, to find the information for the chart.

● The charts should show when and where the religion was started, who started it, how it was spread, and where most of the followers of each religion live today.

● Use the charts to start a classroom discussion about how each religion has been influenced by its early history.

Muhammad is shown below receiving one of the many messages from the angel Gabriel.
► Which of the two figures depicted is Gabriel?

An Angel's Message After spending time traveling with his uncle, Muhammad returned to live in Mecca. Sometimes Muhammad would leave the crowded marketplace of the city and go into the desert to be alone. One night in a desert cave, Muhammad reported that an unusual thing happened. According to Muhammad's account, an angel appeared and told him that it was wrong to worship the images of gods and goddesses in the Kaaba because there was only one true God.

When Muhammad told others about the angel's message, he used the Arabic word *Allah* (AL uh), which simply means "the God." Muhammad reported that the angel said that Allah had sent earlier **prophets** but that he, Muhammad, was the last of them. A prophet is a religious leader who speaks out against wrongdoing and warns that punishments will come to those who break God's laws.

The Koran The message in the desert cave was the first of a number of messages that Muhammad said he received. He repeated the messages to others, who learned them by heart. Later, Muhammad's followers wrote down these messages and gathered them into a book called the *Koran,* an Arabic word meaning "the reading." The Koran, the holy book of the Muslims, contains many teachings, some of which you can read on page 380. Muhammad called his teachings *Islam,* which means "surrender to God." A person whose religion is Islam is known as a *Muslim,* "one who has surrendered to God."

379

Meeting Individual Needs

Concept: Inferring

To better understand the Muslim faith, it is important to understand how the teachings of Muhammad influence the religion today. Below are three activities that will help students infer how the early history of Islam has affected today's Muslim religion.

◆ **EASY** Have students read Sections A, B, and C aloud as a class, stopping after each paragraph to discuss the qualities shown by Muhammad in that paragraph.

List these qualities on the chalkboard and discuss the kind of religion that a person with these qualities might start.

◄► **AVERAGE** Have students skim Section D, listing each fact they find about the Islamic religion as they read.

Then, have students work in pairs to find a historical basis for each fact about present-day Islam in Section A, B, or C.

◄▮► **CHALLENGING** Ask students who need a challenge to write an essay about the influence of Muslim history on the Muslim religion as it is practiced today.

── **Answers to Caption Questions** ──
p. 378 ► One hundred ninety-six
p. 379 ► The figure with the wings

SKILLBUILDER REVIEW

Understanding Comparisons On pp. 352-353 students learned the skill of understanding comparisons. Have them review this skill by making a chart that compares the Bible and the Koran.

● Have students make a chart with two rows, one for the Koran and one for the Bible.

● Have them list specific characterists in a row across the top of the chart.

● Then have students fill in the charts, using a plus when the subject has a certain characteristic, and a minus when it does not have the characteristic.

Writing to Learn

Writing a Letter Ask students to pretend that they have a pen pal who is a Muslim living in North Africa or the Middle East.

● Have them write letters to their imaginary pen pals, describing what they have learned about the Muslim faith from this lesson.

● Have them ask any questions that they may have about the Muslim religion and culture.

● Have them include in their letters any information that they would like their pen pals to know about their own cultural background.

Optional Activities

379

Thinking About Source Material

Background Information

Sacred Book of the Muslims The Muslims believe that this book was revealed to Muhammad by the angel Gabriel. The name *Koran* means "a recitation" or "something to be recited." Muslims believe that Gabriel revealed the Koran a little at a time starting around the time of A.D. 610 and continuing until Muhammad died in 632. The Koran, which is written in rhymed Arabic prose, is, according to Muslim belief, the word of God Himself who keeps the original copy in heaven.

Guided Reading

After students have read the selection from the Koran on p. 380, discuss the teachings of Muhammad. The following questions will aid in this discussion.

1. **Who do Muslims believe that Muhammad was?**
   (A prophet of God)

2. **In how many gods do Muslims believe?**
   (One)

3. **What does the Koran say about how we should treat our parents?**
   (Be good to them; say gentle words to them, and look after them with kindness and love.)

Understanding Source Material

1. Answers may include that you should not give things to people that you would not want to receive yourself.

2. Answers should reflect independent thinking but may include that the Koran's statement about measuring could apply to justice, to giving equally in personal relationships, or to being honest in general.

USING SOURCE MATERIAL

THE TEACHINGS OF MUHAMMAD

Muslims believe that Muhammad was a prophet who served as God's messenger. The messages that Muhammad used as his teachings are contained in the Koran, the holy book of the Muslims. Here are translations of some passages from the Koran.

Muhammad is only a messenger, and many a messenger has gone before him.

Pay homage to God . . . and be good to your parents and relatives, the orphans and the needy and the neighbors who are your relatives, and the neighbors who are strangers, and the friend by your side, the traveler and your servants.

O believers, give in charity what is good of the things you have earned, and of what you produce from the earth; and do not choose to give what is bad as alms [donations], that is, things you would not like to accept yourself.

If you give alms openly, it is well; but if you do it secretly and give to the poor, that is better.

Be good to your parents. . . . say gentle words to them. And look after them with kindness and love. . . .

Give full measure when you are measuring, and weigh on a balanced scale.

You may dislike a thing yet it may be good for you; or a thing may haply [by chance] please you but be bad for you. . . .

God is with those who preserve themselves from evil and do the right.

Understanding Source Material

1. How would you rephrase the Koran's passage about not giving things you would not accept yourself?

2. The Koran's statement about measuring does not just apply to measuring that is done with a ruler, scale, or other instrument. To what other kinds of "measuring" do you think the statement could apply?

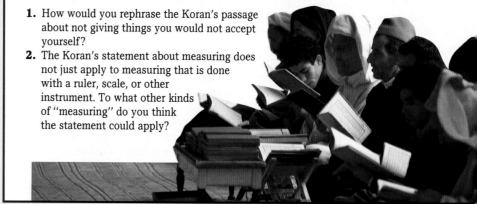

Optional Activities

Using Source Material

- After students have read the selection from the Koran, have them use it as a source for creating a bulletin board.

- Have each student draw a picture or cut out a magazine picture that illustrates one of the teachings found in the Koran.

- Then, have students arrange the pictures on the bulletin board and give their display a title such as "Teachings of the Koran."

Muhammad is shown here completing the Hegira, the journey from Mecca to Medina.
▶ Why, do you think, are these people gathered around him?

C. Muhammad as a Leader

A Religious Leader At first only a few people in Mecca believed Muhammad's account of the angel's message. His wife, his cousin, and a freed slave were among the first to accept it. Most people mocked him. The leaders of Mecca believed that Muhammad had gone mad.

In spite of opposition, Muhammad began to preach about the messages. In time, Muhammad did win followers, and his opponents grew alarmed. They began to abuse and persecute those who believed Muhammad. Muhammad decided to seek safety in another city. So, in A.D. 622, Muhammad left Mecca and went to Medina. The journey from Mecca to Medina is called the *Hegira* (hih JYE ruh). Muslims number the years of their calendar from the Hegira, so that their year 1 is 622 on the Christian calendar.

Defeating Mecca Muhammad became the leader of Medina. When a war broke out between Medina and Mecca, Muhammad led his adopted city into battle and defeated Mecca. He assured the people of Mecca that they would not be harmed if they gave up their old religion.

Muhammad had the Kaaba cleared of the images of the gods and goddesses, but he saw to it that no harm was done to the ancient shrine. He declared that in the future the Kaaba would be dedicated to the worship of Allah. Muhammad instructed his followers to face toward the Kaaba in Mecca whenever they prayed. Muslims still do so today.

Read and Think

Section D

The teachings of Muhammad have been handed down over the centuries making it one of the world's major religions, second only to Christianity in terms of the number of followers. Use these questions to discuss the practice of Islam today:

1. **Where do people practice Islam today?**
(Islam is the major religion of the Middle East and North Africa and is widely practiced in Asia, but there are Muslims on every continent. *p. 382*)

2. **What beliefs do all Muslim groups have in common?**
(That there is one God, that Muhammad was the last of the prophets, and that the Koran is their holy book *p. 382*)

3. **Why did Muhammad speak of helping widows and orphans?**
(Perhaps because his mother had been widowed before he was born and he became an orphan at a very young age. *p. 383*)

Thinking Critically Why, do you think, did Muhammad make the Kaaba an important shrine of Islam, even though it was a shrine of the earlier religion?
(Answers may include that it was a way of wiping out the old religion without upsetting people by destroying a holy place, or that he felt the new religion was an outgrowth of the old beliefs. *pp. 382-383*)

After the conquest of Mecca, other cities of Arabia accepted Muhammad as their leader. Ten years after the journey from Mecca, almost all of Arabia accepted Muhammad as both ruler and prophet.

D. Muslims in the World Today

There are millions of Muslims in the world today. Islam is the religion of most people in the Middle East and North Africa. It is also the faith of large numbers in other parts of Asia. Indeed, there are Muslims on all continents.

Muslims, like Christians, are divided into different groups, but all the Muslim groups share some beliefs. All accept the belief that there is only one God and that Muhammad was the last of the prophets. All regard the Koran as a holy book. Some Muslims memorize the entire Koran,

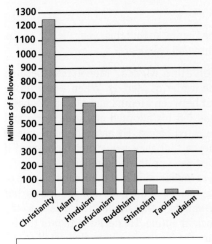

MAJOR WORLD RELIGIONS

Today Islam is the second largest religion in the world.
► What religion has the most followers?

even though the book contains about 78,000 words.

Muhammad taught that faithful Muslims have certain duties. Muhammad said that all should declare their belief in one God and all should pray five times a day, while facing Mecca. Faithful Muslims who could possibly do so had a duty to make a **pilgrimage** to Mecca at least once in their lives. A pilgrimage is a journey to a shrine or other sacred place. Those who make such a journey are called pilgrims. Before pilgrims enter Mecca, they change to simple clothing so that rich and poor are dressed alike. The pilgrims go to the Kaaba, kiss the black stone, and walk around the sacred building seven times,

---

Reteaching Main Objective

⭐ *Describe the role of Muhammad in establishing the Muslim religion.*

Have students work in small groups to make storyboards that show the role of Muhammad in establishing the Muslim religion.

Have students illustrate various stages in Muhammad's life.

Then, have students write a short caption under each frame to explain how that period or episode affected Muhammad.

Display the storyboards in class.

Each year thousands of Muslims from around the world make a pilgrimage to Mecca, Saudi Arabia, the birthplace of Muhammad.
► By what means do modern-day Muslims travel to their holy city of Mecca?

reciting prayers as Muhammad did. Each year large numbers of Muslims from many lands make the pilgrimage to Mecca.

Muhammad taught his followers that they had a duty to help the poor and others in need. He spoke particularly of helping widows and orphans. Perhaps he remembered that his mother had been a widow before he was born and that he became an orphan when he was very young.

LESSON *1* REVIEW

THINK AND WRITE

A. How did Muhammad settle the dispute about placing the black stone in the wall of the Kaaba? **(Recall)**

B. According to Muhammad, what message did he receive in the cave? **(Recall)**

C. What did Muhammad do after the conquest of Mecca? **(Recall)**

D. What are important duties of Muslims? **(Recall)**

SKILLS CHECK

MAP SKILL

Muhammad journeyed from Mecca to Medina to seek safety. Look in the Gazetteer for the coordinates of Medina. Then find Mecca on the political map of Eurasia in the Atlas. About how far did Muhammad travel?

383

---

3 CLOSING THE LESSON

Lesson *1* Review

Answers to Think and Write

A. Muhammad settled the dispute by placing the black stone on a cloth and having the leading man from each of the four disputing families lift a corner of the cloth and carry the stone to its place in the wall, where Muhammad pushed it into place.

B. Muhammad said that an angel came to him in the cave and told him that it was wrong to worship gods and goddesses in the Kaaba because there was only one God, that Allah had sent earlier prophets, and that Muhammad was the last of the prophets sent by Allah.

C. After he conquered Mecca, Muhammad cleared the Kaaba of the images of the gods and goddesses and dedicated the shrine to Allah. He instructed his followers to face toward the Kaaba in Mecca when they prayed.

D. The important duties of Muslims are to declare their faith in one God, to pray — facing Mecca — five times a day, to make a pilgrimage to Mecca, if at all possible, and to help the poor and others in need, especially widows and orphans.

Answer to Skills Check

Mecca and Medina are approximately 200 miles (322 km) apart.

Focus Your Reading

Ask the lesson focus question found at the beginning of the lesson: **How did the Muslim religion begin?**
(The Muslim religion began after Muhammad had a vision telling him that there was only one God, Allah, and that he, Muhammad, was the last of Allah's prophets.)

Additional Practice

You may wish to assign the ancillary materials listed below.

Understanding the Lesson p. 96
Workbook p. 84

┌─ **Answers to Caption Questions** ─┐
p. 382 ► Christianity
p. 383 ► By foot and by car
└─────────────────────────┘

383

CITIZENSHIP AND AMERICAN VALUES

Objectives

1. **Develop** patriotism and American values.

2. **Develop** strong personal integrity and positive self-image.

Guided Reading

1. **From what you have read in this selection, why is Martin Luther King, Jr., considered to be a great person?**
   (He received the Nobel Prize for his role in seeking racial equality and justice.)

2. **What do you think was Sally Ride's greatest accomplishment?**
   (Answers should reflect independent thinking but may include that she was the first American woman to travel in space.)

3. **What do you think makes Beethoven's music great?**
   (Answers should reflect independent thinking but may include that people still enjoy his music 150 years after his death.)

4. **What are two of Thomas Edison's inventions?**
   (The incandescent lamp and the phonograph)

WHAT MAKES A PERSON GREAT?

If you were to ask each person in your class what makes a man or woman great, you would probably get many different answers. These answers would show the different values of the members of your class.

You have just read about Muhammad, who has been called great by many people. All the persons described in the following paragraphs have been called great at one time or another. Of course, not all people have agreed that these persons were great. Do you think they were great? Read about each of them and then make up your mind.

Martin Luther King, Jr.
Martin Luther King, Jr., was born and raised in Atlanta, Georgia. He became a Baptist minister who preached nonviolence and racial integration. Dr. King received the Nobel Peace Prize in 1964 for his role in seeking racial equality and justice. He was assassinated in 1968, in Memphis, Tennessee.

Ludwig van Beethoven
Beethoven was a German composer who wrote some of the world's greatest music. Before he was 30 years old, Beethoven began to lose his hearing. He continued to write music even after he was completely deaf. Now, more than 150 years after Beethoven's death, his music is still enjoyed by many.

Thomas Edison
Thomas Edison, born in Ohio, was the inventor of the incandescent electric lamp and the phonograph. He also improved the inventions of other people, such as the telephone, the typewriter, and the motion picture. Many of Edison's important devices were invented at his workshop in Menlo Park, New Jersey. He was responsible for more than 1,000 inventions in his lifetime.

Sally Ride
Sally Ride, who was born in Los Angeles, California, became the first American woman to travel in space. In 1978 she was one of 35 people chosen from among 8,000 to train as astronauts. In June 1983, Sally Ride and four crew members made a six-day flight on the space shuttle *Challenger*. Ride was later a member of the presidential commission investigating the 1986 *Challenger* accident.

384

◄ Martin Luther King, Jr.

Optional Activities

For Your Information

Thomas Alva Edison   Thomas Edison defined genius as "one percent inspiration, 99 percent perspiration." Ask students what they think the quotation means. Then, share the following example from Edison's life, which illustrates the quotation: When about 10,000 experiments with a storage battery failed to produce results, a friend tried to console Edison, but Edison replied, "I have not failed, I've just found 10,000 ways that won't work." Students may also be interested to hear about a parallel between Edison and Beethoven. Edison was almost completely deaf, yet he still had a keen ear for music. He often claimed that he could hear by placing his head against a phonograph speaker. He personally supervised thousands of recordings, and could instantly detect a wrong note.

Thinking for Yourself

On a separate sheet of paper, answer the following questions in complete sentences.

1. Which of the people described do you consider to be the greatest? Explain your answer.
2. Which of the people described do you think least deserves to be called great? Explain your answer.
3. Name someone living today whom you would include in a list of great people. Why do you consider that person to be great?

◄ Ludwig van Beethoven

Sally Ride ►

Thomas Edison ►

385

Thinking for Yourself

1. Answers should reflect independent thinking but may include Martin Luther King, Jr., because he fought for civil rights; Sally Ride, because she proved to be a great woman in a world where mostly men succeed; Beethoven, because we can still enjoy his music today, or Thomas Edison, because we still use his inventions today.

2. Answers will depend on what students think makes a person great.

3. Answers should reflect independent thinking and should include the reasons why students think the person whom they have chosen is great. Answers may include such people as the President of the United States, other famous politicians, celebrities, or people in the community in which the students live.

Analyzing a Speech

- Bring in a copy of the famous speech entitled "I Have a Dream," given by Martin Luther King, Jr., on August 28, 1963, at the Lincoln Memorial in Washington, D.C. Read excerpts of the speech aloud to the class.

- Based on the speech, students should give reasons why King would be considered great (as an orator, writer, thinker, visionary, leader, and so on).

- Ask students if they think that King's speech would still be appropriate today (that is, do they think anything has changed since August 28, 1963).

- Ask students if they think King's dream will come true.

Curriculum Connection

Music Bring in a recording of some of Beethoven's compositions and play one or two selections for the class. (Students may recognize the opening to the famous Fifth Symphony.)

- Ask students to share their reactions to the music.

- What emotions does the music express?

- Does the music make students picture any visual images in particular?

- For what type of movie would this music be an appropriate soundtrack?

Optional Activities

Caliphs and Crusaders

Objectives

★ 1. **Explain** the causes and results of the Crusades.

2. **Discuss** the development of Islam after the death of Muhammad.

3. **Define** the boundaries of the Ottoman Empire on a map.

4. **Identify** the following people and places: *Abu-Bakr, Omar, Pope Urban II, Saladin, Richard the Lion-Hearted, Suleiman, Medina, Damascus, Baghdad, Istanbul, Edessa, Tripoli,* and *Antioch.*

1 STARTING THE LESSON

Motivation Activity

■ Ask students if they would like to go to a foreign country and why they would go.

■ Make a list on the chalkboard of the students' responses and save the list.

■ Explain that in this lesson they will learn about the first time that large numbers of Europeans traveled to a land that had a different culture.

■ After teaching the lesson, compare the crusaders' reasons for traveling to a land that had a different culture with the students' reasons for wanting to go to a foreign country.

Think About What You Know

■ Assign the THINK ABOUT WHAT YOU KNOW activity on p. 386.

■ Student answers may include reasons for not going, such as the immorality of war, or reasons for going, such as opportunities for travel and adventure.

Study the Vocabulary

■ Have students look up the definitions of the vocabulary words in the Glossary.

■ Have students list synonyms for the terms (ruler, leader, and so on) and discuss whether or not the synonyms describe one or both of the terms.

THINK ABOUT WHAT YOU KNOW
Imagine that you had an opportunity to be part of the First Crusade. Why would or would you not decide to go?

STUDY THE VOCABULARY
caliph   sultan

FOCUS YOUR READING
What brought about the crusades, and what were the results?

A. The Empire of the Caliphs

Abu-Bakr When Muhammad fled Mecca, he was accompanied by his faithful friend Abu-Bakr (ah boo-BAH kur). After Muhammad's death in 632, his followers chose Abu-Bakr as the **caliph** (KAY lihf) of Muhammad. The title *caliph* means "one who comes after." The caliphs acted as religious and political leaders. They used the Koran as the basis for ruling the empire.

Abu-Bakr was a modest man. He is reported to have told the people who chose him caliph,

> *Obey me only so far as I obey God and the prophet [Muhammad]. If I go beyond these bounds, I have no authority over you. If I am wrong, set me right.*

Omar When Abu-Bakr died, the Muslims chose Omar as the caliph. Omar was another of Muhammad's old companions. He was a stern military leader who declared, "The Arabs are like an unruly camel, but I am he who can keep them on the right path." Omar led the Muslims to victories over their foes, but he warned that their triumphs should not make them lazy.

386

Muslim Empire Abu-Bakr and Omar were the first of a long line of caliphs. The Arabs, under the leadership of the caliphs, conquered a large empire, as shown by the map on page 387. The empire included all of North Africa and much of the Middle East. The Muslims also conquered all of the Iberian Peninsula, now divided into Spain and Portugal.

Muhammad and the first four caliphs ruled from the city of Medina, which is located in the heart of Arabia. The fifth caliph made the city of Damascus, in Syria, the capital of the Muslim empire. Damascus is believed to be the oldest existing city in the world.

Later caliphs moved the capital farther east to Baghdad, on the Tigris River in Iraq. At both Damascus and Baghdad, the

Abu-Bakr was a close friend and father-in-law to Muhammad.
► What title was Abu-Bakr given after Muhammad's death?

Writing to Learn

Writing a Diary Have students write a diary entry from the perspective of a 12-year-old Muslim girl or boy on the day in 632 when Muhammad died and his followers chose Abu-Bakr as the caliph.

● As a prewriting activity, read aloud the text in Section A that relates what Abu-Bakr is reported to have told the people who chose him as caliph.

● Judging from the text, what kind of leader do they think Abu-Bakr will be?

● How do they think the death of Muhammad and the choice of Abu-Bakr as caliph will affect them?

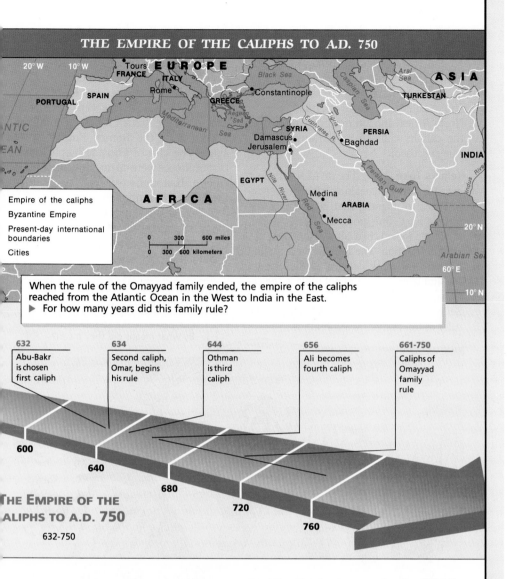

THE EMPIRE OF THE CALIPHS TO A.D. 750

Empire of the caliphs
Byzantine Empire
Present-day international
boundaries
Cities

When the rule of the Omayyad family ended, the empire of the caliphs reached from the Atlantic Ocean in the West to India in the East.
▶ For how many years did this family rule?

632	634	644	656	661-750
Abu-Bakr is chosen first caliph	Second caliph, Omar, begins his rule	Othman is third caliph	Ali becomes fourth caliph	Caliphs of Omayyad family rule

600
640
680
720
760

THE EMPIRE OF THE CALIPHS TO A.D. 750
632-750

caliphs built fine palaces. They and the people of their court enjoyed many luxuries. The later caliphs did not copy Omar's simple way of life. They lived more like kings than like successors to a prophet from the desert.

B. The Turks Appear in the Middle East

Caliphs' Rule Ends The lands conquered by the Muslims contained a variety of peoples. Many of these conquered peoples adopted the Muslim religion. Many spoke

387

2 DEVELOPING THE LESSON

Read and Think
Section A

The Arabs conquered a huge empire, but in time, Turks from Asia conquered the eastern lands. Use the following questions to discuss these developments:

1. **How did the lifestyle of the caliphs change over time?**
   (From a simple lifestyle to living in palaces and and in luxury *pp. 386-387*)

   Thinking Critically How, do you think, did Abu-Bakr's attitude toward his role as caliph compare with Omar's attitude toward his role as caliph?
   (Analyze)
   (Answers may include that Omar saw himself as a powerful leader, whereas Abu-Bakr saw himself as one who could learn from his followers. *p. 386*)

GEOGRAPHY THEMES

Location

■ Have students use the map on p. 387 to answer the following question: **Near which sea are both Medina and Mecca located?** (The Red Sea)

Answers to Caption Questions
p. 386 ▶ Caliph
p. 387 ▶ Eighty-nine years

Curriculum Connection

Language Arts Explain that Omar's comparison of the Arabs to an unruly camel is a *simile*.

● A simile is a figure of speech in which two things are compared, using the words *like* or *as*.

● Have the class make up two or three similes about familiar things, such as the weather or objects in the classroom or the school.

● Then, have students skim through the lesson and write at least three similes about people or places described in the lesson. Examples are "King Richard I was like a lion" and "The Black Sea was like a Turkish lake."

● Ask volunteers to share their similes with the rest of the class.

For Your Information

The Seljuk Turks The Seljuk Turks were tough and hard-riding nomads of Asia who were led by a man named Seljuk. They had been converted to Islam after an earlier conquest by the Arabs (before the political unity of the Arab empire was weakened). The Seljuks, though new to the faith, were fanatic Muslims, and their attacks on the Byzantine Empire were seen as a terrible threat by all Christians. In 1063, a Seljuk named Alp Arslan became sultan. He was known by the Turks as a "strong and fair leader" because he helped the poor and punished corrupt officials. Alp Arslan led the conquest of the Anatolian peninsula and the Byzantine Empire, which led to the Crusades.

Optional Activities

Read and Think
Sections B, C, and D

Use the questions below to discuss the Crusades and their impact on the people of Europe and the Middle East:

1. **After the Seljuks conquered the eastern Muslim lands, who became caliph of Baghdad?**
(No one; the Seljuk sultan became the ruler of the eastern Muslim lands. *p. 388*)

2. **What arguments did Pope Urban II use to persuade the knights of western Europe to join the People's Crusade?**
(The Pope argued that Muslims were robbing and torturing Christian pilgrims journeying to the Holy Land; the war offered the knights a chance for glory and wealth; and it would be better for them to fight Muslims than to fight each other. *p. 389*)

3. **What were the European colonies in the Middle East called, and how were they governed?**
(They were called Jerusalem, Edessa, Tripoli, and Antioch, and were governed like the feudal states of Europe. *p. 390*)

Thinking Critically **Why, do you think, were the Crusades worth or not worth fighting?** (Evaluate)
(Answers may include that they were not worth fighting because nothing was accomplished and many people died, or that they were worth fighting because despite the deaths that they caused, they provided Europeans and Arabs with important information about each other. *pp. 389-392*)

Interpreting a Picture

■ Direct students' attention to the picture on p. 388 to help them complete the following activity: Write a description about what the people in the picture are wearing. **How can you tell what their occupation is?**
(Paragraphs should describe the clothing, including hats and weapons that these rulers are wearing. Students should explain why they know that these people are kings or rulers.)

Arabic, since this was the language of their conquerors. But the empire of the caliphs did not remain united. Many bitter disputes arose among different groups of Muslims. At one time there were three different caliphs, one in Baghdad, one in North Africa, and a third in Spain. Each of the caliphs claimed to be Muhammad's true successor.

Seljuks Take Over The divisions made it easy for Turkish-speaking tribes from central Asia to migrate, that is, move, to the Middle East. One group of Turks, the Seljuks (SEL jooks), had already adopted the Muslim religion. The Seljuks were skillful fighters who took control of the eastern Muslim lands. They did not replace the caliph at the capital city of Baghdad, but the Seljuk leader called the **sultan** became the ruler of the eastern Muslim lands.

The Seljuks conquered the Anatolian peninsula, which was ruled by the Christian emperor at Constantinople. As you have learned in an earlier chapter, Constantinople became the "new Rome." Constantinople became the capital of what was left of the Roman Empire. During the Middle Ages the Roman Empire broke apart. The city of Constantinople and a part of Greece were all that remained of the empire. Historians call this later Roman Empire the Byzantine Empire.

Turkish-speaking tribes other than the Seljuks migrated into Anatolia. In time the peninsula became known as Turkey —land of the Turks.

Turkish nomadic tribes known as the Seljuks migrated to western Asia. Their advance marked the start of Turkish power in the Middle East.
▶ By what means did they travel?

Role-playing

● There are a number of opportunities for creative role-playing in this lesson.

● Divide the class into three groups to role-play groups or individuals discussed in this lesson.

● Have one group role-play members of the First Crusade, another group role-play members of the Children's Crusade, and a third group role-play members of the Third Crusade, including a meeting between Richard the Lion-Hearted and Saladin.

● Give the students 20 minutes to prepare their skits and 20 minutes to act them out.

C. The Call for a Holy War

A Plea for Help After the Seljuk conquest of Anatolia, the Christian emperor at Constantinople sent a message to the pope at Rome asking for help. The emperor probably wanted trained fighting men to help his armies win back lost territory. But Pope Urban II, who received the appeal, had a much more far-reaching plan. The pope wanted to send an army to conquer and rescue from the Muslims the Holy Land, that is, the land where Jesus had lived. Above all, the pope wanted the Christians to capture the Holy City of Jerusalem.

In 1095, Pope Urban called on the knights of western Europe to join in a war against the Muslims. This war was the first of a series of wars that were later called Crusades—wars for the cross—between European Christians and Muslims in the Middle East. The pope declared,

> *It would be far better for the warlike knights of Europe to fight Muslims in the Middle East than to cut each other in pieces in wars at home.*

The pope charged that the Muslim Turks robbed and tortured Christian pilgrims journeying to the Holy Land. He said that Christian knights would win great glory by rescuing the Holy City from the Muslims. They could also win great wealth in the eastern lands. The Holy Land was "fruitful above others." The pope pointed out that the Bible called it a land "flowing with milk and honey."

People's Crusade Even before feudal lords and knights could organize an army, many people in western Europe answered Pope Urban's call for help. These people organized the People's Crusade and started for the Holy Land. The People's

Pope Urban II and Peter the Hermit preach to the crowd about going to war with the Muslims.
▶ How would you describe the reaction of the crowd?

The Granger Collection

Crusade was a crowd, not an army. Most of those who started for the Middle East were not trained fighters. Few of these crusaders had weapons or knew anything about warfare. The result was a disaster. Most of the first wave of crusaders were killed or captured.

D. European Colonies in the Middle East

First Crusade The official army of the First Crusade made up of knights and feudal lords reached Constantinople in 1097. Two years later, in 1099, the crusaders captured Jerusalem.

The fighting between Christians and Muslims was fierce, and neither side showed mercy. When the crusaders took

389

Graphic Organizer

To help students better understand the causes, people involved, and outcomes of the Crusades, you may wish to use the graphic organizer below.

THE CRUSADES

THE FIRST CRUSADE (1095-1099)	THE SECOND CRUSADE (1147-1149)	THE THIRD CRUSADE (1189-1192)	THE CHILDREN'S CRUSADE (1212)
1. Called for by Pope Urban II 2. Knights and feudal lords fought Muslims. 3. Established crusader colonies	1. Called for by a monk 2. Christians in France and Germany fought Muslims. 3. Saladin's army captured Jerusalem.	1. Called for by kings of Germany, France, and England 2. Richard and Saladin make peace for five years. 3. Muslims still held the Holy city, but Christians could visit.	1. Called for by a French boy 2. Children wanted to capture the Holy Land through love rather than by force. 3. Few children returned home.

Optional Activities

Read and Think

Section E

The First Crusade led to other Crusades. Discuss the later Crusades by asking the following questions:

1. **Who was Saladin, and what did he accomplish?**
(Saladin was a ruler who united the Muslims and whose army recaptured Jerusalem from the Europeans. *pp. 391-392*)

2. **Who formed the Third Crusade?**
(Frederick I of Germany, Philip II of France, and Richard I of England *p. 391*)

3. **What happened to the children of the Fourth Crusade?**
(Slave merchants carried them to the slave markets in North Africa. *p. 392*)

Thinking Critically Would you or would you not have joined the Children's Crusade? (Hypothesize)
(Answers may include would, because it was a worthy cause, or would not, because it was a dangerous venture. *p. 392*)

GEOGRAPHY THEMES

Location

■ Ask students to look at the map on this page to help them answer the following questions:

1. **How many crusader colonies are shown on this map, and what are their names?**
(Four; kingdom of Jerusalem, county of Tripoli, principality of Antioch, and county of Edessa)

2. **Which river runs through the empire of the Seljuks?**
(The Euphrates River)

3. **Where is the sultanate of Damascus located in relation to the empire of the Seljuks?**
(It is southeast of the Seljuk Empire.)

Jerusalem, they killed not only fighting men but also many of the women and children. A French priest who accompanied the crusaders later wrote, "War is not beautiful. It is hateful to the innocent and horrible to see."

The crusaders conquered a strip of territory along the eastern Mediterranean shore. There they established four colonies. The crusader colonies were governed like the feudal states in Europe. The largest state, which included the Holy City, was the kingdom of Jerusalem. Two colonies, Edessa and Tripoli, were called counties because they were ruled by counts. Antioch (AN tee ahk) had a prince, so it was a principality. Locate these four colonies on the map below.

Learning New Customs In their colonies the crusaders met people who had different customs and fashions than their own. At first these customs seemed strange, but in time many of the Europeans adopted some of the ways of the Middle East. Those who remained in the conquered lands began to dress in the Middle Eastern fashion. Some crusaders even learned to speak Arabic.

Crusaders who returned home had acquired a taste for Middle Eastern foods, particularly those sweetened with sugar and seasoned with spices. They took back to Europe fine cloth and swords manufactured in the workshops of the east. As Europeans learned more about the products of the Middle East, trade increased. Merchants from such Italian cities as Venice prospered through this trade.

E. Later Crusades

Second Crusade Western Europeans sent later Crusades to the Middle East to support their overseas colonies. When the Muslims recaptured the county of Edessa in 1144, the Second Crusade was organized. This time a fiery monk aroused support for the Crusade. He called upon Christians in France and Germany to leave their homes and go fight for their faith. Many did so, including the kings of France and Germany. Many of those crusaders who left on the Second Crusade never returned home. Both the French and German armies of crusaders were badly beaten by the Muslims.

The First Crusade had succeeded partly because the Muslims were divided. The situation was quite different a half

CRUSADER COLONIES IN THE MIDDLE EAST A.D. 1140

Black Sea
Constantinople
BYZANTINE
EMPIRE OF THE SELJUKS
EMPIRE
Tigris River
KINGDOM OF ARMENIA
COUNTY OF EDESSA
Antioch
PRINCIPALITY OF ANTIOCH
Euphrates River
CYPRUS
COUNTY OF TRIPOLI
Tripoli
Mediterranean Sea
SULTANATE OF DAMASCUS
Damascus
KINGDOM OF JERUSALEM
Jerusalem

Crusader colonies
• Cities
0   100   200 miles
0   100   200 kilometers

One crusader colony, the county of Edessa, was not located along the Mediterranean Sea.
▶ To which two rivers did Edessa have direct access?

Biographical Cartoons

● Ask students to create cartoon-strip biographies of either Omar, Saladin, Suleiman the Magnificent, Richard the Lion-Hearted, or another individual from this lesson.

● Make sure that each of the most important leaders is written about by at least one student.

● Make a classroom display of the completed, colored cartoons.

● Give students a chance to read each other's cartoon strips.

● You may wish to provide the class with samples of cartoon strips from newspapers.

THE MAJOR CRUSADES

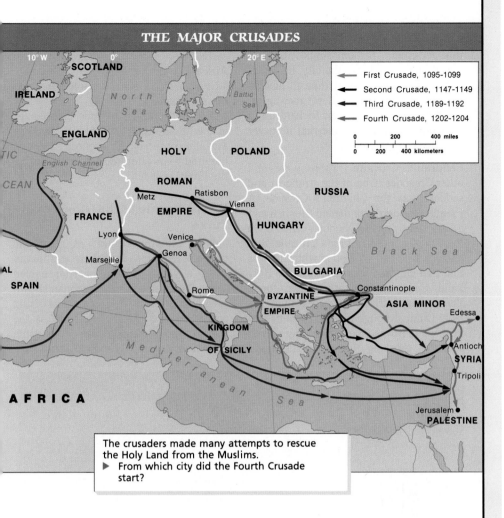

Legend:
- First Crusade, 1095-1099
- Second Crusade, 1147-1149
- Third Crusade, 1189-1192
- Fourth Crusade, 1202-1204

The crusaders made many attempts to rescue the Holy Land from the Muslims.
▶ From which city did the Fourth Crusade start?

century later. A remarkable leader named Saladin (SAL uh dihn) had succeeded in uniting the Muslims under his rule. Like the Christian crusaders, Saladin believed that war for the faith was right. In 1187, Saladin's army captured Jerusalem.

Third Crusade News of the fall of Jerusalem shocked Europeans at home. Three kings, Frederick I of Germany, Philip II of France, and Richard I of England, formed a Third Crusade. Richard, well-known for his bravery in battle, was called Richard the Lion-Hearted.

Christians, although winning some battles, could not recapture Jerusalem. Richard and Saladin agreed to make peace for at least five years. Saladin still held the Holy City, but it was agreed that Christians were free to visit their shrines.

391

Read and Think

Section F

Ask students what makes a ruler great. List student responses on the chalkboard. Then, discuss Suleiman the Magnificent and the Ottoman Empire by asking the following questions:

1. **Describe the extent of the Ottoman Empire under Suleiman.**
   (Much of the Middle East, North Africa, and southeastern Europe *p. 393*)

2. **Why was the Black Sea a Turkish lake during the rule of Suleiman?**
   (The Turks ruled almost all of its shores. *p. 393*)

3. **Why was Suleiman known as the Magnificent?**
   (Because of his great riches and powers *p. 393*)

   Thinking Critically Why, do you think, did the Ottoman Turks change the name of Constantinople to Istanbul? (Infer)
   (Answers may include that the Turks chose a name from their own culture. *p. 393*)

GEOGRAPHY THEMES

Location

■ Direct students' attention to the map on p. 392 to help them answer the following questions:

1. **The Ottoman Empire stretched east and west from approximately 50° E to 2° W. What is the east-to-west distance of the Ottoman Empire?**
   (Approximately 3,000 miles [4,827 km])

2. **What three rivers are located in the Ottoman Empire?**
   (The Nile, the Euphrates, and the Tigris)

3. **Where is Jerusalem located in relation to Istanbul?**
   (Southeast of Istanbul)

Richard sailed for Europe promising that he would return in five years to capture Jerusalem. Saladin supposedly said that if he ever did lose the city, he would rather lose it to Richard than to anyone else. But the two rulers never met again. Saladin died within a year. Richard faced so many problems at home that he never undertook another Crusade.

Children's Crusade There were still other Crusades. One of the strangest and saddest was the Children's Crusade. A French shepherd boy named Stephen and a German boy named Nicholas called upon the children to set out on a Crusade. Stephen said he had a vision in which he was told that children might capture the Holy Land through love rather than force. Thousands of girls and boys set out for the Holy Land, although most of them had no idea where it was. They made their way to seaports, thinking that someone would take them to Jerusalem. Some slave merchants promised to do so, but instead they carried them to the slave markets in North Africa. Few of the children who set out on a Crusade to conquer the Holy Land ever returned home.

In spite of later Crusades, the colonies in the Middle East were finally lost. The Muslims captured the last one in 1291, two hundred years after Pope Urban called for the First Crusade.

F. The Empire of the Ottoman Turks

Fall of Constantinople At about the time the last crusader colony was lost in 1291, a young Turkish warrior named Osman married a beautiful woman known as "Moon Bright." The descendants of that couple replaced the Seljuk Turks as the rulers of the Muslims. Those descendants are known as the Ottoman Turks. The

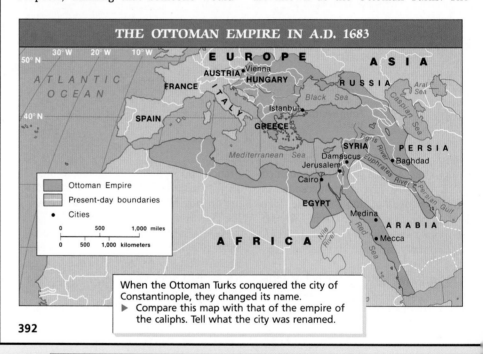

THE OTTOMAN EMPIRE IN A.D. 1683

Ottoman Empire
Present-day boundaries
• Cities

When the Ottoman Turks conquered the city of Constantinople, they changed its name.
▶ Compare this map with that of the empire of the caliphs. Tell what the city was renamed.

392

Optional Activities

Writing to Learn

Writing a Letter Have students imagine that they are participating in the Children's Crusade.

● Have them write a letter to a friend explaining why they are setting out on the Crusade and why their friend should join the Crusade.

● Tell students to use reasons for the Crusades given in the lesson.

The conquest of Constantinople left much of the city in ruins.
► How was the city of Constantinople destroyed?

Ottoman Turks were to build one of the largest and longest-lasting empires of all time.

One of the Ottoman sultans conquered the city of Constantinople in 1453. With the fall of the "city of Constantine," the Christian Byzantine Empire came to an end. The Muslim Ottoman conqueror changed the city's name from Constantinople to Istanbul.

Suleiman In 1517 the Ottoman sultan claimed the title of caliph—successor to Muhammad. One of the greatest leaders of the Ottoman Turks was Suleiman (soo lay-MAHN) the Magnificent—magnificent because of his great riches and power. Suleiman ruled not only much of the Middle East and North Africa but also a good part of southeastern Europe. During the reign of Suleiman, the Black Sea was a Turkish lake; that is, the Turks ruled almost all of its shores.

Ottoman power reached its greatest extent in Suleiman's time, but the Ottoman sultans continued in power for many years. Not until 1922 was the last descendant of Osman and Moon Bright forced from the throne when a group of army officers took over the government.

G. The Armenians

Invading Armenia In ancient time the region around Mount Ararat formed the kingdom of Armenia. It consisted of land that now forms parts of the countries of Turkey and Iran, and the former Soviet Union. A king of Armenia adopted Christianity in A.D. 301, making it the first Christian kingdom in the Middle East.

About 700 years later the Seljuk Turks invaded Armenia. The independent kingdom of Armenia disappeared, but the Armenian people survived. Even after the Turkish conquest of the Middle East, the

393

Lesson 2 Review

Answers to Think and Write

A. North Africa, much of the Middle East, and the Iberian Peninsula were included in the empire of the caliphs.

B. Disputes among the Arab Muslims allowed the Turks to move into the Middle East.

C. Pope Urban II wanted the Holy Land and Jerusalem to be under Christian rule.

D. The crusaders learned to wear Middle Eastern clothing, eat Middle Eastern food, and speak Arabic.

E. The later Crusades resulted in the loss of the European colonies to Muslim rule.

F. The Ottoman Turks conquered Constantinople and changed its name to Istanbul. The sultan claimed the title of caliph.

G. Many Armenians in the Ottoman Empire were massacred in the 1890s and many more were driven from their homes or killed in the early years of World War I. Most survivors fled to Turkey and the Soviet Union.

Answer to Skills Check

Answers should show an understanding of what became of most of the children who embarked on the Children's Crusade.

Focus Your Reading

Ask the lesson focus question found at the beginning of the lesson: **What brought about the Crusades, and what were the results?**

(Pope Urban II's desire to gain control of the Middle Eastern Holy Lands started the Crusades; the results were the spread into Europe of Islamic culture, products, and learning.)

Additional Practice

You may wish to assign the ancillary materials listed below.

Understanding the Lesson p. 97
Workbook pp. 85-86

From 1894 to 1918 the Turks made many attacks on the Armenian people.
▶ By looking at this etching, what can you tell about the advantages the Turks had over the Armenians?

Armenians remained in their mountain homeland, holding onto their language and their Christian religion.

Armenian Massacres In the 1890s the Ottoman sultan became alarmed by the growth of national unity among the Armenians. Attacks were made on the Armenians in Turkey. Thousands were killed in what are known as the Armenian massacres. During the early part of World War I, many Armenians welcomed the Russian invasion of Turkey. The Ottoman government in turn drove Armenians from their homes. Again, many lost their lives. Most Armenians fled Turkey, so few remained in the ancient homeland near Mount Ararat. Many migrated to the Russian empire. When the Communists formed the Soviet Union, the Armenian territory within the Russian empire became the Armenian Soviet Socialist Republic. In 1991, this republic became the independent nation of Armenia.

LESSON 2 REVIEW

THINK AND WRITE

A. What lands were included in the empire of the caliphs? (Recall)

B. Why were the Turks able to migrate to the Middle East? (Recall) (Recall)

C. Why did Pope Urban II call for a holy war?

D. What did the crusaders learn from the colonies they established in the Middle East? (Recall)

E. What were the results of the later Crusades? (Infer)

F. What changes took place during the rule of the Ottoman Turks? (Infer)

G. What happened to the Armenians who lived within the Ottoman Empire? (Recall)

SKILLS CHECK

WRITING SKILL

Imagine that you and some of your friends had joined the Children's Crusade. Write a paragraph or two describing your journey.

Optional Activities

UNDERSTANDING THE LESSON

NAME _____

UNDERSTANDING THE LESSON

CHAPTER **14**

Recalling Facts LESSON 2 CONTENT MASTER

❋ Read each statement below. Write **True** if the statement is true and **False** if it is false. If the statement is false, cross out the part that is incorrect and write the correct words above it.

True 1. Under the caliphs, the Muslims conquered a large empire.

True 2. Bitter disputes began to divide the far-flung Muslim empire.

False 3. During this time, the Seljuk Turks migrated from ~~India~~ into the [Central Asia] Middle East and conquered the eastern Muslim lands.

False 4. After the Seljuk conquest of Anatolia, Pope Urban II sent out a call for a holy war against the ~~Christians~~ [Muslims].

True 5. This crusade, begun in 1095, was the first attempt by Christians to win back the Holy Land.

False 6. The official army of the First Crusade was ~~defeated~~ [captured] outside Jerusalem in 1099.

True 7. The crusaders captured a strip of land along the Mediterranean and established colonies there.

True 8. The crusaders were defeated in 1187 by the Muslim leader Saladin.

False 9. The Ottoman Turks replaced the Seljuks as rulers of the Muslim and built an empire that lasted until ~~1650~~ [1922].

True 10. In 1453, the Muslim Ottomans captured Constantinople.

False 11. When national unity among the Armenians began to grow in the 1890s, the Ottoman sultan ~~let them set up their own country~~ [had them massacred].

Think and Write: Think of an example of people who went to war for their religious beliefs. Write a paragraph explaining whether that war was justified. You may use the back of the sheet.

Answers should reflect independent thinking; suggestions appear in the Answer Key. Use with textbook pages 590–594.

97

◀ **Review Master Booklet, p. 97**

Art and Learning in the Muslim Lands

THINK ABOUT WHAT YOU KNOW

List the numbers from 1 to 10, using our system of Arabic numerals and then using Roman numerals.

STUDY THE VOCABULARY

calligraphy   minaret
mosque

FOCUS YOUR READING

What are the contributions of the people of North Africa and the Middle East?

A. Preserving the Learning of the Greeks

The Arabic language spread with the Muslim religion. Arabic was the language of the Koran and the language of the Muslim rulers. Students throughout the caliph's empire who wanted to get ahead in the world learned the Arabic language. As you have already read in an earlier chapter, Arabic became the language of many of the Middle Eastern and North African countries.

Arabic-speaking Muslims realized that there was much of value written in other languages, particularly in Greek. In order to preserve the learning of the Greeks, Muslim rulers encouraged the translation of Greek books into Arabic.

The caliph at Baghdad established a House of Wisdom, where the work of translation was carried on. The translations made it possible for Muslims to study the works of Greek philosophers, such as Plato and Aristotle, as well as the Koran. Muslim philosophers wrote books about

Greek thinkers that were later studied by Christians in Europe. Some Greek writings that were no longer known in Europe would have been lost had they not been translated into Arabic.

B. The Numerals Borrowed from India

Muslim traders and travelers visited India, and they discovered that the people of that land possessed valuable learning. A poet of Baghdad wrote that there were two things of which the Indians were justly proud: the game of chess and a numeral system that made use of zero.

> *One can write any number, no matter how large, with the ten digits of the Indian numeral system. It is far more convenient than the Roman system of numerals.*

Arabic scholars learned from Greek writings.
▶ For what purpose was the House of Wisdom established?

Curriculum Connection

Language Arts   Bring in a copy of *Arabian Nights* (Mineola, NY: Dover Books, 1969. ISBN 0-486-22289-6) and read a story aloud to the class (for example, the story of Aladdin and his magic lamp, or the story of Ali Baba).

● Discuss the characters and setting of the book.

● Then, ask students to write another story using the same characters and setting, but a different plot.

● Ask volunteers to share their stories with the rest of the class.

● Explain to students that *Arabian Nights* was written in Arabic during the Middle Ages, and that the stories come from many different Middle Eastern countries.

Optional Activities

Art and Learning in the Muslim Lands

Objectives

1. **Identify** Islamic contributions to art, literature, mathematics, and science.

2. **Compare** Arabic numerals with the numerals we use today.

3. **Identify** the following people and places: *Omar Khayyam, the House of Wisdom,* and *the Dome of the Rock.*

1 STARTING THE LESSON

Motivation Activity

■ Ask students to try to perform some moderately difficult mathematics problems, using only Roman numerals.

■ Tell students that in this lesson they will learn about the people who replaced Roman numerals with the more efficient system of numerals that we use today.

Think About What You Know

■ Assign the THINK ABOUT WHAT YOU KNOW activity on p. 395.

■ Our numerals from one to ten are 1, 2, 3, 4, 5, 6, 7, 8, 9, 10; the Roman numerals from one to ten are I, II, III, IV, V, VI, VII, VIII, IX, X.

Study the Vocabulary

■ Have students look up the definitions of the vocabulary words in the Glossary.

■ Ask students to make a chart with the headings *Art, Architecture,* and *Religion.*

■ Have students place each vocabulary word in its appropriate column(s). How many words go under more than one category?

┌─ **Answers to Caption Questions** ─┐
p. 394 ▶ The Turks had the advantages of being on horseback and having weapons.
p. 395 ▶ To translate Greek writings into Arabic

2 DEVELOPING THE LESSON

Read and Think

Sections A and B

The Arabs recognized the value of the knowledge from Greece and India. Use these questions to discuss how the Arabs preserved and developed the knowledge that they gained from those countries:

1. **What activity was carried on in the House of Wisdom?**
   (Translation of Greek works into Arabic *p. 395*)

2. **What important innovation in numbering had the Indians developed?**
   (The use of zero *p. 395*)

3. **What system has been called "the only real universal language?"**
   (The Arabic numeral system *p. 396*)

   Thinking Critically **What attitudes do you think are displayed by the Muslims in their approach to the wisdom of India and Greece?** (Hypothesize) (Answers may include curiosity, toleration of other ways of thinking, and humility in acknowledging that others might be wiser than they are. *pp. 395–396*)

COMPARING NUMERALS

Modern	Arabic	Greek	Roman	Chinese	Hindi
1	١	I	I	一	१
2	٢	II	II	二	२
3	٣	III	III	三	३
4	٤	IIII	IV	四	४
5	٥	Γ	V	五	५
6	٦	ΓI	VI	六	६
7	٧	ΓII	VII	七	७
8	٨	ΓIII	VIII	八	८
9	٩	ΓIIII	IX	九	९
10	١٠	△	X	十	10

There are many similarities among the numerals shown in this table.

► Which numeral systems represented the number ten in the same way as the modern system does?

Arabic-speaking Muslims adopted the convenient system of Indian numerals, and Europeans later borrowed it from them. Because Europeans learned of these numerals from Arabic-speaking people, they called them Arabic numerals. You are familiar with these numerals. They are used in numbering the pages of this book.

Our way of writing the numerals differs somewhat from the Arabic form, as you can see by the chart on this page. It is easy to recognize the Arabic way of writing 1, 9, and 11. The 10 is simple once you understand that a point or dot is used for zero. How do you think 90 or 100 would be written in the Arabic script?

The system of Arabic—or Indian—numerals was one of the world's most important inventions. The system is so

396

---

useful that it has been adopted all over the world. One historian calls it "the only real universal language."

C. Mathematics and Science Among the Muslims

Studying Math The name *Omar Khayyám* (kye YAHM) means "Omar the Tentmaker." But he is not remembered today for his tents—if indeed, he ever made any. Omar Khayyam is known as a poet. He was not only a poet but also an astronomer who studied the movements of the stars and other heavenly bodies. He also wrote an important book on algebra, a field of mathematics. The word *algebra* comes from Arabic. Arabic-speaking Muslims did much to develop this field during the Middle Ages.

As an astronomer, Omar Khayyám changed the Persian calendar.
► What tools and materials is he working with?

Studying Science Muslims also studied a number of sciences, particularly chemistry. It has been said that they originated this field of science. A sign of their influence is found in the number of Arabic words used in chemistry. For example, *alcohol* and *alkali* are Arabic words.

Studying Medicine The Christian crusaders reported that the Muslim doctors were more skillful than those from Europe in caring for wounds and setting broken bones. Muslim physicians had studied medicine by learning from the Greeks, but they also learned through their own observations. By carefully observing the symptoms, or signs, of a disease, Muslim physicians were able to identify diseases more accurately.

In about A.D. 900, a Muslim doctor learned by observation that smallpox and measles were different diseases. He wrote the first book in the world describing these diseases. Muslims also discovered that once a person had had the disease smallpox, he or she became immune to the disease, that is, the person would not get it again. Another doctor observed the diseases of the eye and wrote about them. Both of these books were translated into Latin and studied in western Europe. Careful observations also made it possible to discover the effects of different plants and other medicines in the treatment of diseases.

D. Handwriting as a Fine Art

Calligraphy (kuh LIHG ruh fee) is the art of beautiful handwriting. The Muslim belief that the Koran was a holy book encouraged the development of this art.

Pages from the Koran are decorated with borders and beautiful writing.
▶ What is the art of beautiful writing called?

The Granger Collection

Muslims believed that no other art could be so great as the making of beautiful copies of the Koran, which they held to be the word of God.

Copying the Koran was a religious act somewhat like saying a prayer or going on a pilgrimage. One man made 42 copies of the whole Koran. He worked with great care, using costly inks of different colors. He made one copy entirely in gold. The copies were not given to others to read but instead stored safely in a chest. The man had copied the Koran in order to show how much he loved the words of the holy book. When he died, all 42 copies were buried with him.

Calligraphers took as much care in writing a page as painters do in producing fine pictures. They used the finest materials and decorated the pages. The hand-copied books were bound in fine leather that was often decorated with gold, silver, and precious stones. Among the Muslims a beautifully copied book was considered a truly great work of art.

397

Optional Activities

Read and Think
Sections C, D, and E

It may be said that the Muslims laid the foundations of modern mathematics and science. Use the questions below to discuss these and other contributions by the Muslims:

1. **List Arabic words that are associated with mathematics and science.**
(Algebra, alcohol, and alkali *pp. 396-397*)

2. **Give two examples of medical discoveries made by Muslims.**
(Answers may include the discovery that smallpox and measles are different diseases and that people are immune to smallpox once they have had it. *p. 397*)

3. **How did Muslims artistically show their respect for the words of the Koran?**
(Muslims copied the Koran in beautiful handwriting, or calligraphy, and decorated the pages and covers of the books with fine inks, gold, silver, and precious stones. *p. 397*)

4. **Why were carpets an important means of artistic expression in the Middle East?**
(Carpets could be made with patterns that did not look like any living thing and could be used in place of furniture in mosques and homes. *p. 398*)

Thinking Critically If you had lived during the Middle Ages, would you have allowed or not allowed a Muslim doctor to treat you? (Evaluate)
(Answers may include allowed, because Muslim doctors were well trained, or not allowed, because students might trust European doctors more. *p. 397*)

VISUAL THINKING SKILL

Interpreting a Visual

■ Have students look at the visual on this page to help them answer the following question: **How would you describe these pages from the Koran?**
(Highly decorated, ornate, with beautiful writing)

Answers to Caption Questions
p. 396 *l.* ▶ Arabic and Hindi
p. 396 *r.* ▶ Drawing compass, ruler, paper
p. 397 ▶ Calligraphy

Meeting Individual Needs

Concept:
Analyzing Cultural Transmission

To better understand how the Crusades affected European culture, it is important to understand how ideas spread from culture to culture. Below are three activities that will help students analyze cultural transmission.

◆ **EASY** Have students make a list of the Islamic contributions and innovations discussed in this lesson.

Tell them to put an asterisk by the ones that the Muslims got from another culture.

Then, discuss how each contribution or innovation was passed to the Muslims.

◀▶ **AVERAGE** Have students create a bulletin-board map to show the transmission of ideas and innovations.

Have them devise a symbol for each idea in this lesson and then show the transmission of this idea. (For example, to show the concept of zero, draw a zero in India, and then draw arrows from India to Arabia, and from Arabia to Europe.)

◀▮▶ **CHALLENGING** Tell students who need a challenge to write an essay describing some of the ways that ideas and innovations are passed from culture to culture today.

Decorating Buildings The Muslim religion affected other arts too. Strict Muslims believed it was wrong to make a picture or statue of any living thing. This rule was not in the Koran but came from an old account of Muhammad's teachings. It was said that the prophet had spoken against the making of pictures. He was supposed to have said that no one should try to copy what God has made.

Because of the rule against pictures, artists used other ways to decorate buildings and the things people used. Of course, words from the Koran could be placed on the walls of Muslim places of worship, called **mosques** (mahsks). Artists covered both inside and outside walls of buildings with colorful designs like those used in jewelry and pottery.

Carpets Carpetmaking was an important art in the Middle East. Carpets could be made with patterns that did not look like any living thing. Carpets are made by tying threads tightly together by hand. A carpet maker ties up to 320 knots for each square inch of carpet.

People in the Middle East sometimes used carpets in place of furniture. They sat on cushions or low carpet-covered platforms. Carpets covered the floors of mosques, which had no benches or seats. Instead worshipers sat and kneeled on the carpets. Before worshipers or visitors entered a mosque, they removed their shoes or sandals.

Mosques Mosques and religious shrines were among the most important buildings erected by the Muslims. Except for the Kaaba, the oldest existing shrine is the Dome of the Rock in Jerusalem. It was

This Persian carpet, woven in Tabriz, Iran, is characterized by flowing patterns that feature flowers and leaves.
▶ For what purposes are carpets used in the Middle East?

Making a Bulletin Board

● Have students collect pictures and information on the design and decoration of Islamic mosques and shrines.

● If possible, they should obtain pictures from a consulate, tourist bureau, or travel agent that can be cut out, mounted on construction paper, and displayed.

● Students could also make their own drawings based on information or photographs they find in encyclopedias.

● Ask: **What are some of the most famous mosques of the Arab world?**

● Ask students to create a bulletin board highlighting the features of these buildings.

Reteaching Main Objective

★ *Identify Islamic contributions to art, literature, mathematics, and science.*

● Make a semantic map on the chalkboard to illustrate the Islamic contributions to art, literature, mathematics, and science.

● Write *Islamic contributions* in the center circle.

● Write *art, literature, mathematics,* and *science* in circles that are connected to the center circle with lines.

● Have students take turns going to the chalkboard to write examples of Islamic contributions in the appropriate parts of the semantic map.

The Dome of the Rock is Jerusalem's holiest Muslim shrine.
► How is the shape of this shrine different from that of the Kaaba?

completed 1,300 years ago, and its gilded dome is still seen atop a hill in the old city.

Mosques did not have bell towers like those of many Christian churches. Instead, there were tall and slender towers with balconies, called **minarets**, where people would call others to prayer every day.

In spite of the rule against pictures, some artists did make paintings of living things. Particularly in Iran and Turkey, artists painted pictures not only of animals and plants but also of people. Even the strictest religious beliefs did not affect all of the arts.

LESSON 3 REVIEW

THINK AND WRITE

A. How did the Muslims preserve the learning of the Greeks? **(Recall)**
B. Why are the numerals we use called Arabic? **(Recall)**
C. What developments did the Muslims make in math, science, and medicine? **(Recall)**
D. How did the Muslim religion encourage the development of handwriting as an art? **(Recall)**
E. How did the Muslim religious beliefs affect other arts? **(Infer)**

SKILLS CHECK

THINKING SKILL

Divide a sheet of paper into two columns, leaving space to the left of the columns. On the top of the paper, label one column *Arts* and the other column *Sciences*. Then skim through the lesson and list the contributions of the Muslims on the left side of the paper. Place a check in the column in which each contribution belongs.

399

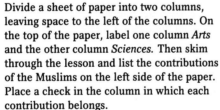
◄ **Review Master Booklet, p. 98**

Optional Activities

Lesson **3** Review

Answers to Think and Write
A. The Muslims preserved the learning of the Greeks by translating Greek works.

B. They were introduced to Europeans by Arabic-speaking people; the numerals originally came from India.

C. Algebra, chemistry, new treatments for diseases resulted from Muslim research.

D. It taught that making beautiful copies of the Koran was the greatest form of art.

E. The Muslim belief that making pictures of living things was wrong encouraged decoration of books, buildings, and carpets with colorful designs.

Answer to Skills Check
The arts column should include checkmarks for translation of Greek works, poetry, calligraphy, book bindings, carpets, mosque architecture, and Iranian and Turkish paintings. The sciences column should include checkmarks for Arabic numerals, algebra, chemistry, and medicine.

Focus Your Reading
Ask the lesson focus question found at the beginning of the lesson: **What are the contributions of the people of North Africa and the Middle East?**
(They preserved the knowledge of the Greeks; used and passed on Arabic numerals; developed the sciences of mathematics, astronomy, chemistry, and medicine; and developed the arts of calligraphy, poetry, carpet making, architecture, and painting.)

Additional Practice
You may wish to assign the ancillary materials listed below.

Understanding the Lesson p. 98
Workbook p. 87

--- **Answers to Caption Questions** ---
p. 398 ► In place of furniture, to cover floors of mosques
p. 399 ► The shape of the Dome of the Rock is a dome and the Kaaba's shape is a cube.

399

Using the Vocabulary

1. caliph
2. shrine
3. pilgrimage
4. minarets
5. prophets

Remembering What You Read

1. A building in the city of Mecca, which is a shrine for the Muslims
2. Muhammad
3. The Koran
4. It is called the Hegira.
5. The Crusades
6. The Ottoman Turks
7. Istanbul
8. Arabic numerals
9. Chemistry
10. Mosques

USING THE VOCABULARY

shrine   caliph
prophets   minarets
pilgrimage

On a separate sheet of paper, write the word from above that best completes each of the sentences.

1. Muhammad's followers made Abu-Bakr the first _____ since he was the first "one who came after" Muhammad.
2. The _____ in Jerusalem is considered a holy place by Christians, Muslims, and Jews.
3. People throughout the world make a _____, or journey, to a religious site.
4. Mosques have tall and slender towers, or _____, instead of bell towers like those of many Christian churches.
5. The angel told Muhammad that he was the last of the _____, or religious leaders who speak out against wrongdoing and warn that punishments will come to those who break God's laws.

REMEMBERING WHAT YOU READ

On a separate sheet of paper, answer the following questions in complete sentences.

1. What is the Kaaba?
2. Who founded the Islamic religion?

3. What is the holy book of the Muslims?
4. What is the journey called that Muhammad made from Mecca to Medina?
5. What were the series of wars between European Christians and Muslims in the Middle East called?
6. Who built one of the largest and longest-lasting empires of all time?
7. What was the name of the city of Constantinople changed to after it was conquered by the Ottoman Turks?
8. What system did the Europeans borrow from the Arabic-speaking Muslims?
9. What field of science is believed to have been originated by the Muslims?
10. What are Muslim places of worship called?

TYING ART TO SOCIAL STUDIES

Muslims used calligraphy, a beautiful form of handwriting, to copy the Koran. They believed that a copied book was truly a great work of art. Look in an encyclopedia to find our alphabet written in calligraphy or look in the library for a book on calligraphy. Then copy a page from a book, newspaper, or magazine, using calligraphy. Be creative by using your imagination and different-colored inks to decorate the page.

400

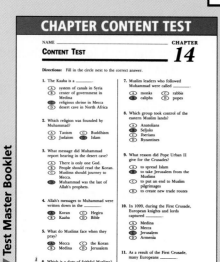

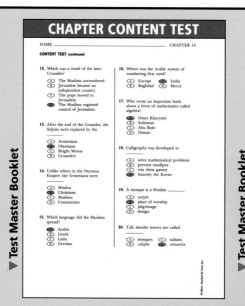

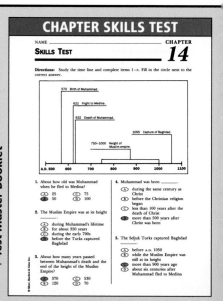

THINKING CRITICALLY

On a separate sheet of paper, answer the following in complete sentences.

1. The Koran is the holy book for the Muslims. What are some holy books that are important to people of other religions?
2. Omar, the second caliph, said, "The Arabs are like an unruly camel, but I am he who can keep them on the right path." What did he mean by that?
3. Pope Urban II pointed out that the Bible called the Holy Land a land "flowing with milk and honey." What do you think that meant?
4. In your opinion, why did children join the Children's Crusade?
5. Muslims worship in mosques. What are some places of worship for other religions?

SUMMARIZING THE CHAPTER

On a separate sheet of paper, draw a graphic organizer like the one shown here. Copy the information from this graphic organizer on the one you have drawn. Under each main idea write three phrases that support it.

CHAPTER THEME → The Middle East has had an important place in the world's history not only because of the universal contributions its people have made but also because it was the birthplace of world religions.

LESSON 1
The Muslim religion began about 1,400 years ago.
1.
2.
3.

LESSON 2
The Crusades brought about many results.
1.
2.
3.

LESSON 3
The people of the Middle East and North Africa have made many contributions.
1.
2.
3.

401

Thinking Critically

1. Answers may include the Bible and the Torah.
2. Answers may include that he was a strict military leader and had plans for creating a well-disciplined army.
3. Answers may include that the land was rich in minerals and agricultural resources.
4. Answers may include because they believed acquiring the Holy Land was a good cause.
5. Answers may include churches, cathedrals, and tabernacles.

Summarizing the Chapter

Lesson 1
1. Muhammad
2. The Kaaba
3. The Koran

Lesson 2
1. The Holy Land
2. Jerusalem
3. Trade

Lesson 3
1. Arabic numerals
2. Algebra
3. Chemistry

CHAPTER SKILLS TEST

NAME _____ CHAPTER 14

SKILLS TEST (continued)

Directions: Study the map and complete items 6–10. Fill in the circle next to the correct answer.

THE EMPIRE OF THE CALIPHS
AND THE BYZANTINE EMPIRE, 750
▢ Empire of the Caliphs
▢ Byzantine Empire
— Present-day national boundaries
• Cities

6. In A.D. 750, the Empire of the Caliphs did *not* include part of present-day
  Ⓐ France Ⓒ Egypt
  Ⓑ Greece Ⓓ India

7. The two largest bodies of water bordering the Byzantine Empire were the
  Ⓐ Atlantic Ocean and the Arabian Sea
  Ⓑ Mediterranean Sea and the Aegean Sea
  Ⓒ Caspian Sea and the Red Sea
  Ⓓ Black Sea and the Mediterranean Sea

8. Muhammad's journey from Mecca to Medina was about
  Ⓐ 200 miles Ⓒ 600 miles
  Ⓑ 400 miles Ⓓ 800 miles

9. The Empire of the Caliphs was located in
  Ⓐ Europe only.
  Ⓑ Africa only.
  Ⓒ Europe and Africa.
  Ⓓ Australia.

10. Which city is located at about 33°N/44°E?
  Ⓐ Constantinople
  Ⓑ Damascus
  Ⓒ Baghdad
  Ⓓ Jerusalem

CHAPTER WRITING TEST

NAME _____ CHAPTER 14

ESSAY TEST

Directions: Write a response to items 1–4.

REMINDER: Read and think about each item before you write your response. Be sure to think of the points you want to cover, details that support your response, and reasons for your opinions. Then, on the lines below, write your response in complete sentences.

1. Describe the beginnings of Islam.
A satisfactory response will explain the following statements.
• Muhammad reported that an angel sent by Allah visited him in a desert cave.
• The angel told Muhammad that he was the last of the prophets and that those who broke Allah's laws would be punished.
• Muhammad instructed his followers with these and other messages from Allah.
• Allah's messages were written down by Muhammad's followers in the Koran.
An excellent response might explain that
• Muhammad's followers in Mecca were persecuted.
• Muhammad fled to Medina and later attacked and defeated Mecca.
• Muhammad and his followers spread Islam throughout the Middle East and North Africa.

2. Who were the Seljuks?
A satisfactory response will explain that the Seljuks were
• Turkish speakers who migrated from Central Asia to the Middle East
• skillful fighters who took control of the eastern Muslim lands.
An excellent response might explain that
• Seljuks made their leader, the sultan, ruler of their lands
• Seljuks conquered the Anatolian peninsula, which became known as Turkey.
• Ottomans eventually replaced the Seljuks.

CHAPTER WRITING TEST

NAME _____ CHAPTER 14

ESSAY TEST (continued)

3. Why did the Crusades take place?
A satisfactory response should explain that Pope Urban II wanted to conquer from the Muslims the Holy Land. He especially wanted the Christians to capture Jerusalem.
An excellent response might explain that
• the pope and many Europeans believed the Muslims were robbing and torturing Christian pilgrims
• knights believed they could win glory and riches by fighting the Muslims.

4. What advances did Muslims make in medicine?
A satisfactory response will explain that Muslim doctors were among the world's most skilled in
• caring for wounds and setting of bones
• identifying and treating diseases.
An excellent response might mention the following.
• Muslim doctors were more knowledgeable than West European doctors.
• Muslim doctors learned from the Greeks and through their own observations.

401

The Middle East and North Africa Today

(pp. 402-428)

Chapter Theme: Modernization has been the aim of most Middle Eastern and North African countries, but wars and political troubles have held back progress.

CHAPTER RESOURCES
Review Master Booklet
    Reviewing Chapter Vocabulary, p. 106
    Place Geography, p. 107
    Summarizing the Chapter, p. 108
Chapter 15 Test

LESSON 1 Iran, Iraq, and Afghanistan

(pp. 402-408)

Theme: In recent history, Iran, Iraq, and Afghanistan have continually been plagued by political and economic problems.

LESSON RESOURCES
Workbook, p. 88
Review Master Booklet
    Understanding the Lesson, p. 102

LESSON 2 Israel and Turkey

(pp. 409-413)

Theme: Despite many wars, Israel has modernized, prospered, and become a democracy while Turkey has come through internal political troubles and has emerged as a republic.

LESSON RESOURCES
Workbook, p. 89
Review Master Booklet
    Understanding the Lesson, p. 103

LESSON 3 Other Countries of the Middle East

(pp. 414-419)

Theme: Political struggles, wars, and large supplies of oil are general characteristics of the countries of the Middle East.

LESSON RESOURCES
Workbook, pp. 90-91
Review Master Booklet
    Understanding the Lesson, p. 104

LESSON 4 Countries of North Africa

(pp. 420-426)

Theme: Crowded conditions, poor foreign relations, tourism, oil, a Mediterranean climate, and the struggle to modernize are some general characteristics of the North African countries.

SOCIAL STUDIES LIBRARY: *Money*

Review Masters

REVIEWING CHAPTER VOCABULARY

15
VOCABULARY MASTER

Review Study the terms in the box. Use your Glossary to find definitions of those you do not remember.

ambassador	embassy	mullah	revenue
asphalt	fez	nonrenewable	shah
ayatollah	hostage	resource	terrorism
causeway	Knesset	phosphate	
crude oil	modernize	reserves	

Practice Complete the paragraphs using terms from the box above. You may change the forms of the terms to fit the meaning.

During this century, the people of the Middle East have made some difficult decisions. Some of these decisions involved questions of how lifestyles should change as countries become more wealthy. In Turkey, for example, President Kemal believed that in order to (1) _modernize_ the country, Turkish people should adopt Western styles of dress. The president made a law to prevent men from wearing the traditional (2) _fez_.

In Iran, modernization led to a revolution and the downfall of the (3) _shah_. Iran has large (4) _reserves_ of petroleum that are exported to other countries in the form of (5) _crude oil_. The (6) _revenue_ earned from these exports gave Iran the opportunity to become a more up-to-date nation. However, the (7) _mullahs_ did not want Iranians to adopt new ways of living. They eventually gained control of the country and formed the Islamic Republic of Iran.

Write Choose ten terms from the box above. Use each term to write a sentence of your own. You may use the back of the sheet.

Sentences should show that students understand the meanings of the terms.

_____

_____

_____

_____

_____

_____

© Silver, Burdett & Ginn Inc.

LOCATING PLACES

15
PLACE GEOGRAPHY MASTER

✳ Listed below are important bodies of water and human-made waterworks in North Africa and the Middle East. Use the Gazetteer in your textbook to find the latitude and longitude of each place. Then locate and label each on the map.

	LAT.	LONG.
1. Suez Canal	30°N	33°E
2. Aswan High Dam	24°N	33°E
3. Dead Sea	32°N	36°E
4. Strait of Hormuz	27°N	56°E
5. San'a	15°N	44°E

© Silver, Burdett & Ginn Inc.

SUMMARIZING THE CHAPTER

15
GRAPHIC ORGANIZER MASTER

✳ Complete this graphic organizer. Under the main idea for each lesson, write four statements that support the main idea.

CHAPTER THEME — Geography, resources, religions, and political policies and conflicts continue to have a strong influence on daily life in the Middle East and North Africa today.

LESSON 1

The recent history of the Middle East is a continuation of many years of problems.

1. Iran's first revolution (1921)
2. Iran's second revolution (1979)
3. Soviet Union seizes control of Afghanistan (1979)
4. Iran-Iraq War (1980s)

LESSON 2

Many political and economic changes have taken place in Israel and Turkey since World War I.

1. British take control of Palestine after World War I.
2. Israel declares independence in 1948.
3. Mustafa Kemal introduces Western ways to Turkey after World War I.
4. Turkey adopts new constitution in 1982.

LESSON 3

Important characteristics shape each of the Arab countries of the Middle East.

1. Jordan—poor land, few resources
2. Syria—some of best land in Middle East
3. Lebanon—torn by civil war
4. Saudi Arabia, Persian Gulf states—much oil

LESSON 4

There are many similarities and differences among the countries of North Africa.

1. Libya, Egypt, and Tunisia all have oil resources.
2. Tunisia, Egypt, Morocco, and Algeria have farming.
3. Tunisia and Morocco have phosphate reserves.
4. Egypt, Libya, and Algeria have large deserts.

© Silver, Burdett & Ginn Inc.

C15-B

Workbook Pages

Page 88 (top left)

IRAN'S PETROLEUM INDUSTRY

Understanding Special-Purpose Maps, Interpreting Information

✳ The map below shows the location of Iran's petroleum resources and industry. The sale of oil and gas to other countries provides about one half of Iran's total income. Study the map; then complete the sentences.

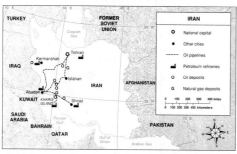

IRAN

- ◉ National capital
- ○ Other cities
- ---- Oil pipelines
- ▬ Petroleum refineries
- O Oil deposits
- G Natural gas deposits

1. Most petroleum and natural gas fields are in the ___southwestern___ part of Iran.

2. The large island port Iran uses to ship oil and gas is ___Kharg Island___

3. Petroleum from Tehran must travel about ___500___ miles by pipeline to reach Abadan.

4. Most of Iran's petroleum is shipped out by tankers sailing on the ___Persian Gulf___

5. The country closest to Iran's main oil fields is ___Iraq___

6. Iran's main refineries are located in ___Tehran, Kermanshah, Abadan, Kharg Island, and Shiraz___

Thinking Further: Write a paragraph explaining how Iran's war with Iraq might have affected the petroleum industry. Answers should note that most of the petroleum industry is located close to Iraq, so the petroleum supply could have been cut off or the refineries and pipelines damaged.

© Silver, Burdett & Ginn Inc.

Page 89 (top right)

MEETING CHALLENGES OF THE FUTURE

Understanding Point of View, Interpreting Information

✳ In 1960, Golda Meir, then the foreign minister of Israel, spoke to the United Nations General Assembly. She described problems and challenges facing Israel and other new nations. Read the paragraphs adapted from Meir's speech shown below; then answer the questions.

There are two dangers that face those of us who have emerged as newly independent states; first, staying too long in the past and, secondly, thinking that independence will instantly solve all our problems. . . .

We, the new countries, have gained our independence in an era of man's greatest achievements. In some parts of the world the standard of living has reached fantastic heights. We should not be told to develop slowly; we should not be told that other countries have taken many years or even centuries to develop. We cannot wait. We must develop quickly. . . .

This challenge is one not only for the new nations, but for the entire world. Much has been done to share extra food from the developed countries with people in the new countries who are hungry. But I wish to say that we will never be really free as long as our children need to be fed by others. Our freedom will be complete only when we have learned to bring forth the food we need from our own soil. The cry that goes out from the African and Asian continents today is: Share with us not only food, but also your knowledge of how to produce it. . . ."

1. What two dangers did Meir see for new independent states? staying too long in the past, and expecting that problems will be solved instantly

2. What rate of development did Meir believe was necessary for new nations? She believed new nations should develop quickly.

3. How did Meir believe other nations could help the new nations? by sharing food and the knowledge of how to produce food

4. When did Meir think the new nations would be truly free? when they are able to produce their own food supply

5. Name two countries Meir may have been thinking about when she spoke of developed countries. possible answer: the United States and Japan

6. Where were most of the new nations located? in Africa and Asia

Thinking Further: Why do you think Golda Meir believed people need knowledge as much as they need food? Write your answer on a separate sheet. Possible answer: She knew that people in new nations would progress only if they knew how to live independently and plan their own future.

© Silver, Burdett & Ginn Inc.

Page 90 (bottom left)

ANALYZING A SPEECH

Inferring Unstated Ideas, Making Observations

✳ Egyptian president Anwar Sadat's visit to Israel in 1977 was an important event in recent Middle East history. Read the paragraphs from Sadat's speech to Israel's leaders and lawmakers; then answer the questions.

"Any life lost in a war is a human life, be it that of an Arab or an Israeli. A wife who becomes a widow is a human being entitled to a happy family life, whether she be an Arab or an Israeli. Innocent children deprived of the care and compassion of their parents are ours. For the sake of them all, for a smile, for a smile on the face of every child born in our land. For all that, I have taken my decision to come to you. . . .

"You want to live with us in this part of the world. In all sincerity, I tell you that we welcome you among us, with full security and safety. . . . We used to reject you, yes. We refused to meet with you anywhere, yes. It is also true that we used to demand . . . a mediator who would meet separately with each party . . . yes, this happened. Yet today I tell you, and I declare it to the whole world, that we accept to live with you in permanent peace based on justice."

1. Where is "this part of the world" referred to by Sadat? the Middle East

2. For many years, Egypt refused to recognize Israel as a country. For whose sake does Sadat now decide to visit Israel? for the sake of Arab and Israeli lives lost in war, and for the sake of the area's children

3. Before Sadat's visit, how did the two nations communicate? through a mediator who met separately with each country

4. On what does Sadat want the peace between Egypt and Israel to be based? on justice

5. With what does Sadat welcome Israel to live with Egypt in the Middle East? with full security and safety

Thinking Further: What do you think can happen to change nations from enemies to friends? Answers may mention the rise of a strong leader such as Sadat who can bring peace and friendly relations, or the decision to cooperate because of economic needs.

© Silver, Burdett & Ginn Inc.

Page 91 (bottom right)

COMPARING OIL RESERVES AND REVENUE

Understanding Tables, Making Inferences

✳ The tables below show petroleum reserves and income for some Middle Eastern countries and the United States. Reserves are oil and natural gas that are still in the ground. Fill in the list beside each chart; then answer the questions.

Country	1988 Income from Petroleum (billions of dollars)
Bahrain	3.0
Kuwait	6.7
Oman	2.2
Qatar	1.9
Saudi Arabia	28.1
United Arab Emirates	3.4
United States	973.6

Top three Middle Eastern countries in income from petroleum:

1. Saudi Arabia
2. Kuwait
3. U.A.E.

Country	Petroleum Reserves as of 1988 (billions of barrels)
Bahrain	.1
Kuwait	91.9
Oman	4.0
Qatar	3.2
Saudi Arabia	167.0
United Arab Emirates	32.8
United States	27.0

Top three Middle Eastern countries in petroleum reserves:

1. Saudi Arabia
2. Kuwait
3. U.A.E.

1. What can you conclude about the relationship between oil reserves and revenue for the countries listed? The nations with the largest reserves have the highest income.

2. Where would the United States rank in income and reserves compared to the Middle Eastern countries listed? first in income and fourth in reserves

3. If the United States consumed 6 billion barrels of petroleum each year and used only its own reserves, how many years would its supply last? 4.5 years

4. Which of the three Middle Eastern countries listed received the smallest income from petroleum in 1988? North Yemen, Qatar, Oman

5. How much larger are the total reserves of the Middle Eastern countries listed than those of the United States? about 273 billion barrels larger

Thinking Further: Why might a country want to produce its own supply of petroleum? Write your answer on a separate sheet. Answers may suggest that a country with its own supply of petroleum would not need any petroleum from foreign sources and would not have to transport oil from distant countries.

© Silver, Burdett & Ginn Inc.

C15-C

Workbook Pages

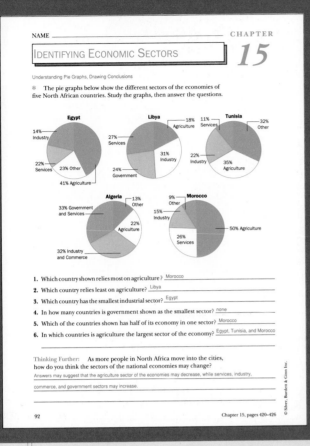

CHAPTER

15

IDENTIFYING ECONOMIC SECTORS

Understanding Pie Graphs, Drawing Conclusions

✳ The pie graphs below show the different sectors of the economies of five North African countries. Study the graphs, then answer the questions.

Egypt
14% Industry
22% Services
23% Other
41% Agriculture

Libya
18% Agriculture
27% Services
31% Industry
24% Government

Tunisia
11% Services
32% Other
22% Industry
35% Agriculture

Algeria
13% Other
33% Government and Services
22% Agriculture
32% Industry and Commerce

Morocco
9% Other
15% Industry
26% Services
50% Agriculture

1. Which country shown relies most on agriculture? _Morocco_

2. Which country relies least on agriculture? _Libya_

3. Which country has the smallest industrial sector? _Egypt_

4. In how many countries is government shown as the smallest sector? _none_

5. Which of the countries shown has half of its economy in one sector? _Morocco_

6. In which countries is agriculture the largest sector of the economy? _Egypt, Tunisia, and Morocco_

Thinking Further: As more people in North Africa move into the cities, how do you think the sectors of the national economies may change?

Answers may suggest that the agriculture sector of the economies may decrease, while services, industry,

commerce, and government sectors may increase.

Chapter 15, pages 420–426

C15-D

Iran, Iraq, and Afghanistan

Objectives

★**1. Compare** the two revolutions that Iran has experienced.

2. Describe the land, people, and resources of Iran, Iraq, and Afghanistan.

3. Explain why Afghanistan was involved in a bloody war during the 1980s.

4. Identify the following people and places: *Reza Khan, Muhammad Reza Pahlavi, Ruhollah Khomeini, Hashemi Rafsanjani, Tehran, Tigris River, Euphrates River, Hindu Kush,* and *Kabul.*

1 STARTING THE LESSON

Motivation Activity

■ Ask students to describe the things that make a country modern.

■ Then ask students what makes a country traditional.

■ Tell students that in this lesson they will learn about a country where the modern and the traditional conflicted.

Think About What You Know

■ Assign the THINK ABOUT WHAT YOU KNOW activity on p. 403.

■ Student answers should reflect independent thinking but may include that it could be good because it would prevent people from wearing clothes that might offend others, or it could be bad because it would take away the freedom to express oneself through the clothes one wears.

Study the Vocabulary

■ Have each student compose a matching quiz based on the vocabulary words and their definitions.

■ Have students exchange quizzes. Each completed quiz should be returned for grading to the student who devised it.

CHAPTER **15** THE MIDDLE EAST AND NORTH AFRICA TODAY

*F*requent conflicts threaten the region of the Middle East and North Africa. Oil has made a number of the countries in this region wealthy in recent years.

402

Optional Activities

Writing to Learn

Writing an Obituary   Have students write an obituary about one of the following twentieth-century leaders of Iran: Reza Khan, Muhammad Reza Pahlavi, or Ruhollah Khomeini.

● Tell students that the obituary should describe how the leader came to power and how he tried to change Iran.

● Have students include in the obituary an evaluation of the leader's accomplishments. Tell them that they can use imaginary quotes from citizens or government officials to lend support to their point of view.

● Conclude the activity by having volunteers read their obituaries to the class.

THINK ABOUT WHAT YOU KNOW

Explain how you would feel if there were a dress code, or a law, in this country that stated what kind of clothing you could and could not wear. How could a law like that be good or bad?

STUDY THE VOCABULARY

shah	embassy
modernize	ambassador
mullah	hostage
ayatollah	crude oil

FOCUS YOUR READING

How is the recent history of the Middle East a continuation of many years of problems?

A. The Scorpion and the Frog: A Tale of the Middle East

A scorpion and a frog met on the banks of the Jordan River. The scorpion, who could not swim, asked the frog to carry him across the river to the other side.

The frog said, "Absolutely not! If I carry you on my back, you might sting me." The scorpion reassured the frog, "If I sting you while we are crossing the river, we will both drown."

The frog thought that the scorpion's argument made sense. Surely the two of them could work together. At last the frog agreed to help the scorpion.

Halfway across the river, the scorpion suddenly stung the frog. As they both started to sink beneath the water, the frog croaked, "Why did you do that? Now we are both going to die." The scorpion sighed and said, "Oh, well, that's life in the Middle East!"

This legendary tale suggests that the nations in the Middle East often find it difficult to get along with one another. Even though they may have many things in common, both old and new rivalries have often led to violence. The Middle East today is one of the most dangerously explosive areas in the world.

B. Two Revolutions in Iran

New Ways of Living The first revolution in Iran happened in 1921, shortly after World War I, when an army officer named Reza Khan overthrew the government. After Reza Khan was declared **shah**, or king, he announced that Iran must **modernize**—that is, adopt up-to-date ways of living. The new shah believed that his people must copy Western ways of thinking. He was convinced that the Muslim religious teachers, known as **mullahs**, encouraged people to cling to their old-fashioned ways. To lessen the influence of the mullahs, the shah established government schools to take the place of religious schools.

When Reza Khan's son, Muhammad Reza Pahlavi, took his father's place as shah, he pushed modernization even faster. He decided that the small villages where most people lived were far too small to have the benefits of modernization. He ordered that many villages be torn down in order to force the people to move to larger and better places.

Things changed very rapidly as a result of the first revolution in Iran. The shah proudly boasted that there had not been so much change in 3,000 years. However, some people did not think that the changes were all for the better.

The mullahs declared that the government schools weakened religion. Even

403

2 DEVELOPING THE LESSON

Read and Think

Section A

Sometimes a story is the best way to illustrate a concept. Help your students understand the meaning of "The Scorpion and the Frog" by asking the following questions:

1. **What is the point that the story makes?** (Even though there might be a common goal, cooperation is difficult to achieve because of mistrust. *p. 403*)

Thinking Critically **What do you think is meant by the statement that the Middle East is one of the "most dangerously explosive areas in the world"?** (Infer)

(Answers should reflect independent thinking but may include that violence can break out in the Middle East at any time. *p. 403*)

Curriculum Connection

Economics Have students examine the data below to determine which nation has the brighter economic future.

- Iran's per capita income is $1,756. Its economy is growing by 1.3 percent per year and its population by 3.3 percent.

- Before the Persian Gulf war, Iraq's per capita income was $2,400. Its economy's growth rate had fallen to −15 percent per year. Its population was growing by 3.8 percent per year.

- Discuss what effect events such as the Iran-Iraq war had on the economies of both nations. Then discuss the effects of the Persian Gulf war on Iraq's economy.

Making Inferences

- Have students make inferences about how the Islamic revolution has affected other areas of life in Iran besides education, dress, and music.

- Ask students what they think television, newspapers, and the movies are like in Iran.

Optional Activities

403

Read and Think
Sections B and C

During the twentieth century, Iran has experienced two revolutions. Summarize the causes and effects of these conflicts by asking students the following questions:

1. **How did Reza Khan and Muhammad Reza Pahlavi want to change Iran?**
(They wanted Iran to modernize. *p. 403*)

2. **What did the mullahs think about the results of the first revolution?**
(They felt that the government schools weakened religion. *p. 403*)

3. **When did Iran's second revolution take place and how did it change life in Iran?**
(1979; the government became based on the Muslim religion and mullahs regulated all parts of life. *pp. 404-405*)

Thinking Critically Why, do you think, did Iran not have good relations with other countries after 1979? (Infer) (Answers should reflect independent thinking but may include that the government feared that relations with other countries would undermine its efforts to keep Iran an Islamic republic. *p. 405*)

GEOGRAPHY THEMES

Location

- Have students refer to the map on this page to answer the following question: Which city on this map is located almost directly on the Tropic of Cancer? (Masqat, Oman)

---

some of the people who favored modernization disliked the shah's undemocratic methods. The shah had secret police who kept close watch on people. Those who spoke out against the government often ended up in prison.

The Second Revolution In 1979, discontent grew so strong that the shah was forced to give up the throne and flee the country. The leader of the revolution was a mullah named Ruhollah Khomeini (roo-HOH luh koh MAY nee), who was often called the **ayatollah** (eye yuh TOH luh), an honorary title for a religious leader in Iran.

C. The Islamic Republic of Iran

Islamic Ways After the revolution in 1979, Iran became an Islamic republic—that is, a government based on the Muslim religion. It had an assembly with a president and prime minister, but final authority rested with the chief religious official. Ayatollah Khomeini was chosen as chief religious official for life.

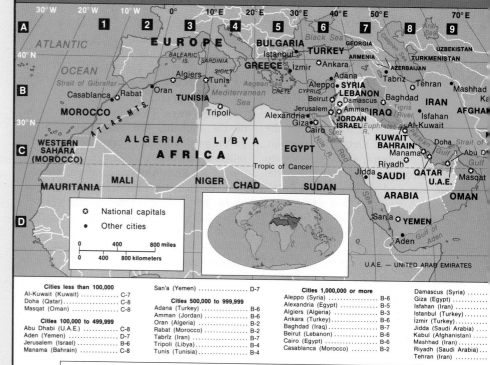

THE MIDDLE EAST AND NORTH AFRICA: POLITICAL

Legend:
- ⊕ National capitals
- • Other cities

0 — 400 — 800 miles
0 — 400 — 800 kilometers

Cities less than 100,000
Al-Kuwait (Kuwait) C-7
Doha (Qatar)..................... C-8
Masqat (Oman)................... C-8

Cities 100,000 to 499,999
Abu Dhabi (U.A.E.) C-8
Aden (Yemen) D-7
Jerusalem (Israel) B-6
Manama (Bahrain) C-8

San'a (Yemen) D-7

Cities 500,000 to 999,999
Adana (Turkey) B-6
Amman (Jordan) B-6
Oran (Algeria) B-2
Rabat (Morocco) B-2
Tabriz (Iran) B-7
Tripoli (Libya)................. B-4
Tunis (Tunisia)................ B-4

Cities 1,000,000 or more
Aleppo (Syria) B-6
Alexandria (Egypt) B-5
Algiers (Algeria) B-3
Ankara (Turkey) B-6
Baghdad (Iraq)................. B-7
Beirut (Lebanon) B-6
Cairo (Egypt) B-6
Casablanca (Morocco) B-2

Damascus (Syria) ....
Giza (Egypt) ....
Isfahan (Iran) ....
Istanbul (Turkey)........
Izmir (Turkey)............
Jidda (Saudi Arabia) ....
Kabul (Afghanistan) ....
Mashhad (Iran)..........
Riyadh (Saudi Arabia)...
Tehran (Iran)............

The Middle East and North Africa are located where three continents come together.
▶ What three continents intersect to form the Middle East and North Africa?

U.A.E. — UNITED ARAB EMIRATES

Graphic Organizer

To help students compare the land, resources, and governments of Iran, Iraq, and Afghanistan, you may wish to use the graphic organizer shown below.

THE LAND, RESOURCES, AND GOVERNMENTS OF IRAN, IRAQ, AND AFGHANISTAN			
	Iran	Iraq	Afghanistan
Land	Seacoast, desert	Dry, with rivers	Landlocked, mountainous
Economic Resources	Crude oil, natural gas, copper	Crude oil, water, farmland	Farming, herding
Government	Islamic republic	One-party republic	Provisional

Optional Activities

In 1979, revolutionary supporters of the Ayatollah Khomeini seized the American embassy in Tehran, Iran.
▶ Who, do you think, is pictured on their signs?

In the Islamic republic, the mullahs supervised all education. Boys and girls attended separate classes. Students entering the universities had to pass a test on the Muslim religion. Rules laid down by the mullahs regulated all parts of life. Neither alcohol nor Western-style music was allowed. Men could not wear T-shirts, short-sleeved shirts, or neckties. Women and girls had to wear long dark garments that covered their hair and body. Anyone suspected of opposing the Islamic republic was severely punished.

The Iranian Islamic Republic did not have good relations with other countries. The ayatollah constantly attacked the United States in speeches. In November of 1979 the Iranian government permitted a group of revolutionaries to take over the American **embassy** in Tehran, the capital. An embassy is where **ambassadors** and their staffs live and work. Ambassadors are officials who represent their governments in foreign countries. The Iranians held more than 50 Americans as **hostages** for more than a year. A hostage is a person held captive until demands of the captor are met. Negotiations between the United States and Iran finally ended the hostage crisis in 1981.

Iran-Iraq War The United States was not the only country that Iran and the ayatollah had conflicts with. In 1980 Iran became involved in a costly war with the neighboring country of Iraq. The war began because of a dispute about the border. Many people, including many children, lost their lives in this struggle. In 1988, Iran and Iraq finally accepted a United Nations plan to end the war. The next year, the Ayatollah Khomeini died at age 89, and a struggle began to see who would lead Iran. Hashemi Rafsanjani (hah SHAYM ee rahf-sahn JAH nee) was elected president of that country in August of 1989.

405

Optional Activities

Read and Think
Sections D and E

The countries of Iran and Iraq are both similar and different. Use the questions below to summarize their similarities and differences:

1. **Why has the population of Iran grown rapidly in recent years?**
(Wars brought in large numbers of refugees from Iraq and Afghanistan. *p. 406*)

2. **What is the chief export of both Iran and Iraq?**
(Crude oil *pp. 406-407*)

3. **How is the government of Iraq different from that of Iran?**
(Iraq is a one-party republic, although much of the power rests with the army. Iran is an Islamic republic, with final authority resting in the hands of the chief religious official. *pp. 404, 407*)

Thinking Critically What risks do you think nations such as Iran and Iraq run when their economies are so dependent on the export of one resource? (Analyze)
(Answers should reflect independent thinking but may include that their wealth will rise and fall with increases and decreases in the price of that resource and that they will also face problems when that resource runs out. *pp. 406-407*)

GEOGRAPHY THEMES

Movement

■ Have students look at the map on this page to help them answer the following question: **Through what important body of water does oil from Iran and Saudi Arabia travel?**
(The Persian Gulf)

D. People and Resources of Iran

Population The population of Iran has grown very rapidly in recent years. Even the war with Iraq did not slow the increase, partly because the war brought in large numbers of refugees from Iraq. Iran also received refugees fleeing from another war in the neighboring country of Afghanistan.

Most of Iran's people live in the northern and western parts of the country, near Tehran. The central region is sparsely populated, because salt deserts cover much of the land.

Land and Resources Iran has long seacoasts. One third of the country's boundaries are formed by the Caspian Sea, Persian Gulf, and the Arabian Sea, which is part of the Indian Ocean. Find the country of Iran on the map below.

Only about one tenth of Iran's land is arable, and much of this must be irrigated to grow crops. At one time Iran produced most of its own food. But the population has grown so much more rapidly than its food supply that the country depends partly on imports.

Iran's great wealth lies in its **crude oil** and natural gas deposits. Crude oil is oil that is found in its natural state—that is, oil that has not been refined, or purified. The war with Iraq greatly affected oil production, yet Iran remained the second largest producer in the Middle East. Iran also has valuable mineral deposits of copper, chromium, and coal.

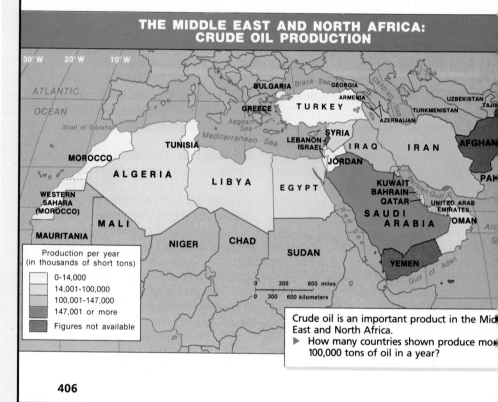

THE MIDDLE EAST AND NORTH AFRICA: CRUDE OIL PRODUCTION

Production per year
(in thousands of short tons)

- 0–14,000
- 14,001–100,000
- 100,001–147,000
- 147,001 or more
- Figures not available

Crude oil is an important product in the Middle East and North Africa.
▶ How many countries shown produce more than 100,000 tons of oil in a year?

Hypothesizing

● Have students hypothesize how the history of Iran might have been different if Shah Reza Pahlavi had not pushed modernization so quickly.

● Ask students if they think it would have made a difference if the shah had not put his critics in prison.

Optional Activities

E. Iraq Today

Oil and a Dictator   Modern Iraq includes ancient Mesopotamia, which you learned about as the land of early civilizations. The people of Mesopotamia depended on the waters of the Tigris and Euphrates rivers. So do the people of Iraq today. The rivers make it possible to irrigate the fields that produce beans, grains, and vegetables. But in recent years Iraq has depended on the sale of oil abroad.

Iraq is a republic, but it has only one political party. Saddam Hussein (sah DAHM hoo SAYN), who became president in 1979, rules as a military dictator. He built up a large army and used it to wage a war against Iran. The war dragged on for eight years and cost many lives.

The Persian Gulf War   The war with Iran left Iraq with enormous debts. Saddam needed funds to maintain the army, which he used to control his country. Neighboring Kuwait, on the Persian Gulf, is a very wealthy land. It has far fewer people than Iraq but nearly twice as much oil. Saddam declared that Kuwait had been wrongfully separated from Iraq after World War I. According to him, this oil-rich land was part of Iraq. On August 2, 1990, Iraqi troops invaded Kuwait and began taking over the country.

The United States and most other countries in the United Nations condemned Iraq's invasion. The United States and a number of other countries sent armed forces to the Persian Gulf. The United Nations repeatedly ordered Iraq to withdraw from Kuwait, but Saddam refused. On January 17, 1991, the United States and its allies began air raids on Iraq. Large ground forces attacked Iraq on February 23. It took the allies about 100

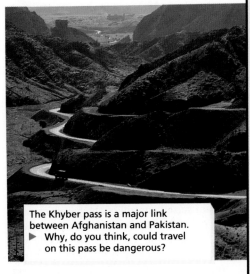

The Khyber pass is a major link between Afghanistan and Pakistan.
▶ Why, do you think, could travel on this pass be dangerous?

hours to defeat the Iraqi army. This was one of the shortest wars in history.

Before the Iraqi forces fled from Kuwait, they set fire to hundreds of oil wells. Firefighters from the United States and other countries were able to put these fires out more quickly than was expected. However, these oil fires have caused considerable damage to the environment.

Iraq suffered much during the Persian Gulf War and during the months that followed. Revolts broke out against the government. Saddam used what was left of his army to suppress these revolts.

F. Mountainous Afghanistan

Land and Resources   In ancient times the land routes across Asia from the Middle East passed through Afghanistan. One route led to China, in the Far East. Another led south to India, through the Khyber Pass. The caravans found it difficult crossing the mountainous country of Afghanistan. Even today, travel is not

407

Summarize the information about Afghanistan by asking students the following questions:

1. **Why is travel difficult in Afghanistan?** (The land is mountainous, and the country has no railroads and only some modern roads. *pp. 407-408*)

2. **What is Afghanistan's chief economic resource?** (The land *p. 408*)

3. **What caused a war to erupt in 1979?** (A Communist group seized control of the government and the Soviet Union sent in troops to support the takeover. Afghans opposed to the Communists went to war with the Soviet army. *p. 408*)

Thinking Critically   Why, do you think, was the Soviet Union interested in seeing a Communist government in control in Afghanistan? (Hypothesize) (Answers should reflect independent thinking but may include to have a buffer nation on its southern border much like it had buffer nations protecting its western border in Eastern Europe. *p. 408*)

┌─ **Answers to Caption Questions** ─
p. 406 ▶ 5 countries
p. 407 ▶ Road has many curves and does not have guard rails or lights

Curriculum Connection

Math   Have students solve the following word problem.

● Tell students that during the war in Afghanistan, the nation's population was reported to have decreased by one third. At least 4 million people fled to Iran or Pakistan and about 1 million were killed in the war.

● Ask students how large Afghanistan's population was before the war. (4 million + 1 million = 5 million; 5 million × 3 = 115 million)

Reteaching Main Objective

★ *Compare the two revolutions that Iran has experienced.*

● Ask students to compare the causes and effects of Iran's two revolutions.

● Make two cause-and-effect charts on the chalkboard.

● Ask students to list the causes of each revolution.

● Then have them list the effects of each revolution.

● Conclude the activity by discussing the ways in which both revolutions were similar and the ways they were different.

3 CLOSING THE LESSON

Lesson 1 Review

Answers to Think and Write

A. Life in the Middle East is dangerously explosive.

B. Government schools took the place of religious schools. Villages were torn down to force people to move to larger cities.

C. Boys and girls attend separate classes, alcohol and Western-style music have been banned, traditional dress must be worn, and anyone suspected of opposing the government faces severe punishment.

D. The war with Iraq increased Iran's population and reduced Iran's oil production.

E. The war with Iran left Iraq with enormous debts. Saddam needed funds to maintain his army. He invaded Kuwait to gain control of its oil.

F. Afghanistan is mountainous and landlocked. Most of the country is at an altitude of at least 2,000 feet (610 m).

Answer to Skills Check

The time lines should include: 1979 — ayatollah starts revolution in Iran; 1979 — war breaks out between Afghanistan and Soviet Union; 1980 — war breaks out between Iran and Iraq; 1989 — Soviets withdraw troops from Afghanistan; 1990 — Persian Gulf War is fought.

Focus Your Reading

Ask the lesson focus question found at the beginning of the lesson: **How is the recent history of the Middle East a continuation of many years of problems?**

(It is a continuation of the struggle between the forces of modernization and tradition and a continuation of the rivalry between Iran and Iraq.)

Additional Practice

You may wish to assign the ancillary materials listed below.

Understanding the Lesson p. 102
Workbook p. 88

---

easy here. Afghanistan has no railroad. There are, however, some modern roads.

Afghanistan is a landlocked country—that is, it has no outlet to the sea. Almost the whole country is at an altitude of at least 2,000 feet (610 m). The Hindu Kush mountains rise much higher. Kabul, the capital, is more than a mile (2 km) above sea level. Throughout their history, the people of Afghanistan have depended on farming small plots of land. They also kept herds of cattle, goats, and sheep.

A Bloody War In 1979, a Communist group seized control of the government of Afghanistan. The Soviet Union sent troops to support the takeover. A bloody war broke out between the Soviet army and Afghans who opposed the Communists. Many people were driven from their homes and fled to Pakistan and Iran. After ten years of costly war, the Soviet troops withdrew. In 1991, in an effort to discourage further fighting in Afghanistan, the United States and the Soviet Union agreed to stop all military aid to either side. In 1992 Afghanistan's communist government collapsed. An alliance of rebels took power.

The Soviets had far better equipment and weapons than the Afghan soldiers.
► What weapon does this soldier have to protect himself?

Today the search for a just peace in all the countries of the Middle East continues. In 1991, the United States and the Soviet Union sponsored a Middle East peace conference in Madrid, Spain. Peace talks in Washington, D.C., and Moscow followed.

LESSON **1** REVIEW

THINK AND WRITE

A. What does the tale of the scorpion and the frog suggest about life in the Middle East?　(Infer)

B. What changes resulted because of the first revolution in Iran?　(Recall)

C. How did life in Iran change after the second revolution?　(Recall)

D. How did the war with Iraq affect Iran's population and resources?　(Infer)

E. How did the results of the Iran-Iraq War lead eventually to the Persian Gulf War?
(Analyze)

F. What are some geographic features of Afghanistan?
(Recall)

SKILLS CHECK

THINKING SKILL

Make a time line for the period from 1975 to 1991. Show the following events: Ayatollah starts revolution in Iran; War breaks out between Afghanistan and Soviet Union; War breaks out between Iran and Iraq; Soviets withdraw troops from Afghanistan; the Persian Gulf War.

408

Optional Activities

UNDERSTANDING THE LESSON

NAME _____

UNDERSTANDING THE LESSON

CHAPTER **15**

Making Comparisons

LESSON 1 CONTENT MASTER

✶ This chart helps you to compare the countries of Iran, Iraq, and Afghanistan. Write the missing information in each blank on the chart. A few have been done for you.

Country	Iran	Iraq	Afghanistan
Present Type of Government	Islamic republic since 1979; final authority rests with chief religious official	Republic; one-party state; president and legislature; the army has much power	Communist government
Farming and Resources	One tenth of land is arable; oil, natural gas, copper, coal, chromium	Irrigated fields of beans, grain, vegetables, dates; crude oil	Farming on small plots of land; herding cattle, goats, and sheep
Major Geographic Features	Deserts cover much of central region; long coasts on Caspian and Arabian seas	Tigris and Euphrates rivers	Landlocked, mountainous; whole country over 2,000 feet high; Hindu Kush rise much higher
Problems Since 1979	War with Iraq; power struggle after death of Ayatollah Khomeini	Long, costly war with Iran	Communists took over government; war between Soviet army and Afghans opposed to Communists

Think and Write: Write a paragraph contrasting the changes resulting from the Iranian revolutions of 1921 and 1979. You may use the back of the sheet.
Answers should reflect independent thinking; suggestions appear in the Answer Key.

102

Use with textbook pages 405–408.

◄ **Lesson Workshee Booklet, p. 102**

LESSON **2**   PAGES 409–413

Israel and Turkey

THINK ABOUT WHAT YOU KNOW
Israel has had many leaders throughout its history. What leaders can you name from ancient Israel?

STUDY THE VOCABULARY
Knesset   **fez**

FOCUS YOUR READING
What political and economic changes have taken place in Israel and Turkey since World War I?

A. The Creation of Modern Israel

Many Rulers   General Yigael Yadin was a leader in Israel's war of independence, in 1948. General Yadin was also an enthusiastic archaeologist, because he believed that ancient remains provided a link between modern Israel and the kingdoms of David and Solomon. As a soldier, Yadin helped win modern Israel's independence. As an archaeologist, he uncovered the remains of the city that Solomon had built in ancient Israel.

The region known today as Israel has had many rulers during its long history. When it was part of the Roman Empire, the Romans called the area *Palestine*. Then Arab caliphs and Ottoman sultans ruled the region throughout the Middle Ages. Palestine was still a part of the Ottoman Empire when World War I began in 1914.

Since Turkey was on the side of Germany during World War I, the British attacked Turkish-ruled lands in the Middle East. Some of the Arabs, wishing to be free of Turkey, helped the British. In return, the British promised that the Turkish Empire would be broken up. Since the majority of the peoples in the Turkish Empire were Arabs, the Arabs took this promise to mean that they would rule Palestine. But the British also made a promise to the Jews. The British said they supported the creation of a national home for the Jews in Palestine.

After World War I, the British took control of Palestine. At that time most of the inhabitants of Palestine were Arabs. But the number of Jews increased rapidly after Adolf Hitler rose to power in Germany in the 1930s. Many more Jewish settlers arrived after World War II. However, the Arabs in Palestine opposed the growing Jewish settlement.

Israel's Independence   In 1947, following World War II, the United Nations proposed to divide Palestine into two states,

Jews celebrated their independence in Israel in 1948.
▶ What is this girl holding in her right hand?

Writing to Learn

Writing a Letter to the Editor   Have students write a letter to the editor of a newspaper in Israel in which they explain what they think should be done to resolve the Arab-Israeli conflict.

- Tell students to begin their letters by explaining what they think is the cause of the conflict.
- Then, have students explain why they think earlier attempts to resolve the conflict have failed.
- Finally, have them describe how they think the conflict could be resolved.
- When students have finished, ask volunteers to read their letters to the class and discuss their proposals with the class.

Optional Activities

Objectives

★1. **List** political and economic changes that have occurred in Israel and Turkey since World War I.

2. **Explain** how the modern state of Israel was created.

3. **Describe** the ways in which Mustafa Kemal modernized Turkey.

4. **Identify** the following people and places: *Yigael Yadin, Golda Meir, Mustafa Kemal, Palestine, Negev,* and *Dead Sea*.

1 STARTING THE LESSON

Motivation Activity

■ Ask students to imagine the following: The government has promised to make your town a homeland for refugees from Asia, although it has promised you that your rights and culture will be protected.

■ Discuss with students how they think their town will change and what they think about these changes.

■ Tell students that a similar situation developed in the land we know as Israel, creating lasting problems for the people who live there.

Think About What You Know

■ Assign the THINK ABOUT WHAT YOU KNOW activity on p. 409.

■ Student answers should reflect independent thinking but may include King Solomon and King David.

Study the Vocabulary

■ Have each student write one question based on each vocabulary word.

■ Have students exchange papers and answer each other's questions.

┌─ **Answers to Caption Questions** ─┐
p. 408 ▶ A gun
p. 409 ▶ Flag of Israel
└──────────────────────────────┘

409

DEVELOPING THE LESSON

Read and Think

Sections A and B

Use the questions below to help students summarize the information about Israel:

1. **Why has Israel been in so many wars?**
   (The Arabs in Palestine and the neighboring Arab countries refuse to accept the Jewish state of Israel. *pp. 409-410*)

2. **Describe Israel's government.**
   (Israel is a democratic republic governed by an elected assembly. *p. 410*)

   Thinking Critically What information would lead you to conclude that **Israel has a high literacy rate?** (Infer)
   (Answers should reflect independent thinking but may include that most Israeli industries require skilled workers. *p. 410*)

GEOGRAPHY THEMES

Regions

- Have students look at the map on this page to help them answer the following questions: **With which countries did Israel go to war in 1967? How do you know?**
  (Egypt, Jordan, and Syria; After the 1967 war, Israel occupied land that was once part of these nations.)

ISRAEL AND ITS NEIGHBORS

- Israel before 1948 war
- Area gained by Israel after 1948 war
- Area occupied by Israel after 1967 war

Israel gave the Sinai Peninsula back to Egypt in 1982.
▶ When had Israel gained the Sinai Peninsula?

one Jewish and one Arab. The Arabs in Palestine and the neighboring Arab countries refused to accept the proposal, but the Jewish state of Israel declared its independence in 1948.

In the year that Israel declared independence, war broke out between Israel and the Arabs. Israel won its war of independence, but victory did not bring peace. There were other Arab-Israeli wars in 1956, 1967, and 1973. Israel won these wars, but there was still no peace agreement.

B. A Modern Country in an Ancient Land

Industry and Resources Israel is a small country—one of the smallest in the Middle East. It is even smaller than the state of Maryland. The southern half of the country, called the Negev, is very dry, but Israelis proudly say that they have "made the desert bloom." Water piped from the north, which has plentiful winter rainfall, is used for irrigation in the Negev. Israeli farmers grow about three fourths of the country's food, and they also produce citrus fruits, avocados, flowers, and other crops for export.

Israel earns more from its industries than does any other Middle Eastern country. Most Israeli industries require skilled workers, such as those who make scientific instruments and electronic equipment and those who cut diamonds. Israel is second only to Belgium in the cutting and polishing of diamonds, an industry that requires highly skilled people. Tourism is also an important industry in Israel. As you have learned, Israel is the Holy Land for Christians and Jews.

Israel is not a country rich in minerals, although it has some copper. There is some oil and natural gas, but not enough to supply the country's needs. The Dead Sea is an important source of minerals, which are used for such products as table salt and fertilizer.

Government Israel is a democratic republic governed by an elected assembly called the **Knesset** (KNES et). The members of the Knesset choose the president and the prime minister. One of the prime ministers, Golda Meir, had studied to be a school teacher in Milwaukee, Wisconsin, before she emigrated to Israel.

Making a Pie Chart

- Have students use the information below to make a pie chart about the people of Israel.
- Tell students to make a pie chart of the religious groups to which the people of Israel belong: 82 percent Jewish, 14 percent Islamic, 2 percent Christian, and 2 percent other.
- Conclude the activity by asking students how they think these percentages have changed since the end of World War I.

Comparing Israel and Turkey

- Have students use the following information to compare the people and economies of Turkey and Israel.
- Ask students to make a bar graph comparing the populations of Israel and Turkey. Tell them that the population of Israel is 4,500,000 and the population of Turkey is 55,400,000.
- Ask students to make a bar graph comparing the GNPs of Israel and Turkey. Tell them that the GNP of Israel is $35 billion and the GNP of Turkey is $67.1 billion.
- Conclude the activity by asking students to look at the bar graphs and visually determine which country has the higher per-capita income (Israel).

C. Modernizing Turkey

Abandoning a Custom For nearly a century, men in Turkey wore a type of hat called a **fez**, a felt hat with a flat top and no brim. The custom began when an Ottoman sultan ordered his soldiers and officials to wear fezzes. The lack of brims on fezzes made it easier for Muslim men to touch their foreheads to the ground when they prayed.

In 1925, Mustafa Kemal (MOOS tah-fah ke MAHL), the powerful president of the Turkish republic, appeared wearing a hat with a brim and other Western clothing. The president told all Turkish men that they, too, must wear such hats. To make sure that they did so, Kemal created a law forbidding the wearing of a fez.

The law against fezzes upset many Turks. They said that wearing a brimmed hat showed that a man had given up the Muslim religion. One man avoided wearing a hat by tying bandages about his head as if suffering great pain.

Turkish Women New laws also changed the lives of the women in Turkey. Turkish women wore veils to hide their faces in public places. But Kemal said that veils could no longer be worn.

Kemal wanted Turkish women to change more than the way they dressed. He said that in a modern nation men and women should be equal. In the past, girls in Turkey had not gone to school outside the home. Kemal ordered them to do so. Women got the right to take jobs in business and government. Women also were given the right to vote.

> Mustafa Kemal changed the Turkish laws of dress.
> ▶ How is this woman's clothing different from the traditional clothing of Turkish women?

411

For Your Information

The Kibbutz Many of the early Jewish settlers in Israel lived on a kibbutz, a community in which all people live and work as a group. The settlers farmed the land and used the money that the farm earned to feed, clothe, house, and educate the members of the kibbutz and their children. Life for these early settlers was not easy. The soil was poor, and they lacked good equipment. Some of the early kibbutzim failed and the members dispersed. However, there were many that succeeded and the kibbutz became the backbone of the nation, providing food for the people and protecting the nation's borders from hostile neighbors. Today, there are more than 250 kibbutzim in Israel. The largest has about 2,000 people. The average kibbutz has about 400 to 500 people.

Read and Think
Sections C and D

Turkey began to modernize after World War I. Discuss the changes Turkey has undergone by asking the following questions:

1. **What changes did Mustafa Kemal introduce in Turkey?**
(He created a law forbidding the wearing of fezzes; he moved the capital to Ankara; he introduced an alphabet based on the Roman alphabet; and he ordered all printed material to use the new alphabet. *pp. 411–413*)

2. **How have the lives of Turkish women changed?**
(They no longer have to wear veils, can go to school, can take jobs in business and government, and can vote. *p. 411*)

3. **How did the government of Turkey change in the twentieth century?**
(It changed from rule by sultans to a republic. *p. 413*)

Thinking Critically Why, do you think, did Mustafa Kemal come to be called "father of the Turks"? (Analyze)
(Answers should reflect independent thinking but may include that he was Turkey's first president or that he instituted many changes that affected Turkish life. *pp. 411–413*)

GEOGRAPHY THEMES

Human-Environment Interactions

■ Have students work in pairs for the following activity: Have students work together to name the countries shown on the maps on this page. This can be done by comparing these maps with the map on p. 406.

■ Then have one student in each pair name one of the countries from the Middle East or North Africa shown on the maps on this page. His or her partner should then name the agricultural products of that country.

■ Have students continue until both students have had a chance to list the products of all of the countries shown.

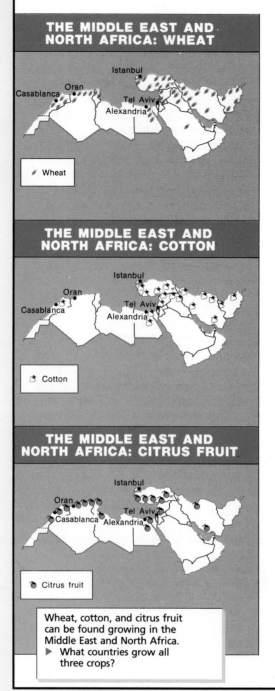

THE MIDDLE EAST AND NORTH AFRICA: WHEAT

Istanbul
Casablanca Oran
Tel Aviv
Alexandria

✦ Wheat

THE MIDDLE EAST AND NORTH AFRICA: COTTON

Istanbul
Oran
Casablanca
Tel Aviv
Alexandria

❀ Cotton

THE MIDDLE EAST AND NORTH AFRICA: CITRUS FRUIT

Istanbul
Oran
Casablanca
Tel Aviv
Alexandria

🍊 Citrus fruit

Wheat, cotton, and citrus fruit can be found growing in the Middle East and North Africa.
▶ What countries grow all three crops?

New Laws, New Ways Why all this fuss about fezzes and veils? It was part of the great changes taking place in Turkey after World War I. A revolution had ended the rule of the Ottoman sultans, and Turkey had become a republic. Mustafa Kemal insisted that Turkey do more than change its government. Turkey had to modernize. The fez was a sign of the past. The president thought that changing what men wore *on* their heads would help change what went on *in* their heads.

Adopting Western-style clothing was only one of the changes introduced by Mustafa Kemal. He moved the capital from Istanbul to Ankara. He introduced an alphabet based on the Roman alphabet used for western European languages. Three months after the introduction of the new alphabet, Kemal ordered all newspapers, books, and street signs to be printed in the new style.

D. Land and People of Turkey

Farming and Resources Even though much of the Anatolian peninsula, where Turkey is located, is dry and mountainous, about one third of the land is cultivated. Wheat and cotton are the largest crops, but Turkey also produces other crops such as citrus fruits, olives, and raisin grapes.

Turkey has the largest coal deposits in the Middle East. It also has other minerals, including chromium, which is used in making stainless steel. Turkey leads the world in the production of an unusual mineral called meerschaum (MIHR shum). It is an easily carved material, used mainly for making tobacco pipes.

Population Turkey lies in both Europe and Asia. Only about 3 percent of Turkey is in Europe, but that part includes its largest

Reteaching Main Objective

★ **List the political and economic changes that have occurred in Israel and Turkey since World War I.**

● Have each student make a time line of events having to do with the political and economic changes that have occurred in Turkey and Israel since World War I.

● Have the students use the text to help them identify the events that should go on the time line.

● To conclude the activity, invite volunteers to use the time lines to give an oral report about the changes in both countries that have occurred since World War I.

Istanbul, Turkey's largest city, has been one of the world's important cities for hundreds of years.
▶ What building in the photograph symbolizes the city's culture?

city, Istanbul, which you learned used to be Constantinople. Turkey's population is spread unevenly over the Anatolian peninsula. The greater number of people live in western Turkey, and they feel they are more like Europeans than like peoples of the Middle East.

Government Mustafa Kemal came to be called Kemal Ataturk. *Ataturk* means "father of the Turks." His title was President of the Republic; but he was, in fact, a

dictator. Although elections were held, only one political party was allowed to run for office.

Mostly because of political unrest, the control of Turkey's government has changed many times over the last five decades, since Ataturk's death in 1938. However, in 1982 a new constitution was adopted. Today the Turkish government is more like a republic of Western Europe, in which voters may choose candidates from among several parties.

LESSON 2 REVIEW

THINK AND WRITE

A. How was the dispute over Palestine after World War I resolved? **(Recall)**
B. What are some of the ways the people of Israel make a living? **(Recall)**
C. In what ways did Mustafa Kemal modernize Turkey? **(Recall)**
D. What are some products produced in Turkey? **(Recall)**

SKILLS CHECK
MAP SKILL

Turn to the map Israel and Its Neighbors on page 410, and answer the following questions: What body of water does Israel share with Jordan? What are the names of the three areas that Israel gained after 1967?

413

Optional Activities

Lesson 2 Review

Answers to Think and Write
A. After World War I, the British took control of Palestine.
B. Israelis make their living by farming, making scientific and electronic equipment, cutting diamonds, and working at tourist-related jobs.
C. Kemal encouraged Turks to wear Western-style clothing; he moved the capital to Ankara; he introduced an alphabet based on the Roman alphabet, and he ordered all newspapers, books, and street signs to be printed using the new alphabet.
D. Turkey produces wheat, cotton, citrus fruits, olives, tobacco, raisin grapes, coal, chromium, and meerschaum.

Answer to Skills Check
Israel and Jordan share the Jordan River and the Dead Sea. Israel gained the Golan Heights, the West Bank, and the Sinai after 1967.

Focus Your Reading

Ask the lesson focus question found at the beginning of the lesson: **What political and economic changes have taken place in Israel and Turkey since World War I?**
(The Jewish state of Israel was given its independence in 1948 and became a democratic republic. Israelis have made the land productive and developed industries that require skilled labor. Turkey became a republic, although political unrest caused the control of the government to change many times. Turkey modernized and has developed its agriculture and mineral resources.)

Additional Practice

You may wish to assign the ancillary materials listed below.

Understanding the Lesson p. 103
Workbook p. 89

--- **Answers to Caption Questions** ---
p. 412 ▶ Morocco, Iran, Turkey, Israel, and Egypt
p. 413 ▶ A mosque

Other Countries of the Middle East

Objectives

★ 1. **List** the main characteristics of each country of the Middle East.

2. **Explain** why Lebanon has been torn by civil war for so long.

3. **Describe** how Saudi Arabia has used its oil wealth to modernize.

4. **Identify** the following places: *Arabian Peninsula, West Bank, Riyadh, Persian Gulf, Strait of Hormuz, Red Sea,* and *Aden.*

1 STARTING THE LESSON

Motivation Activity

■ Ask students to imagine that they are the leaders of a poor land with few resources. Tell them that vast oil reserves are discovered and, practically overnight, their country becomes rich.

■ Discuss with students what they would recommend that their country do with all of this new-found wealth. Tell students that some countries in the Middle East have found themselves in a similar situation.

Think About What You Know

■ Assign the THINK ABOUT WHAT YOU KNOW activity on p. 414

■ Student answers should reflect independent thinking but may include that oil is important because it is used for so many important things, such as heating and transportation fuel.

Study the Vocabulary

■ Have students look up the definition of each of the vocabulary terms for this lesson in the Glossary.

■ Then have students use the terms to write headlines for news articles about oil-rich countries of the Middle East.

LESSON **3**

Other Countries of the Middle East

THINK ABOUT WHAT YOU KNOW

Think of different ways in which we use oil. Then describe why oil is such an important resource.

STUDY THE VOCABULARY

reserve   causeway
nonrenewable resource

FOCUS YOUR READING

What are some of the important characteristics of each of the Arab countries of the Middle East?

A. Jordan and Syria

Jordan   On the northern edge of the Arabian Peninsula are the countries of Jordan and Syria. Jordan was part of the Ottoman Empire before World War I. The British controlled Jordan after the war. Then, in 1928, Jordan gained some control over its own affairs, but Jordan did not get its complete independence until 18 years later, in 1946.

During the 1948 Arab war against Israel, Jordan won territory west of the Jordan River. In 1950 this area, known as the West Bank, became part of Jordan, even though most of the Arab people who lived there called themselves Palestinians. Since 1967, however, all of the West Bank has been under Israel's control. Many of the Arabs who lived on the West Bank fled to Jordan.

Jordan has remained a poor land with very few resources. It has some minerals, but no oil. The removal of minerals from the Dead Sea water is one of the country's important industries.

Only about 5 percent of Jordan's land is arable, yet agriculture is an important occupation. Most of its crops—such as grapes, olives, and citrus fruits—are grown on irrigated land.

Syria   Syria, Jordan's neighbor to the north, has some of the best land in the Middle East. About half of Syria's land is arable. When irrigated, the land produces crops of cotton, wheat, tobacco, and various vegetables. About one fourth of the land in Syria can be used for grazing sheep and goats.

Syria was part of the Ottoman Empire before World War I. France controlled the country between World War I and World War II, but Syria became independent in 1946. Although called a republic, Syria is a one-party state.

Crops such as these chili peppers grow well in the Jordan River valley.
▶ What, do you think, makes the Jordan River valley an important agricultural region?

Optional Activities

Making Comparisons

● Have students make a chart that compares and contrasts Jordan and Syria.

● Tell students to make a chart with two columns. Have them label one column *Jordan* and the other, *Syria*.

● Then tell students to locate the following information for each country: which empire it was part of before World War I, which nation controlled the country after the war, when it gained independence, what percent of the land is arable, and what agricultural and mineral products it produces.

● Conclude the activity by having students study the chart and write sentences that compare and contrast the two nations.

B. Divisions Within Lebanon

Religious Differences Lebanon is a small country — smaller than the state of Connecticut. But in spite of its small size, Lebanon has a varied geography and climate. Winter temperatures along the Mediterranean coast are warmer than those on the French Riviera. And, while basking in the sun on the beach, it is possible to see the snow-covered peaks of the Lebanon Mountains.

Differences in religion have divided the Lebanese people. Part of the population is Christian, and part is Muslim. When Lebanon became independent in 1943, the political offices were divided according to religion. The Christians were then in the majority, so it was agreed that the president would be a Christian and the prime minister, a Muslim. In more recent years, the Muslims say that they have become

the majority, so they have demanded more political power.

A Civil War The dispute about the sharing of power led to civil war in the 1970s. Both Christians and Muslims formed fighting forces. The situation was made more difficult by large numbers of Palestinians who fled north during the Arab-Israeli conflict. The Palestinians had their own military forces and bases. Both of the neighboring countries of Syria and Israel became involved in Lebanon.

At one time a peacekeeping force made up of soldiers from the United States, Britain, France, and Italy was sent into the country of Lebanon. In spite of many efforts to make peace, the fighting in Lebanon continues. Thousands of people have been killed, and much property has been destroyed.

415

Read and Think
Sections A and B

To summarize the information about Jordan, Syria, and Lebanon, ask the following questions:

1. **Why has Jordan remained a poor land while Syria has not?**
   (Jordan has little arable land and few resources, while Syria has some of the best land in the Middle East. *p. 414*)

2. **What differences have caused problems for the people of Lebanon?**
   (Part of the population is Christian and part is Muslim, and these factions have led to power struggles. *p. 415*)

Thinking Critically In what ways, do you think, has Lebanon's economy been affected by the civil war? (Synthesize)
(Answers may include that the economy is in bad shape because people don't want to live there or travel there; much property has been destroyed and it is too risky to do business there. *p. 415*)

— **Answers to Caption Questions** —
p. 414 ▶ The Jordan River
p. 415 ▶ Carrying them on their heads

Negotiating

- Have the class hold a mock United Nations meeting at which the nations of the world try to negotiate a peaceful settlement of the civil war in Lebanon.

- Have small groups of students represent the United States, Great Britain, France, Italy, Lebanese Christians, Lebanese Muslims, Israel, the Palestinians, and Syria.

- Have each group meet separately to develop its own plan for peace in Lebanon.

- Then have the groups meet together, present their plan, and try to persuade the others to support their plan.

- Conclude the activity by discussing with students why peace in Lebanon has been so difficult to achieve.

Curriculum Connection

Economics Tell students that due to falling worldwide demand and rising production of oil, Saudi Arabia has seen its oil wealth decline since 1980.

- Tell students that in 1980, Saudi Arabia's oil revenues were $120 billion, in 1984, they were $43 billion, and in 1985 they were $25 billion.

- Have students make a bar graph showing these statistics.

- Then ask students to write a paragraph explaining how this decline in oil wealth will affect Saudi Arabia's modernization plans.

- Conclude the activity by discussing why a country with a one-resource economy can run into economic problems.

Optional Activities

Read and Think

Section C

To help students understand the changes that oil wealth has brought to Saudi Arabia, ask the following questions:

1. **How have the Saudis used their oil wealth?**
   (To modernize the country through building modern schools, hospitals, roads, and airports; to erect modern industrial plants; and to buy land and businesses abroad *pp. 416–417*)

2. **Why does the fact that only 1 percent of its land is arable not have a negative effect on Saudi Arabia's economy?**
   (Because Saudi Arabia has a wealth of oil reserves)

   Thinking Critically Why, do you think, would the Saudis use their oil wealth to buy land and businesses abroad? (Synthesize)
   (Answers should reflect independent thinking but may include that they feel these purchases are good investments that will help their wealth grow. *p. 417*)

C. Saudi Arabia: Oil in the Desert

Land and Resources Saudi Arabia occupies most of the Arabian Peninsula. Even though Saudi Arabia has a very large land area, it has fewer people than the Netherlands. Saudi Arabia is a monarchy ruled by the Saud family, for whom the country is named.

The kingdom of the Saudis is truly a desert country. Only about 1 percent of the land is arable. Another 39 percent can be used by nomadic Bedouins as pasture for goats, sheep, and camels. But beneath the desert are enormous known oil **reserves**. Reserves are supplies of a natural resource that are known to exist but have not yet been used.

Oil is a **nonrenewable resource**— that is, a resource that cannot be replaced. The graphs below show important facts about the earth's known oil reserves. The greater part of these reserves are in the Middle East and North Africa, and Saudi Arabia has the largest reserves in that region. The largest of the Arabian oil fields is also the largest single reserve in the world.

Modernizing Oil has brought great wealth to Saudi Arabia in recent times. Much of the wealth has been used to modernize the country. The government has built modern schools, hospitals, roads, and airports. Some modern industrial plants have been erected, particularly chemical plants and others that make use of oil. The production of petroleum and petroleum products makes up about 70 percent of what Saudi Arabia produces. Look at the chart on page 418 to see some products that are made from petroleum.

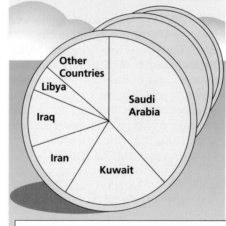

PROVEN OIL RESERVES IN THE MIDDLE EAST AND NORTH AFRICA

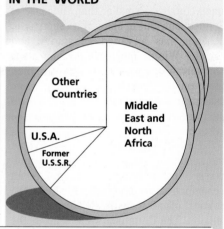

PROVEN OIL RESERVES IN THE WORLD

Most of the world's oil reserves are in the Middle East and North Africa.

► Which country in the Middle East and North Africa has about the same amount of oil reserves as does the United States, the former Soviet Union, and other countries in the world combined?

Supporting Generalizations

● Write the following generalization on the chalkboard: *Religion plays an important role in the life, politics, and economies of the countries of the Middle East.*

● Ask students to skim Sections B and C in order to locate information that would support this generalization.

● Conclude the activity by discussing with students whether they think allowing religion to play such an important role helps or hurts these countries.

Curriculum Connection

Government Tell students that the United Arab Emirates is not one nation but a federation of seven independent emirates, or states, run by a native ruler. These emirates wanted to join together for defense and development, but they wanted to keep control of their own internal affairs.

● Discuss with students what the advantages and disadvantages of such a system of government might be.

● Tell students that at one point in its early history, the United States tried this form of government but it did not work. Ask students why they think this form of government has worked in the Middle East but not in the United States.

Oil has brought wealth to parts of the Middle East. Universities in Saudi Arabia can now buy computers.
► How has money helped these schoolchildren in Qatar?

The Saudis also have used some of the money from oil to buy land and businesses in Europe and the United States.

Oil money has brought many other changes in Saudi Arabia. Pickup trucks have replaced camels among the Bedouins. Riyadh (ree YAHD), the capital, has grown into a modern city with over a million people. But the Saudi leaders do not believe that everything should change. As one Saudi official explained, hospitals and new industries are fine, but they cannot take the place of mosques, the Muslim places of worship. According to this official, "The price we will not pay for development is our religion."

D. Persian Gulf States

Kuwait Kuwait, located on the northwest coast of the Persian Gulf, is smaller than the state of New Jersey. Before 1940, pearls from the Persian Gulf were Kuwait's main export. The discovery of oil in the desert made Kuwait one of the world's richest countries.

It has been said that Kuwait has more oil than it has water. At one time, Kuwait had to import water by boat from Iraq. Kuwait has used part of its wealth to build the world's largest plant for changing sea water into fresh water.

The wealth from their country's oil has also been used to provide Kuwaitis with free education and medical care. As you have read, the desire for Kuwait's oil brought about an invasion by Iraq, which resulted in the Persian Gulf War.

417

Writing to Learn

Writing an Essay After students have read all sections of Lesson 3, ask them to write an essay in which they identify the Middle East nation that they would most like to visit.

● In their essays, students should explain why the country they have selected interests them and what they would hope to see and learn while visiting that country.

● Conclude the activity by having volunteers read their essays to the class.

Optional Activities

Meeting Individual Needs

Concept:
The Future of the Middle East

To help students better understand the countries of the Middle East today, it may be helpful for students to review information about these countries and predict what will happen to them in the future.

◆ **EASY** Ask students to recall what the political situation in Lebanon is like today.

Have students review the information in Section B and ask them to predict what the situation in Lebanon will be like in two years and in five years. Ask them to identify the information they used to formulate their predictions.

◀◆▶ **AVERAGE** Ask students to recall what Saudi Arabia's economy is like today.

Have students review the information in Section C and ask them to predict what will happen to Saudi Arabia's economy when the oil runs out. Ask them to identify the information they used to formulate their predictions.

◀❙▶ **CHALLENGING** Ask students to recall who controls the West Bank today.

Have students review the information in Section A and ask them to predict what will happen to the West Bank in the future. Ask them to identify the information they used to formulate their predictions.

VISUAL THINKING SKILL

Interpreting Graphs

■ Direct students' attention to the graphs on p. 416. Then ask the following question: **Which country in the Middle East and North Africa is second to Saudi Arabia in oil reserves?**
(Kuwait)

Answers to Caption Questions
p. 416 ► Saudi Arabia
p. 417 ► It has provided them with chemistry laboratory equipment.

417

Read and Think

Sections D and E

Use the questions below to summarize the information about the Persian Gulf states, Oman, and Yemen:

1. **How is Bahrain different from the other Persian Gulf states?**
(Its oil reserves have been largely used up, and it consists of a group of about 35 islands. *p. 418*)

2. **What are the major sources of income of Oman and Yemen?**
(Oman—oil; Yemen—coffee, the port of Aden *pp. 418–419*)

Thinking Critically Why, do you think, did Kuwait build a plant for changing sea water into fresh water when it can get water through a pipeline from Iraq? (Analyze)
(Answers should reflect independent thinking but may include that the Kuwaitis did not want to be at the mercy of the Iraqis for their water supply. *p. 417*)

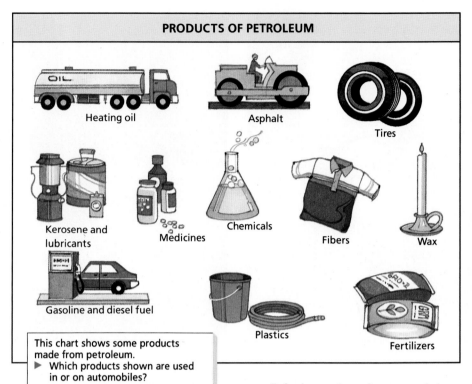

PRODUCTS OF PETROLEUM

Heating oil

Asphalt

Tires

Kerosene and lubricants

Medicines

Chemicals

Fibers

Wax

Gasoline and diesel fuel

Plastics

Fertilizers

This chart shows some products made from petroleum.
▶ Which products shown are used in or on automobiles?

Qatar and United Arab Emirates Qatar is on a peninsula that extends into the Persian Gulf from the Arabian Peninsula. Just to the south, also along the coast, is the state known as the United Arab Emirates. Both Qatar and the United Arab Emirates are sandy, stony deserts that have benefited from the discovery of oil.

Bahrain The countries of Bahrain and Oman are not as rich as are Saudi Arabia, Kuwait, Qatar, and the United Arab Emirates. Bahrain was the first Persian Gulf nation to produce oil, but by the 1970s its reserves were largely used up. Its refineries, however, still operate with oil carried by pipeline from Saudi Arabia.

418

Bahrain consists of a group of about 35 islands just north of Qatar in the Persian Gulf. A **causeway** connects the main island with the coast of Saudi Arabia. A causeway is a raised road across water or swampy land.

E. Oman and Yemen

Oman Ships entering and leaving the Persian Gulf must pass through the Strait of Hormuz (HOR muz). The territory of Oman includes land at the tip of a peninsula overlooking this passageway, which is 24 miles (39 km) wide at this point. Oman also consists of a large stretch of land that forms the southeastern corner of the Arabian Peninsula. Oil is the main source of wealth in Oman.

Reteaching Main Objective

⭐ *List the main characteristics of each country of the Middle East.*

● Pair students who understand the concept with students who need reteaching.

● Have each pair skim the lesson to make up two *Jeopardy*-style questions for each country.

● After students have written their questions and answers, you may wish to have each pair of students work with another pair of students to answer each other's questions.

The sunny beaches of Tunisia attract many tourists each year.
▶ What kind of climate does the coast of Tunisia have?

Muslims. All public signs, including those in airports, must be written in Arabic script only.

Relations between Libya and other countries have been stormy since Colonel Qaddafi came to power. The United States and other countries have charged that Libya has supported terrorism. Terrorism is the use of fear to threaten people or nations to make them do things that they do not want to do.

D. Tunisia: A Land with Variety

Language and Government Tunisia, Libya's neighbor to the west, is also a Muslim country. Arabic is the official language, but many people speak French. This land was part of the French empire before becoming an independent republic in 1957. For a number of years, Tunisia had a one-party government, but today other parties can run for office.

Climate and Land Tunisia is the smallest of the North African countries, yet it has a variety of lands and climates. Tunisia's Mediterranean coast has the same kind of climate as other Mediterranean lands — mild winters and hot summers. Tunisia's sunny Mediterranean beaches attract thousands of tourists, since Tunis, the capital, is only a short flight from Rome and other European cities.

In ancient times, Carthage was a powerful rival of Rome. Today, Carthage is a suburb of Tunis. Only a few ruins remain in modern Carthage to remind travelers that this was the city of Hannibal. You read about Hannibal and the wars of Rome and Carthage in Chapter 3.

Tunisia is basically an agricultural country. Northern Tunisia has forests and fertile farmlands. Farther south there are dry grasslands suitable for grazing sheep, goats, and camels.

423

Curriculum Connection

Science Tell students that the hottest temperature ever recorded in the world was 136° Farenheit in El Azizia, Libya, on September 13, 1922.

● Ask students to convert Fahrenheit temperatures to Celsius. If students are unfamiliar with how to do this, tell them to subtract 32 from the Fahrenheit temperature and then multiply by $5/9$ (or by .556).

● Have students convert 136° F into Celsius (58° C).

● Tell students that the coldest temperature ever reported on the continent of Africa was -11° F in Ifrane, Morocco, on February 11, 1935. Have students convert this temperature into Celsius (-24° C).

Optional Activities

Read and Think
Sections C and D

To summarize the information about Libya and Tunisia, ask students the following questions:

1. **How has a desert land such as Libya been able to pay for the development of modern industries?**
   (Oil was discovered and some of the money gained from selling oil went to the development of modern industries. *p. 422*)

2. **Why does Libya have stormy relations with other countries?**
   (The United States and other countries claim that Libya, under the leadership of Qaddafi, has supported terrorism. *p. 423*)

3. **What are Tunisia's major industries?**
   (Tourism, agriculture, oil, and phosphate *pp. 423-424*)

Thinking Critically How do you think international terrorism can be stopped? (Analyze)
(Answers should reflect independent thinking but may include not giving in to the demands of terrorists and making sure that the terrorists are caught and punished. *p. 423*)

423

Use the questions below to help students summarize the information about Algeria and Morocco:

1. **What are the land and resources of Algeria like?**
(Algeria is mostly desert except for a strip of land along the Mediterranean. The Atlas mountain range separates the desert from the coastal strip. Algeria has a number of valuable minerals as well as oil and natural gas fields. *p. 424*)

2. **Why did a civil war break out in Algeria in the 1950s?**
(Because Algerians had become divided over whether the country should become independent or remain a part of France *p. 425*)

3. **How is the government of Morocco different from that of other North African countries?**
(It is the only monarchy in North Africa. *p. 426*)

Thinking Critically Why, do you think, did the French never consider Morocco to be a part of Greater France, as they did Algeria? (Hypothesize)
(Answers should reflect independent thinking but may include that Morocco was under French control for a shorter period of time than Algeria was and probably had fewer French settlers. *pp. 425–426*)

Algiers is the capital of and the largest city in Algeria. The city has many valuable resources, including its harbor on the Mediterranean coast.
▶ How is the harbor in Algiers a valuable resource?

Tunisia has few minerals. The country has some oil and **phosphate** deposits. Phosphate is a mineral used for fertilizers and detergents.

E. Algeria: The Coast and the Desert

Land and Resources The Trans-Sahara highway runs from the Mediterranean coast of Algeria to Niger in West Africa. Even though it is called a highway, a trip across this desert road is not for your family car. The road has been partly paved with **asphalt**. Asphalt is a substance formed from a combination of oil, sand, and rock. The pavement on one long stretch is so badly broken up that it is better to drive alongside the highway rather than on it.

Algeria is a big country — the biggest in North Africa and the Middle East. Find

it on the map on page 404. Part of Algeria is a strip along the Mediterranean coast where most people live. The climate and crops of this part of the country are typical of the Mediterranean lands. Mountains of the Atlas range separate the coastal strip from the Sahara, which makes up the larger part of the country.

Unlike Tunisia, Algeria has a number of valuable minerals as well as oil and natural gas fields. It is one of the leading natural gas exporters. The natural gas reserves are the fourth largest in the world.

Algeria's History The French began the conquest of Algeria in the 1830s. After they won control of the land, they encouraged French and other Europeans to settle there. The European settlers regarded Algeria as part of a Greater France. At one time the settlers made up 11 percent of the

424

population. Most of the other Algerians did not think of their country as part of France. They were Muslims in religion, and most of them spoke Arabic.

A civil war broke out in the 1950s in which those who wanted independence for Algeria fought against those who wanted to remain with France. After 8 years of fighting, both sides settled the matter by a vote. The majority chose separation from France, and Algeria became an independent republic in 1962. Most of the European settlers left the country. The new government was controlled by one political party, so the people did not have a true choice in electing officials for the republic.

F. Morocco: The Land Farthest West

Land and Resources Morocco, located on the northwest corner of Africa, faces the Atlantic Ocean as well as the Mediterranean Sea. When the Arabs conquered Morocco, they called it "the land farthest west." Morocco is the most mountainous of the North African lands. It contains the highest mountains in the Atlas range. Some peaks are snow-covered from winter until well into the summer months. The high mountains and the Atlantic and Mediterranean beaches are the basis of Morocco's tourist industry.

About half of Morocco's land is arable, and many people depend on farming and herding for a living. The country has various minerals and possesses about two thirds of the world's known phosphate reserves. At present Morocco ranks third among the producers of phosphates.

Moroccan History The Arabs conquered Morocco in the Middle Ages, and Arabic is the official language of this Muslim land. But a third of the people are Berbers, who have a language of their own. The ancestors of the Berbers lived in this part of Africa long before the Arab conquest.

Only mountains separate the lush, fertile land of Morocco from the Sahara desert.
▶ What is this mountain range?

Optional Activities

Reteaching Main Objective

Compare the land, climates, resources, and governments of the countries of North Africa.

- Have students prepare a bulletin-board display about the countries of North Africa.
- Divide a bulletin board into five sections and label each section with the name of a North African country.
- Tell one group of students to illustrate or describe in writing the land of each country. Have other groups do the same with the climates, resources, and governments of the five nations.
- Conclude the activity by asking students to find similarities and differences among the five countries.

Meeting Individual Needs

Concept: Drawing Conclusions About North Africa

To better understand social and economic conditions in North Africa today, it is important to be able to analyze statistics and draw conclusions from them. Below are three activities that will help your students understand this concept.

◆ **EASY** Tell students that Libya's population is growing at a rate of 3.5 percent per year, while its economy is not growing.

Ask students how many new jobs Libya is creating each year if its economy is not growing. Then ask students to draw conclusions as to what effect this will have on Libyans in the future.

◀▶ **AVERAGE** Tell students that 50 percent of Morocco's labor force works in agriculture, while 15 percent works in industry.

Ask students to use these statistics to draw conclusions about whether Morocco has a high or low per-capita income. Have them explain their answers.

Ask students whether they think Morocco has a high or low literacy rate. Have them explain their answers.

◀▮▶ **CHALLENGING** Tell students that Algeria's population is growing at a rate of 3.2 percent per year and its economy is growing at a rate of 2 percent per year. Also, tell students that 30 percent of Algeria's labor force works in agriculture, while 40 percent works in industry.

Ask students to compare Algeria with Libya and draw conclusions as to which country has the stronger economy.

Ask students to compare Algeria with Morocco and draw conclusions as to which country has a higher per-capita income and a higher literacy rate.

┌─ **Answers to Caption Questions** ─┐
p. 424 ▶ It brings oil tankers in and out.
p. 425 ▶ Atlas Mountain range

Lesson *4* Review

Answers to Think and Write

A. The rest of Egypt is desert, which could not support large numbers of people.

B. The dam provided water for new agriculture, made it possible to grow an extra crop each year, and provided new fishing areas. However, the dam stopped rich silt from being carried to the fields where it fertilized the land, and it harmed fishing at the mouth of the Nile.

C. Colonel Qaddafi bases his government's laws on the Muslim religion.

D. Tunisia's Mediterranean coast has a Mediterranean climate. Northern Tunisia has forests and fertile farmlands. Farther south, there is dry grassland.

E. After eight years of fighting, both sides agreed to settle the matter by a vote. A majority chose separation from France, and Algeria became an independent republic.

F. Morocco is the most mountainous of the North African lands and it is the only monarchy in North Africa.

Answer to Skills Check

Answers should reflect independent thinking but should include facts from the lesson.

Focus Your Reading

Ask the lesson focus question found at the beginning of the lesson: **How are the countries of North Africa similar and how are they different?**

(All gained their independence in the twentieth century, yet they differ in their land, resources, and governments.)

Additional Practice

You may wish to assign the ancillary materials listed below.

Understanding the Lesson p. 105
Workbook p. 92

Answers to Caption Questions
p. 426 ▶ Carpets

Although many Moroccan workers are turning to industry, handicrafts are still an important trade.
▶ What famous handicraft are these workers producing?

The French controlled most of Morocco from 1912 to 1956, but they never considered it a part of Greater France. Morocco became independent in 1956. Morocco has a king; it is the only monarchy in North Africa today.

Industry For centuries Moroccan craftspeople have been famous for producing fine carpets, metalwork, and leather goods made from goatskin. This leather is known all over the world. In recent years the country has created modern industrial plants that turn out such products as textiles, soaps, and canned foods. Moroccan workers now assemble automobiles. Morocco seeks to modernize. As you have learned in this chapter, modernization has been the aim of most countries of the Middle East and North Africa.

LESSON *4* REVIEW

THINK AND WRITE

A. Why, do you think, do most people of Egypt live along the Nile River valley and on the delta? **(Infer)**

B. What benefits and problems were created by the Aswan High Dam? **(Recall)**

C. How does Colonel Qaddafi run the government of Libya? **(Infer)**

D. What types of land and climate does Tunisia have? **(Recall)**

E. What was the result of the civil war in Algeria? **(Recall)**

F. Name some of the ways in which Morocco differs from other North African countries. **(Analyze)**

SKILLS CHECK

WRITING SKILL

Write a paragraph or two telling whether, in your opinion, the Aswan High Dam has been more of a benefit or a problem to Egypt.

Optional Activities

UNDERSTANDING THE LESSON

NAME _____
UNDERSTANDING THE LESSON   CHAPTER

Making Comparisons   *15*
                                    LESSON 4 CONTENT MASTER

✽ This chart helps you compare the countries of North Africa. Write the missing information in each blank on the chart. A few have been done for you.

Country	Government	Industries/Resources	Language	Geography/Climate
Egypt	Republic	Aswan Dam, Suez Canal, tourism	Arabic	Desert except for Nile valley and delta
Libya	Dictatorship	Oil, some modern industries	Arabic	Desert except for arable land along coast
Tunisia	Republic	Tourism; forests; farmlands; herding sheep, goats, camels; oil, phosphates	Arabic, French	Forests, farmlands in north; grasslands in south; Mediterranean climate along coast
Algeria	Republic with only one party	Oil, natural gas, minerals	Arabic, French	Mediterranean climate along coast; Atlas Mtns. between coast and desert
Morocco	Monarchy	Farming, herding, minerals, phosphates, tourism, craftwork, textiles, soaps, canned foods, automobiles	Arabic, Berber	Atlas Mtns., Atlantic and Mediterranean beaches, half of land is arable

Think and Write: Write a paragraph comparing how Egypt and Morocco acquired their present forms of government. You may use the back of the sheet. Answers should reflect independent thinking; suggestions appear in the Answer Key.
Use with textbook pages 420–426.   105

◀ **Lesson Workshe Booklet, p. 105**

CHAPTER 15 PUTTING IT ALL TOGETHER

USING THE VOCABULARY

modernize	Knesset
mullah	fez
ayatollah	nonrenewable resource
embassy	terrorism
hostage	phosphate

On a separate sheet of paper, write the word or words from above that best complete the sentences.

1. The use of fear to threaten and manipulate people or nations is called _____.
2. A _____ is a person held captive by someone who has demands.
3. The elected assembly of Israel, called the _____, chooses the president and prime minister.
4. A resource that cannot be replaced, such as oil, is a _____.
5. _____ is an honorary title for a religious leader in Iran.
6. A _____ is a mineral used for fertilizers and detergents.
7. An ambassador to a foreign country lives and works in an _____.
8. A felt hat with a flat top and no brim, worn by men in Turkey, is called a _____.
9. A Muslim religious teacher is called a _____.
10. Many countries are trying to _____, or use up-to-date ways of doing things.

REMEMBERING WHAT YOU READ

On a separate sheet of paper, answer the following questions in complete sentences.

1. Who was the leader of the second revolution in Iran?
2. Why has the population of Iran grown so rapidly in recent years?
3. In what year did the Jewish state of Israel declare its independence?
4. What issue has divided the people of Lebanon?
5. For whom is the country of Saudi Arabia named?
6. What do Saudi Arabia, Kuwait, Qatar, and the United Arab Emirates have in common?
7. What are the beneficial effects of the Aswan High Dam?
8. Who is the head of the Libyan government?
9. What is the biggest country in North Africa and the Middle East?
10. Which country is the only monarchy in North Africa today?

TYING LANGUAGE ARTS TO SOCIAL STUDIES

If you were in charge of writing a peace treaty to be signed by two warring nations, what terms would you include in the treaty? Try writing a one-page treaty that any two countries could follow to maintain peace.

427

Using the Vocabulary

1. terrorism	6. phosphate
2. hostage	7. embassy
3. Knesset	8. fez
4. non-renewable resource	9. mullah
5. ayatollah	10. modernize

Remembering What You Read

1. Ruhollah Khomeini
2. Large numbers of refugees from Iraq and Afghanistan have come into the country.
3. 1948
4. Differences in religion
5. The Saud family
6. The presence of oil
7. It provides water for new agriculture, makes it possible to grow an extra crop each year by holding back the summer flood, and provides new fishing areas.
8. Colonel Muammar al-Qaddafi
9. Algeria
10. Morocco

Thinking Critically

1. Answers might include that prices would go down because oil would be available in larger quantities.
2. Answers might include better negotiation and better security measures.
3. Answers might include that they have oil and that they are strategically located.

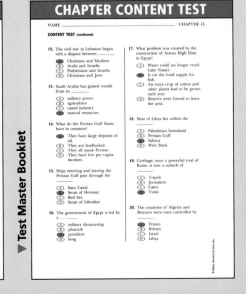

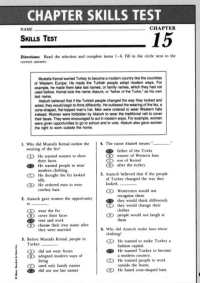

4. Answers might include that the people cannot win their independence any other way.

5. Answers might include jobs in the oil industry, jobs that have to do with shipping, or jobs in tourism.

Summarizing the Chapter

Lesson 1
1. Iran's first revolution (1921)
2. Iran's second revolution (1979)
3. Soviet Union seizes control of Afghanistan (1979)
4. Iran-Iraq War (1980s)

Lesson 2
1. British take control of Palestine after World War I
2. Israel declares independence in 1948.
3. Mustafa Kemal introduces Western ways to Turkey after World War I.
4. Turkey adopts new constitution in 1982

Lesson 3
1. Jordan—poor land, few resources
2. Syria—some of best land in Middle East
3. Lebanon—torn by civil war
4. Saudi Arabia, Persian Gulf states—much oil

Lesson 4
1. Libya, Egypt, and Tunisia all have oil resources.
2. Tunisia, Egypt, Morocco, and Algeria have farming.
3. Tunisia and Morocco have phosphate reserves.
4. Egypt, Libya, and Algeria have large deserts.

THINKING CRITICALLY

On a separate sheet of paper, answer the following questions in complete sentences.

1. How do you think oil prices would be affected if oil were a renewable resource?
2. What nonviolent methods might successfully be used to prevent terrorism?
3. Why are the countries on the Arabian Peninsula of great importance to countries in other parts of the world?
4. Why do so many countries have to win their independence through revolution?
5. What kinds of jobs do you think people have in modern cities in the Middle East and North Africa?

SUMMARIZING THE CHAPTER

On a separate sheet of paper, draw a graphic organizer like the one shown here. Copy the information from this graphic organizer to the one you have drawn. Under the main idea for each lesson, write four statements that support the main idea.

CHAPTER THEME — Geography, resources, religions, and political policies and conflicts continue to have a strong influence on daily life in the Middle East and North Africa today.

LESSON 1
The recent history of the Middle East is a continuation of many years of problems.
1.
2.
3.
4.

LESSON 3
Important characteristics shape each of the Arab countries of the Middle East.
1.
2.
3.
4.

LESSON 2
Many political and economic changes have taken place in Israel and Turkey since World War I.
1.
2.
3.
4.

LESSON 4
There are many similarities and differences among the countries of North Africa.
1.
2.
3.
4.

428

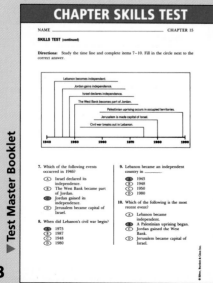

CHAPTER SKILLS TEST

NAME _____ CHAPTER 15

SKILLS TEST (continued)

Directions: Study the time line and complete items 7–10. Fill in the circle next to the correct answer.

▼ Test Master Booklet

428

CHAPTER WRITING TEST

NAME _____ CHAPTER **15**

ESSAY TEST

Directions: Write a response to items 1–4.

▼ Test Master Booklet

CHAPTER WRITING TEST

NAME _____ CHAPTER 15

ESSAY TEST (continued)

▼ Test Master Booklet

COOPERATIVE LEARNING

You may wish to refer to the article on Cooperative Learning found in the front of your Teacher's Edition.

In Chapter 14 you read about Muhammad and the spread of Islam. You learned that the Seljuk Turks conquered Jerusalem and the Holy Land. In 1095 Pope Urban called on the knights of western Europe to join in a war to gain control of the Holy Land and the Holy City of Jerusalem from the Muslims. This was the first of a series of wars that became known as the Crusades.

PROJECT

Work with a group of your classmates to create a board game in which teams of players try to gain control of the Holy Land, especially the Holy City of Jerusalem. Use information from Chapter 14 in your game. Be sure to include people such as Pope Urban, Peter the Hermit, Saladin, and Richard the Lion-Hearted. Think about other board games you have played and about how the boards are designed. Also decide how the pieces in your game will advance. Many board games use spinners, cards, or dice to determine how far a player will move. Sometimes, bonus cards give players extra turns and chances to move ahead; penalty cards cause players to lose turns or move backward. Once your group has discussed and chosen a design, each group member should work to construct part of the game. One person might sketch the board on butcher paper. Others might make the game pieces, dice, cards, or spinner. Each group member could write three bonus cards and three penalty cards.

Finally, your group should meet to put the game together. Don't forget to give it a name!

PRESENTATION AND REVIEW

Your group should test your game by playing it together. By testing the game, you will be able to find and fix any problems. When the group is pleased with the way the game works, present it to the rest of the class. Trade games with another group to see other ideas about how to learn about the Crusades. You might consider having groups each choose a representative for another group whose goal would be to select the best features of each of the game boards and try to put them together into one new game.

REMEMBER TO:
- Give your ideas.
- Listen to others' ideas.
- Plan your work with the group.
- Present your project.
- Discuss how your group worked.

429

Objectives

1. **Explain** the purpose of resource maps.

2. **Interpret** information presented on resource maps.

Why Do I Need This Skill?

To help students better understand the importance of resource maps, ask the following question: **Imagine that you have been asked to help decide the location of new oil refineries. How would you find out where a large concentration of oil deposits was located?**

Tell students that resource maps might help them identify and locate oil deposits.

Learning the Skill

To check students' comprehension of resource maps, ask the following questions:

1. **What information does the map on this page show?**
   (Oil fields and coal deposits in the Middle East and North Africa)

2. **What does each of the colors on the map represent?**
   (Red represents the areas where oil fields are located, and green represents coal deposits.)

3. **Based on this map, what generalizations can you make about oil deposits?**
   (Most of the oil is found along the Persian Gulf.)

4. **What are two uses for resource maps?**
   (Answers may include to show the distribution of a country's natural resources, and to find out what industries, or problems associated with the industries, a country might also have.)

430

A. WHY DO I NEED THIS SKILL?

The kinds of natural resources that countries have has much to do with what products those countries can make. Natural resources, then, are very important for the economies of nations. However, natural resources are not evenly distributed throughout the world. Countries that do not have certain natural resources have to gain them through trade with nations that do have those resources. This has a major effect on the way countries deal with one another. Resource maps show us the distribution of various natural resources in particular areas.

B. LEARNING THE SKILL

At right is a resource map showing areas of coal deposits and oil fields in the Middle East and North Africa. There are a number of colored dots within many of the countries. The red dots represent the areas where oil fields are located. The green dots represent coal deposits.

By looking at this map, you can see that not all of the countries of the Middle East and North Africa have some oil fields. You can also see that only a few of the countries have some coal deposits. However, if you take a closer look at the map, you will learn a great deal of information. For example, some

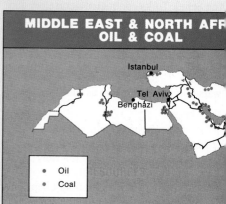

MIDDLE EAST & NORTH AFR
OIL & COAL

Istanbul

Tel Aviv
Benghazi

• Oil
• Coal

countries have oil fields and no areas of coal deposits. Other countries have coal deposits and no oil fields. Some countries have no coal or oil at all.

In addition to showing the distribution of natural resources, resource maps help us figure out what industries a country or region may have. For example, a country with oil fields may have oil refineries. If that is true, then that country might also have a well-developed system for exporting oil. Countries with large coal deposits may rely on coal for fueling their industries. These nations might then have problems associated with air pollution.

430

Homework Activity

● Have students find other resource maps in their texts.

● Ask them to summarize in their own words the information that they see displayed on two of the maps.

● Then ask them to predict what other information those same resource maps might provide, or what conclusions they could draw from the information.

● Answers should reflect independent thinking but should be based on supporting details shown on the maps.

C. PRACTICING THE SKILL

nswer the following questions by using the esource map on the opposite page and the nap of the Middle East and North Africa in ne Atlas of this book.

. Which countries have oil fields?
. List three countries that have no coal deposits or oil fields.
. Which countries have both oil fields and coal deposits?
. Is Saudi Arabia's oil in the western or eastern part of the country?
. Which natural resource can be found in Morocco?

nswer the following questions by using the esource map on this page and the map of ne Middle East and North Africa in the tlas of this book.

. Which two countries are leading producers of phosphates?
. Name three countries that produce neither phosphates nor manganese.
. Which countries produce manganese?
. Which country in this region produces both phosphates and manganese?
. Which is more abundant in this region — phosphates or manganese?

D. APPLYING THE SKILL

Find information about the leading natural resources in your state and where they are located. Next trace or draw a map of your state, then choose at least two of your state's resources and make your own state resource map, using the map below and the one on page 430 as examples. Remember to add a title and a key box to the map. Be creative by using different colors and symbols on your map. When you and the other class members have completed your maps, display them in the classroom.

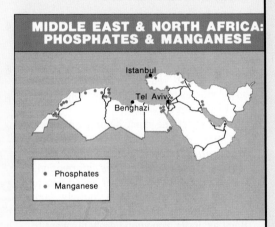

MIDDLE EAST & NORTH AFRICA: PHOSPHATES & MANGANESE

Istanbul
Tel Aviv
Benghazi

● Phosphates
● Manganese

431

Practicing the Skill

Oil and coal map
1. Algeria, Libya, Egypt, Saudi Arabia, Iran, and Iraq
2. Answers may include Israel, Jordan, Syria, Afghanistan, Lebanon, Yemen, and Oman
3. Algeria and Iran
4. Eastern part
5. Coal

Minerals map
1. Morocco and Tunisia
2. Answers may include Libya, Saudi Arabia, Israel, Lebanon, Iraq, Yemen, Oman, Qatar, Kuwait, United Arab Emirates.
3. Morocco, Egypt, Turkey, Iran
4. Morocco
5. Manganese

For students who are still having difficulty with the concept of resource maps, you may wish to use the reteaching activity below.

Applying the Skill

You may wish to direct your students to appropriate resources in your school library, or you may wish to enlist the help of your school librarian for the research portion of this activity. Provide the students with an outline map of your state, help them make a map key showing the major resources, and then assist them as they use appropriate symbols to represent two of your state's resources.

Reteaching Activity

● Have students who are having difficulty with the concept of resource maps look at the resource maps on pp. 430-431.

● Ask students to locate the map key and describe what resources are shown and what symbols are used to represent the resources.

● Then ask students to make two generalizations about each of the maps, based on these symbols and their locations.

● Point out that they are using the resource maps to gather and analyze data about natural resources.

Optional Activities

SKILL TRACE:	Understanding Resource Maps	
INTRODUCE	PRACTICE	TEST
PE pp. 430–431	TE pp. 430–431	Unit 4 Test, TMB
	RMB p. 7	
	WB p. 88	
	TE p. 489	

Selecting
SKILLBUILDER
Resources

Selecting
SKILLBUILDER
Resources

Objectives

1. **Identify** three appropriate resources for locating specific social studies information.

2. **Analyze** situations to determine the best resources for gathering additional information.

Why Do I Need This Skill?

Point out to students that they will often need to consult outside resources to answer questions or gather additional information.

Ask your class to name as many resources as they can. Answers may include atlases, almanacs, encyclopedias, indexes, glossaries, and dictionaries.

Tell students that by knowing which resources to consult, they can save unnecessary research time and obtain the best and most current information possible.

Learning the Skill

To check students' comprehension of the usefulness and importance of selecting appropriate and relevant social studies resources, ask the following questions:

1. **Which two questions should you ask yourself in order to select the most appropriate and helpful resources?**
   (Answers should include these: What sort of information is needed? What resources might have the information I need?)

2. **Where might you find these resources?**
   (Answers may include in the reference section of the school library or public library, or through the card catalog.)

3. **Why would you need to consult outside resources?**
   (Answers may include because students' original resources do not contain enough information for them to answer the questions given, or because they have more questions than the information provided by their resources.)

432

A. WHY DO I NEED THIS SKILL?

Sometimes your teacher may ask you to do special assignments, such as written reports or oral presentations, as a social studies project. The information you need to do these assignments may not be in your textbook. At other times you may have questions that cannot be answered by using your textbook. In these situations, you will need to use other resources. **Resources** are books, articles, and other materials you can use to find the information you need. Knowing how to select the right resources is an important social studies skill.

B. LEARNING THE SKILL

The table on page 433 shows some resources that may help you find information about social studies topics. Study the table on the next page carefully.

To select the most helpful resources, you need to ask yourself two questions: *What sort of information do I need? What resources might contain this information?* For example, if your teacher asked you to compute the distance of a journey from Athens, Greece, through the Suez Canal to Bombay, India, you would probably want to use an atlas. However, if you needed to know the depth of the Suez Canal, you could use an encyclopedia to find the information. To learn about the construction of the Suez Canal, you might look for books on the Suez Canal in the card catalog.

432

C. PRACTICING THE SKILL

Suppose your teacher has asked you to write a report about some important feature of the Middle East and North Africa. You have decided to write about the Aswan High Dam, in Egypt. On a separate sheet of paper, list the resources you would use to complete each of the following parts of the report.

1. Draw a map of Egypt and show the location of the Aswan High Dam.
2. Make a diagram showing the design of the dam.
3. Explain how the dam was constructed, who helped to pay for it, who worked on it, and how long it took to build the dam.
4. Compare the water capacity of the Aswan High Dam with that of other major dams in the world.
5. Find out about any recent events involving the Aswan High Dam.
6. Make a glossary of the new or important words used in the report.
7. Make a bibliography of various sources of information about the dam.

D. APPLYING THE SKILL

Finding information is easy when you know how to select resources. Use the table and ask yourself the two questions for selecting resources whenever you need information for social studies projects. In addition, you can use this skill when you do projects in other subject areas — or whenever you want some information.

Optional Activities

Homework Activity

● Ask students to clip and bring to class one newspaper or magazine article dealing with a current event or a social studies topic. Articles may include international politics, our economy, or other appropriate selections.

● Have students each summarize the information in a paragraph; then have them prepare three questions to which they would like to find the answers.

● Have students read their summaries and questions aloud.

● Have class members recommend appropriate resources for finding answers to the questions.

● Then have them verify the appropriateness of the resources by looking up the answers.

RESOURCES FOR INFORMATION

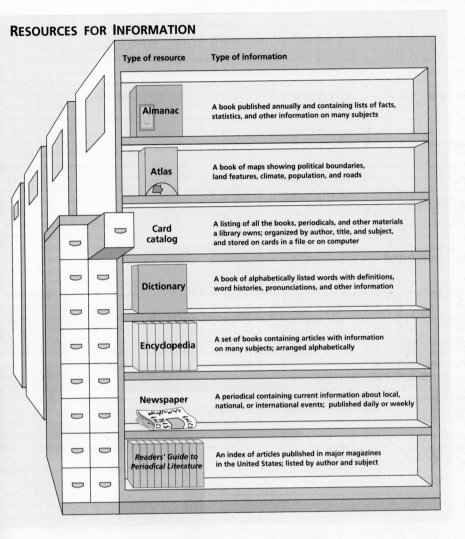

Type of resource	Type of information
Almanac	A book published annually and containing lists of facts, statistics, and other information on many subjects
Atlas	A book of maps showing political boundaries, land features, climate, population, and roads
Card catalog	A listing of all the books, periodicals, and other materials a library owns; organized by author, title, and subject, and stored on cards in a file or on computer
Dictionary	A book of alphabetically listed words with definitions, word histories, pronunciations, and other information
Encyclopedia	A set of books containing articles with information on many subjects; arranged alphabetically
Newspaper	A periodical containing current information about local, national, or international events; published daily or weekly
Readers' Guide to Periodical Literature	An index of articles published in major magazines in the United States; listed by author and subject

433

Practicing the Skill

Answers may include some or all of the following reference materials.

1. Atlas
2. Encyclopedia, almanac
3. Encyclopedia, almanac
4. Almanac
5. *Reader's Guide to Periodical Literature*, almanac
6. Dictionary
7. Card catalog, *Reader's Guide to Periodical Literature*

For students still having difficulty with the concept of selecting resources, you may wish to use the reteaching activity below.

Applying the Skill

Students' responses should reflect the selection of appropriate resources.

SKILL TRACE: Selecting and Using the Appropriate Resources		
INTRODUCE	PRACTICE	TEST
PE pp. 432–433	**TE** pp. 432–433, 450 **WB** pp. 68, 100 **PE** p. 538	Unit 4 Test, TMB

Reteaching Activity

- Have students orally summarize the last lesson of this chapter.
- Ask them to write down two pieces of related information that they would like to know.
- Have them work as a group to list possible resources, including dictionaries, encyclopedias, or almanacs.
- Have students research the information in each of the suggested resources, determine whether or not the source was appropriate, and, if possible, answer the questions.
- Discuss with students the research process that they followed and help them draw conclusions.

Optional Activities

Africa South of the Sahara

Unit Theme Africa south of the Sahara is a land of diverse geography, peoples, languages, and governments.

Chapter 16   Geography of Africa South of the Sahara

(pp. 436-453)

Theme The many different landforms, climates, cultures, and resources found in Africa south of the Sahara affect the way people there live.

Chapter 17   History of Africa South of the Sahara

(pp. 454-473)

Theme Many different African cultures developed in earlier times south of the Sahara. In the 1400s, Europeans began to explore, trade, and form colonies in this part of Africa.

Chapter 18   Africa South of the Sahara Today

(pp. 474-496)

Theme Independence movements in Africa led to the end of European empires. Governments and economies are varied among African countries south of the Sahara.

September Chapters	October Chapters	November Chapters	December Chapters	January Chapters	February Chapters	March Chapters	April Chapters	May Chapters
MSH-1	2-4	5-7	8-9	10-12	13-14	15-17	18-20	21-23

PACING GUIDE

Bulletin Board Idea

LANDS
· deserts
· grasslands
· savanna
· snow covered mountains
· rain forests

RESOURCES
· diamonds
· oil
· peanuts
· coffee
· cacao
· forests

PEOPLES
· many ethnic groups
· multilingual
· proverbs and music
· rapid city growth

Lands, Peoples, and Resources of Africa South of the Sahara

Student Activity

Help students organize the information in Chapters 16-18 by preparing a graphic organizer for students to complete and illustrate. Use the completed organizer to reinforce concepts and information, or to review the entire unit.

Annotated Bibliography

Books for Teachers

Fagle, J.D. *Atlas of African History.* New York: Holmes and Meier, 1978. ISBN 0-8419-0430-9. (Ch. 17) This is a thorough guide to African history, from prehistory to post colonial days.

Kwanmena-Poh. *African History in Maps.* White Plains, NY: Longman, 1982. ISBN 0-582-60331-5. (Ch. 17) Excellent teaching maps fill this useful historical atlas.

Lamb, David. *The Africans.* New York: Random House, 1987. ISBN 0-394-72370-8. (Ch. 16) This is an anecdotal account of Africa south of the Sahara during the years 1975-1980 as seen by an American journalist.

Martin, Phyllis, and Patrick O'Mera. *Africa.* Indianapolis, IN: Indiana University Press, 1986. ISBN 0-253-20392-9. (Ch. 16) The authors provide an anthology of articles on African history and culture, intended for undergraduates and general readers.

Books for Students

Chipoke, F.A. *Ancient Africa.* New York: Holmes & Meier, 1969. ISBN 0-8419-0013-2. (Ch. 17) The history of the people of Ancient Africa, the first humans known to exist, is presented with numerous illustrations.

Appiah, Peggy, trans. *The Anansi Tales.* New York: Pantheon, 1966. (Ch. 17) Readers will enjoy the adventures of Kwaku (Uncle) Anansi, the trickster hero of the Ashanti peoples of Africa.

Creed, Alexander. *Uganda.* New York: Chelsea House, 1987. ISBN 1-55546-189-1. (Ch. 18) The history and heritage of this Central African nation is examined.

Hintz, Martin. *Ghana.* Chicago: Children's Press, 1987. ISBN 0-516-02773-5. (Ch. 18) The geography, culture, and people of Ghana are presented through brief text and photographs.

James, R.S. *Mozambique.* New York: Chelsea House, 1988. ISBN 1-55546-189-1. (Ch. 18) The South African country of Mozambique is explored, and the importance of its natural resources is explained.

Lutz, William. *Senegal.* New York: Chelsea House, 1988. ISBN 1-55546-192-1. (Ch. 18) The people, culture, and geography of Senegal are concisely presented with photographs and maps.

Lye, Keith. *Africa.* Danbury, CT: Franklin Watts, 1987. ISBN 0-531-17065-9. (Ch. 16) The geographic variety of the African continent is examined through numerous illustrations and thorough text.

McKenna, Nancy. *A Zulu Family.* Chicago: Lerner Press, 1987. ISBN 0-8225-1666-7. (Ch. 17) The lifestyles, culture, and heritage of Zulus in Southern Africa are presented for students.

Motley, Mary. *Africa: Its Empires, Nations, and People.* Detroit, MI: Wayne State University Press, 1969. ISBN 0-8143-1399-X. (Ch. 17) The diversity of Africa and its people is explained for students.

Musgrove, Margarat W. *Ashanti to Zulu: African Traditions.* New York: Dial Books for the Young Reader, 1976. ISBN 0-8037-0308-2. (Ch. 17) Beautiful, over-sized illustrations bring the beauty of various African Tribes to life, in alphabetical arrangement.

Ngubane, Harriet. *Zulus of Southern Africa.* Vero Beach, FL: Rourke Publications, 1987. ISBN 0-86625-261-4. (Ch. 17) The daily lives of today's Zulus and the history of their mighty ancestors are explored in this concise book.

Saunders, Renfield. *Malawi.* New York: Chelsea House, 1988. ISBN 1-55546-193-X. (Ch. 18) The people, culture, and geography of the Malawi people are presented through text and numerous illustrations.

Stark, Al. *Zimbabwe: A Treasure of Africa.* Minneapolis, MN: Dillon Press, 1985. ISBN 0-87518-308-5. (Ch. 18) The people and rich natural resources of Zimbabwe are examined, and numerous photographs are included.

Stein, R. Conrad. *Kenya.* Chicago: Children's Press, 1985. ISBN 0-516-02770-0. (Ch. 18) The people and history of Kenya are concisely presented for students.

Stevens, Rita. *Madagascar.* New York: Chelsea House, 1988. ISBN 1-55546-195-6. (Ch. 18) The island of Madagascar, off the east coast of Africa, is examined in this text.

Filmstrips and Videos

A Season in the Sun. 16mm or videocassette. Benchmark Films, 1989. (Ch. 16) The animals and plants that survive in the dry climate of East Africa are profiled.

Children of Apartheid. Videocassette. California Newsreel, 1987 (Ch. 18) This video contrasts the daily lives of black children and white children in South Africa, and shows how the policy of Apartheid affects their lives.

The Ancient African Civilizations

What was Africa like long ago?

Timbuktu, the Kingdom of Kush, and Gao are names that existed in Africa's ancient past. Mali, Zimbabwe, and Ghana are names from its past that have survived until today. Africa was long called the "Dark Continent" because the people outside of Africa knew little about it. In one sense, the ancient civilizations of Africa still belong to that dark past. We know that they existed, we know that they flourished and in many cases, we know why they fell, but any additional information has been lost forever.

Today's world may know little about these ancient kingdoms, but for hundreds of years, they dominated much of Africa. The following activities center around these ancient civilizations.

SOCIAL STUDIES

Economics We may not know everything about Africa's ancient civilizations, but we do know that they flourished. In fact, we have been able to trace many of their trading routes and products. (Popular land routes brought gold and kola nuts from western Africa to the northern kingdoms of Hafsid, Marinid, and Ziyanid. Important sea routes carried gold and ivory from port cities in East Africa to Saudi Arabian and Mediterranean ports.)

■ Have students research these routes and plot them on a map. Label the nations involved as well as the products traded. Some of those items may include Berber grain, glassware, and weapons that were traded for the rock salt of central Africa. Salt was also traded for gold, slaves, ivory, and ebony.

Geography Geography played a great role in deciding where African civilizations flourished and where they did not.

■ Have students research the physical features of the continent of Africa. Make sure that they pay special attention to the Nile, the Atlas Mountains, the Sahara Desert, the rain forests, the grasslands, and the plateaus.

■ Have students create a physical map of Africa and explain in a short, written article how the physical geography of Africa might have affected the growth, development, and evolution of civilizations.

Archaeology Recent archaeological evidence shows that human life originated in Africa and not in Asia as people often thought.

■ Have students research the work of Dr. Richard Leakey and his wife, Mary, using an encyclopedia or books from the library. Historians believe that this information helps explain the rise of the ancient African civilizations. Ask students to write a short report or give oral reports explaining this belief.

Political Science Who owns Africa? For thousands of years, this question has plagued the continent. People have argued, fought, and died attempting to settle the question. For many years, the Europeans claimed to own Africa. They claimed to have discovered the continent, therefore it belonged to them. The Europeans also claimed that since Africans were backward and Europeans were advanced, it was acceptable for them to claim ownership of the underdeveloped continent. Ask students to think about the following:

1. Is it possible to discover a land that has millions of people living on it?

2. Is it possible to claim a land as your own if it has large cities, thriving cultures, and flourishing economic systems?

3. The kingdom of Kush may have been a supreme power for almost one thousand years! How could this land have been "discovered" almost one thousand years later?

■ Have students research the early African civilizations and answer the above questions in written form. You may also wish to have students debate the questions, or review them in a round-table discussion.

Global Awareness The ancient African civilizations started well before the year zero in our calendar. Have students list starting dates for a number of the civilizations, such as the Roman, Aztec, Mayan, and Greek civilizations. Have them compare what was going on elsewhere in the world during these days. Students may want to produce a three- or four-tier time line. One line could stand for Africa, one for Asia, a third for Europe, and a fourth for the Americas.

LANGUAGE ARTS

Ask students to imagine that they are part of a trading caravan traveling through early Africa. Have them write a short folk song that they might have created as they traveled along, describing the places they visit, the landscape they see, and the products they are trading.

ART

■ The people of Nigeria, especially those from the city of Ife, were famous for their sculpting. Sculptures included figures, masks, decorated boxes, and other objects for ceremonial and everyday use. Have students research this art form as well as other types of African art. Students may also wish to research the influence of early African art on the art form known as primitivism.

■ Encourage students to draw examples of the various forms of African art.

SCIENCE

■ Many historians and scientists believe that the land that is now the Sahara Desert was once lush, with plenty of green grass. What factors could cause a savanna to turn into a desert?

■ Have students research this question and apply their answer to both Africa and the rest of the world today. What lessons can we learn from this change?

■ Students may wish to list on a chart the scientific steps that caused this change. Display the chart on a bulletin board for student discussion.

LITERATURE

■ The fertile soils of the Nile Valley supported some of the earliest and richest farming communities in Africa. From there, African civilization continued to all parts of the continent.

■ Students may enjoy reading or listening to the beginnings of African history in J. D. Fagle's book, *Atlas of African History* (New York: Holmes and Meier, 1978. ISBN 0-84419-0450-9.)

Use a Graphic Organizer

INSTRUCTIONS FOR THE TEACHER:

What Is a Graphic Organizer? A graphic organizer can be a chart, diagram, table, or other visual tool that helps students remember or organize information from the text.

Why Use Graphic Organizers? Considerable research on writing, reading, and other thought-demanding activities shows that success depends largely upon organized thinking. Although all students think, not all think in organized patterns that help them retain information, or build understanding. Graphic organizers help them do this.

Graphic organizers also help students "see" what they are thinking. Organizers also help them "see," in a more concrete manner, the information that they must retain, and the ways in which elements of information are related. This can all be accomplished without having to scan several paragraphs of text. These diagrams and charts help students who may have trouble with text or with thinking strategies that are expressed entirely in words.

Some Uses of Graphic Organizers

1. *To organize information in the text* Graphic organizers can be as simple as writing the major industries of Nigeria in boxes next to one another, under the heading *Major Indus-tries of Nigeria.* Main points about each industry can then be written in each respective box.

2. *To assist in forecasting* Often, you will want your students to think of many causes for a real or imagined event and then to think of many subsequent effects.

3. *To "map out" one's thinking; to elaborate* Students will be able to think of more ideas, elaborate on a topic, be able to "see" main ideas and their supporting details, and think of comparisons with a graphic organizer called a *cluster map.* This type of organizer has also been referred to as a *mind-map,* a *semantic map,* and a *web.* Students should write their topic in a central circle, and then ask themselves: *Of what does my topic remind me?* Using this central idea as a starting point, students can write other ideas in smaller circles around the first circle. As students become more proficient in this, they can develop even smaller circles (supporting ideas) radiating from their other circles. You may wish to use the following activity to get students started in the right direction: Tell students: Write a topic, such as *Africa,* on a piece of paper. Draw a circle around it. Now, write another word that relates to *Africa,* such as *Nigeria.* Circle it and connect it to *Africa.* Then, branch out from *Nigeria* by adding words like *coal mining* and *Abuja* (Nigeria's capital). Draw circles around these and connect them to *Nigeria.* Now, how many more branches can you create?

4. *To compare* Students can distinguish similarities and differences between two things by using a Venn Diagram. Two large circles are drawn so that their edges overlap (like two circles of the Olympic logo), and one of the topics to be compared is written above each circle. Students should then write differing characteristics of each topic in the large circles, and similar characteristics in the part where the circles overlap.

5. *To observe* Students can write more detailed descriptions by using a table similar to the one below:

6. *To " walk in someone else's shoes"* For ex-

ample, students who wish to write as though they were the leader of an African country, must first imagine the leader's thoughts and feelings. Students who wish to write to persuade, must first write down what they think the person they are trying to persuade is thinking. Both of these strategies can be accomplished with a thought balloon. The student draws a "balloon" (similar to the one in a comic strip) and writes in it what he or she believes that person is thinking.

ACTIVITY FOR THE STUDENTS:

Have students choose one or more of the following activities. If necessary, use the explanations above to assist students.

1. Have students make a cluster map of Africa's climate.
2. Have students describe Victoria Falls using a graphic organizer that tells how they perceive the falls through their five senses.
3. Have students compare two countries in Africa using a Venn Diagram.
4. Have students write a paragraph persuading two factions in Africa to stop fighting. Students should use a thought balloon to imagine each side's feelings.
5. To forecast what might happen if hunters were allowed free reign to hunt all animals in Africa, have students create a chart.

Visiting Victoria Falls				
Things I might:				
see	hear	smell	taste	feel

Unit Test

CONTENT TEST

Directions: Fill in the circle next to the correct answer.

1. Which of the following continents is larger than Africa?
   - (A) Europe
   - (B) North America
   - (C) Asia
   - (D) Antarctica

2. What type of climate is found on Africa's northern coast and southern tip?
   - (A) an African climate
   - (B) a Saharan climate
   - (C) a Mediterranean climate
   - (D) a desert climate

3. What part of Africa appears to be changing into a desert?
   - (A) the Sahara (C) the Sahel
   - (B) the Horn (D) South Africa

4. What are equatorial lands?
   - (A) places where blacks and whites have equal rights
   - (B) lands along the Equator
   - (C) lands where resources are shared evenly
   - (D) any area that has a tropical climate

5. For most government and business affairs in Kenya and Nigeria, people _____.
   - (A) speak English
   - (B) appoint village chiefs
   - (C) speak Swahili
   - (D) use British currency

6. Foreigners first came to Africa to get _____.
   - (A) slaves
   - (B) wild animals
   - (C) bauxite
   - (D) gold

7. Why do some Africans use the slash-and-burn method?
   - (A) to punish their enemies
   - (B) to kill and cook wild animals
   - (C) to prepare yams and cassava
   - (D) to grow crops

8. Why have African governments created game parks?
   - (A) to protect wildlife
   - (B) to provide tourists with amusements
   - (C) to encourage professional sporting events
   - (D) to encourage citizens to compete

9. Who created the kingdom of Mali?
   - (A) Mansa Musa
   - (B) Alexander the Great
   - (C) Sundiata
   - (D) Anansi

10. In Benin people kept historical records on _____.
    - (A) wooden poles
    - (B) stone tablets
    - (C) bronze plaques
    - (D) animal skins

CONTENT TEST (continued)

11. The people of Zimbabwe were known for building with _____.
    - (A) stone
    - (B) wood
    - (C) thatch
    - (D) straw

12. Who claimed to be the descendants of Solomon?
    - (A) the Boers
    - (B) the Bedouins
    - (C) Ethiopian kings
    - (D) the Queen of Sheba

13. Who sailed around the Cape of Good Hope?
    - (A) Henry the Navigator
    - (B) Kwaku Anansi
    - (C) Sir James Hope
    - (D) Bartholomeu Dias

14. South African Boers wanted the British to _____.
    - (A) give equal rights to all
    - (B) punish David Livingstone
    - (C) keep black Africans in slavery
    - (D) attack the Bushmen of the Kalahari

15. Why did David Livingstone go to Africa?
    - (A) to stop Boers from killing and enslaving African people
    - (B) to teach Africans about the Christian religion
    - (C) to hunt for gold and silver
    - (D) to search for Mr. Stanley

16. Which country established a colony in the Congo?
    - (A) Belgium
    - (B) Mali
    - (C) Britain
    - (D) Ethiopia

17. The Republic of the Congo was renamed _____.
    - (A) Zaire
    - (B) Zimbabwe
    - (C) The Confederation of Congolia
    - (D) Tonga

18. In South Africa the white minority was able to control the country _____.
    - (A) through the use of slavery
    - (B) through the system of apartheid
    - (C) with British assistance
    - (D) by convincing blacks to vote for whites

19. Why does Nairobi have a mild climate?
    - (A) The Equator keeps it warm.
    - (B) The Persian Gulf keeps it cool.
    - (C) It is located in the highlands.
    - (D) It is located in the lowlands.

20. What is Ethiopia's main export?
    - (A) oil
    - (B) telephones
    - (C) helicopters
    - (D) coffee

SKILLS TEST

Directions: Study the maps and complete items 1–5. Fill in the circle next to the correct answer.

SOUTHERN AFRICA: EUROPEAN CLAIMS, 1920

SOUTHERN AFRICA TODAY

1. Which present-day country was *not* controlled by Britain in 1920?
   - (A) South Africa
   - (B) Zambia
   - (C) Angola
   - (D) Zimbabwe

2. What country controlled most of southern Africa in 1920?
   - (A) Britain (C) France
   - (B) South Africa (D) Portugal

3. Northern Rhodesia became a country called _____.
   - (A) Zimbabwe
   - (B) Zambia
   - (C) Malawi
   - (D) Botswana

4. Who controlled Mozambique in 1920?
   - (A) Britain
   - (B) France
   - (C) Belgium
   - (D) Portugal

5. The land known as South-West Africa in 1920 is now called _____.
   - (A) Rhodesia
   - (B) Namibia
   - (C) Zambia
   - (D) Malawi

SKILLS TEST (continued)

Directions: Read this selection and complete items 6–10. Fill in the circle next to the correct answer.

Resources of East and Central Africa

The Land as a Resource When Europeans first began to settle in Africa, one resource that attracted them was the land. Forests were cleared, and plantations were started. The plantations produced cacao, rubber, and coffee.

The Rain Forests Valuable hardwoods, such as ebony and sandalwood, are found in the rain forests. Copal, a tree resin used in varnish, is also a product of the rain forest. Rubber and oil palm trees can be cultivated in the rain-forest climate. Palm oil is used in making soap and margarine.

Mineral Resources Most of the countries of East and Central Africa lack mineral resources. The major exception is Zaire. Zaire supplies most of the cobalt, diamonds, and much of the copper used throughout the world. Cobalt is a mineral used in the production of a very hard kind of steel.

Animal Life Many valuable and unusual animals, from the antelope to the zebra, live in East and Central Africa. They are exported to zoos around the world. Tourists come to this region to see the animals.

6. By scanning the selection you can tell that its main topic is _____.
   - (A) climate (C) resources
   - (B) people (D) history

7. One part of the region you will be learning about is _____.
   - (A) lakes and rivers
   - (B) rain forests
   - (C) volcanoes
   - (D) cities

8. If you wanted to find out whether coal is an important product of the region, you would skim the section with the heading _____.
   - (A) *Animal Life*
   - (B) *The Land as a Resource*
   - (C) *Mineral Resources*
   - (D) *The Rain Forests*

9. If you could not remember what the word *copal* means, what would be the best thing to do?
   - (A) Reread the entire selection.
   - (B) Reread the section with the heading *Animal Life.*
   - (C) Skim for the word and its meaning.
   - (D) Hope that you never need to know the meaning.

10. The purpose of scanning an article is to _____.
    - (A) learn most of the details
    - (B) find out, in general, what the article is about
    - (C) avoid wasting the time it would take to read carefully
    - (D) find out what happens at the end

ESSAY TEST

Directions: Write a response to items 1–4.

> **REMINDER:** Read and think about each item before you write your response. Be sure to think of the points you want to cover, details that support your response, and reasons for your opinions. Then, on the lines below, write your response in complete sentences.

1. Describe the Sahel, the area that separates the Sahara and the savanna.

A satisfactory response should include the following statements:

• The Sahel is the strip of land that separates the Sahara and the savanna.

• When rain is plentiful, the Sahel can support herds of grazing animals.

• There are many dry periods, however, when the region has little to offer these herds.

An excellent response might also

• explain that the term *Sahel* means "border" in Arabic

• explain that the desert has recently been advancing into the Sahel

• cite some of causes of desertification.

2. How has agriculture affected Africa's rain forests?

A satisfactory response should include the following statements:

• In the rain forests, people practice slash-and-burn farming.

• Because this method wears out the soil quickly, farmers must move to new areas every few years.

• Because of increased population, the land is cut and burned too frequently.

• As a result, much of the land can now support neither crops nor forest.

An excellent response might also explain

• that the soil in the rain forest is not rich

• the rationale and procedure for slash-and-burn farming.

ESSAY TEST (continued)

3. What are monsoons, and how did they influence trade?

A satisfactory response should include the following statements:

• Monsoons are the seasonal winds of the Indian Ocean.

• By sailing with the wind, trading ships could travel from Africa to Arabia and India.

• Then, when the winds changed direction, ships could sail back.

An excellent response might also explain

• that from May to September the winds blow from the southwest.

• that from November to March the winds blow from the northeast.

• the results of trade between Africa and the East.

4. What was the purpose of apartheid?

A satisfactory response should include the following statements:

• Apartheid was a system of South African laws designed to separate the races and keep a white minority in power.

• It categorized people into four racial groups: whites, coloreds, Asians, and black Africans.

• Although only one sixth of the population is white, only whites have any real political power.

An excellent response might also include specific examples

• of how blacks were treated under apartheid.

• mention anti-apartheid leaders and protests that brought about changes in this system.

• reflect independent thinking.

TEACHER NOTES

UNIT 5

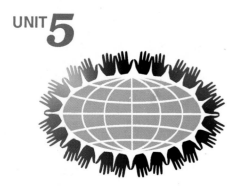

MULTICULTURAL PERSPECTIVES

An African Folk Tale

(pages 455–456)

Every culture has its folk tales. They are designed to give lessons in life or to recount hard-to-explain occurrences. In other instances, folk tales are lessons in cultural values and virtues.

The following short African folk tale resembles a riddle. Read it to your students. Give them time to work out the answer through class discussion. Then read the answer to them.

A certain man was running away from his village. He took with him all of his property. This consisted of a yam, a goat, and a leopard. Now, in time, the man came to a river where he found a canoe. The canoe was too small for the man to take all of his possessions with him at one time. This presented a problem. If he left the yam with the goat, the goat would eat the yam. If he left the goat with the leopard, the leopard would devour the goat. How did the man succeed in getting the yam, the goat, and the leopard safely to the other side?

ANSWER

The man took the goat over first and then the yam. Then he recrossed with the goat which he left on the shore. He ferried back with the leopard. Then he returned to the other shore to bring back the goat.

Source

African Folktales: Traditional Stories of the Black World. Roger Abrahams, ed. New York: Pantheon Books, 1983.

Unit 5

AFRICA SOUTH OF THE SAHARA

Africa south of the Sahara is a land of diverse geography, peoples, languages, and governments.

▶ *Over the centuries, skilled African artisans have used wood, ivory, bronze, beads, and other materials to create masks such as these.*

434

Optional Activities

Current Events

● Ask students to observe the visuals on pp. 434-435.

● Ask: **Which of these pictures represent common images of Africa?**
(Students will probably answer that the giraffe, the mask, and the huts are common images of Africa.)

● Then ask: **Why, do you think, was the picture of Desmond Tutu included here?**
(Student answers should reflect independent thinking but may include that Tutu has become famous for his leadership in the organized resistance to apartheid in South Africa.)

Measurement History

(pages 463–471)

With the age of imperialism came a dramatic increase in trade around the world. Standardized measurement is a result of the increase in trade among peoples.

Cultures throughout time have devised various ways to measure size, distance, time, and weight. Body parts, such as the hand and the arm, were often used as bases for measurement. If a person went to a market to buy cloth, it was to his or her advantage to take along a long-armed friend, since a yard was often measured from the fingertips to the tip of one's nose.

This example helps to explain why standardization became necessary.

- Have two students of different sizes demonstrate this situation for the class.
- Ask students to think of ways in which we continue to estimate measurement today (a pinch of salt, a dash of lemon juice, a splash of ginger ale).

The United States is the only major country that has not adopted the metric system. Of course, scientists in the United States use the metric system. Also, many immigrants have the benefit of knowing the system.

Ask your students to research the history of measurement. They should gather information on at least ten different measurement tools. Instruct students to get information from a number of continents. This will help students understand that different measurement tools were based on different needs and lifestyles.

The Struggle for Human Rights

(pages 484–487)

South Africa has been a land divided by racial tension. Ask students to investigate the civil rights movement of the 1960s in the United States. How does this period in United States history compare with the struggle against apartheid in South Africa?

Ask students to write essays that describe how the people of the United States have worked toward racial harmony. Then have each student take a theme from his or her essay and create an advertisement that promotes peace among the peoples of the world. The ads should have a catchy slogan or thought-provoking question as well as an interesting visual component.

435

Optional Activities

Geography of Africa South of the Sahara

(pp. 436-453)

Chapter Theme: The many different landforms, climates, cultures, and resources found in Africa south of the Sahara affect the way people there live.

CHAPTER RESOURCES
Review Master Booklet
  Reviewing Chapter Vocabulary, p. 112
  Place Geography, p. 113
  Summarizing the Chapter, p. 114
Chapter 16 Test

LESSON *1* A Variety of Lands

(pp. 436-442)

Theme: The continent of Africa contains the Sahara Desert, the savanna or grasslands, the Sahel, rain forests, mountains, three great rivers, and many lakes.

LESSON RESOURCES
Workbook, pp. 93-94
Review Master Booklet
  Understanding the Lesson, p. 109

LESSON *2* A Variety of Peoples

(pp. 443-447)

Theme: Africa is a huge continent with more than one-half billion people of many ethnic and religious backgrounds.

LESSON RESOURCES
Workbook, p. 95
Review Master Booklet
  Understanding the Lesson, p. 110

LESSON *3* Making Use of Resources

(pp. 448-451)

Theme: The important resources found in Africa south of the Sahara are gold, rain forests, farm and ranch land, and wildlife.

 SOCIAL STUDIES LIBRARY: *Money*

LESSON RESOURCES
Workbook, pp. 96-97
Review Master Booklet
  Understanding the Lesson, p. 111

Review Masters

REVIEWING CHAPTER VOCABULARY

Review Study the terms in the box. Use your Glossary to find definitions of those you do not remember.

cacao	savanna	subsistence	Tropic of
commercial farm	sisal	farming	Capricorn
equatorial	slash-and-burn	Tropic of	tropics
multilingual	farming	Cancer	
river basin			

Practice Complete the paragraphs using terms from the box above. You may change the forms of the terms.

Many countries on the continent of Africa were once European colonies. The effects of European rule can be heard in the languages people speak. Many Africans are

(1) __multilingual__ ; they speak several African languages and a European language. The Europeans also brought new farming methods with them. They started

(2) __commercial farms__ , which produced large amounts of crops, such as coffee, for sale.

In many parts of Africa, farming methods have changed little over the years. For example, in the forests along the Equator, most farms are very small. This

(3) __subsistence farming__ only provides enough food for farmers and their families. In

these (4) __equatorial__ rain forests, farmers use (5) __slash-and-burn farming__ methods, because the soil quickly becomes worn out. Poor soil is also the reason why little farming is done on the grasslands south of the Sahara. Here, although the

(6) __savanna__ receives some rain in summer, the soil is thin and not very good for crops.

Write Write a sentence of your own for each term in the box above. You may use the back of the sheet.

Sentences should show that students understand the meanings of the terms.

_____

_____

_____

_____

_____

_____

© Silver, Burdett & Ginn Inc.

LOCATING PLACES

✱ There are more countries in Africa than on any other continent. Listed below are places within Western and Central Africa. Use the Gazetteer in your textbook to find the latitude and longitude of each place. Then locate and label each on the map.

	LAT.	LONG.			LAT.	LONG.
1. Kano, Nigeria	12°N	9°E	5. Brazzaville, Congo		4°S	15°E
2. Lagos, Nigeria	6°N	3°E	6. Libreville, Gabon		0° lat.	9°E
3. Abidjan, Ivory Coast	5°N	4°W	7. Timbuktu, Mali		17°N	3°W
4. Dakar, Senegal	15°N	17°W	8. Accra, Ghana		5°N	1°W

WEST AND CENTRAL AFRICA

○ National capitals
● Other cities

© Silver, Burd

SUMMARIZING THE CHAPTER

✱ Complete this graphic organizer. Under the main idea for each lesson, write five statements that support the main idea.

CHAPTER THEME ➜ The many different landforms, climates, cultures, and resources found in Africa south of the Sahara affect the way people there live.

LESSON 1	*LESSON 2*	*LESSON 3*
There is much variety in the types of land found in Africa south of the Sahara.	**Many different kinds of people live in Africa south of the Sahara.**	**Many important, useful natural resources are found in Africa south of the Sahara.**
1. Deserts	1. Christians	1. Gold
2. Grasslands	2. Muslims	2. Diamonds
3. Sahel	3. Ethnic groups (like the Hausas)	3. Coffee
4. Rain forests	4. Descendants of Indians	4. Cacao
5. Mountains	5. Descendants of Europeans	5. Minerals

© Silver, Burdett & Ginn Inc.

C16-B

Workbook Pages

EXPLORING KENYA

Understanding Facts and Details, Applying Information

✻ The passage below describes a tour of Kenya. Read the passage carefully, and then answer the questions that follow.

The hot-air balloon glides almost silently over the Kenyan landscape. Slowly it floats over the savanna of the Masai Mara Game Preserve. Below, the grassland and scattered trees are colored in shades of yellow and green. The clicking of cameras breaks the cool morning stillness as the tourists riding in the gondola [cabin] suspended under the balloon capture the sights on film. Two giraffes look up from a group of trees. After the balloon lands, the tourists gather for breakfast. As they eat, they watch herds of grazing gazelles, antelopes, and wildebeests.

The next day, the tourists travel by bus from Nairobi to the town of Naivasha. There they take a boat ride on Lake Naivasha. On the lake, pelicans, sea eagles, and hippopotamuses surround the tourists. Two days later, the group flies by airplane to Samburu Park, where elephants and lions roam freely. The visitors watch the elephants and lions, and feed bananas to the baboons.

---

1. Give five examples of African wildlife mentioned in the passage. Students may mention any five of the following: giraffes, gazelles, antelopes, wildebeests, pelicans, sea eagles, hippopotamuses, elephants, lions, baboons.

2. What four means of transportation are mentioned in the passage? The four means of transportation are hot-air balloon, airplane, bus, and boat.

3. At what time of day does the tour begin? The tour begins in the morning.

4. Which two communities does the passage mention by name? The passage mentions Nairobi and Naivasha.

5. What are the balloon passengers doing as they fly into the game preserve? They are taking pictures.

Thinking Further: People all over the world are concerned about protecting endangered animals from extinction. What do you think should be done to make sure these animals have a place to live and remain safe?
Students may suggest stronger law enforcement in areas where poachers operate. They may point out that land should be left alone where endangered animals live. Some may suggest a program of education to make people aware of the problems of animals.

RAINFALL IN ETHIOPIA

Gathering Information from a Map, Hypothesizing

✻ The average yearly precipitation in a region is a major factor that determines where some people live and what they do for a living. Study the precipitation map of Ethiopia below. Then answer the questions.

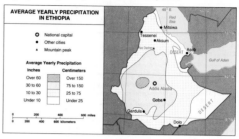

1. The capital of Ethiopia is Addis Ababa. The highest mountain is Ras Dashen. Write these names where they belong on the map.

2. About how much precipitation do the cities of Tessenei and Aksum receive each year? between 10 and 30 inches (25–75 cm)

3. Which region on the map is probably the most populated? The region that receives the most rainfall, around the capital, is probably the most populated.

4. Where would it be easier to farm crops, near Dolo or near Gardular? Give a reason for your answer. Farming would be easier near Gardular, because that area receives more rain.

5. Where are two desert areas in Ethiopia? Write the word *desert* on those places on the map.

Thinking Further: People live in all areas of Ethiopia. How could they use the land to make a living in the driest regions?
Answers may suggest nomadic herding or the use of irrigation.

LEARNING ABOUT THE FOREST PEOPLE

Identifying Details that Support Main Ideas, Drawing Conclusions

✻   Read the paragraph below about the Mbuti. Then answer the questions that follow.

The Mbuti are a group of people who inhabit an area of Zaire's rain forest. They live in huts made of small branches and leaves. They do not grow food because they do not stay long enough in one place to plant and harvest crops. The Mbuti obtain most of their food by hunting, fishing, and gathering. They hunt birds, antelopes, buffalo, elephants, and monkeys. They either trap the animals in nets or they shoot them with bows and poison-tipped arrows. The Mbuti gather berries, nuts, roots, mushrooms, and honey. When the food supply dwindles, the Mbuti move to another place and set up a new camp. In order to obtain things they cannot find in the forest, the Mbuti trade meat and forest products for goods produced by their neighbors. They trade for weapons, tools, and such foods as rice and corn.

---

1. Where do the Mbuti live? The Mbuti live in an area of Zaire's rain forest.

2. Where do the Mbuti find materials to build their homes? They find small branches and leaves in the forest where they live.

3. Why would the Mbuti have to trade for corn and rice? They do not live in one place long enough to grow crops.

4. Why don't the Mbuti live in towns? The Mbuti are hunters and gatherers who need to move around to find new sources of food.

5. What foods do the Mbuti obtain by gathering? They obtain berries, nuts, roots, mushrooms, and honey.

Thinking Further: How do you think road-building and the cutting of the forest could affect the Mbuti and other people who live in the rain forest?
Answers may suggest that it would cut down on their food supply and limit the areas in which they can live and move around.

LEARNING ABOUT AFRICAN COUNTRIES

Understanding Graphs, Interpreting Information

✻   Examine the bar graph and answer the following questions about the percentage of land that is farmed in each African country.

Percent of Usable Land in Farms

Kenya	
Liberia	
Nigeria	
Zaire	
Tanzania	

Percent 0   5   10   15   20   25   30   35   40

1. Which countries have about the same percentage of land in farms? Liberia and Zaire

2. Which country has the smallest percentage of land in farms? Zaire

3. Which country has four times as much land in farms as the country with the smallest percent? Kenya

4. Which country has the highest percentage of land in farms? Nigeria

✻   Use the following clues to find what percentage of the workers in each country work in agriculture. Write the name of the country in the blank under the pie graph that represents it.

- Nigeria has about 55 percent of its labor force working in agriculture.
- In Zaire, 32 percent of the labor force does *not* work in agriculture.
- More of Tanzania's labor force is in agriculture than any other country's.
- Kenya has the least amount of its labor force working in agriculture.
- In Liberia, about three-fourths of the labor force works in agriculture.

Percent of Labor Force Working in Agriculture

Labor Force in Agriculture

Kenya   Liberia   Nigeria   Zaire   Tanzania

Thinking Further: Nigeria has the highest percentage of land in farms. Why do you think it does not have the highest percentage of workers in agriculture? Write your answer on a separate sheet.
Students may suggest that Nigeria has more mechanized farms and fewer subsistence farms than other countries. Others may suggest that industry in Nigeria provides more jobs.

C16-C

Workbook Pages

NAME _____

THE FEATURES OF AFRICA

CHAPTER
16

Knowing Details, Applying Information

✳ Match each term about Africa in Column 1 with its description in Column 2. Write the letter from Column 2 on the line in front of the correct number in Column 1.

Column 1

F   **1.** savanna
E   **2.** Tassili plateau
H   **3.** Kalahari
A   **4.** tropics
B   **5.** Mount Kilimanjaro
D   **6.** Zaire River
K   **7.** Victoria Falls
I   **8.** Great Rift
N   **9.** Lake Victoria
C   **10.** Lake Chad
J   **11.** Senegal
G   **12.** Swahili
P   **13.** Lagos
L   **14.** cacao
M   **15.** wildlife
O   **16.** sisal
S   **17.** Ibos
Q   **18.** Sahel
R   **19.** Africa

Column 2

A. region between $23\frac{1}{2}$°N and $23\frac{1}{2}$°S
B. Africa's highest mountain
C. sometimes shrinks to one third its size
D. "big river," second largest in Africa
E. once fertile, now desert
F. grassland with scattered trees
G. Kenya's national language
H. desert in southern Africa
I. huge crack in earth's surface
J. once ruled by France
K. nearly twice as high as Niagara Falls
L. source of chocolate
M. one of Africa's most valuable natural resources
N. largest lake in Africa
O. fiber plant used to make rope
P. crowded city south of the Sahara
Q. between the Sahara and the grassland
R. second largest continent
S. ethnic group in Nigeria

Thinking Further: People in Africa live in large cities and in small villages. Choose one of these places and write a paragraph describing what living there might be like.

Answers should reflect independent thinking. Life in African cities is much like city life anywhere in the world. Villagers in Africa farm the land, herd livestock, hunt, and fish.

_____

_____

© Silver, Burdett & Ginn Inc.

Chapter 16, pages 437–451

97

TEACHER NOTES

A Variety of Lands

Objectives

★ 1. **Describe** the three types of land found in Africa south of the Sahara.

2. **Locate** the major deserts, mountains, and bodies of water in Africa.

3. **Identify** the following places: *Sahara, Sahel, Tropic of Capricorn, Tropic of Cancer,* and *Great Rift Valley.*

1 STARTING THE LESSON

Motivation Activity

■ Ask students what things come to mind when they think about the Sahara desert.

■ List their answers on the chalkboard. (Answers may include the French foreign legion, mirages caused by heatwaves, camel trains, and so on.)

■ Tell students that in this lesson they will learn about a time when this area was covered by grass and trees and supported a wide variety of wildlife. Tell students that we know this because of rock drawings of animals left behind by people who lived there between 6000 and 2000 B.C.

Think About What You Know

■ Assign the THINK ABOUT WHAT YOU KNOW activity on p. 437.

■ Answers may include deserts, jungles, lions, elephants, and other animals and land formations.

Study the Vocabulary

■ Have students look up the definitions of the new vocabulary words in the Glossary.

■ Then, ask them to locate the Tropic of Cancer and the Tropic of Capricorn on a map or globe.

436

CHAPTER **16**

GEOGRAPHY OF AFRICA SOUTH OF THE SAHARA

*A*frica south of the Sahara has many variation in land and climate. There are rain forests, grassland and deserts. People from all over the world come t see the region's variety o wildlife.

436

Optional Activities

For Your Information

The Sahara Desert   The Sahara is the world's largest desert, extending approximately 3,000 miles (4,827 km) east to west and about 1,200 miles (1,931 km) north to south. At night, the temperature in the desert often falls below freezing, but daytime temperatures of over 135 degrees Fahrenheit (57 degrees Celsius) have been recorded in the shade.

About 15 percent of the desert is sand dunes and about 70 percent is stone and gravel. Huge underground aquifers of water, believed to date from the Pleistocene era, lie beneath vast portions of the desert, which also has deposits of iron ore, phosphates, oil, and natural gas.

A Variety of Lands

THINK ABOUT WHAT YOU KNOW
Suppose you were invited to make a trip to Africa south of the Sahara. What would you expect to see?

STUDY THE VOCABULARY

savanna	tropics
Tropic of Cancer	equatorial
Tropic of Capricorn	river basin

FOCUS YOUR READING
What kind of variety is found in the land south of the Sahara?

A Change in Climate

ncient Drawings It was something of a rprise to a French army officer in 1932 to scover a picture of an elephant on a can-n wall on the Tassili plateau in the heart of the Sahara. Searching further, he found drawings of hippopotamuses, giraffes, antelopes, rhinoceroses, wild oxen, baboons, and ostriches. None of these creatures can be seen today on the plateau. The rocky, windswept land receives little rain. There are no rivers for animals such as hippopotamuses, and elephants would certainly die of thirst. There were also pictures of people on the walls. Some were hunters; others were herders.

Change Over Time Who made these drawings, and how did they know about elephants and hippopotamuses? Scientists believe that the drawings were made by people who lived on the Tassili plateau between 6000 and 2000 B.C. The animals in the drawings also lived there 8,000 years ago. Then this part of Africa had a wetter climate. Trees, grass, and other vegetation grew on the land, and animals as large as

Rock paintings on the walls of caves were made by African people thousands of years ago.
▶ What is shown on this wall?

2 DEVELOPING THE LESSON

Read and Think

Section A

The Sahara was not always a desert. Paintings on the walls of the Tassili plateau attest to this fact. Use these questions to discuss the implications of these paintings:

1. **What was shown in the Tassili plateau rock paintings?**
   (Elephants, hippopotamuses, giraffes, antelopes, rhinoceroses, wild oxen, baboons, ostriches, and people who were hunters and herders *p. 437*)

2. **Why were people in modern times surprised to see these pictures?**
   (Because the climate in the Sahara today is too dry for these animals *p. 437*)

   Thinking Critically Why, do you think, would the people of the Tassili plateau draw pictures on the rocks? (Infer)
   (Answers should reflect independent thinking but may include for decoration or for religious reasons. *p. 437*)

Answers to Caption Questions
p. 437 ▶ People and cattle

Writing to Learn

Arguing for Preservation Have students pretend that they are scientists who have heard about the discovery of drawings on the walls of the Tassili plateau.

● Have them write letters to the French government, urging initiation of a project to further explore the region and study these drawings.

● Their letters should explain why these drawings may be important to scientists.

Preparing a Chart

● Have students prepare a chart that compares the size and population densities of Africa, Asia, Europe, North America, South America, and Australia.

● The charts may also compare the height of the highest mountain and the length of the longest river in each continent.

● Have students use an almanac or atlas to obtain information which is not available in the text.

Optional Activities

Read and Think
Sections B and C

Use the questions below to discuss the land and climate of sub-Saharan Africa:

1. **How much larger than Europe is Africa?**
(Three times as large *p. 438*)

2. **Name the three major deserts of Africa.**
(The Sahara, the Kalahari, and the Namib *p. 438*)

3. **What is the predominant landform outside the deserts of Africa and what kinds of plants and animals are found there?**
(Savanna, or grassland, with scattered trees and bushes, and herds of large animals *p. 438*)

4. **How do people affect the Sahel when they cut trees and bushes for fuel?**
(They rob the land of its cover and help turn the land into desert. *p. 439*)

Thinking Critically Why, do you think, is Africa so sparsely populated in comparison to Europe and Asia? (Infer)
(Answers should reflect independent thinking but may include that extreme climates and poor soil conditions in much of the continent make it difficult to grow enough food to support a large population. *pp. 438-439*)

GEOGRAPHY THEMES

 Place

■ Direct students' attention to the map on this page. Then ask the following question: **What vegetation zone is located at the northern and southern coasts of Africa?**
(Mediterranean)

---

elephants could graze there. Later, herders brought cattle to feed on the plateau.

Sometime after 2000 B.C. the climate became drier. Rivers slowly dried up. Land once covered with grass became a desert, as it is today. No one knows for sure why the climate changed. But the Tassili rock paintings show that it did.

B. The Second Largest Continent

Africa is a large continent. It is two-thirds the size of Asia and three times as large as Europe. Africa's Mediterranean coast and its southern tip are about 5,000 miles (8,045 km) apart. They are nearly the same distance from the Equator, which crosses the continent. Both the northern coast and the southern tip have a Mediterranean climate, with cool, rainy winters and hot, dry summers.

The physical map on page 440 shows some important facts about Africa. Much of the land south of the Equator is a plateau that rises sharply from a narrow plain along the coast. Along the hump, or bulge, of West Africa, the lowland extends farther into the interior.

Although Africa is the second largest continent, it ranks behind Asia in population and Europe in population density. Asia has five times as many people as Africa, and Europe has over five times as many people per square mile.

C. Vegetation Regions

Deserts and Grasslands More than a fourth of Africa is desert. The Sahara is only one of three major deserts found in Africa. In southwest Africa are the Kalahari (kal uh HAHR ee) and Namib (NAHM-ihb) deserts. The Kalahari Desert is drier than the Sahara and covers an area about as large as the state of Oregon in the

---

AFRICA: VEGETATION

Equatorial rain forest
Savanna
Desert or semidesert
Grassland
Mediterranean

0   500   1,000 miles
0   500 1,000 kilometers

The savanna is one of Africa's two largest major vegetation regions.
▶ What is the other very large vegetation region in Africa?

United States. The Namib Desert, located on Africa's southwest coast, is a cool desert. Find all three of these African deserts on the vegetation map on this page. The map shows the great extent of the deserts. These deserts do not support more than a sparse population.

As the map shows, much of the rest of Africa is **savanna**, or grassland with scattered trees and bushes. Herds of large animals, including elephants, giraffes, zebras, and wildebeests, graze here. Some of the savanna is now used for farming, although the soil is thin.

The savanna receives the most rain during the summer months. Winters are usually very dry. Rainfall varies each year.

Optional Activities

For Your Information

Livingstone and Stanley Dr. David Livingstone, a Scottish medical missionary, and Sir Henry Morton Stanley, a British journalist, were the first non-Africans to explore the rivers and lakes of Africa south of the Sahara. Livingstone explored the Zambezi River and Victoria Falls in the 1850s and 1860s, but the world knew little of his discoveries until the *New York Herald* sent Stanley to Africa to look for him and write about his adventures. Stanley located Livingstone in 1871, greeting him with the now famous line, "Dr. Livingstone, I presume?" Together, they traveled to the end of Lake Tanganyika.

The Sahel Between the Sahara and the savanna is a strip of land called the Sahel, which means "border" in Arabic. When rain is plentiful, cattle, sheep, and goats can graze on the Sahel. During times of drought, however, the Sahel has little to offer these herds.

Recently the desert has been advancing into the Sahel. When too many animals are allowed to graze on the dry grasslands, they destroy the vegetation, and the land is left bare. When people cut too many trees and bushes for fuel, this too robs the land of its cover. Strong winds carry away the thin topsoil, leaving stony land on which neither grass nor crops can grow.

> Drought is a constant threat to farmers in nations of the Sahel.
> ► How has drought affected the land shown below?

Climograph: LIBREVILLE, GABON
Location: .30° N/9° E

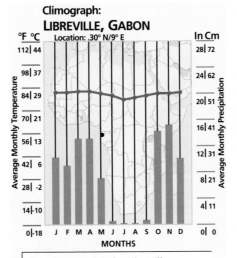

This climograph is for Libreville, Gabon, which is located in an eqatorial rain forest.
► On the average, which month receives the most rainfall?

D. Rain Forests and Snow-Covered Mountains

The Forests A large part of Africa lies on either side of the Equator between the **Tropic of Cancer**, at 23 1/2° north latitude, and the **Tropic of Capricorn**, at 23 1/2° south latitude. This region is known as the **tropics**. The lands along the Equator are called **equatorial**.

The equatorial parts of Central Africa and West Africa receive a lot of rain. Most areas average at least 50 inches (127 cm) of precipitation a year. Look at the climograph to see how much precipitation Libreville receives. The wet equatorial lands are covered by dense rain forests that produce valuable hardwoods such as ebony.

The Mountains The tallest mountains south of the Sahara are in East Africa. Mount Kenya is located on the Equator,

439

Read and Think
Section D

Use the questions below to begin a discussion of Africa's rain forests and mountains.

1. **What is the region between the Tropic of Cancer and the Tropic of Capricorn known as?**
   (The tropics *p. 439*)

2. **What kind of climate is found in the equatorial lands?**
   (Very rainy *p. 439*)

3. **Why does snow cover Mount Kenya throughout the year even though it is located on the Equator?**
   (Because of its elevation *pp. 439-441*)

Thinking Critically Would you rather visit the equatorial rain forests or the mountains of East Africa?
(Evaluate)
(Answers should reflect independent thinking but may include the rain forests because of the adventure that jungles can provide, or the mountains, for their scenic beauty. *pp. 439-441*)

┌─ **Answers to Caption Questions** ─
p. **438** ► Desert or semidesert
p. **439** *l.* ► The land is dry and cracked.
p. **439** *r.* ► November

Curriculum Connection

Science Have students prepare a bulletin board on the desertification of the Sahel.

● Have students use the library card catalogue to locate articles on the causes of desertification.

● Ask them to write brief explanations of the causes of desertification and then illustrate them.

● The bulletin board should include at least one photograph or drawing for each cause.

Cooperative Learning

Planning a Trip Divide students into groups of six in order to plan trips to Africa.

● Each group should agree on a purpose for its trip (for example: to observe desertification in the Sahel).

● Two students in each group should decide which areas and points of interest they wish to visit, two students should plot the route on a map, and two students should make a list of things to take.

● After 45 minutes have one member from each group share that group's plan with the rest of the class.

Optional Activities

Read and Think

Section E

Use the questions below to discuss the rivers and lakes of sub-Saharan Africa:

1. **What does "Zaire" mean?**
   (Big river *p. 441*)

2. **What causes variations in the size and depth of Lake Chad?**
   (Cycles of drought can shrink the lake to one-third of its size during wet years *p. 442*)

3. **What is the Great Rift Valley and what bodies of water are found there?**
   (The Great Rift is a huge crack in the earth's surface; Lake Victoria and Lake Tanganyika are in the Great Rift. *p. 442*)

Thinking Critically Which of the rivers or lakes discussed in this lesson would you most like to visit? (Evaluate) (Answers should reflect independent thinking and be supported by information in the text. *pp. 441-442*)

GEOGRAPHY THEMES

Place

- Have students consult the map on p. 440 to help them do the following activity.

- Assign each student a country in sub-Saharan Africa. Have students draw posters that include a map of their country, and show its major cities, mountains, and bodies of water.

- The posters should also provide information from the text about rainfall, vegetation, population, population density, elevation, and landforms.

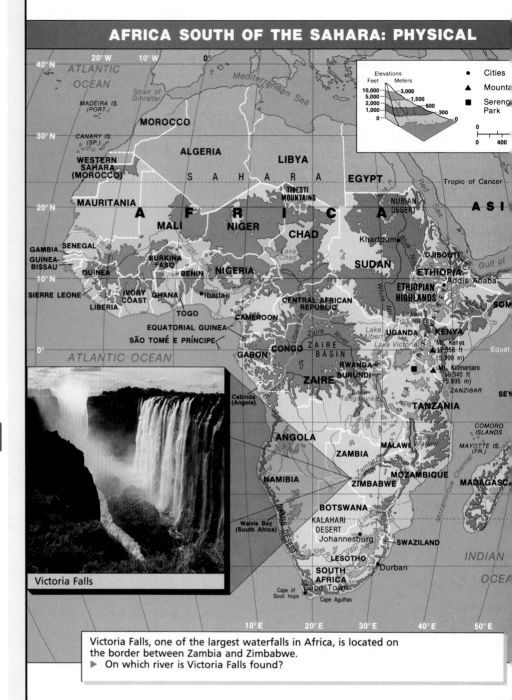

AFRICA SOUTH OF THE SAHARA: PHYSICAL

Victoria Falls

Victoria Falls, one of the largest waterfalls in Africa, is located on the border between Zambia and Zimbabwe.
▶ On which river is Victoria Falls found?

Optional Activities

Drawing Pictures of Landforms

- Have students study the landforms of Africa south of the Sahara by asking them to draw a picture of one of the major landforms.

- Provide students with a list of landforms to choose from. The list should include deserts, grasslands, rain forests, Mount Kilimanjaro or Mount Kenya, the Niger River or Victoria Falls.

- Ask students to make their drawings realistic and include as much detail as possible.

- Display students' drawings in the classroom.

Mount Kilimanjaro, just south of the Equator, is the tallest mountain peak in Africa.
▶ Why is there snow covering the top of the mountain?

possible," flowing lazily through an overgrown swamp "in a what's-it-matter-when-it-comes-out style." Trace the river's course on the map on page 440. Note that its long route to the sea is also winding.

European explorers called the second longest African river the Congo. But to Africans it was known as the Zaire, or "big river." Note on the map on page 440 that the **river basin**, the area drained by the river, is crossed by the Equator.

The Zambezi River, in south central Africa, rises on the high plateau and flows over falls and rapids on its way to the Indian Ocean. The largest of the falls — Victoria Falls — is twice as wide and nearly twice as high as Niagara Falls, in North America.

yet snow covers its summit throughout the year because of its high elevation. Snow-peaked Mount Kilimanjaro (kihl uh mun-JAHR oh), just south of the Equator, is taller than any of the mountains in Europe.

E. Africa's Rivers and Lakes

The Rivers The Niger is the third longest river in Africa. The river rises in the highlands of Guinea and empties into the Atlantic Ocean. Near the Atlantic the Niger divides into many channels that crisscross each other.

Explorers had trouble finding the mouth of the Niger for just this reason. As an early traveler observed, the Niger "comes to sea with as much mystery as

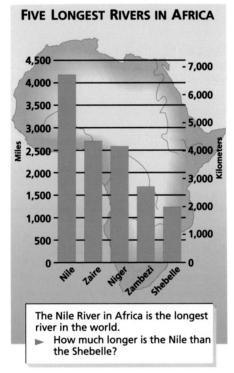

FIVE LONGEST RIVERS IN AFRICA

The Nile River in Africa is the longest river in the world.
▶ How much longer is the Nile than the Shebelle?

441

◆

Meeting Individual Needs
Understanding Landforms

To better understand the geography of Africa, it is important to be able to distinguish among the landforms of the continent. Below are three activities that will help students understand African landforms.

◆ **EASY** Ask students to identify and describe the major landforms of sub-Saharan Africa.

Have students depict one of the landforms, using pictures from magazines or pictures that they have drawn or painted themselves.

◀▶ **AVERAGE** Have students create a physical map that depicts the major landforms, mountains, rivers, and lakes of Africa.

◀▮▶ **CHALLENGING** Ask students to create a chart comparing landforms.

The chart should compare rainfall, vegetation, animals, and other features associated with each landform.

Students may wish to include information from other parts of the text or other sources.

┌─ **Answers to Caption Questions** ─
p. 440 ▶ The Zambezi River
p. 441 *l.* ▶ Because of its high elevation
p. 441 *r.* ▶ About 3,000 miles (4,827 km)

Reteaching Main Objective

Describe the three types of land found in Africa south of the Sahara.

● Have students pretend that they are travelers writing letters about their experiences in Africa.

● Have them write three letters that describe the route they are taking and the landforms that they encounter as they travel this route. They may also invent incidents that might occur while traveling through each landform.

● Students should consult maps to ensure that all three major landforms are encountered in their trips.

Optional Activities

3 CLOSING THE LESSON

Lesson 1 Review

Answers to Think and Write

A. Scientists believe that the climate in the Sahara has changed because drawings of animals that could not survive there today have been found on the walls of the Tassili plateau.

B. Africa is two-thirds the size of Asia and three times the size of Europe. The population of Asia is five times that of Africa and Europe's population is five times as dense as Africa's.

C. The Sahel is a strip of land between the Sahara and the savanna. Although the Sahel can be used for grazing during rainy periods, overgrazing is destroying its plant life. This in turn is causing erosion and the advance of the desert into the Sahel.

D. Equatorial Africa has dense rain forests that contain valuable hardwoods.

E. Three rivers found south of the Sahara are the Niger, the Zambezi, and the Congo (or Zaire). Three lakes found south of the Sahara are Lake Chad, Lake Victoria, and Lake Tanganyika.

Answer to Skills Check

Niger: Guinea, Mali, Niger, Benin, Nigeria; Zaire: Zaire, Congo, Angola; Zambezi: Angola, Zambia, Zimbabwe, Mozambique.

Focus Your Reading

Ask the lesson focus question found at the beginning of the lesson: **What kind of variety is found in the land south of the Sahara?**
(In the land south of the Sahara, one finds deserts, grasslands or savanna, equatorial rain forests, mountains, lakes, and rivers.)

Additional Practice

You may wish to assign the ancillary materials listed below.

Understanding the Lesson p. 109
Workbook pp. 93-94

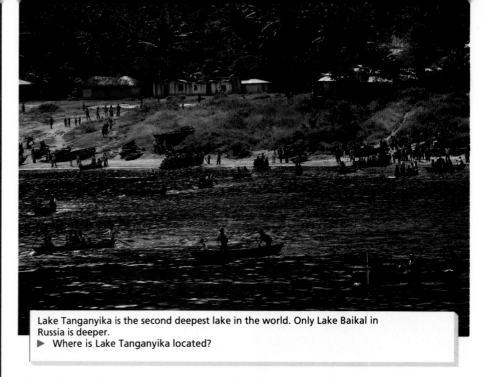

Lake Tanganyika is the second deepest lake in the world. Only Lake Baikal in Russia is deeper.
► Where is Lake Tanganyika located?

The Lakes Africa also has a number of lakes south of the Sahara. Lake Chad is located in the Sahel, on the edge of the desert. The size and depth of Lake Chad vary greatly. In times of drought it shrinks to one third its size in wet years.

Several of Africa's largest lakes are located in the Great Rift Valley. The Great Rift is a huge crack in the earth's surface that extends from East Africa into the Middle East. Lake Victoria, the largest of the African lakes, is here. It is one source of the Nile, Africa's longest river. Lake Tanganyika (tan gun YEE kuh), also in the valley, is deeper than any other lake on the continent. If you dropped a rock at the lake's deepest point, it would sink nearly a mile before reaching the bottom.

LESSON 1 REVIEW

THINK AND WRITE

A. Why do scientists believe that the climate in the Sahara is not the same as it once was? **(Infer)**

B. Compare Africa to Asia and Europe in size and population. **(Recall)**

C. Identify the Sahel and summarize how it is changing. **(Infer)**

D. What type of vegetation is found in equatorial Africa? **(Recall)**

E. Name three rivers and three lakes south of the Sahara. **(Recall)**

SKILLS CHECK

MAP SKILL

Locate the Niger, Zaire, and Zambezi rivers on the physical map of Africa on page 440. List the countries through which each river flows or for which it forms a boundary.

Optional Activities

UNDERSTANDING THE LESSON

NAME _____
UNDERSTANDING THE LESSON   CHAPTER **16**

Organizing Facts   LESSON 1 CONTENT MASTER

❋ The chart can help you describe the physical features of Africa south of the Sahara Desert. Fill in the blank spaces with the specific names of the features, and briefly tell where each feature is located.

Deserts
Sahara—north Africa
Kalahari—southern tip of Africa
Namib—southern tip of Africa

Grasslands and Forests
Savanna—throughout center of Africa
Sahel—border between savanna and desert
Tropical rain forest—equatorial Africa

Mountains
Mount Kenya—East Africa on the Equator
Mount Kilimanjaro—East Africa south of the Equator

Geography of Africa South of the Sahara

Lakes
Lake Chad—in the Sahel
Lake Victoria—East Africa in the Great Rift Valley
Lake Tanganyika—East Africa in the Great Rift Valley

Rivers
Niger River—highlands of Guinea to Atlantic Ocean
Zaire River—equatorial Africa
Zambezi River—south central Africa to Indian Ocean

Think and Write: The climate and vegetation of a region does not stay the same. Write a paragraph supporting this statement. Include examples from the text. You may use the back of this sheet.
Answers should reflect independent thinking; suggestions appear in the Answer Key.

Use with textbook pages 437-442.   109

◄ **Review Master Booklet, p. 109**

THINK ABOUT WHAT YOU KNOW
Think about all the people you know. What different kinds of people live in our country?

STUDY THE VOCABULARY
multilingual

FOCUS YOUR READING
How do people south of the Sahara differ?

A. Some People Who Live in Africa

In Liberia Kama is a 12-year-old girl who lives with her grandmother in a village in Liberia, in West Africa. Kama's grandmother also takes care of Kama's brothers and one of her cousins.

Kama attends a school conducted by Muslims, although she and her family are Christians. Kama is especially interested in learning about faraway places. She has even borrowed an advanced geography book from her teacher to do extra reading.

Often in the evening Kama's grandmother gathers the children into the living room, and they sing songs and hymns. Some of the songs are in English, which is Liberia's official language. Others are in Kpelle, the language of Kama's own people. About 26 African languages are spoken by different groups within Liberia.

In Nigeria Binta also lives in West Africa. Her home is Kano, a large city in northern Nigeria. Even though Binta is only 11 years old, she goes out on the street early each morning to sell bean cakes made by her mother. Binta some- times makes small pancakes to sell to other children.

For an hour or so each day, Binta goes to an Arabic school, where she studies the language of the Koran, which you learned is the holy book of Muslims. There are also public schools in Kano, where subjects are taught in English, the language of Nigeria. But Binta's family, like most people in Kano, are Muslims. They think it is more important for a girl to learn to read the Koran than English.

Binta's family are Hausas, one of the ethnic groups in Nigeria. Members of a particular ethnic group may share language, religion, and customs. In some ways an ethnic group is like a nationality. Most Hausas are Muslims. The Yorubas, Ibos, and Fulanis are other ethnic groups in Nigeria. Each of these ethnic groups has its own language.

People carry goods for sale along the streets of West Africa.
► What are these women carrying on their heads?

Making a Linguistic Map

● Have students use an almanac or atlas to find out the official language of each country south of the Sahara.

● Ask students to devise a color or pattern key for the languages.

● Have students color or code a political outline map of Africa to show the official languages.

A Variety of Peoples

Objectives

★ 1. **Discuss** the concept of ethnic groups and explain how they affect life in Africa.

2. **Explain** why there are so many languages spoken in Africa.

3. **Identify** the following places: *West Africa, East Africa,* and *Lagos, Nigeria.*

1 STARTING THE LESSON

Motivation Activity

■ Ask students to think about some of the advantages and disadvantages of living in a place where many languages are spoken.

■ Tell students that, in this lesson, they will learn about the numerous languages spoken in Africa south of the Sahara.

Think About What You Know

■ Assign the THINK ABOUT WHAT YOU KNOW activity on p. 443.

■ Student answers should reflect particular neighborhoods and experiences.

■ Encourage students to begin thinking about the concept of ethnic groups by identifying public figures with whom students are familiar who have a strong ethnic identity.

Study the Vocabulary

■ Have students look up the definition of *multilingual* in the Glossary.

■ Ask students to name some ethnic groups; choose two or three groups and discuss some features of their identities (language, food, religion, and so on). Be careful to avoid stereotypes when performing this activity.

┌─ **Answers to Caption Questions** ─┐
p. 442 ► In East Africa in the Great Rift Valley
p. 443 ► Fruit on trays
└────────────────────────────┘

DEVELOPING THE LESSON

Read and Think

Sections A, B, and C

Use the questions below to discuss the ethnic groups, languages, and lifestyles of people in Africa south of the Sahara:

1. **Why does Binta study the language of the Koran?**

   (Because Muslims think that it is more important for a girl to read the Koran than English *p. 443*)

2. **In African countries where many languages are spoken, what is usually the official language?**

   (The language of the European country that ruled before the nation became independent *p. 445*)

3. **What are some characteristics of African music?**

   (Africans developed a music style that uses many types of rhythms; their instruments include many kinds of drums, xylophones, string instruments, horns, and flutes. *p. 445*)

   Thinking Critically Why, do you think, were the languages of former European rulers, rather than those of local ethnic groups, chosen as official languages? (Infer)

   (Answers may include that these languages were already used in government and business or that this was to prevent ethnic conflict. *p. 445*)

VISUAL THINKING SKILL

Understanding a Photograph

■ Direct students' attention to the photograph on this page. Then ask them to write a two-paragraph essay in which they describe similarities and differences between this Kenyan classroom and their own classroom.

Children in schoolrooms in Kenya learn how to speak English.
▶ How can you tell that English is being taught?

In Kenya Mr. and Mrs. Munoru and their four children live in Kenya, in East Africa. They are Christians, like the majority of people in Kenya. Mr. Munoru raises coffee beans on a tiny plot of land he inherited. The plot is only half an acre (.2 ha), so it cannot support the family. But Mr. Munoru is a trained stone mason, and he works at his trade in a nearby town whenever he can get a job. Mrs. Munoru earns some money working on large farms.

Mr. and Mrs. Munoru work very hard because they are determined to give their children a good education. The children will learn English in school, although Swahili is Kenya's national language. The Munorus want their children to learn English so that they can get good jobs someday. Most government and business affairs in Kenya are carried on in English.

B. Many Countries, Many Languages

Ethnic Groups Kama, Binta, and the Munoru family are all Africans, but they are not alike. Africa is a huge continent with more than a half billion people. As you would expect, there are many differences among so many people. There are more countries in Africa than on any other continent. Within most of the countries there are different ethnic groups.

Some of the ethnic groups in Africa are descendants of people who came from other continents. In East Africa and South Africa there are people whose ancestors came from India. In South Africa about 18 percent of the people are descendants of Europeans who settled there.

Languages Because of the many different ethnic groups, a variety of languages

Optional Activities

are spoken in most countries south of the Sahara. At least 16 languages are used in Zaire, for example, and 15 in Tanzania. Because various languages are spoken in African countries, many people there are **multilingual**, or able to speak several languages. However, in most countries where there are many different languages the official language is that of the European country that ruled before the nation became independent. France once ruled Senegal, for instance, and French is the official language there.

In addition to being the language of the Muslim religion, Arabic has long been a language for traders in parts of Africa. It is also the official language of several countries. Swahili, an African language widely used in East Africa, includes many Arabic words and is written in Arabic script.

C. Wise Sayings, Works of Art, and Special Music

Proverbs Africans did not develop systems of writing for all the different languages. But they did create a rich variety of poems, songs, stories, and legends. These were passed on by word of mouth. Children learned them from their parents and grandparents, and taught their own children in turn.

Africans are fond of proverbs, or short wise sayings. Here are some samples.

> *He who cannot dance will say the drum is bad.*
> *A loose tooth will not rest until it is pulled out.*
> *He who talks all of the time talks nonsense.*
> *Not to know is bad; not to wish to know is worse.*
> *To try and to fail is not laziness.*

Art and Music One proverb points out that seeing is different from being told. The photograph below tells more than words can tell about the variety of art the peoples of Africa produce. It shows that African artists use all kinds of materials. Today, African artwork is found in museums in many parts of the world.

Africans developed a special style of music that makes use of many different rhythms, or beats. They invented a variety of musical instruments, including many different kinds of drums. One, known as the talking drum, makes sounds somewhat like those of the human voice. African musicians also use many different kinds of xylophones, string instruments, horns, and flutes.

Artists of Africa used antelope skin and other materials to create the ceremonial helmet shown in the photograph below.
▶ What other materials were used?

Writing to Learn

Writing a Letter Have students pretend that they are pen pals with Kama, Binta, or one of the Munoru children.

● Have students write letters to their imaginary pen pals.

● Each letter should include at least three questions about life in Africa and three facts about life in the United States that students think would be interesting to their pen pals.

For Your Information

Liberia Liberia was founded in 1821 by the American Colonization Society, an organization that transported freed black slaves from the United States and settled them in Africa. The first American blacks arrived in Liberia in 1822. By 1847, it had become an independent republic with a constitution modeled after the U.S. Constitution. Although the descendants of the 15,000 American blacks who eventually settled in Liberia are not numerous, they have a great deal of influence. In 1980, a coup ended 100 years of rule by Americo-Liberians. Although English is the official language, Islam and traditional tribal religions and languages play an important role in Liberian culture and society.

Read and Think

Section D

Summarize the growth of African cities south of the Sahara with the following questions:

1. **How are large cities south of the Sahara like large cities on other continents?**
   (They have tall buildings, packed living quarters, and traffic jams. *p. 447*)

2. **What is one of the great changes taking place in this part of Africa?**
   (The rapid growth of cities is making life in Africa more like life in other parts of the world. *p. 447*)

Thinking Critically Why, do you think, are African cities growing so rapidly? (Hypothesize)
(Answers may include the rapidly increasing birthrate in Africa or that African villagers are moving to cities in large numbers to take jobs. *p. 447*)

GEOGRAPHY THEMES

Human-Environment Interactions

- Have students refer to the map on this page and ask the following question: **Generally, where are the most populated areas in each country?**
  (In and around the capital cities of each country.)

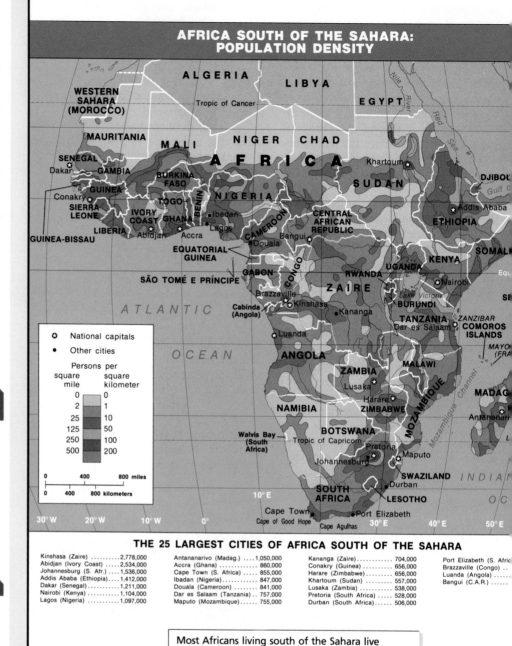

AFRICA SOUTH OF THE SAHARA: POPULATION DENSITY

Persons per

square mile	square kilometer
0	0
2	1
25	10
125	50
250	100
500	200

○ National capitals
● Other cities

THE 25 LARGEST CITIES OF AFRICA SOUTH OF THE SAHARA

Kinshasa (Zaire) 2,778,000	Antananarivo (Madag.) 1,050,000	Kananga (Zaire)............ 704,000	Port Elizabeth (S. Afric
Abidjan (Ivory Coast) 2,534,000	Accra (Ghana) 860,000	Conakry (Guinea) 656,000	Brazzaville (Congo) .....
Johannesburg (S. Afr.) 1,536,000	Cape Town (S. Africa) 855,000	Harare (Zimbabwe) 656,000	Luanda (Angola) ......
Addis Ababa (Ethiopia)....1,412,000	Ibadan (Nigeria)............ 847,000	Khartoum (Sudan) 557,000	Bangui (C.A.R.) ......
Dakar (Senegal)...........1,211,000	Douala (Cameroon) 841,000	Lusaka (Zambia) 538,000	
Nairobi (Kenya) 1,104,000	Dar es Salaam (Tanzania) .. 757,000	Pretoria (South Africa) 528,000	
Lagos (Nigeria) 1,097,000	Maputo (Mozambique)...... 755,000	Durban (South Africa)...... 506,000	

Most Africans living south of the Sahara live in rural areas rather than in cities.
▶ How many of the 25 largest cities have a population of a million or more?

446

Optional Activities

Curriculum Connection

Music Play recordings of African songs and music from Silver Burdett & Ginn's *The World of Music* curriculum.

- Discuss the tribes and locations of the people who sing each song.
- Try to identify the types of instruments being used in each song. Suggested recordings include: "Obwisana" and "Gogo" (*WOM*, grade 1); "Go Well and Safely" and "Kee Chee" (*WOM*, grade 2); "Sante-sana" (*WOM*, grade 3); "As the Sun Goes Down" (*WOM*, grade 4); and "Kum Bah Ya," "Banuwa," and "Johnny's My Boy" (*WOM*, grade 5).

Reteaching Main Objective

★ *Discuss the concept of ethnic groups and explain how they affect life in Africa.*

- Divide students into groups to develop skits involving Kama, Binta, and the Munoru family.
- The skits should emphasize the differences among the characters.
- Remind students that these people all live in different countries, so the skit must account for their being in the same place at the same time.
- Give students about ten minutes to prepare and ten minutes to enact each skit.

446

D. Villagers and City Dwellers

In the past most Africans south of the Sahara lived in small groups. They were villagers who farmed the land, herded livestock, hunted, and fished. Today a majority still live in villages, but the number of city dwellers has been growing rapidly. In some countries more than a fourth of the population is urban.

A number of African cities have more than a million inhabitants. Look at the population density map on page 446 to find out how many African cities south of the Sahara have a population of a million or more. These large cities, like those on other continents, have tall buildings, packed living quarters, and traffic jams. Lagos, Nigeria, has been called the most crowded city south of the Sahara. Its urban area sprawls through suburbs just like the urban areas of many cities in the United States. More people live in the suburbs than in Lagos itself.

The rapid growth of cities is one of the great changes taking place in the lands south of the Sahara. As more and more people live in cities, life in this part of Africa is becoming more like life in other parts of the world.

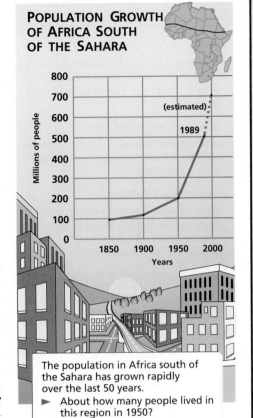

POPULATION GROWTH OF AFRICA SOUTH OF THE SAHARA

The population in Africa south of the Sahara has grown rapidly over the last 50 years.
▶ About how many people lived in this region in 1950?

LESSON 2 REVIEW

THINK AND WRITE

A. What are some of the differences between Kama, Binta, and the Munoru family? **(Analyze)**

B. Name some languages spoken south of the Sahara. **(Recall)**

C. Give an example of a proverb, a piece of art, and a musical instrument from south of the Sahara. **(Recall)**

D. How is African life south of the Sahara changing? **(Infer)**

SKILLS CHECK

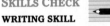

WRITING SKILL

The idea of a proverb can be stated in other words. For example, the idea behind "A proverb is the horse of conversation" is that a wise saying keeps the conversation going. In your own words, write the idea of each proverb given on page 445.

447

Optional Activities

Lesson 2 Review

Answers to Think and Write

A. Some of the differences between Kama, Binta, and the Munoru family are their ethnic backgrounds and the languages that they speak, their religion, their way of earning a living, and their attitudes toward education.

B. Arabic, Swahili and French are some languages spoken south of the Sahara.

C. An example of a proverb is "To try and to fail is not laziness"; of a piece of art is a ceremonial helmet; of a musical instrument is a xylophone.

D. Life south of the Sahara is becoming more like life in other parts of the world because of the growth of cities.

Answer to Skills Check

Possible wordings include: People will be critical of things they cannot do; A problem will continue to be a problem until it is solved; Someone who talks too much is a fool; Not wanting to learn is worse than not knowing anything; If you try and don't succeed, you are still to be commended for trying.

Focus Your Reading

Ask the lesson focus question found at the beginning of the lesson: **How do people south of the Sahara differ?**
(People south of the Sahara are of different ethnic groups, speak different languages, observe different religions, and may live in villages or cities.)

Additional Practice

You may wish to assign the ancillary materials listed below.

Understanding the Lesson p. 110
Workbook p. 95

Answers to Caption Questions
p. 446 ▶ Eight
p. 447 ▶ About 199 million

Making Use of Resources

Objectives

★1. **Explain** how people in Africa south of the Sahara use natural resources.

2. **Explain** why the wildlife population of Africa is declining.

3. **Identify** the following places: *East Africa,* and *the Kalahari.*

1 STARTING THE LESSON

Motivation Activity

■ Show students a bar of soap, a stainless-steel fork or spoon, an aluminum pot or pan, and a chocolate bar.

■ Ask them to talk about how they use these objects in their daily lives.

■ Explain that the chances are good that these objects, or objects like them, are made from materials mined or grown in Africa south of the Sahara.

Think About What You Know

■ Assign the THINK ABOUT WHAT YOU KNOW activity on p. 448.

■ Answers may include that one would expect to find few natural resources because few clues about them are given in Lesson 1.

Study the Vocabulary

■ Have students look up the definitions of the new vocabulary terms in the Glossary.

■ Have students write a paragraph using all the new vocabulary terms correctly.

LESSON 3
Making Use of Resources

THINK ABOUT WHAT YOU KNOW

In Lesson 1 you studied about the lands south of the Sahara. What natural resources would you expect to find in this region?

STUDY THE VOCABULARY

subsistence farming   cacao
slash-and-burn farming   sisal
commercial farm

FOCUS YOUR READING

What important natural resources are found in Africa south of the Sahara, and how are these resources used?

Gold mining is a major industry in South Africa.
► What are these miners wearing for protection?

A. Land of Gold and Other Minerals

Gold first attracted people from other lands to Africa. In early accounts the region south of the Sahara was called "the land of gold." One writer told of an African king who ate from plates of gold, and whose dogs had collars of gold.

Such early accounts no doubt stretched the truth a bit, but there was gold in Africa. There still is. Half of all the gold mined in the world between 1972 and 1987 came from Africa south of the Sahara.

Africa has other minerals that are more useful in the modern world. It is a major source of chromium ore and has one of the world's largest bauxite reserves. Africa also supplies the world with diamonds, uranium, iron, tin, and oil.

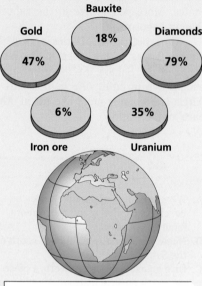

MINERAL PRODUCTION IN AFRICA SOUTH OF THE SAHARA

Bauxite
Gold   18%   Diamonds
47%   79%

6%   35%

Iron ore   Uranium

Africa south of the Sahara produces 79 percent of the world's diamonds.
► How much of the world's gold comes from this part of Africa?

For Your Information

Tsetse Fly The tsetse fly looks much like our common housefly but it carries the one-celled parasite that causes sleeping sickness in humans and animals. Sleeping sickness causes chills and fever, and if the parasite enters the brain, the infected person or animal falls into a deep sleep which leads to a coma, and finally, death if the disease goes untreated. The tsetse fly also carries other diseases that are deadly to cattle.

Optional Activities

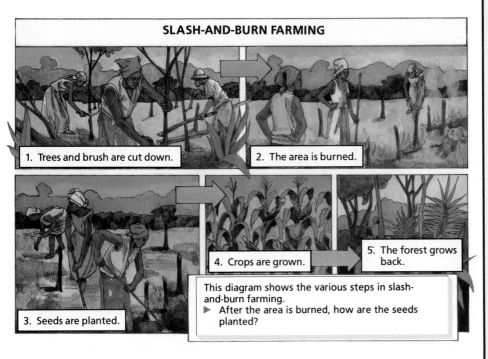

SLASH-AND-BURN FARMING

1. Trees and brush are cut down.
2. The area is burned.
3. Seeds are planted.
4. Crops are grown.
5. The forest grows back.

This diagram shows the various steps in slash-and-burn farming.
▶ After the area is burned, how are the seeds planted?

B. Growing Crops for Family Use

Farming Methods For many centuries **subsistence farming** was the main form of agriculture south of the Sahara. Subsistence farmers grow crops mostly for their own use rather than for sale. About two thirds of African cropland is still used in this way.

There are many small farms in the rain forests. Because these soils are not rich, farmers use **slash-and-burn farming**. First they slash, or cut, the trees and bushes on a patch of land. When the vegetation is dry, they set it on fire. After the fire ashes cover the soil. Farmers then break up the soil with hoes and plant their crops. The ashes serve as fertilizer.

Land Use Farmers in the rain forests plant different crops side by side. Corn,

beans, and peanuts might be grown in the same small field, for example. Africans also grow two important root crops, yams and cassava. The cassava plant, also known as manioc, has a large root that is ground into meal or flour.

Because the soil wears out very quickly, farmers must slash and burn new patches of land every few years. Trees and bushes are allowed to grow up again in the deserted fields. After 20 years or so, the land may be ready to be cut and burned again. In recent times, however, the African population has increased rapidly, and farmers have cut and burned land every few years instead of waiting longer periods. As a result, the soil in some areas has become so poor that it will support neither crops nor forest. Too much farming makes the land nearly useless.

449

2 DEVELOPING THE LESSON

Read and Think

Sections A, B, C, D, and E

Use the questions below to discuss the resources of Africa south of the Sahara:

1. **What first attracted people to Africa?**
   (Gold *p. 448*)

2. **What is the difference between subsistence and commercial farming?**
   (Subsistence farmers grow crops mostly for their own use, while commercial farmers grow crops to sell *pp. 449, 450*)

3. **How have the Bushmen stayed alive in the Kalahari?**
   (By knowing about plants. *p. 450*)

4. **Why is wildlife one of Africa's most valuable resources?**
   (It attracts tourists *p. 451*)

   Thinking Critically Why, do you think, do the Masai measure a family's wealth by the size of its cattle herds?
   (Evaluate)
   (Answers may include that cattle, not money, is the foundation of the Masai way of life. *p. 450*)

— Answers to Caption Questions —
p. 448 *l.* ▶ Hard hats
p. 448 *r.* ▶ 47 percent
p. 449 ▶ Seeds are planted into the ground by people using hoes.

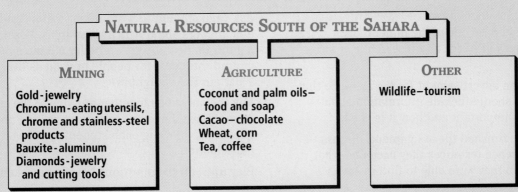

Graphic Organizer

You may wish to use this graphic organizer to help students understand natural resources which are found in Africa south of the Sahara and how they are used.

NATURAL RESOURCES SOUTH OF THE SAHARA

MINING
Gold - jewelry
Chromium - eating utensils, chrome and stainless-steel products
Bauxite - aluminum
Diamonds - jewelry and cutting tools

AGRICULTURE
Coconut and palm oils — food and soap
Cacao — chocolate
Wheat, corn
Tea, coffee

OTHER
Wildlife — tourism

Optional Activities

449

Meeting Individual Needs

Concept:
Describing the Effect of Resources

To understand how resources affect Africa's economy, it is important for students to know how the resources of Africa are used. Below are three activities that will help students understand the resources of Africa.

◆ **EASY** Ask students to make a chart with three headings: *mineral, plant,* and *animal.*

Have them place the resources described in the lesson under the appropriate heading.

◀▶ **AVERAGE** Have students write an essay describing the ways in which the resources of Africa are used.

Encourage them to think about indirect uses.

◀▮▶ **CHALLENGING** Divide students who need a challenge into small groups.

Assign each group a research project on the natural resources of Africa south of the Sahara.

Have groups create posters or bulletin-board displays that show the products derived from, and the uses of, each resource.

C. Growing Crops for Export

In the last century **commercial farms** have taken the place of many subsistence farms. A commercial farm is one that produces crops for sale. Often the crops are exported to other countries.

Products from commercial farms in the rain forest include coconut and palm oils, which are used both in foods and for making soap. **Cacao** (kuh KAY oh) is a very important commercial crop in West Africa. Most chocolate is made from African cacao beans.

Commercial farms in southern Africa and East Africa grow crops such as wheat, corn, tea, and coffee for export. About one fourth of the world's coffee now comes from Africa. East Africa is also the source of **sisal**, a plant with strong fibers used to make rope.

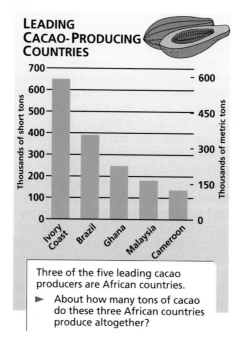

LEADING CACAO-PRODUCING COUNTRIES

Three of the five leading cacao producers are African countries.

► About how many tons of cacao do these three African countries produce altogether?

450

D. Using the Dry Lands

Survival in Deserts Africans make use of much land that is too dry for crops. The Bushmen long ago learned to live in the dry Kalahari. While many work for cattle ranches today, in the past they were food gatherers and hunters. At the end of the short rainy season, they would gather small wild melons and cucumbers to eat. During the long dry season, the Bushmen survived by eating roots. They knew, for instance, where to find a vine that stores water in its thick roots. The Bushmen's knowledge of such desert plants enabled them to stay alive where others would die of hunger and thirst.

Using the Grasslands Herders have long made use of the savanna. Their sheep and goats can graze on the dry grassland. The herders also keep some cattle, although Central Africa is not well suited for these animals because of the tsetse fly. The tsetse fly carries sleeping sickness, a disease that kills cattle.

Herds of cattle are raised on the East African plateau, however, which is largely free of the tsetse fly. The Masai people there depend largely on cattle. A family's wealth, in fact, is measured by the size of its cattle herds.

The Masai have permanent homes, and during the rainy season they are able to pasture their cattle near their villages. But when the dry season comes, the boys and men have to move about with the herds in search of grass for their cattle to eat. The Masai girls and women usually remain in the villages. They raise various vegetables and sorghum, which is a grain that can grow in fairly dry climates. Sorghum seed may be ground into meal for people or used as livestock feed.

SKILLBUILDER REVIEW

Selecting Resources On pp. 432-433, students learned about social studies resources. To practice this skill, ask students to do the following assignment.

● Have each student choose one of the mineral or agricultural resources of Africa and research it in the school library.

● Ask them to write an advertisement for the resource that they chose. The ad should include information about why the resource is important and how it is used.

● After students have finished the assignment, discuss with them the reference resources they used and what types of information they were able to find in each.

Reteaching Main Objective

★ *Explain how people in Africa south of the Sahara use natural resources.*

● Ask each student to write three "What-Am-I" questions and answers about Africa's resources. (Example: Q: I am a grain that can be grown in dry climates and that is ground into meal for people or used as livestock feed. What am I? A: Sorghum)

● Mix the questions together and divide the class into two teams. Have the teams take turns asking and answering questions, allowing each student to take a turn at participation.

● Play until all the questions have been asked.

E. Valuable Wildlife

Wildlife Resources Africa has a wide variety of wildlife. Elephants, giraffes, zebras, and many kinds of antelopes feed on the grasslands. There are big cats — lions, cheetahs, and leopards — that prey on other animals. Chimpanzees, baboons, gorillas, and a number of smaller monkeys add to the variety. Africa has an equally great variety of birds.

Wildlife is one of Africa's most valuable natural resources. For centuries, people hunted the wildlife for food, hides, and ivory. In recent times, wildlife has become valuable in another way. Animals and birds are the basis of a profitable tourist industry. Thousands of people visit Africa mainly to see the animals and birds in their natural setting.

Protecting Wildlife Yet at the same time that tourism has been growing in importance, the wildlife population has been on the decline. As the human population has increased, more and more forestland and grassland has been taken over for farms. Farmers do not want wild animals near their crops. Herders also have been driving wild animals away because they eat grass that cattle could graze on. In addition, although most African countries have laws

Wild animals roam freely in their natural setting in many parts of Africa.
▶ What animals are visible in this photograph?

protecting wildlife, poaching, or illegal hunting, continues.

Because of the declining wildlife population, there is a danger that some animals will become extinct, or die out. To protect this natural resource, game parks and reserves have been created.

LESSON 3 REVIEW

THINK AND WRITE

A. What are some of Africa's mineral resources? (Recall)
B. Summarize why the soil in some areas of the rain forest has become too poor to support crops or forest. (Infer)
C. What crops are grown on African commercial farms for export? (Recall)
D. How have Africans made use of the dry lands? (Recall)

E. Why is the African wildlife population declining? (Recall)

SKILLS CHECK

THINKING SKILL

Look at the cacao graph on page 450. Which of the leading cacao-producing countries are African? What is the leading cacao-producing country in the world? About how many tons of cacao does it produce?

451

◀ Review Master
Booklet, p. 111

Optional Activities

---

3 CLOSING THE LESSON

Lesson 3 Review

Answers to Think and Write
A. Some of Africa's mineral resources are gold, chromium, bauxite, diamonds, uranium, iron, tin, coal, and oil.
B. The soil in some areas of the rain forest has become too poor to support crops because farmers have cut and burned land every few years instead of allowing time for regrowth.
C. Crops grown for commercial export are coconut and palm oils, cacao, wheat, corn, tea, coffee, and sisal.
D. Africans have used dry lands for grazing herds of sheep, goats, and cattle.
E. The wildlife of Africa is declining in numbers because the expanding human population has taken over forests and grasslands and poaching continues.

Answer to Skills Check
Ivory Coast, Ghana, and Cameroon; Ivory Coast; about 650 thousands of short tons

Focus Your Reading
Ask the lesson focus question found at the beginning of the lesson: **What important natural resources are found in Africa south of the Sahara, and how are these resources used?**
(Chromium, bauxite, and diamonds are used to make eating utensils, aluminum, and jewelry. Coconut and palm oils are used for foods and soap; cacao is used for chocolate, and sisal is used to make rope. Twenty-five percent of the world's coffee comes from Africa. Wildlife attracts tourists.)

Additional Practice
You may wish to assign the ancillary materials listed below.

Understanding the Lesson p. 111
Workbook pp. 96-97

┌─ **Answers to Caption Questions** ─
p. 450 ▶ 1,036 thousands of short tons (940 thousands of metric tons)
p. 451 ▶ Lions

451

Using the Vocabulary

1. tropics
2. subsistence farming
3. equatorial
4. sisal
5. savanna
6. river basin
7. commercial farm
8. cacao
9. Tropic of Cancer
10. multilingual

Remembering What You Read

1. Because scientists had no knowledge of a time when that area could have supported such wildlife
2. They have a Mediterranean climate.
3. Africa is more than one-fourth desert.
4. Mount Kilimanjaro is taller than any mountain in Europe.
5. Victoria Falls is on the Zambezi River.
6. Language, religion, and customs
7. They have tall buildings, packed living quarters, and traffic jams.
8. Subsistence farmers grow crops mostly for their own use; commercial farmers produce crops for sale.
9. They gather small, wild melons and cucumbers, eat roots, and use their knowledge of desert plants to help them stay alive.
10. Game parks and reserves have been created.

CHAPTER 16 PUTTING IT ALL TOGETHER

Using the Vocabulary

savanna
Tropic of Cancer
tropics
equatorial
river basin
multilingual
subsistence farming
commercial farm
cacao
sisal

From the list, choose a vocabulary term that could be used in place of the underlined word or words in each sentence. Rewrite the sentences on a separate sheet of paper.

1. A large part of Africa is in the region that lies on either side of the Equator.
2. About two thirds of African cropland is used for the growth of crops mostly for the farmers' own use rather than for sale.
3. The lands of Central Africa and West Africa that are along the Equator receive a lot of rain.
4. East Africa is a source of a plant with strong fibers used to make rope.
5. Between the Sahara and the grassland with scattered trees and bushes is a strip of land called the Sahel.
6. On the Zaire River the area drained by the river is crossed by the Equator.
7. The crops from a farm that produces crops for sale are often exported to other countries.
8. The beans from a very important commercial crop in West Africa are used to make chocolate.
9. A large part of Africa lies between the latitude 23 1/2° north and the Tropic of Capricorn.
10. Because so many languages are used in African countries, many people there are able to speak several languages.

452

Remembering What You Read

On a separate sheet of paper, answer the following questions in complete sentences.

1. Why were the pictures found on rocks on the Tassili plateau surprising?
2. What type of climate do the northern coast and the southern tip of Africa have?
3. What type of land makes up more than a fourth of Africa?
4. Which mountain in East Africa is higher than any mountain in Europe?
5. On which African river is Victoria Falls located?
6. What three things might members of an ethnic group have in common?
7. How are large cities on the African continent similar to large cities on other continents?
8. What is the difference between subsistence farming and commercial farming?
9. How do Africans make use of land that is too dry for farming?
10. What are African countries doing to try to protect the wildlife population?

Tying Language Arts to Social Studies

Scientists have learned about the Tassili plateau from drawings that are about 8,000 years old. Write a paragraph or two describing what you would want scientists 8,000 years from now to know about the place where you live. You could also do a sketch of your ideas for scientists to discover.

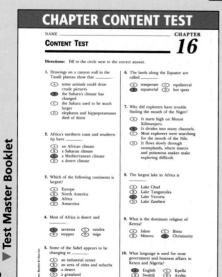

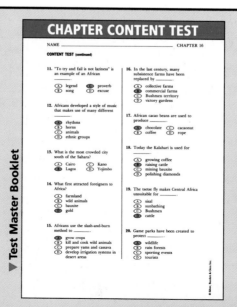

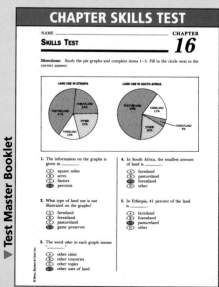

THINKING CRITICALLY

On a separate sheet of paper, answer the following questions in complete sentences.

1. How will the lives of the people of the Sahel change if all the land there becomes desert?
2. Which of the African citizens you read about in Lesson 2 would you trade places with—Kama, Binta, or the Munoru family? Explain.
3. What problems might be created by the use of so many different languages in African countries?
4. How would you restate the proverb "He who cannot dance will say the drum is bad"?
5. What do you think is the most important resource in Africa south of the Sahara? Explain.

SUMMARIZING THE CHAPTER

On a separate sheet of paper, draw a graphic organizer like the one shown here. Copy the information from this graphic organizer to the one you have drawn. Under the main idea for each lesson, write five statements that support the main idea.

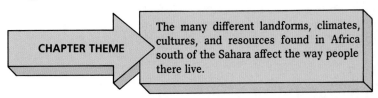

CHAPTER THEME

The many different landforms, climates, cultures, and resources found in Africa south of the Sahara affect the way people there live.

LESSON 1

There is much variety in the types of land found in Africa south of the Sahara.

1.
2.
3.
4.
5.

LESSON 2

Many different kinds of people live in Africa south of the Sahara.

1.
2.
3.
4.
5.

LESSON 3

Many important, useful natural resources are found in Africa south of the Sahara.

1.
2.
3.
4.
5.

453

Thinking Critically

1. The people will most likely have to move to another place.
2. Answers should reflect independent thinking and should be supported by the text.
3. It may result in communication difficulties and a slower exchange of ideas.
4. Envy will often cause people to be critical of skills that they do not have.
5. Answers may include minerals because they are in high demand, cacao or coffee, because they are major agricultural exports, or wildlife, because it attracts tourists.

Summarizing the Chapter

Lesson 1
1. Deserts
2. Grasslands
3. Sahel
4. Rain Forests
5. Mountains

Lesson 2
1. Christians
2. Muslims
3. Ethnic groups (like the Hausas)
4. Descendants of Indians
5. Descendants of Europeans

Lesson 3
1. Gold
2. Diamonds
3. Coffee
4. Cacao
5. Minerals

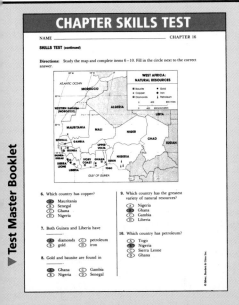

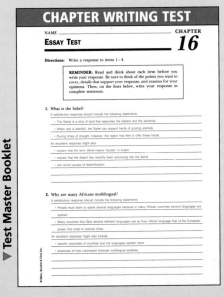

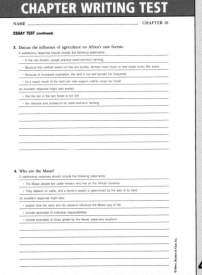

453

History of Africa South of the Sahara
(pp. 454-473)

CHAPTER RESOURCES
Review Master Booklet
  Reviewing Chapter Vocabulary, p. 118
  Place Geography, p. 119
  Summarizing the Chapter, p. 120
Chapter 17 Test

Chapter Theme: Many different African cultures developed in earlier times south of the Sahara. In the 1400s, Europeans began to explore, trade, and form colonies in this part of Africa.

LESSON 1 **West Africa**

(pp. 454-458)

Theme: West Africa's early history was passed down by storytellers.

LESSON RESOURCES
Workbook, p. 98
Review Master Booklet
  Understanding the Lesson, p. 115

LESSON 2 **East Africa**

(pp. 459-462)

Theme: The ruins at Great Zimbabwe have provided information about ancient trade, building structures, city life, and religion in East Africa.

LESSON RESOURCES
Workbook, p. 99
Review Master Booklet
  Understanding the Lesson, p. 116

LESSON 3 **Europeans South of the Sahara**

(pp. 463-471)

Theme: The Europeans, especially the Portuguese, set up trading posts along coast of Africa, captured and sold slaves, and eventually settled and began to rule African countries.

LESSON RESOURCES
Workbook, pp. 100-101
Review Master Booklet
  Understanding the Lesson, p. 117

 SOCIAL STUDIES LIBRARY: *The Slave Ship*

Review Masters

REVIEWING CHAPTER VOCABULARY

Review Study the terms in the box. Use your Glossary to find definitions of those you do not remember.

Boer	missionary	navigator	plaque
dry stone	monsoon	oral history	

Practice Complete the paragraph using terms from the box above. You may change the forms of the terms to fit the meaning.

Portuguese explorers were among the first Europeans to visit Africa. The Portuguese had a school where they trained sailors and explorers. The people from this school were good (1) _navigators_, and they found the best sea routes to Africa. Other explorers and traders were also interested in Africa. They came by ship from India and Arabia, using the (2) _monsoons_ to help blow them to the coast of East Africa. Later, European (3) _missionaries_ followed explorers and traders to Africa. These people came because they wanted to teach African people about the Christian religion. The African people often found the appearance and ways of these foreign visitors very strange. Soon stories about these visitors and the new things they brought were told by storytellers. The stories were handed on from person to person as part of the (4) _oral history_ of Africa.

Write Write a sentence of your own for each term in the box above. You may use the back of the sheet.

Sentences should show that students understand the meanings of the terms.

_____
_____
_____
_____
_____
_____
_____
_____
_____
_____

Use with Chapter 17, pages 455–471.

© Silver, Burdett & Ginn Inc.

LOCATING PLACES

✱ Listed below are places that were of cultural and economic importance to medieval Africa and in later times. Use the Gazetteer in your textbook to find the latitude and longitude of each place. Then locate and label each on the map. (The names of the modern countries are given in parentheses.)

		LAT. ⊖	LONG. ⊕			LAT. ⊖	LONG. ⊕
1.	Timbuktu (Mali)	16°N	2°W	6.	Khartoum (Sudan)	15°N	32°E
2.	Jenné (Mali)	14°N	5°W	7.	Nairobi (Kenya)	1°S	37°E
3.	Great Zimbabwe (Zimbabwe)	20°S	31°E	8.	Mount Kenya (Kenya)	0°	37°E
4.	Lalibella (Ethiopia)	12°N	39°E	9.	Mount Kilimanjaro (Tanzania)	3°N	37°E
5.	Kilwa (Tanzania)	9°S	39°E	10.	Victoria Falls (Senegal)	18°S	26°E

© Silver, Burdett & Ginn Inc.

Use with Chapter 17, pages 455–471.

SUMMARIZING THE CHAPTER

✱ Complete this graphic organizer. Under each question, write four answers from the chapter.

CHAPTER THEME Many different African cultures developed in earlier times south of the Sahara. In the 1400s, Europeans began to explore, trade, and form colonies in this part of Africa.

What was life like in the kingdoms of West Africa?

1. Many people involved in trade
2. Religious education in Mali
3. Most people of Benin were forest farmers.
4. Benin used plaques to tell their history.

What were some of the achievements of people living in East Africa?

1. Built stone structures
2. Used monsoons for tradewinds
3. Built large cities
4. Decorated buildings with carvings

What role did Europeans play in Africa south of the Sahara?

1. Europeans sold Africans into slavery.
2. Europeans took some land away.
3. Europeans made colonies of African lands.
4. Europeans tried to Christianize Africans.

Use with Chapter 17, pages 455–471.

© Silver, Burdett & Ginn Inc.

C17-B

Workbook Pages

THE KINGDOM OF BENIN

Gathering Information from a Map, Hypothesizing

✶ Study the map of trade routes through the sixteenth-century kingdom of Benin. Then answer the questions that follow.

1. Which cities were located in the kingdom of Benin?
Gwato, Benin, Lagos, and Bonny

TRADE ROUTES
THROUGH
SIXTEENTH-
CENTURY BENIN

☐ Kingdom of Benin
● Cities
→ Trade routes
— Present-day boundaries

0   75   150 miles
0   75   150 kilometers

2. Which cities were situated on the trade route to West Africa?
Old Oyo and Ife

3. Which river would a trader bringing dates and figs to Benin from North Africa cross?
Niger

4. In which direction would a trader taking cotton goods and firearms from Benin to the Gold Coast travel?
west

5. How do you think the kingdom of Benin's location helped make it a center for trade?
It was in the path of both land and sea trade routes.

6. At its widest point, east to west, about how many miles across was the kingdom of Benin?
275 miles

7. About how many miles did the kingdom of Benin extend from north to south?
250 miles

8. If a camel caravan from Kano arrived in Gwato, about how many miles had the caravan traveled? 550 miles

Thinking Further: Besides waiting for goods to trade, why else do you think people in the kingdom of Benin might have looked forward to the arrival of camel caravans?
Students might mention that people would look forward to hearing about other parts of the world.

© Silver, Burdett & Ginn Inc.

DISCOVERING THE PAST

Hypothesizing Based on Information, Generating Unstated Ideas

✶ The following statements describe discoveries made by archaeologists in Zimbabwe. What might these discoveries tell us about people of long ago? On the lines beneath each statement, write what the clues might reveal about the people who left them.
Answers should reflect independent thinking. Suggested answers are provided.

1. Archaeologists in Zimbabwe have recovered pieces of Chinese porcelain and Iranian cloth. The people of Zimbabwe traded for goods from faraway places.

2. Huge stone structures, still standing in Zimbabwe after hundreds of years, were built without mortar. The people who built the structures were skilled in construction and design. They may not have had the necessary materials to make a suitable mortar.

3. Carved stone figures and gold ornaments have been found by archaeologists in Zimbabwe. Some of the people were artistic. They may have used gold ornaments for trade.

4. In the Middle Ages, an Ethiopian king had 11 churches carved from solid stone.
Religion was important to the people. The stone carvers were highly skilled engineers.

Thinking Further: If archaeologists discovered your classroom 1,000 years from now, what would the things they found tell them? Choose two objects in your classroom and describe what they would reveal. (Remember that an object would have to be solid and strong to last for 1,000 years.)
Students may mention that a chalkboard would reveal how teachers wrote so all the students could see, and a desk would reveal how students did their work and stored their school supplies.

© Silver, Burdett & Ginn Inc.

FINDING INFORMATION

Selecting and Using Appropriate Resources, Classifying Information

✶ Reference books present information in such a way that people can easily find what they need. If you were doing research on Africa, you might look up the article "Africa" in an encyclopedia. The article would probably be organized in sections, such as those in the following list. Read the questions below and decide in which section you would look *first* to find the information to answer the question. Write the letter of the appropriate section in the blank.

A. Geography
B. Climate
C. Population
D. Language
E. Religion
F. Music and Architecture
G. Natural Resources
H. Agriculture
I. Manufacturing
J. Trade
K. History

K **1.** Which African kingdom remained Christian in the Middle Ages?

J **2.** What are the main exports and imports of Africa?

A **3.** What landforms are found in Zimbabwe?

G **4.** Where is salt found?

D **5.** How did Swahili develop?

I **6.** What kinds of machinery are produced in Egypt?

H **7.** What animals are raised for food in Ghana?

K **8.** Who was the first ruler of Songhai?

G **9.** On what waterway was the city of Gao located?

K **10.** Who defeated the kingdom of Songhai?

H **11.** What is the major crop in southern Nigeria?

J **12.** What metals were exported from Kilwa?

B **13.** What is a monsoon?

F **14.** What do the buildings of Timbuktu look like?

K **15.** What led to the downfall of Ghana?

E **16.** What is the main religion of North Africa?

F **17.** What musical instruments were originally invented in Africa?

C **18.** What is the largest city of modern Africa?

Thinking Further: Besides encyclopedias, what other kinds of resources would be helpful for doing research about Africa? Tell what kinds of information might be obtained from each type of resource you name.
Possible answers: atlas of Africa; collection of African folktales, short stories, or poems; recordings of African music; newspaper and magazine articles; films and videotapes on Africa; person who comes from Africa or has lived there.

© Silver, Burdett & Ginn Inc.

THE BENEFITS OF TRADE

Drawing Conclusions, Understanding Expository Text, Hypothesizing

✶ Read the passage below about trade. In the statements that follow, circle the phrase that best completes each sentence.

Today, if you needed a new notebook, you would go to a store and buy it with money. You would choose one of the many notebooks the store owner had purchased from a supplier, who had bought it from a manufacturer. The manufacturer produced the notebook using paper from a paper mill, which made the paper out of wood supplied by a lumber company. All these steps from tree to notebook to you involved the process of trade. Trade is the buying and selling of goods or services. At each stage in the process, someone should earn a profit. For example, the store owner may have paid $1.00 for the notebook and sold it to you for $1.50, making a profit of 50 cents.

Hundreds of years ago, traders did much more than supply goods and make profits. Before the development of modern communications systems, the business of trade provided a way for people from different parts of the world to exchange information. Trade routes, both overland and by sea, brought peoples of different cultures into contact with one another. As trade increased, trading centers along the major trade routes grew and prospered. In these centers, people who lived thousands of miles apart learned about each other's customs and ideas.

As time passed, people began to look for safer, faster, and more convenient trade routes. The search for better trade routes led Europeans to find a sea route around Africa and to explore lands previously unknown to them.

1. Each step in the process of trade involves (a) a buyer and a seller (b) a manufacturer and a storekeeper (c) a store and a customer.

2. In the process of trade, the goal at each step is that (a) goods are sold (b) the customer is always right (c) someone makes a profit.

3. Trade provided a peaceful means for (a) an exchange of ideas (b) a market (c) a journey.

4. Trading centers grew (a) during times of war (b) as trade increased (c) only if they were on a waterway.

5. People in large trading centers learned more about (a) art and religion (b) other parts of the world (c) remote villages.

6. As some overland trade routes became dangerous or difficult, (a) armies were hired to protect the camel caravans (b) explorers began to search for sea routes to faraway trading centers (c) trade began to decline.

Thinking Further: Besides trade, how else do you think people hundreds of years ago in different parts of the world learned about each other? Write your answer on a separate sheet.
Students may point out that wars brought people in contact; sometimes slaves provided information about their homelands.

© Silver, Burdett & Ginn Inc.

C17-C

TEACHER NOTES

West Africa

Objectives

★ 1. **Compare** life in Mali with life in Benin.

2. **Explain** why Timbuktu became a center for trade.

3. **Identify** the following people and places: *Sundiata, Mansa Musa, Ewuare, Niger River, Mali, Timbuktu, Sahara, Jenné, Benin,* and *Nigeria.*

1 STARTING THE LESSON

Motivation Activity

■ Explain to students that some of the early civilizations of West Africa had no system of writing. Instead, they preserved their history orally or through art.

■ Ask students to imagine that we have no system of writing.

■ Then ask them which events that have occurred in their lives they would like to share with their children.

■ Give students an opportunity to describe these events as they would recount them to their children.

Think About What You Know

■ Assign the THINK ABOUT WHAT YOU KNOW activity on p. 455.

■ Student answers should reflect independent thinking but may include events such as weddings and accomplishments by different family members.

Study the Vocabulary

■ Have students look up each of the new vocabulary words in the Glossary.

■ Challenge students to use the vocabulary words in one sentence that expresses the interrelationship of the terms.

CHAPTER **17**

HISTORY OF AFRICA SOUTH OF THE SAHARA

The climate and land of the continent of Africa produced cultures rich in crafts, music, and dance. African trading states, such as Kilwa, developed in this region in earlier times.

Optional Activities

For Your Information

The Camel Caravans   Commercial caravans carrying trade goods were not the only type of caravan to cross the Sahara. Some caravans were organized to carry people back and forth on religious pilgrimages. Others were organized by armed bandits to raid the commercial caravans, which were loaded with goods. The most common caravan, however, was the commercial one. A large caravan would include between 500 and 2,000 camels and would be about 2 miles (3.2 km) to 8 miles (12.9 km) in length. Small caravans often had fewer than 100 camels.

West Africa

THINK ABOUT WHAT YOU KNOW
Some history, such as that of a family, is handed down by word of mouth. What kinds of things have you heard about that happened in your family before you were born?

STUDY THE VOCABULARY
oral history   plaque

FOCUS YOUR READING
What was life like in the kingdoms of West Africa?

A. Sundiata, the African Alexander

Handing Down History Storytellers were the historians of Africa 700 years ago. Like the Greek poet Homer, they told about the heroes and kings of past times. The storytellers did not find their stories in books, however. Accounts of the past were handed down by word of mouth from one generation to another. Such knowledge is called **oral history**. For this oral history to be remembered, the storyteller had to be entertaining as well as informative. Some of the most famous of these African stories are the Anansi (ah NAHN see) tales. You can read an Anansi tale in the literature selection on page 456.

Stories of the past greatly interested a boy named Sundiata (sun JAHT ah), who was born the son of a king ca. 1210 in a West African village. Most stories Sundiata heard were about African rulers and heroes, but the storytellers also told about Alexander the Great. As you recall from Chapter 2, Alexander was the young king of ancient Macedonia who conquered Greece and other lands and formed an empire. The African storytellers called Alexander "the mighty king of gold and silver whose sun shone over half the world."

Sundiata's Kingdom Sundiata was also curious about faraway places. He liked to talk with travelers who came to his village and often questioned them about the lands on the other side of the Sahara. After Sundiata became king, ca. 1230, he conquered neighboring lands and created the Mali kingdom. The kingdom included most of the land between the Atlantic coast and the great bend of the Niger River. Today seven countries lie in this area.

In later times when storytellers told about Sundiata's kingdom, they called him "the king of kings." They compared him with Alexander the Great. One modern historian has even called Sundiata "the African Alexander."

B. The Wealth of Mansa Musa

Mansa Musa, a descendant of Sundiata, ruled the Mali kingdom from ca. 1307 to ca. 1332. The kingdom was rich in gold. The king of Mali rewarded officials and soldiers with beautiful gold collars, bracelets, and even trousers, much as governments today award medals.

Many of the people of the Mali kingdom followed the old African religions, but Mansa Musa was a Muslim. In 1324 he led a large group of his Muslim subjects on a pilgrimage to Mecca, the Muslim holy city in Arabia.

On the way, Mansa Musa and his party stopped in Cairo, Egypt. The people there were dazzled by Mansa Musa's great wealth, and they were awed by his generosity. Mansa Musa gave away so much gold that its price remained low in Cairo for several years.

455

---

2 DEVELOPING THE LESSON

Read and Think

Sections A, B, C, and D

Summarize what life was like in Mali and Benin by asking the following questions:

1. **Who was Sundiata and what lands were a part of his empire?**
(A West African king who created the Mali empire, which included most of the land between the Atlantic coast and the Niger River *p. 455*)

2. **What was the source of Mali's wealth?**
(Gold *p. 455*)

3. **Why did Timbuktu become a trade center?**
(Its location was perfect for traders traveling by camel or canoe. *p. 457*)

4. **What kinds of work did the people of Benin do?**
(Most were farmers, but some were craftworkers, hunters, soldiers, or entertainers. *pp. 457-458*)

Thinking Critically What kinds of work, do you think, did the people of Mali do? (Infer)
(Answers may include gold mining, making jewelry, and trading. *p. 455*)

Writing to Learn

Writing a Letter Ask students to imagine that they are part of a camel caravan from Cairo that has just arrived in Timbuktu.

- Have students write a letter to their families in Egypt describing what the city and the people of Timbuktu are like.

- Ask student volunteers to read their letter aloud to the class. Discuss how their descriptions are alike and how they are different.

Comparing Leaders

- Divide the class into two groups for a debate.

- Tell students that they will be debating the following statement: Mansa Musa did more for the people of Mali than any other Mali ruler.

- Give students five to ten minutes to prepare their arguments. Then hold the debate.

- When the debate is finished, have students decide which group made the most convincing arguments.

Optional Activities

Use the information below to help students better understand the literature selection found on p. 456.

Selection Summary

The tale of how wisdom was spread throughout the world is only one of a number of stories about Anansi the spider. One tale tells how Anansi acquired the pot of wisdom described in this tale. The people of an Ashanti village came to Anansi for help in catching a python that had been troubling them for years. Anansi developed a clever plan to catch it, using a combination of food and flattery. For his successful efforts, God rewarded Anansi with a pot of wisdom.

Guided Reading

1. **Why was Anansi having a difficult time climbing the tree?**
   (He was carrying the pot of wisdom by a rope around his neck. This prevented him from getting a good grip on the tree.)

2. **Why was Anansi furious with his son?**
   (His son advised him to tie the pot to his back to free his hands. Anansi realized that his son was right, which made him mad.)

3. **How was wisdom spread throughout the world?**
   (As Anansi started to scold his son, he lost his grip on the pot of wisdom. It crashed to the ground, split open, and its contents were scattered far and wide.)

Literature-Social Studies Connection

1. **Why, do you think, were the tales of Anansi such good stories for storytellers to tell?**
   (Answers should reflect independent thinking but may include that not only were they entertaining, but they also ended with a moral that passed wisdom from one generation to another.)

456

FROM:
The Anansi Tales

By: Peggy Appiah
Setting: African forest

Anansi, the spider, sometimes called Kwaku (Uncle) Anansi, is the trickster hero of the Ashanti peoples of Africa. His adventures were passed down orally in the form of folk tales.

In the story "How Wisdom Was Spread Throughout the World," Anansi, sometimes spelled *Ananse*, was the only wise creature in the world. Being greedy, he wished to keep all this wisdom to himself. He asked his wife to store his wisdom in a big pot so he could hide it safely in a big tree in the forest.

Carrying the pot in front of him, he made his way through the forest, followed—unbeknown—by his small son Ntikuma. At last he reached the great tree and started to try climbing it. He hung the pot by a rope around his neck, with the stopper just below his nose so he could make quite sure it did not tip over.

Alas, try as he would, Kwaku Ananse could not climb the tree, for the pot got in the way of his arms and he found he was unable to grip the trunk. He tried, and he tried, and he tried. . .

Ananse's son, watching from behind a tree, advised his father to tie the pot to his back to free his hands.

Ananse was furious. Here his small son was teaching him a lesson—a lesson which he realized was only too true. Shaking with anger and exhaustion he lifted the pot, meaning to take it off and chastise [scold] his son. His hands were slippery with sweat and the great pot was heavy. It slipped through his fingers and crashed to the ground.

The pot burst open and its contents were scattered far and wide. There was a storm coming, and the wind swept through the forest, lifting the wisdom and carrying it on its way. The rain poured down and swept the wisdom into the streams, which carried it into the sea. Thus was wisdom spread throughout the world. . . .

456

Reteaching Main Objective

⭐ *Compare life in Mali with life in Benin.*

- Draw a table on the chalkboard with these headings along the top: *Mali* and *Benin*. Along the side, write these headings: *Sources of Wealth, Occupations, Type of Government, Religion,* and *Leaders.*

- Have students fill in the information as a class activity.

- Conclude by asking several individuals to summarize the comparison chart aloud as all students copy the information into their notebooks for future reference.

C. Centers of Trade and Learning

Trade Timbuktu was one of the most important cities of the Mali kingdom. An old saying described its location on the edge of the Sahara near the Niger River as "the meeting place for all who travel by camel and canoe."

Camel caravans crossed the desert, loaded with silks, brassware, steel weapons, and other goods from North Africa, Europe, and the Middle East. The caravans also carried blocks of salt from salt mines in the Sahara. Salt was scarce south of the Sahara. It was so valuable that in some places it was used for money. Traders exchanged these goods in Timbuktu for gold, copper, ivory, cotton cloth, and other products brought by boats on the Niger River.

Teachers and Students Timbuktu was known for its learned Muslim teachers as well as its traders. The city had several large mosques where people came to study. Because of the many students and teachers, traders brought bundles of books to Timbuktu. It was said that books sold for more money than any other goods.

Jenné was another center of trade and learning in the Mali kingdom. It was located farther upstream on the river.

D. Benin, Kingdom in the Forest

Farm and Town The kingdom of Benin (be NEEN) was located in what is now southern Nigeria. An early king named Ewuare made Benin the most powerful state in this part of Africa.

Most people in the kingdom were forest farmers. They used the slash-and-burn method as some farmers today still do. The king of Benin lived in a walled town. The houses of craftworkers and people who

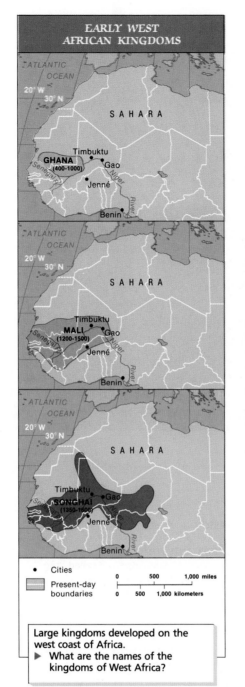

EARLY WEST AFRICAN KINGDOMS

- Cities
- Present-day boundaries

0   500   1,000 miles
0   500   1,000 kilometers

Large kingdoms developed on the west coast of Africa.
► What are the names of the kingdoms of West Africa?

Meeting Individual Needs
Concept: Making Inferences

To better understand the early civilizations of West Africa, it is important to make inferences. Below are three activities that will help your students make inferences.

◆ **EASY** Ask students to discuss possible reasons why most of the Benin people lived in a walled town.

◀▶ **AVERAGE** Have students discuss why the king lived in an enclosed area.

◀▮▶ **CHALLENGING** Have students discuss what the plaques tell us about the Benin people.

GEOGRAPHY THEMES

Place

■ Have students refer to the map of West Africa on this page to answer the following question: **What river formed part of the western boundary of the kingdom of Ghana?**
(The Senegal River)

Answers to Caption Questions
p. 457 ► Ghana, Mali, and Songhai

Curriculum Connection

Literature After students have read the tale of Anansi, ask them to write their own tale about him.

● Tell students that other Anansi tales include: "How Kwaku Ananse was punished for his Bad Manners," "How Kwaku Ananse became Bald," and "How Kwaku Ananse won a Kingdom with a Grain of Corn." Have students write a story that might accompany one of these titles.

● Encourage students to use the characters described in the Anansi tale in their text, as well as any others that they wish to invent.

For Your Information

Cities of the African Empires Although the cities of the various African empires served a variety of different purposes, studies have shown that these cities had a number of characteristics in common. They all were surrounded by walls, made use of passageways, and preserved elements of nature within them. Walls provided protection, privacy, and a place to store things in times of trouble. Passageways directed traffic to places of importance such as the royal palace or the central marketplace. Trees and parks were common sights in African cities and were in keeping with the belief that the earth was the source of life.

Optional Activities

457

3 CLOSING THE LESSON

Lesson 1 Review

Answers to Think and Write

A. Like Alexander the Great, Sundiata conquered many lands, created an empire, and was a great ruler.

B. Answers may include that Mansa Musa was religious, because he led a group of his Muslim subjects on a pilgrimage to Mecca, and that he was generous, because he gave away many gold objects.

C. Timbuktu and Jenné were two important centers of trade and learning in Mali.

D. Most people in Benin were farmers, craftworkers, or people in service to the king.

Answer to Skills Check

Time lines should represent the events and dates in chronological order: Magna Carta is signed, 1215; Sundiata becomes king, 1230; Mansa Musa goes to Mecca, 1324; Gutenberg develops new printing method, ca. 1455; Portuguese traders visit Benin, 1486; Columbus reaches America, 1492.

Focus Your Reading

Ask the lesson focus question found at the beginning of the lesson: **What was life like in the kingdoms of West Africa?**
(The people of Mali made their livings in occupations related to gold or trade. Mali had two great towns that were important centers of trade and learning. In Benin, most people made their living as farmers, but some were craftworkers or worked in service to the king.)

Additional Practice

You may wish to assign the ancillary materials listed below.

Understanding the Lesson p. 115
Workbook p. 98

served the king stood along the town's broad streets. The king and members of his household lived in an enclosed area in the middle of the town. Their houses had wooden pillars decorated with bronze **plaques**, or sheets of metal. The plaques showed kings, queens, hunters, soldiers, musicians, and acrobats. Figures of animals also decorated the plaques.

Ways of Learning The plaques were more than decorations, however. They served as historical records. Benin had no system of writing. Storytellers passed on accounts of the past, and the plaques served as reminders of those events.

In 1486, Portuguese traders visited Benin. They found that the king of Benin was as curious about Portugal as they were about Benin. When the Portuguese ships set sail, one of the king's advisers was on board. He was sent by the king to find out more about the kingdom of Portugal.

Artists from the kingdom of Benin were skilled in sculpting figures from bronze.
▶ Who do you think these bronze statues might depict?

LESSON **1** REVIEW

THINK AND WRITE

A. Why has Sundiata been called "the African Alexander"? (Infer)

B. How would you describe what kind of person Mansa Musa was? (Evaluate)

C. What were two important centers of trade and learning in Mali? (Recall)

D. Give a brief summary of what most people in Benin did for a living. (Recall)

SKILLS CHECK

THINKING SKILL

Make a time line showing the following events: the Magna Carta is signed, 1215; Sundiata becomes king, 1230; Mansa Musa goes to Mecca, 1324; Gutenberg develops new printing method, ca. 1455; Portuguese traders visit Benin, 1486; Columbus discovers America, 1492.

Optional Activities

UNDERSTANDING THE LESSON

NAME _____
UNDERSTANDING THE LESSON
CHAPTER **17**

Organizing Facts   LESSON 1 CONTENT MASTER

✳ The chart shows the main ideas of the lesson. Fill in the blank spaces with the details that support each main idea. The first one has been done for you.
Suggested answers are provided.

Because of his conquests, Sundiata was called "the African Alexander."	Under Mansa Musa, the Mali Empire enjoyed great wealth.
1. He conquered neighboring lands to create the Mali empire.	1. The empire was rich in gold.
2. The empire included most of the land between the Atlantic coast and the great bend of the Niger River.	2. The king rewarded officials and soldiers with golden gifts.
	3. In Cairo, Mansa Musa gave away so much gold that its price dropped.

Great African Empires South of the Sahara

Mali cities became centers of trade.	Benin was a kingdom in the forest.
1. Camel caravans brought silks, brassware, and sea glass to Timbuktu.	1. Ewuare made Benin a powerful African state.
2. Traders from Niger area brought gold, copper, ivory, and cotton cloth.	2. Most of the people were forest farmers.
3. Jenné was also a center of trade.	3. The people used plaques to remember past events.

Think and Write: Write a paragraph describing why books cost so much in Timbuktu. You may use the back of the sheet.
Answers should reflect independent thinking; suggestions appear in the Answer Key.

Use with textbook pages 455–458.   115

◀ **Review Master Booklet, p. 115**

THINK ABOUT WHAT YOU KNOW

If you were an archaeologist, what would you look for that would tell you about people who lived long ago?

STUDY THE VOCABULARY

dry stone   monsoon

FOCUS YOUR READING

What were some of the achievements of people living in East Africa?

A. Clues About the Past in Zimbabwe

Stone Ruins The remains of stone structures in southeast Africa provide many clues about the past. The most famous ruins are those at Great Zimbabwe (zihm BAHB way) National Park, in Zimbabwe. The structures there are the largest built south of the Sahara before modern times.

Huge boulders connected by stone walls cover a hill at Great Zimbabwe. At the foot of the hill is a walled enclosure with a cone-shaped tower inside. The enclosure walls are about 17 feet (5 m) thick at the base. The tower is about 34 feet (10 m) high, although it may once have been taller. All of the structures were built with **dry stones**, that is, stones held together without mortar.

Studying the Ruins Archaeologists who have studied Great Zimbabwe think that the largest stone structure there was built about 500 years ago. They believe it served as the residence of kings who ruled this part of Africa.

Archaeologists have recovered some objects at Zimbabwe that were used by the people who once lived there. They have found carved stone figures and gold ornaments made by African craftworkers. They have also uncovered glassware from the Middle East, and delicate porcelain, or very fine earthenware, from China.

Great Zimbabwe, now lying in ruins, was built by the Shona people.
▶ What material did the Shona use to build these walls?

The Granger Collection

459

Making a Time Line

● Have students make a time line of important events in the history of the city of Great Zimbabwe.

● Put the following dates and events on the chalkboard:
1868—Europeans first discover the ruins of Great Zimbabwe; 1000—Construction begins on the city of Great Zimbabwe; 2—First inhabitants settle on the site that is to become Great Zimbabwe; 1425—Great Zimbabwe is the center of the Monomatapa Empire.

● Have students put these dates and events in correct chronological order on a time line.

Optional Activities

East Africa

Objectives

★1. **List** the ways in which Ethiopia was different from other East African kingdoms.

2. **Explain** how we know about the civilization that lived in Zimbabwe.

3. **Identify** the following people and places: *Vasco da Gama, Solomon, Queen Makeda, King Ezana, King Lalibela, Great Zimbabwe National Park, Indian Ocean,* and *Ethiopia.*

1 STARTING THE LESSON

Motivation Activity

■ Ask students to imagine that they live in an isolated area without access to television or newspapers.

■ Have students discuss how this isolation would affect their lives.

■ Tell students that they will study an isolated culture in this lesson.

Think About What You Know

■ Assign the THINK ABOUT WHAT YOU KNOW activity on p. 459.

■ Student answers should reflect independent thinking but may include tools, weapons, household goods, jewelry, human bones, and the remains of buildings.

Study the Vocabulary

■ Have students look up the new vocabulary words in the Glossary.

■ Then have them categorize the words by asking them which word relates to architecture and which relates to climate.

┌─ Answers to Caption Questions ─┐

p. 458 ▶ Answers may include a king and his attendants.
p. 459 ▶ Dry stones

459

Read and Think

Sections A, B, and C

To summarize the information about the early people of East Africa, ask the following questions:

1. **What purpose do archaeologists think the largest stone structure at Great Zimbabwe served?**
   (The residence of kings *p. 459*)

2. **When would East African traders sail to other continents?**
   (Between May and September *p. 460*)

3. **How did isolation affect Ethiopia?**
   (Ethiopia kept its own language and religious beliefs. *p. 461*)

   Thinking Critically **Which Ethiopian king, do you think, made the greatest contribution to Ethiopian culture?**
   (Evaluate)
   (Answers may include King Ezana, for adopting Christianity, or King Lalibela for building stone churches. *pp. 461-462*)

GEOGRAPHY THEMES

Place

■ Ask students to refer to the map on p. 461 to answer the following question: **Which of the two kingdoms shown on this map is larger?**
(Ethiopia)

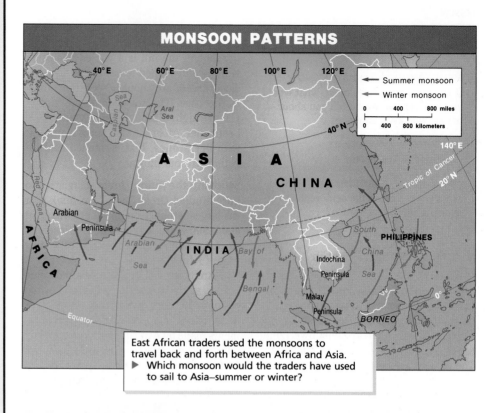

MONSOON PATTERNS

→ Summer monsoon
→ Winter monsoon

0   400   800 miles
0   400   800 kilometers

East African traders used the monsoons to travel back and forth between Africa and Asia.
▶ Which monsoon would the traders have used to sail to Asia—summer or winter?

B. Trade on a Path of Wind

Trade Grows Great Zimbabwe is more than 200 miles (322 km) from the sea. The porcelain found there must have been traded in cities on the East African coast. Goods from Asia came into these ports.

The trading ships often sailed with the seasonal winds of the Indian Ocean. These winds, called **monsoons**, change direction with the seasons. From May to September the summer monsoon blows from the southwest. By sailing with the wind, ships were carried from Africa to Arabia or even farther east to India. From November to March the monsoon blows in the opposite direction, so ships could sail from Arabia or India back to Africa. No

wonder that one writer described a monsoon as a "path of wind."

Ships coming from Arabia and India carried products from those lands and goods from still more distant places. In this way fine cloth from Persia and porcelain from China reached East Africa.

Cities Grow During the Middle Ages, trade increased and the coastal cities grew. When the Portuguese explorer Vasco da Gama reached East Africa, he was surprised to find such well-built cities. He reported that Kilwa had "good buildings of stone." Houses within that walled city rose to three and four stories and stood so close together that one could "run along the tops of them."

460

Optional Activities

Curriculum Connection

Art Have students illustrate on a piece of drawing paper one of the important events in Ethiopian history.

● Tell students to depict the story of Queen Makeda and Solomon, the achievements of King Ezana, or the contribution of King Lalibela.

Reteaching Main Objective

⭐ *List the ways in which Ethiopia was different from other East African kingdoms.*

● Have groups of students prepare a "History Minute" for television that deals with the kingdom of Ethiopia.

● Students' programs should highlight what made this kingdom different from other East African kingdoms.

● Have students first skim the lesson and list these differences. If students need help, tell them to consider religion, livelihood, language, and art. Then, have them write the scripts for their History Minutes.

● Finally, have students present their television programs for the class.

Europeans South of the Sahara

Would you like to be an explorer? If you were one, where would you go? Why?

STUDY THE VOCABULARY
navigator   missionary
Boer

FOCUS YOUR READING
What role did Europeans play in Africa south of the Sahara?

A. Portuguese Exploration

Henry the Navigator Prince Henry of Portugal was called "the Navigator." It was, perhaps, a strange title for a man who seldom went to sea. A **navigator** plans and steers a course through water or air, or on land. Yet although Henry remained in Portugal most of the time, he did plan the courses for the ships he sent to explore the west coast of Africa.

Henry the Navigator set up a school for sailors and explorers on the southwest coast of Portugal. He sent ships to explore the African coast. The captains recorded what they saw as they sailed farther south. Henry had maps for later expeditions made based on this information.

Exploration Continues Prince Henry died in 1460, but the Portuguese continued to travel along the African coast. By 1482 a Portuguese ship had sailed as far south as the Equator. Six years later Bartholomeu Dias (bahr THAHL uh myoo DEE us) discovered the Cape of Good Hope at the southern tip of Africa. This discovery showed that it was possible to sail around

Africa. A few years later, Vasco da Gama sailed around the Cape to the east coast.

Prince Henry sent out ships because he had great curiosity about Africa. Other Portuguese may have shared Henry's desire to know more, but it was not curiosity alone that caused them to explore the African coast. The Portuguese wanted to trade for Africa's gold, ivory, pepper, and slaves.

B. Kidnapped by Slave Traders

One Villager's Tale Slave traders from other countries followed the Portuguese to the African coast. Over the next 350 years, millions of Africans were captured and transported to the Americas.

Prince Henry the Navigator of Portugal established a school for sailors and explorers.
▶ What is Prince Henry holding?

PRINCE HENRY OF PORTUGAL

Writing to Learn

Writing an Obituary Have students write an obituary for Prince Henry the Navigator.

● Ask students to imagine that they are reporters for a Portuguese newspaper in the year 1460. Tell students that their editor-in-chief wants them to write Prince Henry's obituary.

● Remind students that the obituary should include information about the things Prince Henry accomplished and the achievements for which he will be remembered.

● Have volunteers read their obituaries to the class.

Optional Activities

Europeans South of the Sahara

Objectives

★1. **Explain** why European countries became interested in Africa.

2. **List** the reasons why the Portuguese explored the coast of Africa.

3. **Describe** the slave trade.

4. **Identify** the following people and places: *Prince Henry, Bartholomeu Dias, Vasco da Gama, Olaudah Equiano, David Livingstone, Cape of Good Hope, South Africa, Victoria Falls, Kalahari, Ethiopia, Liberia,* and *Gold Coast.*

1 STARTING THE LESSON

Motivation Activity

■ Discuss with students why most American Indians were forced to move from lands they had lived on for hundreds of years.

■ Explain how the attitudes of Indians and whites differed toward land ownership.

■ Tell students that a similar situation developed in Africa in the nineteenth century.

Think About What You Know

■ Assign the THINK ABOUT WHAT YOU KNOW activity on p. 463.

■ Student answers should reflect independent thinking and imagination.

Study the Vocabulary

■ Ask students if they know the definition of any of the new vocabulary words.

■ Have the students use the Glossary to see if they were correct.

Answers to Caption Questions
p. 462 ▶ The shape of a cross
p. 463 ▶ A spear

2 DEVELOPING THE LESSON

Read and Think

Section A

Prince Henry of Portugal's support of the exploration of Africa had a great effect on that continent. Discuss his influence on Africans by asking the following questions:

1. **What navigational contributions did Prince Henry make?**
   (He established a school in Portugal for sailors and explorers, sent out ships to explore the African coast, and had maps made that were based on these voyages. *p. 463*)

2. **Why was Prince Henry called "the navigator"?**
   (He planned the courses for the ships that he sent to explore the west coast of Africa. *p. 463*)

   Thinking Critically Do you think the Portuguese would have explored Africa's coast if they hadn't been interested in trade items and slaves?
   (Hypothesize)
   (Answers may include yes, because they could still use the knowledge for navigational purposes, or no, because there would not have been enough reason to do so. *p. 463*)

Many African slaves died of disease or cruel treatment during voyages in overcrowded ships.
▶ How were the slaves mistreated?

A book written by an African named Olaudah Equiano (oh LOU duh ek wee-AHN oh) tells what it was like to be captured and sold as a slave. Equiano was born around 1745 in a village in Benin. As he remembered it, the village was a very pleasant place. The villagers raised their own food, built their own dwellings, and largely managed their own affairs. The village was far from the king's town and from the sea. Equiano wrote in his book that as a child he had "never heard of white men or Europeans."

The people of Equiano's village had a few slaves. It was the practice to enslave rather than kill persons captured in war. When European traders came to Africa, the demand for slaves increased. Slave traders kidnapped people and took them to the European trading posts, where they were sold and shipped to distant lands.

Sold into Slavery When Olaudah Equiano was 12 years old, he and his sister were stolen from their African home. The kidnappers sold the two young captives to other slave traders, and they were passed from one owner to another. Olaudah was separated from his sister, and after about six months he was taken to the coast. Olaudah was put on board a slave ship, where he was roughly handled and mistreated by the sailors. Many years later, Equiano remembered how terrified he was that day he was carried on board.

I was now persuaded that I had gotten into a world of bad spirits and that they were going to kill me. Their complexions too differing so much from ours, their long hair and the language they spoke (which was very different from any I had ever heard) united to confirm me in this belief.

464

Mapping Routes

- Distribute outline maps of the Eastern Hemisphere to the class.

- Ask students to use the information in Section A and their Atlas maps to help them draw the routes of Portuguese explorers Dias and Da Gama.

- Tell students to label Portugal, Africa, the Cape of Good Hope, the Equator, and the oceans on which the explorers traveled. Remind them to include a map key identifying the routes traveled by Dias and Da Gama.

- Display finished maps on a bulletin board.

Equiano's fears increased when he was shoved below deck of the ship. After a time the badly frightened boy found some of his own people held in chains. From them he learned that "we were to be carried to these white people's country to work for them."

Equiano's Experiences   The first stop was at Barbados, an island in the West Indies. Most of the captives were sold to planters in the islands. They were taken to work in the sugar fields. Equiano was put on another ship and taken to the British colony of Virginia, where he was sold to a planter. Later the planter sold him to a British naval officer.

Equiano served the officer for several years. Equiano had a quick mind, and he learned to speak English well. He also learned to be a barber. He was taken to London, where he found friends who enabled him to attend school for a short time. Equiano managed to make and save some money. When he was 21, he was able to buy his freedom.

As a free man, Olaudah Equiano tried to awaken people in Europe to the cruelty of the slave trade. He wrote the story of his life because he wanted to tell people about "the inhuman traffic of slavery."

C. European Footholds in Africa

In 1481 a large Portuguese fleet set sail from the port of Lisbon. It was headed for the African coast. This time, in addition to traders, it carried carpenters, stone

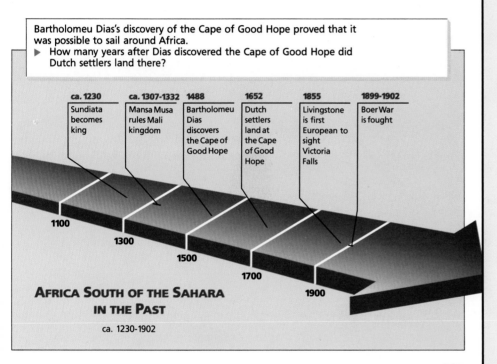

Bartholomeu Dias's discovery of the Cape of Good Hope proved that it was possible to sail around Africa.
▶ How many years after Dias discovered the Cape of Good Hope did Dutch settlers land there?

ca. 1230	ca. 1307-1332	1488	1652	1855	1899-1902
Sundiata becomes king	Mansa Musa rules Mali kingdom	Bartholomeu Dias discovers the Cape of Good Hope	Dutch settlers land at the Cape of Good Hope	Livingstone is first European to sight Victoria Falls	Boer War is fought

1100
1300
1500
1700
1900

AFRICA SOUTH OF THE SAHARA IN THE PAST
ca. 1230-1902

465

Read and Think
Section B
Other European countries followed Portugal's lead and began trading in Africa. Discuss the resulting slave trade with the following questions:

1. **When did the demand for slaves increase?**
(When European traders came to Africa p. 464)

2. **What was the job of a slave trader?**
(To kidnap people and take them to European trading posts where they were sold and shipped to distant lands p. 464)

3. **In the story of Equiano's experiences, where were most of the slaves sent?**
(To the West Indies, working in the planters' sugar fields p. 464)

4. **Why did Equiano decide to write his life story?**
(Because he wanted to tell people about "the inhuman traffic of slavery" p. 465)

Thinking Critically   How, do you think, did Equiano feel about being enslaved? (Evaluate)
(Answers may include frightened, lonely, and terribly mistreated. p. 465)

VISUAL THINKING SKILL

Reading a Time Line

■ Direct students' attention to the time line on this page. Then ask the following question: For how many years was the Boer War fought?
(3 years)

For Your Information

The History of Slavery   As noted in the lesson, slavery did not originate in Africa. Slavery's roots go further back, to ancient Greece and Rome when prisoners taken in battle were kept as slaves. African rulers did the same. In addition, African rulers sometimes enslaved people who broke the law. In times of terrible famine, some people sold themselves and their children in order to get food.

The difference between slavery in Africa and the Americas was one of scale. Most slaves in Africa were household servants. They worked around an owner's house or in the garden. Africans did not have large farms, so they had no need for large numbers of slaves. In the Americas, large numbers of slaves worked on plantations.

Optional Activities

─ **Answers to Caption Questions** ─
p. 464 ▶ They were chained in overcrowded conditions and were treated badly by the sailors who guarded them.
p. 465 ▶ 164 years

Read and Think

Section C

The demand for slaves and valuable African goods led European countries to establish more permanent footholds on the African continent. Discuss these footholds with your students by asking the following questions:

1. **What types of workers were carried by the Portuguese fleet?**
   (Traders, carpenters, stone masons, and a company of soldiers *pp. 465-466*)

2. **In which modern-day African countries were the trading posts located?**
   (Ghana, Angola, Senegal *p. 466*)

   Thinking Critically Why, do you think, were many of the trading posts located on the west coast of the African continent? (Infer)

   (It was closest to Europe and Africa. *p. 466*)

VISUAL THINKING SKILL

Interpreting an Illustration

■ Direct students' attention to the illustration on p. 467. Then ask the students to compare the trek of the Boers across Africa to pictures they have seen of American settlers moving West.

---

masons, and a company of soldiers. The fleet had orders to establish a fort and trading post on the coast.

The Portuguese built Fort St. George at Elmina, which is shown below, on the coast of what is now called Ghana. Later they established other permanent trading stations. One was located at Luanda, on the coast of modern Angola.

The Portuguese were not the only Europeans to seize footholds in Africa. The French built Fort St. Louis at the mouth of the Senegal River, in the country now called Senegal. The Dutch, Danes, and English also built fortified trading posts on African soil.

D. Europeans Settle in South Africa

Dutch Settlers Europeans did not settle in tropical Africa, partly because they were particularly susceptible to, or likely to catch, certain tropical diseases. So many of the early traders and explorers died of these diseases that Europeans called tropical Africa "the white man's grave." South of the tropics, however, at the Cape of Good Hope, Europeans found a land that did attract many settlers. The South African climate was very much like that of the Mediterranean lands.

A group of Dutch settlers landed at the Cape of Good Hope in 1652 and were there to stay. The Cape settlement was to

The fortress of St. George at Elmina, on the coast of what is now called Ghana, was built in 1482 at the order of the king of Portugal as a trading post and supply base for Portuguese navigators.
► What did the Portuguese build at their new settlement?

466

Optional Activities

Current Events

● Have students study the conflicts between blacks and whites in South Africa.

● Ask students to bring to class news magazine and newspaper articles that discuss problems and issues in South Africa today.

● Have students summarize information from the articles and present their summaries to the class.

● If desired, you could make this an extra-credit activity.

Cooperative Learning

Making Public Policy Divide the class into groups of seven students for a portion of one class period.

● Have each group decide who will role-play the following: two members of the British government who oppose slavery, two Boers who support slavery, two Africans who oppose slavery, and want their land returned to them, and an arbitrator who will listen to their opinions and try to make the group members resolve their differences.

● First, the students should present their positions on slavery. Then, the arbitrator should try to get all sides to resolve their differences and come to an agreement.

Dutch settlers, called the Boers, traveled across South Africa in search of land they could farm. They made the trip with large herds of cattle.
► What form of transportation did the Boers use to travel?

To help students summarize important events in the European settlement of South Africa, ask the following questions:

1. **Who were the first Europeans to settle in South Africa?**
(The Dutch *pp. 466-467*)

2. **Why did the Europeans feel no guilt in pushing the Africans off of some of the land?**
(The settlers thought that the land was little used because the Africans did not cultivate crops. *p. 467*)

3. **Why did the Boers go to war with the British at the end of the nineteenth century?**
(The Boers disliked British rule and wanted slavery legalized again. *p. 467*)

Thinking Critically Why, do you think, was life for most Africans no better under British rule than under Dutch rule? (Evaluate)
(Although blacks were free under British rule, they had no land and were forced to work for the white settlers, just as they had done under Dutch rule. *p. 467*)

serve as a supply base rather than a trading post. It would be a place where ships making the long trip from Europe to India could find fresh food and water. The settlers called themselves **Boers** (boorz), a Dutch word meaning "farmers." The Boers planted crops, set out orchards and vineyards, and kept herds of cattle.

Taking Africans' Land South Africa was not an empty land when the Europeans first settled there. It was a homeland for several African peoples. But the settlers thought the land was little used because the Africans did not cultivate crops. Instead they depended on hunting, herding, and food gathering for their living.

The settlers pushed the Africans off some of the land. Fighting broke out between the two groups. African spears were no match for European guns, and soon parts of the African hunting grounds became settlers' farms. The Boers employed black workers on their farms. Many of them were slaves. Those who were free, however, were not treated much better than the slaves.

British Settlers Great Britain seized control of the Cape settlement from the Dutch during a war in 1795. The Boers disliked British rule, and they were outraged when the British abolished slavery within the British Empire in 1834. The British government paid owners for their slaves, but the Boers complained that the payments were far too little. As for the black slaves, they received their freedom but no land, so many of them still had to work for the white settlers.

Because of their differences with the British, a number of Boers left the Cape colony to settle farther inland. At the end of the century, however, the Boers went to war with the British again, over many of the same issues.

467

For Your Information

Boer War The war between the British and the Boers was called the Boer War. It was prompted by the discovery of gold and diamonds in the lands to which the Boers had retreated in the 1850s. After the Boers had migrated inland, they established their own republics and legalized slavery. With the discovery of valuable minerals in Boer land, the British wanted to reestablish control over the Boers. The Boer War, from 1899 to 1902, was a bloody battle. The Boers put up a strong fight despite being outnumbered. In the end, the Boers and their lands came under British control. However, it only took a few years before the Boers made up an elected majority in the South African government.

Optional Activities

── **Answers to Caption Questions** ──
p. 466 ► A large fort and smaller storage homes
p. 467 ► Covered wagons

467

Read and Think
Section E

Some Europeans who came to Africa were interested in missionary work, not trade. David Livingstone was one such person. Discuss his accomplishments with students by asking the following questions:

1. **How did Livingstone show respect for the ways of the Africans?**
   (He lived among them and learned their languages and customs. *p. 468*)

2. **How did Livingstone help open up Africa?**
   (He explored the continent, visiting lands that no white person had seen, and he wrote books about his travels. *p. 468*)

Thinking Critically What, do you think, did Livingstone mean when he called the slave trade "the open sore of Africa"? (Infer)
(He meant that the slave trade was hurting Africa and that if it continued, it would permanently damage the continent. *p. 468*)

Henry Stanley was an American reporter who went to Africa in 1869 to find David Livingstone, a famous explorer of the time who was feared to be missing.
▶ Besides exploring, for what other work was Livingstone known?

E. A Missionary Explorer in Africa

David Livingstone David Livingstone did not come to South Africa from Scotland in 1841 to settle or trade. He was a doctor who was also a **missionary**, so he came to teach the African people about the Christian religion.

After arriving in Africa, Livingstone decided that he could best serve the Africans by helping open up the continent to the outside world. Livingstone respected the ways of the Africans. He lived among them and learned their languages and customs. But he was convinced that Africans needed to learn about modern science and business. He by no means gave up the hope of bringing Christianity to Africa. He simply decided that the faith could best be spread by Africans who knew more about the outside world.

To help open up Africa, Livingstone spent much of his life exploring the continent. He traveled hundreds of miles by boat and on foot, visiting lands no white person had seen. He explored the Kalahari, traveled to Africa's great lakes, and discovered Victoria Falls.

Teaching About Africa Livingstone not only taught Africans about the outside world, he also taught the outside world about Africa. He wrote books about his travels that were widely read in Europe and America. He told the world about the slave trade, which he called "the open sore of Africa."

Livingstone died in 1873 in a central African village in what is now Zambia. His African friends buried his heart in African soil before carrying his body to the coast to be sent back to Britain.

468

Optional Activities

Graphic Organizer

● To help students better understand the extent of European influence and control in Africa, you may wish to use the graphic organizer shown below.

EUROPEAN COLONIES IN AFRICA

GREAT BRITAIN
1. Egypt
2. South Africa
3. Nigeria
4. Other lands in East Africa and West Africa

FRANCE
1. Algeria, Tunis, and most of Morocco in North Africa
2. French Equatorial Africa
3. Madagascar
4. French West Africa

PORTUGAL
1. Angola
2. Mozambique
3. Portuguese Guinea

ITALY
1. Libya (in North Africa)
2. Eritrea and part of Somaliland (in East Africa)

BELGIUM
1. Belgian Congo

F. European Rule in Africa

Colonial Africa Europeans first established footholds in Africa so they could trade. They did not try to rule the continent. After 1880, however, European governments claimed large areas of Africa for their empires. Within a very short time, they had divided Africa into colonies.

The map on this page shows which countries ruled in Africa in 1920. Only two lands, Ethiopia and Liberia, were independent. Find these lands on the map below.

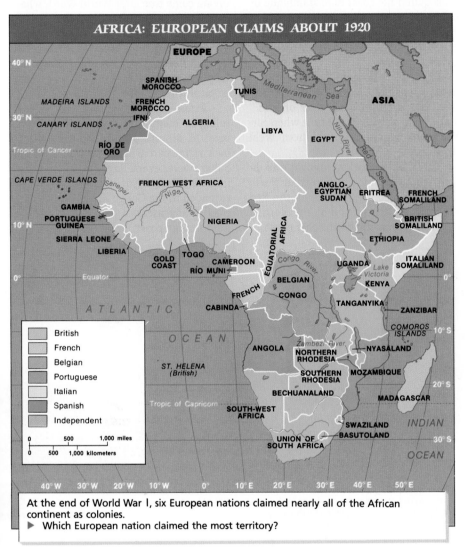

AFRICA: EUROPEAN CLAIMS ABOUT 1920

Legend:
- British
- French
- Belgian
- Portuguese
- Italian
- Spanish
- Independent

At the end of World War I, six European nations claimed nearly all of the African continent as colonies.
▶ Which European nation claimed the most territory?

469

Optional Activities

Interviewing

- Ask students to imagine that they have the opportunity to interview the great missionary and explorer, David Livingstone.

- Have each student write down five questions that they would like to ask Livingstone. These questions could relate to his missionary work, his travels, or his writings.

- You may wish to conclude this activity by asking some students to read their questions to the class and having other class members answer the questions the way that Livingstone might have.

◆◆◆◆

Meeting Individual Needs

Concept: European Influence on Africa

To better understand the effect Europeans had on Africans south of the Sahara, it is important to draw conclusions from the information in the lesson. Below are three activities that will help your students draw conclusions about the impact of Europeans on Africa.

◆ **EASY** Ask students to recall what the source of conflict was between the British and the Boers in South Africa in the 1830s.

Have them draw conclusions about whether slavery was made legal or illegal in the new lands where the Boers settled.

Have students explain the basis for their conclusions.

◀▶ **AVERAGE** Ask students to recall the accomplishments of David Livingstone.

Have them draw conclusions about whether Livingstone changed European perceptions of Africa and the African people.

Have students explain the basis for their conclusions.

◀▮▶ **CHALLENGING** Ask students to recall what life was like for many Africans in South Africa.

Have them draw conclusions about the lifestyle of many black South Africans in the twentieth century.

Have students explain the basis for their conclusions.

Answers to Caption Questions
p. 468 ▶ Missionary work
p. 469 ▶ Britain

469

Read and Think

Section F

European governments divided most of Africa into colonies after 1880. Discuss how and why Africa was colonized by asking students the following questions:

1. **Why did European governments begin to claim large areas of Africa after 1880?**
(To expand their empires *p. 469*)

2. **Which countries ruled the largest part of Africa?**
(Great Britain and France *p. 470*)

Thinking Critically **Why, do you think, did Great Britain acquire some of Germany's colonies in Africa after World War I?** (Infer)
(When Germany lost World War I, it was forced to hand over its colonies to Great Britain and the other winners of the war. *p. 470*)

Portugal, Spain, and Italy Portugal was the first country to explore the African coast, and the first to establish colonies. Portuguese Guinea and Angola had grown from forts built to protect trade—particularly the slave trade. The Portuguese had acquired the coast of Mozambique by conquering the trading cities of East Africa. They later extended their control along the Zambezi. Spain's holdings were confined to northwest Africa.

Spain held Ifni and Río de Oro on the Atlantic coast of the Sahara desert. The name *Río de Oro* means "river of gold." The name went back to the time when caravan merchants traded gold from West Africa there.

Italy's largest colony, Libya, was directly across the Mediterranean in North Africa. Italy also held Eritrea on the Red Sea coast and Somaliland on the Horn of Africa, the peninsula on the east coast.

Britain and France Great Britain and France ruled the largest part of Africa. Before World War I some British leaders had dreamed that Britain would someday rule a strip of land "from the Cape to Cairo," that is, from South Africa to Egypt. This dream came true after World War I, when Britain acquired some German colonies. The British Empire also included Nigeria and other lands in West Africa. The name of one of these lands, Gold Coast, recalls why it was that Europeans first came to tropical Africa.

France held much of North Africa, ruling or controlling Algeria, Tunis, and most of Morocco. The French flag flew over a large part of the Sahara. South of the Sahara were several large French colonies, including French Equatorial Africa, which extended to the Congo River. France also ruled Madagascar, a large island off the East African coast.

The Foreign Legion is made up of volunteers from different countries. One of its original purposes was to assist in the conquest of Algeria. Later many of the Legion's units served in North Africa.
▶ Under which government do you think the Foreign Legion serves?

Optional Activities

Hypothesizing

- Tell students that although the Europeans carved Africa into colonies, few Europeans came to the colonies to make new lives for themselves.

- Have students hypothesize why this was the case (climate was different and inhospitable; reluctance to live among people who were so different).

- Conclude this activity by asking students to find factual information in the lesson that would support their hypotheses.

Reteaching Main Objective

★ *Explain why European countries became interested in Africa.*

- Ask students to imagine that they have been asked to write an entry in an encyclopedia which describes the part of Africa's history that deals with the role of Europeans south of the Sahara.

- Tell students to write the first paragraph of this imaginary article in which they explain why European countries became interested in Africa.

- Conclude this activity by asking volunteers to read their paragraphs to the class.

Belgium Belgium, one of Europe's smallest countries, ruled one of the largest colonies in tropical Africa. The Belgian Congo was 77 times as large as Belgium itself. Belgium had acquired this land because the Belgian king Leopold II had organized an international business company to develop the resources of the Congo Basin.

Although Leopold made a large fortune from ivory and rubber, he could not convince many Europeans to move to the Congo. Leopold used extreme cruelty in his attempt to get as much labor as he could from the people who lived in the Congo. Countries around the world loudly protested Leopold's methods. Largely due to the international pressure, the Belgian government took over the colony and made reforms. Today this area is the independent country of Zaire.

The division of Africa among European nations took place quickly, but the European countries did not hold on to their colonies long. The Gold Coast became independent in 1957 and took the name Ghana. Other African colonies soon gained their independence.

King Leopold's treatment of the Congo people angered many nations.
▶ How does the artist portray King Leopold?

LESSON **3** REVIEW

THINK AND WRITE

A. What reasons did the Portuguese have for exploring the coast of Africa? (Recall)

B. What effect do you think Olaudah Equiano's book had on people during his lifetime? (Evaluate)

C. What European countries built forts along the African coast? (Recall)

D. Summarize the development of the colony in South Africa. (Recall)

E. What effects did David Livingstone's mission in Africa have on Africans and Europeans? (Infer)

F. How did European activity in Africa change after 1880? (Recall)

SKILLS CHECK

MAP SKILL

Compare the map of European colonies in Africa, on page 469, with that of Africa today in the Atlas, on page 624. Write the modern name of each of these former colonies: Gold Coast, Belgian Congo, Bechuanaland, Southern Rhodesia, Tanganyika. Name at least three countries created out of what had been French West Africa.

471

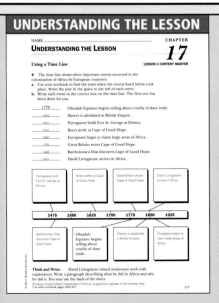
Optional Activities

---

3 CLOSING THE LESSON

Lesson **3** Review

Answers to Think and Write

A. They were curious and wanted to trade for gold, ivory, pepper, and slaves.

B. Equiano's book probably awakened people to the cruelty of the slave trade.

C. Portugal, France, the Netherlands, Denmark, and England built forts.

D. South Africa's Cape colony began as a supply base and was settled by Dutch farmers called Boers. The British seized control of the Cape settlement in 1795. Disliking British rule and opposing the abolition of slavery, the Boers left the colony and moved farther inland.

E. David Livingstone's mission in Africa brought Christianity to Africa, taught Africans about the world, and taught Europeans about Africa through his books.

F. After 1880, Europeans began to claim large areas of Africa for their empires.

Answer to Skills Check

They are Ghana, Zaire, Botswana, Zimbabwe, and Tanzania. Benin, Guinea, Ivory Coast, Mali, Mauritania, Niger, and Senegal were created from French West Africa.

Focus Your Reading

Ask the lesson focus question found at the beginning of the lesson: **What role did Europeans play in Africa south of the Sahara?** (Europeans explored the coast, set up trading posts, took part in the slave trade, and made colonies of many African nations.)

Additional Practice

You may wish to assign the ancillary materials listed below.

Understanding the Lesson p. 117
Workbook p. 100

┌─ **Answers to Caption Questions** ─┐
p. 470 ▶ French government
p. 471 ▶ As a tough, proud military leader

471

Using the Vocabulary

1. Boer
2. navigator
3. monsoon
4. oral history
5. missionary

Remembering What You Read

1. Mansa Musa was going to Mecca.
2. It was a center of trade and learning.
3. They served as historical records.
4. Huge boulders connected by stone walls, a walled enclosure with a cone-shaped tower inside, carved stone figures and bowls, gold ornaments, glassware, beads, and porcelain
5. They sailed to Asian countries between May and September, when the monsoon blows from the southwest.
6. It caused them to grow.
7. In small villages, if they were farmers, or, if they were herders, they wandered with their animals.
8. It showed that it was possible to sail around Africa.
9. To tell people about "the inhuman traffic of slavery"
10. Europeans pushed Africans off some of the land, some made slaves of the Africans, and they claimed large areas of Africa for their empires.

USING THE VOCABULARY

oral history	monsoon
navigator	Boer
missionary	

On a separate sheet of paper, write the word or words from above that best complete the sentences.

1. A Dutch farmer who settled at the Cape of Good Hope in the 1600s had the name _____ .
2. Prince Henry of Portugal was a _____ who planned the courses for ships he sent to explore the west coast of Africa.
3. The summer _____ on the Indian Ocean blows from the southwest.
4. An account of the past that African storytellers handed down by word of mouth is called _____ .
5. Dr. David Livingstone was a _____ who went to Africa to teach people there about the Christian religion.

REMEMBERING WHAT YOU READ

On a separate sheet of paper, answer the following questions in complete sentences.

1. Where was Mansa Musa going when he stopped to spend time in Cairo, Egypt?
2. Why was the African city of Timbuktu important?
3. What were the purposes of the plaques on houses in the kingdom of Benin?
4. What objects have archaeologists found at Great Zimbabwe?
5. How did sailing ships from Africa make use of the monsoons to trade with Asian countries?

6. How did increased trade affect cities on the coast of East Africa during the Middle Ages?
7. Where did most people in Ethiopia live during the Middle Ages?
8. Why was Bartholomeu Dias's discovery of the Cape of Good Hope important?
9. Why did Olaudah Equiano write a book about his experiences?
10. What changes did European settlers make in Africa south of the Sahara?

TYING ART TO SOCIAL STUDIES

Use the maps and the information in this chapter to create a map showing goods that were traded in Africa south of the Sahara. First draw or trace the outline of the continent. Then design your own symbols for some of the traded goods and draw the symbols on your map to show areas where those goods were traded. Label any cities or countries in the appropriate areas of trade.

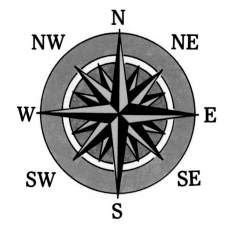

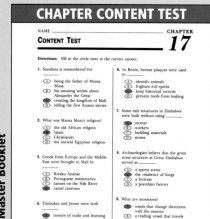

CHAPTER CONTENT TEST

NAME _____

CONTENT TEST CHAPTER *17*

Directions: Fill in the circle next to the correct answer.

1. Sundiata is remembered for _____
   (A) being the father of Mansa Musa
   (B) his amusing stories about Alexander the Great
   (C) creating the kingdom of Mali
   (D) telling the first Anansi stories

2. What was Mansa Musa's religion?
   (A) the old African religion
   (B) Islam
   (C) Christianity
   (D) the ancient Egyptian religion

3. Goods from Europe and the Middle East were brought to Mali by _____
   (A) Kwaku Ananse
   (B) Portuguese missionaries
   (C) canoes on the Nile River
   (D) camel caravans

4. Timbuktu and Jenne were both _____
   (A) centers of trade and learning
   (B) meeting places for camels
   (C) powerful city-states
   (D) heroes of the Ashanti people

5. The kingdom of Benin was located in what is now _____
   (A) Egypt
   (B) eastern Portugal
   (C) southern Nigeria
   (D) western Mali

6. In Benin, bronze plaques were used to _____
   (A) identify animals
   (B) frighten evil spirits
   (C) keep historical records
   (D) prevent roofs from leaking

7. Some early structures in Zimbabwe were built without using _____
   (A) mortar
   (B) workers
   (C) building materials
   (D) stones

8. Archaeologists believe that the great stone structure at Great Zimbabwe served as _____
   (A) a sports arena
   (B) the residence of kings
   (C) a fortress
   (D) a porcelain factory

9. What are monsoons?
   (A) winds that change directions with the seasons
   (B) a trading vessel that travels to India
   (C) a type of African ape that lives on the coast
   (D) people of mixed Indian and African descent

10. The dominant religion in Ethiopia was _____
    (A) Islam (C) Christianity
    (B) Ananse (D) Judaism

CHAPTER CONTENT TEST

NAME _____

CONTENT TEST (continued) CHAPTER 17

11. What enabled Ethiopia to keep its own language and beliefs?
    (A) its isolation
    (B) a book called *The Glory of Kings*
    (C) loyalty to the Queen of Sheba
    (D) the army loyal to King Ezana

12. Ethiopian kings claimed to be the descendants of _____
    (A) Alexander the Great
    (B) monsoons
    (C) Solomon
    (D) Vasco da Gama

13. During the Middle Ages most Ethiopians were _____
    (A) traders and priests
    (B) craftspeople
    (C) fishermen and hunters
    (D) farmers or herders

14. Prince Henry of Portugal encouraged _____
    (A) slavery
    (B) exploration
    (C) wars
    (D) Columbus

15. The voyage of Bartholomeu Dias showed that it was possible to sail around _____
    (A) Europe
    (B) Ethiopia
    (C) Nigeria
    (D) Africa

16. Slave traders from other countries captured Africans and transported them to _____
    (A) the Americas
    (B) Ethiopia
    (C) Portugal
    (D) Benin

17. In 1481 who built forts on the coast of what is now Ghana?
    (A) Olaudah Equiano
    (B) King Lalibela
    (C) the Portuguese
    (D) the Dutch

18. The Boers were outraged when the British _____
    (A) sent Livingstone to Africa
    (B) treated Africans like slaves
    (C) abolished slavery
    (D) made them speak English

19. David Livingstone went to Africa to _____
    (A) stop Boers from killing and enslaving people
    (B) teach Africans about the Christian religion
    (C) hunt for gold and silver
    (D) make King Leonardo end slavery in the Congo

20. What leader organized a company to develop resources in the Belgian Congo?
    (A) King Leonardo
    (B) Leopold II
    (C) David Livingstone
    (D) Olaudah Equiano

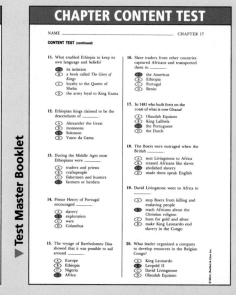

CHAPTER SKILLS TEST

NAME _____

SKILLS TEST CHAPTER *17*

Directions: Study the map and complete items 1–5. Fill in the circle next to the correct answer.

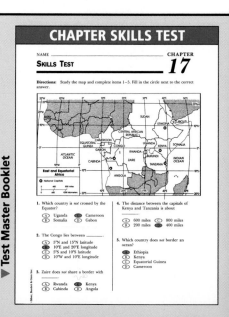

1. Which country is *not* crossed by the Equator?
   (A) Uganda (C) Cameroon
   (B) Somalia (D) Gabon

2. The Congo lies between _____
   (A) 5°N and 15°N latitude
   (B) 10°E and 20°E longitude
   (C) 5°S and 15°S latitude
   (D) 10°W and 10°E longitude

3. Zaire does *not* share a border with _____
   (A) Rwanda (C) Kenya
   (B) Cabinda (D) Angola

4. The distance between the capitals of Kenya and Tanzania is about _____
   (A) 600 miles (C) 800 miles
   (B) 200 miles (D) 400 miles

5. Which country does *not* border an ocean?
   (A) Ethiopia
   (B) Kenya
   (C) Equatorial Guinea
   (D) Cameroon

▶ Test Master Booklet

▶ Test Master Booklet

▶ Test Master Booklet

THINKING CRITICALLY

On a separate sheet of paper, answer the following questions in complete sentences.

1. What are some of the ways in which we have learned about earlier times in Africa south of the Sahara?
2. Why would people have paid more money for books than for any other goods traded in Timbuktu?
3. What do you think the cone-shaped tower at Great Zimbabwe might have been used for?
4. Why, do you think, did so many different countries come to explore Africa south of the Sahara?
5. Why, do you think, did David Livingstone want to teach people outside of Africa about this continent?

SUMMARIZING THE CHAPTER

On a separate sheet of paper, copy the graphic organizer shown below. Beside each question, write four answers from the chapter.

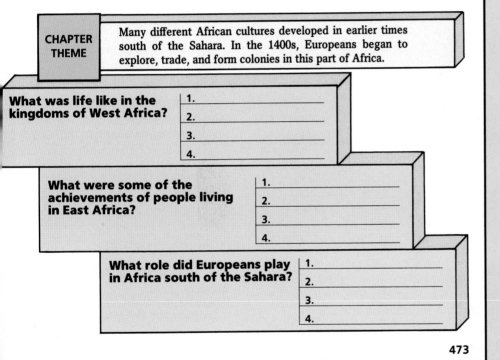

CHAPTER THEME

Many different African cultures developed in earlier times south of the Sahara. In the 1400s, Europeans began to explore, trade, and form colonies in this part of Africa.

What was life like in the kingdoms of West Africa?
1. _____
2. _____
3. _____
4. _____

What were some of the achievements of people living in East Africa?
1. _____
2. _____
3. _____
4. _____

What role did Europeans play in Africa south of the Sahara?
1. _____
2. _____
3. _____
4. _____

Thinking Critically

1. Answers may include by studying the ruins of structures, objects, and art.
2. Books were rarer and more precious than any other goods traded in Timbuktu.
3. Possible answers include an observation tower to watch the people who approached.
4. Africa south of the Sahara possessed many valuable resources.
5. Livingstone wanted people outside of Africa to regard the land and people of Africa with respect.

Summarizing The Chapter

What was life like in the kingdoms of West Africa?
1. Many people involved in trade
2. Religious education in Mali
3. Most people of Benin were forest farmers.
4. Benin used plaques to tell their history.

What were some of the achievements of people living in East Africa?
1. Built stone structures
2. Used monsoons for tradewinds
3. Built large cities
4. Decorated buildings with carvings

What role did Europeans play in Africa south of the Sahara?
1. Europeans sold Africans into slavery
2. Europeans took some land away.
3. Europeans made colonies of African lands.
4. Europeans tried to Christianize Africans.

473

Africa South of the Sahara Today

(pp. 474-496)

Chapter Theme: Independence movements in Africa led to the end of European empires. Governments and economies are varied among African countries south of the Sahara.

CHAPTER RESOURCES
Review Master Booklet
  Reviewing Chapter Vocabulary, p. 125
  Place Geography, p. 126
  Summarizing the Chapter, p. 127
Chapter 18 Test

LESSON *1* West Africa

(pp. 474-479)

Theme: West African countries faced political and economic problems after they gained independence.

 SOCIAL STUDIES LIBRARY: *Money*

LESSON RESOURCES
Workbook, p. 102
Review Master Booklet
  Understanding the Lesson, p. 121

LESSON *2* Central Africa

(pp. 480-483)

Theme: Most of the countries in Central Africa became independent around 1960 and their economies rely on cash crops, oil, mining, and diamonds.

LESSON RESOURCES
Review Master Booklet
  Understanding the Lesson, p. 122

LESSON *3* Southern Africa

(pp. 484-490)

Theme: The discovery of diamonds laid the foundation for a prosperous mining industry in South Africa, but poor relations between races has caused political unrest.

 SILVER WINGS WORKSHOP: The Courage of Your Convictions

LESSON RESOURCES
Workbook, p. 103
Review Master Booklet
  Understanding the Lesson, p. 123

LESSON *4* East Africa

(pp. 491-494)

Theme: East Africa has faced political, population, and economic problems, but tourism has been a source of income in some East African countries.

LESSON RESOURCES
Workbook, pp. 104-106
Review Master Booklet
  Understanding the Lesson, p. 124

Review Masters

REVIEWING CHAPTER VOCABULARY

CHAPTER
18
VOCABULARY MASTER

Review Study the terms in the box. Use your Glossary to find definitions of those you do not remember.

Africanized	cash crop	groundnut	pyrethrum
apartheid	economic boom	high veld	teff

Practice Complete the paragraphs using terms from the box above.
You may change the forms of the terms to fit the meaning.

Some African agricultural products are similar to those in the United States, but some are quite different. The grasslands of the (1) ___high veld___ are similar to the Great Plains in the United States; they both are good for raising cattle and grain. Another important African product familiar to people in the United States is the (2) ___groundnut___. It is one of the most important (3) ___cash crops___ grown in Gambia and Senegal.

Few American farmers, however, would be familiar with (4) ___teff___, a grain grown mainly in Ethiopia. This crop provides Ethiopians with a type of bread, an important part of their diet. Another unusual African crop is (5) ___pyrethrum___, which is grown mainly in Kenya. It is used to produce insect poison.

Write Write a sentence of your own for each term in the box above.
You may use the back of the sheet.
Sentences should show that students understand the meanings of the terms.

_____

_____

_____

_____

_____

_____

_____

_____

_____

_____

_____

_____

© Silver, Burdett & Ginn Inc.

LOCATING PLACES

CHAPTER
18
PLACE GEOGRAPHY MASTER

✻   Listed below are places in Southern and Eastern Africa. Use the Gazetteer in your textbook to find the latitude and longitude of each place. Then locate and label each on the map.

	LAT. ⊖	LONG. ⟲			LAT. ⊖	LONG. ⟲
1. Harare, Zimbabwe	18°S	31°E	5. Addis Ababa, Ethiopia		9°N	39°E
2. Victoria Falls, Zambia	18°S	26°E	6. Luanda, Angola		9°S	13°E
3. Pretoria, South Africa	26°S	28°E	7. Lusaka, Zambia		15°S	28°E
4. Nairobi, Kenya	1°S	37°E	8. Cape of Good Hope		33°S	19°E

© Silver, Burdett & Ginn Inc.

SUMMARIZING THE CHAPTER

CHAPTER
18
GRAPHIC ORGANIZER MASTER

✻   Complete this graphic organizer. Under the main idea for each lesson, write three statements that support the main idea.

CHAPTER THEME Independence movements in Africa led to the end of European empires. Governments and economies are varied among African countries south of the Sahara.

LESSON 1
West African countries faced problems after gaining their independence.

1. Civil war in Nigeria in the 1960s

2. Drop in the price of oil

3. Democracy has been hard to establish.

LESSON 3
Relations between different races have affected the countries of Southern Africa.

1. Foreign nations disapprove of apartheid.

2. Zambia and Botswana disapprove of apartheid.

3. Civil war in Mozambique

LESSON 2
The countries of Central Africa have many things in common.

1. Most people are employed in agriculture.

2. Common history of European rule

3. Place names have been Africanized.

LESSON 4
In many ways the countries of East Africa are alike.

1. They are mainly agricultural.

2. Resource allocation problems

3. All have diverse populations.

© Silver, Burdett & Ginn Inc.

C18-B

Workbook Pages

GEOGRAPHY OF NIGERIA

Understanding Coordinates, Analyzing Information

※ The following statements tell about the location of important places and physical features of Nigeria. Using the information in the statements, write each underlined name on the map below.

1. The capital of Nigeria is <u>Abuja</u>.

2. Most of <u>Lake Chad</u> is located between 13°N and 15°N and 13°E and 15°E.

3. <u>Onitsha</u> is situated at about 6°N/7°E.

4. <u>Jos</u> is located at 10°N/9°E.

5. In Nigeria, the <u>Niger River</u> flows to the south between about 3°E and 7°E.

6. <u>Makurdi</u> is located on the <u>Benue River</u>.

7. <u>Maiduguri</u> is southwest of Lake Chad at about 12°N/13°E.

8. The city located at approximately 12°N/8°E is <u>Kano</u>.

9. <u>Ibadan</u> is located approximately 2° to the south and about 3° west of the capital.

10. <u>Sokoto</u> is located at 13°N, just east of 5°E.

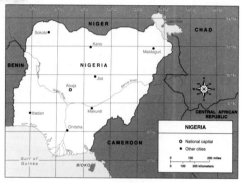

Thinking Further: Identify an important feature of the geography of Nigeria and tell why it is significant. Write your answer on a separate sheet. Answers should reflect independent thinking. Students may mention the Niger and Benue rivers, which link much of the country, or the coastline along the Atlantic.

102   Chapter 18, pages 475–479

INDEPENDENCE IN AFRICA

Making a Time Line, Hypothesizing

※ Use the information in the list of African countries below to complete the time line. Write the name of each country on the line connected to its independence year. Note that more than one country achieved independence in 1960 and 1964. Refer to the time line to complete the sentences that follow.

African Independence Dates

Botswana 1966	Ghana 1957	Sudan 1956
Cameroon 1960	Ivory Coast 1960	Tanzania 1964
Central African Republic 1960	Kenya 1963	Zaire 1960
Congo 1960	Mozambique 1975	Zambia 1964
Gabon 1960	Nigeria 1960	Zimbabwe 1980
Gambia 1965	Senegal 1960	

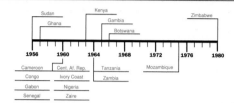

1. _____Sudan_____ has been independent longer than the other countries shown on the time line.

2. The country with the most recent independence date is _____Zimbabwe_____

3. The majority of countries shown gained independence in _____1960_____

4. The only country on the time line that achieved independence in the 1970s was _____Mozambique_____

5. The countries that became independent in 1964 are _____Tanzania and Zambia_____

Thinking Further: Why do you think many African nations changed their names when they gained independence? (For instance, Northern Rhodesia became Zambia at independence.) Write your answer on a separate sheet. Students may suggest that it was important to the people to establish their own African identity and to erase reminders of colonialism.

Chapter 18, pages 484–490   103

AFRICAN ANIMALS

Solving a Puzzle, Writing Persuasively

※ Choose the correct African animals from the box to fill in the puzzle below. The first letter of each animal is given. Then, unscramble the circled letters in the puzzle to find the mystery word. This word tells you something about the animals underlined in the box. The first letter is given.

baboon	leopard	giraffe	aardvark	ibis	<u>rhinoceros</u>
flamingo	lion	<u>zebra</u>	crocodile	<u>ostrich</u>	hippopotamus
ape	jackal	python	impala	dromedary	monkey
serval	gnu	<u>elephant</u>	cheetah	chimpanzee	

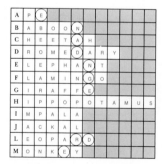

MYSTERY WORD: E N D A N G E R E D

Thinking Further: Imagine that you are a Kenyan in charge of finding ways to educate the public about preserving the animal population. On a separate sheet, write a paragraph that you think will help people understand the importance of saving the animals. Some students may mention that the economy will suffer if the animals are killed or driven away. The animals attract many tourists to Kenya, and the tourists spend money. Others may mention the importance of saving animals from extinction.

104   Chapter 18, pages 491–494

AFRICAN ECONOMIES

Unscrambling Words, Making Observations

※ The paragraph below contains information about natural resources and other products that contribute to African economies. The scrambled names of these important items are in the word box. As you read the paragraph, unscramble the names of the products or resources and write them on the lines. The first has been unscrambled for you.

lio	aloc	glod	tontoc	miadonds	burber	brimet
artulan ags	roppec	axbiute	lassi	accoa	feft	
triceelicty	neseamang	nit	ofecef	tactel	roundstung	

_____Oil_____ is an important resource in Congo, Gabon, and Nigeria. Nigeria also has vast amounts of _____natural gas_____. Ghana exports _____electricity_____ and _____coal_____ is found in Mozambique. Important metals found in Africa south of the Sahara include _____copper_____ in Botswana, Zambia, and Zaire; _____manganese_____ in Gabon; _____gold_____ in South Africa; _____bauxite_____ in Mozambique, and _____tin_____ in Zaire. Fine _____cotton_____ is grown in Sudan and Tanzania. Tanzania is also known for its _____sisal_____ _____Coffee_____ is an important product in Cameroon, Ethiopia, Ivory Coast, and Tanzania. _____Diamonds_____ are found in the Central African Republic and South Africa. _____Cacao_____ is a leading export of Cameroon, Ivory Coast, and Ghana. Other African agricultural resources include _____cattle_____ in Botswana, _____rubber_____ in Cameroon, _____teff_____ in Ethiopia, and _____groundnuts_____ in Zambia and Senegal. _____Timber_____ is a valuable asset in Gabon and Congo.

Thinking Further: Identify an important natural resource of the region where you live and tell why it is important. Answers should reflect the resources of your region. A possible answer: Salmon is an important resource of Washington State. Fishers who catch salmon earn much money by selling them.

Chapter 18, pages 475–494   105

Workbook Pages

TOWARD COOPERATION IN AFRICA

Interpreting Information, Making Observations

✳ In 1963 foreign ministers from 32 African states gathered in Addis Ababa, Ethiopia. They met to establish a new international organization called the Organization of African Unity, or OAU. The following articles are part of the OAU Charter, or constitution. Read the articles and answer the questions.

Article I. Establishment of the Organization of African Unity. The Organization to include continental African states, Madagascar, and other islands surrounding Africa.

Article II. Aims of the OAU.
1. To promote unity and solidarity among African states
2. To intensify and coordinate efforts to improve living standards in Africa
3. To defend sovereignty, territorial integrity, and independence of African states
4. To eradicate [do away with] all forms of colonialism from Africa
5. To promote international cooperation in keeping with the Charter of the United Nations

Article IV. Each independent sovereign African state shall be entitled to become a member of the Organization.

Article V. All member states shall have equal rights and duties.

1. What areas other than the continent of Africa are included in the OAU? _Madagascar and__ other islands surrounding Africa

2. Who can become a member of the OAU? _Any independent sovereign African state can join.___

3. What is the relationship of member states within the organization? _All member states have__ equal rights and duties.

4. What is the main goal of the OAU? _The main goal is to promote unity and solidarity among African__ states.

5. Which other charter does the organization want to follow? _the Charter of the United Nations__

Thinking Further: Describe an international organization other than the OAU or the United Nations.
Students may mention the Red Cross, which helps people and nations in times of disaster, or the European
Community, which promotes close economic cooperation among European nations.

     Chapter 18, pages 475–494   © Silver, Burdett & Ginn Inc.

TEACHER NOTES

West Africa

Objectives

★ **1. Describe** the countries of West Africa.

2. Explain the problems faced by the countries of West Africa after they became independent of their colonial rulers.

3. Identify the following people and places: *Jomo Kenyatta, Kwame Nkrumah, Ghana, Nigeria, Cote d'Ivoire, Senegal,* and *Gambia.*

1 STARTING THE LESSON

Motivation Activity

- Tell students to imagine that they are rulers of a country which has just gained its independence.

- Ask students whether or not they would want to keep close ties with their former colonial rulers.

- Discuss the factors that would influence their decisions. (Examples include citizens' feelings towards the former colonial rulers and the economic status of both countries.)

Think About What You Know

- Assign the THINK ABOUT WHAT YOU KNOW activity on p. 475.

- Answers may include Saudi Arabia, Kuwait, and Bahrain.

Study the Vocabulary

- Have students look up the definitions of the vocabulary words in the Glossary.

- Then ask them to make a rebus for each term. (In a rebus, students use pictures or symbols to represent words or parts of words.)

- Have individual students share their rebus pictures with the rest of the class.

474

CHAPTER **18** AFRICA SOUTH OF THE SAHARA TODAY

*T*he nations of Africa struggle to build strong economies despite differences in cultures, languages, and customs. Africa's cities, like big cities everywhere, have modern buildings, theater and museums.

474

Optional Activities

Writing to Learn

Writing a Letter to the Editor   Have students pretend to be Nigerians in the late 1950s, just before independence, who are writing letters to the editor of a Nigerian newspaper expressing their attitudes toward British rule.

- The letter should include at least one *analogy* comparing Britain and Nigeria to a parent and child, a master and slave, or a yoke and an ox.

- You may wish to have students review earlier chapters on African history, slave trade, and colonization to find information on how Nigerians might have felt about British rule.

THINK ABOUT WHAT YOU KNOW
You will learn in this lesson that oil has had a great influence in the development of the country Nigeria. What other countries have you learned about that have prospered from oil?

STUDY THE VOCABULARY
economic boom   groundnut

FOCUS YOUR READING
What problems did West African countries face after independence?

A. Independent Ghana

At the time European countries ruled Africa, some Africans went to Europe or America for an education. Among them were Jomo Kenyatta (JOH moh ken YAHT-uh) and Kwame Nkrumah (KWAH mee un-KROO muh). Both returned to Africa to lead movements for African independence in the 1950s. Kenyatta was named the first president of Kenya. Nkrumah became Ghana's first president.

When Ghana became independent, it kept ties with Great Britain. English remains the official language, and Ghana is a member of the Commonwealth of Nations.

Nkrumah was not in office for very long. He grew impatient with those who opposed him and finally had himself declared president for life. In 1966, however, a group of army officers took over the government. Though it is called a republic, Ghana is still under military rule.

Ghana has remained an agricultural country, although the government has taken steps to develop industry. Cacao is the country's most valuable export. Ghana also sells electricity to neighboring countries. Electric power is produced at a large dam on the Volta River.

B. A Better Tomorrow for Nigeria

Independent Nigeria The British invented the name Nigeria for the different regions along the Niger River that were part of their empire. When British rule ended, the African leaders had to create a Nigerian nationality. At one time it seemed that they might fail. A bloody civil war broke out between some of Nigeria's many ethnic groups in the 1960s. In the end, however, Nigeria remained one country. As a member of the Commonwealth of Nations, it has kept some ties with Britain.

Independent Nigeria has had several types of governments. There were two efforts to establish elected governments, but army officers seized power each time. In

Kwame Nkrumah (right) talks with Dwight D. Eisenhower, President of the United States from 1953–1961.
▶ Of what country was Nkrumah president?

2 DEVELOPING THE LESSON

Read and Think
Section A

To discuss the political and economic life of independent Ghana, ask the following questions:

1. **In what two ways are Ghana's continuing ties with Great Britain reflected?**
   (English remains the official language, and Ghana belongs to the Commonwealth of Nations. *p. 475*)

2. **Name two exports of Ghana.**
   (Cacao and electricity *p. 475*)

   Thinking Critically **Why, do you think, did a group of army officers take over the government of Ghana in 1966?** (Infer)
   (Answers should reflect independent thinking but may include that Nkrumah provoked the coup by declaring himself president for life. *p. 475*)

Answers to Caption Questions
p. 475 ▶ Ghana

Giving Oral Reports

- Divide the class into small groups to research information on African countries not covered in this lesson.

- Have each group prepare and present an oral report on the country that they have chosen.

- Individual students can collect information on the country's location, population, capital city, form of government, major crops, major industries, and other means of employment for the population.

- The group can elect one or two members to present the report orally to the rest of the class.

Optional Activities

Concept: Understanding An Economic Boom

To better understand the economy of Africa, it is important to understand how an economic boom affects a country or region. Below are three activities that will help students understand an economic boom.

◆ **EASY** Ask students to create a cause-and-effect chart for the economic boom in Nigeria.

A box on the left should show what caused the boom (high oil prices), and a box on the right should list some of its effects (people left farms for cities).

◀▮▶ **AVERAGE** Have students work in groups of two or three to create a "boom diary."

Ask each group to select a specific Nigerian character (farmer, son or daughter of a farmer, restaurant owner, or government official) and write diary entries that depict the way his or her life might have changed between 1970 and 1985.

◀▮ **CHALLENGING** Ask students who need a challenge to write an essay comparing the effect of oil on the Nigerian economy with the effect of oil on the Saudi Arabian economy.

VISUAL THINKING SKILL

Interpreting a Photograph

- Direct students' attention to the photograph on this page which shows children working on a plantation.

- Ask students to write two or three sentences describing the photograph.

- Then, make a list on the chalkboard of adjectives that students have used to describe the visual.

Oil has had a great influence on Nigeria's development.
▶ What are these oil drillers wearing for protection?

1989, however, the military rulers promised that there would be an elected government again in the future.

Nigeria's Economy Nigeria has rich soil, forests, and deposits of oil and natural gas. Oil has had the greatest influence on the country's development. When oil prices were high in the 1970s, Nigeria enjoyed an **economic boom**, a period of great prosperity. Many people left the farms to take higher-paying jobs in the cities. As a result, a land that had once fed itself had to import food. Nigeria borrowed large amounts of money from foreign banks, believing that oil prices would stay high or even rise.

The price of oil fell sharply in the early 1980s, however, and the boom was followed by hard times. Nigeria could not repay the foreign loans. In the meantime the population kept on growing, so the standard of living fell. But Nigeria's leaders have not given up hope. They believe "tomorrow can be better."

C. Ivory Coast, Senegal, and Gambia

Ivory Coast Côte d'Ivoire (koht deev-WAHR) is the French name for "Ivory Coast" and the nation's official name. French is the official language in Ivory Coast, as it is in nine other West African nations that were once part of the French empire. Ivory Coast is a republic, but it has only one political party.

Good soil is the main natural resource of Ivory Coast, and most people work on farms or in the forests. Most of those who work in industry process agricultural and forest products. Ivory Coast leads the world in the export of coffee and cacao. It also exports pineapples, bananas, palm oil, and timber.

Senegal Senegal, another former French colony, kept close ties with France after

These children are working on a plantation in the Ivory Coast.
▶ What crop are the children harvesting?

Creating a Bulletin Board

- Have students create a bulletin-board display which provides information about at least three other "booms" besides Nigeria's oil boom.

- The display should provide information about a boom that took place near the students' homes, if possible.

- The display could include gold, silver, industry, or trade booms as well as oil booms.

- Examples of other specific booms include the silver and gold rushes in the American West; 20th-century oil and gas booms in Texas, Oklahoma, Wyoming, and Montana; and the Florida real-estate boom of the 1920s.

AFRICA SOUTH OF THE SAHARA: COFFEE PRODUCTION

**Production per year
(thousands of tons)**

- 0-60
- 61-140
- 141-250
- 251 or more
- Figures not available

400   800 miles

400   800 kilometers

...is a leading export for many countries in ...south of the Sahara.
...ich country in Africa south of the Sahara ...duces the most coffee?

MAURITANIA, MALI, NIGER, CHAD, SUDAN, SENEGAL, BURKINA FASO, BENIN, GUINEA, IVORY COAST, NIGERIA, DJIBOUTI, ETHIOPIA, GHANA, TOGO, LIBERIA, EQUATORIAL GUINEA, CAMEROON, CENTRAL AFRICAN REPUBLIC, SOMALIA, SÃO TOMÉ E PRÍNCIPE, GABON, CONGO, ZAIRE, UGANDA, KENYA, RWANDA, BURUNDI, TANZANIA, MALAWI, SEYCHELLES, COMOROS IS., ANGOLA, ZAMBIA, MOZAMBIQUE, ZIMBABWE, MAURITIUS, MADAGASCAR, RÉUNION (FRANCE), NAMIBIA, BOTSWANA, Walvis Bay (S. Africa), LESOTHO, SWAZILAND, SOUTH AFRICA

Cabinda (Angola)

ATLANTIC OCEAN

INDIAN OCEAN

Red Sea, Gulf of Aden, Equator, Tropic of Capricorn

---

becoming independent. Dakar, the capital city, has been called the cultural center for all French-speaking West Africa.

Senegal is somewhat more democratic than many African states. It has a number of political parties. All but one,

however, are so small that they have never held power.

Gambia   Gambia, the smallest African country, was once a British colony. English is the official language of Gambia. There are several parties in Gambia. One,

477

■ Have students look at the map on this page to answer the following question: **What country produces 251,000 tons or more of coffee?** (Ivory Coast)

Read and Think
Section B

Discuss the political system and economy of Nigeria with the following questions:

1. **What are the origins of the name *Nigeria?***
   (The British invented the name to describe the different regions along the Niger River that were part of their empire. *p. 475*)

2. **Name four resources of Nigeria.**
   (Rich soil, forests, oil, and natural gas *p. 476*)

   Thinking Critically How, do you think, did high oil prices help or hurt Nigeria in the long run? (Hypothesize) (Answers should reflect independent thinking but may include that the economic boom appears to have hurt the country by disrupting agriculture and encouraging indebtedness. *p. 476*)

Answers to Caption Questions
p. 476 *l.* ▶ Hard hats and gloves
p. 476 *r.* ▶ Pineapples
p. 477 ▶ Ivory Coast

Curriculum Connection

Economics   Have students prepare a chart comparing the economies of the countries of West Africa.

- Tell them to use an almanac or encyclopedia to find information about population densities, resources, electricity production, and literacy rates.

- Based on the information they find, ask them to rank the five countries according to their economic health.

- Then, have students write one or two paragraphs explaining why they ranked the countries as they did.

For Your Information

Cote d'Ivoire   The Ivory Coast officially adopted the French version of its name, Cote d'Ivoire, in October 1985. Cote d'Ivoire is the most prosperous nation in West Africa and is among the most prosperous nations in tropical Africa because of its rich agricultural resources, its close ties to France, and its encouragement of foreign investment.

President Felix Houphouet-Boigny (oo FWAY BWAHN-yee), who took power in 1960, has been criticized by the leaders of other black African states for recognizing Biafra during the Nigerian civil war and for advocating dialogue with the white rulers of South Africa. The country leads the pro-Western bloc in Africa.

Optional Activities

Location

■ Direct students' attention to the political map of Africa found on this page to help them answer the following question:

1. **Locate the city in Botswana that is located near the Tropic of Capricorn.**
(Gaborone)

Read and Think

Section C

To discuss the West African nations of Ivory Coast, Senegal, and Gambia, ask the following questions:

1. **Which crops does Ivory Coast lead the world in exporting?**
(Coffee and cacao *p. 476*)

2. **Give two names for an important export crop in Gambia and Senegal.**
(Peanuts, groundnuts *p. 479*)

Thinking Critically Why, do you think, have Gambia and Senegal joined to form the Confederation of Senegambia? (Infer)
(Answers should reflect independent thinking but may include that the two nations perceived a mutual military threat to be deterred or mutual economic advantages to be gained through the alliance. *p. 479*)

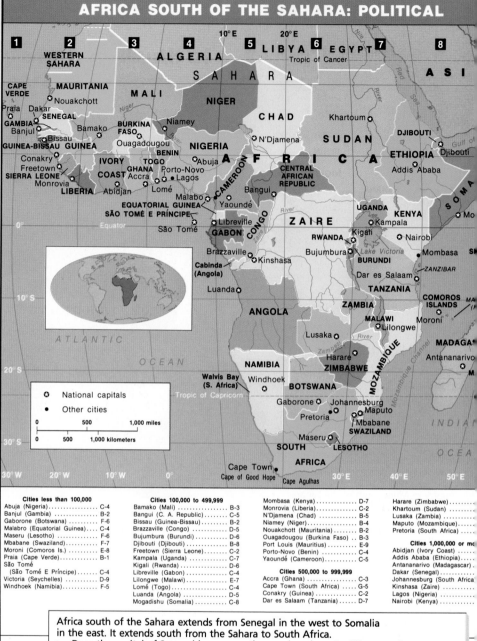

AFRICA SOUTH OF THE SAHARA: POLITICAL

⌖	National capitals
•	Other cities

0   500   1,000 miles
0   500   1,000 kilometers

Cities less than 100,000
Abuja (Nigeria) C-4
Banjul (Gambia) B-2
Gaborone (Botswana) F-6
Malabro (Equatorial Guinea) C-4
Maseru (Lesotho) F-6
Mbabane (Swaziland) F-7
Moroni (Comoros Is.) E-8
Praia (Cape Verde) B-1
São Tomé
   (São Tomé E Príncipe) C-4
Victoria (Seychelles) D-9
Windhoek (Namibia) F-5

Cities 100,000 to 499,999
Bamako (Mali) B-3
Bangui (C. A. Republic) C-5
Bissau (Guinea-Bissau) B-2
Brazzaville (Congo) D-5
Bujumbura (Burundi) D-6
Djibouti (Djibouti) B-8
Freetown (Sierra Leone) C-2
Kampala (Uganda) C-7
Kigali (Rwanda) D-6
Libreville (Gabon) C-4
Lilongwe (Malawi) E-7
Lomé (Togo) C-4
Luanda (Angola) D-5
Mogadishu (Somalia) C-8

Cities 500,000 to 999,999
Accra (Ghana) C-3
Cape Town (South Africa) G-5
Conakry (Guinea) C-2
Dar es Salaam (Tanzania) D-7

Cities 1,000,000 or more
Mombasa (Kenya) D-7
Monrovia (Liberia) C-2
N'Djamena (Chad) B-5
Niamey (Niger) B-4
Nouakchott (Mauritania) B-2
Ouagadougou (Burkina Faso) . . B-3
Port Louis (Mauritius) E-9
Porto-Novo (Benin) C-4
Yaoundé (Cameroon) C-5

Harare (Zimbabwe) . . . .
Khartoum (Sudan) . . . .
Lusaka (Zambia) . . . .
Maputo (Mozambique) . . . . . .
Pretoria (South Africa) . . . . . .

Cities 1,000,000 or more
Abidjan (Ivory Coast) . . . . . .
Addis Ababa (Ethiopia) . . . . .
Antananarivo (Madagascar) . .
Dakar (Senegal) . . . .
Johannesburg (South Africa . .
Kinshasa (Zaire) . . . .
Lagos (Nigeria) . . . .
Nairobi (Kenya) . . . .

Africa south of the Sahara extends from Senegal in the west to Somalia in the east. It extends south from the Sahara to South Africa.
▶ Does the capital of Senegal have more than, or less than, 1 million people?

478

Reteaching Main Objective

★ *Describe the countries of West Africa.*

● Provide students with an outline map of the countries of West Africa.

● Have them work together to label the countries on the map and list, either within the outline of each country or in a separate map key, the form of government and principal resources of each country.

PRODUCTS OF PEANUTS

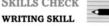

Peanuts
Peanut oil
Peanut butter
Soap
Cookies
Furniture polish
Paint
Ink
Margarine
Flour
Cosmetics

This chart shows some of the products that come from peanuts.
▶ Where on the peanut plant do the pods, or the shells that contain the nuts, grow?

however, has had more political power than the others.

Gambia's main export is peanuts. Peanuts are also called **groundnuts** because they grow underground rather than on trees or bushes. Groundnuts are an important crop in Senegal, too.

One village in Gambia is known to many through the book *Roots* by Alex Haley. The village of Juffere was the home of Haley's ancestor Kunta Kinte. Like Haley, other African Americans have looked for their ancestors' homelands.

Gambia and Senegal are separate countries, but they have joined to form the Confederation of Senegambia. Under this arrangement the nations have agreed to act together on defense and other matters.

LESSON 1 REVIEW

THINK AND WRITE

A. How did Ghana's government change after it became independent? **(Recall)**

B. What problems did Nigeria face when British rule ended? **(Infer)**

C. Summarize the similarities and differences between the governments of Ivory Coast, Senegal, and Gambia. **(Analyze)**

SKILLS CHECK

WRITING SKILL

Imagine that you have traveled to West Africa to find your "roots." Write a brief letter to a friend in the United States describing your emotions on discovering the village where your ancestors were born.

479

Optional Activities

3 CLOSING THE LESSON

Lesson 1 Review

Answers to Think and Write

A. After independence, the government of Ghana was taken over by a group of army officers. Though the country is called a republic, it is under military rule and its people cannot choose their government.

B. When British rule ended, Nigeria faced the problem of uniting people of many different ethnic groups. Despite civil war, Nigeria has remained one country.

C. Only one political party has any real power in Ivory Coast, Senegal, and Gambia, but other parties do exist in Senegal and Gambia.

Answer to Skills Check

Answers will vary but should reflect an understanding of the importance of discovering one's ancestral home.

Focus Your Reading

Ask the lesson focus question found at the beginning of the lesson: **What problems did West African countries face after independence?**

(After independence, the countries of West Africa had the problems of unifying different ethnic groups within their countries, maintaining stability, and establishing democratic governments.)

Additional Practice

You may wish to assign the ancillary materials listed below.

Understanding the Lesson p. 121
Workbook p. 102

┌ **Answers to Caption Questions** ┐
p. 478 ▶ More than 1 million
p. 479 ▶ On the underground part of the plant

479

Central Africa

Objectives

★1. **Explain** what the Central African countries discussed in this lesson have in common.

2. **Discuss** the histories of Zaire and Cameroon.

3. **Identify** the following people and places: *Pygmies, Albert Schweitzer, Belgian Congo, Mount Cameroon, Zaire, Congo, Gabon,* and *Central African Republic.*

1 STARTING THE LESSON

Motivation Activity

■ Ask students what they know about Pygmies.

■ Tell students that in this lesson they will learn about the country where Pygmies live and what their lives are like.

Think About What You Know

■ Assign the THINK ABOUT WHAT YOU KNOW activity on p. 480.

■ Student answers should reflect independent thinking but may include problems of unifying different groups and establishing democratic forms of government.

Study the Vocabulary

■ Have students look up the definitions of the vocabulary words in the Glossary.

■ Ask them to list words that are similar to *Africanized* but that refer to other countries or cultures (for example, *Anglicized*).

LESSON **2**

Central Africa

THINK ABOUT WHAT YOU KNOW
Most of the nations of Central Africa became independent around 1960. What problems, do you think, would a new country face?

STUDY THE VOCABULARY
Africanized   cash crop

FOCUS YOUR READING
What do the countries discussed in this lesson have in common?

A. Zaire: The Importance of Names

Zaire is one of the largest countries south of the Sahara. It is also one of the largest on the African continent. Because of its size, Zaire is easy to locate on a map of Africa. But you would not find Zaire on a map made in 1970. Instead you would see a land labeled *Republic of the Congo.* You would also discover cities with different names. Kinshasa (keen SHAH sah), which is the capital of Zaire today, was then called Léopoldville. Kisangani (kee sun GAYN ee) was Stanleyville.

The names of both the country and its cities were **Africanized** — changed to African forms. The African names were one way to show that the country was completely independent. The old names reminded people of a time when Europeans had ruled. Léopoldville was named after King Leopold II of Belgium. Stanleyville was named for Henry Stanley, the first white man to explore the Congo River, now known as the Zaire.

Even though place-names have been Africanized, French remains the official

language in Zaire. It was used during the years of Belgian rule and is understood by leaders in all parts of the country. Zaire's different ethnic groups, however, have their own languages.

B. Different Ways of Life in Zaire

Zaire's Economy The peoples of Zaire have varied ways of living. Most work on the land. Many are subsistence farmers; others grow **cash crops** such as cacao and peanuts. These crops are grown for sale rather than for the farmer's own use.

A number of people make their living as miners. Zaire produces copper, tin, zinc, and uranium. It is the world leader in the production of industrial diamonds, which are needed in industry for grinders, glass cutters, and oil drills.

AFRICA SOUTH OF THE SAHA CACAO AND PEANUTS

- Cacao
- Peanuts

Cacao and peanuts are two main crops grown in southern Africa.
▶ Which crop is more abundant in Africa south of the Sahara?

Writing to Learn

Writing an Informational Letter Have students pretend that they are Zairian officials in the early 1970s.

● Ask students to write letters to the citizens of Zaire, explaining why the names of the country and its cities are being changed.

● The letter should explain how the name changes will affect the attitudes of Zairians and people of other countries.

The Mbuti of Zaire live by hunting and gathering in the rain forests.
▶ How would you describe the rain forests shown above?

City Dwellers and Forest Dwellers
About 44 percent of the people in Zaire live and work in cities. Very different from the city dwellers are a group of people who live in the rain forest. Outsiders have called these people Pygmies because adults in the group average between 4 feet and 5 feet (between 1 m and 1.5 m) in height. The people themselves consider the name Pygmy to be offensive and prefer to be called by the name of their ethnic group. These names include Mbuti (em BOOTEE) and Efe (AY fay).

These forest people live by hunting and food-gathering. Their size makes it easy for them to move through the thick tropical forest. They do not grow crops or have permanent villages. Instead they move from one forest camp to another.

Officials have encouraged these forest dwellers to adopt a more settled way of life, but with little success. The building of roads and the cutting of the forests make their way of life increasingly difficult. A member of one of these ethnic groups has observed, "When the forest dies, we die."

C. Cameroon: A Mountain and a Country

Cameroon's History Cameroon is one of five independent countries that were once French colonies in equatorial Africa. The country takes its name from Mount Cameroon, an active volcano on its coast. One side of this mountain is one of the wettest places on earth. It receives about 400 inches (1,016 cm) of rain a year. The southern part of Cameroon lies in the tropical rain forest. The north is dry savanna.

481

Optional Activities

② DEVELOPING THE LESSON

Read and Think
Sections A, B, C, and D

Use the questions that follow to discuss the histories and economies of the countries of Central Africa:

1. **Why does French remain the official language in Zaire?**
   (It is understood by leaders in all parts of the country. *p. 480*)

2. **Compare the lifestyle of the Pygmies to the lifestyle of city dwellers in Zaire.**
   (The lifestyle of city dwellers is much more settled than the lifestyle of the Mbuti. *p. 481*)

3. **How do most people in Cameroon make a living?**
   (Farming *p. 482*)

4. **What vegetation regions are located in the Central African Republic?**
   (Savanna and forest *pp. 480-483*)

   Thinking Critically What do the many changes in the names and borders of the countries and cities in this lesson tell you about the recent history of Central Africa? (Infer)
   (The countries of this region have undergone many changes in leadership. *pp. 480, 482*)

GEOGRAPHY THEMES

Human-Environment Interactions

■ Direct students' attention to the map on the facing page. Then ask the following question:

1. **What region of Africa produces the most cacao and peanuts?**
   (The northwest)

481

Meeting Individual Needs

Concept:
Understanding a Hunting-and-Gathering Culture

Below are three activities that will help students understand a hunting-and-gathering economy like that of the Pygmies.

◆ **EASY** Ask students to imagine that they live in a forest which is located in an area with a warm climate.

Have them think of three things that they use every day. Discuss how students could obtain these items if they had to depend solely on the forest for all of their needs.

◀▶ **AVERAGE** Ask students to write an essay explaining what they think the Pygmy who was quoted in this lesson meant when he or she said, "When the forest dies, we die."

◀▮▶ **CHALLENGING** Have students write an essay comparing and contrasting life on a farm with life in a hunting-and-gathering society.

Tell them to include in their essays the advantages and disadvantages of each way of life.

Germany ruled Cameroon before World War I. After Germany's defeat in the war, Great Britain and France divided the country. When Cameroon became independent, one part of the British territory chose to become part of neighboring Nigeria. The remainder of the British territory joined with the French territory to form one country. Both French and English are official languages in Cameroon.

Cameroon's Economy About eight out of ten people in Cameroon are farmers. Many are subsistence farmers. At one time, Cameroon supplied most of its own food. Now it depends partly on imports to feed its growing population. Some farmers in Cameroon produce crops for export. Among these cash crops are cacao, coffee, and rubber.

D. Congo, Gabon, Central African Republic

Congo Before 1960 two African states had the name Congo. One was the Belgian Congo, the other the French Congo. The first became Zaire; the other is still called Congo. Brazzaville, the capital of Congo, is located directly across the Zaire River from Kinshasa.

About half of the people in Congo now live in cities. Only a small part of the land is arable. Timber was once the principal export, but oil has replaced it in recent years.

Gabon Gabon (ga BOHN), like Congo and Cameroon, was created from French Equatorial Africa. Libreville, Gabon's capital, is located almost on the Equator. *Libreville* means "free town." It was established by the French about 150 years

Gabon became independent in 1960. Presidential Guard members celebrate Gabon National Day.
▶ To what American national holiday can this celebration be compared?

Cooperative Learning

Assessing the Effects of Independence Divide students into five groups and assign each group a country in this lesson.

- Ask each group to research conditions in its country before and after independence.
- Have each student take responsibility for information for a different phase of life in that country (for example, education, health care, or transportation).
- Ask groups to compile their findings and use a television-documentary format with visual aids to present the information to the class.

Reteaching Main Objective

★ ***Explain what the Central African countries discussed in this lesson have in common.***

- Ask students to write facts about the countries of Central Africa on small slips of paper.
- Mix up the slips and have students take turns selecting facts.
- Discuss which facts apply to more than one country in Central Africa.
- Then, have volunteers pin the slips of paper on the appropriate country or countries on a wall map. (Students will need to make multiple copies of some facts.)

ago as a town for freed slaves. Another town in Gabon, Lambaréné (lahm buh RAY-nee), is known as the place where Albert Schweitzer, a Christian missionary, set up a hospital in 1913. It has room for 600 patients and their families. Schweitzer was a famous musician and philosopher in addition to being a medical doctor.

Gabon has forests, oil, and other mineral resources. Mining is the most important industry. About one fourth of the manganese used in the Western industrial countries is mined in Gabon. As you have learned in an earlier chapter, manganese is used to harden steel.

Central African Republic The Central African Republic is mostly savanna, although it has some forest. Diamonds are the leading export, but most people are employed in agriculture.

In 1976 a military leader had himself crowned emperor and changed the country's name to Central African Empire. But his empire did not last long. He was driven from power in 1979, and the nation again became a republic. The republic, however, has but one political party. Congo and Gabon are also one-party states.

Albert Schweitzer is shown above working in his hospital office.
▶ Besides medicine, what other fields was Albert Schweitzer famous for?

LESSON **2** REVIEW

THINK AND WRITE

A. Why did the Republic of the Congo change its name and the name of its capital? **(Recall)**

B. What are some different ways that people live in Zaire? **(Recall)**

C. Which European countries ruled Cameroon at different times in the past? **(Recall)**

D. What are the natural resources of Congo, Gabon, and the Central African Republic? **(Recall)**

SKILLS CHECK

MAP SKILL

Gabon's capital, Libreville, is one of the three capitals of African countries that lies almost on the Equator. Look at the political map of Africa in the Atlas on page 624 and name the other two African capitals.

483

Optional Activities

---

3 **CLOSING THE LESSON**

Lesson 2 Review

Answers to Think and Write

A. After independence, the Republic of the Congo used African words for its name and the name of its capital to show that it was completely independent of the European rulers who had previously named it.

B. People in Zaire live as subsistence farmers, commercial farmers, miners, city dwellers, and hunters and gatherers.

C. Cameroon has been ruled by Germany, Great Britain, and France.

D. Forests, oil, manganese, other minerals, and diamonds are the natural resources of Congo, Gabon, and the Central African Republic.

Answer to Skills Check

São Tomé is the capital of São Tomé e Príncipe, and Kampala is the capital of Uganda.

Focus Your Reading

Ask the lesson focus question found at the beginning of the lesson: **What do the countries discussed in this lesson have in common?**
(All were once colonies of European nations; most people in these countries make their living as farmers; French is an official language of all the countries, but different ethnic groups have their own languages.)

Additional Practice

You may wish to assign the ancillary materials listed below.

Understanding the Lesson p. 122

Answers to Caption Questions
p. 482 ▶ Fourth of July
p. 483 ▶ Music and philosophy

483

Southern Africa

Objectives

★ **1. Discuss** how relations between different races have affected the countries of Southern Africa.

2. Describe the resources of Southern Africa.

3. Identify the following people and places: *Afrikaners, South Africa, Zimbabwe, Botswana, Zambia,* and *Mozambique.*

1 STARTING THE LESSON

Motivation Activity

■ Ask students what problems would be caused by total racial segregation in the United States (would need to have two or more of everything; many people's skills and abilities would not be fully utilized, tension and violence could result).

Think About What You Know

■ Assign the THINK ABOUT WHAT YOU KNOW activity on p. 484.

■ Student answers should reflect independent thinking but may include that the history of the slave trade and of the Boers enslaving black Africans can help explain the tensions between races in Southern Africa today.

Study the Vocabulary

■ Pronounce the vocabulary words aloud for students before they read them.

■ Explain that these words come from another language that is similar to English. Ask students to guess the meanings of the words based on their sounds.

■ Have students find the meanings of the words in the Glossary.

■ Discuss the similarities of the sounds of these words and their English meanings.

LESSON 3

Southern Africa

THINK ABOUT WHAT YOU KNOW

Relations between different races are poor in many parts of Southern Africa today. What have you learned about the history of the region that would help to explain the racial situation there today?

STUDY THE VOCABULARY

apartheid   high veld

FOCUS YOUR READING

How have relations between different races affected the countries of Southern Africa?

A. Peoples of South Africa

Language and History Monuments usually honor great people or are set up in memory of great events. But in one of the nations of Southern Africa there is a monument to a language. The monument, which is in South Africa, honors Afrikaans (af rih KAHNZ), one of the two official languages of the country. The other official language is English. Afrikaans is based on the Dutch that was spoken by the earliest European settlers. It also includes many words from French, German, and a number of African languages.

The language monument was erected by Afrikaners, the descendants of the early settlers. The Afrikaners held fast to their own ways and language after the British acquired South Africa. Defeat in the Boer War only strengthened their desire to remain Afrikaners. The monument was a way to show pride in their culture. The majority of the white South Africans today are Afrikaners.

Whites are a minority in South Africa. Nevertheless, they have controlled the government. Only whites have had any real political power, although they make up just one-sixth of the population.

The white government of South Africa divided the population into four racial groups. The groups were white descendants of Europeans; black Africans; people of mixed race, called coloreds; and Asians, mostly of Indian descent.

The classification by race was used to keep whites in power and blacks powerless. More than two out of three South Africans are black, but they have had no voice in government. Coloreds and Asians have had only a limited part.

WHITE PERSONS ONLY
THIS BEACH & THE AMENITIES THEREOF HAVE BEEN RESERVED FOR WHITE PERSONS ONLY   BY ORDER PROVINCIAL SECRETARY

NET BLANKES
HIERDIE STRAND EN DIE GERIEWE DAARVAN IS NET VIR BLANKES AANGEWYS.   OP LAS PROVINSIALE SEKRETARIS

Apartheid laws restricted the freedom of blacks in South Africa.
▶ What people were permitted to use this beach?

Current Events

● Have students find newspaper and magazine articles about the racial and political situation in South Africa.

● Ask them to read the articles to find out what kinds of alternatives to apartheid have been proposed by different people or groups in South Africa.

● Have small groups work together to create a bulletin board or poster display about the current situation and its proposed alternatives in South Africa.

Optional Activities

B. History of Laws to Keep Races Separate

A Divided Nation In 1948 the South African government adopted a policy called **apartheid** (uh PAHR tayt). *Apartheid* means "apartness" or "separateness" in Afrikaans. The apartheid laws segregated people according to race. People of different races could not live in the same area, go to the same school, or eat in the same restaurant. Marriage between people of different races was illegal.

According to the white South African government, apartheid was supposed to provide for "the separate development of the races." Certain areas were set aside as "homelands" for blacks. But these areas were small, making up only 13 percent of the land. The large black majority could not possibly make a living there. Black people had to go to work on white-owned farms and in white-owned industries. As a result, many black workers have been forced to travel long distances to work each day. Some laborers, such as miners, have had to leave their families for long periods and live in camps near their jobs.

Protest In 1960 the South African government banned the African National Congress, the main black political party. Many people, however, continued to speak out against apartheid and were put in jail. One of the best known is Nelson Mandela. In 1962 he was sentenced to five years in prison. Later he was sentenced to life in prison.

Several black leaders urged black South Africans to use nonviolent protest to end apartheid. One of the most highly respected is Archbishop Desmond Tutu, who is now the leader of the Anglican Church in several African countries.

C. The Beginning of Change

Improvements Almost all blacks and some South African whites opposed apartheid. The policy was also condemned by people all over the world. Partly as a result of this condemnation, the South African government made some changes in the 1980s. Marriage between people of different races was no longer illegal. Segregated eating places were no longer required by law. Schools for blacks and whites were still separate, but funds for black schools were increased.

In 1990, the South African government realized it must do more to meet black demands. It lifted the ban on the African National Congress. It released Nelson Mandela from prison, a step that met with worldwide approval. The apartheid laws were finally repealed in 1991; but not all customs have changed. There is still much segregation in practice.

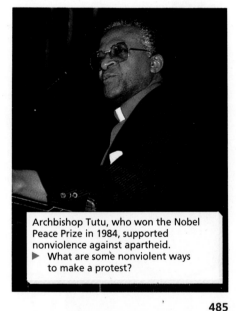

Archbishop Tutu, who won the Nobel Peace Prize in 1984, supported nonviolence against apartheid.
▶ What are some nonviolent ways to make a protest?

485

2 DEVELOPING THE LESSON

Read and Think
Sections A and B

Use the questions that follow to discuss South Africa and apartheid:

1. **What proportion of the population of South Africa is black African?**
   (More than two out of three South Africans are black. *p. 484*)

2. **What group in South Africa holds real political power?**
   (White descendants of Europeans *p. 484*)

3. **How did apartheid disrupt the family life of black South Africans?**
   (Rules about where blacks could live forced many to travel long distances to work or to live away from their families. *p. 485*)

   Thinking Critically What effect do you think worldwide condemnation had on the South African government's decision to repeal the apartheid laws? (Analyze)
   (Answers should reflect independent thinking but may include that economic and political pressure from the world community probably contributed to the government's decision to repeal the apartheid laws. *p. 485*)

--- **Answers to Caption Questions** ---
p. 484 ▶ Whites only
p. 485 ▶ Answers may include speeches, rallies, and boycotts.

Role-playing

● Divide the class into small groups. Within each group, have some students role-play South African whites, and some students role-play South African blacks.

● Tell each group to imagine that they are a commission appointed to rewrite South African laws to eliminate apartheid.

● Ask them what laws they would abolish and what new laws they would write.

● Remind students that even though some white people may want black people to be free, they may fear that black people would take revenge if they gained control of the government.

For Your Information

Apartheid The policy of racial separation in South Africa became official in 1948. In 1959, laws were passed providing for separate development, separate residential areas, and eventual political independence for each of the four racial groups of South Africa.

At least 600 people, mostly black, were killed in protests against apartheid in 1976. Among the most notable of the more recent protests was a strike by some 2 million black workers in June 1988.

Under apartheid laws, South African blacks and whites had separate schools, parks, buses, and restaurants. There were separate entrances and service areas in post offices and libraries.

Optional Activities

CITIZENSHIP AND AMERICAN VALUES

Objectives

1. **Explain** the meaning of apartheid.

2. **Develop** an awareness of and skills in resolving social issues.

Guided Reading

1. **How many years did Nelson Mandela spend in prison?**
   (27)

2. **What does apartheid mean?**
   (It is a system in which people of different races have different rights.

3. **Why did the African National Congress leaders turn to violent methods?**
   (Because after the police killed 69 peaceful demonstrators, the ANC saw that these peaceful demonstrations were not effective.)

4. **What subjects did Mandela study while in prison?**
   (Law, economics, and history)

5. **Why did people begin to call the prison "Mandela University"?**
   (Because younger prisoners followed Mandela's example and began studying)

6. **What did South Africa's new president, F.W. de Klerk, promise?**
   (He promised that he would work for change with black leaders if he were elected.)

7. **How did the blacks of South Africa react to Mandela's release?**
   (With joyous celebrations)

NELSON MANDELA: SYMBOL OF THE STRUGGLE AGAINST APARTHEID

"**O**ur march to freedom is irreversible. We must not allow fear to stand in our way." With those words, Nelson Mandela, a 71-year-old black South African leader was freed after almost 30 years in prison. In February of 1990 the South African government released Mandela. His freedom has raised the hope among millions of black South Africans living in that troubled country.

As you have just learned, the mostly-black nation of South Africa has been ruled by the white National Party for more than 40 years. This party began a system of apartheid, or apartness, where people of different races in South Africa have different rights.

Nelson Mandela, the son of a tribal chief who was born in a tin-roofed house, became involved with a black nationalist party called the African National Congress (ANC). The ANC and Mandela fought against the system of apartheid, starting with nonviolent demonstrations. Then, in 1960, after the police killed 69 peaceful demonstrators in the town of Sharpeville, the ANC saw that these peaceful demonstrations were not effective. ANC leaders set off bombs in four cities and made plans to overthrow the government. The South African government banned, or outlawed, the ANC, and Mandela and others were arrested for trying to overthrow the government. Mandela was sentenced to life in prison.

For the first ten years of his confinement, Mandela broke boulders into gravel with a pick-ax. In later years, he woke up every morning at 3:30, exercised for two hours, and then spent the rest of the day studying. He took correspondence courses in law and read about economics and history. Mandela was a role model to the younger prisoners. People began to call the prison Mandela University.

In 1989 the people of South Africa elected a new president, F. W. de Klerk, who had promised in his campaign that he would work for change with black leaders. Mandela had repeatedly refused

486

Optional Activities

For Your Information

One of Nelson Mandela's partners in the antiapartheid movement over the years was his wife, Winnie. She married Nelson in 1958 and became more and more involved in the movement after he was imprisoned.

The government forced her to leave her home in 1976 and move to Brandfort in the Orange Free State. She founded a rural health clinic there and became a symbol of the antiapartheid movement.

government offers of freedom on the condition that he leave the country or limit his activities against apartheid. After months of negotiations under the new president, Mandela was finally freed unconditionally, that is, without any reservations.

Nelson Mandela became a symbol of the struggle against the system of apartheid in South Africa. Mandela's release set off joyous celebrations among the blacks of South Africa. His dignity in his many years as a prisoner transformed him into a national figure who commands the respect of whites as well as blacks.

Thinking for Yourself

1. Why, do you think, has Nelson Mandela gained worldwide respect?
2. What characteristics does Mandela possess that helped him endure almost 30 years in prison?
3. Why, do you think, did Mandela become a symbol for the struggle against the policy of apartheid?

Thinking for Yourself

1. Answers should reflect independent thinking but may include because of his selfless devotion to the cause of racial equality.

2. Answers should reflect independent thinking but may include dignity, determination, and faith.

3. Answers should reflect independent thinking but may include that his leadership of the African National Congress and his devotion to the cause of racial equality during the long years of his imprisonment have made him a symbol of the struggle against apartheid.

Current Events

● Have students check newspapers and news magazines for articles about apartheid.

● Have students bring the articles they find to class and give summaries of them.

● Discuss the subject of apartheid from the black national point of view and from the South African government's point of view.

● Ask students to share their personal reactions to what they have learned from the articles.

Optional Activities

487

■ Direct students' attention to the map found on this page. Then ask the following question: **In what region of Africa is the most gold found?** (Southern Africa)

Meeting Individual Needs

Concept:
Understanding Apartheid

Below are three activities that will help students understand the impact of apartheid and how it works.

◆ **EASY** Have students list their daily activities and put a star by the ones that would change or not exist if they were black Africans in an apartheid system.

◀▶ **AVERAGE** Ask students to make a list like the one above and write a fictional account of a day in the life of a black South African sixth grader.

◀▮▶ **CHALLENGING** Have students write a skit in which non-South Africans try to bring about change in South Africa.

Give students a chance to rehearse and present their skit.

VISUAL THINKING SKILL

Interpreting a Graph

■ Have students use the graph on this page to help them answer the following question: **Which country is the second leading gold-producer in the world?** (Former Soviet Union)

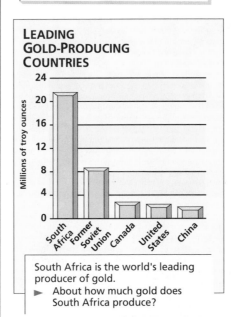

AFRICA SOUTH OF THE SAHARA: OIL, GOLD, AND DIAMONDS

▮	Oil
•	Gold
•	Diamonds

Some countries in southern Africa are rich in resources.
▶ What important energy resource is found in Africa south of the Sahara?

LEADING GOLD-PRODUCING COUNTRIES

South Africa is the world's leading producer of gold.
▶ About how much gold does South Africa produce?

488

C. South Africa's Resources

Valuable Minerals It is said that the discovery of diamonds in South Africa was an accident. Children playing on the banks of the Orange River in 1866 found some pebbles, which they took home. Later someone discovered that the pebbles would scratch glass. This is one way to test diamonds, which are the hardest of stones.

The discovery of diamonds, followed later by the discovery of gold, laid the foundation for South Africa's important mining industry. South Africa has half of the world's known gold reserves. It also has other minerals, including iron, chromium, nickel, tin, platinum, and coal.

Industry South Africa today is one of the continent's most industrialized countries. Its factories turn out automobiles, farm machinery, tires, and electrical equipment. Mining, agriculture, and industry all depend on black workers. Mining is a major South African industry, and most of the miners are black. They dig the country's gold, diamonds, copper, and other useful minerals. They do most of the heavy work in cities where whites live. This is one reason why complete separation of the races has not worked.

Tourism has also been an important industry. South Africa has a mild climate, striking scenery, beaches on two oceans, and large national parks where visitors can see animals in the wild. However, a number of people from other lands avoided going to South Africa because they disapproved of apartheid.

Agriculture South Africa is a major agricultural country in Africa. Early settlers discovered that the Mediterranean climate of the Cape colony was great for growing

Curriculum Connection

Science Mohs's scale, devised by German mineralogist Friedrich Mohs, ranks minerals in order of increasing hardness. Diamonds are the hardest mineral on the scale. The hardness of a mineral is determined by how difficult it is to scratch its surface.

● Find Mohs's scale in a dictionary. If possible, obtain samples of some minerals on the scale from a geology teacher or rock collector and bring the samples to class.

● With the teacher's or the collector's permission, let students experiment with the rocks to determine hardness. Then, have them compare their findings with the rankings on Mohs's scale.

Optional Activities

The high veld is valuable grassland that helps to make South Africa one of the important agricultural countries of Africa.
▶ How can you tell from the photograph above that the high veld is an agricultural area?

Read and Think
Sections C, D, and E

Use the questions that follow to discuss the countries and resources of Southern Africa:

1. **How does the economy of South Africa differ from the economies of the other countries of Southern Africa?**
   (It is more industrialized than the other countries and has more agricultural and mineral resources. *p. 488*)

2. **Why might Zimbabwe be important to black South Africans?**
   (Because black leaders now control this country that was once ruled by a white minority, as South Africa is today *p. 489*)

3. **What are the new names of the countries that were called Bechuanaland and Northern Rhodesia before they won independence from British rule?**
   (Botswana and Zambia *p. 490*)

Thinking Critically Why, do you think, did many white Zimbabweans leave after black leaders took control? (Hypothesize)
(Answers may include that they feared blacks would take revenge on their former rulers. *p. 489*)

wine grapes. When the settlers later moved out on the **high veld** (velt), they found land well suited for cattle and grain. The high veld is a region of open grassland with a good water supply and is similar to the Great Plains of the United States.

D. Zimbabwe: An Old Name Brought Back

Before it became independent, Zimbabwe was called Rhodesia. Then it was ruled by a very small white minority. When black leaders finally got control of the country in 1980, they proudly chose a name connected with Africa's past. The name Zimbabwe reminded the world that people in this land had built the stone structures of Great Zimbabwe long before white Europeans arrived in this part of Africa.

Many whites left the country after it became Zimbabwe. Today only about 1 percent of the population is white. Whites still own much of the best land. Some black families have received land from the government, but many are still waiting.

Harare (hah RAH ree), a large, modern city, is the capital and business center of Zimbabwe. The country has mines and some industrial plants, but agriculture is the most important industry. Zimbabwe usually produces enough food to feed its people and to export.

Answers to Caption Questions
p. 488 *t.* ▶ Oil
p. 488 *b.* ▶ About 22 million troy ounces
p. 489 ▶ There are cows grazing on the land, and rows of crops can be seen in the background.

Lesson 3 Review

Answers to Think and Write

A. South African laws divide the country's population into whites of European descent, Asians, blacks, and people of mixed race, or coloreds.

B. The purpose of apartheid is to keep people of different races separated from each other.

C. South Africa's resources include diamonds, gold, and other minerals; agricultural products such as grapes, wheat, and cattle; industrial products like automobiles, farm machinery, and electrical equipment; and tourist attractions.

D. Rhodesia took the name Zimbabwe as a reminder of the native Africans of that country who built the stone structures of Great Zimbabwe long before Europeans colonized Africa.

E. Civil war would drain a country's resources, cause damage, and affect jobs and production. Drought would affect agriculture.

Answer to Skills Check

Answers will vary but should reflect an understanding of the arbitrary and unfair nature of such a law.

Focus Your Reading

Ask the lesson focus question found at the beginning of the lesson: **How have relations between different races affected the countries of Southern Africa?**

(The apartheid policies of South Africa have affected relations between that country and other black-majority-ruled nations of Southern Africa who disapprove of apartheid.)

Additional Practice

You may wish to assign the ancillary materials listed below.

Understanding the Lesson p. 123
Workbook p. 103

E. Botswana, Zambia, and Mozambique

Botswana Before winning its independence from Great Britain in 1966, Botswana (baht SWAH nuh) was called Bechuanaland (bech oo AHN uh land). A large part of the country is desert or dry grassland. Copper mining and cattle raising are the most important industries. Although it has had close economic ties with South Africa, Botswana has strongly disapproved of apartheid.

Zambia Zambia was Northern Rhodesia under British rule. The leaders of this land also chose an African name when the country became independent in 1964. Zambia takes its name from the Zambezi River, on which it is located. The country recently changed from a one-party government to a multiparty government.

Victoria Falls and copper are two of Zambia's natural resources. The great falls are a tourist attraction. Copper is the most valuable export.

Mozambique Mozambique, as you learned in Chapter 17, was once a Portuguese colony. Located on the Indian Ocean, it offers an outlet to the sea for both Zimbabwe and Zambia. Mozambique

This African worker is mining copper in Zambia, where copper is the most valuable export.
▶ What piece of equipment is he working with?

has rich agricultural land and deposits of diamonds, copper, lead, and tin. But a long civil war, combined with drought, makes it one of the world's poorest countries.

LESSON 3 REVIEW

THINK AND WRITE

A. Into what four groups do South African laws divide the population? **(Recall)**

B. Summarize the purpose of apartheid. **(Infer)**

C. What are some of South Africa's resources? **(Recall)**

D. Why did Rhodesia take the name Zimbabwe when it became independent? **(Recall)**

E. In your opinion, why might civil war and drought make a country poor? **(Infer)**

SKILLS CHECK

WRITING SKILL

Imagine there was a law that separated students into different schools based on their hair color. Write a paragraph or two describing how that law would make you feel.

Optional Activities

UNDERSTANDING THE LESSON

◀ Review Master Booklet, p. 123

THINK ABOUT WHAT YOU KNOW

Tourism is important in East Africa. What are some sights that tourists to your state visit?

STUDY THE VOCABULARY

pyrethrum   teff

FOCUS YOUR READING

In what ways are the East African countries described in this lesson alike?

A. Kenya on the Equator

Nairobi, the capital of Kenya, is located just south of the Equator, yet it has a mild climate. Even during the hottest months, temperatures are not as high as on most July days in New York or Boston. Nairobi has a mild climate because it is located in the Kenyan highlands.

The climate of the highlands attracted white European settlers to Kenya when it was part of the British Empire. Whites made up only a minority of the population, but a large area, called the White Highlands, was reserved for them.

The black majority in Kenya felt it was unfair that so much of the best land was reserved for the white settlers. Blacks rose up against white rule in the 1950s. Kenya became an independent republic in 1964. Kenya's first president, Jomo Kenyatta, urged all races to help build the new nation. He gave the country its motto, *Hamambee*, "Pull together!"

The new government invited European and American companies to establish businesses in Kenya. A number of foreign companies did so, but agriculture and cattle raising remain the main occupations in Kenya. Cash crops that are grown mainly for export include coffee, tea, cotton, and **pyrethrum**. Pyrethrum is a plant used to make insect poison.

B. Tourism and a Growing Population

Kenya is one of the most visited countries in Africa, so tourism is a big business. People come partly to see the scenery, but mainly to see the marvelous variety of African animals and birds there. Kenya has a

This plantation worker is picking tea on the highlands in Kenya.
▶ Why, do you think, is it useful for the worker to carry the basket on his back?

491

Role-playing

- Divide students into groups of six or seven and have them role-play the conflict between white and black Kenyans over the use of the highlands.

- Have one or two students in each group portray white settlers and have the other students portray native Kenyans, including one who is Jomo Kenyatta.

- Tell students to use the library to get information about the characters that they are portraying. Tell them that their role-playing should include facts such as the year and place of the revolt.

Optional Activities

LESSON 4   PAGES 491–494

East Africa

Objectives

★1. **Discuss** the similarities of the countries of East Africa.

2. **Describe** the tourist attractions of East Africa.

3. **Identify** the following person and places: *Jomo Kenyatta, Kenya, Nairobi, Tanzania, Mount Kilimanjaro, Ethiopia, Addis Ababa, Sudan*, and *Khartoum*.

1 STARTING THE LESSON

Motivation Activity

■ Tell students that in this lesson they will learn about the countries that attract the most tourists to Africa.

■ Ask students what they think draws tourists to these nations. Write their answers on the chalkboard and leave them for reference during the lesson.

Think About What You Know

■ Assign the THINK ABOUT WHAT YOU KNOW activity on p. 491.

■ Answers will vary from state to state, but students might refer to historic sites, national parks, recreational resources, or museums.

Study the Vocabulary

■ Have students look at the vocabulary words and ask what they think these words describe. (For example, are they places, types of animals, or buildings?) Give hints that will encourage students to guess that these are resources and/or plants.

■ Then, have students find the meanings of the words in the Glossary.

┌─ **Answers to Caption Questions** ─┐
p. 490 ▶ Some type of drill
p. 491 ▶ Answers may include to keep his hands free.
└──────────────────────────────┘

Read and Think

Sections A and B

Use the questions that follow to discuss the nation of Kenya:

1. **What was the attitude of Jomo Kenyatta toward whites?**
(He wanted them to help build the newly independent Kenya. *p. 491*)

2. **Why do tourists visit Kenya?**
(To see the scenery and the variety of African animals and birds *p. 491*)

Thinking Critically Do you think Kenya's population growth is likely to slow down or speed up? (Infer)
(Answers should reflect independent thinking but may include that it will speed up because most of its people are young. *p. 492*)

Meeting Individual Needs

Concept: Understanding a Population Explosion

These three activities will help students understand rapid population growth in countries such as Kenya.

◆ **EASY** Work with students to create a family-tree chart showing how, in two or three generations, two people can develop into more than 60 people if each person in each generation has three children.

◀▶ **AVERAGE** Tell students that more than half of Kenya's approximately 24 million people are under the age of 15.

Ask each student to list three ways that these approximately 12 million people will strain Kenya's resources as they reach adulthood (more food, more land, and more housing will be needed).

◀▐▶ **CHALLENGING** Ask students who need a challenge to propose a way to slow Kenya's population growth.

Have students present their proposals to the class.

Many tourists go to Tsavo National Park to see the wildlife of Africa.
▶ What animal herd is shown below roaming the park?

number of parks. Tsavo National Park outside Nairobi is the largest national park in the world.

Kenya's population has been growing rapidly. More than twice as many people live in Kenya today as in 1964. The nation's population is also very young, with more than half under the age of 15. A young and growing population needs land and jobs. Farmland in Kenya is limited because more than half of the country is desert. The number of jobs in industry has grown, but not as fast as the population.

C. Two Countries Unite

When Tanganyika and the island of Zanzibar joined together to form one country in 1964, they took the name Tanzania.

Tanganyika was a German colony until Great Britain took it over after World War I. Zanzibar was already under British rule. Both countries had become independent in the early 1960s.

Farmers in Tanzania raise cotton, coffee, and sisal. Zanzibar and nearby islands are referred to as the Clove Islands because they produce that spice.

Mount Kilimanjaro, Africa's highest mountain, is in Tanzania. When the first European explorer to see it reported that there was a snowcapped mountain on the Equator, people did not believe him. Today large numbers of tourists travel to Tanzania to see the mountain and to visit the national parks. Almost one fourth of the country is parkland.

Optional Activities

Curriculum Connection

Ecology Have students research the animals found in Kenya's Tsavo National Park or in the parks of Tanzania.

● Ask them to prepare a visual display on the animals of these parks, either in the form of a poster or a bulletin board.

● The display should indicate which of these animals are threatened or endangered.

● You may wish to have students describe efforts to preserve each species.

Changes in an Old Country

History and Economy About 100 years ago, Menelik II, emperor of Ethiopia, lived on top of a mountain near the center of his empire. It was cold there, and Taitu, the empress, persuaded Menelik to build a new residence farther down the mountain, near a hot spring. This was the beginning of a city. Taitu called it Addis Ababa, or "Little Flower." Addis Ababa is now a city of more than a million people.

Ethiopia is largely an agricultural country. Coffee is its main export. A grass-like grain called **teff**, which is little known in other parts of the world, is another important crop. The Ethiopians make a thin, flat bread from teff, which is used to scoop up hot, spicy stews.

Famine and Civil War In 1974 the last Ethiopian emperor, Haile Selassie (HYE lee suh LAS ee), was overthrown. Mengistu, a military leader, became president of Ethiopia. He was a harsh Communist ruler with ties to the Soviet Union. A long civil war against him ended in May 1991, when he was forced to flee the country. Drought conditions that have brought famine persist, but now that the war has ended, more food aid may get through to the people.

E. Sudan: A Meeting Place

Sudan is the largest country in Africa, extending from Zaire to Egypt. Here Africa south of the Sahara meets North Africa and the Middle East.

FROM BERRIES TO COFFEE

2. Berries are dried and sorted.

3. Beans are removed from the berries.

4. Beans are roasted and ground.

5. Coffee is tested.

6. Coffee is packed for sale.

Unroasted coffee beans are often exported to the country where the final product will be sold.
► What is done to the unroasted beans before the product can be sold?

Read and Think
Sections C, D, and E

Use the questions that follow to discuss the other countries and conflicts of East Africa:

1. **How is Tanzania similar to Kenya?**
(Both have large national parks and important tourist industries. *pp. 491-492*)

2. **How did political problems combine with drought to bring hardship to Ethiopians?**
(Opposition to President Mengistu led to a long civil war. Drought conditions led to a famine, which resulted in many deaths. *p. 493*)

Thinking Critically Why, do you think, is the capital of Sudan located where it is? (Hypothesize)
(Answers should reflect independent thinking but may include that it is located in the major agricultural region, which is the richest region of the country. *p. 494*)

VISUAL THINKING SKILL

Interpreting a Flow Chart

■ Direct students' attention to the flow chart on this page. Then ask the following question: **What happens to the coffee beans immediately after they are removed from the berries?**
(They are roasted and ground.)

— Answers to Caption Questions —
p. 492 ► Elephants
p. 493 ► They must be roasted, ground, tested, and packed for sale.

For Your Information

The Origins of Human Beings Many anthropologists believe that the first human beings may have lived in the Great Rift Valley of southern Kenya and northern Tanzania some two million years ago. These people (*Australopithecus* and *Homo habilis*) knew how to control fire, made tools out of chipped stone, and probably had some type of language.

Louis, Mary, and Richard Leakey (father, mother, and son, respectively) are the archaeologists whose discoveries in East Africa have been most noteworthy. Although their findings have often been controversial, their work has convinced many that the evolution of humans took place in Africa rather than in Asia.

Reteaching Main Objective

⭐ ***Discuss the similarities of the countries of East Africa.***

● Divide students into four groups. Assign each group a country from this lesson.

● Have students use the text (and other reference books, if you wish) to assemble lists of facts about their assigned country.

● Ask each group to read its lists aloud, while members of other groups check off facts that also appear on their lists.

● Then, ask students how many facts on their lists matched items on the other lists.

Optional Activities

Lesson 4 Review

Answers to Think and Write

A. The White Highlands was an area that Europeans restricted to white settlement, causing resentment among blacks.

B. Kenya's growing population affects tourism because people need the land used by animals that the tourists come to see.

C. Tanzania's name combines Tanganyika and Zanzibar, the countries that formed it.

D. After the overthrow of Haile Selassie, Ethiopia faced a long civil war, a drought, and a famine.

E. Sudan has been called a meeting place because it includes the climates and cultures of sub-Saharan Africa and the Middle East.

Answer to Skills Check

Graphs should reflect the following information: Mt. Kilimanjaro, 19,340 ft (5,895 m); Mt. Olympus, 9,570 ft (2,917 m); Mont Blanc, 15,771 ft (4,807 m); Mt. Ararat, 16,945 ft (5,165 m); and Mt. Damāvand, 18,934 ft (5,771 m).

Focus Your Reading

Ask the lesson focus question found at the beginning of the lesson: **In what ways are the East African countries described in this lesson alike?**

(They are all mainly agricultural, and all face problems regarding allocation of resources.)

Additional Practice

You may wish to assign the ancillary materials listed below.

Understanding the Lesson p. 124
Workbook pp. 104–106

Answers to Caption Questions
p. 494 ▶ Khartoum

The White Nile and the Blue Nile join at the place shown here.
▶ What city is located where these rivers meet?

Northern Sudan, like Egypt, is desert. The climate is also similar to that of Egypt. Khartoum, the capital of Sudan, is located where the White Nile and Blue Nile flow together. The irrigated land between the rivers is Sudan's major agricultural region. Fine cotton is one crop grown there. In southern Sudan the desert gives way to savanna and woodlands.

People in north Sudan speak Arabic and are Muslims. Black Africans in the south have many languages. Some are Christians, but most follow African religions.

Blacks make up the largest group, but Arabic-speaking Muslims have controlled the government. When the government ruled in 1962 that the nation's laws would be based on Muslim laws, civil war broke out between the north and the south. To this day the meeting of Africa and the Middle East in Sudan has brought more conflict than understanding.

LESSON 4 REVIEW

THINK AND WRITE

A. What are the White Highlands, and why were they a cause of conflict? **(Infer)**

B. How does Kenya's growing population affect tourism? **(Infer)**

C. How does Tanzania's name explain the country's origin? **(Recall)**

D. What problems did Ethiopia face after Haile Selassie was overthrown? **(Recall)**

E. Why has Sudan been called a meeting place? **(Infer)**

SKILLS CHECK

THINKING SKILL

You have learned that Mount Kilimanjaro is Africa's highest peak. In earlier chapters you have read about mountain peaks in other regions of the world. Look in the Gazetteer to find the heights for the following: Mount Kilimanjaro, Mount Olympus, Mont Blanc, Mount Ararat, and Mount Damāvand. Then make a graph using the information you found.

Optional Activities

UNDERSTANDING THE LESSON

NAME _____ CHAPTER
UNDERSTANDING THE LESSON 18

Organizing Facts LESSON 4 CONTENT MASTER

✱ The chart shows the main ideas of the lesson. Fill in the blank spaces with the details that support each main idea. One has been done for you.
Suggested answers are provided.

Kenya's climate helps agriculture and tourism prosper.	Tanzania contains many farms, parks, and Africa's highest mountain.
1. The Kenyan highlands are near the Equator but have a mild climate.	1. Farmers raise cotton, coffee, sisal, and cloves.
2. Agriculture and cattle raising are the main occupations in Kenya.	2. Many people visit Mount Kilimanjaro and the national parks.
3. Many tourists come to see Kenya's scenery, animals, and birds.	3. One fourth of the country is parkland.

Countries in East Africa

Ethiopia is an agricultural country that has faced problems in recent years.	Sudan contains a mixture of regions, peoples, and religions.
1. Coffee and teff are important crops in Ethiopia.	1. Northern Sudan is desert, while the south is savanna and woodlands.
2. Quarrels and conflicts broke out within Ethiopia and with neighboring Somalia.	2. Some people in Sudan speak Arabic; others speak African languages.
3. Because of drought, many people left home to search for food.	3. People in Sudan follow Muslim, Christian, and African religions.

Think and Write: Write a paragraph describing some of the tourist attractions in East Africa. You may use the back of the sheet.
Answers should reflect independent thinking; suggestions appear in the Answer Key.

124 Use with textbook pages 491–494.

◀ **Review Master Booklet, p. 124**

USING THE VOCABULARY

Africanized
cash crop
apartheid
high veld
teff

Each of the following sentences is an answer to a question about a term above. On a separate sheet of paper, write a question to go with each answer.

Example:
Answer: They are Gambia's main export.
Question: What are groundnuts?

1. This open grassland is well suited for cattle and grain.
2. Some African nations did this to their place-names to show independence.
3. Bread is made from this grasslike grain.
4. People throughout the world think this policy is unfair.
5. A profit can be made if this agricultural product is sold.

REMEMBERING WHAT YOU READ

On a separate sheet of paper, answer the following questions in complete sentences.

1. What two people led movements for African independence in the 1950s?
2. What caused the economic boom to end in Nigeria?
3. What is the principal natural resource of the Ivory Coast?
4. What two countries form the Confederation of Senegambia?
5. What is the largest country south of the Sahara?
6. Why have the names of many countries and cities been Africanized?
7. How do the Pygmies of Zaire live?
8. How did Cameroon get its name?
9. What three nations were created from French Equatorial Africa?
10. What two discoveries laid the foundation for South Africa's mining industry?
11. What was Zimbabwe called before it became independent?
12. Why is Kenya one of the most visited countries in the world?
13. What country did Tanganyika and the island of Zanzibar join to form in 1964?
14. Where is Mount Kilimanjaro located?
15. What caused civil war to break out in Sudan?

TYING LANGUAGE ARTS TO SOCIAL STUDIES

Imagine you are on a five-day photographic safari, taking pictures of African birds and animals. You will keep a journal of your trip. First, you need to do some reading about African wildlife. Now you are ready to begin your journal. Tell where in Africa you are. Write about some of the photographs that you take each day. You may choose to describe some of the animals, what they were doing, or what you think will make your photographs special.

495

Using the Vocabulary

1. What is the high veld?
2. What is Africanized?
3. What is teff?
4. What is apartheid?
5. What is a cash crop?

Remembering What You Read

1. Jomo Kenyatta and Kwame Nkrumah
2. A fall in the price of oil during the 1980s
3. Good soil
4. Senegal and Gambia
5. Zaire
6. To show that they are completely independent of European rule
7. As hunters and gatherers
8. From Mount Cameroon, an active volcano on its coast
9. Congo, Gabon, and the Central African Republic
10. Diamonds and gold
11. Before it became independent, Zimbabwe was called Rhodesia.
12. Because of the marvelous variety of African animals and birds found there
13. Tanzania
14. Tanzania
15. The government's 1962 ruling that the nation's laws would be based on Muslim laws

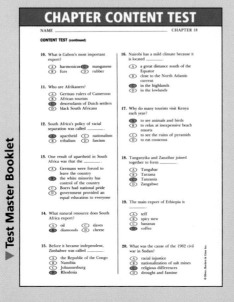

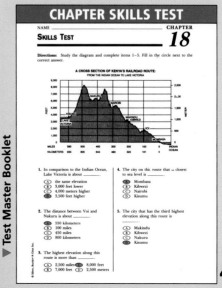

Thinking Critically

1. Answers may include because African lands were rich in resources.

2. Botswana's large areas of desert and dry grassland make cattle raising one of its most important industries.

3. Answers may include that it would harm it because most people work on farms or in the forests.

4. Answers may include manganese because Western industrial countries use this mineral to harden steel.

5. Answers may include by developing programs to control both the human population and the animal population.

Summarizing the Chapter

Lesson 1
1. Civil war in Nigeria in the 1960s
2. Drop in the price of oil
3. Democracy has been hard to establish.

Lesson 2
1. Most people are employed in agriculture.
2. Common history of European rule
3. Place names have been Africanized.

Lesson 3
1. Foreign nations disapprove of apartheid.
2. Zambia and Botswana disapprove of apartheid.
3. Civil war in Mozambique

Lesson 4
1. They are mainly agricultural.
2. Resource allocation problems
3. All have diverse populations.

THINKING CRITICALLY

On a separate sheet of paper, answer the following questions in complete sentences.

1. Why, do you think, were the countries of Europe interested in ruling African lands?

2. How can you explain the fact that cattle raising is one of Botswana's most important industries?

3. If the soil of the Ivory Coast were suddenly to become poor and unable to support plant life, how do you think that would affect the Ivory Coast's economy?

4. Which product of Gabon do you think is most important to Western countries? Explain why.

5. How do you think Kenya could resolve the conflict between its people's demand for land and its animals' need for land?

SUMMARIZING THE CHAPTER

On a separate sheet of paper, draw a graphic organizer like the one shown here. Copy the information from this graphic organizer to the one you have drawn. Under the main idea for each lesson, write three statements that support the main idea.

CHAPTER THEME Independence movements in Africa led to the end of European empires. Governments and economies are varied among African countries south of the Sahara.

LESSON 1
West African countries faced problems after gaining their independence.
1. _____
2. _____
3. _____

LESSON 3
Relations between different races have affected the countries of Southern Africa.
1. _____
2. _____
3. _____

LESSON 2
The countries of Central Africa have many things in common.
1. _____
2. _____
3. _____

LESSON 4
In many ways the countries of East Africa are alike.
1. _____
2. _____
3. _____

CHAPTER SKILLS TEST

NAME _____ CHAPTER 18

SKILLS TEST (continued)

Directions: Read the paragraphs and complete items 6–10. Fill in the circle next to the correct answer.

The Serengeti National Park in Tanzania is one of the largest in Africa. It has a wonderful variety of wild animals and birds. The Serengeti National Park is located east of Lake Victoria and extends to the border with Kenya. It covers an area as large as the state of Connecticut, and touches other partly protected reserves in neighboring Tanzania and Kenya.

The Serengeti National Park is mostly savanna with many scattered trees in the higher elevations. It contains some of the best grazing land in East Africa. Thousands of wildebeests are among the animals who feed upon its rolling high plains. The name wildebeest means "wild cattle," but the wildebeests are really a type of antelope. Visitors to the park not only see wildebeests but many other types of antelopes. There are gazelles, impalas, and even small dik-diks who get their name

from the sounds they make. A visitor to the park can see striped zebras mixing in with the huge wildebeest herds for protection.

The grazing animals need protection, for Serengeti is also a home for lions. There are several thousand in the park. Visitors being driven through sometimes see small groups of lions, called prides, hiding in the tall grass. It would be dangerous for a wildebeest to wander away from the herd when the lions are hungry.

There are other animals of prey in the park. Packs of wild dogs, hyenas, and jackals also hunt in the tall grass. If visitors are lucky, they might see a leopard draped over a limb in a tree. Cheetahs, large cats that are the fastest running animals for short distances, also live in the park. But these creatures are harder to see during the daytime.

6. The park is located in _____.
   (A) Kenya
   (B) South Africa
   ● Tanzania
   (D) Connecticut

7. The park is mostly _____.
   (A) tropical jungle
   ● savanna
   (C) rolling desert
   (D) mountain forest

8. A dik-dik is a type of _____.
   (A) wildebeest   (B) zebra
   (C) ostrich   (D) antelope

9. The animals of prey mentioned in this article include _____.
   (A) lions and wildebeests
   ● jackals and cheetahs
   (C) gazelles and cheetahs
   (D) impalas and antelopes

10. The best title for this article would be _____.
   ● Tanzania's Serengeti National Park
   (B) The Lion: King of the Savanna
   (C) Endangered Species of East Africa
   (D) Seeing Tanzania: A Guide for the Tourist

▶ Test Master Booklet

CHAPTER WRITING TEST

NAME _____ CHAPTER **18**

ESSAY TEST

Directions: Write a response to items 1–4.

REMINDER: Read and think about each item before you write your response. Be sure to think of the points you want to cover, details that support your response, and reasons for your opinions. Then, on the lines below, write your response in complete sentences.

1. What are groundnuts, and why are they important to the people of Gambia?
   A satisfactory response should include the following statements.
   · Groundnuts is another name for "peanuts"
   · They are an important crop and the main export of Ghana.
   An excellent response might also
   · explain that peanuts are called groundnuts because they grow underground, rather than on trees and bushes.
   · explain that the nuts are also an important crop in Senegal.

   _____
   _____
   _____
   _____

2. Who are the Mbuti?
   A satisfactory response should include the following statements.
   · The Mbuti are a group of small people who live in the forests of Zaire.
   · They live by hunting and food gathering.
   · They do not grow crops but move from one camp to another.
   · They have resisted attempts to have them adopt a more settled life, but the development of roads and the cutting of forests threaten their way of life.
   An excellent response might also include
   · the average size of the Mbuti and how that makes it easy for them to move through the forest.
   · a reference to the Mbuti statement "When the forest dies, we die."

   _____
   _____
   _____

▶ Test Master Booklet

CHAPTER WRITING TEST

NAME _____ CHAPTER 18

ESSAY TEST (continued)

3. What happened to Germany's African colonies?
   A satisfactory response should include the following statements.
   · Germany had colonies in Africa until the end of World War I.
   · After the war, Allied countries such as Great Britain and France took control of Germany's African possessions.
   · These colonies eventually gained their independence.
   An excellent response might also
   · identify former German possessions, such as Cameroon and Tanganyika (now part of Tanzania)
   · reflect independent thinking.

   _____
   _____

4. What was apartheid?
   A satisfactory response should include the following statements.
   · Apartheid was a system of South African laws designed to separate the races and keep a white minority in power.
   · It categorized people into four racial groups: whites, black Africans, coloreds, and Asians.
   · Although only one sixth of the population is white, only whites have any real power.
   An excellent response might also
   · include specific examples of how blacks were treated under apartheid.
   · mention the leaders and effects of protest against the policy.
   · reflect independent thinking.

   _____
   _____
   _____

▶ Test Master Booklet

REVIEW

COOPERATIVE LEARNING

You may wish to refer to the article on Cooperative Learning found in the front of your Teacher's Edition.

In Unit 5 you learned about the geography of Africa south of the Sahara. You also read about the economies, cultures, and governments of countries in this region.

A good way to present facts about these and other characteristics of a country is to make a bulletin-board display. Work with a group of classmates to design and make a bulletin-board display of information for one country you read about in Unit 5.

PROJECT

When your teacher assigns a country to your group, hold a group meeting to plan your bulletin board. Discuss what information you want to include in the display. As a group, decide what kinds of facts you think are most interesting and useful. You might want to do some research to add to information presented in your textbook.

After you have decided on the information to be included in the display, divide tasks among group members. Your group might divide tasks such as the following.

● One group member could draw and label a map of the country.

● Another group member could make a table or chart telling the country's size, population, chief exports, and capital city.

● One person could find magazine or newspaper articles about recent events in the country and write a one-page summary of these events.

● Another group member could research and write a one-page biography about the country's leader.

● A group member could draw some pictures illustrating interesting places in the country.

PRESENTATION AND REVIEW

When each person has finished his or her part of the project, hold another group meeting. Decide on a background color and talk about how you will arrange your bulletin board. Then set up your bulletin-board display in your classroom.

Look at the displays designed by the other groups in your class. Are the bulletin-board displays attractive and fun to look at? Do they present clear, interesting, useful facts about countries in Africa south of the Sahara? Could your group's display be improved?

REMEMBER TO:
- Give your ideas.
- Listen to others' ideas.
- Plan your work with the group.
- Present your project.
- Discuss how your group worked.

Objectives

1. **Analyze** how political boundaries can change over time.

2. **Summarize** changes in the political divisions of Africa in the twentieth century.

Why Do I Need This Skill?

Political maps show boundaries and cities. By comparing political maps, one can see how boundaries have changed over a period of time, and if countries or cities have changed names from past to present.

Political maps are useful tools for making comparisons. One can compare political divisions or subdivisions of long ago with contemporary ones, or compare the size of nations at different periods in history.

Learning the Skill

To check students' comprehension of political maps, ask the following questions:

1. **How are countries and other divisions usually shown on political maps?**
   (In different colors)

2. **What might a star within a circle indicate on a political map?**
   (A capital city)

A. WHY DO I NEED THIS SKILL?

In Unit 5 you learned that the nations of Africa have undergone many changes in the twentieth century. Some of these changes are reflected on maps that show political divisions. By comparing political maps that show a particular region during different periods, you can quickly see how boundaries and other features of countries have changed over time. Comparing the political maps presented in your social studies textbook will help you remember some of the changes you have read about.

B. LEARNING THE SKILL

Political maps show the boundaries of countries within a region or the divisions within a country, such as states, countries, provinces, or republics. Countries and other divisions on a political map are usually shown in different colors so that the divisions can be easily distinguished from one another.

Political maps may also show cities within a political division. A symbol, usually a dot, is placed on a map to show where a city is located. A capital city may be indicated by a star within a circle. As on other types of maps, a map key on a political map often explains what particular symbols on the map stand for.

In Chapter 17 and Chapter 18, you read about changes that occurred in Africa. By comparing political maps that show Africa at different times in the twentieth century, you can see what some of those changes were.

The map on page 469 of Chapter 17 shows European claims in Africa in 1920. Turn to that page and study the map. The different colors on the map show the claims in Africa by various European colonial powers. Notice the colonial names of each area within the various claims.

Now turn to page 478 in Chapter 18 and study the map that shows Africa today. Flip back and forth between the two maps to see if you can notice any differences between what is shown on the maps. Which African countries retained the same name following the departure of the colonists? Which African countries were independent in 1920?

By comparing these two maps, you can see how the continent of Africa changed after these individual African countries became independent.

SKILL TRACE: Comparing Political Maps		
INTRODUCE PE pp. 498–499	**PRACTICE** TE pp. 498–499 WB p. 65 TE p. 536	**TEST** Unit 5 Test, TMB

Optional Activities

Homework Activity

- Ask students to look at two of the maps of Europe in Chapter 8 (p. 228, *Europe in 1914*; p. 231, *Europe After World War I*).

- Have each student write five questions that compare the political divisions or subdivisions shown on the maps. Also tell students to provide the answers to each question on a separate sheet of paper.

- Have students bring their prepared list of questions and answers to class, and exchange questions with one another.

- Students should then compare the two political maps, read and answer the questions, and check their responses against the answer key.

C. PRACTICING THE SKILL

On a separate sheet of paper, copy the table shown below. Next, turn to the map on page 469 and use it to find ten countries that existed in Africa in 1920. List the countries in the first column of the table. Then compare this map with the map on page 478. Indicate in the second column the present-day name of the country (in some cases there has been no change). In the third column list the empire of which the country was a part or with which it was associated. For example, if you listed Belgian Congo in the first column, you would write Zaire in the second column. In the third column you would write Belgian.

D. APPLYING THE SKILL

As you read this textbook, take the opportunity to compare political maps that show any particular region in different periods. Looking at the maps as you read about changes in the region will help you visualize the results of the changes. Looking back at the maps later on will help you recall the changes you have read about.

THE CHANGING MAP OF AFRICA

African Countries in 1920	Present-day Country	European Empire

499

Reteaching Activity

- Ask students who have difficulty analyzing the political changes between the maps compared in the Skillbuilder activity on pp. 498-499 to review with you as you provide them with additional skills practice.
- Have students compare the map *Europe in 1914* with the map *Europe After World War I.* Ask students to use the map keys to identify key political divisions on each map.
- Write students' responses on the chalkboard, making a Venn diagram to help students visualize the changes between the two maps.
- Encourage students to summarize their findings orally, and to use analysis to distinguish between the two maps.

Optional Activities

Practicing the Skill

The following answers represent ten possible combinations.

African Countries in 1920:

1. Algeria	6. Cameroon
2. Libya	7. Rio de Oro
3. Egypt	8. Basutoland
4. Angola	9. Ethiopia
5. Tanganyika	10. Italian Somaliland

Present-day Country:
1. Algeria
2. Libya
3. Egypt
4. Angola
5. Tanzania
6. Cameroon
7. Western Sahara
8. Lesotho
9. Ethiopia
10. Somalia

European Empire:
1. French
2. Italian
3. British
4. Portuguese
5. British
6. French
7. Spanish
8. British
9. Independent
10. Italian

For students who are still having difficulty with the concept of comparing political maps, you may wish to use the reteaching activity listed to the left.

Applying the Skill

As students read this textbook, they should compare political maps in regions where changes occurred to help them visualize those changes.

Objectives

1. Identify the steps in skimming and scanning.

Why Do I Need This Skill?

To help students better understand the importance of skimming and scanning ask the following question: **Can you describe what you do when you flip through television channels in order to select one?** (Answers may include skimming or scanning.)

Then tell students that they can apply the same skills when they read.

Learning the Skill

To check the students' comprehension of skimming and scanning ask the following questions:

1. **When do you skim a lesson and when do you scan a lesson?**
   (You skim before you read the lesson and you scan after you have read a lesson.)

2. **What is the purpose of skimming?**
   (The purpose is to get a general idea of what the lesson is about.)

3. **What is the purpose of scanning?**
   (The purpose is to look for specific information.)

SKILL TRACE: Skimming for Main Idea		
INTRODUCE PE pp. 500–501	**PRACTICE** TE pp. 500–501 WB pp. 56–57 PE p. 587 TE p. 545	**TEST** Unit 5 Test, TMB

SKILL TRACE: Scanning for Specific Facts or Ideas		
INTRODUCE PE pp. 500–501	**PRACTICE** TE pp. 500–501 WB pp. 42–43 PE p. 539 TE p. 545	**TEST** Unit 5 Test, TMB

500

A. WHY DO I NEED THIS SKILL?

Sometimes as you read your social studies textbook, you may want to get an overview of a particular lesson or chapter. At other times you may be looking for a specific fact or idea. In these cases, you can use the skills of skimming and scanning to get the information you want. Knowing how to skim and scan will help you to do a better job of locating needed information and studying social studies materials.

B. LEARNING THE SKILL

Skimming is reading a selection quickly to get a general idea of what it is about. Skimming a selection before you read it carefully will help you identify the main ideas and most important information.

Scanning is looking quickly over a selection to find some specific information. Readers usually scan material after they have read it. Scanning is especially helpful when you must answer questions about what you have read.

The table on the next page lists five steps to follow when you skim through a reading selection and four steps to follow when you scan for information. Study the skimming and scanning table carefully.

C. PRACTICING THE SKILL

Turn to page 505 and skim through Lesson 1 of Chapter 19, "Geography of South and East Asia," to see if you can get a general idea of what it is about. Follow the five steps in the table. Write a sentence that tells the topic of the first lesson.

What did you write? Did you mention the variety of land areas in South Asia?

Now turn back to Lesson 1 of Chapter 16, "Geography of Africa South of the Sahara," to practice scanning. See if you can find the European name for the second longest river in Africa.

How did you do? Did you find on page 441 that the Europeans called this river the Congo? Did the heading "Africa's Rivers and Lakes" help you find this information?

Turn to Lesson 2 in Chapter 19. Skim the lesson, following the steps on the chart. What is the topic of Lesson 2?

Now scan all of Chapter 16 to answer these questions.

1. What is bauxite?
2. Where does sisal grow?
3. How is sleeping sickness spread?
4. What is the deepest lake in Africa?
5. In what part of Africa are its tallest mountains found?

500

Optional Activities

Homework Activity

- Have students skim magazine or newpaper articles.
- Have them follow the steps on the skimming and scanning chart to summarize the article which they have read.

D. APPLYING THE SKILL

Skimming and scanning are important reading skills that you can use as you continue reading your social studies textbook. Before you read any chapter, skim through it to get an idea of what the chapter is about. After you have read a chapter, scan it to find facts you need to answer questions and to remember the important topics in the chapter.

SKIMMING AND SCANNING FOR INFORMATION				
What?	**When?**	**Why?**	**How?**	
Skim	Usually **before** you read a selection	To get a general idea of what a selection is about	1. Read the lesson title and the FOCUS YOUR READING question. 2. Read the first paragraph of the lesson. 3. Quickly glance through the rest of the lesson. Read the first sentence in each paragraph.	4. Pay attention to boldfaced vocabulary terms, headings, and other key words in the lesson. 5. Read the last paragraph in the lesson and see if you can summarize the lesson in your own words.
Scan	Usually **after** you have read a selection	To look for specific information	1. Decide what question you have and what information you need to find. 2. Read through the section headings until you find a section related to information you need.	3. Move your eyes quickly through the section until you come to a key word related to your question. 4. Read the nearby text to try to find the answer to your question.

501

Practicing the Skill

1. Bauxite is the ore from which aluminum is made.

2. Sisal grows in East Africa.

3. Sleeping sickness is spread by the tsetse fly.

4. Lake Tanganyika

5. East Africa

For students that are still having difficulty with the concepts of skimming and scanning, you may wish to use the reteaching activity listed below.

Applying the Skill

Since this activity does not require an answer, you may wish to have students review the steps in skimming and scanning listed on the table on p. 501 and apply these steps to their study of Chapter 19.

Reteaching Activity

● Pair students who have mastered the concepts with students who need reteaching.

● Have students practice skimming and scanning by answering the following questions from Chapter 20.

1. **What are some inventions and discoveries of the ancient Chinese?**
   (Making paper, inventing gunpowder, and making silk)

2. **Why did Japan close its door to European trade?**
   (The shogun feared that Europeans who came to trade would later try to rule.)

3. **What is a mausoleum?**
   (A large tomb)

South and East Asia

Unit Theme Influences from outside and within the countries in South and East Asia have caused dramatic changes in these countries' governments and cultures throughout history.

Chapter 19 Geography of South and East Asia

(pp. 504-521)

Theme A variety of lands and climates exist in South Asia and East Asia.

Chapter 20 History of South and East Asia

(pp. 522-539)

Theme East Asia and South Asia were affected by new religions, trade, and empire builders from Europe, the Middle East, and from within the regions themselves.

Chapter 21 South and East Asia Today

(pp. 540-564)

Theme The governments and economies of countries in South Asia and East Asia are varied.

September	Chapters	October	Chapters	November	Chapters	December	Chapters	January	Chapters	February	Chapters	March	Chapters	April	Chapters	May	Chapters
	MSH-1		2-4		5-7		8-9		10-12		13-14		15-17		18-20		21-23

PACING GUIDE

Bulletin Board Idea

CAN YOU NAME ME?

PAPER   SILK   GUNPOWDER

SAMURAI   TAJ MAHAL   MARCO POLO

Student Activity

Motivate students to identify and remember outstanding achievements relating to South and East Asia by having them research reports and post the reports with pictures of these items on the bulletin board.

Annotated Bibliography

Books for Teachers

Clayre, Alasdair. *The Heart of the Dragon.* Boston: Houghton Mifflin, 1985. ISBN 0-395-41837-2. (Ch. 21) This beautifully illustrated companion book for the PBS television series of the same name discusses themes such as remembering, believing, eating, working, creating, and trading.

MacDonald, C.A. *Korea, the War Before Vietnam.* New York: Free Press, 1987. ISBN 0-02-919621-3. (Ch. 20) The American involvement in the war in Korea is detailed.

Shapiro, Michael. *Japan: In the Land of the Brokenhearted.* New York: Henry Holt and Co., 1989. ISBN 0-8050-0395-9. (Ch. 21) Shapiro describes the national characteristics, ethnic relations, and other aspects of life in Japan.

Books for Students

Bahree, Patricia. *The Hindu World.* Morristown, NJ: Silver Burdett Press, 1983. ISBN 0-382-06718-5. (Ch. 20) The world's oldest living faith and third largest religion is presented in detail through text, time lines, photographs, and illustrations.

Barrett, G.W. *Ancient China.* White Plains, NY: Longman, 1969. ISBN 0-582-20453-4. (Ch. 20) The rich histories of ancient Chinese dynasties are presented.

Blumberg, Rhoda. *Commodore Perry in the Land of the Shogun.* New York: Lothrop, Lee, & Shepard Books, 1985. ISBN 0-688-3723-2. (Ch. 20) Fascinating illustrations and engrossing text combine to bring to life the opening of Japan and the resulting cultural clash.

Burland, Cottie. *Ancient China.* Chester Springs, PA: Dufour, 1974. ISBN 0-7175-0018-7. (Ch. 20) The culture and legacies of ancient China are given thorough coverage in this excellent text.

Caldwell, John C. *Let's Visit India.* Bridgeport, CT: Burke Publishing Co., 1984. ISBN 0-222-00914-4. (Ch. 21) The rich ethnic and religious diversity of the Indian subcontinent is presented through brief text and illustrations.

Carter, Alden R. *Modern China.* Danbury, CT: Franklin Watts, 1987. ISBN 0-531-10124-X. (Ch. 21) Life in modern-day China is presented for students in this concise book.

Farly, Carol. *Korea: A Land Divided.* Minneapolis, MN: Dillon Press, 1984. ISBN 0-87518-244-5. (Ch. 21) The histories, geographies, and cultures of the two Koreas are illustrated with photographs.

Greene, Carol. *Japan.* Chicago: Children's Press, 1983. ISBN 0-516-02769-7. (Ch. 20) Color photographs and useful maps add to this coverage of the land, history, and people of Japan.

Lawson, Don. *The War in Vietnam.* Danbury, CT: Franklin Watts, 1981. ISBN 0-531-04331-2. (Ch. 21) The author gives a clear description of the events leading to the war in Vietnam, the involvement of the United States, and the peace process.

Lepthein, Emilie U. *The Philippines.* Chicago: Children's Press, 1984. ISBN 0-531-602782-4. (Ch. 21) The history, geography, and culture of the islands of the Philippines up to the assassination of Begnino Aquino are illustrated with color photographs and maps.

Lye, Keith. *Asia & Australia.* Danbury, CT: Glouchester Press, 1987. ISBN 0-531-17067-5. (Ch. 19) The rich natural resources and diversity of climate in these areas are presented for students through many illustrations and maps.

Lyle, Garry. *Let's Visit Indonesia.* London: Burke Publishing Co., 1988. ISBN 0-222-01035-5. (Ch. 21) Photographs illustrate discussions of the cultures, lifestyles, economies, and histories of the 13,000 islands that compose Indonesia.

Verne, Jules. *Around the World in Eighty Days.* New York: Lancer Books, Inc., 1968. (Ch. 19) Phileas Fogg bets his life's savings that he and his valet, Passepartout, can travel around the world by balloon in only 80 days.

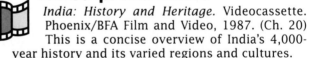

Filmstrips and Videos

India: History and Heritage. Videocassette. Phoenix/BFA Film and Video, 1987. (Ch. 20) This is a concise overview of India's 4,000-year history and its varied regions and cultures.

China Since Mao. Videocassette. BBC Films, 1988. (Ch. 21) The history of the world's most populous nation is traced from the death of revolutionary leader Mao to the changes brought about by Deng Xiaoping.

Children of Japan. Videocassette. Great Plains Instructional Television Library, 1987. (Ch. 21) This video presents the daily life of children in Japan during the mid-1980s and how the country's culture interfaces with the technological changes brought about by the modern world.

China: A Nation in Transition. Filmstrips. United Learning, 1989. (Ch. 21) Viewers are introduced to the history, culture, economy, and politics of China and the changes being made in the 1980s.

Japan's Amazing Success Story

An overnight success?

Modern Japan has been labeled an amazing, "overnight" success, but the truth is that Japan's success did not happen overnight at all. Since the early days of Japanese history, the Japanese have shown a particular talent for assimilating new ideas into their culture. They have not only been able to accept new ideas but they have often been able to improve upon them. Japan's post-World War II success is really only the latest chapter in an ongoing story. The following activities center around that story.

SOCIAL STUDIES

Economics Students can easily find evidence of Japan's success in stores throughout the United States today.

■ Have students find examples of Japanese products available on the market today.

■ Students may want to clip advertisements from magazines and newspapers and create a scrapbook or bulletin-board display of the items found.

■ You may wish to have students check news magazines or newspapers of 20 and 30 years ago to see how Japanese products have increased over the years.

■ Ask students to write an answer to the following question: **Why do you think Japanese products sell so well in the United States and in other countries?**

History Two major examples of countries that influenced Japan are China and the United States. The Chinese influence came very early — in the sixth, seventh, and eighth centuries. The Japanese took four principal ideas from the Chinese — writing, Buddhism, government, and art.

■ Have students produce a time line showing when the Japanese

adopted each of these ideas. Then mark the point of Western influence on the time line.

■ In the mid-nineteenth century, Japan once again made a major shift. Ask the students to find out how Western nations influenced Japan, in the mid-nineteenth century and again in the mid-twentieth century.

■ Students may want to produce a play or role-playing activity that shows the influence of the Chinese and the Americans on the Japanese.

Geography The geography of Japan helped shape the character of the country. Have students work in groups of four or five to create physical maps of the four main islands of Japan. You may wish to have students make their maps from papier-mâché, using a mixture of newspaper strips, wallpaper paste, and water. When maps are dry, have students color the mountains, rivers, plains, and other geographical features with tempera or poster paint.

LANGUAGE ARTS

■Many students mistakenly think that the language and writings of Japan are the same of those of China. Actually, they are completely different. It is true that hundreds of years ago the Japanese borrowed the Chinese way of using characters, but then they developed their own system — another example of borrowing an idea and changing it. Actually, the Japanese have a system of writing that resembles printed English letters. Have students study the ways in which the writing systems of China and Japan are alike and different. Students may wish to learn how to draw some of the Japanese characters.

SCIENCE

■The concepts of research and development have played a major role in Japan's success. Have students select items that the Japanese have successfully marketed, such as stereo equipment, cars, televisions, and cameras. Then have students research the answers to the following questions.

1. What role might research have played in the successful development of each of these items?

2. What technological or scientific principle is involved with each of these products?

3. What lessons can the United States learn from Japan's success?

■After students have written down their answers, have a discussion about the issues that they have raised.

LITERATURE

■Japanese literature is among the greatest in the world. It reflects many characteristics of the Japanese people, such as their appreciation of tradition and their sensitivity to nature. One popular and original form of Japanese verse is called *haiku.* A haiku poem consists of three unrhymed lines containing five, seven, and five syllables respectively. This type of poem refers to aspects of nature and merely suggests ideas and feelings, leaving the reader to use his or her own imagination to interpret them.

■Obtain books of Japanese haiku from a local library and read several poems to the class. Encourage students to write their own haiku and share them with the class.

ART

■The art of Japan is unique, although it, too, was strongly influenced by other cultures. Students may want to study the various forms of Japanese art: architecture, plays (including the Kabuki), paper folding (or Origami), flower arranging, paintings, calligraphy, and ceramics.

■Divide students into groups and assign each team one aspect of Japanese art to study and re-create. Have the students display their works to the class.

■Challenge students to research the foreign influence on their particular Japanese art form.

MUSIC

■Traditional Japanese music is often hard for students to understand and enjoy. It may sound very thin compared to the rich harmonies of Western music. It usually features only one instrument or voice at a time, rather than blending many harmonies together.

■Have students research and present orally reports describing the traditional instruments of Japan: the *biwa* (lutelike), *koto* (zitherlike), and *simisen* (banjolike). Encourage students to find illustrations or draw pictures of the instruments, and, if possible, bring in musical selections featuring them to play for the class.

Use an Atlas

INSTRUCTIONS FOR THE TEACHER:

Why Focus Attention on the Atlas? After a few years in school, many students may feel that they have given the atlas all the thought that is needed. For many, the atlas has been scanned and summarily dismissed. However, an atlas can be so much more than just a group of maps at the back of the book.

Unit 6 focuses on the lands, peoples, and histories of South and East Asia. The study of these topics can be greatly enhanced by the use of an atlas. This is an excellent chance to share with students the fact that an atlas can be a valuable source of information.

Different Types of Atlases Before distributing the atlases, ask students to list at least four different kinds of atlases and the information found in each. Some responses may include political atlases (which show divisions and subdivisions of continents, nations, states, cities, and so on), historical atlases (which show important leaders and events in specific segments of time), world atlases (which show cities, roads, countries, rivers, mountains, the size and relationship of land and water areas, and names of features and places), physical atlases (which show terrain, mountains, lakes, volcanoes, and other physical features), cultural atlases (which show the characteristics of different cultures of the world), United States atlases (which contain the same information as a world atlas but are limited to the United States), atlases of the ocean floor (which show the elevations and contours of ocean floors), and atlases of the solar system (which contain information about the sun, planets, and stars).

ACTIVITY FOR THE STUDENTS:

Discovering the Atlas One way to help students understand the value of the atlas is to conduct a class "atlas search" (or "atlas scavenger hunt"). This can be done in the classroom or in the library and is designed to help students understand the types of information available in various atlases, as well as understanding that there is more than one type of atlas. (Enlist the assistance of the school librarian, if possible.)

■ Gather as many atlases as possible for students to examine and use.

■ Divide students into small teams or groups and let each team examine one atlas or one type of atlas. Their task will be to share with the class the type and range of information contained in their atlas. If you have chosen to call this an atlas "scavenger hunt," provide students with a list of things they must find in their atlas such as: something interesting, something I already knew, something I didn't know, something that might help a weatherperson, something that might help a historian, something that might help a politician, something that might be found in a *Believe It or Not*-type of book, something that might be found in a "world records"-type of book, and so on.

■ If time allows, you may wish to ask students to list the types of skills needed to read the various maps contained inside their particular atlas. Students could then design a new cover or dust jacket for their atlas, using the words, *DO NOT OPEN UNTIL YOU KNOW HOW TO...* followed by the skills one would have to possess. Skills needed to use most atlases include understanding how to use scale, read a chart, read a graph, use a grid, read latitude and longitude, read a legend or key, and comprehend boundary lines and symbols.

An Atlas Bee After students have familiarized themselves with atlases in general, they might enjoy having an "atlas bee."

■ Divide the class into two teams.

■ Give students (individually, in groups, or in pairs) an atlas to use. (This can be the one in the back of their text, or can be several copies of the same paperback atlas that you have obtained from a library. It may also help to know that some insurance agencies, banks, and other businesses often give away small atlases to their customers.)

■ Prepare a list of places in the Eastern Hemisphere.

■ Call out the name of one of the places on your list.

■ Have the teams race to see who can first locate in the atlas the place that you have named. The first team to identify the place's latitude and longitude, grid marking, or page number wins a point.

■ At the end of the "atlas bee" the team with the most points for locating places wins.

Unit Test

CONTENT TEST

Directions: Fill in the circle next to the correct answer.

1. What separates the subcontinent from the rest of Asia?
   - (A) the Great Wall of China
   - (B) mountains
   - (C) the Indian Ocean
   - (D) rivers

2. What type of weather do summer monsoons bring to South Asia?
   - (A) rainy
   - (B) dry
   - (C) cold
   - (D) hot

3. Why do farmers in Southeast Asia build terraces?
   - (A) to entertain their guests outdoors
   - (B) because the land is very steep
   - (C) because rice requires lots of water
   - (D) to keep out wild birds and animals

4. Which of the following materials is used to produce rubber?
   - (A) latex
   - (B) plastic
   - (C) velcro
   - (D) bamboo

5. What is the world's second-largest desert?
   - (A) the Sahara
   - (B) the Mekong
   - (C) the Himalayas
   - (D) the Gobi

6. Which of the following countries is an island?
   - (A) Tibet
   - (B) Taiwan
   - (C) Thailand
   - (D) Vietnam

7. Which of the following countries is an archipelago?
   - (A) Japan
   - (B) China
   - (C) Vietnam
   - (D) Korea

8. Marco Polo is remembered for
   - (A) leading the Mongol invasion of China
   - (B) teaching Genghis Khan about Europe
   - (C) inventing a game played with horses
   - (D) describing his journey to China

9. The fibers used to make silk come from the _____.
   - (A) stomach of a sheep
   - (B) cocoon of a caterpillar
   - (C) leaves of a willow
   - (D) snout of a camel

10. Which port did the Japanese government allow to remain open to foreigners?
    - (A) Nagasaki
    - (B) Hiroshima
    - (C) Tokyo
    - (D) Hong Kong

CONTENT TEST (continued)

11. President Fillmore asked the Japanese to _____.
    - (A) visit Pearl Harbor
    - (B) surrender to Commodore Perry
    - (C) become Christians
    - (D) open ports to trade

12. The Taj Mahal was built as a
    - (A) temple
    - (B) mausoleum
    - (C) palace
    - (D) museum

13. Because it collected no taxes on goods landed there, the British base in Singapore was called a _____.
    - (A) free port
    - (B) tax haven
    - (C) port of call
    - (D) free base

14. What is a Chinese commune?
    - (A) a government official
    - (B) an unofficial government located on Taiwan
    - (C) a place where criminals are sent for punishment
    - (D) a farm on which people live and work together

15. Why did Deng Xiaoping allow people to make profits?
    - (A) to encourage increased production
    - (B) to stop the spread of democracy
    - (C) to create a wealthy class in China
    - (D) to please his capitalist opponents

16. Which country controls the island of Taiwan?
    - (A) the United States
    - (B) the People's Republic of China
    - (C) the Nationalist Republic of China
    - (D) Japan

17. Which country has the world's second highest gross national product?
    - (A) the People's Republic of China
    - (B) the United States
    - (C) Japan
    - (D) India

18. Because a high percentage of its population can read and write, South Korea is said to have a
    - (A) low ignorance level
    - (B) high per capita intellect
    - (C) high literacy rate
    - (D) low standard of illegibility

19. Who led the movement to gain India's independence from Britain?
    - (A) Ho Chi Minh
    - (B) Benazir Bhutto
    - (C) Mohandas Gandhi
    - (D) Winston Churchill

20. Which country took control of the Philippines in 1898?
    - (A) Spain
    - (B) Japan
    - (C) the United States
    - (D) the Soviet Union

SKILLS TEST

Directions: Read the paragraphs and complete items 1–5. Fill in the circle next to the correct answer.

A. For many years, the Chinese wanted no foreign embassies in Peking, the city of the emperor. The emperor saw no need to trade with foreign countries. "China lacks no product within its own borders," he said.

B. The Chinese were very proud of their fine tea, beautiful silk, and delicate porcelain. These goods were not available in Europe. The Chinese could understand that Europeans would want such things.

C. One of the emperors agreed to allow a limited trade between China and Europe. However, he laid down strict rules for trade.

The most important rule was that Europeans should not mix with the Chinese.

In 1793, the British king sent a message to the emperor asking that the British be allowed to have an embassy in Peking and that there be more trade.

D. The emperor refused both requests. Differences between China and Britian led to quarrels. The British complained that the Chinese did not treat British merchants fairly. The Chinese charged that the British merchants broke Chinese laws. In 1839, war broke out between China and Britian.

1. Which paragraph would allow you to predict that the emperor would resist foreign trade?
   - (A) A
   - (B) B
   - (C) C
   - (D) D

2. From the events in part B, you could predict that trade between China and Europe would
   - (A) stop
   - (B) shrink
   - (C) open
   - (D) help China

3. From the events in part C, you could predict that _____.
   - (A) war would not break out
   - (B) the emperor would refuse the ambassador's requests
   - (C) the British would leave
   - (D) a British embassy would be set up in Peking

4. From the events in part D, you could predict that part E would probably deal with _____.
   - (A) the growth of industry in China
   - (B) new trade ventures for the United Kingdom
   - (C) Chinese handcrafts
   - (D) the outcome of the war

5. Which of the following is *not* a good strategy for making predictions as you read?
   - (A) Use knowledge you have learned from other sources.
   - (B) Always stick with your first prediction.
   - (C) Consider how the events might cause something to happen.
   - (D) Consider how the people involved might react.

SKILLS TEST (continued)

Directions: Study the charts and complete items 6–10. Fill in the circle next to the correct answer.

National Currencies			Exchange Rates	
Country	**Monetary Unit**	**Symbol**	$1 = £1.49	$1 = 6.9 Fr
United States	dollar	$1	$1 = Y1.55	$1 = Can$1.39
United Kingdom	pound	£1	$1 = DM 2.09	$1 = HK$7.80
Japan	yen	Y1		
Germany	Deutsche Mark (German mark)	DM1		
France	franc	1 Fr		
Canada	dollar	Can$1		
Hong Kong	dollar	HK$1		

6. The kind of currency used in Japan is the _____.
   - (A) dollar
   - (B) franc
   - (C) pound
   - (D) yen

7. The symbol for the Hong Kong dollar is _____.
   - (A) DM1
   - (B) HK$1
   - (C) £1
   - (D) 1 Fr

8. What is a United States dollar worth in Japan?
   - (A) Y1.55
   - (B) 6.9 Fr
   - (C) £1.49
   - (D) HK$7.80

9. How much would it cost you in United States dollars to buy a product in Hong Kong that cost HK$49?
   - (A) $382.20
   - (B) $1.95
   - (C) $64.77
   - (D) $6.28

10. If a Japanese visitor to the United States wanted to buy a jacket that cost $64.95, how much money would the person exchange to pay for the jacket?
    - (A) Y43.59
    - (B) Y96.76
    - (C) Y100.67
    - (D) Y41.90

NAME _____

ESSAY TEST

Directions: Write a response to items 1–4.

> **REMINDER:** Read and think about each item before you write your response. Be sure to think of the points you want to cover, details that support your response, and reasons for your opinions. Then, on the lines below, write your response in complete sentences.

1. How do the monsoons affect the climate of the South Asian subcontinent?

A satisfactory response should include the following statements:

- Monsoons are seasonal winds.
- They blow from the land to the water in winter.
- They blow from the water to land in the summer.
- Summer monsoons bring moist air and heavy rain to the South Asian subcontinent.

An excellent response might also include

- examples of damage caused by floods resulting from summer monsoons.
- specific locations and examples.

2. Explain the difference between the governments of the People's Republic of China and the Nationalist Republic of China.

A satisfactory response should include the following statements:

- The People's Republic, located on the Chinese mainland, has a Communist government.
- The Nationalist Republic, located on the island of Taiwan, has a non-Communist government.

An excellent response might also explain that

- most businesses and many farms in the People's Republic are government-owned.
- businesses and farms in the Nationalist Republic are privately owned.
- each government considers itself the lawful government of China.

© Silver, Burdett & Ginn Inc.

NAME _____

ESSAY TEST (continued)

3. How did Emperor Meiji modernize Japan?

A satisfactory response should include the following statements:

- To help modernize Japan, the government sent young people to study in Europe and the United States.
- When the young people returned, they applied what they had learned by developing modern machinery, a modern military, and schools.

An excellent response might also

- mention that Japan became the most powerful country in East Asia
- explain how Japan demonstrated its power by defeating China and Russia.

4. Why was India partitioned after the end of British rule?

A satisfactory response should include the following statements:

- Religious differences prevented the citizens of India from reaching an agreement about a new government.
- Muslim leaders feared that the Hindu majority might become too powerful.
- These Muslim leaders wanted to partition the subcontinent into the separate Muslim and Hindu countries of Pakistan and India.

An excellent response might describe how Pakistan and India were established in 1947, Sri Lanka (then Ceylon) became independent in 1948, and Bangladesh became a separate nation in 1971.

© Silver, Burdett & Ginn Inc.

TEACHER NOTES

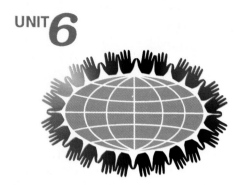

MULTICULTURAL PERSPECTIVES

The Indochina Peninsula
(pages 512–514)

Point out to students that people throughout the ages have moved about, forming different groups, and adopting and blending cultures and customs to form new cultures and customs.

Direct students' attention to the Atlas map on pages 616–617, which shows Eurasia. Have students locate Indochina, the peninsula south of China. Explain that its earliest inhabitants were Austronesian peoples who had migrated north from the islands of the Pacific.

Have students look at the physical map of Eurasia on pages 618–619. Ask them to describe the topography of Indochina, based on the map.

Long ago, Indochina became the focus of competition between Asia's two great civilizations, India and China. Merchants and missionaries from both countries set out to leave their distinctive influence on the religions, commerce, languages, art, and customs of the area.

The *Khmer*, the name that the Cambodians call themselves, may have come from western India. The Lao, who are related to the Thai, came from the highlands of southern China. The Vietnamese came south from China's lower Chang Jiang valley.

Bring in colorful pictures of the peoples and countries of the Indochina peninsula. See if students can identify Chinese influences and Indian influences.

Optional Activities

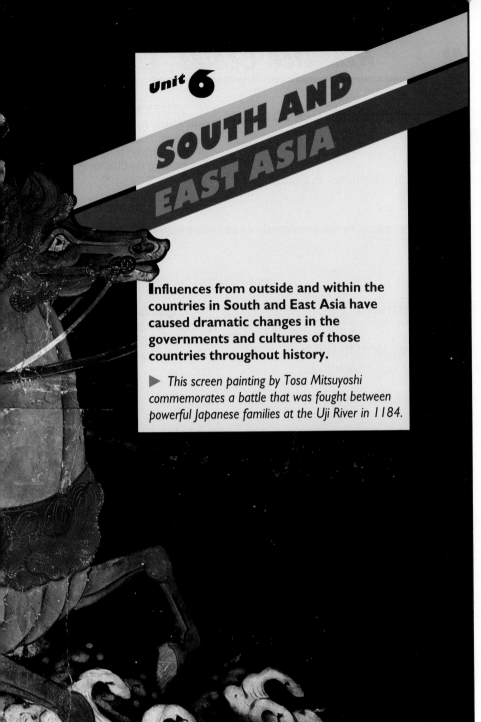

SOUTH AND EAST ASIA

Influences from outside and within the countries in South and East Asia have caused dramatic changes in the governments and cultures of those countries throughout history.

▶ *This screen painting by Tosa Mitsuyoshi commemorates a battle that was fought between powerful Japanese families at the Uji River in 1184.*

China's Ancient Traditions
(pages 523–526)

Ambassadors, merchants, and missionaries who traveled to China in the 1700s and 1800s found a civilization rich in ancient traditions. Many of those traditions live on today.

The ancient Chinese lunar calendar is based on the cycles of the moon and is divided into 12 months of either 29 or 30 days each. Each year is associated with the name of one of twelve animals—the rat, ox, tiger, hare, dragon, snake, horse, sheep, monkey, rooster, dog, and pig.

In China, both the Gregorian, or western, calendar and the lunar calendar are used. The lunar calendar is used to set dates for traditional festivals.

The Chinese New Year, Xin Nian, begins at the second new moon after winter begins. The first day of the celebration falls between January 21 and February 19 of the Gregorian calendar year. The Chinese celebrate Xin Nian for 4 days.

The *World Almanac* entry for the Chinese lunar calendar includes a chart showing years and their corresponding animal designations. For example, someone born in 1953 was born in the Year of the Snake.

Bring a copy of the almanac to class and have students identify their Chinese birth years by animal. They can also identify other important events, such as historical dates with which they are familiar.

Chinese Names
(pages 541–544)

Most Chinese names have three parts. The family name comes first, followed by the personal, or first, name. The first name usually has two parts.

Because there are only a few hundred family names in China, millions of people have the same surname.

Geography of South and East Asia

(pp. 504-521)

Chapter Theme: There are a variety of lands and climates in South Asia and East Asia.

CHAPTER RESOURCES
Review Master Booklet
   Reviewing Chapter Vocabulary, p. 131
   Place Geography, p. 132
   Summarizing the Chapter, p. 133
Chapter 19 Test

LESSON **1 The South Asian Subcontinent**

(pp. 504-511)

Theme: The South Asian subcontinent has three large rivers, monsoons, which affect its climate, and a very large population.

SILVER WINGS WORKSHOP: The Walls Came Tumbling Down

LESSON RESOURCES
Workbook, p. 108
Review Master Booklet
   Understanding the Lesson, p. 128

LESSON **2 Southeast Asia**

(pp. 512-514)

Theme: Southeast Asia has many characteristics, including an archipelago, two peninsulas, many ethnic groups, many religions, a generally hot and humid climate, and great forests.

LESSON RESOURCES
Workbook, p. 109
Review Master Booklet
   Understanding the Lesson, p. 129

LESSON **3 East Asia**

(pp. 515-519)

Theme: East Asia is twice as large as the South Asian subcontinent; it has mountains and deserts, three great rivers, and many climates.

LESSON RESOURCES
Workbook, pp. 107, 110
Review Master Booklet
   Understanding the Lesson, p. 130

Review Masters

REVIEWING CHAPTER VOCABULARY

Review   Study the words in the box. Use your Glossary to find definitions of those you do not remember.

archipelago	artery	latex	terrace
	Deccan	teak	

Practice   Complete the paragraphs using words from the box above. You may change the forms of the words to fit the meaning.

Agricultural and forest products play an important part in the economies of Southeast Asian countries. These products provide food for the large population of the region and valuable resources that can be exported to other countries. Because of the hot, humid climate, tropical rain forests cover much of the land in Southeast Asia that has not been cleared for farming. These forests, unlike the great coniferous forests of Russia, are made up of hardwood trees. The timber from these trees is in great demand, particularly (1) _____teak_____, used to make furniture. Another important forest product is (2) _____latex_____, collected from rubber trees. These trees are not native to Southeast Asia, but were introduced from South America, which has a similar climate.

In places where the land has been cleared for farming, rice is an important crop. Rice paddies can be found in both lowland and upland regions in Southeast Asia and China. Even farmers in steep mountain regions grow rice on the flat (3) _____terraces_____ they cut into the steep slopes. The great rivers of the region also play a part in the production and transportation of rice. Lowland farmers use water from rivers to flood their rice paddies and to irrigate their crops. The rivers are often the main (4) _____arteries_____ along which rice and other crops are transported to market.

Write   Write a sentence of your own for each word in the box above. You may use the back of the sheet.

Sentences should show that students understand the meanings of the words.

_____
_____
_____
_____
_____
_____

LOCATING PLACES

✳   The nations of East Asia include China, Japan, North and South Korea, and Taiwan. The British possession of Hong Kong and the Portuguese colony of Macao are also part of East Asia. Listed below are some places in East Asia. Use the Gazetteer in your textbook to find the latitude and longitude of each place. Then locate and label each on the map.

	LAT. ⊖	LONG. ⊕			LAT. ⊖	LONG. ⊕
1. Beijing	40°N	116°E	6. Seoul		37°N	127°E
2. Guangzhou	23°N	113°E	7. Nagasaki		33°N	130°E
3. Harbin	46°N	126°E	8. Hiroshima		34°N	132°E
4. Taipei	25°N	122°E	9. Tokyo		36°N	140°E
5. Hong Kong	22°N	114°E	10. Shanghai		31°N	121°E

EAST ASIA

⊙ National capitals
● Other cities
■ Other location

0   200   400 miles
0   200   400   600 kilometers

SUMMARIZING THE CHAPTER

✳   Complete this graphic organizer. Under the main idea for each lesson, write four statements that support the main idea.

CHAPTER THEME   There are a variety of lands and climates in South Asia and East Asia.

LESSON 1

South Asia has a variety of geographical features.

1. Tall mountains
2. Long rivers
3. Plateaus
4. Islands

LESSON 2

Many differences can be found among the people and lands of Southeast Asia.

1. Languages
2. Religions
3. Climates
4. Natural resources

LESSON 3

East Asia has a variety of geographical features.

1. Deserts
2. Rivers
3. Peninsulas
4. Mountains

C19-B

Workbook Pages

MAJOR CITIES OF ASIA

Making a Bar Graph, Making Observations

※ The list below shows the largest cities in ten Asian countries. Complete the bar graph of the populations of these cities.

a. Write the names of the cities in the blanks next to the chart. Put the cities in the order of their populations, with the most populous city at the top.

b. Shade in a bar to the right of each city's name to show its population. The first one has been done for you.

Bangkok, Thailand: 5,363,000	Rangoon, Myanmar: 2,458,000
Calcutta, India: 3,305,000	Seoul, South Korea: 9,639,000
Dhaka, Bangladesh: 4,470,000	Shanghai, China: 7,100,000
Ho Chi Minh City, Vietnam: 2,441,000	Taipei, Taiwan: 2,575,000
Jakarta, Indonesia: 7,829,000	Tokyo, Japan: 8,354,000

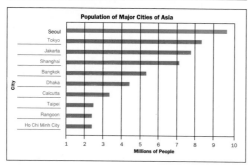

Population of Major Cities of Asia

Cities (top to bottom): Seoul, Tokyo, Jakarta, Shanghai, Bangkok, Dhaka, Calcutta, Taipei, Rangoon, Ho Chi Minh City

X-axis: Millions of People (1–10)

Y-axis: City

Thinking Further: How might cities like Seoul and Tokyo be different from cities like Rangoon and Ho Chi Minh City?

Students should mention that Seoul and Tokyo are about four times larger than Rangoon and Ho Chi Minh City, and so may be more highly developed but may also have greater problems.

ANALYZING STATISTICS

Reading a Graph, Hypothesizing

※ The pictograph below compares health and education statistics for the countries of the South Asian subcontinent and the United States at the end of the 1980s. Study the graph; then complete the sentences that follow by circling the correct answer in parentheses.

COUNTRY	UNITED STATES	INDIA	BANGLADESH	PAKISTAN	SRI LANKA	KEY
POPULATION (in millons)	246	802	108	109	17	
Birthrate per 1,000						○ 10
Death rate per 1,000						● 5
Life expectancy at birth						☺ 20 years
Number of people per doctor						■ 300
Literacy rate						□ 10 percent

1. Of the Asian countries shown on the graph, the country with the smallest population has the (**highest**/lowest/fastest) literacy rate.

2. A person in India will probably live (**more years than**/fewer years than/the same number of years as) someone in Bangladesh.

3. The country with the (highest/**lowest**/slowest) death rate also has the largest number of people for each doctor.

4. The birthrates in Bangladesh and (India/**Pakistan**/Sri Lanka) are almost three times that of the United States.

5. The South Asian country that appears to be the most developed in the areas of health and education is (India/Bangladesh/**Sri Lanka**).

Thinking Further: What might statistics on the number of people per doctor tell you about the quality of health care in a country?

Answers should reflect independent thinking. On the whole, the fewer people per doctor, the more likely that the entire population benefits from the health-care system. However, the graphs shows that Sri Lanka, which has the largest number of persons per doctor in South Asia, nonetheless has the lowest death rate, indicating that its health-care system is quite good.

ISLAND NATIONS OF ASIA

Gathering Information from a Chart, Evaluating Information

※ Study the chart about five Asian island nations. Then read the following sentences and circle the nation or nations described.

Country	Area	Neighbor Countries	Topography
Indonesia	741,101 sq. mi.	Malaysia to the northwest, Papua New Guinea to the east	13,667 islands; 3,000 are inhabited
Maldives	115 sq. mi.	India to the northeast	2,000 islands; 220 are inhabited
Papua New Guinea	178,703 sq. mi.	Indonesia to the west, Australia to the south	Eastern half of New Guinea plus other islands
Philippines	115,800 sq. mi.	Malaysia and Indonesia to south; Taiwan to the north	7,109 islands; most people live on the 11 largest
Singapore	240 sq. mi.	Indonesia to the southeast, Malaysia to the north	Small island at the end of Malay Peninsula

1. This country contains the fewest square miles:
   Singapore   (Maldives)   Papua New Guinea   Philippines   Indonesia

2. This country contains the most square miles:
   Singapore   Maldives   Papua New Guinea   Philippines   (Indonesia)

3. This country has an area nearest 200,000 square miles:
   Singapore   Maldives   (Papua New Guinea)   Philippines   Indonesia

4. These countries have an area of 100,000 to 200,000 square miles:
   Singapore   Maldives   (Papua New Guinea)   (Philippines)   Indonesia

5. These countries have Indonesia as a neighbor:
   (Singapore)   Maldives   (Papua New Guinea)   (Philippines)   Indonesia

6. This country is a neighbor of Australia:
   Singapore   Maldives   (Papua New Guinea)   Philippines   Indonesia

7. This country is a neighbor of India:
   Singapore   (Maldives)   Papua New Guinea   Philippines   Indonesia

8. This country is made up of the most islands:
   Singapore   Maldives   Papua New Guinea   Philippines   (Indonesia)

Thinking Further: Imagine that you meet a person who wants to learn about Indonesia. What three or four facts about Indonesia would you mention? Write your answer on a separate sheet. Answers should reflect independent thinking. Students might point out that the country is made up of islands, some of which are very large. The inhabitants are mostly Muslim. Rice is an important crop. Petroleum is produced.

TEMPERATURES IN ASIA

Understanding Bar Graphs, Applying Information

※ Use the information in the bar graph to help you answer the questions below about January temperatures in Asia.

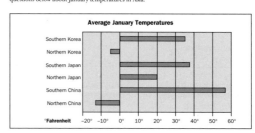

Average January Temperatures

Areas (top to bottom): Southern Korea, Northern Korea, Southern Japan, Northern Japan, Southern China, Northern China

X-axis: °Fahrenheit (−20° to 60°)

1. Which of the areas listed on the chart has the highest average temperature in January? southern China

2. On average, how much colder is northern China than southern China in January? 70°

3. If a group of people traveled from southern Japan to southern Korea in January, how could they expect the temperature to change? It would probably drop several degrees.

4. If you were planning a trip to both northern and southern areas, in which country would you find the combined average temperature the highest? Japan

5. In which country on the graph is the temperature change from north to south greatest? China, because it is the largest country

6. If you traveled the length of all the countries from north to south in January, what would you discover about the change of temperature? The temperature becomes warmer as you travel from north to south.

7. In which country is the difference between temperatures between north and south the smallest? Japan

Thinking Further: Describe two or three aspects of geography that can affect an area's temperature. Write your answer on a separate sheet. An area's temperature can be affected by its latitude (distance from the Equator), altitude, proximity to large bodies of water or mountains, or nearness to the path of a jet stream.

The South Asian Subcontinent

Objectives

★ 1. **Describe** the land of the South Asian subcontinent.

2. **Explain** how the monsoons affect the climate of the South Asian subcontinent.

3. **Name** population characteristics of the South Asian subcontinent.

4. **Identify** the following people and places: *Jules Verne, Phileas Fogg, Himalayas, Hindu Kush, Mount Everest, Ganges River, Indus River,* and *Brahmaputra River.*

1 STARTING THE LESSON

Motivation Activity

- Tell students that in this lesson they will be reading about a mountain chain, the Himalayas, which contains 30 of the world's highest mountains.

- Ask students to guess how tall Mount Everest, the tallest mountain, is. Have one of the students record the guesses.

- After students have read the lesson, have them determine whose guess came closest to the actual height of the mountain.

Think About What You Know

- Assign the THINK ABOUT WHAT YOU KNOW activity on p. 505.

- Student answers should reflect independent thinking but may include the ruins of Mohenjo-Daro and Harappa.

Study the Vocabulary

- Have students look up the meaning of the new vocabulary word in the Glossary.

- Ask students to use the word correctly in a sentence.

504

CHAPTER *19*

GEOGRAPHY OF SOUTH AND EAST ASIA

*S*outh and East Asia form a region of many geographic contrasts. Some parts are very rainy, others are deserts. The highest mountains in the world and some of the lowest delta lands are found in this region.

Optional Activities

Curriculum Connection

Language Arts Divide the class into groups of three students for a word challenge game.

- Tell the groups to find as many words as possible from the letters in the word *subcontinent*. Give the groups about 10 minutes to come up with their list of words.

- When the 10 minutes are up, have a student from each group read the group's list and have the rest of the class verify that the words can be found in *subcontinent*.

- Determine which group is the winner and give the students in that group an appropriate reward or prize.

The South Asian Subcontinent

THINK ABOUT WHAT YOU KNOW
In an earlier chapter, you studied ancient India. Based on what you have already learned, what would you expect to see if you visited India?

STUDY THE VOCABULARY
Deccan

FOCUS YOUR READING
What are the principal geographical features of South Asia?

A. Around the World in 80 Days

A trip around the world in 80 days would not seem fast now. One could make the trip in far less time today by airplane. However in 1873, when author Jules Verne wrote a book entitled *Around the World in Eighty Days*, such a trip seemed an improbable adventure.

Phileas Fogg, the main character of Verne's book, and his servant, Jean Passepartout, use various modes of transportation on their round-the-world trip from London. They use a hot-air balloon to fly to the Mediterranean and then travel by steamship and railroad. Their trip would have been even shorter if they had been able to travel straight east across Europe and Asia. But in 1873 no railroad crossed Asia, the world's largest continent. In order to make the story believable, the author has Fogg and Passepartout use steamship and railroad routes that existed at the time. The travelers go through the Suez Canal and make their way along the southern and eastern edges of Asia.

Around the World in Eighty Days is a travel adventure book to be read with a map in hand. Fogg and Passepartout's route through Asia is accurately described. The travelers sail through the Red Sea and across the Indian Ocean to Bombay, on the west coast of India. They travel overland across India to Calcutta, on the Bay of Bengal. From there they take a ship to Singapore, in Southeast Asia. Another ship then takes them to Hong Kong, on the Chinese coast.

After a number of difficulties, the travelers reach Japan. They take a ship to the United States, travel across the country by rail, and eventually cross the Atlantic to London. To learn more about the adventures in Jules Verne's *Around the World in Eighty Days*, read the literature selection on the next page.

B. The Mountain Wall

In the story of Phileas Fogg's journey, Jules Verne describes India as a "great reversed triangle of land, with its base in the north and its apex [peak] in the south." A look at the map on page 508 explains why Verne describes India this way. The triangle is actually the South Asian subcontinent; India is only one country located on it. The other five countries are Pakistan, Bangladesh, Nepal, Bhutan, and the island of Sri Lanka. Locate these countries on the physical map on page 508. The subcontinent is part of Asia, but it is separated from the rest of the continent by a mountain wall formed by the Himalaya and Hindu Kush mountain ranges.

The Himalayas include 30 of the world's highest mountains. The name *Himalaya* means "abode, or home, of snow." Snow covers the high peaks throughout

505

---

2 DEVELOPING THE LESSON

Read and Think

Sections A and B

To help students summarize what the land of the South Asian subcontinent is like, ask the following questions.

1. **Why couldn't travelers go straight across Europe and Asia in the nineteenth century?**
   (Because no railroad crossed Asia at that time *p. 505*)

2. **How many of the world's highest mountains are in the Himalayas?**
   (30 *p. 505*)

   Thinking Critically Why, do you think, is *Himalaya* a good name for the mountain chain? (Evaluate)
   (Snow covers the high peaks of the Himalayas throughout the year, and *Himalaya* means "abode, or home, of snow." *p. 505*)

Curriculum Connection

Math Ask students to compute the difference between the highest and lowest places on earth.

- Tell students that the highest place on earth is Mount Everest, at 29,028 feet (8,848 m), and the lowest place is the Dead Sea, at 1,290 feet (393 m) below sea level.
- Have students determine the difference between these two places (30,318 feet, or 9,241 m).
- Conclude the activity by asking students to explain how they arrived at this figure (by adding the two distances).

For Your Information

The Himalayas The world's highest and longest east-west chain of mountains is in northern India. Many peaks are more than 20,000 feet (6,096 m) high. More ice and snow cover the Himalayas than cover any place on earth except the North Pole and South Pole. The height of the mountains prevents India from becoming a desert and keeps its climate tropical. Clouds from the south drop moisture on the plains as they move to the mountains, and cold winds from the north and east are kept out.

Mount Everest has presented a challenge to mountain climbers for many years. The first people to reach the top of the mountain were Edmund Hillary of New Zealand and Tenzing Norgay of Nepal on May 29, 1953.

Optional Activities

Use the information below to help students better understand the literature selection found on p. 506.

Selection Summary

French novelist Jules Verne used his adventurous imagination and knowledge of geography in writing *Around the World in Eighty Days*. In the novel, Phileas Fogg bets his friends that he can travel around the world in 80 days. Fogg and his valet use a variety of transportation methods, including steamships, railroads, elephants, and a hot-air ballon, among others, to complete their journey and win the bet. The novel was Verne's most popular book.

Guided Reading

1. **Why were elephants "far from cheap in India"?**
   (Because they were becoming scarce)

2. **Why did Phileas Fogg want to buy or hire the elephant?**
   (Because elephants can travel rapidly and for a long time, and there was no other transportation available)

3. **How many people rode the elephant?**
   (Four)

Literature-Social Studies Connection

1. **What fact about transportation in Asia in 1873 does this selection reflect?**
   (In 1873, no railroad crossed Asia.)

LITERATURE SELECTION

FROM: **Around the World in Eighty Days**

By: Jules Verne
Setting: India

Even as a boy, Jules Verne dreamed of exciting voyages. At the age of 12, he stowed away on a ship bound for India. His father retrieved him, and from then on, Verne's adventures took place in his imagination. Verne researched his books carefully, blending fantasy with facts. Before writing *Around the World in Eighty Days*, he plotted realistic courses for his characters to take.

Phileas Fogg, the book's main character, bets his friends that he can travel around the world in eighty days. In the excerpt below, Fogg, his servant, Passepartout, and Sir Francis Cromarty, a passenger, are on a train traveling through India when it suddenly comes to a halt because the railway has ended.

"I shall go afoot," said Phileas Fogg.
Passepartout . . . said, "Monsieur, I think I have found a means of conveyance [transportation]. . . . An elephant! An elephant that belongs to an Indian who lives but a hundred steps from here."
. . . Kiouni — this was the name of the beast — could doubtless travel rapidly for a long time, and, in default of any other means of conveyance, Mr. Fogg resolved to hire him. But elephants are far from cheap in India, where they are becoming scarce. . . . When, therefore, Mr. Fogg proposed to the Indian to hire Kiouni, he refused point-blank. . . .

Finally, after Mr. Fogg made many offers to hire or to buy the elephant, the Indian sold the beast at a costly price.

. . . The elephant was led out and equipped. The Parsee, who was an accomplished elephant driver, covered his back with a sort of saddle-cloth, and attached to each of his flanks some curiously uncomfortable howdahs [seats].
. . . While Sir Francis and Mr. Fogg took the howdahs on either side, Passepartout got astride the saddle-cloth between them. The Parsee perched himself on the elephant's neck, and at nine o'clock they set out from the village, the animal marching off through the dense forest of palms by the shortest cut.

Optional Activities

Curriculum Connection

Language Arts Have students make up metaphors about the South Asian subcontinent.

● Tell students that a metaphor is a figure of speech in which a word or phrase that refers to one kind of object is used to suggest a likeness to another object.

● For example, tell students that Tibet is often called the "roof of the world" because Tibet is a high plateau surrounded by higher mountains.

● Ask students to make up metaphors for the subcontinent of South Asia, Mount Everest, and the Deccan Plateau.

Making a Bar Graph

● Have students make a bar graph that compares the three longest rivers in South Asia with the three longest rivers in North America.

● Tell students that, in South Asia, the Ganges is 1,557 miles (2,505 km) long, the Brahmaputra is 1,800 miles (2,896 km) long, and the Indus is 1,800 miles (2,896 km) long.

● In North America, the Mississippi-Missouri-Red Rock is 3,880 miles (6,243 km) long, the Mackenzie is 2,635 miles (4,240 km) long, and the Yukon is 1,979 miles (3,184 km) long.

● Ask students to summarize the comparison verbally.

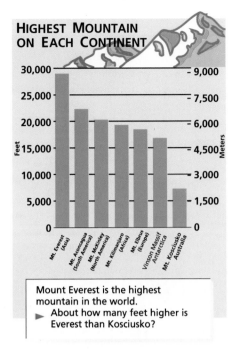

HIGHEST MOUNTAIN ON EACH CONTINENT

Mountains on graph (left to right): Mt. Everest (Asia), Mt. Aconcagua (South America), Mt. McKinley (North America), Mt. Kilimanjaro (Africa), Mt. Elbrus (Europe), Vinson Massif Antarctica, Mt. Kosciusko Australia

Mount Everest is the highest mountain in the world.
► About how many feet higher is Everest than Kosciusko?

(brahm uh POO truh). All three rivers have their sources in the high mountains and plateaus that set the subcontinent apart from the rest of Asia. The Indus and Brahmaputra both begin on the Tibetan plateau but flow to different sides of the continent. The Indus goes to the Arabian Sea. The Brahmaputra empties into the Bay of Bengal. The waters of the Ganges come from melting snow and ice high in the Himalayas. The river flows eastward across its broad plain and joins the Brahmaputra. The two rivers form a large delta in what is now the country of Bangladesh.

Islands are located near the southern tip of the subcontinent. Sri Lanka, the largest, was once called Ceylon. The Maldives are a chain of more than 1,000 small islands, located southwest of the South Asian subcontinent. Only about 200 of these islands are inhabited.

the year. Mount Everest, the tallest mountain in the world, is in the Himalayas. It rises 29,028 feet (8,848 m) above sea level. As the map on page 508 shows, Mount Everest is on the border between the countries of Nepal and China.

The southern part of the subcontinent contains a low plateau called the **Deccan**. Two mountain ranges, the Western Ghats (gawts) and the Eastern Ghats, form the edges of the Deccan Plateau.

C. Rivers and Islands

On their tour, Verne's characters travel along the plain of the Ganges River. The plain is a very fertile and densely populated region of the subcontinent.

The Ganges is one of the three longest rivers in South Asia. The other two rivers are the Indus and the Brahmaputra

This fertile plain runs along the Ganges River.
► How can you tell that people travel on the plain?

Optional Activities

Read and Think
Section C

To cover the material on the rivers and islands of the South Asian subcontinent, ask the following questions.

1. **What are some features of the plain of the Ganges River?**
   (The broad plain is a very fertile and densely populated region. *p. 507*)

2. **What are the three longest rivers?**
   (The Ganges, the Indus, and the Brahmaputra *p. 507*)

3. **Where do the Indus and Brahmaputra rivers begin?**
   (On the Tibetan plateau *p. 507*)

4. **Where do the waters of the Ganges originate?**
   (They come from melting snow and ice high in the Himalayas. *p. 507*)

   Thinking Critically Why, do you think, is the plain of the Ganges River densely populated? (Infer)
   (Answers should reflect independent thinking but may include that because it is a very fertile area, many people may live there to farm the land. *p. 507*)

VISUAL THINKING SKILL

Understanding a Bar Graph

■ Direct students' attention to the bar graph on this page. Ask the following questions.

1. **What is the tallest mountain on the continent of Europe?**
   (Mt. Elbrus)

2. **What is its elevation?**
   (About 18,000 feet)

— **Answers to Caption Questions** —
p. 507t. ► About 21,500 feet (6,600 m) higher
p. 507b. ► In the background of the photograph, there is a road; there is also a bridge across the river.

Read and Think

Sections D and E

To summarize material on South Asia's rivers, climate, and people, ask the following questions.

1. **How do the monsoons affect the climate?**
   (Summer monsoons bring rain, and winter monsoons bring dry weather. *p. 509*)

2. **What kind of population growth is South Asia experiencing?**
   (Rapid population growth *p. 509*)

   Thinking Critically **How do you think the many languages, faiths, and ethnic groups affect South Asian relations?** (Evaluate)
   (Answers may include that they are often a source of tension. *p. 511*)

GEOGRAPHY THEMES

Place

■ Have students look at the maps on pp. 508 and 509 for help in answering the following questions.

1. **What two landforms are found on and along the southern coast of Asia?**
   (Peninsulas and islands)

2. **Which mountain range in India has the lowest elevation?**
   (Eastern Ghats)

3. **Which part of India gets the most rain in the winter?**
   (The southern tip)

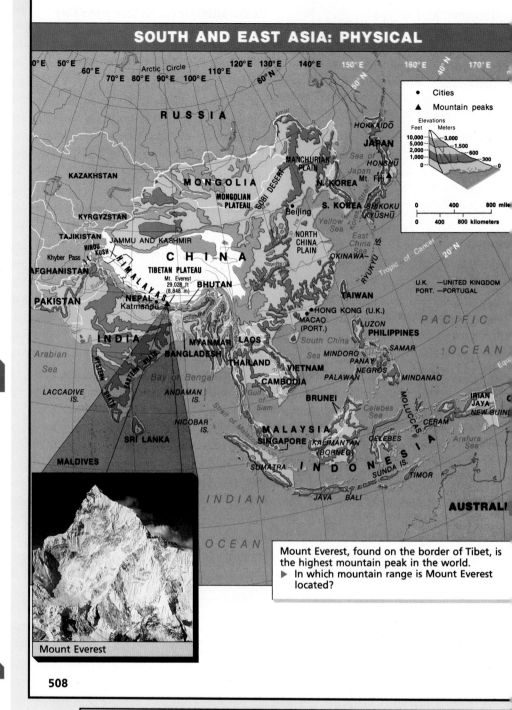

SOUTH AND EAST ASIA: PHYSICAL

Cities
▲ Mountain peaks

Elevations
Feet   Meters
10,000 — 3,000
5,000 — 1,500
2,000 — 600
1,000 — 300
0 — 0

0   400   800 miles
0   400   800 kilometers

U.K. —UNITED KINGDOM
PORT. —PORTUGAL

Mount Everest, found on the border of Tibet, is the highest mountain peak in the world.
▶ In which mountain range is Mount Everest located?

Mount Everest

508

Writing to Learn

Writing a Descriptive Paragraph Ask students to imagine that they are in Cherrapunji in the summertime when the summer monsoons are blowing.

● Tell them to write descriptive paragraphs in which they describe what the weather is like and how it is affecting the land and the daily activities of the people.

● Encourage students to be expressive so that readers can visualize what a summer monsoon is like.

● Conclude the activity by asking volunteers to read their paragraphs to the class.

Optional Activities

D. How the Monsoons Affect Climate

Monsoon winds, which moved early sailing ships across the Indian Ocean from Africa, greatly affect the subcontinent's climate. Summer monsoons, blowing from the southwest, pick up moisture as they pass over the ocean. As the air moves over highlands and mountains on the subcontinent, it cools and drops moisture in the form of rain or snow. As you can see on the map at the right, heavy precipitation falls on the Western Ghats and Himalayas. Cherrapunji (cher uh PUN jee), in northeastern India, is 4,300 feet (1,311 m) above sea level and averages 450 inches (1,143 cm) of rainfall a year. Most of this rain falls between April and September. Delhi, on the central plain of the subcontinent, also receives most of its rain during the summer, but much less than Cherrapunji. You will note on the map above that Pakistan receives very little summer rain. Can you explain why?

The winter monsoons blow from the northeast, off the Asian continent. These winds bring dry, sunny weather to the subcontinent. Even Cherrapunji usually receives less than an inch of rain in January.

E. A Crowded Land

Asia is the home of most of the human race. About 60 percent of the world's people live in Asia. One third of Asia's population lives on the subcontinent.

The population of the subcontinent is growing rapidly. Between 1965 and 1990 the total number of people more than doubled. The population is spread unevenly over the land. There is a high density of population in the Ganges valley and delta and also along the southwestern coast of the subcontinent.

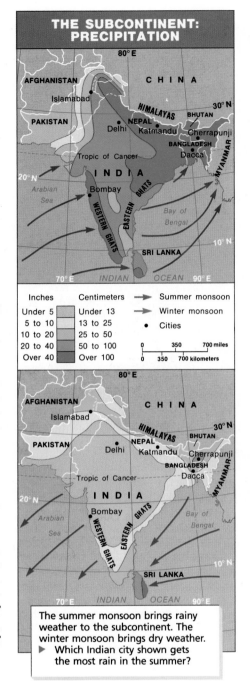

THE SUBCONTINENT: PRECIPITATION

Inches	Centimeters
Under 5	Under 13
5 to 10	13 to 25
10 to 20	25 to 50
20 to 40	50 to 100
Over 40	Over 100

→ Summer monsoon
→ Winter monsoon
• Cities

The summer monsoon brings rainy weather to the subcontinent. The winter monsoon brings dry weather.
▶ Which Indian city shown gets the most rain in the summer?

GEOGRAPHY THEMES

Human-Environment Interactions

■ Have students refer to the map on this page in order to answer the following questions.

1. How many of the listed cities in India have a population of 1 million or more? (4)

2. How many of the listed cities in China have a population of 1 million or more? (8)

3. How many of the listed cities in Japan have a population of 1 million or more? (3)

4. Which of these countries—India, China, Japan, or Pakistan—is most densely populated? (Japan)

5. How many of the listed cities in Pakistan have a population of 1 million or more? (2)

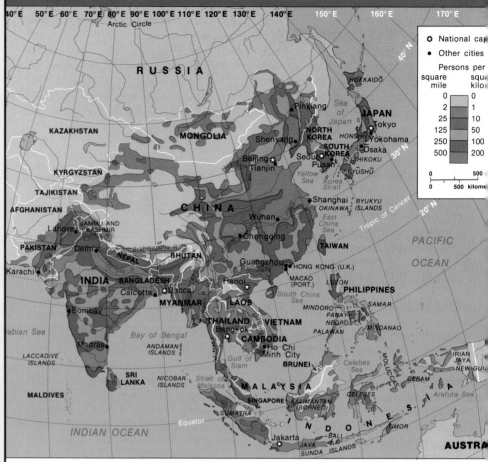

SOUTH AND EAST ASIA: POPULATION DENSITY

Legend:
- ⊙ National capital
- • Other cities

Persons per square mile	square kilometer
0	0
2	1
25	10
125	50
250	100
500	200

THE 25 LARGEST CITIES OF SOUTH ASIA AND EAST ASIA

Seoul (South Korea) 9,501,000	Bangkok (Thailand) 5,018,000	Pusan (South Korea) 3,160,000
Tokyo (Japan) 8,355,000	Delhi (India) 4,884,000	Yokohama (Japan) 2,993,000
Bombay (India) 8,227,000	Shenyang (China) 4,135,000	Lahore (Pakistan) 2,922,000
Jakarta (Indonesia) 7,348,000	Dacca (Bangladesh) 3,459,000	Chongqing (China) 2,734,000
Shanghai (China) 6,881,000	Ho Chi Minh City (Vietnam) ... 3,420,000	Ōsaka (Japan) 2,636,000
Beijing (China) 5,755,000	Wuhan (China) 3,338,000	Pinkiang (China) 2,592,000
Hong Kong (United Kingdom) ... 5,553,000	Calcutta (India) 3,305,000	Hanoi (Vietnam) 2,571,000
Tainjin (China) 5,312,000	Madras (India) 3,277,000	
Karachi (Pakistan) 5,103,000	Guangzhou (China) 3,222,000	

Some of the most populated cities in the world are in South Asia and East Asia. China has many of the most populated cities in this region.
▶ How would you describe the difference in the population densities of eastern and western China?

510

Optional Activities

Reteaching Main Objective

★ *Describe the land of the South Asian subcontinent.*

● Ask students to write a brochure for South Asia that will show the principal geographic features of the subcontinent.

● Tell students to begin by making a list of the geographic features of the subcontinent.

● Then have them refer to a map to determine the route than their tour will take.

● Finally, have them write the brochure, describing the geographic sights and the route of the tour.

Calcutta, with a population of 11 million, is India's second largest city.
▶ By looking at the photograph above, how can you tell that this is a very crowded city?

The subcontinent's large population is made up of many ethnic, language, and religious groups. There are 14 major languages, plus hundreds of dialects. Each of the major languages is spoken by millions and has its own ancient literature. Differences between religious groups have had a great effect on the history of the subcontinent. You will read about some of these religious groups in Chapters 20 and 21.

LESSON 1 REVIEW

THINK AND WRITE

A. Why did Fogg and Passepartout not travel straight east across Europe and Asia? **(Recall)**

B. What separates the South Asian subcontinent from the rest of Asia? **(Recall)**

C. Name the three main rivers and some of the islands of South Asia. **(Recall)**

D. Summarize how monsoons affect the climate of the subcontinent. **(Infer)**

E. Why, do you think, is the population spread unevenly across the subcontinent? **(Analyze)**

SKILLS CHECK

MAP SKILL

Use the precipitation maps on page 509 to answer these questions: (a) How much rain does Delhi usually receive during the summer monsoon? During the winter monsoon? (b) Does Pakistan receive more or less rain than Bangladesh in the summer? (c) Which country receives about the same amount of precipitation in the winter as it does in the summer?

511

Optional Activities

---

3 CLOSING THE LESSON

Lesson 1 Review

Answers to Think and Write

A. No railroad crossed Asia at that time.

B. A mountain wall formed by the Himalaya and Hindu Kush mountain ranges separates the South Asian subcontinent from the rest of Asia.

C. The three main rivers are the Ganges, Indus, and Brahmaputra. Some islands in South Asia are Sri Lanka and the Maldives.

D. The summer monsoons bring rain to the subcontinent, and the winter monsoons bring dry weather.

E. One third of Asia's population lives on the subcontinent.

Answer to Skills Check

(a) Delhi receives 20 to 40 inches (51 to 102 cm) in the summer, and under 5 inches in the winter; (b) Pakistan receives less rain than Bangladesh in the summer; and (c) Sri Lanka receives about the same amount of precipitation in the winter as it does in the summer.

Focus Your Reading

Ask the lesson focus question found at the beginning of the lesson: **What are the principal geographical features of South Asia?** (The Himalaya and Hindu Kush mountain ranges; the Ganges, Indus, and Brahmaputra rivers; the Deccan Plateau; and the islands of Sri Lanka and the Maldives)

Additional Practice

You may wish to assign the ancillary materials listed below.

Understanding the Lesson p. 128
Workbook p. 108

Answers to Caption Questions

p. 510 ▶ Eastern China has a much greater population density than western China.
p. 511 ▶ It is so crowded that people are walking in the streets.

511

Southeast Asia

Objectives

★1. **Describe** the climate and resources of Southeast Asia.

2. **Explain** what makes the people of Southeast Asia such a varied group.

3. **Identify** the following places: *Indochina, Malay Peninsula, Mekong River, South China Sea,* and *Malay Archipelago.*

1 STARTING THE LESSON

Motivation Activity

■ Ask students why the United States is sometimes referred to as a "melting pot."

■ Write students' answers on the chalkboard.

■ Explain that in this lesson they will read about Southeast Asia, a region of the world that is also referred to as a "melting pot" and for many of the same reasons that apply for the United States.

Think About What You Know

■ Assign the THINK ABOUT WHAT YOU KNOW activity on p. 512.

■ Answers should reflect independent thinking but may include questions about the climate, geography, schools, and forms of entertainment.

Study the Vocabulary

■ Have students read the definitions of the new vocabulary words in the Glossary.

■ Have each student compose a quiz based on these terms and their definitions.

■ Have students exchange quizzes. After each quiz has been completed, it should be returned to the student who created it. Have students check their classmates' answers to their quizzes.

LESSON 2

Southeast Asia

THINK ABOUT WHAT YOU KNOW
Suppose some students from Southeast Asia visited your class. What questions would you ask them? What kinds of questions do you think they would want to ask you?

STUDY THE VOCABULARY

archipelago   teak
terrace   latex

FOCUS YOUR READING
What variety can be found among the peoples and across the lands of Southeast Asia?

A. A Peninsula and Islands

Indochina Fogg and Passepartout traveled around the large peninsula formed by Southeast Asia. Because this peninsula lies between India and China, Europeans called it Indochina.

Indochina has many interesting sights, but Fogg did not care about that. He simply wanted to take the shortest sea route to the Chinese coast. If you look at the map on page 508, you can easily figure out the route the travelers took. From the subcontinent they sailed to Singapore. As the map shows, Singapore is located at the tip of the Malay Peninsula, which is part of the Indochina peninsula. It reaches almost to the Equator and is the southernmost part of the continent.

Tiny Singapore is only one of the countries of Indochina. Today the peninsula holds seven countries. Look at the physical map of South Asia and East Asia on page 508. Can you name the other six countries?

Southeast Asia's longest river, the Mekong, runs through all of these lands except Singapore. The sources of the Mekong are on the Tibetan plateau. As it nears the South China Sea, the Mekong River forms a large delta.

Malay Malay is also the name of an **archipelago** (ahr kuh PEL uh goh), or group of islands, off the coast of Southeast Asia. The Malay Archipelago is the world's largest group of islands. It extends more than 3,800 miles (6,114 km) along the Equator and includes thousands of islands. Some are very small and have no inhabitants. Others are among the largest islands in the world. New Guinea, for instance, the world's second largest island, is bigger than the state of Texas. Two of the world's largest islands belong to the Malay Archipelago.

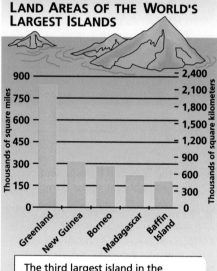

LAND AREAS OF THE WORLD'S LARGEST ISLANDS

Thousands of square miles: 900, 750, 600, 450, 300, 150, 0
Thousands of square kilometers: 2,400, 2,100, 1,800, 1,500, 1,200, 900, 600, 300, 0

Greenland, New Guinea, Borneo, Madagascar, Baffin Island

The third largest island in the world is part of Indonesia.
► What is the name of this island, and how many square miles is it?

Holding a Geography Contest

● Have students prepare location questions for a Map Meet.

● Divide the class into four teams and direct each team to come up with ten location questions and their answers, based on the maps on pp. 508 and 510. For example, "What country borders Singapore to the south?" (Indonesia)

● Collect the questions and conduct a Map Meet in which each team answers the questions that the other teams created.

● The team with the most correct answers at the end of the meet is the winner.

B. Many Peoples

Different Languages The Malay Archipelago of Southeast Asia is divided into four countries. Indonesia is the largest country. The others are the Philippines, Brunei, and part of Malaysia. These, added to those of Indochina, make up the 11 nations of Southeast Asia.

Each country has a variety of ethnic groups that speak different languages. Singapore has four official languages. English is one of the official languages in Singapore, the Philippines, and Brunei. Chinese is spoken throughout the region.

Many Religions A number of the world's major religions have followers in this part of Asia. Many of the people in Indochina are Buddhists. Indonesia is a Muslim country. In fact, it has more Muslims than any country in the Middle East or North Africa. On the Indonesian island of Bali the people are Hindus. Christianity is the religion of the large majority of people in the Philippines. Some of the people of Southeast Asia also hold to religious beliefs and practices that originated in the region.

C. Climate and Natural Resources

Farming Southeast Asia lies within the tropics and has a generally hot and humid climate. Yet the climate offers one great advantage: crops can be grown all year.

Much land is mountainous and hilly, although there is some flatland, such as that on the Mekong delta. Through hard work and skill, the people of Southeast Asia farm even steep mountainsides. They construct **terraces**, flat areas built up like steps on steep slopes. Crops are planted and tended on each terrace. Rice is Southeast Asia's most important crop, but farmers also grow sugarcane and fruits.

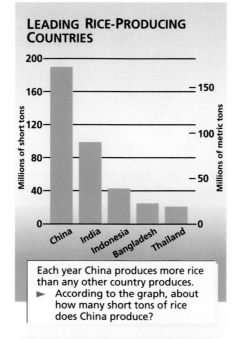

LEADING RICE-PRODUCING COUNTRIES

Millions of short tons — China, India, Indonesia, Bangladesh, Thailand — *Millions of metric tons*

Each year China produces more rice than any other country produces.
► According to the graph, about how many short tons of rice does China produce?

This photograph shows rice terraces in the Philippines.
► How can you tell that this land is used for terrace farming?

2 DEVELOPING THE LESSON

Read and Think
Sections A, B, and C

To summarize information about the land, people, climate, and resources of Southeast Asia, ask the following questions:

1. **Why is the large peninsula in Southeast Asia called Indochina?**
   (Because it lies between India and China *p. 512*)

2. **Southeast Asia comprises how many nations?**
   (Eleven *p. 513*)

3. **What important minerals are found in Southeast Asia?**
   (Tin, copper, lead, and iron *p. 514*)

Thinking Critically Why, do you think, are there so many different languages and religions in Southeast Asia? (Evaluate)
(Answers should reflect independent thinking but may include that many people migrated from other areas, bringing their languages and religions with them. *p. 513*)

Answers to Caption Questions
p. 512 ► Borneo; 300,000 sq. mi
p. 513 t. ► About 190 short tons
p. 513 b. ► Because the land is built up like steps on steep slopes

---

Lesson 2 Review

Answers to Think and Write

A. Indochina is a large peninsula located between India and China. The Malay Peninsula is part of the Indochina peninsula, and is located in the southernmost part of the continent. The Malay Archipelago, located off the coast of Southeast Asia, is the world's largest group of islands, extending more than 3,800 miles (6,114 km) along the Equator.

B. The people of Southeast Asia speak many different languages, are members of a variety of ethnic groups, and are followers of a number of the world's major religions.

C. Southeast Asia's hot, humid climate allows crops to be grown throughout the year; natural resources include timber, rubber trees, oil, natural gas, tin, copper, lead, and iron.

Answer to Skills Check

Burma is the largest; Vietnam has the largest population.

Focus Your Reading

Ask the lesson focus question found at the beginning of the lesson: **What variety can be found among the peoples and across the lands of Southeast Asia?**
(In terms of people, there is variety in languages, ethnic groups, and religions. In terms of land, there are peninsulas, islands, mountains, and flatlands.)

Additional Practice

You may wish to assign the ancillary materials listed below.

Understanding the Lesson p. 129
Workbook p. 109

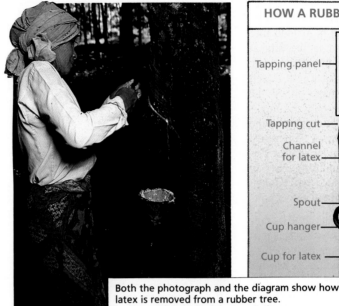

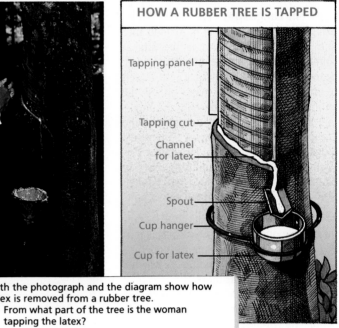

HOW A RUBBER TREE IS TAPPED

Tapping panel
Tapping cut
Channel for latex
Spout
Cup hanger
Cup for latex

Both the photograph and the diagram show how latex is removed from a rubber tree.
▶ From what part of the tree is the woman tapping the latex?

Valuable Resources Tropical forests cover much of the land that has not been cleared for crops. The forests provide valuable timber, such as **teak**, a hardwood once used for building ships. Teak is still used for making furniture.

Rubber trees were brought to Southeast Asia from Brazil, a country in South America. Natural rubber is produced by cutting slits in the bark of the rubber trees and collecting **latex**, the milky sap that drips from the cuts.

Southeast Asia also has oil and natural gas fields. In addition, important deposits of such minerals as tin, copper, lead, and iron are found in the region.

LESSON 2 REVIEW

THINK AND WRITE

A. Locate and describe the peninsulas and islands of Southeast Asia. **(Recall)**

B. Why can it be said that no one person is (**Infer**) typical of the people in Southeast Asia?

C. What climate and natural resources does Southeast Asia offer? **(Recall)**

SKILLS CHECK

THINKING SKILL

Turn to the Countries of the Eastern Hemisphere charts on pages 32–43 and find the seven countries that make up the Indochina peninsula. Use the information on the table to answer the following questions: Which country is the largest? Which country has the highest population?

514

UNDERSTANDING THE LESSON

NAME
UNDERSTANDING THE LESSON

CHAPTER
19

Finding the Main Idea

LESSON 2 CONTENT MASTER

✷ The chart shows the main ideas of the lesson. Fill in the blank spaces with the details that support each main idea. Some have been done for you.

The countries of Indochina are on a peninsula.
1. Myanmar
2. Thailand
3. Laos
4. Kampuchea
5. Vietnam
6. Malaysia
7. Singapore

The Malay Archipelago includes four countries.
1. Indonesia
2. Philippines
3. Brunei
4. Part of Malaysia

Southeast Asia: A Land of Variety

The region has many religions.
1. Buddhists in Indochina
2. Muslims in Indonesia
3. Hindus in Bali
4. Christians in Philippines
5. Native religions throughout region

The area has many natural resources.
1. Crops are grown all year round.
2. Tropical forests provide timber.
3. Rubber trees provide latex.
4. Oil fields
5. Natural gas fields
6. Minerals: tin, copper, lead, iron

Think and Write: If you were going to move to Southeast Asia, would you rather live on the peninsula or in the archipelago? In a paragraph, give reasons for your choice. You may use the back of the sheet. Answers should reflect independent thinking; suggestions appear in the Answer Key.

Use with textbook pages 512–514.

129

◀ **Review Master Booklet, p. 129**

THINK ABOUT WHAT YOU KNOW
You have already learned about the three most important rivers in China in Chapter 4. Can you name them?

STUDY THE VOCABULARY
artery

FOCUS YOUR READING
What are the principal geographical features of East Asia?

A. Different Maps of the World

Matteo Ricci, a Roman Catholic priest from Italy, went to China in 1582. Father Ricci was a Christian missionary. He took some religious books with him, but he also took some works on science and a world map. When the Chinese first saw the map, they scarcely knew what to make of it. It was not that they had never seen a map before. The Chinese had made maps since ancient times, and they had mapped areas within China quite accurately. But the Europeans' map differed greatly from any world map they had ever seen.

The Chinese people called their land the Middle Kingdom. On Father Ricci's map, however, China did not appear in the middle, but was placed near the edge. The Chinese showed Ricci a map of their own, which was entitled *Picture of All Under Heaven*. It represented the world as a square, with China filling most of the square. Japan and Korea were squeezed into one corner, India and Arabia into another. All of the foreign lands put together were smaller than the smallest part of the Chinese empire.

Father Ricci explained that since the earth was a sphere, there really was no Middle Kingdom. A map drawn on a flat sheet could be made to show different parts of the world. He made a map locating China at the center of the page, with the Americas on the right and Europe and Africa on the left. The new map correctly showed that China was a large land, but smaller than all the other lands combined.

B. China's Lands

The Gobi China is by no means as large as it appeared on the Chinese map *Picture of All Under Heaven*, but it does make up the greater part of East Asia. It is more than twice as large as the South Asian subcontinent.

The world's second largest desert lies partly in northwestern China and partly in the neighboring country of Mongolia. It is a stony wasteland with very few shady

Nomads have set up camp here in the Gobi—a vast desert area.
► What homes of other groups of people are similar in shape to these houses?

515

Curriculum Connection

Art Have students draw maps showing how they think the *Picture of All Under Heaven* (discussed on this page) might have looked.

● First, have students reread Section A and make a list of the features that the Chinese map contained.

● For example, students should note that the world was drawn as a square and that China filled most of the square.

● Then have students draw their maps. Remind them to label places that the Chinese would have considered to be important.

● Hang some of the completed maps on a bulletin board.

Optional Activities

East Asia

Objectives

★1. **Compare** the geographic features of China, Korea, Taiwan, and Japan.

2. **Explain** why a large part of China's population lives near rivers or on river deltas.

3. **Discuss** why the Japanese need to make careful use of their resources.

4. **Identify** the following people and places: *Matteo Ricci, the Gobi, Chang Jiang, Huang He, Xi Jiang, Honshū, Hokkaidō, Kyūshū, Shikoku,* and *Mount Fuji.*

1 STARTING THE LESSON

Motivation Activity

■ Have students look at a map of East Asia. Ask them to make generalizations about East Asia from the map.

■ Tell students that in this lesson they will find out if their generalizations were correct.

Think About What You Know

■ Assign the THINK ABOUT WHAT YOU KNOW activity on p. 515.

■ The rivers are the Huang He, the Chang Jiang, and the Xi Jiang.

Study the Vocabulary

■ Have students look up the new vocabulary word in their Glossary. Tell students that *artery* has another meaning.

■ Have students use each meaning of the word in a separate sentence.

--- **Answers to Caption Questions** ---
p. 514 ► From the bark of the tree's trunk
p. 515 ► Answers may include igloos and wigwams.

DEVELOPING THE LESSON

Read and Think

Sections A, B, and C

Use the questions below to help students summarize the information about the geography of China:

1. **Why were the Chinese confused by the map that Matteo Ricci brought to China?**
   (Chinese maps depicted the earth as a square, with China filling most of it; Ricci's map showed that China was a large land, but smaller than all the other lands combined. *p. 515*)

2. **Why is only one tenth of China cultivated?**
   (Two thirds of the land is either mountainous or desert. *p. 516*)

3. **Why is "Gobi" a good name for the desert?**
   (*Gobi* means "waterless place," and the desert is a stony, dry wasteland. *pp. 515-516*)

4. **Why do so many of China's people live near rivers or on the river deltas?**
   (Rivers provide irrigation and are used for travel and shipping. *p. 516*)

   Thinking Critically **Why, do you think, was China's map of the world in the 1500s so inaccurate?** (Infer)
   (Answers should reflect independent thinking but may include that the Chinese had done little exploring and relied on the word of visitors to make their map. *p. 515*)

VISUAL THINKING SKILL

Understanding a Photograph

■ Ask students to study the photograph on p. 517 and discuss how it shows that Japan has modern and metropolitan areas.

---

areas. It is called the *Gobi*, which means "waterless place." It is well named. The Gobi has an extreme continental climate. Temperatures there may fall to −40°F (−40°C) in the winter and rise as high as 113°F (45°C) in the summer. Those who think that all deserts are sandy, hot lands would learn otherwise if they crossed the Gobi in January.

Tibetan Plateau Only about one tenth of China is cultivated. Two thirds of the land is either mountainous or desert. Southwestern China consists of very high mountains and plateaus. The Tibetan plateau, called Zizang (shee SHAHNG) by the Chinese, rises as high as 15,000 feet (4,572 m). It is the highest inhabited plateau in the world.

C. China's Three Great Rivers

Huang He All of China's large rivers flow from west to east. The Chang Jiang (chahng jee AHNG), formerly known as the Yangtze, and the Huang He (hwahng-hih) begin on the Tibetan plateau. They run down from the highlands and across the broad North China Plain. Both rivers carry silt to the plain. You may recall that silt is fine particles of soil carried by water. The Huang He flows through areas of yellow soil, and its muddy yellow water gives the river its name. *Huang He* means "Yellow River." The Huang Hai (hwahng hye), or "Yellow Sea," into which the river empties, also takes its name from the silt-filled water.

Chang Jiang The course of the Chang Jiang runs south of the Huang He. After crossing the North China Plain, the Chang Jiang empties into the East China Sea. It is China's longest river and the world's fourth longest. The Chang flows for over 3,000 miles (4,827 km).

The Huang He, or Yellow River, is 2,903 miles (4,671 km) long.
► Why, do you think, is Yellow River a good name?

Xi Jiang The Xi Jiang (shee jee AHNG), the third of China's great rivers, has its sources in the hills of southern China. The river is called *Xi Jiang*, which means "West River," because it flows from the west toward the South China Sea. The Xi Jiang is not as long as the other great rivers, but it serves as a main **artery**, or transportation route, for southern China. The important port of Guangzhou (GUAHNG joh), which was formerly known as Canton, is located on the delta formed by the Xi Jiang.

A very large part of China's population lives along or on the deltas of the three great rivers. The rivers are used for irrigation and for travel and shipping. They also flood from time to time and have destroyed many lives and much property. It is because of this that the Huang He is known as "China's sorrow."

Optional Activities

Cooperative Learning

Researching Volcanoes Divide the class into groups of four students.

● Have each group research volcanoes. Assign the following questions so that each group member is responsible for one answer: (a) Why do volcanoes erupt? (b) What happens when a volcano erupts? (c) What do scientists look at to determine when a volcano will erupt and what tools do they use to study volcanoes? (d) Where are some of the world's active volcanoes located?

● Give students about 20 minutes to finish the research. Then, have them present their information orally or in writing.

D. The Korean Peninsula and Taiwan

The Korean peninsula juts out from the northern coast of China. It separates the Yellow Sea from the Sea of Japan, on the east. The Korean peninsula is mountainous, particularly in the east. Most of the level and rolling land is on the west side. Forests cover much of the mountainous land. At one time, overcutting nearly destroyed the forests. In more recent times the forests have been replanted and are carefully conserved.

The island of Taiwan lies about 90 miles (145 km) off the Chinese coast. When the Portuguese first arrived on this island in 1590, they called it *Formosa*, which means "beautiful." For many years the country was labeled *Formosa* on maps.

Taiwan, like Korea, has rugged mountains on its eastern side, with more gently sloping land on the west. Taipei, the capital, and Taiwan's other large cities are located on the western half of the island.

This bridge links Kōbe, located on Honshū, with the island of Awaji.
► Why, do you think, is this bridge important to Awaji?

E. The Japanese Archipelago

Main Islands The Japanese archipelago stretches for 1,500 miles (2,414 km) along the coast of East Asia. There are four main islands and numerous smaller ones. Honshū, on which Japan's capital, Tokyo, is located, is the largest. It is a little larger than Utah. Hokkaidō, the second largest, has over one fifth of Japan's land but only one twentieth of its people. Many Japanese think of Hokkaidō as an "icebox" because it receives so much snow. Kyūshū is located farthest to the south and has the warmest climate. The smallest of the four main islands is Shikoku.

There are bridges and tunnels that now link the main islands of Japan. Trains glide 33.5 miles (54 km) through the tunnel between the islands of Honshū and Hokkaidō. A series of six bridges connect Honshū and Shikoku. Kyūshū and Honshū are joined by both a bridge and a tunnel.

517

Read and Think
Sections D, E, and F

Summarize the information about the geographies of Korea, Taiwan, and Japan, and the climates of East Asia by asking the following questions:

1. **How are the geographical features of the Korean peninsula and Taiwan similar?**
(Both have mountains in the east and more gently sloping land in the west. *p. 517*)

2. **Why do Japanese farmers need to cultivate the land so carefully?**
(Only 13 percent of the land is arable. *p. 518*)

3. **Why is East Asia a region of many climates?**
(Because it covers a large area and because of the effect of monsoons *pp. 518-519*)

Thinking Critically Why, do you think, would *Formosa* also be a good name for Japan? (Analyze)
(Answers may include because Japan has many beautiful mountains' including Mount Fuji. *pp. 517-518*)

┌─ **Answers to Caption Questions** ─┐
p. 516 ► Because the water looks muddy and has a yellow color to it
p. 517 ► It is its link to the main islands of Japan.

Graphic Organizer

To help students better understand the geography of East Asia, you may wish to use the graphic organizer below.

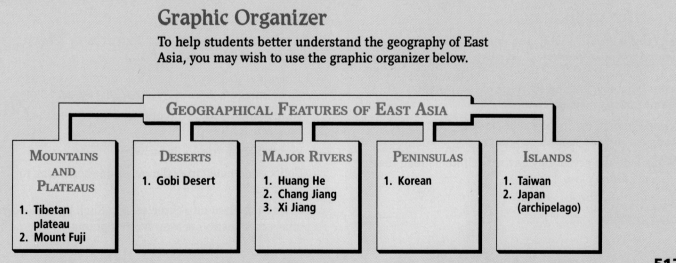

GEOGRAPHICAL FEATURES OF EAST ASIA

MOUNTAINS AND PLATEAUS	DESERTS	MAJOR RIVERS	PENINSULAS	ISLANDS
1. Tibetan plateau 2. Mount Fuji	1. Gobi Desert	1. Huang He 2. Chang Jiang 3. Xi Jiang	1. Korean	1. Taiwan 2. Japan (archipelago)

Concept:
Geographic Comparisons

To better understand the diversity of the geography and climate of East Asia, it is important to be able to compare and contrast. Below are three activities that will help your students relate the concept of comparing and contrasting to East Asia.

◆ **EASY** Have students make a chart with the headings *China* and *Japan*.

Ask students to complete the chart with information about the climate and land.

Finally, have students write a paragraph in which they explain how the two nations are similar and how they are different.

◀▶ **AVERAGE** Have students make a chart with the headings *Huang He*, *Chang Jiang*, and *Xi Jiang*.

Ask students to fill in the chart with information that points out similarities and differences among these three rivers.

◀▮▶ **CHALLENGING** Have students make a chart with the headings *South Asia*, *Southeast Asia*, and *East Asia*.

Ask students to fill in the chart with information comparing and contrasting the geographical features, climates, and resources of these regions.

Mount Fuji is 12,388 feet (3,776 m) high. It was once a volcanic mountain but is no longer active. Its last eruption was almost 300 years ago.
▶ For what purpose is the land shown in the foreground of the photograph used?

Mountains Mount Fuji, in Japan, may well be the world's most-pictured mountain. It has been drawn, painted, and photographed countless times. Because it has been pictured so often, millions of people who have never been to Japan are familiar with Mount Fuji's snowy, cone-shaped peak. The cone was formed by the eruption of the volcano, which is no longer active. There are, however, a number of active volcanoes in Japan.

Mountains cover most of Japan, so only about 13 percent of the land is arable. This island country is slightly smaller than California, but its population is more than four times larger. Because space is so limited, the Japanese have learned to make use of every bit of land. The farmers carefully cultivate the small plots of arable soil. Well-managed forests, covering about two thirds of the country, grow on the mountain slopes. The forests supply timber and bamboo. Bamboo is not a tree but a type of grass that, like trees, is used to make houses, furniture, and paper.

F. The Climates of East Asia

East Asia has many climates because the region covers such a large area. Hong Kong, on the coast of China, is located in the tropics, and Harbin, in northeastern China, is as far from the tropics as Minneapolis, Minnesota, is. A large part of China has a continental climate, but Japan and Taiwan have a maritime climate, one influenced by winds blowing from the sea.

The seasonal monsoon winds affect the climates of East Asia just as they affect those of the South Asian subcontinent. From May to October, winds generally

Writing to Learn

Writing a Poem Tell students that the Japanese created a type of poetry called *haiku*, a nonrhyming poem of 17 syllables, arranged in a line of five syllables, a line of seven syllables, and another line of five syllables. These poems usually concern nature.

● Have students write haiku poems in which they describe some aspect of Japan's geography.

● Conclude the activity by having volunteers read their poems to the class.

Reteaching Main Objective

★ *Compare the geographic features of China, Korea, Taiwan, and Japan.*

● Tell students they will play a *Jeopardy*-style game with these categories: China, Korea, Taiwan, and Japan.

● Have students make up one question for each of the categories.

● Remind them to supply answers.

● Collect and categorize the questions according to country.

● Divide the class into three teams. Each team to correctly answer a question is awarded ten points.

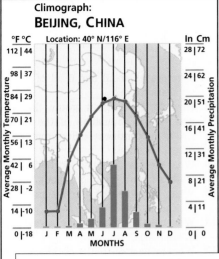

Climograph:
BEIJING, CHINA

Location: 40° N/116° E

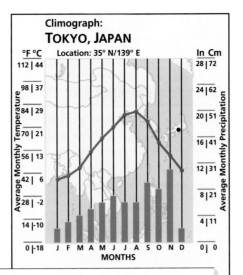

Climograph:
TOKYO, JAPAN

Location: 35° N/139° E

Although Beijing has a continental climate and Tokyo has a maritime climate, both cities are affected by seasonal monsoons.

▶ How does the temperature during the winter months in Tokyo differ from that of Beijing?

blow off the Pacific Ocean. These summer monsoons bring rain. In the northern part of the country, China's capital, Beijing (BAY JING), once known as Peking, receives most of its yearly rainfall in the summer.

The winter monsoon winds blow from the heart of Asia and bring cold, dry weather. Beijing receives little rainfall from October to May, but on the Japanese islands, the winter is neither as dry nor as cold. The winter winds from Asia blow over the Sea of Japan, which warms the air.

The monsoons affect all the climates of East Asia, but their effects vary from place to place. As a result, East Asia is a region not of one climate, but of many.

LESSON 3 REVIEW

THINK AND WRITE

A. Why did the Chinese think that Father Ricci's map was strange? **(Recall)**

B. What is the difference between the climate on the Tibetan plateau and that in the Gobi? **(Analyze)**

C. What are the names and courses of the three great rivers of China? **(Recall)**

D. In what way is the geography of the Korean peninsula like that of Taiwan? **(Analyze)**

E. What are the names of the four main islands of the Japanese archipelago?

F. What two factors explain the variety of climates in East Asia? **(Recall)**

SKILLS CHECK

WRITING SKILL

Describe in a short paragraph why the Tibetan plateau has been called "the roof of the world."

519

Optional Activities

◀ **Review Master Booklet, p. 130**

---

3 CLOSING THE LESSON

Lesson 3 Review

Answers to Think and Write

A. The Chinese thought Father Ricci's map was strange because it showed the earth as being round and China as being smaller than they thought.

B. The climate in the Gobi is very cold in winter and very hot in summer. The climate on the Tibetan plateau is cold, snowy, and dry.

C. They are the Huang He, Chang Jiang, and Xi Jiang. All three flow from west to east.

D. Both are mountainous in the east and have rolling land in the west.

E. They are Honshū, Hokkaidō, Kyūshū, and Shikoku.

F. East Asia has a variety of climates because it covers such a large area and because of the seasonal monsoon winds.

Answer to Skills Check

Answers should reflect independent thinking but may include that the Tibetan plateau is the highest plateau in the world.

Focus Your Reading

Ask the lesson focus question found at the beginning of the lesson: **What are the principal geographical features of East Asia?** (Mountains, plateau, desert, rivers, peninsulas, and islands)

Additional Practice

You may wish to assign the ancillary materials listed below.

Understanding the Lesson p. 130
Workbook pp. 107, 110

Answers to Caption Questions

p. 518 ▶ The cows in the foreground indicate that the land is used for dairy farming.
p. 519 ▶ It is warmer in the winter in Tokyo than in Beijing.

519

Using the Vocabulary

1. teak
2. archipelago
3. latex
4. Deccan
5. bamboo

Remembering What You Read

1. *Around the World in Eighty Days*
2. The Himalaya and the Hindu Kush
3. On the border between China and Nepal
4. The Ganges, the Indus, and the Brahmaputra
5. Sri Lanka
6. Monsoons
7. In the South Asian subcontinent
8. In ethnicity, language, and religion
9. The Malay Archipelago
10. Rice, sugarcane, fruits, timber, rubber trees, oil, natural gas, tin, copper, lead, and iron
11. China
12. The Gobi
13. It is a main transportation route.
14. Four
15. It covers a large area and has monsoons.

USING THE VOCABULARY

On a separate sheet of paper, write the letter of the term that best matches each numbered statement.

a. Deccan   d. latex
b. archipelago   e. bamboo
c. teak

1. A hardwood used for building ships and furniture
2. A chain or group of islands
3. The milky sap that drips from slits cut into the bark of rubber trees
4. The low plateau that is located on the southern part of the South Asian subcontinent
5. A type of grass used to make houses, furniture, and paper

REMEMBERING WHAT YOU READ

On a separate sheet of paper, answer the following questions in complete sentences.

1. What book tells about Phileas Fogg and his worldwide travels?
2. What two mountain ranges separate the South Asian subcontinent from the rest of Asia?
3. Where is the tallest mountain in the world located?
4. What are the three longest rivers in South Asia?
5. Which is the largest island located off the tip of the subcontinent?
6. What kinds of winds greatly affect the climate of the subcontinent?

7. Where does about one third of Asia's population live?
8. How do the different groups that are part of the population of the South Asian subcontinent differ from each other?
9. What are the name and location of the world's largest group of islands?
10. What are some of the resources of Southeast Asia?
11. What country makes up the largest part of East Asia?
12. What is the name of the world's second largest desert?
13. Why is the Xi Jiang an important river in China?
14. How many main islands make up the country of Japan?
15. Why is East Asia a region of many different climates?

TYING SCIENCE TO SOCIAL STUDIES

Imagine that you are planning a trip around the world. Make a copy of a world map, or perhaps your teacher can provide a copy for you. Choose at least six countries that you would like to visit. Mark these locations on the map to show where you will stop on your trip. Then use an encyclopedia or another reference book to find the average temperatures and average precipitation levels for the time of year you plan to visit these countries. Indicate the temperature and rainfall levels on the map. Of all the countries you have chosen, which is the warmest? Which is the wettest? Which is the coldest?

520

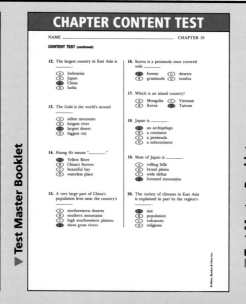

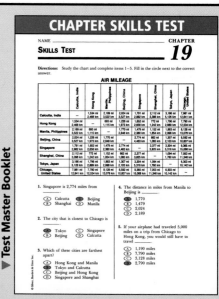

THINKING CRITICALLY

On a separate sheet of paper, answer the following questions in complete sentences.

1. Why did so many people in 1873 find the book *Around the World in Eighty Days* exciting and interesting?
2. Why, in your opinion, is the population of the South Asian subcontinent spread unevenly over the land?
3. How do you suppose so many of the world's major religions came to have followers in the Malay Archipelago?
4. The Chinese had designed an incorrect map of the world. How would you explain this?
5. What differences are there between the Malay Archipelago and the Japanese archipelago?

SUMMARIZING THE CHAPTER

On a separate sheet of paper, draw a graphic organizer like the one shown here. Copy the information from this graphic organizer to the one you have drawn. Under the main idea for each lesson, write four statements that support the main idea.

CHAPTER THEME — A variety of lands and climates exist in South Asia and East Asia.

LESSON 1

South Asia has a variety of geographical features.

1.
2.
3.
4.

LESSON 2

Many differences can be found among the people and lands of Southeast Asia.

1.
2.
3.
4.

LESSON 3

East Asia has a variety of geographical features.

1.
2.
3.
4.

Thinking Critically

1. Answers may include that it seemed like such an improbable adventure.
2. Answers may include that people tend to live where water and natural resources are present.
3. Answers may include that many different people traveled through and settled in the islands over the years.
4. Answers may include that the Chinese were mainly interested in their own culture and therefore overestimated the size and importance of their country.
5. The Malay Archipelago is spread out over thousands of miles, while the Japanese archipelago is more compact.

Summarizing the Chapter

Lesson 1
1. Tall mountains
2. Long rivers
3. Plateau
4. Islands

Lesson 2
1. Peninsulas and islands
2. Ethnic groups, languages, and religions
3. Climates
4. Natural resources

Lesson 3
1. Desert
2. Rivers
3. Peninsulas and islands
4. Mountains and plateau

▶ Test Master Booklet

CHAPTER SKILLS TEST

NAME ______________________ CHAPTER 19

SKILLS TEST (continued)

Directions: Read this section of a gazetteer and complete items 6–10. Fill in the circle next to the correct answer.

Hiroshima (hihr uh SHEE muh) Industrial city in Japan. On August 6, 1945, the city was destroyed by an atomic bomb. This was the first time an atomic bomb was ever used in warfare. (34°N/132°E)
Hokkaidō (hoh KYE doh) Northernmost of the four main islands of Japan. p. 508.
Honshū (HAHN shoo) Largest of Japan's four main islands. p. 508.
Kyūshū (kee OO shoo) Southernmost of the four main islands of Japan. p. 508.
Shikoku (SHEE koh koo) Smallest of the four main islands of Japan. p. 508.
Tokyo (TOH kee oh) Capital of Japan. Located on the island of Honshū on Tokyo Bay. Second most populated city in the world. (36°N/140°E) p. 545.

6. Which two entries are both islands?
   (A) Hokkaidō and Tokyo
   (B) Shikoku and Hokkaidō
   (C) Tokyo and Hiroshima
   (D) Hiroshima and Shikoku
7. For which of these places does the gazetteer give the most exact location?
   (A) Honshū (C) Hokkaidō
   (B) Kyūshū (D) Hiroshima
8. You *cannot* find out from these entries ______.
   (A) the country in which each place is located
   (B) where to look for more information about each place
   (C) the current population of each place
   (D) how to pronounce the name of each place
9. Which statement is false?
   (A) Kyūshū is larger than Shikoku.
   (B) Tokyo is farther north than Kyūshū.
   (C) Hokkaidō is smaller than Honshū.
   (D) Shikoku is farther north than Hokkaidō.
10. Which entry or entries include information about the history as well as the geography of the place?
   (A) Tokyo and Hiroshima
   (B) only Hiroshima
   (C) Hokkaidō and Tokyo
   (D) only Tokyo

▶ Test Master Booklet

CHAPTER WRITING TEST

NAME ______________________ CHAPTER 19

ESSAY TEST

Directions: Write a response to items 1–4.

REMINDER: Read and think about each item before you write your response. Be sure to think of the points you want to cover, details that support your response, and reasons for your opinions. Then, on the lines below, write your response in complete sentences.

1. Describe the land of the South Asian subcontinent.

A satisfactory response should explain that the subcontinent
- is shaped like an upside-down triangle
- is separated from the rest of Asia by the Himalaya and Hindu Kush mountains in the north
- has a low plateau to the south called the Deccan, which is bordered by the Eastern Ghats and the Western Ghats.

An excellent response might add that the
- subcontinent has three major rivers—the Ganges, Indus, and Brahmaputra
- Ganges creates a fertile plain
- Ganges and Brahmaputra form a large delta in what is now Bangladesh
- islands of Sri Lanka and the Maldives are near the southern tip of the subcontinent.

2. Where do most of the people of South and East Asia live?

A satisfactory response should state the following:
- Asia's population is not spread out evenly.
- Population is concentrated in the river valleys and deltas of the South Asian subcontinent and China.

An excellent response might add that
- population is very dense in the Ganges valley and delta and along the southwestern coast of the subcontinent
- on East Asia's mainland, a very large part of the population lives in the valleys or deltas of the three great rivers of China—the Chang Jiang, the Xi Jiang, and the Huang He
- since Japan has little good land, its people must live on every bit of available land
- the population of the subcontinent is growing especially rapidly.

▶ Test Master Booklet

CHAPTER WRITING TEST

NAME ______________________ CHAPTER 19

ESSAY TEST (continued)

3. Compare and contrast the climates of South Asia, Southeast Asia, and East Asia.

A satisfactory response should make the following points:
- On the South Asian subcontinent, summer monsoons bring wet weather to northeastern India and to the central plain, and winter monsoons bring dry, sunny weather.
- Southeast Asia has a hot, humid climate.
- East Asia has many climates, including continental and maritime areas and areas affected by summer and winter monsoons.

An excellent response might also explain that
- summer monsoons blow off the ocean, where they pick up moisture
- winter monsoons blow from the continent, bringing dry weather
- the climate of the Japanese islands is moderated by the ocean
- the hot, humid climate of Southeast Asia is good for year-round farming
- the Gobi has extremely hot summers and cold winters.

4. What is "China's sorrow"?

A satisfactory response should explain that the Chinese people call the Huang He "China's sorrow" because of its floods.

An excellent response might
- explain that many people live in the Huang He valley, where there is farming and shipping
- state that the Huang He's floods destroy much property and many lives.

History of South and East Asia

(pp. 522-539)

Chapter Theme: East Asia and South Asia were affected by new religions, trade, and empire builders from Europe, the Middle East, and from within the regions themselves.

CHAPTER RESOURCES
Review Master Booklet
  Reviewing Chapter Vocabulary, p. 137
  Place Geography, p. 138
  Summarizing the Chapter, p. 139
Chapter 20 Test

LESSON 1 China

(pp. 522-526)

Theme: Chinese culture, inventions, and discoveries attracted visitors and trade from European countries, and China was forced to open its doors to trade.

 SILVER WINGS WORKSHOP: The Walls Came Tumbling Down

 SOCIAL STUDIES LIBRARY: *Money*

LESSON RESOURCES
Workbook, pp. 112-113
Review Master Booklet
  Understanding the Lesson, p. 134

LESSON 2 Korea and Japan

(pp. 527-531)

Theme: Both Korea and Japan borrowed greatly from Chinese culture, but the Japanese government was more like the feudal governments of Europe in the Middle Ages.

 SILVER WINGS WORKSHOP: The Walls Came Tumbling Down

 SOCIAL STUDIES LIBRARY: *The Cat Who Went to Heaven*

LESSON RESOURCES
Workbook, p. 111
Review Master Booklet
  Understanding the Lesson, p. 135

LESSON 3 South Asia

(pp. 532-537)

Theme: Outsiders have influenced South and East Asia's customs, religion, art, and government throughout the region's history.

 SOCIAL STUDIES LIBRARY: *The Cat Who Went to Heaven*
Ferdinand Magellan

LESSON RESOURCES
Workbook, p. 114
Review Master Booklet
  Understanding the Lesson, p. 136

Review Masters

REVIEWING CHAPTER VOCABULARY

20

VOCABULARY MASTER

Review   Study the terms in the box. Use your Glossary to find definitions of those you do not remember.

cocoon	mausoleum	shogun	typhoon
free port	samurai	successor	

Practice   Complete the paragraphs using terms from the box above. You may change the forms of the terms to fit the meaning.

    European traders always looked to Asia for many of the things European people wanted. Spices and tea were popular items in Europe, and they could be found only in Asia. In time, traders returned with beautiful cloths that no one in Europe had seen before. These cloths were made of silk, which the Chinese began to produce after they discovered how to unwind fibers from the (1) _cocoons_ of silkworms. Europeans were willing to pay high prices for Asian goods, and traders would undertake long sea voyages to bring them back. On these dangerous trips, ships would sometimes encounter bad weather and even (2) _typhoons_. Many ships never returned with their precious cargoes.

    Sometimes it was difficult to obtain goods from Asia for other reasons. For many years, Europeans could not trade with China at all. The emperor Kublai Khan and his (3) _successors_ did not want to open China to foreign trade. Later, trade was allowed, but only in the city of Guangzhou. Not until 1793 would the Chinese receive ambassadors from European countries. Eventually, these countries controlled trade in China. Europeans traded at (4) _free ports_ where their goods were not taxed, and they had unlimited access to Chinese goods.

Write   Write a sentence of your own for each term in the box above. You may use the back of the sheet.

Sentences should show that students understand the meanings of the terms.

_____

_____

_____

_____

_____

_____

_____

_____

LOCATING PLACES

20

PLACE GEOGRAPHY MASTER

✳   In earlier times, people from China, the South Asian subcontinent, and even the Middle East came to Southeast Asia to trade and settle. With them they brought their own religions, languages, and customs. Listed below are some present-day cities in Southeast Asia. Use the Gazetteer in your textbook to find the latitude and longitude of each place. Then list the country in which each city is located. Finally locate and label each on the map.

		COUNTRY	LAT. ⊖	LONG. ⊕
1.	Rangoon	Myanmar	17°N	96°E
2.	Hanoi	Vietnam	21°N	106°E
3.	Singapore	Singapore	1°N	104°E
4.	Manila	Philippines	15°N	121°E
5.	Jakarta	Indonesia	6°S	107°E
6.	Bangkok	Thailand	14°N	101°E
7.	Phnom Penh	Cambodia	12°N	105°E

SUMMARIZING THE CHAPTER

20

GRAPHIC ORGANIZER MASTER

✳   Complete this graphic organizer. Next to the main idea for each lesson, write four statements that support the main idea.

CHAPTER THEME — East Asia and South Asia were affected by new religions, trade, and empire builders from Europe, the Middle East, and from within the regions themselves.

LESSON 1

Outsiders affected the development of China.

1. Marco Polo
2. Popularity of Chinese inventions
3. European trade limited
4. War with the British

LESSON 2

Korea and Japan differed from China.

1. Very different languages
2. Feudal government in Japan
3. Japanese interest in Europe
4. Japanese desire to modernize

LESSON 3

Newcomers affected the South Asian subcontinent and Southeast Asia.

1. Mogul invasions
2. Moguls affect culture
3. Asian traders
4. European colonies

Workbook Pages

WRITING WITH STYLE

Appreciating Cultural Differences, Making Observations

✳ The Chinese people have kept written records for thousands of years. During this time, different writing styles have developed. Three of these styles are shown below. The seal style was used to copy ancient images found on bone, stone, or bronze. Most people used the broad strokes of the regular style for normal writing. The flowing grass style can express the writer's personality and mood in poetry and in letters to friends. All three columns read the same: "house full of precious things." Choose one of the three styles below. Copy it into the blank column to the right. Label it with the name of the style you have copied.

Seal Style	Regular Style	Grass Style

Thinking Further: Where do you think the phrase you have copied might have been found?

Answers may suggest a temple, a shrine, or a place of burial.

_____

_____

THE TRAVELS OF MARCO POLO

Understanding a Historical Map, Understanding Stated Facts and Details

✳ The map below shows the areas traveled by Marco Polo. Using the description, mark the course of his journey on the map. Show the direction he traveled with arrows.

MARCO POLO'S JOURNEY
- ○ Marco Polo's route
- ● Imperial capital
- ● Other cities

0   500   1000 miles
0   500   1000 kilometers

In 1271, 17-year-old Marco Polo left his home in Venice and sailed to Acre. From there, he rode in a camel caravan through Tabriz to the port city of Hormuz. He then traveled across Asia, passing through Balkh and Kashgar on his way to Shangdu. After three years of traveling he reached Shangdu, where he was welcomed into the summer palace of Kublai Khan by the emperor himself. During his stay in China, Marco Polo went to Beijing, visited Pagan, then returned to Beijing. He went to Yangzhou, where he served as a government official for three years.

After 21 years in China, Marco Polo began the trip back to Venice, traveling by sea. He departed from the port city of Zaitun and sailed through the South China Sea, around the peninsula north of Sumatra, and into the Bay of Bengal. The ships sailed between Ceylon and India, then across the Arabian Sea to Hormuz. From there, Marco Polo rode in a camel caravan through Tabriz to Trebizond, a port on the Black Sea. Boarding a ship once again, he sailed to Constantinople, then home to Venice.

THE TRAVELS OF MARCO POLO CONTINUED

✳ During Marco Polo's travels in China, he visited the palace of Kublai Khan. The passage below is from *The Travels of Marco Polo*. It describes what Marco Polo saw at the palace. Read the passage, and then answer the questions.

The sides of the great halls and the apartments are ornamented with dragons in carved work and gilt, figures of warriors, of birds, and of beasts, with representations of battles. . . . The grand hall is extremely long and wide, and admits of dinners being there served to great multitudes of people. The palace contains a number of separate chambers, all highly beautiful, and so admirably disposed that it seems impossible to suggest any improvement to the system of their arrangement. The exterior of the roof is adorned with a variety of color, red, green, azure, and violet, and the sort of covering is so strong as to last for many years. The glazing of the windows is so well wrought and so delicate as to have the transparency of crystal. In the rear of the body of the palace there are large buildings containing several apartments, where is deposited the private property of the monarch, or his treasure in gold and silver bullion, precious stones, and pearls, and also his vessels of gold and silver plate.

1. What is Marco Polo's overall opinion of the palace? He says that it is very large and beautiful.

2. Where might a feast take place in the palace? It would be held in the grand hall.

3. What words does Marco Polo use to say that a certain part of the palace is without equal? "It seems impossible to suggest any improvement."

4. What things are represented in the decorations on the palace walls? Dragons, birds, beasts, warriors, and battle scenes are depicted.

5. Where is the private treasure of Kublai Khan kept? It is kept in apartments in large buildings at the rear of the palace.

Thinking Further: Why did many people think Marco Polo's stories were so fantastic?

Europeans knew little about Asian countries and thought they were uncivilized, not rich and advanced as Marco Polo described.

FACTS ABOUT SOUTH ASIA

Reviewing Facts About South Asia, Hypothesizing Based on Information

✳ This worksheet reviews some important facts about South Asia. After completing the sentences, decode two messages. Fill in the missing word or words to complete the statements below. Place one letter in each blank.

1. The first Portuguese explorer to arrive in South Asia was V A S C O   D A   G A M A.
(10)

2. The Mogul leader who invaded the Asian subcontinent was B A B U R.
(4)(12)

3. The noisy Mogul weapon that frightened the elephants was the C A N N O N.
(16)

4. Akbar tried to unite two religious groups: the H I N D U S and the M U S L I M S.
(3)(17)(23)

5. The temple built by Shah Jahan as a memorial to his wife was the T A J   M A H A L.
(5)(1)(25)

6. Europeans went to Asia looking for pepper, ginger, and other S P I C E S.
(2)(13)

7. The Moguls gave great encouragement to writers, craftspersons, and A R T I S T S.
(8)

8. India gradually came under the control of G R E A T   B R I T A I N.
(21)(24)

9. The Spanish conquered the Philippines, which they named after their K I N G.
(26)(14)

10. Vietnam, Laos, and Cambodia were conquered by F R A N C E.
(6)

✳ Use the numbered letters above to decode the messages below.

A K B A R was T H E   G R E A T E S T of the
(1)(26)(4)(1)(21)   (5)(3)   (14)(21)(6)(1)(5)(8)

M O G U L   R U L E R S.
(12)(16)(14)(23)(25)   (21)(3)(23)(6)(21)(8)

Many E U R O P E A N   C O U N T R I E S
(6)(23)(21)(16)(2)(6)(1)(24)   (16)(16)(23)(24)(5)(21)(13)(6)(8)

E S T A B L I S H E D   S E T T L E M E N T S in
(6)(8)(5)(1)(4)(25)(13)(8)(6)(17)   (8)(6)(5)(5)(25)(6)(12)(6)(24)(5)(8)

S O U T H   A S I A.
(8)(16)(23)(5)(3)   (1)(8)(13)(1)

Thinking Further: Akbar tried to unite people of different faiths by inventing a new religion. Why do you think this idea failed?

Answers may suggest that religion was part of the culture of these groups, and people were not willing to give up something familiar for something new.

C20-C

China

Objectives

★1. **Explain** the attitudes of the British and the Chinese toward foreign trade and how these attitudes led to conflicts.

2. **Describe** some inventions of the ancient Chinese.

3. **Identify** the following people and places: *Kublai Khan, Marco Polo, Ch'ien Lung, Beijing, Guangzhou,* and *Hong Kong.*

1 STARTING THE LESSON

Motivation Activity

■ Ask students to imagine that they are the richest ruler in the world.

■ Ask students how they would use their power and wealth. What things would they do for the people of their kingdom?

■ Tell students that in this lesson they will learn about the richest kingdom on earth 700 years ago.

Think About What You Know

■ Assign the THINK ABOUT WHAT YOU KNOW activity on p. 523.

■ Student answers may include that the Mongols might have forced the Chinese to adopt their nomadic way of life.

Study the Vocabulary

■ Have students look up the definition of the new vocabulary word in the Glossary.

■ Tell students what a metaphor is. Ask students to think about the ways *cocoon* could function as a metaphor. (Give students examples, such as: Being happily wrapped in his *cocoon* of books, the librarian was unaware of what was happening outside the library.)

CHAPTER 20

HISTORY OF SOUTH AND EAST ASIA

*A*sia is the home of s‹ of the world's oldest cultures. Inventions and ideas that were develop‹ here have influenced all the world. Europeans ca‹ to South and East Asia t‹ trade and to settle.

Optional Activities

Creating a Bulletin Board

● Have students create bulletin boards showing the processes by which silk, paper, and gunpowder are made.

● Displays should provide information about how these things were made in ancient China and how they are made today.

● Bulletin boards should also show how these products are used—for example: silk is used for clothing; paper is used for printing books, cardboard, and packing material; and gunpowder is used for guns, cannons, and fireworks.

China

THINK ABOUT WHAT YOU KNOW
You have already read about the conquests of the Mongol emperor Genghis Khan. How, do you suppose, did life in early China change with the arrival of the Mongols?

STUDY THE VOCABULARY
cocoon

FOCUS YOUR READING
How did outsiders affect the development of China?

A. Marco Polo Visits China

Kublai Khan's Empire When Niccolò and Maffeo Polo visited China in 1265, they were presented to the ruler Kublai Khan (KOO blye kahn). The Polo brothers had left their home in Venice, Italy, five years earlier. After many delays and difficulties, they had made their way overland across Asia to northern China.

Kublai Khan was the grandson of Genghis Khan, the Mongol chief whose armies had conquered the world's largest empire. Kublai Khan, also known as the Great Khan, conquered China. Kublai Khan had never met a European.

Marco Polo's Book Niccolò's son, Marco, accompanied the Polo brothers on their second trip to China, almost ten years later. Marco Polo set about learning the language of the Great Khan's people. This so pleased Kublai Khan that he took Marco into his service and sent him on missions to various parts of the empire.

Marco Polo served Kublai Khan for 17 years before returning to Venice. He took careful notes on his travels and later wrote

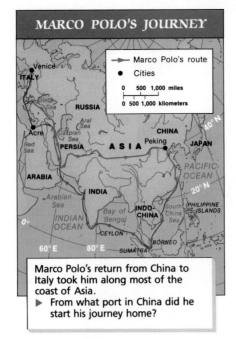

MARCO POLO'S JOURNEY

→ Marco Polo's route
● Cities

0 500 1,000 miles
0 500 1,000 kilometers

Marco Polo's return from China to Italy took him along most of the coast of Asia.
▶ From what port in China did he start his journey home?

about them in a book now known as *The Travels of Marco Polo*.

Much of the book is about Kublai Khan. Marco Polo describes the Great Khan as the richest and most powerful ruler in the world. His empire was larger than any other, and his palace was the biggest ever known.

B. Chinese Discoveries and Inventions

Making Paper Europeans knew little about China in Marco Polo's day, but they did know about Chinese discoveries and inventions. Paper, as we know it today, was invented in China about A.D. 100, and knowledge of papermaking spread to the Middle East and to Europe. The first paper mills in Italy were being built about the time that Marco Polo arrived in China.

523

For Your Information

Ts'ai Lun The name of the man who invented paper is well-known in China, though it is not terribly familiar in the West. Chinese records indicate that around the year 105, Ts'ai Lun, a court official, presented Emperor Ho Ti with a sample of paper that he had made. Although the emperor was pleased with Ts'ai Lun's achievement and rewarded him generously, Ts'ai later became involved in a court scandal and committed suicide. Before Ts'ai Lun, most Chinese books were made of bamboo, although a few special books were written on silk. In the West, vellum, or parchment made of sheep or calfskin, was used. All of these options were heavy, bulky, unwieldy, and expensive.

Optional Activities

---

2 DEVELOPING THE LESSON

Read and Think

Sections A and B

To cover the time period from the journeys of Marco Polo to the opening of China to foreign trade, ask the following questions:

1. **Why did Kublai Khan welcome the Polo brothers?**
   (He had never met a European and had many questions. *p. 523*)

2. **How was it that Europeans had knowledge of Chinese silk, paper, and gunpowder and yet knew so little about China?**
   (They obtained Chinese goods from a series of traders, not directly from China. *p. 525*)

Thinking Critically **What do you think Europeans during Marco Polo's time thought of the Chinese?** (Hypothesize)
(Answers may include that they were impressed with Chinese discoveries and inventions and probably thought that the Chinese must have been very intelligent. *p. 525*)

GEOGRAPHY THEMES

Movement

■ Have students refer to the map on this page in order to answer the following question: **Did Marco Polo travel more miles by water on the journey to China, or on the return trip to Italy?**
(He covered more miles by water on the return trip to Italy.)

Answers to Caption Questions
p. 523 ▶ From Peking

Thinking About Source Material

Background Information

Chinese Inventions Paper money is not the only Chinese invention that amazed Marco Polo. In his writings, he also described Kublai Khan's kingdom-wide postal system, in which riders on horseback relayed messages from one courier station to another. Polo also detailed how the Chinese mined and used coal, a resource not used in Europe at that time.

Polo's writings were widely read in Europe. Many historians feel that his works may be responsible for the European introduction of such Chinese inventions as the compass, papermaking, and printing.

Guided Reading

1. **What type of trees did the Chinese use to produce paper?**
   (Mulberry trees)

2. **What did the money look like?**
   (It was black, nearly square, came in different sizes, and was signed and stamped by a number of officials.)

3. **Name an act in this selection that was punishable by death.**
   (Answers may include counterfeiting or refusing to accept the paper money.)

4. **Why did Kublai Khan's subjects accept the money without hesitation?**
   (Because it could be used to purchase whatever they wanted)

Understanding Source Material

1. Like Kublai Khan's money, the paper money we use today is made of paper, is rectangular, bears the signatures of government officers, is circulated widely, and is used to purchase all types of goods.

2. One can tell from this passage that Kublai Khan was a powerful man because he authorized the operation of the mint, the distribution of the money, and the punishment of counterfeiters and those who would not accept the currency.

USING SOURCE MATERIAL

MARCO POLO DISCOVERS PAPER MONEY

Kublai Khan

The Granger Collection

Marco Polo spent nearly two decades serving Kublai Khan. Polo spent much of that time traveling throughout the Mongol Empire. During his travels, Polo kept careful notes, which he later used to write *The Travels of Marco Polo.* In the following passage from his book, Polo describes how paper money is made and used in the empire.

> In this city of Kanbalu [now Beijing] is the mint of the Great Khan, who may truly be said to possess the secret of the alchemists, as he has the art of producing money. . . . He causes the bark to be stripped from . . . mulberry-trees. . . . This . . . is made into paper, resembling, in substance, that which is manufactured from cotton, but quite black. When ready for use, he has it cut into pieces of money of different sizes, nearly square, but somewhat longer than they are wide. . . . The coinage of this paper money is authenticated with as much form and ceremony as if it were actually of pure gold or silver; for to each note a number of officers, specially appointed, not only subscribe their names, but affix their seals also. . . . The act of counterfeiting it is punished as a capital offence. When thus coined in large quantities, this paper currency is circulated in every part of the Great Khan's dominions; nor dares any person at the peril of his life, refuse to accept it in payment. All his subjects receive it without hesitation, because, wherever their business may call them, they can dispose of it again in the purchase of merchandise they may require; such as pearls, jewels, gold, or silver. With it, in short, every article may be procured.

Understanding Source Material

1. How does the paper money that Polo described in his book compare with ours today?
2. How can you tell from the above passage that Kublai Khan was truly a powerful man?

Optional Activities

Using Source Material

Drawing Ancient Chinese Money Have students use details from the Source Material selection to draw pictures of what they think Kublai Khan's paper money might have looked like.

● Encourage students to focus on details such as the size, shape, and color of the money, and to represent these details in their drawings.

● After students have finished their drawings, display a United States dollar bill and discuss the ways in which it differs from their drawings of the ancient Chinese money.

Inventing Gunpowder When the Mongols invaded eastern Europe, they used gunpowder, which may have been another Chinese invention. Many historians believe that the Chinese had gunpowder by the tenth century. If so, they used it mainly for fireworks. Cannons and guns were probably invented later.

Making Silk Since ancient times the Chinese have known how to make silk cloth from fibers spun by silkworms. A silkworm is a caterpillar that spins an especially light, strong covering. This covering, which protects the silkworm while it is changing into a moth, is called a cocoon. The Chinese discovered how to unwind the thin fibers of cocoons, spin them into thread, and weave the thread into cloth. Silk cloth was valuable and easily transported. Passing from trader to trader, it was being carried across Central Asia 1,200 years before Marco Polo wrote his book.

C. European Traders Reach China

Chinese emperors after Kublai Khan did not welcome visitors from Europe and saw no reason for China to open its doors to foreign trade. They thought that China lacked nothing within its own borders.

One of the emperors, however, understood why foreigners wanted Chinese silk, tea, and porcelain. For this reason he permitted foreigners to enter the city of Guangzhou for limited trading.

The Chinese laid down strict rules for trading at Guangzhou. European traders had to come during the summer, and they could do business with only a few Chinese merchants. All Europeans had to stay within a district set aside for foreigners. The European traders were not supposed to mix with the Chinese.

SILK: FROM SILK MOTHS TO TIE

1. A silkworm moth lays hundreds of eggs.

2. Silkworms hatch from the eggs.

3. Silkworms spin cocoons of silk fibers.

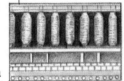
4. The silk fibers are spun into yarn.

5. The yarn is woven into fabric.

6. A silk garment is made from the fabric.

Silk was first used by the ancient Chinese, who kept the secret of the silkworm for thousands of years.
▶ What happens after the silkworm moth lays its eggs?

Meeting Individual Needs
Concept:
Understanding the Role of Ambassadors

To better understand the history of China, it is important to understand the role of ambassadors in foreign relations. Below are three activities that will help students understand what ambassadors do.

◆ **EASY** Have students review the definitions of *ambassador* in the text and the Glossary.

Ask them to list three reasons why governments might use ambassadors.

◆▶ **AVERAGE** Ask students to work in small groups to create charts showing the advantages and disadvantages of receiving ambassadors from other countries.

◀▮▶ **CHALLENGING** Place students who need a challenge into two groups and have them conduct a debate.

Ask one group to argue that the Chinese were right to refuse to let Britain open an embassy.

Have the other group argue that the British were right to demand that China allow them to establish an embassy in China.

Read and Think
Sections C and D

Use the following questions to discuss the effects that foreign trade had on China:

1. **Why did Chinese emperors not want to open China to foreign trade?**
   (They thought that China lacked nothing within its own borders. *p. 525*)

2. **What did the British ask of the Chinese emperor in 1793?**
   (Permission to open an embassy and for freer trade *p. 526*)

Thinking Critically How, do you think, might the British and the Chinese have avoided fighting a war? (Evaluate)
(Answers may include by negotiation and compromise. *p. 526*)

— **Answers to Caption Questions** —
p. 525 ▶ Silkworms hatch from the eggs.

3 CLOSING THE LESSON

Lesson 1 Review

Answers to Think and Write

A. Marco Polo learned about the empire because he learned the language and he also traveled extensively throughout China.

B. The Chinese invented ways to make silk fabric, paper, and gunpowder.

C. Kublai Khan welcomed European traders, but subsequent emperors restricted trade because they felt that China did not need anything from other countries.

D. Quarrels between the British and the Chinese led to war in 1839. The British won the war, forced China to open its ports to trade, and established a British colony on the island of Hong Kong.

Answer to Skills Check

Letters should include descriptions of Marco Polo's activities from the text.

Focus Your Reading

Ask the lesson focus question found at the beginning of the lesson: **How did outsiders affect the development of China?**
(European merchants and traders who wanted to obtain Chinese products eventually forced China to open its ports to trade and, in time, came to control the country.)

Additional Practice

You may wish to assign the ancillary materials listed below.

Understanding the Lesson p. 134
Workbook pp. 112-113

D. The Opening of China's Doors

A Special Favor In 1793 the British sent a representative to Ch'ien Lung (chee UN lung), the Chinese emperor. The emperors had never received ambassadors, or official representatives, from European countries, but Ch'ien Lung agreed to do so as a special favor to the British.

The ambassador carried a message from the British king, George III. The king asked that the British be allowed to open an embassy in Peking and that there be freer trade between the two countries. In his reply to the king, Ch'ien Lung said that the Chinese did not need such contacts.

The Chinese officials thought the British were very rude to ask for more favors after the emperor had been kind enough to meet their ambassador. The British viewed Ch'ien Lung's refusal to allow an embassy very differently. They thought civilized countries exchanged ambassadors. But there were other differences between China and Britain. The British complained that the Chinese did not treat their merchants at Guangzhou fairly. The Chinese charged that British merchants broke Chinese laws.

The Granger Collection

The British are shown here attacking the Chinese in the First Opium War, in 1839.
▶ What caused the war?

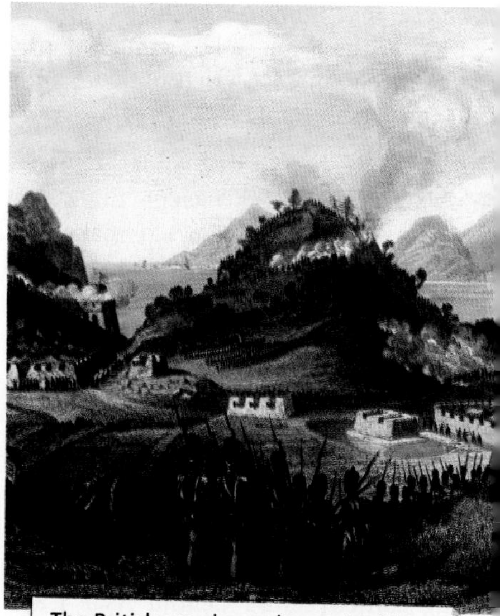

China Defeated These quarrels led to a war in 1839, in which the British defeated the Chinese. Britain forced China to open more of its ports to trade. The British also acquired Hong Kong, off the coast of southern China, where they set up a colony.

Once the British forced China to open its doors, other countries did the same. China was not divided up into colonies, as Africa was, but by 1900, European countries largely controlled the country.

LESSON 1 REVIEW

THINK AND WRITE

A. How was Marco Polo able to learn so much about Kublai Khan's empire? (Infer)

B. What were some Chinese discoveries and inventions? (Recall)

C. How did the views of Chinese emperors change regarding European trading in China? (Infer)

D. Summarize the results of the quarrels between the Chinese and the British. (In

SKILLS CHECK

WRITING SKILL

Suppose you were a Venetian who listened to Marco Polo tell about his years in China. Write a letter to a friend, describing what you heard.

Optional Activities

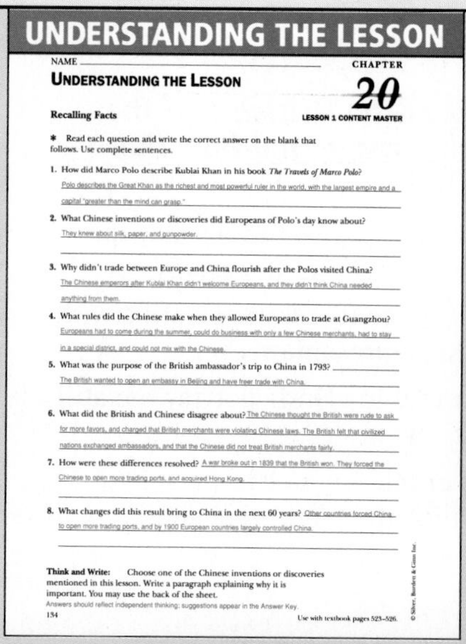

UNDERSTANDING THE LESSON

NAME ______ CHAPTER 20

UNDERSTANDING THE LESSON

Recalling Facts LESSON 1 CONTENT MASTER

* Read each question and write the correct answer on the blank that follows. Use complete sentences.

1. How did Marco Polo describe Kublai Khan in his book *The Travels of Marco Polo?* Polo describes the Great Khan as the richest and most powerful ruler in the world, with the largest empire and a capital "greater than the mind can grasp."
2. What Chinese inventions or discoveries did Europeans of Polo's day know about? They knew about silk, paper, and gunpowder.
3. Why didn't trade between Europe and China flourish after the Polos visited China? The Chinese emperors after Kublai Khan didn't welcome Europeans, and they didn't think China needed anything from them.
4. What rules did the Chinese make when they allowed Europeans to trade at Guangzhou? Europeans had to come during the summer, could do business with only a few Chinese merchants, had to stay in a special district, and could not mix with the Chinese.
5. What was the purpose of the British ambassador's trip to China in 1793? The British wanted to open an embassy in Beijing and have freer trade with China.
6. What did the British and Chinese disagree about? The Chinese thought the British were rude to ask for more favors, and charged that British merchants were violating Chinese laws. The British felt that civilized nations exchanged ambassadors, and that the Chinese did not treat British merchants fairly.
7. How were these differences resolved? A war broke out in 1839 that the British won. They forced the Chinese to open more trading ports, and acquired Hong Kong.
8. What changes did this result bring to China in the next 60 years? Other countries forced China to open more trading ports, and by 1900 European countries largely controlled China.

Think and Write: Choose one of the Chinese inventions or discoveries mentioned in this lesson. Write a paragraph explaining why it is important. You may use the back of the sheet.
Answers should reflect independent thinking; suggestions appear in the Answer Key.

134 Use with textbook pages 523–526.

◀ Review Master Booklet, p. 134

THINK ABOUT WHAT YOU KNOW

f you visited a class in North Korea or apan and were asked to tell something bout the history of your country, what vould you talk about?

STUDY THE VOCABULARY

amurai   typhoon
hogun

FOCUS YOUR READING

Iow did Korea and Japan differ from China?

Korea and Chinese Civilization

The people of Korea have a proverb: er the house has burned, pick up the ls. By this they mean, if you suffer a s, take what is left and start over. The reans have done this a number of times. e Korean peninsula, located between ina and Japan, was occupied by both : Chinese and the Japanese at different es during Korea's long history.

In early times the Koreans borrowed ny things from Chinese civilization. The ddhist religion, which originated in lia, was taken to Korea by the Chi- se. The Koreans studied ancient Chi- se writings, particularly those of nfucius. They also used the Chinese stem of writing.

The Korean language is very different m Chinese, however. As long as the reans wrote with borrowed Chinese aracters, only a few people could learn read and write. Most people did not ve time to memorize the thousands of ferent Chinese characters.

To solve this problem, in the mid-1440s the Korean king, Sejong (SAY ZHONG) introduced an alphabet of 28 letters. The alphabet represented the sounds of the Korean language and so provided a simpler way to write and read. Some officials who knew the Chinese characters continued to use them. Today, however, Korean students learn King Sejong's alphabet.

B. Japan and the Chinese

Chinese Influence   Japan was influenced by Chinese civilization, too. Buddhism was taken to Japan from China by way of Korea. Japanese nobles went to China to learn Chinese ways. Like the Koreans, Japanese scholars in early times wrote with Chinese characters and read Confucius. Later a simpler writing system was invented that was better suited to the Japanese language.

About 550 years ago, King Sejong introduced the Korean alphabet that is used today.
► Why did he invent the alphabet?

Courtesy Korean Cultural Service

For Your Information

King Sejong   The ruler of Korea in the mid-fifteenth century, King Sejong was strongly influenced by the ideas of Confucius, and his rule was marked by progressive ideas. He is known for introducing a sliding scale of taxation, the creation of a simple Korean alphabet, invention of the pluviometer (rain gauge), concern for the health of his people, and interest in astronomical science. He also instigated the creation and later revision of notation for Korean and Chinese music. King Sejong strengthened his country, opened ports to Japanese trade, emphasized scholarship and literature, and evoked a national consciousness among the people.

Optional Activities

Korea and Japan

Objectives

★**1. Explain** Japan's development from a feudal society to the most powerful country in East Asia.

2. Discuss the influence of China on the Japanese and Korean cultures.

3. Identify the following people and places: *King Sejong, Commodore Matthew Perry, Emperor Meiji, Korea,* and *Japan.*

1 STARTING THE LESSON

Motivation Activity

■ Show students a map of East Asia (China, Japan, and Korea). Locate the East Asian countries in this chapter on the map.

■ Ask students which of the three countries they would expect to be the most powerful (most will probably answer China). Explain that by the end of the nineteenth century, Japan had become the strongest.

Think About What You Know

■ Assign the THINK ABOUT WHAT YOU KNOW activity on p. 527.

■ Student answers may include the American Revolution, the development of our government, and various events that took place during westward expansion.

Study the Vocabulary

■ Have students look up the definitions of the new vocabulary words in the Glossary.

■ Ask students to make up movie titles using the vocabulary words.

Answers to Caption Questions

p. 526 ► Quarrels over the right of Britain to open an embassy in China and over the right to free trade

p. 527 ► So that his people would not have to memorize thousands of different Chinese characters; his alphabet also provided a simpler way to write and read.

527

Read and Think

Sections A, B, and C

Although foreigners have had an important influence on Korean and Japanese history, both countries have retained their own culture and identity. Ask the questions below to discuss Chinese and European influence on Korea and Japan:

1. **What did King Sejong do to solve the problem of learning the Chinese system of writing?**
   (He introduced an alphabet of 28 letters that represented the sounds of the Korean language and provided a simpler way to read and write. *p. 527*)

2. **How did the Japanese learn about Chinese culture?**
   (Through Korea, and by studying Confucius and sending nobles to China *p. 527*)

3. **What did the early Europeans offer that was of most interest to the Japanese?**
   (Clocks, musical instruments, clothes, science, geography, and the Christian religion *p. 529*)

   Thinking Critically Do you think the shogun was wise to fear the growing interest in European ideas and products? (Evaluate)
   (Answers may include yes, the shogun was wise to see that the Europeans might try to dominate Japan just as they eventually did China, or no, the shogun was foolish to close his country off from trade and modern ideas. *p. 529*)

VISUAL THINKING SKILL

Reading a Time Line

■ Direct students' attention to the time line on p. 529. Then ask the following question: **In what year did Commodore Matthew Perry arrive at Nagasaki?**
(1853)

Ancient samurai warriors wore very elaborate suits of armor that were considerably lighter in weight than those worn by European knights.
▶ With what weapons are these samurai warriors equipped?

Feudalism Like China, Japan had emperors. But the Japanese government was much more like the feudal governments of the European countries during the Middle Ages. Real power belonged to the nobles, who had large estates. Each noble ruled the people who lived on his land. Many nobles had their own bands of fighting men called **samurai** (SAM uh rye). The most powerful of the nobles was a military leader called the **shogun**. For nearly seven centuries the shoguns held real power, although the emperors supposedly ruled.

Takeover Attempts When Kublai Khan ruled China, he heard tales about Japan's great wealth and decided to add Japan to his empire. He sent a message to the Japanese, demanding that they pay tribute to him. If they did not, he would invade their islands. When the Japanese refused, Kublai Khan sent a fleet to attack them. Fortunately for the Japanese, a storm wrecked part of the Mongol fleet, forcing it to return to the mainland.

Kublai Khan did not give up his dream of conquering Japan. In 1281 he sent an even larger force. Once again bad weather favored the Japanese. A **typhoon**, or severe hurricane, destroyed most of the Mongol fleet. Japan remained independent. Although the Japanese borrowed ideas and customs from China, Japan was never part of China's empire.

528

Optional Activities

Making a Bar Graph

● Ask students to predict, based on what they have learned about systems of writing, where literacy rates would be highest and lowest in East Asia today.

● Ask students to use an almanac to find the literacy rates of China (70%), Japan (99%), North Korea (99%), and South Korea (92%).

● Have them create bar graphs to chart the literacy rate in each country.

● Students might also wish to chart additional statistics, reflecting newspaper circulation per thousand or years of compulsory education in each country.

C. Japan Closes the Door to Foreigners

Japan's Fear Portuguese merchants and Christian priests were the first Europeans to visit Japan. At first the Japanese welcomed the Europeans, although they thought them rather rude. Japanese nobles bought European goods from merchants from the West. The nobles particularly liked clocks and musical instruments. Some bought European clothes to wear.

Christian priests reported that the Japanese were eager to hear about new things. They were especially interested in European science and geography. Some Japanese were interested in the Christian religion. By the 1630s the shogun in power became worried about the growing interest in European ways and ideas. He feared that Europeans who came to trade would later try to rule the country. He knew that European countries had established colonies on the subcontinent and in the Philippines.

Closing the Door The shogun decided that Japan should follow China's example and close the door to foreigners. Yet, although most Europeans had to leave the country, the shogun did agree to leave the door ajar. A few Dutch traders were allowed to stay at the port of Nagasaki. Rules for the traders at Nagasaki were much like those set by the Chinese for traders at Guangzhou.

The Japanese left this opening because they wanted to know what was going

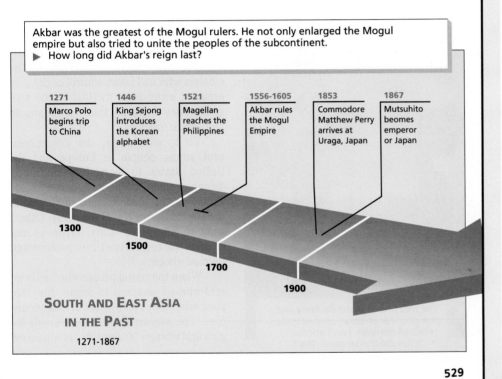

Akbar was the greatest of the Mogul rulers. He not only enlarged the Mogul empire but also tried to unite the peoples of the subcontinent.
▶ How long did Akbar's reign last?

1271 Marco Polo begins trip to China

1446 King Sejong introduces the Korean alphabet

1521 Magellan reaches the Philippines

1556-1605 Akbar rules the Mogul Empire

1853 Commodore Matthew Perry arrives at Uraga, Japan

1867 Mutsuhito beomes emperor or Japan

1300
1500
1700
1900

SOUTH AND EAST ASIA IN THE PAST
1271-1867

529

Read and Think
Sections D and E

Although the Japanese closed their doors to everything except limited trade with the Europeans for several centuries, they changed their policy in the mid-nineteenth century. Use the questions below to discuss how the Japanese benefited from contact with foreigners:

1. **What was the attitude of the Japanese toward Commodore Perry's 1853 visit?**
(Some feared that future visits might not be as peaceful, but others felt that Japan had to learn from the West in order to remain independent. *p. 530*)

2. **How had the Japanese government changed by the time Emperor Meiji took the throne?**
(The shoguns had lost power to officials who believed in rapid modernization. *p. 530*)

Thinking Critically How was the Japanese attitude toward Western culture in the nineteenth century similar to its attitude toward China centuries earlier? (Synthesize)
(Answers may include that in both instances, the Japanese were eager to learn new ways and incorporate them into their own culture, but they were careful to protect their own independence. *p. 530*)

on in the world. Every year when a new Dutch officer came to take over the post at Nagasaki, he had to write a newsletter about the important events of the past year. The Dutch were required to supply the Japanese with European books, which a few Japanese could read.

D. The United States Navy Opens the Door

A few years after the British forced China to open its doors to trade, the United States sent a small fleet to Japan. Commodore Matthew Perry was in command of the fleet, which included the first steamships ever seen in Japan. Perry arrived at Uraga in 1853 with a letter from President Millard Fillmore to the emperor of Japan. The letter said that the United States wanted nothing more than friendship and trade between the two countries.

The meeting of Matthew Perry and the emperor of Japan opened trade relations between two nations.
► What did the Japanese fear?

Matthew Perry's visit was friendly. The Japanese feared, however, that in the future the fleets might be less peaceful. They knew that China had fought and lost against foreigners. Some Japanese leaders, however, believed that to remain independent, Japan had to learn from the Western countries.

E. "Knowledge from the Whole World"

A 15-year-old boy named Mutsuhito became the emperor of Japan in 1867. As emperor he became known as *Meiji*, which means "enlightened government." On taking the throne, Emperor Meiji read this statement:

> *My country is now undergoing a complete change from old to new ideas, which I sincerely desire. To speed the change people should seek knowledge from the whole world.*

The views in the statement read by the young emperor were really those of the officials who had taken control of the government away from the last of the shoguns. They believed that Japan should modernize quickly.

To speed change, the government sent young people to Europe and the United States to learn Western ways. Young women attended colleges in the United States. One young man studied at the United States Naval Academy. Others went to Europe to study. Japanese mechanics worked in American machine and railroad shops.

When the young people who had been sent abroad returned to Japan, they applied what they had learned in other countries. The women established schools for girls and women. Young officers organized

圖之道鐵縄高

The Japanese built their first railway as part of their plan to modernize.
▶ Where did the Japanese learn to build locomotives?

and trained modern armed forces. Mechanics built modern locomotives.

How well the Japanese had learned their lessons became plain when Japan defeated the much larger country of China in 1895. Ten years later, Japan surprised the world by defeating the Russians in East Asia. These victories showed that Japan had become the most powerful country in all of East Asia.

LESSON 2 REVIEW

THINK AND WRITE

A. What did the Koreans borrow from the Chinese? **(Recall)**

B. How was Japan like Europe during the Middle Ages? **(Infer)**

C. Why did Japan not close the door to the West completely? **(Recall)**

D. What did the United States want from Japan? **(Recall)**

E. How did the Japanese promote change under Emperor Meiji? **(Recall)**

SKILLS CHECK

THINKING SKILL

Make a time line for the years 1400–1900. Look in the lesson for the dates of the following events and show them on the time line: King Sejong introduces an alphabet; Japan closes the door to foreigners; Perry lands at Nagasaki; Emperor Meiji comes to the throne; Japan defeats China.

531

Optional Activities

Lesson 2 Review

Answers to Think and Write

A. The Koreans borrowed the Buddhist religion, the ideas of Confucius and other Chinese thinkers, and, for a time, the Chinese system of writing.

B. Japan was like medieval Europe because it had a feudal society, in which powerful nobles owned large estates and had their own bands of warriors.

C. Japan agreed to limited trade with the Dutch because they wanted to know what was going on in the rest of the world.

D. The United States said it wanted only friendship and trade with Japan.

E. Under Emperor Meiji, the Japanese promoted change by sending young people to Europe and the United States to learn Western ways and by sending Japanese mechanics to work in American machine and railroad shops.

Answer to Skills Check

Events listed in the Skills Check correspond respectively to the following dates: 1446; 1630s; 1853; 1867; and 1895.

Focus Your Reading

Ask the lesson focus question found at the beginning of the lesson: **How did Korea and Japan differ from China?**
(Although Korea and Japan borrowed ideas from China, they had different languages and adopted simpler writing systems; Japan, like China, finally opened the door to foreign trade but, unlike China, was able to resist foreign domination.)

Additional Practice

You may wish to assign the ancillary materials listed below.

Understanding the Lesson p. 135
Workbook p. 111

Answers to Caption Questions

p. 530 ▶ Japanese feared that future fleets would be less peaceful.
p. 531 ▶ In the United States

South Asia

Objectives

★1. **Explain** the ways that outsiders influenced the history and culture of South Asia.

2. **Describe** the goals and achievements of Akbar.

3. **Identify** the following people and places: *Vasco da Gama, Babur, Akbar, Goa, Taj Mahal, Burma, Cambodia, Thailand, India, Vietnam, Malay Peninsula, Indonesia, the Philippines,* and *Laos.*

1 STARTING THE LESSON

Motivation Activity

■ Ask students why Columbus called the people that he found living in America "Indians." (He thought that he had found India.)

■ Ask students to describe how they think India might have differed from North America during Columbus's time.

■ Tell students that Columbus did not reach India, but other explorers did. In this lesson they will learn what India was like in the years following Columbus's voyages.

Think About What You Know

■ Assign the THINK ABOUT WHAT YOU KNOW activity on p. 532.

■ Answers may include in cooking and for fragrances.

Study the Vocabulary

■ Have students look up the definitions of the vocabulary words in the Glossary.

■ Ask students to make and exchange crossword puzzles that include the vocabulary words and names of important people and places from all three lessons in this chapter.

THINK ABOUT WHAT YOU KNOW

Europeans first went to South Asia seeking spices. Name some of the ways that spices are used today.

STUDY THE VOCABULARY

successor   free port
mausoleum

FOCUS YOUR READING

How did people from outside the South Asian subcontinent and Southeast Asia affect these regions?

A. Newcomers Enter the Subcontinent

Vasco da Gama In 1498 the Portuguese explorer Vasco da Gama landed on the west coast of the South Asian subcontinent. Da Gama erected a stone pillar as proof of Portugal's claim to the land. The people living there did not think that the newcomers had any claim to the land. But the Portuguese went on to take the port of Goa a few years later, declaring it a Portuguese colony. It was the first European colony on the subcontinent.

Mogul Invasions Another group of newcomers entered the subcontinent through the Khyber Pass from Afghanistan. They were raiders led by Babur, a descendant of the Mongol conqueror Genghis Khan. People of the subcontinent called the invaders Moguls, their word for Mongols.

Babur's followers were fierce and skillful fighters. At first they came only to raid the land. Later, however, Babur decided he wanted an empire, and in 1526 he set out to win one.

On the subcontinent, Babur faced armies far larger than his own. His opponents had thousands of foot soldiers, many horses, and even war elephants. But Babur's men were better fighters and better armed. A Mogul could shoot a bow while riding at full speed. More important, Babur's men had cannons. Even if the cannonballs did not hit the elephants, the noise so frightened the large animals that they often trampled their handlers.

Babur conquered the northern part of the subcontinent. His **successors,** those who came after him, enlarged the empire. Mogul emperors, known as the Great Moguls, came to rule an empire that stretched from Afghanistan to the country now called Bangladesh.

Babur's army invaded the land of Afghanistan in 1507.
▶ What animals did the Moguls use in fighting?

Optional Activities

Making a Map

● Distribute outline maps of the world and have students show the route taken by Vasco da Gama from Portugal to Goa in 1497 and 1498.

● Have students use the scale of miles/kilometers on the world map in the Atlas to estimate the distance of the trip from Lisbon to Goa. Tell them to transfer this information to their maps.

● Later in the lesson, you may ask students to show the route traveled by Magellan's ships on their voyage around the world. How much farther did Magellan's men travel than Da Gama's?

Christian priests and Muslims are debating religion before Akbar ca. 1605.
▶ What books do you suppose are shown in this picture?

B. Akbar: Greatest of the Great Moguls

Akbar's Accomplishments Akbar, the grandson of Babur, was the greatest of the Mogul rulers. He ruled for 49 years, from 1556 to 1605. He not only enlarged the Mogul Empire, he also tried to unite the different peoples of the subcontinent. The peoples of the empire spoke different languages and followed different religions.

The Moguls were Muslims, but the majority of the people on the subcontinent were Hindus. Akbar took steps to win the support of the Hindus. He placed Hindus in high positions and arranged the marriage of his son to the daughter of a Hindu noble. He also did away with a special tax that people who were not Muslims had been forced to pay.

Akbar's Religion Religions greatly interested Akbar. He built a hall of worship to which he summoned teachers of different faiths. Among others, Akbar invited Christian priests from Goa. Akbar questioned the priests for hours, not only about their religion but also about Europe.

Akbar did not adopt any of the existing religions. Instead he invented a religion that borrowed ideas from other religions. Akbar thought that such a religion would help to unite the peoples of his empire. But when Akbar died in 1605, his new religion died too.

C. The Moguls and the Arts

Akbar encouraged artists, craftspeople, and writers. He set up studios for the artists and gave prizes for the best works.

533

2 DEVELOPING THE LESSON

Read and Think

Sections A, B, and C

Discuss the contributions of Mogul rulers to South Asian culture with these questions:

1. **What advantages did Babur's Moguls have in fighting the armies of the subcontinent?**
   (Babur's men were better trained, better armed, and had cannons. *p. 532*)

2. **Why did Akbar invent a new religion?**
   (He hoped that a religion that borrowed ideas from many religions would help to unite the people of his empire. *p. 533*)

3. **Describe the Taj Mahal.**
   (It is built of white marble and combines Persian and subcontinental art styles. *p. 534*)

Thinking Critically How, do you think, might encouraging the arts encourage unity among a people? (Evaluate)
(Answers might include that as people develop a body of artistic achievement together, they will see themselves as a people sharing a common heritage. *pp. 533-534*)

Answers to Caption Questions
p. 532 ▶ Horses and camels
p. 533 ▶ Probably holy books, such as the Bible and the Koran

Graphic Organizer

After students have read the lesson, you may wish to have them use the graphic organizer below as an aid to help them understand the impact of outsiders on South Asia.

OUTSIDERS' IMPACT ON SOUTH ASIA			
PORTUGAL: Established colony at Goa; first to arrive in Indonesia	**MOGULS:** Conquered subcontinent; brought Islam; enriched arts	**SPAIN:** Conquered Philippines, named after Philip I	**FRANCE:** Fought with British for control of subcontinent; conquered Vietnam, Laos, and Cambodia
DUTCH: Gained control of Indonesia from the Portuguese	**ENGLISH:** Gained control of subcontinent; conquered Burma, Singapore, and Malay Peninsula	**UNITED STATES:** Took control of Philippines after Spanish-American War	**OTHERS:** Peoples from China, the subcontinent, and the Middle East went to trade and settled in Southeast Asia

Optional Activities

533

Concept:
Understanding European Colonization

To better understand the history of South Asia, it is important to understand how European nations colonized these countries. Below are three activities that will help students examine how European countries controlled South Asia.

◆ **EASY** Divide the class into six small groups. Assign each group an empire (Portugal, the Netherlands, Spain, the United States, Britain, or France).

Ask students to review Section E. Then, on a map of Southeast Asia, have them find the place(s) where their empire had colonies or control. A different color should be used to indicate each empire's holdings.

◀▶ **AVERAGE** Have students color-code maps of colonial South Asia to indicate areas controlled by individual European countries.

Have them trace maps showing present-day national boundaries and compare them with the older colonial divisions.

◀▮▶ **CHALLENGING** Ask students who need a challenge to write essays summarizing the ways that European empires gained control of different areas of South Asia.

VISUAL THINKING SKILL

Describing a Photograph

■ Direct students' attention to the picture of the Taj Mahal found on this page. Then have each student write a descriptive paragraph about this famous building.

The Taj Mahal stands at Agra, in northern India. It is made of white marble and was built by about 20,000 workers between 1630 and 1650.
▶ For what purpose was the Taj Mahal built?

Akbar's successors did the same. The Moguls also invited Persian artists and craftspeople to the subcontinent. Persian and subcontinental styles were often combined in the paintings.

These two styles can also be seen in one of the world's most famous buildings, the Taj Mahal. The Taj Mahal was built by Akbar's grandson, Shah Jahan, as a **mausoleum** (maw suh LEE um), or large tomb, for his beloved wife. Shah Jahan told the builders that he wanted a building "as beautiful as she was beautiful."

D. Trading Companies and Empires

Trading Posts Other Europeans followed the Portuguese to the subcontinent. Dutch, English, and French trading companies sought sugar, spices, cotton, yarn, and cloth.

Europeans went to trade rather than to settle, but they established permanent trading posts. The European companies needed places where their employees could live and do business. The first trading posts were enclosures with offices, warehouses, living quarters, and usually a chapel, or small church. As trade increased, the companies fortified their posts and hired troops to protect them. Although the officers of the troops were Europeans, most of the common soldiers were Asians.

British India As the power of the European companies increased, the power of the Moguls declined. After 1700 the Great Moguls lost control of the subcontinent. Wars broke out between local rulers, and the trading companies entered into these struggles with their armies.

534

Optional Activities

Making a Time Line
● To help students see the relationships of the events presented in this chapter, ask volunteers to make a large time line for the classroom wall.
● Have them skim Chapter 20 for important dates to place on the time line.
● You may wish to have students extend the time line as other dates are presented in the remainder of the unit.

French and British companies clashed on the subcontinent. This conflict was part of a much larger struggle between France and Britain, fought in Europe and North America. The British defeated the French and became even more powerful on the subcontinent. Although a Mogul remained on the throne until 1857, the subcontinent had become part of the British Empire and was known as British India.

E. Peoples of Southeast Asia

Peoples from China, from the subcontinent, and even from the Middle East went to Southeast Asia to trade and to settle. All of these groups had their own religions, languages, and customs.

Peoples from the subcontinent settled in many parts of the Indochina peninsula and the Indonesian archipelago. They spread Buddhism and Hinduism throughout these regions. Today, Buddhism is the main religion in Burma, Cambodia, and Thailand. Remains of famous Hindu temples in these countries show that Hinduism was once common there.

Chinese traders and settlers moved south along the coast of East Asia. They, too, spread their language and culture. The Vietnamese adopted Chinese characters to write their language. When Marco Polo visited Vietnam, he reported that although the country had its own king, it paid tribute every year to the Great Khan.

Arab leaders from the Middle East also journeyed to Southeast Asia. They introduced the Muslim religion, which largely replaced Hinduism and Buddhism on the Malay Peninsula, the Indonesian archipelago and in the Philippines.

Angkor Wat, a Hindu temple, was built in Cambodia in the 1100s.
▶ What does this ruin tell about the history of Cambodia?

To review the information on the influences of European companies and different Asian peoples on South Asia, ask the following questions:

1. **Which European countries followed the Portuguese to the subcontinent and what goods were they seeking?**
(Dutch, English, and French trading companies sought sugar, spices, cotton yarn, and cloth. *p. 534*)

2. **What religions were introduced to Indochina and the Malay Peninsula by outsiders?**
(Buddhism, Hinduism, and the Muslim religion *p. 535*)

Thinking Critically How do you think South Asian history might have changed if the French had defeated the English on the subcontinent? (Hypothesize)
(Answers may include that it might have changed greatly, because the French would have ruled differently, or that it might not have changed much, because France was also a colonial power. *p. 535*)

Answers to Caption Questions
p. 534 ▶ As a mausoleum
p. 535 ▶ That Hinduism was once common in Cambodia

For Your Information

The Seven Years' War During the years 1756–1763, a worldwide conflict pitted France, Austria, Russia, Saxony, Sweden, and Spain against Great Britain, Prussia, and Hannover. The French and British fought for supremacy in North America and India; in Europe, Austria and Prussia battled for power. Major battles were fought at Louisbourg and Quebec in Canada, and at Plassey and Pondichéry in India. By the end of the war, France had lost nearly all of its overseas possessions, England had become the world's chief colonial power, and Prussia had emerged as a major European power.

Optional Activities

Read and Think
Section F

Europeans first visited Southeast Asia in the sixteenth century, and later, established many colonies there. Discuss European activity in Southeast Asia with the following questions:

1. **Why was Singapore an important center of trade?**
   (It was a free port that did not collect taxes on goods that were shipped there. *p. 537*)

   Thinking Critically **What types of conflicts, do you think, might be likely to occur in Southeast Asia?** (Evaluate)
   (Answers may include conflicts between followers of different religions or of different nationalities, between European colonizers and Asian peoples, or between separate European colonizers. *p. 537*)

GEOGRAPHY THEMES

Location

■ Have students refer to the map on this page in order to answer the following question: **What is the latitude and longitude of Bangkok?**
(13° N/100° E)

F. Europeans in Southeast Asia

Portugal Europeans first went to Southeast Asia seeking pepper, ginger, nutmeg, and other spices. Spices were popular in Europe because they made food tastier and helped to preserve it.

The Portuguese were the first to arrive in Indonesia, where many of the spices grew. The Dutch later drove the Portuguese out. By 1750 the Dutch controlled the more important islands of Indonesia, which they called the Dutch East Indies. They were part of the Dutch Empire until after World War II. Locate the islands in the Dutch East Indies on the map.

Spain A Spanish fleet commanded by Ferdinand Magellan reached the Philippines in 1521. Magellan was attempting to sail around the world. He had sailed west from Europe, across the Atlantic, and around the tip of South America into the Pacific. Magellan did not complete his voyage though. He was killed in the Philippines. But one of his ships did make it back to Spain. It was the first ship to sail around the world.

The Spanish conquered the Philippines, which they named after their king, Philip II. The islands were under Spanish rule until after the Spanish-American

SOUTHEAST ASIA PRIOR TO WORLD WAR II

Legend:
- Independent
- British
- French
- Dutch
- American
- Portuguese
- • Cities

0 200 400 miles
0 200 400 kilometers

The United States and some European countries controlled parts of Southeast Asia prior to World War II.
▶ What country in the area was independent?

536

SKILLBUILDER REVIEW

Comparing Political Maps On pp. 498–499, students learned about political maps. To help students practice this skill in a different context, ask them to look at the political map of Southeast Asia prior to World War II, on p. 536, and the political map of Eurasia found in their Atlas.

● Have each student list five countries found on the map on p. 536.

● Then have students list the status of each country prior to World War II (whether it was independent, or controlled by another country).

● Finally, have students name the present-day country that corresponds to each of the five countries on their list.

536

Reteaching Main Objective

★ ***Discuss the ways that outsiders influenced the history and culture of South Asia.***

● Divide the class into groups of two or three. Have each group review the lesson and list how each group of outsiders influenced the areas of South Asia that they settled.

● Have each group choose a group of outsiders and create a poster showing the influences of its chosen group.

● Ask each group to accompany its poster with a brief oral presentation explaining what the students have learned about the subject of each picture.

War, in 1898. At that time, Spain had to turn the islands over to the United States. The Philippines became independent in 1946, shortly after World War II.

Britain The British conquered Burma and ruled it as part of their empire in India. The British Empire also included Singapore, an island at the tip of the Malay Peninsula. At first, Singapore was the location of a British naval base. The naval base grew into a busy trading city, partly because it was a **free port**. A free port is one that does not collect taxes on goods landed there. Singapore became a profitable place to do business. The British also made the entire Malay Peninsula part of their empire. British rule of Singapore and the Malay Peninsula lasted until the late 1950s.

France French priests as well as traders went to Indochina more than 300 years ago. The priests went to teach people about the Christian religion. One priest also invented an alphabet that is still used today for the Vietnamese language. Between 1862 and 1893 the French conquered Vietnam, Laos, and Cambodia. These lands remained part of the French empire until after World War II.

British troops are shown here entering Singapore in 1824, making it part of their empire.
▶ By what means did they enter?

LESSON *3* REVIEW

THINK AND WRITE

A. How did the Portuguese and the Moguls establish their holds on the subcontinent? **(Recall)**

B. How did Akbar attempt to unite the peoples of his empire? **(Recall)**

C. Explain how the Moguls encouraged the arts. **(Recall)**

D. Why did Europeans go to the subcontinent? **(Recall)**

E. Why does Southeast Asia have so many different cultures? **(Recall)**

F. What European countries had empires in Southeast Asia before World War II? **(Recall)**

SKILLS CHECK

MAP SKILL

Singapore was a key port on a vital sea route. Use the map on page 536 to answer the following questions: What is the shortest sea route from the subcontinent to East Asia? Where is Singapore located in relation to this route?

537

◀ **Review Master Booklet, p. 136**

Optional Activities

Lesson *3* Review

Answers to Think and Write

A. The Portuguese and the Moguls established their holds on the subcontinent through military force.

B. Akbar attempted to unite the peoples of his empire by placing Hindus in high positions and by arranging his son's marriage to a Hindu noblewoman. He also did away with a special tax paid by non-Muslims and tried to create a new religion that everyone could accept.

C. The Moguls encouraged the arts by setting up studios, giving prizes for the best works, and inviting Persian artists to the subcontinent to share their ideas.

D. Europeans went to trade for sugar, spices, cotton yarn, and cloth.

E. Southeast Asia has many different cultures because peoples from Asia and Europe went there to trade and to settle.

F. Portugal, the Netherlands, Spain, the United States, Britain, and France had empires in Southeast Asia before World War II.

Answer to Skills Check

The shortest route is through the Strait of Malacca, and Singapore is at the mouth of the strait.

Focus Your Reading

Ask the lesson focus question found at the beginning of the lesson: **How did people from outside the South Asian subcontinent and Southeast Asia affect these regions?** (Outsiders colonized South Asia, and brought different religions, languages, and artistic styles to the area.)

Additional Practice

You may wish to assign the ancillary materials listed below.

Understanding the Lesson p. 136
Workbook p. 114

┌ Answers to Caption Questions ┐

p. 536 ▶ Thailand
p. 537 ▶ By elephant and by horse

Using the Vocabulary

1. a
2. e
3. c
4. b
5. d

Remembering What You Read

1. His travels and his 17 years spent in the service of Kublai Khan

2. Silk

3. China's refusal to open its ports to trade and its refusal to allow the British to open an embassy in Peking

4. The Korean king, Sejong

5. For nearly seven centuries

6. Because he was worried about the growing interest in European ways and ideas, and he feared that Europeans who came to trade would later try to rule

7. Commodore Matthew Perry

8. Emperor Meiji

9. Portugal

10. The Moguls

11. Babur's soldiers were better fighters, better armed, and they had cannons.

12. Akbar

13. It was built by Shah Jahan as a mausoleum for his wife.

14. From Spain

15. Vietnam, Laos, and Cambodia

USING THE VOCABULARY

On a separate sheet of paper, write the letter of the term that best matches each numbered statement.

a. cocoon
b. samurai
c. shogun
d. typhoon
e. mausoleum

1. The strong, light covering that protects the silkworm while it changes into a moth
2. A large tomb
3. A military leader who was the most powerful noble in Japan
4. Bands of Japanese fighting men
5. A severe hurricane

REMEMBERING WHAT YOU READ

1. What did Marco Polo write about in his book?
2. What valuable cloth did the Chinese make?
3. What quarrels or conflicts led to a war between the Chinese and the British in 1839?
4. Who invented the alphabet that Korean students use today?
5. How long did the shoguns rule Japan?
6. Why did the shogun decide to close Japan's door to foreigners?
7. Who was the leader of the American fleet that visited Japan in 1853?
8. What was the name of the emperor who believed that Japan should be modernized?
9. What country established the first European colony on the subcontinent?
10. What group of raiders led by Babur invaded the subcontinent?
11. Why was Babur able to defeat his opponents, even though he faced armies far larger than his own?
12. Who was the greatest of the Mogul rulers?
13. Why was the Taj Mahal built?
14. From what country was the first ship to sail around the world?
15. What lands in Southeast Asia were part of the French empire until after World War II?

TYING SCIENCE TO SOCIAL STUDIES

What spice is used in your favorite food? Prepare an oral report to share with your classmates, telling about the spice in your favorite food. Use a reference book to find out what part of the plant the spice comes from, the country and climate in which the spice grows, and what other foods it is used to flavor. You could also show on a map where the spice is grown.

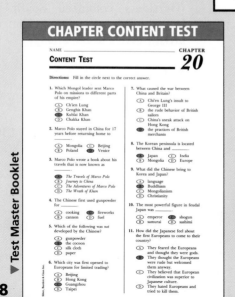

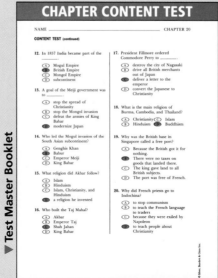

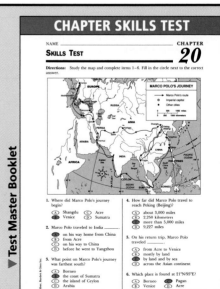

THINKING CRITICALLY

1. How do we know that Marco Polo was very impressed with Kublai Khan?
2. Do you think China was right to be fearful of visitors from Europe?

3. Why did Christian priests visit Japan?
4. Why have spices played an important role in history?
5. Do you think that countries have a right to claim other lands?

SUMMARIZING THE CHAPTER

On a separate sheet of paper, copy the graphic organizer shown below. Beside the main idea for each lesson, write four statements that support the main idea.

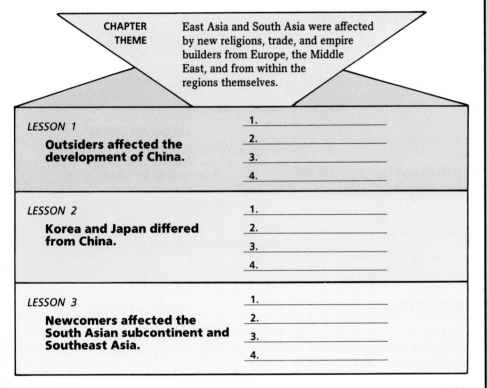

CHAPTER THEME — East Asia and South Asia were affected by new religions, trade, and empire builders from Europe, the Middle East, and from within the regions themselves.

LESSON 1
Outsiders affected the development of China.
1. _____
2. _____
3. _____
4. _____

LESSON 2
Korea and Japan differed from China.
1. _____
2. _____
3. _____
4. _____

LESSON 3
Newcomers affected the South Asian subcontinent and Southeast Asia.
1. _____
2. _____
3. _____
4. _____

539

South and East Asia Today

(pp. 540-564)

Chapter Theme: The governments and economies of countries in South Asia and East Asia are varied.

LESSON *1* China and Taiwan

(pp. 540-547)

Theme: The Communists have tried to revolutionize the Chinese way of life so that loyalty to the state would replace loyalty to the family.

 SILVER WINGS WORKSHOP: The Courage of Your Convictions

SOCIAL STUDIES LIBRARY: *Young Fu of the Upper Yangtze*

LESSON *2* Japan and Korea

(pp. 550-553)

Theme: After World War II, Japan was rebuilt and became one the world's richest countries; Korea became two separate states.

SOCIAL STUDIES LIBRARY: *Money*

LESSON *3* The South Asian Subcontinent

(pp. 554-557)

Theme: The independent countries of India, Sri Lanka, Pakistan, and Bangladesh were created after World War II.

SILVER WINGS WORKSHOP: The Courage of Your Convictions

SOCIAL STUDIES LIBRARY: *The Cat Who Went to Heaven*

LESSON *4* Southeast Asia

(pp. 558-562)

Theme: Southeast Asia has undergone many governmental and political changes in the last half of the twentieth century.

 SOCIAL STUDIES LIBRARY: *A Boat to Nowhere*
Ferdinand Magellan
Money

Review Masters

REVIEWING CHAPTER VOCABULARY

Review   Study the terms in the box. Use your Glossary to find definitions of those you do not remember.

civil disobedience	Diet	incentive	pagoda
commune	finance	jute	partition
copra	gross national product	literacy rate	warlord

Practice   Complete the paragraphs using terms from the box above. You may change the forms of the terms to fit the meaning.

    Many Asian countries have experienced changes in their governments and economic systems during this century. In China, for example, the power once held by local (1) ___warlords___ and enforced by their armies is now held by a Communist government. Under this government, Chinese life has changed. Families were forced to give up ownership of their lands, and farmers had to join (2) ___communes___.

    Although some recent changes have occurred, such as the use of (3) ___incentives___ to increase production, China is still tightly controlled by its Communist government.

    Japan and South Korea have both emerged from times of conflict with strong economies. Japan has developed many modern industries, and it now has the second highest (4) ___gross national product___ in the world. More recently, South Korea has developed rapidly from being an agricultural country to a modern industrial nation. Good education, which led to a high (5) ___literacy rate___, and a hard-working labor force have helped South Korea's progress.

    Pakistan and Bangladesh are countries that still struggle with poverty. Both countries were part of India before India was (6) ___partitioned___ in 1947. Today, these countries remain among the poorest in the world.

Write   Write a sentence of your own for each term in the box above. You may use the back of the sheet.

Sentences should show that students understand the meanings of the terms.

_____
_____
_____
_____
_____

 Use with Chapter 21, pages 541–562.

LOCATING PLACES

✴   Pakistan and India became independent from Great Britain in 1947. In 1971, East Pakistan won its independence from Pakistan and became the country of Bangladesh. Listed below are places on the South Asian subcontinent. Use the Gazetteer in your textbook to find the latitude and longitude of each place. Then locate and label each on the map.

	LAT. ⊖	LONG. ◐			LAT. ⊖	LONG. ◐
1. Calcutta, India	22°N	88°E	6. Karachi, Pakistan		25°N	66°E
2. Bombay, India	19°N	73°E	7. Goa (Panaji), India		15°N	74°E
3. Delhi, India	29°N	77°E	8. Katmandu, Nepal		28°N	85°E
4. Islamabad, Pakistan	33°N	73°E	9. Mount Everest, Nepal		28°N	87°E
5. Dacca, Bangladesh	24°N	90°E	10. Mohenjo-Daro, Pakistan		28°N	69°E

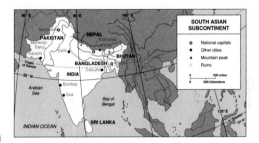

SOUTH ASIAN SUBCONTINENT

- ◎ National capitals
- ● Other cities
- ▲ Mountain peak
- ◌ Ruins

M6-EH-PM-21

Use with Chapter 21, pages 541–562.

SUMMARIZING THE CHAPTER

✴   Complete this graphic organizer. Under the main idea for each lesson, write three statements that support the main idea.

CHAPTER THEME

The governments and economies of countries in South Asia and East Asia are varied.

LESSON 1

Revolutions and civil wars have affected China.

1. Revolution forced the last emperor from the throne in 1912.
2. The Communist takeover in 1949 made all industry and land property of the state.
3. After 1976, reforms included incentives to increase production.

LESSON 3

Independent countries were created on or near the South Asian subcontinent after World War II.

1. Gandhi led India to independence in 1947.
2. Pakistan became independent in 1947; East Pakistan became Bangladesh in 1971.
3. Ceylon won independence in 1948 and later changed its name to Sri Lanka.

LESSON 2

Many changes took place in Japan and Korea after World War II.

1. Japan adopted a new constitution after World War II.
2. Korea was divided in 1950.
3. South Korea had free elections in 1987.

LESSON 4

Southeast Asia has undergone changes in the last half of this century.

1. Malaysia and Singapore won independence.
2. North Vietnam conquered South Vietnam.
3. The Philippines elected their first woman president.

Use with Chapter 21, pages 541–562.

C21-B

Workbook Pages

A Changing China

Understanding Time Lines, Analyzing Information

✻ The People's Republic of China was formed in 1949. In the years since then, some of China's Communist leaders have tried to follow socialism strictly, while others have worked to modernize China by allowing more individual freedom and trade with other nations. Ten important events in Communist China's history are listed below. Place the letter of each event in the correct box on the time line. Then answer the questions that follow.

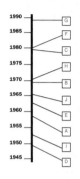

1990	G
1985	F
1980	C
1975	H
1970	B
1965	J
1960	E
1955	A
1950	I
1945	D

A. Communists launch the Great Leap Forward, a plan to make China a developed nation quickly—1958

B. Premier Zhou Enlai begins to expand China's diplomatic and trade contacts with other nations—1969

C. The United States and China establish normal diplomatic relations—1979

D. Mao Zedong proclaims establishment of the People's Republic of China—1949

E. Friendly relations between the Soviet Union and China end—1963

F. Deng Xiaoping becomes China's most powerful leader and begins program of modernization—1980

G. Student demonstration in Tiananmen Square crushed—1989

H. People's Republic of China admitted to the United Nations in place of Taiwan—1971

I. Under Communist rule, China begins its first Five-Year Plan for industrial development—1953

J. Cultural Revolution brings a return to strict socialism—1966

1. Which two events brought less freedom to the Chinese people? the Cultural Revolution and the crushing of the demonstration in Tiananmen Square

2. How long did it take for the United States to establish diplomatic relations with the People's Republic of China? 30 years

3. Which economic program was designed to get immediate results? the Great Leap Forward

Thinking Further: Why could it be difficult to lead a nation like China?
Answers may mention the vast size of the country, the many different peoples who live there, or the underdeveloped areas.

© Silver, Burdett & Ginn Inc.

Chapter 21, pages 541–547   115

Understanding Japan's Trade Success

Understanding Bar Graphs, Hypothesizing Based on Information

✻ Since World War II, Japan has become a world economic leader. One of the reasons for its success has been the strength of its foreign trade. The graphs below show Japan's main trading partners. Study the graphs and underline the correct answer to each question.

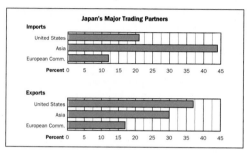

Japan's Major Trading Partners

Imports — United States, Asia, European Comm. — Percent 0 5 10 15 20 25 30 35 40 45

Exports — United States, Asia, European Comm. — Percent 0 5 10 15 20 25 30 35 40 45

1. From where does the largest percentage of Japan's imports come?
United States   <u>Asia</u>   European Community

2. What percent of Japan's exports go to the United States and the European Community?
12%   37%   <u>54%</u>   72%

3. What percent of Japan's imports come from Asia?
12%   30%   37%   <u>44%</u>

4. With which partner does Japan have the most even balance of imports and exports?
United States   Asia   <u>European Community</u>

5. Which partner has the greatest total trade with Japan?
United States   <u>Asia</u>   European Community

Thinking Further: Japan exports many more goods than it imports. Is this good or bad for Japan? Explain your reasons.
Answers should suggest that it is good, since Japan receives more money for its exports than it has to pay for its imports.

© Silver, Burdett & Ginn Inc.

116   Chapter 21, pages 550–553

We, the People

Recognizing and Understanding Constitutional Texts, Inferring Unstated Ideas

✻ The constitution of a country is a written plan for the country's government. It describes how leaders will be chosen, how laws will be made, and who will make sure the laws are obeyed. Most constitutions also have a preamble, or opening statement that explains the purpose of the government. Read the preamble to India's constitution. Then answer the questions.

Preamble to the Constitution of the Republic of India

We, the people of India, have solemnly resolved to constitute [form] India into a sovereign [free] democratic republic and to secure to all its citizens: JUSTICE, social, economic and political; LIBERTY of thought, expression, belief, faith and worship; EQUALITY of status and of opportunity; and to promote among them all FRATERNITY assuring the dignity of the individual and the unity of the Nation; in our Constituent [authorized to make a constitution] Assembly this 26th day of November 1949 do hereby adopt, enact and give to ourselves this Constitution.

1. Who made the decision to set up a new government for India? The people of India made this decision.

2. When did India adopt its constitution? November 26, 1949

3. What four main things do the people of India want for all India's citizens? justice, liberty, equality, and fraternity

4. What type of government does the constitution of India set up? It establishes a sovereign democratic republic.

5. What do you think equality of opportunity means? It means having the same chance as everyone else to get an education, find a good job, or have a decent place to live.

6. What will happen if the people of India have fraternity, or common interests and goals? Individuals will have dignity and the nation will be unified.

7. Who adopted this constitution for the people of India? The Constitution was adopted by a Constituent Assembly.

Thinking Further: Why is it important to know the purposes of an organization?
Possible answer: You can tell whether or not the organization is working in the way it should if you know what its purposes are.

© Silver, Burdett & Ginn Inc.

Chapter 21, pages 554–557   117

Communicating in Asia

Categorizing, Interpreting Information

✻ In some countries people have ready access to telephones, radios, televisions, and other means of communication, while in other countries these items are not widely available. The chart below shows how many people there are for each radio, television, and telephone in six Asian countries. Study the chart and answer the questions.

| Country | Number of people for each . . . | | |
	Radio	Television	Telephone
China	4.2	12.0	149.0
South Korea	1.1	4.9	4.5
Japan	1.3	3.9	1.8
Pakistan	20.0	57.0	168.0
Taiwan	1.4	3.2	3.2
India	15.0	84.0	192.0

1. How many radios would an average group of 100 Pakistani people have? 5

2. About how many radios would an average group of 100 South Koreans have? 91

3. Which nation listed has the fewest televisions per person? India

4. Do people in Japan have more televisions or more telephones? telephones

5. The six countries listed can be divided easily into two groups. List the countries in each group and describe the difference between them. China, Pakistan, and India have many people for each radio, television, and telephone. South Korea, Japan, and Taiwan have few people for each radio, television, and telephone.

6. Why do you think there is such a difference between these two groups? China, Pakistan, and India are much larger and less developed than South Korea, Japan, and Taiwan.

Thinking Further: How do you think the United States compares to the nations above in the number of radios, televisions, and telephones?
Answers may note that the United States has more of each than any of the nations listed.

© Silver, Burdett & Ginn Inc.

118   Chapter 21, pages 541–557

Workbook Pages

POLITICAL CHANGES IN ASIA

Understanding a Historical Map, Sequencing

❋ After World War II, many nations in Asia gained their independence from Western nations. Using the map, draw a line from each Asian nation listed below to the nation from which it became independent.

WESTERN CONTROL IN ASIA

	Great Britain
	France
	Netherlands
	United States
	Independent
	Present-day boundaries

Date of Independence	Nation	Became Independent From
August 15, 1947	India	
August 14, 1947	Pakistan	Great Britain
March 1971	Bangladesh	
January 1948	Burma (Myanmar)	Netherlands
July 1954	Vietnam	
July 1949	Laos	France
November 1953	Cambodia	
July 1946	Philippines	United States
February 1948	Sri Lanka	
December 1949	Indonesia	

❋ List the nations above in the order they became independent.

Philippines, Pakistan, India, Burma (Myanmar), Sri Lanka, Laos, Indonesia, Cambodia, Vietnam, Bangladesh

Thinking Further: Why did some areas controlled by Western nations divide into smaller countries after they became independent?

Answers may suggest differences in language, religion, and culture of the people in an area.

© Silver, Burdett & Ginn Inc.

Chapter 21, pages 550–562

119

THE RELIGIONS OF SOUTH ASIA

Understanding Special-Purpose Maps

❋ Religion has been a vital part of life in South Asia for centuries. In many countries, most people follow one religion. Study the chart and complete the map. (An asterisk [*] on the chart means that none or only a few people are of that religion.)
a. Color each box in the map key a different color.
b. Using the chart, put the correct color in each country on the map.

| Country | Number of people (in millions) who follow ... | | |
	Islam	Hinduism	Buddhism
India	88.4	643.4	5.5
Pakistan	105.9	*	*
Bangladesh	93.4	13.1	*
Nepal	0.5	16.1	1.0
Myanmar	1.5	*	35.7
Bhutan	*	0.3	1.0
Thailand	2.1	*	52.1
Sri Lanka	1.2	2.6	11.5

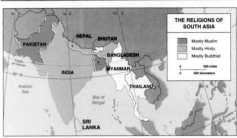

THE RELIGIONS OF SOUTH ASIA

	Mostly Muslim
	Mostly Hindu
	Mostly Buddhist

Thinking Further: How do you think religion has influenced political boundaries in South Asia?

Answers may suggest that religious differences have often led to political divisions in South Asia, since most people

in each country follow one religion.

© Silver, Burdett & Ginn Inc.

120

Chapter 21, pages 554–562

TEACHER NOTES

*A*sia has more of th[e] world's largest cities t[han] any other region. Som[e] cities, such as Tokyo, Japan, are very moder[n]

LESSON 1 PAGES 540–547

China and Taiwan

Objectives

★ **1. Compare** the economies of China and Taiwan.

2. Explain how the Communists came to power in China.

3. Describe how the Communists revolutionized the Chinese way of life.

4. Identify the following people and places: *Mao Zedong, Chiang Kai-shek, Deng Xiaoping, Dalai Lama, Beijing, Hong Kong, Macao,* and *Tibet.*

1 STARTING THE LESSON

Motivation Activity

- Ask students to bring to class one article of clothing that contains a label indicating where it was made.

- Make a list on the chalkboard of the countries where the clothing was manufactured.

- Ask students to make some generalizations based on the list. Tell students that a great deal of our clothing and other goods come from China and Taiwan.

Think About What You Know

- Assign the THINK ABOUT WHAT YOU KNOW activity on p. 541.

- Student answers should reflect independent thinking but may include new forms of government and greater rights.

Study the Vocabulary

- Have students look up each of the new vocabulary words in the Glossary.

- Then have them use the vocabulary words to write headlines for news articles about China.

Optional Activities

Curriculum Connection

Math   Tell students that in 1989, China's population was estimated at 1,103,900,000, and that population forecasters predict that China's population will rise to 1,631,800,000 by the year 2100.

- Have students figure out the percentage of growth that this represents. If students need help, tell them to:
  1. Subtract to find the difference between the two population figures.
     $(1,631,800,000 - 1,103,900,000 = 527,900,000)$
  2. Divide that number by the 1989 figure.
     $(527,900,000 \div 1,103,900,000 = .478)$
  3. Multiply this answer by 100 for the correct percentage. $(.478 \times 100 = 47.8 \text{ or } 48\%)$

China and Taiwan

THINK ABOUT WHAT YOU KNOW
In previous chapters you have read about revolutions in such places as England, France, and Russia. What are some changes that revolutions can bring?

STUDY THE VOCABULARY
warlord   incentive
commune

FOCUS YOUR READING
How have revolutions and civil wars affected China?

A. Revolutions and Civil Wars

China is about the same size as the United States, but it has four times as many people. About a billion people live in China. No other country in the world has such a large population.

The people of China have experienced many changes during the last century. A revolution forced the last of China's emperors, a 6-year-old boy, from the throne in 1912. A republic was established, but the new government was not able to control the land. Local rulers known as **warlords** held most of the country. The warlords had their own small armies, much like the feudal lords in Europe during the Middle Ages. Wars between the government and the warlords weakened China.

Japan took advantage of this weakness and invaded China in the 1930s. In 1941, Japan's war in East Asia became part of World War II. Peace did not come to China with the defeat of Japan in 1945, however. A civil war broke out between the Nationalists, who controlled the Chinese government, and the Communists.

By 1949 the Communists, who were led by Mao Ze-dong (mou DZU-doong), had control of the Chinese mainland. The Nationalists and their leader, Chiang Kai-shek (chang kye SHEK), fled to Taiwan.

B. The People's Republic of China

The Nationalists called their government, on Taiwan, the Republic of China. The Communists named their government, on the mainland, the People's Republic of China. Both the Nationalists and the Communists claimed that theirs was the lawful government of all China.

The Communists wanted to revolutionize the Chinese way of life. Loyalty to the state was to take the place of loyalty to family or friends. Neither families nor individuals could own land. Farmers had to join **communes**, farms on which people

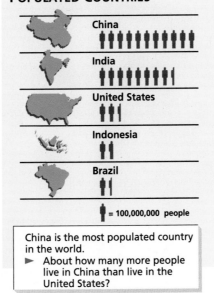

THE WORLD'S FIVE MOST POPULATED COUNTRIES

China
India
United States
Indonesia
Brazil

 = 100,000,000 people

China is the most populated country in the world.
► About how many more people live in China than live in the United States?

Read and Think
Sections A and B

The Chinese government has undergone many changes in this century. Discuss these with students by asking the following questions:

1. **Why did the republican government fail?**
   (Warlords waged war against the government. *p. 541*)

2. **How did the Communists revolutionize the Chinese way of life?**
   (Loyalty to the state was required, all people were equal, and all industries and land became property of the state. *pp. 541-542*)

   Thinking Critically Why, do you think, did the Communists not allow individuals to own land? (Infer)
   (Answers should reflect independent thinking but may include that the Communists wanted complete loyalty to the state; if the state owned all the land, the people's allegiance would be to the state. *p. 541*)

Answers to Caption Questions
p. 541 ► About 750,000,000 people

For Your Information

The Pragmatists The leaders who took control of the Communist party after Mao Zedong's death were known as pragmatists. As people who believed in being practical, they were willing to implement any plan that would help China's economy. Their approach worked. Between 1978 and 1984, peasants raised a record amount of grain. The standard of living rose, too. Brick and tile houses replaced many mud huts. More people were able to buy such luxuries as television sets, cassette recorders, and refrigerators. To keep China's economic recovery going, many students were sent abroad to learn about Western technology and management techniques.

Optional Activities

Read and Think
Section C

After Mao Zedong's death, some Communist leaders decided that the revolution should be reformed. To discuss those reforms, ask the following questions:

1. **Why were reforms made after 1976?**
(Communes and state-owned factories were not producing enough. *p. 542*)

2. **How did some peasants become prosperous after 1976?**
(Farmers and factory workers were allowed to sell some of their goods for a profit, and could own small businesses. *p. 542*)

Thinking Critically **Why, do you think, was the Communist government unwilling to allow reform of the political system?** (Analyze)
(Answers should reflect independent thinking but may include that those in positions of authority feared that they would lose their power. *pp. 541-542*)

lived and worked together. All people were to be equal. So, an individual farmer was not allowed to make a profit by growing and selling extra vegetables.

All industries became property of the state. Factory workers who worked hard and produced more were not paid more money. Instead they were awarded red stars and banners as symbols of China.

The Communist government under Mao Ze-dong crushed all opposition to the revolutionary changes. Special courts were set up to rid anyone thought to be against the revolution. These courts condemned many people. Thousands were killed; no one knows exactly how many.

C. Reforming the Revolution

Increasing Production The communes and state-owned factories failed, however, to produce the food and goods so badly needed by the large population of China.

After Mao Ze-dong's death in 1976, some of the Communist leaders decided that the revolution should be reformed. Under the leadership of Deng Xiaoping (dung shou-pihng), the government made use of **incentives** to increase production. Incentives are rewards for people who work harder or do more. For example, a farmer who grew extra food could sell it for a profit. Factory workers who produced more would be paid more. People could again own small businesses.

The offering of incentives did increase production. Both agricultural and industrial production rose. Farmers grew more when they could sell for a profit. Workers produced more when they could earn more. In some areas of China the peasants grew prosperous. Fortunately, China has an abundance of coal, which is used to fuel its industries. China is one of the world's leading producers of coal.

In December 1989, Brent Scowcroft, the United States National Security Adviser, met with Deng Xiaoping.
▶ Who is Deng Xiaoping?

542

Optional Activities

Making a Time Line

- Have students make a time line of important events that have happened in China in the twentieth century.

- Tell students to skim the first three sections of this lesson to locate important events in China's history since 1912. Ask them to write these dates and events on a sheet of paper.

- Then have students organize this information in chronological order and transfer it to a time line.

- Conclude this activity by having students decide on a good title for this time line.

SOUTH AND EAST ASIA: COAL PRODUCTION

Production per year
(in thousands of tons)

- 0-6,100
- 6,101-51,700
- 51,701-154,600
- 154,601 or more

- Figures not available

0   250   500 miles

0   250   500 kilometers

RUSSIA

KAZAKHSTAN

MONGOLIA

NORTH KOREA

JAPAN

Sea of Japan

SOUTH KOREA

Yellow Sea

CHINA

East China Sea

TAIWAN

PACIFIC OCEAN

Tropic of Cancer

NEPAL   BHUTAN

INDIA   BANGLADESH

MYANMAR   LAOS

THAILAND   VIETNAM

CAMBODIA

HONG KONG (U.K.)

South China Sea

PHILIPPINES

Equator

PAPUA NEW GUINEA

Bay of Bengal

ANDAMAN ISLANDS

Gulf of Siam

BRUNEI

Celebes Sea

ACCADIVE ISLANDS

SRI LANKA   NICOBAR ISLANDS

MALAYSIA

Arafura Sea

MALDIVES   INDIAN OCEAN

SINGAPORE

INDONESIA

AUSTRALIA

70° E   80° E   90° E   100° E   110° E   120° E

160° E   150° E   140° E   130° E

40° N   30° N   20° N   10° N   10°

y countries in South and East Asia
uce coal.
Which country has the most coal in
outh and East Asia?

South and East Asia: Leading Producers of Coal

China	India	North Korea	South Korea	Japan

700
600
500
400
300
200
100
0

543

GEOGRAPHY THEMES

Human-Environment Interactions

■ Have students look at the map and graph on this page to answer the following questions:

1. **How much coal does China produce per year?**
   (About 550,000,000 tons or more)

2. **Which country produces more coal per year, Japan or Thailand?**
   (Japan)

3. **List the countries that produce between 6,101,000 tons and 51,700,000 tons per year.**
   (Japan, South Korea, North Korea)

Role-Playing

- Divide the class into groups of five or six students.

- Ask each group to prepare a short skit in which some farmers discuss the effects that the new incentives have made on their lives.

- Remind students to include mention of the old ways as well as the new ways.

- Allow one class period for the groups to prepare scripts, props, and, if possible, costumes for their skits.

- Conclude this activity by asking each group to present its skit to the class.

Optional Activities

Answers to Caption Questions
p. 542 ▶ The Communist leader of China
p. 543 ▶ China

To summarize the information about Taiwan, ask the following questions:

1. Why do the Chinese on Taiwan have a higher standard of living?
(Because they export more and earn more than those on the mainland *pp. 544-546*)

Thinking Critically Why, do you think, are the people of Taiwan able to export more goods? (Analyze)
(Answers should reflect independent thinking but may include that the businesses are privately owned, so the people have incentives to keep increasing their profits. *p. 544*)

Meeting Individual Needs
Concept:
Understanding Chronology

To better understand the history of the Chinese territories, it is important to understand chronology. Below are three activities that will help students understand the concept of chronology.

◆ **EASY** Ask students to put the events in Sections D and E in chronological order.

◀▶ **AVERAGE** Ask students to make a time line of the events in Sections D and E.

◀▮▶ **CHALLENGING** Ask students to make a bulletin-board display that illustrates the sequence of events described in Sections D and E.

VISUAL THINKING SKILL

Interpeting a Photograph

■ Ask students to study the photograph on this page and describe in their own words the work that these people are doing in the Taiwanese factory.

More Reforms Reforms on the farms and in factories led to demands for other kinds of reforms. People not only wanted freedom to sell their goods, they also wanted freedom to speak out about what was on their minds. University students spoke of the need for democracy, the freedom of people to choose their government. In 1989 a large number of students in Beijing, the capital of China, demonstrated peacefully for more freedom. Other groups joined the student demonstrations.

The Communist government was by no means willing to allow this type of freedom and demonstration. The government used the army to clear the city's squares and streets of demonstrators. A number of people were killed, and the leaders of the demonstration were hunted down and arrested.

D. The Republic of China on Taiwan

The Nationalist Republic of China has continued to hold Taiwan since 1949. Taiwan appears small when compared with mainland China, but it has a larger population than many Western European countries. Both the Nationalists and the Communists consider the island to be part of China. As explained earlier, each group considers its government the lawful government of all China, both the mainland and Taiwan.

On Taiwan, businesses are privately owned. They produce a variety of goods. The United States is a major trading partner of the Republic of China. The Chinese on Taiwan export more and earn more than those on the mainland. Because of this, they also enjoy a higher standard of living than the people on the mainland.

These people are working in a factory in Taiwan.
▶ What product are the workers assembling?

Curriculum Connection

Language Arts Ask students to imagine that they are on a visit to China.

● Have them write a letter home describing the visit, including such information as how people live, what they do, what they eat, and how they spend their leisure time.

● To conclude this activity, ask students to read their letters to the class.

● You may also wish to display the letters on a bulletin board.

Optional Activities

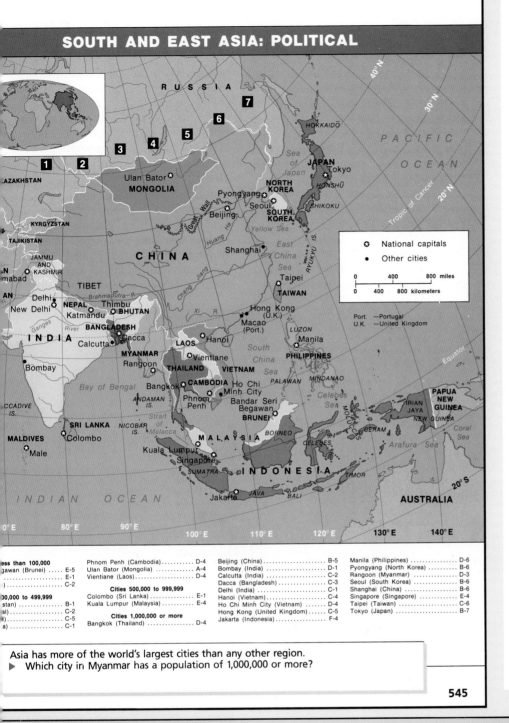

SOUTH AND EAST ASIA: POLITICAL

National capitals ⊕
Other cities •

| 0 | 400 | 800 miles |
| 0 | 400 | 800 kilometers |

Port. —Portugal
U.K. —United Kingdom

Cities less than 100,000

Bandar Seri Begawan (Brunei) E-5
Thimbu (Bhutan) E-1
Male (Maldives) C-2

Cities 100,000 to 499,999

Islamabad (Pakistan) B-1
Katmandu (Nepal) C-2
Macao (Portugal) C-5
Vientiane (Laos) C-1

Phnom Penh (Cambodia).......... D-4
Ulan Bator (Mongolia) A-4
Vientiane (Laos) D-4

Cities 500,000 to 999,999

Colombo (Sri Lanka) E-1
Kuala Lumpur (Malaysia) E-4

Cities 1,000,000 or more

Bangkok (Thailand) D-4

| Beijing (China) .... B-5 |
| Bombay (India) .... D-1 |
| Calcutta (India) .... C-2 |
| Dacca (Bangladesh) .... C-3 |
| Delhi (India) .... C-1 |
| Hanoi (Vietnam) .... C-4 |
| Ho Chi Minh City (Vietnam) .... D-4 |
| Hong Kong (United Kingdom)...... C-5 |
| Jakarta (Indonesia)................ F-4 |

| Manila (Philippines) .... D-6 |
| Pyongyang (North Korea) .... B-6 |
| Rangoon (Myanmar) .... D-3 |
| Seoul (South Korea) .... B-6 |
| Shanghai (China) .... B-6 |
| Singapore (Singapore) .... E-4 |
| Taipei (Taiwan) .... C-6 |
| Tokyo (Japan) .... B-7 |

Asia has more of the world's largest cities than any other region.
▶ Which city in Myanmar has a population of 1,000,000 or more?

545

GEOGRAPHY THEMES

Location

■ Have students look at the map on this page to help them answer the following questions:

1. **What is the population of Hanoi?**
(1,000,000 or more)

2. **Does Male have a larger or smaller population than Colombo?**
(Smaller)

3. **Where is Sri Lanka located in relation to Thailand?**
(Sri Lanka is located southwest of Thailand.)

4. **What body of water would you have to cross if you were to travel in a straight line from Bombay to Bangkok?**
(The Bay of Bengal)

5. **Which country shown on this map has the greatest number of cities with populations of 1,000,000 or more?**
(India)

— **Answers to Caption Questions** —
p. 544 ▶ Bicycles
p. 545 ▶ Rangoon

Read and Think
Section E

To compare and contrast the territories of Hong Kong, Macao, and Tibet, ask the following questions:

1. **What countries govern Hong Kong, Macao, and Tibet?**
   (Britain governs Hong Kong, Portugal governs Macao, and China governs Tibet. *pp. 546-547*)

2. **Which of these territories was ruled by Buddhist Monks?**
   (Tibet *p. 546*)

3. **What do Hong Kong and Macao have in common?**
   (Both territories will be given back to China in this century. *p. 546*)

Thinking Critically Why, do you think, did the Communists try to destroy the Buddhist religion in Tibet, after they had taken over China? (Analyze)
(Answers should reflect independent thinking but may include that they wanted the people to be loyal to the state above all else. *pp. 546-547*)

E. Three Territories

Hong Kong Great Britain and Portugal both hold land in China. As you recall, the British took over the island of Hong Kong in the 1840s. They later leased territory on the nearby Chinese mainland. Under British rule, Hong Kong grew into one of the great business centers of East Asia and world's major ports. Many of its people work in factories that make textiles and clothing.

The British lease on the mainland runs out in 1997. The British government and the Chinese Communist government agreed that Hong Kong would become part of China again in 1997. However, private businesses will be allowed to continue to operate there for 50 additional years.

Macao Near Hong Kong is the Portuguese colony of Macao (muh KOU), located on the mainland of China covering 6 square miles (16 sq km). The Portuguese have also reached an agreement with China about Macao's future. The territory will be given back to China in 1999, but, as in Hong Kong, private businesses can continue for another 50 years.

Tibet Tibet, which is located on a high plateau northeast of the South Asian subcontinent, has long been cut off from the outside world. The Chinese emperors claimed that Tibet was part of China, but Buddhist monks actually ruled the land. The leader of the Buddhists was known as the Dalai Lama (dahl EYE LAH muh).

Hong Kong is a center of international trade and finance.
▶ How can you tell that Hong Kong is a modern territory?

546

Reteaching Main Objective
⭐ *Compare the economies of China and Taiwan.*

- Divide the class into two groups for a debate.
- Tell students that they will be debating the following statement: People's lives are better in China than in Taiwan.
- Have one group defend the statement and the other group refute it. Give students 20 minutes to prepare.
- Use the remainder of the class period for the debate.
- When the debate is finished, let the students know which group was more convincing.

The Dalai Lama, spiritual leader of Tibet's Buddhists, accepted the 1989 Nobel Peace Prize for his nonviolent acts to free Tibet from China.
▶ How did the Dalai Lama escape the Communists?

After the Communists took over China, they occupied Tibet. The Communists attempted to destroy the Buddhist religion in Tibet. They wrecked monasteries and imprisoned monks and nuns. To escape the Communists, the Dalai Lama fled the country.

When the Communist leaders decided to reform their revolution, they realized that the old policy in Tibet had failed. The Chinese government still insisted that Tibet was part of China, but it released the monks and nuns. It also allowed some monasteries to be rebuilt.

LESSON 1 REVIEW

THINK AND WRITE

A. What changes took place in the government of China after 1912? **(Recall)**

B. How did the Communists revolutionize China? **(Recall)**

C. Summarize the kinds of reforms of the revolution that the Chinese did and did not allow. **(Infer)**

D. How do businesses on Taiwan differ from most businesses on the Chinese mainland? **(Analyze)**

E. What is China's political position with regard to Tibet, to Hong Kong, and to Macao? **(Infer)**

SKILLS CHECK

MAP SKILL

Look at the political map on page 545. Find the territories of Hong Kong, Tibet, and Macao on the map to answer the following questions. Which is landlocked? Which is under British rule? Which is at the mouth of the Xi Jiang?

547

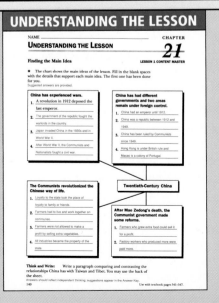

UNDERSTANDING THE LESSON

NAME _____ CHAPTER

UNDERSTANDING THE LESSON **21**

Finding the Main Idea LESSON 1 CONTENT MASTER

◀ **Review Master Booklet, p. 140**

Lesson 1 Review

Answers to Think and Write

A. A republic was established, but wars and Japanese occupation weakened the government. By 1949, the Communists had taken control.

B. The Communists required loyalty to the state above all else; they made farmers join communes; all people were made equal, and all industries became the property of the state.

C. The Chinese allowed the use of incentives to increase production, but would not permit greater political freedom.

D. Businesses on Taiwan are privately owned.

E. China regards Tibet, Hong Kong, and Macao as part of China.

Answer to Skills Check

Tibet is landlocked. Hong Kong is under British rule. Macao is at the mouth of the Xi Jiang.

Focus Your Reading

Ask the lesson focus question found at the beginning of the lesson: **How have revolutions and civil wars affected China?** (Revolutions have brought changes in the Chinese government and way of life. Civil war has divided the country into two groups, the Nationalists on Taiwan, and the Communists on mainland China. Both claim that theirs is the legitimate government of all of China.)

Additional Practice

You may wish to assign the ancillary materials listed below.

Understanding the Lesson p. 140
Workbook p. 115

┌─ **Answers to Caption Questions** ─┐
p. 546 ▶ The tall skyscrapers indicate that Hong Kong is modern.
p. 547 ▶ He fled the country.
└───────────────────────────────────┘

547

CITIZENSHIP AND AMERICAN VALUES

Objectives

1. **Participate** in the democratic process.

2. **Develop** patriotism and American values.

Guided Reading

1. **What was life like in China after Communist rule began in 1949?**
(China's people were not allowed to travel outside the country and few foreigners were allowed to visit China.)

2. **What changes did the Chinese people who were demonstrating at Tiananmen Square want?**
(The right to participate in their government and the right to openly express their desire for change)

3. **According to Machiavelli, what constituted a healthy, powerful nation?**
(One that was orderly and united under a strong government and ruler)

4. **What freedoms do we enjoy under the First Amendment of our Constitution?**
(Freedom of speech, freedom of the press, freedom to assemble, and freedom to petition)

You Decide: Should People Have the Right to Demonstrate Against Their Government?

When Communist rule began in the People's Republic of China in 1949, the country was closed to the outside world. Things began to change in the 1970s. Foreigners were encouraged to visit China, and the Chinese people were allowed to travel to other countries. Many came to study in the United States.

As time went by, many people in China were inspired by the democratic ideas of other countries. These people felt they, too, should be able to participate in their own country's government and to express openly their desire for change.

Finally, in May 1989, thousands of students, workers, and other supporters of democracy gathered in Tiananmen Square, in Beijing, to show the government that the people of China wanted a change. As you read on page 544, the Chinese government eventually sent in the army to break up the demonstration. Why did the Chinese government react so strongly to a peaceful demonstration?

On the next page are two different points of view about the relationship between a nation's government and its citizens. Read both and decide for yourself whether people should have the right to demonstrate against their government.

Optional Activities

For Your Information

Great Thinkers You may wish to share with the class a review of the great thinkers who began to question old ideas about systems of government.

● Voltaire fought against religious intolerance.

● John Locke believed that if a government did not protect the rights of its people, the people had the right to find other rulers. He wrote about educational reforms, freedom of the press, and religious intolerance.

● Thomas Jefferson believed in freedom of speech, freedom of the press, freedom of religion, and other civil liberties. He believed in "eternal hostility against every form of tyranny over the mind of man."

The Government Must Be in Control

During the Renaissance, which you read about in Chapter 6, an important political thinker, Niccolò Machiavelli, wrote a book describing how leaders could build and maintain powerful nations. He said a healthy, powerful nation is one that is orderly and that is united under a strong government and ruler. Machiavelli went on to say that when the people of a nation are divided and order is disrupted, the government should use any means necessary—including force—to control the nation.

In the twentieth century, Niccolò Machiavelli's influence could still be seen in countries where success would be measured by the strength of the central government and its leaders. During the demonstration in Tiananmen Square in May 1989, China's premier, Li Peng, made the following statement to the demonstrators.

In the last few days, Beijing has fallen into a kind of anarchy [lack of government]. I hope you will think it over. What will result from the situation? China's government is responsible to the people. We will not sit idly by, doing nothing. We have to safeguard people's property and our students' lives. We have to safeguard our factories. We have to defend our socialist system. . . .

Thinking for Yourself

1. Which is more important to the success of a nation—a strong government or personal freedom?
2. What examples of successful demonstrations against governments can you think of from history?

The People Have a Right to Speak

During the seventeenth and eighteenth centuries, great thinkers such as John Locke, Thomas Jefferson, and Voltaire began to question old ideas about systems of government. The result was new ideas about "government by the people" and basic natural rights. Among these rights were those of freedom of thought and the expression of thought. These were revolutionary ideas that had significant effects on political revolutions and new governments.

The idea of a right to freedom made its way into the First Amendment of the United States Constitution.

Congress shall make no law . . . abridging the freedom of speech, or of the press; or the right of the people peaceably to assemble, and to petition the government for a redress of grievances.

According to this amendment, the United States government cannot stop the American people from speaking or writing their thoughts. It also cannot stop people from demonstrating or sending petitions to let the government know what the people think.

Voltaire said, "Liberty of thought is the life of the soul." Today the right to free thought and expression is common to democratic societies and is a growing spirit in societies around the world.

549

Thinking for Yourself

1. Answers should reflect independent thinking but may include that personal freedom is more important because people are happier, which makes the nation, as a whole, prosper, or that a strong government is more important because it can protect the nation from outside threats.

2. Answers should reflect independent thinking but may include the solidarity demonstrations in Poland and the peaceful demonstrations led by Mohandas Gandhi in India.

Current Events

● Discuss with students the freedoms mentioned in the First Amendment of our Constitution.

● Give some examples of how we exercise these rights in the United States today.

● You may wish to bring a newspaper to class to find examples of how we exercise these freedoms. (Editorials against the government and articles about demonstrations are two examples.)

● Discuss recent examples of countries that are fighting for these rights that we enjoy.

Optional Activities

Japan and Korea

Objectives

★1. **Compare** economic growth in Japan and in South Korea after World War II.

2. **Describe** Japan's government.

3. **Explain** how Korea became a divided peninsula.

4. **Identify** the following people and places: *Emperor Hirohito, Emperor Meiji, Tokyo, Hiroshima, Nagasaki, North Korea, South Korea,* and *Seoul*.

1 STARTING THE LESSON

Motivation Activity

■ Ask students to name several automobile makers. Write student answers on the chalkboard.

■ Ask students to identify which automobile makers are Japanese or Korean.

■ Tell students that automobiles are just one industry in which the Japanese and Koreans have become major competitors of the United States.

Think About What You Know

■ Assign the THINK ABOUT WHAT YOU KNOW activity on p. 550.

■ Student answers should reflect independent thinking but may include automobiles and various kinds of electronic equipment such as televisions and stereos.

Study the Vocabulary

■ Have students look up the vocabulary terms for this lesson in the Glossary and list the definitions for the terms on a separate sheet of paper.

■ Then ask students to develop a word search puzzle using the vocabulary words for this lesson.

■ Have students exchange and solve each other's puzzles.

550

Japan and Korea

THINK ABOUT WHAT YOU KNOW
Name any products made in Japan or Korea that your family or friends use.

STUDY THE VOCABULARY

Diet	finance
gross national product	literacy rate

FOCUS YOUR READING
What changes took place in Japan and Korea after World War II?

A. Old and New in Government

Japan is by far the oldest monarchy in the world, with 125 emperors in the course of its long history. But the position of the emperor of Japan has changed greatly over the years. In the past it was said that the emperors were descendants of the Sun Goddess. In 1946, Emperor Hirohito informed his people that this was only a myth. "The emperor," he said, "is not a living god." Today the emperor of Japan is considered the symbol of the state. The emperor's position is similar to that of the British monarch.

After its defeat in World War II, Japan adopted a new constitution. The constitution was based on suggestions made by the Americans who occupied Japan for a time after the war. It provides for a prime minister as the head of the government. The prime minister is chosen by the **Diet**, a legislature made up of representatives elected by the people. The Diet is similar to Parliament in England.

Emperor Hirohito was the symbolic leader of Japan at the time of his death in 1989. His son, Akihito, followed him to the throne.
► Who actually heads the Japanese government?

550

Writing to Learn

Expressing a Point a View Ask students to think about their point of view regarding opening up baseball's World Series to teams from other countries.

● Have students make a list of reasons why they would be for or against such a proposal.

● Then ask them to organize their arguments into a persuasive paragraph.

● Conclude the activity by asking volunteers to read their paragraphs to the class.

B. Japan's Economic Growth

Rebuilding Japan During World War II the Japanese suffered heavy losses. Fire-bombs destroyed almost half of the buildings in Tokyo and killed nearly 100,000 people. The atomic bombs dropped on the cities of Hiroshima and Nagasaki took even more lives.

With the help of the United States, the Japanese rebuilt the war-damaged cities and industries in a remarkably short time. Only eight years after the war ended, Japan was producing more goods than it had been producing when the war began.

Japanese Business Today, Japan is one of the world's richest countries. It produces and exports many different goods. Japanese automobiles, cameras, and television sets, for instance, are used in many parts of the world.

In fact, Japan has the second highest **gross national product** (GNP) in the world. A nation's gross national product is the total value of all the goods and services it produces in a year. We can use this figure to show economic growth from one year to the next. Only the United States has a larger GNP than does Japan.

Japan has also become a world leader in **finance**, or the management of money. Japanese banks lend money to foreign businesses. Japanese-owned companies have bought land and built industrial plants in a number of other countries, including the United States.

C. Literature and Sports

Poetry Although the Japanese have borrowed from others, they also cling to parts of their own culture. For example, the Japanese have long written and read *haiku* (HYE koo). A haiku is a three-lined poem

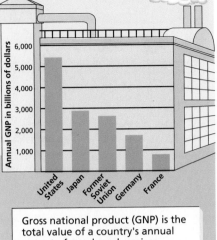

FIVE COUNTRIES WITH HIGHEST GROSS NATIONAL PRODUCT (GNP)

Annual GNP in billions of dollars
6,000
5,000
4,000
3,000
2,000
1,000

United States / Japan / Former Soviet Union / Germany / France

Gross national product (GNP) is the total value of a country's annual output of goods and services.

► Which country has about the same GNP as the former Soviet Union?

that draws attention to something that has moved the poet. Here are some samples of translated Japanese haiku.

How the mulberry leaves
shine, as I trudge along the way
toward my parents' home!

Even the rabbit
droops one of her ears—
midsummer heat!

After killing
a spider how lonely I feel
in the cold of the night!

Baseball The Japanese have wisely followed Emperor Meiji's advice "to seek knowledge from the whole world." They have studied the sciences, business methods, and ways of other countries, and they have adopted what they like or find

551

Concept:
Economic Success in Japan and South Korea

To better understand the extent of Japan's and South Korea's industrial and economic success, it is important to be able to make inferences and draw conclusions from economic data. Below are three activities that will help students understand this concept.

◆ **EASY** Tell students that of the world's 50 largest banks, 25 are Japanese.

Discuss with students why this data supports the statement in their text which says that Japan is a world leader in finance.

◀▶ **AVERAGE** Tell students that in 1975, no Japanese cars were made in the United States. By 1985, 695,020 Japanese autos were made in the United States.

Ask students what conclusions they can draw about the number of Japanese industrial plants in the United States. Then ask why the Japanese are manufacturing so many cars in the United States.

◀▮▶ **CHALLENGING** Tell students that South Korea's GNP rose from $90.6 billion in 1986 to $118 billion in 1987.

Discuss with students what effect this GNP growth probably had on the standard of living in South Korea.

Baseball is a favorite pastime in the United States and in Japan.
▶ How do Japanese fans differ from American fans?

useful. They have even made a foreign sport their own. That sport is baseball.

Japan now has both school and professional baseball teams. More than half of the Japanese are devoted baseball fans. Every year the winning teams in the two professional leagues play in the Japan Series. Some Japanese fans would like to see teams from around the world participate in the American World Series.

D. How One Korea Became Two

Japan ruled Korea as a colony from 1910 until the end of World War II. When Japan surrendered, the United States occupied the southern part of the Korean peninsula, and the Soviet Union took over the north. The 38th parallel (38°N) served as a boundary between the occupation zones. No agreement was ever reached concerning the future of Korea, so two separate states were created in 1948. A Communist country was established in North Korea. South Korea became a republic.

North Korea invaded South Korea in 1950. The United Nations sent troops, most of them Americans, to help South Korea defend itself. Communist China sent troops to help North Korea, and the Soviet Union also gave support to North Korea. After more than three years, the fighting ended. Korea was still divided, and no permanent peace treaty was signed.

North Korea is called the Democratic People's Republic of Korea, but it is actually a Communist dictatorship. South Korea is a republic, but for years military leaders ran the government. In 1987 a free election was held. In 1991 the two Koreas signed agreements that may lead to a permanent peace treaty and eventual reunification.

E. Modernization in South Korea

Education South Korea has twice as many people as North Korea. South Korea's skilled and educated population is its main resource. Large numbers of South Koreans attend the country's modern schools and colleges. South Korea has a high **literacy rate**, or percent of the population able to read and write.

Industry When South Korea became independent, it was a land of peasant

Comparing Literacy Rates

● Have students determine the number of people in South Korea who can read and write.

● Tell students that South Korea's literacy rate is 92 percent and its total population is 43,200,000. Ask students to figure out how many South Koreans can read and write (43,200,000 × .92 = 39,744,000).

● Have students compute the number of literate citizens in Japan by telling them that Japan's literacy rate is 99 percent and its total population is 123,300,000 (123,300,000 × .99 = 122,067,000).

Reteaching Main Objective

★ *Compare economic growth in Japan and in South Korea after World War II.*

● Divide the class into two groups.

● Have one group make a mobile showing how Japan's economy has changed since World War II. Have the other group make a mobile showing the changes in South Korea's economy.

● Mobiles of Japan should show the rebuilding after the war, the goods that Japan produces for export, and the role Japan plays in the world's economy. Mobiles of South Korea should show how the Korean work force has changed and the goods that South Korea produces.

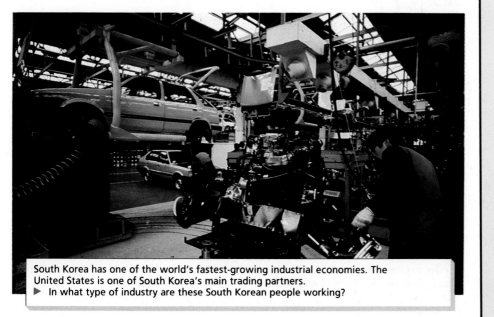

South Korea has one of the world's fastest-growing industrial economies. The United States is one of South Korea's main trading partners.
► In what type of industry are these South Korean people working?

farmers. Today it still grows much of its own food, but it also has modern industries that turn out automobiles, television sets, videocassette recorders, microwave ovens, and a host of other products.

South Korea's industrial success is due only in part to the education of its labor force. South Koreans also work longer hours than workers in most other industrial countries. For example, the average workweek in the United States is 40 hours, whereas, the average workweek in Korea is 54 hours. Yet, although incomes have risen rapidly in South Korea, wages are still lower than in Japan or the Western countries. By the late 1980s, Korean workers were demanding a larger share of the wealth they helped to create.

As a result of South Korea's shift from agriculture to industry, more Koreans live in cities today. Seoul, the capital, is one of the world's largest cities.

LESSON 2 REVIEW

THINK AND WRITE

A. How did the government of Japan change after World War II? (Recall)

B. Summarize Japan's economic growth after World War II. (Infer)

C. What does the popularity of baseball and haiku say about the Japanese? (Evaluate)

D. Why is the Korean peninsula divided into two states? (Recall)

E. Briefly explain the causes of South Korea's industrial success. (Infer)

SKILLS CHECK

WRITING SKILL

Write a haiku that has three unrhymed lines. The first line should have five syllables, the second line seven syllables, and the third line five syllables.

553

◄ **Review Master Booklet, p. 141**

Optional Activities

---

3 CLOSING THE LESSON

Lesson 2 Review

Answers to Think and Write

A. After World War II, Japan adopted a new constitution that provided for a prime minister to head the government.

B. After World War II, Japan rebuilt its industries in a remarkably short period of time. Today, Japan is one of the world's richest countries.

C. The Japanese have adopted what they find useful from other countries, but they also cling to parts of their own culture.

D. After World War II, the United States occupied the south, and the Soviet Union took over the north. No agreement could be reached, so two states were created.

E. South Korea's industrial success is due to its educated labor force, the long hours that people work, and the relatively low wages that the people earn.

Answer to Skills Check

Answers should reflect independent thinking but should demonstrate proper haiku structure.

Focus Your Reading

Ask the lesson focus question found at the beginning of the lesson: **What changes took place in Japan and Korea after World War II?**

(Japan adopted a new constitution, rebuilt its industries, and became one of the world's richest countries. Korea was divided, with the north controlled by a Communist dictatorship and the south controlled by a republic. South Korea has experienced industrial success.)

Additional Practice

You may wish to assign the ancillary materials listed below.

Understanding the Lesson p. 141
Workbook p. 116

┌─── **Answers to Caption Questions** ───┐
p. 552 ► Most of the Japanese fans are dressed much more formally than the American fans are dressed.
p. 553 ► Automobile industry

553

The South Asian Subcontinent

Objectives

★1. **List** the countries that were created on or near the South Asian subcontinent after World War II.

2. **Compare** the populations and economies of Pakistan and Bangladesh.

3. **Identify** the following people and places: *Mohandas Gandhi, Benazir Bhutto, Calcutta, Bombay, Islamabad, Nepal, Bhutan,* and *Sri Lanka.*

1 STARTING THE LESSON

Motivation Activity

■ Tell students that religion has played an important role in the history of the South Asian subcontinent in the twentieth century. Ask students why they think this is so. (Religion is an important part of the peoples' lives.)

■ Then ask them what has played an important role in our history in this century (spreading democracy).

■ Discuss what might account for the difference in influential factors.

Think About What You Know

■ Assign the THINK ABOUT WHAT YOU KNOW activity on p. 554.

■ Student answers may include trying to change the rule by talking to the principal or to parents.

Study the Vocabulary

■ Have each student compose a matching quiz based on the vocabulary words and their definitions.

■ Tell students to look up any words with which they are unfamiliar in their Glossary.

■ Have students exchange quizzes. Each completed quiz should be returned for grading to the student who devised it.

554

LESSON **3**

The South Asian Subcontinent

THINK ABOUT WHAT YOU KNOW

Imagine that your teacher made a classroom rule that you thought was unfair. Would you obey the rule? What could you do to try to change it? Would you refuse to obey the unfair rule, even if it meant being expelled, or dismissed, from school?

STUDY THE VOCABULARY

civil disobedience   **jute**
partition

FOCUS YOUR READING

What independent countries were created on or near the South Asian subcontinent after World War II?

A. The End of An Empire

Gandhi Before World War II the South Asian subcontinent was part of the British Empire. Britain also ruled the island of Ceylon, now called Sri Lanka, off the southern tip of the subcontinent. Within a few years after the war, all of these lands became independent nations.

Mohandas Gandhi (MOH hun dahs GAHN dee) was one of the leaders of the movement for India's independence. When Gandhi was a young man, he went to London to study law. He returned home after 3 years, and then he went to South Africa. Many other Indians had gone to live there. But they were treated unfairly by the white people who ruled that land.

Gandhi believed that British rule was unjust, but he did not call for an armed revolt. He strongly opposed the use of violence. Instead, Gandhi urged the use of

554

---

civil disobedience. By this he meant that people should refuse to obey unjust laws, even if it meant going to prison. Gandhi set an example by cheerfully going to prison when he was convicted of refusing to obey laws he believed unjust.

Dividing the Subcontinent Most people on the subcontinent wanted an end to British rule, but they did not agree about what should take its place. The majority of people were Hindus, but there was a large Muslim minority. Some Muslim leaders feared that if the subcontinent became a single country, Hindus would have too much power. These leaders wanted to **partition**, or divide, the subcontinent into independent Muslim and Hindu countries. Hindu leaders did not want this but accepted it to secure independence.

Mohandas Gandhi led the movement for the independence of India.
▶ How are these people showing their respect for Gandhi?

Optional Activities

Writing to Learn

Writing an Editorial Ask students to imagine that they are the editor of a newspaper in India at the time of the partition of the South Asian subcontinent.

● Remind students that the differences between Muslims and Hindus are threatening to cause a civil war.

● Ask students to take a stand for or against partition and to write an editorial supporting their position.

● Conclude the activity by having volunteers read their editorials to the class.

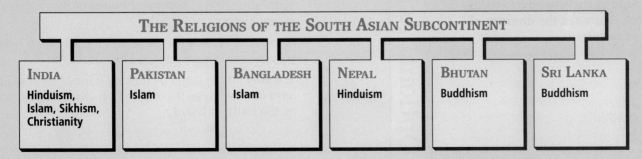

This Hindu man is meditating, or reflecting, while sitting on a platform that overlooks the Ganges River.
▶ Why, do you think, did he choose this place to meditate?

The independent countries of Pakistan and India were created in 1947. Pakistan was made up of two regions. West Pakistan was on the Indus River plain; East Pakistan was located at the mouth of the Ganges and Brahmaputra rivers. A thousand miles (1,609 km) separated the two parts of Pakistan. The two regions were separated by more than distance, however. Although the majority of the people in the two regions were Muslims, they were of different ethnic groups and spoke different languages. These differences led to a civil war in 1971. East Pakistan won its independence and became the country of Bangladesh.

The island of Ceylon became independent in 1948. It later changed its name to Sri Lanka. The name *Sri Lanka* comes from a Hindu epic. India, Bangladesh, Sri Lanka, and Pakistan all chose to belong to the Commonwealth of Nations.

B. The People of the World's Largest Democracy

Religion and Language India is the largest country on the subcontinent. It is also the second most populous country on earth, with more people than any of the continents except Asia. Most people in India still work the land, but many live in the cities.

A variety of ethnic groups live in India, and the Indian people speak a number of languages. Both Hindi and English serve as official languages. There are also many different religions in India. The majority of people are Hindus, but Hinduism includes various beliefs and practices. Hindus are also divided into numerous castes. You learned earlier that a caste is a way of separating people into classes, or groups, based on birth. Castes have existed for centuries in India, but there are now many more than in ancient times.

555

2 DEVELOPING THE LESSON

Read and Think

Sections A, B, C, and D

Use the questions below to help students summarize the information about the South Asian subcontinent:

1. **Who was Mohandas Gandhi?**
   (One of the leaders of the movement for India's independence *p. 554*)

2. **How do most people in India make a living?**
   (Farming *p. 556*)

3. **What do Pakistan and Bangladesh have in common?**
   (Both are poor countries; both have Muslim majorities. *pp. 555-556*)

4. **What type of government do Nepal and Bhutan have?**
   (Monarchies *p. 557*)

   Thinking Critically What problems, do you think, will India face in the future? (Hypothesize)
   (Answers may include overpopulation and ethnic and religious conflicts. *pp. 554-556*)

Answers to Caption Questions

p. 554 ▶ By hugging him and kneeling at his feet
p. 555 ▶ Answers may include that it is a peaceful place.

Graphic Organizer

To help students better understand the diversity of the South Asian subcontinent, you may wish to use the graphic organizer shown.

THE RELIGIONS OF THE SOUTH ASIAN SUBCONTINENT

INDIA	PAKISTAN	BANGLADESH	NEPAL	BHUTAN	SRI LANKA
Hinduism, Islam, Sikhism, Christianity	Islam	Islam	Hinduism	Buddhism	Buddhism

Optional Activities

555

Human-Environment Interactions

- Have students work in pairs, using the maps on this page and the political map on p. 545 for the following activity.

- Have one student in each pair name a country in South or East Asia. His or her partner should then name which of the four crops (wheat, rice, cotton, and tea) are grown in that country.

- Have students alternate between naming countries and naming crops.

Meeting Individual Needs

Concept:
The Diversity of Peoples in South Asia

To better understand the diversity of peoples in South Asia, it is useful to put information into pie charts. Below are activities that will help your students visualize this diversity.

◆ **EASY** Tell students that 85% of the people in India are Hindus, 10% are Muslims, 3% are Christians, and 2% are Sikhs.

Have students use this information to make a pie chart of India's major religions.

◆▶ **AVERAGE** Tell students that there are 16.9 million Sri Lankans. Of these, 2.6 million are Tamils, 12.7 million are Sinhalese, and the rest are of other ethnic backgrounds.

Have students use this data to make a pie chart of Sri Lanka's ethnic groups.

◀▶ **CHALLENGING** Have students consult an almanac or an encyclopedia to make a pie chart that illustrates the diversity of the South Asian peoples.

One tenth of India's population is Muslim. There are also other religious groups, such as the Sikhs (seeks). The Sikh religion began as a movement to combine the Hindu and Muslim religions. Christians make up about 3 percent of the population of India.

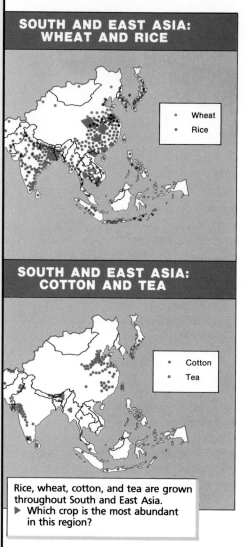

SOUTH AND EAST ASIA: WHEAT AND RICE

- Wheat
- Rice

SOUTH AND EAST ASIA: COTTON AND TEA

- Cotton
- Tea

Rice, wheat, cotton, and tea are grown throughout South and East Asia.
▶ Which crop is the most abundant in this region?

556

Government India is a republic made up of separate states. Voters elect the officials who govern. Indians enjoy freedom of religion, speech, and the press. They proudly point out that their country is the world's largest democracy. Yet, even though India is a democracy, one party has usually controlled the government.

Farming More than half of the Indian people still earn their living from agriculture. Rice is the most important crop. India is second only to China in rice production. Wheat and other grains are also major crops. India is a leading producer and exporter of spices, tea, and cashew nuts.

C. Pakistan and Bangladesh

Pakistan Pakistan is a poor country. Most people are farmers, although there is a limited amount of arable land. Many Pakistanis work in other countries and send part of their earnings home to their families. Pakistan is officially called an Islamic republic, and its laws are based on the Muslim religion. The name of the capital, *Islamabad,* means "city of Islam." Army leaders controlled the republic for years. In 1988, Benazir Bhutto (BOO toh), the daughter of a former prime minister, was elected prime minister. She was replaced by Nawaz Sharif in 1990.

Bangladesh Bangladesh is only about one-fifth the size of Pakistan, but it has a larger population. It is one of the most densely populated countries in the world, and one of the poorest.

Most of the land of Bangladesh is a delta, formed by the Ganges and Brahmaputra rivers. Farmers grow rice, vegetables, tea, and **jute** (joot) on this fertile land. The fibers of the jute plant are used for making rope, twine, and burlap fabric.

Optional Activities

Reteaching Main Objective

★ *List the countries that were created on or near the South Asian subcontinent after World War II.*

- Have students skim the lesson and make a bulletin-board time line of important events in South Asia's recent history.

- Have them include the dates and names of the new countries that were created after World War II.

- Tell students to begin by making a list of events. Then have them arrange these events in chronological order on the bulletin board.

Tea is a major crop on the island country of Sri Lanka.
► How are these people carrying the tea that they picked?

D. Nepal, Bhutan, and Sri Lanka

Nepal and Bhutan are located in the Himalayas. Both are monarchies. Hinduism is Nepal's official religion, and Buddhism is the religion of Bhutan.

Few outsiders came to these lands before 1951 because they were so difficult to reach. Now roads and air flights connect both Nepal and Bhutan with India.

The island country of Sri Lanka has been influenced by the civilization of nearby India since ancient times. The ancestors of most Sri Lankans migrated from India. Sri Lanka's major languages are related to those of India. It is said that Buddhism, the religion of the largest part of the population, was brought to Sri Lanka by a son of Asoka, the ancient Indian emperor.

LESSON 3 REVIEW

THINK AND WRITE

A. Why was the subcontinent divided after British rule ended? **(Recall)**

B. Describe the people and government of India. **(Recall)**

C. How does Bangladesh differ from Pakistan? **(Analyze)**

D. What links do Nepal, Bhutan, and Sri Lanka have with India? **(Infer)**

SKILLS CHECK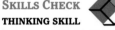

THINKING SKILL

After Gandhi was killed, the first prime minister of India told his people, "The light has gone out of our lives, and there is darkness everywhere." What do you think he meant by this?

557

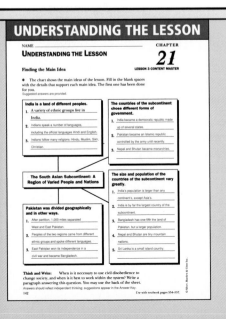
Optional Activities

Lesson 3 Review

Answers to Think and Write

A. The subcontinent was divided in order to give Muslims and Hindus their own separate countries.

B. A variety of ethnic groups live in India, and the Indian people speak a number of languages. The majority of people are Hindus, but there are also Muslims, Sikhs, and Christians. India is a republic made up of separate states.

C. Bangladesh is much smaller than Pakistan, but it has a larger population. Bangladesh also has more arable land.

D. Nepal and Bhutan are located along India's northern border. Sri Lanka has been influenced by India since ancient times. Also, the ancestors of most Sri Lankans came from India.

Answer to Skills Check

Answers should reflect independent thinking but may include that Gandhi was a source of inspiration to the Indian people. When this man of peace was killed, the hope that he gave to others was snuffed out.

Focus Your Reading

Ask the lesson focus question found at the beginning of the lesson: **What independent countries were created on or near the South Asian subcontinent after World War II?**
(India, Pakistan, Bangladesh, and Sri Lanka were created on or near the South Asian subcontinent after World War II.)

Additional Practice

You may wish to assign the ancillary materials listed below.

Understanding the Lesson p. 142
Workbook pp. 117–118

Answers to Caption Questions

p. 556 ► Rice is the most abundant.
p. 557 ► In woven baskets on their backs

557

Southeast Asia

Objectives

★1. **List** changes that Southeast Asia has undergone in the last half of this century.

2. **Compare** the resources of the countries of Southeast Asia.

3. **Describe** the governments of the countries of Southeast Asia.

4. **Identify** the following people and places: *King Rama the Strong, Corazon Aquino, Rangoon, Irrawaddy River, Malay Peninsula, Borneo, Hanoi, Saigon, Java, Jakarta,* and *Bali.*

1 STARTING THE LESSON

Motivation Activity

■ Tell students that of the 20 most populous countries in the world, nine are in Asia.

■ Ask students which Asian countries these might be. If students need help, tell them that four of the nine are in Southeast Asia.

■ The countries include China, India, Indonesia, Japan, Bangladesh, Pakistan, Vietnam, the Philippines, and Thailand.

Think About What You Know

■ Assign the THINK ABOUT WHAT YOU KNOW activity on p. 558.

■ Student answers should include the types of clothing one would wear in a tropical climate.

Study the Vocabulary

■ Have students look up the new vocabulary words in their Glossary.

■ Then ask them to use each word in a sentence to make sure they understand its meaning.

558

LESSON 4
Southeast Asia

THINK ABOUT WHAT YOU KNOW

Suppose you were going to take a trip to Southeast Asia. What kinds of clothing would you pack?

STUDY THE VOCABULARY

pagoda   copra

FOCUS YOUR READING

What changes has Southeast Asia undergone in the last half of this century?

A. Myanmar and Thailand

Changes on the Map Many changes have taken place in Southeast Asia. The country that was once called Burma is now called Myanmar. At one time it was part of British India. Today it is an independent state that does not even belong to the Commonwealth of Nations. Although it is called a republic, Myanmar has been controlled by army leaders.

Myanmar is a Buddhist country. Its most famous building is the gold-covered Shwe Dagon **pagoda** (puh GOH duh). A pagoda is a tower that serves as a religious building. The Shwe Dagon pagoda rises 326 feet (99 m) in the midst of Rangoon, Myanmar's capital city.

Except for the low-lying Irrawaddy River plain, most of Myanmar is mountainous. Rice is the main crop, and tropical forests provide valuable hardwoods, such as teak. The center of a teak log is so hard that even termites will not eat it. Teak beams in some Buddhist temples are more than 1,000 years old.

Thailand On old maps, Thailand appears as Siam. The name *Thailand* means "land

558

---

of the free." The Thais are proud that their country was never a European colony, as were the other lands in Southeast Asia.

Thailand, like Myanmar, is a Buddhist country and has many famous shrines. The Thais have tried to preserve their ancient culture. Their alphabet was invented over 700 years ago by King Rama the Strong. Thailand still has a king, but the army has run the government in recent years.

Thailand has good farmland along its rivers and is a rice-exporting country. The Thais also export other resources such as hardwoods and tin. Thailand is the world's fifth leading producer of tin.

B. Malaysia and Singapore

Malaysia Malaysia appears as part of the British Empire on maps printed before 1963. It was in that year Malaysia became independent. The country includes the

The Shwe Dagon pagoda is the most famous Buddhist temple in Myanmar.
▶ With what material is the pagoda covered?

Cooperative Learning

Making an Informational Display   Divide the class into groups of four students and have each group prepare an informational display about a Southeast Asian country.

● Have each group decide who will be responsible for the following duties: drawing a map of the country and labeling important places, making an illustrated list of the country's resources, illustrating the major religions, illustrating the form of government and the foreign countries that have played a role in the country's history.

● When groups are finished, put their displays on a bulletin board for the rest of the class to see.

southern part of the Malay Peninsula and the northern coast of the island of Borneo. Nearly 400 miles (644 km) of ocean separate the two parts of Malaysia.

Malaysia's population is made up of several ethnic and religious groups. Over half of the people are Muslim Malays. A third of the population is of Chinese descent. There are also Hindus from India and Muslims from Pakistan. A variety of languages are spoken, but Malay is the official language.

Malaysia has valuable resources. More than half of its cultivated land is planted in rubber trees, making Malaysia the world's chief supplier of natural rubber. Malaysia produces more tin than any other country in the world. The country also exports considerable amounts of petroleum and palm oil, used as a preservative in many foods. Look at the distribution of tin, oil, and rubber in Malaysia on the map on this page.

Singapore Singapore was part of Malaysia before 1965. It is now an independent state, even though it is only a city built on islands off the tip of the Malay Peninsula. Singapore is the smallest independent country in Asia; it is also the most densely populated. Chinese make up the largest ethnic group in Singapore.

Singapore may be small, but it is not poor. It has one of the highest standards of living in Southeast Asia. Singapore makes good use of its two great resources: its location and its people. By taking advantage of its location on a major sea route, Singapore has become the largest port in Southeast Asia. It has also developed industries that make use of the skills of its people. Singapore manufactures goods that are exported to many parts of the world. It is a city that lives on trade.

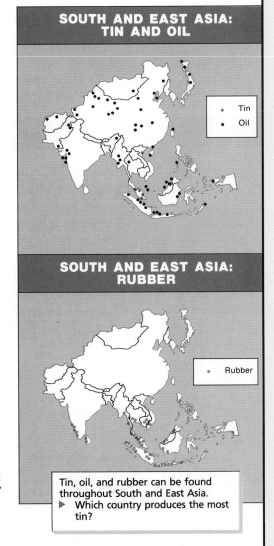

SOUTH AND EAST ASIA: TIN AND OIL

• Tin
• Oil

SOUTH AND EAST ASIA: RUBBER

• Rubber

Tin, oil, and rubber can be found throughout South and East Asia.
▶ Which country produces the most tin?

C. Vietnam, Laos, and Cambodia

Vietnam After World War II, there was a long and costly struggle for control of Vietnam, Laos, and Cambodia. France withdrew from the area in 1954; however, a war continued between the Communist

559

For Your Information

Military Rule in Myanmar The army has ruled Myanmar (formerly Burma) since 1962, when it seized power in a bloodless coup. Army leaders promised the people prosperity through their economic plan called the "Burmese Way to Socialism." This plan combined Buddhism, socialism, and isolationism. In actual practice, the army's plan has destroyed Myanmar's economy. At one time, Myanmar was Asia's largest rice exporter and had a flourishing trade in oil, gems, and timber. Because of mismanagement and an attempt to make the nation self-sufficient, the country's per capita income dropped from $670 in 1960 to $210 in 1989. In fact, Myanmar is now listed as one of the least developed countries in the world.

Optional Activities

2 DEVELOPING THE LESSON

Read and Think

Sections A and B

Use the questions below to summarize the information about Myanmar, Thailand, Malaysia, and Singapore:

1. **How are the governments of Myanmar and Thailand similar?**
   (Both are Buddhist countries, and both are run by army leaders. *p. 558*)

2. **What are the most valuable resources of Malaysia and Singapore?**
   (Malaysia's are rubber, tin, and oil; Singapore's are its location and people. *p. 559*)

   Thinking Critically What, do you think, would happen to Singapore if it decided to ban trading with other countries? (Hypothesize)
   (Answers should reflect independent thinking but may include that since the economy depends on trade, it would go into a decline. *p. 559*)

GEOGRAPHY THEMES

Human-Environment Interactions

■ Direct students' attention to the maps on this page. Then ask the following questions:

1. **Which of these three resources are found in Papua, New Guinea?**
   (Oil and Rubber)

2. **Which country produces more rubber, Sri Lanka or India?**
   (India)

3. **If you were the president of an oil company and you wanted to move your company to South or East Asia, which countries would appeal to you most?**
   (Answers should reflect independent thinking but should include countries in South and East Asia that produce oil.)

Answers to Caption Questions
p. 558 ▶ Gold
p. 559 ▶ Malaysia

GEOGRAPHY THEMES

Human-Environment Interactions

■ Have students use the map on this page to help them answer the following question: **Which country in South Asia and East Asia is still under foreign control?** (Tibet)

Read and Think

Sections C and D

To understand the vast differences among the various countries in Southeast Asia, ask the following questions:

1. **Why are Cambodia, Laos, and Vietnam so poor?**
   (Because of the long years of war *pp. 559-561*)

2. **What are Indonesia's resources?**
   (Oil, natural gas, gold, tin, and tropical timber *p. 561*)

Thinking Critically Why, do you think, are the major religions of Indonesia and the Philippines so different? (Analyze)
(Answers may include that the people who occupied and controlled these lands brought very different faiths with them. *p. 561*)

Vietnamese government at the capital city of Hanoi in the north, and an anti-Communist government at the capital city of Saigon in the south. The Soviet Union and Communist China backed the north. The United States supported the south.

At first the United States sent only advisors and supplies, but then in 1965,

American forces went to fight in Viet▮ At one time the United States had ▮ than half a million troops in Viet▮ United States troops pulled out of Viet▮ in 1973, but the war continued for ano▮ two years. North Vietnam finally ▮ quered South Vietnam and brought▮ entire country under Communist rule▮

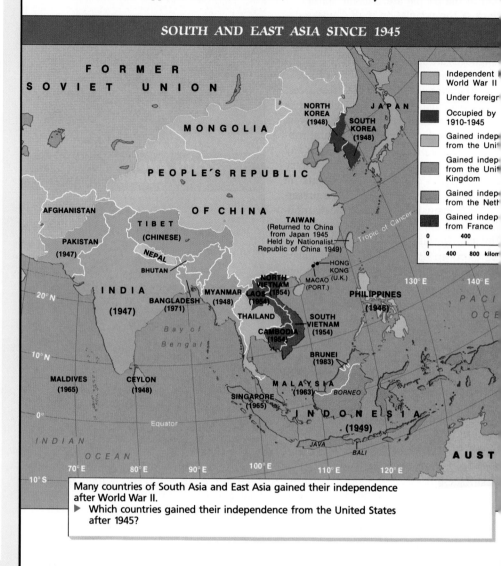

SOUTH AND EAST ASIA SINCE 1945

Many countries of South Asia and East Asia gained their independence after World War II.
▶ Which countries gained their independence from the United States after 1945?

Laos and Cambodia Communists also took control of the countries of Laos and Cambodia. Thousands of people fled from the lands taken over by the Communists. Many came to the United States.

Even though Vietnam and Cambodia are both Communist-ruled lands, war broke out between them in 1978 when Vietnam invaded Cambodia. The world's two largest Communist states took different sides in this conflict. The Soviet Union supported Vietnam; Communist China helped Cambodia. The long years of war have left Vietnam, Laos, and Cambodia very poor.

D. Indonesia and the Philippines

Indonesia Indonesia and the Philippines are island countries. Indonesia consists of more than 13,000 islands, and there are more than 7,000 islands in the Philippines. Indonesia is about 50 times as large as the Netherlands. As you know, it was once part of the Dutch empire. Since becoming independent in 1949, Indonesia has been ruled by military leaders.

Among the countries of Asia, only China and India have more people than Indonesia. The island of Java is the most heavily populated Indonesian island. Jakarta, Indonesia's capital, is on Java.

Indonesia is the largest Muslim country in the world. It has more Muslims than Iran, Iraq, and Egypt combined. There were once important Buddhist kingdoms on the islands, and the remains of Buddhist temples may still be seen. Hinduism was also introduced into Indonesia in early times. It still survives on the island of Bali.

Indonesia is rich in resources. It has oil, natural gas, gold, tin, and tropical timber. Manufacturing has grown in importance, but most of the labor force is still employed in farming. Densely populated

This woman is planting rice seedlings in Java, Indonesia.
▶ What condition must the soil be in before planting?

Java is a very carefully cultivated food-producing island. Rice, coffee, and sugar are among the country's exports.

Philippines Spain established its rule in the Philippines 50 years after Ferdinand Magellan visited the islands in 1521. During the period of Spanish rule, Christianity spread. Today the Philippines is the only country of Southeast Asia in which Christianity is the main religion.

As you may recall, the United States acquired the Philippines as a result of a war with Spain in 1898. The United States controlled the Philippines for a much shorter time than Spain, but American influence has been important. English and Pilipino are both official languages. The

561

Reteaching Main Objective

List changes that Southeast Asia has undergone in the last half of this century.

- Write the names of the countries of Southeast Asia as column headings on the chalkboard.

- Ask students to list the major changes that have occurred in each country in the last 50 years in the appropriate column.

- Then ask students questions that require them to compare and analyze the changes that have occurred in these countries. For example: **Why is Singapore described as having the highest standard of living in Southeast Asia?** (Its population is more highly skilled.)

Optional Activities

Lesson 4 Review

Answers to Think and Write

A. Myanmar and Thailand are both Buddhist countries ruled by army leaders. They both grow rice and hardwoods. Myanmar was once a part of British India. Thailand was never a European colony.

B. Malaysia's resources are rubber, tin, and oil, while Singapore's are its location and people.

C. A war continued between the Communist Vietnamese government in the north and an anti-Communist government in the south. The war lasted until 1977.

D. Indonesia is ruled by military leaders and is largely Muslim. The Philippines is a democracy and Christianity is its main religion.

Answer to Skills Check

For Myanmar, check Buddhism; for Thailand, check Buddhism; for Malaysia, check Hinduism and Islam; for Indonesia, check Islam; for Philippines, check Christianity.

Focus Your Reading

Ask the lesson focus question found at the beginning of the lesson: **What changes has Southeast Asia undergone in the last half of this century?**

(With the exception of Thailand, which has always been independent, the countries of Southeast Asia have achieved their independence from foreign control. Also, some countries have developed strong manufacturing and trade industries.)

Additional Practice

You may wish to assign the ancillary materials listed below.

Understanding the Lesson p. 143
Workbook pp. 119-120

The Filipinos voted on a new constitution in 1987, which gave them more democracy and granted Corazon Aquino the presidency until 1992.
▶ In what year was Aquino elected?

Philippine government is similar to that of the United States. The president and the members of Congress are elected by the people. The Congress has a Senate and a House of Representatives. There is also a Supreme Court. In 1986, Filipinos elected their first woman president, Corazon Aquino (KOR uh zahn uk KEE noh). In 1992, Aquino was succeeded by Fidel V. Ramos.

The Philippine islands are mountainous, but about one third of the land is arable and produces sugar, rice, corn, and coconuts. Coconuts are exported largely in the form of vegetable oil or as **copra** (KAH-pruh), dried coconut. The country also manufactures products ranging from watches to clothing. The United States is its most important trading partner.

LESSON 4 REVIEW

THINK AND WRITE

A. Summarize the similarities and differences between Myanmar and Thailand. **(Analyze)**
B. How do the resources of Malaysia and Singapore differ? **(Analyze)**
C. What conflict developed in Vietnam after World War II? **(Recall)**
D. Compare the religions and governments of Indonesia and the Philippines. **(Analyze)**

SKILLS CHECK

THINKING SKILL

Divide a sheet of paper into four vertical columns and five horizontal rows to make a chart. Assign each column one of the following religions: *Christianity, Buddhism, Hinduism, Muslim*. Assign each row one of the following Southeast Asian countries: *Myanmar, Thailand, Malaysia, Indonesia, Philippines*. Use a check (✔) in each row to show the main religion of each country.

562

Optional Activities

UNDERSTANDING THE LESSON

NAME _____
UNDERSTANDING THE LESSON

CHAPTER
21

Making Comparisons

LESSON 4 CONTENT MASTER

✳ This chart helps you to compare some of the countries in Southeast Asia. Write the missing information in each blank on the chart. A few have been done for you.

Country	Colonial Ruler	Present Government	Major Religions	Agricultural Products	Other Products
Myanmar	Britain	Republic controlled by military	Buddhism	Rice	Teak
Thailand	Never a colony	Monarchy controlled by military	Buddhism	Rice	Hardwoods, tin
Indonesia	Netherlands	Military rule	Islam, Hinduism	Rice, coffee, sugar	Oil, natural gas, gold, tin, timber
Philippines	Spain, United States	Democratic republic	Christianity	Sugar, rice, corn, coconuts, copra	Watches, clothing

Think and Write: Write a paragraph explaining why the countries of Vietnam, Cambodia, and Laos remain poor while the standard of living of other Asian countries has risen. You may use the back of the sheet.
Answers should reflect independent thinking; suggestions appear in the Answer Key.

Use with textbook pages 558–562.

143

◀ **Review Master Booklet, p. 143**

USING THE VOCABULARY

warlord	jute
civil disobedience	finance
commune	pagoda
partition	literacy rate
gross national product	copra

From the list, choose a vocabulary term that could be used in place of the underlined word or words in each sentence. Rewrite the sentences on a separate sheet of paper.

1. Some Muslim leaders wanted to <u>divide</u> the subcontinent into independent Muslim and Hindu countries.
2. Farmers in Bangladesh grow <u>a plant that has fibers which are used for making rope, twine, and burlap fabric.</u>
3. <u>Refusing to obey unjust laws even if it means going to jail</u> is the opposite of violent opposition.
4. The <u>percent of the population able to read and write</u> is high in South Korea.
5. In China a <u>local ruler</u> had his own army.
6. The most famous building in Myanmar is the Shwe Dagon <u>tower</u>.
7. The Chinese Communists forced farmers to join a <u>farm on which people live and work together</u>.
8. The <u>total value of all the goods and services produced by a country in one year</u> is used to show the economic growth of a country from one year to the next.
9. Japan's banks and companies have helped Japan become a world leader in <u>the management of money</u>.
10. The Philippine Islands export coconuts in the form of <u>dried coconut</u>.

REMEMBERING WHAT YOU READ

On a separate sheet of paper, answer the following questions in complete sentences.

1. What weakened China and caused Japan to decide to invade China?
2. What did the Communists want to do in China?
3. What other kinds of reform do the people of China want in addition to reforms on the farms and in factories?
4. What is the agreement between Britain and the Communists about Hong Kong?
5. Explain how the government of Japan is organized.
6. What is South Korea's main resource?
7. How did Mohandas Gandhi encourage his followers to make changes in their government?
8. What religions exist in India?
9. What is the only country of Southeast Asia in which Christianity is the main religion?
10. How is the Philippine government similar to that of the United States?

TYING LANGUAGE ARTS TO SOCIAL STUDIES

Haiku is a lovely form of Japanese poetry that often deals with nature. Find a picture in a magazine that shows something from nature. Mount the picture on construction paper. Below the picture, write a haiku using these guidelines: The haiku has three lines. The first line has five syllables, the second line seven syllables, and the third line five syllables. Display your haiku in the classroom.

563

Using the Vocabulary

1. partition	6. pagoda
2. jute	7. commune
3. civil disobedience	8. gross national product
4. literacy rate	9. finance
5. warlord	10. copra

Remembering What You Read

1. Wars between the government and the warlords weakened China.
2. The Communists wanted to revolutionize the Chinese way of life. Loyalty to the state was to replace loyalty to family or friends.
3. They want freedom to speak out against the government.
4. Hong Kong will become part of China in 1997; private businesses will be allowed to operate for 50 more years.
5. A prime minister is chosen by the Diet, or legislature.
6. A skilled and educated population is South Korea's main resource.
7. He urged the use of civil disobedience.
8. The Hindu, Muslim, Sikh, and Christian religions exist in India.
9. The Philippines is the only Southeast Asian country in which Christianity is the main religion.
10. The president is elected by the people; the congress is made up of a senate and house of representatives; there is also a supreme court.

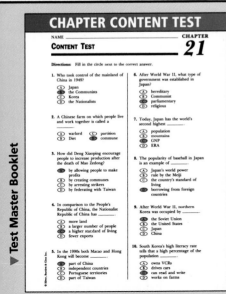

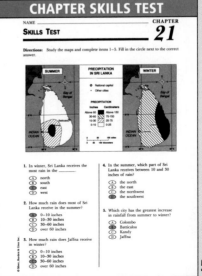

563

Thinking Critically

1. The Chinese mainland is the area of China that does not include Taiwan.

2. Answers may include that Emperor Meiji's advice has proved valuable in Japan because the Japanese have studied what other countries do and adapted the best of those ways to Japanese life.

3. There is little work and a limited amount of land for farming.

4. Thailand was never a European colony.

5. It is located on a major sea route and manufactures goods for export.

Summarizing the Chapter

Lesson 1
1. Revolution forced the last emperor from the throne in 1912.
2. Communist takeover in 1949
3. Reforms to increase production

Lesson 2
1. Japan adopted a new constitution after World War II.
2. Korea was divided in 1950.
3. South Korea had free elections in 1987.

Lesson 3
1. Gandhi led India to independence.
2. Pakistan became independent in 1947.
3. Ceylon won independence in 1948.

Lesson 4
1. Malaysia and Singapore won independence.
2. North Vietnam conquered South Vietnam.
3. The Philippines elected their first woman president.

THINKING CRITICALLY

1. What do you think is the meaning of the term *Chinese mainland.*
2. What is your opinion of Emperor Meiji's advice to his country?
3. Why have many Pakistanis sought work in other countries?
4. What about Thailand's history makes it different from the other countries in Southeast Asia?
5. What has helped Singapore become the largest port in Southeast Asia?

SUMMARIZING THE CHAPTER

On a separate sheet of paper, draw a graphic organizer like the one shown here. Copy the information from this graphic organizer to the one you have drawn. Under the main idea for each lesson, write three statements that support the main idea.

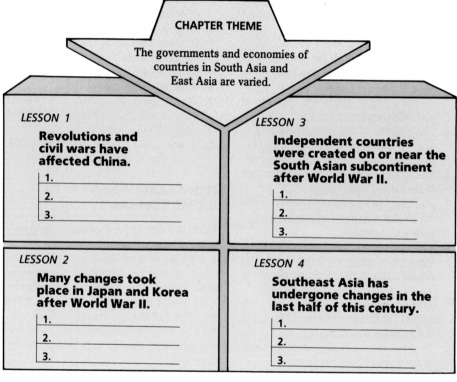

CHAPTER THEME

The governments and economies of countries in South Asia and East Asia are varied.

LESSON 1
Revolutions and civil wars have affected China.
1.
2.
3.

LESSON 3
Independent countries were created on or near the South Asian subcontinent after World War II.
1.
2.
3.

LESSON 2
Many changes took place in Japan and Korea after World War II.
1.
2.
3.

LESSON 4
Southeast Asia has undergone changes in the last half of this century.
1.
2.
3.

564

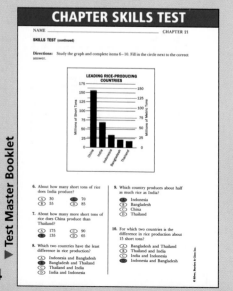

▶ Test Master Booklet

564

▶ Test Master Booklet

▶ Test Master Booklet

COOPERATIVE LEARNING

In this unit you learned about important people, places, and events in South and East Asia. Sometimes, people, places, and events from history are the bases for works of literature, such as plays. Do you think you and your classmates could write a historical play?

PROJECT

Work with a group of classmates to plan, write, and perform a play about some real person, place, or event from South or East Asia. For example, a play could be written about Marco Polo's return to Venice. The characters in this play could be Marco, his father, and several Venetian nobles. The setting for your play could be a banquet hall in Venice, and the plot could tell how Marco and his father convinced the Venetians that their stories about China were true.

There are many other stories in Unit 6 that could be subjects of plays. Meet as a group and look through the chapters to select a subject for your play. Be sure to discuss each other's ideas politely and try to stay on the job.

Once you have chosen the subject for your play, discuss specific ideas for the characters, setting, and plot. Take notes to record each group member's ideas.

Once you have planned your play, the group is ready to begin writing. Divide the play's characters among the group members. Then as you write, each group member should suggest what lines his or her assigned character or characters might say. You may also want to write lines for a narrator to introduce and explain the action of your play. Give your play a title.

PRESENTATION AND REVIEW

When your play is written, decide together which group member will play each role. Rehearse your play. When you are ready, present your play in front of your classmates. Watch other groups' plays. Think about how plays can make history come to life.

Meet again with your group to evaluate your project. How well did your group members work together? How could your play have been improved?

REMEMBER TO:
- Give your ideas.
- Listen to others' ideas.
- Plan your work with the group.
- Present your project.
- Discuss how your group worked.

565

You may wish to refer to the article on Cooperative Learning found in the front of your Teacher's Edition.

Objectives

1. **Identify** the monetary units of the countries of South and East Asia.
2. **Apply** the conversion process to monetary units of South and East Asia.

Why Do I Need This Skill?

Ask your students if they have ever tried to use American money in another country. If they have not, ask them to imagine what it would be like to try to use an American dollar in France or in Mexico. Elicit the idea that they would need to use the money of each nation.

Continue the discussion by asking how they would know the value of an item even if they had some of the money of the country they were visiting. Explain that the value of our own money differs in various countries. We need to know the exchange rate in order to know how much we are spending.

Learning the Skill

1. **What is the first thing you should know when you decide to visit another country?**
   (You need to know the name of that country's monetary unit and the exchange rate for U.S. dollars.)

2. **How do you find out the exchange rate?**
   (Watch the newspapers or inquire at banks and major hotels.)

3. **How would you figure out the cost in American dollars of an item that costs 1,500 yen when the exchange rate is 1:150?**
   (Divide 1,500 by 150 because each American dollar is worth 150 yen. The item would cost ten American dollars.)

SKILL TRACE: Budgeting and Banking		
INTRODUCE PE pp. 566–567	**PRACTICE** TE pp. 566–567 TE p. 584	**TEST** Unit 6 Test, TMB

566

A. WHY DO I NEED THIS SKILL?

Each country has its own currency, or system of money. It is important when traveling and doing business with other countries of the world to know what the currencies are and how to exchange them with ours.

B. LEARNING THE SKILL

Each currency has its own monetary unit. For example, the dollar is the monetary unit for the United States. In this unit you have learned about South and East Asia. The chart below shows the monetary units for most of the countries in that region.

Country	Monetary Unit
India	Rupee
Pakistan	Rupee
Bangladesh	Taka
Sri Lanka	Rupee
China	Yuan
Taiwan	Dollar
Japan	Yen
South Korea	Won
Myanmar	Kyat
Thailand	Baht
Malaysia	Ringgit
Singapore	Dollar
Vietnam	Dong
Laos	Kip
Indonesia	Ruphiah
Philippines	Peso

566

The currency of each country has its own exchange rate. The exchange rate is the amount that the currency can be exchanged for in other currencies. Since exchange rates vary from day to day, it is important to check a newspaper for the exchange rate for a particular day. Banks and major hotels also have this information.

The following chart shows exchange rates for some of the currencies in South and East Asia on a particular day. For example, the chart shows that one United States dollar was worth 150 yen.

Monetary Unit	Monetary Unit per U.S. Dollar
Yen	150.00
Rupee	11.50
Won	668.00
Peso	21.60

C. PRACTICING THE SKILL

Use the tables on this page to answer the following questions on a separate sheet of paper.

1. If you exchanged 5 dollars for each of the currencies listed on the table above, how much would you receive? For example, multiply the exchange rate for 1 yen by 5: $150 \times 5 = 750$ yen.
2. What is the monetary unit for India?
3. What other countries use the same monetary unit that India uses?

Optional Activities

Homework Activity

● Have students make a list of items that they would take on a trip to India or Japan.

● Ask the students to use newspaper ads to find out the prices of the items that they need to take. Allow them to estimate the cost if necessary. Ask students to round off the prices to the nearest dollar.

● Then have the students convert the cost of the items to yen or rupees, depending on which country they chose to visit.

● Discuss with students how different the totals are.

4. What countries in Southeast Asia use the dollar as their monetary unit?

5. How many Indian rupees would you get by exchanging 100 United States dollars?

6. If you were in Japan and wanted to buy a product that cost 7,500 yen, how much would that be in United States money?

7. If wheat sold at 2.60 dollars a bushel and could be bought at the same price in South Korea, what would it cost?

8. What country uses the peso as its monetary unit?

9. According to the table, how many pesos would be exchanged for 2 United States dollars?

10. How many different monetary units are used in the South and East Asia region?

D. APPLYING THE SKILL

As you read a newspaper, check to see what the exchange rates are on a particular day. Check again a week later to see if there were any changes in those rates.

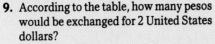

Practicing the Skill

1. 57.50 rupees; 3,340 won; 108 pesos

2. The monetary unit for India is the rupee.

3. Pakistan and Sri Lanka use the same monetary unit that India uses.

4. Taiwan and Singapore use the dollar as their monetary unit.

5. 1,150

6. $50

7. 1,736.80 won

8. The Philippines uses the peso.

9. 43.20 pesos

10. Thirteen monetary units are used.

For students who are still having difficulty with the concept of exchanging currency, you may wish to use the reteaching activity below.

Applying the Skill

Students should bring in their newspaper clippings.

567

Reteaching Activity

For students having difficulty converting currency, offer the following simple exercise.

● Have students draw some pretend American dollar bills.

● Then have them create some imaginary paper money called "moneybills."

● Tell them that for every American dollar they give you, you will give them two moneybills.

● After actually exchanging their money, explain that this is the same as exchanging American money for foreign currency.

Optional Activities

Objectives

1. **Identify** the steps for making predictions while reading.
2. **Apply** the predicting process to social studies reading.

Why Do I Need This Skill?

Ask your students if they have ever tried to make a prediction about something in their lives. If they do not come up with any answers immediately, ask if they have tried to predict their parents' behavior on such occasions as asking their parents if they could spend the night with a friend or asking for a certain toy. In both of these instances, students probably tried to predict an outcome before they asked the question.

Tell students that learning to make predictions will help them understand historical and social forces that propel events. This skill is valuable in their study of social studies and other subjects, and has lifelong application to other situations.

Learning the Skill

1. **What is the first thing you should do when making predictions while reading?** (Read the first paragraph and think about what might happen next.)

2. **What are three effective strategies in making predictions?** (Use what you already know, think about an event that might cause something else to happen, and think of the people involved and what they might do next.)

3. **What should you do if your prediction turns out to be incorrect?** (Change it or make a new one; then verify it.)

SKILL TRACE: Making and Verifying Predictions		
INTRODUCE PE pp. 568–569	**PRACTICE** TE pp. 568–569, 589 WB pp. 20, 92 TE p.589	**TEST** Unit 6 Test, TMB

A. WHY DO I NEED THIS SKILL?

While you are reading a story, do you ever try to guess what will happen next in the story? If so, you are making a **prediction**. Trying to make predictions makes reading more interesting and enjoyable. Knowing how to make predictions will also help you understand the information you read in your social studies textbook.

B. LEARNING THE SKILL

You can use these four steps to make predictions when you read.

1. **Read** the first paragraph. As you read, think about what is happening and what might happen next.

2. **Predict** what will happen next or what additional information you might be presented with. You can try the following strategies to make predictions.
   - Think about what you already know about the subject of your reading.
   - Think about how events you have read about might cause something else to happen.
   - Think about people you have read about and how they might behave or what they might do next.

3. **Verify** your predictions. Continue reading to see if your guesses were correct.

4. **Change** your predictions or make new predictions if necessary. Then read on to verify them.

568

C. PRACTICING THE SKILL

Use the four steps for making predictions as you read the following selection from Chapter 22.

1. **Read** the beginning of the selection.

> When Elsie was eight years old, she went to a school run by Christian missionaries. She lived with other students in a building called a dormitory. She learned English and worked in the school garden. At first, Elsie hated school and living in a dormitory. She particularly disliked working in the garden. She thought it was far better to gather food in the bush [sparsely settled land], as her people had always done.

2. **Predict** what will happen next. Can you guess what might happen to Elsie? Are there any clues that her life might change? Write one or two predictions on a separate sheet of paper. Then read the next section.

> Later, Elsie changed her mind about school, at least partly. She grew to like life in the dormitory. She became a good runner and won prizes on school sport days. She never, however, learned to like working in the garden.
>
> The mission school closed during World War II, and Elsie, who was then 18, returned to her family. She now found life in the bush hard. When the school reopened after the war, Elsie went back to work there as a teacher's aide.

Optional Activities

Homework Activity

- Have students follow an ongoing news story for five days in a row. Students may wish to select a current-events article or a recurring topic, such as a sports story.
- Ask them to make a daily oral report on their story, including a prediction about the way that the situation may develop.
- At the end of the five-day period, review the four steps of prediction-making, outlined on pp. 568-569.
- Discuss with students how they used these guidelines to make and revise their predictions.

3. **Verify** your predictions. Were your guesses correct? Did you guess correctly about what life was like for Elsie? Were there any clues that helped you?

4. **Change** your predictions or make new ones. Can you predict what Elsie did after returning to the missionary school? Write down your new predictions. Now turn to pages 573–574 and read all of Elsie's story to again verify your predictions.

D. APPLYING THE SKILL

Use the four-step predicting strategy as you read all of Chapter 22. See if making predictions helps you to better understand what you read.

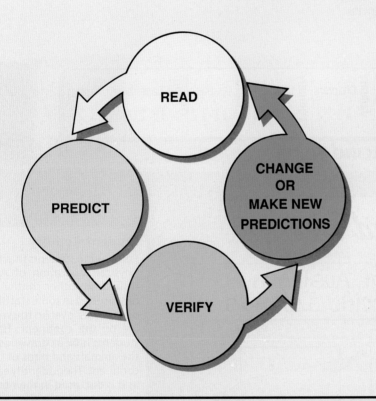

569

Practicing the Skill

Students should follow the outlined steps and check their predictions against the text on pp. 573–574. After the students have finished reading these pages, you may wish to have them share their predictions with the rest of the class.

For students who are still having difficulty with the concept of making predictions, you may wish to use the reteaching activity listed below.

Applying the Skill

Have students follow the four-step predicting strategy as they read Chapter 22. After they have read the chapter, you may wish to discuss students' predictions and ask students if the strategy of making predictions helped them to better understand what they read.

Reteaching Activity

- For students having difficulty practicing the skill of making predictions, review the four steps involved in making a prediction, found on pp. 568–569.

- Provide students with a sample reading that is at least four paragraphs in length. If possible, have each paragraph of the text appear on a separate page or use an overhead projector to show only one paragraph at a time.

- Ask students what step they should follow with the next paragraph. (Read it and think about what comes next.)

- Continue the process with each paragraph, expanding on the prediction-making strategies.

Optional Activities

Australia, New Zealand, and the Pacific Islands

Unit Theme Australia, New Zealand, and the Pacific Islands make up one of the world's most unique regions, with a wealth of interesting people, animals, plants, and landforms.

Chapter 22 Geography of Australia, New Zealand, and the Pacific Islands

(pp. 572-587)

Theme Australia, New Zealand, and the Pacific Islands have a variety of geographic features.

Chapter 23 Past and Present in Australia, New Zealand, and the Pacific Islands

(pp. 588-604)

Theme There are close economic and political ties between Australia, New Zealand, the islands of the Pacific, and other nations.

September Chapters MSH-1	October Chapters 2-4	November Chapters 5-7	December Chapters 8-9	January Chapters 10-12	February Chapters 13-14	March Chapters 15-17	April Chapters 18-20	May Chapters 21-23

PACING GUIDE

Bulletin Board Idea

Student Activity
Point out to students that the physical separation of Australia from other continents has resulted in some startling differences, even in the wildlife on the continent. Have students look at drawings of the animals and birds of this continent. Then, identify each as it is discussed in their text.

Books for Teachers

Anderson, A. Grant. *New Zealand in Maps.* New York: Holmes and Meier, 1978. ISBN 0-8419-0324-7. (Ch. 22) This geographic guide to New Zealand offers unique maps of the country that are useful in teaching.

Conlon, Dalys. *Presenting Australia.* Salem, NH: Salem House, 1985. ISBN 0-88162-118-8. (Ch. 22) This richly illustrated book presents Australia's past and present.

Hughes, Robert. *The Fatal Shore.* New York: Knopf, 1987. ISBN 0-394-50668-5. (Ch. 23) Written in conjunction with Australia's bicentennial, this book explains how the country began as a place for outcasts from the British Empire.

Karnow, Stanley. *In Our Image.* New York: Random House, 1989. ISBN 0-394-54975-9. (Ch. 23) This is a thoroughly researched look at the Philippines and the effect of the United States' domination of its society over the past 80 years.

Books for Students

Arnold, Caroline. *Australia Today.* Danbury, CT: Franklin Watts, 1987. ISBN 0-531-10377-3. (Ch. 23) Life in today's Australia, from its cosmopolitan cities to its rustic outback, is detailed through text and pictures.

Armitage, Ronda. *New Zealand.* Danbury, CT: Franklin Watts, 1988. ISBN 0-531-18158-8. (Ch. 23) The people, culture, and geography of the island nation of New Zealand are presented through brief text and numerous illustrations.

Bell, John. *We Live in New Zealand.* Danbury, CT: Franklin Watts, 1984. ISBN 0-531-04781-4. (Ch. 23) Daily life in New Zealand is examined in this well-illustrated text.

Bjener, Tamiko. *Philippines.* Minneapolis, MN: Gareth Stevens, 1987. ISBN 1-55532-167-4. (Ch. 23) The rich heritage and culture of the Filipino people are examined in this concise book.

Cornelia, Elizabeth. *Australia.* Morristown, NJ: Silver Burdett Press, 1988. ISBN 0-382-06182-9. (Ch. 22) Another in the "Nations of the World" series, this book examines the geography and people of Australia.

Harrington, Lyn. *Australia and New Zealand: Pacific Community.* Toronto, Canada: Thomas Nelson and Sons, 1969. (Ch. 23) Harrington summarizes the history of two interesting and unusual countries in the South Pacific.

Henderson, W.F. *Looking at Australia.* New York: Harper & Row, 1977. ISBN 0-397-31703-4. (Ch. 23) The author gives his views on the people of Australia and how their distance from the rest of the world gives them a unique perspective.

Heyerdahl, Thor. *Kon-Tiki: Across the Pacific by Raft.* Skokie, IL: Rand McNally, 1960. (Ch. 22) Six South American men board a primitive raft and set sail for the the Pacific Islands in an effort to prove that the islands were originally settled by others who made the same journey centuries earlier.

Keyworth, Valerie. *New Zealand: Land of the Long, White Cloud.* Minneapolis, MN: Dillon Press, 1989. ISBN 0-87518-414-6. (Ch. 22) This colorful guide to the nation of New Zealand features many excellent photographs.

Lepthein, Emilie U. *Australia.* Chicago: Children's Press, 1982. ISBN 0-516-02751-4. (Ch. 22) The diversity of Australia, its people, and its landscape are captured in this discussion of the history, geography, and inhabitants of the country.

Rau, Margaret. *Red Earth, Blue Sky: The Australian Outback.* New York: Harper & Row, 1981. ISBN 0-690-04080-6. (Ch. 22) Life in the rustic Outback region of Australia is presented along with facts about many of its unique features.

Stark, Al. *Australia.* Minneapolis, MN: Dillon Press, 1987. ISBN 0-87518-365-4. (Ch. 22) This is a slim yet thorough guide to the Australian people and their culture.

Trezise, Percy J. *The Peopling of Australia.* Minneapolis, MN: Gareth Stevens, 1987. ISBN 1-55532-950-0. (Ch. 23) This book seeks to explain how Australia grew from a country of outcasts into one of the world's foremost economic powers.

Warner, Oliver. *Captain Cook and the South Pacific.* New York: American Heritage Publishing Co., Inc., 1963. (Ch. 22) Warner details the life and voyages of Captain James Cook, the British navigator who was the first European to visit many of the Pacific islands, and who claimed the east coast of Australia for Great Britain.

Filmstrips and Videos

VolcanoScapes. Videocassette. Tropical Visions Video, 1988. (Ch. 22) The eruption of the Kilauea Volcano, on the island of Hawaii, from 1983 to 1987 is profiled along with a look at how volcanic eruptions formed the Hawaiian Island chain.

Studying Australia

Life "Down Under"

Referring to Australia as "down under" seems very appropriate to most Americans. In relationship to the United States, Australia seems to be very far down under. Many students are quite surprised to learn the size of Australia and the scope of its geography. The following activities are designed to help students understand more about Australia and the people from "down under."

SOCIAL STUDIES

Economics   The geography of Australia contributes greatly to the nation's tourist industry, which in turn aids its economy. Wildlife sanctuaries, sandy beaches, the Great Barrier Reef, and the Australian Alps are just a few natural features that attract over 1,000,000 foreign tourists each year.

■ Have students research tourist attractions and recreational activities in Australia. Then have them explain how Australia's geography influences each.

Geography   Have students draw a political map of Australia, showing the states, their capitals and their largest city, and the population of each city.

■ Then have students research the total population of Australia. Ask students to answer the following questions:

1. Why do the people of Australia live where they do?
2. Why are the cities located where they are?

■ Ask students to discuss their findings with the class.

Global Awareness   Obtain or create an upside-down map. Place the South Pole at the top and draw the other land masses accordingly. Students will most likely note that the world looks strange

upside down. Discuss the concept of an upside-down world with students. Have them draw their own maps and then ask them the following questions:

1. Can the world really be upside down?
2. In space, does the earth really have a top or a bottom?
3. How does this map look strange to you?
4. In what ways does it change your thinking about the placement of the continents?
5. What might be different if all the maps you have been studying in school looked like this? How might your thinking be different?

■ Have students share their answers in a classroom discussion.

History   Immigration played a large role in the history of Australia. In particular, two waves of immigration dominate its history. The first was the immigration of the Aborigines, some time around 25 B.C. The second major wave was the arrival of the Europeans, beginning with the Portuguese in the 1400s.

■ Have the students write a report about the Aborigines.

■ Students may wish to debate the wisdom of the Europeans' policy toward the Aborigines. They may wish to draw comparisons between this and the way the Native Americans were treated in the United States.

SCIENCE

■ Australia is different from the United States in some very important ways. Australia has different animals, different vegetation, and even different seasons from the United States.

■ Explain to students that Australians head north to find warm weather and south to find cold weather. Have students make a diagram explaining why this is true and why the seasons are reversed in the Northern and Southern hemispheres.

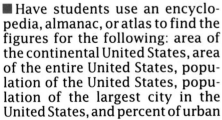

MATHEMATICS

■ Have students use an encyclopedia, almanac, or atlas to find the figures for the following: area of the continental United States, area of the entire United States, population of the United States, population of the largest city in the United States, and percent of urban

versus rural dwellers. Then have them do the same for Australia.

■ Have the students create graphs comparing the two countries. Tell students to use one color of marker for the United States and a different color of marker for Australia. Have students use their graphs to explain how the two countries are similar and how they are different.

LANGUAGE ARTS

■ Australians speak English, but students may have trouble understanding everything that they hear in Australia. Provide the students with a glossary of Australian terms and have them guess the meaning of each word. Then have them guess how each word came to have that meaning. The glossary could include the following terms*:

Outback — the interior of Australia

Going inside — heading for a city from the outback

Bush — rural areas

Good on you — a term of approval

Willy-willy — a cyclone or high wind storm

Digger — an Australian soldier

Hard yacker — hard exhausting work

Up a gum tree — in trouble or in a mess

Barney — an argument

Ropeable — angry, irritable or upset

Sticky beak — an inquisitive person

The big smoke — a city

■ Have students translate: "That sticky beak digger from the bush caused a barney. He got me ropeable, he did! He'd better head inside, or he'll be up a gum tree." (That curious soldier from the country caused an argument. He got me angry, he did! He'd better head for the city, or he'll be in trouble.)

*Source: Australia and New Zealand, Life World Library editors. New York: Time, Inc., 1966. ISBN 64-25755.

LITERATURE

■ Students may enjoy learning more about the diversity of Australia, its people, and its landscape from Valerie Keyworth's *Australia* (Chicago: Children's Press, 1982. ISBN 0-516-02751-4).

■ After obtaining the book from a local library and sharing excerpts from it with the class, ask students to write a one-page creative story reflecting a day in the life of an Australian youth.

Develop an Outline

INSTRUCTIONS FOR THE TEACHER:

What Is an Outline?   An outline organizes information into main ideas and supporting details. An outline can also be a skeleton of a lesson or chapter.

In addition, an outline may be a written plan for a report. It can help students organize a report by showing them how information goes together. An outline can tell a student if he or she has enough details for each main idea.

Why Have Students Make Outlines? By outlining a chapter, students can more easily remember its main ideas and the supporting details. An outline cuts through interesting, but often unimportant, details to help students get "the big picture" or the "meat" of a chapter. Students are also practicing the important skill of finding the main idea.

ACTIVITY FOR THE STUDENTS:

Preparing to Make an Outline   Explain to students that outlining text is very easy because all of the units are divided into chapters, which are divided into lessons, which are divided into sections. Each section has a title under which subheadings tell the section's main idea.

Students just beginning to outline can practice this valuable skill by writing the lesson title, the section titles, and so on, in proper outline form. At this stage, students should only copy boldface words or words printed in blue. Later students can move on to find main ideas and supporting details from within the paragraphs in the text.

Outlining a Lesson   Select a lesson in this unit, "Australia, New Zealand, and the Pacific Islands." After students have read the lesson, tell them that before the author ever wrote this lesson, he or she had a plan of what to write. It is the students' job to read all of the paragraphs in the lesson and discover the plan or outline. Emphasize that the plan contained all of the main ideas and supporting details that the author wanted to get across.

You may wish to give students a blank outline form to fill in as they search for the author's original plan.

The Outline Itself   Below is an example of a "skeleton" outline that you may wish to give to your students. Students should fill in the blanks. For your reference, appropriate answers have been provided in parentheses. (NOTE: Lesson 1 is outlined as part of the entire chapter; therefore, there is no "II," because the "II" would be Lesson 2. "III" would be Lesson 3, and so on.):

Chapter 22 — "Geography of Australia, New Zealand, and the Pacific Islands":

I. Australia

  A. Australia's First Inhabitants

    1. Bush Life

      a. _____ (Aborigines were Australia's earliest inhabitants.)

      b. _____ (Aborigines are only a small part of today's population.)

    2. New Ways

      a. _____ (Life in a Christian school is strange for an Aborigine.)

      b. _____ (An Aborigine returns to the mission school as an adult.)

    3. Valuable Knowledge

      a. Aborigine lore is usually passed down orally.

      b. An aborigine writes a book to preserve his or her heritage.

  B. The World's Smallest Continent

    1. _____ (Flat Land)

      a. Australia is about the size of the United States.

      b. _____ (The flattest of the continents)

    2. _____ (Unusual Features)

      a. _____ (Ayer's Rock is in the center of Australia.)

      b. _____ (The Great Barrier Reef stretches along Australia's east coast.)

  C. A Mostly Dry Continent

    1. _____ (Precipitation)

      a. The second driest continent

      b. The eastern part is moist.

      c. The center part is very dry.

      d. _____ (The northern coast has a tropical climate.)

      e. The southwestern coast has a Mediterranean climate.

    2. _____ **(Temperature)**

      a. The southern part is cooler.

      b. _____ (The coldest area is in the Australian Alps.)

      c. _____ (Cities are on the coast.)

  D. _____ **(Australia's Animals and Birds)**

    1. _____ (Unique Creatures)

      a. The kangaroo is unlike any European animal.

      b. _____ (Gliders are sometimes called "flying possums.")

      c. _____ (Koalas look like bears, but are not bears.)

    2. Egg-layers

      a. The duckbill platypus has webbed feet.

      b. _____ (The echidna is a spiny anteater.)

      c. _____ (The emu is a flightless bird.)

      d. _____ (The kookaburra is also called "the laughing jackass.")

The above activity can be done with students working in groups or individually. Students may feel less threatened by filling in the blanks than they would if they were told to develop an outline of Chapter 22.

Unit Test

CONTENT TEST

Directions: Fill in the circle next to the correct answer.

1. What is Australia's bush?
   - (A) sparsely settled land far from settlements ●
   - (B) the Great Barrier Reef
   - (C) a small shrub in Queensland
   - (D) land with small trees near the coasts

2. Which continent receives less precipitation than Australia?
   - (A) Africa
   - (B) Asia
   - (C) Antarctica ●
   - (D) North America

3. A platypus is a mammal that can _____.
   - (A) change color
   - (B) change shape
   - (C) fly
   - (D) lay eggs ●

4. Because the Australian interior is so dry, _____.
   - (A) aborigines must import their water
   - (B) it is a popular tourist attraction
   - (C) it has no large cities ●
   - (D) crocodiles live in sand

5. What are typhoons?
   - (A) hurricanes in the Pacific ●
   - (B) Polynesian business leaders
   - (C) spears used to kill whales
   - (D) coral atolls

6. Mount Cook is the highest peak in _____.
   - (A) Australia
   - (B) New Zealand ●
   - (C) Tasmania
   - (D) Polynesia

7. Much of the Hot-Water Belt gets its heat from _____.
   - (A) hydroelectric power
   - (B) geothermal energy ●
   - (C) petroleum
   - (D) coal-fired water heaters

8. Which of the following is an important product in New Zealand?
   - (A) buttons
   - (B) sheep ●
   - (C) umbrellas
   - (D) porcupine quills

9. The Pacific islands in the tropics can be divided into three groups: Polynesia, Micronesia, and _____.
   - (A) Indonesia
   - (B) Melanesia ●
   - (C) Fantasia
   - (D) Amnesia

10. Abel Tasman is remembered for _____.
    - (A) building and governing the nation of Tasmania
    - (B) bringing hundreds of English convicts to Australia
    - (C) inventing the tassel
    - (D) exploring New Zealand ●

CONTENT TEST (continued)

11. Who landed on Australia's southeast coast and named the place New South Wales?
    - (A) Captain James Cook ●
    - (B) Admiral Matthew Flinders
    - (C) Lieutenant Dick Roughsey
    - (D) Captain James Kirk

12. Why did the first European settlers come to Australia?
    - (A) to bring Christianity to Aborigines
    - (B) to find religious freedom
    - (C) as a punishment ●
    - (D) to hunt for gold

13. Which of the following is an Australian state?
    - (A) Victoria ●
    - (B) Brisbane
    - (C) New Zealand
    - (D) Wales

14. What is the national capital of Australia?
    - (A) Canberra ●
    - (B) Sydney
    - (C) New South Wales
    - (D) Brisbane

15. Who were the first people to settle on New Zealand?
    - (A) English
    - (B) Maoris ●
    - (C) Dutch
    - (D) Native Zealanders

16. To drive birds from the forest, the Maoris _____.
    - (A) made loud noises
    - (B) removed all leaves from the trees
    - (C) made large scarecrows
    - (D) started forest fires ●

17. Who or what is the symbolic head of New Zealand's national government?
    - (A) the sheep
    - (B) Queen Elizabeth II ●
    - (C) Chief Kupe
    - (D) the kiwi

18. Which country took control of Tahiti in the nineteenth century?
    - (A) Britain
    - (B) France ●
    - (C) Spain
    - (D) Japan

19. Which country took control of eastern Samoa?
    - (A) France
    - (B) the Soviet Union
    - (C) Germany
    - (D) the United States ●

20. Nauru is an island country that is a source of _____.
    - (A) low-calorie sweetener
    - (B) high-grade phosphate ●
    - (C) soft-shelled coconuts
    - (D) high-octane gasoline

SKILLS TEST

Directions: Read this section of a textbook and complete items 1–5. Fill in the circle next to the correct answer.

> The Aborigines of Australia did not farm the land, but they were skilled food gatherers. They knew where to find fruits, berries, birds' eggs, nuts, and grass seeds. They also gathered shellfish, crabs, and insects that were fit to eat.
>
> The Aborigines hunted as well as gathered their food. They made weapons from sticks, stones, shells, and bones. They hunted with spears and boomerangs. The boomerangs they used for hunting were flat, curved sticks that returned to the thrower.
>
> In places where there were no streams or ponds, the Aborigines were able to get moisture from the roots of certain plants. They could cut the bark of the paperbark trees and draw as much as two cups of water in ten minutes.
>
> The search for food kept the Aborigines on the move. They did not build permanent houses. Instead they made shelters of sticks, grass, and bark, which they left behind as they moved from place to place.

1. The best way for you to summarize each paragraph would be to write down the _____.
   - (A) details
   - (B) main idea ●
   - (C) paragraph
   - (D) last sentence

2. Which sentence belongs in a summary of this textbook section?
   - (A) Boomerangs are curved sticks.
   - (B) Aborigines ate grass.
   - (C) The Aborigines got water from streams, ponds, or roots. ●
   - (D) The life of an Aborigine must have been exciting.

3. The best title for a summary of this textbook section would be _____.
   - (A) An Aborigine Adventure
   - (B) Aborigine Hunting Methods
   - (C) Australia's Natural Resources
   - (D) How the Aborigines Lived ●

4. Which sentence best summarizes the first paragraph?
   - (A) The Aborigines were not farmers.
   - (B) Some insects make delicious food.
   - (C) The Aborigines gathered food from the land. ●
   - (D) The Aborigines picked nuts and berries.

5. Which sentence best summarizes the second paragraph?
   - (A) The Aborigines made spears.
   - (B) The Aborigines hunted for food. ●
   - (C) The Aborigines used shells to make weapons.
   - (D) The Aborigines' boomerangs returned to the thrower.

SKILLS TEST (continued)

Directions: Read the paragraphs from James Cooks's journal and complete items 6–10. Fill in the circle next to the correct answer.

> The natives of this country are of middle stature, straight bodied, and slender limbed. Their skins are the color of wood soot or of dark chocolate, their hair mostly black. . . .
>
> I do not look upon them to be a warlike people. On the contrary, I think them a timorous (shy) and inoffensive race, no way inclined to cruelty. . . . Neither are they numerous. They live in small parties along by the sea coast, the banks of lakes, rivers, and creeks. They seem to have no fixed habitations, but move about from place to place like wild beasts in search of food, and I believe depend wholly upon the success of the present day for their subsistence (livelihood).
>
> From what I have said of the natives of New Holland, they may appear to some to be the most wretched people on earth, but in reality they are far happier than we Europeans. Being wholly unacquainted not only with the unnecessary but the necessary conveniences so much sought after in Europe, they are happy in not knowing the use of them. They live in a tranquillity (peacefulness) which is not disturbed by the inequality of condition. The earth and the sea of their own accord furnish them with all things necessary for life. . . . In short, they seemed to set no value upon any thing we give them, nor would they ever part with any things of their own for any one article we could offer them.

6. From whose point of view are the Aborigines being described?
   - (A) an ancestor of the Aborigines
   - (B) a newspaper reporter in 1770
   - (C) an explorer who observed the Aborigines ●
   - (D) an archaeologist who studied Aborigine artifacts

7. In Cook's description of the Aborigines' way of life, he expresses an attitude of _____.
   - (A) amusement
   - (B) disgust
   - (C) sympathy
   - (D) admiration ●

8. Cook felt that the Aborigines were _____.
   - (A) warlike
   - (B) mysterious
   - (C) peaceful ●
   - (D) artistic

9. What is Cook's point of view on the modern conveniences of his day?
   - (A) They were all unnecessary.
   - (B) They were destroying the environment.
   - (C) They did not bring happiness. ●
   - (D) Everyone should have them.

10. Which sentence states an opinion about the Aborigines?
    - (A) They were happier than Europeans. ●
    - (B) Their hair was mostly black.
    - (C) They were few in number.
    - (D) They lived in small groups.

NAME _____ U N I T **7**

ESSAY TEST

Directions: Write a response to items 1–4.

> **REMINDER:** Read and think about each item before you write your response. Be sure to think of the points you want to cover, details that support your response, and reasons for your opinions. Then, on the lines below, write your response in complete sentences.

1. Explain how atolls are formed from coral reefs.

A satisfactory response should include the following statements:

- Coral reefs form ridges in shallow water.
- Reefs often build up slowly along the edges of volcanic islands.
- When pressures under the ocean floor cause shifts on the surface, the centers of some islands sank and the surrounding reefs were thrust up, creating atolls.

An excellent response might also include

- an explanation of how coral is formed from the skeletons of sea creatures
- examples of coral islands, such as Bikini.

_____

2. What type of climate is found in the Pacific Islands?

A satisfactory response should include the following statements:

- There is no winter in the Pacific Islands; they are warm and humid throughout the year.
- Rain falls throughout the year, but it usually comes in short, heavy showers.
- Although the temperature is warm, ocean breezes make the air comfortable.

An excellent response might also

- provide specific examples
- cite specific average temperatures
- mention typhoons.

_____

NAME _____ UNIT 7

ESSAY TEST (continued)

3. How did the European settlement of Australia affect the lives of Aborigines?

A satisfactory response should include the following statements:

- The Europeans changed the continent and made life difficult for the Aborigines.
- Settlers turned sheep and cattle loose on the grasslands.
- The settlers moved onto lands occupied by Aborigines.
- Europeans brought diseases such as smallpox that killed large parts of the Aboriginal population.
- When arguments broke out between the two populations, the Europeans used their guns.

An excellent response might also

- include specific examples and analogies
- mention that today most Aborigines live in urban areas.

_____

4. Why was raising sheep a profitable way of using land for early settlers in Australia?

A satisfactory response should include the following statements:

- Early settlers discovered that there were few predatory animals in Australia.
- Herding required fewer laborers than farming did.
- Before the development of refrigeration, it was much easier to ship wool than to ship food products.

An excellent response might also explain that Australia

- still supplies 30 percent of the world's wool
- is the second largest exporter of mutton.

_____

Year-End Test

CONTENT TEST

Directions: Fill in the circle next to the correct answer.

1. In 1989, what event allowed many East Germans to visit West Germany for the first time?
   - (A) the opening of the German Autobahn
   - (B) the opening of the Berlin Wall
   - (C) the election of Chancellor Willy Feldheim
   - (D) the Bedouin revolution

2. Who are the Bedouins?
   - (A) desert nomads
   - (B) German anti-communists
   - (C) Polish labor-union members
   - (D) Lebanese terrorists

3. What type of government does Iran have?
   - (A) an Islamic republic
   - (B) a terrorist government
   - (C) a limited monarchy
   - (D) an oil-producing dictatorship

4. The Suez Canal connects the Red Sea with the _____.
   - (A) Dead Sea
   - (B) Mediterranean Sea
   - (C) Persian Gulf
   - (D) Gulf of Suez

5. The Islamic faith was founded by the prophet _____.
   - (A) Koran
   - (B) Suleiman
   - (C) Hegira
   - (D) Muhammad

6. During the Crusades, European knights and lords tried to capture Jerusalem from the _____.
   - (A) Muslims
   - (B) Jews
   - (C) Christians
   - (D) pope

7. To increase the amount of arable land in the Middle East, many countries have _____.
   - (A) drilled for oil and natural gas
   - (B) revived the Dead Sea
   - (C) imported moist earth
   - (D) built irrigation systems

8. The area that lies between Africa's desert and savanna is called the _____.
   - (A) bush
   - (B) Great Divide
   - (C) jungle
   - (D) Sahel

9. Central Africa is unsuitable for raising cattle because of the danger from the _____.
   - (A) lion
   - (B) wildebeest
   - (C) wild jackal
   - (D) tsetse fly

10. Winds that change direction with the seasons are called _____.
    - (A) winds of change
    - (B) gusts
    - (C) squalls
    - (D) monsoons

CONTENT TEST (continued)

11. The South African system of apartheid separated races in order to _____.
    - (A) conserve Africa's dwindling resources
    - (B) give freedom and justice to all citizens
    - (C) improve the living conditions of workers
    - (D) keep the white minority in power

12. Mohandas K. Gandhi is remembered for _____.
    - (A) partitioning Indian Muslims in Pakistan
    - (B) being the father of Mahatma and Indira Gandhi
    - (C) leading India's struggle for independence
    - (D) fighting a war against British imperialists

13. Where is the Deccan plateau?
    - (A) Mecca
    - (B) India
    - (C) Tanganyika
    - (D) Kukamonga

14. China's Yellow River is called the _____.
    - (A) Hsien-yang
    - (B) Huang He
    - (C) Chung Ming Woo
    - (D) Chiang Kai-shek

15. Babur was the leader of the _____.
    - (A) Mongol invasion of China
    - (B) Mogul invasion of the subcontinent
    - (C) British invasion of Burma
    - (D) Chinese Communists

16. Who led China's Communist revolution?
    - (A) Deng Xiaoping
    - (B) Chiang Kai-shek
    - (C) Babur
    - (D) Mao Ze-dong

17. In 1997 Hong Kong will _____.
    - (A) gain its independence
    - (B) become part of China
    - (C) surpass China in population
    - (D) host the Olympic games

18. Kenya established game parks to _____.
    - (A) provide a hunting ground for sportsmen
    - (B) protect birds and animals
    - (C) attract European and Asian tourists
    - (D) hold the upcoming Olympic games

19. Which of the following is a series of mountains in Australia?
    - (A) the Great Dividing Range
    - (B) the Great Barrier Reef
    - (C) the Mountains of the Bush
    - (D) the Tasmanian Rockies

20. Why did the first English settlers come to Australia?
    - (A) They were seeking religious freedom.
    - (B) They wanted to teach Christinaity to the Aborigines.
    - (C) They were convicts sent as punishment.
    - (D) They were seeking a shorter route to Asia.

ESSAY TEST

Directions: Write a response to items 1–4.

> **REMINDER:** Read and think about each item before you write your response. Be sure to think of the points you want to cover, details that support your response, and reasons for your opinions. Then, on the lines below, write your response in complete sentences.

1. Who was Muhammad?

   A satisfactory response should identify Muhammad as the prophet and founder of Islam, and it should provide some specific details about his life or about Islam.

   An excellent response might also

   - include the terms *Koran, Mecca, Allah,* and *Hegira*
   - identify geographic locations on the Arabian Peninsula
   - describe Muhammad's journey from Mecca to Medina
   - provide examples of Muhammad's teachings.

2. What was Britain's role in the creation of Israel?

   A satisfactory response will include the following statements:

   - Rather than giving Palestine its independence, Britain took control of the country from the Ottoman Empire after World War I.
   - The British supported the idea of creating a national home for Jewish people in Palestine and encouraged Jews to settle there.
   - After World War II, thousands of Jews came to Palestine from Europe, which caused a conflict with Arab residents.
   - Britain turned the matter over to the United Nations, which called for the creation of separate Jewish and Arab states.

   An excellent response might also

   - discuss the resulting conflicts between Israel and its Arab neighbors
   - reflect independent thinking.

ESSAY TEST (continued)

3. How did monsoons affect trade between Africa and the Orient?

   A satisfactory response should include the following statements:

   - The monsoons provided steady winds for sailing ships.
   - During the summer, the winds blow from the southwest, allowing travel from Africa to India.
   - Winter winds blow from the northeast, allowing ships to return to Africa.

   An excellent response might also include

   - the phrase *path of wind*
   - an explanation of the influence that trade with the East had on Africa.

4. Discuss the creation of the People's Republic of China.

   A satisfactory response should include the following statements:

   - Japan controlled China during World War II.
   - After the defeat of Japan, a civil war broke out in China.
   - The Nationalists, who controlled the government, were defeated by the Communists.
   - The Communists took control of mainland China and renamed it the People's Republic; the Nationalists fled to the island of Taiwan.

   An excellent response might also

   - identify Mao Zedong and Chiang Kai-shek
   - provide examples of reforms and changes made by the Communists
   - reflect independent thinking.

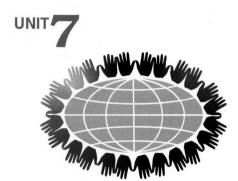

MULTICULTURAL PERSPECTIVES

Australia's First Inhabitants

(pages 573–574)

Much like Native Americans in the United States, the Aborigines of Australia have been displaced people in their own land. In response, the Department of Aboriginal Affairs was formed, based on much the same principles as the United States' Bureau of Indian Affairs.

Charles Nelson Perkins, an Aborigine born in Alice Springs, Australia, in 1936, became well known as a radical protester who championed the cause of Aboriginal equality during the 1960s. Aborigines were not legally recognized as Australian citizens until 1967.

Perkins was the first Aborigine to attend Sydney University. As head of the Department of Aboriginal Affairs from 1984 to 1989, he was the highest-ranking Aborigine in Australia. Perkins's vision of Australia would "incorporate Aboriginal culture into Australian culture—giving Australian culture a uniqueness that it has lacked."

Ask students to go to the library to research Aborigines. Have them find out about the Aboriginal belief that people are descendants of the soil. They should also look into other aspects of Aboriginal culture, such as Aboriginal contributions to medicine.

Ask students to compare the treatment of the Aborigines in Australia with that of Native Americans and African Americans in the United States.

Optional Activities

Unit 7

AUSTRALIA, NEW ZEALAND, AND THE PACIFIC ISLANDS

Australia, New Zealand, and the Pacific Islands make up a unique region, with a wealth of interesting peoples, animals, plants, and landforms.

▶ *Akaroa Harbor, which can be seen in the background, lies at the base of the lush hillsides of Banks Peninsula on New Zealand's South Island.*

Kiri Te Kanawa *(pages 579-581)*

Kiri Te Kanawa is one of the most acclaimed opera singers in the world. Her soprano voice has been described as warm and opulent.

Kiri Te Kanawa was born in Gisborne, on New Zealand's North Island, in 1944. Her father was a Maori, and her mother was of European origin. Shortly after her birth she was adopted by a New Zealand couple. Her adoptive father, a building contractor, was also a Maori. Her adoptive mother was of Irish descent. They named her *Kiri*, which means "bell" in Maori.

Kiri Te Kanawa exhibited vocal potential before she was three years old and was encouraged to sing, with her mother at the piano. In 1955 the Te Kanawas moved to Auckland, where Kiri became a student of a distinguished voice teacher. In 1966, Te Kanawa placed first in a prestigious competition in Australia. With the prize money, the funds she and her parents had saved, and a grant from the New Zealand Arts Council, Kiri Te Kanawa moved to London with her mother to continue her voice training.

Her first major operatic success came in 1971 at Covent Garden in London. In 1974 she made her debut with the Metropolitan Opera in New York City. The performance helped her to gain international recognition.

Proud of her mixed ancestry, Te Kanawa maintains contact with her homeland. Late in 1987, a reunion in New Zealand of all the Te Kanawas evoked in the singer such powerful memories of her childhood that she decided to share with children throughout the world the Maori myths and legends that she loved as a child. Two years later her book *Land of the Long White Cloud* was published.

Play for the class two recorded selections in which Kiri Te Kanawa is the soloist. Choose one selection from a musical such as *My Fair Lady* or a collection of folk songs such as *Come to the Fair*. Choose the second selection from a collection of classical works such as *French Opera Arias* or *Song Recital*. Discuss with students what the recordings reveal about Te Kanawa as an artist.

Source
Fingleton, David. *Kiri Te Kanawa: A Biography*. New York: Atheneum-Macmillan, 1983.

Optional Activities

571

Geography of Australia, New Zealand, and the Pacific Islands

(pp. 572-587)

Chapter Theme: Australia, New Zealand, and the Pacific Islands have a variety of geographical features.

LESSON 1 **Australia**

(pp. 572-578)

Theme: Australia is the world's smallest continent, and it has flat land, mountains, a huge coral reef, the world's largest monolith, a dry climate, and some very unusual wildlife.

LESSON 2 **New Zealand**

(pp. 579-581)

Theme: New Zealand is a hilly and mountainous land with a temperate climate, hot-water springs, and many unusual animals and birds.

LESSON 3 **The Pacific Islands**

(pp. 582-585)

Theme: The Pacific Islands were formed by volcanoes and coral reefs and have a temperate climate and lush vegetation.

 SOCIAL STUDIES LIBRARY: *Lost Star: The Story of Amelia Earhart*

Review Masters

REVIEWING CHAPTER VOCABULARY

Review Study the terms in the box. Use your Glossary to find
definitions of those you do not remember.

Aborigine	bush	geothermal	monolith
atoll	coral reef	energy	temperate
			climate

Practice Complete the paragraphs using terms from the box above.
You may change the forms of the terms to fit the meaning.

Australia's varied landscape and its unusual wildlife attract many visitors each year.

Most visitors travel through part of Australia's mostly uninhabited (1) __bush__
region, where they may be lucky enough to see kangaroos, gliders, and koalas in their
natural environments. Other visitors come to see the fascinating undersea life of the

(2) __coral reef__ along Australia's eastern coast. After leaving Australia, some

people may travel to Micronesia. Here, they can visit (3) __atolls__, also formed
by tiny sea creatures.

Those who prefer cooler weather may prefer to visit New Zealand. The

(4) __temperate climate__ of these islands provides pleasant weather most of the year.
Visitors come to New Zealand in both the winter and the summer. Winter temperatures
are cold enough to attract skiers to the high peaks of the northern island. In the Hot-
Water Belt, the temperatures are cold enough for people to need the

(5) __geothermal energy__ that is used to heat houses.

Write Write a sentence of your own for each term in the box above.
You may use the back of the sheet.

Sentences should show that students understand the meanings of the terms.

_____

_____

_____

_____

_____

_____

_____

_____

LOCATING PLACES

✱ Although New Zealand and Australia are neighbors, they are not close.
About 1,200 miles (1,931 km) of ocean lies between the two countries.
Listed below are places in each country. Use the Gazetteer in your textbook
to find the latitude and longitude of each place. Then locate and label each
on the map.

	LAT.	LONG.			LAT.	LONG.
1. Perth, Australia	32°S	116°E	6. Ayers Rock, Australia		25°S	131°E
2. Sydney, Australia	34°S	151°E	7. Canberra, Australia		35°S	149°E
3. Melbourne, Australia	38°S	145°E	8. Auckland, New Zealand		37°S	174°E
4. Brisbane, Australia	28°S	153°E	9. Wellington, New Zealand		41°S	175°E
5. Adelaide, Australia	35°S	139°E	10. Christchurch, New Zealand		44°S	173°E

SUMMARIZING THE CHAPTER

✱ Complete this graphic organizer. Under the main idea for each
lesson, write four statements that support the main idea.

CHAPTER THEME

Australia, New Zealand, and the Pacific Islands
have a variety of geographical features.

LESSON 1
**Australia is a land of
varied geographical
features and animals.**

1. Kangaroo

2. Duckbill platypus

3. Ayers Rock

4. Great Barrier Reef

LESSON 2
**New Zealand is a
land of varied
geographical
features and
animals.**

1. Hot-Water belt

2. Hilly and mountainous

3. Moa

4. Kiwi

LESSON 3
**The Pacific Islands
share a similar
climate with one
another.**

1. Volcanoes

2. Atolls

3. Tropical

4. Typhoons

C22-B

Workbook Pages

Page 121 — The Great Barrier Reef

THE GREAT BARRIER REEF

Understanding Stated Facts and Details, Hypothesizing

✳ Read the following paragraphs about Australia's Great Barrier Reef. Then answer the questions based on the passage.

The Great Barrier Reef lies off the northeast coast of Australia. It is a series of coral islands, reefs, and shoals that extend for about 1,250 miles (2,000 km). The reef is made up of billions of live corals and shells of dead corals. Scientists believe that the Great Barrier Reef began forming millions of years ago during the Ice Age.

The Aborigines were the reef's earliest human inhabitants. Many of them moved to the Australian continent when a rising ocean covered their homes on the reef. Pictures painted on the walls of caves and rocks, many of them now under water, were drawn by Aborigines thousands of years ago.

The reef was first explored and charted by Captain James Cook in 1770. His ship, the *Endeavor*, ran aground on the reef. Cook navigated his way out of the reef by discovering a channel of deeper water. This channel was named Cook's Passage. It is still used today.

The Great Barrier Reef is a big tourist attraction. At high tide, it is 90 percent under water. At low tide, people can walk on the reef and observe the plant and animal life. Some people scuba dive or fish. More species of plant and animal life live on the reef than almost anywhere else in the world.

Unfortunately, the reef is now threatened. Sewage and pesticides from coastal cities and farms are released into the reef area. Companies have come to explore for oil. To help prevent further damage to the reef, the Australian government passed the Great Barrier Marine Park Act, in 1975, to protect life on the reef.

1. What are the islands and reefs of the Great Barrier Reef made of? _living corals and shells of dead corals_

2. When did the reef begin forming? _millions of years ago, during the Ice Age_

3. How do we know about the reef's first inhabitants? _The Aborigines painted pictures on the walls of caves and rocks on the reef._

4. Why is Captain Cook important to the history of the reef? _He was the first to explore and chart the reef; he discovered Cook's Passage._

5. What do people enjoy doing on the reef? _walking at low tide, fishing, scuba diving_

6. How is the reef being threatened today? _It is threatened by pollution from pesticides and sewage, and by oil drilling._

Thinking Further: Why is it important to preserve a natural feature like the Great Barrier Reef and protect its wildlife? Use a separate sheet. _Answers may mention recreation and plant, animal, and marine life, or may point out that natural features may take millions of years to form but can be destroyed in only a few years._

Chapter 22, pages 573–578   121

Page 122 — Changes in New Zealand's Trade

CHANGES IN NEW ZEALAND'S TRADE

Examining Relevant Information, Defending a Choice

✳ The pie graphs below show New Zealand's main trading partners in 1984 and 1988. Use the information for 1988 to complete the 1988 graph; then answer the questions that follow.

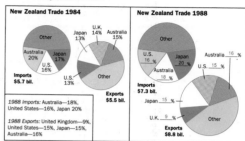

New Zealand Trade 1984 — Imports $5.7 bil., Exports $5.5 bil.

New Zealand Trade 1988 — Imports $7.3 bil., Exports $8.8 bil.

1988 Imports: Australia—18%, United States—16%, Japan 20%

1988 Exports: United Kingdom—9%, United States—15%, Japan—15%, Australia—16%

1. How did the total value of imports and exports change from 1984 to 1988? _Both imports and exports increased._

2. Did imports or exports show a greater increase? _Exports showed a greater increase._

3. How did New Zealand's import partners change during the period shown? _Japan replaced Australia as New Zealand's most important import partner._

4. How did export partners change? _New Zealand exported more to the United States than to the United Kingdom in 1988. Exports to Japan and Australia increased slightly by 1988._

5. How did New Zealand's imports from the United States change during the four-year period? _The percentage of imports remained the same._

6. How did New Zealand's exports to the United States change? _The percentage of goods exported to the United States increased slightly._

Thinking Further: Based on the information above, do you think New Zealand's trade with the United States changed greatly between 1988 and 1992? Explain your answer. Use a separate sheet. _Answers may suggest little change in export and import trade between the United States and New Zealand. A stable pattern of trade has been established, and the distance between the two countries is so great that rapid change is not likely._

122   Chapter 22, pages 579–581

© Silver, Burdett & Ginn Inc.

Page 123 — Wildlife of Australia and New Zealand

WILDLIFE OF AUSTRALIA AND NEW ZEALAND

Using Context Clues, Classifying Information

✳ The statements below describe some of the many interesting birds and animals that live in Australia and New Zealand.
a. Write the name of the correct bird or animal in the blank next to each description.
b. Place each name on the correct line in the puzzle below. Use the length of the names and the letters given on the puzzle as clues.

1. This marsupial has short front legs and large back legs. _KANGAROO_
2. This egg-laying animal has a bill like a duck. _PLATYPUS_
3. Like the ostrich, this large bird can run fast but cannot fly. _EMU_
4. This furry, tree-dwelling animal looks like—but is not—a bear. _KOALA_
5. This noisy bird is nicknamed the "laughing jackass." _KOOKABURRA_
6. This egg-laying animal is also known as the "spiny anteater." _ECHIDNA_
7. This large New Zealand bird is now extinct. _MOA_
8. This animal is also known as the "flying possum." _GLIDER_
9. This small flightless bird is New Zealand's national symbol. _KIWI_

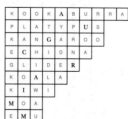

K O O K **A** B U R R **A**
P L A T Y **P** U S
K A N G **A** R O O
E C H I D N A
G L I D E **R**
K O **A** L A
K I W I
M O A
E M U

Thinking Further: Why do you think Australia and New Zealand have so many birds and animals that appear nowhere else on the earth? _Answers may mention Australia's and New Zealand's distance from other land areas and the difficulty of animal migration from Australia and New Zealand to other places._

© Silver, Burdett & Ginn Inc.

Chapter 22, pages 573–581   123

Page 124 — Geography of the Pacific Islands

GEOGRAPHY OF THE PACIFIC ISLANDS

Understanding Main Ideas, Analyzing Information

✳ Complete the sentences below to decode a message about the origin of the South Pacific Islands.
a. Complete each sentence by choosing the correct word from the word box. Write one letter of the word in each blank.
b. Use the numbered letters to decode the message. Some letters have been given.

> TROPICAL   MELANESIA   ATOLLS
> TYPHOON   NEW GUINEA
> POLYNESIA   DATELINE   MICRONESIA

1. M I C R O N E S I A means "small islands."
2. The climate of the Pacific Islands is T R O P I C A L.
3. Ringlike islands formed by coral are called A T O L L S.
4. In the Pacific a hurricane is called a T Y P H O O N.
5. P O L Y N E S I A means "many islands."
6. The 180° meridian is called the International D A T E L I N E.
7. N E W   G U I N E A is the largest of the Pacific Islands.
8. M E L A N E S I A means "black islands."

M O S T   I S L A N D S   W E R E
F O R M E D   B Y   V O L C A N O E S
O R   C O R A L   R E E F S

Thinking Further: Why do you think the Pacific Islands have been called the "lands of endless summer?" _Students may mention that the islands have a tropical climate. High and low temperatures are generally the same all year. There are no freezing temperatures._

124   Chapter 22, pages 582–585

© Silver, Burdett & Ginn Inc.

Australia

Objectives

★ **1. Describe** the physical characteristics of Australia.

2. Identify the first inhabitants of Australia.

3. Identify the following people and places: *Elsie Roughsey, Australia, Great Dividing Range, Mount Kosciusko, Ayers Rock,* and *Great Barrier Reef.*

1 STARTING THE LESSON

Motivation Activity

■ Play a recording of the song "Kookaburra," which can be found in Silver Burdett & Ginn's *World of Music* (grade 4).

■ Write the words of the song on the chalkboard. Underline the words *kookaburra, gum tree,* and *bush.*

■ Ask students to discuss the meaning of the song and the underlined words. Then, explain that in this lesson they will learn about the kookaburra's world, the continent of Australia.

Think About What You Know

■ Assign the THINK ABOUT WHAT YOU KNOW activity on p. 573.

■ Answers may include that it has kangaroos, koala bears, and nice beaches.

Study the Vocabulary

■ Have students look up the definitions of the vocabulary words in the Glossary.

■ Ask students to make a prediction about the subject of this lesson, based on the vocabulary words. (The geography and original inhabitants of Australia)

■ After students have read the lesson, have them check to see whether their predictions were accurate.

CHAPTER

22

GEOGRAPHY OF AUSTRALIA, NEW ZEALAND, AND PACIFIC ISLANDS

*S*cattered across the Pacific Ocean are thousands of islands. They range in size from the continent of Australia to tiny islands so small that no one has ever lived on them. Mount Kosciusko is the tallest peak in the Australian Alps.

572

Optional Activities

Comparing Native Peoples

● Have students write reports that compare the past and present of Australian Aborigines with that of Native Americans.

● Suggest that students narrow their comparison to one Native American tribe or group of related tribes.

● Some students might prefer to research and compare myths of the Native Americans and Australian Aborigines.

● Others might create a visual display of native arts and crafts of America and Australia.

THINK ABOUT WHAT YOU KNOW
Suppose that you are going to take a vacation in Australia. What do you know about Australia that will make your visit there particularly interesting?

STUDY THE VOCABULARY
Aborigine   **monolith**
bush   **coral reef**

FOCUS YOUR READING
What are the characteristics of the Australian continent?

A. Australia's First Inhabitants

Bush Life   The **Aborigines** (ab uh RIHJ uhneez) are the earliest known inhabitants of Australia. They have lived on the continent for thousands of years. Today, however, Aborigines make up only a small part of Australia's population. White Australians form the large majority. Their ancestors started arriving in Australia from Europe 200 years ago.

Elsie Roughsey is an Aborigine. She was born in 1923 on Mornington Island, off the northern coast of Australia. As a child, Elsie lived with her family in the **bush**, which is what Australians call sparsely settled land far from any settlement. Elsie remembers these early years as a happy period, when her people spent their time "hunting, dancing, gathering for tribal meetings, [and] gathering together for great feasts."

New Ways   When Elsie was eight years old, she went to a school run by Christian missionaries. She lived with other students in a building called a dormitory. She learned English and worked in the school garden. At first, Elsie hated school and living in a dormitory. She particularly disliked working in the garden. She thought it was far better to gather food in the bush, as her people had always done.

Later, Elsie changed her mind about school, at least partly. She grew to like life in the dormitory. She became a good runner and won prizes on school sport days. She never, however, learned to like working in the garden.

The mission school closed during World War II, and Elsie, who was then 18, returned to her family. She now found life in the bush hard. When the school reopened after the war, Elsie went back to work there as a teacher's aide. Elsie married a carpenter at the mission named Dick Roughsey. Dick was a skilled craftsperson who carved wood and painted pictures on bark in the Aboriginal fashion.

Although most Aborigines have adopted modern ways, some groups have kept their traditional culture.
▶ Why, do you think, is this Aborigine wearing paint?

2 DEVELOPING THE LESSON

Read and Think
Section A

European settlers in Australia, like those who went to North America, found people already living there. Discuss the life of Elsie Roughsey, an Australian Aborigine, using the questions that follow:

1. **Compare the ways that white Australians and Aborigines learn about their ancestors.**
   (White Australians read about their ancestors, while Aborigines orally pass down knowledge about their ancestors. *p. 574*)

2. **Why did Elsie Roughsey write a book?**
   (She wanted to preserve the customs of her people. *p. 574*)

   Thinking Critically   How do you think Elsie Roughsey's book might help Aborigines? (Infer)
   (Answers might include that descriptions of their culture would preserve the Aborigines' pride and might help white Australians understand and respect them. *pp. 573–574*)

   ┌─ **Answers to Caption Questions** ─┐
   p. 573 ▶ Some type of tribal tradition

For Your Information

Australia's Aborigines   There are about 50,000 fullblooded Aborigines and about 150,000 people who are part Aborigine in Australia today. Most are detribalized, but there are several preserves in the Northern Territory. Approximately 130,000 people speak what are known as Australian languages. It is estimated that there are between 100 and 600 Australian languages; many of these are already or nearly extinct. None of these languages appears related to any other linguistic group, and none has a writing system of its own. Although racially discriminatory immigration policies officially ended in 1973, most Aborigines are economically disadvantaged.

Optional Activities

GEOGRAPHY THEMES

Location

■ Direct students' attention to the physical map of Australia to help them answer the following questions:

1. **Where is the Simpson Desert located?**
   (In the central part of Australia)

2. **Name the oceans that surround Australia.**
   (The Indian Ocean and the Pacific Ocean)

3. **Where is the island of Tasmania located?**
   (Off the southeastern coast of Australia)

4. **Which is farther east, the Great Artesian Basin or the Gibson Desert?**
   (The Great Artesian Basin)

5. **On what coast is the Great Dividing Range located?**
   (On the east coast)

Valuable Knowledge At the mission and in the cities that she and Dick visited, Elsie learned much about the ways of the white Australians. But she continued to respect the ways of her own people. She worried because the young Aborigines knew so little about their ancestors.

White Australians, Elsie knew, learned of their European ancestors through books that made "a history of the adventures of great men of the past [and] scenes of the past." Elsie's own people, however, did not pass on their knowledge in that way. Instead, she observed, they "sit in circles around the bush or camps and yarn about which is the right way to keep all their laws, customs, and legends and cultures." Since children rarely lived in the bush as she had done, they had little chance to learn about the "men and women of rich wisdom" among the Aborigines. To prevent all knowledge of her people from being lost, Elsie wrote a book about "some of the customs [that] were finally ruined and forgotten by [the Aborigines] when the white men came."

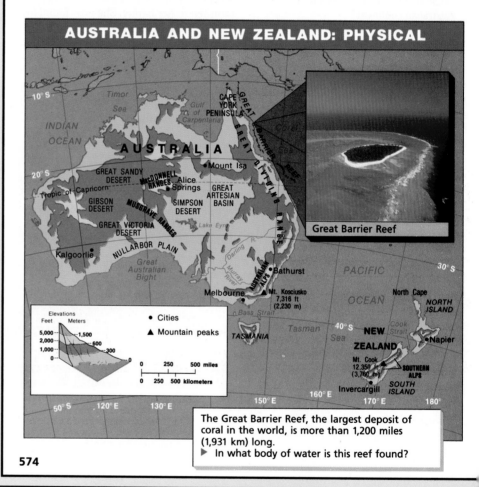

AUSTRALIA AND NEW ZEALAND: PHYSICAL

Great Barrier Reef

The Great Barrier Reef, the largest deposit of coral in the world, is more than 1,200 miles (1,931 km) long.
▶ In what body of water is this reef found?

574

Optional Activities

Writing to Learn

Inventing a Myth Ask students to look at the picture of Ayers Rock on p. 575.

● Have them make up stories about how the rock was formed, or about magical properties that it has, or about events that might have occurred near the rock.

● Ask students to read their stories aloud.

● You may wish to find a "real" myth or legend about the rock that is told by the Aborigines. Read it to students after they have finished writing and reading their stories.

Predicting Outcomes

● Ask students to brainstorm a list of the advantages and disadvantages of living in a country that is an island and write their suggestions on the chalkboard.

● Advantages may include the unlikelihood of being attacked by another country. Disadvantages may include having to import many products.

● Then, organize students into small groups of three or four. Ask them to discuss the item from each column that they consider most important.

● Have students write brief essays predicting areas in which they would expect Australia to be especially successful and areas that would challenge the nation.

Ayers Rock runs about 1 1/2 miles (2 km) long and rises to a height of 1,143 feet (348 m). It also has numerous small caves, many of which Aborigines covered with rock paintings long ago.
► Why, do you think, is Ayers Rock such a popular tourist attraction?

B. The World's Smallest Continent

Flat Land Australia, the land where Elsie Roughsey lives, is located south of the Equator, in the Southern Hemisphere. It is the smallest of the seven continents. It is about the size of the United States without Alaska and Hawaii. The distance from east to west across Australia is almost the same as the distance between the Atlantic and Pacific coasts of the United States. Australia has coasts on the Indian and the Pacific oceans.

Australia is also the flattest of the continents, although there are some mountains. The Great Dividing Range runs along the eastern and southeastern edges of the continent. Since this range rises from a coastal plain, it appears high and rugged. Part of the Great Dividing Range is

even called the Australian Alps. But Mount Kosciusko (kahs ee US koh), the tallest peak, is less than half as high as the Alpine peaks in Europe.

Unusual Features Perhaps the most famous feature of Australia's landscape is Ayers Rock. Ayers Rock is a large mass of stone that rises 1,143 feet (348 m) above the desert in the center of the continent. It is said to be the world's largest **monolith**, or single stone. Ayers Rock is a sacred place for the Aborigines.

The Great Barrier Reef, the largest **coral reef** in the world, stretches more than 1,250 miles (2,011 km) along Australia's eastern coast. A coral reef is a ridge built up in shallow ocean water by the skeletons of countless tiny sea creatures.

575

For Your Information

History and Government of Australia Australia attracted little interest from Europeans until Captain James Cook sailed into Botany Bay, named for its unusual plants. Eventually, Great Britain claimed the entire continent. At first, it served as a penal colony for British convicts. The first shipment of "transported" convicts arrived in 1788. By about 1850, voluntary colonization had begun, and gold rushes in 1851 and 1892 attracted more settlers. In 1901 the Commonwealth of Australia was formed, but Australia has remained a close ally of Britain. Australia has a popularly elected parliament with two houses, a prime minister and cabinet, and a governor general who represents the British monarch.

Optional Activities

Read and Think

Section B

Use the questions below to discuss the land features of Australia:

1. **What are some of Australia's most notable landforms?**
   (The Great Dividing Range, Mount Kosciusko, Ayers Rock, and the Great Barrier Reef *p. 575*)

2. **On which oceans does Australia have coasts?**
   (The Indian and the Pacific oceans *p. 575*)

3. **Why is part of the Great Dividing Range called the Australian Alps?**
   (Because the mountains appear high and rugged *p. 575*)

Thinking Critically If you had to choose one, which of Australia's land features would you like to visit? (Analyze)
(Answers may include Mount Kosciusko, because it is the highest peak in Australia; Ayers Rock, because it is the world's largest monolith; or the Great Barrier Reef, because it is the world's largest coral reef. *p. 575*)

VISUAL THINKING SKILL

Interpreting a Picture

■ Direct students' attention to the picture on p. 575 to help them answer the following question: **Would you like to visit Ayers Rock?**
(Answers should reflect independent thinking but may include yes, because it is so large, famous, and unusual, or no, because it is just a rock.)

— **Answers to Caption Questions** —
p. 574 ► The Coral Sea
p. 575 ► Answers may include that it is popular because it is so large and unusual.

575

Read and Think

Section C

Explain that only Antarctica is drier than Australia. Then ask the following questions to discuss Australia's climate:

1. **Why is the center of Australia thinly populated?**

   (Because it is very dry *p. 576*)

   Thinking Critically Which area of Australia is most similar to the area where you live? (Synthesize)

   (Answers will depend upon the area where your students live. *pp. 576-577*)

GEOGRAPHY THEMES

Human-Environment Interactions

■ Have students look at the population-density map on this page to answer the following question: **Other than a wetter climate, what might account for the population density on the east coast of Australia?**

(Answers may include harbors and the continent's likely dependence upon imported goods, which would lead to job opportunities; a mountain range blocks westward migration; and it is close to New Zealand.)

C. A Mostly Dry Continent

Precipitation Australia is the second driest continent. Only Antarctica receives less precipitation. Two thirds of Australia is either desert or too dry to support any vegetation but scattered plants and dryland grass.

The eastern and southeastern parts of the continent receive the most moisture, and it is there that most people live. The center of the continent is very dry and thinly populated. The northern coast has a tropical climate; the southwestern coast has a Mediterranean climate.

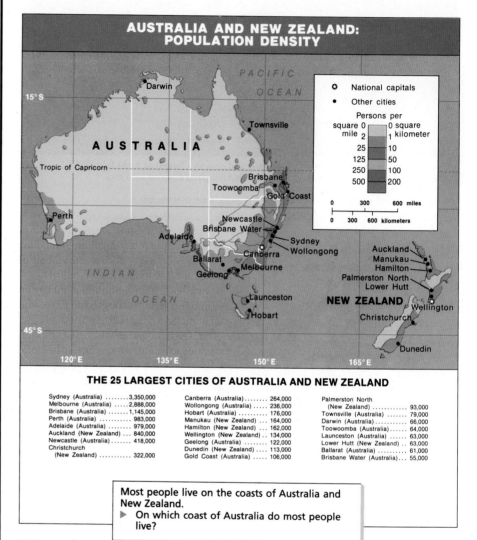

THE 25 LARGEST CITIES OF AUSTRALIA AND NEW ZEALAND

Sydney (Australia) 3,350,000	Canberra (Australia) 264,000	Palmerston North
Melbourne (Australia) 2,888,000	Wollongong (Australia) 236,000	(New Zealand) 93,000
Brisbane (Australia) 1,145,000	Hobart (Australia) 176,000	Townsville (Australia) 79,000
Perth (Australia) 983,000	Manukau (New Zealand) . . . 164,000	Darwin (Australia) 66,000
Adelaide (Australia) 979,000	Hamilton (New Zealand) . . . 162,000	Toowoomba (Australia) 64,000
Auckland (New Zealand) . . 840,000	Wellington (New Zealand) . . 134,000	Launceston (Australia) 63,000
Newcastle (Australia) 418,000	Geelong (Australia) 122,000	Lower Hutt (New Zealand) . . 63,000
Christchurch	Dunedin (New Zealand) 113,000	Ballarat (Australia) 61,000
(New Zealand) 322,000	Gold Coast (Australia) 106,000	Brisbane Water (Australia) . . . 55,000

Most people live on the coasts of Australia and New Zealand.

▶ On which coast of Australia do most people live?

Optional Activities

Curriculum Connection

Science Have a small group of students present oral reports on marsupials, or pouched mammals. These animals are found almost exclusively in Australia and New Guinea.

● Ask students to include photographs or drawings of different types of marsupials with their report.

● Suggest that students try to develop a "family tree" to show how marsupials fit into the class Mammalia.

Writing to Learn

Writing a Letter Ask students to imagine that they are Australian Aborigines visiting the United States for the first time.

● Ask them to think of something that they might see which would seem odd or strange (just as the kangaroo seemed to the European explorer).

● Have them write a letter home to Australia, describing some of the strange sights of the United States, using comparisons and examples that an Aborigine would understand.

Perth is the capital and business center of the state of Western Australia. Two of Perth's attractions are its warm, sunny climate and cultural center.
▶ What, do you think, is an important industry in Perth?

Read and Think
Section D

Use the questions below to discuss some of Australia's more intriguing animals:

1. **Why are there animals in Australia that are not found anywhere else?**
   (Because Australia is an island and is cut off from other continents *p. 577*)

2. **Why is the duckbilled platypus so unusual?**
   (Because it combines the characteristics of birds and mammals *pp. 577–578*)

   Thinking Critically **Why, do you think, might the animals of Australia be especially interesting to scientists?** (Infer)
   (Answers may include that these animals provide information about the ways that animals adapt to an environment. *pp. 577–578*)

Temperature Southern Australia has a cooler climate than northern Australia because it is farther from the Equator. But no part of the continent has a truly cold climate. The coldest areas are in the high elevations of the Australian Alps. One range within the Alps receives enough snow to be called the Snowy Mountains.

Climate has greatly affected the locations of Australia's cities. As you can see on the map on page 576, there are no large cities in the dry interior. The five largest cities are on the coastal rim. Four of the five are on the eastern and southeastern coasts. Perth, the fifth, is in the southwest.

D. Australia's Animals and Birds

Unique Creatures The animals and birds of Australia differ from those found elsewhere because Australia is an island and was cut off from the other six continents. One European explorer noted that the kangaroo "bears no sort of resemblance to any European animal I ever saw." Another European said of a large kangaroo, "It is as tall as a man with a head of a rabbit [and] a tail as big as a bed-post." Actually, not all kangaroos are nearly so large. There are more than 47 different kinds of kangaroos, some smaller than a rabbit.

A number of other Australian animals appeared strange to European eyes. There are gliders, sometimes called "flying possums," which have flaps of skin between their front and hind legs. When they spread their legs, they can glide for long distances between the tops of trees. The small, furry koalas (koh AH luhz) look like tiny bears, although they are not related to bears at all.

Egglayers The so-called duckbill platypus (PLAT ih pus) is one of Australia's most unusual animals. The nickname duckbill is given to the platypus because it

577

Reteaching Main Objective
Describe the physical characteristics of Australia.

● Divide students into eight groups and assign each group a state in Australia.

● Have each group locate its state on a map and create a poster that shows the state's climate, population, area, and any outstanding physical characteristics.

● Have students use almanacs, encyclopedias, and other reference sources to locate information about their state.

● Put the completed maps and posters together to create a giant wall display of Australia's characteristics.

Meeting Individual Needs
Concept
Understanding How Climate Affects Population Density

To better understand how the settlement of Australia has been affected by climate zones, it is important to understand how climate affects population density. Below are three activities that will help students understand this concept.

◆ **EASY** Have students look at the population density map on p. 576. Ask them to notice where most people live and to write a statement about their findings.

◀▶ **AVERAGE** Provide students with an outline map of Australia and have them color-code it to show the climatic zones. Then, have them use lines or dot codes to show population density on the same map.

◀▮▶ **CHALLENGING** Have students write a paragraph explaining why they think it is a good idea or a bad idea to find ways to support a large population in the deserts of Australia.

Answers to Caption Questions
p. 576 ▶ Southeast coast
p. 577 ▶ Tourism

3 CLOSING THE LESSON

Lesson 1 Review

Answers to Think and Write

A. Aborigines live on sparsely settled land and spend their time dancing, hunting or gathering food, holding feasts and tribal meetings, or telling stories.

B. Australia is the smallest and flattest continent.

C. Australia has no cold climates except in the high elevations of its mountains. The interior of the continent is dry; the northern coast has a tropical climate, and the southwestern coast has a Mediterranean climate.

D. The kangaroo, the glider, the koala, the duckbill platypus, the echidna, the emu, and the kookaburra are among the unusual animals of Australia.

Answer to Skills Check

Australia has a relatively sparse population because a large portion of the continent is desert.

Focus Your Reading

Ask the lesson focus question found at the beginning of the lesson: **What are the characteristics of the Australian continent?**
(The Australian continent is generally dry and flat, with most major cities located on the southeastern coast. It has some unusual landforms, including Ayers Rock and the Great Barrier Reef, and it has many unique animals.)

Additional Practice

You may wish to assign the ancillary materials listed below.

Understanding the Lesson p. 147
Workbook p. 121

578

Australia has some unique birds and animals, including the kookaburra (top left), the emu (bottom left), and the koala bear (right).
▶ Which of these creatures resembles an ostrich?

has webbed feet and a bill like that of a duck. Its tail is similar to a beaver's, and it has poison spurs on its hind feet. The platypus is a mammal, but it lays eggs. The echidna, also called the spiny anteater, is another Australian animal that lays eggs.

Europeans discovered that some of Australia's birds were unusual. The emu is a large flightless bird that looks similar to an ostrich. European settlers called the kookaburra, another Australian bird, "the laughing jackass" because of its hoarse cry.

LESSON 1 REVIEW

THINK AND WRITE

A. Briefly describe how life among Aborigines in the bush in Australia differs from life in the cities and other settled areas. **(Analyze)**

B. How does Australia compare in size and surface with other continents? **(Recall)**

C. What kinds of climates does Australia have? **(Recall)**

D. What unusual animals and birds are found in Australia? **(Recall)**

SKILLS CHECK

THINKING SKILL

Find Australia and New Zealand on the charts on pages 32–43. Notice the land area and population of these two countries. Considering that Australia has almost 30 times the amount of land that New Zealand has, how can you explain why Australia only has about five times the number of people that New Zealand has?

578

Optional Activities

UNDERSTANDING THE LESSON

NAME _____
UNDERSTANDING THE LESSON

CHAPTER
22

Organizing Facts

LESSON 1 CONTENT MASTER

✱ The chart helps you describe the people, physical features, climate, and animals of Australia. Fill in the blank spaces with the details that describe each aspect of Australia.

Population
Large majority of whites; small minority of Aborigines

Location and Size
Southern Hemisphere, between Pacific and Indian oceans; smallest of continents, about size of continental United States

Physical Features
Flattest of continents; Great Dividing Range along eastern and southeastern edges; Ayers Rock in center of continent; Great Barrier Reef along eastern coast

Australia

Climates
Most precipitation in east and southeast; center very dry; tropical climate on northern coast; Mediterranean climate on southwestern coast; south cooler than north

Unique Animals
Forty-seven kinds of kangaroos; gliders, or "flying possums"; furry koalas; mammals that lay eggs, such as the duckbill platypus and echidna

Unusual Birds
Emu: large, flightless, looks like ostrich; kookaburra

Think and Write: Write a paragraph explaining why Elsie Roughsey decided to write a book about the customs of the Aborigines. You may use the back of the sheet.
Answers should reflect independent thinking; suggestions appear in the Answer Key.
Use with textbook pages 575–578.

147

◀ Review Master Booklet, p. 147

THINK ABOUT WHAT YOU KNOW

Like Australia, New Zealand is separated from other lands. What does this suggest to you about the kinds of animals that are found in New Zealand?

STUDY THE VOCABULARY

geothermal energy   temperate climate

FOCUS YOUR READING

What are the main geographical features of New Zealand?

A. The Islands of New Zealand

High Land Abel Tasman, a Dutch explorer, discovered New Zealand in 1642. Tasman named New Zealand after a province in the Netherlands. The two Zealands are different from each other. The province in the Netherlands is low and flat; New Zealand is hilly and mountainous.

New Zealand appears small when compared with Australia, but it is actually larger than the United Kingdom. Like the United Kingdom, New Zealand is an island country. No part of it is more than 70 miles (113 km) from the sea. Its two main islands are North Island and South Island. South Island is larger in area, but North Island has a larger population. Both Auckland, the largest city, and Wellington, New Zealand's capital, are on North Island.

Both North Island and South Island are mountainous, but the highest and most jagged peaks are on South Island. Some are snow-covered all year. At 12,349 feet (3,764 m), Mount Cook is the highest peak and can be seen from the sea. There are also large glaciers on South Island.

Natural Resources The Hot-Water Belt, an area where heat from within the earth is close to the surface, is located on North Island. Water seeping into the hot earth there boils and turns to steam. The steam escapes through cracks in the earth's surface. Hot springs flow from other openings, and geysers shoot steam into the air. People in this region are able to heat their homes with the steam by driving pipes deep into the earth. The underground steam is also piped to a powerhouse and used to generate electricity. Heat from within the earth is called **geothermal energy**. It is one of New Zealand's natural resources.

Forests once covered the greater part of New Zealand. There are still forests, but much of the land has been cleared and turned into pastures for sheep and cattle to graze. New Zealand has far more sheep than people.

Hot springs create geysers that shoot steam into the air.
► How are geysers useful natural resources in New Zealand?

579

Writing to Learn

Writing a Business Letter Ask students to pretend that they are visiting New Zealand as representatives of a company that is considering opening a branch there.

● Have students describe what company or type of business they want to represent.

● Then ask students to write a letter, using proper business-letter format, to their main office in America.

● The letter should describe the features of New Zealand and outline the advantages and disadvantages of opening a branch of their company there.

Optional Activities

Objectives

★**1. Describe** the climate and physical characteristics of New Zealand.

2. Explain how the people and animals of New Zealand have been affected by their nation's physical isolation.

3. Identify the following people and places: *Abel Tasman, New Zealand, North Island, South Island, Auckland, Wellington,* and *Hot-Water Belt.*

1 STARTING THE LESSON

Motivation Activity

■ Have students locate New Zealand on the map on p. 574.

■ Ask them to use the map key to estimate the distance from New Zealand to Australia. (Approximately 1,200 miles [1,931 km]).

■ Ask students to use a map of the United States to locate a city that is 1,200 miles from the city where they live.

Think About What You Know

■ Assign the THINK ABOUT WHAT YOU KNOW activity on p. 579.

■ Answers should include that the animals of New Zealand might be unique.

Study the Vocabulary

■ Have students look up the definitions of the vocabulary words in the Glossary.

■ Ask students to create other terms from the individual words in the vocabulary phrases. Then have them define them.

Answers to Caption Questions

p. 578 ► Emu
p. 579 ► They are used for heating and electricity.

579

Read and Think

Sections A, B, and C

Use the following questions to discuss the geography and climate of New Zealand:

1. **How do New Zealanders use geothermal energy?**
   (To heat their homes and to generate electricity *p. 579*)

2. **Who was living in New Zealand when European explorers first arrived?**
   (Maoris *p. 580*)

3. **What are some unique birds of New Zealand?**
   (The moa and the kiwi *p. 580*)

4. **Where is the warmest part of New Zealand?**
   (North Island *p. 581*)

Thinking Critically   What, do you think, are some of the advantages and disadvantages of heating a home by driving pipes into the earth to tap geothermal energy? (Hypothesize)
(Answers may include that it is cheap to use but could be hard to rely on or control. *p. 579*)

B. A Land Set Apart

People   New Zealand and Australia are neighbors, but they are not close to each other. About 1,200 miles (1,931 km) of ocean lies between them. Today that distance can be flown in a short time, but for centuries, New Zealand was isolated from other lands. Few plants or living creatures from other places reached the islands.

When Europeans arrived in New Zealand, the Maoris (MAH oh reez) inhabited the land. The Maoris were the first inhabitants of New Zealand. They had been living in New Zealand long before any Europeans had reached the island. Europeans knew almost nothing about the Maoris. Today, historians believe that the Maoris originally came to New Zealand by way of sea from other Pacific Islands. You will read and learn more about the Maoris in Chapter 23.

Wildlife   The first Europeans in New Zealand found few living creatures they recognized except the small dogs of the Maoris. Later the Europeans discovered that there were some bats and one kind of rat inhabiting the islands. But they found no other animals like those on other continents.

There were, however, large numbers of birds, including some that lived on the ground and could not fly. The largest of these birds, the moa, had already been killed off by the Maori people, but there were still kiwis. A kiwi is about the size of a chicken. Some kiwis still survive, but they are not often seen, because they feed at night and spend the day in their burrows, or underground homes.

Seagulls (top left), wallabies (bottom left), possums (top right), and kiwis (bottom right) live in New Zealand.
▶ Which belongs to the kangaroo family?

580

Graphic Organizer

To help students better understand the differences and similarities between Australia and New Zealand, you may wish to use the graphic organizer shown below.

AUSTRALIA AND NEW ZEALAND

AUSTRALIA	NEW ZEALAND
Located in southwestern Pacific	Located in southwestern Pacific
Claimed and settled by Great Britain	Claimed and settled by Great Britain
About the size of USA	About the size of Colorado
Mostly flat desert	Mountainous, temperate

580

Reteaching Main Objective

⭐ *Describe the climate and physical characteristics of New Zealand.*

- Tell small groups of students to pretend that they are some of the first European settlers in New Zealand. The year is 1850, and they have made a trip to England to try to attract new settlers to New Zealand.

- Ask them to make oral presentations, which may be in the form of skits, songs, or talks, that will tell people in England about life in New Zealand.

- They will want to make New Zealand sound as interesting and attractive as possible without misleading people.

South Island has a mostly mild climate as well as sufficient precipitation throughout the year.
▶ Why, do you think, are there snowcapped mountains in South Island if the climate there is generally mild?

C. New Zealand's Climate

Mostly Mild The country of New Zealand has a **temperate climate**, one that is neither very hot nor very cold. North Island is generally warmer than South Island. Look at the map on page 574. Can you explain why this is so?

No part of New Zealand is within the tropics. New Zealanders call the peninsula north of Auckland, on North Island, "the winterless north." It is warm enough there to grow oranges and other citrus fruits.

Winters are also mild elsewhere on the islands except in the mountains.

Enough Rain New Zealand has no deserts. The whole country generally receives adequate rainfall, which is distributed throughout the year. Snow is not common except on South Island's high peaks.

The plain on the eastern side of South Island, around the city of Christchurch, is one of the drier parts of the country. Most of New Zealand's wheat is grown here.

LESSON *2* REVIEW

THINK AND WRITE

A. Describe the two main islands of New Zealand. **(Recall)**
B. How did New Zealand's location affect plant life and wildlife there? **(Recall)**
C. What sort of climate does New Zealand have? **(Recall)**

SKILLS CHECK

MAP SKILL

Find the latitude of Wellington in the Gazetteer. Turn to the map on page 620 in the Atlas and find a city in North America that is located at about the same latitude north of the Equator.

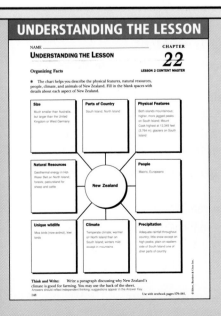
Optional Activities

---

3 CLOSING THE LESSON

Lesson *2* Review

Answers to Think and Write

A. North Island is the most populated island of New Zealand, while South Island is the larger island. Both islands are mountainous, but South Island is more mountainous.

B. New Zealand's isolation meant that few plants or living creatures from other places reached the islands.

C. New Zealand has a temperate climate with adequate rainfall throughout the year.

Answer to Skills Check

The latitude of Wellington is 41° S. Cities in North America at about 41° N include New York, Pittsburgh, and Salt Lake City.

Focus Your Reading

Ask the lesson focus question found at the beginning of the lesson: **What are the main geographical features of New Zealand?** (The main geographical features of New Zealand are its mountains and hills, large glaciers, the Hot-Water Belt, its isolation, and its temperate climate.)

Additional Practice

You may wish to assign the ancillary materials listed below.

Understanding the Lesson p. 148
Workbook pp. 122-123

Answers to Caption Questions
p. 580 ▶ The wallaby
p. 581 ▶ Because of the high altitude

The Pacific Islands

Objectives

★**1. Explain** two ways that the Pacific Islands were formed.

2. Locate the International Date Line and explain its function.

3. Identify the following places: *the Pacific Ocean, Polynesia, Micronesia, Melanesia, New Guinea, the Hawaiian Islands, Tahiti, International Date Line,* and *Prime Meridian.*

1 STARTING THE LESSON

Motivation Activity

■ Ask students what they think of when they think of "paradise." Record their answers on the chalkboard.

■ Explain that for many Europeans and North Americans, the Pacific Islands, with their pleasant climates, attractive and friendly people, and beautiful trees and flowers, have come to symbolize paradise.

■ Tell students that they will learn about these beautiful islands in this lesson.

Think About What You Know

■ Assign the THINK ABOUT WHAT YOU KNOW activity on p. 582.

■ Students should be able to predict that volcanoes would emit rock and lava that could form an island.

Study the Vocabulary

■ Have students look up the definition of the vocabulary word in the Glossary.

■ Ask students to write a poem about what they imagine life on a Pacific island would be like, using the letters of *atoll* to begin each line. (The first line should begin with *a*, the second line with *t*, and so on.)

Answers to Caption Questions

p. 582 ▶ Its clear blue-green water, lush mountainsides, volcanic mountains, and palm trees

582

LESSON **3**

The Pacific Islands

THINK ABOUT WHAT YOU KNOW

On the basis of what you have already learned about volcanoes, describe how you think a volcanic eruption might result in the formation of an island.

STUDY THE VOCABULARY

atoll

FOCUS YOUR READING

What are the land and the climate of the Pacific Islands like?

A. Stories About the Pacific Islands

Many stories have been told about the Pacific Islands. One story was written by Herman Melville about 150 years ago. As a young man, Melville lived for a time on a Pacific island. Afterwards he painted a very favorable picture of island life in a book called *Typee* (tye PEE). Melville wrote that the island was a place of delightful beauty. He describes one scene here.

> *As the ship approached the beach, the crew saw a stirring of the water. At first I imagined it to be a shoal [large group] of fish sporting on the surface, but our friends assured us that it was a shoal of young girls, who in this manner were coming off from the shore to welcome us. As they drew nearer, and I watched the rising and sinking of their forms . . . I almost fancied they could be nothing else than so many mermaids.*

The Pacific Islands were enchanting to Melville. It should be noted that writers sometimes exaggerate when telling of faraway places. They often draw more from their imagination than from memory.

582

B. How the Islands Were Formed

Island Groups The Pacific Ocean is the world's largest body of water. It contains thousands of islands, many uninhabited. Geographers divide the islands located within the tropics into three large groups: Polynesia, Micronesia, and Melanesia.

Polynesia, which means "many islands," extends from New Zealand to the Hawaiian Islands, in the central Pacific. Read the literature selection on the next page to learn about Tahiti, a Polynesian island. Micronesia, meaning "small islands," is an area in the western Pacific, north of the Equator. Melanesia, or "black islands," is south of the Equator and west of Polynesia. Europeans gave Melanesia its name because of the dark skin of most islanders in that region. Melanesia includes New Guinea, the largest of the Pacific Islands and the second largest island in the world.

Tahiti is one of the scenic islands of French Polynesia.
▶ What makes this island so picturesque?

Curriculum Connection

Literature Ask students to look again at the excerpt from *Typee*, on p. 582. You may ask one or more students to read the selection aloud.

● Have students write one or two more paragraphs continuing Melville's description of the Pacific island and using information from the lesson and photographs.

● Encourage students to try to imitate Melville's style as they write.

● Ask some students to read their continuations aloud. What features do their continuations have in common?

LITERATURE SELECTION

FROM: Kon-Tiki
Across the Pacific By Raft

By: Thor Heyerdahl
Setting: Tahiti

In 1947, Thor Heyerdahl and five companions sailed on a balsa-wood raft named *Kon-Tiki* from Peru, South America, to the Tuamotu Archipelago, in eastern Polynesia. They made the voyage to test Heyerdahl's theory that the islands of Polynesia could have been settled centuries ago by Indians from South America. Heyerdahl tells of the voyage in his book *Kon-Tiki*. In this literature selection, Heyerdahl describes the island of Tahiti.

*F*our days later Tahiti rose out of the sea. Not like a string of pearls with palm tufts. As wild jagged blue mountains flung skyward, with wisps of cloud like wreaths round the peaks.

As we gradually approached, the blue mountains showed green slopes. Green upon green, the lush vegetation of the south rolled down over rust-red hills and cliffs, till it plunged down into deep ravines and valleys running out toward the sea. When the coast came near, we saw slender palms standing close packed up all the valleys and all along the coast behind a golden beach. Tahiti was built by old volcanoes. They were dead now and the coral polyps had slung their protecting reef about the island so that the sea could not erode it away.

Early one morning we headed through an opening in the reef into the harbor of Papeete. When we came into the harbor, the population of Tahiti stood waiting. . . . The pae-pae [raft] which had come from America was something everyone wanted to see. The Kon-Tiki *was given the place of honor alongside the shore promenade, the mayor of Papeete welcomed us, and a little Polynesian girl presented us with an enormous wheel of Tahitian wild flowers. . . . Then young girls came forward and hung sweet-smelling white wreaths of flowers round our necks as a welcome to Tahiti, the pearl of the South Seas.*

583

Use the information below to help students better understand the literature selection found on p. 583.

Selection Summary
The author of *Kon-Tiki* takes the reader along on the daring voyage of six men on the Pacific. The men eat plankton and cook the flying fish that jump into the raft. They make sport of catching sharks by the tail, and they devise a basket in which a man can go under the raft and see the extraordinary beauty of the shoals of fish in the sunlit blue sea. Eventually the raft smashes on a reef, but the men survive the wreck and are welcomed by the natives of Tahiti.

Guided Reading
1. **Which of the Pacific Islands is described in this selection?**
   (Tahiti)

2. **How did Heyerdahl and his crew get from Peru to Tahiti?**
   (On a balsa-wood raft named *Kon-Tiki*)

3. **Why, do you think, does Heyerdahl describe Tahiti as the "pearl of the South Seas"?**
   (Answers may include because of Tahiti's lush vegetation, beautiful mountains, and golden beaches.)

Literature-Social Studies Connection
1. **Based on what you have read about the Pacific Islands in this lesson, how accurate is Heyerdahl's description of Tahiti?**
   (Answers should include that it is a very accurate description.)

Drawing a Picture
- Ask students to draw pictures of Tahiti, based on the literature selection on p. 583.
- Allow students time to review the description of Heyerdahl's first view of Tahiti before drawing their pictures.
- Display students' art on the bulletin board.

For Your Information
Herman Melville One of America's greatest writers, Herman Melville, spent five years at sea. A whaling ship, he said, was his Yale College and his Harvard, and to his own generation he was known as "the man who lived among cannibals." He jumped ship while serving on a whaler in the Marquesas and was captured by natives, but he escaped to Tahiti and finally to Hawaii, where he shipped back to the United States. His adventures in the South Seas were the basis for his immensely popular novels, *Typee* and *Omoo*. Today, Melville's name is most closely associated with his masterpiece, *Moby Dick*, but the book was poorly received when it was first published, and Melville died with little sense of its impact on fiction.

Optional Activities

2 DEVELOPING THE LESSON

Read and Think

Sections A, B, C, and D

Use the questions that follow to discuss the geography and climate of the Pacific Islands:

1. **What are the three major groups of Pacific islands?**
   (Polynesia, Micronesia, and Melanesia *p. 582*)

2. **How did plants first grow on the Pacific Islands that were formed by volcanoes?**
   (Seeds were brought by birds or washed up by the sea. *p. 584*)

3. **What is a typhoon?**
   (A Pacific hurricane *p. 584*)

4. **Where is the International Date Line in relation to the Prime Meridian?**
   (Halfway around the world *p. 585*)

   Thinking Critically How does a tropical climate differ from a desert climate? (Analyze)
   (A tropical climate is warm all the time and very humid; a desert climate is extremely hot during the day, very cold at night, and extremely dry. *p. 584*)

Some coral reefs (inset) form ringlike islands, called atolls. The French Polynesian island of Motu, shown, is an atoll.
► How did the coral reef form the atoll?

Island Types Most Pacific islands were formed by volcanoes. Eruptions on the floor of the ocean threw up lava, which rose above the surface. In time, seeds brought by birds or washed up by the sea took root and grew in the volcanic soil. The Hawaiian Islands and Tahiti are volcanic. Some of the island volcanoes are still active and erupt from time to time.

Some islands were formed partly by coral reefs. The reefs were built up slowly in the shallow water along the edges of volcanic islands. Later, pressures under the ocean's floor caused shifts on the surface. The centers of some islands sank, and the surrounding reefs were thrust up. These coral rims formed ringlike islands, called **atolls** (A tawlz). A number of islands in Micronesia are coral islands.

584

C. The Climate of the Islands

There is no winter season in the tropical islands of the Pacific. High and low temperatures are about the same throughout the year. For example, the daily high in the Gilbert Islands usually reaches 88° or 90°F (31° or 32°C). The low is about 75° or 74°F (24° or 23°C). Freezing weather is unknown in the Pacific.

Rain falls throughout the year, but all the islands have much sunshine. Rains usually come in short, heavy showers, even during the rainy seasons.

Although the islands are very warm and humid, daytime ocean breezes make the air comfortable. Sometimes the islands are hit by very strong winds. Typhoons, as hurricanes are called in the Pacific, sometimes sweep over the islands.

west set their watches back an hour when they enter another time zone, because they gain an hour. People traveling east do the opposite. They set their watches ahead one hour when they enter another time zone, because they lose an hour. If one circles the entire earth from east to west, one will cross all 24 zones and gain 24 hours—a whole day.

Date Change So that everyone gains or loses a day at the same place, it has been agreed that the 180th meridian serves as the International Date Line. This imaginary line runs from the North Pole to the South Pole, through the Pacific Ocean. As you can see on the map on page 350, in some places the date line runs east or west of the 180th meridian so that neighboring regions will have the same date. Note that the date line is halfway around the world from the Prime Meridian.

People going west across the International Date Line gain a day. For example, if it is Sunday east of the line, it is Monday west of the line. Those going east across the line lose a day. If it is Sunday west of the date line, they go back to Saturday when they cross.

D. The International Date Line

Time Zones You have already learned that the earth is divided into 24 time zones. The time changes when one travels from one time zone to another. People traveling

---

LESSON **3** *REVIEW*

THINK AND WRITE

A. What led Melville and others to write stories about the Pacific Islands? *(Infer)*

B. What are two ways that some of the Pacific islands were formed? *(Recall)*

C. What kind of climate do the Pacific Islands have? *(Recall)*

D. What is the International Date Line, and what happens there? *(Recall)*

SKILLS CHECK

WRITING SKILL

Use your imagination to write a two-paragraph story about an experience in the Pacific Islands. You may also draw on the photographs and text of the lesson for material for your story.

585

---

3 CLOSING THE LESSON

Lesson 3 Review

Answers to Think and Write

A. They were enchanted by the delightful beauty of the islands.

B. Most Pacific islands were formed by volcanoes, but some were formed by the accumulation of coral.

C. The Pacific Islands have a tropical climate; there is no winter, and though there is a good deal of rainfall, the islands receive plenty of sunshine.

D. The International Date Line is the 180th meridian. It is the point at which those traveling west gain a day and those traveling east lose a day.

Answer to Skills Check

Paragraphs should reflect understanding of the information in the lesson regarding climate and geography of the islands and include details shown in the photographs.

Focus Your Reading

Ask the lesson focus question found at the beginning of the lesson: **What are the land and the climate of the Pacific Islands like?** (Most of the Pacific islands were created either from volcanic debris or coral reefs; they have a tropical climate with plenty of rainfall and pleasant breezes, which occasionally become hurricanes or typhoons.)

Additional Practice

You may wish to assign the ancillary materials listed below.

Understanding the Lesson p. 149
Workbook p. 124

UNDERSTANDING THE LESSON

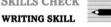

◄ Review Master Booklet, p. 149

Optional Activities

Answers to Caption Questions

p. 584 ▶ The centers of the islands sank, and the surrounding reefs were thrust up.

585

Using the Vocabulary

1. monolith
2. geothermal energy
3. temperate climate
4. bush
5. atoll

Remembering What You Read

1. The Aborigines
2. South of the equator, in the Southern Hemisphere
3. It is about the size of the United States without Alaska and Hawaii.
4. Ayers Rock
5. The Great Barrier Reef
6. On the eastern, southeastern, and southwestern coasts
7. Because Australia is an island, cut off from the other six continents
8. North Island and South Island
9. They use geothermal energy.
10. By volcanic eruptions
11. Winter
12. The sea breezes
13. People traveling west gain an hour when they travel to another time zone. People traveling east lose an hour when they enter another time zone.
14. So that everyone gains or loses a day at the same place
15. From the North Pole to the South Pole

USING THE VOCABULARY

bush
monolith
geothermal energy
temperate climate
atoll

On a separate sheet of paper, write the word or words from the above list that best complete the sentences.

1. Ayers Rock, the world's largest _____, is a sacred place for Aborigines.
2. _____, or heat from within the earth, is one of New Zealand's natural resources.
3. A country that has weather that is neither very hot nor very cold has a _____.
4. The Australian word for "sparsely settled land far from any settlement" is _____.
5. An _____ is a ringlike island that has formed from coral reefs.

REMEMBERING WHAT YOU READ

On a separate sheet of paper, answer the following questions in complete sentences.

1. Who are the earliest known inhabitants of Australia?
2. Where is Australia located?
3. How does the size of Australia compare with that of the United States?
4. What is the most famous feature of Australia's landscape?
5. What is the name of the largest coral reef in the world?
6. Where are the five largest cities in Australia located?
7. Why are the animals and birds of Australia different from the animals and birds found in other parts of the world?
8. What are the two main islands that make up the country of New Zealand?
9. How do the people in the Hot-Water Belt region of North Island heat their homes?
10. How were most of the Pacific Islands formed?
11. Which season of the year does not exist in the tropical islands of the Pacific?
12. What makes the air comfortable in the tropical islands of the Pacific, even though the climate is warm and humid?
13. How does the time change when a person travels from one time zone to another time zone?
14. Why has everyone agreed on the location of the International Date Line?
15. From what two points does the International Date Line run?

TYING ART TO SOCIAL STUDIES

The Great Barrier Reef is known around the world for the beauty of its animal life. Billions of coral animals live on top of the skeletons of the coral animals that have died there. Corals grow in many brilliant colors. Giant clams, sea turtles, and exotic fish and birds also inhabit the Great Barrier Reef. Find a science book or another reference book that has photographs of the Great Barrier Reef. Then, paint a picture that shows the beautiful underwater sea life of the Great Barrier Reef.

586

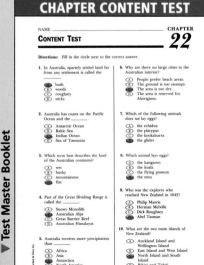

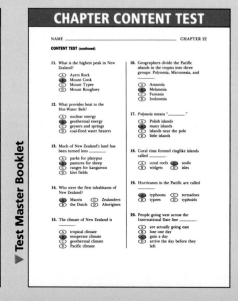

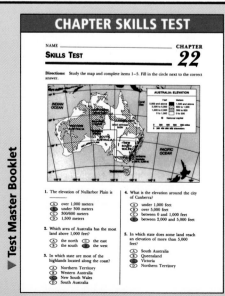

THINKING CRITICALLY

On a separate sheet of paper, answer the following questions in complete sentences.

1. What did Elsie Roughsey think that the Aboriginal children were in danger of losing?
2. What, do you think, is most unusual about the duckbill platypus?
3. If you lived on a Pacific island, would the climate there affect any of your favorite activities?
4. Coconut palm trees grow on tropical islands. These trees often lean out over the water's edge. Why, do you think, do the trees grow this way?
5. Where do the International Date Line and the Prime Meridian meet?

SUMMARIZING THE CHAPTER

On a separate sheet of paper, draw a graphic organizer like the one shown here. Copy the information from this graphic organizer onto the one you have drawn. Under the main idea for each lesson, write four statements that support the main idea.

CHAPTER THEME

Australia, New Zealand, and the Pacific Islands have a variety of geographical features.

LESSON 1
Australia is a land of varied geographical features and animals.

1.
2.
3.
4.

LESSON 2
New Zealand is a land of varied geographical features and animals.

1.
2.
3.
4.

LESSON 3
The Pacific Islands share a similar climate with one another.

1.
2.
3.
4.

587

Thinking Critically

1. Knowledge of their ancestors and past
2. That it has features of a duck, including the laying of eggs, although it is a mammal
3. Answers may include yes, because snow skiing would not be possible, or no, because they can continue doing their favorite activities on the islands.
4. Answers may include that the soil is sandy and softer near the water, making the trees lean in that direction.
5. At the North Pole and at the South Pole

Summarizing the Chapter

Lesson 1
1. Ayers Rock
2. Great Barrier Reef
3. Kangaroo
4. Duckbilled platypus

Lesson 2
1. Hot-Water belt
2. Hilly and mountainous
3. Moa
4. Kiwi

Lesson 3
1. Tropical
2. Rainy season
3. Ocean breezes
4. Typhoons

CHAPTER SKILLS TEST

NAME _____ CHAPTER 22
SKILLS TEST (continued)

Directions: Read the paragraphs and complete items 6–10. Fill in the circle next to the correct answer.

There are more than 10,000 islands in the Pacific Ocean. These islands are not near any continent. Geographers divide these islands into three groups—Melanesia, Micronesia, and Polynesia. The islands of the southwestern Pacific are known as Melanesia. The western Pacific islands north of the Equator are called Micronesia. The many islands of the central Pacific are called Polynesia.

The climate of most of the Pacific Islands is warm, with plenty of rain. It is much the same throughout the year. For example, on the island of Saipan in Micronesia, there is little change between the average temperatures in January and in July. The average temperature is 78°F (24°C) in January and 78°F (25°C) in July.

6. The islands of the central Pacific are called _____.
   Ⓐ Melanesia Ⓒ Polynesia
   Ⓑ Micronesia Ⓓ Macronesia

7. Some of the Pacific islands lie _____.
   Ⓐ in the northeastern Pacific
   Ⓑ near continents
   Ⓒ north of the Equator
   Ⓓ near the North Pole

8. You can conclude from the paragraphs that the Pacific islands have _____.
   Ⓐ few mountains
   Ⓑ no snow
   Ⓒ poor soil
   Ⓓ little animal life

9. You *cannot* conclude from the paragraphs that _____.
   Ⓐ the weather in the islands is usually comfortable
   Ⓑ drought is often a problem in the islands
   Ⓒ the exact number of Pacific islands is unknown
   Ⓓ some of the islands lie south of the Equator

10. These paragraphs do not discuss the islands' _____.
    Ⓐ climate
    Ⓑ population
    Ⓒ locations
    Ⓓ names

CHAPTER WRITING TEST

NAME _____ CHAPTER
ESSAY TEST **22**

Directions: Write a response to items 1–4.

REMINDER: Read and think about each item before you write your response. Be sure to think of the points you want to cover, details that support your response, and reasons for your opinions. Then, on the lines below, write your response in complete sentences.

1. What is Ayers Rock, and why is it unusual?
   A satisfactory response should include the following statements:
   • Ayers Rock is a large mass of stone that rises above the desert in the center of Australia.
   • It is the world's largest monolith, or single stone.
   An excellent response might also mention
   • the height of Ayers Rock (1,143 feet).
   • that the rock is considered a sacred place by the Aborigines.

2. How do coral reefs influence the formation of islands?
   A satisfactory response should include the following statements:
   • A coral reef is a ridge built up in shallow water by the skeletons of sea creatures.
   • Reefs often build up slowly along the edges of volcanic islands.
   • When pressures under the ocean floor caused shifts on the surface, the centers of some islands sank and the surrounding reefs were thrust up.
   An excellent response might include
   • the term atoll.
   • an example of coral islands, such as Bikini.

CHAPTER WRITING TEST

NAME _____ CHAPTER 22
ESSAY TEST (continued)

3. Describe the differences between New Zealand's North Island and South Island.
   A satisfactory response should include the following statements:
   • South Island is bigger, and it contains glaciers and New Zealand's highest and most rugged peaks.
   • South Island is generally cooler than North Island.
   • North Island has a larger population, and it contains New Zealand's capital and largest city.
   • The Hot-Water Belt is located on North Island.
   An excellent response might also
   • mention Mount Cook, Auckland, Wellington, and geothermal energy.
   • provide specific examples.

4. Describe the climate of the Pacific Islands.
   A satisfactory response should include the following statements:
   • There is no winter in the Pacific Islands; they are warm and humid throughout the year.
   • Rain falls throughout the year, but it usually comes in short, heavy showers.
   • Although the temperature is warm, ocean breezes make the air comfortable.
   An excellent response might also
   • provide specific examples.
   • cite specific average temperatures.
   • mention typhoons.

587

Past and Present in Australia, New Zealand, and the Pacific Islands
(pp. 588-604)

Chapter Theme: There are close economic and political ties between Australia, New Zealand, the Pacific Islands, and other nations.

CHAPTER RESOURCES
Review Master Booklet
  Reviewing Chapter Vocabulary, p. 156
  Place Geography, p. 157
  Summarizing the Chapter, p. 158
Chapter 23 Test

LESSON *1* **Australia**
(pp. 588-593)

Theme: Australia has undergone many changes in agriculture, industry, and government since Europeans arrived in the 1700s.

LESSON RESOURCES
Workbook, p. 125
Review Master Booklet
  Understanding the Lesson, p. 153

LESSON *2* **New Zealand**
(pp. 594-597)

Theme: New Zealand has a double heritage handed down from both the Europeans and the Maoris.

LESSON RESOURCES
Workbook, p. 126
Review Master Booklet
  Understanding the Lesson, p. 154

LESSON *3* **The Pacific Islands**
(pp. 600-602)

Theme: After World War II, there were great changes in the political status of the Pacific Islands.

LESSON RESOURCES
Workbook, pp. 127-128
Review Master Booklet
  Understanding the Lesson, p. 155

 SOCIAL STUDIES LIBRARY: *Lost Star: The Story of Amelia Earhart*

Review Masters

REVIEWING CHAPTER VOCABULARY

CHAPTER

23

VOCABULARY MASTER

Review Study the terms in the box. Use your Glossary to find definitions of those you do not remember.

boomerang	food processing	heritage	protectorate smelting

Practice Complete the paragraphs using terms from the box above. You may change the forms of the terms to fit the meaning.

The history of Australia may be divided into two periods: the time before European settlers arrived and the time since European settlement. Unlike Tahiti, which was a (1) _protectorate_ controlled by France, Australia became a colony of Great Britain. Although it has its own independent government today, Australia still has strong links with Great Britain.

Before Europeans arrived in Australia, the Aborigines had been living there for thousands of years. The older Aborigines tried hard to pass on their (2) _heritage_ to the younger people. In this way, they hoped their traditional ways of life, such as the use of the (3) _boomerang_ for hunting, would not be lost. Most Aborigines now live in cities and have jobs in Australia's big industries, such as (4) _food processing_ or manufacturing.

Write Write a sentence of your own for each term in the box above. You may use the back of the sheet.

Sentences should show that students understand the meanings of the terms.

_____
_____
_____
_____
_____
_____
_____
_____
_____
_____
_____

156   Use with Chapter 23, pages 589–602.   © Silver, Burdett & Ginn Inc.

LOCATING PLACES

CHAPTER

23

PLACE GEOGRAPHY MASTER

✻ In 1959, Hawaii, a group of Pacific Ocean islands, became the fiftieth state of the United States. Listed below are places in the Pacific Ocean, and in Australia and its neighbors, which lie between the Pacific and Indian oceans. Use the Gazetteer in your textbook to find the latitude and longitude of each place. Then locate and label each on the map.

	LAT. ⊖	LONG. ⓘ		LAT. ⊖	LONG. ⓘ
1. Honolulu, Hawaii	21°N	158°W	6. Fiji	18°S	178°E
2. Canberra, Australia	35°S	149°E	7. Mount Cook, New Zealand	43°S	173°E
3. Auckland, New Zealand	37°S	174°E	8. Brisbane, Australia	28°S	153°E
4. Bikini	11°N	165°E	9. Tahiti	18°S	149°W
5. Nauru	30°S	167°E	10. Perth, Australia	32°S	116°E

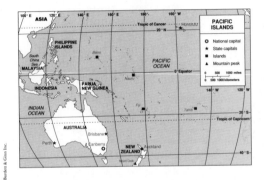

157   Use with Chapter 23, pages 589–602.   © Silver, Burdett & Ginn Inc.

SUMMARIZING THE CHAPTER

CHAPTER

23

GRAPHIC ORGANIZER MASTER

✻ Complete this graphic organizer. Next to the main idea for each lesson, write four statements that support the main idea.

CHAPTER THEME There are close economic and political ties between Australia, New Zealand, the islands of the Pacific, and other nations.

LESSON 1

Australia has changed since Europeans arrived on the continent.

1. Farms and ranches
2. Diseases wiped out much of the Aboriginal population.
3. A government was established.
4. Towns and cities

LESSON 2

The Maoris and the European settlers have affected New Zealand.

1. Forest fires were used to clear the land.
2. New crops, birds, and wild animals
3. Commonwealth of Nations
4. Most New Zealanders live in cities.

LESSON 3

The governments of the Pacific countries changed after World War II.

1. Many countries became independent.
2. Tahiti became a French territory.
3. American Samoa became a territory of the United States.
4. Hawaii became a state of the United States.

158   Use with Chapter 23, pages 589–602.   © Silver, Burdett & Ginn Inc.

C23-B

Workbook Pages

Page 1 (125)

FINDING DISTANCES IN EASTERN AUSTRALIA

Understanding a Special-Purpose Map, Understanding Scale

✳ The map below shows eastern Australia. Use the map scale to determine the distance between the places mentioned in the statements. Underline or fill in the best answers.

1. The distance from Brisbane to the Tropic of Capricorn is about

   450 miles   <u>275 miles</u>

2. The distance between Canberra and Mount Kosciusko is just under

   200 miles   <u>100 miles</u>

3. The distance from Melbourne to the northern tip of Tasmania is about

   <u>350 km</u>   500 km

4. The distance from the tip of the Cape York Peninsula to the Mitchell River is about

   250 miles   <u>350 miles</u>

5. The distance from the capital city of Victoria to the capital city of New South Wales is about

   600 miles   <u>450 miles</u>

6. The distance from Newcastle to Canberra is about

   375 km   <u>275 km</u>

7. The distance from Hobart in Tasmania to Melbourne is about __375__ miles.

8. The distance from Broken Hill to the Murray River is about __250__ km.

EASTERN AUSTRALIA

◎ National capital
★ State capitals
● Other cities

Thinking Further: What things would you like to see if you visited Australia?

Answers may mention beaches, cattle ranches, desert areas, large cities such as Melbourne and Sydney, or native animals such as koalas and kangaroos.

Page 2 (126)

AUSTRALIA AND NEW ZEALAND

Building Vocabulary, Using Words in Context

✳ Can you figure out the words that help describe Australia and New Zealand? If so, you can complete the statements below.
a. Unscramble the words under each blank in the left column.
b. Complete the sentences in the right column by putting the unscrambled letters in the correct blank.

1. ___CANBERRA___
   A R A N B C E R

2. ___MAORIS___
   R O M A I S

3. ___TASMANIA___
   A M A I A T S N

4. ___SYDNEY___
   N D S Y E Y

5. ___COOK___
   K O C O

6. ___BEEF___
   E F E B

7. ___WELLINGTON___
   W N G E L T L I O N

8. ___CONTINENT___
   N T I N C O N E T

9. ___ABORIGINES___
   G O A B R I I N E S

10. ___GOLD___
    L O G D

11. ___BOOMERANG___
    N R E O M B A O G

12. ___VOTE___
    E O T V

a. The oldest and largest Australian city is ___SYDNEY___

b. ___TASMANIA___ is an island that is part of Australia.

c. ___ABORIGINES___ lived in Australia before Europeans came.

d. The capital, ___CANBERRA___, is located in the Australia Capital Territory.

e. A curved, flat throwing stick is a ___BOOMERANG___

f. A valuable mineral discovered in Australia in 1851 was ___GOLD___

g. The early settlers of New Zealand were ___MAORIS___

h. Australia leads the world in the production of ___BEEF___

i. New Zealand was the first country in the world to give women the right to ___VOTE___

j. The capital of New Zealand is ___WELLINGTON___

k. ___COOK___ explored the coasts of Australia and New Zealand.

l. Australia is both a country and a ___CONTINENT___

Thinking Further: Do you think the vast interior of Australia will remain unsettled? Give reasons for your answer.

Some students may say it will probably be settled as the population increases and more land is needed. Others may think the vast open spaces should be preserved for animals and native tribes.

Page 3 (127)

LANDS OF THE PACIFIC

Using Context Clues, Identifying Points of View

✳ Use the clues below to complete the crossword puzzle about Australia, New Zealand, and the Pacific Islands.

ACROSS

4. Disease brought by Europeans
6. Native people of Australia
8. Important resource of Papua New Guinea
11. Fruit grown in New Zealand, named after a bird
12. Gilbert Islands are reefs made of this
14. Meat from sheep
15. Australia leads the world in the export of this
17. Culture handed down from the past
18. Native Australian throwing stick

DOWN

1. Became our fiftieth state in 1959
2. Used to clear the forests of New Zealand
3. Vast Pacific region of small islands
5. Large city on south coast of Australia
7. Wind blows this away when ground is dry
9. British colony in Melanesia that became independent in 1974
10. First English explorer of Australia
13. Most productive mine of this metal is in Australia
16. A leading export of Australia since the days of early settlers

Thinking Further: Explain how the statement "Australia is the land down under" is both correct and incorrect.

Answers should mention that from the United States, Australia is "down under" the Equator, but from Australia, the United States is down under.

Page 4 (128)

SETTLEMENT OF THE PACIFIC ISLANDS

Understanding Sequence, Analyzing Information

✳ People from Asia had settled in the Pacific region long before the European explorers arrived. The map shows when people arrived on the islands of the Pacific. Use the map to number the places in each box in the order they were settled.

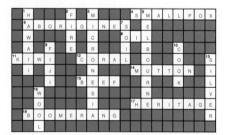

SETTLEMENT OF THE PACIFIC

→ Before 3000 B.C.
⋯▶ 3000 B.C. – A.D. 300
-▶ A.D. 300 – A.D. 1000

__4__ Easter Island
__1__ Borneo
__2__ Fiji Islands
__3__ Marquesas Islands

__4__ Society Islands
__2__ New Guinea
__1__ Philippines
__3__ Fiji Islands

__6__ Chatham Islands
__1__ Asia
__5__ New Zealand
__2__ New Guinea
__3__ Fiji Islands
__4__ Marquesas Islands

Thinking Further: Why do you think it took so long to settle the Pacific Islands?

Answers may mention the vast size of the region or the difficulty of traveling on the seas.

TEACHER NOTES

Australia

Objectives

★1. **Explain** how Australia was settled by Europeans.

2. **Describe** how the European settlers affected the lives of the Aborigines.

3. **Discuss** the government of Australia.

4. **Identify** the following people and places: *Aborigines, William Dampier, James Cook, Matthew Flinders, Sydney, New South Wales, Victoria, South Australia, Queensland, Western Australia, Tasmania, Northern Territory,* and *Canberra*.

1 STARTING THE LESSON

Motivation Activity

■ Remind students that the early Aborigines had no written language, so we are not sure where they came from.

■ Ask students where they think the later inhabitants of Australia came from. Put their answers on the chalkboard.

■ Tell students to keep their answers in mind as they read this lesson.

Think About What You Know

■ Assign the THINK ABOUT WHAT YOU KNOW activity on p. 589.

■ Student answers should reflect independent thinking but may include that much of the land is dry and barren.

Study the Vocabulary

■ Ask students if they know the definition of any of the lesson's new vocabulary words.

■ Have the students look up each of the words in their Glossary to see if they were using the correct definitions.

CHAPTER *23* PAST AND PRESENT IN AUSTRALIA, NEW ZEALAND, AND THE PACIFIC ISLANDS

$\mathcal{M}$ost of the islands in region are either independent or mostly self-governing. The isolated location of this region attracts many tourists from other lands.

Optional Activities

Writing to Learn

Writing a Petition   Ask students to imagine they are Aborigines living in Australia in the 1800s.

● Have each student write a petition asking the British Parliament to put a halt to more settlement.

● Tell students that they should include a list of reasons why settlement is hurting the Aborigines' way of life.

● Remind students that the petition needs to be persuasive enough to win the signatures of other Aborigines as well as persuasive enough to convince the British that the Aborigines are right.

● You may wish to display the students' petitions around the classroom.

THINK ABOUT WHAT YOU KNOW
Europeans regarded Australia as an "empty continent." What have you learned about Australia that would explain this point of view?

STUDY THE VOCABULARY
boomerang   smelting
food processing

FOCUS YOUR READING
How has Australia changed since Europeans arrived on the continent?

A. Aborigines and Europeans Meet

The Dutch As you know, the Aborigines had been living in Australia for thousands of years when the Europeans arrived. The Dutch explored the north and west coasts of Australia and called the land New Holland. But they did not establish colonies. They were interested only in trade.

William Dampier, an English seafarer who landed on the west coast of Australia in 1688, had an unfavorable view of the continent. He wrote that the land was barren and that the Aborigines were "the miserablest people in the world."

English Explorers In 1770, the English explorer Captain James Cook landed on the southeast coast. Cook had read Dampier's description of Australia, so he was surprised and pleased to find "a green and woody land." It should be noted, however, that Cook arrived in the fall, the wettest season of the year in southeastern Australia. Cook also found the Aborigines to be different from Dampier's description. Cook observed that the Aborigines were

"far happier than we Europeans," taking "all things necessary for life" from the earth and sea.

Cook named the place where he landed New South Wales and claimed the east coast for Great Britain. In 1803 another English explorer, Matthew Flinders, sailed around the continent and mapped much of the coast. He suggested that New Holland might better be called Australia, which means "southern land."

B. European Settlement

The first group of Europeans who came to Australia did not want to come. They were convicts sent to work far from home as punishment for breaking the law. The first fleet carrying convicts, together with marines to guard them, reached New South Wales in January 1788.

January is summer in Australia. It was a dry summer, so the country did not appear as green as Cook had described it. The convicts were made to plant crops, but because of the dry conditions, they had little success. They nearly starved during the first year. The convicts were also set to work constructing the buildings of the first settlement, which was named Sydney.

Other Europeans besides convicts eventually came to Australia. Many wanted to own farms. The discovery of gold in 1851 brought more immigrants. Some who failed to strike it rich in the 1849 California gold rush came to try their luck in Australia. Many gold seekers stayed.

C. Settlers Change a Continent

Land Use The Europeans brought animals, seeds, tools, ideas—and diseases—to Australia. All of these changed the continent and greatly affected the lives of

---

2 DEVELOPING THE LESSON

Read and Think
Sections A and B

European settlers began arriving on the Australian continent in 1788. They came for a variety of reasons. Discuss this with students by asking the following questions:

1. **Why were Dampier's and Cook's impressions of Australia so different?**
   (Dampier landed on the west coast, which is barren; Cook landed on the southeast coast, where everything looked green and wooded. *p. 589*)

2. **Why did Australia's first European settlers come to Australia?**
   (They were convicts who were sent there as punishment, because they broke the law in England. *p. 589*)

Thinking Critically Historians have told us that the first European settlers were unhappy in Australia. Why, do you think, might they have been unhappy? (Infer)
(Students' answers will reflect independent thinking but may include that they were far from home, they did not come voluntarily, they nearly starved, and they had to do hard work. *p. 589*)

SKILLBUILDER REVIEW

Making Predictions On pp. 568–569 the students learned how to make predictions as they read. Ask them to use this skill with the information on how settlers changed the Australian continent on pp. 589–590.

● After reading this section, have the students predict what might happen in any society when new settlers arrive.

For Your Information

The Australian Language Due to the large number of British settlers, English became the official language of Australia. However, the settlers soon discovered that English had no words for some of the plants and animals they encountered and some of the activities they engaged in. As a result, the settlers borrowed some words from the Aborigines and invented some of their own. *Kangaroo* and *koala* were Aborigine words for native animals, while *brumbies* (wild horses) and *buckjumpers* (bucking broncos) were words invented by the settlers. The title of Australia's most famous song, "Waltzing Matilda," does not have to do with a woman or dancing. A *matilda* is a backpack; *waltzing matilda* refers to tramping the roads.

Optional Activities

Read and Think
Section C

The European settlers changed the Australian land in many ways. Discuss with students how the coming of the settlers affected Australia by asking the following questions:

1. **What did the settlers bring to Australia?**
   (They brought animals, seeds, and tools, as well as ideas and diseases. *p. 589*)

2. **How did the European settlers change the way Australia's land was used?**
   (They turned their livestock loose and cleared the land to plant crops, taking away the lands the Aborigines had used for hunting and gathering. *p. 590*)

Thinking Critically Which problem brought to Australia by the settlers, do you think, was the most harmful?
(Evaluate)
(Answers should reflect independent thinking but may include diseases. *p. 590*)

GEOGRAPHY THEMES

Human-Environment Interactions

■ Have students look at the map on p. 591 to help them answer the following question: **Why, do you think, are most of Australia's cities on the coastlines?**
(The settlers arrived by ship and settled along the coast; mountain ranges and deserts inland inhibited travel; cities need harbors for transportation.)

---

the Aborigines. The settlers turned cattle and sheep loose on the grasslands. The Europeans used steel axes and plows to clear the land and plant crops.

The European settlers' farms and ranches occupied lands where the Aborigines had hunted and gathered food. When troubles broke out between settlers and Aborigines, the settlers used their guns. Guns were far more deadly than the Aborigines' spears and their throwing sticks, called **boomerangs**.

Imported Problems Europeans did not intend to bring diseases to Australia, but they did. Some diseases, such as smallpox, wiped out a large part of the Aboriginal population. The settlers also brought animals they would rather have left behind. Mice and rats arrived on European ships and escaped when the ships were in port.

Europeans did bring some animals on purpose, however. Camels were imported to pull wagons in dry areas where horses could not survive. Settlers brought wild animals that they could hunt for sport. In 1859 a man turned 24 English rabbits loose on his estate. Since there were no foxes or other beasts of prey, the number of rabbits increased rapidly. The 24 rabbits quickly became a horde of rabbits.

The rabbits spread over the country and destroyed crops, orchards, and even pastures. In dry years the rabbits strip the land of its cover. Then winds blow away the topsoil. Various methods have been used to control the rabbit population, but not with complete success.

D. The Commonwealth of Australia

Government The British established separate colonies in Australia. In 1901 the colonies united to form the independent

---

Commonwealth of Australia. Each colony became a state in a federal government somewhat like that of the United States.

There are six states: New South Wales, Victoria, South Australia, Queensland, Western Australia, and Tasmania. The thickly populated Northern Territory has self-government, but it is not a state. The national capital, Canberra, is not located within any state but in a federal territory, like Washington, D.C.

The governments of the Commonwealth and the states are elected by the people. Australia has chosen to remain a member of the Commonwealth of Nations, the organization of countries that were once part of the British Empire. Queen Elizabeth II of the United Kingdom, who is head of the Commonwealth of Nations, is also queen of Australia. However, she serves only as the symbol of government.

Canberra was chosen as the site for Australia's federal capital in 1909.
► How is Canberra similar to Washington, D.C.?

Optional Activities

Graphic Organizer

To help students better understand the people, government, and economy of Australia, you may wish to use the graphic organizer shown.

ALL ABOUT AUSTRALIA

EARLY SETTLERS	AUSTRALIANS TODAY	AUSTRALIA'S GOVERNMENT	AUSTRALIA'S ECONOMY
1. The first European settlers were convicts sent to Australia as punishment.	1. Most of Australia's newest settlers have come from Asia.	1. Australia has a federal government.	1. Australia leads the world in the export of beef and supplies 30 percent of the world's wool.
2. Other Europeans came to get farms of their own or to look for gold.	2. Most Australians live in towns and cities.	2. Australia has six states.	2. Wheat is Australia's largest export crop.
3. Most early settlers came from the British Isles.		3. Australia has chosen to remain a member of the Commonwealth of Nations.	3. Leading industries include food processing, mining, and manufacturing.

AUSTRALIA, NEW ZEALAND, AND THE PACIFIC ISLANDS: POLITICAL

Legend:
- ✪ National capitals
- • Other cities

0   500   1,000 miles
0   500   1,000 kilometers

AUST. —AUSTRALIA
FR. —FRANCE
JAP. —JAPAN
N.Z. —NEW ZEALAND
U.K. —UNITED KINGDOM
U.S. —UNITED STATES

Cities less than 100,000	
...ern Samoa) C-5	
...bati) B-4	
...stralia) C-2	
...olomon Islands) C-3	
...(Tonga) D-5	
...Vanuatu) C-4	
...valu) C-4	

Cities 100,000 to 499,999	
Canberra (Australia) D-3	
Christchurch (New Zealand) E-4	
Dunedin (New Zealand) E-4	
Honolulu (United States) A-6	
Port Moresby (Papua New Guinea) C-3	
Wellington (New Zealand) E-4	

Cities 500,000 to 999,999	
Adelaide (Australia) D-2	
Auckland (New Zealand) D-4	
Perth (Australia) D-1	

Cities 1,000,000 or more	
Brisbane (Australia) D-3	
Melbourne (Australia) D-3	
Sydney (Australia) D-3	

There are more than 20,000 islands scattered across the Pacific Ocean.
▶ Which islands are included in the territory of French Polynesia?

Curriculum Connection

Language Arts   Review the three degrees of comparison, using the word *wet* (wet, wetter, wettest).

● Tell students that these three variations show the positive, comparative, and superlative degrees of the adjective *wet*.

● Remind students that the comparative forms of some adjectives cannot be made by adding *-er* and *-est* to the end of the word.

● Have students identify the three degrees of comparison of the following adjectives found in Sections A and B: *happier, better, dry,* and *new* (happy/happier/happiest; good/better/best; dry/drier/driest; new/newer/newest).

Optional Activities

Meeting Individual Needs

Concept:
The Government of Australia

To understand the government of Australia, it is important to be able to put information in chart form. The activities below will help your students do this.

◆ **EASY** Have students make a chart about the government of Australia.

Ask students to complete the chart by listing the date of independence, the number of states, the national capital, and how the government is chosen.

◀▶ **AVERAGE** Have the students make an organizational chart about the Australian government, using the following information:

The head of the government is the Prime Minister, who is chosen from the party that wins the most votes at election time, when the people vote for members of the House of Representatives and Senate.

◀▮▶ **CHALLENGING** Have students use the information in the activities above to make a chart comparing the governments of Australia and the United States.

Read and Think
Sections D and E

Use the questions below to summarize the information about Australia's government and economy:

1. **What kind of government did Australia establish when it became independent in 1901?**
   (A federal government *p. 590*)

2. **What are Australia's leading exports?**
   (Wool, beef, mutton, wheat, processed foods, manufactured goods, and minerals *pp. 592-593*)

   Thinking Critically Why, do you think, do most Australians live in cities and towns? (Infer)
   (Answers should reflect independent thinking but may include that most people work in factories or mines and the factories and mines are located near cities and towns. *p. 592*)

GEOGRAPHY THEMES

Place

- Direct students' attention to the maps on p. 592 to help them answer the following questions:

1. **Where are Australia's coal deposits located?**
   (In the east)

2. **Which of the natural resources shown on these maps is found offshore?**
   (Oil)

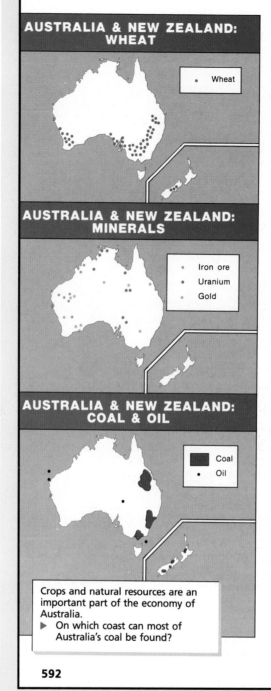

AUSTRALIA & NEW ZEALAND: WHEAT

Wheat

AUSTRALIA & NEW ZEALAND: MINERALS

- Iron ore
- Uranium
- Gold

AUSTRALIA & NEW ZEALAND: COAL & OIL

- Coal
- Oil

Crops and natural resources are an important part of the economy of Australia.
▶ On which coast can most of Australia's coal be found?

Population Most of the early settlers in Australia came from the British Isles. Later groups came from other European countries, such as Germany, Italy, and Greece. In recent years a growing number have come from Asia. Today, people of Asian descent outnumber the Aborigines.

Most Australians live in towns and cities. Most of the Aborigines are now city dwellers. Sydney, the oldest city, is also the largest. Other large cities are Melbourne, Brisbane, Adelaide, and Perth. Locate these cities on the map on page 591.

E. Australia's Economy

Crops European settlers introduced crops they had known at home—wheat, barley, oats, potatoes. Wheat is the largest export crop today. Australia also produces other grains, including corn and rice.

Sugarcane and various kinds of tropical fruit are grown in Queensland. In the southeast, wine grapes and other fruit have become important products.

Industry Although Australia's agricultural exports are numerous, more people work in factories and mines than on farms or ranches. Many workers have jobs in **food processing**. They can or freeze agricultural products. Others work in manufacturing, turning out machinery, electrical equipment, and other goods.

Mining and **smelting** make up a number of jobs in Australia. Smelting is the process of separating a metal from other materials in its ore. Gold is still mined, as are a number of other minerals. The continent has large deposits of coal, iron, copper, and bauxite. The world's most productive silver and lead mine is in Australia. Almost all opals, beautiful gemstones, come from this continent.

Curriculum Connection

Science Have students make a list of the minerals found in Australia.

- Next to each mineral, have students list some of the products made from the mineral. For example, gold is used to make jewelry, coins, and dentures.

- Tell students to consult a dictionary if they do not know what products are made from the minerals on their lists.

- Conclude this activity by having students make a master list of minerals and products on the chalkboard.

Reteaching Main Objective

⭐ ***Explain how Australia was settled by Europeans.***

- Ask students to imagine they are Europeans who have gone to settle in Australia in the late 1700s or 1800s.

- Have students write a brief biography of their lives in which they describe what life was like for them in Europe and what circumstances caused them to leave their homes and come to Australia.

- Also have students describe how they are making their living in Australia.

- Conclude the activity by having volunteers read their biographies to the class.

PRODUCTS OF SHEEP

PRODUCTS:

1. Wool for clothing and blankets
2. Food
3. Leather
4. Soap
5. Tennis racket strings
6. Fertilizer
7. Glue

Thirty percent of all the world's wool comes from Australia. Wool is used to make clothing.
▶ What sheep product besides wool can make something people wear?

Livestock The early settlers found that raising sheep was a profitable way to make use of the land. There were few predatory animals; Australia had no wolves or bears. Herding required fewer laborers than did farming. It was easier to export wool than

food products. The first Australian wool was shipped to England in 1812.

The use of refrigerators on ships opened new markets. Frozen meat was first shipped to England in 1879. Australia now leads the world in the export of beef, and it ranks second after New Zealand in shipping mutton, or meat from sheep.

LESSON 1 REVIEW

THINK AND WRITE

A. How did Dampier's and Cook's views of the Aborigines differ? **(Recall)**
B. What different reasons did Europeans have for coming to Australia? **(Recall)**
C. What intended changes and what unplanned changes did European settlers make in Australia? **(Recall)**

(Analyze)
D. Summarize how the government of Australia is like that of the United States.
E. What are some of Australia's products?

(Recall)

SKILLS CHECK

WRITING SKILL

Write a letter to an Australian student, telling about your country and the place where you live. Point out similarities to and differences from Australia.

593

◀ Review Master Booklet, p. 153

Optional Activities

---

3 CLOSING THE LESSON

Lesson *1* Review

Answers to Think and Write

A. Dampier thought the Aborigines were horrible people, while Cook described them as happy, self-sufficient people.

B. Some Europeans came to Australia because they were forced to as punishment for breaking the law at home. Others came seeking farms of their own. Still others came seeking gold and riches.

C. Europeans intentionally turned the land into grazing land and farm land. They unintentionally brought diseases, which wiped out a large part of the Aboriginal population.

D. Both governments consist of states that are ruled by a federal government.

E. Some of Australia's products include wool, beef, mutton, wheat, corn, rice, sugar cane, tropical fruits, wine grapes, processed foods, machinery, electrical equipment, gold, and other minerals.

Answer to Skills Check

Answers should reflect independent thinking.

Focus Your Reading

Ask the lesson focus questions found at the beginning of the lesson: **How has Australia changed since Europeans arrived on the continent?**

(Europeans brought their ways of life and changed Australia into a leading agricultural and industrial nation. In 1901, Australia became an independent nation, with a federal government. Australia has become an urban nation, with many of its newer immigrants coming from Asia.)

Additional Practice

You may wish to assign the ancillary materials listed below.

Understanding the Lesson p. 153
Workbook p. 125

Answers to Caption Questions
p. **592** ▶ On the eastern coast
p. **593** ▶ Leather

593

New Zealand

Objectives

★1. **Explain** what brought European settlers to New Zealand.

2. **Describe** how the Maoris and Europeans changed the land of New Zealand.

3. **Examine** the government and economy of New Zealand.

4. **Identify** the following people and places: *Maoris, Kupe, Abel Tasman, James Cook,* and *Auckland.*

1 STARTING THE LESSON

Motivation Activity

■ Ask students to think of nicknames that are used to describe Americans or American things. For example, Americans are often referred to as "Yankees," and the flag is often called "Old Glory."

■ Then ask students to think of a good nickname for New Zealanders, based on what they have learned about New Zealand. Tell students that New Zealanders are often called Kiwis, after their national symbol, which is a bird.

Think About What You Know

■ Assign the THINK ABOUT WHAT YOU KNOW activity on p. 594.

■ Answers should reflect independent thinking but may include that they lie below, or south of, the Equator.

Study the Vocabulary

■ Have the students look up the vocabulary word in their Glossary.

■ Ask them to identify the cultures that make up their heritage.

■ Finally, have students use the vocabulary word in a sentence.

THINK ABOUT WHAT YOU KNOW

Australia and New Zealand are sometimes referred to as lands "down under." Try to explain this reference on the basis of what you know about the location of Australia and New Zealand.

STUDY THE VOCABULARY

heritage

FOCUS YOUR READING

How did the Maoris and the European settlers affect New Zealand?

A. The People of New Zealand

Maoris The Maoris tell a story about a great chief named Kupe who sailed in a large canoe to New Zealand from one of the Polynesian islands. Kupe later returned home and gave his people directions for sailing to Aotearoa, the Maori name for New Zealand.

Historians believe that the story Kupe is a legend, but it is a legend par based on fact. The ancestors of the Mao did come to New Zealand by canoe fro Polynesia about a thousand years ago.

Europeans The Dutch explorer Ab Tasman arrived in New Zealand long af the first Maoris. Although Tasman fou the islands beautiful, he thought they h little value for Europeans. Captain Jam Cook, who arrived in New Zealand in 176 had a different view. He thought it wou be a good place for settlers.

After 1790 many Europeans fou their way to New Zealand. Whaling shi stopped there. Some hunted seals alo the coasts. A few convicts from Austral escaped to the islands. Other Europea traded with the Maoris, who wanted gun

Missionaries came to teach th Maoris about the Christian religion. Sin the Maoris had no system of writing, th missionaries introduced the alphabet ar printed the New Testament of the Bible i the Maori language.

The Maori people today use canoes as their ancestors did about a thousand years ago, when they came to New Zealand.
► What do you think the man at the front of the canoe is doing?

Writing to Learn

Writing a Speech Ask students to imagine they are Kupe, the great Maori chief, who has just returned from his first trip to New Zealand, or as he called it, Aotearoa.

● Have each student write a speech that Kupe might have given to his people to convince them that they should leave their Polynesian island and resettle in Aotearoa.

● Remind students that a good speech is one that persuades and inspires people to take action. Encourage students to use language that would convince the Maoris that Aotearoa was an ideal place to live.

● When students are finished, ask volunteers to read their speeches to the class.

USING SOURCE MATERIAL

CAPTAIN JAMES COOK'S JOURNAL

In 1769 Captain James Cook became the first European to visit New Zealand. The next year he explored the east coast of Australia. British claims to both New Zealand and Australia were based on his expeditions. This passage about the Maoris of New Zealand is from Cook's journal.

> The natives of this country are a strong, raw-boned, well-made, active people rather above than under the common size especially the men. They are all of a very dark brown color with black hair, thin black beards and white teeth. . . . They seem to enjoy a good state of health and many of them live to a good old age. . . .
>
> Whenever we were visited by any number of them that had never heard or seen anything of us before, they generally came off in the largest canoes they had. . . . In each canoe were generally an old man, in some two or three, these used always to direct the others, and generally carried a halberd or battle ax in their hands. . . . As soon as they came within about a stone's throw of the ship, they would there lay and call out, . . . come ashore with us and we will kill you with our patoos [fighting axes]. . . . Musketry they never regarded unless they felt the effect, but the great guns they did because these threw stones farther than they could comprehend. After they found that our arms were so much superior to theirs and that we took no advantage of that superiority, . . . they ever after were our very good friends and we never had an instance of their attempting to surprise or cut off any of our people when they were ashore. . . .

Understanding Source Material

1. Do you think Captain Cook was favorably impressed by the Maoris? Explain.
2. Why, do you think, did the Maoris become friends with Captain Cook and his crew?

Thinking About Source Material

Background Information
The Maori At the time of Captain James Cook's visit in 1769, the Maori population was an estimated 100,000 to 250,000. The Maoris now number about 250,000, roughly 12 percent of New Zealand's population. They have many, but not all, of the same rights as other New Zealanders.

Guided Reading
1. **What did the Maoris look like?**
   (Strong, tall, healthy-looking people with black hair and brown skin.)
2. **How did the Maoris greet the Europeans?**
   (They would come near them in large canoe-type boats, carrying up to 100 men. They would come near the ship and call out to the Europeans to come ashore, threatening to kill them.)

Using Source Material
1. Answers should reflect independent thinking but may include that Cook was favorably impressed because of their general good health and their intelligence in realizing the superior military strength of the Europeans.
2. Answers should reflect independent thinking but may include that they realized the Europeans had superior military strength and it would be useless to fight them.

┌─ **Answers to Caption Questions** ─
p. 594 ▶ He is probably guiding the others.

Making Pie Charts

- Have students make a series of pie charts about the people of New Zealand, using the following statistical information: 70 percent of all New Zealanders live on North Island, while the rest of the population lives on South Island and the other small islands; about 85 percent of the population of New Zealand lives in urban areas, while the rest of the people live in rural areas; 87 percent of New Zealanders are of European ancestry, 12 percent are Maoris, and the rest are of other ancestry.
- Conclude the activity by having students make generalizations about New Zealanders, based on the pie charts.

Using Source Material

- Ask students to imagine they are members of Captain Cook's crew on his voyage to Australia and New Zealand.
- Have students write a letter to their families in England in which they describe what the Maoris are like.
- Remind students that the information in their letters should be based on a factual source, such as Captain Cook's journal.
- Conclude this activity by asking volunteers to read their letters to the class. Discuss the accuracy of the letters with the class.

Optional Activities

Read and Think

Sections A, B, and C

To summarize information about the people, government, and economy of New Zealand, ask the following questions:

1. **Name some of the occupations of the Europeans who came to New Zealand after 1790.**
   (Whalers, convicts, traders, and missionaries *p. 594*)

2. **Why did conflicts develop between the Maoris and the British government?**
   (The Maoris felt that the British were cheating them out of their lands, and British settlers felt the Maoris were inhibiting development. *p. 596*)

3. **Describe New Zealand's government.**
   (A one-house parliament elected by the people *p. 597*)

   Thinking Critically **Why would you expect to see women taking an active role in government in New Zealand?** (Synthesize)
   (Because they have been allowed to participate in government for such a long time *p. 597*)

VISUAL THINKING SKILL

Interpreting a Time Line

- Have students look at the time line on this page and ask: **How many years passed between Captain Cook's arrival in New Zealand and the formation of the Commonwealth of Australia?**
  (132)

Great Britain made New Zealand part of the British Empire in 1840. The Maoris were promised protection of their lands if they accepted British authority, or rule. Conflicts arose between the Maoris and the government, in spite of this promise. The Maoris felt that they were being cheated. The European settlers thought that the Maoris stood in the way of the development of New Zealand. These conflicts led to warfare in which the Maoris were defeated.

Ancestry The Maoris make up about 12 percent of New Zealand's population. A number of New Zealanders have both Maori and European ancestors. Modern New Zealand has a double **heritage** (HER-ih tihj), that is, a culture handed down from the past.

Many immigrants in recent years have come from Polynesia, as the ancestors of the Maoris did long ago. A large number of these recent immigrants have settled in Auckland, which is called the largest Polynesian city in the world.

B. People Change the Land

Forest Fires Both the Maoris and the Europeans changed the New Zealand landscape. The Maoris set fires in the forest to drive out the birds they hunted and to clear the land for planting. Perhaps as much as one third of the forests in New Zealand had been cleared by fire before the Europeans arrived there.

The European settlers also used fire to clear the forests. Much of what is now green pasture was once covered with trees.

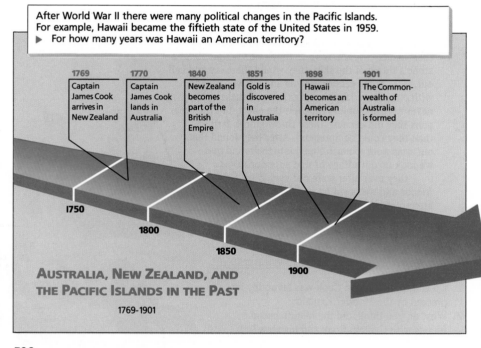

After World War II there were many political changes in the Pacific Islands. For example, Hawaii became the fiftieth state of the United States in 1959.
▶ For how many years was Hawaii an American territory?

1769 Captain James Cook arrives in New Zealand

1770 Captain James Cook lands in Australia

1840 New Zealand becomes part of the British Empire

1851 Gold is discovered in Australia

1898 Hawaii becomes an American territory

1901 The Commonwealth of Australia is formed

1750   1800   1850   1900

AUSTRALIA, NEW ZEALAND, AND THE PACIFIC ISLANDS IN THE PAST
1769-1901

596

Curriculum Connection

Government Tell students that there are 97 members in New Zealand's one-house parliament and that of these 97 members, four are always Maoris.

- Discuss with students whether they think this is fair.
- Remind students that Maoris make up about 12 percent of New Zealand's population. Tell them that their representation in New Zealand's parliament constitutes about 4 percent.
- Conclude the activity by discussing whether Maori representation in New Zealand's parliament should be changed and, if so, how it should be changed.

596

Reteaching Main Objective

⭐ ***Explain what brought European settlers to New Zealand.***

- Have students make a bulletin board display illustrating why Europeans settled in New Zealand.
- Before students begin, review with them what kinds of Europeans came to settle in New Zealand and what attracted them to the land.
- Then assign students to illustrate specific groups of European settlers.
- Conclude the activity by having students label their pictures and make a title for the bulletin board display.

European Imports Like the Europeans who settled in Australia, settlers in New Zealand brought animals, seeds, and tools, as well as ideas and diseases. Diseases killed off at least half of the Maoris in the 1840s and 1850s. In addition to farm animals, the settlers brought birds and wild animals from Europe. They thought the songs of familiar birds would make them feel more at home. They introduced grouse, rabbits, pheasants, and deer for hunting. They even imported fish for the streams.

Almost all the food grains and vegetables grown in New Zealand today were brought by early settlers. Even many of the plants sown for pasture, such as white clover, were imported. The settlers also brought bees to fertilize the clover.

C. New Zealand Today

Government Today, New Zealand is an independent member of the Commonwealth of Nations. As in Australia, Queen Elizabeth II is the symbolic head of state, but she does not rule.

New Zealand is governed by a one-house parliament elected by the people. New Zealand was the first country in the world to allow women to vote in national elections. The women of New Zealand have been voting for nearly a century.

Sheepherding is still an important industry in New Zealand.
▶ Why, do you think, does the shepherd use a motorcycle to do his job?

Economy New Zealand's main exports come from its farms and ranches, although 85 percent of the people live in cities and towns. Wool, meat, dairy products, and fruit are leading exports. New Zealand is known for the kiwi fruit. Its name supposedly comes from its shape, which is like that of the flightless bird called the kiwi.

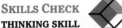

LESSON 2 REVIEW

THINK AND WRITE   (Infer)
A. Explain New Zealand's double heritage.
B. How did the Maoris and the European settlers change New Zealand? **(Recall)**
C. Describe the government and economy of New Zealand. **(Recall)**

SKILLS CHECK
THINKING SKILL

Compare the flags of Australia and New Zealand, found on the charts on pages 32–43, with the flag of the United Kingdom also found on these charts. What element do the flags share? Why do they have this common element?

597

UNDERSTANDING THE LESSON

NAME

UNDERSTANDING THE LESSON   CHAPTER **23**

Organizing Facts   LESSON 2 CONTENT MASTER

✱ The chart shows the main ideas of the lesson. Fill in the blank spaces with the details that support each main idea. The first one has been done for you.

All New Zealanders originally came from other lands.
1. Ancestors of the Maoris came from Polynesia about 1,000 years ago.
2. After 1790 many Europeans found their way to New Zealand.
3. Many immigrants in recent years have come from Polynesia.

New Zealanders clear forests.
1. Maoris set fires in forests to drive out birds they hunted and to clear land for planting.
2. Europeans used fire to clear forests for pasture land.

People from Other Lands Shape New Zealand

Europeans brought animals and seeds to New Zealand, and developed an agricultural economy.
1. Animals included farm animals, rabbits, grouse, pheasants, and deer.
2. Almost all food grains and vegetables grown in New Zealand were brought by early settlers.
3. New Zealand's main exports come from farms and ranches.

New Zealand's government has ties with Great Britain.
1. New Zealand is a member of the Commonwealth of Nations.
2. Queen Elizabeth II is the symbolic head of state.
3. New Zealand is governed by a one-house parliament elected by the people.

Think and Write: Write a paragraph telling how the Maoris of New Zealand have been treated by European settlers and their descendants. You may use the back of this sheet.
Answers should reflect independent thinking; suggestions appear in the Answer Key.
154   Use with textbook pages 594–597.

◀ **Review Master Booklet, p. 154**

Lesson 2 Review

Answers to Think and Write
A. New Zealand was settled first by the Maoris and later by Europeans. This has given New Zealand a double heritage.

B. Both used fire to clear the forests. Much of what is now pasture land was once covered with trees.

C. New Zealand is governed by a one-house parliament elected by the people. New Zealand's economy is dependent on the products that come from its farms and ranches. Its main exports are wool, meat, dairy products, and fruit.

Answer to Skills Check
The pattern of the flag of the United Kingdom can be found in the upper left-hand corner of the flags of Australia and New Zealand. The flags share this common element because Australia and New Zealand were once colonies of the United Kingdom and still remain members of the Commonwealth of Nations.

Focus Your Reading
Ask the lesson focus question found at the beginning of the lesson: **How did the Maoris and the European settlers affect New Zealand?**
(They changed the landscape of New Zealand by burning down the forests to clear the land, and they gave the country a double heritage.)

Additional Practice
You may wish to assign the ancillary materials listed below.

Understanding the Lesson p. 154
Workbook p. 126

Answers to Caption Questions

p. 596 ▶ For 61 years
p. 597 ▶ He can cover more territory more quickly on a motorcycle.

CITIZENSHIP AND AMERICAN VALUES

YOU DECIDE: SHOULD THE LAWS OF A COUNTRY REPLACE ITS TREATIES?

You learned in Chapter 23 that New Zealand is a relatively small island country in the Pacific Ocean. It is about 1,000 miles (1,609 km) southeast of Australia and 6,500 miles (10,500 km) away from the United States. During the days of the British Empire, New Zealand was a British colony. It gained its independence in 1907.

New Zealand fought on the side of the Allies during World War II. About 140,000 troops traveled all over the world to fight the enemy.

Following World War II, New Zealand, Australia, and the United States signed the Australia–New Zealand–United States (ANZUS) defense treaty. The name combines the first letter of each word in the names of the member countries. This treaty recognized that an armed attack on any of the nations would be dangerous to them all.

The government of New Zealand adopted a new policy in 1984, which later became a law. This law banned nuclear weapons and ships powered by nuclear energy from the nation's ports and territorial waters. On the next page are two different points of view about whether New Zealand has the right to deny the United States and Australia access to its shores if their ships are carrying nuclear weapons or are powered by nuclear energy. Read them both and decide for yourself.

Objectives

1. **Explain** the point of view of New Zealand's government and of the United States government on the nuclear issue.

2. **Develop** an awareness of and skills in resolving social issues.

Guided Reading

1. **Why did Australia, New Zealand, and the United States form the ANZUS treaty?**
   (They recognized that an armed attack on any of the nations would be dangerous to them all.)

2. **What new policy did the government of New Zealand adopt in 1984?**
   (One which banned nuclear weapons and ships powered by nuclear energy from the nation's ports and territorial waters)

3. **Who denied the United States Navy destroyer access to New Zealand?**
   (David Lange, New Zealand's prime minister)

4. **Why did the United States government not want to announce whether or not the ship was carrying nuclear weapons?**
   (Because officials argued that the country cannot announce such information because it would expose its operations to the enemy)

5. **How did the United States government respond to New Zealand's actions?**
   (In 1986 the government announced that it would no longer guarantee the security of New Zealand; in effect, breaking the alliance and isolating New Zealand as an ally.)

Optional Activities

For Your Information

The United States Navy commissioned its first nuclear submarine, the *Nautilus,* in 1954. Nuclear submarines can travel long distances underwater because, unlike conventional submarines, which burn fuel oil, they do not require air for combustion. The navy had about 125 nuclear submarines in the early 1980s.

Nuclear-powered surface ships have also been developed by the Navy. These ships can travel at high speeds for long distances without refueling. More than 33 percent of the United States Navy's ships were nuclear-powered by the mid-1980s.

View_____

New Zealanders Have the Right to Protect Their Country from Nuclear Weapons

Based on the provisions of the ANZUS treaty, the United States Navy and United States ships were free to move about the waters and ports of New Zealand. However, New Zealanders began to object to visits by American ships that carried nuclear weapons or were powered by nuclear energy.

Relations between the United States and New Zealand became strained when, in 1985, New Zealand's Prime Minister, David Lange, denied a United States destroyer access to a New Zealand port. Lange issued the denial after United States officials refused to give assurances that the ship carried no nuclear weapons. According to reports, the Prime Minister had the support of the people of New Zealand.

Polls have shown decided support for the antinuclear ships policy, although most New Zealanders, like their government, prefer to keep ANZUS intact.

Thinking for Yourself

1. Do you think New Zealanders had the right to keep United States ships from visiting their ports?
2. Do you think the United States should isolate New Zealand as an ally because of government policies?

The Security of New Zealand Cannot Be Guaranteed

The United States government was very unhappy with these developments. United States officials argued that the country cannot announce whether its ships do or do not carry nuclear weapons. That would expose its operations to the enemy. "An alliance partner," they said, "cannot pick and choose the nature of its contributions." Also, since 40 percent of the United States Navy is nuclear powered, it would be very impractical to comply with New Zealand's demands.

The United States government reacted very strongly to the position of New Zealand. Because of the policy, the United States announced in 1986 that it would no longer guarantee the security of New Zealand under the ANZUS treaty. In other words, the United States broke the alliance and isolated New Zealand as an ally.

Thinking for Yourself

1. Answers should reflect independent thinking but may include yes, New Zealanders had the right to deny access to United States ships because the ports belong to New Zealand, or no, because as allies receiving United States protection, they were obliged to help the United States military.

2. Answers should reflect independent thinking but may include no, the United States should still protect New Zealand, or yes, because New Zealand did not uphold its side of the treaty.

Current Events

- Bring encyclopedias and news magazines to class to have students research recent military alliances. (Prime examples include the North Atlantic Treaty Organization [N.A.T.O.] and the Warsaw Pact.)

- Have students list the primary responsibilities of each party under the alliance.

- You may wish to have students further research problems that have developed between alliance members and the methods by which the members tried to resolve them.

Optional Activities

The Pacific Islands

Objectives

★ **1. Explain** what changes occurred in the Pacific Islands after World War II.

2. Describe what happened to many Pacific islands between 1850 and World War I.

3. Identify the following people and places: *Queen Pomare, Queen Victoria, Tahiti, Hawaii, Papua New Guinea, Fiji, American Samoa, Western Samoa, Tuvalu, Nauru,* and *Kiribati.*

1 STARTING THE LESSON

Motivation Activity

■ Put the following sentences on the chalkboard: *Mi stap hir. Disfela meri inaisfela.*

■ Ask students if they can figure out what these sentences mean. (*I am here. This woman is pretty.*) Tell them that reading them aloud may help.

■ Ask students if the language is familiar. Tell them that these sentences are Melanesian Pidgin, a language that developed when Europeans and Melanesians met and needed to communicate.

Think About What You Know

■ Assign the THINK ABOUT WHAT YOU KNOW activity on p. 600.

■ Students' answers should reflect independent thinking but may include good year-round weather and few pollution problems as advantages, and little protection against tropical storms and limited access to foreign cultural output as disadvantages.

Study the Vocabulary

■ Have students look up the vocabulary word in their Glossary.

■ Ask them to skim the lesson to find the way the word is used in context.

600

LESSON **3**

The Pacific Islands

THINK ABOUT WHAT YOU KNOW

Most of the Pacific Islands are small and located in the tropics. What, do you think, would be the advantages and disadvantages of living on a small tropical island?

STUDY THE VOCABULARY

protectorate

FOCUS YOUR READING

How did the governments of the Pacific Island countries change after World War II?

A. Empires in the Pacific

Foreign Possessions In 1838, Queen Pomare of Tahiti sent a message to Queen Victoria of Great Britain, asking for protection. Queen Pomare made the request because a French warship had delivered a message demanding that the French be allowed to settle in Tahiti.

Victoria replied that Great Britain could not defend Tahiti at that time. In the meantime a French representative managed to get four Tahitian chiefs to sign a request that Tahiti be made a French **protectorate** (proh TEK tur iht). A protectorate is a land at least partly controlled by a stronger country. Queen Pomare protested the French action, but in the end, Tahiti became a French protectorate.

Between 1850 and World War I, many Pacific Islands were taken over by France, Great Britain, Germany, and the United States. Some islands became colonies in large empires. The United States took over the island of Hawaii in 1898 and declared it an American territory.

600

Independence World War I had little effect on the Pacific Islands. Major battles, however, were fought in the Pacific during World War II.

After the war there were great changes in the political status, or situation, of the Pacific Islands. Hawaii became the fiftieth state of the United States in 1959. A number of islands became independent, or self-governing.

B. Countries of Melanesia

Papua New Guinea is the largest of the Pacific Island countries, occupying the eastern half of the island of New Guinea. It became independent in 1975.

Much of Papua New Guinea is mountainous and heavily forested. Since becoming independent the country has changed rapidly. The discovery of gold and

In the mid-1800s, Queen Pomare tried to protect Tahiti from becoming a French protectorate.
► How can you tell that she was a queen?

Optional Activities

Cooperative Learning

Debating Divide the class into groups of five students.

● Have each group decide who will be responsible for the following positions: two members of the British Parliament who feel that Queen Victoria should come to the aid of Queen Pomare of Tahiti, two members of Parliament who feel that Queen Victoria should not help Queen Pomare, and one member of Parliament who must be convinced of which course of action to follow.

● In a 15-minute debate, the four members of Parliament must try to sway the opinion of the fifth member.

● After the debate the fifth member must tell the class if he or she is for or against helping Queen Pomare and why.

oil has speeded change. One government official noted, "In the 14 years since independence, our people have gone from village huts and caves to skyscrapers."

Fiji was a British colony for nearly a century before it became independent, in 1970. Years ago, people were brought from India to work in the sugar fields. Today, Indians outnumber Fijians.

Other independent countries in Melanesia include the Solomon Islands, Tonga, and Vanuatu. These three countries and Papua New Guinea are members of the Commonwealth of Nations.

C. Countries of Polynesia

The island country of Tahiti is no longer a French protectorate. Tahiti and 130 other countries make up the French overseas territory of French Polynesia. As

Papua New Guinea lies on the eastern half of the second largest island in the world.
▶ To what island group does Papua New Guinea belong?

an overseas territory, French Polynesia has its own elected assembly.

The Samoan Islands were divided by Germany and the United States in 1900. The eastern islands, known as American Samoa, are a territory of the United States. The people elect a governor and legislature. Western Samoa became independent in 1962.

Tuvalu is one of the smallest states in Polynesia. It is less than half the size of Manhattan Island in New York City, yet it is an independent country.

601

Lesson 3 Review

Answers to Think and Write

A. Before World War I, many Pacific islands were taken over by France, Great Britain, Germany, and the United States.

B. Papua New Guinea is the largest Pacific island country. It became independent in 1975 and has changed rapidly as a result of discoveries of oil and gold. Fiji became independent in 1974. Today, Indians outnumber Fijians. The Solomon Islands, Tonga, and Vanuatu are independent countries and members of the Commonwealth of Nations.

C. Tahiti is an overseas territory of France, American Samoa is a territory of the United States, and Western Samoa and Tuvalu are independent countries.

D. It is a large region of small islands.

Answer to Skills Check

Hawaiian Islands are a state of the United States. Fiji is independent. Tokelau Islands is administered by New Zealand. Western Samoa is independent. Nauru is independent. Pitcairn Island is a dependency of Great Britain.

Focus Your Reading

Ask the lesson focus question found at the beginning of the lesson: **How did the governments of the Pacific Island countries change after World War II?**
(Many of the Pacific Island countries became independent or self-governing.)

Additional Practice

You may wish to assign the ancillary materials listed below.

Understanding the Lesson p. 155
Workbook pp. 127-128

Phosphate mining is an important industry on the island of Nauru.
▶ What equipment is used to mine the phosphate?

D. Countries of Micronesia

Micronesia is truly a vast region of small islands. Some are independent countries. Tiny Nauru has an area of only 8 square miles (21 sq km). The center of the island is a deposit of high-grade phosphate rock. Phosphate is a valuable fertilizer. The country has been living by exporting parts of itself. Over the years many millions of tons of phosphate have been mined and shipped abroad. Nauru is now independent, but it has close ties with Australia.

Kiribati was once a British colony called the Gilbert Islands. The country consists of 33 coral islands that rise no more than 12 feet (4 m) above sea level. The islands of Kiribati are scattered over about 2 million square miles (5 million sq km) of the Pacific Ocean. Kiribati has been independent since 1979.

The United States has ties with several groups of islands in Micronesia. These include the Commonwealth of Northern Mariana Islands, the Federated States of Micronesia, the Republic of the Marshall Islands, and the Republic of Palau. All are self-governing, but the United States is responsible for their defense.

LESSON **3** REVIEW

THINK AND WRITE

A. Which countries took over Pacific Islands before World War I? (Recall)

B. Briefly describe the following five countries of Melanesia: Papua New Guinea, Fiji, the Solomon Islands, Tonga, and Vanuatu. (Synthesize)

C. What is the difference in the political status of Tahiti, American Samoa, Western Samoa, and Tuvalu? (Analyze)

D. Why, do you think, is Micronesia an appropriate name for the island group in the Pacific? (Analyze)

SKILLS CHECK

MAP SKILL

Locate the following Pacific Islands on the Atlas map on pages 610–611: Hawaiian Islands, Fiji Islands, Tokelau Islands, Western Samoa, Nauru, Pitcairn Island. Determine whether each is independent or a possession of another country.

UNDERSTANDING THE LESSON

NAME _____
UNDERSTANDING THE LESSON
CHAPTER **23**

Organizing Facts
LESSON 3 CONTENT MASTER

* The chart shows the main ideas of the lesson. Fill in the blank spaces with the details that support each main idea. The first one has been done for you.

Before World War I, foreign powers controlled many Pacific islands.
1. Tahiti became a French protectorate.
2. Some islands became colonies in large empires.
3. Hawaii became an American territory.

Most countries of Melanesia became independent after World War II.
1. Papua New Guinea became independent in 1975.
2. Fiji gained its independence from Great Britain in 1974.
3. Other independent countries include Solomon Islands, Tonga, and Vanuatu.

The Pacific Island Nations in the Twentieth Century

Polynesian countries include territories and independent nations.
1. Tahiti and 130 other countries are part of French Polynesia.
2. American Samoa is a territory of the United States.
3. Western Samoa became independent in 1962.
4. Tuvalu, one of the smallest states in Polynesia, is an independent nation.

Many Micronesian countries are self-governing, but some maintain ties with larger countries.
1. Nauru is independent but has close ties with Australia.
2. Kiribati became independent in 1979.
3. Commonwealth of Northern Mariana Islands, Federated States of Micronesia, Republic of the Marshall Islands, Republic of Palau are selfgoverning, but the U.S. is responsible for their defense.

Think and Write: What advantages have some Pacific Island nations gained by close ties with the countries that were their colonial rulers? Write a paragraph answering this question. You may use the back of the sheet. Answers should reflect independent thinking; suggestions appear in the Answer Key.
Use with textbook pages 600–602.

155

◀ **Review Master Booklet, p. 155**

USING THE VOCABULARY

boomerang   heritage
food processing   protectorate
smelting

On a separate sheet of paper, write the word or words from the list above that best complete the sentences.

1. Many people in Australia have jobs in _____, the procedure in which agricultural products are canned or frozen.
2. The Maoris and the Europeans have given New Zealand a double _____, or culture handed down from the past.
3. Tahiti is no longer a French _____, a land at least partly controlled by a stronger country.
4. An Aborigine used a throwing stick, called a _____, for defense.
5. Mining and _____, which is the process of separating a metal from other materials in its ore, provide Australians with many jobs.

REMEMBERING WHAT YOU READ

On a separate sheet of paper, answer the following questions in complete sentences.

1. Why did the Dutch come to Australia?
2. What name did the Dutch give the land that we now know as Australia?
3. Who were the first group of Europeans to settle in Australia?
4. What did the Europeans bring to Australia that changed the continent?
5. Why did trouble break out between the Aborigines and the settlers?
6. What weapons did the Aborigines use to fight the Europeans?
7. Explain how the government of Australia is organized.
8. What is the oldest and largest city in Australia?
9. What animal did the early settlers make good use of in Australia?
10. What industries provide jobs for people in Australia?
11. What promise did the British authorities make to the Maoris?
12. What products do the farms and ranches of New Zealand produce?
13. What happened to many of the Pacific islands in the time period between 1850 and World War I?
14. What is the largest of the Pacific Island countries?
15. What islands of Polynesia are a territory of the United States?

TYING MATH TO SOCIAL STUDIES

You read that 24 English rabbits were released in Australia in 1859. If 50 percent of those rabbits were does, or female rabbits, how many does were released? A female rabbit usually produces about 20 young a year. How many baby rabbits could the does have produced in one year? In two years? In three years?

Using the Vocabulary

1. food processing
2. heritage
3. protectorate
4. boomerang
5. smelting

Remembering What You Read

1. The Dutch came to Australia to trade.
2. *New Holland*
3. British convicts
4. Animals, seeds, and tools, as well as ideas and diseases.
5. Because the settlers' farms and ranches occupied lands where the Aborigines hunted and gathered food
6. The Aborigines used boomerangs.
7. The government of Australia is similar to that of the United States.
8. Sydney is the oldest and largest city.
9. They made good use of sheep.
10. The food processing, manufacturing, and mining and smelting industries
11. Protection of their lands if they accepted British authority
12. Wool, meat, dairy products, and fruit
13. Many Pacific islands were taken over by France, Great Britain, Germany, and the United States.
14. Papua New Guinea is the largest.
15. The islands called American Samoa are a territory of the United States.

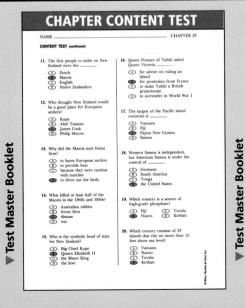

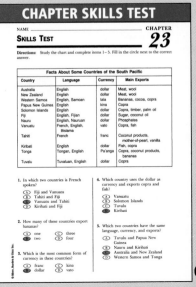

Thinking Critically

1. Answers might include that in both places the native populations were treated poorly and denied their rights.
2. It enabled them to transport beef and mutton to England.
3. Answers should reflect that Tasman did not like the Aborigines because they were not traders and that Cook was pleased to find a pleasant land.
4. Answers may include that the nations might want to decide their own fate.
5. Answers may include that the United States wants to maintain ties with several island groups in Micronesia because it wants to have military bases there.

Summarizing the Chapter

Lesson 1
1. Farms and ranches
2. Diseases wiped out much of the Aboriginal population.
3. A government was established.
4. Towns and cities

Lesson 2
1. Forest fires were used to clear the land.
2. New crops, birds, and wild animals
3. Commonwealth of Nations
4. Most New Zealanders live in cities.

Lesson 3
1. Many countries became independent.
2. Tahiti became a French territory.
3. American Samoa became a territory of the United States.
4. Hawaii became a state of the United States.

THINKING CRITICALLY

On a separate sheet of paper, answer the following questions in complete sentences.

1. Do you think there are any similarities between how Aborigines were treated in Australia and how Native Americans were treated in America?
2. How did the invention of refrigerated ships help the economy of Australia?
3. If you had been an explorer, do you think you would have agreed with Abel Tasman's view of New Zealand or with Captain James Cook's view of New Zealand? Explain your answer.
4. Why, in your opinion, would some Pacific Island countries choose to become independent, or self-governing?
5. What reasons could the United States have for maintaining ties with several island groups in Micronesia?

SUMMARIZING THE CHAPTER

On a separate sheet of paper, copy the graphic organizer shown below. Beside the main idea for each lesson, write four statements that support the main idea.

CHAPTER THEME — There are close economic and political ties between Australia, New Zealand, the islands of the Pacific, and other nations.

LESSON 1
Australia has changed since Europeans arrived on the continent.
1. ___
2. ___
3. ___
4. ___

LESSON 2
The Maoris and the European settlers have affected New Zealand.
1. ___
2. ___
3. ___
4. ___

LESSON 3
The governments of the Pacific Island countries changed after World War II.
1. ___
2. ___
3. ___
4. ___

604

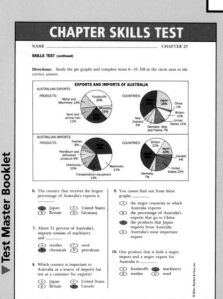

REVIEW

COOPERATIVE LEARNING

In Unit 7 you learned about Australia, New Zealand, and the Pacific Island nations. Each area has unique characteristics.

A report is a beneficial way for your group to learn more about a country or island.

PROJECT

Work with a group of classmates to write a report about a country or island in Unit 7. The purpose of the report will be to learn more about a certain place and teach the other students in your class.

The first step in the project will be brainstorming. Hold a group meeting to talk about all the interesting and exciting material about your area. Try to come up with at least ten different ideas. Choose one member to write down all your group's ideas. When you are finished brainstorming, the person should read the list aloud and ask group members to vote on what they think are the five best ideas to research.

After you have decided on the five best ideas to write about, divide the tasks among group members.

● One group member will be the presenter. This leader will gather all the information from the others and present the report to the class.

Each member in the group will gather information. Information can be found in your textbook and different encyclopedias.

● One person should draw and label the location studied. This could be the cover for the report.

● One group member will be responsible for writing or typing the report.

● One person should gather interesting photographs for the report.

PRESENTATION AND REVIEW

The group leader will present the report to the class. The students in other groups should ask questions based on the report. The members of the group will answer these questions.

After the presentation is over, your group should meet to evaluate your project. The following questions will help you in your evaluation: How well did your group's members work together? How could your project have been improved? Did everyone in the group do his or her job?

REMEMBER TO:
- Give your ideas.
- Listen to others' ideas.
- Plan your work with the group.
- Present your project.
- Discuss how your group worked.

605

You may wish to refer to the article on Cooperative Learning found in the front of your Teacher's Edition.

Objectives

1. **Explain** the uses of a summary.
2. **Summarize** a lesson in your social studies textbook.

Why Do I Need This Skill?

To help students better understand the importance of summarizing information, ask the following question: **Do you think it is easier to understand written material if it is broken down into smaller pieces?** (Most students will probably answer that material broken down into manageable pieces is easier to understand.)

Then tell students that they will use this concept in writing a summary.

Learning the Skill

To check the students' comprehension of writing a summary, ask the following questions:

1. **What is the first step in writing a summary of a section of a lesson?**
   (Write down the section heading as the title of the summary.)

2. **What are the second and third steps in writing a summary of a section of a lesson?**
   (Second step: Decide what the main idea is for each paragraph in the section. Write it down under the summary title. Third step: Read through the summary. Take out unimportant information and add important ideas that might have been left out.)

SKILL TRACE:	Summarizing Information	
INTRODUCE PE pp. 606–607	**PRACTICE** TE pp. 606–607 **WB** pp. 82–83	**TEST** Unit 7 Test, TMB

A. WHY DO I NEED THIS SKILL?

Your social studies textbook contains so much information that it would be impossible for you to remember it all. Therefore, it is important for you to remember the main points of your reading. One way to do this is to write a **summary**. A summary is a short way of stating, in your own words, the important ideas from a piece of writing.

B. LEARNING THE SKILL

It would be very difficult to summarize all the information in this book in just a few sentences or even in a few pages. Such a summary would leave out many important ideas. This is why you need to break the material you are summarizing into manageable pieces. A good way of doing this is to summarize one section of a lesson at a time.

To write a summary for a section of a lesson in your social studies textbook, follow these steps.

1. Write the section heading as the title for your summary.
2. Decide what the main idea is for each paragraph in the section. Write the main ideas under the summary title.
3. Read through your section summary. Take out any information that is not important. Add any important ideas that you left out.

Here is a summary for the section of Chapter 23 called "New Zealand Today." Reread the section, found on page 597, and then compare it with this summary. Notice that the summary includes the title and the main ideas of the section.

New Zealand Today

- New Zealand is part of the Commonwealth of Nations, with Queen Elizabeth II serving as the symbolic head of state.

- New Zealand is governed by a one-house parliament elected by the people.

- Although most New Zealanders live in cities, farming and ranching are very important; the country's main exports come from farms and ranches.

Certain information in this section of the book has been left out of the summary. For example, the information that you read about the kiwi is interesting, but it is not the main idea for the paragraph. A summary contains only the most important information.

C. PRACTICING THE SKILL

On a separate sheet of paper, write a summary for the section called "Australia's

Optional Activities

Homework Activity

- As a homework activity, ask students to write a summary of a newspaper article.

- Remind students to (1) write down the title of the article, (2) write the main idea under the title, and (3) take out information that is not important and add any important ideas that they might have left out.

Economy," found on pages 592–593, in Chapter 23. The summary title and the first main idea have been written for you. Copy the parts of the summary shown and then write the main ideas for the rest of the section.

Australia's Economy
● Growing crops is an important industry in Australia, which is a leading exporter of such products as wheat, other grains, and fruit.

D. APPLYING THE SKILL

You can also summarize larger sections in your social studies textbook. For example, you can summarize an entire lesson by writing one or two sentences that tell the main ideas in each section. Try writing a summary of the first lesson in Chapter 23, which begins on page 589. See if making a summary helps you remember the main points in the lesson. Then try writing a summary of the entire chapter.

Practicing the Skill
Students' sample summaries will vary.

Australia's Economy
■ More people work in factories and mines than on farms or ranches.

■ Many people work in processing metals.

■ Sheep raising is an important industry in Australia, which is a leading exporter of wool and mutton.

■ Refrigeration opened new markets for Australia, as Australia now leads the world in the export of beef.

Applying the Skill
Students' sample summaries will vary.

Australia
■ In 1770, Captain James Cook landed in Australia and claimed it for Great Britain.

■ The first group of Europeans to live in Australia were British convicts sent there as punishment.

■ Settlers established farms and clashed with the Aborigines.

■ Australia became independent from Great Britain in 1901.

■ Many Australian workers are employed in manufacturing and agriculture.

Reteaching Activity

Students who are still having difficulty with the concept of writing a summary should summarize shorter sections of a lesson (such as "Enough Rain" in Section C of Lesson 2 of Chapter 22). You may wish to do one example with these students and then have them do another on their own.

Enough Rain
● Generally receives enough rainfall

● The plain on the eastern side of South Island is one of the drier parts of the country.

Optional Activities

Objectives

1. **Explain** why it is important to understand different points of view.

2. **Develop** an awareness of and skills in resolving social issues.

Why Do I Need This Skill?

To help students understand that people can have different points of view on a subject, ask: **How did the English point of view on settlement of New Zealand differ from the Maori point of view?**
(The British felt that the Maoris were standing in the way of development of New Zealand; the Maoris felt that they were being cheated.)

Learning the Skill

The writer's point of view is probably factual because the Europeans had never seen animals unique to Australia. The writer uses the words *unusual* and *strange* several times. The writer presents quotes from European explorers and scientific theory to support the point of view that many of Australia's animals are unusual. The quotes describing kangaroos support what the author has written.

A. WHY DO I NEED THIS SKILL?

Two writers describing the same person or event may create two totally different impressions of that person or event. This is because writers each have their own beliefs and feelings that may be reflected in their writing. These beliefs and feelings are a writer's point of view. You, too, have your own point of view. As a reader, you need to be aware of any writer's point of view so that you can decide how much of what you read is strictly factual and how much is the writer's own beliefs and feelings. From there, you can decide if you agree with the writer's point of view.

B. LEARNING THE SKILL

Writers often express a point of view when they write to persuade — that is, to get the reader to feel a certain way, to believe in something, or to buy something. A letter to an editor, an editorial, and an advertisement are examples of persuasive writing.

Writers may also express a point of view when they write to inform, or give information about a topic. Your social studies textbook is an example of something written to inform. However, writers generally try to just present facts, not a point of view, when they write to inform.

When you read, your job is to try to decide if what you are reading reflects facts and reason rather than the writer's own point of view. A point of view may be based

on emotions or faulty arguments and may not be logical. The table on the next page describes four steps to follow to recognize and understand a point of view.

In Chapter 22 you read, "A number of other Australian animals appeared strange to European eyes." Do you think this statement is the writer's point of view alone or is it factual as well? Turn back to pages 577 and 578 and reread the selection "Australia's Animals and Birds." Use the steps in the table as you read.

Does the textbook author express a particular point of view? If so, does the author also provide facts to support that point of view? Do the quotes from European explorers describing kangaroos express a point of view? Do those quotes support what the author has written?

C. PRACTICING THE SKILL

Using the steps in the table, try to determine if there is a point of view expressed in the following paragraph, which is related to early European settlement in Australia.

The first group of Europeans who reluctantly came to Australia did not want to come. They were savage convicts sent to do backbreaking work far from home as harsh punishment for breaking the law. The first fleet carrying villainous convicts, together with law-abiding marines to guard them, reached New South Wales in January 1788.

Reteaching Activity

- To review this skill, you may wish to assign students the following activities.

- Provide each student with a photocopy of the excerpt in this Skillbuilder and the "European Settlement" section, on page 589.

- As you read aloud, have students underline each sentence with a red marker if it expresses an opinion and a blue marker if it expresses a fact.

- Remind students that opinions are often expressed with adjectives and that facts are the same, no matter who is describing them.

On a separate sheet of paper, answer the following five questions in complete sentences.

1. What point of view does the writer express?
2. What words or phrases are clues that the writer has a point of view?
3. What reasons might the writer have for expressing that point of view?
4. What, if any, facts are there to support the writer's point of view?
5. Do you agree with the writer's point of view?

Now turn back to Chapter 23 and read the first paragraph in the section called "European Settlement," on page 589. Does your textbook author express a point of view? If so, how does it differ from that expressed in the paragraph that you read on page 608?

D. APPLYING THE SKILL

Whenever you read, try to determine if the writer is expressing a point of view. Remember, it is all right for a writer to express a point of view. Just be certain that you recognize a point of view and try to determine if there are facts that support it. Then you can decide for yourself if you agree or disagree with the point of view.

POINT OF VIEW
Steps for Understanding Point of View
1. As you read, look for descriptive words or phrases that may express a particular belief or feeling.
2. Think about how those words and phrases tell what the writer's attitude toward a person, event, or topic may be.
3. Determine if any facts are presented to support the writer's point of view.
4. Decide if you agree or disagree with the writer's point of view.

Homework Activity

● For homework, have students identify fact and opinion in current news magazine articles.
● Provide students with photocopies of new articles.
● Ask students to mark words, phrases, and sentences that express a point of view with a red marker.
● Have students mark factual words, phrases, and sentences with a blue marker.
● Review students' homework orally in class.

Optional Activities

Practicing the Skill

1. The writer's point of view is that the first Europeans to live in Australia were dangerous convicts who deserved their punishment.
2. Descriptive words or phrases that indicate a point of view include: "reluctantly," "did not want to come," "savage," "harsh," "villainous," and "law-abiding."
3. The writer may express that point of view because the first Europeans to settle Australia were convicts.
4. The only fact given is the date that the first prison ship reached Australia.
5. Answers should reflect independent thinking.

For students who are having difficulty with the concept of point of view, you may wish to use the reteaching activity listed below.

Applying the Skill

Encourage students to practice this skill in all types of reading that they do.

SKILL TRACE: Understanding an Author's Point of View		
INTRODUCE PE pp. 608–609	**PRACTICE** TE pp.608–609 WB pp. 53, 89	**TEST** Unit 7 Test, TMB

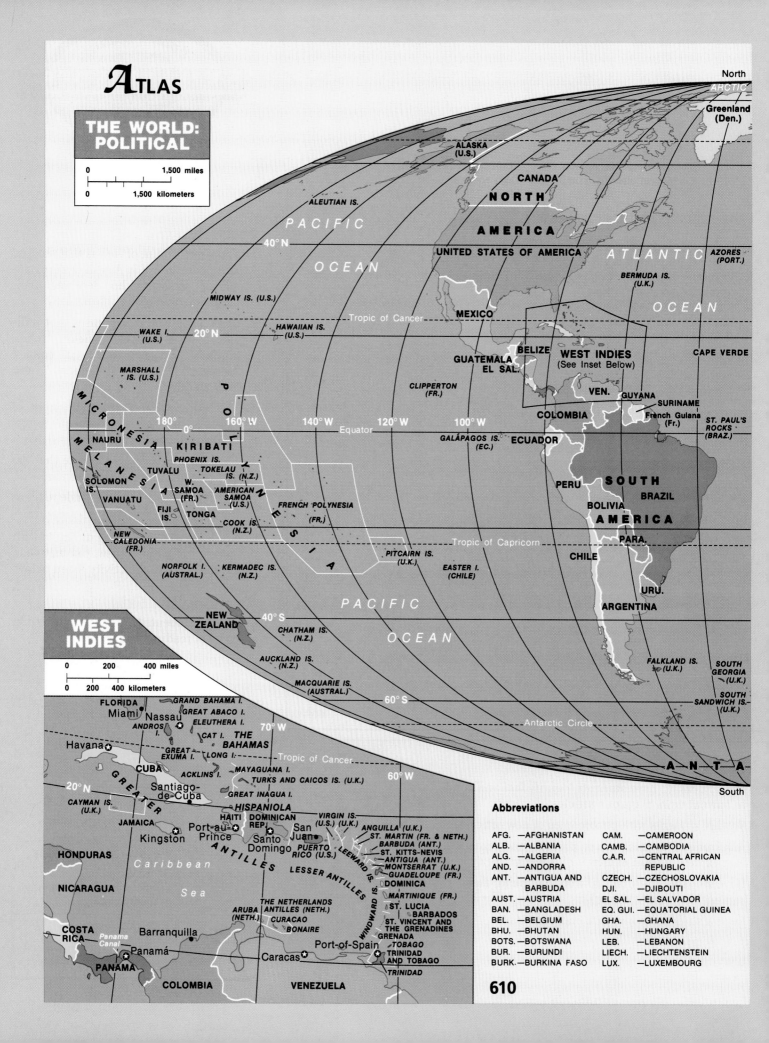

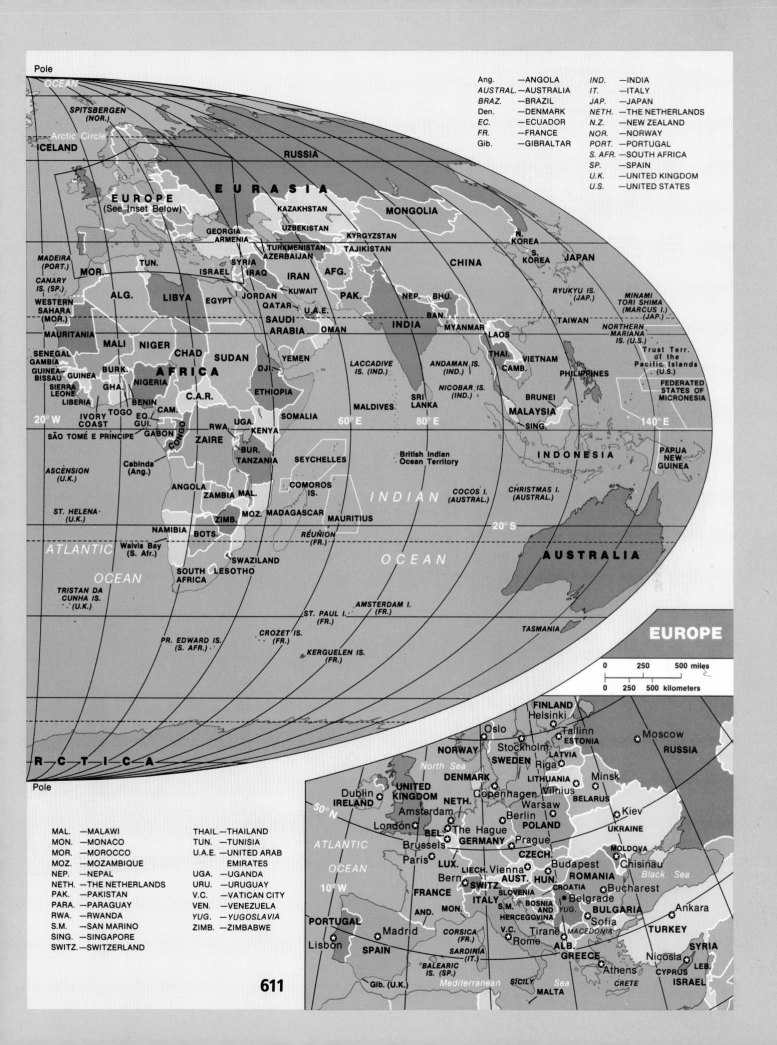

Pole

OCEAN

SPITSBERGEN
(NOR.)

Arctic Circle

ICELAND

RUSSIA

EURASIA

EUROPE
(See Inset Below)

MADEIRA
(PORT.)

CANARY
IS. (SP.)

WESTERN
SAHARA
(MOR.)

MAURITANIA

MOR.

ALG.

TUN.

LIBYA

EGYPT

SENEGAL
GAMBIA
GUINEA-
BISSAU GUINEA
SIERRA
LEONE
LIBERIA

MALI

NIGER

CHAD

BURK.

GHA.

NIGERIA

BENIN

TOGO

IVORY
COAST

EQ.
GUI.

CAM.

SÃO TOMÉ E PRÍNCIPE

GABON

CONGO

ASCENSION
(U.K.)

ANGOLA

Cabinda
(Ang.)

ST. HELENA
(U.K.)

AFRICA

C.A.R.

SUDAN

ZAIRE

RWA.

BUR.

UGA.

ZAMBIA

MAL.

ZIMB.

NAMIBIA

BOTS.

Walvis Bay
(S. Afr.)

TRISTAN DA
CUNHA IS.
(U.K.)

SWAZILAND

SOUTH
AFRICA LESOTHO

ATLANTIC

OCEAN

GEORGIA
ARMENIA

TURKMENISTAN

AZERBAIJAN

SYRIA

ISRAEL

IRAQ

JORDAN

QATAR

SAUDI
ARABIA

U.A.E.

OMAN

IRAN

KUWAIT

YEMEN

DJI.

ETHIOPIA

SOMALIA

KENYA

TANZANIA

SEYCHELLES

COMOROS
IS.

MOZ. MADAGASCAR

KAZAKHSTAN

UZBEKISTAN

TAJIKISTAN

AFG.

PAK.

MONGOLIA

KYRGYZSTAN

CHINA

N.
KOREA

S.
KOREA

JAPAN

NEP.

BHU.

BAN.

INDIA

MYANMAR

LAOS

THAI.

RYUKYU IS.
(JAP.)

TAIWAN

LACCADIVE
IS. (IND.)

SRI
LANKA

MALDIVES

ANDAMAN IS.
(IND.)

NICOBAR IS.
(IND.)

British Indian
Ocean Territory

CAMB.

VIETNAM

PHILIPPINES

BRUNEI

MALAYSIA

SING.

MINAMI
TORI SHIMA
(MARCUS I.)
(JAP.)

NORTHERN
MARIANA
IS. (U.S.)

Trust Terr.
of the
Pacific Islands
(U.S.)

FEDERATED
STATES OF
MICRONESIA

INDONESIA

PAPUA
NEW
GUINEA

INDIAN

OCEAN

MAURITIUS

RÉUNION
(FR.)

COCOS I.
(AUSTRAL.)

CHRISTMAS I.
(AUSTRAL.)

20° S

AUSTRALIA

ST. PAUL I.
(FR.)

AMSTERDAM I.
(FR.)

PR. EDWARD IS.
(S. AFR.)

CROZET IS.
(FR.)

KERGUELEN IS.
(FR.)

TASMANIA

20° W

20° W

60° E

80° E

140° E

A R C T I C A

Pole

Ang.   —ANGOLA
AUSTRAL.—AUSTRALIA
BRAZ. —BRAZIL
Den.   —DENMARK
EC.   —ECUADOR
FR.   —FRANCE
Gib.   —GIBRALTAR

IND.   —INDIA
IT.   —ITALY
JAP.   —JAPAN
NETH. —THE NETHERLANDS
N.Z.   —NEW ZEALAND
NOR.   —NORWAY
PORT. —PORTUGAL
S. AFR.—SOUTH AFRICA
SP.   —SPAIN
U.K.   —UNITED KINGDOM
U.S.   —UNITED STATES

MAL.   —MALAWI
MON.   —MONACO
MOR.   —MOROCCO
MOZ.   —MOZAMBIQUE
NEP.   —NEPAL
NETH. —THE NETHERLANDS
PAK.   —PAKISTAN
PARA. —PARAGUAY
RWA.   —RWANDA
S.M.   —SAN MARINO
SING. —SINGAPORE
SWITZ. —SWITZERLAND

THAIL. —THAILAND
TUN.   —TUNISIA
U.A.E. —UNITED ARAB
        EMIRATES
UGA.   —UGANDA
URU.   —URUGUAY
V.C.   —VATICAN CITY
VEN.   —VENEZUELA
YUG.   —YUGOSLAVIA
ZIMB. —ZIMBABWE

EUROPE

0   250   500 miles

0   250   500 kilometers

FINLAND
Helsinki

Oslo

Stockholm

Tallinn
ESTONIA

Moscow

NORWAY

SWEDEN

Riga

LATVIA

RUSSIA

North Sea

DENMARK

LITHUANIA

Minsk

Dublin
IRELAND

UNITED
KINGDOM

NETH.

Copenhagen

Vilnius

BELARUS

Amsterdam

Warsaw

Kiev

London

Berlin

POLAND

UKRAINE

BEL.

The Hague

GERMANY

Prague

Brussels

Paris

LUX.

CZECH.

MOLDOVA

ATLANTIC

OCEAN

LIECH. Vienna

Budapest

Chisinau

Bern

AUST. HUN.

ROMANIA

Black Sea

FRANCE

SWITZ.

SLOVENIA

CROATIA

Belgrade

Bucharest

AND.

MON.

S.M.

BOSNIA
AND
HERCEGOVINA

YUG.

BULGARIA

Ankara

PORTUGAL

ITALY

V.C.

Tirane

Sofia

MACEDONIA

TURKEY

Lisbon

Madrid

Rome

ALB.

Nicosia

SPAIN

CORSICA
(FR.)

GREECE

Athens

SYRIA

LEB.

SARDINIA
(IT.)

CYPRUS

ISRAEL

BALEARIC
IS. (SP.)

SICILY

Sea

CRETE

Gib. (U.K.)

Mediterranean

MALTA

50° N

10° W

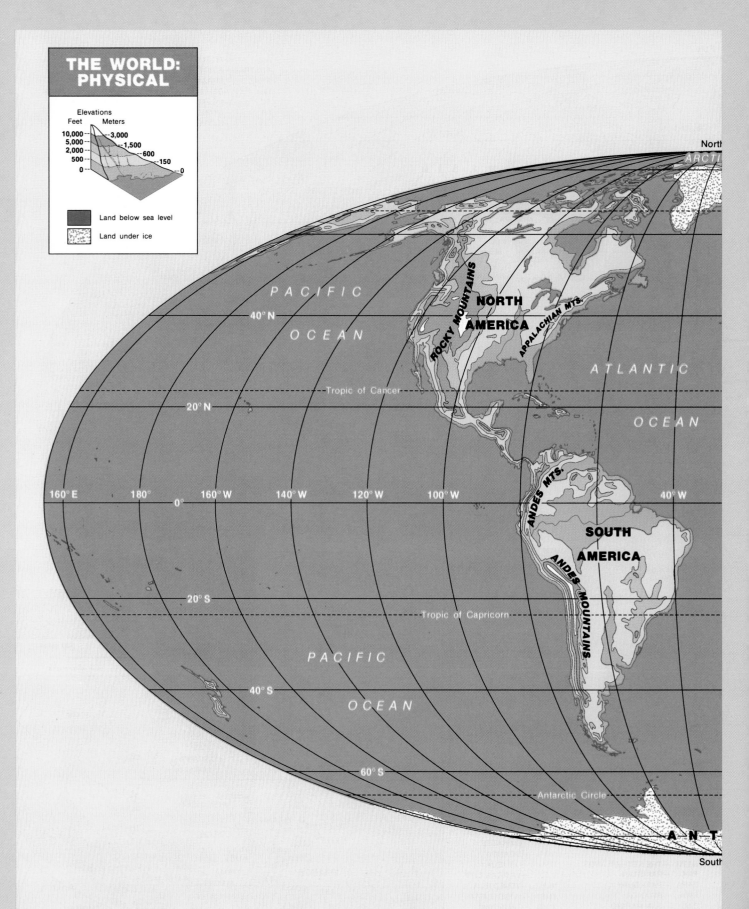

THE WORLD:
PHYSICAL

Elevations
Feet   Meters
10,000 --- --3,000
5,000 ---   --1,500
2,000 ---   --600
500 ---   --150
0 ---   --0

Land below sea level

Land under ice

PACIFIC

OCEAN

40° N

Tropic of Cancer

20° N

160° E   180°   160° W   140° W   120° W   100° W   40° W

0°

20° S

Tropic of Capricorn

PACIFIC

40° S

OCEAN

60° S

Antarctic Circle

North

ARCTI

NORTH
AMERICA

ROCKY MOUNTAINS

APPALACHIAN MTS.

ATLANTIC

OCEAN

ANDES MTS.

SOUTH
AMERICA

ANDES MOUNTAINS

A N T

South

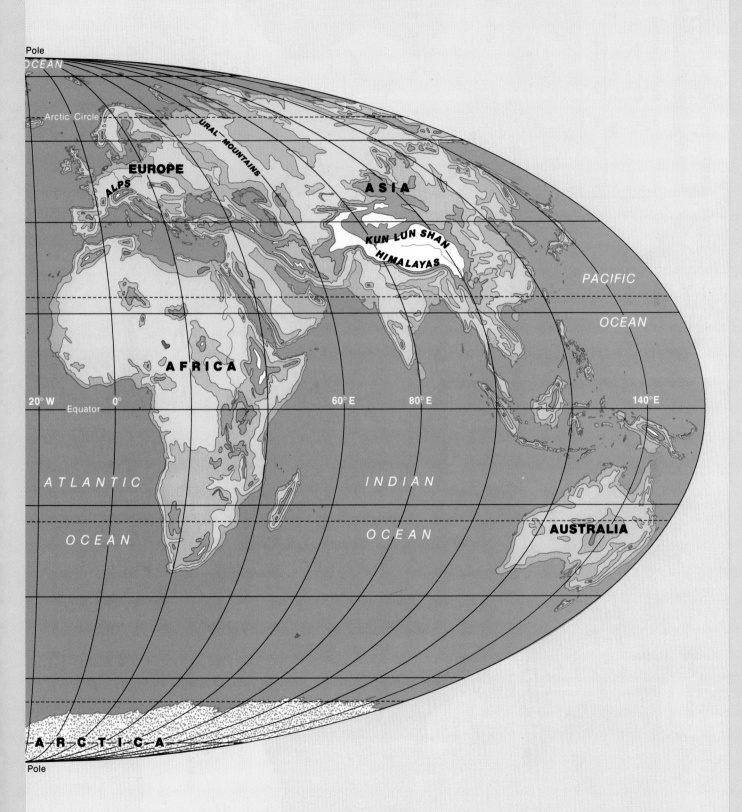

Pole

OCEAN

Arctic Circle

EUROPE

URAL MOUNTAINS

ALPS

ASIA

KUN LUN SHAN

HIMALAYAS

PACIFIC

OCEAN

AFRICA

20° W   0°   60° E   80° E   140° E

Equator

ATLANTIC   INDIAN

OCEAN   OCEAN   AUSTRALIA

ANTARCTICA

Pole

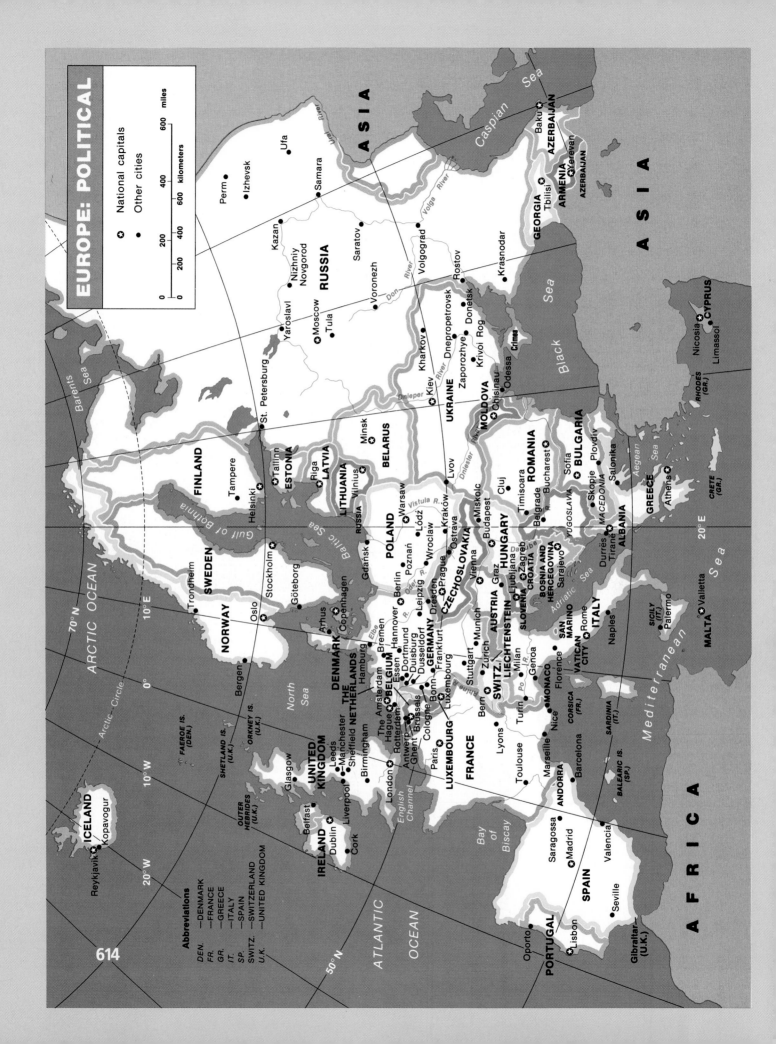

EUROPE: POLITICAL

National capitals ✪
Other cities •

| 0 | 200 | 400 | 600 | kilometers |
| 0 | 200 | 400 | 600 | miles |

Abbreviations

DEN. —DENMARK
FR. —FRANCE
GR. —GREECE
IT. —ITALY
SP. —SPAIN
SWITZ. —SWITZERLAND
U.K. —UNITED KINGDOM

614

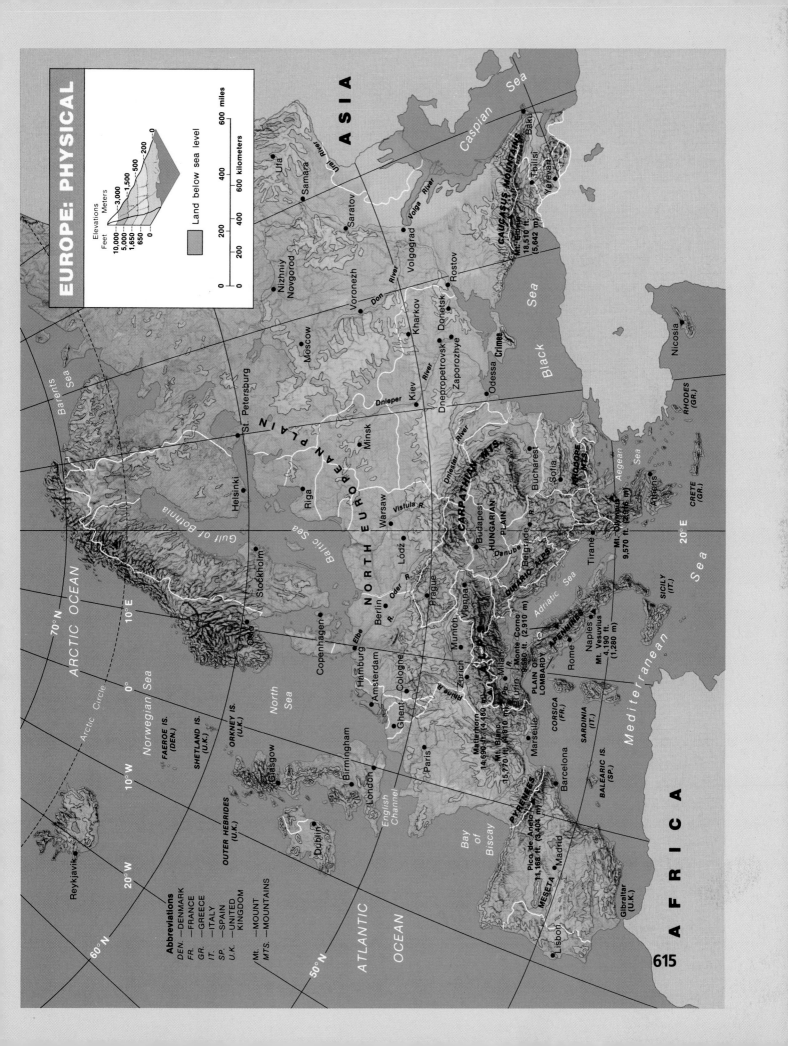

EUROPE: PHYSICAL

Elevations
Feet   Meters
10,000 — 3,000
5,000 — 1,500
1,650 — 500
650 — 200
0 — 0

Land below sea level

600 miles
600 kilometers

ASIA

AFRICA

ARCTIC OCEAN

ATLANTIC OCEAN

Norwegian Sea

North Sea

Mediterranean Sea

Barents Sea

Baltic Sea

Gulf of Bothnia

Black Sea

Caspian Sea

Adriatic Sea

Aegean Sea

Bay of Biscay

English Channel

NORTH EUROPEAN PLAIN

CAUCASUS MOUNTAINS
Mt. Elbrus
18,510 ft.
(5,642 m)

CARPATHIAN MTS.

HUNGARIAN PLAIN

DINARIC ALPS

RHODOPE MTS.

Mt. Olympus
9,570 ft.
(2,916 m)

APENNINES

Mt. Vesuvius
4,190 ft.
(1,280 m)

PLAIN OF LOMBARDY

Monte Corno
9,560 ft. (2,910 m)

Matterhorn
14,690 ft. (4,480 m)

Mt. Blanc
15,770 ft. (4,810 m)

PYRENEES
Pico de Aneto
11,168 ft. (3,404 m)

MESETA

Reykjavik

Dublin

Glasgow

Birmingham

London

Paris

Amsterdam

Ghent

Cologne

Hamburg

Copenhagen

Berlin

Munich

Zurich

Turin

Milan

Venice

Rome

Naples

Marseille

Barcelona

Madrid

Lisbon

Gibraltar (U.K.)

Tirané

Sofia

Bucharest

Belgrade

Budapest

Vienna

Prague

Warsaw

Łódź

Minsk

Riga

Helsinki

Stockholm

St. Petersburg

Moscow

Nizhniy Novgorod

Samara

Ufa

Saratov

Voronezh

Volgograd

Rostov

Donetsk

Kharkov

Dnepropetrovsk

Zaporozhye

Kiev

Odessa

Baku

Tbilisi

Yerevan

Athens

Nicosia

FAEROE IS. (DEN.)

SHETLAND IS. (U.K.)

ORKNEY IS. (U.K.)

OUTER HEBRIDES (U.K.)

CORSICA (FR.)

SARDINIA (IT.)

SICILY (IT.)

BALEARIC IS. (SP.)

CRETE (GR.)

RHODES (GR.)

Crimea

Volga River

Ural River

Don R.

Dnieper

Dniester River

Danube

Vistula R.

Oder R.

Elbe R.

Rhine R.

Po R.

Arctic Circle

70° N

60° N

50° N

20° W

10° W

0°

10° E

20° E

Abbreviations
DEN. —DENMARK
FR. —FRANCE
GR. —GREECE
IT. —ITALY
SP. —SPAIN
U.K. —UNITED KINGDOM

Mt. —MOUNT
MTS. —MOUNTAINS

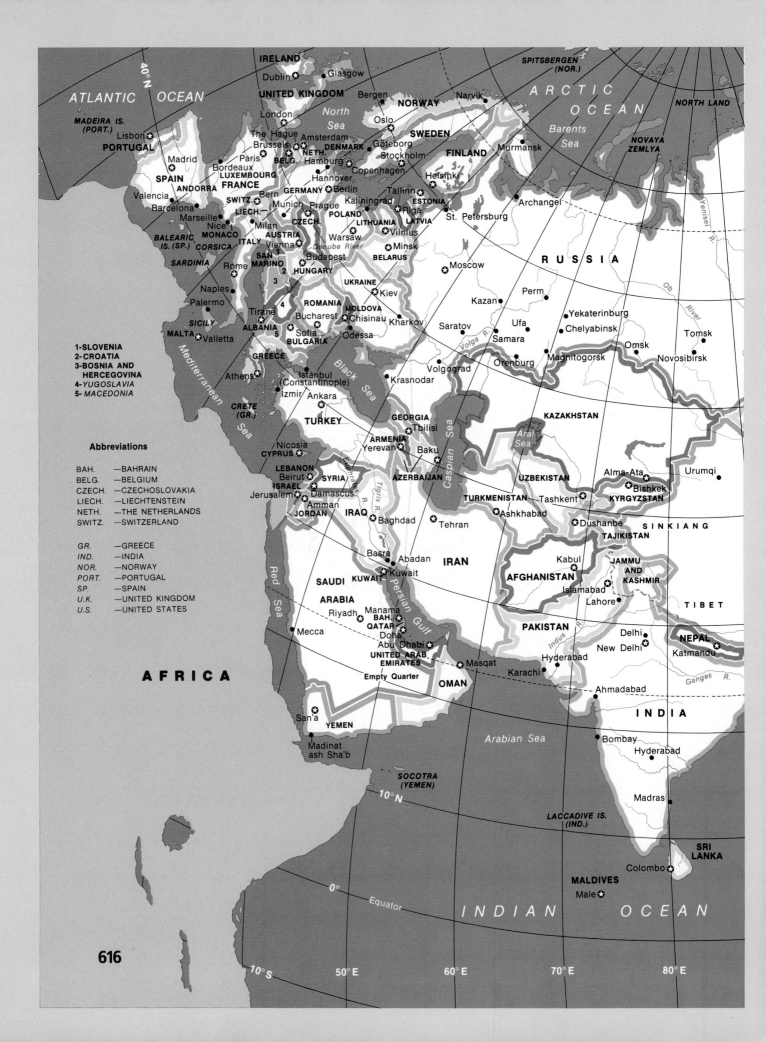

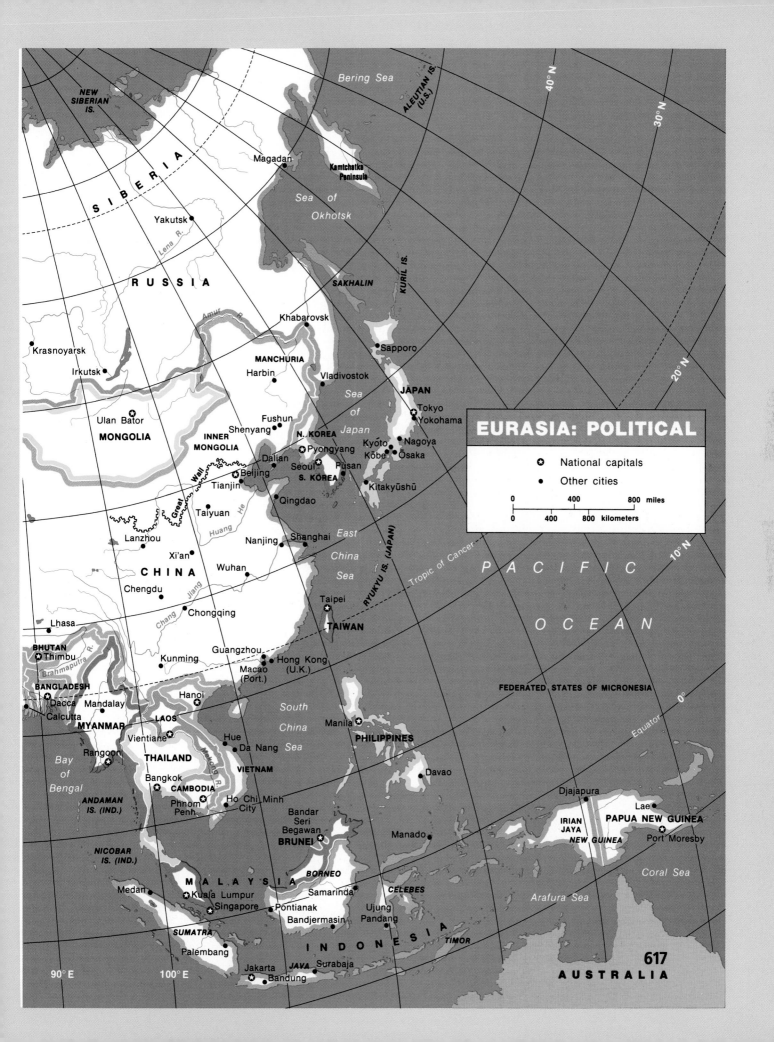

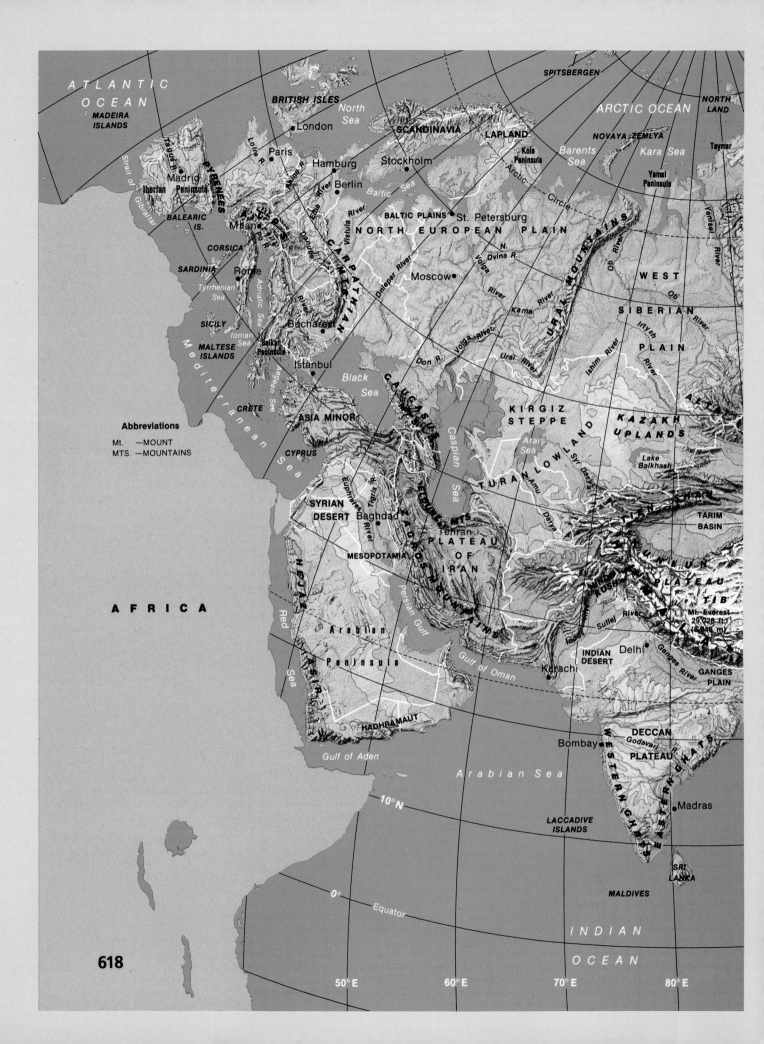

ATLANTIC
OCEAN

MADEIRA
ISLANDS

SPITSBERGEN

BRITISH ISLES

North
Sea

London

SCANDINAVIA

LAPLAND

ARCTIC OCEAN

NORTH
LAND

NOVAYA ZEMLYA

Kola
Peninsula

Barents
Sea

Kara Sea

Taymar

Paris

PYRENEES

Loire R.

Madrid

Iberian Peninsula

Rhine R.

Hamburg

Berlin

Stockholm

Baltic
Sea

Arctic

Circle

Yamal
Peninsula

Yenisei

River

BALEARIC
IS.

Milan

Elbe R.

Po R.

CORSICA

SARDINIA

Rome

Tyrrhenian
Sea

Adriatic Sea

Vistula

River

Danube

BALTIC PLAINS

NORTH EUROPEAN PLAIN

St. Petersburg

Moscow

N.
Dvina R.

Volga

Kama

River

WEST

SIBERIAN

PLAIN

URAL MOUNTAINS

Ob River

Ob

River

Irtysh

River

SICILY

Ionian
Sea

Bucharest

Balkan
Peninsula

Mediterranean

MALTESE
ISLANDS

Aegean Sea

Sea

CRETE

Istanbul

Black
Sea

CAUCASUS

ASIA MINOR

CYPRUS

Dnieper River

Don R.

Volga River

Ural River

Caspian Sea

KIRGIZ
STEPPE

Aral
Sea

TURAN LOWLAND

KAZAKH
UPLANDS

Lake
Balkhash

ALTA

Syr Darya

Amu Darya

TIAN SHAN

TARIM
BASIN

AFRICA

HEJAZ

ASIR

Red Sea

SYRIAN
DESERT

Baghdad

Euphrates River

Tigris R.

MESOPOTAMIA

ZAGROS MTS

Tehran

PLATEAU
OF
IRAN

Persian Gulf

Arabian

Peninsula

Gulf of Oman

HADHRAMAUT

Gulf of Aden

HINDU KUSH

KUNLUN

PLATEAU

TIB

Mt. Everest
29,028 ft.
(8,848 m)

INDIAN
DESERT

Delhi

Karachi

Indus

Sutlej
River

Ganges River

GANGES
PLAIN

Arabian Sea

10°N

DECCAN

PLATEAU

Bombay

Godavari R.

WESTERN GHATS

EASTERN GHATS

LACCADIVE
ISLANDS

Madras

0°

Equator

MALDIVES

SRI
LANKA

618

INDIAN

OCEAN

50°E   60°E   70°E   80°E

Abbreviations

Mt. —MOUNT
MTS. —MOUNTAINS

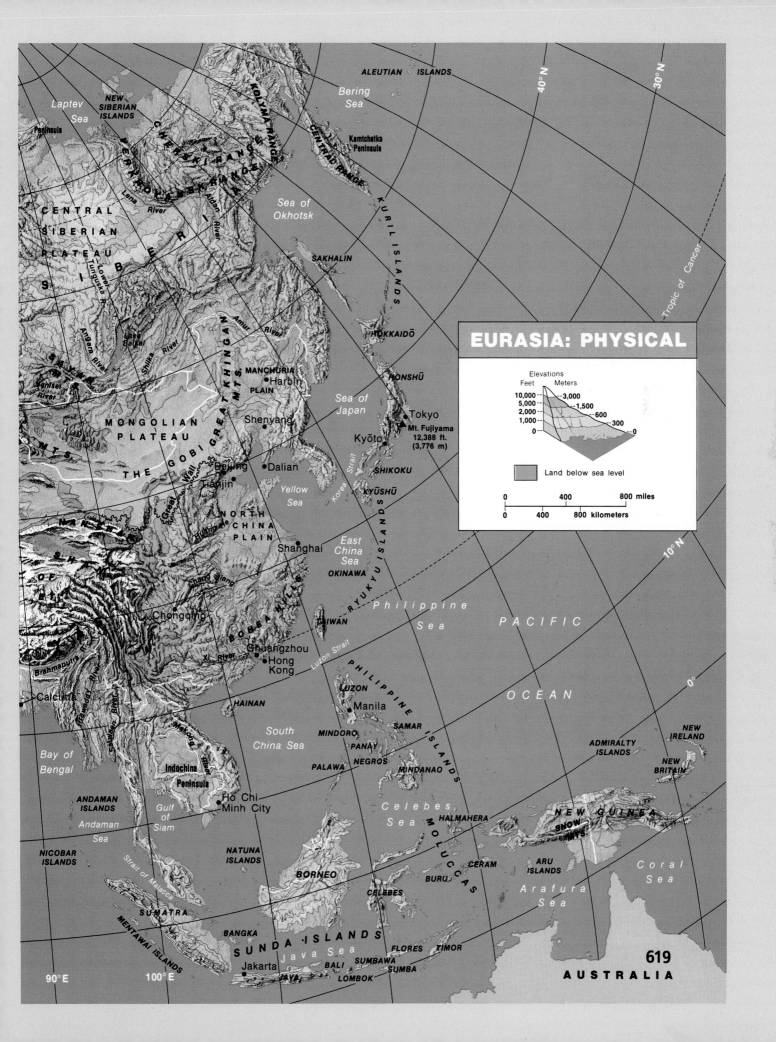

EURASIA: PHYSICAL

Elevations

Feet	Meters
10,000	3,000
5,000	1,500
2,000	600
1,000	300
0	0

Land below sea level

0   400   800 miles

0   400   800 kilometers

ALEUTIAN   ISLANDS

Laptev Sea

NEW SIBERIAN ISLANDS

Peninsula

CHERSKI RANGE

KOLYMA RANGE

Bering Sea

CENTRAL RANGE

Kamtchatka Peninsula

CENTRAL SIBERIAN PLATEAU

Lena River

Aldan River

Sea of Okhotsk

KURIL ISLANDS

SIBERIA

VERKHOYANSK RANGE

Lower Tunguska R.

Angara River

Shilka River

Amur River

SAKHALIN

Lake Baikal

SAYAN MTS.

Yenisei River

HOKKAIDŌ

GREAT KHINGAN MTS.

MANCHURIA PLAIN

• Harbin

HONSHŪ

MONGOLIAN PLATEAU

• Shenyang

Sea of Japan

Tokyo •

▲ Mt. Fujiyama
12,388 ft.
(3,776 m)

THE GOBI

Great Wall

• Beijing

• Dalian

Kyōto •

MTS.

NAN SHAN

• Tianjin

Yellow Sea

Korea Strait

SHIKOKU

KYŪSHŪ

OF

• Chongqing

NORTH CHINA PLAIN

Huang He R.

• Shanghai

East China Sea

RYUKYU ISLANDS

BETS

BOREA HILLS

OKINAWA

• Calcutta

Chang Jiang R.

Xi River

• Guangzhou
• Hong Kong

TAIWAN

Luzon Strait

Philippine Sea

PACIFIC

Brahmaputra R.

HAINAN

PHILIPPINE ISLANDS

LUZON

OCEAN

Bay of Bengal

Mekong River

South China Sea

• Manila

SAMAR

Irrawaddy R.

ANDAMAN ISLANDS

Gulf of Siam

Indochina Peninsula

MINDORO

PANAY

NEGROS

MINDANAO

ADMIRALTY ISLANDS

NEW IRELAND

• Ho Chi Minh City

PALAWA

Andaman Sea

NEW BRITAIN

NICOBAR ISLANDS

NATUNA ISLANDS

Celebes Sea

MOLUCCAS

HALMAHERA

NEW GUINEA

SNOW MTS.

ARU ISLANDS

Coral Sea

CERAM

BURU

Strait of Malacca

BORNEO

SUMATRA

CELEBES

Arafura Sea

MENTAWAI ISLANDS

BANGKA

SUNDA ISLANDS

Java Sea

FLORES

TIMOR

Jakarta •

BALI

SUMBAWA

SUMBA

JAVA

LOMBOK

Tropic of Cancer

40° N

30° N

10° N

0°

90°E

100°E

619

AUSTRALIA

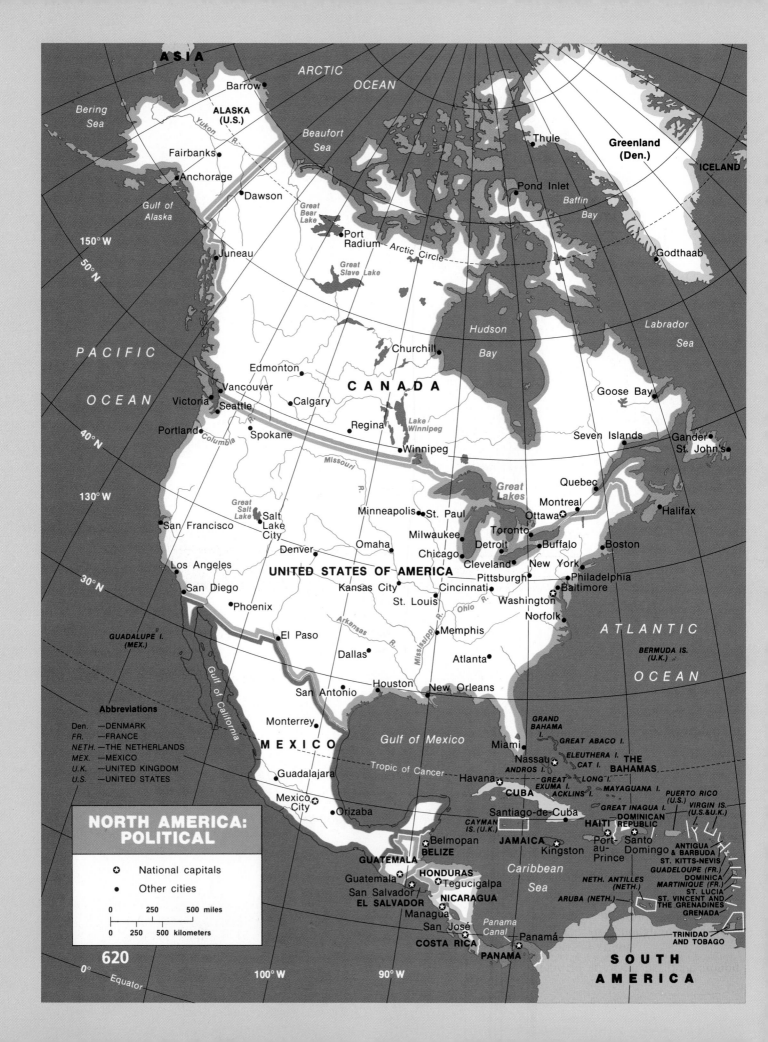

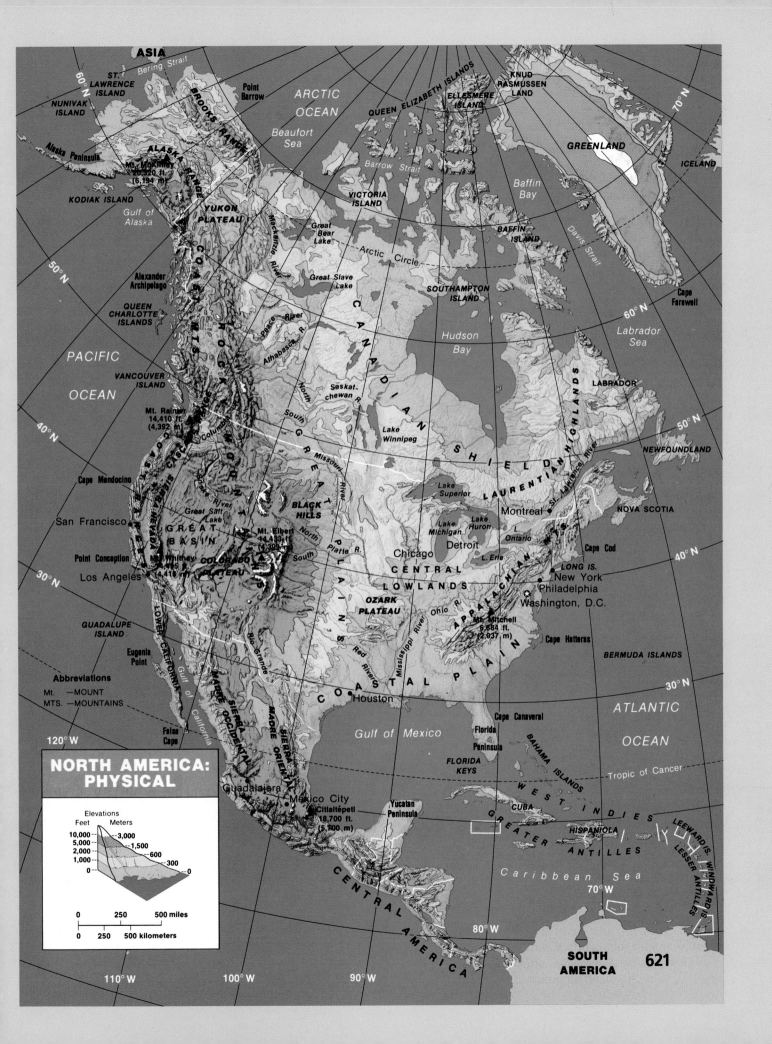

NORTH AMERICA: PHYSICAL

Elevations

Feet	Meters
10,000	3,000
5,000	1,500
2,000	600
1,000	300
0	0

0   250   500 miles

0   250   500 kilometers

Abbreviations
Mt. —MOUNT
MTS. —MOUNTAINS

ASIA

ARCTIC OCEAN

Bering Strait

St. LAWRENCE ISLAND

NUNIVAK ISLAND

Point Barrow

Beaufort Sea

Alaska Peninsula

KODIAK ISLAND

Gulf of Alaska

ALASKA RANGE

Mt. McKinley 20,320 ft. (6,194 m)

BROOKS RANGE

YUKON PLATEAU

Alexander Archipelago

QUEEN CHARLOTTE ISLANDS

PACIFIC OCEAN

VANCOUVER ISLAND

Cape Mendocino

San Francisco

Point Conception

Los Angeles

GUADALUPE ISLAND

Eugenia Point

False Cape

LOWER CALIFORNIA

Gulf of California

CASCADE RANGE

COAST RANGES

Mt. Rainier 14,410 ft. (4,392 m)

Columbia R.

Snake River

Great Salt Lake

GREAT BASIN

SIERRA NEVADA

Mt. Whitney 14,495 ft. (4,418 m)

COLORADO PLATEAU

Rio Grande

SIERRA MADRE OCCIDENTAL

SIERRA MADRE ORIENTAL

Guadalajara

Mexico City

Citlaltépetl 18,700 ft. (5,700 m)

ROCKY MTS.

Peace River

Athabasca R.

Mackenzie River

North Saskatchewan R.

South Saskatchewan R.

Missouri River

North Platte R.

South Platte R.

Mt. Elbert 14,433 ft. (4,399 m)

BLACK HILLS

GREAT PLAINS

CENTRAL LOWLANDS

OZARK PLATEAU

Red River

Arkansas R.

Mississippi River

Ohio R.

Houston

COASTAL PLAIN

Gulf of Mexico

Yucatan Peninsula

CENTRAL AMERICA

QUEEN ELIZABETH ISLANDS

ELLESMERE ISLAND

KNUD RASMUSSEN LAND

Barrow Strait

VICTORIA ISLAND

Arctic Circle

Great Bear Lake

Great Slave Lake

CANADIAN SHIELD

SOUTHAMPTON ISLAND

Hudson Bay

Lake Winnipeg

Lake Superior

Lake Michigan

Lake Huron

Chicago

Detroit

L. Ontario

L. Erie

Montreal

LAURENTIAN HIGHLANDS

LABRADOR

APPALACHIAN MTS.

Mt. Mitchell 6,684 ft. (2,037 m)

Cape Cod

LONG IS.

New York

Philadelphia

Washington, D.C.

Cape Hatteras

Florida Peninsula

Cape Canaveral

FLORIDA KEYS

BAHAMA ISLANDS

WEST INDIES

GREATER ANTILLES

CUBA

HISPANIOLA

Caribbean Sea

LEEWARD IS.

WINDWARD IS.

LESSER ANTILLES

GREENLAND

ICELAND

Baffin Bay

BAFFIN ISLAND

Davis Strait

Cape Farewell

Labrador Sea

NEWFOUNDLAND

NOVA SCOTIA

ATLANTIC OCEAN

BERMUDA ISLANDS

Tropic of Cancer

SOUTH AMERICA

60° N, 70° N, 50° N, 40° N, 30° N

120° W, 110° W, 100° W, 90° W, 80° W, 70° W

Barranquilla
Cartagena
Valencia
Maracaibo
Caracas
Barquisimeto
Cúcuta
San Cristóbal
Medellín
Bucaramanga
VENEZUELA
GUYANA
Georgetown
Paramaribo
Cayenne
SURINAME
French Guiana (Fr.)

Bogotá
COLOMBIA
Cali

MALPELO I. (COL.)

Quito
ECUADOR
Guayaquil
Iquitos

Equator

Belém
São Luis
Fortaleza

Manaus

River
Amazon
River

PERU

BRAZIL

Trujillo

Recife
Maceió

10° S

Callao
Lima
Cuzco

Lake Titicaca
Arequipa
BOLIVIA
La Paz

Salvador

Brasília
(Federal District)

Sucre

PACIFIC

Belo Horizonte

20° S

Chuquicamata

PARAGUAY

Rio de Janeiro
São Paulo
Niterói

OCEAN

Antofagasta

Asunción

Curitiba
Santos

Tropic of Capricorn

SAN FELIX I. · SAN AMBROSIO I.
(CHILE)   (CHILE)

Tucumán

ATLANTIC

CHILE

Paraná
River

Pôrto Alegre

Valparaiso
Santiago

Córdoba
Santa Fe
Paraná

URUGUAY

OCEAN

JUAN FERNÁNDEZ IS.
(CHILE)

Rosario
Buenos Aires
La Plata

Montevideo

Rio de la Plata

Concepción

ARGENTINA

Bahía Blanca
Mar del Plata

FALKLAND IS. (U.K.)
(MALVINAS IS.)

Strait of Magellan

Punta Arenas

10° N
0°
10° S
20° S
30° S
40° S
50° S

90° W   80° W   60° W   50° W
40° W   30° W

622

SOUTH AMERICA: POLITICAL	
✪	National capitals
●	Other cities

0   500 miles

0   500 kilometers

Caribbean Sea

Guajira Pen.

MARGARITA I.

Caracas

Orinoco River Delta

Orinoco R.

Angel Falls

DEVILS I.

C. Orange

G. of Panama

Mt. Tolima
18,425 ft.
(5,616 m)

Bogotá

LLANOS

GUIANA HIGHLANDS

MALPELO I.

Orinoco Rio

ANDES MOUNTAINS

Meta R.

Caqueta R.

Negro

Amazon River Delta

MARAJÓ I.

Equator

10° N

Amazon R.

C. São Roque

AMAZON

Mt. Chimborazo
20,561 ft.
(6,267 m)

0°

Japura R.

Marañón R.

Tapajóz R.

Xingu R.

Tocantins R.

Parnaíba R.

BASIN

Gulf of Guayaquil

Juruá

R.

Purus

Araguaia R.

Tocantins R.

Aguja Pt.

Ucayali R.

Madeira R.

São Francisco R.

Mt. Huascarán
22,205 ft.
(6,768 m)

Beni R.

10° S

Lima

Mamoré R.

Lake Titicaca

MATO

GROSSO

Brasília

BRAZILIAN

Mt. Ancohuma
21,490 ft.
(6,612 m)

Poopó

PLATEAU

HIGHLANDS

Mt. Bandeira
9,495 ft.
(2,894 m)

Pilcomayo R.

GRAN

Paraguay R.

São Paulo

São Francisco

20° S

Tropic of Capricorn

ATACAMA DESERT

CHACO

Paraná R.

C. Frio

SAN FELIX I.

SAN AMBROSIO I.

Rio de Janeiro

PACIFIC

Salado R.

Mt. Aconcagua
22,834 ft.
(6,960 m)

Uruguay R.

ATLANTIC

30° S

Santiago

Buenos Aires

Montevideo

JUAN FERNÁNDEZ IS.

PAMPAS

Rio de la Plata

OCEAN

OCEAN

Colorado R.

Blanca Bay

40° S

San Matías Gulf

CHILOÉ I.

Valdés Pen.

CHONOS ARCH.

PATAGONIA

Gulf of San Jorge

Taitao Pen.

C. Tres Puntas

FALKLAND IS. (U.K.)
(MALVINAS IS.)

50° S

Grande Bay

Strait of Magellan

623

Strait of Magellan

TIERRA DEL FUEGO

Cape Horn

90° W

80° W

60° W

50° W

SOUTH AMERICA: PHYSICAL

Elevations
Feet   Meters

10,000 — 3,000
5,000 — 1,500
2,000 — 600
1,000 — 300
0 — 0

0   500 miles

0   500 kilometers

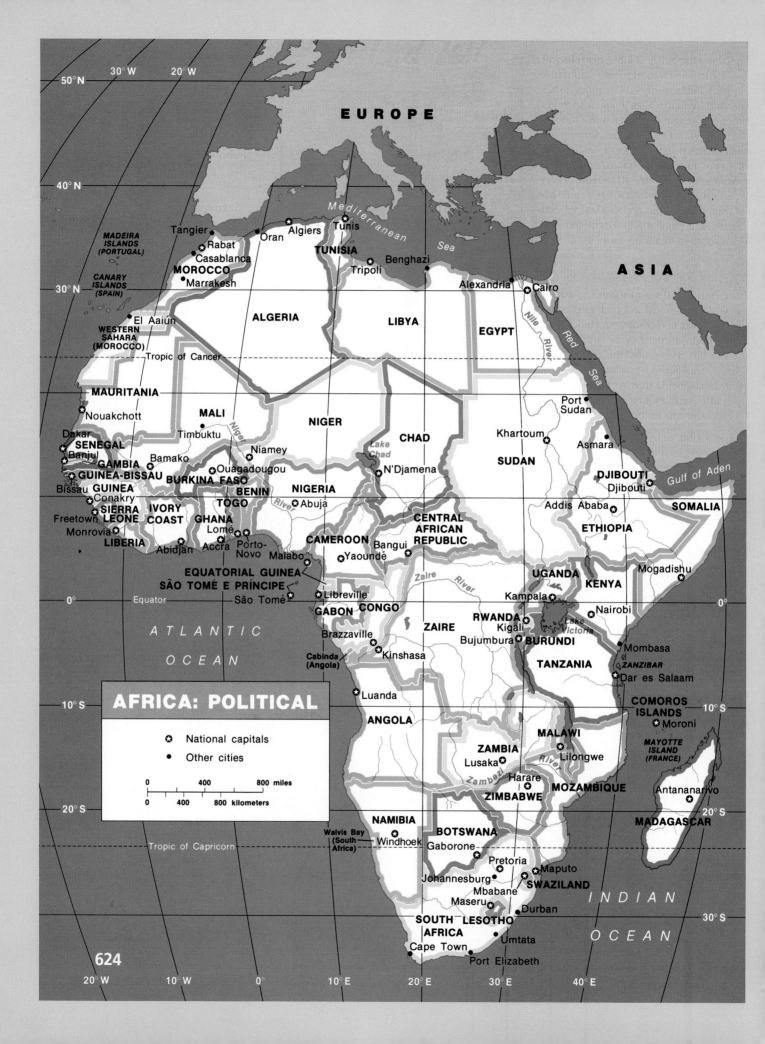

AFRICA: POLITICAL

⊛ National capitals
● Other cities

0   400   800 miles
0 400 800 kilometers

EUROPE

ASIA

MADEIRA ISLANDS (PORTUGAL)

CANARY ISLANDS (SPAIN)

Tangier
Rabat
Casablanca
MOROCCO
Marrakesh

Oran
Algiers
Tunis
TUNISIA
Tripoli

Benghazi

Mediterranean Sea

Alexandria
Cairo

Nile River

Red Sea

WESTERN SAHARA (MOROCCO)

El Aaiún

ALGERIA

LIBYA

EGYPT

Tropic of Cancer

MAURITANIA

Nouakchott

MALI
Timbuktu

NIGER

CHAD

Port Sudan

Dakar
SENEGAL
Banjul
GAMBIA
GUINEA-BISSAU
Bissau **GUINEA**
Conakry
SIERRA LEONE
Freetown
Monrovia
LIBERIA

Niger

Bamako
Niamey
Ouagadougou
BURKINA FASO
BENIN
NIGERIA
IVORY COAST
GHANA
TOGO
Lomé
Abidjan Accra Porto-Novo
Malabo

Khartoum
Asmara

SUDAN

DJIBOUTI
Djibouti

Lake Chad
N'Djamena

Addis Ababa

SOMALIA

Abuja
River

CENTRAL AFRICAN REPUBLIC

Bangui

ETHIOPIA

Mogadishu

CAMEROON
Yaoundé

EQUATORIAL GUINEA
SÃO TOMÉ E PRÍNCIPE
São Tomé

Equator

Libreville
GABON **CONGO**

Brazzaville
Cabinda (Angola)
Kinshasa

Luanda

ANGOLA

Zaire River

ZAIRE

UGANDA
Kampala

RWANDA
Kigali
BURUNDI
Bujumbura

KENYA
Nairobi

Lake Victoria

Mombasa
ZANZIBAR
Dar es Salaam

TANZANIA

COMOROS ISLANDS
Moroni

MAYOTTE ISLAND (FRANCE)

ATLANTIC OCEAN

MALAWI
Lilongwe

ZAMBIA
Lusaka

River
Zambezi
Harare
ZIMBABWE

MOZAMBIQUE

Antananarivo

MADAGASCAR

NAMIBIA
Walvis Bay (South Africa)
Windhoek

BOTSWANA
Gaborone

Pretoria
Maputo
SWAZILAND
Johannesburg
Mbabane
Maseru
LESOTHO
Durban

Tropic of Capricorn

INDIAN OCEAN

SOUTH AFRICA
Cape Town
Umtata
Port Elizabeth

624

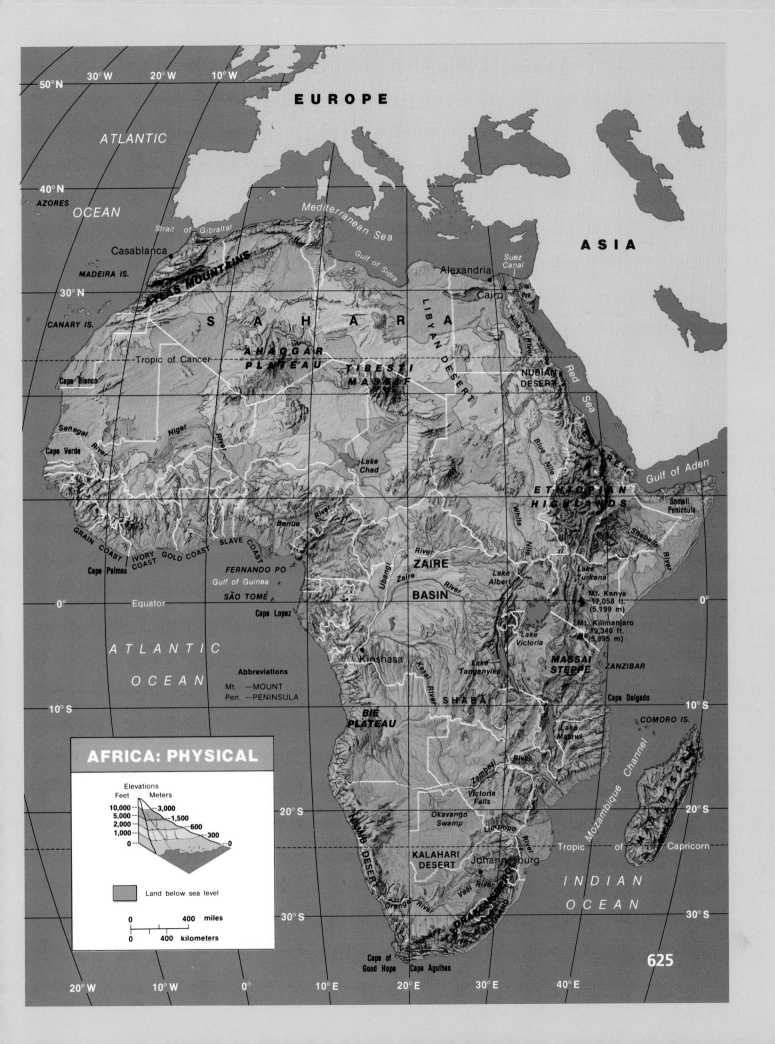

AFRICA: PHYSICAL

EUROPE

ATLANTIC

ASIA

ATLANTIC
OCEAN

AZORES

OCEAN

Mediterranean Sea

MADEIRA IS.

Strait of Gibraltar

Casablanca

ATLAS MOUNTAINS

Gulf of Sidra

Suez Canal

Alexandria

Cairo

Sinai Pen.

CANARY IS.

S A H A R A

LIBYAN DESERT

Nile River

Red Sea

NUBIAN DESERT

Tropic of Cancer

AHAGGAR PLATEAU

TIBESTI MASSIF

Cape Blanco

Senegal River

Niger River

Cape Verde

Lake Chad

Blue Nile

ETHIOPIAN HIGHLANDS

Gulf of Aden

Somali Peninsula

GRAIN COAST

IVORY COAST

GOLD COAST

SLAVE COAST

Benue River

Shebelle River

Cape Palmas

FERNANDO PO

Gulf of Guinea

SÃO TOMÉ

Cape Lopez

Ubangi River

Zaire River

ZAIRE BASIN

River

White Nile

Lake Albert

Lake Turkana

Mt. Kenya
17,058 ft.
(5,199 m)

Equator

Kinshasa

Lake Victoria

Mt. Kilimanjaro
19,340 ft.
(5,895 m)

ATLANTIC

OCEAN

Abbreviations

Mt. —MOUNT
Pen. —PENINSULA

Kasai River

Lake Tanganyika

MASSAI STEPPE

ZANZIBAR

SHABA

Cape Delgado

BIE PLATEAU

Lake Malawi

COMORO IS.

Elevations

Feet   Meters

10,000 — 3,000
5,000 — 1,500
2,000 — 600
1,000 — 300
0 — 0

Land below sea level

NAMIB DESERT

Zambezi

Victoria Falls

Okavango Swamp

Limpopo

Mozambique Channel

Tropic   of   Capricorn

MADAGASCAR

KALAHARI DESERT

Johannesburg

INDIAN OCEAN

0   400   miles

0   400   kilometers

Vaal River

Orange River

DRAKENSBERG

Cape of Good Hope

Cape Agulhas

625

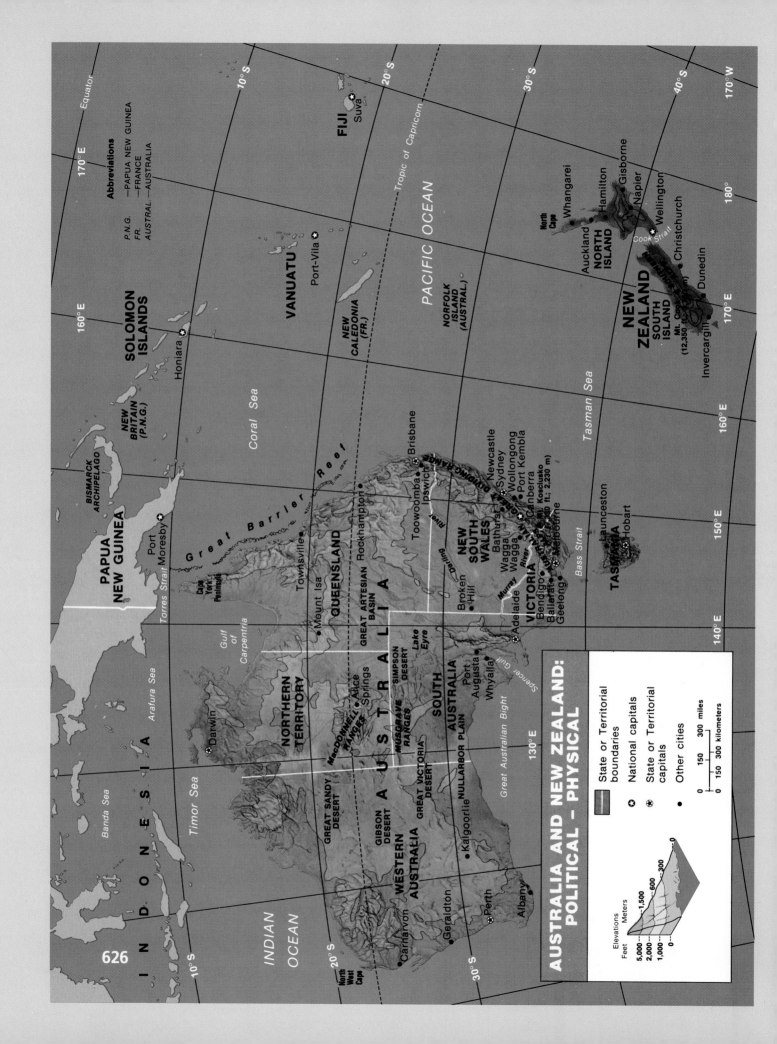

AUSTRALIA AND NEW ZEALAND: POLITICAL – PHYSICAL

626

INDONESIA

Banda Sea

Timor Sea

Arafura Sea

PAPUA NEW GUINEA

Port Moresby

BISMARCK ARCHIPELAGO

NEW BRITAIN (P.N.G.)

Torres Strait

Cape York Peninsula

Gulf of Carpentaria

Coral Sea

SOLOMON ISLANDS

Honiara

VANUATU

Port-Vila

NEW CALEDONIA (FR.)

PACIFIC OCEAN

Tropic of Capricorn

FIJI
Suva

NORFOLK ISLAND (AUSTRAL.)

INDIAN OCEAN

North West Cape

Carnarvon

Geraldton

Perth

Albany

Kalgoorlie

WESTERN AUSTRALIA

GREAT SANDY DESERT

GIBSON DESERT

GREAT VICTORIA DESERT

NULLARBOR PLAIN

Great Australian Bight

NORTHERN TERRITORY

Darwin

Alice Springs

MacDONNELL RANGES

MUSGRAVE RANGES

SIMPSON DESERT

A U S T R A L I A

QUEENSLAND

Mount Isa

Townsville

Rockhampton

GREAT ARTESIAN BASIN

Toowoomba

Ipswich Brisbane

SOUTH AUSTRALIA

Lake Eyre

Port Augusta

Whyalla

Spencer Gulf

Adelaide

Broken Hill

NEW SOUTH WALES

GREAT DIVIDING RANGE

Newcastle

Sydney

Wollongong

Port Kembla

Canberra

Bathurst

Wagga Wagga

Murray River

Darling River

Mt. Kosciusko (7,310 ft.; 2,230 m)

VICTORIA

Bendigo

Ballarat

Geelong

Melbourne

Bass Strait

Launceston

TASMANIA

Hobart

Tasman Sea

NEW ZEALAND

North Cape

Whangarei

Auckland

Hamilton

NORTH ISLAND

Gisborne

Napier

Wellington

Cook Strait

SOUTH ISLAND

Mt. Cook (12,350 ft.)

Christchurch

Dunedin

Invercargill

Equator

10° S

20° S

30° S

40° S

170° E

180°

170° W

160° E

10° S

20° S

30° S

160° E

150° E

140° E

130° E

120° E

Abbreviations

P.N.G. —PAPUA NEW GUINEA
FR. —FRANCE
AUSTRAL. —AUSTRALIA

State or Territorial boundaries

✪ National capitals

⊛ State or Territorial capitals

• Other cities

0   150   300 miles
0   150   300 kilometers

Elevations
Feet   Meters
5,000   1,500
2,000   600
1,000   300
0   0

THE WORLD: CLIMATE REGIONS

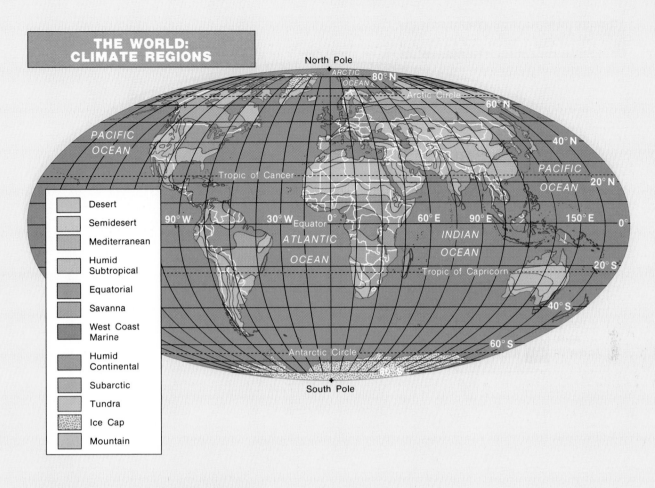

North Pole

ARCTIC OCEAN

80° N

Arctic Circle

60° N

40° N

PACIFIC OCEAN

PACIFIC OCEAN

20° N

Tropic of Cancer

90° W

30° W

0°

Equator

60° E

90° E

150° E

0°

ATLANTIC OCEAN

INDIAN OCEAN

Tropic of Capricorn

20° S

40° S

60° S

Antarctic Circle

80° S

South Pole

Legend:
- Desert
- Semidesert
- Mediterranean
- Humid Subtropical
- Equatorial
- Savanna
- West Coast Marine
- Humid Continental
- Subarctic
- Tundra
- Ice Cap
- Mountain

THE WORLD: FORESTS

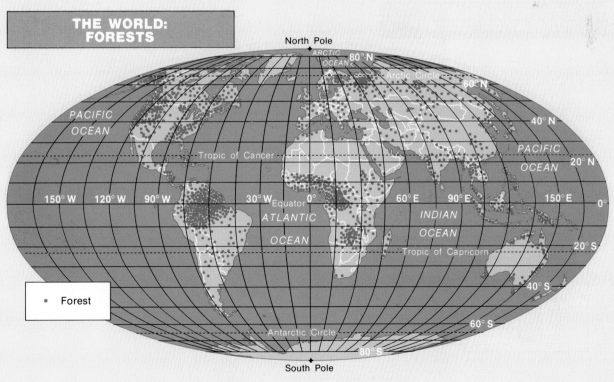

North Pole

ARCTIC OCEAN

80° N

Arctic Circle

60° N

40° N

PACIFIC OCEAN

Tropic of Cancer

PACIFIC OCEAN

20° N

150° W

120° W

90° W

30° W

0°

Equator

60° E

90° E

150° E

0°

ATLANTIC OCEAN

INDIAN OCEAN

Tropic of Capricorn

20° S

40° S

60° S

Antarctic Circle

80° S

South Pole

- • Forest

627

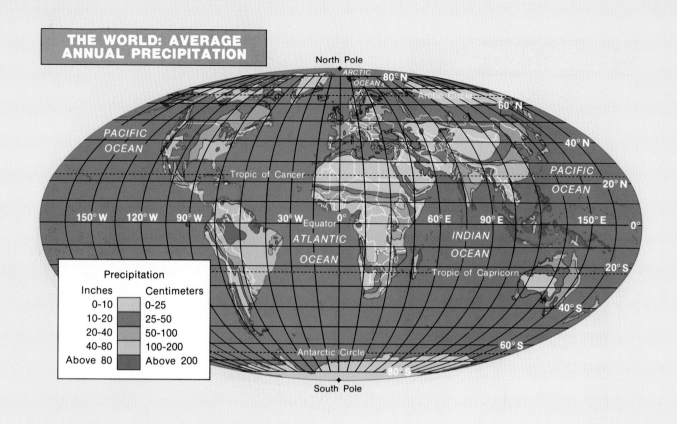

THE WORLD: AVERAGE ANNUAL PRECIPITATION

North Pole

ARCTIC
OCEAN

80° N

Arctic Circle

60° N

40° N

PACIFIC
OCEAN

Tropic of Cancer

PACIFIC

OCEAN

20° N

150° W   120° W   90° W   30° W   0°   60° E   90° E   150° E   0°

Equator

ATLANTIC

OCEAN

INDIAN

OCEAN

Tropic of Capricorn   20° S

Precipitation

Inches	Centimeters
0-10	0-25
10-20	25-50
20-40	50-100
40-80	100-200
Above 80	Above 200

40° S

60° S

Antarctic Circle

80° S

South Pole

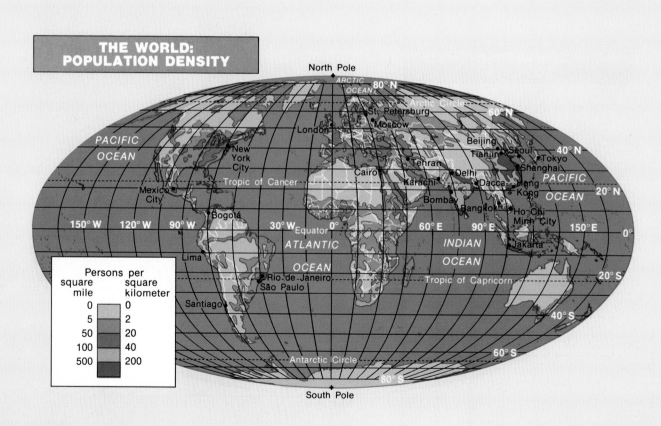

THE WORLD: POPULATION DENSITY

North Pole

ARCTIC
OCEAN

80° N

Arctic Circle

60° N

St. Petersburg
London   Moscow

Beijing   Seoul   40° N
Tianjin   Tokyo
Tehran   Shanghai
Delhi   PACIFIC
Karachi   Dacca   Hong   OCEAN
Cairo   Kong

PACIFIC
OCEAN

New
York
City

Mexico
City

Tropic of Cancer

20° N

Bombay   Bangkok
Ho Chi
Minh City

Bogotá

150° W   120° W   90° W   30° W   0°   60° E   90° E   150° E   0°

Equator

Lima   ATLANTIC   INDIAN   Jakarta

OCEAN   OCEAN

Santiago

Rio de Janeiro
São Paulo

Tropic of Capricorn   20° S

Persons per

square mile	square kilometer
0	0
5	2
50	20
100	40
500	200

40° S

60° S

Antarctic Circle

80° S

South Pole

628

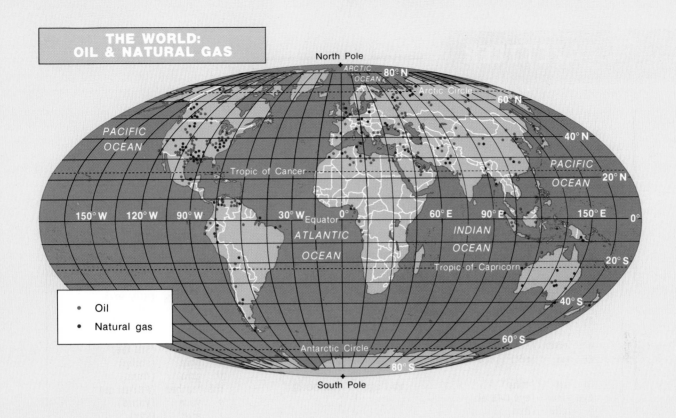

THE WORLD: OIL & NATURAL GAS

PACIFIC OCEAN

North Pole

ARCTIC OCEAN

80° N

Arctic Circle

60° N

40° N

PACIFIC OCEAN

Tropic of Cancer

20° N

150° W   120° W   90° W

30° W

Equator

0°

60° E   90° E   150° E   0°

ATLANTIC OCEAN

INDIAN OCEAN

20° S

Tropic of Capricorn

40° S

• Oil

• Natural gas

60° S

Antarctic Circle

80° S

South Pole

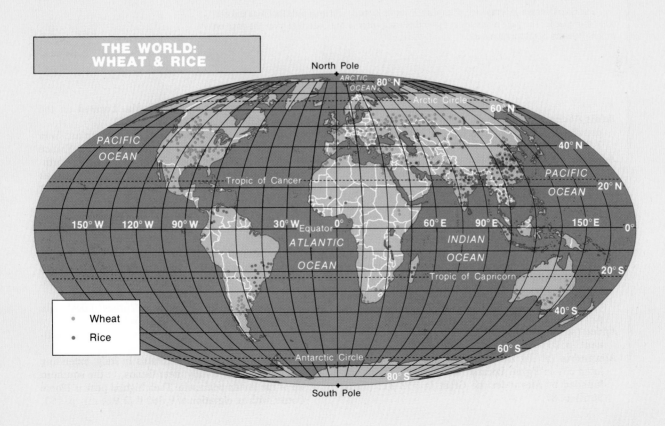

THE WORLD: WHEAT & RICE

PACIFIC OCEAN

North Pole

ARCTIC OCEAN

80° N

Arctic Circle

60° N

40° N

PACIFIC OCEAN

Tropic of Cancer

20° N

150° W   120° W   90° W

30° W

Equator

0°

60° E   90° E   150° E   0°

ATLANTIC OCEAN

INDIAN OCEAN

20° S

Tropic of Capricorn

40° S

• Wheat

• Rice

60° S

Antarctic Circle

80° S

South Pole

629

GAZETTEER

Some words in this book may be new to you or difficult to pronounce. Those words have been spelled phonetically in parentheses. The syllable that receives stress in a word is shown in small capital letters.

For example: **Chicago** (shuh KAH goh)

Most phonetic spellings are easy to read. In the following Pronunciation Key, you can see how letters are used to show different sounds.

PRONUNCIATION KEY

a	after	(AF tur)	oh	flow	(floh)	ch	chicken	(CHIHK un)
ah	father	(FAH thur)	oi	boy	(boi)	g	game	(gaym)
ai	care	(kair)	oo	rule	(rool)	ing	coming	(KUM ing)
aw	dog	(dawg)	or	horse	(hors)	j	job	(jahb)
ay	paper	(PAY pur)	ou	cow	(kou)	k	came	(kaym)
						ng	long	(lawng)
e	letter	(LET ur)	yoo	few	(fyoo)	s	city	(SIH tee)
ee	eat	(eet)	u	taken	(TAY kun)	sh	ship	(shihp)
				matter	(MAT ur)	th	thin	(thihn)
ih	trip	(trihp)	uh	ago	(uh GOH)	thh	feather	(FETHH ur)
eye	idea	(eye DEE uh)				y	yard	(yahrd)
y	hide	(hyd)				z	size	(syz)
ye	lie	(lye)				zh	division	(duh VIHZH un)

The Gazetteer is a geographical dictionary. It shows latitude and longitude for cities and certain other places. The page reference at the end of each entry in the Gazetteer gives the page on which the entry is shown on a map.

A

Addis Ababa (AD ihs AB uh buh). Capital of and most populated city in Ethiopia. Located at an elevation of 7,900 ft (2,408 m). (9°N/39°E) p. 478.

Adelaide (AD ul ayd). Capital of the Australian state of Victoria. Located near a gulf of the Indian Ocean. (35°S/139°E) p. 591.

Aden (AHD un). Port city in Yemen. Located on the Gulf of Aden. (13°N/45°E) p. 404.

Adriatic Sea (ay dree AT ihk see). Arm of the Mediterranean Sea, between Italy and the Balkan Peninsula. p. 157.

Aegean Sea (ee JEE un see). Part of the Mediterranean Sea, between the eastern coast of Greece and the western coast of Turkey. Bounded on the north by the Greek mainland and on the south by Crete. p. 77.

Africa (AF rih kuh). The earth's second largest continent. p. 23.

Alexandria (al ihg ZAN dree uh). Second most populated city in Egypt. Located in the Nile Delta. It was founded by Alexander the Great in 332 B.C. (31°N/30°E) p. 87.

Algiers (al JIHRZ). Capital of Algeria. Located on the Mediterranean Sea. (37°N/3°E) p. 361.

Alps (alps). Mountain system extending in an arc from the Mediterranean coast between Italy and France through Switzerland and Austria and into the northwest coast of the former Yugoslavia. The highest peak is Mont Blanc, with an elevation of 15,771 ft (4,807 m). p. 157.

Amsterdam (AM stur dam). Capital of the Netherlands. Connected to the North Sea by a canal. (52°N/5°E) p. 166.

Anatolian plateau (an uh TOH lee un pla TOH). Plateau on which Asian Turkey is located. This plateau lies between the Black and the Mediterranean seas. p. 359.

Ankara (ANG kuh ruh). Capital of Turkey. Located in central Anatolia. (41°N/33°E) p. 361.

Antarctica (ant AHRK tih kuh). The earth's third smallest continent. p. 23.

Apennines (AP uh nynz). Mountains in Italy, extending from northwestern Italy, near Genoa, to the southern tip of the Italian peninsula. Their highest peak is Monte Corno, with an elevation of 9,560 ft (2,914 m). p. 157.

Arabian Peninsula (uh RAY bee un   puh NIHN suh luh). Large peninsula located east of the Red Sea. p. 359.

Arabian Sea (uh RAY bee un   see). Arm of the Indian Ocean, between India and the Arabian Peninsula. p. 359.

Aral Sea (AR ul   see). Inland body of salt water in the southwestern Asian area of the former Soviet Union, east of the Caspian Sea. p. 285.

Arctic Circle (AHRK tihk   SUR kul). Line of latitude located at 66 1/2° north latitude. p. 10.

Arctic Ocean (AHRK tihk   OH shun). Large body of water north of the Arctic Circle. p. 285.

Asia (AY zhuh). The earth's largest continent. p. 23.

Asia Minor (AY zhuh   MYE nur). Asian peninsula on which most of Turkey is located. It is bounded on the north by the Black Sea, on the west by the Aegean Sea, and on the south by the Mediterranean Sea. p. 77.

Aswan (ahs WAHN). City on the Nile River. Site of Aswan High Dam. (24°N/33°E) p. 51.

Athens (ATH unz). City-state in ancient Greece. Today it is the capital of and largest city in Greece. (38°N/24°E) p. 166.

Atlantic Ocean (at LAN tihk   OH shun). Large body of water separating North America and South America from Europe and Africa. p. 23.

Atlas Mountains (AT lus   MOUNT unz). Mountains located in Morocco, Algeria, and Tunisia, along the northern edge of the Sahara. The highest peak is Jebel Toubkal, with an elevation of 13,665 ft (4,165 m). p. 359.

Auckland (AWK lund). Seaport in northern New Zealand. (37°S/175°E) p. 576.

Australia (aw STRAYL yuh). The earth's smallest continent. p. 23.

Australian Alps (aw STRAYL ee un   alps). Mountain range in southeastern Australia. The southern end of the Great Dividing Range. p. 574.

B

Babylon (BAB uh lun). Ancient city in the country of Mesopotamia. Located on the Euphrates River. The city's ruins are near the present-day city of Baghdad, Iraq. (33°N/44°E) p. 51.

Baghdad (BAG dad). National capital of and most populated city in present-day Iraq. Located on the Tigris River. One-time capital of the empire of the caliphs. (33°N/44°E) p. 359.

Bali (BAH lee). Island of Indonesia, east of Java. p. 508.

Balkan Peninsula (BAWL kun   puh NIHN suh luh). Peninsula in southeastern Europe, between the Adriatic and Ionian seas on the west and the Aegean and Black seas on the east. Usually thought to consist of Greece, Albania, Bulgaria, Romania, the former Yugoslavia, and European Turkey. p. 157.

Baltic Sea (BAWL tihk   see). Arm of the Atlantic Ocean, south and southeast of Sweden. p. 157.

Barbados (bahr BAY dohs). Country that is the easternmost island of the West Indies. pp. 610–611.

Barcelona (bahr suh LOH nuh). Large port city in northeastern Spain, on the Mediterranean Sea. (41°N/2°E) p. 166.

Bay of Bengal (bay   uv   ben GAWL). Arm of the Indian Ocean, between the eastern coast of India and the Malay Peninsula. p. 508.

Beijing (BAY JING). Capital of China. Formerly known as Peking. (40°N/116°E) p. 545.

Belfast (BEL fast). Seaport and the capital of Northern Ireland. (55°N/6°W) p. 255.

Belgrade (BEL grayd). Capital of Serbia. Formerly capital of Yugoslavia. Located where the Sava River joins the Danube River. (45°N/21°E) p. 326.

Benin (be NEEN). Former native kingdom located in what is now southern Nigeria. p. 457.

Bering Strait (BER ihng   strayt). Narrow body of water that connects the Arctic Ocean and the Bering Sea. Separates Asia from North America. p. 285.

Berlin (bur LIHN) The capital of Germany. Formerly a divided city located in East Germany. East Berlin was the capital of East Germany. West Berlin, although surrounded by East Germany, was a part of West Germany. (53°N/13°E) p. 228.

Black Sea (blak   see). Large sea located on the southern divide between Europe and Asia. p. 285.

Bombay (bahm BAY). City in western India. (19°N/73°E) p. 510.

Bonn (bahn). City in Germany; located on the Rhine River. Formerly capital of West Germany. (51°N/7°E) p. 249.

Borneo (BOR nee oh). Large island in the East Indies, southwest of the Philippines. p. 508.

Boston (BAWS tun). Capital of and most populated city in Massachusetts. Located on Massachusetts Bay. (42°N/71°W) p. 620.

Brahmaputra River (brahm uh POO truh   RIHV ur). River that rises in southwestern Tibet. Joins the Ganges River near Dacca, India, before flowing into the Bay of Bengal. p. 508.

Brazzaville (BRAH zuh vihl). Riverport and capital of the Congo. (4°S/15°E) p. 446.

Brisbane (BRIHZ bayn). Capital of the Australian state of Queensland. Port city located on the east coast of Australia. (28°S/153°E) p. 591.

British Isles (BRIHT ihsh   EYE ulz). Group of islands northwest of France. Includes Great Britain, Ireland, and several smaller islands. p. 255.

Brussels (BRUS ulz). Capital of Belgium. (51°N/4°E) p. 249.

Budapest (BOOD uh pest). Capital of Hungary. Located on both sides of the Danube River. (48°N/19°E) p. 326.

C

Cairo (KYE roh). Capital of Egypt. Most populated city in Africa. Located on the eastern side of the Nile River. (30°N/31°E) p. 404.

Calcutta (kal KUT uh). City in northeastern India, on the Hooghly River. (23°N/88°E) p. 510.

Canberra (KAN bur uh). Capital of Australia. Located in southeastern Australia. (35°S/149°E) p. 591.

Cape of Good Hope (kayp uv good hohp). Cape located on southeast coast of South Africa. (31°S/23°E) p. 440.

Carpathian Mountains (karh PAY thee un MOUNT unz). Mountains that stretch from the Alps in the west to the Balkans in the east. Highest peak is Gerlachovka Peak, with an elevation of 8,737 ft (2,663 m). p. 285.

Carthage (KAHR thihj). Ancient city and nation on coast of North Africa, near present-day city of Tunis, Tunisia. (37°N/10°E) p. 110.

Caspian Sea (KAS pee un see). Largest totally inland body of water in the world. Except for its southern shore, which borders Iran, the Caspian Sea is completely within the former Soviet Union. p. 285.

Caucasus Mountains (KAW kuh sus MOUNT unz). Very high mountains in the former Soviet Union. They form part of the southern divide between Europe and Asia. Highest peak is Mount Elbrus, with an elevation of 18,481 ft (5,633 m). p. 285.

Central America (SEN trul uh MER ih kuh). The narrow part of America between Mexico and South America. Central America includes Guatemala, Belize, El Salvador, Honduras, Nicaragua, Costa Rica, and Panama. pp. 610–611.

Chang Jiang (chahng jee AHNG). One of the world's longest rivers. Rises in Tibet and flows into the East China Sea near Shanghai, China. Formerly called Yangtze River. p. 508.

Cherrapunji (cher uh PUN jee). Village in northeast India. One of the wettest places on earth. Averages 450 in. (1143 cm) of rain a year. (25°N/92°E) p. 509.

Christchurch (KRYST CHURCH). City in New Zealand. Located on South Island. (44°S/173°E) p. 576.

Congo River (KAHNG goh RIHV ur). River that rises in southeastern Zaire as the Lualaba River. Flows into the Atlantic Ocean at Matadi, Zaire. One of the world's longest rivers. Former name of the Zaire River. p. 461.

Constantinople (kahn stan tuh NOH pul). City built by Emperor Constantine in A.D. 325 on the site of the ancient Greek city of Byzantium. Renamed Istanbul in 1930. (41°N/29°E) p. 390.

Copenhagen (koh pun HAY gun). Capital of and largest city in Denmark. Important port. (56°N/13°E) p. 249.

Corsica (KOR sih kuh). French island in the Mediterranean, southeast of France. p. 157.

Crimea (kry MEE uh). Peninsula in the Black Sea. Located in Ukraine. p. 285.

Cyprus (SYE prus). Country on an island in the Mediterranean, south of Turkey. p. 157.

D

Dakar (duh KAHR). Capital and seaport of Senegal, in western Africa. (15°N/17°W) p. 478.

Damascus (duh MAS kus). Capital of Syria. (34°N/36°E) p. 404.

Danube River (DAN yoob RIHV ur). Second longest river in Europe. It begins in the Alps and in Romania and flows into the Black Sea. The Danube passes through or borders many European countries. p. 285.

Dardanelles (dahr duh NELZ). Narrow strait in Turkey. Connects the Sea of Marmara and the Aegean Sea. Called the Hellespont in ancient times. p. 77.

Dead Sea (ded see). Salt lake located on the border between Israel and Jordan. (32°N/36°E) p. 65.

Deccan Plateau (DEK un pla TOH). Most of the peninsula of India, south of the Narbada River. pp. 618–619.

Delhi (DEL ee). City in India. Located on the Jumna River. Once the capital of Mogul India. (29°N/77°E) p. 510.

Dnieper River (NEE pur RIHV ur). Located in Russia. Rises in the Valdai Hills and flows into the Black Sea. p. 285.

Don River (dahn RIHV ur). Located in the former Soviet Union. Rises south of Moscow and flows into the Sea of Azov, which is part of the Black Sea. Connected by canal to the Volga River. p. 285.

Dublin (DUB lun). Seaport and capital of Ireland. Located on the Irish Sea. (53°N/6°W) p. 255.

E

East China Sea (eest CHYE nuh see). Arm of the Pacific Ocean, east of China and west of Kyūshū, Japan, and the Ryukyu Islands. pp. 618–619.

Eastern Ghats (EES turn gawts). Mountains located along the eastern coast of India. Highest peak is Mount Doda Betta, at an elevation of 8,640 ft (2,633 m). p. 508.

Eastern Hemisphere (EES turn HEM ih sfihr). The half of the earth east of the Prime Meridian. p. 9.

Edessa (ee DES uh). Greek city in western Macedonia. A capital of Macedonian kings in ancient times. (41°N/22°E) p. 391.

Edinburgh (ED un bur uh). The capital of Scotland. Located in the southeastern part of Scotland. (56°N/3°W) p. 255.

Elbe River (EL buh RIHV ur). Flows 724 miles (1,165 km), mostly through Germany, and empties into the North Sea. p. 285.

Elburz Mountains (el BOORZ MOUNT unz). Mountain range located in northern Iran. Separates the Plateau of Iran from the Caspian Sea. p. 359.

English Channel (IHNG glihsh CHAN ul). Arm of the Atlantic Ocean, between southern England and northwestern France. p. 157.

Equator (ee KWAYT ur). 0° latitude. A line drawn on maps that circles the earth halfway between the North Pole and the South Pole. p. 8.

Euphrates River (yoo FRAYT eez RIHV ur). River that rises in mountains in eastern Turkey and flows through Syria into Iraq, where it joins with the Tigris River near Al-Qurna to form the Shatt-al-Arab, which flows into the Persian Gulf. p. 51.

Eurasia (yoo RAY zhuh). Name often given to the total area covered by Europe and Asia. pp. 616–617.

Europe (YOOR up). The earth's second smallest continent. p. 23.

F

Florence (FLOR uns). City in Italy, located on the Arno River at the base of the Apennines. (44°N/11°E) p. 249.

G

Ganges River (GAN jeez RIHV ur). Sacred river of India. Rises in the Himalayas. Joined by the Brahmaputra River near Dacca before flowing into the Bay of Bengal. p. 129.

Gaul (gawl). Historical name for area that consisted of northern Italy and part of southern France. p. 110.

Gdańsk (guh DAHNSK). City in Poland. Located on Baltic Sea. Formerly known as Danzig. (54°N/19°E) p. 326.

Genoa (JEN uh wuh). City in Italy. One of the most important Italian seaports. (44°N/9°E) p. 166.

Gilbert Islands (GIHL burt EYE lundz). Group of islands in the west central Pacific Ocean. p. 591.

Gobi, The (GOH bee). The world's second largest desert. Located in northwestern China and Mongolia. p. 508.

Gold Cost (gohld kohst). Former British territory located along the Gulf of Guinea. Named for large amounts of gold once mined in the area. p. 469.

Great Barrier Reef (grayt BAR ee ur reef). World's largest deposit of coral. Located in the Coral Sea, off the northeast coast of Australia. p. 574.

Great Dividing Range (grayt duh VYD ihng raynj). Mountain area of Australia. Extends from north to south near most of the east coast. Highest peak is Mount Kosciusko, at 7,305 ft (2,226 m). p. 574.

Great Hungarian Plain (grayt hung GER ee un playn). Plain located mostly in Hungary. The Danube River crosses this plain. p. 285.

Great Lakes (grayt layks). Chain of five large lakes in central North America. Except for Lake Michigan, the lakes are on the Canada–United States boundary. p. 620.

Great Plains (grayt playnz). Large plain area located in the western part of the Central Plains of the United States. p. 621.

Great Rift Valley (grayt rihft VAL ee). Huge crack in the earth's surface that runs about 4,000 mi (6,436 km) from the Middle East into East Africa. p. 440.

Greenland (GREEN lund). Large island off the coast of northeastern North America belonging to Denmark. It is the largest island in the world with the exception of the continent of Australia. p. 21.

Greenwich (GREN ihch). Place in London, England, designated as 0° longitude. The Prime Meridian runs from the North Pole through Greenwich to the South Pole. (51°N/0°long) p. 9.

Guangzhou (GUAHNG joh). Large seaport city in southeastern China. Formerly known as Canton. (23°N/113°E) p. 510.

Gulf of Mexico (gulf uv MEKS ih koh). Large bay of the Atlantic Ocean. Bounded by Mexico on the west and south, Cuba on the east, and the United States on the north. p. 162.

Gulf Stream (gulf streem). Warm ocean current, about 50 mi (80 km) wide, that flows from the Gulf of Mexico along the United States coast and across the Atlantic to Europe. p. 162.

H

Hague, The (hayg). City in western Netherlands and capital of South Holland province. (52°N/4°E) p. 249.

Hamburg (HAM burg). Busy port city in Germany, on the Elbe River. (54°N/10°E) p. 157.

Hanoi (hah NOI). Capital of Vietnam. Located on the Red River. (21°N/106°E) p. 545.

Harappa (huh RAP uh). Site of ancient city in the Indus Valley. (31°N/73°E) p. 129.

Harare (hah RAH ree). Capital of Zimbabwe, in southern Africa. (18°S/31°E) p. 478.

Harbin (HAHR bihn). City in northeastern China, on the Songhua River. (46°N/127°E) p. 617.

Hawaiian Islands • Lagos

Hawaiian Islands (huh WAH eeun EYE lundz). Group of islands in the North Pacific Ocean that together form a state of the United States. p. 591.

Hellespont (HEL us pahnt). Historical name for the Dardanelles, a strait in Turkey. p. 77.

Himalayas (hihm uh LAY uz). World's highest mountain system. Located in central Asia. Mount Everest, at 29,028 ft (8,848 m) the highest peak in the world, is located in the Himalayas. p. 508.

Hindu Kush (HIHN doo kush). Mountain range located mostly in Afghanistan. Its highest point, Tirich Mir, has an elevation of 25,260 ft (7,699 m). p. 129.

Hokkaidō (hoh KYE doh). Northernmost of the four main islands of Japan. p. 508.

Hong Kong (HAHNG KAHNG). British colony in southeastern China. (22°N/114°E) p. 508.

Honolulu (hahn uh LOO loo). Capital of and most populated city in Hawaii. Located on the island of Oahu. (21°N/158°W) p. 591.

Honshū (HAHN shoo). Largest of Japan's four major islands. p. 508.

Huang He (hwahng hih). River in north central and eastern China that flows into the Yellow Sea. p. 508.

Iberian Peninsula (eye BIHR ee un puh NIHN suh luh). European peninsula southeast of the Pyrenees. Spain and Portugal are on this peninsula. p. 157.

Iceland (EYE slund). Island between the Atlantic and Arctic oceans and between Norway and Greenland. p. 157.

Indian Ocean (IHN dee un OH shun). Large body of water between Africa, Asia, Antarctica, and Australia. p. 508.

Indonesia (ihn duh NEE zhuh). Island group located between Southeast Asia and Australia. Made up of Java, Sumatra, most of Borneo, and other islands. p. 545.

Indus River (IHN dus RIHV ur). River that arises in Tibet and flows into the Arabian Sea in Pakistan, near the border with India. p. 129.

Ireland (EYE ur lund). Large island west of Great Britain. An independent country, the Republic of Ireland, takes up most of the island, but a small part in the north (Northern Ireland) is a part of the United Kingdom. p. 157.

Iron Gate (EYE urn gayt). Gorge, or pass, between the Carpathian and the Balkan mountains, through which the Danube River flows. (45°N/23°E) p. 283.

Islamabad (ihs LAHM uh bahd). Capital of Pakistan. (34°N/73°E) p. 545.

Istanbul (ihs tan BOOL). Most populated city in Turkey. Located on both sides of the Bosporus. Part of the city is in Europe, and part is in Asia. Formerly known as Constantinople. (41°N/29°E) p. 361.

Ivory Coast (EYE vuh ree kohst). Country in western Africa, along the Gulf of Guinea. p. 478.

Jakarta (juh KAHR tuh). Capital of Indonesia. One of the world's most populated cities. Located on the northwest coast of Java. (6°S/107°E) p. 545.

Java (JAV vuh). Island that is part of Indonesia. Located between the Java Sea and the Indian Ocean. p. 508.

Jerusalem (juh ROOZ uh lum). Capital of Israel. Holy city for Jews, Christians, and Muslims. (32°N/35°E) p. 404.

Jordan River (JORD un RIHV ur). River that rises in Syria and flows south through the Sea of Galilee and into the Dead Sea. p. 51.

Jutland Peninsula (JUT lund puh NIHN suh luh). Peninsula located between the North and Baltic seas. Denmark and part of Germany are located on it. p. 157.

Kabul (KAH bool). Capital of and most populated city in Afghanistan. (35°N/69°E) p. 361.

Kalahari Desert (kal uh HAHR ee DEZ urt). Dry plateau region located in Botswana, South Africa, and Namibia. p. 440.

Khartoum (kahr TOOM). Capital of Sudan, on the Nile River. (16°N/33°E) p. 478.

Khyber Pass (KYE bur pas). Narrow pass through the Hindu Kush, along the border between Pakistan and Afghanistan. (34°N/71°E) p. 129.

Kiev (kee EV). Capital of Ukraine. Located on the Dnieper River. (50°N/31°E) p. 296.

Kilwa (KIHL wah). Ancient town on a small island off the coast of Tanzania. Known for its excellent harbor. (9°S/39°E) p. 461.

Kinshasa (keen SHAH sah). Capital of Zaire. Located on the Zaire River. Formerly known as Léopoldville. (4°S/15°E) p. 478.

Kyūshū (kee OO shoo). Most southern of the four main islands of Japan. p. 508.

Lagos (LAY gahs). Most populated city in Nigeria. Formerly the capital. Located on the Gulf of Guinea. (6°N/3°E) p. 478.

Lake Baikal (layk bye KAWL). The world's deepest lake. It is 5,712 ft (1,741 m) deep. Located in Siberia, in Russia. p. 285.

Lake Chad (layk chad). Lake located on the borders between Niger, Chad, Nigeria, and Cameroon. The size of this lake varies, depending on the season. p. 440.

Lake Superior (layk suh PIHR ee ur). Lake located along the boundary between Canada and the United States. Largest of the five Great Lakes. Its coastline is in Minnesota, Wisconsin, and Michigan. p. 621.

Lake Tanganyika (layk tan gun YEE kuh). Lake in east central Africa. Four African nations—Tanzania, Zaire, Zambia, and Burundi—have coastlines on this lake. p. 440.

Lake Victoria (layk vihk TOR ee uh). One of the largest bodies of fresh water in the world. Located in eastern Africa. Kenya, Uganda, and Tanzania all have coastlines on this lake. p. 440.

Leningrad (LEN un grad). *See* St. Petersburg.

Libreville (LEE bruh veel). Seaport and capital of Gabon, in western equatorial Africa, on the Gulf of Guinea. (0°lat./9°E) p. 478.

Liechtenstein (LIHK tun styn). Country in west central Europe, on the Rhine River. p. 157.

Lisbon (LIHZ bun). Capital of Portugal. Mainland Europe's westernmost port city. (39°N/9°W) p. 249.

London (LUN dun). Capital and most populated city in the United Kingdom. Located on the Thames River. (52°N/0°long.) p. 157.

Luanda (loo AHN duh). Capital of and seaport in Angola, in southwestern Africa (9°S/13°E) p. 478.

M

Macedonia (mas uh DOH nee uh). Part of ancient Greece, once ruled by Alexander the Great. It was located in northern Greece. p. 77.

Madagascar (mad uh GAS kur). Island located in the Indian Ocean, off the southeast coast of Africa. Excluding Australia, it is the world's fourth largest island. The nation of Madagascar is on this island. p. 440.

Madrid (muh DRIHD). Capital of Spain. Second most populated city in Europe. (40°N/4°W) p. 249.

Malta (MAWL tuh). Country on a group of islands in the Mediterranean, south of Sicily. p. 157.

Manchester (MAN ches tur). City in northwestern England. (54°N/2°W) p. 255.

Manila (muh NIHL uh). Capital of and most populated city in the Philippines. Located on Manila Bay, on the island of Luzon. (15°N/121°E) p. 545.

Mecca (MEK uh). Birthplace of Muhammad. Holy city for Muslims. Located in Saudi Arabia. (21°N/40°E) p. 392.

Medina (muh DEE nuh). City in Saudi Arabia. Muhammad's trip from Mecca to Medina in A.D. 622 is called the Hegira. (24°N/40°E) p. 392.

Mediterranean Sea (med ih tuh RAY nee un see). Large body of water surrounded by Europe, Africa, and Asia. It is the largest sea in the world. p. 157.

Mekong River (MAY kahng RIHV ur). River in Southeast Asia. Rises in Tibet. Forms most of the boundary between Thailand and Laos. Flows into the South China Sea in southern Vietnam. p. 508.

Melanesia (mel uh NEE zhuh). Group of islands in the South Pacific, northeast of Australia. pp. 610–611.

Melbourne (MEL burn). Capital of the Australian state of Victoria. Located in southeastern Australia, near the coast. (38°S/145°E) p. 591.

Mesopotamia (mes up puh TAY mee uh). Region between the Tigris and Euphrates rivers. p. 51.

Micronesia (mye kruh NEE zhuh). Group of islands in the Pacific, east of the Philippines. pp. 610–611.

Milan (mih LAN). Industrial city in northern Italy. Second most populated city in Italy. (45°N/9°E) p. 166.

Minneapolis (mihn ee AP ul ihs). Most populated city in Minnesota. Located on the Mississippi River. (45°N/93°W) p. 162.

Mohenjo-Daro (moh hen joh DAHR oh). Site of an ancient city in the Indus plain. (28°N/69°E) p. 129.

Mongolia (mahng GOH lee uh). Country in east central Asia, north of China. p. 508.

Mont Blanc (mohn blahn). Highest peak in the Alps. Located in the French Alps, near the border with Italy. Elevation is 15,771 ft (4,807 m). p. 157.

Moscow (MAHS koh). Capital of Russia. Former capital of Soviet Union. The most populated city in Europe. (56°N/38°E) p. 326.

Mount Ararat (mount AR uh rat). Highest point in Turkey, at 16,945 ft (5,165 m). (40°N/44°E) p. 359.

Mount Cook (mount kook). Peak in west central South Island. The highest peak in New Zealand, with an elevation of 12,349 ft (3,764 m). (44°S/170°E) p. 574.

Mount Damāvand (mount DAM uh vand). Highest peak in Iran. Located in the Elburz Mountains. Elevation is 18,934 ft (5,771 m). (36°N/52°E) p. 359.

Mount Elbrus (mount EL broos). Peak in the Caucasus Mountains. Highest peak in Europe, with an elevation of 18,481 ft (5,633 m). (43°N/42°E) p. 285.

Mount Everest (mount EV ur ihst). Highest peak in the world. Located in the Himalayas, with an elevation of 29,028 ft (8,848 m). (28°N/87°E) p. 508.

Mount Fuji (mount FOO jee). Highest peak in Japan. Located on Honshū island. Elevation is 12,388 ft (3,776 m). (35°N/138°E) p. 508.

Mount Kenya (mount KEN yuh). Peak in central Kenya. Second highest point in Africa, with an elevation of 17,058 ft (5,199 m). (0° lat./37°E) p. 440.

Mount Kilimanjaro (mount kihl uh mun JAHR oh). Highest mountain peak in Africa, with an elevation of 19,340 ft (5,895 m). Located in northeastern Tanzania, near the Kenyan border. (3°S/37°E) p. 440.

Mount Kosciusko (mount kahs ee US koh). Highest peak in the Australian Alps. Located in southeastern Australia. Elevation is 7,316 ft (2,230 m). (36°S/148°E) p. 574.

Mount Olympus (mount oh LIHM pus). Highest peak in Greece, with an elevation of 9,570 ft (2,917 m). In ancient Greek mythology it was supposed to be the home of the gods. (40°N/22°E) p. 77.

Mount Vesuvius (mount vuh SOO vee us). Only active volcano on the European mainland. Located near Naples, Italy. (41°N/14°E) p. 110.

Murray River (MUR ee RIHV ur). Most important river in Australia. Rises in the Great Dividing Range and flows into the Indian Ocean near Adelaide. p. 574.

N

Nairobi (nye ROH bee). Capital of and most populated city in Kenya. (1°S/37°E) p. 478.

Namib Desert (NAHM ihb DEZ urt). Dry area along the coast of Namibia. p. 440.

Naples (NAY pulz). Important port city in Italy. Located on the Tyrrhenian Sea, which is part of the Mediterranean Sea. (41°N/14°E) p. 166.

New Delhi (noo DEL ee). Capital of India. Located on the Jumna River. (29°N/77°E) p. 545.

New Guinea (noo GIHN ee). Large island north of Australia. The western half is part of Indonesia; the eastern half is the country Papua New Guinea. p. 508.

New South Wales (noo south waylz). State of southeastern Australia. p. 591.

New York City (noo york SIHT ee). Most populated city in the United States. Located at the mouth of the Hudson River, in the state of New York. (41°N/74°W) p. 621.

Nice (nees). Resort city on Mediterranean coast of France. (44°N/7°E) p. 249.

Niger River (NYE jur RIHV ur). River that rises in southern Guinea, near the Sierra Leone border. Flows into the Gulf of Guinea in Nigeria. p. 440.

Nile River (nyl RIHV ur). Longest river in the world. Flows into the Mediterranean Sea at Alexandria, Egypt. p. 359.

Nineveh (NIHN uh vuh). Ancient capital in northern Mesopotamia, on the Tigris River. (36°N/43°E) p. 51.

North America (north uh MER ih kuh). The earth's third largest continent. p. 23.

North China Plain (north CHYE nuh playn). Large plain located in eastern China. p. 508.

Northern Hemisphere (NOR thurn HEM ih sfihr). The half of the earth that is north of the Equator. p. 8.

North European Plain (north yoor uh PEE un playn). Large area of flat land stretching from southwestern France through Belgium, the Netherlands, Germany, and Poland into the former Soviet Union. The southeastern part of the United Kingdom is also part of this plain. p. 285.

North Island (north EYE lund). Northernmost of the two major islands of New Zealand. p. 574.

North Pole The most northern place on the earth. Located at 90° north latitude. p. 8.

North Sea (north see). Part of the Atlantic Ocean between Great Britain and the European continent. p. 157.

O

Ob River (ohb RIHV ur). River that rises in the Altai Mountains and flows north into the Arctic Ocean. Located in Russia. p. 285.

Oder River (OH dur RIHV ur). River that flows north through Poland. In Germany, it is joined by the Neisse River. It then flows north to the Baltic Sea, forming the boundary between Poland and Germany. p. 249.

Olympia (oh LIHM pee uh). City in ancient Greece. Located in western Peloponnesus. Site of the ruins of the temple of Zeus. Ancient Greeks held their Olympian Games here every four years. (38°N/22°E) p. 77.

Orange River (OR ihng RIHV ur). Longest river in South Africa. Part of the river forms the boundary between South Africa and Namibia. Flows into the Atlantic Ocean at Alexander Bay. p. 440.

Oslo (AHS loh). Capital of Norway. Located on Oslo Fjord. (60°N/11°E) p. 249.

P

Pacific Ocean (puh SIHF ihk OH shun). The earth's largest body of water. Stretches from the Arctic Circle to Antarctica and from the western coast of the Americas to the eastern coast of Asia. p. 23.

Palestine (PAL us tyn). Region on the eastern coast of the Mediterranean. It was the country of the Jews in biblical times and is now divided into Arab and Jewish states. p. 391.

Paris (PAR ihs). Capital and river port of France. (49°N/2°E) p. 249.

Pennines (PE nynz). Range of mountains in northern England, extending from the Cheviot Hills southward to Derbyshire and Staffordshire. p. 255.

Persia (PUR zhuh). Ancient kingdom in the area that today is called Iran. p. 87.

Persian Gulf (PUR zhun gulf). Arm of the Arabian Sea. Separates Iran and Saudi Arabia. Connected with the Gulf of Oman and Arabian Sea by the Strait of Hormuz. p. 359.

Perth (purth). Capital of the Australian state of Western Australia. Located on the southwest coast of Australia. (32°S/116°E) p. 591.

Philippines (FIHL uh peenz). Country in the Pacific, north of Indonesia, made up of more than 7,000 islands. p. 508.

Polynesia (pahl uh NEE zhuh). Scattered group of many islands in the central and southern Pacific, including Hawaii and Tahiti. pp. 610–611.

Pompeii (pahm PAY ee). Ancient Roman city at the base of Mount Vesuvius. Destroyed in A.D. 79 by an eruption of Mount Vesuvius. (41°N/15°E) p. 110.

Po River (poh RIHV ur). Longest river in Italy. Starts in the Alps and flows into the Adriatic Sea south of Venice. p. 157.

Prague (prahg). Capital of Czechoslovakia. Located on the Vltava River. (50°N/14°E) p. 326.

Prime Meridian (prym muh RIHD ee un). 0° line of longitude that passes through Greenwich, England. It divides the earth into the Eastern Hemisphere and the Western Hemisphere. p. 9.

Prussia (PRUSH uh). Former state of northern Germany. p. 226.

Pyrenees (PIHR uh neez). Mountains along the border between France and Spain. Highest peak is Pico de Aneto, at 11,168 ft (3,404 m). p. 157.

R

Rangoon (ran GOON). Capital of and most populated city in Myanmar. Located on the Rangoon River. (17°N/96°E) p. 545.

Red Sea (red see). Large sea separating part of eastern Africa from Asia. p. 359.

Rhine River (ryn RIHV ur). River that starts in the Alps in Switzerland. Flows north through the Netherlands into the North Sea. p. 157.

Rhone River (rohn RIHV ur). River that starts from a glacier in the Alps in Switzerland and flows through France and into the Mediterranean Sea near Marseilles, France. p. 157.

Riyadh (ree YAHD). Capital of Saudi Arabia. (25°N/47°E) p. 404.

Rocky Mountains (RAHK ee MOUNT unz). Longest mountain chain in Canada and the United States. Stretches from Alaska to Mexico. Its highest peak in Canada is Mount Robson, British Columbia, with an elevation of 12,972 ft (3,954 m). p. 621.

Rome (rohm). Capital of and most populated city in Italy. Located on the Tiber River. Most important city in the Roman Empire. (42°N/12°E) p. 249.

Rotterdam (RAHT ur dam). Seaport in the southwestern Netherlands (52°N/4°E) p. 166.

S

Sahara (suh HAR uh). Largest desert in the world. Located in North Africa. p. 359.

Saigon (SYE gahn). Seaport in South Vietnam. Saigon was the capital of South Vietnam when Vietnam was a divided country. The new name is Ho Chi Minh City. (11°N/107°E) p. 536.

St. Petersburg (saynt PEET urz burg). City in Russia built by Peter the Great in 1703. Located on the mouth of the Neva River. At different times known as Petrograd and Leningrad. Today it is the second most populated city in Russia. (60°N/30°E) p. 326.

Salamis (SAL uh mihs). Greek island in the Saronic Gulf, near Piraeus. Ancient Greeks won an important naval battle near here against the Persians in 480 B.C. (38°N/23°E) p. 77.

San'a (sah NA). Capital of Yemen. (15°N/44°E) p. 404.

Sarajevo (sar uh YAY voh). City in Bosnia and Hercegovina. Site of 1984 Winter Olympics. (44°N/18°E) p. 228.

Sardinia (sahr DIHN ee uh). Italian island in the Mediterranean. It is just south of the island of Corsica. p. 157.

Scandinavian peninsula (scan duh NAY vee un puh NIHN suh luh). Large peninsula in northern Europe, consisting of Norway and Sweden. p. 157.

Sea of Japan (see uv juh PAN). Arm of the western Pacific Ocean, between Japan and eastern Asia. p. 508.

Sea of Marmara (see uv MAHR muh ruh). Body of water between European Turkey and Asian Turkey. Connects the Bosporus and the Dardanelles. (41°N/28°E) p. 77.

Senegal River (sen ih GAWL RIHV ur). River that rises in Guinea and flows into the Atlantic Ocean at Saint-Louis, Senegal. Forms boundary between Senegal and Mauritania. p. 440.

Seoul (sohl). Capital of South Korea. One of the world's most populated cities. (38°N/127°E) p. 545.

Serbia (SUR bee uh). State in the eastern part of the former Yugoslavia. Formerly a kingdom. p. 228.

Shikoku (SHEE koh koo). Smallest of the four main islands of Japan. p. 508.

Siberia (sye BIHR ee uh). Region mostly in Russia, covering much of the area between the Ural Mountains and the Pacific Ocean. p. 285.

Sicily (SIHS ul ee). Largest island in the Mediterranean Sea. Part of Italy. p. 157.

Singapore (SIHNG uh por). City on the island of Singapore. Also the capital of the nation of Singapore. One of the world's busiest ports. Located on Singapore Strait. (1°N/104°E) p. 545.

Sofia (SOH fee uh). Capital of Bulgaria. (43°N/23°E) p. 326.

South America (south uh MER ih kuh). The earth's fourth largest continent. p. 23.

South China Sea (south CHYE nuh see). Arm of the Pacific Ocean, west of the Philippines and Borneo. p. 508.

Southern Hemisphere (SUTH urn HEM ih sfihr). The half of the earth that is south of the Equator. p. 8.

South Island (south EYE lund). Largest of New Zealand's islands. p. 574.

South Pole (south pohl). The most southern place on the earth. Located at 90° south latitude. p. 10.

Sparta (SPAHRT uh). City-state in ancient Greece. Today a small town on the Eurotas River, on the southern part of the Peloponnesian peninsula. (37°N/22°E) p. 74.

Sri Lanka (sree LAHNG kuh). Country in the Indian Ocean, off the southern tip of India. At one time called Ceylon. (7°N/81°E) p. 508.

Stockholm (STAHK hohm). Capital of Sweden. On the Baltic Sea. (59°N/18°E) p. 166.

Strait of Gibraltar (strayt uv jih BRAWL tur). Narrow neck of water separating the Iberian Peninsula from North Africa. Connects the Mediterranean Sea with the Atlantic Ocean. p. 157.

Strait of Hormuz (strayt uv HOR muz). Narrow body of water connecting the Persian Gulf and the Gulf of Oman. (27°N/56°E) p. 361.

Suez Canal (soo EZ kuh NAL). Waterway that joins the Red and Mediterranean seas. Construction started in 1859 and was completed in 1869. (30°N/33°E) p. 359.

Sydney (SIHD nee). Capital of the Australian state of New South Wales. Most populated city in Australia. Port city located on Tasman Sea, which is part of the Pacific Ocean. (34°S/151°E) p. 591.

T

Tahiti (tuh HEET ee). French island in the South Pacific, south of Hawaii. (18°S/149°W) p. 591.

Taipei (tye PAY). Capital of and most populated city in Taiwan. (25°N/122°E) p. 545.

Taiwan (tye WAHN). Island off the southeastern coast of China. This island country is called the Republic of China. p. 508.

Tashkent (tash KENT). Capital of Uzbekistan. (41°N/69°E) p. 326.

Tasmania (taz MAY nee uh). Island off the coast of Australia. Also, one of Australia's states. p. 574.

Tehran (te RAHN). Capital of Iran. Located at the base of the Elburz Mountains. (36°N/51°E) p. 404.

Thames River (temz RIHV ur). River in Great Britain on which London is located. p. 157.

Thebes (theebz). City-state in ancient Greece. (38°N/23°E) p. 77.

Thermopylae (ther MAHP uh lee). Narrow pass in eastern Greece, where ancient Greeks fought Persians in 480 B.C. (39°N/23°E) p. 77.

Tiber River (TYE bur RIHV ur). River in Italy. It rises in the Apennines and flows through Rome to the Mediterranean Sea. p. 110.

Tibet (tih BET). High mountainous area in western China, north of India and Nepal. p. 545.

Tigris River (TYE grus RIHV ur). River that rises in Turkey and flows into Iraq, where it joins with the Euphrates River near Al-Qurna to form the Shatt-al-Arab, which flows into the Persian Gulf. p. 51.

Timbuktu (tihm buk TOO). Town in central Mali, near the Niger River. (17°N/3°W) p. 457.

Tokyo (TOH kee oh). Capital of Japan. Located on the island of Honshū on Tokyo Bay. Second most populated city in the world. (36°N/140°E) p. 545.

Tripoli (TRIHP uh lee). Capital of Libya. Port city on the Mediterranean Sea. (33°N/13°E) p. 404.

Tropic of Cancer (TRAHP ihk uv KAN sur). Line of latitude located at 23 1/2° north latitude. p. 21.

Tropic of Capricorn (TRAHP ihk uv KAP rih korn). Line of latitude located at 23 1/2° south latitude. p. 21.

Troy (troi). Ancient city on the coast of Asia Minor. (40°N/26°E) p. 77.

Tunis (TOO nihs). Capital of Tunisia. Seaport located on the Mediterranean Sea. (37°N/10°E) p. 361.

U

Uruk (OO ruk). Ancient Sumerian city in southern Babylonia, on the Euphrates River. (31°N/45°E) p. 51.

Ural Mountains (YOOR ul MOUNT unz). Mountains located in Russia. They form the east-west divide between Asia and Europe. p. 285.

V

Vatican City (VAT in kun SIHT ee). Independent state inside the city of Rome, with the pope as its head. (42°N/12°E) p. 157.

Venice (VEN ihs). City in Italy. (45°N/12°E) p. 224

Victoria (vihk TOR ee uh). State in the southeastern part of Australia. p. 591.

Victoria Falls (vihk TOR ee uh fawlz). Falls located on the Zambezi River, on the boundary between Zambia and Zimbabwe. More water flows over these falls than over any others in Africa. (18°S/26°E) p. 440.

Vienna (vee EN uh). Capital of and largest city in Austria. Located on the Danube River. (48°N/16°E) p. 249.

Vistula River (VIHS choo luh RIHV ur). Longest river in Poland. Rises in the Carpathians and flows into the Baltic Sea near Gdańsk. p. 285.

Vladivostok (vlad ih VAHS tahk). City in Russia. Eastern end of the Trans-Siberian Railroad. Located on the Sea of Japan. (43°N/132°E) p. 285.

Volga River (VAHL guh RIHV ur). Longest river in Europe. Rises in the Valdai Hills of Russia and flows into the Caspian Sea. p. 285.

W

Wales (waylz). One of the four major political divisions of the United Kingdom. p. 255.

Warsaw (WOR saw). Capital of Poland. Located on the Vistula River. (52°N/21°E) p. 326.

Washington, D.C. (WAWSH ing tun dee see). Capital of the United States. Located on the Potomac River. (39°N/77°W) p. 620.

Waterloo (WAWT ur loo). Village in Belgium where Napoleon met his final defeat, in 1815. (51°N/4°E) p. 218.

Wellington (WEL ing tun). Capital of New Zealand. Located on North Island and Cook Strait. (41°S/175°E) p. 591.

Western Ghats (WES turn gawts). Mountains located along the western coast of India. Highest peak is Anai Mudi, at an elevation of 8,841 ft (2,695 m). p. 508.

Western Hemisphere (WES turn HEM ih sfihr). Hemisphere in which all of South America and North America are located. The half of the earth west of the Prime Meridian. p. 9.

X

Xi'an (SHEE AHN). Capital of the Shaanxi province in east central China, on the south bank of the Wei River. Formerly called Sian. (34°N/109°E) p. 617.

Xi Jiang (shee jee AHNG). River in southeastern China. Formerly known as Hsi Chiang. p. 144.

Y

Yenisei River (yen uh SAY RIHV ur). River in Russia. One of the world's longest rivers. Rises in the Sayan Mountains and flows into the Kara Sea, which is part of the Arctic Ocean. p. 285.

Z

Zagros Mountains (ZAG rus MOUNT unz). Mountains that stretch from northwestern Iran to near the southern end of the Persian Gulf. Highest peak is Zardeh Kuh, with an elevation of 14,921 ft (4,548 m). p. 359.

Zanzibar (ZAN zuh bahr). Island belonging to Tanzania. Located in the Indian Ocean, off the coast of Tanzania. Also the name of the chief city on the island. (6°S/39°E) p. 440.

A

abdicate (AB dih kayt). To give up a position of power, such as a kingship. p. 315.

Aborigine (ab uh RIHJ uh nee). A member of the first inhabitants of Australia. p. 573.

acid rain (AS ihd rayn). Rain or snow that has a high amount of certain acids due to air pollution. p. 271.

Africanized (AF rih kuh nyzd). Changed to reflect African names. p. 480.

alliance (uh LYE uns). An agreement by persons, groups, or nations to act together for some special purpose or benefit. p. 80.

altitude (AL tuh tood). The height above sea level. p. 14.

ambassador (am BAS uh dur). An official who represents his or her government in a foreign country. p. 405.

amphitheater (AM fuh thee ut ur). A large open-air theater built in a semicircular pattern, with ascending rows of seats built into a hillside. p. 95.

anarchy (AN ur kee). The complete lack of government or law. p. 315.

ancestor (AN ses tur). A person from whom a family or a group of people descends. p. 65.

anno Domini (AH noh DOH mee nee). Latin words that mean "in the year of the Lord." Usually shortened to the letters A.D., the term is used to mark the years after the birth of Jesus. p. 27.

apartheid (uh PAHR tayt). The policy of racial segregation that the Republic of South Africa had until 1991. Apartheid means "apartness." p. 484.

apprentice (un PREN tihs). A person learning a trade or an art. p. 182.

aqueduct (AK wuh dukt). A structure or an artificial channel used to transport water. p. 114.

arable (AR uh bul). Suitable for growing crops. p. 343.

archaeologist (ahr kee AHL uh jihst). A scientist who studies objects, ruins, and other evidence of human life in the past. p. 49.

archipelago (ahr kuh PEL uh goh). A group of islands. p. 512.

armistice (AHR muh stihs). A halt to fighting by agreement between warring nations. p. 230.

artery (AHRT ur ee). A main road or channel. p. 516.

ascetic (uh SET ihk). A person who chooses to live without the comforts of life, especially one who lives this way for religious reasons. p. 132.

asphalt (AS fawlt). A substance formed from a combination of oil, sand, and rock. p. 424.

assassination (us sas sih NAY shun). The murdering of someone by secret or sudden attack. p. 107.

astronomy (uh STRAHN uh mee). The scientific study of the sun, moon, planets, and stars. p. 201.

atheism (AY thee ihz um). The belief that there is no God. p. 342.

atlas (AT lus). A collection of maps. p. 22.

atoll (A tawl). A ring-shaped coral island enclosing or partly enclosing a lagoon. p. 584.

axis (AK sihs). The imaginary rod around which the earth turns. p. 4.

Axis (AK sihs). The name given to Italy, Japan, and Germany, the countries that fought against the Allies in World War II. p. 241.

ayatollah (eye yuh TOH luh). An honorary title for a Muslim religious leader in Iran. p. 404.

B

Bedouin (BED oo ihn). A wandering Arab herder. p. 360.

bilingual (bye LIHNG gwel). Having two languages. p. 267.

Blitzkrieg (blihts KREEG). A war conducted with great speed. From German words meaning "lightning" and "war." p. 236.

Boer (boor). An early Dutch settler in South Africa; Dutch word for "farm worker." p. 467.

boomerang (BOOM ur ang). A bent throwing stick that can be thrown in such a way that it comes back to the thrower. p. 590.

Brahman (BRAH mun). A class of priest under the Aryans' caste system. p. 134.

bush (boosh). Sparsely settled land far from any settlement. p. 573.

C

cacao (kuh KAY oh). The tree and the seeds from which cocoa and chocolate are made. p. 450.

caliph (KAY lihf). The Arabic title given to Muslim religious leaders. p. 386.

calligraphy (kuh LIHG ruh fee). The art of handwriting. p. 397.

capital (KAP ut ul). Wealth in the form of goods or money used for making more goods. p. 210.

cartographer (kahr TAHG ruh fer). A person who makes maps. p. 16.

cash crop (kash krahp). A crop grown for sale. p. 480.

caste (kast). A class or group into which people are separated based on birth. p. 134.

causeway (KAWZ way). A raised roadway across a body of water. p. 418.

central planning (SEN trul PLAN nihng). A system in which the government decides what and how much should be produced by industries. p. 325.

century (SEN chu ree). A period of 100 years. p. 28.

circa (SUR kuh). The Latin word meaning "about" or "approximately." Used to refer to dates. p. 28.

city-state (SIHT ee stayt). A state made up of an independent city and the nearby countryside, as in ancient Greece. p. 78.

civil disobedience (SIHV ul dihs oh BEE dee uns). Nonviolent opposition to a government law by refusing to obey the law. p. 554.

civilization (sihv ul luh ZAY shun). The stage of cultural development marked by the presence of cities, trade, government, art, writing, and science. p. 48.

civil war (SIHV ul wor). A war between two or more groups of people within a country. p. 107.

climate (KLYE mut). The kind of weather a place has over a long period of time. p. 24.

climograph (KLYE muh graf). A graph that shows both the average temperature and the average precipitation for a certain place over a period of time. p. 161.

cocoon (kuh KOON). The silky case, or covering, that caterpillars spin to shelter themselves while they are changing into butterflies or moths. p. 525.

collective farm (kuh LEK tihv fahrm). A farm that a group of people operate together to produce and to share the products. p. 323.

collectivism (kuh LEK tuh vihz um). A system of ownership by all the people together. p. 323.

colony (KAHL uh nee). A settlement in one land ruled by the government of another land. p. 86.

commercial farm (kuh MUR shul fahrm). A farm that produces crops for sale. p. 450.

Commonwealth of Nations (KAHM un welth uv NAY shunz). An association of countries that were once part of the British Empire. p. 258.

commune (KAHM yoon). Land that is worked together by a team of people. p. 541.

communism (KAHM yoo nihz um). A social and economic system in which most property is owned by the government and shared by the governed. p. 316.

Confucianism (kun FYOO shun ihz um). A religion based on the teachings of the philosopher Confucius. Confucianism teaches respect for the past and one's ancestors and stresses the importance of having only superior people rule a well-ordered society. p. 141.

coniferous (koh NIHF ur us). Having cones. p. 160.

constitutional monarchy (kahn stuh TOO shuh nul MAHN ur kee). A kind of government in which the monarch's powers are limited by a constitution. p. 213.

consul (KAHN sul). The annually elected chief magistrate of the Roman republic. The magistrate was given the powers of a king. p. 102.

consumer goods (kun SOOM ur goodz). Things that are grown or made by producers and used by people. p. 389.

continental climate (kahn tuh NENT ul KLYE mut). A climate with extreme changes of temperature, and with hot summers and cold winters. p. 287.

contour line (KAHN toor lyn). A line that is used to show elevation on a topographical, or physical, map. p. 15.

convent (KAHN vunt). A building or buildings in which a group of nuns live. p. 180.

copra (KAH pruh). Dried coconut meat. p. 562.

Coptic (KAHP tihk). An Egyptian language no longer used except in the services of the Egyptian Christian Church. p. 59.

coral reef (KOR ul reef). A line or ridge of coral lying at or near the surface of the water. p. 575.

coronation (kor uh NAY shun). The crowning of a king or queen. p. 311.

crest (krest). The highest point. p. 286.

crude oil (krood oil). Oil in the form in which it comes from the earth, before impurities are removed. p. 406.

Crusade (kroo SAYD). A Christian military expedition to take control of the Holy Land from the Muslims. p. 178.

culture (KUL chur). The way of life of a group of people, including their customs, traditions, and values. p. 88.

cuneiform (kyoo NEE uh form). A form of writing with wedge-shaped symbols that was used in Mesopotamia. p. 49.

current • forestry

current (KUR unt). A stream that flows in the ocean. p. 162.

czar (zahr). The title of any of the former emperors of Russia. p. 310.

D

decade (DEK ayd). A period of 10 years. p. 28.

Deccan (DEK un). A low plateau occupying most of the peninsula of India. Two mountain ranges, the Western Ghats and the Eastern Ghats, form the edge of the Deccan. p. 507.

deciduous (dee SIHJ oo us). Dropping off; losing leaves at the end of a growing season. Oak and maple trees are deciduous. p. 160.

delta (DEL tuh). The land formed by mud and sand in the mouth of a river. p. 55.

democracy (dih MAHK ruh see). A government in which power is held by the people. p. 78.

depression (dee PRESH un). An economic condition in which business is very bad and large numbers of people are unemployed. p. 233.

despot (DES put). A person who rules with total and unlimited control. p. 77.

dialect (DYE uh lekt). A form of a language that is used only in a certain place or among a certain group. p. 138.

dictator (DIHK tayt ur). One who has absolute power of rule in a country. p. 102.

Diet (DYE ut). The legislature of Japan. The Diet is made up of representatives elected by the people and is similar to Parliament in England. p. 550.

dike (dyk). A wall or bank built to control or hold back the water of a river or sea. p. 51.

distortion (dih STOR shun). A twisting or stretching out of shape. p. 20.

divine right (duh VYN ryt). A belief during the Middle Ages that kings received their powers from God. p. 195.

dry stone (drye stohn). A stone held together with another stone without the use of mortar. p. 459.

E

economic boom (ek uh NAHM ihk boom). A period of great prosperity. p. 476.

economy (ih KAHN uh me). The way in which natural resources and workers are used to produce goods and services. p. 175.

elevation (el uh VAY shun). The height of something. The elevation of land is its distance above or below sea level and is usually measured in feet or meters. p. 14.

embassy (EM buh see). The buildings where the ambassador of a country lives and works. p. 405.

emperor (EM pur ur). A supreme ruler of an empire. p. 109.

epic (EP ihk). A long narrative poem about great heroes and their deeds. p. 71.

equatorial (ee kwuh TOR ee ul). Near the Equator. p. 439.

ethnic group (ETH nihk groop). A group of people who share many traits and customs. p. 341.

explorer (ek SPLOR ur). A person who searches for new things and places. p. 190.

export (EKS port). **1.** Something that is sent to another country, usually for sale there. **2.** To send something to another country for sale. p. 257.

ex post facto law (eks pohst FAK toh law). The rule that no law can be used to punish a person for something done before the law was made. p. 121.

F

factory (FAK tuh ree). An industrial plant. p. 207.

Fascist (FASH ihst). A member of a group that believes in a political system that supports a single party and a single ruler, and involves total government control of political, economic, cultural, religious, and social activities. p. 232.

feudalism (FYOOD ul ihz um). The system of mutual rights and duties between lords and vassals. The system existed in the Middle Ages. p. 174.

fez (fez). A felt hat with a flat top and no brim once worn by Turkish men. p. 411.

fief (feef). Land granted by a lord to his vassal in return for military service. p. 174.

finance (FYE nans). The management of money. p. 551.

fjord (fyord). A long, narrow, often deep inlet of the sea, lying between steep cliffs. p. 261.

folk tale (fohk tayl). A story handed down from one generation to another that often reflects the ideas and traditions that a nationality values. p. 294.

food processing (food PRAH ses ihng). The canning, freezing, or drying of agricultural products. p. 592.

forestry (FOR ihs tree). The science and work of planting and taking care of forests. p. 160.

free enterprise (free ENT ur pryz). A type of economy in which people have many choices about how to make and spend their money. p. 211.

free port (free port). A port or place with no taxes on imports or exports. p. 537.

G

genocide (JEN un syd). The planned killing of a whole group of people because of their race, religion, or nationality. p. 239.

geothermal energy (jee oh THUR mul EN ur jee). The heat from within the earth. p. 579.

geyser (GYE zur). An underground stream that sends forth a gush of hot steam or hot water. p. 262.

gladiator (GLAD ee ayt ur). A person who fought another person or an animal for the entertainment of an audience in ancient Rome. p. 115.

glasnost (GLAHS nust). A policy of "openness" in the former Soviet Union, which resulted in less secrecy about problems and weaknesses of Soviet society. p. 329.

gorge (gorj). A narrow passage through land. p. 291.

grid (grihd). A network of lines that form a pattern of crisscrosses. p. 8.

gross national product (grohs NASH uh nul PRAHD ukt). The total value of all the goods and services produced in a year by a nation. p. 551.

groundnut (GROUND nut). Nuts that grow underground, rather than on trees or bushes. p. 479.

ground water (ground WAWT ur). Water that has seeped below the ground and has collected in layers of soil, sand, and rock. p. 369.

guild (gihld). An organization of people in a craft or trade. p. 182.

guillotine (GIHL uh teen). A machine for beheading people that was introduced in France during the French Revolution. p. 217.

Gulf Stream (gulf streem). The currents that flow north and east from the Gulf of Mexico. p. 162.

H

hemisphere (HEM ih sfihr). Half of a sphere, or ball. Half of the earth. p. 5.

heritage (HER ih tihj). Ways and beliefs handed down from one generation to the next. p. 596.

hieroglyphics (hye ur oh GLIHF ihks). A form of picture writing used by the early Egyptians. p. 60.

high veld (hye velt). The upland grassland area of South Africa. p. 489.

historical source (hihs TOR ih kul sors). A person or thing that tells about the past. p. 116.

Holocaust (HAHL uh kawst). The destruction of more than 6 million European Jews by the Nazis. p. 239.

hostage (HAHS tihj). A person held captive until demands of the captor are met. p. 405.

humidity (hyoo MIHD uh tee). The amount of water or dampness in the air. p. 24.

I

incentive (ihn SENT ihv). Anything that makes a person work harder or do more. p. 542.

Industrial Revolution (ihn DUS tree ul rev uh LOO shun). The period of great change in the way people worked and lived, brought about by the invention of power-driven machines. p. 207.

Inquisition (ihn kwuh ZIHSH un). A special court of the Roman Catholic Church, established in the thirteenth century. p. 204.

International Date Line (ihn tur NASH uh nul dayt lyn). The line at roughly 180° longitude that marks the place where each day begins. p. 9.

irrigate (IHR uh gayt). To bring water to crops, usually through canals, ditches, or pipes. p. 51.

isthmus (IHS mus). A narrow strip of land connecting two larger bodies of land. p. 23.

J

jury (JOOR ee). A group of people called into court to give a verdict, or decision, in a dispute. p. 80.

jute (joot). A plant, raised mostly in the Ganges Delta, from which the fiber for burlap and twine is obtained. p. 556.

K

Knesset (KNES et). The Israeli parliament. p. 410.

knight (nyt). A warrior of the Middle Ages. p. 174.

L

labor force (LAY bur fors). The working population. p. 360.

landlocked ● odometer

landlocked (LAND lahkt). Not having a seacoast. p. 248.

latex (LAY teks). The milky sap that drips from cuts made in the bark of rubber trees. p. 514.

latitude (LAT uh tood). The distance measured in degrees north and south from the Equator to the earth's poles. Lines of latitude are imaginary lines used to locate places on the earth. p. 8.

League of Nations (leeg uv NAY shunz). An international organization, formed after World War I, of nations interested in preventing war. p. 231.

legend (LEJ und). A story handed down from earlier times, which may be no more than partly true. p. 103.

literacy rate (LIHT ur uh see rayt). The percentage of the population able to read and write. p. 552.

longitude (LAHN juh tood). The distance measured in degrees east and west of the Prime Meridian. Lines of longitude are used to locate places on the earth. p. 8.

M

manor (MAN ur). A large medieval farm. p. 175.

maritime climate (MAR ih tym KLYE mut). A climate influenced by winds blowing off the sea. p. 256.

market economy (MAHR kiht ih KAHN uh mee). An economy in which the choices of buyers decide what shall be produced. p. 327.

mausoleum (maw suh LEE um). A large tomb. p. 534.

Mediterranean climate (med ih tuh RAY nee un KLYE mut). A warm, temperate climate occurring on the western margins of continents in the latitudes 30° to 40°. It is marked by hot, dry, and sunny summers and moist, warm winters. p. 264.

meridian (muh RIHD ee un). Another name for a line of longitude. p. 8.

metropolitan area (me troh PAHL ih tun ER ee uh). An area made up of a large city or several large cities and the surrounding towns, cities, and other communities. p. 167.

migration (mye GRAY shun). The movement of people from one place to another. p. 360.

minaret (mihn uh RET). A tall, slender tower, with a balcony, on a mosque. p. 399.

missionary (MIHSH un er ee). A person who tries to spread his or her religion. p. 468.

modernize (MAHD urn eyes). To change over to the use of up-to-date ways of doing things. p. 403.

monarchy (MAHR ur kee). A government headed by one ruler, usually a queen or a king. p. 78.

monastery (MAHN uh ster ee). Building(s) where monks live together. p. 179.

monolith (MAHN uh lihth). A large block of stone, or a statue or monument carved from a single large stone. p. 575.

monopoly (muh NAHP uh lee). The exclusive possession or control of a commodity or service. p. 182.

monsoon (mahn SOON). A seasonal wind that blows from the land to the water in one season and from the water to the land in the other. p. 460.

mosque (mahsk). A Muslim place of worship. p. 398.

mullah (MUL uh). A Muslim religious teacher. p. 403.

multilingual (mul tih LIHNG gwel). Having several languages. p. 445.

mummy (MUM ee). A body treated for burial with preservatives to keep it from decaying. p. 55.

myth (mihth). An ancient story that usually explains something in nature. p. 71.

N

nationalism (NASH uh nul ihz um). A feeling of loyalty and devotion to one's country. p. 223.

natural resource (NACH ur ul REE sors). Something useful to people that is supplied by nature, such as land, minerals, water, and forests. p. 160.

navigator (NAV uh gayt ur). A person who plans and steers a course through water or air or on land. p. 463.

nomad (NOH mad). A person who moves from place to place. p. 129.

nonrenewable resource (nahn rih NOO uh bul REE sors). A resource that will not be replaced by nature, such as oil. p. 416.

North Atlantic Drift (north at LAN tihk drihft). A large movement of water made up of the Gulf Stream and other warm currents. p. 162.

O

oasis (oh AY sihs). A green place in a desert where wells provide water. p. 55.

odometer (oh DAHM ut ur). An instrument that tells how far one has traveled. p. 11.

oligarchy (AHL ih gahr kee). A government by a few. p. 78.

oral history (OHR ul HIHS tuh ree). The history or tradition of a people handed down from one generation to another by word of mouth. p. 455.

orbit (OR biht). The path that one body travels as it goes around another body, such as the path of the earth around the sun. p. 4.

P

pagoda (puh GOH duh). A tower that serves as a religious building. p. 558.

papyrus (puh PYE rus). A tall reed that grows in the Nile Valley. The pith (spongy center part) was used to make a paperlike substance. p. 61.

parable (PAR uh bul). A short, simple story that teaches a moral lesson, as in the teachings of Jesus. p. 117.

parallel (PAR uh lel). An imaginary line of latitude running in an east-west direction on a map. p. 8.

Parliament (PAHR luh munt). The lawmaking body of the United Kingdom. p. 212.

partition (pahr TIHSH un). A division into parts. p. 554.

patrician (puh TRIHSH un). A member of one of the original citizen families of ancient Rome. A member of the upper class. p. 101.

peninsula (puh NIHN suh luh). A piece of land almost surrounded by water and connected to a large body of land. p. 102.

per capita income (per KAP ih tuh IHN kum). The amount of income (money received) that each person in a country would have if the country's total income were divided equally among all of its people. p. 367.

perestroika (per es TROI kuh). The reform of government and economy in the former Soviet Union. p. 330.

permafrost (PUR muh frawst). Permanently frozen ground. p. 286.

petroleum (puh TROH lee um). An oily liquid found in the earth, from which gasoline and many other products are made. p. 367.

pharaoh (FAR oh). A ruler of ancient Egypt. From the Egyptian word for "Great House." p. 55.

philosophy (ful LAHS uh fee). The study of human behavior, thought, and knowledge. The word *philosophy* originally meant "the love of wisdom." p. 90.

phosphate (FAHS fayt). A mineral used in making fertilizers and detergents. p. 424.

pictograph (PIHK toh graf). A kind of graph that uses symbols, instead of numbers, to represent fixed amounts of a particular thing. p. 50.

pilgrimage (PIHL grihm ihj). A journey to a shrine or other sacred place. p. 382.

Pinyin (pihn YIHN). A system of spelling and writing Chinese words, using the Roman alphabet. p. 138.

plaque (plak). A thin, flat piece of metal or wood with decoration or lettering on it. p. 458.

plateau (pla TOH). A large, high, rather level area that is raised above the surrounding land. p. 248.

plebeian (plee BEE un). One of the common people in any country, such as in ancient Rome. p. 101.

pollution (puh LOO shun). The unclean condition of the earth's soil, air, and water. p. 251.

population density (pahp yoo LAY shun DEN suh tee). The average number of people living in a unit of land area. p. 25.

precipitation (pree sihp uh TAY shun). Moisture that falls on the earth's surface: rain, snow, sleet, and hail. p. 24.

Prime Meridian (prym muh RIHD ee un). The line of 0° longitude that passes through Greenwich, England. p. 9.

prime minister (prym MIHM ihs tur). The chief official of a country. p. 224.

principality (prihn suh PAL uh tee). A territory ruled by a prince. p. 254.

profit (PRAHF iht). The gain made from selling a product or service over the cost of producing or purchasing the product or service. p. 211.

projection (proh JEK shun). The representation on a map of all or part of the earth's grid system. p. 19.

prophet (PRAHF ut). A person who was believed to have a message from God. p. 379.

protectorate (proh TEK tur iht). A place or country under the protection of another country. p. 600.

proverb (PRAHV urb). A short saying that expresses some truth or fact. p. 295.

province (PRAHV ihns). A division of a country. p. 106.

pyramid (PIHR uh mihd). A massive four-sided structure built on a broad base and narrowing gradually to a point at the top. p. 58.

pyrethrum (pye RETH rum). A plant used to make insect poison. p. 491.

raw material • *subsistence farming*

R

raw material (raw muh TIHR ee ul). A natural material that can be processed into finished products. p. 251.

Reformation (ref ur MAY shun). The religious movement during the sixteenth century that aimed at reforming the Roman Catholic Church and resulted in establishing the Protestant churches. p. 192.

Renaissance (ren un SAHNS). The great revival of art and learning in Europe in the 1300s, 1400s, and 1500s. The word **Renaissance** means "a new birth." p. 184.

republic (rih PUB lihk). A government in which citizens choose representatives to run the country. p. 101.

reserve (rih ZURV). A reserve is a supply of a natural resource that is known to exist but has not yet been used. p. 416.

revenue (REV uh noo). Income. p. 422.

revolution (rev uh LOO shun). **1.** A complete change in the way a country is governed. p. 201. **2.** The movement of the earth around the sun. One complete *revolution* takes 365 1/4 days. p. 201.

river basin (RIHV ur BAYS un). The area drained by a river. p. 441.

Romance language (roh MANS LANG gwihj). Any language that grew out of Latin: Spanish, Portuguese, French, Italian, and Romanian. p. 122.

rural (ROOR ul). Having to do with the countryside; nonurban. p. 167.

S

samurai (SAM uh rye). The military class in feudal Japan. p. 528.

sanctuary (SANGK choo er ee). A place where birds and animals are protected from hunters and others who would disturb them. p. 291.

satellite (SAT uh lyt). An object made to go around the earth. p. 18.

savanna (suh VAN uh). Land covered with coarse grass and, sometimes, scattered trees and bushes. p. 438.

scale (skayl). The relationship between real size and size used on a map or model. Also, the line, drawn on maps, that shows this relationship. p. 12.

schism (SIHZ um). A split or division between the members of a church or other group when they no longer agree on what they believe. p. 304.

scribe (skryb). A person who copied manuscripts and records and wrote letters. p. 61.

Senate (SEN iht). An assembly or council, as in ancient Rome. Only patricians could be part of the Roman Senate. p. 102.

serf (surf). A person who lived and worked on a manor. p. 175.

service industry (SUR vihs IHN dus tree). A business that provides some kind of useful work for another business or a person. p. 257.

shah (shah). A Persian word meaning "king." p. 403.

shogun (SHOH gun). A military leader in feudal Japan. p. 528.

shrine (shryn). A place considered to be holy. p. 377.

silt (sihlt). Fine particles of earth that are carried and deposited by water and wind. p. 55.

sisal (SYE sul). A plant with strong fibers used for making rope. p. 450.

slash-and-burn farming (slash un BURN FAHRM ihng). A system of farming in which farmers slash, or cut, tree branches and other plant growth and let the vegetation dry so that it will burn. Then the farmers burn the dried vegetation, clearing the ground and enriching the soil at the same time. After this, they plant crops. p. 449.

smelting (SMELT ihng). The process of separating a metal from other materials in its ore. p. 592.

socialism (SOH shul ihz um). A system that calls for ownership of land and industry by the government. p. 316.

Solidarity (sahl uh DAR uh tee). The large free union of Polish workers. The word *solidarity* means "unity." p. 337.

sphere (sfihr). A three-dimensional figure that is round or nearly round. p. 4.

standard of living (STAN durd uv LIHV ihng). A measure of how well people live. p. 210.

steppe (step). One of the belts of grassland in Europe and Asia, somewhat like the prairie of North America. p. 288.

strait (strayt). A narrow waterway connecting two larger bodies of water. p. 78.

subcontinent (SUB kahnt un unt). A landmass of great size but smaller than the continents. p. 127.

subsistence farming (sub SIHS tuns FAHRM ihng). The growing of crops by farmers for their own use rather than for sale. p. 449.

successor (suk SES ur). A person who succeeds, or follows, another. p. 532.

sultan (SULT un). A ruler of a Muslim country. p. 388.

T

taiga (TYE guh). The great coniferous forest region of the northern and western parts of the former Soviet Union. p. 287.

tax (taks). Money paid to a ruler or government and spent on providing government services. p. 173.

teak (teek). A hard wood used in building ships and furniture. p. 514.

teff (tef). A grasslike grain native to northern Africa and grown for its edible seeds. p. 493.

temperate climate (TEM pur iht KLYE mut). A climate that is moderate, neither very hot nor very cold. The temperate zones of the earth are usually called the middle latitudes. p. 581.

terrace (TER us). A flat shelf of land, arranged like a wide step on a mountainside. p. 513.

terrorism (TER ur ihz um). Surprise violent attacks against people's lives. p. 423.

time line (tym lyn). A line representing a period of time, on which dates and the order of events are shown. p. 28.

time zone (tym zohn). A geographic region where the same standard time is used. p. 289.

tributary (TRIHB yoo ter ee). A stream or river that flows into a larger body of water. p. 284.

Tropic of Cancer (TRAHP ihk uv KAN sur). A line of latitude that circles the earth at 23 1/2° north latitude. p. 439.

Tropic of Capricorn (TRAHP ihk uv KAP rih korn). A line of latitude that circles the earth at 23 1/2° south latitude. p. 439.

tropics (TRAHP ihks). The zone between the Tropic of Capricorn and the Tropic of Cancer. p. 439.

tundra (TUN druh). A rolling plain without trees, found in the Arctic area of the high latitudes. p. 286.

typhoon (tye FOON). A tropical storm accompanied by strong winds and heavy rain. p. 528.

U

unification (yoon uh fih KAY shun). The uniting of separate regions and cities into one nation. p. 223.

United Nations (yoo NYT ihd NAY shunz). An organization set up to settle disputes between nations. p. 242.

urban (UR bun). Having to do with a town or city. p. 167.

V

volcano (vahl KAY noh). An opening in the earth, usually at the top of a cone-shaped hill or mountain, out of which steam and other gases, stone, ashes, and melted rock may escape from time to time. p. 112.

W

wadi (WAH dee). The bed of a stream that is dry most of the time. p. 363.

warlord (WOR lord). A general who controls an area by force. p. 541.

Z

ziggurat (ZIHG oo rat). A platform in the form of a terraced pyramid, with each story smaller than the one below it. p. 52.

INDEX

CREDITS

PEOPLE in Time and Place

PROGRAM SCOPE & SEQUENCE CHART

I. Acquiring and Providing Information

	Grade 1	2	3	4	5	6/7
A. Map and Globe Skills						
Understanding directions: up, down, left, right, North, South, East, West	●	●	●	●	●	●
Understanding the globe	●	●	●	●	●	●
Understanding cardinal directions	●	●	●	●	●	●
Using the globe to explain night and day				●	●	●
Comparing maps and the globe	●	●	●	●	●	●
Comparing maps with photographs	●	●	●	●	●	●
Understanding symbols	●	●	●	●	●	●
Understanding the legend (key)	●	●	●	●	●	●
Identifying landforms	●	●	●	●	●	●
Understanding relative size		●	●	●	●	●
Understanding latitude: Equator			●	●	●	●
Arctic Circle				●	●	●
Antarctic Circle				●	●	●
Tropic of Cancer				●	●	●
Tropic of Capricorn				●	●	●
Understanding longitude: Prime Meridian			●	●	●	●
Understanding continents and oceans	●	●	●	●	●	●
Understanding hemispheres			●	●	●	●
Understanding intermediate directions			●	●	●	●
Understanding the compass rose			●	●	●	●
Understanding scale			●	●	●	●
Using scale to measure distance			●	●	●	●
Understanding coordinates (grid system)			●	●	●	●

	1	2	3	4	5	6/7
A. Map and Globe Skills (continued)						
Understanding elevation tints				●	●	●
Understanding contour lines				●	●	●
Understanding special-purpose maps:						
Relief map				●	●	●
Population map				●	●	●
Product map			●	●	●	●
Precipitation map				●	●	●
Physical-Political map			●	●	●	●
Road map				●	●	●
Historical map			●	●	●	●
Understanding movements of the earth: rotation, revolution				●	●	●
Understanding time zones				●	●	●
Understanding seasons		●	●	●	●	●
Understanding map projections				●	●	●
B. Graphic Skills						
Understanding charts	●	●	●	●	●	●
Understanding diagrams	●	●	●	●	●	●
Understanding graphs:						
Pictograph	●	●	●	●	●	●
Pie graph		●	●	●	●	●
Bar graph	●	●	●	●	●	●
Line graph			●	●	●	●
Climograph			●	●	●	●
Understanding time lines	●	●	●	●	●	●
Understanding cartoons					●	●
C. Learning Social Studies [Reading Skills] **1. Vocabulary**						
Using context clues (synonym, antonym, definition) to understand word meanings	●	●	●	●	●	●
Using illustrations or objects to understand word meanings	●	●	●	●	●	●
Using a dictionary or glossary to understand word meanings	●	●	●	●	●	●
Classifying and categorizing words (semantic maps and feature analysis)	●	●	●	●	●	●
Understanding the multiple meanings of words		●	●	●	●	●
Recognizing roots and affixes			●	●	●	●

	Grade					
	1	2	3	4	5	6/7
1. Vocabulary (continued)						
Understanding denotations and connotations of words			●	●	●	●
Identifying abbreviations and acronyms			●	●	●	●
Understanding etymology			●	●	●	●
2. Comprehension						
Understanding stated facts and details	●	●	●	●	●	●
Inferring unstated ideas	●	●	●	●	●	●
Understanding main ideas and details:						
Identifying stated main ideas	●	●	●	●	●	●
Generating unstated main ideas	●	●	●	●	●	●
Identifying details that support main ideas	●	●	●	●	●	●
Using headings and prereading questions to aid in main idea identification	●	●	●	●	●	●
Understanding sequence	●	●	●	●	●	●
Understanding cause and effect	●	●	●	●	●	●
Making and verifying predictions	●	●	●	●	●	●
Drawing conclusions	●	●	●	●	●	●
Understanding word referents				●	●	●
Relating text information to prior knowledge	●	●	●	●	●	●
Recognizing an author's purpose			●	●	●	●
Distinguishing fact from opinion		●	●	●	●	●
Understanding an author's point of view			●	●	●	●
Detecting bias:						
Propaganda techniques			●	●	●	●
Emotionally laden words			●	●	●	●
Evaluating arguments:						
Detecting illogical reasoning			●	●	●	●
Detecting faulty generalizations			●	●	●	●
Recognizing comprehension breakdowns					●	●
Employing reading comprehension fix-up strategies (summarizing, paraphrasing, rereading/retelling)		●	●	●	●	●
Recognizing and understanding the characteristics of various text types (informational/expository, narrative, historical fiction, biography/autobiography, journal/diary, essay, letter, speech, legend/myth)	●	●	●	●	●	●
Recognizing and using various text structures to aid comprehension (description, simple listing, sequence/time order, cause/effect, problem/solution, explanation, comparison/contrast, definition/examples)	●	●	●	●	●	●

	Grade					
	1	**2**	**3**	**4**	**5**	**6/7**
D. Speaking and Listening						
Listening to and following oral directions	●	●	●	●	●	●
Preparing and giving oral reports	●	●	●	●	●	●
Preparing and engaging in a debate			●	●	●	●
Expressing a point of view	●	●	●	●	●	●
Critical listening:						
Recognize a speaker's purpose/point of view			●	●	●	●
Distinguishing fact from opinion			●	●	●	●
Detecting bias (propaganda, emotionally laden words)			●	●	●	●
Evaluating oral arguments (illogical reasoning, faulty generalizations)			●	●	●	●
E. Study Skills						
Alphabetical order	●	●	●	●	●	●
Understanding and following written directions	●	●	●	●	●	●
Understanding and using book parts (table of contents, glossary, index, bibliography, appendices, gazetteer, footnotes)	●	●	●	●	●	●
Understanding and using graphic and typographical features (boldface, headings, captions, dictionary respellings)	●	●	●	●	●	●
Understanding and using textbook study features (prereading, questions, graphic organizers, preview statements, summary statements, postreading questions)	●	●	●	●	●	●
Learning and using a study/reading technique		●	●	●	●	●
Note-taking			●	●	●	●
Outlining a selection			●	●	●	●
Summarizing a chapter or section	●	●	●	●	●	●
Skimming for main ideas	●	●	●	●	●	●
Scanning for specific facts or ideas			●	●	●	●
Adjusting reading rate to accommodate the purpose for reading, a reader's prior knowledge, and the difficulty/content of the material			●	●	●	●
F. Reference Skills						
Using the community as a resource	●	●	●	●	●	●
Selecting and using the appropriate resources:						
Atlas and gazetteer	●	●	●	●	●	●
Encyclopedia			●	●	●	●
Dictionary and thesaurus		●	●	●	●	●
Newspaper and periodicals		●	●	●	●	●

	Grade 1	2	3	4	5	6/7
F. Reference Skills (continued)						
Other resources (almanac, vertical files, telephone book, films, audio and video recordings, art, artifacts, microfiche)			●	●	●	●
Using a manual and electronic card catalog			●	●	●	●
Using a computer to run instructional and reference software			●	●	●	●

II. Organizing and Using Information

	Grade 1	2	3	4	5	6/7
A. Writing Skills						
Report writing		●	●	●	●	●
Writing a biography/autobiography			●	●	●	●
Writing a journal/diary	●	●	●	●	●	●
Writing book reports			●	●	●	●
Persuasive writing (editorials, commentaries, opinions)			●	●	●	●
Writing letters: Friendly letter	●	●	●	●	●	●
Business letter			●	●	●	●
Writing other forms common to social studies (essay, historical fiction, legend, myth, news report, research paper, speech, bibliography)			●	●	●	●
B. Thinking Skills						
Making observations	●	●	●	●	●	●
Classifying information	●	●	●	●	●	●
Interpreting information	●	●	●	●	●	●
Analyzing information	●	●	●	●	●	●
Summarizing information	●	●	●	●	●	●
Synthesizing information	●	●	●	●	●	●
Hypothesizing information	●	●	●	●	●	●
Evaluating information	●	●	●	●	●	●
Applying information	●	●	●	●	●	●

III. Interpersonal Skills

Grade

	1	2	3	4	5	6/7
A. Personal Skills						
Being sensitive to needs, problems and aspirations of others	●	●	●	●	●	●
Being courteous to others	●	●	●	●	●	●
Accepting and giving constructive feedback	●	●	●	●	●	●
Developing friendships	●	●	●	●	●	●
Developing respect for others as individuals (not stereotyping)	●	●	●	●	●	●
B. Group Interaction Skills						
Listening to differing views	●	●	●	●	●	●
Participating in group discussions	●	●	●	●	●	●
Participating in making decisions in a group setting	●	●	●	●	●	●
Being able to lead	●	●	●	●	●	●
Showing willingness to follow	●	●	●	●	●	●
Showing skills in persuading, compromising, debating, negotiating, and solving conflicts	●	●	●	●	●	●

IV. Citizenship

Grade

	1	2	3	4	5	6/7
A. Social and Political Participation Skills						
Keeping informed on social issues	●	●	●	●	●	●
Showing commitment toward the improvement of society	●	●	●	●	●	●
Showing willingness to work to influence those in power to preserve and extend justice, freedom, equality, and human rights	●	●	●	●	●	●
Working with others towards the solution of social problems	●	●	●	●	●	●
B. American Beliefs and Values						
Respecting the multicultural nature of our society	●	●	●	●	●	●
Abiding by the majority rule	●	●	●	●	●	●
Respecting and protecting the rights of the minorities	●	●	●	●	●	●
Respecting peaceful solutions	●	●	●	●	●	●
Respecting society's rules and laws	●	●	●	●	●	●
Striving for equality and freedom for all	●	●	●	●	●	●

B. American Beliefs and Values (continued)	1	2	3	4	5	6/7
Working for the common good	●	●	●	●	●	●
Recognizing and protecting the rights of the individual	●	●	●	●	●	●
Recognizing and protecting the freedom of the individual	●	●	●	●	●	●
Recognizing the responsibilities of the individual in a democracy	●	●	●	●	●	●
Developing pride in one's own work	●	●	●	●	●	●
Accepting the dignity in all occupations	●	●	●	●	●	●
Developing good work and job habits	●	●	●	●	●	●

C. Seven Strands of Citizenship	1	2	3	4	5	6/7
Participate in the democratic process	●	●	●	●	●	●
Develop patriotism and American values	●	●	●	●	●	●
Develop an awareness of and skills in interdependence	●	●	●	●	●	●
Develop an awareness of and skills in resolving social issues	●	●	●	●	●	●
Develop an awareness of and skills in relating to public officials	●	●	●	●	●	●
Learn how to use resources wisely	●	●	●	●	●	●
Develop strong personal integrity and positive self-image	●	●	●	●	●	●

V. Life Skills

	1	2	3	4	5	6/7
Practicing pedestrian safety	●	●	●	●		
Reading traffic signs	●	●	●	●		
Being able to say full name and address	●	●	●			
Explaining fire drill procedures	●	●	●			
Being able to tell when and how to call for fire and police help	●	●	●	●		
Using a telephone	●	●	●	●	●	●
Being able to dial emergency telephone numbers	●	●	●	●	●	●
Budgeting and banking		●	●	●	●	●
Addressing an envelope		●	●	●		●
Using a telephone directory		●	●	●		●
Reading a schedule	●	●	●	●	●	●
Reading a calendar	●	●	●	●	●	●
Filling out forms and applications			●	●	●	●
Reading newspaper ads		●	●	●	●	●
Using leisure time appropriately	●	●	●	●	●	●

TEACHER NOTES

TEACHER NOTES